Worldmark
Encyclopedia of
Cultures and
Daily Life

Worldmark Encyclopedia of Cultures and Daily Life

VOLUME 3 Asia & Oceania
Second Edition

Editors

Timothy L. Gall and Jeneen Hobby

GALE
CENGAGE Learning

Detroit • New York • San Francisco • New Haven, Conn • Waterville, Maine • London

Worldmark Encyclopedia of Cultures and Daily Life, Second Edition

Editors: Timothy L. Gall and Jeneen Hobby

Product Management: Julia Furtaw and Carol Nagel

Manufacturing: Rita Wimberley

Gale
27500 Drake Rd.
Farmington Hills, MI 48331-3535

ISBN 978-1-4144-4882-4 (set)
ISBN 978-1-4144-4883-1 (vol. 1)
ISBN 978-1-4144-4890-9 (vol. 2)
ISBN 978-1-4144-4891-6 (vol. 3)
ISBN 978-1-4144-4892-3 (vol. 4)
ISBN 978-1-4144-6430-5 (vol. 5)

ISSN 0196-2809

© 2009 Gale, Cengage Learning

For product information and technology assistance, contact us at Gale Customer Support, 1-800-877-4253.
For permission to use material from this text or product, submit all requests online at www.cengage.com/permissions.
Further permissions questions can be emailed to permissionrequest@cengage.com

This publication is a creative work fully protected by all applicable copyright laws, as well as by misappropriation, trade secret, unfair competition, and other applicable laws. The authors and editors of this work have added value to the underlying factual material herein through one or more of the following: unique and original selection, coordination, expression, arrangement, and classification of the information.

While every effort has been made to ensure the reliability of the information presented in this publication, Gale, a part of Cengage Learning, does not guarantee the accuracy of the data contained herein. Gale accepts no payment for listing; and inclusion in the publication of any organization, agency, institution, publication, service, or individual does not imply endorsement of the editors or publisher. Errors brought to the attention of the publisher and verified to the satisfaction of the publisher will be corrected in future editions.

EDITORIAL DATA PRIVACY POLICY: Does this product contain information about you as an individual? If so, for more information about our editorial data privacy policies, please see our Privacy Statement at www.gale.cengage.com.

Library of Congress Cataloging-in-Publication Data

Worldmark encyclopedia of cultures and daily life / Timothy L. Gall, editor. -- 2nd ed.
    p. cm.
  Includes bibliographical references and index.
  ISBN 978-1-4144-4882-4 (set) -- ISBN 978-1-4144-4883-1 (vol. 1) -- ISBN 978-1-4144-4890-9 (vol. 2) -- ISBN 978-1-4144-4891-6 (vol. 3) -- ISBN 978-1-4144-4892-3 (vol. 4) -- ISBN 978-1-4144-6430-5 (vol. 5)
  1. Ethnology--Encyclopedias, Juvenile. 2. Manners and customs--Encyclopedias, Juvenile. [1. Ethnology--Encyclopedias. 2. Manners and customs--Encyclopedias.] I. Gall, Timothy L. II. Title: Encyclopedia of cultures and daily life.
  GN333.W67 2009
  305.8003--dc22
                                                2009004744

This title is also available as an e-book.
ISBN: 978-1-4144-4893-0
Contact your Gale sales representative for ordering information.

Printed in Mexico
3 4 5 6 7 13 12 11

CONTENTS

For entries on the Kyrgz through Zhuang *see* Vol. 4

JUSTIN CORFIELD. Department of History, Geelong Grammar School.

DIANNE K. DAEG DE MOTT. Researcher/Writer, Tucson, Arizona.

CATHARIN DALPINO. Department of Asian Studies, Georgetown University

MICHAEL DE JONGH. Professor, Department of Anthropology, University of South Africa.

GEORGI DERLUGUIAN. Senior Fellow, Ph.D., U. S. Institute of Peace.

CHRISTINE DRAKE. Department of Political Science and Geography, Old Dominion University.

ARTURO DUARTE. Guatemalan Mission to the OAS.

CALEB DUBE. Department of Anthropology, Northwestern University.

BRIAN DU TOIT. Professor, Department of Anthropology, University of Florida.

LEAH ERMARTH. Worldspace Foundation, Washington, DC.

NANCY J. FAIRLEY. Associate Professor of Anthropology, Department of Anthropology/Sociology, Davidson College.

GREGORY A. FINNEGAN, Ph.D. Tozzer Library, Harvard University.

ALLEN J. FRANK, Ph.D.

DAVID P. GAMBLE. Professor Emeritus, Department of Anthropology, San Francisco State University.

FREDERICK GAMST. Professor Emeritus, Department of Anthropology, University of Massachusetts, Harbor Campus.

PAULA GARB. Associate Director of Global Peace and Conflict Studies and Adjunct Professor of Social Ecology, University of California, Irvine.

HAROLD GASKI. Associate Professor of Sami Literature, School of Languages and Literature, University of Tromsø.

STEPHEN J. GENDZIER.

FLORENCE GERDEL.

ANTHONY P. GLASCOCK. Professor of Anthropology; Department of Anthropology, Psychology, and Sociology; Drexel University.

LUIS GONZALEZ. Researcher/Writer, River Edge, New Jersey.

JENNIFER GRAHAM. Researcher/Writer, Sydney, Australia.

MARIE-CÉCILE GROELSEMA. Doctoral candidate, Comparative Literature, Indiana University.

ROBERT GROELSEMA. MPIA and doctoral candidate, Political Science, Indiana University.

MARIA GROSZ-NGATÉ. Visiting Assistant Professor, Department of Anthropology, Northwestern University.

ELLEN GRUENBAUM. Professor, School of Social Sciences, California State University, Fresno.

N. THOMAS HAKANSSON. University of Kentucky.

ROBERT HALASZ. Researcher/Writer, New York, New York.

MARC HANREZ. Professor, Department of French and Italian, University of Wisconsin-Madison.

ANWAR UL HAQ. Central Asian Studies Department, Indiana University.

LIAM HARTE. Department of Philosophy, Loyola University, Chicago.

FR. VASILE HATEGAN. Author, Romanian Culture in America.

BRUCE HEILMAN. Doctoral candidate, Department of Political Science, Indiana University.

JIM HENRY. Researcher/Writer, Cleveland, Ohio.

BARRY HEWLETT. Department of Anthropology, Washington State University.

SUSAN F. HIRSCH. Department of Anthropology, Wesleyan University.

MARIDA HOLLOS. Department of Anthropology, Brown University.

HALYNA HOLUBEC. Researcher/Writer, Cleveland, Ohio.

YVONNE HOOSAVA. Legal Researcher and Cultural Preservation Officer, Hopi Tribal Council.

HUIQIN HUANG, Ph.D. Center for East Asia Studies, University of Montreal.

MARCEL IONESCU-HEROIU. Teaching Assistant, Cornell University

ASAFA JALATA. Assistant Professor of Sociology and African and African American Studies, Department of Sociology, The University of Tennessee, Knoxville.

STEPHEN F. JONES. Russian Department, Mount Holyoke College.

THOMAS JOVANOVSKI, PH.D. Lorain County Community College.

A. KEN JULES. Minister Plenipotentiary and Deputy Head of Mission, Embassy of St. Kitts and Nevis.

GENEROSA KAGARUKI-KAKOTI. Economist, Department of Urban and Rural Planning, College of Lands and Architectural Studies, Dar es Salaam, Tanzania.

EZEKIEL KALIPENI. Department of Geography, University of Illinois at Urbana-Champaign.

DON KAVANAUGH. Program Director, Lake of the Woods Ojibwa Cultural Centre.

SUSAN M. KENYON. Associate Professor of Anthropology, Department of History and Anthropology, Butler University.

ALLA GOLOVINA KHADKA. PhD Candidate, University of Pittsburgh

MARIA GROSZ-NGATÉ. Visiting Associate Director of the African Studies Program, Indiana University.

ADEL ISKANDAR. Center for Contemporary Arab Studies, Georgetown University

ASAFA JALATA. Professor of Sociology, The University of Tennessee, Knoxville.

THOMAS JOVANOVSKI, Ph.D. Lorain County Community College.

EZEKIEL KALIPENI. Associate Professor of Geography, University of Illinois at Urbana-Champaign.

SUSAN M. KENYON. Associate Professor of Anthropology, Butler University.

WELILE KHUZWAYO. Department of Anthropology, University of South Africa.

PHILIP L. KILBRIDE. Professor of Anthropology, Mary Hale Chase Chair in the Social Sciences, Department of Anthropology, Bryn Mawr College.

RICHARD O. KISIARA. Doctoral candidate, Department of Anthropology, Washington University in St. Louis.

SARAH KLUMP. Center for Eurasian, Russian and East European Studies, Edmund A. Walsh School of Foreign Service, Georgetown University .

KAREN KNOWLES. Permanent Mission of Antigua and Barbuda to the United Nations.

MELISSA KERR. Eurasian, Russian, and East European Studies, Georgetown University.

IGOR KRUPNIK. Research Anthropologist, Department of Anthropology, Smithsonian Institution.

LEELO LASS. Secretary, Embassy of Estonia.

ROBERT LAUNAY. Professor, Department of Anthropology, Northwestern University.

BENJAMIN LAZARUS. Eurasian, Russian, and East European Studies, Georgetown University.

CHARLES LEBLANC. Professor and Director, Center for East Asia Studies, University of Montreal.

RONALD LEE. Author, Goddam Gypsy, An Autobiographical Novel.

PHILIP E. LEIS. Professor and Chair, Department of Anthropology, Brown University.

MARIA JUKIC LESKUR. Croatian Consulate, Cleveland, Ohio.

RICHARD A. LOBBAN, JR. Professor of Anthropology and African Studies, Department of Anthropology, Rhode Island College.

DERYCK O. LODRICK. Visiting Scholar, Center for South Asian Studies, University of California, Berkeley.

NEIL LURSSEN. Intro Communications Inc.

GREGORIO C. MARTIN. Modern Language Department, Duquesne University.

HOWARD J. MARTIN. Independent scholar.

HEITOR MARTINS. Professor, Department of Spanish and Portuguese, Indiana University.

ADELINE MASQUELIER. Assistant Professor, Department of Anthropology, Tulane University.

DOLINA MILLAR.

EDITH MIRANTE. Project Maje.

ROBERT W. MONTGOMERY, Ph.D. Indiana University.

THOMAS D. MORIN. Associate Professor of Hispanic Studies, Department of Modern and Classical Literatures and Languages, University of Rhode Island.

CHARLES MORRILL. Doctoral candidate, Indiana University.

CAROL A. MORTLAND. Crate's Point.

FRANCIS A. MOYER. Director, North Carolina Japan Center, North Carolina State University.

MARIE C. MOYER.

NYAGA MWANIKI. Assistant Professor, Department of Anthropology and Sociology, Western Carolina University.

KENNETH NILSON. Celtic Studies Department, Harvard University.

MARTIN NJOROGE. PhD. SRF/UPenn Postdoctoral Fellow, Graduate School of Education, University of Pennsylvania.

JANE E. ORMROD. Graduate Student, History, University of Chicago.

JUANITA PAHDOPONY. Carl Perkins Program Director, Comanche Tribe of Oklahoma.

TINO PALOTTA. Syracuse University.

ROHAYATI PASENG.

PATRICIA PITCHON. Researcher/Writer, London, England.

STEPHANIE PLATZ. Program Officer, Program on Peace and International Cooperation, The John D. and Catherine T. MacArthur Foundation.

MIHAELA POIATA. Graduate Student, School of Journalism and Mass Communication, University of North Carolina at Chapel Hill.

MANSAH PRAH. Dean, Faculty of Social Sciences, University of Cape Coast, Ghana.

LEOPOLDINA PRUT-PREGELJ. Author, Historical Dictionary of Slovenia.

J. RACKAUSKAS. Director, Lithuanian Research and Studies Center, Chicago.

J. RAKOVICH. Byelorussian-American Cultural Center, Strongsville, Ohio.

HANTA V. RALAY. Promotions, Inc., Montgomery Village, Maryland.

SUSAN J. RASMUSSEN. Associate Professor, Department of Anthropology, University of Houston.

RONALD REMINICK. Associate Professor of Anthropology, Cleveland State University.

BRUCE D. ROBERTS. Associate Professor of Anthropology, Department of Anthropology & Earth Science, Minnesota State University, Moorhead.

LAUREL L. ROSE. Philosophy Department, Carnegie-Mellon University.

ROBERT ROTENBERG. Professor of Anthropology, International Studies Program, DePaul University.

CAROLINE SAHLEY, Ph.D. Researcher/Writer, Cleveland, Ohio.

VERONICA SALLES-REESE. Associate Professor, Department of Spanish and Portuguese, Georgetown University.

MAIRA SARYBAEVA. Kazakh-American Studies Center, University of Kentucky.

DEBRA L. SCHINDLER. Institute of Arctic Studies, Dartmouth College.

KYOKO SELDEN, Ph.D. Department of Asian Studies, Cornell University.

ELIZABETH SERLEMITSOS. Chief Advisor, National AIDS Council, Zambia.

ENAYATULLAH SHAHRANI. Central Asian Studies Department, Indiana University.

ROBERT SHANAFELT. Department of Sociology & Anthropology, Georgia Southern University.

TUULIKKI SINKS. Teaching Specialist for Finnish, Department of German, Scandinavian, and Dutch, University of Minnesota.

JAN SJÅVIK. Professor, Scandinavian Studies, University of Washington.

MAGDA SOBALVARRO. Press and Cultural Affairs Director, Embassy of Nicaragua.

PAMELA SODHY. History Department, Georgetown University

MICHAEL STAINTON. Researcher, Joint Center for Asia Pacific Studies, York University.

RIANA STEYN. Department of Anthropology, University of South Africa.

PAUL STOLLER. Professor, Department of Anthropology, West Chester University.

CRAIG STRASHOFER. Researcher/Writer, Cleveland, Ohio.

SANDRA B. STRAUBHAAR. Assistant Professor, Nordic Studies, Department of Germanic and Slavic Languages, Brigham Young University.

DAVID STRAUB. Masters Program in Central Eurasian Studies, Indiana University.

VUM SON SUANTAK. Author, Zo History.

MURAT TAISHIBAEV. Kazakh-American Studies Center, University of Kentucky.

CHRISTOPHER C. TAYLOR. Associate Professor, Anthropology Department, University of Alabama, Birmingham.

FATIMA TLISOVA. Kennedy School at Harvard.

EDDIE TSO. Office of Language and Culture, Navajo Division of Education.

DAVID TYSON. Foreign Broadcast Information Service, Washington, D.C.

NICOLAAS G. W. UNLANDT. Assistant Professor of French, Department of French and Italian, Brigham Young University.

GORDON URQUHART. Professor, Department of Economics and Business, Cornell College.

CHRISTOPHER J. VAN VUUREN. Associate Professor, Department of Anthropology, University of South Africa.

DALIA VENTURA-ALCALAY. Journalist, London, England.

CATHERINE VEREECKE. Assistant Director, Center for African Studies, University of Florida.

CAMILA VERGARA. Journalist, New York.

KORA BATTIG VON WITTLESBACH. Department of Romance Studies at Cornell.

GREGORY T. WALKER. Associate Director, Office of International Affairs, Duquesne University.

GERHARD WEISS. Department of German, Scandinavian, and Dutch, University of Minnesota.

PATSY WEST. Director, The Seminole/Miccosukee Photographic Archive.

WALTER WHIPPLE. Associate Professor of Polish, Germanic and Slavic Languages, Brigham Young University.

ROSALIE WIEDER. Researcher/Writer, Cleveland, Ohio.

JEFFREY WILLIAMS. Professor and Chair, Department of Sociology, Anthropology, & Social Work, Texas Tech University.

KOSTAS YIAVIS. Lecturer in Modern Greek, Cornell University.

GUANG-HONG YU. Associate Research Fellow, Institute of Ethnology, Academia Sinica.

RUSSELL ZANCA. Associate Professor of Anthropology, Northeastern Illinois University.

COUNTRY INDEX

PREFACE

The *Worldmark Encyclopedia of Cultures and Daily Life, Second Edition,* contains over 500 articles exploring the ways of life of peoples of the world. Arranged in five volumes by geographic regions—*Africa, Americas, Asia & Oceania* (two volumes), and *Europe*—the volumes of this encyclopedia parallel the organization of its sister set, the *Worldmark Encyclopedia of the Nations.* Whereas the primary purpose of *Nations* is to provide information on the world's nation states, this encyclopedia focuses on the traditions, living conditions, and personalities of many of the world's culture groups. Entries emphasize how people live today, rather than how they lived in the past.

Defining groups for inclusion was not an easy task. Cultural identity can be shaped by such factors as geography, nationality, ethnicity, race, language, and religion. Many people, in fact, legitimately belong in two or more classifications, each as valid as the other. For example, the citizens of the United States all share traits that make them distinctly American. However, few would deny the need for separate articles on Native Americans or African Americans. Even the category Native American denies the individuality of separate tribes like the Navajo and Paiute. Consequently, this encyclopedia contains an article on the Americans as well as separate articles on the Native Americans and the Navajo. Closely related articles such as these are cross-referenced to each other to help provide a more complete picture of the group being profiled. Included in this encyclopedia are articles on groups as large as the Han of China, with over one billion members, and as small as the Jews of Cochin, with only a few dozen members. Unfortunately, although the vast majority of the world's peoples are represented in this encyclopedia, time and space constraints prevented many important groups from being included in the first edition. Twenty-three new groups have been added to this second edition, and the editors look forward to including many more culture groups in future editions of this work.

New entries include in Americas: Sudanese Americans ("Lost Boys"); in Africa: Afar, Berbers, Ewe, Guineas of Guinea Bissau, Jola, Maldivians, San (Bushmen), Sao Tomeans, and Twa; in Asia and Oceania: Brunei, Coptic Christians, Kashmiris, Moro, Rajasthanis, and Timorese; and in Europe: Alsatians, Kosovars, Maltese, Montenegrins, Serbs, Tyrolese, and Vlachs.

Over 175 contributors and reviewers participated in the creation of this encyclopedia. Drawn from universities, consulates, and the press, their in-depth knowledge and first-hand experience of the profiled groups added significantly to the content of the articles. A complete listing of the contributors and reviewers together with their affiliations appears in the front of each volume.

ORGANIZATION

Each volume begins with an introduction that traces the cultural developments of the region from prehistoric times to the present. Following the introduction are articles devoted to the peoples of the region. Within each volume the articles are arranged alphabetically. A comprehensive table cross referencing the articles by country follows the table of contents to each volume.

The individual articles are of two types. The vast majority follow a standard 20-heading outline explained in more detail below. This structure allows for easy comparison of the articles and enhances the accessibility of the information. A smaller number do not follow the 20-heading format, but rather present simply an overview of the group. This structure is used when the primary purpose of an article is to supplement a fully rubriced article appearing elsewhere in the set.

Whenever appropriate, articles begin with the **pronunciation** of the group's name, a listing of **alternate names** by which the group is known, the group's **location** in the world, its **population,** the **languages** spoken, the **religions** practiced, and a listing of **related articles** in the five volumes of this encyclopedia. Most articles are illustrated with a map showing the primary location of the group and photographs of the people being profiled. The twenty standard headings by which most articles are organized are presented below.

INTRODUCTION: A description of the group's historical origins provides a useful background for understanding its contemporary affairs. Information relating to migration helps explain how the group arrived at its present location. Political conditions and governmental structure(s) that typically affect members of the profiled ethnic group are also discussed.

LOCATION AND HOMELAND: The population size of the group is listed. This information may include official census data from various countries and/or estimates. Information on the size of a group's population located outside the traditional homeland may also be included, especially for certain groups with large diaspora populations. A description of the homeland includes information on location, topography, and climate.

LANGUAGE: Each article lists the name(s) of the primary language(s) spoken by members. Descriptions of linguistic origins, grammar, and similarities to other languages may also be included. Examples of common words, phrases, and proverbs are listed for many of the profiled groups, and some include examples of common personal names and forms of address.

FOLKLORE: Common themes, settings, and characters in the profiled group's traditional oral and/or literary mythology are highlighted. Many entries include a short excerpt or synopsis of one of the group's most noteworthy myths, fables, or legends. Some entries describe the accomplishments of famous heroes and heroines or other prominent historical figures.

RELIGION: The origins of traditional religious beliefs are profiled. Contemporary religious beliefs, customs, and practices are also discussed. Some groups may be closely associated with one particular faith (especially if religious and ethnic identification are interlinked), while others may have members of diverse faiths.

MAJOR HOLIDAYS: Celebrations and commemorations typically recognized by the group's members are described. These holidays commonly fall into two categories: secular and religious. Secular holidays often include an independence day and/or other days of observance recognizing important dates in history that affected the group as a whole. Religious holidays are typically the same as those honored by other peoples of the same faith. Some secular and religious holidays are linked to the lunar cycle or to the change of seasons. Some articles describe unique customs practiced by members of the group on certain holidays.

RITES OF PASSAGE: Formal and informal episodic events that mark an individual's procession through the stages of life are profiled. These events typically involve rituals, ceremonies, observances, and procedures associated with birth, childhood, the coming of age, adulthood, and death. The impact of twenty-first century communications and global media on customs are addressed here.

INTERPERSONAL RELATIONS: Information on greetings, body language, gestures, visiting customs, and dating practices is included. The extent of formality to which members of a certain ethnic group treat others is also addressed, as some groups may adhere to customs governing interpersonal relationships more/less strictly than others.

LIVING CONDITIONS: General health conditions typical of the group's members are cited. Such information includes life expectancy, the prevalence of various diseases, and access to medical care. Information on urbanization, housing, and access to utilities is also included. Transportation methods typically utilized by the group's members are also discussed.

FAMILY LIFE: The size and composition of the family unit is profiled. Gender roles common to the group are also discussed, including the division of rights and responsibilities relegated to male and female group members. The roles that children, adults, and the elderly have within the group as a whole may also be addressed.

CLOTHING: Many entries include descriptive information (size, shape, color, fabric, etc.) regarding traditional clothing (or a national costume), and indicate the frequency of its use in contemporary life. A description of clothing typically worn in the present is also provided, especially if traditional clothing is no longer the usual form of dress. Distinctions between formal, informal, and work clothes are made in many articles, along with clothing differences between men, women, and children.

FOOD: Descriptions of items commonly consumed by members of the group are listed. The frequency and occasion for meals is also described, as are any unique customs regarding eating and drinking, special utensils and furniture, and the role of food and beverages in ritual ceremonies. Many entries include a sample recipe for a favorite dish.

EDUCATION: The structure of formal education in the country or countries of residence is discussed, including information on primary, secondary, and higher education. For some groups, the role of informal education is also highlighted. Some articles may include information regarding the relevance and importance of education among the group as a

whole, along with parental expectations for children. In addition, literacy levels are described where appropriate.

CULTURAL HERITAGE: Since many groups express their sense of identity through art, music, literature, and dance, a description of prominent styles is included. Some articles also cite the contributions of famous individual artists, writers, and musicians.

WORK: The type of labor that typically engages members of the profiled group is discussed. For some groups, the formal wage economy is the primary source of earnings, but for other groups, informal agriculture or trade may be the usual way to earn a living. Working conditions are also highlighted.

SPORTS: Popular sports that children and adults play are listed, as are typical spectator sports. Some articles include a description and/or rules to a unique type of sport or game.

ENTERTAINMENT AND RECREATION: Listed activities that people enjoy in their spare time may include carrying out either structured pastimes (such as public musical and dance performances) or informal get-togethers (such as meeting for conversation). The role of popular culture, movies, theater, and television in everyday life is also discussed.

FOLK ARTS, CRAFTS, AND HOBBIES: Entries describe arts and crafts commonly fabricated according to traditional methods, materials, and style. Such objects may often have a functional utility for everyday tasks.

SOCIAL PROBLEMS: Internal and external issues that confront members of the profiled group are described. Such concerns often deal with fundamental problems like war, famine, disease, and poverty. A lack of human rights, civil rights, and political freedom may also adversely affect a group as a whole. Other problems may include crime, unemployment, substance abuse, and domestic violence.

GENDER ISSUES: New to this edition is a section focusing on women's issues including cultural attitudes, discrimination, status, health, sexual issues, education, and work and employment. Some discussion on the group's attitudes toward homosexuality may be included in this section, where relevant.

BIBLIOGRAPHY: References cited include works used to compile the article, as well as benchmark publications often recognized as authoritative by scholars. Citations for materials published in foreign languages are frequently listed when there are few existing sources available in English.

A glossary of terms and a comprehensive index appears at the end of each volume.

ACKNOWLEDGMENTS

The editors express appreciation to the members of the Cengage Gale staff who were involved in a number of ways at various stages of development of the *Worldmark Encyclopedia of Cultures and Daily Life, Second Edition:* Christine Nasso, Barbara Beach, and Leah Knight, who helped the initial concept of the work take form; and Larry Baker and Allison McNeill, who supported the editorial development of the profiles for the first edition. Carol Nagel and Ellen McGeagh were instrumental in the planning and scheduling of the second edition of this work. Anne Marie Hacht selected the photo illustrations and provided valuable review of the entries. Marybeth Trimper,

Evi Seoud, and Shanna Heilveil oversaw the printing and binding process.

In addition, the editors acknowledge with warm gratitude the contributions of the staff of Eastword Publications—Debby Baron, Dan Lucas, Brian Rajewski, Kira Silverbird, Maggie Lyall, Karen Seyboldt, Tajana G. Roehl, Janet Fenn, Cheryl Montagna, Jeneen Hobby, Dan Mehling, Karen Ellicott, Alexander Barnes, and Elizabeth Gall—who managed interactions with contributors; edited, organized, reviewed, and indexed the articles; and turned the manuscripts into the illustrated typeset pages of these five volumes.

SUGGESTIONS ARE WELCOME: Maintenance of a work the size and scope of *Worldmark Encyclopedia of Cultures and Daily Life, Second Edition, is a daunting undertaking; we appreciate any suggestions that* will enhance future editions. Please send comments to:

Editor
Worldmark Encyclopedia
of Cultures and Daily Life
Cengage Gale
27500 Drake Rd.
Farmington Hills, MI 48331-3535

INTRODUCTION

by
Rhoads Murphey

The first humans, or their immediate ancestors, seem clearly to have evolved in East Africa. By about two million years ago these creatures had spread to Asia and Europe. Archeologists have labeled them Homo erectus, and their bones and tools have been found in China, Java, and elsewhere in Asia. Over the time since their arrival in Asia, the minor physical differences that distinguish modern Asians from Africans or Europeans gradually emerged. The cold areas of Siberia were penetrated by people later and more slowly, but by about half a million years ago, that migration had also been accomplished. Australia was settled by people from Asia, probably via a land bridge linking the two continents at a time of lower sea level, by about 50,000 years ago. By about the same time, people also spread via Southeast Asia into Oceania (the islands of the Pacific east of Indonesia).

The native people of Siberia—Yakuts, Tungus, Kazakhs, Uzbeks, and many others—spoke different languages and had quite separate cultures. The Uzbeks and a few others who occupied dry areas had developed irrigated farming in scattered oases by about the beginning of the Christian era. The other Siberian groups remained dependent on hunting, gathering, and trapping in the vast forests.

AUSTRALIA AND OCEANIA

Most of the inhabitants of Oceania also practiced hunting, gathering, and trapping until quite late, although they practiced rudimentary agriculture, based on cultivation of coconuts and taro and including the raising of pigs and fishing, by the second millennium BC. There are three major groups of the peoples of Oceania, each speaking a different language. (In the case of New Guinea, by far the largest unit of Melanesia, the people spoke many different languages). The groups are Melanesians, so called from their dark skin color, since mela means black; Micronesians, inhabiting a great number of small islands south and east of Melanesia; and Polynesians, settled over a huge arc of the Pacific on smaller islands as far east as Hawaii, speaking a common language, and sharing a common culture. (Polynesians of New Zealand have been known as Maoris since the fourteenth century AD.) The Polynesians are renowned for their long sea voyages in small outrigger canoes, which carried them over great distances in search of new islands to settle.

The aborigines of Australia are a different group that migrated from the Asian mainland much earlier than those who peopled Oceania. Thus, these Australian aborigines are largely unrelated to the Melanesians, Micronesians, or Polynesians; they survived in Australia with a relatively primitive technology centered on hunting and gathering without even domesticated animals.

In Siberia there was little change in culture or technology until the coming of Russian people in their expansion across Asia, beginning in the fifteenth and sixteenth centuries AD.

Russian explorers and conquerors crossed the Ural Mountains, the conventional boundary between Europe and Asia, seized Kazakstan and Astrakhan immediately east of the Caspian Sea by the early seventeenth century, and reached the Pacific by 1639. Their chief objective was to obtain furs, long Siberia's major export, but they also sought to colonize this vast area in the name of the Czar (the ruler of Russia). Russians became, and remain, the dominant settlers of Siberia in a narrowing wedge of patches as far east as Irkutsk near Lake Baikal, with a further extension in the valley of the Amur River that forms the boundary with China. Siberia is the center of the route followed by the Trans-Siberian Railway, completed by 1905, and the cities along it are dominated by Russian inhabitants. Although they have been drawn into the web of commerce, they are still hunting and gathering, mining for gold, and producing timber for export from the huge Siberian forests.

Oceania was penetrated by Westerners beginning in the late eighteenth century. These Westerners were largely explorers and whalers, many of the latter from New England. The cultures and peoples of Oceania were not too affected until the advent of missionaries and permanent white settlers, who (in Hawaii especially) attempted to convert the Polynesians to evangelical and puritanical Christianity, which condemned many aspects of their traditional culture. Europeans, including missionaries, had invaded New Zealand by 1820 AD, although the islands were not formally taken over by Great Britain until 1840. Many of the Maori inhabitants there were killed in small wars with the new arrivals. However, Maoris still constitute about five percent of the total population, with a number of mixed Maori-white descent.

Australia was first settled by whites, predominantly British, late in the 1780s. They quickly drove off or killed aborigines who lived in the better-watered areas along the coasts, pushing their settlements inland, where large areas of wheat and other crops were planted, and even larger areas were converted to grazing for sheep and cattle. Aborigines now survive on reservations in the driest and most remote areas, but are dwindling in numbers. Most now hold low-paying jobs in the dominant white economy, in areas including the big cities along the coast.

SOUTH AND SOUTHEAST ASIA

The rest of Asia south of the former USSR and east of Afghanistan—sometimes called Monsoon Asia—is composed of the modern states of Pakistan, India, Nepal, Bhutan, Sikkim, Bangladesh, and Sri Lanka (together constituting what is called South Asia); Burma, Thailand, Laos, Cambodia, Vietnam, Malaysia, Singapore, Indonesia, and the Philippines (together constituting Southeast Asia); China, Korea, and Japan. Peoples of the Paleolithic or Old Stone Age were settled in all of these areas from about one million BC to about 25000 BC. The early habitation by Homo erectus, including Peking Man and Java Man, gradually gave way to the universal spread of Homo sapiens, or Modern Man. But the pace of other change remained slow until about 30000 BC, when the last phase of glacial ice advanced and its subsequent retreat changed the physical environment and stimulated new adaptations. Fire had been used since about one million BC, but after about 30000 BC stone tools slowly improved and population probably increased.

The big change was the Neolithic revolution from about 10000 BC, including the appearance of settled agriculture. Neolithic means New Stone Age and finer and finer stone tools continued to be made. These were increasingly supplemented by tools of bone, including such delicate items as bone needles for sewing and bone fishhooks. Clothing— leather suits, suits or jackets made of fur pelts sewn together, fur hats, and leather boots—could now be made much less crudely and fitted to each individual. Hunting could now be supplemented on a larger scale by fishing, and population again increased. Agriculture began in two quite different and widely separated areas: the uplands of southwest Asia surrounding the Tigris-Euphrates lowland of Mesopotamia, and the coastal or near-coastal areas of mainland Southeast Asia, especially in what are now Thailand and Vietnam.

Neolithic settlements in what is now Turkey, Palestine, Syria, northern Iraq, and Iran began the transition from gathering grains, including the ancestors of wheat, in the wild to planing the seeds in tended fields. Wheat, barley, and other steppe (dry climate) grasses were native to this area of winter rains. Neolithic stone-toothed sickles, dated to about 10000 BC, have been found there with a sheen on them from cutting such grasses with their grain heads. Dating from a little later, small hoards of stored grain have been found. It must have been a longish process of adaptation from gathering grains in the wild to planting them, perhaps originally by accident, in fields that could be prepared and tended until harvest. Fields growing only the desired plants could obviously yield far more than could be gathered in the wild. But they did require care, and hence a permanent settlement was developed, usually one where a supplement of water was available. Soon after 10000 BC stone mortars (grinders) appeared, indicating that the grain was ground into flour and that it helped support a population beginning to grow well beyond what could be sustained by hunting and gathering.

By about 7000 BC there were large and numerous storage pits for grain, and clay pots for the same purpose and for storing and carrying water. By this time cultivated wheat, barley, and peas had evolved into more productive forms than their wild ancestors, probably through purposeful selection of the best seeds by the cultivators. Sheep, goats, and dogs were domesticated instead of being hunted, and in the case of dogs, used as hunting assistants. A thousand years later cattle and pigs had joined the list of domesticates. By about 4000 BC or slightly earlier agricultural techniques were advanced enough and populations large enough to allow the expansion of settlements into the different environment of the Tigris-Euphrates lowland, and somewhat later to the Indus valley in what is now Pakistan. Most of these areas were desert or near-desert, but the river floodplains, with their fertile soils and long growing seasons of high temperatures, were very productive if they could be given water through controlled irrigation. Both rivers are fed by rains and melting snow in their mountain source ar-

eas, and are thus subject to seasonal flooding, which had to be protected against. Techniques of irrigation and flood control were developed at about the same time in Egypt. The names of the cities supported by the newly productive agriculture are recorded in the world's first written texts, scratched on clay tablets while they were still wet: Ur, Eridu, Nippur, and others.

The Neolithic revolution was completed with the development of metalworking and the production of bronze tools and weapons. In Mesopotamia by about 4000 BC successive experiments mixing copper with tin and lead in varying proportions produced bronze, which made all these innovations possible, including the division of labor whereby some people were able to pursue non-farm occupations such as smelting and working metals. Perhaps through trade, agricultural and irrigation techniques spread east from Mesopotamia and western Iran, and by about 3500 BC were fully developed in eastern Iran, Afghanistan, and the fringes of the Indus valley. By or before 3000 BC irrigated agriculture was established on the floodplain of the Indus and its major tributaries, where the first true cities of monsoon Asia arose, growing out of Neolithic villages and towns. There and in Mesopotamia and Egypt cities had bureaucrats, tax collectors, priests, metalworkers, scribes, schools, and traffic problems, almost all the features of our own times.

In mainland Southeast Asia, the other equally early hearth of agriculture, upland fringes of river valleys and areas along the coast had probably begun to practice farming soon after 10000 BC. On the coast, gathering and early cultivation could be supplemented by fishing and by collecting from shellfish beds. This is an area of warm temperatures, ample rainfall, and an unbroken growing season. Rice and several tropical root crops such as taro and yams were native there in wild form. Root crops are easily cultivated in this tropical climate by setting cuttings in the ground. Rice was probably domesticated somewhere to this area. Unlike the dry Middle East, the constant humidity and high temperatures meant that no organic remains lasted very long, and we thus cannot date any of these developments accurately. But stone tools and the evidence from charcoal fires suggest that by at least 8000 BC, in what is now northern Vietnam, local people had moved from gathering to agriculture. By about 4000 BC, as in Mesopotamia, bronze objects had begun to appear there and in nearby northern Thailand (although this was long before the Thais, migrating south from south China, occupied the area). Chickens and pigs, both native to mainland Southeast Asia, are also identifiable at these sites, and at one there is a large cemetery, suggesting a large population. Later, perhaps by about 2000 BC, agriculture, by then further evolved, moved down from the early upland sites to the fertile floodplains of the great Southeast Asia rivers, Irrwaddy (in Burma), Mekong, and others, a move which paralleled the earlier one in Mesopotamia.

Most of the modern inhabitants of Southeast Asia came originally from what is now China, including Tibet, many thousands of years ago, although they surely interbred with other people already there. It seems to have been other waves of migrants from the Chinese course area that produced the people called Malays, who became the dominant inhabitants of the Malay Peninsula, what is now Indonesia, and the Philippines. Ethnically and physically the varied Malay people are broadly similar, speaking related languages and sharing a generally common culture, but they did not penetrate beyond what is now eastern Indonesia. The areas east of there belong within Oceania, outlined above as Melanesia, Micronesia, and Polynesia. As they migrated south and east, the Malays brought agriculture and domesticated animals with them. The fertile volcanic island of Java came to support by far the greatest concentration of population.

INDIA (SOUTH ASIA)

The Indus civilization collapsed by about 2000 BC, but we do not know for sure who its people were. We cannot read the script they wrote on clay tablets, but it seems likely that they were relatively dark-skinned ancestors of the present inhabitants of southern India. Beginning about 1700 BC or slightly later, the north was invaded over several centuries by a lighter-skinned central Asian or Iranian people who called themselves Aryans, speaking an early form of Sanskrit, the ancestor of the modern languages of the north, and through its Iranian (Persian) connection also those of modern Europe. In the years following 2000 BC these Indo-European people, as they are called, migrated both east into India and west into what is now Greece and Turkey from an original homeland probably in what is now Iran, bringing their language with them. In India they intermarried with the people already there, but although they remained a minority their military skills conquered the north, while mountain barriers and southern resistance kept them largely out of the south. The new rulers of the north evolved the religion of Hinduism, a blend of the ideas of the Indus civilization with those brought in from Iran, centered on the supreme gods Vishnu, Brahma, and Shiva, with many lesser gods, but basically monotheistic (one god) in its belief in a single creative principle and the sanctity of all life, or the great chain of being. According to Hindus, the faithful following of *dharma* or duty produces a good *karma* or character, which in turn determines identity in the next re-birth; a bad karma may result in re-birth as an animal or insect, while a good one can even result in escape from the endless cycle of re-birth to a bodiless reunion with the godhead, or *moksha*, equivalent to the Buddhist *nirvana*. Hinduism spread to all parts of India and remains the dominant religion even in the south.

Buddhism is a later offshoot from Hinduism that was developed in the sixth century BC, sharing most of its beliefs but centered on denial of worldly preoccupations, following the four noble truths announced by the Buddha: Life is full of pain, suffering, and impermanence. This is caused by desire. To end suffering, end desire. To end desire, end worldly attachments and live a charitable and holy life. Buddhism gradually was reabsorbed into Hinduism by the thirteenth century AD, and the few remaining Buddhists were slaughtered by the Islamic invaders early in that century. By the beginning of the Christian era Buddhism had spread to Southeast Asia and China, and from China to Korea and Japan, although it was later extinguished in the land of its birth. Most Indians, both Hindus and Muslims (followers of Islam) take religion far more seriously than any people elsewhere, and religion is still a major part of South Asian life.

The Mauryan empire, which ruled the north from 322 BC to about 180 BC, was followed by fresh invasions by several central Asian groups including those who formed the Kushan kingdom which ruled north India from about 100 BC to about 200 AD. Before the Mauryas Alexander the Great of Macedon had also invaded India and left behind several Greek kingdoms in the northwest. Trade with the Mediterranean continued for several centuries thereafter, and early Christianity was carried to India in the first century AD. After the fall of the Kushans India relapsed into its more normal pattern of separate regional kingdoms until the rise of the Gupta empire which ruled the north from about 320 AD to about 550 AD. It was destroyed by new invaders from central Asia, probably Iranians, one more in the long succession of ethnically and culturally different outsiders drawn into India through its western passes and woven into the Indian fabric to form a hybrid population and culture. Outside groups however never conquered the south, which still speaks languages of the north. In the sixth century BC, the island of Ceylon (now Sri Lanka) off the southern tip of India was settled by the Sinhalese from north India largely displacing the original less technically developed inhabitants, the Veddas. Later Dravidian migrants from south India, the Tamils, settled in the north of the island, with their Hindu faith, but the Sinhalese had earlier been converted to Buddhism, which remains the major religion.

Beginning in the twelfth century AD India was again invaded, this time by Afghans and Turks from central Asia who brought with them the crusading religion of Islam. They were fiercely intolerant of other religions, and forced many Indians to convert to Islam while oppressing Hindus, but never conquered the south. The Delhi Sultanate, which ruled most of the north from 1206 to 1526, was replaced by the Mughal Dynasty which conquered Delhi and established a new empire that lasted into the new colonial order established by the British. The Mughals also came from central Asia, but were the carriers of a largely Persian culture as well as of Islam. Originally tolerant of Hindus, still the great majority of Indians, they later became less so and thus helped to sow the seeds of antagonism between Hindus and Muslims, although they never conquered the south. By 1600 the population of undivided India was about 100 million.

The last invaders of India were the British, never more than 100,000 in total but the dominant group after about 1800 out of a population which reached 200 million by 1800 and 400 million by the end of the Colonial period. The British transformed the country in partnership with many Indians. Some of the British married Indian wives and produced a new hybrid group of Anglo-Indians, while building a huge rail network and stimulating the beginnings of industrialization. Their early coastal trade bases: Calcutta, Bombay, and Madras, became the biggest cities in India, as Calcutta and Bombay still are, while Madras was overtaken after independence in 1947 by the capital of Delhi-New Delhi, a twin city where the Mughals had also ruled. South India had been ruled in Mughal times, as under the Delhi Sultanate, by many independent kingdoms, and it still preserves a distinct regional culture, distinguished from the north also by its different languages, collectively known as Dravidian. Modern India is thus a mixture of peoples, languages, and religions, more diverse than in any modern state. At independence in 1947, India was partitioned at Muslim insistence into Pakistan in the northwest, where there was a Muslim majority, and, later, Bangladesh in the east, also a largely Muslim area, leaving what is now the Republic of India occupying the largest share of the sub-continent. South Asia as a whole now has a population well over one billion, larger even than China's.

The small Himalayan kingdom of Nepal, independent since 1923, also has a mixed population, including Tibetans with both Hinduism and Buddhism practiced. The neighboring kingdoms of Bhutan and Sikkim remain under Indian supervision while nominally independent. There is a long list of people called "tribals," by no means all of them primitive and some highly developed. "Tribals" are concentrated in mountainous central India and along the mountain borders of India, Pakistan, and Bangladesh.

Ceylon (called Sri Lanka since 1975) had never been politically united with India but in larger terms belongs within Indian culture, except for its continued adherence to Buddhism. It became independent in 1948, but then was torn by violence between the dominant Sinhalese and the minority Tamils, about 18 percent of the population. Roughly half of the Tamils have lived there for some 2000 years after migrating from nearby south India. The other half are more recent arrivals in the nineteenth century who came to work on the tea and rubber plantations, and remain an underprivileged group. Tamil terrorism in support of their demands for regional autonomy has been met by harsh reprisal in an atmosphere close to civil war.

SOUTHEAST ASIA

The label of Southeast Asia is a term of convenience rather than one that suggests regional coherence. It includes nine modern states: Burma, Thailand, Laos, Cambodia (Kampuchea), Vietnam, Malaysia, Singapore, Indonesia, and the Philippines, which have never operated as a political unit. Most of them also contain a variety of minority peoples, and most won their independence from Western colonialism only after the World War II. Burma (which the military dictatorship there renamed Myanmar) is dominated by the lowland Burmese who settled in the valley of the Irrawaddy before recorded history. Burma contains in its hill and mountain fringes a number of separate people who have similar origins in southwestern China but different cultures and languages; Shans, Kachins, and Karens are the largest such groups, in the past beyond the control of the Burmese government and now in chronic rebellion. The traditional capital was at Mandalay (earlier at Paga) in the mid-Irrawaddy valley. Thailand (formerly Siam) is numerically more dominated by the lowland Thais of the Menam or Chao Praya River, even though they seem to have become the main inhabitants more recently than the Burmese; they too came originally from south China, but probably in successive waves over many centuries, the last being in the thirteenth century AD. Laos is a small mountain country chronically split into factions, but the inhabitants are preponderantly Thai. Cambodia is what remains of the once far more extensive Khmer empire, which included much of what is now southern and central Thailand and southern Vietnam. The Khmers also originated in south China, following the valley of the Mekong River.

The Vietnamese are closely related to the Chinese and were for a thousand years incorporated into the Chinese empire. They reclaimed their independence in the tenth century AD and have always been a separate people with their own language. Their early center was in the valley of the Red River with their capital at Hanoi, but beginning in the thirteenth century AD they extended their occupation and rule southward, at the expense of the Khmers, and by the fifteenth century were the dominant inhabitants of the lower course of the Mekong River and its delta in southern Vietnam. The western mountain borders of Vietnam have long been occupied by a variety of different peoples, called by the French, who ruled Vietnam from 1886 to 1954, simply "Montagnards." Malaya (known as Malaysia since 1963), occupying the tail of mainland Southeast Asia, was until recently thinly settled by Malays, with the towns being populated primarily with people who originated in China. As a British colony, Malaya boomed after 1890, when the discovery of tin and the developed of new rubber plantations produced major exports. As such, Malaya attracted large numbers of migrant Chinese and Indians as laborers, who became a dominant presence in the country. Chinese entrepreneurs prospered, handling much of Malaya's trade with Indonesia. Following Malaya's independence in 1957, Singapore was separated from the new state in 1965 and at the same time other formerly British areas in northern Borneo were added, to form the new state of Malaysia, primarily to reduce the proportion of Chinese and to give Malays a stronger majority. North Borneo includes some Chinese, but also more tribal groups such as Dyaks, Bugis, and others. Independent Singapore remains as a tiny city-state, 80 percent Chinese and 8 percent Indian.

Indonesia is both the largest and the most diverse country of Southeast Asia, composed of some 3000 islands inhabited by a great variety of people and never governed as a unit until the Dutch colonial rulers took over most of it at the end of the nineteenth century. The island of Java has always been by far the most populous and most developed; its language, Javanese, was not shared by the other islands, although its Malay culture was. Cultural influences from classical India were formative from the third century BC to the fourteenth century AD and survive in the Hindu-Buddhist religion of the island of Bali. From the fifteenth century Islam began to spread into what is now Indonesia via the trade routes from India, and is now the official state religion, but Christianity was established especially in the outer islands beyond Java by Portuguese, Dutch, and American missionaries, and original animism remains vigorous in many areas.

Modern Indonesia includes the large islands of Sumatra and Borneo (except for its northern coast), Celebes or Sulawesi farther east, the several small islands of the Muluccas or Spice Islands beyond, and many others directly east of Java, including Bali, each of these with its own original language. In 1960 the new Indonesian state, independent of Holland from 1949, forcibly took over the western half of New Guinea and named it Irian, thus adding a veritable welter of unrelated aborigines in hundreds of different tribal groupings. To try to give the new state some coherence, the Indonesian government created a new national language, Indonesian, based almost entirely on Malay, long the universal trade language of maritime Southeast Asia. It was taught in all schools, and most people in Indonesia necessarily became bi-lingual, retaining their own languages among themselves. The capital remained at Djakarta in west Java, where the Dutch had ruled. Java has long been extremely densely settled but also highly productive with its rich volcanic soils and unbroken growing season. The other islands, except for parts of Sumatra and Bali, are by contrast thinly populated. The Javanese may be regarded as a single people, but the rest of Indonesia, with a total population now of about 200 million, is made up of a very long list of separate cultural and language groups, including tribal groups.

The Philippines is even more fragmented than Indonesia—some 7000 islands rather than only 3000—and thus preserves many regional cultural differences. But conquest by Spain in the sixteenth century, and by the United States in the twentieth, have brought nearly universal conversion to Christianity, a high literacy rate, and the rise of strong national consciousness, despite the survival of many small tribal groups and their separate cultures in the mountainous areas, even on the main island of Luzon, where Manila, the capital is also located. There is a somewhat larger community of Muslims on the southernmost island of Mindanao, a group known as Moros, relics of the early spread of Islam. Otherwise English has replaced Spanish as the major common language, although the official state language is Tagalog, a Malay-related language of lowland Luzon.

CHINA

This most populous country in the world is dominated by ethnic Chinese called Han, but also includes a great number of ethnic and cultural minorities, altogether 6 percent of the total. The main non-Han groups are the Tibetans, Mongols, and Uighurs (in Sinkiang-Kinjiang), but others include the Manchus of Manchuria, the Khirghiz and Kazaka of Kinjiang, and a great number of groups scattered around south and southwest China too numerous to mention. The latter were the original inhabitants of most of south China but have been pushed off the best lands and into the mountains by the advancing wave of Han Chinese migration from the north, spread over the period from the fourth century BC to the present. There were several centers of early civilization in China where settled agriculture, bronze-making, and writing were gradually evolved. The best preserved evidence is in the dry north, in the middle Yellow River valley, where a fully developed late Neolithic site has been excavated at Banpo near modern Sian (Xian). Southern sites are less well preserved in a warm humid climate, but equally early developments with some archeological evidence have been found in the lower Yangtze valley and south of there. By about 2000 BC the Black Pottery Culture or Lung Shan in the north was building cities with pounded earth walls, making bronze, and producing early writing, while such developments were also present in the south.

Given the early evolution of agriculture, bronze, and domesticated animals in adjacent Southeast Asia, it seems probable that these techniques spread early into south China and were diffused northward from there. This included rice, the water buffalo, pigs, and chickens, all native to mainland Southeast Asia. There are no major mountain barriers between Thailand or Vietnam and south China, and until more modern times it is best to think of this area as a single cultural unit. It is hard to imagine Chinese agriculture without even one of these imports from Southeast Asia, something which strengthens the case for origins in south China as early as those in the north. By 1600 BC the first authenticated Chinese dynasty, the Shang, had emerged in the Yellow River valley, leaving behind written records using characters close to those still in use. Bronze making reached a height of perfection never surpassed elsewhere, and the Shang capitals, which were frequently moved, became true cities. Shang technology was probably matched in all respects in central and south China, which belonged to different cultures. The Shang were overthrown in 1027 BC by the Chou (Zhen) who founded a new dynasty which lasted until 221 BC when it was in turn overthrown by the Ch'in (Qin) conquest. The last several centuries of the Chou however were marked by the rise of rival regional states in north, central, and south China as central control weakened. This was the period of Confucius (c. 551–c. 79 BC), who aimed to treat the chaos of his time by a return to order, following what he called the rules of an earlier golden era. His rough contemporary Lao Tzu rejected the Confucian prescriptions in favor of a philosophy based on inaction and contemplation, the heart of the religion he founded known as Taoism (Daoism), or simply "The Way."

The Ch'in conquered all of the other rival states in a series of lightening campaigns culminating in 221 BC, and imposed its own imperial model on what had heretofore been a wide variety of regional cultures, including both spoken and written languages. Until this occurred, one could not speak of China or the Chinese as a single people but as a collection of separate groups united for the first time by the Ch'in as the first all-China empire. The Ch'in conquered much of the south plus northern Vietnam, but its rule was oppressive and it fell in a series of revolts, to be succeeded by the Han dynasty in 202 BC. Under the Han, which ruled until 220 AD, most of the area now within China's modern borders was conquered, and the movement of the Chinese southward acquired new momentum. The Chinese still call themselves "people of Han." The Han empire included southern Manchuria, settled in large numbers by Han Chinese, northern Vietnam, parts of Inner Mongolia, and the far western desert of Sinkiang (Xinjiang), through which the silk road ran, guarded by Han watchtowers and garrisons. To begin with, most of the south was still occupied by non-Han people, but over the following centuries they were displaced by the movement of Hans from the north, especially after the fall of the dynasty in 220 AD and the invasion of the north by barbarians from the steppe. The Han census recorded a total population of 60 million, but the real total was almost certainly at least 80. We have only guesses for earlier periods, but the population of the whole of China in Shang times has been estimated at 5–10 million, and by mid-Chou at 20–30 million.

Buddhism had spread to China under the Han, via central Asia, and in the "time of troubles" after 220 its other-worldly message of salvation attracted many followers, although in many cases it blended with the Taoism already there. With the revival of empire under the T'ang dynasty (618–907) there was new resistance to this alien religion with its denial of the material world, and in the ninth century the T'ang government confiscated the large Buddhist landholdings as a threat to the state. From that time on Buddhism remained a small minority religion, merged with Taoism, in a society where Confucianism was again dominant. The T'ang reclaimed the empire won by the Han, and established new contacts with central Asia, while briefly occupying Tibet, although Chinese control there was not achieved until the eighteenth century. Korea, occupied as part of the Han empire, was not obliged to accept status as a tributary state, as was Vietnam after the fall of the T'ang. The Sung (Song) dynasty (960–1279) continued this arrangement but gave up the costly and unprofitable effort to hold Inner Mongolia, Sinkiang, and Tibet—until it was overwhelmed by the Mongol invasion which also conquered most of the rest of Asia and swept even into Europe. By 1350 the hated Mongols had largely been driven out of China, and the Ming dynasty (1368–1644) reaffirmed the traditional Chinese system, as did its successor the Ch'ing (Qing-1644–1911). Population totals reached 100 million in the Sung, 150 in the Ming, and 450 by the end of the Ch'ing.

With the fall of the Ch'ing in 1911, China lapsed into the chaos of the warlord years, briefly and incompletely relieved by the nationalist government from its capital at Nanking (Nanjing) for the ten years between 1927 and the full-scale Japanese attack on China in 1937. The long and bloody anti-Japanese war helped to destroy the nationalist government and to build up support for the Chinese Communist Party with its effective guerrilla resistance to the hated Japanese in north China. The Japanese had taken Manchuria in 1931 and developed its rich resources to create the largest industrial complex in East Asia, but Manchuria had been massively settled by Han Chinese from the late nineteenth century and was reclaimed by the communist guerrillas at the end of the war. The remnants of the nationalist government and its army, defeated by the communist advance into south China, fled to the offshore island of Taiwan, where the nationalists still rule.

Taiwan had been settled by Han Chinese from the early seventeenth century, slowly displacing the aboriginal occupants who now live largely on reservations, distantly related to but basically different from the Han. Taiwan had been ruled as part of the Japanese empire from 1895, but under nationalist control it experienced vigorous economic growth on foundations laid by the Japanese in industry, agriculture, and communications. Meanwhile the new communist government on the mainland declared the founding of the People's Republic in 1949, and announced a new policy toward the many non-Han minorities, who were to be given recognition as members of the greater Chinese family. Tibet, brutally re-occupied in the 1950s, Sinkiang, and Inner Mongolia were designated as "Autonomous Areas," but the hand of the Chinese state was strong and the people of these areas continued to be dominated by Han Chinese, who held all power together with their local collaborators. Smaller areas in mountainous south China where non-Hans remained numerically important were designated as "Autonomous Regions," including large sections of Kiangsi (Jiangxi) Province. But "autonomy" remained a cruel joke, and there were pressures on all non-Hans to conform to the standard Chinese way if they were to succeed in the new society.

One reason for Chinese reassertion of control was that most of these areas, especially Tibet, Sinkiang, and Inner Mongolia, lay along the country's international borders and hence had some strategic significance, especially after China and Russia became adversaries rather than allies in the late 1950s. Another reason was the new government's determination to reclaim all of the territory held by the great Chinese empires of the past, and thus to establish its credentials as their successor. Chinese behavior in Tibet, where there has been an effort to suppress Tibetan Buddhism and to root out other elements of Tibetan identity, has been so brutal, especially toward Tibetan protests, that it has attracted international censure. In Inner Mongolia, the tide of Han Chinese settlers has engulfed the remaining Mongol population and now outnumbers it by at least twenty to one, replacing the traditional pastoral nomadic economy with commercial agriculture and industrialization. Outer Mongolia, where Mongols are still the (slight) majority, declared its independence from China in 1921, but there too the trend is toward agriculture and industry rather than the traditional pastoral nomadism. In Sinkiang, Chinese technicians, managers, and political bosses are almost as numerous as the indigenous Uighurs, and the capital at Urumchi (Ulumuqi) has become a major industrial center. Wherever a technically more advanced, more powerful, and more numerous people has become dominant over another population, it tends to overwhelm the latter and to force it to accept the rule and ways of the dominant group. (We have ample evidence in the fate of the North American Indians.) Non-Hans are about 6 percent of the total Chinese population, but the numbers have become vaguer as many Hans marry non-Hans in order to get the benefits reserved for the latter. Muslims are listed as by far the largest minority, although nearly all are in fact Han Chinese. Total population of China doubled between 1949 and 1982 and is now over one billion.

KOREA

The Korean people came originally from eastern Siberia and northern Manchuria, as their spoken language, unrelated to Chinese but akin to Japanese, suggests. We do not know when this migration into the mountainous Korean peninsula may have taken place, but it was well before the beginning of any written records. By 2000 BC agriculture and domesticated animals spread to Korea from China; bronze-making was diffused from China somewhat later. The early Koreans were tribal peoples dependent on hunting, gathering, and fishing. As their culture merged into farming, permanent villages and towns arose, and bronze weapons and ornaments began to be made. Northern Korea, adjacent to Manchuria, was incorporated in the Han empire and settled significantly by Han Chinese, who introduced most elements of Chinese culture, at least to the Korean upper classes. Chinese influences continued after the fall of the Han dynasty, but Korea divided into three rival kingdoms which were later unified by the state of Koryo (the origin of the name Korea) in the tenth century. Buddhism had spread to Korea from China during the Han dynasty and spread widely, but after the founding of the Yi dynasty in 1392 Confucianism was favored and Korean Buddhism declined. Korea, especially its upper class culture, became a faithful echo of China while retaining its Korean distinctiveness. Koreans referred to China as "Elder Brother" and looked up to the Chinese model in all things, producing their own accomplishments in ceramics, printing, and the early use of moveable type as well as a magnificent art in the Chinese style but recognizably Korean.

The early tribes at the beginning of Korean history slowly merged into a single Korean people, and no traces of any early distinctions remain. Korea was conquered by the Mongols and was terribly exploited, including the forcing of its army and navy to aid in the Mongol conquest of China and its fruitless attempt to conquer Japan. After the Mongol collapse, Korea slowly recovered but then had to fight a Japanese invasion by the warlord Hideyoshi from 1592 to 1598 which devastated the country. There were some Korean successes against the Japanese, but Hideyoshi died in 1598 and his troops quickly returned to Japan. The Yi dynasty slowly lost effectiveness and was crippled by factional fighting among different upper class groups. It stubbornly resisted foreign pressures to open the country to trade and clung to traditional Korean culture, trying to prevent the disruption that inevitably comes with change. In the end, the Japanese took over Korea in 1895 and ruled in oppressively until their defeat in the second world war in 1945. Korea's population grew from an estimated five million in 1669 to 9 million by 1800 and continued to rise slowly during the nineteenth and twentieth centuries to a 1995 total of over 60 million in north and south Korean combined.

In 1945, the newly independent Korea was partitioned between a Russian puppet government in the north and an American puppet regime in the South, as a reflection of the Cold War. This led directly to war when the North invaded the South in 1950, a campaign that was halted just short of success by an American-dominated United Nations force in aid of their South Korean allies, who drove slowly north, devastating the country yet again as they advanced. A stalemate was reached, and the armistice signed in 1953 returned matters almost exactly to where they had been before, the country still divided roughly along the 38th parallel. Since then the South, still a police state, has seen strong economic growth, while the even more repressive communist government in the North was less successful. Dangerous tensions between the two halves of the artificially divided country remained.

JAPAN

As an island country—four main islands and many smaller ones—120 miles off the coast of Korea at the nearest point, Japan has preserved a separate identity and its culture has remained a distinctive variant from those on the Asian mainland. Like the Koreans, the present-day Japanese people can be traced back to migrants from northeast Asia or eastern Siberia, speaking an Altaic language related to Korean but not to Chinese. There were probably, however, some movements of people into Japan from south China and perhaps from the south Pacific. Paleolithic cultures were widespread in Japan by at least 50000 BC, and by about 6000 BC a variety of Neolithic cultures had arisen, of which the best known is called Jomon. Some Jomon groups had begun to practice a rudimentary agriculture about 300 BC, presumably diffused from China via Korea. They made cord-marked pottery, lived in sunken pit shelters, and engaged in hunting, gathering, and fishing. But the direct and principal ancestors of the modern Japanese did not begin to arrive, again via Korea, until some time between 300 BC and 200 AD, in successive waves. Other and unrelated groups already inhabiting the Japanese islands, including those of the Jomon culture, were absorbed by conquest and intermarriage, and the survivors of the Japanese invasion were slowly driven northward. The principal group among the aborigines was the Ainu, related to the Causasian family and with more facial and body hair than most East Asians. The Ainu seem to have been the principal opponents of the advancing wave of Japanese invaders as they moved north from their original beachheads in the southern island of Kyushu, closest to Korea, and by about 500 AD had established their chief center on the mainland of Honshu, on the Yamato Plain between modern Osaka, Nara, and Kyoto. For a long time the boundary with the Ainu lay just north of Kyoto along the line of Lake Biwa, although there was doubtless some interbreeding that may help to explain the greater hairiness of most Japanese than other East Asians.

Meanwhile the Jomon culture was progressively displaced beginning in the third century BC by an early agricultural culture called Yayoi. It is likely that the transition into settled agriculture was hastened by the arrival of the Japanese via Korea, bringing with them other new techniques used by the Yayoi people: the potter's wheel, cultivated rice, irrigation, and the beginnings of bronze and then iron tools and weapons, all diffused from China. A few Chinese coins found at Yayoi sites show that there was trade with China, but we do not know for sure who the Yayoi people were, most probably a mix of the early Japanese and those already there. By the third century AD, with the Japanese migration largely complete, Yayoi sites included large earthen mounds over the tombs of prominent men, a practice that seems clearly to have been derived from earlier Korean models. Much of Yayoi culture, and its people, may most accurately be seen as provincial Korean. By the fifth century iron swords and armor appeared that were similar to or identical with Korean equivalents, as were the jeweled crowns and other ornaments found in some of the tombs. Houses were now raised off the ground, agriculture was becoming more productive with the help of iron tools, and pottery had become harder and more highly fired. Kyushu and Honshu had reached the technological levels achieved in China some 2000 years earlier and in Korea perhaps 1000 years thereafter. But Japan still lacked writing and we have no evidence of true cities or what the population totals may have been.

The earliest written accounts of Japanese and Chinese, compiled in the third century AD, describe the route via Korea. The country was shown as divided into a hundred "kingdoms"—probably better called "clans"—of about a thousand households each. The earliest Japanese written accounts, using the characters adopted from China, did not appear until the eighth century, strikingly late. They are a mixture of pious and often contradictory myths, especially for the early periods, with some more factual accounts of later events. They recount the story of the divine creation of the Japanese islands, and the descent of the Japanese emperor from Amterasu, the sun goddess. We can infer that by the fifth century the earlier clan basis of Japanese society was giving way to an infant state called Yamato, on the Yamato plain, a label that the Japanese came to apply to themselves as a nation. The emperor was both a temporal and a spiritual ruler who presided over the worship of the sun goddess and the forces of nature. In later times this nature worship came to be called Shinto, or the "Way of the Gods," but it was never a fully developed religion and had no coherent philosophy or moral code.

Immigration from Korea continued into the ninth century, and until the sixth century the Japanese retained a foothold on the southeast Korean coast. There may have been some form of alliance between groups on both sides of the Tsushima Straits, which now separate the two countries. Large numbers of Koreans lived in Japan, where they seem to have dominated or at least been prominent in Japanese society. A genealogical record of 815 AD, one of the earliest Japanese written texts, listed over a third of the aristocracy as claiming Korean or Chinese ancestry, clearly a mark of distinction. Koreans also served in Japan as skilled artisans, metallurgists, and other technologists. For some centuries there seem to have been periodic raids in both directions across the Straits of Tsushima, but by the fifth century such violent interactions faded. Those remaining in Japan continued to move northward, mainly against the Ainu, who were slowly overcome and now live as a tiny and dwindling group on reservations in the northernmost island of Hokkaido.

Buddhism came to Japan from Korea in the sixth century and brought with it further elements of Chinese and Korean culture. The pace and scope of such influences accelerated on a major scale with the rise of the T'ang dynasty of China in 618. The T'ang model of cultural brilliance powerfully attracted the Japanese, who had by now reached a level in their own development where they were ready to move from a tribal and pre-literature state to a Chinese-style civilization. Successive embassies were sent from Japan to China beginning early in the seventh century, to bring back all they could learn about Chinese ways, including writing and city-building.

Japan is smaller than France or California and somewhat larger than the British Isles, but it is mainly covered with mountains. Settlement has thus remained heavily concentrated on the narrow coastal plain between modern Tokyo and Osaka, in a series of disconnected basins over an area roughly equivalent to the coastal corridor between Boston and Washington, D.C. in the United States. In practice this makes Japan an even smaller country since so much of it, in the mountains, is thinly populated. Hokkaido, the northernmost island, was occupied by the Japanese very late, mainly after World War I. Mountains retarded Japanese economic development and political unification came late, not until 1600, after many centuries of disunity and chronic fighting among rival regional groups. Agriculture too has been hampered by the shortage of level land. Japan's great agricultural advantage is its mild maritime climate, the gift of the surrounding sea, which keeps it humid, mild in winter, and largely free of the droughts that plague north China. The mountains are steep and come down close to the sea so that nowhere are there extensive plains where soil can build up. Fish from the surrounding seas have always formed an important part of the diet, especially convenient since the bulk of the population lives close to the coast. The Chinese, in their superior attitude toward other peoples, called the Japanese "hairy sea dwarfs," since they were also generally shorter than the Chinese norm (perhaps the result of a different diet, lower in meat); the "sea" is a reference to the highly successful Japanese piracy along the coasts of China.

Beginning in 710, a Chinese-style capital city was built at Nara, midway on the Yamato Plain, a direct copy of the T'ang capital, and including many Buddhist temples, the first real city in Japan. This was still a small country, and over half of the original plan for Nara was never built. A Chinese-style law code was also issued, and a census taken, but the results it reported were not clear. In 794 a new emperor began the building of a new capital at modern Kyoto (then called Heian), also on the Chinese model, as its checkerboard pattern still shows. The Japanese, despite their admiration of Chinese civilization, altered that system of government wherever necessary to fit Japan's quite different circumstances. But on the whole they successfully transplanted Chinese culture on a major scale, including T'ang music and dance, architecture, gardens, and the tea ceremony, most of these things long since gone in China. If you want to get a glimpse of T'ang China you must go to Japan, where these and other adoptions have been carefully preserved.

One important difference between Japan and China was the persistence in Japan of an hereditary and privileged aristocracy, as in Korea, where China had long before abolished it and set up a system of competitive examinations as a basis for selecting officials. Officials in Korea and Japan came only from the aristocracy. For other reasons, Japanese art, architecture, and literature slowly diverged to some extent from their Chinese origins, as was only to be expected. Japan also produced a number of outstanding women writers, including Lady Murasaki, author of the world's first psychological novel, *The Tale of Genji* written about 1000 AD. Court women, such as Murasaki was, where literate, in both Chinese and the soon-developed Japanese phonetic system called *kana,* which represented the sounds of spoken Japanese. But the splendor of court life at Kyoto (Heian) was limited to a fortunate few. Most of the Japanese remained poor villagers, with limited exchange through barter, and many, perhaps most of them were, in effect, serfs. This may help also to explain the relatively slow movement of Japanese northward beyond Kyoto, not only because of Ainu resistance but because northern Japan was not a desirable place to live during this period. The Japanese had arrived at the sub-tropical island of Kyushu, and southern or western Honshu was not dramatically different. Northern Honshu, let alone Hokkaido, was cold and snowy. Japanese culture had adapted to a mild winter climate with hot summers. Their traditional houses could be opened to the breezes on all sides by sliding panels, there was minimal provision for heating, and people wore loose-fitting clothes, although all of this could be related, as some argue, to cultural or migratory influences from south China or the south Pacific.

The spread of Buddhism led to the building of many large monasteries as well as temples, and armed monks began to take part in fighting rival groups. Japanese Buddhism moved far from the Buddha's message of non-violence, and acquired magic elements such as the recitation of the Buddha's name as a means of salvation. At the same time, Japan became torn by warfare between rival secular groups. This was the age of the samurai or warriors, who destroyed the rule of Heian and set up successive military regimes headed by a *shogun,* who claimed to be the emperor's military lieutenant but was in fact the real power. The chronic fighting came to a climax in the civil wars of the sixteenth century, but was finally ended by the victory of a new shogunate, the Tokugawa, in 1600. The Tokugawa shoguns largely unified the country for the first time but tried to suppress change of any kind as threatening their feudal-style rule. Nevertheless pressures for change built up, and by the 1850's were ready to break out as trade had thrived and merchants had grown newly prosperous. In 1853, the U.S. government sent Matthew Perry to demand free trade access to Japan. His mission, resulting in a commercial treaty, sparked a new wave of change, and in 1868 a largely nonviolent revolution toppled the Tokugawa and put in power a new group of radical reformers who were determined to save Japan from western pressures by building up its military and by pushing wholesale westernization as a source of strength.

This change was called the Meiji Restoration, from the title of the new boy emperor, who in fact he remained, as in the past, an essentially powerless symbol, as the emperor still is today. Under the direction of the new Meiji era leaders, Japan quickly industrialized and became a major world power, defeating China in 1894 (and acquiring Korea and Taiwan as a result), and Russia in 1904. Japan was now acknowledged by the Western powers as an equal, but Western sentiment began to turn against the Japanese as pride in their military successes and their growing ambition led them to make plans for the conquest of China, beginning with Manchuria in 1931, and leading gradually to an all-out confrontation with the United States and Britain at Pearl Harbor and Singapore in 1941. World War II destroyed most of Japan's cities and factories, as well as killing over three and a half million Japanese, soldiers, sailors, and civilians, including those who died in the nuclear bombing of Hiroshima and Nagasaki in the closing days of the war.

The recovery of Japan from such a disaster has been almost miraculously rapid. By 1965 Japan had become the world's third industrial power, thanks to its newly rebuilt factories but even more to the hard work and determination of its people. High quality Japanese goods won buyers all over the world. The American Occupation from 1945 to 1952 helped to push Japan away from militarism and in the direction of American-style democracy, which has struck deep roots in Japan, in part no doubt because rapid economic growth has created a new middle class and because general prosperity means that people are not seeking radical alternatives. Population growth has leveled off, as tends to happen when the survival of children can be assumed and families concentrate instead on providing well for their children. At nearly 130 million, Japan is clearly a dominant country, but the huge increase in population has been accompanied by a steep rise in living standards. The pop-ulation in 1000 AD has been estimated at about 5 million, in the late sixteenth century at 15 million, and by the mid-nine-teenth perhaps 30 million, but at each period most Japanese re-mained poor. Now most Japanese are affluent, and enjoy a wide range of social services plus a highly effective education sys-tem, which in turn is a major key to economic growth. Perhaps Japan's major shortcoming now is its limited living space. Over 80 percent of Japanese live in cities—Tokyo being the world's largest at over 30 million—and most of them live in tiny apart-ments. Space is at a premium, and very few Japanese begin to have the living space many Americans take for granted. The countryside, although very beautiful, tends to be horrendously crowded on weekends and holidays by urbanites anxious for a break. But Japanese know that in other respects they are very well off on any comparative scale.

The remainder of this Asia volume treats in more detail each of the major areas: South Asia, Southeast Asia, China, Korea, and Japan.

ACEHNESE

PRONUNCIATION: AH-cheh-neez
LOCATION: Indonesia (Sumatra)
POPULATION: 2–3 million
LANGUAGE: Acehnese
RELIGION: Islam
RELATED ARTICLES: Vol. 3: Indonesians

¹ INTRODUCTION

Located at the northernmost tip of Sumatra, Aceh has been the region of Indonesia most exposed to influences from the Islamic Middle East and Islamized India. Even the physical appearance of the coastal population reflects this: a great many Acehnese have Arab or Indian features. The Acehnese seem always to have played a key role in the trade linking India and China. Their closest linguistic relatives are the Cham of central Vietnam; their languages preserve a common fund of Austro-Asiatic loanwords that indicate intimate contacts with Mon-Khmer peoples. A network of kindred communities may have run from Vietnam to Sumatra through the Malay Peninsula, particularly as the earliest trade passed over the Isthmus of Kra instead of rounding the peninsula, as it did later.

The most renowned early state recorded in the Acehnese region is Samudra (meaning "ocean," from which the name "Sumatra" probably comes). Still pagan when Marco Polo stopped there in 1292, it was already Muslim in 1323 when the famous Arab traveler Ibn Battuta passed through. Under a new name, Pasai, the kingdom became the model Islamic court in the archipelago. In its immediate vicinity, however, were other independent states: Barus, Daya, Lamri, and Aru. In the territory of Lamri, Sultan Ali Mughayat Shah established the kingdom of Aceh at the beginning of the 16th century. The new power profited from the Portuguese capture of Malacca; Muslim merchants (and later Protestant Dutch and English) sought refuge at Aceh, and the sultanate carried on a holy war against Malacca's new Catholic rulers from 1540 to 1630.

These years, particularly during the reign of the autocratic Sultan Iskandar Muda ("Young Alexander"), constituted Aceh's Golden Age. Acehnese ships carried pepper to ports in the Red Sea, providing half of Europe's supply. Acehnese power extended far south on Sumatra (sultan's viceroys were placed over the Minangkabau, Simalungan Batak, and Karo Batak) and into the Malay peninsula (Kedah, Perak, Johor, and Pahang fell under its sway).

In 1629 an Acehnese armada was destroyed in an attempt to take Malacca; from that point, Acehnese power began a slow decline. Bloody succession struggles led the Acehnese aristocracy to accept a series of female rulers in the 17th century, despite the conflict with Islam's male bias. The power of the central government weakened as that of local lords (*uleebalang*, who controlled river mouths and thus the trade of the interior) grew.

The diffusion of political power to regional overlords did not harm Aceh's economic vitality. Its wealth, particularly in pepper, attracted attacks by foreigners, such as the Americans and French, in the 1820s and 1830s. Because of a mutual defense treaty between Aceh and Britain, the Dutch did not launch a major invasion until 1871. Warfare with the Acehnese lasted from 1873 to 1906 and cost the Dutch much in money and men.

The Indonesian Revolution took a particularly bloody form in Aceh; *ulama* (Muslim religious leaders) directed popular fury against the uleebalang, who were virtually exterminated as a class. In 1953, not wanting to be included with Christian Batak in the province of North Sumatra, Acehnese began a revolt against Jakarta that lasted for 10 years. In the end, the central government granted Aceh the status of "Special Region" (*Daerah Istimewa*), with autonomous jurisdiction over religion, education, and customary law. This special status notwithstanding, Suharto's New Order regime (1966–1998) exploited Aceh's natural resource bounty (natural gas, petroleum, gold, silver, and copper) without benefiting the rural majority of Acehnese, provoking the emergence of a separatist Free Aceh Movement (GAM—Gerakan Aceh Merdeka) that went into armed rebellion in the late 1980s; this in turn was answered by brutal military repression that killed 2,000 Acehnese in 1989–1991 and made thousands of others refugees within their own homeland or in neighboring provinces. The years immediately after the fall of the Suharto regime in 1998 were marked by Acehnese continuing to mobilize to demand autonomy and the central government going back and forth between conceding greater autonomy and resuming military offensives against GAM insurgents.

The guerilla war was again in full swing when a massive earthquake and tsunami devastated Aceh on 26 December 2004, killing 230,000 and leaving over 500,000 homeless. The epicenter of the earthquake was right off Aceh's coast, though the resulting tsunami struck as far as Thailand and Sri Lanka. The catastrophe led GAM and the Indonesian government, under the mediation of Finnish ex-president Martti Ahtisaari, to reach a peace agreement (signed on 15 August 2005). With financial help for reconstruction coming from many foreign governments and organizations, Aceh is recovering. In 2006 the economy began to experience positive growth (7.7%). Aceh now enjoys the expanded autonomy granted in 2002, including the implementation of Sharia (Islamic law), the right to retain 80% of revenues from petroleum and natural gas production and receive foreign direct investment and not via the central government, and a new official name, "Nanggroe Aceh Darussalam" (literally, "The State of Aceh, Abode of Peace," i.e. "domain of Islamic government").

² LOCATION AND HOMELAND

The Acehnese inhabit coastal lands along the northernmost end of Sumatra, as well as river valleys leading into the interior (the high mountains and thick forests of the interior are the home of another ethnicity, the Batak-related Gayo people). Acehnese comprise 50-70% of the population of the Nanggroe Aceh Darussalam, or 2–3 million people. There being no large cities (the capital of Banda Aceh counts only 80,000 inhabitants), the majority of Acehnese live in small towns in the fertile coastal plain, most hugging the modern 600-km (375-mi) road between Banda Aceh and Medan in neighboring North Sumatra province, Indonesia's greatest metropolis west of Jakarta.

³ LANGUAGE

The Acehnese language is related to Malay but is even closer to the Cham languages of central Vietnam. The vocabulary of Acehnese and Cham includes some basic words adopted from

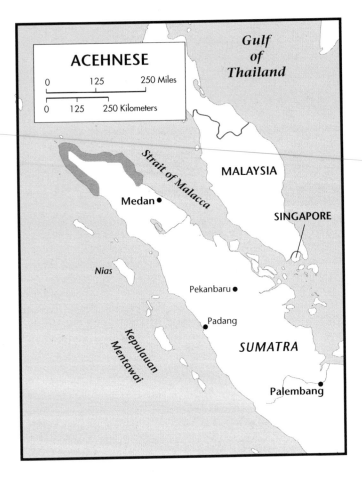

ACEHNESE

0   125   250 Miles

0   125   250 Kilometers

Gulf of Thailand

Strait of Malacca

MALAYSIA

Medan ●

SINGAPORE

Nias

Pekanbaru ●

Padang ●

SUMATRA

Kepulauan Mentawai

Palembang ●

Austro-Asiatic languages (modern representatives of that family are Khmer, Mon, and Vietnamese). Until the 17th century, Acehnese used Malay in Arabic script as their sole written language; in the 17th century they began to produce literature in their own language.

4 FOLKLORE

Traditional Acehnese believe evil spirits reside in forests, swamps, river mouths, and banyan trees. The *jen aphui* (fire spirit) appears as a light in the night. The *sibujang itam* is a coarse, scary, but magically potent being whom one can enlist for evil purposes. The *geunteut* is a giant who squeezes down on sleeping people. The *burong* are women who have died in childbirth. They are clothed in white and have unnaturally long fingernails and a hole in their back. The *burung tujuh* are seven sisters who died in childbirth whose spirits threaten those giving birth.

5 RELIGION

As befits a region long known as the "front porch (*srambi*) of Mecca," the region where all Southeast Asian Muslims used to embark on the Haj (the pilgrimage to Mecca), the Acehnese are regarded as among the most devout Muslims in the archipelago and their culture as the most inseparable from Islam. A saying expresses this: "*adat ngon hukom lagee zat ngon sifeuet,*" meaning, "[Acehnese] custom is to [Islamic] law as the essence is to manifestation." Islamic law (Sharia) influences every aspect of family life: weddings, marital conflicts, civil suits, funerals, and inheritance.

The lowest-level religious court is held after Friday prayer. The Acehnese support the national Islamic political parties such as, formerly, the modernist Muhammadiyah.

The Acehnese are zealous in their observance of three of Islam's five pillars: going on the pilgrimage to Mecca (Hajj); paying the tithe (*zakat*); and fasting (*puasa*) during the month of Ramadan. Many are less consistent in performing the five daily prayers. Pantheistic mysticism has been widespread, and it is common to make pilgrimages of the graves of famous mystics.

Outside the scope of Islamic orthodoxy is the use of magic to ensure success in agriculture and other enterprises. Ritual meals to bless rice cultivation (*kenduri blang*) and fishing (*kenduri laut*) include Islamic elements, such as Arabic prayers and the chanting of the surah "Yasin" from the Qur'an. There is a tradition of female shamanism. *Dukun* (spirit healers) issue *sijunde*, spells that can cause sickness or death or that can counteract the action of other spells. Healing includes exorcistic practices aiming to "cool" the sick person. Dukun also specialize in interpreting dreams and omens.

6 MAJOR HOLIDAYS

See the article entitled **Indonesians**.

7 RITES OF PASSAGE

Rites of passage generally resemble those of the Malays (see **Malays**). A boy's placenta is buried under the spot where rainwater draining from the roof comes down, and a girl's placenta is buried under the entry ladder. Features of the wedding process specific to Acehnese are as follows: the representative (*teulangke*) of the man's side presents the woman's side with gold and other valuables (*kongnarit*); if the latter accepts them, this renders the betrothal binding. In addition, the man's side must deliver a bride-price (*jeunamee*) of 50–100 g (1.75–3.5 oz) of gold; alternatively, the bride-price may be given to the couple later as a *peunalang* to buy a separate house or rice land. Preparatory to the wedding are the *malam berinai*, during which the bride is made as beautiful as possible and the bridal dais is decorated; and the *mandi berlimau*, in which an old woman gives the bride her last bath as a single woman. The procession (*intat linto*) of the groom to the bride's house is accompanied by noisemakers and the chanting of the *Barzanji* and *selawat Nabi* (tales of the life of Muhammad).

Children are buried in their father's family burial place (*bhom*). Modernist Muslims (Muhammadiyah) do not perform the post-funeral prayers for the deceased that others do.

8 INTERPERSONAL RELATIONS

Under the sultanate, the following hierarchy of political units existed: several *gampong* (villages) led by a *keusyik* (*geucik*), grouped into a *mukim* led by an *imeum*. A number of mukim fell under the jurisdiction of an *uleebalang* or, in the capital region, formed into one of three *sagoe* each under a *panglima*, kin of the sultan. Originally, the title *imeum* indicated the head official of a mosque, but its bearers gradually gained worldly power; sultans recognized the more powerful ones as *uleebalang* (regional lords, hereditary, and largely autonomous). The uleebalang appointed and could dismiss the keusyik; the latter was responsible for ensuring village security and prosperity and for arbitrating disputes. In addition, each village had a *teungku* (a person knowledgeable in Islam to head religious observances and take charge of the *meunasah*), *ureung tua* (an elected village council), and a *tuha peut* (an expert on customary law). Of this structure, only the gampong and mukim remain under the Indonesian bureaucracy.

In the 19th century, society divided into the following classes: the sultan and those of royal blood; nobles (*uleebalang);* peasants; slaves; and *ulama,* a group of religious leaders not tied to a particular locale. Sultans' descendants carried the titles *ampon* for males and *cut* for females; the uleebalang, *teuku;* and the ulama, *teungku.* Nowadays, the only distinction recognized is that between the wealthy and the non-wealthy.

Touching the head, especially that of an older or higher-status person, is a grave insult. When meeting people, one must always greet them. One must speak politely and softly, especially with an older or higher-status person. Guests must be offered betel to chew before drinks are brought out. The duty to participate in community works binds villagers together: they cooperate to build the village mosque and other common buildings and, on Fridays, repair water channels and roads and clear away underbrush. Villagers also help each other build houses and establish wet-rice fields.

Traditionally, there was no free interaction between young men and young women. According to social norms, a man may not enter a house if the husband is not there. In the husband's absence, a visitor may not enter even the yard. If he has happened to, or must, enter the yard, he coughs to signal his approach so the women of the house can withdraw to the interior. These strictures are changing, one major reason being the fact that boys and girls are not separated in school. Nonetheless, censorship of sex-related material from films is considerably stricter in Aceh than elsewhere in Indonesia (where films edited by Jakarta authorities are screened).

⁹ LIVING CONDITIONS

A village (*gampong*) consists of 50–100 houses, with the houses of kin clustering or lining up with no more than a fence separating them. Each village has at least one *meunasah,* a structure that is open on all sides and raised on piles. It serves as a prayer hall and school, and as a place where the village's young men and houseguests sleep and public ceremonies are held.

Facing the sea or the south, houses are raised on 20–24 posts, each 30 cm (12 in) in diameter and 2.5–3 m (8–10 ft) in height (either wooden or bamboo, depending on family wealth). Floors are usually made of wooden planks, sometimes of bamboo; older houses employed rattan cording instead of nails. Roofs are two-sloped, 2–6 m (6.5–20 ft) high, and of plaited sago palm-leaf, lasting 20 years. The front room (*seuramoe keue*) is an open veranda where the children sleep, as do guests during weddings, funerals, and other celebrations. The middle room (*tungai*) contains a central corridor with the *romoh inong* on the left and *anjong* to the right (sleeping quarters for the women of the family and the parents respectively). The kitchen is in the back room (*seuramoe likot*) or in a room of its own (*tiphik*). Poorer families house their married daughters in annexes to the main dwelling. Harvested rice is stored inside the house in a *krong pade* or *berandang.* The garden contains coconut, citrus, and banana trees.

Nanggroe Aceh Darussalam has a Human Development Index (combining measures of income, health, and education) of 69 (2005 score), almost as high as Indonesia's national score of 69.6. Nanggroe Aceh Darussalam's GDP per capita is US$7,752, moderately high for Indonesia (cf. US$10,910 for North Sumatra, US$6,293 for Central Java and US$2,919 for North Maluku, with income from petroleum and natural gas production added, Aceh's GDP per capita reaches US$12,679, among the highest in the country). In 2000, the level of infant mortality, at 39.71 deaths per 1,000 live births, was the fourth lowest in the country (after the national capital region of Jakarta, the highly urbanized Yogyakarta region, and North Sulawesi). Neglect by the central government and the effects of insurgency and military repression, compounded now by the devastation of the earthquakes and tsunamis of December 2004 and March 2005, have long denied Aceh a level of development fully commensurate with its resource wealth, a situation slowly being corrected since the post-tsunami peace agreement.

¹⁰ FAMILY LIFE

Following Islamic strictures, marrying an uncle or aunt or a nephew or niece is taboo. Nor should first cousins, especially the children of two brothers or of two sisters (parallel cousins), marry each other; this, however, occurs often, despite being thought very unlucky.

Except in some areas where the choice depends on whose parents are wealthier, in general a newly married couple lives with the wife's parents. As part of the marriage contract, the wife's parents pledge to support the couple until the first child is born, or for 3–4 years (the exact duration depends on the amount of the bride-price). In the case of poorer families, the husband does not reside in but rather only visits his wife in his in-laws' house, still regarding his own mother's village as his home. If the spouses are from the same village, the man will sleep in the *meunasah* when not with his wife. In some regions, many husbands trade or grow coffee far from home and only return for Ramadan festivities.

Parents-in-law and sons-in-law are very formal with each other until the birth of the first child. Parents-in-law will sleep in a back room to avoid hearing or running into a son-in-law; they will even speak to him only through the wall. A man feels much closer to his younger siblings-in-law; the latter can act as intermediaries between the man and his parents-in-law if the wife is out.

Children tend to be closer to their mother than to their father and are more likely to bring up their problems with the former (mothers raise the children, while the fathers are usually away all day working). Relations between fathers and grown children tend to be rather distant, with the father often appearing as an "autocratic" authority figure. Moreover, although the father's siblings are responsible for his children should the father die, children still tend to feel more intimacy with the mother's siblings. Grandparents love to spoil their grandchildren; because of this, parents prefer that their children not stay with their grandparents.

Only wealthy men take more than one wife at a time (a legitimate reason, according to Islam, would be the first wife's failure to bear children). Interference by parents-in-law in a couple's affairs constitutes the most frequent cause for divorce. If a wife dies while the couple is still being supported by the parents, her parents give the husband a refund of half of the bride-price or, alternatively, give one of their other daughters to him as a wife. If a husband dies, one of his brothers almost always takes the widow as his wife.

¹¹ CLOTHING

Everyday wear for men consists of a shirt, sarong, and *peci* cap. Some women wear Acehnese-style black pants and the *baju tukok,* a short-sleeved shirt; most wear a long-sleeved shirt and a sarong, with a sash over the shoulder.

For ceremonies, men put on a collared jacket, long pants *(cekak musang),* a sarong *(pendua)* over it, a peci cap *(makutup),* and a *rencong* (a slightly curved blade) tucked in the front. Women attire themselves in a cekak musang, with a pendua of silk woven on a traditional *pok teumpeun* loom over it, a shirt covering the hips, a waist sash *(pending),* and jewelry (necklaces, bracelets, and anklets). A bride wears a *kulah kama* crown with golden hairpins, and flower blossoms. The groom wraps a head cloth around the peci and puts a kulah kama on the front.

¹² FOOD

Meals consist of rice and fish. Supplementary foods include cassava, sweet potato, maize, and *jeneng* (a kind of wild tuber). Jeneng are mixed with grated coconut or granulated sugar and eaten with coffee as breakfast. Acehnese prepare sticky rice in various ways: as *bu leukat keurabee,* mixed with grated coconut and salted; as *bu leumak,* cooked with coconut milk; as *bu leukat kuneng,* steamed with coconut milk and turmeric; and as *bu leukat meukuah,* cooked in a coconut milk sauce and optionally mixed with banana or durian. They also enjoy *kanji* (congee, a gruel of rice or sticky rice) cooked with coconut milk and sometimes mixed with mung beans.

Foods for special occasions include the following: *timphan,* rice flour boiled with grated coconut and sugar; *pulut panggang,* sticky rice mixed with coconut milk and grilled; and *guleeplei,* a combination of *maninjau* fruit, green pepper, banana blossoms, young *maninjau* leaves, tamarind leaves, string beans, and small shrimp, eaten with rice. One special Ramadan food is *ibupeudah,* rice gruel mixed with 44 kinds of edible leaves and sprinkled with grated or finely chopped coconut.

Because Islam forbids the consumption of alcohol, those who do so must drink it secretly. Popular drinks include sweet palm-saps, sugarcane water, and coconut juice. Rather more exotic is *air madu,* the "honey" secreted by an *uno,* a kind of spider; *dukun* specialize in collecting this fluid.

¹³ EDUCATION

In Aceh, religious education is compulsory from age seven. This entails first instruction in reciting the Qur'an at a village *meunasah* then goes on to further education at a *pesantren. In 2005, North Sulawesi's level of literacy stood at 95.98%, high by Indonesian national standards.*

¹⁴ CULTURAL HERITAGE

Traditional dances include the *tari ranub lampuan,* depicting young women offering betel to guests; the Arab-influenced *seudati agam* for males and *seudati inong* for females; the *saman,* where dancers sit in a row on the ground, performing coordinated hand and body movements in a dynamic rhythm; and the *ramphak,* a female dance displaying courage in fighting the Dutch. One type of musical performance is *rapa-i,* playing the *rebana* tambourine to accompany chanting.

Many of the classics of Malay literature were created in Acehnese cities, e.g., the Pasai royal chronicle *Hikayat Raja-*

Acehnese students read the Quran at a mosque in Banda Aceh, Indonesia. (AP Images/Binsar Bakkara)

Raja Pasai; the heretical mystical poems of Hamzah Fansuri; and the Nuruddin ar-Raniri's *Bustan as-Salatin* (the Garden of Kings), an encyclopedic work on history and politics. Prose and poetry in the Acehnese language only began to be written in the 17th century. One classic is the *Hikayat Perang Sabil* (Chronicle of the Holy War), a narrative of the Dutch war.

¹⁵ WORK

The majority of Acehnese support themselves through wet-rice agriculture. Most fields begin as sectioned-off swampland; only some rely on irrigation from rivers and streams. Men, working cooperatively, manage irrigation, while women plant and weed. Swidden (shifting-cultivation) fields far from the village provide supplementary crops, such as dry rice, chilies, papayas, sweet potatoes, and vegetables. Formerly, pepper was the primary cash crop; now it is coffee. An alternative to farming is life as a trader, marketing agricultural produce.

Fishing is another major source of livelihood; traditionally, *pawang* guilds, each consisting of a chief and a boat crew, partitioned a stretch of coast among themselves. Acehnese also keep cattle and water buffalo, selling their animals as far away as Medan. A dairy industry exists, though it was introduced and remains in the hands of Bengali immigrants.

In the past, the primary exports were plantation-produced rubber and palm oil. Nowadays, oil and natural gas production supports local development.

16 SPORTS

Pencak silat, a Malay-style martial art characterized by the dance-like grace of its hand movements, is a popular sport; many women practice it.

17 ENTERTAINMENT AND RECREATION

See the article entitled **Indonesians**.

18 FOLK ART, CRAFTS, AND HOBBIES

See the article entitled **Indonesians**.

19 SOCIAL PROBLEMS

See the article entitled **Indonesians**.

20 GENDER ISSUES

Nanggroe Aceh Darussalam's Gender-Related Development Index (combining measures of women's health, education, and income relative to men's) is 62.1, higher than Indonesia's national GDI of 59.2. The province's Gender Empowerment Measure (reflecting women's participation and power in political and economic life relative to men's) is 55.5, also higher than the national GEM (54.6).

The position of women is relatively high. For instance, a wife does not automatically submit to her husband's wishes. She takes an active part in wet-rice cultivation and within the home wields much power (the children fear her more than the often-absent father). Women have exercised leadership roles in Acehnese history; there were several queens in the 17th century, as well as a female military commander, Malahajati. However, a woman, especially one about to be married, cannot leave the house without her parents' supervision. When parents die, daughters inherit the house while sons get the rice fields, which usually end up under women's control, in any case, as men seek their livelihood away from the village. The ideal is for parents to build a house for each of their daughters as she marries, often spending their last years in a shack surrounded by the houses of their married daughters; if they cannot afford to build a separate house for a married daughter, they may leave their house to her and move into the kitchen (a separate structure).

Acehnese women suffered greatly during the struggle between GAM guerrillas and the Indonesian military. Many were brutalized, driven from their homes, and forced, with their children, to endure life in refugee camps (where they were even denied control of a kitchen of their own, the one place they were master in a society where Islamic teaching is interpreted to support patriarchy). Worse yet, many were raped by government soldiers. In the wake of the war, over 377,000 households are headed by widows. Women played an active role in promoting peace, from organizing regency-wide days of communal prayers to negotiating with the Indonesian army and presenting statements to the United Nations Committee in Geneva.

21 BIBLIOGRAPHY

Bertrand, Jacques. *Nationalism and Ethnic Conflict in Indonesia*. Cambridge, UK: Cambridge University Press, 2004.

Data Statistik Indonesia. http://demografi.bps.go.id/ (November 9, 2008).

Kamaruzzaman, Suraiya. "Violence, Internal Displacement and Its Impact on the Women of Aceh." In Charles A. Coppel, ed., *Violent Conflicts in Indonesia: Analysis, Representation, Resolution*. London: Routledge, 2006.

LeBar, Frank M., ed. *Ethnic Groups of Insular Southeast Asia*. Vol. 1 *Indonesia, Andaman Islands, and Madagascar*. New Haven, Conn.: Human Relations Area Files Press, 1972.

Oey, Eric. *Sumatra: Island of Adventure*. Lincolnwood, IL: Passport Books, 1991.

Profil Propinsi Republik Indonesia. Vol. 1, "Aceh." Jakarta: Yayasan Bhakti Wawasan Nusantara, 1992.

Project for the Study and Recording of Regional Cultures. *Adat Istiadat Daerah Istimewa Aceh*. Jakarta: Department of Education and Culture, 1978.

Rosantini, Triana. "Aceh, suku bangsa." In *Ensiklopedi Nasional Indonesia*, Vol. 1. Jakarta: Cipta Adi Pustaka, 1988.

Sjamsudin, Teuku. "Kebudayaan Aceh." In *Manusia dan Kebudayaan di Indonesia* (Man and Culture in Indonesia, edited by Koentjaraningrat). Jakarta: Djambatan, 1975.

Waterson, Roxana. *The Living House: An Anthropology of Architecture in South-East Asia*. Singapore: Oxford University Press, 1990.

—revised by A. J. Abalahin

AFGHANIS

PRONUNCIATION: af-GHAN-eez
LOCATION: Afghanistan
POPULATION: 31.9 million (2007)
LANGUAGE: Dari; Pashto (Pushto); Turkish
RELIGION: Islam (Sunni, 80–90%; Shia, 10–20%)
RELATED ARTICLES: Vol. 3: Hazaras; Kafirs; Vol. 4: Pashtuns

¹ INTRODUCTION

Throughout history, the territory that is now Afghanistan has been a crossroads for conquering armies and a jumping-off point for invasions of India. This pattern seems to have begun when the Indo-European-speaking Aryans first began to penetrate the Indus Valley in about 1800 BC. The Persian Empire of Cyrus was established in 545 BC. Persian rule lasted for the next two centuries. From 330 BC to 327 BC, Alexander the Great campaigned in Afghanistan. In 307 BC, Seleucus, one of Alexander's successors, traded Alexander's conquest in India and eastern Afghanistan to an Indian ruler named Chandragupta for 500 war elephants. This deal introduced a millennium during which Afghanistan was divided along often-shifting frontiers between a part ruled from the East, with an Indic culture, and a part ruled from the West, with a Hellenic and later Persian culture.

The armies of the Islamic invasion of the 7th century AD conquered Afghanistan in AD 699. In 1220, Genghis Khan brought his hordes into Afghanistan. For the next century and a half, parts of Afghanistan were under the control of various descendents of Genghis Khan. Then, after a time of rule by other conquerors, a central Asian ruler named Babur established a base in Kabul in 1504. From there he marched into India in 1525 and founded the Moghul Empire that dominated India for nearly 200 years. Until 1739, the moghuls controlled parts of Eastern Afghanistan, although they were often resisted by indigenous tribal groups. Western Afghanistan came under the control of the Persian dynasty. For 150 years, Afghanistan was divided between two empires.

The Afghan Empire took shape when Ahmed Khan, a young Pashtun (or Pushtun) cavalry leader, led his 4,000 troops to Kandahar where he was elected leader of a group now renamed Durrani. The Durranis set out on a campaign of conquest and brought much of Afghanistan under control by 1750. At its height, the empire of Ahmed Shah Durrani covered modern Pakistan and Kashmir, Afghanistan, and the northeastern province of Iran. Modern Afghanistan can be considered the part of this empire that was not subsequently whittled away.

The existence of a national entity that we can recognize as Afghanistan dates from the reign of Amir Adbur Rahman in 1880–1901. The country came to have its present boundaries during this period. However, Afghanistan was still under the heavy influence of various foreign powers. It was not until 1919 that the Afghan government succeeded in gaining independence in conducting its foreign affairs. In 1964 a new constitution was adopted that looked toward development of a parliamentary democracy. In a coup in 1973, the king was ousted by his first cousin, Daoud, who declared the country a republic, with himself as president. Five years later, Daoud was killed in a leftist coup in April 1978. Within a year, the widespread perception of the new regime as anti-Islamic and pro-Russian led to uprisings in most parts of the country. At least 400,000 refugees crossed over into Pakistan, and another 600,000 fled to Iran. Soviet military aid for the suppression of insurgency was not succeeding, so in December 1979 the Soviet army marched into Kabul. Thousands more Afghanis fled across the border. By late 1981, there were about 3 million Afghanis in Pakistan, and 250,000 in Iran. Ten years later, the number of refugees had climbed to 5 million.

The Soviet army left Afghanistan in 1989 and fighting among tribal and ethnic groups intensified. In the mid-1990s a Pakistan-supported mercenary army of Islamic fundamentalists called the Taliban (Arabic for "students") began taking control of large swathes of the country. Many Taliban fighters were Arabs who had come to Afghanistan in the 1980s to repel the Soviet occupation of a Muslim land. Their deeply traditional brand of Islam was welcomed in many parts of the country, particularly in the southern provinces around Kandahar. They were less successful in the Hazara lands to the east and the Tajik part of the north. By 1996 the Taliban had taken control of most of the country. A tiny pocket of Afghanistan was still ruled by a coalition of Uzbek, Hazara, and Tajik forces called the Northern Alliance.

After the al Qaeda-led attacks on Washington D.C. and New York on 11 September 2001, the United States and the United Kingdom began a bombing campaign of Afghanistan to overthrow the Taliban and to capture leaders of the al Qaeda terrorist network who were being protected by the government. The Taliban forces fell quickly and an interim government was established and backed militarily by a large contingent of American and North Atlantic Treaty Organization (NATO) forces. Partial peace returned to regions of the country held by NATO and the United States, and a democratic government, headed by Hamid Karzai, was established in 2004. The Taliban, however, were never fully defeated and beginning in 2005 they began a counter-offensive in the south, attacking from the mountainous border areas with Pakistan. By 2007 and 2008, suicide bombings were becoming common throughout the country, even in Kabul, by that time a heavily fortified and militarized city.

² LOCATION AND HOMELAND

Afghanistan is a relatively inaccessible, mountainous, land-locked country of southwestern Asia. It is bounded by Pakistan; Iran; the republics of Uzbekistan, Tajikistan, and Turkmenistan; and, for less than 65 km (40 mi), China. Afghanistan is about the same size as the U.S. state of Texas. The mountain ranges of the Hindu Kush cover most of the country, with elevations rising to 7,300 m (24,000 ft). In the northeast, the mountains are perpetually covered with snow, while in the southwest there are rocky or sandy deserts. Most of Afghanistan's water supply comes from the snow that falls on the mountains between December and April, which only amounts to the equivalent of 38 cm (15 in) of rain. Without irrigation, little of Afghanistan's land can be cultivated. The climate varies widely according to altitude and regional weather patterns. The range between high summer and low winter is large. Almost all places have some freezing weather, and those below actual mountain zones have temperatures above 32°C (90°F). In some areas, temperatures can go above 38°C (100°F). A wide day-to-night range of temperature is also typical. The area along both sides of the Afghanistan-Iran border is very windy—a south wind blows continuously from June through September, at speeds of up to 160 kph (100 mph). Wheat is harvested during the windy period and is ground with the aid of windmills with vertical vanes and a vertical shaft, an ancient invention of this region.

The 2007 population of Afghanistan was estimated to be 31.9 million. Since the U.S.-led invasion in 2001 and the overthrow of the Taliban regime, many of the estimated population of 6 million Afghanis have returned home from years as refugees in, primarily, Pakistan, Iran, and Tajikistan. Aid agencies differ as to how many Afghanis have returned home.

Ethnically, Afghanis are very mixed. Racially, there are Caucasians, Mongoloids, and Australoids. Pashtuns (or Pushtuns) make up about half the Afghani population and consider themselves the true Afghanis. Of Aryan stock, they appear to have lived in Afghanistan since the earliest recorded history. Pashtuns are tall and fair-skinned, with black or brown hair and brown eyes (hazel or blue eyes are also common). Tajiks are Persian, of Mediterranean stock. They are tall with fair skin and black hair (though some have red or blond hair). Afghanis of Mongoloid descent include Hazaras, Turkmen, and Kirghiz. Mongoloid races have Asian features. The Uzbeks, along with several small nomadic tribes, are of Turkish origin and have Turkish features and fairer skin than other Afghanis. There are also many groups of Afghanis who claim to be of Arab descent. They call themselves *sayyid* and speak a form of Arabic. Through centuries of intermarriage, most Afghanis are a blend of these different races. One more isolated group is the Nuristanis, about whom little is known. They seem to be of Mediterranean descent, with light-brown skin, thin straight noses, and black to brown or even blond, hair.

³ LANGUAGE

The principal languages of Afghanis are Dari, a variety of Persian; and Pashto (or Pushto), a language shared with the residents of the North West Frontier Province of Pakistan. Both are official languages of the country, and most educated Afghanis can use both. Schools use whichever is most common in the area and teach the other as a second language. The languages are related, though they probably split into two distinct languages millennia ago, before the Christian era. Speakers of Pashto, called Pashtuns (or Pushtuns), have been the ruling group in Afghanistan and have tended to set the tone for the entire nation. The Pashtuns constitute a single ethnic group, while the Dari-speakers are more diverse. Geographically, Dari is the predominant language of the Kabul area and the regions to the northwest of the Hindu Kush Mountains; while Pashto is principally located to the southeast of the mountains. Dari is a much more urban language, and is the language in which business is most frequently conducted. Both Dari and Pashto are written using adaptations of the Arabic alphabet. Dari adds four extra consonants for sounds not occurring in classical Arabic, and Pashto adds those four plus eight more letters. In written form, Dari and Pashto are closer than when spoken.

There are many other languages spoken by the various ethnic groups in Afghanistan. After Dari and Pashto, the major language family is Turkish. Turkic languages are spoken mostly in the northern regions of Afghanistan. Ancient Indo-European languages are also spoken, by small groups living in

isolated areas. Each language may have only a few thousand speakers.

Afghani names are for the most part Islamic. The Pashtun population uses non-Arabic names frequently. The father's oldest brother is usually the person to pick a child's name. The name is then officially conferred by a religious leader on the third day after birth. Surnames are a recent innovation in Afghanistan. Where they have been adopted, they usually have a geographic reference, or a connection with the professional interests of those using them. Since the choice of a surname is personal, close relatives (even brothers) may opt for different names. Pashtuns normally identify themselves by the tribal lineage-division to which they belong. Most Afghanis only use their given names in public. Within the privacy of the home, they call each other by nicknames, or *laqubs*. All nicknames are made up of combinations of the same few words—candy, flower, lion, uncle, dear, etc.—like "Lion Uncle," or "Flower Dear."

⁴ FOLKLORE

Afghanis love to tell stories, and they all have quite a repertoire that they know by heart to tell at a gathering. Stories for children are usually teaching stories about foolish people who get what they deserve, such as the Three Sons of Mah'madyar, or Bachey Kul (the "Bald Boy"). Another favorite character for Afghani stories is Mullah Nasruddin. Mullahs are respected Islamic religious teachers or leaders, but they are not sacred like the Quran, so people often poke fun at them in a friendly way. The Mullah frequently figures as a "wise fool" in Afghani stories, appearing foolish but turning out to be very smart.

Adult Afghanis enjoy stories of love and/or heroism. The most popular love story is that of Leilah and Majnun, two doomed lovers who are separated when young and then cannot reconnect when old. They both die of grief and unfulfillment. Many hero-tales come from the *Shahnama, the Book of Kings,* written in Afghanistan for a Turkish emperor about the rise of the Iranian people. Other tales are about real-life heroes, such as the warrior Habibullah Ghazi who overthrew the Pashtun government in 1929 and ruled for nine months. The Pashtuns, on the other hand, call him Bachey Saqao, "the Water Carrier's Boy," and paint him as a fool.

Afghanis believe in *jinns,* spirits who can change shape and be either visible or invisible. Jinns are usually evil, or at least out to do no good. Many Afghanis wear amulets around their necks to protect them from jinns. Stories of jinns are often told at night, like ghost stories around a campfire.

5 RELIGION

Afghanistan is one of the most solidly Muslim countries in the world. The overwhelming majority follow the mainstream branch of Islam, the Sunni tradition. About 10–20% of Afghanis are Shia Muslims, of both the Imami and Ismaili sects. There are also sufis (or dervishes), members of the mystical branch of Islam. Afghani Sufis generally belong to the Qadiri order or "path," the most ancient and widespread of sufi paths. For the most part it is the folk level of Islam that is important to Afghanistan. The local religious leaders are not usually well-instructed. They are mostly peasants with other part-time work. In upper valleys of the tributaries that run into the Kabul River from the north between Kabul and the Pakistan border, there used to be a pocket of paganism. It was called Kariristan ("land of the heathen") until 1896 when Abdur Rahman invaded it and forcibly converted the inhabitants to Islam. He then renamed these valleys Nuristan ("land of light"). The Nuristanis of today are a very distinct ethnic group in Afghanistan.

6 MAJOR HOLIDAYS

Probably the most important annual observance in Afghanistan is the ancient Persian New Year celebration, Nawruz (or Now Ruz), meaning "new day," at the beginning of spring on March 21. It is marked by special foods, including *samanak,* a dessert made of wheat and sugar, and *haft miwa,* a mixture of seven fruits and nuts symbolizing spring; sporting events; and attempts to secure good fortune for the following year. The ceremonial raising of the flag at the tomb of Muhammad's son-in-law, Ali, occurs on Nawruz at Mazar-e-Sharif. The standard of Ali, a staff, is raised in the courtyard there. For 40 days, pilgrims flock to touch it and gain merit or be cured of disease and injury. On the fortieth day after Nawruz, the staff is lowered and a particular red species of tulip blooms, disappearing soon after. Fairs and carnivals brighten Nawruz, as does the custom of dyeing farm animals—green chickens and purple sheep abound.

Most major holidays in Afghanistan are religious, following the Islamic lunar calendar (causing the dates to vary on the standard Gregorian calendar). The main Muslim holidays are Ramadan (or Ramazan in Afghani pronunciation), the month of fasting (called *ruzah* by Afghanis) from dawn to dusk; Ayd Al-Fitr, a three-day festival at the end of Ramadan; Ayd Al-

Adha, a three-day feast of sacrifice at the end of the month of pilgrimage to Mecca (known as the Hajj); the First of Muharram, or the Muslim New Year; Mawoulid An-Nawabi, the prophet Muhammad's birthday; and Ayd Al-Isra wa Al-Miraj, a feast celebrating the nocturnal visit of Muhammad to heaven. Ashura is celebrated by Shia Muslims, after the first 10 days of the new year that are spent in mourning to commemorate the killing of Hussein, the grandson of the prophet Muhammad on 10 October 680. Ashura is an optional fast day.

Nonreligious holidays in Afghanistan include Jeshn, or Independence Day, on August 18, a week-long festival celebrating Afghanistan's independence from Britain in 1919; Workers' Day, or Labor Day, on May 1; and Revolution Day on April 27, the date in 1978 when President Daoud was overthrown by the leftist regime.

7 RITES OF PASSAGE

Weddings are the greatest occasions for celebration in Afghanistan. After several preliminary observances, the ceremonies connected with the actual wedding are spread over a three-day period, except in cities, where they are all condensed into one day. The most popular time for weddings is late summer or early fall. Most marriages are arranged by the parents and relatives, often when children are still very young. Men generally marry between the ages of 18 and 20; and women, between the ages of 16 and 18. Marriage between cousins, especially paternal ones, is preferred. A bride-price is paid by the groom's family to pay for the loss of a valuable family member. A dowry of household goods, etc., is paid by the bride's family to help with the initial setting up of a home. The groom's family pays for the wedding, which involves much feasting and dancing. The official ceremony is called *nikah-namah* and consists of the signing of the marriage contract before witnesses, readings from the Quran by the *mullah* (local religious leader), and the tossing of sugared almonds and walnuts onto the bridegroom.

The birth of a first child is the occasion for a day-long celebration; most elaborate if the child is a boy. Children are named on the third day after birth. The name is chosen by a paternal uncle who then becomes the child's guardian, responsible for the child if the father dies. The sixth night after a birth is observed with an "open house" for friends of the family, who bring small gifts. Boys are usually circumcised at about the age of seven (after which they begin wearing turbans). The circumcision is the occasion for a feast, likely to involve wrestling contests and other demonstrations of manliness.

Large-scale food distributions connected with funerals were made illegal in the 1950s. Now, commemorative meals take place several times in the year following a death.

8 INTERPERSONAL RELATIONS

Interpersonal relations among Afghanis are largely ruled by *Pashtunwalli* (or *Pushtunwalli*), unwritten laws and codes belonging to the Pashtuns but followed by almost all Afghanis. The laws and codes deal mostly with honor and self-pride. Hospitality is required for honor's sake, so travelers and guests never go without food or shelter. Pashtunwalli involves *melmatia,* being a good and generous host; *ghayrat,* upholding personal and family honor; *namus,* defending women's honor; *nanawati,* providing shelter to anyone who needs it; *sabat,* or loyalty; and *badal,* avenging blood with blood. Other requirements of Pashtunwalli are never to kill a woman, a minstrel, a

Hindu, or an uncircumcised boy; to pardon any wrong—except for murder—when asked to by a woman, the wrongdoer's family, a *sayyid* (an Afghan who claims Arab descent), or a *mullah* (local religious teacher or leader); to punish adultery with death; and to spare the life of anyone who takes refuge in a mosque or shrine, or anyone in battle who begs for mercy.

Afghanis are very expressive with their bodies, using extravagant gestures and facial expressions to communicate. There is also a lot of physical affection expressed between members of the same sex. It is forbidden in Islam to touch members of the opposite sex who are not intimately related. Afghani men greet friends and acquaintances by clasping both hands in a firm handshake, hugging, and kissing each other on the cheeks. They often walk together, arm in arm. Business contracts are sealed with a nod of the head.

⁹ LIVING CONDITIONS

Nomadic Afghanis, called *kochis,* live in tents and move from place to place to find grazing grounds for their herds of camel and sheep. In the north, the Turkoman nomads have red dome-shaped tents. In the south, the Pashtun or Balūchī nomads live in black tents that look like huge bats. The Pashtun or Balūchī nomads keep large dogs with heavy shoulders and big heads; they are known as *kochi* dogs. Afghanistan is one of the few places left in the world with a sizable number of nomads. There are about 2 million nomads in Afghanistan.

Settled Afghanis mostly live in small villages with a few hundred to a few thousand people. They generally make their living as farmers. Some wealthier Afghanis live in *qalas,* or country forts, with other farmers working their land. Some 70% of Afghanis are farmers, even though the country is very dry, and only a tenth or less of the land is arable. Constant warring has prevented the Afghanis from developing and maintaining effective irrigation systems, so most of them barely scratch a living out of the soil. Afghanistan is one of the poorest countries in the world. With the harsh terrain and destruction from the continual conflicts, Afghanis have not been able to move very far beyond a medieval world of poverty and hardship. Many of the few major roadways in the country have been destroyed in the wars. Hydroelectric power is only readily available in the springs when the mountain streams swell with melting snow. During the dry summers, dams and reservoirs must provide this power.

Village houses are made of bricks plastered with a mixture of mud and straw. Most are flat-roofed, but in some regions domed roofs are preferred. An enclosed compound holds the livestock and storage sheds, as well as the cooking area and the general living area. Women carry water from nearby streams or pools (some wealthier Afghanis have artificial streams or pools called *juy*). Bathing and laundry are also done in these streams and pools. Households have the bare minimum of furniture, with mattresses spread on the floor at night for beds. The mattresses are then stacked in a corner during the day. In summer, Afghanis sleep on their flat roofs where it is cooler. Dung patties—made by the women and children, who collect the manure, shape it into patties, and slap them on the walls to dry—are used for fuel. Two uniquely Afghani ways to keep warm are *tawkhanah* and *sandali. Tawkhanah* are hot-air tunnels built under the floor with a fire at one end. The heat from the fire travels through the tunnels and warms the whole floor. These tawkhanah are used mostly in villages south of the Hin-

du Kush mountains. In other places, a small, low table with a blanket over it is placed above a charcoal brazier. The blanket holds in the heat, and the family then sits around the table to keep warm. This is known as the *sandali* system.

Villages in Afghanistan are circled around larger towns that act as commercial, communication, and administrative centers. Farm goods, crafts, and raw materials are brought to the towns from the villages. The goods are then sent to the cities. Horse-carts are used for transportation in the towns. From the towns to the cities, trucks are used. The trucks are often brightly painted with elaborate designs. *Caravanserais,* or inns, are located in the towns, as well as teahouses where men gather to smoke water-pipes, talk, and drink strong tea. The teahouses are known as *chaykhanas.* Markets, or bazaars, are located on the main street of the town. Most shop-owners live above their shops.

Where major routes intersect, cities have sprung up. The five major cities in Afghanistan are Kabul, Kandahar, Herat, Mazar-e-Sharif, and Kunduz. The first four all have populations of over 100,000 people, and Kabul has some 2 million residents. Kabul has become almost a separate nation, with a very different lifestyle and flavor than the rest of the country. High-rise buildings with bricks are found in cities to house their ever-growing populations. Though the standard of living is somewhat better than in villages and towns, it is still not modernized or consistently comfortable. Plumbing and water-supply are particularly iffy. Afghanistan has one of the highest infant mortality rates in the world.

¹⁰ FAMILY LIFE

Afghani life revolves around the family, and "family" includes all extended relations. Traditionally, Afghani society was tribal, and tribal affiliation is still the most significant organizing principle in parts of rural Afghanistan. Tribal units have a strong patrilineal organization, which is supported by Islam. "Modern" extended family units are still patrilineal, consisting of men related through their fathers, the men's wives, and unmarried female relatives. Extended families often live together in the same household, or in separate households clustered together. Even large cities are made up of small "villages" of extended family units. The women of the households form a single work group and care for and discipline the children. The senior active male member, typically the grandfather, controls all expenditures, and the grandmother controls all domestic work assignments.

Women have a great deal of say in the home, but little authority in public. Strong, courageous, and hard-working, women are primary members of the Afghani household. But Islamic tradition requires that they be veiled and kept separate in public, so they play little part in society outside the home. In Kabul, some women are leaving behind the traditions of Islam and venturing out to take jobs, serve in government (though very few women have gained prominence politically), and attend higher education classes alongside men.

Divorce is fairly simple in Islamic law—a man merely has to say "I divorce you" three times in front of witnesses to divorce his wife. A woman has to appear before a judge with reasons for divorcing her husband. Despite the ease of divorce, however, few Afghanis end their marriages. Polygamy is also allowed but rarely practiced. Adultery is punishable by death.

A young boy holds onto his mother's burqa while walking through a market in Kabul, Afghanistan. Despite the fall of the Taliban regime, most Afghan women still opt to wear the burqa. (AP Images/Farzana Wahidy)

Children are cherished in Afghani society, particularly boys. Girls are not openly abused, but often the needs of their brothers' come first, to the point where some girls may seem to be neglected. All children are raised in the women's quarters, and a baby is nursed until the next child is born or the child becomes too old. Children are expected to grow up quickly and learn to take care of themselves. They are toilet-trained and taught to feed themselves at a very early age. After a boy is circumcised, usually at age seven, he is treated like a man and is expected to behave like one. Girls have no rite of passage into adulthood, but by the time they are 9 or 10 years old they know all the skills necessary to be a wife and mother. They can grind wheat and corn, fetch water, cook, clean, and sew, and make dung patties for fuel.

Marriages are almost always arranged by the families, often when the couple are still young children. A match between paternal cousins is preferred. Boys usually marry at age 18–20, and girls at 16–18.

11 CLOTHING

The ordinary clothing of Afghani men is a rather baggy pair of trousers with a drawstring at the waist, and a loose, long-sleeved shirt reaching about to the knees. Over this (when it is cool), a vest is worn. Coats worn in rural areas are often brightly striped, and they are quilted for winter warmth. Turbans—traditionally white, but now of any color—are wound around the locally favored type of turban caps. Pashtuns (or Pushtuns), and others who imitate them, leave some of the turban cloth hanging down, while most of those in the rest of the country tuck the end in. Pashtun men customarily have their hair cut off square at earlobe length. Other groups have their heads shaved about once a month. In villages and rural areas, men follow the Islamic custom of wearing beards and moustaches. In Kabul, many men are clean-shaven. The *pakol* hat has become popular recently. Originally a Nuristani hat, it was adopted as a sign of the Mujahideen resistance to the government. However, now even the president that the Mujahideen are fighting sometimes wears the pakol.

Women often wear pleated trousers under a long dress and cover their heads with a shawl. Urban women traditionally wore a *chadri,* an ankle-length cloth covering, like a sack over the whole body, with a mesh insert over the eyes and nose. Though the chadri was officially banned in 1959, some women continue to wear them. In the countryside, hard-working village and tribal women could not go about so encumbered, so they have never worn chadris.

In large cities, particularly Kabul, Western-style clothing is becoming increasingly popular, for both men and women.

12 FOOD

Afghani cuisine is a blend of all the different cuisines of the peoples who have occupied their country over the millennia. The strongest influences are from India and Iran. Staple foods are rice, a flatbread known as *naan,* and dairy products. A variety of fruits and vegetables are also available.

Afghan bread, leavened or unleavened, is baked thin on a very hot fired-clay surface. Typically, a round pottery vessel whose sides come in toward the bottom is buried in the earth and heated by coals in the middle of the bottom. The dough is formed and slapped onto the hot concave sides where it bakes rapidly. Bread is eaten at every meal, often serving as a utensil for scooping up the food, since Afghanis generally eat with their fingers.

The main feature of a major meal is a rice *pilau,* which is rice cooked with meats or vegetables. There are as many kinds of pilaus as there are cooks, though certain combinations are common. For example, an honored guest would be served *qabli*—rice with raisins, shredded carrot, almonds, and pistachios. *Kala-pacheh* is rice with the head (including the eyeballs) and feet of a sheep. In rural Afghanistan, regular meals are not eaten between breakfast and supper, but people carry nuts and dried fruit to eat during the day for energy.

The usual beverage is tea, usually drunk without milk. Black tea is generally preferred south of the Hindu Kush mountains, while green tea is preferred in the north. Sugar is expensive in Afghanistan, but many Afghanis will pay the extra price to soak a sugar cube in their tea and then either eat the cube or hold it between their teeth while they drink the tea. Alcohol is forbidden by Islam (as is pork).

Meals are spread on a cloth placed on the floor. The family and any guests sit on the floor around the cloth. A bowl is carried to each guest with fresh water poured into it for each person to wash their hands before and after eating. Most families have a special pot and bowl for this purpose, called an *aftawa-lagan.* Women and girls do the cooking.

A special soup served only on *Nawruz,* or the Persian New Year, is *haft miwa.* This soup is made of seven fruits and nuts to symbolize spring. In the recipe that follows, peaches are substituted for a locally grown Afghani fruit known as *sanje.*

Haft Miwa
(Seven Fruits)

1 cup skinned almonds (unsalted)
1 cup skinned walnuts (unsalted)
1 cup skinned pistachios (unsalted)
1 cup dried peaches
1 cup red raisins
1 cup green raisins
1 cup dried apricots
6 cups water

If you only have salted nuts, rinse off the salt with water. Put the nuts in one bowl and the fruits in another. Add 3 cups of cold water to each bowl. Stir, cover the bowls, and put them in the refrigerator. After two days, combine the ingredients from the two bowls into one large bowl. Stir, cover the bowl, and put it in the refrigerator for two or three more days. Serve cold.
(Adapted from Ansary, p. 59)

¹³ EDUCATION

Western-style education has never been widely accepted in Afghanistan, and the literacy rate is still very low. Literacy in Dari is much more prevalent than literacy in Pashto (or Pushto).

Before 1903, the only education available was in mosque schools taught by the local *mullah* (religious leader or teacher). The mosque schools, or *madrassas,* were just for boys. Girls were taught at home by elderly women. At the madrassa, boys learned Islamic subjects and were taught to read and write using the Quran. The first modern school was established in 1903 in Kabul by King Habibullah. Both religious and secular subjects were taught there, and foreign teachers were brought on the staff by World War II (1939–45). King Habibullah also founded a military training academy and a teachers' college. Under King Amanullah in the 1920s, more schools were opened in both urban and rural areas. The first high school class graduated in 1923. The first school for girls was founded in 1924 in Kabul. The 1931 constitution made primary education mandatory and free for all children, but this aim was not realized for decades. With the constant warring, formal education has been erratic. The University of Kabul was founded in 1946, with separate faculties for men and women. By 1960, all faculties had become coeducational.

Before the Communist takeover in 1978, there were 3,404 schools with 83,500 teachers. After two decades of civil war, however, the number of schools and teachers had both been slashed dramatically. After the Taliban came to power, education of girls was banned and virtually all non-religious education was forbidden. After the Western allied powers installed the Karzai government, education was reformed (the 2004 constitution guarantees education to all Afghans) and by 2007 the government reported that there were 5.4 million children enrolled in schools, 35% of whom were girls.

Education in Afghanistan is conducted strictly, with few frills. Students sit in rigid rows of desks, with a blackboard and perhaps a map or two on the walls. There is no playground equipment—at recess, if there is no shooting or bombing going on, students play simple games, or sit and talk with each other. Learning is by rote; the students repeat lessons back to the teacher. There are no group projects or "learning centers," etc. Grades are based solely on oral and written exams given several times a year in each subject. Exam grades are added up at the end of the year, and students who pass move on to the next grade. Failing students repeat the grade, which is not uncommon. The educational system of Afghanistan consists of six years of primary school, and six years of *lycee,* or high school. Refugee students may receive no formal education at all.

¹⁴ CULTURAL HERITAGE

Persian is a language with a vast cultural and literary tradition (Dari is a form of Persian). The first shoots of classical Persian literature began to appear in the 9th century AD. During the late medieval period, a Persian civilization developed that embraced Iran, Afghanistan, and the Muslim-ruled parts of India. It also included much of Central Asia. Throughout this region, Persian became the language of administration. The small world of the literate also made it their principal medium of expression, whatever their native language, much as Latin dominated Western Europe. It was presumably during this period that Persian replaced other Iranian languages as the common speech in much of northern Afghanistan. Contemporary prose and poetry are most often written in Dari and often imitate classical Persian style and form.

Pashto (or Pushto) literature was essentially created by Khushal Khan Khattak, who lived from 1613 to 1690. He was a brilliant warrior who opposed the Moghul emperor. He was also a poet of wide-ranging interests. Pashto literature has not been cultivated since then to the extent that Dari literature has been. There has been little new or original art, literature, or architecture of any sort produced since the 17th century, when the rivalry between the Persians and Moghuls began. Almost constant warring, with no significant periods of peace, has prevented the Afghanis from giving their attention to the arts.

The Islamic reverence for poetry continues to inspire poetic recitals and some original writing. The greatest modern Afghani poet, Khalilullah Khalili, died recently. Mujahideen resistance fighters often quote his poems. The most popular theme in Afghani poetry is war, followed by love and jealousy, then religion and folklore (though almost all poems have some religious sentiment in them). There is also some nature poetry. Traditionally, Afghanis have not been known for writing fiction or other prose. After the 2001 war and its violent aftermath brought the world's attention to the country, a few notable books were produced by the Afghani Disapora, as well as internationally renowned films. *The Kite Runner,* written by the Afghan-American writer Khaled Hosseini and published in 2003, was an international best seller. The Siddiq Barmak film of 2003, *Osama,* was the first film shot in Afghanistan since the Taliban had taken power. The film, which won several international awards, is a rather bleak assessment of life in modern Afghanistan .

Visual arts reached their peak in the 15th century AD. Since then, no exceptional painters or sculptors have emerged, and no new styles or content have been developed. Most painting is done in the form of calligraphy, illumination, or functional decoration. Muslim architecture continues to be beautifully realized, particularly in the design of mosques. Tall minarets with bulbous domes and colorful, intricate tile-work make for one of the most graceful and elegant architectures in the world.

15 WORK

Most Afghanis (about 80%) are farmers and herders. Even those who engage in crafts such as pottery, weaving, shoemaking, and housebuilding are also part-time agriculturalists. The army and government administration are the only large-scale employers outside the agricultural sector. Wheat is the principal crop. For trade purposes, grapes and orchard fruit (dried or fresh), together with walnuts and almonds, are important. Cotton is also a commercial crop. Perhaps the most profitable crop in Afghanistan is opium derived from poppies grown in the northwest provinces near the Pakistani border. Opium is the base for morphine and heroin. Efforts have been made from time to time to curtail the illegal drug trade, but political instability, the power of local warlords, and continuing Taliban insurgency make it difficult to supervise people's activities effectively. By 2006 Afghanistan was the world's largest producer of opium.

Sheep are raised in most parts of the country. Some 14% of Afghanis are still nomads, traveling from grazing ground to grazing ground. Goats are often herded together with the sheep. The skins of the Karakul sheep ("Persian lamb") of northern Afghanistan are the country's most profitable product. Wool is also exported.

In towns there are traders and full-time craft specialists, teahouses, and schools, but only about 300 such communities exist in Afghanistan. Only the few large cities, and particularly the capital, Kabul, have a modernized economic sector. Besides these, there are a very small number of factories and mining centers in other locations. Some small industries begun by the government include tanneries; machine-repair shops; cotton-ginning mills; bakeries; fruit-processing plants; and oil, soap, shoe, and ceramics factories. Larger government industries include cotton, rayon, and wool mills; the production of domestic construction materials and chemical fertilizers; and mining, especially for natural gas and lapis lazuli. Afghanistan is the leading producer of the precious stone lapis lazuli. Some Afghanis also find jobs as truck drivers, transporting goods from towns to cities and vice versa.

In 2008 more than 50% of the population lived below the official poverty line. The country's economy was growing, but was largely dependent on foreign aid.

16 SPORTS

Afghanis are very competitive and take their sports very seriously. Winning is a question of personal, family, and tribal honor. Afghani sports also tend to be violent, although injuries are rare. A favorite Afghani sport is called *buzkashi,* or "goat pulling," though these days a calf is usually used. In this contest, a headless calf carcass is placed in the center of a circle formed by two teams of horsemen (known as *chapandaz*). Only men participate. Teams have been known to number up to 1,000 players A signal is given and all the chapandaz move to the center to try to lift the carcass onto their horse. Once someone captures the carcass, he rides to a point 1.5 km to 5 km (1–3 mi) away, then returns to the starting point and drops

the carcass where he picked it up. During all this, the other chapandaz are trying to grab the carcass away from him. The Afghan Olympic Federation laid down rules to buzkashi, limiting teams to no more than 10 players and games to 1 hour, with a 10-minute break at halftime. Two declared fouls are intentionally hitting an opponent with a whip, and forcing an opponent off his horse. Horses must be trained for the sport for at least five years. These rules are only used at official games. Buzkashi is to Afghanis what baseball is to Americans.

Another popular Afghani sport is wrestling, or *pahlwani,* where the only rule is that one cannot grab one's opponent's legs. Some modern sports were introduced in the 20th century, including tennis, golf, cricket, basketball, soccer, and field hockey.

17 ENTERTAINMENT AND RECREATION

Afghani children do not have much time for play, nor do their families have the money to buy manufactured toys (which are not widely available in their war-torn country). So children play simple games with basic toys, such as dolls made from natural objects, or slingshots. *Buzul-bazi* is a game like marbles or dice, played with sheep's knucklebones. Girls play a game very similar to hopscotch or amuse themselves for days with *mara-yadast-tura-furamosh* ("I remembered, you forgot"). When a family cooks a chicken, the girls take the wishbone and break it in half, giving one half to each girl. Then they try to trick each other into looking at their half of the wishbone, for example by tying it up in a bandage on their finger and asking the other one to look at the injury. When one succeeds in tricking the other into looking at her wishbone, she shouts, "Mara yadast, tura furamosh!" One sighting does not end the game; rather, a game can continue for days with repeated successes.

Boys enjoy kite-fighting, or *gudi-paran jungi* (literally, "flying-doll fighting"). Each boy makes his own kite from tissue paper stretched over bamboo sticks, decorated with other tissue-paper cutouts glued on the surface (often to give the appearance of a face). The point of the game is to cross strings with another kite-flyer and saw your string back and forth on his to cut the string and set his kite loose. To make their strings more lethal, boys "glass" them by soaking them in a mixture of ground glass and paste. Each boy has his own jealously guarded method of "glassing."

Adults love to sing and dance, and do both often. Afghanis do not dance with partners; instead, they either dance alone or in circles. Once a party gets going, Afghanis can dance outside for hours. Men spend time in teahouses listening to music, drinking tea, and talking. They also indulge in a more violent entertainment—animal-fighting. Cocks (roosters) are used most often, but partridges, dogs, goats, and even camels are sometimes pitted against each other as well. The two animals fight to the death, and men bet on the outcome.

What movie theaters there are in the cities usually show movies from India and Pakistan.

18 FOLK ART, CRAFTS, AND HOBBIES

The main folk art, and the most profitable one, is carpet-weaving. The weaving is done by young girls and women (except in Turkoman, where men weave, too). Patterns are passed down from generation to generation. Carpet patterns, like recipes elsewhere, are considered "family secrets." The best carpets are from Meymaneh, woven from Karakul wool. These carpets have as many as 55 knots per sq cm (355 per sq in), whereas coarser ones have only 20–30 knots per sq cm (129–194 per sq in). The finest work takes four weavers three months to finish a 6-sq-m (6.6-sq-yd) rug.

Embroidery is widely practiced. Indeed, Afghani women have raised embroidery to an art form, embroidering nearly everything around them. The skullcaps around which men's turbans are wound are usually decorated according to designs that are characteristic of the region. Shirts, vests, and coats may be embroidered—particularly ones for wear on special occasions.

Metalworking has produced silver jewelry and elaborately designed dagger handles, as well as trays and bowls. Lapis lazuli, which Afghanistan has produced for millennia, is made into jewelry. Folk artists paint colorful scenes on the body-panels of trucks. Herat is noted for glassware, and Istalif (in the mountains not far from Kabul) produces a special blue-glazed type of pottery.

¹⁹ SOCIAL PROBLEMS

Continual warfare is the biggest social problem facing the Afghanis. It is hard to talk of any social problems that are not related to the fighting that has been going on for centuries. A country made up of separate tribes of people who are historically warriors seems almost doomed to drown in conflict. The Communists hoped to end that conflict by creating a unified state, but the devoutly Islamic Afghanis rebelled against an "atheistic" government. Without a significant period of peace, there has been no time for Afghanis to give their attentions to improving their standard of living. In Kabul, the only extensively modernized city in Afghanistan, the more-Westernized lifestyle has led to a disintegration of traditional family and tribal values. The elderly, who are respected and revered in villages, are neglected in the cities and turn to drugs for comfort, becoming heroin and opium addicts. Education, health care, employment opportunities, and even the basic food and shelter needs for survival have been severely disrupted by the fighting.

Even the relative peace that was imposed on the north of Afghanistan, in and around Kabul, after the U.S.-led invasion of 2001 has started to unravel. Suicide bombings, unheard of in Afghanistan just a few years prior, had become by 2007 and 2008 nearly commonplace.

Refugee resettlement is also a significant problem. Western countries have been encouraging Afghans to return to their homeland, but as violence has increased, the government has faced delays in finding homes for the returnees.

Opium cultivation also contributes to the lawlessness of Afghanistan. International agencies estimate that Afghanistan's crop, by far the world's largest, has the potential to create more than 500 metric tons of processed heroin annually. Money from the trade is used to arm local warlords and Taliban fighters. The Kabul administration has tried for years to eradicate opium crops, but simply doesn't have the resources, even with United States and NATO support, to make a significant dent in the trade.

²⁰ GENDER ISSUES

Women in Afghanistan face great difficulties at nearly every stage of their lives. By nearly every internationally used measure of quality of life Afghani women rank near the bottom.

Their life expectancy in 2007 was 46 years, 1,600 women die in childbirth for every 100,000 births (it is reported that an Afghan woman dies in childbirth every 30 minutes), and only 12% of women over 15 years are literate. Although the constitution guarantees equality between the sexes, this has made few dents into centuries of traditional oppression. Women in much of the country must still cover themselves in a *burqa* to appear in public and can rarely go anywhere without a male relative accompanying them.

Violence against women is widespread. Most estimates suggest 30–50% of women experience physical, psychological, or sexual violence. It is estimated that between 70–80% of Afghan women are forced into marriage, often at a very young age. The 2004 constitution sets the legal age of marriage at 16 for girls and 18 for boys, but the laws are widely ignored. In villages, it is not uncommon for girls to be married at 11 or 12, often to men in their 40s, 50s, or even older.

²¹ BIBLIOGRAPHY

Ali, Sharifah Enayat. *Cultures of the World: Afghanistan.* New York: Marshall Cavendish, 1995.

Ansary, Mir Tamim. *Afghanistan: Fighting for Freedom.* New York: Dillon Press, 1991.

Crews, Robert D. and Amin Tarzi. *The Taliban and the Crisis of Afghanistan.* Cambridge, MA: Harvard University Press, 2008.

Ewins, Martin. *Afghanistan: A Short History of its People and Politics.* New York: Harper Perennial, 2002.

Stewart, Rory. *The Places in Between.* Washington, PA: Harvest Books, 2006.

—revised by J. Henry

AHIRS

PRONUNCIATION: uh-HIRS
ALTERNATE NAMES: Goala; Gaura; Gopal; Rawat
LOCATION: India (middle Ganges valley; states of Bihar, Orissa, and Uttar Pradesh)
POPULATION: About 45–50 million
LANGUAGE: Language of the region of India in which they live
RELIGION: Hinduism
RELATED ARTICLES: Vol. 3: People of India

¹ INTRODUCTION

The Ahirs are a traditional cattle-keeping caste distributed widely throughout northern and western India. They are thought to be the descendants of an immigrant, probably non-Aryan, tribe of ancient India. One first hears of this tribe, the Abhiras, around the 3rd or 2nd century BC. Abhiras are mentioned in the epic *Mahabharata* as "slaves" and "barbarians" coming from the northwest. Some authorities see them as nomads of Central Asian origin, perhaps entering India in the troubled times that followed Alexander's death. Their early settlements were limited to the Punjab, Rajasthan, and Sind, but in the centuries following the beginning of the Christian Era they migrated towards the south and east. Abhira rulers established extensive kingdoms in Gujarat and nearby areas during this period. Abhiras may even have reached southern India, as legends of the Ayars (Abhiras) appear in the ancient Tamil literature. Eventually the nomadic Abhiras gave up their migratory ways and began to integrate with the surrounding communities. The Sanskrit *Abhira* becomes *Ahir* in the vernacular language.

Ahirs today are mainly cattle-keepers and dairy farmers. They are known locally by names such as Goala, Gaura, Gopal, and Rawat. Although their precise rank varies according to region, Ahirs are usually placed among the Sudras, the third of the four major caste groupings in Hindu society.

² LOCATION AND HOMELAND

Because of the variety of names by which they are known and the lack of caste data in the modern census, any estimate of the Ahir population is, at best, crude. The 1931 census placed the number of Ahirs and related castes at just over 14 million people, or roughly 4% of the population. Assuming that this percentage has not changed significantly, with an estimated population of 1.13 billion in India (March 2008), the Ahir population would lie between 45 million and 50 million people. *Ahir* defines numerous cattle-keeping communities with the same (or related names) distributed throughout India. These usually fall into regional groupings who are not interconnected and do not intermarry. Ahirs are most numerous on the alluvial plains of the middle Ganges valley. Significant Ahir communities are found in the states of Bihar, Orissa, and areas of Uttar Pradesh. Ahirs are also found in central India, and in the western states of Rajasthan and Gujarat.

³ LANGUAGE

Over time, Ahirs have adopted many of the cultural traits—including language—of the regions in which they have settled. Thus Ahirs in Gujarat speak Gujarati, in western Uttar Pradesh they speak Braj, and in Bihar their language is Bihari. Ahirs in other parts of India speak the language current in the areas they inhabit. In some areas, the importance of Ahirs in the local population is reflected in the names of local dialects. Khandeshi, a dialect of the Gujarati language, is also known as Ahirani. Malvi, a Rajasthani dialect, bears the name Ahiri. Ahirwal (Ahirwati) is the name of a folk region southwest of Delhi in which Ahirs dominate and in which the local dialect is called Ahirwati.

⁴ FOLKLORE

The legend of Lorik is one of the most popular in Ahir mythology. Several versions of the legend exist, but the following is told in Mirzapur District in eastern Uttar Pradesh. Lorik is an Ahir who elopes with Chandani, his neighbor's wife. He defeats her husband in a fight and then goes on to meet Mahapatiya Dusadh, chief of the gamblers. Lorik loses everything, including Chandani, but the girl argues her jewelry was not part of the stake and induces Lorik to play again. This time Chandani distracts the chief of the gamblers by displaying her ankles, and Lorik wins everything back. Chandani tells Lorik she has been insulted by his opponent, so Lorik cuts off the gambler's head with his magic sword. The head and the body are turned to stone.

In his subsequent wanderings, Lorik gains a kingdom and marries the girl (not Chandani) to whom he had been betrothed. He eventually incurs the displeasure of the god Indra, and after giving in to temptation by Indra's wife who assumed the form of Chandani, Lorik dies in shame in Varanasi (Banaras). Several elements of this tale—the gambling match, the magic sword, the body turning into stone, and the fidelity test—are common motifs in folk tales in both the East and the West.

⁵ RELIGION

The majority of Ahirs are Hindu and share in the basic beliefs and practices of Hinduism. They belong mostly to the Vaishnava sect, i.e., they worship the god Vishnu rather than Shiva. (In Bihar, however, many are Shaivites or worship the Mother Goddess). Ahirs pay particular respect to, and are closely identified with, the legendary god Krishna. Krishna is regarded as the eighth incarnation of Vishnu, although he is also worshiped in his own right. The name *Krishna* (meaning "black") occurs in the Vedas, but not in reference to any deity. The dark-skinned god of later times is basically non-Vedic in origin, with a later Aryan overlay. Some scholars have argued that Krishna was a pastoral deity of the Ahirs, whose worship was spread throughout northern India during their migrations and subsequently absorbed into Hinduism. Others see aspects of Krishna (e.g., Krishna as child-god) as reflecting knowledge of Christ acquired by Ahirs from early Christian missionaries in India.

Many legends of Krishna, for example, his birth and childhood, his exploits as a cowherd, and his amorous dalliance with the *gopis* (cowgirls), are set in Braj, the region of western Uttar Pradesh State around Mathura and Vrindavan. Even today, many Ahir groups in northern India have a tradition that their ancestors came from this region of India. The cow is regarded as the favorite animal of Krishna, and Krishna-worshipers are among the most ardent supporters of the Hindu concept of the sanctity of the cow. Not only is the cow revered as a deity, Ahirs also worship various local gods who are linked in some way with cattle and cattle-keeping.

6 MAJOR HOLIDAYS

Ahirs celebrate all the major festivals of Hinduism. Of particular importance among the community, however, are the festivals dedicated to Krishna. These include Holi, Divali, Janamastami (Krishna's birthday), and cattle festivals such as Gopashtami and Govardhan Puja. Gopashtami, literally "Cow Eighth," falls on the eighth day of the Hindu month of Kartik (October-November). It marks the occasion when the child Krishna first took his father's cattle out to graze in the forests of Braj. Cattle are washed and decorated at this time, processions of cattle are taken through the streets of towns and villages, and cows are worshiped (the *go-puja* ceremony). Govardhan Puja, another cattle-related festival, falls on the day after the Divali festival. The centerpiece of this ritual is the worship of an image made of cow dung said, in certain areas of the country, to represent Krishna. An unusual custom of the Ahirs of Bihar and West Bengal at Govardhan Puja is a ritual involving the goading of village cattle to trample a pig to death.

7 RITES OF PASSAGE

In the Chhattisgarh region of central India, Rawats (i.e. Ahirs) follow a rite known as *sidhori* during pregnancy. This involves feeding the pregnant woman special foods so that the unborn child will not hunger for these foods in its later life. If the birth is delayed, a line of men and boys is formed between the house and a well. A pitcher is then passed rapidly along the line, filled with water, and returned to the house. The speed acquired by the water on its trip to the house, it is believed, will be communicated to the woman and give rise to a quick delivery. The father is not allowed to see the mother or child until purificatory rites are performed on the sixth day. If a child is born on an inauspicious day, its ears are pierced in the fifth month after birth to protect it from possible harm.

Ahirs cremate their dead, after performing the appropriate funeral rites. One unusual ritual in Chhattisgarh involves bringing the soul back to the house. On the third day after death, women place a lamp on a red, earthen pot and go to a pond, river, or stream at night. Fish are attracted to the light and one is caught, placed in water in the pot, and taken home. The son of the deceased, or a close relative, takes a stone and washes it with water from the pot. After the sacrifice of a cock or hen, the stone is enshrined in the house as a family god. It is believed that the dead person's soul is brought back to the house in the fish and then transferred to the stone by the act of washing it in the water. The sacrifice of a fowl is repeated annually before the stone.

8 INTERPERSONAL RELATIONS

Ahirs follow the greeting patterns and visiting customs of the local communities among whom they reside.

9 LIVING CONDITIONS

Wherever Ahirs settled, they adopted many local customs concerning caste, kinship, and material culture. Ahir villages in Rajasthan, for example, differ little in form and appearance from other villages in the region. Settlements are nucleated, located in the center of the village lands. Houses, constructed

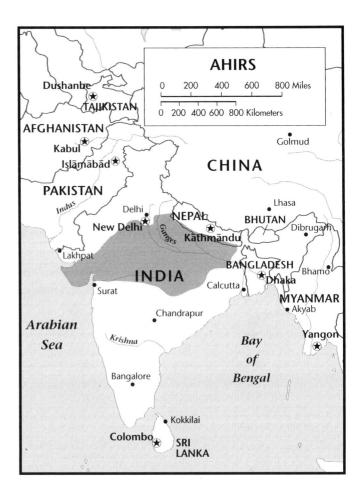

haphazardly along winding, unpaved lanes, are built of mud or sun-dried brick. Attached to the houses are small compounds, enclosed by low mud walls or thorn fences, used for keeping cattle at night. Residences contain living quarters and several small rooms used for storage. People sleep on the floor on mats or on low wooden cots. In the hot season, it is common to sleep outdoors or on the roof. Most houses lack sanitary facilities, with villagers going to the fields to perform daily bodily functions. In general, creature comforts and standards of living reflect the economic status of individual families.

10 FAMILY LIFE

Ahirs fall into several broad regional groupings which are not connected and which do not intermarry. In any given region, there are endogamous groups of Ahirs, each divided into exogamous clans (*gotra*). Marriage rituals do not differ much from those of other Hindu castes. The rules of marriage conform to broader regional practices. In Uttar Pradesh, for example, marriage is forbidden between a member of a clan and the clans of one sisters' relations up to three generations. In Bihar, marriage is regulated according to territorial-based categories called *muls*. The marriage of first cousins is prohibited. Marriages are arranged. Ahir girls are wed around the time of puberty, although some groups prefer infant marriage. Residence is patrilocal, i.e., the bride moves into the household of her husband's family. Family structure conforms to regional patterns, with the extended family being the norm. Divorce is possible under certain circumstances, although it requires the approval of the caste's *panchayat* or council. Widow remarriage is allowed.

11 CLOTHING

Just as they have adopted local languages, Ahirs have assumed the regional dress of their locality. Thus Ghosis (Ahirs who have converted to Islam) in central India wear tight, short pants of white cotton, a waist band with a fringe on either end, a short jacket, and a tight, saucer-shaped turban. Ghosi women wear a long bodice over a petticoat. Women wear a variety of jewelry. Rawat women favor large, cylindrical leg-ornaments called *churas*. Ahir girls are commonly tattooed immediately after marriage.

12 FOOD

Most Ahirs are nonvegetarian, eating goat, chicken, and, in some cases, pork. There are reports from central India that local Ahirs will even eat field mice and rats. Ahirs do not eat beef, however, and their special relationship with the cow is reflected in their good social standing in many communities. Many higher-caste communities will accept food and water from Ahirs. Milk and dairy products are important in the Ahir diet, which generally mirrors regional dietary patterns. Ahirs also consume local "country" liquor in fair quantities.

13 EDUCATION

In such a numerous and widely distributed community, literacy and educational levels vary. Although Ahirs have access to government schools, the nature of their occupation and their predominantly rural character is reflected in generally low levels of literacy and educational achievement.

14 CULTURAL HERITAGE

The folk songs and dances of the Ahirs reflect their pastoral traditions and their historical associations with Krishna. Known as *birhas,* Ahir songs are accompanied by the flute and tell of past heroes or of the carefree life of the cowherds. Some are love songs, expressing the longings of Ahir youth. Love is also the theme of the *rasas,* the folk dances depicted in early paintings and sculptural representations of Krishna. These often show the cowherd god playing on his flute, surrounded by a ring of dancing *gopis* (cowgirls). The *garba* dance of Gujarat and many of the folk dances of Uttar Pradesh and other areas are derived from the rasas of old.

15 WORK

The hereditary occupation of Ahirs is tending milk cattle and dealing in dairy products such as milk, butter, and *ghi* (clarified butter). In the past, Ahir women sometimes entered domestic service. One group, the Dauwa Ahirs of central India, are descended from the illegitimate offspring of Rajput fathers and Ahir women employed as wet-nurses. Today, perhaps no more than one-third of the Ahirs breed cattle or are dairy farmers, and even less cling to their old nomadic ways. The majority of Ahirs are now engaged in cultivation, either as farmers or as laborers. Those few who have acquired some education may work in offices or other low-level clerical jobs.

16 SPORTS

As might be expected, many of the traditional pastimes of Ahirs focus on their cattle. At the time of the Gopashtami festival, bull fights are staged in honor of Krishna. Two bulls are set on each other, and they lock horns in a test of strength until one submits to the other. The animals are separated before they hurt each other. Cattle sports represent an ancient tradition in India, with evidence suggesting "bull-jumping" took place in the Harappan culture nearly 4,000 years ago. Another modern practice found in rural areas is the "running of the herds." At the time of Govardhan Puja, village cattle are taken outside the settlement then stampeded towards their pens in the village. The men of the village try to stop them from reaching their pens. It is considered a sign of good fortune for the next year if the herds manage to reach their pens safely.

17 ENTERTAINMENT AND RECREATION

In addition to their folk activities, Ahirs seek recreation and entertainment at the numerous fairs and festivals of rural India. One of the biggest and best-known of these is the Pushkar Camel and Cattle Fair in Rajasthan, which is attended by livestock breeders and farmers from a wide area. The fair has even become an attraction for Western tourists. Depending on their individual circumstances and where they live, Ahirs have radios and televisions and can visit movie theaters in nearby towns for entertainment.

18 FOLK ART, CRAFTS, AND HOBBIES

Although pastoral themes and the legends of the cowherd god Krishna are prominent motifs in Indian art, paintings and sculptures depicting such subjects are produced by professional artisan castes. The Ahirs themselves have not developed folk arts or crafts that can be considered unique to the community.

19 SOCIAL PROBLEMS

Given the extensive geographic distribution and variation in culture of Ahir communities in India, it is difficult to make generalized statements about their social conditions. Ahirs are usually ranked as the highest of the cultivating castes and thus do not face the problems of discrimination, etc., encountered by Untouchables and tribal groups. However, in central India many Ahirs are hardly considered Hindu because they live in Gond villages.

There are many among the Ahir community who face problems typical of the rural peasant in India today, such as landlessness, poverty, debt, illiteracy, and alcoholism. In general, however, Ahirs are placed with the Jat and Gujar as being among the most successful cultivating castes of northern India.

20 GENDER ISSUES

Ahir women, like most women in India, occupy a low social status. They are involved in agricultural activities (many are agricultural laborers), collect fuel and run the household, but have little say or control in the social arena. Literacy among them is low, despite recent central government attempts to remove gender barriers in education. (Until 1976, education was solely the concern of states but a Constitutional Amendment permitted the Union Government to legislate educational reforms , viz the 2001 Sarva Shihska Abhiyan (SAA) was which aimed at providing schooling for all 6-14 year-olds by the year

2005, at bridging all gender and social gaps by 2007, and at universal retention by 2010). Although formerly practicing child marriage (this still occurs, though it has been made illegal by the Union Government), there is a tendency among Ahirs for the age of marriage to be delayed to between 15 and 20 years for women. Customs regarding widow remarriage and divorce vary among Ahir groups. Occasionally, due to illness or the inability of a wife to bear children, a man is allowed to take a second wife, provided this act is approved by the local *panchayat* or tribal council.

[21] BIBLIOGRAPHY

India 2007: A Reference Annual. Reserch and Reference Division, Ministry of Information and Broadcasting, Government of India, 2007.

Lodrick, Deryck O. "Gopashtami and Govardhan Puja: Two Krishna Festivals of India." *Journal of Cultural Geography* 7, no. 2 (Spring/Summer 1987): 101–16.

Russell, R. V., and Hira Lal. "Ahir." In *The Tribes and Castes of the Central Provinces of India.* Vol. 2. Nagpur: Government Printing Press, 1916.

Singh, S. "Distribution Patterns of the Major Agricultural Communities (Ahirs, Gujars, Jats and Rajputs) in their Traditional Abode of the Northwestern Indian Subcontinent." *Population Geography* 10, nos. 1-2 (Jun-Dec 1988), 1-17.

Suryavanshi, Bhagwansingh. *The Abhiras: Their History and Culture.* Baroda: M. S. University of Baroda, Dept. of Archaeology and Ancient History, 1962.

Yadava, S. D. S. *Followers of Krishna.* New Delhi: Lancer's Publishers, 2006.

—by D. O. Lodrick

AINU

PRONUNCIATION: EYE-noo
LOCATION: Japan (Hokkaidô)
POPULATION: 25,000 (Official figure for Hokkaidô; some believe that the numbers are substantially higher for Japan as well as for Hokkaidô)
LANGUAGE: Japanese; Ainu (few present speakers)
RELIGION: Pantheistic beliefs
RELATED ARTICLES: Vol. 3: Japanese

[1] INTRODUCTION

Until 400 years ago, the Ainu, a hunting and fishing people, controlled Hokkaidô, which in the late 19th century was incorporated as the northernmost of Japan's four main islands. Today they are a small minority group of Japan. Their origins remain in dispute. It was long believed that they came from Siberia or from the southern Pacific, originally comprising different groups; recent DNA studies seem to indicate, however, that the Ainu have approximately the same genes as mainstream Japanese and Ryukyuans, all stemming from north Asia. After centuries of developing Ainu culture in interaction with, but distinctive from, that of the Japanese, in recent centuries, they have faced Japanese government policy of modernization and integration. As with indigenous people in the United States and many other nations, the Ainu have largely assimilated. And like many other such groups, there have been signs of cultural revival in recent decades.

The oldest ruins found in Hokkaidô, the Ainu homeland, date from 20,000 to 30,000 years ago in the Old Stone Age. Iron was introduced approximately 2,000 years ago from either southern Japan or the continent, probably by ancestors or groups related to the Ainu. Between the 8th and 13th centuries, earthenware unique to Hokkaidô and the northern mainland appeared. Its producers were the direct ancestors of the Ainu. The subsequent 300 to 400 years saw the development of the culture known today as uniquely Ainu.

[2] LOCATION AND HOMELAND

Hokkaidô is 83,520 sq km (32,247 sq mi)—one-fifth of Japan, and twice as large as Switzerland. A small number of Ainu live on southern Sakhalin. Earlier, the Ainu also lived in the southern Kuril Islands, along the lower reaches of the Amur River, and in Kamchatka, as well as the northern part of the Northeast region of Honshû. Their ancestors may once have lived all over Japan.

Hokkaidô is surrounded by beautiful coasts. There are many mountains, lakes, and rivers. Into the 20th century its land was densely wooded with ancient trees. Two major mountain ranges, Kitami in the north and Hidaka in the south, divide Hokkaidô into the eastern and western regions. The Saru River basin area in southeastern Hokkaidô is known as a historical center of Ainu culture.

An 1807 survey reported the Hokkaidô and Sakhalin Ainu population as 23,797. Mixed marriages between Ainu and mainland Japanese became more common over the last century. In 1986 the total number of people in Hokkaidô identifying themselves as Ainu was 24,381. A 2006 Hokkaidô survey found 23,782 Ainu in 72 municipalities, of which 59.5% resided in Hidaka and Iburi districts. There is Ainu population in mainland cities as well, including some 2,700 in Tokyo. The survey numbers represent only those who identified themselves as Ainu. In the past many people of Ainu ancestry may have preferred not to identify themselves as Ainu.

In the late 19th century, the central government created a colonial office for Hokkaidô's economic development and encouraged settlers from other parts of Japan. A similar government office now continues to promote Hokkaidô's development. With the loss or in some cases the deliberate destruction of their land, their livelihood, their language and their traditional culture, the Ainu had to adapt to a rapidly industrializing society.

³ LANGUAGE

Ainu is said to belong either to a Paleo-Asiatic or a Paleo-Siberian group of languages. It divides into Hokkaidô and Sakhalin dialects, and each can be subdivided into minor dialects. The Saru region dialect is said to be especially refined, rich with oral traditions. The Ainu language was first systematically studied by the British missionary John Batchelor (1854–1944), the Japanese linguist Kindaichi Kyôsuke (1882–1971), and the Ainu linguist Chiri Mashio (1909–1961).

Interesting characteristics of the Ainu language include: (1) p-, b-, k- sounds are interchangeable with b-, d-, g- sounds, and c-, s- sounds are close to ch-, sh- sounds; (2) instead of stress accents, as in English, a pitch accent system, as in Japanese, is found in most Hokkaidô dialects; (3) word order is similar to Japanese: the subject, the object, then the verb; (4) verbs and some nouns, instead of conjugating and declining as in Latin and other European languages, have affixes that that indicate the first person ("I") and second person (informal "you" and formal "you").

To explain the fourth point, the noun *tek*, meaning "hand," takes the form *ku-tek-e* when the hand(s) belonging to the speaker is meant (*ku-* indicating the first person and -*e* indicating the possessive mode). The verb *kore*, meaning "give," takes the form *e-en-kore* if the giving occurs from "you" (second person singular informal) to "us" (first person plural). Affixing is a distinctive aspect of Ainu. Adding prefixes and suffixes can produce long words, even so long that they correspond to whole sentences in English or Japanese.

Ainu and Japanese share many single words. God (male or female) is *kamui* in Ainu and *kami* in Japanese. Chopstick(s) is *pasui* in Ainu and *hashi* in Japanese. The word *sirokani* (silver) and *konkani* (gold) in literary Ainu correspond to *shirokane* and *kogane* in literary Japanese (see quotation below). The two languages, however, are unrelated. Two well-known Ainu words still commonly used refer to venerated Ainu individuals: *ekasi* (grandfather or sire) and *huci* (grandmother or grand dame).

The Ainu historically had no written language. It can no longer be said, however, that there is no written Ainu language. It is the same situation as when the Japanese adopted Chinese characters to create the Japanese phonetic system of hiragana and katakana, or borrowed the Roman alphabet to write "Romaji," Ainu adopted the alphabet and katakana, improving both systems over the years to represent Ainu language. Now "Ainu-go" is one of the language choices on the computer. Extended katakana (the Japanese phonetic syllabaries with some modifications) or the Roman alphabet is used to transcribe

or write Ainu. Few people now speak Ainu as their primary language. The folklorist from the Saru region Kayano Shigeru (1926–2006) called himself the youngest living Ainu able to speak fluent Ainu. In 1982 Kayano, a leading figure in the Ainu cultural preservation and revival movement, founded the first Ainu Language School. By 1993 the number of Ainu language schools had increased to 11; by 2007 the number had risen to 14 in Hokkaidô and a few in Kantô.

Traditional Ainu names are single names without surnames. For example, Kayano Shigeru's grandfather was named Totkaram ("may he grow well"), and his grandmother Tekatte ("an added hand"). Starting in 1876, the Ainu were forced to adopt Japanese names. A few Ainu people today have reclaimed their Ainu names, using a single name or combining it with a Japanese name. Thus, an Ainu embroiderer calls herself Chikap Mieko, "Chikap" being an Ainu name meaning "bird."

The name Ainu comes from a common noun *ainu,* meaning "human(s)." Once the term was felt to be derogatory, but more Ainu now use the name positively, taking pride in their ethnic identity. Their land is called "Ainu Mosir"—peaceful land of humans. The phrase *ainu nenoan ainu* means "human-like human." The following is a famous refrain from a poem about the owl deity:

> *sirokanipe ranran piskan*
> (fall, fall, silver drops, all around)
> *konkanipe ranran piskan*
> (fall, fall, golden drops, all around)

In 2001 Kayano Shigeru opened a small Ainu language FM radio station *called FM Nibutani Broadcast (nicknamed "FM Pipausi" after the name of the old village, meaning* "a place where there are many marsh snails," now part of present-day Nibutani). It only reached listeners in the Nibutani area then, but back numbers are now available on RealPlayer, a cross-platform media player. The radio not only provides local news and recalls Ainu tradition mostly in Japanese, but also offers Ainu lessons and airs recordings of old recitations by Ainu bards. The quarterly *Ainu Times* is a bilingual newspaper, with Ainu and Japanese printed side by side. STV (Sapporo Television) started an Ainu language lesson program in 1999 with Kayano Shigeru as the original instructor. It continues today with elderly and younger Ainu lecturers from different areas of Hokkaidô presenting Ainu local dialects. Kayano Shigeru was the driving force behind all these activities, along with Kayano Shirô, his second son.

⁴ FOLKLORE

The world was created, according to mythic poetry, when floating oil in the ocean rose like a flame and became the sky. What was left turned into land. Vapor gathered over the land and a god was created. From the vapor of the sky, another god was created and descended on five colored clouds. Out of those clouds, the two gods created the sea, soil, minerals, plants, and animals. The two gods married and produced many gods including two shining gods—the sun god and the moon god, who rose to Heaven in order to illuminate the fog-covered dark places of the world.

Okikurmi of the Saru region is a semi-divine hero who descended from Heaven to help humans, who lived in a beautiful land but did not know how to build fire or make bows and arrows. Okikurmi taught them how to build fire, to hunt, to catch salmon, to plant millet, to brew millet wine, and to worship the gods. He married and stayed in the village, but eventually returned to the divine land.

Ainu historical heroes include Kosamainu and Samkusainu. Kosamainu, who lived in eastern Hokkaidô, led an Ainu rebellion against the mainland Japanese ruling the southern tip of Hokkaidô, called Matsumae. He destroyed 10 out of the 12 Japanese bases but was killed in 1457. Samkusainu organized Ainu in the southern half of the island during a 1669 uprising, but after two months they were destroyed by Matsumae forces armed with guns.

⁵ RELIGION

Ainu religion is pantheistic, believing in many gods. In the mountains dwell the god of mountains and in the river dwells the god of water. The Ainu hunted, fished, and gathered food in modest quantities so as not to disturb these gods. Animals were visitors from the other world who temporarily assumed animal shapes. The bear, striped owl, and killer whale received the greatest respect as divine incarnations.

The most important god in the home was the female god of fire. Every house had a fire pit where cooking, eating, and rituals took place. The main offerings made to this and to other gods were wine and *inau*, a whittled twig or pole, usually of willow, with shavings still attached and decoratively curled. A fence-like row of taller *inau* stood outside between the main house and the raised storehouse. Outdoor rituals were observed before this sacred altar area.

⁶ MAJOR HOLIDAYS

The spirit-sending festival, called *i-omante,* either for a bear or striped owl, was the most important Ainu festival. The bear *i-omante* was observed once in 5 or 10 years. After three days of reverence to a bear cub, accompanied by prayers, dancing, and singing, it was shot with arrows. The head was decorated and placed at the altar, while the meat was enjoyed by the members of the village community. The spirit, while visiting this world, had temporarily adopted the form of a bear; the bear ritual released the spirit from the form so it could return to the other land. Similar festivals are observed by many northern peoples.

Another important festival is boat-launching, called *cip-sanke.* A newly built canoe (or canoes) is brought from the place of construction to the river. The festival is still celebrated in Nibutani around August 20. In April 1996, the Nibutani dam was filled with water but the Ainu won their legal battle to have the water drained and the festival occurred one last time in the original Saru river. More recently, it has been celebrated in a lower reach of the Saru. It has become a festivity welcoming mainland Japanese as well, and the launching preceded by prayers and dances is followed by Japanese Bon-dances joined by all who wish to participate.

There are also youthful attempts to create new forms that combine traditional Ainu oral performances with contemporary music and dance. "Ainu Rebels," formed in 2006, is constituted mostly of Ainu youth but also including wajin and foreigners, is active, singing and dancing. They draw on Ainu oral tradition adapted to hip hop and other modern forms, as well as engaging in artistic activities that combine traditional Ainu art with contemporary artistic elements.

⁷ RITES OF PASSAGE

In preparation for adulthood, boys traditionally learned hunting, carving, and making tools like arrows; girls learned weaving, sewing, and embroidery. Girls, usually in their mid-teens, were tattooed around the mouth in stages by a skilled older woman; long ago they were also tattooed on the forearms. The Japanese government banned tattooing in 1871.

The gift of a knife mounted in carved wood from a young man indicated both his skill and his love. The gift of embroidery from a young woman similarly indicated her skill and her willingness to accept his proposal. In some cases, a young man visited the family of a woman he wished to marry, helping her father in hunting, carving, and so forth. When he proved himself an honest, skilled worker, the father approved the marriage.

A death was mourned by relatives and neighbors, fully dressed in embroidered costume, men wearing a ceremonial sword and women a necklace of beads. The important elements of a funeral were prayers to the fire deity and verse laments that included wishes for a smooth journey to the other world. Items to be buried with the dead were first broken or cracked so that the spirits would be released and travel together to the other world. Sometimes burial was followed by the burning of the dwelling. The funeral for an unnatural death could include a tirade against the gods.

⁸ INTERPERSONAL RELATIONS

A formal greeting, *irankarapte,* which corresponds to "how are you" in English, means "let me softly touch your heart."

It is said that Ainu people always shared food and drink with neighbors, even a cup of wine. As the host and the guests seated themselves around the fire pit, the host dipped his ceremonial chopstick in the cup of wine, sprinkled a few drops onto the fire pit giving thanks to the fire god (goddess of fire), then he and the guests shared the wine. The first catch of salmon of the year in early fall was a special item to be shared with neighbors.

There was a custom, called *ukocaranke* (mutual argumentation), for settling differences by debating instead of fighting. The disputants sat and argued for hours or even days until one side was defeated and agreed to compensate the other. Representatives with oratorical skills and endurance were chosen to resolve disputes between villages. Kayano Shigeru repeatedly emphasized the importance of this tradition, and the term is now widely known to mainlanders as well.

⁹ LIVING CONDITIONS

In the old days the Ainu house was made of poles and thatch plant and warmly insulated for the northern climate, with a fire pit at the center of the main room and an opening below each end of the ridge for smoke to escape. Between 3 and 20 such houses, built at appropriate distances from one another so that fire would not spread but a voice would reach in case of emergency, formed a village community called *kotan*. A *kotan* was usually located by water for convenient fishing but also in the woods to remain safe from floods and close to gathering grounds. As necessary, the *kotan* moved from place to place in search of a better livelihood.

Tatsue Sato, wearing traditional Ainu clothing, in her Tokyo restaurant. To many Japanese, the Ainu remain a target of discrimination. In the summer of 1997, a law was passed to officially recognize the Ainu as a minority.
(AP Images/Shizuo Kambayashi)

¹⁰ FAMILY LIFE

Besides weaving and embroidering, women farmed, gathered wild plants, pounded grains with a pestle, and cared for babies, while men hunted, fished, and carved. Some accounts suggest that married couples lived in separate houses, others that they stayed with the husband's parents. A bilineal descent system was observed until recently. Males traced descent through different animal crests (such as a killer whale insignia) and females through hereditary chastity belts and forearm tattoo designs. The inheritance could include the art of a bard (male or female), a midwife, or a shaman. The midwife and shamaness Aoki Aiko (1914–1995) inherited her arts as the fifth generation offspring of the female line of the family. Dogs were favorite animals. In one scene of an epic poem describing the descent of a divine youth to this world, a dog is mentioned as guarding millet grains. Dogs were also used in hunting.

¹¹ CLOTHING

The Ainu traditional robe made of a textile woven of inner elm bark fibers and worn with a woven sash is similar in shape to the mainland Japanese kimono. The male robe was calf-length. In winter a short sleeveless jacket of deer or other animal fur was also worn. The female robe was ankle-length and worn over a long undershirt with no front opening. The robes were hand-embroidered or appliquéd with rope-like designs. A

pointed edge at the tip of each front flap was characteristic of the Saru region.

The traditional costume is still worn on special occasions by some, but in everyday life the Ainu wear international-style clothing like other Japanese.

¹² FOOD

Traditional staple foods were salmon and deer meat, in addition to millet raised at home and herbs and roots picked in the woods. Millet was largely replaced by rice earlier in this century. During the season, fresh salmon was cut up and boiled in soup. A rice porridge called *ciporosayo* was prepared by adding heaping servings of salmon roe to boiled grains.

As in other cold regions, Ainu children used to enjoy making maple ice candy. On a late March or early April evening, when a cold night was expected, they made cuts in the bark of a big sugar maple and placed containers of sorrel stalks (sorrel is hollow inside) at the roots of the tree to collect dripping syrup. In the morning, they found the sorrel cylinders filled with frozen white syrup.

Sito, dumplings made of vegetable starch, usually eaten with kelp-based sweet sauce, are still commonly enjoyed today.

Among the many traditional utensils and artifacts are the poison arrow, unattended trap arrow, rabbit trap, fish trap, ceremonial sword, mountain knife, canoe, woven bag, and loom.

In the early 1960s Kayano Shigeru began privately collecting many such genuine items in and around his village in the Saru region, when he realized that what was left of the Ainu cultural heritage were scatterings from the communities. His collection developed into the Biratori Township Nibutani Ainu Cultural Museum and the Kayano Shigeru Ainu Memorial Museum. Also famous is the Ainu Museum established in 1984 in Shiraoi in southeastern Hokkaidô on the Pacific.

¹³ EDUCATION

Traditionally children were educated at home, with grandparents reciting poems and tales while parents taught practical skills and crafts. From the late 19th century, the compulsory education emphasized the use of Japanese by Ainu children. According to a 2006 survey conducted by Hokkaidô, in the municipalities inhabited by Ainu, the rate of Ainu children advancing from junior to senior high school increased from 41.6% in 1972 to 93.5% in 2006. The rate of Ainu advancing to college increased from 8.8% to 17.4% in the same period. Nevertheless, the 2006 Ainu ratios are below those of mainstream Japanese in the same areas, which are, respectively, 98.3% (to senior high) and 38.5 % (to college).

¹⁴ CULTURAL HERITAGE

The Ainu have handed down a vast body of oral traditions. The main categories are *yukar* and *oina* (longer and shorter epic poems in literary Ainu), *uwepekere* and *upasikma* (old tales and autobiographical stories, both in prose), lullabies, and dance songs. *Yukar* usually refers to heroic poetry, chanted mainly by men, dealing with demi-gods and humans, but it also includes *oina,* or *kamui yukar,* shorter epics chanted principally by women about the gods. The Saru region, in south central Hokkaidô, is especially known as the homeland of many bards and storytellers.

Yukar was narrated by the fireside for a mixed gathering of men, women, and children, with men sometimes reclining and beating time on the belly. Depending upon the piece, it lasted all night or even for a few nights. There were also festival songs, group dance-songs, and stamping dances.

The best known Ainu musical instrument is the *mukkuri,* a mouth harp made of wood. There were also coiled-bark horns, straw flutes, skin drums, five-string zithers, and a type of lute.

15 WORK

Since the mid-19th century, hunting, fishing, and gathering of wild plants, accompanied by millet raising, have been replaced by rice and dry-crop cultivation and commercial fishing. Other activities in Hokkaidô include dairy farming, forestry, mining, food processing, wood working, pulp, and paper industries. The Ainu contribute to all of these. In 2006, 28.6% of the Hokkaidô Ainu population worked in the agricultural sector, decreasing over one half from 1972; 27.7% worked in manufacturing, increasing 1.4 times more from 1972; and 41.1% in small and medium-sized service-oriented enterprises, the latter increasing over 2.5 times.

16 SPORTS

Traditional sports for children included swimming and canoeing. In the early 20th century there was a children's game called *seipirakka* (shell clogs). A hole was bored through the shell of a large surf clam and a thick rope passed through it. Children wore two clams each, with the rope between the first two toes, and walked or ran about on them. The shells made a clicking noise like horseshoes. Another indigenous Ainu game was making toy *pattari* in the creek when the snow thawed in spring. They were made from hollow stalks of sorrel filled with creek water. With the accumulation of water, one end of the stalk dropped to the ground under the weight. On the rebound, the other end hit the ground with a thump. Adults used real *pattari* to pound millet grains.

17 ENTERTAINMENT AND RECREATION

The Ainu enjoy many forms of modern entertainment similar to those enjoyed by mainland Japanese, such as television, movies, theater, concerts, and karaoke. Appreciation of seasonal changes and holiday festivals are traditional pastimes that remain popular. Major festivals attract huge crowds, and famous sites for admiring plum and cherry blossoms, irises, azaleas, chrysanthemums, and the bright leaves of fall draw many visitors who come to view the sights and to party outdoors among the flowers.

18 FOLK ART, CRAFTS, AND HOBBIES

Weaving, embroidery, and carving are among the most important forms of folk art. Some types of traditional Ainu weaving were once almost lost, but were revived around the 1970s. Chikap Mieko, a second generation professional embroiderer, builds her original embroidery on the foundation of the traditional art. Carved trays and bears are treasured tourist items. Ainu influence on modern Japanese music has been observed in recent years. Again recently, two traditional musical instruments have become better known: *tonkori,* a five-stringed Sakhalin string instrument revived the musician by the name of OKI, and *mukkur,* a mouth harp. At Shiraoi Museum, tonkori lessons are given.

19 SOCIAL PROBLEMS

The 1899 Ainu law that treated the Ainu as "former aborigines" remained in effect into the 1990s. As a representative to the National Diet between 1994 and 1998, Kayano Shigeru took the lead in fighting to eliminate this law. A new Ainu law, called "A Law Related to the Promotion of Ainu Culture as well as Spread and Enlightenment of Knowledge related to Ainu Traditions," was enacted in 1997, replacing the 1899 law. The recent construction of a dam in Kayano's homeland, Nibutani village in Biratori town, exemplifies forceful development of Hokkaidô at the cost of the Ainu's civil rights. Despite the resistance led by Kayano Shigeru and Kaizawa Tadashi, construction proceeded and in early 1996 the village was buried under water. In a speech delivered in February 1988 at a meeting held in Hokkaidô's capital city on the use of Hokkaidô lands, Kayano stated that he would accept the Nibutani dam construction plan if only the salmon fishing rights be returned to the Nibutani Ainu in exchange for the destruction of their homes and fields. His request was ignored.

20 GENDER ISSUES

Ainu society traditionally was organized around clear cut divisions among men and women. Typically men went out to hunt or fish, and women wove, maintained the household, and ground grains. Traditionally, men chanted long heroic verses while women chanted shorter songs of the gods. By mid-20th century, with few male chanters available, women chanters replaced them.

21 BIBLIOGRAPHY

Ainu and Their Culture: A Critical Twenty-First Century Assessment, http://japanfocus.org/products/details/2589 (May 2008).

Ainu no sato Nibutani ni ikite (Living in Nibutani, an Ainu village). Hokkaidô Shinbunsha. 1987.

Encyclopedia of Japan. New York: Kôdansha, 1983. Hanazaki, Kôhei. *Shimajima wa hanazuna* (A Wreath of islands). Tokyo: Shakai Hyôronsha, 1990. Hokkaidô Government Official Site, http://www.pref.hokkaido.lg.jp/foreign/english.htm (May 2008).

Hokkaidô Utari Kyôkai (Hokkaidô Ainu Association) http://www.ainu-assn.or.jp/ (May 2008).

Honda, Katsuichi. *Harukor: An Ainu Woman's Tale* (trans. Kyoko Selden). Berkeley: University of California Press, 2000.

Howell, David. *Geographies of Identity in Nineteenth-Century Japan.* Berkeley: University of California Press, 2005.

Japan: An Illustrated Encyclopedia. New York: Kôdansha, 1993.

Kamuiyukar to mukashibanashi (Divine epics and old tales). Tokyo: Shôgakukan, 1988.

Kayano, Shigeru. *Our Land Was a Forest: An Ainu Memoir* (trans. Kyoko Selden and Lili Selden). Boulder, CO: Westview Press, 1994.

Nibutani Museum of Ainu Culture, Biratoty City, http://www.ainu-museum-nibutani.org/html/mainN.htm (May 2008).

Philippi, Donald L. *Songs of Gods, Songs of Humans: The Epic Tradition of the Ainu.* Princeton: Princeton University Press, 1979.

—by Kyoko Selden

'ALAWIS

PRONUNCIATION: ah-LOW-eez
ALTERNATE NAMES: 'Alawite
LOCATION: Syria; Lebanon; Turkey.
POPULATION: 1.4 million in Syria; 100,000 in Lebanon; indeterminate numbers in Israel-occupied Syrian Golan Heights, uncounted numbers in Turkey, and a small diaspora in Australia
LANGUAGE: Arabic
RELIGION: Secret 'Alawi faith; a branch of Shia Islam

OVERVIEW

'Alawi (or 'Alawite) means "a follower of 'Ali," the Prophet Muhammad's cousin and son-in-law. The 'Alawis (and all Shia Muslims) believe that 'Ali was Muhammad's rightful heir to political and spiritual leadership of the Muslim community. Originally calling themselves "Nusairis," they became known as 'Alawis only in 1920 after the French colonizers dubbed them as such. As part of their colonial strategy, the French normally allied with the minority of any particular territory they occupied. The minority would then greatly benefit from the occupation of the country, as the French would promote them to positions from which they otherwise would be banned. This was true of the 'Alawis as well.

During the Abbasid Empire of the 12th century AD, Nusairi views became increasingly differentiated from mainstream Shia views. This resulted in increasing persecution by the Sunni government of the Abbasids. The Nusairis were forced to flee from Iraq and Arabia farther and farther west, until they reached the mountains in western Syria on the Mediterranean coast. There they survived, despite continuing persecution, for centuries.

The French granted the people they called 'Alawis a strong measure of autonomy in 1920 when the French occupation of Syria was formalized by the League of Nations. However, when the French left in 1946, the new Syrian government sent troops into the 'Alawi villages to squelch their autonomy and forcibly assimilate them into becoming fully integrated Syrian citizens. Although some 'Alawis moved down from the mountains to the Latakia province on the coast, they rarely mingled with the rest of Syrian society, even in their new urban environments.

The 'Alawi are believed to be remnants of an ancient Canaanite people, who were then influenced by both Islam and Christianity. They adopted the Arabic language and Islamic faith over the course of the Muslim domination of the region beginning in the 7th century AD. However, they broke away to form their own religion during the reign of the Abbasids. Sunni and Shia Muslims refuse to accept 'Alawis as true Muslims because of their belief in a holy trinity: the Imam 'Ali as the most important figure; Muhammad; and Salman al-Farisi, one of Muhammad's companions. In Syria, the president is required to be a Muslim by law, and as an 'Alawi, the first Asad had a religious cleric issue a fatwa, a Muslim religious pronouncement, that 'Alawis were Muslim. The head of state as of 2008, Bashar al Asad, relies also upon this fatwa for his legitimacy.

Location and homeland. In 2008 there were estimated to be about 2.6 million 'Alawis in the world. Most (about 1.4 mil-

lion) were concentrated in the Latakia province on the western coast of Syria though there are small numbers in Turkey, Israel (2,000 in Israel-occupied Golan Heights), Lebanon, and Australia. In Lebanon, they live in a small area just to the south of the Syrian border; in Turkey they occupy rather larger settlements near Antioch, the al-Kuysar plateau, and in the plains formed by the Lower Orontes river.

The ancient 'Alawi stronghold is the Jabal an Nusayriyah mountain range, which is named for them ("Mountains of Nusairi," as the 'Alawis were formerly known). The mountain range runs north-to-south along the Mediterranean coastal plain of Syria. It is sometimes called Jabal 'Alawite. The wetter western side of the range supports some farming, but the drier eastern side is good only for sheep-herding. It is a poor region, and the 'Alawis have for centuries been a poor, struggling people. Over 60% of the rural population along the coast in the Latakia province is 'Alawi. The largest ethno religious minority group in Syria, 'Alawis made up between 10% and 12% of the total Syrian population according to 2004 estimates; reliable, more precise figures are unavailable.

'Alawis are not considered by some to be true Arabs; they converted to Islam centuries after the majority of modern-day Syrians. Thus, 'Alawis have historically felt a sense of estrangement from the Sunni Arab majority that surrounds them. Centuries of persecution and life hidden away in tiny mountain strongholds has also led to a sense of separation and isolation for the 'Alawis. Their society is organized tribally, with most 'Alawis belonging to one of four main tribal confederations: the Haddadin, the Matawira, the Khaiyatin, and the Kalbiya. Three smaller tribes—the Darawisa, Mahaliba, and 'Amamira—settled at the northern end of the Jabal an Nusayriyah range. Some detribalized 'Alawis settled on the plains surrounding the mountain area. Modern 'Alawis are trying to replace tribal notions with notions of citizenship in the state, but all 'Alawis, even the children, still know which tribe is theirs.

Language. The 'Alawis adopted Arabic as their language during the period known in the West as the Middle Ages. Arabic, spoken by at least 300 million people worldwide, has many dialects. Nevertheless, most Arabs can understand each other's speech, although certain words may have different nuances in different countries. Written Arabic comes in two varieties: the classical Arabic of the Quran and Modern Standard Arabic (MSA). The latter is the version of the language printed in newspapers and books in all Arab countries. Arabic is written and read from right to left. "Hello" (*marhaba* or *ahlan*) in Arabic is a very informal greeting one rarely hears. Far more common is the traditional *As-salam alaykum*, "Peace be with you," with the reply of *Walaykum as-salam*, "and to you peace." *Ma'assalama* means "Go in peace." "Thank you" is *Shukran* and "You're welcome" is *Afwan*. These greetings and pleasantries are known not only in the Arab world but by virtually all Muslims around the world who use them daily. "Yes" is *na'am*, and "no" is *la'a*. The numbers one to ten in Arabic are *wahad, itnin, talata, arba'a, khamsa, sitta, saba'a, tamania, tisa'a*, and *ashara*.

Religion. The precise details of the tenets of the 'Alawi faith, its rituals and practices are somewhat mysterious. After decades of persecution by Muslims who considered their veneration of saints and other rituals and beliefs heretical to orthodox Islam, the 'Alawis began to carefully guard their holy books and practice their rituals in private. The 'Alawi story of creation tells of

An 'Alawi child makes a victory sign as women hold red flags and banners during a protest in Istanbul, Turkey. The people marched to commemorate deadly riots that happened in 1995 between police and 'Alawi residents. (AP Images/Murad Sezer)

a spirit world inhabited by beings of light who worshiped God but who began over time to deny his divinity. This caused their exile from paradise and condemned to the mundane existence of suffering humanity. The 'Alawis worshipped a pantheon of prophets and minor deities throughout their history, but in the Islamic era they have embraced devotion to a trinity consisting of the Imam Ali, the Prophet Muhammad, and Salman al-Farisi, one of the Companions of the Prophet, the men and women who were Islam's first converts and are held in great esteem all over the Muslim world. It is speculated that they perform a ritual using bread and wine to represent the body and blood of the incarnate God, much as Christians do in their Eucharist or Holy Communion. Only men take part in worship and are initiated into the faith. The initiation is a long process that begins no earlier than age 19, and involves tremendous study and the passing of trials and tests.

The 'Alawis believe that God has appeared on the earth seven times, the most recent being in the form of the greatly revered Imam Ali.

The most authoritative book for the 'Alawi faith is not the Muslim holy book of the Quran, which they interpret largely allegorically, unlike virtually all other Muslims, who consider it to be the direct words of Allah transmitted through the Prophet Muhammed. Rather, the 'Alawis' holy book is the Kitab al-Majmu, which has 16 *surahs* (chapters) and almost certainly was compiled over many years by many writers. 'Alawi ritual and belief appears to involve the worship of sacred springs and trees, etc., probably descending from their ancient Phoenician pagan heritage. They also worship stars, planets, and other heavenly bodies, believing as they do that they began their existences as beams of light not unlike the heavenly bodies. Through successive reincarnations, 'Alawis believe humans may eventually return their souls to the heavens, becoming celestial bodies once again, healing the rift with God created by their doubting his divinity at the beginning of time.

The 'Alawis do not worship in mosques in a symbolic protest and recognition of the fact that their highly revered Imam Ali was killed in a mosque. Most 'Alawis gather in friends' houses for prayers. There is no prohibition against drinking alcohol among the 'Alawis. In addition, they do not, generally, adhere to the controversial topic among Islamic scholars as to the meaning of Allah's command that the wives of and daughters of the Prophet cover their heads and chests.

Other aspects of their beliefs relate to objects of light, including the belief by one 'Alawi sect, known as the Shamsis, that the Imam Ali lives in the sun; the Qamaris believe he lives on the moon. The Alawis believe in reincarnation and the existence of more than the world they currently inhabit. They believe that after death, 'Alawis that practiced goodness are reborn into another human form: the wicked are reborn as animals seen as unclean or predatory.

Major holidays. As the 'Alawis keep their faith so secret, it is difficult to discover their major holy days. It is said they do not observe the Muslim month-long fast of Ramadan or make a pilgrimage to Mecca (some believe doing so constitutes a form of idol worship), though the traditional Persian new year festival, known as Nowruz, is widely celebrated. There is good evidence they do celebrate something very similar to the Catholic mass and partake in the ritual of the Eucharist though the wine they drink is not meant to represent the blood of the Christian prophet Jesus but that of the Imam Ali. They may celebrate some Christian holy days such as Christmas, Easter, and Epiphany.

Living conditions. 'Alawis have traditionally been very poor. Living in marginal mountain villages, most families grow wheat and raise goats to provide their bread, bulghur (cracked wheat), yogurt, and butter. Wealthier families might have grapevines, fruit trees, and sheep. Since Hafiz al-Asad, an 'Alawi, ascended to the presidency of Syria, conditions have improved for his people. After his death in 2000 his son Bashar took over the country, with few expecting him to do other than follow his father's policies of preferences to the 'Alawis. In 1970, for example, only 10% of houses in the Latakia province had piped-in drinking water; in 2004, more than 90% did. Roads have been built to every village. Communications and technology have improved and Internet cafes are spreading in the major cities, though the state keeps close watch on their use. In 2007 Syria had 119 Internet providers and 1.5 million regular users. Its country domain code is .sy. Government power projects have supplied electricity to even the most remote corners of Syria. However, high inflation rates and a struggling economy eat away at the gains made in the 'Alawis' standard of living. Also, any change in government (if an 'Alawi is no longer in power) could, and probably would, return the 'Alawis to their former days of hardship and poverty.

Education. Through much of their history, 'Alawis were illiterate mountain dwellers. There were no schools in the mountain villages until the 1930s, when the French started some elementary schools there. After the Ba'ath Party takeover in 1963 with 'Alawi Hafiz al-Asad at the helm, 'Alawis poured into the educational system. By 1985, under the first al-Asad regime, 'Alawis were strongly represented in Syrian professions and upper-level government. Under the second al-Asad's Democratic Socialist regime, education has been made available to everyone at all levels of society. Between 40% and 62% of 'Alawi girls now attend school, a significant increase from earlier times.

Work. Before the Ba'ath Party takeover in 1963 when the 'Alawis came into power, many 'Alawis joined the military because it was the only opportunity for employment readily available to them in the Sunni-dominated society. It is these 'Alawis who joined forces to overthrow the government in 1963. The 'Alawis continue to be the largest ethno religious group in the Syrian military. Prior to the 1960s and 1970s, the only industry in the 'Alawi mountain area was tobacco, and it employed just a few dozen workers. By the mid-1980s, however, under President al-Asad's Democratic Socialist reform program, 40,000 'Alawi workers were employed in public sector companies in food processing and the manufacture of aluminum, cement, textiles, and carpets. Under the second al-Asad administration, tentative steps toward economic liberalization have been instituted and in 2007 the country experienced a real economic growth rate of 3.5%.

Social problems. 'Alawis continue to be looked down upon by the Sunni Muslim majority. Their current good fortunes are largely due to the fact that an 'Alawi, Bashar al-Asad, is president of Syria. Any change in government resulting in a loss of 'Alawi power would probably reverse their situation and send them back to the struggling, persecuted poverty that they knew for so many centuries. In Turkey, where 'Alawis hold no political power, their situation is worse. The Turkish state does not even recognize them as a distinct ethno religious group from the Kurds.

Gender Issues. 'Alawi society is patriarchal in ways not dissimilar to most non-Western cultures around the world. Religiously, there are gender practices and rituals worth noting: for example, women are excluded from the priestly classes and are not allowed to participate in rituals intended to return the 'Alawis to their former existence as beacons of semidivine lights in the presence of God. This is justified by the belief that women are born of the devil. Some extreme 'Alawis even consider that women have no souls. On the other hand, Syria is a secular, quasi-socialist state where strict interpretations of Islam common in other parts of the Arab world, particularly in the Gulf and the Maghrib (western part of North Africa), are not adhered to. In this sense, women enjoy greater personal freedoms in Syria. They are highly visible in the public sphere, most do not cover their heads and, like all 'Alawis, are free to drink alcohol.

BIBLIOGRAPHY

Abd-Allah, Dr. Umar F. *The Islamic Struggle in Syria*. Berkeley, CA: Mizan Press, 1983.

Beaton, Margaret. *Enchantment of the World: Syria*. Chicago: Childrens Press, 1988.

Dymond, Johnny. "Turkish Journey: A Town called Trouble," *BBC News Online*, http://news.bbc.co.uk/2/hi/europe/4025895.stm (14 March 2008).

Mulloy, Martin. *Syria*. New York: Chelsea House, 1988.

Patterson, Charles. *Hafiz al-Asad of Syria*. Englewood Cliffs, NY: Julian Messner, 1991.

Seale, Patrick. *Asad: The Struggle for the Middle East*. Berkeley and Los Angeles: University of California Press, 1988.

Sinai, Anne, and Allen Pollack, ed. *The Syrian Arab Republic: A Handbook*. New York: American Academic Association for Peace in the Middle East, 1976.

South, Coleman. *Cultures of the World: Syria*. New York: Marshall Cavendish, 1995.

Ziser, Eyal. Commanding Syria: Bashar al-Asad and the First Years in Power. New York: Tauris, 2007.

—revised by J. Henry

AMBONESE

PRONUNCIATION: AHM-bawn-eez
LOCATION: Indonesia (Moluccas)
POPULATION: Over 800,000
LANGUAGE: Ambonese; Ambon Malay
RELIGION: Christianity; Islam
RELATED ARTICLES: Vol. 3: Indonesians

¹ INTRODUCTION

No later than 40,000 years ago, the first humans entered the Moluccas, the same basic stock that would go on to settle Papua New Guinea, the Melanesian islands, and Australia. However, with the exception of parts of Halmahera (including the important former sultanate on Ternate), the present population of the Moluccas ("Maluku" in Indonesian) speaks Austronesian languages brought by farming and seafaring people from Sulawesi beginning 4,500 years ago. In physical terms, the Ambonese and other Moluccan groups represent a mixture of the aborigines and these newcomers.

Produced exclusively in the Moluccas until the late 18th century AD and traded as far as Syria as early as the 18th century BC, cloves first came into high international demand during the Han dynasty in China and the Roman Empire in the West. Traders en route between the north Javanese ports and the clove-trading sultanate of Ternate (Muslim since the 15th century) made stopovers at Hitu on the north coast of Ambon island. A year after capturing Malacca in 1511, the Portuguese sent an expedition under Antonio de Abreu to the famed Spice Islands, landing at Hitu. They set up a fort there in 1522, from which Hitu Muslims (with Ternatan aid) were to drive them in 1575. In the meantime, however, the first conversions to Catholicism occurred in 1538, to be greatly augmented by the work of St. Francis Xavier in 1565 (three decades later, 50,000 converts are recorded).

After their expulsion from Hitu, the Portuguese transferred to the south coast where they established the fort that would become Kota Ambon (Ambon City). This the Dutch captured in alliance with the Hitu Muslims in 1605, desecrating the Catholic churches and deporting the "white" and "black" *(mestizo)* Portuguese. The single-minded Dutch pursuit of the spice monopoly led to the notorious massacre of English traders in 1623 and to the *hongi tochten,* annual sweeps to locate and destroy spice trees (and growers) outside the monopoly areas. Cloves were permitted to grow only on Ambon, no longer on Ternate and Tidore. The Dutch pressed Ambonese men and boats into service on the hongi tochten, offering villages land rights in proportion to their contribution.

The spice monopoly made Kota Ambon a rich town, the "Queen of the East" beside which Batavia and Manila were said to pale. Fond of European dance and dress, the local notables shared this wealth and some of the power, joining a representative council in the archipelago at the side of Dutch East India Company officials. As coffee, tea, and sugar came to overshadow spices in the 18th-century European market, the city began to decline. In any case, the British occupation of Ambon from 1796 to 1802 released cloves for cultivation elsewhere.

The Ambonese played a prominent role in the expansion of Dutch power in the archipelago, forming half of the colonial military (KNIL) and a disproportionate percentage of the bureaucracy. Priding themselves on their loyalty and discipline, Ambonese soldiers received higher pay and rations than non-Ambonese; the Javanese called them "dogs of the Dutch" and "black Dutchmen." From the 1880s on, Ambonese (as many as 10% by 1930) migrated to fill jobs as soldiers, clerks, and minor professionals for which Ambon's educational system, the best in Netherlands Indies, qualified them. Christian Ambonese in particular felt more tied to the Dutch than to other "native" peoples.

Strategic to both the Japanese and the Allies, Ambon, especially Kota Ambon, was devastated in World War II. After the war, Christian Ambonese, having identified more with the Dutch than with other "native" peoples, tried to set up an independent nation, the Republic of the Southern Moluccas (RMS), waging a guerilla war against the Indonesian national army until the capture of the RMS president in 1956. After the 1950 transfer of sovereignty to Indonesia, the Dutch government brought ex-KNIL soldiers to refugee camps in the Netherlands; with their expectation to return home to fight for the RMS frustrated, the soldiers and their families continued as a neglected minority in the "mother country." It was only after some Moluccan youth resorted to terrorism in the 1970s that the Dutch government focused its attention on the problems of this 40,000-strong community, beginning programs for bicultural education and job procurement.

Under the New Order regime (1966–1998), the government policies promoting the emergence of a Muslim technocratic elite in the country as a whole as well as the largely spontaneous, non-government-directed influx of Muslim transmigrants into Maluku (especially Bugis and Butonese from their poorer provinces) threatened the fragile balance in the region between Christians and Muslims, heretofore evenly matched in numbers (a situation almost unique in Indonesia). Christian Ambonese, whose high education level gave them dominance in the bureaucracy, resented the Muslim newcomers from Sulawesi for taking increasing control over the regional economy (though they had not begrudged local Christian Chinese their economic power). Moreover, Christian Ambonese feared they would be pushed out of the bureaucracy by increasingly educated and increasingly numerous Muslims, who for their part saw the Christians as continuing to shut them out of positions of power in the province.

Post-Suharto democratization and decentralization intensified competition and tension between the two groups; hostility erupted into mass inter-ethnic/inter-religious violence, beginning in Kota Ambon (initially only between Protestant Ambonese and Muslim transmigrants but eventually involving Catholic and Muslim Ambonese) and then spreading to other parts of the province and to neighboring North Maluku. News of the conflict provoked many Muslims in other parts of Indonesia. Mass rallies in Jakarta called for jihad in Maluku, thousands of Laskar Jihad vigilantes streamed into the province to fight Christians (even as the Ambonese themselves, Christians and Muslims, were becoming tired of the violence), and anti-Christian/Chinese and anti-Hindu/Balinese rioting broke out on Lombok. The conflicts in Maluku and North Maluku ultimately killed 3,000-4,000 people; these constituted the worst episode of collective violence in Indonesia since the 1965–1966 anti-leftist massacres, surpassing even the Dayak-Madurese conflict in Kalimantan in 1997. The "Maluku wars" displaced

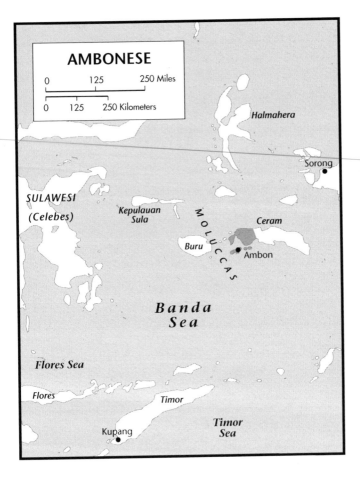

AMBONESE

0   125   250 Miles

0   125   250 Kilometers

Halmahera

Sorong

SULAWESI (Celebes)

Kepulauan Sula

M O L U C C A S

Ceram

Buru

Ambon

B a n d a Sea

Flores Sea

Flores

Timor

Kupang

Timor Sea

ruined by people fishing with dynamite or digging for sand to make cement.

The population of Ambon has grown very rapidly: in 1971, Central Maluku counted 378,870 people; by 1980, Ambon island alone had 651,000 inhabitants. In 2005, the two regencies corresponding to the Ambonese homeland plus Ambon city had a combined population of nearly 700,000. The growth of Kota Ambon appears even more dramatic when one considers that the population of 234,000 (up from 209,000 in 1980 and 80,000 in 1959) must squeeze into 4 sq km (1.5 sq mi) between the shore and the hills, with only some relief from reclaiming land from the sea and building houses up the hillsides.

Since colonial days, when they were disproportionately represented in the military and bureaucracy, the Ambonese have settled in cities throughout the archipelago, particularly Makassar and Jakarta. In addition, there are 40,000 Ambonese in the Netherlands, mostly former soldiers of the KNIL (Dutch colonial army) and their families who came for "temporary" refuge after Indonesian independence.

³ LANGUAGE

A member of the Central Malayo-Polynesian branch of the Austronesian language family (and thus more distant from Bahasa Indonesia than the languages of Madagascar and the Philippines), the Ambonese language is closely related to dialects in West Seram and, on a higher level, groups with the Austronesian languages in Timor.

At the end of the colonial period (1950), Dutch was widely known in Kota Ambon. As the city has always attracted migrants and sojourners from elsewhere in the archipelago, the dominant language, however, has been a version of the Malay lingua franca, Bahasa Melayu Ambon. Malay in its local variant, as well as Bahasa Indonesia, is displacing the indigenous speech.

⁴ FOLKLORE

A Christianized origin myth places the first people on the slopes of Mount Nunusaku in western Seram. There they lived in abundance until the Fall (as in Genesis), when they scattered to Ambon and other islands.

The short British occupation during the Napoleonic Wars produced two heroes whose resistance to the reimposition of Dutch rule earned them national honor. Thomas Matulessy, a.k.a. Pattimura, had served the British as a sergeant major before leading an uprising against the returning Dutch. The daughter of another rebel leader, Martha Christina Tiahahu, continued her father's struggle after his death and, when captured, refused to inform on her co-rebels; she eventually starved herself on the way to exile on Java.

An example of a ghost story is the legend of Soya Atas village. The daughter of the head of the village fell in love with a Dutch official. Because of her father's disapproval, she drowned herself. Her ghost is said to kidnap foreign men or small babies; the victims disappear, only to be found after a few days either dead or in shock. Only a drink of water given by the present head of the village can revive them.

In order to deter thieves, farmers put up *matakau* figures in their fields suggestive of a curse (e.g., a grasshopper symbolizes stomach pains like an insect crawling about inside the body). The owners of young coconut trees have the church council

between 123,000 and 370,000 people, comparable to the numbers displaced by Indonesia's far more murderous 1975 invasion of East Timor. Since hostilities subsided in 2002 after a peace accord, Kota Ambon, heavily devastated by the fighting (including its state and Christian universities), remains segregated along religious lines (with people not being able to return to their homes if they are not of the majority religion of their neighborhood), but commerce and other contacts have resumed between Christians and Muslims.

² LOCATION AND HOMELAND

For Indonesians from outside the region, "Ambon," including the island, the city, and the people, *is* the "Moluccas," hence, anyone hailing from any of this diverse array of islands is likely to be called an "Ambonese" (*orang Ambon*). However, in the strict sense, the Ambonese ethnic group comprises the populations of the islands of Ambon, Haruku, Saparua, and the western portion of the much larger "mother island" of Seram. The two "peninsulas" of Ambon Island itself, Hitu and Leitimur, were once separate islands but are now linked by an extremely narrow isthmus. The long bay formed by the joining of the two land masses provides excellent shelter for ships, and it was on the southern shore of the bay that the city of Ambon (Kota Ambon) rose. The relatively high precipitation level and the quality of the volcanic soils favor agriculture, although much of the land is too steep for cultivation. Off the long stretches of beach are coral reefs that, however, have in many places been

pray for their protection; a potential thief knows that theft will lead to misfortune.

5 RELIGION

The Ambonese divide almost evenly into Christians (51%) and Muslims (49%). Except for five mixed villages, the rest (42) are either exclusively Christian or Muslim. Traders from Ternate and the north Java coast introduced Islam to Hitu (north Ambon) well in advance of the Portuguese, who in turn brought Catholic missionaries such as St. Francis Xavier. The Dutch uprooted these early Catholic communities. Conversions to Protestantism (the Dutch Reformed Church) accelerated only in the 19th century.

Indigenous beliefs focusing on ancestral spirits remain strong, though they coexist more harmoniously with Islam than with Protestantism. Village halls (baileu), which formerly one could enter only after asking permission of the spirits dwelling there, contain a mystically charged stone (batu pamali) used as an altar for sacrifices and other offerings. In some places, the heads of goats slaughtered in Islamic rites are placed on the stone in the baileu, alongside skulls from previous years. When getting wood from the forest for a school, church, or the baileu itself, one hangs the head of a sacrificed goat from an old baileu pillar. Before the Dutch forbade the practice, the taking of human heads was crucial to traditional rituals, including weddings (as part of the bride-price).

Coexisting with Muslim and Christian religious authorities, the mauweng mediates between humans and ancestral spirits, particularly in rites for success in agriculture. This folk religious specialist also heals the sick by employing divination techniques to learn the underlying cause of disease, i.e., what is displeasing the ancestors (modern medicines are considered effective only for treating symptoms).

Since the 1863 abolition of the clove monopoly deprived village heads of the basis of much of their power, in Christian villages, ministers (always originally outsiders to the village) have challenged their authority. The mauweng have supported the village heads, but the balance tends now to favor the minister.

6 MAJOR HOLIDAYS

In villages, the most important festival is the cuci negeri, the annual village cleansing. The baileu, as well as every house and yard, is thoroughly cleaned; one family's failure to do so would invite fatal illness or crop failure for the whole community. Village leaders make speeches to the ancestors who established the baileu, the springs, and the holy places and pray to God to grant well-being. Eating, drinking, and general merrymaking follow the ceremonies. In Soiya, however, scheduling the cuci negeri for the Friday before Christmas reduces the scale of the celebration.

Seven days after Idul Fitri, the end of the Muslim fasting month of Ramadan, young men in Mamala village strike each other with rattan brooms (consisting of the sharp central spines of pine fronds) until they draw blood. The wounds disappear after the application of a locally made coconut oil.

7 RITES OF PASSAGE

There are three ways to get married: by proposal (kawin minta); by elopement (kawin lari or lari bini); or by the man's "moving in" (kawin masuk).

For kawin minta, a young man first informs his family of his choice for a bride. His famili (all his paternal and maternal relatives) gathers to discuss arrangements for the bride-price, the wedding ceremony, etc. Once agreed, they send a delegation to the young woman's parents asking for a time when they can issue the marriage proposal. The man's kin sends a spokesperson at the time set by the woman's kin. After paying the customary forms of respect to the woman's kin, giving the young man's full name (including those of his family and clan) the spokesperson of his kin negotiates the amount of the bride-price and other arrangements with the young woman's kin. The bride-price must be paid in full before a Christian or Muslim wedding ceremony can be held; otherwise, the ancestors will be offended and may cause death to the couple's children. The slowness of the woman's father in accepting the man's side's terms often results in a postponement of the religious ceremony and in the birth of children out of wedlock, a situation very unsatisfactory to Christian authorities.

Marriage by elopement avoids all these negotiations and, thus, is by far the most popular form of wedding. The young man may prefer this method in order to avoid rejection, or his family might prefer it in order to spare themselves the shame of a refused proposal. Although the woman's kin do not prefer elopement in principle, they sometimes agree to it beforehand as a way for them to reduce the bride-price without losing face. The young man's brothers or friends help him to "abduct" his bride and carry away all her clothes and other things. If the young woman's family knows beforehand, the young man leaves a letter in a white envelope on the girl's bed explaining in flowery language who has taken their daughter and that she is safe. After a week in hiding, the young woman is brought to the young man's house for the wedding rite and feast. During the feast, the bride offers around a tray of cigarettes and drinks to show that she is officially a wife. All friends and neighbors are invited so that the marriage will be public.

While generally it is the bride who comes to live with the groom's family, under the third type of wedding, kawin masuk, the groom moves in with the bride's family. He may choose this if his own family cannot afford the bride-price (in which case he himself must work for his in-laws in lieu thereof), if his family does not approve of the match because of differences in status between the sides, or if the woman is an only child and the man must join the woman's clan.

8 INTERPERSONAL RELATIONS

Before the Dutch, related lineages originating in Seram formed soa, headed by an upu who was assisted by a military commander (malessi) and a religious leader (mauweng). Under Ternatan hegemony, soa formed federations (uli). Ambonese also applied the Javanese terms for "state" (negeri) and "king" (raja) to their own villages and village headmen.

The Dutch abolished these federations, replacing them with a system of independent villages run by councils (saniri). The highest council was the Saniri Rajapatih, consisting of the village head and the soa heads. The next lower council, the Saniri Negeri Lengkap, added to the above the various village officials: the tuan tanah, an expert on traditional land inheritance law; the panglima, formerly a military leader; the kewang, forest police; and the marinyo, the town-crier. Finally, the Saniri Negeri Besar included all adult males but was convened very rarely, usually only for village-head elections. In recent times, the once-hereditary village headmanship has become largely ceremonial, with the soa heads rotating de facto governing duties among themselves.

While the distinction persists between a village's "original inhabitants" (the descendants of the village founder, as such the village elite) and "newcomers," Ambonese society recognizes many translocal organizations. Every village belongs to either the Patasiwa or the Patalima faction, a division tracing back to the manipulations of the Sultan of Ternate and referring to federations on either side of the Mala River on Seram. More significant is the *pela,* an alliance linking two villages, often very distant and of different religions. The allies draw blood with knives and dip the bloody knives in water. They seal an oath of alliance by drinking the water containing each other's blood. The villages provide famine relief to each other and refuge in war; a Muslim village will contribute funds to its pela partner's Christian church and vice versa.

⁹ LIVING CONDITIONS

While traditional dwellings were built on wooden piles, contemporary Muslim and Christian houses sit on the ground. These houses have a square floor plan with an open veranda (*dego-dego*) in the front. The frame consists of tree trunk sections or wooden beams, while the walls are made of plaited sago-palm leaf (*gaba-gaba*). As most houses lack windows, the steep roofs have holes in the corners to release smoke. Sometimes there is a room in back serving as a kitchen. The houses of village leaders are in the European style, partially brick with windows and separate rooms inside.

Villages usually consist of houses grouped closely along a main road, though houses may also be separated by fenced yards. Each village includes a *baileu,* the village head's house, a church or mosque, the clergy's house, and small shops.

In Kota Ambon, in addition to buses, *becak* pedicabs provide the most common means of transport; the city has more than 2,000 becak that, not all being able to share the streets at a single time, are divided into three color-coded groups (red, white, and yellow). Of the local boat types, the *patakora* from Ternate is regarded as the best. Big boats (*jungku* and *orambi*) carry merchandise to Kota Ambon.

Maluku province has a Human Development Index (combining measures of income, health, and education) of 69.2 (2005 score), almost as high as Indonesia's national HDI of 69.6. Kota Ambon's HDI is considerably higher at 76.2, while the two surrounding regencies, Central Maluku (a portion of the earlier province of that name) and Western Seram, have lower HDIs (respectively, 67.7 and 64.8). Maluku has a higher HDI than all the nearby provinces other than North Sulawesi. The closest, North Maluku, at 67, has one of the country's lowest. However, this is despite the fact that Maluku's GDP per capita is only us$3,637, among the lowest in Indonesia (us$9,784 for West Sumatra, us$8,360 for North Sulawesi, but us$6,293 for Central Java and us$6,151 for West Nusa Tenggara). Kota Ambon's GDP per capita (us$5,699) was higher, but still rather low. In 2000, the province's rate of infant mortality stood at 60.63 deaths per 1,000 live births (though only almost half this in Kota Ambon).

¹⁰ FAMILY LIFE

Perhaps under Muslim and Christian influence, kinship is patrilineal as expressed, for instance, in newlywed couples' residing with the groom's family.

A household includes parents, unmarried children, and married sons with their wives and children. An individual belongs to a clan (*rumah tau, matarumah,* or *fam*) of patrilineally related kin who has a name and possesses rights to titles (political office), land, and sacred stones and springs; one must marry outside the clan. Women join their husband's clan (unless she is an only child, in which case the man joins his wife's clan). The rumah tau has a meeting house built by the clan founder containing weapons, cloth, and other heirlooms, which are under the hereditary stewardship of a clan leader.

¹¹ CLOTHING

Elements of traditional Ambonese clothing preserve influences from 16th century Portuguese fashion. While younger women wear bright pink, yellow, and blue Western-style dresses to church, older women wear long black dresses with long sleeves and a highly prized sash made of beads.

¹² FOOD

As the sago palm grows abundantly in the local swamps, sago-palm starch is the staple; rice supplements sago-palm starch but does not displace it. A 6- to 15-year-old tree can be cut down for food. The preparer beats the tree core to loosen the flour-rich fibers. These are then washed and squeezed through a filter to obtain the starch, which is formed into squares (*tuman*). The tuman are either grilled or made into a thick porridge (*pepeda*).

Other foods are bananas and papayas, available all year round. Freshly grilled fish is served with *colo-colo,* a sauce of chopped onions, chili, and tomatoes. *Kohu-kohu* is a pungent salad of shredded tuna meat, bean sprouts, onions, and cabbage. Also eaten with a spice mixture are *laor,* seaworms who come to shore to breed in March and April. Local menus do not announce it, but black dog is also cooked. From the sap of the lontar palm, local people distill wine (*moke*).

¹³ EDUCATION

Since the 19th century, when Christian missionaries built schools, Ambon has enjoyed one of the highest education levels in the archipelago. This has allowed many local Ambonese to migrate to other parts of the country as office workers. In 2005, Maluku province's level of literacy stood at 96.16%, very high by Indonesian national standards and comparable or superior to provinces with much higher GDPs per capita. (*See also* the article entitled **Indonesians.**)

¹⁴ CULTURAL HERITAGE

Throughout Indonesia, the Ambonese are famous for singing (Western-style) music. Cassettes of local songs and singers are popular nationwide. Traditional instruments include the *tifa* (a single-membrane drum) and the ukulele. The latter forms part of the *kroncong* ensemble, a sentimental Portuguese-derived musical style, one of whose cradles was Ambon. Bamboo flutes are also played; orchestras of bamboo flutes open church services. Famous dances are the *lenso* and the *cakalele* (a war dance).

Ambonese men perform a traditional war dance in Ambon, Indonesia. There has been religious turmoil between Muslims and Christians on this small eastern Indonesian island since 1999. (AP Images/Vonny Litamahuputty)

15 WORK

Most people continue to obtain a living by agriculture, which involves slash-and-burn cultivation of tubers and peanuts. The Dutch brought potatoes, which remain a minor crop, grown on mountain slopes. Other crops are coffee, sugarcane, cassava, maize, and fruits (bananas, mango, mangosteen, durian, and gandaria, the last having medicinal value). Coconut production satisfies regional consumption. Farmers grow tobacco for their own use under the eaves of their houses, where they can benefit from rainwater coming off the roof; the leaves are dried on the roof itself. Although a Dutch clove monopoly no longer confines clove cultivation to Ambon, the spice continues to be grown, requiring little work from the farmer but yielding a substantial profit on the market (as an ingredient in Indonesian-made cigarettes, *kretek*). Farmers sell their surplus crops to obtain money for taxes, school fees, and daily necessities that they cannot produce themselves.

People hunt for deer, wild boar, and cassowary birds using traps that may endanger unwary humans. Fishing by hook, harpoon, and net also adds protein to the diet.

16 SPORTS

Children's toys include hoops from old bicycle wheels and stilts from palm trunks. Billiards is a popular pastime. Children play in the early evening, as the afternoon is too hot.

17 ENTERTAINMENT AND RECREATION

See the article entitled **Indonesians**.

18 FOLK ART, CRAFTS, AND HOBBIES

"Paintings" (usually intricate still-lifes of flowers) are fashioned from thin slices of mother-of-pearl. Large models of boats made entirely of cloves and wire are common souvenirs. Embroidered *baju kurung* (long shirts) are also produced. The woodcarvings and *ikat* (tie-dyed) cloth available in Kota Ambon generally come from the more traditional Tanimbar islands to the southeast.

19 SOCIAL PROBLEMS

See the article entitled **Indonesians**.

20 GENDER ISSUES

Maluku's Gender-Related Development Index (combining measures of women's health, education, and income relative to men's) is 62.6, somewhat higher than Indonesia's national GDI of 59.2 (2002 scores). The province's Gender Empowerment Measure (reflecting women's participation and power in political and economic life relative to men's), however, is 51.8, rather lower than the national GEM of 54.6. Kota Ambon itself, however, has a GDI of 71.3, higher than Jakarta's (which is the highest among the country's province-level administrative divisions) and a GEM of 59.4, higher than North Sulawesi's (which is number one among province-level administrative divisions). This contrasts sharply with the immediately surrounding province of Maluku Tengah, which has a GDI of 54.1 and a GEM of 34.3.

21 BIBLIOGRAPHY

Bertrand, Jacques. *Nationalism and Ethnic Conflict in Indonesia*. Cambridge, UK: Cambridge University Press, 2004.

Data Statistik Indonesia. http://demografi.bps.go.id/ (November 9, 2008).

Harsrinuksmo, B. "Ambon, Pulau." In *Ensiklopedi Nasional Indonesia*, vol. 1. Jakarta: Cipta Adi Pustaka, 1988.

Jonge de Nico, ed. *Indonesia in Focus: Ancient Traditions—Modern Times*. Meppel: Edu'Actief, 1988.

Kamsteeg, A., Marianne Hehuat, and Han Hehuat. *Ambon nu, Ambon sekarang*. n.p.: J. H. Kok-Kampen, 1984.

Klinken, Gerry van. "The Maluku Wars: 'Communal Contenders' in a Failing State." In Charles A. Coppel, ed., *Violent Conflicts in Indonesia: Analysis, Representation, Resolution*. London: Routledge, 2006.

LeBar, Frank M., ed. *Ethnic Groups of Insular Southeast Asia*. Vol 1; *Indonesia, Andaman Islands, and Madagascar*. New Haven, CT: Human Relations Area Files Press, 1972.

Loveband, Anne and Ken Young. "Migration, Provocateurs and Communal Conflict: The Cases of Ambon and West Kalimantan." In Charles A. Coppel, ed., *Violent Conflicts in Indonesia: Analysis, Representation, Resolution*. London: Routledge, 2006.

Muller, Kal. *Spice Islands: The Moluccas*. Berkeley: Periplus, 1991.

Subyakto. "Kebudayaan Ambon" (Ambonese culture). In *Manusia dan kebudayaan di Indonesia* (Man and Culture in Indonesia, edited by Koentjaraningrat). Jakarta: Djambatan, 1975.

—revised by A. J. Abalahin

ANDAMANESE

PRONUNCIATION: an-duh-mun-EEZ
ALTERNATE NAMES: Great Andamanese, Jarawas, Onge, Sentinelese
LOCATION: India (Andaman Islands)
POPULATION: 429 (2001 Census of India)
LANGUAGE: Andamanese
RELIGION: Animism

1 INTRODUCTION

The Andamanese are the original inhabitants of the Andaman Islands, which lie in the Bay of Bengal some 1,000 km (640 mi) southeast of the mouth of the Ganges River. Of Negrito (Asian pygmy) stock, this population consists of hunting-and-gathering tribes who are related physically and culturally to the peoples of Southeast Asia. Little is known of their origins, but the Andamanese most probably reached the islands from the Malay and Burmese coasts. The northernmost point of the Andaman Islands is only 300 km (190 mi) from the mainland of Burma (Myanmar).

Various explanations of the name *Andaman* have been proposed, but it possibly comes from the Malay *Handuman*, i.e., Hanuman, the monkey god of Hindu mythology. Lying astride the trade routes across the Indian Ocean, the Andamans have been known from early times. Among those who have mentioned the islands are Ptolemy, the Greek geographer, 7th-century Chinese Buddhist monks, 9th-century Arab travelers, and Marco Polo. A common theme in historical reports of the islands is the hostility and ferocity of the native peoples. In 1789, the colonial government of Bengal established a penal colony on the islands, though it was subsequently abandoned. The British returned in 1858 to found Port Blair and maintained a presence in the islands (except during Japanese occupation in World War II) until control of the islands passed to India when that country gained its independence from Britain. Today, the Andamans are administered by New Delhi as part of the Union Territory of the Andaman and Nicobar Islands.

2 LOCATION AND HOMELAND

In the early years of the 20th century, 13 distinct indigenous tribes were present in the Andaman Islands. By the mid-1960s, however, only 4 groups remained. These were the Great Andamanese of Strait Island, the Jarawas of Middle Andaman, the Onge of Little Andaman Island, and the Sentinelese of North Sentinel Island. The Andamanese are few in number compared to the rest of the islands' population, who are largely immigrants and descendants of immigrants from mainland South Asia. The total tribal population of the Andaman Islands was estimated to be 429 according to the Cennus of India, 2001, but this number is unreliable.

The tribal populations of the Andamans appeared to survive the tsunami of December 2004 relatively untouched, although at first there was concern that they had perished in the disaster. Their survival has been attributed to a knowledge of ancient lore and an understanding of the behavior of birds, wind and the sea. Apparently the tribal groups moved inland and thus escaped the worst of the tsunami, which ravaged much of the coast of the Andamans. Forty one of the 43 Great Andamanese reported in the 2001 Census of India were sighted after the tsunami, as were 73 Onge of the 98 reported in the Census. The Jarawa, reported as having a population of 240 in the 2001 Census, are thought to number about 300, while the Sentinelese are reported as having 39 people (clearly an undercount—the population is actually estimated at around 300) in 2001

The Andamans are a group of 204 islands, 6,340 sq km (2,448 sq mi) in total land area, located in the Bay of Bengal. Centered at about 12°N latitude, they form an arc running north–south for 500 km (300 mi). North, Middle, and South Andaman Islands, known collectively as Great Andaman, are the chief islands of the group. Many of the other islands are uninhabited. Great Andaman consists of a jumble of hills rising to 740 m (2,427 ft) at Saddle Peak that enclose narrow valleys covered in dense tropical forest. Little Andaman, the southernmost island in the chain, is relatively flat. The climate is tropical, with heavy rainfall in the summer during the southwest monsoon.

3 LANGUAGE

The aboriginal tongues of the Andaman Islands are grouped together in the Andamanese family of languages. They are clearly related, though early accounts of the Andamanese indicate that the tribes spoke languages that could not be understood by other tribal groups on the islands. The Andamanese languages have yet to be classified in relation to the major linguistic families of South and Southeast Asia. They fall into two main groups. Proto-Little Andamanese includes Onge, Jarawa, and Sentinelese, the tongues of the tribes in the southern islands. The various languages spoken by the tribes that once inhabited North, Middle, and South Andaman Islands fall into the category of Proto-Great Andamanese.

4 FOLKLORE

The following legend, from one of the Great Andaman tribes, accounts for the origin of night. In the early days of the world, the tale goes, in the time of the ancestors, there was no night; it was always day. Sir Monitor Lizard went into the jungle, where he found yams, resin, and a cicada (a type of insect). He brought them to the camp of the ancestors. He rubbed the cicada between his hands, crushing it. At this, the cicada let out its cry, and day became night. It remained dark for several days. The ancestors tried to get the day to return, lighting torches of resin, singing, and dancing, but with no success. Various types of birds also sang to try to get the day to return, but all in vain. Finally, after an ant sang, morning came. Ever since that time, day and night have followed one another.

5 RELIGION

The Andamanese religion is animistic in nature. Among the Onge, the supreme being (Eiugia) takes the shape of a lizard that is bigger than a crocodile. The thunder is his voice, and the wind is his breath; if he becomes angry, he breathes out storms and sets fire to the forest. In addition, two broad categories of spirits inhabit the Onge universe. There are the spirits associated with natural phenomena such as earthquakes, rainbows, and waterspouts, or which control the reproduction of plants and animals useful to humans. There are also the spirits of the dead, who may be benign or evil in nature. The Onge do not revere the spirits, but rather fear them. Their anger is to be

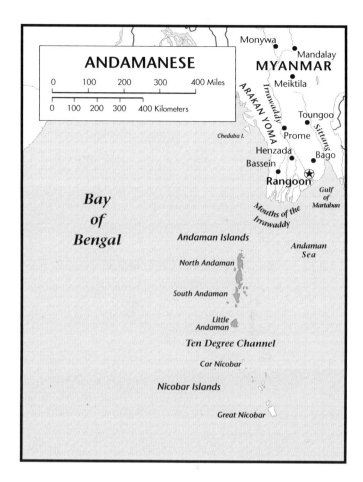

avoided, but the Onge do not hesitate to deceive or trick them if they can get away with it. The spirits of the ancestors are seen to be in direct competition for the resources of the islands.

Certain individuals among the Andamanese can communicate with the spirits while in a trance. Frequent contact with the supernatural is thought to enhance the powers of these shamans or medicine men. The medicine man is consulted to deal with the spirit world, to diagnose illness and effect cures, to help the community find food, and to determine its ceremonial activities.

6 MAJOR HOLIDAYS

Lacking any formal religious system, the Andamanese also lack a calendar of festivals or holidays. Celebrations revolve around ceremonies accompanying events such as birth or marriage. For the Onge, even a successful hunt is an occasion for gorging oneself and painting the body in white clay.

7 RITES OF PASSAGE

There is a complete absence of ritual surrounding the birth of children. Women do not go through any period of isolation or purificatory ceremonies after childbirth, returning to their normal activities within a few days. The Onge interchange or adopt children freely, perhaps reflecting both strong maternal instincts and the low birth rates among the group. Such children may be kept temporarily, for a number of years, or even permanently if the birth parents do not ask for their return. Matrilineal relatives assume responsibility for raising children in their early years, and after menstruation a girl's ties with her mother's family become even stronger. Following his initiation, however, a boy's training and education lie in the hands of his father and paternal relatives.

Just as initiation makes an adult out of the child, so funeral ceremonies complete the transformation of the human to the spirit. In fact, the Onge believe that if the proper burial rites are not completed, the spirit becomes malevolent and will return to cause harm. The dead are buried underneath the floor of the communal hut. A second burial occurs later when the lower jaw is exhumed, colored with red ochre, and carefully reburied in the floor. Some of the bones are kept and worn as necklaces and ornaments around the neck. The spirits of the dead, which stay near the bones, are thus kept near their relatives to protect them and help them in their daily lives.

8 INTERPERSONAL RELATIONS

In the past, it was customary for the Andamanese to kill all outsiders who landed on their shores. Early encounters between Europeans and the Andamanese tribes resulted in bloody conflicts that frequently left casualties on both sides. The Jarawas, in particular, have an implacable hatred for outsiders. This hostility extends even to other Andamanese groups. Even today, the Jarawas have not been totally subdued and remain isolated from the rest of the islands' population.

9 LIVING CONDITIONS

During the dry winter season, the Andamanese migrate to coastal areas where they fish and hunt sea turtles and dugongs (sea cows). Groups of families set up camp, constructing flimsy lean-to huts and shelters (korale) in a circle around a central campground. With the onset of the rains in early summer, the Andamanese move into the interior. Breaking up into smaller groups of four or five families, they build temporary huts or live in rock shelters as they move through the forests in search of pigs and other game. At the end of the wet season, families gather at the circular clan hut (berale), which is tended throughout the year by men from the clan. This structure has a thatched roof and side walls, and contains permanent sleeping platforms for each family in the clan. Individuals sleep on mats, using log headrests as pillows. These, along with a few living utensils and weapons, are carried by the families on their yearly migrations between the coasts and the forests. Territory is identified with specific bands which generally hunt and fish within their own lands. Little Andaman, which is inhabited solely by the Onge, is divided into four divisions each of which is identified with one of the four Onge clans.

10 FAMILY LIFE

Clan and lineage might determine where one hunts, but the basic social and economic unit among the Andaman islanders is the family. This is nuclear in character, consisting of husband, wife, and children, both birthed and adopted. Women have an important role in Andaman society, with descent being reckoned by both male and female lines. Most rights and obligations are inherited through the female line, although items such as weapons and canoes may be passed down from the father's side.

Marriage is highly valued among the Andamanese. Marriages are arranged by tribal elders, with a man's patrilineal relatives approaching his matrilineal family for a suitable girl.

Given the relatively small populations of the surviving Andaman tribes, there is often some difficulty in finding a match. The actual marriage ceremony is simple. The man and woman take possession of each other in the presence of the group, and he leads her to a new bed built for the occasion in the group's sleeping quarters. The event is celebrated by dancing late into the night.

The Onge are passionately fond of dogs, which were introduced to the Andamans in 1850. They are kept as pampered pets, and puppies are even suckled by Onge women. A family may have 10 or 12 dogs. The animals are used for hunting pigs and other wild game.

11 CLOTHING

Traditionally, the tribes of the Andaman Islands went completely naked. The Jarawas still follow this practice, although Onge women have adopted a small apron to cover their genitals.

12 FOOD

The Andamanese subsist on a diet of seafood, wild game, and products gathered in the forest. The importance of fish to the Onge is seen in the fact that their word for fish (cioghe) also means food in general. Men fish with harpoons or bows and arrows, hunting sea turtles, dugongs (sea cows), and large fish. Men also collect turtle eggs. Women use nets, catching pilchards (sardines), crabs, and a variety of other fish. The pig is the favorite game of the Andamanese, who often gorge themselves to excess after a successful hunt. For the Onge, birds harbor the spirit of the dead and are never eaten. Honey is a favorite food, being gathered in considerable quantities during the dry season. When an Onge finds a beehive, he or she marks its location as a sign of ownership. No other would then dare to take possession of it. When convenient, the finder returns with others to help get at the nest and open it up. Other foods gathered in the forest include wild fruits, edible roots and tubers, and wild berries. The larvae of insects such as the cicada are regarded as delicacies. The Andamanese have no knowledge of salt or alcoholic drinks.

13 EDUCATION

As might be expected among relatively primitive hunting-and-gathering tribes, the traditional Andamanese have no written script and are totally illiterate, i.e., they have no ability to read or write. They also have no access to formal education. Individuals who have had contact with Bengālīs and other peoples may have learned some Bengali or other Indian languages. The highest literacy rate is found among the Onge, who have taken advantage of development programs.

14 CULTURAL HERITAGE

Dancing is a common feature of Andaman culture. It is almost always done at night and marks occasions such as marriage or the end of a mourning period. In the past, a dance was held before going to battle, as well as to mark peace between warring groups. Among the coastal Great Andamanese, males and females form lines on either side of a man who beats out the rhythm of the dance on a type of convex shield made of a hard and aromatic red wood. Onge and Jarawa men dance in single file, hitting the ground first with the right heel, then with the left, the toes raised just above the ground and moving forward a short way each time. Women clap their hands, then grasping the wrist of one hand with the other, slap one thigh with the open palm of the hand. Dances are accompanied by songs, each person composing his or her own song for the occasion.

15 WORK

Agriculture is unknown to the Andamanese, who survive entirely by hunting and gathering. Their weapons include the bow and arrow, and harpoons with detachable points. Fishing is carried out from dugout canoes with a single pontoon as an outrigger. Though they frequently capsize, the canoes rarely sink and are easily righted. The Onge use digging sticks to uproot yams and other tubers. As these have to be "stolen" from the spirits who own them, the Onge collect tubers some distance from the main stem and cover all traces of their activities. The traditional Andamanese had no knowledge of how to create fire, although they utilized it and carried it wherever they went.

The Jarawa and Sentinelese are still totally dependent on hunting and gathering. Some Onge, however, are employed gathering coconuts from plantations introduced into their area in 1958. They are paid for their services with food and manufactured items from the mainland. The Great Andamanese are furthest removed from their hunting-and-gathering roots, being paid a regular allowance by the government and also wages for taking care of citrus fruit plantations.

16 SPORTS

Children are introduced to skills they will need as adults through play and toy nets, shelters, canoes, and weapons. Hunting is a means of survival, rather than a pastime as it is among many other tribal groups in South Asia.

17 ENTERTAINMENT AND RECREATION

The Andamanese have no access to modern recreation and entertainment and rely on traditional activities such as dancing, singing, and feasting for their enjoyment.

18 FOLK ART, CRAFTS, AND HOBBIES

As is to be expected, the graphic or visual arts are poorly represented among the Andamanese.

Although some tribes resort to tattooing, the Onge do not, painting geometrical designs on their bodies with white clay instead. This seen as a protection from evil spirits (as well as from the attention of mosquitoes). The Andamanese have acquired a knowledge of pottery. Their pots have pointed bases, so they do not stand upright and are carried in baskets. Basket-making is practiced by the Andamanese, with the Onge being particularly adept in the art. The Andamanese fashion dugout canoes from single tree trunks. The Jarawas, however, appear to have lost their ability to make seaworthy craft. The Andamanese are skilled in making bows, arrows, and other weapons.

19 SOCIAL PROBLEMS

The Andamanese are unique in that they represent a contemporary example of perhaps the earliest form of society known to humans. Subsisting by hunting and gathering, and without even the means of making fire, they have survived undisturbed in their island refuge for thousands of years. Today, they face

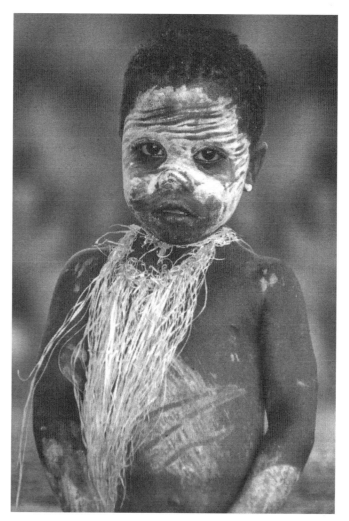

An Andamanese boy in Nicobar, India. (AP Images/ Anthropological Survey of India, HO)

a situation that it seems will almost inevitably lead to a loss of tribal identity. Contact with the large population of immigrants from the mainland of India and their more complex economic systems has already begun to erode the traditional Andamanese way of life. This will continue in spite of—or perhaps because of—attempts to promote development among the tribals by government and quasi-government agencies. For example, in 2002 the Supreme Court of India ordered the Andaman Trunk Road, the road that crossed the territory of the Jarawas, closed, though it still remains open. Similarly, in an effort to protect the Jarawas, tour operators have been warned that arranging "sightings" of the Jarawas also violates a Supreme Court order. But the most telling problem is simply a matter of numbers. The Andamanese population has been declining in recent decades. It may well be that the critical mass has already been passed, and that within a few generations the Andamanese people and their culture will no longer exist.

20 GENDER ISSUES

Given the nature of the Andamanese, it is not surprising that women occupy the traditional roles typically associated with primitive societies and do not participate in the "gender" advancement associated with other women's groups in South

Asia. There are reports of sexual exploitation of Andamanese women.

[21] BIBLIOGRAPHY

Basu, B. K. *The Onge.* Calcutta: Seagull Books, 1990.

Cipriani, Lidio. *The Andaman Islanders.* New York: Praeger, 1966.

Jana, Bijaykrishna. *Unprecedented Earthquake and Dreadful Tsunami.* New Delhi : Mohit Publications, 2005.

Mukerjee. Madhusree. *The Land of Naked People: Encounters with Stone Age Islanders.* Boston: Houghton Mifflin, 2003.

Radcliffe-Brown, A. R. *The Andaman Islanders; a Study in Anthropology.* Cambridge: The University Press, 1922.

Sharma, A. N. *Tribal Development in Andaman Islands.* New Delhi: Sarup and Sons, 2003.

—by D. O. Lodrick

ANDHRAS

PRONUNCIATION: AHN-druz
ALTERNATE NAMES: Telugu
LOCATION: India (Andhra Pradesh State)
POPULATION: About 81 million
LANGUAGE: Telugu
RELIGION: Hinduism
RELATED ARTICLES: Vol. 4: People of India

[1] INTRODUCTION

The Andhras, who are also known as Telugu, are a Telugu-speaking people of India. Ancient Sanskrit texts describe them as non-Aryans *(Anarya).* In later times, however, some Andhras claimed Brahman descent and added the suffix *-ayya* to indicate their high status. The Hindu epic literature refers to them as a primitive, indigenous tribe inhabiting wild, inaccessible forests to the south of the Aryan region. The traditional home of the Andhra people is the land between the Godavari and Kistna (Krishna) rivers in southeastern India. Today, Andhras make up the dominant element in the population of the Indian state of Andhra Pradesh.

Over 2,000 years ago, the Andhra region formed part of Ashoka's Mauryan Empire. It was strongly Buddhist and remained so for several centuries after the decline of the Mauryas. The 1st century BC saw the emergence of the earliest in a line of Andhra dynasties that were to rule much of central India. The Andhras subsequently came under the control of most of the important states that arose in southern India. These included the Pallavas, the Eastern Chalukyas, and the Cholas. At the time the Europeans arrived in India, the northern areas of Andhra country were in the Muslim state of Golkonda, while southern areas lay in Hindu Vijayanagara. During the colonial period, the British gained control of most of the Andhra region and administered it as part of their Madras Presidency. Northwestern areas remained under the Muslim princely state of Hyderabad, which accepted British paramountcy (overall British rule in India). Princely states in British India were supposed to accede to either India or Pakistan in 1947, but the Nizam of Hyderabad—ruler of the largest Muslim princely state in India—refused to join India. Hyderabad was invaded by the Indian army and integrated into the Indian Republic in 1949. Andhra pressure for a Telugu-speaking state resulted in the creation of Andhra Pradesh in its present form in 1956.

[2] LOCATION AND HOMELAND

The population of Andhra Pradesh was reported at 76.3 million people in the 2001 census. To this number should be added Telugu-speakers who live in the border areas of the surrounding states, as well as a substantial Telugu population in Tamil Nadu State. Telugu-speakers are also found among the various immigrant Indian communities in Africa, Asia (especially Malaysia), and the West.

Andhra Pradesh falls into three geographic regions: the coastal plains, mountains, and interior plateaus. Running for some 800 km (500 mi) along the Bay of Bengal, the coastal lowlands are intensively cultivated and support dense populations. The central region is formed by the alluvial deltas of the Godavari and Kistna rivers. To the west, the plains are bounded by the Eastern Ghats, the hills that mark the edge of the Deccan Plateau. These reach an elevation of 1,680 m (5,513 ft) in the north, decreasing to around 1,000 m (3,300 ft) in the south. The Ghats are not a continuous mountain system, but are broken up by numerous rivers flowing eastwards to the ocean. West of the Ghats lie the interior plateaus of the Deccan, averaging about 500 m (1,600 ft) above sea level. This area is drier than the rest of the state (annual rainfall is less than 75 cm or 30 in) and supports only scrub vegetation. Parts of the Eastern Ghats, however, have an extensive cover of tropical deciduous forest and thorn forest. Annual rainfall in coastal areas, associated mostly with the summer monsoon, approaches 125 cm (50 in). Summers along the coast are hot, with maximum temperatures exceeding 40°C or 104°F. Minimum temperatures in winter, especially in the plateau region, can fall as low as 10°C (50°F).

3 LANGUAGE

The language of the Andhra people is Telugu. It is a Dravidian tongue which, along with Tamil, Kannada, and Malayalam, is one of the four major languages of this linguistic family. There are several regional Telugu dialects such as Andhra (spoken in the delta), Telingana (the dialect of the northwestern region), and Rayalasima (spoken in southern areas). There are also specific dialects identified with social categories, i.e., Brahmans, non-Brahmans, and Untouchables. Literary Telugu is quite distinct from the spoken forms of the language. Telugu is written in its own script. This script is allied to Sanskrit but, because it was originally written on palm leaves, developed a cursive (i.e., rounded, flowing) form. Telugu is the official language of Andhra Pradesh, as well as being one of the regional languages officially recognized by the Indian constitution.

4 FOLKLORE

Hero worship is a significant element in Andhra culture and folklore. Andhra warriors who died on the battlefield defending their king, or who sacrificed their lives for great or pious causes, were deified and worshiped by the common people. Stone pillars or *lingams* (phallic symbols) commemorate their deeds. These memorials or "hero stones," called *Viragallulu* in the Telugu language, are found all over Andhra country. Hero worship has become something of a cult in Andhra Pradesh and is observed by annual rituals in various parts of the region. The *Katamaraju Kathala,* one of the oldest ballads in Telugu, celebrates the heroic exploits of the 12th-century warrior, Katamaraju.

5 RELIGION

Andhras are mostly Hindu by religion. They accept the fundamental philosophy of Hinduism, from the concept of *dharma* (right conduct) and its related beliefs, to ideas of ritual pollution, concepts of sin *(pap)* and merit *(punya),* and the caste system. The Brahman castes, as everywhere in Hindu society, have the highest social status, and Brahmans serve as priests in temples dedicated to the gods of the Hindu scriptures. Andhras worship Shiva, Vishnu, Hanuman, and other Hindu deities. At the popular level, however, Andhra religion is distinctly South Indian in character. Worship of *ammas* or village goddesses is as important as that of the major gods of Hinduism. Durgamma presides over the welfare of the village, Maisamma protects the village boundaries, and Balamma is

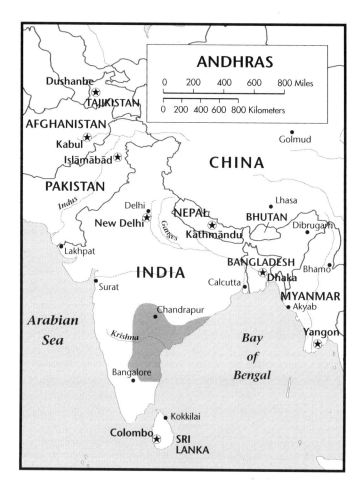

a goddess of fertility whose anger causes sterility in women. These deities play a much more immediate role in daily life and are to be respected and feared. They are all forms of the great Mother Goddess, and their rites invariably require blood sacrifices. The lesser deities often have priests drawn from the lower castes, and low castes may use their own priests rather than Brahmans. Ancestor spirits have to be appeased, and ghosts and evil spirits cause trouble for the living. Ritual specialists are called on to deal with spirits, and also to protect against sorcery and witchcraft.

6 MAJOR HOLIDAYS

Important events on the Andhra festival calendar include Ugadi (the Telugu New Year's Day), Shivaratri (honoring Shiva), and Chauti (Ganesha's birthday). This is in addition to celebrations such as Holi, Dasahara, and Divali. Different castes also have their own caste festivals. For example, Rath Saptami is observed only by Brahmans and is an occasion for the worship of the Sun. In the northwestern Telingana region, the annual worship of Pochamma, the goddess of smallpox, is an important village festival. As described by Dube (1955) in a village near Hyderabad, the day before the festival the village drummers go around the village announcing the plans for the festival. Members of the potter caste clean the shrines of the village goddesses, and those of the washerman caste paint them with whitewash. Village youths construct small leaf sheds in front of the shrines, and women of the sweeper caste smear the ground around the booths with red earth. On the day of the festival, every household prepares rice in a new, decorated earthenware pot called *bonam*. The Madigas, the Untouchable caste that act as village drummers, worship and perform sacrifices at their own Pochamma shrine, then return to participate in the main ceremony. They lead the village in procession to the Pochamma shrine, where a member of the potter caste (Kummari) officiates as priest at the ceremony. Every family, in strict order of caste and standing within the caste, offers some rice to the goddess. Goats, sheep, and fowl are sacrificed at the shrine. Following the ceremony, families return to their houses where they feast on the rice and meat. Even Muslims, though they do not participate in the worship, take part in the ceremony and offer sacrifices. They, just like the Hindus, feel the need to propitiate the goddess Pochamma.

7 RITES OF PASSAGE

Although the specifics of life-cycle rituals vary among castes, in outline they follow the forms set out by the Hindu texts. On the birth of a child, the mother and other family members are considered impure. Rituals are performed to remove this impurity, which last up to 30 days for the mother. In villages, women from the barber caste act as midwives for the "clean" Hindu castes. A Brahman may be consulted to cast the infant's horoscope. The name-giving ceremony is held within three to four weeks, with the occasion marked by a feast for family and friends. Infants are raised by the women in the household, though young children are often left in the care of older siblings. As they grow up, children accompany their parents in their daily tasks and begin to learn their household duties and caste occupation at an early age. Higher castes often perform the sacred thread ceremony for males before puberty is reached. A girl's first menstruation is accompanied by elaborate rituals, including a period of seclusion, worship of household gods, and a gathering of village women for singing and dancing.

The higher Hindu castes usually cremate their dead, except in the case of death from snakebite and smallpox. Children are normally buried, and burial is also common among low-caste and Untouchable groups. The corpse is bathed, dressed, and carried to the cremation ground or graveyard on a bier. On the third day after death, the first of several purifying rituals takes place. This involves cleansing the house, washing all the linens, and discarding all earthen pots used for cooking or storing water. On the eleventh or thirteenth day, rites for removing the impurity of family members are performed. This includes shaving the head and face if the deceased were one's father or mother. Food and water are offered to the soul of the deceased, and a feast is given. The higher castes collect bones and ashes from the funeral pyre and immerse them in a holy river such as the Godavari. In exceptional cases, they are taken to the sacred Ganges in North India.

8 INTERPERSONAL RELATIONS

Andhras tend to be hypercritical and very sensitive in their interpersonal relations, especially in rural areas. There is a great tradition for argument that can easily progress to noisy quarrels or confrontations. There is a pervasive attitude of fault-finding, and people do not easily let pass the opportunity to criticize their neighbors. However, in situations that demand generosity and good neighborliness, Andhras are quick to rise to the occasion.

9 LIVING CONDITIONS

In northern Andhra Pradesh, villages are usually linear in form, with occasional isolated outlying hamlets. Settlements in the southern areas of the state can be either linear or square, but they also may have tributary hamlets. House types and creature comforts vary according to the economic circumstances of the owner. The average cultivator in a village in Telingana typically has a square house built around an internal courtyard. The walls are made of stone, the floor is made of mud, and the roof is tiled. There are two or three rooms, used for living, sleeping, and housing livestock. There is invariably one room used for the family shrine, where family valuables are also kept. The doors are often carved, and designs are painted on the walls. Most houses lack latrines, the inhabitants using the fields for their natural functions. There may be a backyard used for growing vegetables and keeping chickens. Furnishings are sparse and may consist of a few bedsteads, wooden stools, and a crude chair or two. Kitchen utensils, except for metal plates for eating, are usually of earthenware and are made by the village potters. In cities, houses are more substantial, have modern conveniences such as running water, and are better furnished.

10 FAMILY LIFE

Andhras must marry within their caste or subcaste. These endogamous social units are divided into exogamous clans (*gotram*), each of which may be further subdivided into lineages (*vansham*). One must marry outside one's own clan. And, as different clans have lineages of the same name, one has to make sure to marry outside one's own lineage. (Members of the same lineage, even though of different clans, are regarded as brother and sister. A sexual union between members of the same lineage is viewed as incestuous.) Marriages are arranged, and cross-cousin marriage is common. The details of marriage practice vary according to caste, but in outline they follow normal Hindu practices. Newlyweds usually move into the household of the groom's father. The extended family structure is regarded as ideal, although the nuclear family is also found.

Women occupy a subordinate role in Andhra society, being responsible primarily for rearing children and household chores. Among the cultivating castes, women also engage in agricultural activities. Divorce and widow remarriage are permitted by lower castes, though not by Brahmans and other high castes. Property is equally divided among sons.

11 CLOTHING

Male clothing consists of the Indian loincloth, or *dhoti*, tied in a distinctive Andhra manner and worn with a long *kurta* that comes down to the knees. In many rural areas, the material used is a slightly brownish, village-made *khadi* (handspun cloth). A cloth with a colored border is also thrown around the shoulders. Villagers commonly wear a turban. Women favor the *sari* and a bodice, the latter often brightly colored and embroidered. Saris are traditionally dark blue, parrot green, red, or purple in color. Young people, especially in urban areas, are turning to synthetic fabrics and ready-made, Western-style clothes. The sari is the preferred formal wear of women.

Andhra Pradesh folk artists get ready to perform during the India International Trade Fair in New Delhi, India.
(AP Images/Manish Swarup)

12 FOOD

The basic diet of the Andhras consists of rice, millets, pulses, and vegetables. Nonvegetarians who can afford it eat meat or fish. All Hindus avoid beef (although Untouchable castes eat carrion meat), and Brahmans and other high castes abstain from any kind of meat, fish, or eggs. Economic standing also influences the diet of individuals. The relatively well-to-do eat three meals a day. A typical meal would be rice or *khichri* (rice cooked with lentils and spices) or *paratha* (an unleavened bread made from wheat flour and fried in oil); this would be taken with a meat or vegetable (e.g., eggplant or okra) curry, hot pickles, and tea. Coffee is a popular drink in coastal areas. Savories are preferred to sweets. Betel leaves, twisted into rolls and filled with nuts, are served after a meal and considered a delicacy. In a poor household, a meal might consist of millet bread, eaten with boiled vegetables, chili powder, and salt. Poorer-quality rice would be eaten, and meat would only rarely be consumed. As is common throughout South Asia, men dine first and the women eat only after the men have finished. Children are served as soon as the food is ready.

13 EDUCATION

Literacy in Andhra Pradesh is relatively low. Recent data are not available, but the 1981 census records a literacy rate of only 29.72% for the state. Even though this figure includes children and can be expected to have risen over the last few years, it still compares unfavorably with many Indian states. Variations in literacy rates range from 14.10% among women in rural areas to a high of 61.05% for urban males. Hyderabad, Andhra Pradesh's largest city and the state capital, is an important center of learning with several universities and institutions of higher education.

14 CULTURAL HERITAGE

The Andhra people have made major contributions to India's culture in the areas of art, architecture, literature, music, and dance. The early Andhra rulers were great builders and patrons of religion and the arts. From the 1st century BC on, they developed a style of architecture that led to the creation of some of the greatest Buddhist monuments of Central India. The *stupa* (a monument built to hold a relic of Buddha) at Sanchi, and the ruins at Amaravati and other sites, attest to the achievements of the Andhras. Many critics see sculptures of the mature Andhra period (c. 3rd century AD) as among the finest in India. Some of the paintings of the famous Buddhist caves at Ajanta are ascribed to Andhra artists.

The Andhras developed a style of classical dance known as *kuchipudi*. This is a dance-drama, presenting religious themes, that is performed by certain Brahman families and passed down from generation to generation. The Andhra region and its people have contributed greatly to the development of South Indian classical music. South Indian compositions are mostly written in Telugu because of the smooth, rich, flowing sound of the language. Telugu literature dates to the 11th century AD. Major contributions were made by Shaiva (followers of Shiva) poets of the 13th century. However, Telugu literature reached it greatest heights under the patronage of the Vijayanagara kings around the 16th century.

15 WORK

Over three-quarters (76.75%) of Andhras live in rural areas, making their living mostly from agriculture. Rice is the dominant food grain. Sugarcane, tobacco, and cotton are grown as cash crops, in addition to chilies, oilseeds, and pulses. Periodic village markets throughout the region afford the opportunity for selling and trading one's goods.

Once basically agricultural in nature, Andhra Pradesh has emerged as one of the most highly industrialized states in India. Industries such as aeronautics, light engineering, chemicals, and textiles are found in the Hyderabad and Guntur-Vijayawada areas. As well as being an important port, Visakhapatnam has India's largest shipbuilding yard.

16 SPORTS

Young girls play with dolls, dressing them and celebrating doll marriages. Boys play ballgames and indulge in the usual pastimes of tag, hide-and-seek, and similar children's games. Playing with dice is common among men and women, and traditional amusements such as cockfighting and shadow plays are popular in rural areas. Modern sports such as cricket, soccer, and field hockey are played in educational institutions across the state.

17 ENTERTAINMENT AND RECREATION

Folk culture predominates in rural areas. Wandering entertainers put on puppet shows for the amusement of villagers. Professional ballad singers recount the exploits of past heroes, or tell stories from mythology. Modern media such as the radio have been used to make urban dwellers aware of folk traditions, as well as to expose rural people to Andhra's classical heritage. Andhra Pradesh has its own movie industry, making films in the Telugu language. The late N. T. Rama Rao, a popular movie idol who starred in over 300 Telugu films, rose to become chief minister of Andhra Pradesh.

18 FOLK ART, CRAFTS, AND HOBBIES

Andhra has a variety of traditional handicrafts. It is known for its wooden toys, which are carved and skillfully decorated. The subjects include birds, animals, human beings, gods and goddesses, and legendary beings from Hindu mythology. Other crafts include lacquer ware, hand-woven carpets, hand printed textiles, and tie-dyed fabrics. Bidri ware (silver inlay on metal), filigree silver work, embroidery, painting on ivory, basketry, and lace work are also products of the region. The making of leather puppets was developed in the 16th century under the Vijayanagara rulers.

19 SOCIAL PROBLEMS

With a population exceeding that of many of the larger European nations, Andhras are subject to the full range of economic and social problems that afflict India in the late 20th century. In contrast to the emerging middle classes, rural populations are frequently faced with excessive population growth, poverty, indebtedness, illiteracy, and lack of social infrastructure. Consumption of *arrack* or country liquor has been such a problem that pressure from women in recent years has led to the imposition of prohibition in the state. Economic problems are worsened by the destructive cyclonic storms (the last occurred in 1996) that sweep in from the Bay of Bengal. Currently, Andhra Pradesh State is involved in a longstanding dispute with Karnataka over the use of the waters of the Kistna River. Sporadic outbreaks of crime and violence are associated with the Peoples War Group (PWG), a quasi-political Maoist leftist organization that assassinates local government officials and political leaders as "class enemies" and "caste oppressors." Through all of this, however, the Andhras retain a very evident pride in being Andhra and have a strong sense of identity with Telugu culture.

20 GENDER ISSUES

Telegu women face the same gender issues as other women in South Asia—arranged marriages, child marriage, complaints over dowries and dowry deaths. In April 2008, SIFF (Save Indian Family Foundation) filed a memorandum with the Chief Minister of Andhra Pradesh complaining about the inadequacies of IPC (Indian Penal Code) Section 498A and the Dowry Prohibition Act by which people have been arrested without the complainant's charges having been investigated by police and demanding that laws (e.g. adultery laws, laws against rape and sexual harassment, domestic violence laws, divorce laws, child maintenance laws and child custody laws) should be gender neutral. The memorandum claims that innocent women have been incarcerated and even committed suicide because of the arrests made under these laws.

Despite the fact that Andhra Pradesh's performance in schooling of girls is better than many other Indian states, gender bias in schooling for girls still persists in the state.

21 BIBLIOGRAPHY

Innaiah, N. *A Century of Politics in Andhra Pradesh: Ethnicity & Regionalism in Indian State.* Hyderabad: Rationalist Voice Publications, 2002.

Krishna, G. *The Story of the Telugus and Their Culture.* Hyderabad, India: International Telugu Institute, 1983.

Krishna Kumari, M. *Facets of Andhra Culture.* Delhi: Gyan Sagar Publications, 1998.

Parthasarathy, R., ed. *Andhra Culture: A Petal in Indian Lotus.* Hyderabad, Andhra Pradesh: District Gazetteers Department, Government of Andhra Pradesh, 1984.

Subramiah Pantulu, G. R. *Folklore of the Telugus : a Collection of Forty-two Highly Amusing and Instructive Tales.* New Delhi: Rupa & Co., 2003.

Tapper, Bruce Elliott. *Rivalry and Tribute: Society and Ritual in a Telugu Village in South India.* Delhi: Hindustan Publishing Corp., 1987.

—by D. O. Lodrick

ANGLO AUSTRALIANS

PRONUNCIATION: AN-glo aw-STRAY-lee-uhns
LOCATION: Australia
POPULATION: 19.3 million (2007)
LANGUAGE: English
RELIGION: Christianity (majority); Islam; Buddhism; Judaism

¹ INTRODUCTION

Australia is a relatively young country in the world community. Yet it is also a very ancient land, where for over 40,000 years the Aboriginal people had lived in harmony with their environment. When England first settled Australia in 1788, however, and made it a penal colony for its overcrowded prison population, all that was to change.

Australia was rich in mineral wealth and became a leading world producer of wool and wheat. But links with Britain kept it isolated until World War II, after which it turned more and more towards the United States. Today, Australia is becoming a multicultural society that is seeking to establish itself as a leading nation in the Asia-Pacific region.

Throughout the 20th and into the 21st century, Australia has had a democratic form of government in which individual freedom has been prized above all else. It is considered a safe, peaceful country that has never experienced internal war. Its standard of living is high and the country has some of the world's most uniquely beautiful environments. Consequently, one of its fastest-growing industries today is tourism.

Australia's identity is a result of its English and European past and its multicultural (i.e., a European and Asian mix of cultures) present. In a speech in Indonesia in 1992, the Australian prime minister Paul Keating said that Australia's identity in the 1990s was changing "due to the multi-cultural reality of our society, and the final passing of … our colonial past."

Australia today is a foremost member of APEC, the Asia Pacific Economic Cooperation forum, and looks to forge free trade agreements with China and ASEAN, the Association of Southeast Asian Nations.

² LOCATION AND HOMELAND

Australia is both a continent and an island, situated in the southern hemisphere between the Pacific and Indian oceans. It measures about the same in area as the United States (excluding Alaska), yet it has a total population of only about 21 million people. Of those 21 million people, about 80% live in just 10 cities, all by the sea. By far the largest of these are Sydney and Melbourne. Approximately 92% of the population (about 19.3 million) is of European descent. In the 2006 Australian Census, about 25% of Australians specifically listed themselves as having English ancestry while another 29% listed themselves simply as Australian.

Most of the country is empty of people. In fact, Australia has one of the lowest population densities in the world. The state of Western Australia, for example, is three times the size of the US state of Texas, yet has only about 1.5 million people. The main reason for the low population density is that Australia is an extremely dry continent—two-thirds of the continent is desert.

Apart from the flat desert lands, however, the country's geography is quite varied. It includes large areas of tropical rain forests in the northeast, a long mountain range running along the eastern coast (the Great Dividing Range), snowfields in the southeast, and flat tablelands in the west.

The climate varies tremendously, from the tropics in the north with their "wet" and "dry" seasons to the much colder climates of Tasmania.

Because the country was first settled by England in 1788, most Australians were of English origin and, until 1950, about 90% of Australians were born there. Some 9% were immigrants from Britain. However, after World War II, the country took in more than 5 million immigrants from Europe and, in the post-Vietnam-War years, Australia was a major recipient of refugees from Indochina. The population in the early 21st century has become more international.

Immigration dropped dramatically in the late 1990s. Almost all immigrants have chosen to live in the ever-growing cities and have not populated the sparse country areas as was hoped.

³ LANGUAGE

The language of Australia is English, brought by the first English settlers. However, the accent is far more nasal and less clipped than the British English accent.

Since World War II, the culture of the United States has had a large influence on Australia, so that Australians are using many American expressions introduced by movies and television shows. However, a typical Australian greeting is still "G'day," and men routinely call each other "mate." To congratulate someone, Australians say, "Goodonya" ("Good on you"), and to reassure someone, they say, "She'll be right, mate." And, of course, there is what is known as the Great Australian Adjective—"bloody"—before almost everything, as in, "Oh bloody hell! I'm going to be bloody late for school again!"

⁴ FOLKLORE

Australia is an ancient land and for more than 40,000 years its Aboriginal people had lived there undisturbed, until the Europeans came over. Over time, a complex and rich Aboriginal mythology has evolved and has been passed down from generation to generation. This mythology is known as the Dreamtime Legends—the Dreamtime being the mystical time during which the Aborigines' ancestors established their world. These myths from ancient times are accepted as a record of absolute truth, and dominate the cultural life of the people.

There are many myths of the Dreamtime. One tells how the sun was made: Long ago in Dreamtime there was no sun, and the people had to search for food in the dim light of the moon. One day, an emu and a crane started quarreling. In a rage, the crane ran to the emu's nest and snatched one of its huge eggs. She flung the egg high into the sky, where it shattered and the yolk burst into flames, causing such a huge fire that its light revealed for the first time the beauty of the world below. When the spirits up in the sky saw this great beauty, they decided that the earth inhabitants should have this light each day. So, every night, the sky-people collected a pile of dry wood, ready to be set afire as soon as the morning star appeared. But a problem arose—if the day was cloudy, the star could not be seen and no one lit the fire. So the sky people asked the Kookaburra, who had a loud, braying laugh, to call them every morning. When

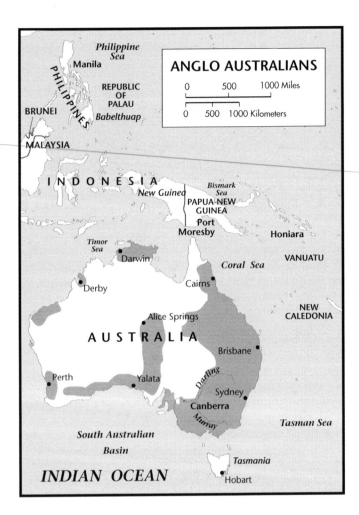

ANGLO AUSTRALIANS

```
0        500      1000 Miles
0    500   1000 Kilometers
```

tralia, accounting for 19% of the total population in the 2006 Australian Census. The Roman Catholic Church, however, is the largest denomination in the country with about 25% of the population claiming membership. The Uniting Church in Australia was established in 1977 through the union of the Congregational Union of Australia, the Methodist Church of Australia, and the Presbyterian Church of Australia. The Uniting Church, which embraces doctrines and confessions from all three of its founding traditions, was the third largest single denomination in the country in 2006 with a membership of about 1.1 million. About 18% of the total population claimed no religion in the 2006 Census.

⁶ MAJOR HOLIDAYS

Apart from those holidays celebrated throughout the Christian world, such as Christmas and Easter, Australia celebrates some of its own.

ANZAC Day on April 25 each year is set aside to honor Australians who died in all wars. ANZAC stands for the Australian and New Zealand Army Corps. Veterans of the armed forces march through the streets of Australian cities and towns in the morning and share drinks and memories in the afternoon. It is a solemn and patriotic day when the country remembers its war heroes.

Australia Day is celebrated on January 26, commemorating the day in 1788 when the English soldiers raised their flag and declared Australia a new colony. Today it is celebrated with street fairs, parties, picnics, and fireworks. It coincides with the last days of the long summer vacation from school and is a fun time for families. Backyard barbecues are very traditional on this day—followed by time on the beach or in the pool.

Boxing Day (December 26) is also a public holiday in Australia. It is known as a traditional day to spend at the beach and in practical terms it makes for a longer Christmas break.

⁷ RITES OF PASSAGE

At age five, children begin kindergarten at their local state or private primary school, which they attend through the sixth grade. There is usually a ceremony celebrating the child's graduation from primary to secondary school, consisting of a ceremony at the school with a guest speaker. There is usually a family celebration as well. The child then enters the high school (grades 7 to 10), followed by senior school (grades 11 and 12), and graduates from senior school at about age 18.

When students are in the twelfth grade they attend a senior school dance called the Formal. This is like the American tradition of prom night, when students hire limousines to attend a formal function sponsored by their school, usually held at some reasonably glamorous location. Just as in the US, the students place much emphasis on having the "right" clothes and the "right" date.

The 18th birthday party is a large, peer-group party celebrating entry into the adult world. At age 18 the young adult is given all legal rights. The 21st birthday celebration, a much more traditional family-and-friend celebration party, often is held in a hotel or restaurant. Gifts are traditionally given and this celebration often marks the time the young person leaves home to live independently.

the bird's laugh was first heard, the fire in the sky was lit but threw out little heat or light. By noon, when all the wood was burning, the heat was more intense. Later, the fire slowly died down until the sun had set.

It is a strict rule of the Aboriginal tribes that nobody may imitate the Kookaburra's call, because that could offend the bird and he could remain silent. Then darkness would again descend upon the earth and its inhabitants.

There are some folklore tales regarding the early European settlers. Many stories have been inspired by the figure of William Buckley, an English convict sent to Australia who escaped from prison and lived among the Aboriginals. There are legends and folk songs about "bushrangers," escaped convicts that were wild enough to be unwilling or unable to live in mainstream communities. Ned Kelly represents one such popular folk hero. Some stories about gold diggers from the mid-1800s have survived as folk lore, painting these rugged men, who generally showed disdain for authority, as heroes of the land. Other folk tales relate to the drovers and shearers (cattle and sheep herders) of early European settlers. Romanticized tales of life in the bush or outback continue to be popular in modern culture.

⁵ RELIGION

Australia is predominantly a Christian country. Most Anglo-Australians are members of the Anglican Church of Aus-

⁸ INTERPERSONAL RELATIONS

Men shake hands when introduced to each other or to a woman. Women often greet other women with a kiss on the cheek.

Pub life—the sharing of drinks with friends at a hotel bar—plays a large role in most Australians' social lives. The "shout" system is used—i.e., one person in a small circle of friends buys a drink for themselves and for everyone else in the circle. When it comes time for the next round, another person in the circle does the same—and so on, until each person has "shouted a round" of drinks for their group.

When invited to dinner, guests are usually asked to come at "7:30 for 8:30" which means the guests should arrive somewhere between 7:30 and 8:30 pm for pre-dinner drinks, with dinner to be served at 8:30.

Young people in Australia usually begin dating around age 14 or 15 and make their own choices of friends and partners in life. They tend to marry in their mid-20s.

⁹ LIVING CONDITIONS

At the 2006 Australian Census, an estimated 33% of all dwellings were owner-occupied, with an additional 32% of dwellings being purchased by the occupant, either through a loan or rent-to-own plan. The most popular home is the freestanding brick house with a red tiled roof, a front lawn, and a back garden. Most people want to own a home and usually rent until they can afford one. There is a trend toward larger houses and prices of houses vary according to the desirability of the location. However, housing prices in all cities have increased steadily over the years. The average household size was 2.6 persons in 2006.

Australia does not have the extremes of wealth and poverty that the US does, and therefore does not have extravagant mansions or slum dwellings. Instead, homes tend to be more like those found in a typical American middle-class suburban dwelling. Young people in cities live in flats (apartments) or townhouses close to the inner city, where there is a great deal of night-life. Cities are usually busy centers of life at night, with restaurants, bars, theaters, and activities at the harbor.

Australia has a universal public health system called Medicare, under which a broad range of medical and hospital services are available either for free or with substantial government rebates. Private health care providers are free to determine their own fees and to choose what rebateable services they will provide. The Pharmaceutical Benefits Scheme pays for some physician services as well as most prescription medications. The 2006 National Health Survey reported that about 50% of the population aged 15 years and older had private health insurance.

Life expectancy for Australians at birth is about 80 years (2008); 77.8 years for men and 83.7 years for women. A majority of Australians are considered to be in very good or excellent health, according to a 2005 National Health Survey. Excessive weight was the most common health problem in the survey, with about 62% of men and 45% of women being in the category of overweight or obese.

¹⁰ FAMILY LIFE

Family life in Australia is changing, as the nuclear family unit of two married parents and two children with the father in the workforce and the mother at home is becoming a thing of the past. In 2006 only 49.6% of Australians aged 15 and old-

A boy and his father celebrating Australia Day.
(© Sean Davey/Corbis)

er were married; representing a decrease from 51.4% in 2001. About 33.2% of the population had never married and 11.3% were separated or divorced. About 5.9% of the population was widowed. In 2005 the marriage rate was listed as about 5.4 marriages for every 1,000 people. This figure represents a downward trend in the number of marriages. In 1986, for example, the marriage rate was at about 7.2 marriages per 1,000 people. It was estimated that about 33% of all marriages entered into in 2000–2002 would end in divorce within about 14 to 16 years. In 2005 the median age for marriage was 30 years old for men and 28 years old for women. The number of couples choosing to cohabitate without a registered marriage has been increasing. In 2006 about 7.7% of the population aged 15 years and over were in such a de facto marriage. This figure represents an increase from 5.3% in 1996 and 6.4% in 2001. The decrease in the number of marriages and increase in the number of divorces translates into a larger number of children being raised in single-parent households, primarily with the mother as head of household.

Australian families have seen an increase in the number of adult children who remain living with their parents after leaving secondary school or university. This is due in part to unem-

Bindi Irwin poses with a snake during a promotional tour for her show, "Bindi the Jungle Girl," at the Australia Zoo, Beerwah, Australia. (Bradley Kanaris/Getty Images)

ployment, as some new graduates have a difficult time getting a job. However, the dreams of most young people remain the same as those their parents had at that age—to travel "overseas" (which means England, then Europe) usually for about a year, before returning and settling down.

¹¹ CLOTHING

Australia's temperatures are generally far milder that those found in the US. Australians favor easy-to-wear, light clothing in the summer. To stay cool, many Australians wear long socks and long tailored shorts instead of slacks. This is acceptable apparel even in the workplace. Clothing styles are a mixture of European and American fashions. People tend to dress stylishly in the city and the office but wear jeans and sneakers on the weekends.

All school children wear uniforms. School caps are now almost compulsory. These are usually "legionnaire"-style cloth caps with a flap covering the back of the neck for protection from the sun. All children also wear sunscreen all year round, as Australia has one of the highest rates of skin cancer in the world. In fact, having a suntan is regarded as a sign of foolishness. Most people are very careful to protect their skin from the fierce Australian sun.

¹² FOOD

Good seafood is abundant along Australia's coastline, and is very popular. Australians also eat a lot of meat—especially beef or lamb roasts.

The tropical north of Australia offers wonderful fruits and vegetables and there is also an excellent local wine industry with vineyards in the south of the country. Typically, a family would have cereal and toast or eggs and bacon for breakfast; sandwiches, salad, and fruit for lunch; and either meat or seafood with vegetables and dessert for the main meal in the evening, around 7:30 pm.

The influx of European and Asian immigrants over the past 20 to 30 years has led Australians to enjoy foods from all cultures, and Australian families now incorporate Chinese, Thai, or Indian foods into their weekly meal planning. European foods, particularly Greek and Italian, have always been favorites.

One food remains an Australian tradition—a black spread called Vegemite. This is made from yeast extract plus salt and is spread on toast and butter for breakfast or eaten in sandwiches for lunch—all children are brought up eating it from babyhood. The other famous Aussie meal is meat pie. Approximately 260 million meat pies are eaten by Australians every year. Favorite desserts include the Australian Pavlova—a cake-sized soft meringue filled with fruits and cream—and a small treat called Lamingtons, which are sponge cake cubes coated with chocolate and grated coconut.

¹³ EDUCATION

Education is compulsory for students aged 6 to 15. School children enter kindergarten at about age five or six. Primary school covers grades 1 to 6. High school consists of middle school (grades 7 to 10) and senior school (grades 11 and 12). At the end of the twelfth grade, when student are about 18 years old, the student takes a public exam called the Higher School Certificate. From this exam alone the student is ranked against others in the country and his or her grade determines which university, if any, the student may enter and which course of study to follow. If the student does not plan to enter a university, he or she needs the exam to enter any other higher education institution or to show a prospective employer. Therefore, this is a very stressful exam for the student.

University entrance is extremely competitive. Fees are very low by US standards, though up until the 1980s all university courses were free. Nearly all universities are government-run. In 2003 it was estimated that nearly 74% of the adult population was enrolled in some type of higher education program. At the university level, students enter their chosen field of study immediately, without needing to complete an undergraduate degree first. Students often live in large shared houses with other students around the universities, but many also continue to live at home. Apart from the universities, there are many institutions of adult education and career training, mostly government-run, with minimal fees, where students can study for other careers.

The literacy rate among Australians is about 99%.

¹⁴ CULTURAL HERITAGE

Australia has a growing film industry that is fast gaining international respect. In the 1980s and 1990s it produced such hits as *Babe*, *Muriel's Wedding*, *Mad Max*, The Piano, and *Crocodile*

Dundee. Most celebrities must travel to Hollywood, however, to gain worldwide fame—e.g., Errol Flynn, Paul Hogan, Olivia Newton-John, Mel Gibson, and Nicole Kidman. Australian television shows that have been exported and well-received in the UK and the US include *The Crocodile Hunter, The Wiggles, and A Country Paradise.*

Sydney's Opera House is world-famous, designed by the Danish architect Utzen to resemble sails on the ocean. It houses the Australian Opera Company, theaters, concert halls, and restaurants, and attracts hundreds of thousands of tourists each year.

The country has wonderful wildlife and many natural attractions. The Great Barrier Reef is one of these—a world heritage coral reef, the longest and most complex living system in the world. Farther inland is the beautiful Kakadu National Park. This park has 275 bird species, and many ancient examples of Aboriginal folk art, and is classified by the UN Educational, Scientific and Cultural Organization (UNESCO) as a world heritage area, as are Cradle Mountain in Tasmania and Shark Bay in Perth. Also classified as a world heritage area is Ayers Rock—a giant red rock sacred to the Aborigines that stands majestically in the Olgas in the middle of the dessert.

Famous Anglo-Australian writers include Patrick White, the author of *The Eye of the Storm* and winner of the 1973 Nobel Prize for Literature, and Germaine Greer, known for her feminist writings and her career in journalism. The composers Percy Grainger and Arthur Benjamin were both born in Australia.

15 WORK

Australians work in a wide variety of professional fields and trade occupations. In 2005 about 76% of the population aged 15 to 64 was employed. About 75% of the work force is employed in service-related professions and occupations, 21% in industry, and about 4% in agriculture. The unemployment rate in 2007 was estimated as 4.4%. The standard minimum wage in 2005 was at about us$362.35 per week. Full-time workers usually receive four weeks annual vacation and belong to a superannuation scheme which will give them income when they retire. The working week is Monday to Friday, 9:00 am to 5:00 pm. Workers' rights are protected by numerous laws, and Australia has an attractive union system.

16 SPORTS

Australians love sports—both playing and watching them on television. The all-time favorite is football. Australians follow three different types, depending on which part of the country they come from: The Rugby League, played in N.S.W., Queensland, and Canberra; Australian Rules, played in Victoria, Southern Australia, Western Australia, and Tasmania; and Rugby Union, played in N.S.W. and Queensland (also played internationally, and usually the football game played by schoolboys, along with soccer).

In summer, Australians enjoy cricket. Within Australia, the states play each other to see who will win that year's Sheffield's Shield; teams also play internationally. Australia plays countries such as Britain and the West Indies to see who will win the Ashes.

Other popular sports include swimming, tennis, surfing, and sailing. However, the fastest growing new sport in Australia today is baseball.

17 ENTERTAINMENT AND RECREATION

In the cities, many forms of entertainment are offered. Theaters, movies, bars, and discos, plus every type of restaurant imaginable, are common. Australians enjoy a pub life similar to that found in England. But mostly they enjoy the ocean. On summer weekends the beaches are packed with surfers, and the harbors are full of boats of all types. Australians love to spend weekends outdoors near the water.

During their vacations, Australians travel within the country, usually by car, exploring the tourist attractions and the "Outback," as the dry, flat inland areas are called. When vacationing outside the country, favorite places are Bali, Fiji, and New Zealand.

Sunday afternoon barbecues at home are very popular. Traditionally, friends arrive around 2:00 pm for a barbecue lunch. The host cooks steaks, sausages, or seafood on a grill and friends talk, eat, and drink into the evening. Entertainment in Australia is mostly relaxed and informal.

Many Australians enjoy gambling, especially on horse-racing. This culminates in an event that takes place on the first Tuesday of November each year, at exactly 3:00 pm—the running of the Melbourne Cup. This event brings the country to a standstill—it is even broadcast live over loudspeakers in most offices. Everyone has a small bet on the outcome—usually "sweeps" are run among friends and at offices.

18 FOLK ART, CRAFTS, AND HOBBIES

Australian hobbies are very similar to those pursued by people in the US and just as varied. There is a rich culture of Aboriginal art and wood carvings in Australia—often using various hues of clay color. Aboriginal rock paintings and carvings are found in many of the states' National Parks and reserves.

19 SOCIAL PROBLEMS

As of 2008 the question of when and how Australia might become a republic was a source of political and social debate. Australia is still part of the British Commonwealth, with the queen of England serving as the official head of state. However, many citizens and politicians have argued that the government should reorganize into a republic with a president taking over the roles currently held by the queen and a governor-general. Concerns arise as to how power will be apportioned within the new style of government. These issues have yet to be decided.

Immigration is a further concern. Many people feel that Australia cannot support more people, because of the nature of the land. Others are concerned that the country is becoming multicultural too fast. The country has maintained a strict policy on unauthorized arrivals. Asylum seekers are held in detention centers, which have been criticized at home and abroad, until their cases are heard. However, in February 2008 Australia ended its policy of sending asylum seekers into detention on small Pacific islands, with the last refugees leaving Nauru.

20 GENDER ISSUES

An increase in the rate of divorces and decrease in the number of marriages has caused an increase in the number of single-parent households. Most single-parent households are headed by women. In 2006 approximately 87% of all single-parent households with children under the age of 15 years were headed by mothers. Education and employment are issues of concern for single parents, both male and female. In 2006 about 39% of all single parents had left school before year 12. About 19% of all single mothers were employed full-time in 2006, compared to about 24% of married mothers. Approximately 32% of single-mothers worked part-time, compared to 39% of married mothers. Nearly 40% of all single mothers were unemployed and seeking employment. About 48% of single fathers worked full-time while 15% worked part-time and 10% were unemployed. About 85% of married fathers worked full-time while 6% worked part-time and 2% were unemployed. It has been estimated that 51% of all single-parents do not receive weekly income from child support or maintenance payments.

While women can and do participate in a wide variety of profession, women in the workforce tend to earn less money than men in similar employment positions. In 2007 it was estimated that women's full-time average weekly earnings were about 83.6% of those of men. Women can and do participate at all levels of government.

21 BIBLIOGRAPHY

Australian Bureau of Statistics. http://www.abs.gov.au (21 April 2008).

Coppell, Bill. *Australia in Fact and Fiction*. Sydney: Penguin Books, 1994.

Cue, Kerry. *Australia Unbuttoned*. Sydney: Penguin Books, 1996.

Dale, David. *The 100 Things Everyone Needs to Know About Australia*. Sydney: Pan Macmillan, 1996.

Docherty, J. C. *Historical Dictionary of Australia*. Lanham, MD: Scarecrow Press, 2007.

Roberts, A., and C. P. Mountford. *Legends of the Dreamtime*. Sydney: International Limited Editions, 1975.

Weiss, Johann Peter. *In Search of an Identity: Essays and Ideas on Anglo-Australians, German-Australians, and Others*. New York: Peter Lang, 2000.

—revised by K. Ellicott

ANGLO INDIANS

PRONUNCIATION: AN-glo IN-dee-uhns
ALTERNATE NAMES: Domiciled Europeans
LOCATION: India
POPULATION: 100,000–125,000
LANGUAGE: English
RELIGION: Christianity (Roman Catholic, Church of England [Anglican], other Protestant sects)
RELATED ARTICLES: Vol. 3: Goans; Vol 4: People of India

1 INTRODUCTION

"Anglo Indian" has two meanings, one essentially historical and one in use today. In the past, the term described Europeans (usually British) who had made India their permanent home and lived there for generations. They were sometimes known as Domiciled Europeans. In its modern usage, however, Anglo Indian refers to people of mixed European and Indian ancestry. This sense of the word received official government recognition in India in 1911. Prior to that, various designations such as "Eurasian" or "Indo-Briton," or more derogatory terms such as "half-caste" or "mixed-breed," were used to describe this population.

The Anglo Indian community has existed in India for almost 500 years. Its beginnings go back to AD 1498 when Vasco da Gama established a Portuguese colony on the Malabar coast of southwestern India. The Portuguese established a formal policy of encouraging Portuguese men to marry Indian women. This was seen as a way of spreading the Christian faith, as the women were required to be baptized before the marriage was approved by the authorities. During the 17th and 18th centuries, other Europeans established themselves in India. However, the Dutch presence was temporary and the French were defeated by the British, so few people today can claim a Dutch or French ancestry. The British East India Company, however, followed policies that encouraged mixed marriages and sexual unions between British men and Indian women. In the early 1700s, Anglo Indians in India outnumbered overseas British. Anglo Indians were in a favored position, filling many military and commercial posts as British interests in India expanded. At the same time, the British East India Company had a supply of trained recruits who were "Western" in their outlook who could be employed in the Company's service.

This situation changed following 1785. Fears that the Anglo Indians were becoming too powerful led the East India Company to prohibit their employment and dismiss those already working with the company. The next 50 years was a period of economic hardship for Anglo Indians, who had few alternate sources of employment. It also saw the alienation of the Anglo Indian community from the British, and the emergence of a sense of communal identity within the group. Anglo Indian fortunes changed again when the East India Company's policy of nonemployment was reversed after 1833. This was also the time when the railroad and telegraph were introduced into India, and Anglo Indians were closely involved in the construction and operation of these systems. As might be expected, the Anglo Indian community supported the British during the 1857 Sepoy Mutiny, and Anglo Indian military leaders played a prominent role in this conflict.

During the early decades of the 20th century, Anglo Indians in India were faced with growing economic and political pressures. A rising tide of Indian nationalism saw government reforms open occupations formerly reserved for Anglo Indians to Indians. The political concerns of the Anglo Indian community were largely ignored by the British government in England as it grappled with the problems of larger minorities such as the Muslims. As independence for India approached in 1947, many Anglo Indians, especially the more affluent and better educated, emigrated rather than remain in the country. Even though Anglo Indians fought for and received certain rights and special political representation in the Constitution of the newly independent India, the community remains a small and marginal one in the context of modern India.

2 LOCATION AND HOMELAND

Reliable data concerning the size of the Anglo Indian population in India today are unavailable. Leaders of the community suggest the population numbers 250,000 people, but a more realistic estimate is between 100,000 and 125,000.

The Anglo Indian community is essentially urban in nature, and this is clearly seen in its modern distribution in India today. The largest concentration of Anglo Indians is found in Calcutta, with sizable communities living in Madras, Bombay, Bangalore, and the Delhi area. In addition, there are small Anglo Indian communities in towns around the country, such as Ajmer, Jhansi, and Bilaspur, that are important centers on India's rail system. In many of these towns, Anglo Indians lived in "railway colonies." These were planned settlements, with housing constructed specifically for employees of the railways. They created de facto Anglo Indian neighborhoods which set the community apart from the surrounding population. With the decline in numbers of Anglo Indians employed by the railways since independence, this informal segregation is less noticeable today.

One group in India that is viewed as belonging to the Anglo Indian community by some, and not by others, is the Goans. Of mixed Portuguese and Indian descent, they are technically Anglo Indian. Many Anglo Indians of British descent, however, do not see them as "proper" Anglo Indians and do not accept them into their communities.

In 1947, there were approximately 300,000 Anglo Indians in India. Over the next 25 years, this number was reduced dramatically by a mass exodus of Anglo Indians from India. Even though Frank Anthony, a prominent leader of the Anglo Indian community in India, was able to negotiate two nominated representatives in Parliament, jobs for Anglo Indians, and educational concessions, many Anglo Indians saw little future for themselves in the new India. A first wave of emigration, in the years following 1946, took many Anglo Indians to Britain. A second wave of emigration occurred in the 1960s. By this time, however, British immigration laws were more restrictive, so many Anglo Indians relocated to Canada, Australia, and New Zealand. Studies have shown that although these overseas Anglo Indians continue to preserve a sense of their past, they integrate very quickly into their new societies.

3 LANGUAGE

A distinguishing feature of the Anglo Indian community, and also a matter of considerable pride, is the use of English as the mother tongue. While members of the group may be bilingual,

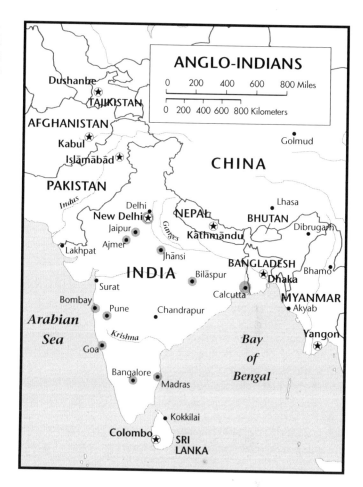

speaking Hindi or another regional language in addition to English, English is the language of choice used in the home. English is the medium of instruction in Anglo Indian schools. The use of the language has come to be a symbol of the "separateness" of the Anglo Indian community.

Some writers have identified an accent and speech patterns in the English spoken by Anglo Indians that set it apart from standard English. This includes a mincing or sing-song intonation of words and phrases that has been called *chee-chee*. This term was also used by the British in India as a derisive word for a member of the Anglo Indian community.

4 FOLKLORE

Anglo Indians are neither Europeans nor Indians. In the areas of culture and lifestyle, they are Western in outlook. They reject the Indian part of their heritage, yet they are not British or European, either. During colonial times, Anglo Indians were regarded as a separate and socially inferior community by the British. Any direct links with their British (or Portuguese) heritage are long gone. What remains is a sense of identity with a British past—perhaps, if one disregards genetics, more semimythical than real—that is reinforced by the consciously Westernized way of life followed by Anglo Indians in India today. For many of the older generation, even though they had never lived there, "Home" was Britain, not India.

5 RELIGION

All Anglo Indians are Christians, and the church plays an important role in the religious and social life of the community.

Anglo Indians often attend church on a regular basis and also participate in the church's organized social and recreational activities. There is no one particular Christian denomination that is exclusively identified with the Anglo Indian community. Catholics form the most numerous group, but non-Catholic denominations such as Church of England (also known as Anglican or Episcopalian), Methodist, Baptist, and Presbyterian are also represented. Of the Protestant sects, the Church of England is the most prestigious and attracts Anglo Indians of the middle and upper classes.

In the years since independence, the Anglo Indian Christian community in India has had to accommodate inevitable changes in their church life. One is the presence of Indian Christians in their churches. Historically, Indians who had accepted Christianity were looked down upon by Anglo Indians. The reality of declining numbers has meant that Indian Christians have been accepted into the congregations of churches that were formerly almost exclusively attended by Anglo Indians. However, subtle forms of discrimination against Indian Christians continue. Another major change since 1947 is the reorganization of the Christian Churches in the subcontinent as independent entities (e.g., the United Church of Northern India and the Church of South India). In addition, the clergy and church hierarchy are now almost exclusively Indian.

6 MAJOR HOLIDAYS

Anglo Indians observe the traditional Christian holidays with great enthusiasm. Attendance at church on holy days such as Good Friday, Easter Sunday, or Christmas is customary, to be followed by visits to friends and relatives, socializing, and entertaining. Children are given chocolate or marzipan Easter eggs at Easter. During the Christmas season, homes are decorated with Christmas trees and colored streamers, Christmas gifts are exchanged, and a traditional "English" Christmas lunch is eaten. Christmas is also a time when clubs and social organizations hold parties for children and dances for adults.

7 RITES OF PASSAGE

The rites of passage of the Anglo Indian community follow those of the Christian Church, with specific details being determined by the denomination involved. Infants are baptized in church, with godparents standing witness. Children attend Sunday School to receive religious instruction and at the appropriate time are confirmed and receive their First Communion. Marriages are performed in church and, with so many Anglo Indians being Catholic, the divorce rate is low. Death ceremonies follow the normal Christian pattern, with funeral services held in church, followed by burial in a cemetery.

8 INTERPERSONAL RELATIONS

Anglo Indians greet each other in the Western fashion, men shaking hands and women embracing and kissing each other on both cheeks. Young children address any adult visitor as "Auntie" or "Uncle" as a matter of respect, regardless of the relationship. Visiting and entertaining, especially at times such as Christmas and other holidays, is a common practice. Visitors are offered tea, snacks, or, should the occasion demand it, drinks such as beer, rum, or whiskey.

9 LIVING CONDITIONS

Anglo Indian homes are usually furnished in a Western style, with decor and furniture showing a marked British influence. Among the middle classes, furniture typically consists of overstuffed sofas and chairs, oak or mahogany tables, and carpets, mixed together with objects of local manufacture. Pictures on the wall may consist of European landscapes, with perhaps portraits of the British royal family, along with family photographs.

The living conditions of Anglo Indians reflect, by and large, their economic standing and social status. The affluent live in spacious, well-furnished houses with several bedrooms and modern conveniences, and servants to perform household tasks. By contrast, there are many Anglo Indians who, through force of economic circumstances, are forced to live in slum-like conditions. One writer cites an instance in which three families numbering a total of 23 people were living in a two-room house in Bangalore. In the area of Ripon Street in Calcutta, many Anglo Indians live in one- or two-room homes lacking running water, electricity, and modern toilet facilities. Large numbers of this community depend on the financial support of various welfare organizations.

10 FAMILY LIFE

Anglo Indian family structure has been described as the modified-extended family. This ordinarily consists of husband, wife, and children, and sometimes other dependents such as grandparents residing in the same household. The actual number residing in any given household, of course, depends to a large extent on economic circumstances.

Young adults are permitted to mix relatively freely with members of the opposite sex, and the selection of a spouse is a matter of individual choice, unlike the arranged marriages of Hindu society. Young married adults try to set up their own household if their finances permit it. In the past, Anglo Indians were a strongly endogamous community. The British would not marry Anglo Indians, while it was unthinkable for an Anglo Indian to marry an Indian (as it was for an Indian to marry an Anglo Indian). The great majority of Anglo Indians continue to marry within the community today, but intergroup marriage is evidently becoming more common. Increasing numbers of Anglo Indian girls are marrying Indians, both Indian Christians and men of other religious communities. This is partly economic, reflecting high unemployment among Anglo Indian males and their inability to support a family. It is partly a matter of choice, as economic security and a comfortable life with an Indian husband for some girls is more attractive than the possibility of years working as the main wage-earner to support an Anglo Indian husband. It should be noted that Anglo Indian girls marrying an Indian often face resistance and resentment from the husband's family. Because of their lifestyles and dress, Anglo Indian girls are viewed as loose and promiscuous by traditional Indians.

11 CLOTHING

Dress in South Asian society is of considerable symbolic significance, and the cultural orientation of the Anglo Indian community is clearly reflected in its dress styles. Men invariably wear Western attire. Among the older generation, the "solar topi" or sun helmet is worn as a sign of one's European descent. Women wear dresses, blouses, and skirts and follow Western fashion fads such as miniskirts. Whereas Indian women traditionally wear their hair long, Anglo Indian women follow hair fashions prevailing in Western countries. Differences in hair styles, however, are becoming less apparent as more Indian women are adopting cosmopolitan fashions. Anglo Indian women and girls may wear the Indian *sari* for formal occasions or for work situations. Western dress, nonetheless, remains a symbol of Anglo Indian cultural identity.

12 FOOD

In few areas of life are Anglo Indians more Western than in food preferences and dining customs. The inevitable Indian influences are, of course, seen in a taste for curries and a liking for local "sweets." But the kinds of food eaten, the methods of preparing food, and the style of eating show marked Western influences. Unlike Hindus and Muslims, who have strong religiously based food taboos, Anglo Indians have few restrictions on their diet. They are usually nonvegetarians, eating beef, pork, chicken, and other meat if they can afford it. They dine seated at the table, using plates, cups, and saucers, and eating with knives, forks, and spoons. The traditional Indian practice of eating with one's hands is totally unacceptable in Anglo Indian society. In addition, alcohol may be served as an aperitif or taken along with the meal.

A typical day begins with early morning tea ("bed tea"), followed around 8:00 or 9:00 am by an English breakfast of porridge or cereal, eggs, toast, and tea. Lunch is curry and rice. Afternoon tea is taken around 4:00 pm, accompanied by biscuits or cake. Dinner, which is eaten quite late, usually starts with a soup course. Mulligatawny, a spicy "pepper-water" soup, is a standard on the Anglo Indian menu. The main course might consist of roast meat or cutlets, served with potatoes and vegetables. Dessert or cheese and crackers, perhaps followed by coffee, completes the meal.

The modern diet of Anglo Indians depends largely on financial circumstances. Wealthier families with having the resources to buy meat and other expensive foodstuffs may keep to traditional Anglo Indian menus. The less fortunate, who may not be able to afford meat, tend to eat Indian-style vegetarian dishes, and their diet more closely resembles that of the local Indian population.

13 EDUCATION

Literacy among Anglo Indians is high. This is a measure of the pride the community takes in English as a symbol of its European heritage. English-language schools, often church-run and staffed by Anglo Indian teachers, provide education of a relatively high standard. However, these schools are private institutions, and their fees are often out of the reach of the lower-class Anglo Indian. Competition for entrance is fierce, as middle-class non-Anglo Indians see English-language schooling as essential for their children to succeed in government service and the professions. A common perception is that many Anglo Indian students—especially boys—lack the motivation to pursue higher education.

14 CULTURAL HERITAGE

As a small, isolated community that has rejected its Indian heritage, Anglo Indians lack cultural traditions of their own. They live a consciously Western lifestyle and share, secondhand, in Western trends in fashions, dance, and popular culture. In the

1960s, for example, young Anglo Indians formed rock-and-roll bands that performed at dances and social events. Some Anglo Indians achieved fame in the West as pop singers, notably Engelbert Humperdinck and Cliff Richards. Other famous Anglo Indians include the movie stars Merle Oberon and Ben Kingsley.

Although it can hardly be said that there is an Anglo Indian literary tradition, many British writers have dealt with Anglo Indian society in their works. A few, such as John Masters, focus specifically on the Anglo Indian community, notably in his novel *Bhowani Junction*. Others paint a picture—of varying degrees of accuracy and bias—of Anglo Indians as part of their overall consideration of relations between the British and Indians in India. Such authors include Rudyard Kipling, E. M. Forster, and Paul Scott.

15 WORK

Under British rule, Anglo Indians fulfilled an important occupational role in the economy of India. They were well represented in the Indian railways, posts and telegraph service, customs, and police. Anglo Indians reached high rank in the British Indian Army and other branches of the armed forces. Following the policy of Indianization initiated in 1919, however, Anglo Indians lost their advantage over Indians in terms of employment in the civil sector. This process was speeded up following Indian independence in 1947.

As a community, Anglo Indians have not fared well in terms of their accomplishments in modern India. Some individuals have gained national recognition. Melville de Mellow, for instance, was a broadcaster of international fame on All-India Radio. Many Anglo Indians served with distinction in the armed forces during India's wars with Pakistan and China. But these were of another generation. The picture for Anglo Indian youth today is bleak. Girls have traditionally become secretaries, teachers, and nurses. Unemployment among Anglo Indian men is high, with many reluctant to accept employment they feel is beneath their status. Many Anglo Indians also see discrimination by Indian society at large as a barrier to their advancement.

16 SPORTS

Anglo Indians had the reputation, particularly in the early decades of this century, of being the best athletes in India. They raised field hockey to new levels of play and dominated India's representative teams at the time. Hockey teams dominated by Anglo Indians were fielded by railway departments, customs, and other organizations. They regularly swept national tournaments such as the Aga Khan Cup in Bombay and the All-India Scindia Gold Cup. Cricket and soccer were also popular sports.

17 ENTERTAINMENT AND RECREATION

Anglo Indians have full access to the recreational amenities of urban India. These include radio, television and movie theaters. Church-related social and recreational activities are important in many communities. In the past, clubs such as Railway Institutes were the focus of social life, but these are no longer exclusively the preserve of Anglo Indians.

18 FOLK ART, CRAFTS, AND HOBBIES

There are no folk arts or crafts that can be said to be unique to the Anglo Indian community.

19 SOCIAL PROBLEMS

Anglo Indians form a small and isolated community in India. Western in outlook and lifestyle, they reject their Indian background. Yet the question remains how long Anglo Indians, as a minority cut off from their European roots, will be able to maintain their separate identity in Indian society. A few Anglo Indians have prospered in post-Independence India and lead lives similar to other Indian elites. The majority, however, still clinging tenaciously to their non-Indian identity, have not fared so well. Anglo Indian men are typically identified with poor educational qualifications, high unemployment, poverty, and a high incidence of alcoholism. This has led to Anglo Indian women seeking partners outside the community, forcing men in turn to look elsewhere for their wives. Should the trend of marrying outside the community continue, the erosion in numbers of an already small group could threaten its very existence within the next few generations. With strong leadership, schools, and cultural organizations, and their focus on the English language, Anglo Indians may survive in India as a distinct entity. An equally likely scenario, however, is the gradual integration of the community into Indian society, as has happened to so many "alien" peoples in India in the past.

20 GENDER ISSUES

Anglo-Indian women, being more exposed to feminism and gender issues current in the West, are much more familiar with such issues than other women's groups in India. However, with more Anglo-Indian women marrying into Indian families, they tend to face discrimination because, to do so, they flout indigenous customs of arranged marriages and specific caste rules. However, once they bear male children, much of this discrimination disappears. Their children tend to be raised according to the customs of the caste into which they marry.

21 BIBLIOGRAPHY

Abel, Evelyn. *The Anglo-Indian Community.* Delhi: Chanakya Publications, 1988.

Anthony, Frank. *Britain's Betrayal in India: The Story of the Anglo-Indian Community.* Bombay: Allied Publishers, 1969.

Caplan, Lionel. *Children of Colonialism: Anglo-Indians in a Postcolonial World.* Oxford, New York: Berg, 2001.

Gist, Noel P., and Wright, Roy Dean. *Marginality and Identity: Anglo-Indians as a Racially-mixed Minority in India.* Leiden, Holland: E.J. Brill, 1973.

Hawes, Cristopher J. *Poor Relations: The Making of a Eurasian Community in British India, 1773-1833.* Richmond, Surrey: Curzon Press, 1996.

Maher, James, Reginald. *These Are The Anglo Indians.* London: Simon Wallenberg Press, 2007.

Schermerhorn, R. A. "Anglo-Indians: An Uneasy Minority." *In Ethnic Plurality in India.* Tucson, AZ: University of Arizona Press, 1978.

—by D. O. Lodrick

ASMAT

PRONUNCIATION: AWZ-mot
LOCATION: Indonesian province of Papua on the island of New Guinea
POPULATION: Approximately 70,000
LANGUAGE: Asmat-Kamoro language family; Bahasa Indonesia (national language of Indonesia)
RELIGION: Christianity; Asmat religion based on spirit worship

1 INTRODUCTION

The Asmat are a Melanesian, or Papuan, people who live within the Indonesian province of Papua that occupies most of the western half of the island of New Guinea. They are widely known for the quality of their wood sculptures, and they are also notorious for their traditional practices of headhunting and cannibalism, which have been linked to the unsolved disappearance of Michael Rockefeller, 23-year-old son of former New York governor Nelson Rockefeller, in 1961 while touring the region to collect indigenous artwork.

The Asmat's first European contact was with the Dutch in 1623. Some 150 years later, Captain James Cook arrived on their shores. For many years, due to their fearsome reputation, the group had few outside visitors, and another 150 years passed before the Dutch began to settle the Asmat area in the 1920s, bringing in the first Catholic missionaries. The first permanent Dutch colonial post, at Agats, was established in 1938. During World War II, Asmat lands lay on the border between Allied-controlled Papua and Japanese-controlled West New Guinea, and some skirmishes occurred between the Japanese and the Asmat. Contact with the West has expanded steadily since the 1950s, and traditional Asmat warfare and cannibalistic practices have declined.

2 LOCATION AND HOMELAND

The Asmat have traditionally been a coastal people occupying a low-lying swampy region that covers approximately 25,000 square kilometers in southwestern Papua. The swamps are punctuated by stands of sago palms, mangroves, and patches of tropical rain forest. Numerous streams and tributaries that overflow their banks in the rainy season provide the primary means of transportation for the Asmat. The Asmat population is estimated at around 70,000, living in about 120 villages with populations of up to 2,000. There are five main cultural groups of the Asmat: Central Asmat, Casuarina Coast Asmat, Yaosakor Asmat, North Asmat, and Citak. In the remainder of this entry, Asmat will refer to the Central Asmat unless otherwise specified.

The Indonesian government granted Papua "special autonomy" status in November of 2001, along with a promise to provide limited autonomy and control to the indigenous peoples there such as the Asmat as long as they can substantiate their traditional land claims.

3 LANGUAGE

The Asmat languages belong to a larger language family known as Asmat-Kamoro. This language family is classified by linguists as being non-Austronesian or Papuan. There are around 70 different language families within the non-Austronesian grouping, but their internal relationships to each other have not yet been determined. The Asmat-Kamoro family has over 50,000 speakers, which is fairly large by Papuan standards. Because of missionary involvement in the region, central Asmat now have a written form of the spoken language. A modest publishing effort in the language exists that produces children's readers and religious literature. A form of Bahasa Indonesia, the national language of the Republic of Indonesia, is spoken by many Asmat men.

⁴ FOLKLORE

A significant body of mythology surrounds the origins of headhunting among the Asmat. According to the origin myth, two brothers were the original inhabitants of the Asmat region. The older brother convinced the younger brother to cut off his head, and the decapitated head instructed the younger brother about how to go headhunting, process the trophy head, and use it in initiation rituals for young males. The name of the older brother was also transferred to the younger brother, an event mirrored in the practice of an Asmat taking the name of a person he has decapitated. The number of names a man has reflects the number of heads he has taken in his lifetime. In accord with the great power traditionally accorded to the spirits of the deceased, the skull of a deceased relative was traditionally kept as a desirable protection against evil spirits.

⁵ RELIGION

Prior to the introduction of Christianity into the territory, the Asmat religion was based on a belief in spirits that inhabited things in the natural world, as well as the fear of the ghosts of the dead. It was also believed that the deaths of all persons except the very young or very elderly were deliberately caused by some malevolent outside force. The ancestral spirits, to whom great powers were generally attributed, were said to demand that tribe members avenge a wrongful death by killing and decapitating an enemy and offering his body to the community for cannibalistic consumption. Headhunting and other male activities associated with that endeavor were the focus of many Asmat rituals.

⁶ MAJOR HOLIDAYS

In traditional Asmat societies, there were elaborate cycles of ceremonial feasting that occurred throughout the year. Feasts that celebrate the feast-givers' deceased kinfolk are still very important celebrations. Other events that required a feast were the opening of a new men's house, the dedication of the tall ancestor poles (bis), the dedication of twenty or more war canoes, a celebration of masks, and a celebration of shields. In the past, most of the feasting events centered on male activities associated with raiding and headhunting.

Missionary activity has introduced Christianity into the Asmat area. Now some Asmat are professed Christians and celebrate the major Christian holidays. Although Islam is the major religion of Indonesia, it not practiced among the indigenous population.

⁷ RITES OF PASSAGE

Male initiation was one of the most important rites of passage in pre-colonial Asmat society, although it has lost some of its importance today. In the past, initiates were given a decapitat-

ed head that they would contemplate. The power of the warrior, which was believed to reside in his decapitated head, was to be absorbed by the initiate. The initiates would fast during this time. They would then take a canoe trip to the sea. Their sponsors would eventually plunge the initiates into the sea, symbolically killing them. The initiates were reborn as warriors. Male prowess is still highly valued in Asmat society, although male initiation rites no longer involve decapitation.

Death is accompanied by grieving by family and friends of the deceased, who roll in the mud of the riverbanks to hide their scent from the ghost of the deceased. Ceremonies are performed to ensure that the ghost passes to the land of the dead, referred to as "the other side." The skull of a person's mother is often used as a pillow.

⁸ INTERPERSONAL RELATIONS

Precontact Asmat life is only sketchily known to anthropologists. The earliest reliable accounts date from the 1950s around the time of pacification. These accounts focus more on ritual behaviors and practices than they do on the mundane.

Little is known about the Asmat's everyday life, and the current Indonesian practice of limiting the amount of time researchers may spend in Asmat country does not facilitate the acquisition of such information.

Missionary and governmental influence has affected practices relating to greetings and other forms of social etiquette. In precontact times, sexual relations between unmarried males and females were not prohibited, and there were extensive ritual contexts in which promiscuity was expected.

⁹ LIVING CONDITIONS

The southern coast of Papua is an ideal setting for the proliferation of malaria, which is endemic to the region. The debilitating aspects of the disease take their toll on the Asmat population. Death due to crocodile attack is also common in parts of the Asmat territory. In one region, these deaths occur frequently enough to warrant the carving of special commemorative poles called "crocodile poles."

Houses are elevated on stilts to prevent them from flooding during the rainy season. There is no running water or electricity in a traditional Asmat house. Mission and government posts in the area typically do have these services, and Asmat who work with those institutions do have some access to these comforts. Most houses have an outside porch area where people can congregate to talk, gossip, smoke, or just watch their neighbors.

The coastal Asmat groups travel extensively by canoe along the coast and inland along rivers and tributaries. Most of their travel has traditionally been related to inter-village feasting and the visitation of relatives in other communities. Transportation for the Asmat is primarily by dugout canoe and also by foot on trails through the rain forest. There are different kinds of canoes constructed for different activities. War canoes of the Asmat are about 21 m (70 ft) long and can hold around 30 people. Paddling is done from a standing position, and the narrowness of the hull demands that each person maintain their balance; otherwise, the canoe could easily capsize. This is extremely dangerous in the crocodile-infested rivers, lakes, and streams.

10 FAMILY LIFE

Marriage among the Asmat is traditionally defined in terms of the village and the kin group. Asmat society is divided into two complementary and contrasting halves termed "moieties" by anthropologists. A person is supposed to marry someone from within their village who belongs to the opposite half of the society: the other moiety. In the past, men were allowed to have more than one wife. A groom had to pay a "bride price" to his prospective father-in-law to negotiate a marriage. In some cases, the price would be so high that he would have to make installment payments on the total amount due. However, he was also given rights to harvest a portion of his in-laws' sago trees. Before the introduction of European goods, the payments consisted of animal furs, bird of paradise feathers, triton shells, dogs' teeth necklaces, stone axes, and other weapons. In modern times, tobacco, money, and other Western goods are included in the payments. After the marriage, the bride moves in with her husband's family. Extended families occupy large houses built of bamboo, sago bark, and sago frond thatching.

Men sleep apart from their wives in the men's longhouse (*yew*). Ceremonial activities that take place inside the men's house are prohibited to women. Menstruating women stay in a separate house that is off-limits to men.

11 CLOTHING

The Asmat traditionally have worn little or no clothing. Footwear is not often owned. The Asmat women wore a fiber skirt, while men went completely naked. Men among the eastern Asmat wore rattan bands around their waists and a small hollow tube covering their penises. Plaited cane bands were also worn around the wrists and just below the knees. Because of missionary and governmental influence, many Asmat today wear Western-style clothing, often consisting of rugby shorts for men and floral, cotton dresses for women. Objects of bodily adornment that are still seen today include the tusks of wild pigs or boars that are worn in the pierced nasal septum of men. On ceremonial occasions, men and women have their bodies decorated with paints made from natural products and dyes including mud and ochre.

12 FOOD

Fish and the sago palm are the staple foods of all Asmat groups. The larva of a butterfly that is often found in the rotting carcasses of fallen sago palms is an important ritual food and a delicacy among the Asmat. Canned meats and fish, as well as flour, tea, and sugar have become important food items for the Asmat. These items are obtained from trade stores set up by Indonesians or from mission stores.

As opposed to other groups on the island of New Guinea, the Asmat did not have trading relationships with neighboring groups that would have allowed for specialization in foodstuff production in pre-colonial times. In other areas, one group would produce sago and trade it for the fish caught by another group. Instead, Asmat villages attempted to monopolize the food resources in their area. The Asmat went to great lengths to provide for the fertility of the sago palm stands in their territory. The heads of headhunting victims were frequently hung in the sago palm stands to promote the fertility of the trees. Ancestor poles (*bis*) were also erected in the sago stands to promote the sago palms' fertility. Although the fertility of the sago stand is still important to the Asmat, they are no longer permitted to engage in headhunting activities.

13 EDUCATION

Outside influences on the Asmat include formal education. Missionaries and colonial administrations have set up various schools in the region. Agats, the regional administrative center in the coastal Asmat area, has schoolhouses for mass education. In precontact times, children would learn from their elders those tasks that were specific to their sex.

14 CULTURAL HERITAGE

As is the case with other Melanesian peoples, drums are important instruments. Asmat drums are similar in shape to drums produced in other parts of insular New Guinea. They have an hourglass shape and a single, lizard skin-covered head that is struck with the palm of the hand. The other hand is used to hold the drum by a carved handle. Ceremonial horns were also used by the Asmat. Although the Asmat regard drums as sacred objects, they do not define the sounds produced by instruments as music; only singing is classified as music in Asmat culture.

Dance was an important part of ceremonial life in precontact Asmat villages, although missionary activity has discouraged dancing among the Asmat. Written literature was not available to the Asmat, since their language was exclusively an oral one. However, they have an extensive body of oral literature. Epic songs that often lasted for several days and metaphorical love songs are still important forms of expression among the Asmat.

15 WORK

The Asmat are hunters and gatherers who gather and process the pulp of the sago palm and hunt crocodiles and other animals. Some also grow vegetables or raise chickens, which have been imported to the area in small numbers. There is a traditional division of labor along gender lines. Women are responsible for net fishing, gathering, and other domestic tasks. Men are responsible for line and weir (fence or enclosure) fishing, hunting, horticulture, and the felling of trees. Tree felling is an important job since canoes, ancestor poles, and domestic structures are all constructed from forest wood. An export market in crocodile skins and tropical hardwoods has been developing among the Asmat, and the sale of wood carvings to outsiders represents an additional source of income.

16 SPORTS

Traditionally, male competition among the Asmat was intense. This competition centered on the demonstration of male prowess through success in headhunting, the acquisition of fishing grounds and sago palm stands, and the cultivation of a number of feasting partners. Males still compete in these areas, except headhunting, which is now prohibited.

17 ENTERTAINMENT AND RECREATION

The Asmat region of Papua is still very isolated. Agats is the major administrative center for the entire southwestern coastal region. Amenities are available on a limited basis, but Western forms of entertainment and recreation are not available.

An Asmat tribe from Papua perform their traditional dance during the Fifth Indonesia Art Festival in Sanur, Bali. The festival is held to promote tourism on the resort island. (Sonny Tumbelaka/AFP/Getty Images)

18 FOLK ART, CRAFTS, AND HOBBIES

Asmat art has been highly valued by European and American art collectors ever since it was brought to the attention of the outside world. During the 1960s there was a move to collect Asmat art following pacification efforts throughout the entire region. It was known that much of Asmat artistic production was tied to the practice of headhunting, and with pacification and the prohibition of headhunting, the proliferation of artifact production declined.

Art from the central and coastal Asmat is the most widely known in museums in Europe and the United States. Groups in these areas produced decorated shields, spears, digging sticks, canoes, bows and arrows, and a wide range of figurative carvings. The most famous ritual carving of the central and coastal Asmat is the ancestor pole, called *bis* in the Asmat language. These elaborately carved and decorated poles commemorated the deaths of those killed in battle or by sorcery. They were erected during a feast that preceded a headhunting raid to avenge those deaths. Phallic symbolism is evident in the *bis* poles.

Birds and flying foxes were important motifs on shields and other objects because of their association with headhunting. In Asmat cosmology, trees and human beings are viewed as similar entities. The head of a human being is equivalent, symboli-

cally, with the fruit of a tree; therefore, creatures that eat the fruit of trees are equivalent to men who take the heads of other men. The praying mantis is also an important motif in Asmat sculpture.

The Asmat Woodcarving Festival is an annual event held in October. The purpose of the festival is to promote the development of Asmat art and culture for the Asmat people. It is a mechanism to support the continuation of traditional wood working. The carvings are judged and the one that is awarded the top prize is put on permanent display in the Asmat Museum of Culture and Progress in Agats. Many of the other carvings and poles are sold at auction during the festival.

19 SOCIAL PROBLEMS

The Asmat are fighting to retain their traditional ways of life in the face of pressure by Indonesian administrators. As of the 1990s, many Asmat had converted to Christianity and were being educated in Western-run schools. However, they have had limited influence on Indonesian government's policy regarding the use of their land.

A native-run cultural center and museum in Agats called the Asmat Museum of Culture and Progress is striving to collect artifacts from all areas of Asmat culture. It also produces catalogues and cultural monographs on Asmat culture, mythology, and history to preserve these bodies of knowledge for future generations of Asmat.

20 GENDER ISSUES

By all accounts, Asmat women experience difficult lives in many regards. Wife beating is sanctioned within the society, although the influence of missionaries and the presence of local law enforcement officials currently mitigates this practice. Unmarried women and girls can be beaten by their fathers or brothers for promiscuity. A woman's property is transferred to her husband at the time of marriage, and, as a result, she loses control over any resources that she might derive from it. Traditionally, wife-swapping was a common practice, either to confirm a bond of friendship between two men or as a community-wide phenomenon in times of crisis. Women were directly involved with the fertility cult within the community. Sorcery was attributed to women only among the central Asmat.

The Asmat also engage in a practice called "wife exchange," or *papisj* in Asmat. In this practice, two men—or the families of two unmarried boys— determine that a *papisj* relationship needs to be established. In the case of married, adult men, the men rub sago powder on each other's foreheads and then return to their respective wives to convince them of the agreement. Once convinced, the wives will exchange households for one day/night where they will prepare a meal for the exchange family and sleep with the exchange husband. The following morning, the woman will be decorated with sago flour and feathers and will return to her husband and family.

Unlike neighboring South Coast cultures of Papua, the Central Asmat males did not engage in ritualized homosexuality. However, the Asmat did engage in ritualized heterosexuality especially as a means to calm disturbances in either nature or the village itself. There is evidence among the Casuarina Coast Asmat had ritualized homosexual relationships between males called *mbai*. The *mbai* relationship of the Casuarina Coast Asmat is very similar in many respects to the *papisj* relationship of the Central Asmat.

21 BIBLIOGRAPHY

Knauft, Bruce. *South Coast New Guinea Cultures*. New York: Cambridge University Press, 1993.

Muller, Kal. *New Guinea: Journey into the Stone Age*. Lincolnwood, Ill.: NTC Publishing Group, 1990.

Schneebaum, Tobias. *Asmat Images: From the Collection of the Asmat Museum of Culture and Progress*. Minneapolis: Crosier Missions, 1985.

———. *Secret Places: My Life in New York and New Guinea*. Madison: University of Wisconsin Press, 2000.

Smidt, Dirk, ed. *Asmat Art : Woodcarvings of Southwest New Guinea*. New York: George Braziller, 1993.

Van Arsdale, Peter, and Kathleen van Arsdale. "Asmat." *Encyclopedia of World Cultures*. Boston: G. K. Hall, 1992.

—by J. Williams

ASSAMESE

PRONUNCIATION: as-suh-MEEZ
LOCATION: India (Assam state)
POPULATION: c. 20 million
LANGUAGE: Assamese
RELIGION: Hinduism
RELATED ARTICLES: Vol. 3: Hindus; People of India

1 INTRODUCTION

In referring to people, the word "Assamese" is used in two senses. It can identify the entire population of the state of Assam in northeastern India (numbering 26, 655,528 according to the Census of India, 2001). Used in this manner, it includes not only the majority ethnic group found in the Brahmaputra Valley, but also all the tribal groups (e.g., Bodo, Mikir, Miri, and Naga) and immigrants from other parts of India living in the state. In its more restricted sense, "Assamese" refers to the peoples of the Brahmaputra plains whose native language is Assamese and who developed what may be considered Assamese culture. Unless otherwise stated, it is this latter group that is the focus of this article.

The Assamese of the plains are mainly of Indo-Iranian stock, with some Mongoloid physical characteristics. This reflects the complex history of migrations into the area over many centuries. Early Indian texts identify Assam as Kamarupa, and the 7th-century Chinese traveler Hsuan-tsang has left a detailed account of the region. The Assam valley fell under various regional and local dynasties until the Ahom, a Shan people from Burma (Myanmar), assumed power in the 13th century. The Ahoms ruled Assam for four centuries, until their kingdom fell to Burma in 1821. The former Ahom lands were ceded to Britain in 1826 following the First Anglo-Burmese War (1824–26). Assam was administered as part of British India until India gained its independence in 1947. The modern state of Assam is much reduced in area from colonial times, reflecting the separation of many of the tribal areas of the northeast as states in their own right.

2 LOCATION AND HOMELAND

Assamese are the dominant ethnic group in Assam, making up some 48.8% of the state's population. The Census of India 2001 gives a population of 26,655,528 which, at current growth rates, would be projected to over 29 million people today.

The geographical and historical heartland of the Assamese people lies on the lowlands of the Brahmaputra Valley. One of India's great rivers, the Brahmaputra (literally, "Son of Brahma") emerges from the Himalayas in eastern Assam. It then flows in a southwesterly direction for 650 km (400 mi) through the length of the state. As it leaves Assam, the river swings south into Bangladesh where it joins the Ganges and flows into the Bay of Bengal. The Brahmaputra and its valley are the dominant physical features of Assam. The river is over 8 km (5 mi) wide during flood stage, and widespread and destructive flooding is common in the area. The valley, lying at elevations generally below 100 m (330 ft), averages about 100 km (60 mi) in width. To the north lie the foothills of the Himalayas. South of the valley are the Meghalaya Plateau and the hills that form India's eastern border with Burma. Climate is monsoonal. Annual rainfall varies from 160–320 cm (65–125 in) and falls mainly between May and September. Mean monthly temperatures range from 16°C (61°F) in January to 29°C (84°F) during the summer months.

3 LANGUAGE

Assamese is the language spoken by the Assamese people. It belongs to the Indo-Aryan language family but has been influenced in its vocabulary, pronunciation, and structure by its contact with the Tibeto-Burman dialects spoken in the region. Assamese is closely related to Bengali and is written in a script that shows only minor deviations from the Bengali script. Assamese has emerged as the *lingua franca* of northeastern India. A lingua franca is a language that is widely used for communication by peoples who do not understand each other's languages. Currently, there are about 20 million Assamese speakers, of whom perhaps 13 million reside in Assam (the remainder are found on the borders of Assam and in the Indian State of West Bengal. In 2001, for the first time, Assamese speakers accounted for less than half the population (48.8%) of Assam.

4 FOLKLORE

The *Mahabharata* and *Kalika Purana* relate numerous stories concerning Kamakhya, the site of an important temple near Gauhati, in Assam. According to legend, when the goddess Sati died, her distraught husband, Shiva, carried her body on his head as penance. Vishnu, fearing this would give Shiva excessive powers, cut Sati's body into numerous bits with successive throws of his discus. Each place on earth where a piece of Sati's body fell became a sacred center of pilgrimage. Tradition has it that Sati's sexual organs landed at Kamakhya, where a temple was built to mark the spot. There is no image of the goddess—who is also called Kamakhya—at the temple, but in the depths of the shrine is a cleft in the rock that is worshiped as the *yoni* (female organ) of the goddess. Kamakhya is one of the most important *sakti* or Mother Goddess temples in India. (*Sakti,* or "energy," refers to the power of a deity manifested through his female counterpart.) Rites of worship at the temple include animal sacrifice.

5 RELIGION

The Assamese are Hindu and follow the basic observances of the religion. They worship many Hindu gods, are organized into castes, and have ritual specialists (the Brahmans) to perform religious functions. Within this overarching structure, however, there exists considerable diversity in practice. Vaishnavism has a strong following among the peoples of the plains, and Krishna (an incarnation of Vishnu) is by far the most popular deity among the Assamese. Villagers gather at *namghars* (prayer halls) to recite Krishna's name as part of the rituals of this devotional *(bhakti)* sect. Shiva, too, has his following, while the importance of Kamakhya has already been noted [see "Folklore"]. At the level of folk religion, local deities such as Manasa, the snake goddess, and Shitala, the goddess of small pox, are revered. Assamese believe in spirits who inhabit trees, water, and other elements in nature. Some are good, but some are evil and cause disease and other problems for humans. Various charms, spells, and rituals are used to deal with the spirit world.

6 MAJOR HOLIDAYS

The Assamese have three principal festivals known as Bihu. Baisakh Bihu is celebrated in mid-April to usher in the New Year. It also marks the end of the unlucky month of Chait, and the beginning of Baisakh which is considered auspicious. Cows are worshiped and bathed in the sacred Brahmaputra. They have their horns painted, are garlanded with flowers, and are then driven through the village streets in procession. It is a time for visiting friends and relatives, for singing and dancing, and for general rejoicing. The other Bihu festivals, Magh Bihu and Kati Bihu, are also occasions for feasting and merriment. Other major Hindu festivals such as Holi, Durga Puja, and Janamashtami (Krishna's birthday) are also celebrated.

7 RITES OF PASSAGE

The Assamese follow the basic life-cycle rituals as set out by the ancient Hindu lawgivers. Some specific customs, however, are unique to Assam. When a baby is born, for example, a knife is kept under the mother's bed to keep evil spirits away. Iron is believed to have certain magical properties. Similarly, fish play an important role in Assamese culture. When a baby is born, and particularly if it is a son, the Assamese distribute fish to friends and relatives. Fish is invariably served at the feast that accompanies the naming ceremony, which is usually held when the baby is around six months old. The period of pollution for a woman after childbirth lasts for a month. A girl attaining puberty is also considered unclean and is confined in a room during her first period.

At death, the corpse is removed from the house. It is rubbed with oil and turmeric paste, before being bathed and dressed in new clothes. The dead person is thus ready for his or her last journey. The body is carried to the cremation grounds, where it is burned according to Hindu custom. The man who performs the *sraddha* (funeral) rites carries a knife, the metal being protection against evil spirits. The mourners returning from the cremation have to bathe, place their feet on stones, and step over a fire before they can enter the house. If it is late at night, they cannot enter until the next morning, in case the spirit of the dead person follows them into the house.

8 INTERPERSONAL RELATIONS

As a rule, Assamese have two names. One is known publicly, but the real one, which is given in accordance with astrological calculations, is kept secret. This is for fear that harm might befall the person if the true name is divulged. Names are often given after popular gods and goddesses in the hope of receiving protection from them, or of children acquiring their godly qualities.

9 LIVING CONDITIONS

The Assamese are mostly rural people, living in villages and hamlets on the alluvial lowlands of the Brahmaputra River valley. Traditional houses are built of wood, bamboo, and other available materials. The walls are plastered with a mixture of cow dung and clay, with the roof thatched with grasses or reeds. A residence typically consists of a building containing the living quarters and kitchen, a separate structure for cattle, and a storehouse—often built on piles—for keeping paddy rice and other items. Wealthier families may have a separate guest house, and a small hut for daily worship. Furnishings depend

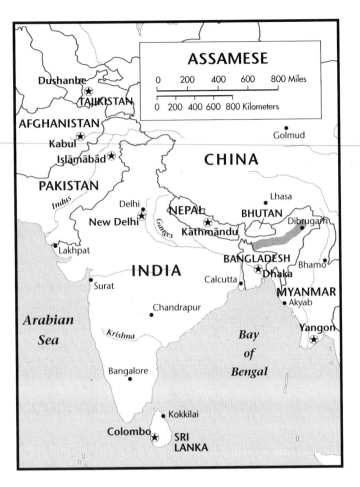

ASSAMESE

0   200   400   600   800 Miles

0   200 400 600 800 Kilometers

on the means of the individual family but in villages typically consist of cane mats, wooden stools and beds, and the usual cooking and eating utensils.

10 FAMILY LIFE

The Assamese follow North Indian marriage patterns. They practice caste endogamy and clan (*jati*) exogamy. Marriages are arranged, and among castes such as the Brahmans and Kayasthas child marriage is still prevalent, particularly in rural areas. The marriage rituals last for two or three days and follow the Vedic rites, although certain practices reflect local customs and beliefs. In an Assamese marriage, for example, a conical structure called a *bei* is built of bamboo and bark, and the bride and groom bathe under it. A couple of eggs are buried at the spot of the bathing, and sometimes the bride has to carry two eggs to her new home. The egg is a symbol of fertility, and this custom may have been acquired from local tribal peoples for whom the egg has great ritual significance.

As with all Hindu groups, the bearing of male children is the desired outcome of any union. Divorce and widow remarriage are not permitted by most groups. The extended family system is traditional among the Assamese, with residence being patrilocal (i.e., the bride resides at the home of her new father-in-law). Although women are assigned an honored position in Assamese society, inheritance passes down the male line.

11 CLOTHING

The typical clothing of Hindu men on the Assam plains is the *dhoti,* the long cotton loincloth that is wrapped around the body, then drawn between the legs and tucked in at the waist. Villagers might go bare-chested, but the higher castes wear upper garments. The *kurta* and the Western-style shirt are common dress nowadays. Villagers of social standing often wear a turban. Female dress consists of a blouse, with a long cloth wrapped around the body just above the breasts like a sarong. Alternatively, the traditional *choli* (bodice) and *sari* are worn. Ornaments favored by women include earrings, necklaces, nose studs, armlets, bangles, and anklets. The use of scented oil is a common practice among both men and women.

12 FOOD

Rice is the staple food of the Assamese, eaten with a variety of fish or meat curries. A particular favorite is sour fish curry. Most Hindus in Assam, even the Brahman castes, eat fish and meat. However, all except the lowest Hindu castes avoid beef. At certain times, such as the period of mourning following a death, fish and meat are avoided. Caste Hindus usually do not eat chicken, eggs, or pork. The rice and curried dishes are served with vegetables, pulses, and condiments such as chutneys and pickles. Fruits such as bananas, pineapples, and oranges are also eaten. A type of rice pudding prepared with milk and sugar is a particular favorite of the Assamese. Rice beer is brewed and consumed in quantities, especially at celebrations such as the Bihu festivals. The chewing of areca nut and betel leaf is universal in Assam.

13 EDUCATION

Education in Assam is compulsory up to the age of 12, and free through the secondary level. However, actual educational levels of the Assamese vary considerably, according to factors such as openness to modernization, economic circumstances, and location. The literacy rate for the population of Assam 7 years and older was reported as 64.28% in the 2001 census. Literacy among males (71.93%) was higher than among females (56.03%). There are universities at Gauhati and Dibrugarh, as well as the Assam Agricultural University at Jorhat.

14 CULTURAL HERITAGE

The earliest indisputable work in the Assamese language dates to the 13th century AD. Literature of this period was mostly derived from Sanskrit sources, but by the 16th century the *buranjis,* the chronicles of the Ahoms, were being written in Assamese. The writings of Shankaradeva and other poets of the devotional Vaishnava sect greatly enriched Assamese literature during the 15th and 16th centuries. Modern literature in Assamese dates to the late 19th century but has done little more than mirror Western writing.

The Assamese have a rich tradition of oral literature, folk music, and dance. Of particular note are the songs (*nam*) associated with the Bihu festivals and weddings. Some folk songs are lullabies and nursery rhymes for children, others deal with love, while still others focus on the god Krishna and his life. In addition, there are ballads on both popular and historical themes. Dance is as important a part of Assamese culture as is music. Special Bihu dances are performed at the time of the Bihu festivals. *Ojha-Pali* is a group of dancers and singers that

Assamese Bihu dancers perform in Gauhati, India. (AP Images/Anupam Nath)

presents stories from the Hindu epics and the Puranas. *Deodhas* are temple dancers who are believed to become possessed and dance in honor of the snake-goddess Manasa and other deities.

15 WORK

Most Assamese are cultivators, with rice being the dominant food crop produced in the region. Vegetables, pulses (peas, beans, lentils), and oilseeds are also grown. Sugarcane and jute are important cash crops. Tea is grown on estates on the flanks of the Brahmaputra Valley. However, these are often corporate ventures operated with immigrant labor from other parts of India. Assamese also work in the important forest industries, in the limited industries of the region, and in the service sector of the economy.

16 SPORTS

The amusements of Assamese children are relatively few. For the most part, they play with balls, cowry shells (which pass for money), tops, kites, and the like. They play hide-and-seek, games of tag, individual wrestling, and team wrestling *(kabaddi).* At the time of the spring Bihu, fighting with eggs is a game popular with children. In the past, elephant-fights and buffalo-fights formed part of the Bihu festivities. Modern sports such as soccer, cricket, volleyball, basketball, and track-and-field are played in the schools, colleges, and universities of Assam.

17 ENTERTAINMENT AND RECREATION

The Assamese are essentially a rural people. They rely mainly on festivals, fairs, and traditional forms of folk entertainment for their recreation. Modern entertainment such as radio, television, and movie houses are available in urban centers to those with the means to access it.

18 FOLK ART, CRAFTS, AND HOBBIES

Assamese women are skilled in the art of weaving, producing fine cotton cloth and gold-colored *muga* and rough *endi* silks. Nearly every household has its hand-loom, and every young girl is taught the art of weaving. Embroidery is also a local art. Artisan castes work gold and silver; produce pottery, metal goods, and brassware; and make items of cane and bamboo. Wood from Assam's abundant forests is carved into both domestic items and religious icons.

19 SOCIAL PROBLEMS

Since India became independent in 1947, separate states have been created for many of the tribal peoples of the "old" Assam. Despite this, the Assamese face serious social and political problems arising from ethnic tensions in the state. Since the 1980s, resentment among the Assamese against outsiders has led to widespread communal violence and the loss of hundreds of lives. The so-called "foreigners" targeted in this campaign are Bengali villagers who have lived in Assam for many years but still retain their Bengali identity; more recent immigrants from Bangladesh; Biharis; and Nepalis. The situation is further complicated by other ongoing conflicts. Disaffected Bodo tribespeople have been agitating for a separate state of their own within Assam. In addition, some Assamese are advocating outright secession from India. Indian security forces operating against the militant United Liberation Front of Assam (ULFA) are facing numerous charges of violating the civil rights of Assamese civilians.

The Assam Accord was a Memorandum of Settlement (MoS) signed between representatives of the Government of India and the leaders of the Assam Agitation in New Delhi in 1985. The accord brought an end to the Assam Agitation and paved the way for the leaders of the agitation to form a political party and form a government in the state of soon after. Some of the key clauses of the Accord have yet to be implemented, which has kept some of the issues festering, and violence from insurgent groups remains a problem in Assam.

20 GENDER ISSUES

Assamese society has traditionally treated women with disdain, and the plight of women (mostly poor and low-caste or tribals) is one of exploitation. As a result of poverty, age, custom, and terrorism many women, out of dire need, are forced to sell their bodies and are engaged in the sex trade throughout India. In 2005, Javed Akhtar, a noted Assamese lyricist, raised a firestorm with his alleged remark on Assamese women on a private TV channel in Guwahati—"Assamese women are known for frequently changing husbands and can be purchased in any city of the country." Police are far too involved in fighting insurgents to turn their attention to the thousands of women and girls in Assam who go missing every year, many of these ending up as "sex slaves" for wealthy landowners in other parts of the country.

Despite this, a UNIFEM (United Nations Development Fund for Women) report finds greater gender equality in Assam than elsewhere in India. The society doesn't suffer from practices like dowry, child-marriage and bride-burning.

21 BIBLIOGRAPHY

Barkataki, S. *Assam*. New Delhi, India: National Book Trust, 1969.

Baruah, B. K. *A Cultural History of Assam*. Gauhati, Assam: Lawyer's Book Stall, 1969.

Cantlie, Audrey. *The Assamese*. London: Curzon Press, 1984.

Das, Jogesh. *Folklore of Assam*. New Delhi, India: National Book Trust, 1972.

Hussain, Wasbir. Homenakers without the Men: Assam's Widows of Violence. New Delhi: Indialog Publications, 2006.

Kunda, Bijan Kumar. Politics in the Brahmaputra Valley, since the Assam Accord. New Delhi: Om Publications, 2007.

Where is Assam?: Using Geographical History to Locate Current Social Realities. Guwahati: Centre for Northeast India, South and Southeast Asia Studies, Omeo Kumar Das Institute for Social Change and Development, 2003.

—by D. O. Lodrick

AUSTRALIAN ABORIGINES

PRONUNCIATION: aw-STRAYL-yuhn ab-bor-RIDGE-in-eez
LOCATION: Australia; Tasmania
POPULATION: Approximately 517,000
LANGUAGE: Western Desert language; English; Walpiri and other Aboriginal languages
RELIGION: Traditional Aboriginal religion; Christianity

1 INTRODUCTION

Australian Aborigines, the original inhabitants of the continent of Australia, took up residence there at least 40,000 years before Europeans landed at Botany Bay in 1788. In 1788, the Aborigines were clearly the majority, numbering around 300,000. In 1996, they were a minority struggling to claim rights to their traditional lands and financial compensation for lost lands and resources. Relations between Aboriginal and non-Aboriginal inhabitants of Australia have not been very good, and there is a great deal of resentment on the part of many Aboriginal people for the treatment their ancestors received from the European colonists. In February 2008, Prime Minister Kevin Rudd formally apologized to Aboriginal peoples for mistreatment by the Australian government in the past. Prime Minister Rudd singled out the "Stolen Generations" who were children forcibly removed from their families to attend boarding schools where they were punished for speaking their native languages and following their native traditions. Australian Aborigines face many of the same problems that Native Americans face in the United States.

2 LOCATION AND HOMELAND

Australian Aborigines traditionally lived throughout Australia and Tasmania. As Australia and Tasmania lie south of the equator, the seasons are reversed from those of North America. The varied climatic zones gave rise to local cultural adaptations among populations. In Central and Western Desert regions, Aboriginal groups were nomadic hunters and gatherers. They had no permanent place of residence, although they did have territories and ate whatever they could catch, kill, or dig out of the ground. The Australian desert is an extremely harsh environment with hot days and cool nights and very few permanent water sources. In the southern parts of the island continent, winter is cold and Aboriginal populations had to shelter themselves from the cold wind and driving rain. Although many Aboriginal people move frequently within Australia, very few emigrate. Approximately 33% of the total population of the Northern Territory is Aboriginal according to the 2006 Australian Census of Population and Housing. This is the highest percentage of any Australian state/territory.

3 LANGUAGE

There were approximately 300 different Aboriginal languages spoken in 1788 when Captain James Cook claimed the island continent for England. Now, there are only about 145 Aboriginal languages still spoken. Only about 18 of these, like Walpiri, spoken in and around Alice Springs in the center of the continent, have a good prognosis. Walpiri is taught in schools and a growing body of written literature is produced in the language daily. Other languages such as Dyirbal are dying out. Of the 145 language still spoken, 110 are severely and critically endangered. This category indicates languages that are spoken only by small groups of people, mostly over 49 years old. Aboriginal Australian languages are very different in structure from Indo-European languages such as English. Linguists believe that all of the languages of the Australian continent are genetically related to each other; however, there is some disagreement about the genetic relationship of the language of the Tasmanians, which is now extinct. The largest language in terms of number of speakers is called the Western Desert language, spoken by several thousand Aboriginal people in the Western Desert region of the continent. Most Aboriginal people speak English as their first or second language. In parts of Australia, distinctive kinds of English have developed within Aboriginal communities. In the Northern Territory there is a kind of English spoken by Aboriginal people that is called Kriol.

4 FOLKLORE

Australian Aborigines have a large body of folklore and oral history that is often referred to as "the Dreaming." This body of verbal art relates humans to the natural and mystical landscape in which they find themselves. "The Dreaming" is the time when everything came into being and the rules of social relations and behavior were instituted by ancestral beings. It is the means by which Aboriginal people identity themselves with their territory and their heritage. "The Dreaming" is also the mechanism by which Aboriginal people claim traditional ownership of land through the display of intimate knowledge of the terrain and its inhabitants. Myths of "the Dreaming" often have cultural heroes as central characters. These cultural heroes, like those of most cultures of the world, have greatly exaggerated powers.

5 RELIGION

Traditional Aboriginal religion revolves around "the Dreaming." Totems are also an important part of Aboriginal religious identity. Totems are symbols from the natural world that serve to identify people and their relationships with one another in the social world. These totems both defined social groups, such as clans and lineages, as well as individual totems. The conceptual landscape was inhabited by ghosts of the dead as well as a variety of spirits who controlled certain aspects of the natural world, such as the Rainbow Serpent, who brought rain. Rituals were performed to placate these spirits and also to increase the fertility of certain species of animals that were important.

Since the colonization of Australia, many Aboriginal people have converted to Christianity either by choice or by the influence of education in mission schools. About 75% of Aborigines indicate that Christianity is their primary religion. One aspect of the conversion of Aboriginal people to Christianity is that very few, if any, traditional elements of Aboriginal spirituality have been incorporated into Aboriginal Christianity.

6 MAJOR HOLIDAYS

As part of the larger Australian society, Australian Aborigines can participate in major holidays. Australia Day, January 26, is the equivalent of Independence Day in the United States. This holiday often invokes public protests on the part of Aboriginal people. Many Aboriginal people participated in major protests on the event of the Bicentennial in 1988. Traditional Aboriginal society, however, had no holidays as such.

7 RITES OF PASSAGE

In some Aboriginal societies, there were both male and female initiation rituals that marked the passage of the child into adulthood. Male initiation still takes place among groups like the Aranda in central Australia. Circumcision is an important part of male initiation among the Aranda. Exclusion of young males is also an integral part of the initiation process; however, school schedules have to be taken into account in a modern context.

Death in Aboriginal Australian societies was accompanied by complex rituals. Among the Walpiri of central Australia, a wife would have to isolate herself from the rest of the community upon the death of her husband. She would live in a "widows' camp" for a period of one to two years. During that time she would communicate through an intricate system of sign language. She was not permitted to speak during this period of mourning and seclusion. If a woman chose not to follow these traditions, her husband's ghost could steal her soul, which would lead to her death.

8 INTERPERSONAL RELATIONS

Behavior and interpersonal relations among Australian Aboriginals are defined by who one is related to and who one is descended from. In many Aboriginal societies, certain kinfolk stand in avoidance relationships with each other. For instance, in some groups a son-in-law must avoid his mother-in-law completely. Individuals will often change course entirely and go out of their way to avoid a prohibited in-law. In these complete avoidance relationships, he must not have any contact with her at all. In other types of relationships, a son-in-law can only speak to his mother-in-law by way of a special language, called "mother-in-law language." The opposite of avoidance relationships are joking relationships. These are relationships between potential spouses that typically involve joking about sexual topics.

Aboriginal people comment that non-Aboriginal people say "thank you" all the time. Aboriginal social organization is based on a set of reciprocal obligations between individuals that are related by blood or marriage. Such reciprocal obligations do not require any thanks: If I am related to you and you ask me to share my food with you, I am obligated to do so without any expectation of gratitude on your part. Anglo-Australians often misconstrue this behavior as rude.

9 LIVING CONDITIONS

Health care is a central problem for most Aboriginal people. For rural groups, access to health care may be extremely limited. In precontact times, they would have relied on traditional health practices to cure illness and limit disease. However, through European influence, many rural societies have lost knowledge of traditional medicine and now must rely on Western medicine, which is often available only sporadically.

Aboriginal people receive a monthly allowance in restitution from the Australian government in the same way that Native Americans receive a monthly payment from the United States government. Aboriginal people buy various kinds of goods with this money. Often in rural communities, the majority of the check goes to food in the form of tea, flour, and

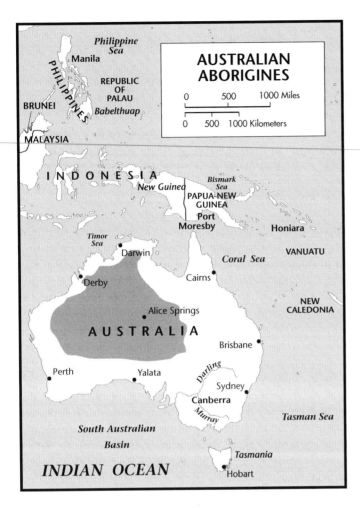

AUSTRALIAN ABORIGINES

0   500   1000 Miles

0   500   1000 Kilometers

tinned meat. Some Anglo-Australians visit outstations after the checks are delivered to these communities. They then will set up a type of bank/general store from the back of a utility truck and sell products to the people at extremely inflated prices.

Housing varies between urban and rural Aboriginal people. The national, state, and local governments have encouraged nomadic groups to settle in houses in the European manner, and, to this end, they have built houses for some groups that live in the desert regions of central and western Australia. Aboriginal people have adapted these structures to their own design, using them as a place to store things, but generally regarding them as too small and too hot to actually eat, sleep, or entertain in.

¹⁰ FAMILY LIFE

Marriage in traditional Aboriginal societies is a complicated matter that has interested and perplexed anthropologists ever since they encountered the marriage prescriptions of Australian Aborigines. In many societies, first marriages were arranged. Husbands were often much older than their wives. Among the Tiwi of Melville and Bathurst islands off the northern coast of Australia, female infants were betrothed at birth. Females in this society were always married. This practice was related to Tiwi belief that females became impregnated by spirits; human males were not active participants in the process

of human procreation. Tiwi society also required that every individual needed to have a "social father." Since the biological father was a spirit and could not provide for the child, and since procreation could occur at any time in a female's life, it was necessary to ensure that any child that might be produced would have a social father: the husband of the female.

¹¹ CLOTHING

Australian Aborigines were one of the only groups of people in the world to not wear any type of clothing. Both men and women went naked. Nowadays things have changed considerably. Urban Aborigines wear modern clothes appropriate to their age group. Rural groups dress like the Anglo-Australians who also live there: many of these people dress like American cowboys. Aborigines from the southeastern coast wear large blankets made from kangaroo hide to protect them from the cold, wind, and rain that characterize winter in that region.

¹² FOOD

Since many Aboriginal groups were nomadic hunters and gatherers, they did little in the area of food preparation. Meals were simple. Almost all Aboriginal groups made a conceptual distinction between meat and non-meat foodstuffs. This is reflected in the terminology of the various languages. In Walpiri, the term *kuyu* refers to meat or any game animal or bird that is killed for meat. In contrast, the term *miyi* refers to vegetables or fruit.

¹³ EDUCATION

Most urban Aboriginal children have the opportunity to attend public school. They often encounter discrimination in the classroom in terms of their culture and their language. Some communities have developed their own educational programs to help Aboriginal children achieve in the educational system. At Yuendumu in central Australia, the Walpiri have a very well-developed educational system that provides both European-style education and education in the areas of traditional language and culture. As is the case for Anglo-Australians, school is mandatory through the tenth grade, with grades 11 and 12 being optional. There have been attempts to develop institutions of higher education targeted to Aboriginal people, for the most part in rural areas of the country.

¹⁴ CULTURAL HERITAGE

Traditional Aboriginal societies possessed little in the way of material objects due to their nomadic lifestyles. As a result, Aboriginal groups did not have many musical instruments. The most well-known Aboriginal musical instrument is the *dijeridoo,* a long, hollow tube made from a piece of wood that had been hollowed out by termites. These instruments were traditionally only found in groups in the Top End region of the continent, in the areas around Arnhem Land, Cape York Peninsula, and the Kimberleys. These long trumpets produce a characteristic drone that accompanies ritual dancing. Dijeridoos have become popular instruments in the production of modern world music. A few Aboriginal people teach dijeridoo to non-Aboriginal people who want to learn to play it.

In many Aboriginal societies men used a "bullroarer" to frighten women and uninitiated males at ceremonial events. The bullroarer is a decorated and shaped piece of flat wood that is attached to a line and swung around and around above a person's head to produce a whirring sound. The sound is usually said to be the voice of important spirits of the land. As opposed to their Oceanic neighbors, Australian Aborigines did not use drums.

Dance is an extremely important part of Aboriginal ceremonial life. Many Aboriginal dances mimic the movements and behaviors of animal species such as the *brolga* crane of the northern wetlands. Typically, men and women had separate rituals and, as a result, separate dances and dance performances. There are several Aboriginal performance troupes in Australia that travel to urban centers to perform traditional dances as well as newly created pieces.

15 WORK

In traditional Aboriginal societies there was a division of labor according to age and sex. Women and children were responsible for gathering vegetables, fruit, and small game such as *goannas* (a large lizard). Men were responsible for obtaining meat by hunting both large and small game. Men in Aranda society hunted with a variety of implements including spears, spear throwers, and non-returning boomerangs.

Aboriginal people in urban areas are employed in a variety of jobs. However, gaining employment is often difficult due to discrimination.

16 SPORTS

Rugby, Australian-rules football, and cricket are important spectator and participant sports in Australia, though basketball has been a fast-growing sport for some time now. Aboriginal people play for some of the semi-professional rugby teams.

17 ENTERTAINMENT AND RECREATION

In some parts of Australia, Aboriginal people have established their own broadcasting stations for radio and television. These establishments have been most successful in the central region of Australia in and around Alice Springs. In these communities, elders have realized that if they do not provide alternative programming for their youth, they will turn away from the traditional ways of life under the influence of American and Australian television programs. Aboriginal bands also produce music videos for these programs, as well as for distribution to the larger society.

18 FOLK ART, CRAFTS, AND HOBBIES

Australian Aboriginal art has been extremely popular on the world art market for some time now. The pointillist acrylic paintings of "dreamings" from the Central Desert region bring a high price, especially if the artist is one of the well-known Aboriginal artists. In the Walpiri community of Yuendumu, the elders decided to paint the doors of the classrooms of the school with various "dreamings."

There are regional differences in the art of Aboriginal Australia. Arnhem Land in the northern part of the Northern Territory is renowned for bark painting, weaving, rock art, and sculpture. The use of cross-hatched patterns is a distinctive characteristic of Arnhem Land art. Even within the Arnhem Land region, there are subregions whose art can be distinguished, demonstrating the complexity and variation in traditional Aboriginal artistic expression.

An Australian Aborigine in New South Wales, Australia. (Tim Graham/Getty Images)

19 SOCIAL PROBLEMS

The retention of the right to pursue traditional ways of life is one of the biggest social problems facing Aboriginal people. To pursue traditional lifestyles, language and folklore must be maintained in the face of societal pressure to modernize. Many Aboriginal communities have hired linguist-teachers to help in the efforts to preserve the traditional language for future generations; however, there are more languages in need of preservation than there are linguist-teachers willing to take on the task of aiding in the preservation and transmission of these languages.

Life in urban areas, where the standard of living is very low and prospects for further education and meaningful employment are minimal, has fostered a high incidence of domestic violence and alcoholism. In an attempt to reverse this trend, some older males have "kidnapped" young men and taken off to traditional lands to participate, involuntarily, in a kind of "scared straight" rehabilitation program. There have been mixed reactions to this kind of behavior both within Aboriginal society and the larger Australian society as a whole.

20 GENDER ISSUES

Most Aboriginal societies recognize two genders: male and female. Some Aboriginal languages encode gender grammatically through a system of noun classes. While somewhat similar to the use of gender in many Indo-European languages, the Aboriginal systems are more complex and have provided some interesting semantic relationships. For instance, in Dyirbal, which was once spoken in far northern Queensland, there were four noun classes. The first class included men and animate objects. The second class included women, water, fire, and violence; all of which were considered dangerous by the Dyirbal. The third class was composed of edible fruits and vegetables, while the fourth class included everything that was not in the first three classes.

In traditional Aboriginal ritual and social life, male and female were sharply demarcated and differentiated. Any ritual that was sacred and secret to one gender was held out of eye and ear shot from the rest of the group. There are strict punishments for any females who transgress a male ritual. While the punishments were less extreme for men, they still avoid going near female rituals. In social life, gender and kinship also dictated behavior and decorum. There are precise rules that govern the interactions of men and women who are related to each other either by blood or marriage. To avoid contravening these rules, men and women tend to gather together in gender-exclusive groups when in public places.

For groups like the Mardu of Western Australia, the strong egalitarian nature of the society means that men and women feel equally able to make decisions and express opinions on most matters important to the well-being of the group. However, this does not mean that women and men have equal rights within Mardu society. For instance, women are not free to divorce their husbands, to have more than one husband at a time, or to engage in "husband-lending." Mardu men, on the other hand, are free to engage in the equivalent activities within the society. Older male relatives often make major decisions that will affect the lives of women, the most influential being infant betrothal. Infant betrothal is a social practice whereby an older male relative negotiates a husband for a baby girl, although the formal marriage does not take place until the girl attains puberty. The practice typically results in young girls being married to much older men.

21 BIBLIOGRAPHY

Bell, Diane. *Daughters of the Dreaming.* Minneapolis: University of Minnesota Press, 1993.

Berndt, R.M., and C.H. Berndt. *The World of the First Australians.* Sydney: Ure Smith, 1964.

Contested Ground: Australian Aborigines Under the British Crown. St. Leonards, Australia: Allen & Unwin, 1995.

Hiatt, Lester R. *Arguments about Aborigines: Australia and the Evolution of Social Anthropology.* Cambridge, New York: Cambridge University Press, 1996.

Holmes, Sandra Le Brun. *The Goddess and the Moon Man: The Sacred Art of the Tiwi Aborigines.* Roseville East, Australia: Craftsman House, 1995.

In the Age of Mabo: History, Aborigines, and Australia. St. Leonards, Australia: Allen & Unwin, 1996.

Kohen, James L. *Aboriginal Environmental Impacts.* Sydney, Australia: University of New South Wales Press, 1995.

Morphy, Howard. *Aboriginal Art.* London: Phaidon Press, 1998.

—by J. Williams

AZERBAIJANIS

PRONUNCIATION: ah-zer-bye-JAHN-eez
LOCATION: Azerbaijan; Iran
POPULATION: Estimated about 40-45 million worldwide: Republic of Azerbaijan, 8.2 million; Iran, estimated 30 million; Georgia, Dagestan, Russia, China, Iraq, Germany, Sweden, United Kingdom, Canada, United States and Australia.
LANGUAGE: Azeri (also called Azerbaijani)
RELIGION: Islam (majority); Christianity (Orthodox and Evangelical); Judaism

1 INTRODUCTION

The word Azerbaijan means "land of fire." Even today, it is possible to find places in Azerbaijan where fires ignite and burn spontaneously on the surface of the earth. These fires seem to burn eternally because they are fed by gas that seeps through cracks in the surface of the earth. The fires indicate that this land has vast oil reserves deep beneath the surface of the earth; geologists and geophysicists are discovering that Azerbaijan has more oil hidden below its surface than ever imagined before.

Azerbaijan is an ancient land. Some of the earliest evidence of all human civilization can be traced to this region. For example, in 1960 archeologists discovered a prehistoric cave (Azikh) that dates to the Neanderthal period. A human jawbone found there is believed to be 350,000–400,000 years old. Stone tools were also unearthed that date back to the Paleolithic and Mesolithic periods, which would make them approximately 1–1.5 million years old.

In ancient times, Azerbaijanis were believed to be skilled mariners who lived along the western coast of the Caspian Sea. The people of this advanced culture navigated, explored, and colonized many waterways, from the Volga and Dvina rivers in present-day Russia to the Black, Baltic, and North seas. Some archeologists believe that the ancestors of modern Azerbaijanis may have even traveled as far east as China and as far west as Norway and Sweden and that even modern Scandinavians themselves may have descended from ancient, fair-skinned Azerbaijani explorers and colonists.

Azerbaijan is located at the crossroads of Europe and Central Asia along what used to be called the Silk Road, which was a famous web of roads between Europe and China traveled by traders in mule and camel caravans. The Italian explorer and adventurer Marco Polo passed through Azerbaijan in about 1270. He wrote about the eternal fires burning from the earth and about a special oil that was used as medicine for skin diseases and other ailments in people and cattle. He observed that people came from neighboring countries, often from great distances, to obtain oil for their lamps.

Because visitors from many countries and nationalities passed through this region, not only were goods, such as silk and tea, traded, but also many ideas about music, literature, medicine, and science were exchanged. Even today, this openness to foreigners and this curiosity about other parts of the world is part of the Azerbaijani legacy.

Azerbaijan is a tiny country squeezed between three major economic and political powers—Russia, Iran, and Turkey.

Azerbaijan is bordered by Russia to the north, the Caspian Sea to the east, Iran to the south, and Armenia and Georgia to the west. There is also a 10-km (6.2-mi) strip that touches Turkey on the western border of Nakhchivan, an autonomous republic in Azerbaijan. Each of these countries (except Georgia) has, at different times in history, tried to gain control over Azerbaijan and to benefit from its vast natural resources, especially oil. Some people say Azerbaijan lives in a "tough neighborhood" because of the political pressures it has to deal with from all sides but as writer Yusif Vazir Chamanzaminli (1887–1943) described, Azerbaijan was located between "Two Fires"—Russia and Iran.

Over the centuries, many kingdoms and empires have fought to gain control over the region, including the Romans, Greeks, Mongols, Persians, and Russians. For example, Arabs from the south conquered this region in AD 642 and imposed the Muslim religion. Then Mongols from the east dominated the region from 1236 to 1498. The country was ruled by Safavids beginning in the 16th century. During the 18th century, Russians from the north began their territorial expansion into the region, only to be countered by Turks from the West.

By the beginning of the 19th century, the region was again under Russian jurisdiction. In 1918 Azerbaijan gained its independence and became known as the Democratic Republic of Azerbaijan. But, freedom was very short-lived. Less than two years later, in 1920, Soviet army troops invaded and occupied Baku. Azerbaijan then lived under the domination of the Soviet Union until 1991, when the Soviet Union collapsed and Azerbaijan was able to regain its independence. The country is now known as the Republic of Azerbaijan. Since 1988, the Armenians have been fighting with Azerbaijanis. As of 1994, Armenians occupied about 15% of Azerbaijan's territory.

2 LOCATION AND HOMELAND

Azerbaijan is a small country. The map of Azerbaijan somewhat resembles an eagle flying eastward. The Republic of Azerbaijan covers 86,600 sq km (33,430 sq mi), making it about the size of the U.S. state of Maine. The land has many contrasts in temperature and terrain, from coastal lowlands (along the Caspian Sea and at the basins of the Kura and Araz rivers) to high mountain ranges of the Greater and Lesser Caucasus and Talish mountain chains. The mountain regions are extremely cold, but other regions in Azerbaijan are nearly as hot as tropical or desert regions. These vast temperature differences mean that many kinds of foods can be grown here. Azerbaijan grows cotton, grapes for wine, and a wide range of garden vegetables. The population of the Republic of Azerbaijan is approximately 8.2 million people. However, three times as many Azerbaijanis live to the south in Iran (an estimated 30–35 million). More Azerbaijanis live in Iran because of a treaty signed between Russia and Persia in 1828, splitting the country into two sections, northern (now the Azerbaijan Republic) and southern (now part of Iran).

Azerbaijanis also live in other parts of the former Soviet Union, especially Georgia, Dagestan, and Russia. Azerbaijanis also live in China (Xinjiang Province) and Iraq. An estimated 200,000 Azerbaijanis used to live in Armenia, but according to UNHCR about 182,000 Azerbaijanis fled Armenia in 1988 before the war started between these two countries. In the 1970s, many Azerbaijanis immigrated from Iran to Western Europe (especially Germany, Sweden, and England) and to Canada

(Toronto) and the United States (Los Angeles, Washington, D.C., and New York City). Also, a considerable number of Azerbaijanis from Iran have settled in Australia. An estimated 40–45 million Azerbaijanis live throughout the world.

3 LANGUAGE

Azerbaijanis speak Azeri (sometimes called Azerbaijani). It is a Turkic language belonging to the Altaic-Turkic language group, which also includes Anatolia Turkish and other Central Asian languages. For centuries, Azerbaijanis wrote their language using the Arabic alphabet. However, a Latin-based alphabet was adopted in 1923 in a purge by the Soviet government to rid Azerbaijan and other Muslim countries of the influence of Islam.

In the Muslim republics of the Soviet Union, the people were forced to burn books that were written in Arabic script into giant bonfires in the middle of their villages and towns; these books were not only religious books, but also books of poetry and medicine. It was tragic for Azerbaijanis and for the rest of the world that these books and manuscripts were destroyed. The Soviets wanted to destroy these books primarily because they associated the Arabic script with Islam (particularly the holy book, the Quran) and wanted to stamp out all religious influences in the region.

In 1939, Soviet dictator Josef Stalin (1879–1953) feared that the people of Azerbaijan and the other Central Asian Turkic Republics, who spoke Turkic languages, might join together and rebel against the Soviet government. In order to make it impossible for them to communicate with each other through writing, he imposed the Cyrillic alphabet that was used for the Russian language. Azerbaijan and the other Turkic republics (Kazakhstan, Turkmenistan, Uzbekistan and Kyrgyzstan) in the Soviet Union had no choice. Almost overnight, works were published, not in Latin any more but Cyrillic script. Furthermore, to confound the situation, Stalin assigned different letters for some of the identical sounds in their Turkic languages that did not exist in the Russian language. For example, there were seven different letters created in Turkic Cyrillic script to represent the "ng" sound (as in "English"). Thus, it became nearly impossible for speakers of related languages to read each other's languages.

One of the first things that Azerbaijan's parliament did after Azerbaijan gained its independence in 1991 was to readopt a Latin-based alphabet for their language. However, the enormous task of rewriting everything from street signs to textbooks to computer keyboards, as well as teaching in a new alphabet, has been daunting.

But, Azerbaijanis, who have changed their alphabet three times in the 20th century, feel that the new alphabet represents their new, independent country and that they are no longer under control of anyone else. It also reflects the desire of Azerbaijanis to develop friendships with people in Europe and the United States, countries where a similar Latin alphabet is also used.

4 FOLKLORE

Azerbaijanis have close family ties, spending much of their time talking with one another. Therefore, a rich tradition of oral folklore has developed in this region. Many songs, stories, proverbs, and expressions have been passed down over hundreds and thousands of years. The oldest known story in the

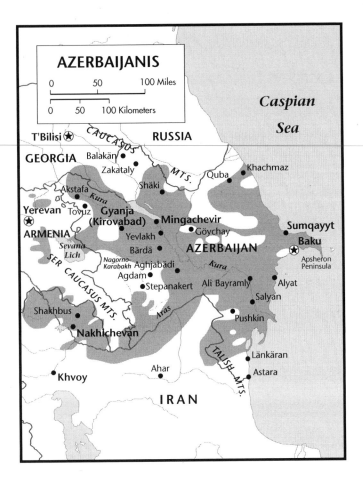

AZERBAIJANIS

0 50 100 Miles

0 50 100 Kilometers

Caspian Sea

RUSSIA

T'Bilisi ⍟
GEORGIA Balakän
Zakataly Quba Khachmaz
Akstafa Shäki
Yerevan Tovuz Gyanja
⍟ (Kirovabad) Mingachevir
ARMENIA Yevlakh Göychay Sumqayyt
Sevana Bärdä AZERBAIJAN Baku
Lich Nagorno- Aghjabädi Apsheron
Karabakh Agdam Kura Peninsula
Stepanakert Ali Bayramly Alyat
Shakhbus Salyän
Nakhichevan Pushkin
Aras Länkäran
Khvoy Ahar Astara
IRAN

Turkic languages is Dede Gorgud. It was first written down in the 11th century, but its origin dates to the 7th century. Dede Gorgud is believed to have been a real person who entertained others with stories, many of which bear a resemblance to tales in the Greek Odyssey.

Azerbaijanis have many legends. One of the most famous is about an ancient tower, called Maiden Tower, which still stands today as the most famous landmark in Baku. According to the legend, a young girl ordered the tower to be built and threw herself from its heights into the sea below when her father wanted to marry her off. Legends like this have become favorite themes in the works of many Azerbaijani artists and poets. There is even a ballet based on the Maiden Tower legend.

Azerbaijanis have many proverbs, such as: "Wish your neighbor two cows so that you may have one for yourself" (In other words, wish good fortune for others so that you also may benefit); "Laughter is the remedy for 1,001 illnesses;" "The dog barks, the caravan passes" (Don't get discouraged and distracted when people criticize you); "The more you know, the less you should talk;" and "Even the ground has ears" (There is no such thing as a secret).

Like other people of the region, Azerbaijanis love the humor and wisdom of Molla Nasraddin stories. There are hundreds of stories, many set in the 13th century, that deal with social issues that are fundamental to human nature. Molla Nasraddin stories often point to an obvious truth taken for granted. Molla appears to be the fool but, in reality, he exposes other people's foolishness. Some of the stories are very short and witty. For

example, one story is as follows: "One day Molla was asked the secret to his long life. He replied, 'Keep your feet warm, your head cool, be careful what you eat, and don't think too much!'"

5 RELIGION

Some historians believe that Zoroastrianism (which involves the worship of sacred fire), which originated in the 6th century BC, was prevalent in ancient Azerbaijan because of the presence of underground oil and natural gas. Zoroastrianism is believed to have influenced Christianity, Judaism, and Islam.

It appears that Christianity was popular in the region from the 2nd through 6th centuries when the area was called Albania. Numerous archeological sites and churches date to this period. Recently, Dr. Zaza Alexidze (born 1935) of the Institute of Manuscripts in Tbilisi, Georgia, discovered a palimpsest manuscript in St. Catherine's Monastery at Mt. Sinai, Egypt, that proves that early Christians in the region known as Caucasian Albania (now Azerbaijan) had parts of the Bible available in the Caucasian Albanian script. This alphabet dates back to 5th–7th century. There are still people known as Udins in Azerbaijan and Georgia who speak this language.

In the 7th century, when the Arabs invaded the region, Islam was imposed. By the end of the 9th century, it is believed that most Azerbaijanis had become Muslims of the Shi'ite branch (as in Iran).

During the Soviet period, religious worship was discouraged, and most mosques and churches were either destroyed or converted into cultural centers or music halls. Atheism was the official religion. Today, Azerbaijan enjoys freedom of religion—Muslims, Christians (Orthodox and Evangelical), and Jews can all worship openly and freely. The constitution ratified by the Azerbaijan Parliament in 1995 guarantees freedom of religion to all. The state has no official religion, though most people are traditionally Muslim. The Constitution provides for separation of the powers of church and state. A person does not have to belong to a certain religion to be elected or hold an office. However, especially since 2000, more and more Azerbaijanis are becoming devout, practicing Muslims, and more women are wearing head scarves and modest apparel associated with Islam.

6 MAJOR HOLIDAYS

The most anticipated and joyful holiday of the year is Novruz (meaning New Year). Novruz is an ancient tradition marking the Spring Solstice (March 21) or the coming of spring. This holiday is not only celebrated by Azerbaijanis, but by others throughout the region, including Iranians, Afghanis, Turks, and people in the Central Asian countries. During the Soviet period, Novruz was officially banned because the holiday was thought to be too nationalistic. Soviets wanted to emphasize the unity of the 15 republics of the Soviet Union, not the distinctive characteristics of individual states. Nevertheless, many Azerbaijanis commemorated Novruz in the privacy of their homes. Since 1990, Novruz has been an official holiday in Azerbaijan and is celebrated openly.

Novruz is always associated with the colors red and green and the newness of spring. One of the most vivid symbols of Novruz is a plate of green wheat seedlings that each family grows (or these days, often buys) that is tied up with a red ribbon. On the Tuesday before Novruz, young boys build bonfires in their yards and in the streets and dare each other to jump over the flames without getting burned. Women bake cookies and sweets, and friends and relatives visit each other at home. Shops and government offices are closed, as are schools.

Azerbaijanis in the republic celebrate January 1 as New Year's Day, though in Iran, Novruz officially ushers in the new calendar year.

Since 1992, the Azerbaijan Republic has celebrated Independence Day on May 28, which commemorates the first period of independence from 1918–1920 before the Bolsheviks took power and Azerbaijan became a part of the Soviet Union.

The saddest public holiday of the year for Azerbaijanis is January 20. It commemorates "Black January" when Soviet troops attacked Baku in 1990 with tanks and machine guns and killed hundreds of civilians in the streets. Mikhail Gorbachev, then president of the Soviet Union, was afraid that Azerbaijanis would rise up and demand independence. He sent troops to Baku to squelch the rebel movement. Now on this day, people visit cemeteries and place red flowers on the graves of those who have died for Azerbaijan.

7 RITES OF PASSAGE

The most significant Azerbaijani rites of passage are connected with birthdays, marriage, and death. The birthdays of famous people, such as artists, musicians, scholars, or statesmen, are called Jubilees and become significant events in the life of the nation. Usually, jubilees occur on the person's 60th, 70th, or other decade birthdays. If a person has made an incredible contribution to the nation, his or her jubilee may be celebrated even after he has died. For example, the 120th jubilee of the famous composer, Uzeyir Hajibeyov, was celebrated in 2005 although he had died in 1948. Hajibeyov is honored as the founder of classical music in Azerbaijan.

The color red is associated with both marriage and death. Often, the bride wears a white wedding gown with a red sash tied around her waist. Weddings are important celebrations. In the countryside, weddings can continue for three days. In cities wedding celebrations usually take place in restaurants with big halls with ample space for dancing.

Thursdays are days for visiting cemeteries. Mourners place red flowers, usually carnations in pairs (for example, two or four) on the grave. When a person dies, the funeral is usually held the next day. Friends also gather again one week later, 40 days later, and then on the annual date of the death. When a person dies who has never married, a cracked mirror wrapped with a red ribbon is often placed near the grave. The red ribbon is a reminder that the person never had the chance to enjoy the joyous occasion of getting married and starting his own family.

8 INTERPERSONAL RELATIONS

Azerbaijanis are generally expressive with their emotions. They are not shy in expressing their love. People feel very comfortable holding hands and touching. When people meet each other, generally they kiss each other on the cheeks—men with men and women with women. Young girls often walk down the street holding hands, or arm in arm. Parents often hold the hands of their children, even older ones. Personal relations are highly nurtured and, in general, people are very courteous to one another.

Azerbaijanis are known for their kind hospitality to strangers. They love to invite guests from the international community to their homes for dinner. They enjoy traveling to other countries and making friends throughout the world. For about 70 years (1920–1991) Azerbaijan was under the control of the Soviet Union and lived behind what was called the "Iron Curtain," which restricted them from being able to meet or communicate easily with people from other countries. Since Azerbaijan became an independent country, Azerbaijanis have been able to continue their tradition of international friendship. Now they travel abroad frequently.

9 LIVING CONDITIONS

The average life expectancy for Azerbaijanis in the Republic is not as high as in established industrialized nations. As in many of the other former Soviet republics, there has been a shortage of modern medical equipment and pharmaceuticals in Azerbaijan, especially during the transitional years since the collapse of the Soviet Union as Azerbaijan works to establish a market economy.

Azerbaijanis, however, especially those living in the Caucasus Mountains, are famous for their extreme longevity. Many people live to be over 100-years-old. Throughout Azerbaijan, there are numerous regions where longevity is the norm, including Lerik, Lankaran, Gazakh, Tovuz, Ismayilli, Jalilabad, Shamakhi, Lachin, Kalbajar, and Aghdam. Azerbaijanis credit their longevity to a variety of factors best described as a combination of heredity, environment, and psychological, social, and cultural patterns. They believe longevity is basically inherited; many of the oldest Azerbaijanis had parents who also lived long lives. Centenarians living in the mountains typically are poor and eat yogurt and vegetables that they grow themselves. Most say they have spent much of their lives involved in hard physical work.

The leading cause of death in Azerbaijan is heart disease, followed by cancer, respiratory infections, and accidents. Diabetes, tuberculosis, hepatitis A, and acute respiratory infections also pose serious public health problems.

The war with Armenians over the Karabakh territory in Azerbaijan began in late 1988. It has resulted in more than 25,000 deaths and many permanent injuries to people who stepped on land mines.

Much of the water supply is unsafe due to high levels of chemical and biological pollution. Much of the pollution comes from oil leaks at petroleum plants and from the dumping of raw sewage into the Caspian Sea. In Baku, for example, it is essential to boil any water intended for drinking.

10 FAMILY LIFE

Older people are greatly esteemed in Azerbaijan and are given high positions in the family and community. The elderly are never left to feel useless or unneeded. Traditional Azerbaijani social organization, including extended kinship and inter-generational bonds, makes aging less stressful. Children are greatly revered among the Azerbaijanis, as well.

11 CLOTHING

Clothing is very similar to Western styles. Women, especially, try to look as attractive as possible. Azerbaijani women rid themselves of the traditional Muslim veil (chador) in 1928. The event is even commemorated by various statues in Baku.

An Azerbaijani shepherd with his sheep, standing between Dahana and Dagestan in the Caucasian mountains. Despite oil contracts and foreign investment, Azerbaijanis still live with low incomes. (Manoocher Deghati/AFP/Getty Images)

However, the influence of Islam is becoming more evident, and more and more women do wear head scarves and long-sleeved jackets and long clothing.

12 FOOD

Food consists primarily of bread, grains, fruits, and vegetables but is supplemented by meats, such as lamb, chicken, and fish. Pilaf (rice) and dolma (grape leaves stuffed with meat) is one of the favorite dishes. In Iran, Azerbaijanis eat rice nearly every day. In the Republic, the cuisine is patterned more on Russian-style food during the Soviet republics. In Russian meals there is more emphasis on bread, potatoes, and cabbage. The traditional beverage is black tea with sugar cubes. Azerbaijanis are excellent hosts and love to invite people to their homes to share meals. Dinners often last three hours or longer.

13 EDUCATION

The Soviet period placed great emphasis on education. Azerbaijanis have achieved a high level of literacy, estimated at about 99%. Today, even though Azerbaijan has gained its independence, the education system is severely challenged. Nearly 800,000 refugees lost their homes in the early 1990s because of the ethnic conflicts with Armenia. This placed severe pressure on the education system. Many refugee children had no schools to attend. Sometimes, school buildings were used to house the

refugees, which meant that children from families who were not refugees also suffered. Salaries for teachers and professors still have not been adjusted to reflect current living standards and, therefore, enormous bribing goes on in the education system at all levels. This is beginning to have an enormous impact on the society. Many Azerbaijanis admit that education standards were higher during the Soviet period.

During the Soviet period, Russian was the predominant language taught in Azerbaijan. Today, young people have the greatest chances of getting the best jobs if they are trilingual—fluent in Azeri, Russian, and English. Great emphasis is being placed on learning English. Popular music in English is played on local radio stations.

14 CULTURAL HERITAGE

Since ancient times, Azerbaijanis have held their poets and literary figures in highest esteem. The city of Baku has many statues devoted to Azerbaijani poets and literary figures, such as Nizami, Fuzuli, and Nasimi.

Baku is a charming city known for its architectural diversity, which is a unique synthesis of both Eastern and Western styles. An incredible architectural transformation took place during the relatively short period of the oil boom years (1880–1920) that completely altered the physical features and character of Baku, converting it from a sleepy, medieval feudal city into a bustling international metropolis comparable to its European sister cities. One of the primary reasons so many Western-style buildings appeared was that a number of prominent European architects were hired by oil barons and brought to Baku from countries such as Poland, Germany, Austria, Italy, and Russia. Naturally, they drew upon their own experience and training. They introduced a wide range of European styles; for example, Neo-Classical, German, and Italian Renaissance Revival, French Islamic Maghrib, Venetian Gothic Revival, etc.

However, the architecture of the oil boom period in Baku is becoming overpowered by hundreds of modern apartment towers. The city has taken on a new skyline.

Azerbaijanis are famous for their music. It is impossible to truly understand Azerbaijani culture without understanding their deep love of music. The majority of Azerbaijanis have either been trained in music or perform it on Western or traditional Eastern stringed instruments, such as tar or kamancha, or wind instruments such as zurna and balaban.

Classical Azerbaijani music is a rich blend of eastern melodies, rhythms, and modes blended with Western forms and styles like symphonies, ballets, and opera. Azerbaijani world-class composers include Uzeyir Hajibeyov, Gara Garayev, Fikrat Amirov, and Agshin Alizade. The world-renown cellist Mstislav Rostropovich was also born in Baku

15 WORK

The greatest sources of employment are the oil industry, construction and agriculture. Enormous reserves of oil have been discovered in the Azerbaijan sector of the Caspian Sea. Many international companies are already helping Azerbaijan drill for oil and gas and building pipelines that will transport the oil and gas to international markets.

New Azerbaijan oil began reaching the international market in 2005. Already Azerbaijan is exporting about 1 million barrels of oil per day. However, the recent conflicts between Russia and Georgia have already impacted oil export because Azerbaijan's BTC (Baku–Tbilisi–Ceyhan) pipeline travels more than 1000 miles from Baku to Tbilisi (Georgia) before it reaches the Mediterranean port in Ceyhan (pronounced Jeyhan), Turkey.

The most serious challenge facing the economy is to make sure that the proceeds from the oil benefit the entire country and that the infrastructure within the country is built up for the benefit of all. In other words, that wealth is not concentrated in the hands of only a few.

16 SPORTS

Azerbaijanis love sports and excel at wrestling. They are famous for chess, as well. World chess champion Garry Kasparov grew up playing chess in Baku.

17 ENTERTAINMENT AND RECREATION

It is a rare Azerbaijani home that does not have a television. The few exceptions would occur in remote mountain villages. Satellite dishes are becoming popular throughout the country, many of which are affixed to the narrow balconies above the streets. Western television programs are well-liked among the Azerbaijanis, as are Russian and Turkish programs. Azerbaijanis, especially elderly people spend their leisure time playing nard (backgammon), dominoes and chess. Educational insti-

tutions, work places are computerized. Many homes now have personal computers. More than half the population has mobile phones.

18 FOLK ART, CRAFTS, AND HOBBIES

In Azerbaijan more emphasis is placed on music than on folk arts and hobbies, though during the Soviet period, many people enjoyed collecting postcards, stamps, and other memorabilia that made them feel more connected to the world.

19 SOCIAL PROBLEMS

Since the mid 1980s, Armenians and Azerbaijanis have been fighting over the territory of Nagorno-Karabakh within the borders of Azerbaijan. The region has a large percentage of Armenians who wanted to separate from Azerbaijan and join with Armenia. The Nagorno-Karabakh region has some of the most productive farmland in the area, favoring a wide cultivation of products including cotton, wheat, tobacco, grapes, tomatoes, and other fruits and vegetables. It also has gold mines. The fighting has caused a tragic loss of life (an estimated 25,000 people), and many have been permanently injured.

As of the late 1990s, the Armenian military occupied about 15% of Azerbaijan's territory. Approximately 800,000 Azerbaijanis who lived in this region were forced to flee their communities, their homes, their schools, and their workplaces. The refugees used to live scattered throughout the countryside in refugee camps, hostels, schools, and anywhere else they can find shelter but now there are no refugee camps left in Azerbaijan. Refugees move to special communities with buildings constructed by government. Azerbaijan wants to reclaim the Nagorno-Karabakh area so that the people can go back and rebuild their homes, schools, and factories that were burned down during the war. A cease-fire agreement has been in place since May 1994, but Azerbaijanis are eager to resolve the problem and bring about a permanent peace. At the same time, they are unwilling to give up their lands. The problem will probably take a long time to resolve.

20 GENDER ISSUES

Many women hold down office jobs as well as manage their households and raise the children. The work load on women is extremely heavy.

21 BIBLIOGRAPHY

Alexidze, Zaza and Betty Blair, "Caucasian Albanian Alphabet Ancient Script Discovered in the Ashes," *Azerbaijan International*, Autumn 2003 (11.3), 38-41.

Azerbaijan International Magazine. Los Angeles: Azerbaijani International. AZER.com.

Goltz, Thomas. *Azerbaijan Diary: A Rogue Reporter's Adventures in an Oil-Rich, War-Torn, Post-Soviet Republic.* Sharpe: Armonk, New York, 1998.

Said, Kurban. *Ali & Nino.* New York: Anchor, 2000

—revised by B. Blair

BAHRAINIS

PRONUNCIATION: bah-RAIN-eez
LOCATION: Bahrain
POPULATION: 727,000 (2006)
LANGUAGE: Arabic (official); English; Farsi (Persian); Hindi; Urdu
RELIGION: Islam (Shia, 70%; Sunni, 24%); Christianity; Hinduism; Judaism; Baha'i

¹ INTRODUCTION

Bahrain (meaning "two seas") has been the only safe port on the Persian Gulf throughout history because of prevailing wind and weather patterns. Therefore it has played an important part in the life of the Gulf since civilization began there. This tiny island nation has been of strategic significance since Sumerian times (4000 BC) to the present. Despite this, it has had a relatively peaceful history.

The entire northern coastal region of the Arabian peninsula was once known as Bahrain, with present-day Bahrain known then as Dilmun. It is described in the Sumerian hero-tale *The Epic of Gilgamesh* as an island of immortals where heroes went after death to live in eternal bliss. In fact, Bahrain hosts the largest cemetery in the world: more than 170,000 burial mounds, dating from 2500–1800 BC, are located on the island of Bahrain. They range from slight lumps in the ground to mounds as high as 12 m (40 ft). The mounds have been pillaged by grave robbers for 3,000 years, however, and few archaeological artifacts remain.

For a time in ancient history, and later in modern days, Persia (now Iran) claimed Bahrain as its territory. The Portuguese laid claim to it in 1521, but they were forced back out by the Bahrainis in 1602. In 1782, the al-Khalifa Arab family took over the islands and have been the ruling family ever since. (They are cousins of the al-Sabah ruling family of Kuwait and are distantly related to the al-Saud ruling family of Saudi Arabia.) Pirates long used Bahrain as a base for attacking ships in the Gulf. In 1820, Bahrain signed an agreement with Britain to become a British-protected state, meaning that Britain would protect Bahrain's sovereignty in return for safe sailing up the Gulf for Britain's ships. Therefore, while Bahrain kept the pirates from attacking Britain's ships, Britain kept the Iranians (and others) from attacking Bahrain. This agreement lasted until Britain decided to terminate it in 1968. By 1971, all British troops had left Bahrain, although British soldiers still supervise Bahrain's army and security forces. On 15 August 1971, Bahrain proclaimed independence. The constitution of 1972 provided for a parliament, or National Assembly, the first in the nation's history, and elections were held in 1973. Two years later, in 1975, the Assembly was disbanded by the king for security reasons; the king claimed that some Assembly members were involved in subversive activities.

In 1993 the king created a 40-member Consultative Council, all of whose members serve by appointment. The 2002 constitution also created a 40-member Chamber of Deputies, whose members are directly elected by universal adult suffrage. Women have not only the right to vote but can also stand for office, and the Bahraini Chamber of Deputies typically has a few elected female members.

Known as "the land of sweet waters," Bahrain's first wealth was in the form of fresh water that bubbled up in artesian wells and springs, even through the saltwater of the Gulf just off the islands' shores. Bahrain had more easily available fresh water than anywhere else on the Gulf coast. Pearls were the other big moneymaker, collected from offshore oyster beds. When the Japanese introduced cultured pearls in the 1930s, Bahrain's economy was in danger. However, oil was discovered in 1931, giving Bahrain the first oil well, and then the first oil refinery, on the Arab side of the Arabian Gulf. Although Bahrain has always produced less oil than other Arab states, oil continues to be the major source of income for the tiny island nation.

² LOCATION AND HOMELAND

Bahrain is an archipelago in the Persian Gulf, lying 24 km (15 mi) off the northeast coast of Saudi Arabia, and 21 km (13 mi) northwest of the Qatar Peninsula. Of the 33 islands, only 5 are inhabited. The six major islands are Bahrain (also known as as-Awal), Muharraq, Sitrah, Umm al-Nassan, Jidda (used as the Bahraini prison), and Nabi Salih. The 27 minor islands include the Muhammadiyah and Hawar groups. There is dispute between Bahrain and Qatar over the possession of the Hawar Islands. The total area is 678 sq km (262 sq mi), of which 85% is the island of Bahrain. There are 126 km (78 mi) of coastline. The capital city, Manama, is located on the north coast of Bahrain island. A causeway 2 km (1.5 mi) long connects the islands of Bahrain and Muharraq (the second-most important island, where the ruling family lives). A bridge joins the islands of Bahrain and Sitrah. There is also a long bridge, the King Fahd Causeway, linking Bahrain to mainland Saudi Arabia.

Bahrain is essentially a desert surrounded by water. Although freshwater springs bubble up from beneath the sea floor just offshore (these "wells" are marked with iron posts that rise above the surface of the water), and other artesian wells flow out of the ground at the north end of Bahrain Island, the land is otherwise dry and sandy. The climate ranges from hot (up to 48°C [120°F]) and humid in the summer to chilly (down to 10°C [50°F]) and damp (as high as 90% humidity) in the winter. Only about 7.6 cm (3 in) of rain fall per year, always during the winter. In recorded history there has never been any rain during the months of June through September. The *shamal* is a wind from the southeast in the winter that brings damp air and occasional dust storms. In the summer, *gaws* blow from the southwest, bringing hot air and frequently blinding sandstorms. The climate has probably changed over time. In Sumerian times (4000 BC), the prevailing winds were most likely from the northeast, bringing more temperate weather.

There are no forests in Bahrain, and the plant life is restricted to date palms and desert plants. Wildlife includes desert rats, gazelles, mongooses, snakes, lizards, and rabbits. A large wildlife refuge at al-Andareen provides protected space for various exotic birds, gazelles, oryx, and ibex.

In 2006 the Bahraini population was estimated at about 727,000, with 63% Bahraini Arabs; 27% Pakistanis, Indians, and Iranians; 5% other Arabs; and 4% Europeans. The population is increasing rapidly, but as more women enter the workforce, the birth rate is expected to slow. Bahrain is a largely urban nation. A full 85% of Bahrainis live in cities, and only 15% live in rural areas. The largest city is Manama, the capital, with a population of more than 150,000. Muharraq is the second largest city with 75,000 people.

³ LANGUAGE

The official language of Bahrain is Arabic. English, introduced during the time Bahrain was a British-protected state (1820–1968), is also spoken by many Bahrainis. Farsi (Persian) is spoken by the Iranians in Bahrain. The Indian population speaks Hindi and the Pakistanis speak Urdu.

Arabic, spoken by 300 million people worldwide, is spoken in different dialects from country to country, and the same words may have different shades of meaning in different areas. Even within the small nation of Bahrain, the Arabic dialect used by the rural population sounds "uncultured" to urban Bahrainis. The written form of Arabic is called Classical Arabic or Modern Standard Arabic. It is the same for all literate Arabs, regardless of how different their spoken forms are. Arabic is written from right to left in a unique alphabet that has no distinction between upper and lower cases. It is not necessary for the letters to be written on a straight line, as English letters must be. Punctuation conventions are also quite different from English.

Arabic speakers tend to use emotional appeal, exaggeration, and repetition in their language. They are very interested in the poetry of the language. "Hello" in Arabic is *marhaba* or *ahlan*, to which one replies, *marhabtayn* or *ahlayn*. Other common greetings are *As-salam alaykum* ("Peace be with you"), with the reply of *Walaykum as-salam* ("and to you peace"). *Ma'assalama* means "goodbye." "Thank you" is *Shukran,* and "You're welcome" is *Afwan;* "yes" is *na'am,* and "no" is *la'a.* The numbers one to ten in Arabic are: *wahad, itnin, talata, arba'a, khamsa, sitta, saba'a, tamania, tisa'a,* and *ashara.*

Arabs have very long names, consisting of their first name, their father's name, their paternal grandfather's name, and finally their family name. Following Islamic tradition, women do not take their husband's name when they marry but rather keep their father's family name. Popular Arabic names include Mohammad, Abdullah, Hamad, and Ahmad for boys and Fatima, Laila, Hessa, and Shaima for girls. Because the majority of Bahraini Muslims are Shia, many are named for the great Shia Imams such as Ali and Husayn.

⁴ FOLKLORE

Bahrainis tell their children a popular legend that explains how the freshwater springs or wells bubble up from beneath the sea just off their shores. According to the story, falling stars knocked holes in the ground and Allah, the One God, cupped them up for his faithful followers to use. The ancient Sumerians (4000 BC) believed that the springs came from a freshwater sea that lay beneath the regular saltwater sea. This submarine sea was called *Abuz,* and it was ruled by a god known as *Abyss,* whom it was very important to please. In English, the word *abyss* has come to mean any bottomless depth. Geologists now believe the freshwater springs come from the Tuwaiq Mountains in Saudi Arabia—the water seeps through the porous layers of rock to flow towards Bahrain.

Pearls, long a source of wealth for the Bahrainis, have also inspired much folklore. Bahraini parents like to tell their children that pearls are created when a mermaid's tears fall into an open oyster shell. Certain "magic" pearls have supernatural powers, such as helping to find lost objects or to bind love (if a young woman rubs her eyes with a pearl, she can make a man her slave simply by gazing on him).

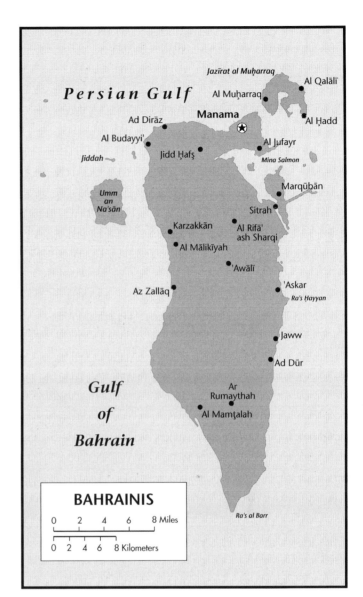

⁵ RELIGION

At least 94% of the Bahraini population is Muslim. About 70% of Bahrainis are Shia, and 24% Sunni. A small percentage (5%) of the population is Christian, and the remaining 1% is Hindu, Jewish, Baha'i, or other faiths. Although Sunni Muslims are numerically in the minority, they have been the dominant religious community in Bahrain since the 17th century or before. The royal family of Bahrain and the majority of its wealthy merchant class are Sunnis. This has created many conflicts between the majority Shia and the ruling Sunnis. Even among the Sunnis and Shia there are various groups who are not always in agreement with one another, so Bahrain is beset with constant religious conflicts.

Islam is one of the youngest of the world's main monotheistic religions, having only begun in the early 7th century AD when the prophet Muhammad received his revelations from Allah (which means "God" in Arabic). Muslims believe that Jews, Christians, and Muslims all worship the same God but by different names. Within just a few years of Muhammad's death in AD 632, Islam had spread through the entire Middle East. The Arab tribes were the first to convert.

Born into the Koreish tribe of Mecca (c. AD 570) in what is now Saudi Arabia, Muhammad was later driven from the city because of his outspoken denunciation of the pagan idols worshipped there (idols that attracted a lucrative pilgrim trade). The year of Muhammad's flight from Mecca, AD 622 (July 16), called the *Hegira*, is counted as Year One in the Muslim calendar. Muhammad fled to the city now known as Medina, another of the holy sites of modern-day Saudi Arabia. Eventually Muhammad returned to Mecca as a triumphant religious and political leader, destroyed the idols (saving the Black Stone, an ancient meteorite housed in the *Kaaba* [or Cube] building, which has become a focal point of Muslim worship), and established Mecca as the spiritual center of Islam. All prayers are said facing Mecca, and each Muslim is expected—and greatly desires—to make a pilgrimage there (called a *Haj* or *Hadj*) at least once in his or her lifetime. Islam is a simple, straightforward faith with clear rules for correct living. Religion, politics, faith, and culture are all linked together for Muslims.

The difference between Sunni and Shia Muslims, which has played an important role in Bahraini history, has to do with the early history of the religion. After the Prophet Muhammad's death, the entire Muslim community was divided over who should become the first political successor, or *caliph*. A strong minority believed that Ali, Muhammad's cousin and son-in-law, should be caliph. The rest accepted Abu Baker as the first caliph. Abu Baker assumed the caliphate and eventually obtained the allegiance of Ali.

Ali did not become caliph until after the death of Uthman, the third caliph. At that time, Mu'awiyah, the governor of Syria and a relative of Uthman, challenged Ali for the caliphate using Syrian troops personally loyal to him. The battles between the caliph and Mu'awiyah were inconclusive, and Ali remained in control over most areas except Greater Syria until his death. At that time, Mu'awiyah was able to defeat a number of challenges from Muslims of Muhammad's family and friends to firmly establish himself as caliph. He instituted a system of hereditary rule for his family, thus establishing the Umayyed dynasty. Those Muslims who refused to recognize the legitimacy of Mu'awiyah's caliphate and the Umayyed dynasty were called the followers of Ali, or *Shi'iat Ali*, while the supporters of the Umayyeds were known as *Shi'iat Uthman*. Eventually the followers of Ali became known as the Shia.

Although there are doctrinal differences, the fundamental difference between the sects is an argument about authority, not doctrine. The Shia believe that the successors of Muhammad should have come from his close family (or *Ahl al-Bayt*) and that Ali should have been the first caliph. The Sunnis believe that although Ali was justified in defending the caliphate from Mu'awiyah, once the Umayyeds took control it was more important to maintain political stability than to risk the chaos that might have resulted from a civil war. These political differences have developed into substantial theological differences over the centuries.

In present-day Bahrain, there is political tension between the Sunni ruling elites (including the royal family) and the majority Shia population. Many boycotted the 2002 parliamentary elections, and street demonstrations, which can turn violent, are common.

⁶ MAJOR HOLIDAYS

Secular holidays include New Year's Day on January 1 and National Day on December 16. Because 94% of Bahrainis are Muslim, their holidays are the official ones. Muslim holidays follow the lunar calendar, which moves back by 11 days each year, so their dates are not fixed on the standard Gregorian calendar. The main Muslim holidays are: *Ramadan*, the ninth month of the Muslim year, during which Muhammad received his first revelations, and which is celebrated by complete fasting from dawn until dusk each day of the entire month; *Ayd Al-Fitr*, a three-day festival at the end of *Ramadan*; *Ayd Al-Adha*, a three-day feast of sacrifice at the end of the month of pilgrimage to Mecca known as the *Haj* (families who can afford it slaughter a lamb and share the meat with poorer Muslims); the First of *Muharram*, or the Muslim New Year; *Mawoulid An-Nabawi*, the prophet Muhammad's birthday; and *Ayd Al-Isra wa Al-Miraj*, a feast celebrating the nocturnal visit of Muhammad to heaven. Friday is the Islamic day of rest, so most businesses and services are closed on Fridays. All government offices, private businesses, and schools are also closed during *Ayd Al-Fitr* and *Ayd Al-Adha*.

Ashura is only commemorated by Shia. It is a formal day of mourning marking the anniversary when Muhammad's grandson, Husayn, and a small band of loyal followers were massacred by Yazid, the son of Mu'awiyah, who was named caliph by the Umayyeds after Mu'awiyah's death. Yazid was almost universally despised by the Muslims for his impiety and oppression but maintained a strong army personally loyal to him. The massacre occurred at Karbala' in Iraq. The Muslims who had asked Husayn to oppose Yazid failed to show up at Karbala' to help him against Yazid's army. Today the holiday has political overtones as Shia cry and lament the failure of the Muslims to defend Muhammad's family and as they celebrate the bravery of Husayn in opposing an unjust ruler despite terrible odds.

⁷ RITES OF PASSAGE

Bahraini rites of passage are similar to those in other Arab and Islamic cultures. Marriage and family are the focus of most Bahrainis' lives. Typically, marriages are arranged, although young men and women are consulted about prospective partners and in most cases can refuse a potential spouse.

⁸ INTERPERSONAL RELATIONS

Arab hospitality reigns in Bahrain. An Arab will never ask personal questions, as that is considered rude. It is expected that a person will say what he or she wishes without being asked. Food and drink are always taken with the right hand, because the left hand is used for "unclean" purposes, such as cleaning oneself. When talking, Arabs touch each other much more frequently and stand much closer together than Westerners do. People of the same sex will often hold hands while talking, even if they are virtual strangers. Members of the opposite sex, however, even married couples, rarely touch in public. Arabs talk a lot, speaking loudly, repeating themselves often, and interrupting each other constantly. Conversations are highly emotional and full of gestures.

⁹ LIVING CONDITIONS

Bahrain has one of the highest standards of living in the Persian Gulf region. A rapidly increasing population is beginning to put a strain on housing and water supplies, however, raising the cost of living and causing poorer Bahrainis to live in substandard conditions. To help alleviate overcrowding in other cities, the government built a new town in the center of Bahrain Island called Madinat Hamad (Madinat is Arabic for " city" or " town" and Hamad is the name of the king who initiated the project). It encompasses 1,300 hectares (3,212 acres) of desert land, reaching 8 km (5 mi) from north to south and 2.5 km (1.5 mi) east to west. A road was built to connect Madinat Hamad to Manama and also gives access to the causeway linking the islands of Bahrain and Muharraq. After the first Gulf War (1990–91) many Kuwaiti refugees were resettled in Madinat Hamad. In 2001 the new city had a population of 126,000.

Bahrain's oil wealth has enabled the government to make many improvements in Bahrain's standard of living, including better health care, housing, and education. Technologically advanced medical care has led to the eradication of smallpox. There are government-subsidized medical facilities, as well as private ones. Bahrainis needing specialized care not available at home are flown abroad at the government's expense. The government also provides social security coverage for pensions, industrial accidents, illness, unemployment, maternity, and a family allowance.

Although there is no railway system in Bahrain, there are now 225 km (140 mi) of paved roads, which is more than adequate for such a small country. Bahrain also has one of the most modern communications systems in the world, with two communications satellites in space (the first launched in 1968, the second in 1980). A state-of-the-art international airport serves more than 3 million passengers per year, and Mina Salman, located east of the capital city of Manama, is one of the most modern and efficient ports in the Middle East. Members of the older generation can still remember making their own shoes—that is how quickly the "industrial revolution" has happened in Bahrain.

Traditionally, Bahraini homes were made from palm fronds, or *barasti*. Modern homes are made of cement and lime brick. Rooms are built around an inner courtyard, and houses are built vertically (rather than horizontally, like ranch houses) to catch the breezes that blow higher in the air. "Wind towers" on the upper floors of many houses and other buildings catch these breezes and funnel the air down to the lower floors through air shafts. The most prized furnishings in Bahraini households are handwoven rugs, either imported from Iran or locally crafted.

¹⁰ FAMILY LIFE

Bahraini women are more publicly active than in most other Arab countries. With the increase in higher education and paid employment for women, traditional women's roles are beginning to change. Fewer marriages are arranged by the couple's parents as more couples choose their own partners. The dowry or "bride-price" paid by the groom to the bride's family is disappearing. These changes are taking place only among the upper-middle and upper classes, however. Only those with sufficient money can afford to send their daughters for higher education, and only wealthy women can afford to hire domestic help so that they may work outside the home. The lower and lower-middle classes of Bahrain remain much more traditional.

The family is the center of life for Bahrainis. Family lineage is very important, extending out to the whole tribe. Bahrainis continue to be fiercely loyal to their tribes. Children live with their parents until they are married, and sometimes after marriage as well. Polygamy (up to four wives) is legal, but few men practice it. Divorce is fairly simple, for both men and women, but it rarely occurs.

¹¹ CLOTHING

Bahrainis have never been as conservative as many of their Saudi neighbors. Women were never as strict about covering themselves completely in public, and many modern Bahraini women no longer veil their faces at all. (Most do still choose to wear some sort of head covering and long sleeves.) Bahraini men wear a *thawb*, which is a long outer robe reaching from neck to ankles, made of white cotton, to keep them cool in the hot sun. They also wear a *ghutra*, a large rectangular piece of material draped over the head and held in place with an *agal*, a thick, black woven band. This headscarf protects them from the sun as well as from sandstorms (it can quickly be drawn across the face).

Western-style clothing is becoming more popular in the larger cities of Bahrain. The large numbers of expatriate workers normally dress as they do in their homelands, so it is a common sight in Bahrain to see, for example, cinema lines containing women in black abayas, Indians in saris, Pakistanis in shalwars, and Westerners in jeans and t-shirts.

¹² FOOD

Meals are taken very seriously by Bahrainis. All talking is done during the hour or so before sitting down to eat; there is no conversation during dinner. After the meal, coffee is served, and then any guests leave. Coffee is also always served as a welcome to guests when they first arrive. It is most often drunk unsweetened and flavored with cardamom. Fresh vegetables, lamb, fish, chicken, and beef are common foods. (Pork is forbidden by Islam, as is alcohol.)

Meals always include a dish made with basmati rice. *Khoubz* is the name of the local flatbread, and *samouli* is a white bread (like French bread) that is glazed with water or egg and then sprinkled with salt or sesame or caraway seeds.

One of the most popular dishes is *ghouzi*, which was developed by the Bedu (or Bedouin) nomadic Arabs (*see* Bedu). A lamb is slaughtered and left whole, and then a chicken stuffed with rice, nuts, onions, spices, and shelled hard-boiled eggs is placed inside the lamb. The lamb is sewn up, trussed, and cooked on a spit. To serve ghouzi, the chicken and stuffing are removed and arranged around the lamb. Diners break off chunks of meat with their right hands (the meat is not carved).

Date groves, fruit orchards, and vegetable gardens are located along the well-watered northern and northwestern coasts of Bahrain island. Bananas, citrus fruits, pomegranates, and mangoes are grown there, along with dates and other produce.

Bahrainis love desserts, and they love dates. Here is a recipe that combines both:

Bahraini women in Manama wear traditional dress to celebrate the last day of Ayd Al-Fitr, which ends the Muslim holy month of Ramadan. (AP Images/Mohamed El-Dakhakhny)

Date Bars

1 cup rolled oats, plain or instant
1 cup melted butter or margarine
½ cup all-purpose flour
2 eggs, well beaten
½ teaspoon baking powder
1 cup finely chopped pitted dates
½ cup dark brown sugar
1 cup chopped nuts (walnuts, peanuts, or pecans)
½ teaspoon salt
½ cup confectioner's sugar for garnish
1 teaspoon cinnamon

Preheat oven to 350°F. Grease 8-inch-square baking pan. Put oats, flour, baking powder, brown sugar, salt, and cinnamon in large mixing bowl and mix well. Add butter or margarine, eggs, dates, and nuts, and mix well using clean hands. Put mixture into greased baking pan and bake in oven for about 35 minutes, until firm. Remove from oven and cut while still warm into 1½-inch squares. Sprinkle with confectioner's sugar. Makes 16 date bars.

[Adapted from Albyn and Webb, *The Multicultural Cookbook for Students*, p. 73]

¹³ EDUCATION

Bahrain has had the highest literacy rate in the Arab world for decades. More than 90% of Bahrainis are literate. The public school system was established in the early years of the 20th century. The first school for boys in the Persian Gulf region, the Hadiyya al-Khalifiya school, was opened in Bahrain in 1919. The first school for girls in Bahrain opened in 1929. Education is compulsory and free for all children. Government primary and secondary education facilities are still segregated by sex, but the education received by boys and girls is comparable. Private institutions have mixed gender classrooms. Primary education runs from the age of 6 to the age of 11. Almost 100% of Bahraini children attend primary school. Secondary education lasts from age 12 to age 17. The University of Bahrain and the College of Health Sciences are two of the older universities in Bahrain. Foreign universities from the west have branch campuses in Bahrain, as they do in many other Gulf countries. The New York Institute of Technology, for example, has a campus in Manama.

¹⁴ CULTURAL HERITAGE

Bahrain has a well-established artistic community, including some of the most respected writers in the Persian Gulf region. Ibrahim al-'Urayyid and Ahmad Muhammad Al Khalifah write lyrical poetry about heroes and romance in the classical Arab style. Younger poets have developed a more Westernized style, writing non-rhyming poems on personal and political subjects. Qasim Haddad (b.1948) is the best-known contemporary Bahraini poet. He has published several collections of poetry, including *The Good Omen* (1970), *Doomsday* (1980), and *Shrapnel* (1983). Hamdah Khamis (b.1946) is a journalist and a contemporary poet. Her collection of poetry, published in 1978, is called *An Apology for Childhood*.

Arab music is much like the Arab language—rich, repetitive, and exaggerated. The *oud* is a popular instrument; it is an ancient stringed instrument that is the ancestor of the European lute. Another traditional instrument is the *rebaba*, a one-stringed instrument. A traditional Arab dance is the *ardha*, or men's sword dance. Men carrying swords stand shoulder to shoulder, and from among them a poet sings verses while drummers beat out a rhythm.

Islam forbids the depiction of the human form, so Bahraini art focuses on geometric and abstract shapes. Calligraphy is a sacred art, with the Quran being the primary subject matter. Muslim art finds its greatest expression in mosques.

¹⁵ WORK

The pearl trade was the big money-maker for Bahrain until the Japanese introduced cultured pearls in the 1930s. Before that, divers would go down to depths of 30 to 120 ft, with just a nose clip and earplugs, to collect oysters. The best divers could hold their breath for up to two minutes. It was a dangerous trade for the divers, and not a lucrative one. Although profits were supposed to be shared by all on the pearl boat, the captains kept the largest share and gave the divers a minimal share, not even enough to repay their captain for the cost of food and expenses he had advanced to them. In this way, pearl divers were kept in virtual slavery by debts that were passed down through the generations.

Since 1931, oil has been a major industry in Bahrain, as well as natural gas. Although small in comparison to other oil-producing nations in the region, the income from oil and natural gas has paid more than 70% of the Bahraini government's expenses in the past few decades. Unfortunately, Bahrain's oil reserves are quickly being depleted. Its offshore natural gas reserves are somewhat more plentiful, but still small in comparison to major producers in the area, in particular Qatar. Therefore, the government is attempting to diversify the industrial sector to prepare for the depletion of the oil and gas reserves. Bahrain has developed state-of-the-art technology for petrochemical plants and oil refineries that it will be able to sell to other oil-producing nations. It has also begun manufacturing plastics and producing aluminum.

International offshore banking has also become one of Bahrain's mainstays, in these days of large economic transactions. Like Dubai in the United Arab Emirates and Qatar, Bahrain has become an important banking center in the region. Many international financial institutions have set up offices in the kingdom. A stock exchange was opened in 1989.

Shipbuilding has long been a respected trade in Bahrain. Some of the shipbuilders of today can trace their lineage back through many generations, with skills passed down from father to son. Bahrain currently constructs everything from huge, industrial oil tankers to small wooden *dhows*, which are built in the same style that has been used since ancient times (with motors added today).

Because of the desert climate, there is not much farming in Bahrain, but fishing is a significant industry. Bahrain is known for its fist-sized shrimp.

16 SPORTS

Football (known as soccer in the United States) is the national sport of Bahrain. It was introduced during the time when Bahrain was a British-protected state (1820–1968). Other popular modern sports include tennis, water sports, and dune-buggy racing. Ancient sports that are still greatly enjoyed are horse-racing and -breeding (the famous Arabian horses, probably the oldest domesticated breed, date from 1500 BC or before), camel-racing, and falconry. Falconry is a sport for the rich because birds are very expensive; a well-trained falcon can cost up to $15,000.

Bahrain has hosted a Formula One race, the Bahrain Grand Prix, since 2004. It was the first Formula One Grand Prix in the Middle East.

17 ENTERTAINMENT AND RECREATION

Camping is perhaps the favorite Bahraini family recreation. Men spend a great deal of time in coffeehouses, drinking tea and chatting. Educated and upper class women also congregate in coffee shops in upscale districts. There are many cinemas in Manama and they provide an important cultural gathering point. On weekends, Saudis drive across the causeway and fill the cinemas (movie houses are banned in Saudi Arabia), creating a lively, energetic atmosphere. Restaurants in malls are filled on weekends with young people from the upper classes, who have time and money to spare. Because of the intense heat in Bahrain, people spend a lot of time in their air conditioned cars and many young people spend their free time simply driving around and listening to the latest Arabic pop music.

18 FOLK ART, CRAFTS, AND HOBBIES

The government supports traditional arts with generous subsidies. Bahrain is known for its elaborate and uniquely designed coffee servers. Metalworking is an ancient traditions in Bahrain, as are ceramics and basket-weaving. Folk music is popular and the traditional music of the pearl divers, called fijeri, is widely performed. Bahrain is home to an important Islamic museum, the Beit al Quran (the House of the Quran). It has a large collection of Islamic holy books, some dating to the 8th century.

19 SOCIAL PROBLEMS

The rapidly increasing population has put a tremendous strain on Bahrain's water supply. In 1968 daily consumption of water was less than 4 million gallons; by 1982, consumption had risen to over 30.4 million gallons per day. Freshwater sources are unable to provide for the increasing demand and by 2005, three-fifths of Bahrain's water supply was from desalinization plants. These plants, powered primarily with natural gas, are a great cost to the country and also cause significant environmental stresses. They contribute to global warming by burning fossil fuels and they alter the salinity of the Persian Gulf.

The increase in population has also put housing at a premium, driving the cost of living up. With the focus on new home construction, old homes are not given the attention or repairs they need and are becoming run-down and dilapidated. Many Bahrainis, therefore, are forced to live in overcrowded, substandard conditions.

Bahrain has experienced serious challenges to its ruling regime stemming from the lack of full democracy and from sectarian tensions. Although the new constitution did create a democratically elected chamber in parliament, the king retains the most power both through executive powers left to him in the constitution and by his power to appoint all the members of the Consultative Council. The politically and economically marginalized Shia majority regularly engages in street demonstrations and other forms of political protest, but the government typically responds with force. Some Shia look to predominantly Shia Iran for political inspiration, and this also causes great fear in Bahrain, a tiny island not too many miles distant from large, militarily powerful Iran. The United States maintains an enormous naval presence on the Island, and this also has caused social strains. This tension has increased since the U.S.-led War on Terror led to war in neighboring Shia-majority Iraq.

20 GENDER ISSUES

The status of Bahraini women is better than in some Islamic societies, but remains far behind the rights and privileges typical in Western countries. Women have the right to vote and to stand for political office (in 2007 there were two female cabinet ministers), but the Bahraini judicial system is based on Islamic (Sharia) law and women therefore face obstacles in obtaining divorces and in securing custody of their children after being divorced. A major problem is the lack of a personal status system of laws that would ensure some degree of rights to women. In the absence of such a system, legal matters are left to the discretion of judges who are free to interpret Islamic law and issue rulings. The judiciary is made up of conservative, religious men.

²¹ BIBLIOGRAPHY

Albyn, Carole Lisa, and Lois Sinaiko Webb. *The Multicultural Cookbook for Students*. Phoenix, AZ: Oryx Press, 1993.

Cooper, Robert. Bahrain: Cultures of the World. New York: Benchmark Books, 2000.

Cordesman, Anthony. Bahrain, Oman, Qatar, and the UAE: Challenges of Security. Boulder, CO. Westview Press, 1997.

Fox, Mary Virginia. *Enchantment of the World: Bahrain*. Chicago: Childrens Press, 1992.

Lawson, Fred H. *Bahrain: The Modernization of Autocracy*. Boulder, CO: Westview Press, 1989.

Sluglett, Peter, and Marion Farouk-Sluglett. *Tuttle Guide to the Middle East*. Boston: Charles E. Tuttle Co., 1992.

Wheatcroft, Andrew. *Bahrain in Original Photographs, 1880–1961*. London and New York: Kegan Paul International, 1988.

Winkler, David F. *Amirs, Admirals, and Desert Sailors: Bahrain, the US Navy and the Arabian Gulf*. Annapolis, MD. U.S. Naval Institute Press, 2007.

—revised by J. Henry;

BAI

PRONUNCIATION: BYE
ALTERNATE NAMES: Bo
LOCATION: China
POPULATION: 1.6 million
LANGUAGE: Bai; Chinese
RELIGION: Polytheism; some combinations of Buddhism and indigenous beliefs
RELATED ARTICLES: Vol. 3 : China and Her National Minorities

¹INTRODUCTION

The ancestors of the Bai people were called Bo and were descendants of the ancient Qiang (Tibeto-Burman group), who lived around present-day Sichuan more than 2,000 years ago. After unifying China, the Qin Dynasty (221–206 BC) planned to carve out a way to India through the area inhabited by the Bo. For this reason the Bo gradually migrated to Yunnan and joined the other Bo already living there. In 109 BC, the King of Yunnan pledged allegiance to the Han Dynasty (206 BC–AD 220), placing the Bo under the latter's authority. From the 1st century AD the Bo oscillated between submission and rebellion. Gradually the Chinese character that was in ancient times pronounced "Bo" came to be pronounced "Bai," both pronunciations meaning "white." This is an example of the different pronunciations of the same character in north (Bai) and south (Bo) China.

In the 8th century, following the unification of six small principalities, the powerful kingdom of Nanzhao was established with Dali (in northwest Yunnan) as its capital and ruled Yunnan for 247 years. Ten of the 13 successive kings received titles granted by the Tang Dynasty (618–907). Later, Nanzhao was replaced by Dali, which acknowledged allegiance to the Song Dynasty (960–1279) and ruled Yunnan for more than 300 years. In 1253, the Mongolian aristocrats conquered Dali. Before long, the Yuan Dynasty (1271–1368) set up a system appointing Bai headmen under the jurisdiction of the former royal court of the Dali Kingdom. In the following centuries, hundreds of thousands of Chinese, Mongolians, and Manchus moved from the central provinces into the areas of Yunnan inhabited by the Bai. There was much cross-cultural exchange and intermarriage. Chinese culture exerted a strong influence on the Bai.

²LOCATION AND HOMELAND

Today over 80% of the Bai live in the Dali Bai Autonomous Prefecture. There are small communities dispersed in other counties of the Yunnan Province. Bai are also found in Sichuan and Hunan. Two rivers, Lancang and Nu, flow south through the Dali prefecture, which is located in the Yunnan-Guizhou Plateau. The deep river valleys are thickly forested. The snow-capped Cang Mountain and limpid Er'hai Lake in the suburbs of Dali inspired many beautiful legends of the Bai people. The Bai population was 1.86 million in 2000.

³LANGUAGE

Bai is classified as belonging to the Sino-Tibetan family in the Tibeto-Burman group of languages. In 1990, it was estimated that 900,000 people speak Bai. Scholars still debate the exact place of Bai as a branch of the Tibeto-Burman group. There are three Bai dialects. Bai is a self-given name. Most of the Bai speak Chinese.

⁴FOLKLORE

Bai myths are usually long and complex. Most of them are related to daily life, love, and religious beliefs. A famous one, called "Husband-expecting Cloud" was transformed into a dance drama and a Bai opera. In short, a princess of Nanzhao Kingdom fell in love with a young hunter. They escaped to Cang Mountain and married in a cavern. During a snowstorm, the hunter left the cavern to find a suit of thick clothes for his chilled wife. Unfortunately, he was discovered by a Buddhist priest of the royal court. The priest turned the hunter into a stone mule, which was sunk into the Er'hai Lake. Dying from cold and hunger, the princess transformed herself into a cloud. If it suddenly appeared around the peak of Cang Mountain in winter, the stone mule in the deep water always cried in response. Then a strong gale blew abruptly, the water split, and the stone mule appeared in an awe-inspiring manner.

⁵RELIGION

The Bai are polytheistic, believing in many gods. Each village enshrines and worships a certain god as the master and protector of the village. The villagers carve an idol made of wood or clay and put it in the temple. Most of the masters are famous personages of the kingdoms of Nanzhao or Dali. Some are part of their respective myths, while others are gods related to agriculture. After the 9th century, Buddhism became prevalent in areas around Er'hai Lake. The three Buddhist temple pagodas at the foot of Cang Mountain date from the Tang Dynasty. The stone relief sculpture of the Buddha and of the Kings of Nanzhao in the grottoes of Shibao Mountain are a combination of Buddhism and of Bai traditional belief in the Master God.

The Bai revere conch and fish. The Bai believe in the Fish God: whenever a fisherman catches a big fish, he puts it back in the water at once and prays while burning incense.

⁶MAJOR HOLIDAYS

The Spring Festival extends from the last day of the old year to January 15 (lunar calendar; Western calendar, from February 6 to March 6) during the slack season. Each family cleans the house and prepares fine dishes for the holidays. A great variety of recreational activities are held, such as the Lion Dance, the Dragon Lantern Festival, walking on stilts, flying kites, playing the "tossing the silk ball" game, etc. Some villages devote most of the holiday to "meeting the Master."

The Third Month Fair is a grand festival of the Bai, held March 15 to 21 (lunar calendar; Western calendar, from April 6–12 to May 4–10). It has a history of more than 1,000 years. On the occasion, the endless array of native products and the dazzling articles of daily use are exhibited on the streets and squares. The number of participants may reach hundreds of thousands, including various neighboring nationalities.

The "Memorial Ceremony for the Dead" in February, the "Torch Festival," the "Rao San Ling," and the "Yu Tan Hui" are also distinctive and colorful festivals celebrated in the areas inhabited by the Bai.

⁷RITES OF PASSAGE

Gifts are important on the birth of a child, the engagement of two young people, and the birthday of a senior person. On these occasions, money or items that come in sixes are always welcome. For instance, a gift of 160 *yuan* (Chinese currency) will be gladly received, while 500 *yuan* might be refused. The reason for the prominence of the number "six" is that the Bai are descendants of six tribes. When, in the past, their king presented gifts to the Emperor of imperial Tang, each tribe prepared a gift of its own—altogether six. The gifts from the Emperor in return were also six and each tribe took one gift as its own. Moreover, in Bai language, the pronunciation of "six" is the same as that of "enough" or "handsome salary," so six is an auspicious number.

A rite of "seeing off the soul" is held after the death of a senior person. In the eyes of the Bai, the soul will come back to its native house again and again. Therefore, on the first, third, seventh, thirtieth, and hundredth day after death, family, relatives, and friends perform the rite of "seeing off the soul." On the occasion, the family will receive relatives or neighbors to dinner. It is believed that after the last ritual performance, the soul will definitely go to the "other side" to unite with the ancestors.

⁸INTERPERSONAL RELATIONS

In addition to public festivals, every happy event of the family or clan is an occasion to pay a congratulatory visit. Gifts are absolutely necessary. When they are about to leave, guests usually receive a gift in return from the host.

Young people used to express their feelings for the opposite sex by blowing on a tree leaf. The addressee tried to understand the meaning from the melody and the tune. This is a rather indirect method of courtship as compared with the antiphonal singing prevalent among neighboring ethnic groups.

⁹LIVING CONDITIONS

Most Bai houses are two-story, made of wood and bricks (or adobes), usually roofed with tiles. The walls on two sides are often higher than the roof; this is to keep fire from spreading. The house is oriented toward the east. The family lives downstairs; the central room is for daily life and receptions. Rooms upstairs are for storage. In some areas, wooden houses on stilts still exist; in that case, pigs and chickens are kept on the ground floor, while the family lives on the second floor. Bai dwelling in mountainous areas have thatched-roof cottages; the family sleeps in the firepool room. Bai inhabiting the plains and valleys have a much higher standard of living than mountain-dwellers. Bai cities and towns have flourished since 1949. Many endemic (sometimes epidemic) diseases, such as schistosomiasis (a parasitic disease carried by certain types of snails) have been practically eliminated after years of treatment.

¹⁰FAMILY LIFE

Bai family is patrilineal (traced through the fathers), with two generations usually living under the same roof. Parents live with the youngest son, because the older ones leave the house after marriage. A son-in-law is allowed to live with his wife's parents if they lack a son. Childless families are allowed to adopt a child from brothers of the same clan. In those cases, the names of the son-in-law and the adopted son should be

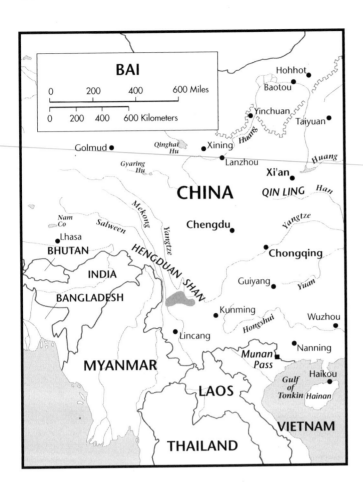

changed to the family's surname; otherwise, they do not have the right of inheritance. Bai families are monogamous, but there exist cases of polygamy. The position of women is socially lower than that of men. People with the same surname or of the same clan are not allowed to marry. The marriage of cousins, however, is prevalent. Arranged marriage is common, although "love marriages" are increasing. Betrothal gifts are usually expensive.

11 CLOTHING

Men wear multi-buttoned Chinese-style upper garments in white or blue, sometimes with a vest, and long white trousers. They wrap their heads with white or blue cloth and carry a decorated bag over the back of the shoulder. Most women wear white tops with a black or purple velvet vest and loose trousers in blue. A short apron with embroidered ribbons is fastened to the waist. A string of silver ornaments is hung on the right of the garment. Unmarried girls have a braid on their back or coil the braid on the top of the head. Married women comb their hair into a bun, which they wrap with an embroidered or printed scarf with the tassels hung over one side of the head. Some of them put together the four angles of the scarf on the back of the head, then fix them with string. They are fond of embroidered shoes. Their costumes for special occasions are not much different from their daily dress. Various ornaments are put on during the festival.

12 FOOD

Rice and flour are the staple foods of the Bai. Mountain dwellers live on corn and buckwheat. All have a liking for sour, cool, and spicy dishes, as well as for a medium roast pork, which is shredded and seasoned. They are good at making salted fish, ham, and snail sauce. Baked tea is a distinctly favorite dish. As a rule, they take three meals a day.

13 EDUCATION

There are primary schools, middle schools (junior and senior), and universities in Bai villages, counties, and cities respectively. Illiteracy, however, is still prevalent in the rural areas. The intensive manual labor in the fields often requires the participation of the children. As a result, many girls are usually obliged to drop out of primary or middle school. The overall cultural and educational level of the Bai is higher than the average for national minorities, but it is still below the average for the whole country.

14 CULTURAL HERITAGE

The "Bai Melody" is a kind of national folk song. Although slightly different in various Bai districts, it is always a poem with five or seven characters to a line, accompanied by three stringed instruments (sometimes the opening bars are accompanied by a woodwind instrument). It is part of every important Bai festival.

Bai opera, as a combination of music, song, and dance, developed under the influence of Chinese models. The famous Lion Dance, however, was borrowed from the Bai by the Chinese during the Tang Dynasty. The works of Bai poets of Nanzhao Kingdom were included in the great Chinese poetry anthology called *Quan Tang Shi* (Complete poetry of the Tang).

15 WORK

Bai economy rests principally on rice culture, complemented by barley, wheat, millet, and beans. Fruit growing, stock raising, and fishing on Lake Er'hai provide important sideline economic activities. Bai workers, with heavy slabs of marble on their backs, descend from a quarry in the Cang Mountain, just as their ancestors did 1,000 years ago; but, the processing of the slabs is now carried out with mechanical devices by Bai factory workers. The fine texture and natural designs have made Dali marble famous for more than 2,000 years and continues to inspire craftsmen in carving ingenious landscape scenes. Dali horses and knives carved by Bai artists are also much sought after by connoisseurs.

16 SPORTS

"Tossing the silk ball" and "rattle stick dance" are traditional popular Bai sports and spectator sports as well. The game of "tossing the silk ball" is usually played on festivals. The ball is actually a small bag padded with cottonseed or rice husk, ½ to 1 lb in weight, and variable in size. Two teams, one of boys and one of girls, oppose each other, but are separated by a mat shelter. A member of one team tosses the ball over the top of the mat shelter; the ball should be caught by a member of the receiving team. If the ball is missed, a negative mark will be recorded. This game offers the occasion for boys and girls to meet and get acquainted socially.

The rattle stick is a 3 ft bamboo stick, thicker than one's thumb. There are nine openings on the shaft, each of which is pierced by a bamboo nail. Two-holed copper coins are hung on each bamboo nail. Each player taps his or her own shoulders, arms, knees, and feet with the rattle stick while dancing, jumping, marching, or squatting, but without letting the coins drop from the stick. The one who loses the least coins is the winner.

17 ENTERTAINMENT AND RECREATION

The Bai people have complete access to movies, television, and other recreational equipment in their cities and towns, especially in Dali. More traditional forms of entertainment are mainly singing and dancing. Singing contests are held around Mount Wudiao in the fall of each year. Torches are kindled. The rising and falling sounds of songs fill the night like waves. Young boys and girls in Jianchuan, north of Dali, sing all night long in antiphonal style, accompanied by three-string instruments. When the busy season of transplanting rice shoots is finished, the Bai people have a festive dinner party in the temple of the Master. They dress as fishermen, woodcutters, peasants and scholars, participate in the procession of the "rattling stick dance," and tour their village for fun.

18 FOLK ART, CRAFTS, AND HOBBIES

The artistic sense of the Bai is exemplified in their lacquerware and wood carvings, for which they are famous. More than 1,000 years ago, their lacquerware entered China proper. The lacquerers chosen by the central government of the Yuan and Ming dynasties were all Bai artists. The Bai also excel at wood carving, as may be seen in the exquisite birds, flowers, and personages carved on the doors and windows of Jizushan Buddhist Monastery. The continuation of their skills in all kinds of wood carving can be also found in present-day private house decorations.

19 SOCIAL PROBLEMS

The economic cleavage of Bai society is quite prominent. On the one hand, urban Bai have a markedly improved living standard, especially in recent decades; on the other hand, mountain-dwellers still live in abject poverty. There is no easy solution to this problem, which is not specific to the Bai, but it is shared by every nationality whose people are divided into urbanites, valley dwellers, and mountain dwellers.

20 GENDER ISSUES

The Chinese constitution states that women have equal rights with men in all areas of life, and most legislation is gender neutral. However, there are continued reports of discrimination, sexual harassment, wage discrepancies, and other gender related problems. The gap in educational level between women and men is narrowing with women making up 47.1% of college students in 2005, but only 32.6% of doctoral students. China has strict family planning laws, and it is illegal for women to marry before 20 years of age (22 for men) and it is illegal for single women to give birth. The Family Planning Bureau can require women to take periodic pregnancy tests, and enforce laws that often leave women with no real options other than abortion or sterilization. Prostitution and the sex trade is a significant problem in China involving between 1.7 and five million women. It involved organized crime, businessmen, the

Bai women in traditional dress.
(© Steven Vidler/Eurasia Press/Corbis)

police and government workers, and as a result prosecution against prostitution has limited success. In 2002, the nation removed homosexuality from its official list of mental illnesses, and though it is still a taboo topic, homosexuality is increasingly accepted, especially in large, international cities.

21 BIBLIOGRAPHY

Chiao, Chien, Nicholas Tapp, and Kam-yin Ho, ed. "Special Issue on Ethnic Groups in China." *New Asia Bulletin* no 8 (1989).

Dreyer, June Teufel. *China's Forty Millions.* Cambridge, MA: Harvard University Press, 1976.

Eberhard, Wolfram. *China's Minorities: Yesterday and Today.* Belmont: Wadsworth Publishing Company, 1982.

Heberer, Thomas. *China and Its National Minorities: Autonomy or Assimilation?* Armonk, NY: M. E. Sharpe, 1989.

Lebar, Frank, et al. *Ethnic Groups of Mainland Southeast Asia.* New Haven: Human Relations Area Files Press, 1964.

Lemoine, Jacques. "Les Pai." In *Ethnologie régionale II* (Encyclopédie de la Pléiade). Paris: Gallimard, 1978.

Ma Yin, ed. *China's Minority Nationalities.* Beijing: Foreign Languages Press, 1989.

Miller, Lucien, ed. *South of the Clouds: Tales from Yunnan.* Seattle: University of Washington Press, 1994.

Ramsey, S. Robert. *The Languages of China.* Princeton: Princeton University Press, 1987.

Wiens, Harold J. *Han Chinese Expansion in South China.* New Haven: The Shoestring Press, 1967.

—by C. Le Blanc

BAJAU

PRONUNCIATION: BAH-jau (Indonesian pronunciation) or bah-JOW (Philippine pronunciation)
ALTERNATE NAMES: Badjao (Philippine spelling), "Sea Gypsies"
LOCATION: Philippines (Sulu Archipelago), Malaysia, Indonesia
POPULATION: Over 200,000
LANGUAGE: Samal
RELIGION: Islam; indigenous beliefs
RELATED ARTICLES: Vol. 3: Filipinos; Vol 4: Tausug

¹INTRODUCTION

The Bajau (or Badjao) of the Sulu Archipelago are one of several groups of Sea Nomads who not only make their living from the region's waters but also spend most of their lives on them. Little used in Sulu itself, the name "Bajau" seems to derive from the Wajo kingdom of the Bugis, who have had a long history of association with Sea Nomads. The Bajau of southern Philippine waters, however, were claimed as vassals by the Sulu sultanate of the Tausug people, rivals of the Bugis. Traditionally, Tausug *datus* extended their protection to particular Bajau groups in exchange for various services, such as delivering tribute in dried fish. Stressing a common origin with the land-dwelling Samal peoples of the archipelago, such as the Yakan and the Jama Mapun, the Sulu Bajau call themselves *Sama Laut,* or *Sama Mandelaut* (Sea Samal).

The term "Sea Gypsies" popularly applied to the Bajau is apt insofar as it reflects their position as outcasts within the wider Sulu society. Although it was Samal peoples, such as the Balangingi, who carried out (as clients of Tausug, Bugis, and Malay aristocrats) most of the piracy and slave-raiding that plagued Southeast Asian waters until the late 19th century, the Bajau themselves are a peaceable people whose response to exploitation or victimization by non-Bajau has been to take flight. Despising Bajau nomadism, passivity, and paganism, neighboring peoples refer to them with derogatory names, such as the Tausug *Luwa'an* ("that which has been spat out") and *kuto dagat* ("lice of the sea").

Occupied with the more assertive Tausugs, Spanish, American, and still to some extent Filipino governments have left the small numbers of Bajau largely to themselves. Over the last century, Bajau have more and more been abandoning the boat-dwelling life for a more sedentary one on land, as well as dropping animistic practices for a more orthodox Islam; these trends are reducing their distinctiveness from the other peoples of the Sulu archipelago. Devastated by the Moro separatist conflict, Tawi-Tawi province (where Samal peoples predominate) was separated from Sulu province in 1973 and was one of the four provinces that formed the Autonomous Region in Muslim Mindanao in 1989. Samal remain wary of reassertion of Tausug dominance, even to the extent of more readily identifying themselves as Filipino rather than Moro and on insisting on addressing Tausug in English rather than in Tausug as they can and the Tausug expect. In recent years, Muslims (commonly referred to as Badjao) have become highly visible in Manila, often as peddlers of pirated DVDs.

²LOCATION AND HOMELAND

The Bajau communities, collections of either houseboats or houses raised above the water, lie mainly in a zone stretching from Zamboanga Bay through the Sulu archipelago to Semporna on the Sabah coast; the islands within this region are dominated, however, by non-Bajau. Other more distantly related Bajau communities can be found on or off the shores of eastern Kalimantan; northern, western, and southern Sulawesi; Flores; and Sumbawa; as well as the Togian, Bangga, and Sula island groups.

In the early 1970s, the Sulu Bajau numbered perhaps 20,000. In 2000, there were 13,180 Badjao and 49,000 Samal in Sulu province, while in Tawi-Tawi province a number of Samal groups were distinguished (Sama Dilaya, 115,400; Sama Abakon, 49,000; and Jama Mapun, 18,800). Among the Samal (including those outside Tawi-Tawi province), various dialect-groups are also identified (2000 figures): Jama Mapun, 40,600; Central Samal, 90,000; Southern Samal, 120,000). The largest group on Basilan island (35.8% of the population), the Yakan, speak a Sama-type language. About 6.37% of households in the Autonomous Region in Muslim Mindanao identified Samal (Sama/Abakon) as their first language (that could mean as many as 125,000 people). Bajau in Malaysian Sabah numbered 40,000 in 1980 and in eastern Indonesia 90,000 in 2000 (cf. early 1970s estimate of 10,000–15,000).

Sea Nomads can also be found in a zone stretching from the east Sumatra coast and the islands off it, up along the shores of the Malay peninsula as far as southern Thailand and beyond to Burma's Mergui archipelago. Generally known as *Orang Laut* (Sea People), the groups there are often called "Bajau," though their relation to the Sulu Bajau is unclear as they do not (at least presently) speak Samal but rather a dialect of Malay close to that of the land-dwelling Kubu.

³LANGUAGE

The Bajau speak a single, largely homogeneous dialect of Samal. The Samal languages are Austronesian but form a group distinct from Tausug (a Visayan language) and the languages of mainland Mindanao and Borneo.

⁴FOLKLORE

The Bajau believe in a variety of supernaturals *(saitan),* e.g., *pangguah* (ghosts), *umagad* (spirits), *balbalan* (vampires), and *ah-ah inggai tandah mata* (sorcerers).

They are careful not to trespass on the territory of *tungguh* (watcher), guardians of both animate and inanimate objects, who live in areas such as clumps of mangrove trees. If a family fishes in a particular area without asking permission of the tungguh, a member may suffer punishment, such as stomach pains. One appeases the tungguh by leaving offerings of betel or cigarettes or by placing small green or white flags at the spot. Such pennants also mark the roofs of the houses of village headmen who have the favor of an *ombolh,* an illness-curing spirit; in the corner of such a house is a *bangku,* the ombolh's place, including a bed and a trunk holding a multicolored piece of cloth donated by the community.

Saitan also take the form of animals or fish, invading villages and spreading disease. Rites to combat epidemics include the launching of a spirit boat; thanksgiving celebrations require seven nights of dancing *(igal)* to entertain the ombolh.

⁵RELIGION

Most Bajau consider themselves Muslim, although they rarely perform the daily prayers, nor do their communities usually have mosques. Neighboring Muslim peoples look down on them as pagans. Nonetheless, *imam,* and older men with some knowledge of scriptures, lead prayer during ceremonial occasions and oversee life-crisis rituals.

Among the Bajau, mediums, both male and female, commune with spirits through dreams and trances in order to affect cures and predict the future. Several times a year, mediums renew their relations with their supernatural patrons in a nightlong public dance, a rite benefiting the entire community. Once a year, a village's women and children bathe in the sea to fortify themselves against spirits.

To cure an ill person, members of his or her *pagmundah* (a group of boats traveling together) gather at his or her houseboat while a knowledgeable person leads a curing ritual, burning incense to call the spirits and making food offerings to them. In case of serious illness, relatives swear to hold a *magtimbang* ceremony. The recovered individual is put into a sling hanging at one end of an improvised scale. At the other end are placed goods (bananas, sugarcane, and firewood) equal to his or her weight, which, after the scale is rotated several times while chanting, are distributed to those attending the ceremony.

Another important rite is thanking Omboh Dilaut, the Lord of the Sea, after a bountiful catch; one drops a plate, bowl, or saucer into the part of the sea where the fish were caught so the spirit will not be angry and will provide more fish in the future.

The college-educated among the Samal are those who tend to be the most interested in Islam. Many have been attracted to the teachings of the Ahmadi sect, which has been considered heretical by many Muslims worldwide for recognizing a prophet after Muhammad, the late 19th century Indian figure, Mirza Ghulam Ahmad. However, in Tawi-Tawi, ahmadi generally means anyone who questions traditions.

⁶MAJOR HOLIDAYS

The Bajau observe the Muslim festivals, but seldom fast for Ramadan. In July or August, a *dakampungan* celebrates the *maggomboh* to avert disaster in the coming year. Each family obtains rice and places it in a special basket that they put at one end of the boat; everyone sleeps with their heads towards the basket. The next day the rice is cooked and formed into a cone. The families bring these cones to a central houseboat. A medium invites the spirits to partake of the rice, then takes some rice from each cone and mixes the handfuls in a common bowl for all the children of the dakampungan to eat. After this, the families take the cones home to consume with the next meal.

⁷RITES OF PASSAGE

All infant girls undergo a first ear-piercing rite, accompanied by the chanting of an old man. Circumcision for boys can be a very simple ceremony, although wealthier families host elaborate celebrations, decorating the houseboat and making merry with music and dancing on the reef top or beach throughout the afternoon and evening.

For marriage, a boy indicates his preferred partner, or his parents persuade (but never force) him to accept a girl of their choice. Siblings of the boy's parents, rather than the parents themselves, convey the proposal to siblings of the girl's par-

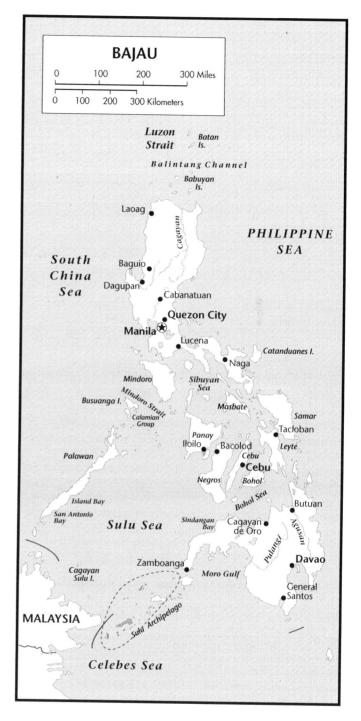

ents. The boy's representatives present family jewelry and other valuables to the girl's side. After discussion, and with the girl's consent, her family announces the bride-price, setting an unreasonably high one if they are not interested in the union. As a single nuclear family cannot generally afford the bride-price, the boy's parents receive contributions from their siblings.

The engagement period commences with a *pag-angbat* announcement celebration, including a fluvial parade of the boy's kin to the girl's residence, to the accompaniment of gongs. The boy sends cash and goods to the girl's family but is not to speak to the girl during the engagement period.

Members of the Bajau fish on the Sulu Sea in the Philippines.
(© Ted Spiegel/Corbis)

For one to two weeks before the wedding, there is merry-making every night, with relatives and well-wishers dancing to display their grace and skill. It is also a chance for young men to check out young women. To announce the wedding, a pole on which a multicolored blanket hangs is raised in front of the house. After the Islamic ceremony itself, three days of celebration begin, the highlight of which is the *paglibuhan*. Young women (15 from either kin-group) take turns dancing in front of the couple (earning a fee); at the end, the bride herself dances. The guests sometimes push the groom to join in as well.

A forced marriage (when a man abducts a woman or impregnates her) merits much less ceremony. The *imam* solemnizes the wedding, but subjects the couple to seven lashes to wash away the sin of premarital sex; the man, moreover, must pay a fine.

Formerly, at his death a man's boat was disassembled to make his coffin. All through the night following the death, most adults of the moorage or village drop in to chant prayers and sing laments. The next morning, a flotilla of boats accompanies the body to the cemetery islands where it is buried with the deceased's personal belongings. The surviving family makes periodic visits to the grave, leaving small offerings of betel nuts.

8 INTERPERSONAL RELATIONS

A consensus of a community's household heads selects a headman *(panglima)*. The headman's duty is to call meetings when there is a dispute or breach of custom. He collects fines from an offending party, which he shares with the offended party. However, such penalties cannot be imposed without the voluntary submission of both parties. Those who have antagonized their neighbors can just move away to another community until the incident is forgotten.

9 LIVING CONDITIONS

Communities are either permanent villages of houses raised over water just off islands or reefs or, alternatively, are semi-permanent or seasonal collections of houseboats (as many as 40) moored together with or without onshore houses nearby. A channel open during low tide runs through a village like a main street; a complicated network of gangplanks connects most houses. Houseboat groups exhaust one fishing ground then move on.

The living space in a houseboat measures 3 m (10 ft) long, 1.2 m (4 ft) wide, and 1.2 m (4 ft) high. A portable bamboo framework with a plaited nipa roof provides the shelter. At the stern, food and water are stored, and meals are cooked and eaten.

A pile house is 6–9 m by 4.5 m (20–30 ft by 15 ft) and consists of a single large room; in front, an open platform for docking boats juts out, and the kitchen occupies a separate smaller building.

Average family income in the Autonomous Region in Muslim Mindanao, of which Tawi-Tawi province is a part, amounted to 89,000 pesos (us$1,745) in 2006, the lowest in the country, cf. the national average of ₱173,000, the National Capital Region's ₱311,000, Southern Tagalog's ₱198,000, and those of the neighboring Davao and Zamboanga regions, ₱135,000 and ₱125,000 respectively. In 2000, Tawi-Tawi, however, had the second lowest Human Development Index, 0.391 (combining measures of health, education, and income) in the country (above Sulu and below Basilan, its fellow provinces in the Sulu archipelago, cf. the Philippines' national HDI of 0.656)

According to the 2000 census, the proportion of houses in Tawi-Tawi with a roof of galvanized iron/aluminum reached 52.2% (a great increase over just 37.9% ten years earlier) and the percentage of homes with a roof of grass or palm thatch was at 38.3% (down from 55.88%); 67.5% of houses had wooden outer walls, and another 21.3% walls of bamboo or thatch. 4.7% of households had access to a community faucet, 7.5% to a faucet of their own, and 21.6% to a shared deep well, while 39.3% obtained their water from a well, and 34.9% from springs, lakes, rivers, or rain. 41.3% of households disposed of their garbage by burning it, 25.6% by dumping it into a household pit, 5.8% by burying it, and 3.3% by feeding it to their animals; only 3.5% had it picked up by a collection truck. 71% of houses were lit with kerosene lamps, 17.2% with electricity, and 7.2% with firewood. 61.9% possessed a radio, 9.7% a television, 4.8% a refrigerator, 8.5% a VCR, 2.8% a telephone or cell phone, 2.3% a washing machine, and 14.7% a motorized vehicle.

10 FAMILY LIFE

For boat-dwelling Bajau, the *mataan,* consisting of a man, his wife, and their children, is the most important social group; this nuclear family may include, in addition, other relatives: a widowed parent, a divorced sister, or a husband's adult nephew. The widowed remarry quickly, as houseboat life is too difficult without a partner. Sometimes, incomplete *mataan* will join forces, such as when two widowed second cousins with children set up a single household.

Most marriages are between cousins (excepting the children of brothers); marrying a relative of another generation or a close same-sex kin of one's former spouse is regarded as incestuous. The ideal, rarely achieved given such a mobile lifestyle, is for a new couple to settle in the wife's moorage after a few months of moving between the two parental houseboats (or after a year of living with the wife's parents).

Spending most of a day's 24 hours at sea cut off from other families, the members of the *mataan* develop extremely strong bonds. Bajau tend to trust only their own siblings and form the next-higher unit of economic and ritual cooperation, the *pagmundah* (literally, a group of boats traveling or moored together) by uniting, on average, four sets of siblings, spouses, and unmarried children (a member leaves the *pagmundah* once he has married children who can form a *pagmundah* among themselves). Among house-dwelling Bajau, a house will shelter an entire *pagmundah,* with the senior male as the leader. Upon partition of the household, the youngest sibling stays with the original house while the others set up their own houses adjacent to it.

Most Bajau marry more than once, usually divorcing before the third year, once the romantic feeling is lost.

The Bajau keep no animals other than (occasionally) cats and fighting cocks.

¹¹CLOTHING

Bajau clothing is similar to Tausug clothing [see **Tausugs**]. Young children are left naked so that they can get used to the extremes in temperature that they will encounter as fisher-folk. Once prestigious but now regarded as signs of ignorance were the filing, blackening, and gold capping of teeth. To preserve their complexion from the sun, women apply a thick coating of white *burak* rice powder to their faces.

¹²FOOD

The staple food is ground cassava root from which the juice has been squeezed; the resulting powder is wrapped in banana leaf as is, or it is fried or steamed. When they can afford it, people eat rice (often mixed with corn). Boiled or grilled fish is the main accompaniment; shark meat, sea urchins, and shellfish (crabs) are also eaten. Bajau prefer to sell the better-quality seafood such as shrimp and lobsters. Considering it unclean, Bajau avoid the meat of land animals. They rarely eat vegetables other than seaweed. There are no set mealtimes—the family eats when the father returns with the catch.

¹³EDUCATION

The Bajau take less advantage of modern educational opportunities (which in any case remain very limited) than Tausugs or other Samal.
A ccording to the 2000 census, the literacy level in the Autonomous Region of Muslim Mindanao was 68.9%, very low by national standards. In Tawi-Tawi province, 39.9% had completed elementary school, 23.7% high school, and one in 8.6% college or university (the latter two percentages were actually higher than in Sulu).

¹⁴CULTURAL HERITAGE

Melodious, sentimental songs *(leleng, lolo,* and *tenes-tenes)* are performed by a young man and young woman alternating parts to the accompaniment of a *gabbang* xylophone. For exercise and relaxation and as a part of ceremonies and celebrations, Bajau perform *igal,* dancing to the beat of *kulintangan* and *agong* [see **Tausugs**].

¹⁵WORK

Fishing (by men) provides subsistence and a product to trade for (or sell for cash to buy) necessities available from non-Bajau (agricultural produce, cooking hearths, metal utensils, nipa matting). All year round, groups of siblings and siblings-in-law cooperate in fishing; large seasonal fish drives, however, bring as many as 60 boats together. One method, the *pag-ambit,* involves a group of boats encircling a shoal of fish with a net. Women and children gather shellfish at low tide. Some Bajau have recently begun to tend onshore gardens on borrowed land.

Respected specialists include *imam,* herb doctors, midwives, woodcarvers, and boat builders.

¹⁶SPORTS

Popular sports include swimming and running races or playing volleyball on a sand bar at low tide, there being no suitable areas for basketball or softball.

¹⁷ENTERTAINMENT AND RECREATION

Bajau spend what little leisure time they have chatting, picking lice, playing cards, tossing coins, and enjoying water-splashing games. Today, they also like to record and play back their own and their children's singing on cassette recorders, as well as to go to movies in town.

¹⁸FOLK ART, CRAFTS, HOBBIES

Women weave mats that are in high demand in local and tourist markets.

¹⁹SOCIAL PROBLEMS

See the article entitled **Filipinos**.

²⁰ GENDER ISSUES

In 2000, in Tawi-Tawi the ratio between men and women was 99 men for every 100 women (a dramatic decline from 106 men for every 100 women just five years earlier); women were more numerous in the age group 0 to 39 years, men more numerous in the age group 40 and above (which may be partly the result of male insurgent casualties in recent years and high rates of women's deaths in childbirth in earlier years). Literacy levels in the Autonomous Region of Muslim Mindanao, low by national standards, were somewhat higher for men (69.8%) than for women (67.7%). In Tawi-Tawi (differing in this regard from the ARMM and the Philippines as a whole), despite there being more women than men, men were still somewhat more numerous among those completing all levels of education except in post-secondary education. In contrast to other parts of the country, such as Southern Tagalog, more overseas workers from the ARMM were female (56%) than male; the median age of those female overseas workers was 24 years. There are hiring quotas for Muslim domestic workers employed in Saudi Arabia and other Muslim Middle Eastern states.

21 BIBLIOGRAPHY

Gordon, Raymond G., Jr. (ed.). *Ethnologue: Languages of the World,* 15th ed.. Dallas: Texas: SIL International, 2005. http://www.ethnologue.com (November 16, 2008).

Horvatich, Patricia. "The Ahmadiya Movement in Simunul: Islamic Reform in One Remote and Unlikely Place. In *Islam in an Era of Nation-States: Politics and Religious Renewal in Muslim Southeast Asia,* edited by Robert W. Hefner and Patricia Horvatich. Honolulu: University of Hawai'i Press, 1997.

_____. "The Martyr and the Mayor: On the Politics of Identity in the Southern Philippines." In *Cultural Citizenship in Island Southeast Asia: Nation and Belonging in the Hinterlands,* edited by Renato Rosaldo. Berkeley, CA: University of California Press, 2003.

LeBar, Frank M., ed. *Ethnic Groups of Insular Southeast Asia.* Vol. 2, *The Philippines and Formosa.* New Haven, Conn.: Human Relations Area Files Press, 1972.

Melalatoa, M. Junus. "Bajau, suku bangsa." In *Ensiklopedi Nasional Indonesia,* vol 3. Jakarta: Cipta Adi Karya, 1989.

National Statistics Office: Republic of the Philippines. "Autonomous Region in Muslim Mindanao: Nine Out of Ten Persons Were Muslims." http://www.census.gov.ph/data/pressrelease/2003/pr0301tx.html (November 21, 2008).

_____. "Tawi-Tawi: Population Growth Rose More than Threefold." http://www.census.gov.ph/data/pressrelease/2002/pr02138tx.html (November 21, 2008).

Nimmo, H. Arlo. *The Sea People of Sulu: A Study of Social Change in the Philippines.* San Francisco: Chandler, 1972.

Teo, Saladin S. *The Lifestyle of the Badjaos: A Study of Education and Culture.* Manila: Centro Escolar University Research and Development Center, 1989.

—revised by A. J. Abalahin

BALINESE

PRONUNCIATION: BAHL-uh-neez
LOCATION: Indonesia (Bali)
POPULATION: 3 million
LANGUAGE: Balinese
RELIGION: Indigenized version of Hinduism
RELATED ARTICLES: Vol. 3: Indonesians

1 INTRODUCTION

Although, as Southeast Asia's prime tourist destination, Bali provides much of Indonesia's image to the outside world, Balinese culture deviates widely from the national mainstream, most crucially in its unique Hindu-animist religion. Created from the early 1st millennium AD on, huge stone sarcophagi and bronze drums attest to the fertile island's ability to support social stratification and attract long-distance trade. Inscriptions from the 9th to 10th centuries record the emergence of Hinduized kingdoms that would later fall under the domination, political and cultural, of the great east Javanese realms. In 1334, Gajah Mada, the prime minister of the Javanese kingdom of Majapahit, conquered Bali, laying the foundations for the later transplantation of Hindu-Javanese culture by refugees from Majapahit after its fall to Islamized rival states. In the 16th century, King Batu Renggong of Gelgel unified Bali (acquiring also Lombok, Sumbawa, and parts of East Java) and in partnership with the high priest Nirartha established the socioreligious order that continues to the present day.

By the 18th century, Gelgel's domain had fragmented into nine competing kingdoms. Beginning in the 1840s, the Dutch, initially on the pretext of punishing the Balinese for plundering shipwrecks, involved themselves more and more in the island's internal affairs, imposing direct rule on north and west Bali in 1853. Between 1894 and 1908, the Dutch subdued the Balinese kingdoms first in Lombok and then in south Bali; bloody resistance by the royal courts ended in *puputan* (suicide charges) into Dutch fire. However, the Dutch ruled Bali through the surviving aristocrats; the latter became administrators and major landowners, as well as playing up their religious authority. Colonial legislation rigidified caste hierarchies at the expense of rising commoner families. After Indonesia won its independence from the Dutch in 1950, increasing competition over land in an overpopulated island (suffering, moreover, the effects of the catastrophic eruption of Gunung Agung, Bali's most sacred volcano in 1963) and the penetration of rival nationwide political networks into Balinese rural society intensified social conflicts, culminating in the anticommunist massacres of 1965–66 that claimed 100,000 lives and annihilated whole villages.

Suharto's New Order regime (1966–1998) promoted Bali as a destination for international tourism, seeing the resulting income flow as essential to achieving its development goals for Indonesia as a whole. At the same time, the government sought to minimize what it considered to be the erosive effects of tourism on traditional Balinese culture by confining large-scale tourist infrastructure (especially high-class hotels) to a zone on Bali's southern peninsula; towns there, such as Kuta, are barely distinguishable from beach resort areas in other parts of the world, including the appearance of some European nude bathing. Catering to foreign "hippies" and other budget travelers, cheap guesthouses have proliferated beyond the official tourist zone, and domestic tourism into Bali, particularly among urban middle-class Javanese and Chinese-Indonesians discouraged from travel abroad by heavy airport departure taxes, has grown massively.

Still, tourism is only one of the phenomena transforming contemporary Balinese culture: the same economy- and nation-building program pursued by the government in the rest of the country, including everything from the Green Revolution to the institutionalization of religion, has been a more important one as have been generic industrialization and urbanization. Balinese indigenous culture is changing and thriving, driven by internal dynamics to which tourist consumption of such things as abbreviated dance shows is peripheral. The complex situation is captured in the following paradox: while, in the cities, preparation of daily offerings to gods and demons has become a noticeably rushed affair with women and girls often simply buying offerings at market before heading to work, at the same time, the productivity of workers in the garment industry is lowered by the time and energy they spend on traditional rituals, ignoring workplace rules.

Bali has remained largely free of the violence that has afflicted some other parts of Indonesia during and since the fall of Suharto, though it was the site of the most murderous terrorist attacks in the world since the 11 September 2001 attacks in the United States, the suicide bombings of Denpasar tourist bars by (ethnically Javanese) Islamic militants on 12 October 2002 (202 people were killed, of which 88 were Australians and 38 Indonesians). The assertion of Islamism in Indonesia as a whole, though restrained by moderate Muslim, secular, and Christian counter-pressure, has caused some concern for the Balinese: a recent "anti-pornography" bill has been viewed as potentially threatening traditional Balinese religious art.

²LOCATION AND HOMELAND

Separated by narrow straits from Java to the west and Lombok to the east, the island of Bali covers 5,808 sq km (2,243 sq mi), or an area slightly larger than the state of Delaware. Its population of 3.4 million is, however, four times as high as that of Delaware. Population density (2005 figures) reaches 601 people per sq km., three times as high as in neighboring West Nusa Tenggara, more than six times than in East Nusa Tenggara, and 79% that of East Java. An unbroken east–west chain of volcanoes leaves a narrow plain along the north coast. A series of valleys carved by swiftly flowing rivers stretches south to the Indian Ocean; the southernmost tip of the island is an arid limestone peninsula.

The axis between the mountains and the sea dominates the Balinese sense of orientation. For instance, custom dictates that one should sleep with one's head facing *kaja*, the direction of the divine mountains, and one's feet facing *kelod*, the direction of the demonic sea (the soles of the feet should not face a party that must be shown respect, in this case the mountains). *Kaja* can mean "north" or "south" depending upon the location.

The Balinese have not been known as a seafaring people nor, before the 20th century, as migrants (except in western Lombok). Overpopulation, however, has forced many Balinese to participate in government-sponsored transmigration to South Sumatra, Central Kalimantan, Sulawesi, and Nusa Tenggara

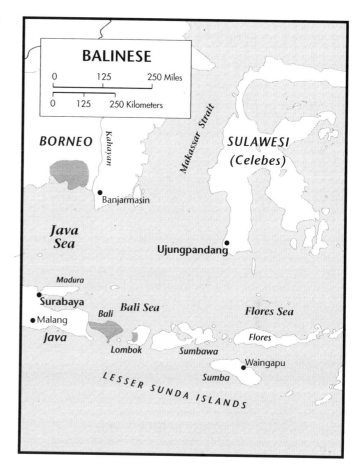

(Balinese form 3% of the population of West Nusa Tenggara province). On the other hand, Bali attracts people from other islands, especially Java; 11% of the population of Bali is ethnically non-Balinese.

³LANGUAGE

The Balinese speak an Austronesian language whose closest relative is Sasak, the language of Lombok. Although now they increasingly use Latin letters, their traditional script was a calligraphically distinct version of the Javanese alphabet. From its earliest recorded form (in an inscription from AD 882), the Balinese language shows profound influences from Sanskrit and Kawi (Old Javanese).

Balinese linguistic etiquette employs a system of politeness levels (High, Refined, Middle, and Low). Most words only have one form in all levels, but a few hundred of the most basic words, ranging from conjunctions to names of body parts, do have more than one form, e.g., "to eat" can be *ngunggahang* (referring to a Brahmana priest); *ngajeng* (referring to other high-caste people); *nglungsur* (referring to common people); *naar* (referring to family members); or *ngamah* (referring to animals).

Nowadays, the High (*tinggi*) language is spoken only to Brahmana priests; in most families, no more than one member is fluent in it, and so he or she alone approaches Brahmana with requests. The Refined (*alus*) level is used when addressing higher-status people, older people, and one's parents. The Low (*rendah, also referred to as* Ordinary, *biasa, or Coarse,*

Balinese dancers take part in a peace parade in Denpasar on Bali island. The peace parade took part one day before the anniversary of the bomb blasts that ripped through a night club in Legian Kuta, killing about 200 people in October 2002.
(Sonny Tumbelaka/AFP/Getty Images)

kasar) level serves for talking to those one considers of equal or inferior status: children; relatives; intimate friends; and lower-status people, such as maids; men address their wives with the Low language. Strangers whose status is as yet unknown are addressed with a mixture of Refined and Ordinary levels. The Middle *(madia)* level is used to people of equal status with whom one is not intimate. When two Balinese meet for the first time, they begin the conversation in the Middle level, and then, once it becomes clear who is of higher status than the other, each speaker adjusts his level accordingly.

Although the old etiquette is scrupulously observed in the context of religious rituals and other customary activities, in other contexts this is becoming less and less the case. In recent times, higher-caste people have been using the Refined level with lower-caste people, particularly if the latter rank high in the national bureaucracy. Classmates converse in the Ordinary level, regardless of caste differences. In schools in the provincial capital of Denpasar, teachers address students using the Middle level (in conservative east Bali, the medium of instruction is the Refined level, which is also what strangers there will use the first time they meet). As in Java, the national language, Bahasa Indonesia, taught in school at all levels, offers a means of communication whereby people can avoid locating themselves and others within the traditional hierarchy

(though not necessarily evading any of modern society's status differences).

One common way of referring to adults is by a name that places them in relation to a child or grandchild, e.g., "Father *(Pan)* of X," "Mother *(Men)* of Y," or "Grandfather *(Kak)* of Z." Moreover, custom assigns names according to birth order among siblings. For Sudra families, the first-born will receive the name "Wayan," the second "Made," the third "Nyoman," the fourth "Ketut," and the fifth "Putu." To these, the Wesya will prefix "Gusti" for males and "Gusti Ayu" or "Ida"/"Ni," for females; the Satrya "Dewa" (males) and "Dewa Ayu" (females) or "Agung Gede," and the Brahmana "Ida Bagus" (males) or "Ida Ayu" (females).

⁴FOLKLORE

Leyak are witches who are ordinary people by day but who leave their bodies at night, taking any shape (a monkey, a bird, a disembodied head, a ghostly light). Haunting cemeteries and crossroads, leyak can cause disease or crop failure, poison food, or introduce foreign objects into their victims' bodies. Amulets or *mantra* (incantations) acquired from a priest or shaman can combat them. A person who dies without any apparent cause is regarded as having been a leyak whose spirit, for whatever reason, never returned to the body after a night's roaming.

⁵RELIGION

Unlike the vast majority of Indonesians, the Balinese are not Muslims but Hindu (except for tiny Christian and Buddhist minorities). Their Hinduism is not a wholesale transplant of the Indian religion but rather consists of the grafting of Indian elements onto an indigenous stem. Balinese believe that *kesaktian,* "potency" or "magical power," is present in ritual objects, trees, stones, mountains, etc., and must be respected. The object of their religious practices is to maintain the equilibrium between the "upper" (pure, good, constructive) forces and the "lower" (impure, evil, destructive) forces. Thus, Balinese make offerings to both gods and demons, e.g. prepared food, especially rice cakes, or leaf-weavings for the former and the blood of freshly slaughtered animals for the latter.

The Balinese recognize an immense range of supernatural beings, ranging from demons to ancestral spirits to divinities, such as the sun god Surya (a manifestation of the Hindu deity Siwa [Shiva]) and the rice goddess Dewi Sri. Since the Indonesian state philosophy Pancasila emphasizes monotheism, the organization Parisada Hindu Dharma (founded in 1959) has promoted the worship of Sang Hyang Widhi Wasa, a supreme being of which all the other deities are lesser manifestations. This "reform" has not altered everyday practices other than to install Sang Hyang Widhi Wasa's shrine, an empty lotus seat, in every temple.

All rituals aim to purify and thus require holy water that people can only obtain from priests. Other religious specialists include several types of *balian,* "shamans" (masseuses, healers, augurs, spirit mediums, and so-called "literate" balians who use *lontar,* palm-leaf manuscripts, in their magic).

⁶MAJOR HOLIDAYS

Each of the thousands of temples on Bali celebrates its own *odalan* or festival, usually lasting three days. The timing of these festivals is determined by a calendrical system including a 210-day ritual cycle and a 12-month lunar cycle, the latter numbered according to the Indian *Saka* year, the first of which corresponded to AD 78. In addition, there are three "week" cycles: a Balinese market week (three days: Pasah, Beteng/Tegeh, Kajeng); a Javanese market week (five days: Umanis, Paing, Pon, Wage, Kliwon) and the seven-day week.

Galungan, a festival celebrated throughout the island, runs for 10 days, beginning with the first day of the eleventh week of the 210-day year; the Balinese invite the gods and deified ancestors to descend from heaven, which is directly above the island's greatest mountain, Gunung Agung. As Galungan originated as a harvest festival, *penjor,* high bamboo poles bending with decorations, are raised in front of each house and temple to represent fertility.

Nyepi occurs on the first day of the Saka year. While on the eve people make a great deal of noise, either to drive demons away or call their attention to offerings laid out for them, on Nyepi itself people observe absolute quiet—not even vehicles may travel.

Eka Dasa Rudra occurs only once every 100 years, the last time being in 1979. This entails several weeks of ceremonies at Bali's supreme temple, Besakih, on the slopes of Gunung Agung, whose aim is to purify the entire universe by exorcising Rudra, the chaotic aspect of Siwa.

⁷RITES OF PASSAGE

Depending on the caste or wealth of a family, as many as 13 life-cycle rituals *(manusa yadnya)* can be performed: the sixth month of pregnancy; birth; the falling off of the umbilical cord; the 12th, 42nd, and 105th days after birth; the 210th day after birth, marking the child's first "touching of the earth"; the emergence of the first adult tooth; the loss of the last baby tooth; the onset of puberty (first menstruation for girls); tooth-filing; marriage; and purification for study.

Great care is taken to show respect to a newborn infant's "spiritual siblings": the placenta, the amniotic fluid, the blood, and the *lamas* or *banah,* a natural yellow salve covering the skin; the placenta is buried under a river stone at the entrance of the sleeping house. These "four companions" (kanda empat) can, if properly treated, protect the child in life, but, if neglected, may harm it.

As a necessary prerequisite to adulthood, tooth-filing is performed on teenagers to purge them of the "animal" nature, associated with the evils of lust, greed, anger, drunkenness, confusion, and jealousy, that are symbolized by the fang-like upper canines.

Full adulthood, in the sense of complete social responsibility, begins only with marriage. Wedding protocol involves roughly three stages: a ceremony whereby the boy's family asks for the hand of the girl from her family; the wedding ceremony itself; and a formal visit by the new couple and the groom's family to the bride's family so that the bride may "ask leave" of her own ancestors. This would also be the time for the groom's family to deliver the bride-price, a custom largely dropped by educated people. Such "weddings by proposal" involve many expensive rituals and feasts, to which kin, neighbors, and *banjar* will contribute aid. A cheaper and very popular alternative is "elopement" *(mamaling or nyogotin).* A boy and a girl spend a night at a friend's house, a publicly known deed after which they must marry. The boy's family holds a wedding ceremony to which the girl's family are not invited, since the latter are obliged to appear angry even if they secretly consented to the match. Some time afterwards, bringing gifts, the boy's family pays a formal visit to the girl's family in hopes of reconciling her family to the union. After this, the girl's side can publicly accept the marriage.

As a proper cremation ceremony is extremely expensive, the family may take months or even years to accumulate the necessary funds, installing the body in a special pavilion or burying it temporarily in a cemetery. Many families wait until a high-caste family holds a cremation, in conjunction with which they can perform ceremonies for their own deceased at a much reduced cost. For the cremation itself, the body is placed in an ornate animal-shaped coffin installed in a portable tower, whose number of levels (roofs) reflects the status of the deceased (as many as 11 for royalty). Dozens of mourners carry the tower to the cremation field, rotating it at each crossroads so that the deceased's spirit cannot find its way back home to haunt the living. Under the supervision of a priest, the body, coffin, tower, and offerings are burned; the ashes are collected and with further ceremony cast into the sea. Only after all this has been done can the deceased become a deified ancestor.

One striking exception to the above pattern is the Bali Aga people of Trunyan: after mourning, the body is laid under a tree in a forest-cemetery and allowed to rot away.

[8]INTERPERSONAL RELATIONS

Following the Hindu scriptures, Balinese society has been divided since the Majapahit period into four castes (which do not correspond to occupation in any straightforward way): Brahmana, Satria, Wesia, and Sudra. Comprising 15% of the Balinese, the first three (the Triwangsa) claim direct descent from transplanted Majapahit nobility, the privileged "insiders" of the pre-colonial kingdoms, while the Sudra majority were literally the "outsiders" *(Jaba)*. However, a small minority, the Bali Aga or Bali Turunan, claiming to be the "original [pre-Majapahit] Balinese," have kept themselves apart in mountain villages. The position of the castes relative to each other has always been a matter of great dispute. Only under colonial rule have the Brahmana been able to assert a certain superiority, a status unconceded, for example, by a Sudra subcaste, the Pande (blacksmiths in origin), who take holy water from priests of their own subcaste.

Balinese society divides into a great variety of organizations; an individual belongs to several of these groups at once (their memberships never completely overlap). All these organizations have a leader and a set of written regulations *(awig-awig* or *sima,* passed down through the generations). Agriculture, house repair, rituals, emergencies, and other major tasks require the cooperation of members of these organizations (though nowadays, hiring workers is often cheaper than feeding helpers).

The *banjar* is a subvillage residential unit, which in the lowlands may include as many as 100 families or 500–600 people; it is led by a *klian banjar,* elected by the membership (though often from a hereditary line), who is responsible for arbitrating conflicts falling under the jurisdiction of customary law, as well as leading the banjar's religious activities. Eligible to join upon marriage, men may have to pay a fee for banjar membership; a man can expect aid from fellow members in staging his own family's rituals and feasts.

The *subak* is an association of individuals who depend on the same irrigation network (which does not match village or banjar boundaries). Subak join other subak in reliance upon one of several mountain-lake temples from which their water ultimately derives.

Sekaha are associations for specific purposes, temporary or permanent, e.g., music, dance, and theater ensembles, or separate clubs for young men and young women.

Traditional etiquette, now increasingly confined to ceremonial occasions, requires that people of higher status (including greater age) sit on a physically higher place and closer to the *kaja* direction and the east. For Brahmana priests and in ceremonies, the greeting is *"Ohm Swastiastu,"* with a small bow and the palms put together at the chest (this is now being promoted as an equivalent to the Muslim *"Assalamu alaikum"*). In opening conversation with higher-status people, one also bows; but to children and lower-status people, one simply nods. One takes advice, instruction, or criticism with *"nggih"* (a deferential "yes") or with silence and without contradicting; one does everything possible to comply with a request or command. Adults correct children indirectly, e.g., a mother will tell her children that she herself will be scolded if the child misbe-

haves, or that misconduct is "low-caste" behavior. High-caste wives do not dare to correct older people; they either let them do as they will or appeal to another older third party, such as a mother-in-law. Self-deprecation (referring humbly to one's own person, property, or achievements) is essential to polite conversation.

Between adolescents of the opposite sex, only chatting at food stalls in the presence of others is acceptable. Balinese joke freely about sex but take great care to keep the genitals covered and to keep garments that have been in contact with them (especially those of menstruating women) in a place where they will not be above people's heads.

[9]LIVING CONDITIONS

Inhabited by a group of brothers and their respective families, a residential compound *(uma)* is surrounded by a wall pierced by a narrow gate. Within it, grouped around a central courtyard, are separate pavilion-like buildings on the *kelod* side for cooking (one for each nuclear family), storing rice, and keeping pigs, and in the other directions ones for sleeping (on the *kaja* side for grandparents, parents, or the senior brother; on the east for guests; on the west for children). Each compound has a shrine *(sanggah)* in the kaja-east corner. A thatched pavilion *(bale)* serves for meetings and ceremonies, and a walled-in pavilion *(bale daja)* stores family heirlooms. Rivers serve for toilet and bathing functions. The compounds of *banjar* members cluster around a meeting pavilion *(bale banjar),* which nowadays often has a television and ping-pong tables.

Villages *(desa)* may be compact (in the mountains) or dispersed among fields and gardens (in the lowlands). Each village has three, usually separate, temples: the most kaja is the *pura puseh,* associated with the god Wisnu and the purified ancestors; at the center is the *pura bale agung* or *pura desa,* dedicated to Brahma; and most kelod is the *pura dalem,* associated with Siwa and the not-yet-purified dead.

Bali has a Human Development Index (combining measures of income, health, and education) of 69.8 (2005 score), slightly higher than Indonesia's national HDI of 69.6. The province's GDP per capita is us$10,033, relatively high for Indonesia (cf. us$9,784 for West Sumatra and us$8,360 for North Sulawesi, two regions with much higher HDIs, us$6,293 for Central Java, which has the same HDI, and us$6,151 for West Nusa Tenggara, which has among the lowest HDIs in the country). In 2000, the rate of infant mortality stood at 35.72 deaths per 1,000 live births, the lowest in the country after Jakarta, Yogyakarta, and North Sulawesi (by contrast, neighboring West Nusa Tenggara's infant mortality rate was 88.55, the highest in the country).

[10]FAMILY LIFE

Marriage between members of different castes is now common, although before Indonesian independence a woman marrying a man of inferior caste would be banished with her spouse from their locality. Unions between a husband's sisters and a wife's brothers remain taboo. With some exceptions, a newlywed couple remains in the groom's compound; children belong to the clan or subclan of the compound where they live (either the father's or mother's as the case may be). Households include married sons and their families until they are able to establish their own households. At least one son must stay behind to care for the parents in their old age.

Clan organizations (*warga*) for the Triwangsa include branches scattered all over the island. The senior family (of most direct descent from the common ancestor) keeps the clan history and genealogy (*babad*).

¹¹ CLOTHING

In work outside the home, especially for office and store jobs, Balinese wear Western-style clothes. Around the house, men wear shorts and a tank-top or, alternately, a sarong. Men's traditional clothing includes a *kamben sarung* (a tube sarong) of *endek* or *batik* cloth. In temples, a *songket* cloth (woven with gold- or silver-thread designs) is worn over the kamben; for rite-of-passage ceremonies, the kamben itself would be of songket. Men are very particular about how the kamben and the head cloth (*udeng*) required for formal occasions are tied. The lower edge of the kamben hangs longer in the front (held up while walking) and may be hitched up trouser-like for work in the fields.

Women wear a *kamben lembaran* (a nontube sarong), usually of mass-produced batik cloth, often with a sash (*selempot*) when outside the house; going about outside the house with breasts exposed has long been rare. When carrying things on the head (the usual method), women put a cloth between the load and the head. For temple ceremonies, women wear a *sabuk* belt wrapped around the body up to the armpits and put a *kebaya* jacket over this (but no kebaya or selempot for rite-of-passage ceremonies). As most women now wear their hair too short for traditional coiffures, they wear wigs to complete ritual dress.

¹² FOOD

Balinese consume their ordinary meals individually, silently, quickly, and at no fixed times, snacking very frequently. Everyday food consists of rice and vegetable side dishes, sometimes with a bit of chicken, fish, tofu, or tempeh, and seasoned with chili sauce (*sambel*) made fresh daily. Many dishes require *basa genep*, a standard spice mixture (sea salt, pepper, chili, shallots, garlic, shrimp paste, ginger, galangal, tamarind, candlenuts, sugar, coriander, and citrus).

For ceremonial feasts, much male labor goes into the making of *ebat*, chopped pig or turtle meat (including innards) mixed with spices, grated coconut, and *lawar* (slices of turtle cartilage or unripe mango). Other Balinese specialties are *sate lembat* (barbecue skewers consisting of ground meat rather than pieces of whole meat), *babi guling* (stuffed pig turned over a fire), and *bebek betutu* (stuffed duck wrapped in banana leaves and cooked in ashes).

¹³ EDUCATION

In 2005, the level of literacy stood at 86.22%, low by Indonesian national standards but comparable to provinces with high population densities and high numbers of poor, such as Central Java, East Java and South Sulawesi. (*See* also the article entitled **Indonesians.**)

¹⁴ CULTURAL HERITAGE

An essential part of religious ceremonies as well as entertainment (for Balinese and tourists), traditional performing arts are highly developed and vigorously pursued. A great range of musical ensembles exist, variants of the *gamelan* orchestra (drums, flutes, and bronze instruments or their substitutes of iron or bamboo). Examples are the *gong gede*, which plays slow, stately, and very old temple music; the delicate *gamelan semar pegulingan* accompanying court dances (also said to have once provided music for the palace bedchamber); and the dynamic *gong kebyar*, dating only from the beginning of the 20th century, also accompanying dance, theater, and rituals. A vast array of dances are performed, the most famous being the *Baris* dance, depicting drilling warriors; the *Legong* dance, depicting dueling princesses (sometimes girls in trance execute its intricate movements without previous instruction); and the *Barong*, in which a mythical lion, symbol of the good, combats the witch Rangda. Several dramatic genres are practiced: the *wayang kulit* shadow play (differing from the Javanese version in the form of the puppets and in the accompaniment by four *gender* instruments) and various forms of masked and unmasked theater (*topeng, wayang wong, gambuh, and arja*).

Balinese literature has been preserved incised on *lontar*, palm-leaf books. It divides into the epics of the gods and heroes of the previous world (in Kawi, Old Javanese) and tales of the old Balinese kingdoms (in Literary Balinese).

¹⁵ WORK

Some 70% of the Balinese earn a living from agriculture, which, where water is sufficient (as in the south), means wet-rice cultivation and elsewhere means nonirrigated crops, such as dry rice, maize, cassava, and beans. Sharecropping has become common in the most densely populated areas. Coconuts are grown along the coasts; fruits, such as citrus and *salak* (snakefruit), are grown for the off-island market. Pigs, ducks, and cattle are kept; fish are raised in flooded paddies as well as caught in the sea.

Many Balinese find employment in cottage and medium-scale industries. Since the 1970s, the garment industry has expanded dramatically; there are also factories for printing, canning, and coffee and cigarette processing. With a flood of foreign and domestic visitors every year, tourism provides work in hotels, travel bureaus, guide and taxi services, and craft shops, as well as money for performing and visual arts.

¹⁶ SPORTS

Although officially banned in 1981 as a venue for intense gambling, cockfights are still permitted as a necessary part of temple rituals (three rounds to appease demons). Cricket fighting continues as a milder substitute.

¹⁷ ENTERTAINMENT AND RECREATION

See the article entitled **Indonesians**.

¹⁸ FOLK ART, CRAFTS, AND HOBBIES

Painting, stone carving, and woodcarving in traditional and modernist styles, puppet making, mat- and basket weaving, and gold- and silver working are the most prominent crafts, with much production now directed towards the tourist market.

The most popular locally made cloth is *endek*, a kind of *ikat* (tie-dyed weft and solid warp). Particularly precious is another kind of ikat, *geringsing*, whose complicated dyeing process takes months to complete.

[19] SOCIAL PROBLEMS

See the article entitled **Indonesians**.

[20] GENDER ISSUES

Bali's Gender-Related Development Index (combining measures of women's health, education, and income relative to men's) is 61.2, significantly above Indonesia's national GDI of 59.2 and dramatically above that of both neighboring provinces, East Java (56.3) and West Nusa Tenggara (51.6, the second lowest in the country). The province's Gender Empowerment Measure (reflecting women's participation and power in political and economic life relative to men's), however, is among the lowest in the country, 45.6, compared to the national GEM of 54.6.

Although menstruating women are considered ritually impure and may not enter temples, discrimination against women is not pronounced. However, there is a clear division of labor: women buy and sell in the markets, cook, wash, care for the pigs, and prepare offerings; men work for the *banjar,* prepare spices and meat for feasts, play in orchestras, attend cockfights, and drink together in the early evenings. Women join the caste of their husbands; the wife of a Brahmana priest succeeds to his duties upon his death. Wives have control over their dowries and over their own and their husbands' earnings, have ownership of their clothing and jewelry and of family's small livestock (a form of capital, and a significant one, in itself), and in general manage family finances.

If a husband abuses his wife, is impotent, does not support his family, or takes a co-wife (madu) without his first wife's approval, she may return to her own family and, if she is able to convince a court of her husband's guilt, she gets custody of the children. Upon divorce a wife has rights to a share of assets jointly acquired with her husband. A wife who neglects her duties, commits adultery, or remains childless may be "thrown away" by her husband only if they had married by elopement. If they had married with familial consent or arrangement from the very beginning, it is much more difficult for him to do this, and he may go live with his lover while continuing to support his wife. In principle, inheritance goes only to men, but women can be classified as "males" for legal purposes and thus inherit (while their husbands become classified as legally "female").

[21] BIBLIOGRAPHY

Ayotrahaedi, et al. *Tatakrama di Beberapa Daerah di Indonesia* [Etiquette in Some Regions of Indonesia].Jakarta: Department of Education and Culture, 1989.

Badan Pusat Statistik: Statistik Indonesia. http://demografi. bps.go.id (November 9, 2008).

Eiseman, Fred B. *Bali, Sekala and Niskala*. Vol. 1, *Essays on Religion, Ritual, and Art*. Berkeley: Periplus, 1989.

———*Bali, Sekala and Niskala*. Vol. 2, *Essays on Society, Tradition, and Craft*. Berkeley: Periplus, 1990.

Hobart, Angela, Urs Ramseyer, and Albert Leeman. *The People of Bali*. Oxford, UK: Blackwell, 1996.

Hobart, Mark. "Engendering Disquiet: On Kinship and Gender in Bali." In "Male" and "Female" in *Developing Southeast Asia*, edited by Wazir Jahan Karim. Oxford, UK: Berg, 1995.

Koentjaraningrat, ed., *Manusia dan Kebudayaan di Indonesia* [Man and Culture in Indonesia]. Jakarta: Djambatan, 1975.

LeBar, Frank M., ed. *Ethnic Groups of Insular Southeast Asia.* Vol 1, *Indonesia, Andaman Islands, and Madagascar.* New Haven, CT: Human Relations Area Files Press, 1972.

Oey, Eric, ed. *Bali: Island of the Gods.* Berkeley: Periplus, 1990.

—revised by A. J. Abalahin

BALŪCHĪ

PRONUNCIATION: bal-OOCH-i
ALTERNATE NAMES: Baloch; Balochi
LOCATION: Pakistan (Province of Baluchistan); Iran;
    Afghanistan; Turkmenistan; Oman; East African coast
POPULATION: 7.5–11 million
LANGUAGE: Baluchi
RELIGION: Islam (mostly Sunni Muslim; also the Zikrī sect)
RELATED ARTICLES: Vol. 4: Pakistanis

¹ INTRODUCTION

The Balūchī (also Baloch, or Balochi) are a semi-nomadic tribal people inhabiting the southern mountains and coastal regions of South Asia's west+ern borderlands. Though united by a common language and culture, they have suffered the fate of many groups in the region in that their traditional homeland is divided between several political units—Pakistan, Iran and Afghanistan.

The Balūchī, who believe they are descendants of Amir Hamza, an uncle of the Prophet Muhammad, trace their origins to tribes living in the region of Aleppo, in Syria. Migrating eastward, these tribes reached the southern shores of the Caspian Sea and from there settled in their present homeland sometime between the 5th and 7th centuries AD. Isolated by the remoteness and inhospitable nature of their lands, they existed for several centuries as more or less independent groups organized along clan lines. Persians, Arabs, Hindus, and others have laid claim to parts of Balūchīstan, the traditional Balūchī homeland, at various times. None, however, succeeded in effectively establishing political control over the area. In the 12th century, Mir Jalal Han succeeded in uniting some of the Balūchī tribes under the short-lived First Balūchī Confederacy. Tribal conflict and intertribal rivalries were commonplace throughout the region, often instigated by competition for land, revenues, and resources. By the 16th century, the Balūchī were organized into three political entities—the Makran State, the Dodai Confederacy, and the Kalat Confederacy. In the 18th century, virtually all of the Balūchī tribes were united in a loose confederacy under the banner of Mir Abdullah Khan of Kalat.

The British annexation of Sind in 1843 pushed the frontier of British India to the borders of Balūchīstan. Concerned with a possible Russian threat to their Indian Empire, and also with gaining access to the strategic Afghanistan frontier, the British sought to extend their influence over the Balūchī. They achieved this by playing local leaders against each other, exploiting the Balūchī through a policy of divide and conquer. Tribal chiefs were guaranteed local autonomy and cash payments in return for allowing British garrisons in their territory. Some areas along the Afghanistan border were brought under direct British administration. By the early 20th century, British control over the region extended to the borders of Afghanistan and Iran.

The British Province of Balūchīstan passed to Pakistan when that country came into being in 1947. Pakistan also inherited the problems of the region, with the fiercely independent and warlike Balūchī tribes resisting integration into the new political state. Opposition to the central government led to brutal confrontations with the Pakistani military in the mid-1970s. Indiscriminate air attacks were mounted on villages and civilian populations in an effort to subdue the Balūchī dissidents. Today, the Balūchī see themselves as a neglected minority in a country, whose government is dominated by non-Balūchī ethnic groups such as the Punjabis.

² LOCATION AND HOMELAND

Balūchī speakers today are estimated to number about 8 million people. This figure is based on linguistic data, as census information from the countries in which the Balūchī live is unreliable. (The 2002 Pakistan Census estimate for the population of Balūchīstan Province is 7,215,700.) In addition, there are perhaps half as many people again who, though essentially Balūchī in culture, have adopted the language of their neighbors. Thus, if cultural rather than linguistic criteria are used, the Balūchī in Pakistan could total around 11 million in number.

The traditional homeland of the Balūchī extends west from the borders of the Punjab and Sind, across a small section of Afghanistan, to the areas of the Iranian Plateau southeast of Kirman. The southern boundary of the region is defined by the coast of the Arabian Sea and the Gulf of Oman. The section of this territory falling within Pakistan makes up the Pakistani Province of Balūchīstan, in which some 7 million people or 70% of the total Balūchī population live in Balūchīstan.. Some 1-2 million Balūchī reside within the borders of Iran, and a further 300,000 are found in Afghanistan. Balūchī communities are also found in Turkmenistan in Central Asia, in Oman in Arabia, and along the coast of East Africa, and also in the Pakistani city of Karachi.

Apart from the fringing coastal lowlands in the south and the arm of the Indus flood plain that extends towards Sibi in Pakistan, the entire region is characterized by harsh, inaccessible terrain. Rugged mountain ranges are interspersed with upland plateaus and desert basins. In Pakistan, the eastern margins of Balūchīstan are defined by the north–south-running Kirthar Hills and the Sulaiman Ranges. The latter average 1,800–2,100 m (6,000–7,000 ft) in elevation, but in places mountain peaks exceed 3,000 m (10,000 ft). Zargun, near Quetta, reaches a height of 3,591 m (11,738 ft). In southern Balūchīstan Province, the mountain ranges swing westward to parallel the Makran coast. The northwest of the province is made up of the desert basin of the Hamun-i-Mashkel, a region of bare sun-cracked clay, sand dunes, and marshes. The entire region experiences an arid climate, with the hot summers and cold winters typical of desert regions.

The Province of Balūchīstan is rich in natural resources, though its inhabitants perceive that they receive little benefit from this and that they are exploited by the central government.

³ LANGUAGE

The Balūchī language is an Indo-Iranian language of the Indo-European linguistic family. Related to Kurdish and Pashto, its origins are apparently to be found in the civilization of the ancient Medes or Parthians. Modern Balu chi shows borrowings from Persian, Arabic, Sindhi, and other languages. Distinctions are made between Western, Southern, and Eastern Balu chi, and six individual dialects of Balūchī are identified. No written form of the language existed before the early 19th century. Persian was used for official purposes until that time.

Subsequently, Balūchī was written in the Persian and Urdu scripts. With the rise of Balūchī nationalism, an adaptation of the Arabic script known as Nastaliq has been adopted for writing purposes.

4 FOLKLORE

Bravery and courage are respected by the Balūchī, and many tribal heroes who remained true to Balūchī values are revered and honored in folk songs and ballads. Doda, for example, is remembered for defending the principle of *bāhot,* or protection. Legend tells of a wealthy widow, Sammi, who sought protection in the village of Doda Gorgez. One day, Beebagr, a relative of Sammi's deceased husband, carried off some of Sammi's cows. Even though Doda had just been married, he pursued the thieves because he was honor-bound to safeguard the property as well as the life of the widow. Doda was killed in the ensuing battle (a similar tale is found in Rajasthani folklore). In keeping with Balūchī tradition, Doda's death was eventually avenged by his brother Balach.

Balūchī culture incorporates many elements that pre-date Islam. The veneration of tribal heroes and belief in the power of ancestral spirits reflect these ancient practices. In the past, it was customary for the Balūchī to perform certain rituals and even sacrifice at the graves of heroes. No doubt under later Islamic influence, such rites are now undertaken at the shrines of Muslim saints.

5 RELIGION

The Balūchī are Muslim, mostly Sunni but also including members of the Zikrī sect. Zikrīs (pronounced "Zigris" in Balūchī) were estimated to number over 750,000 people in 1998. If they increased in numbers at the same overall rate as Pakistan's population, today they would number close to 1 million people. They live mostly in Makran and Las Bela in southern Pakistan and are followers of a 15th-century *mahdi,* an Islamic messiah, called Nur Pak ("Pure Light"). Zikrī practices and rituals differ from those of orthodox Islam. For example, they do not observe the month of fasting during Ramadan. Zikrīs see themselves as Muslim, but in the eyes of Sunnis they are nonbelievers. This is because they place the teachings of their mahdi above those of Muhammad. As a result, Zikrīs are discriminated against by the dominant Sunni majority in Pakistan. They are also subjected to personal violence as well as attacks on their places of worship by Muslim extremists.

Balūchī Sunnis follow the teachings of Muhammad, keeping to the practices and principles of Islam as set out in the Koran *(Quran).* Religious instruction and the performance of religious ritual and observances lie in the hands of the *mullahs* (priests). However, many Baluch, and particularly the Zikrīs, are ardent followers of Sufi saints or *pirs.* These mystics, who can cure illnesses, foretell the future, and are reputed to perform miracles, are seen as evidence of the direct hand of God in the affairs of humans. For the Balūchī, religious beliefs and practices are very much an individual matter. The Balūchī do not support the idea of the religious state that underlies national policies implemented by Pakistani governments in recent years.

6 MAJOR HOLIDAYS

The Balūchī observe the festivals of Id ul-Fitr, which marks the end of Ramadan, and Id ul-Adha, the Feast of Sacrifice that falls at the end of the Islamic year. On these occasions, clean clothes are worn in honor of the occasion. The day begins with prayer, and the rest of holiday is spent in gambling, horse-racing, and general merry-making. Id ul-Adha is celebrated with the sacrifice of goats and sheep and the distribution of the meat to relatives, friends, and the poor. Alms are distributed at this time. The tenth day of Muharram is observed by visits to the graves of relations, followed by prayers and the distribution of alms to the poor. In general, the Balūchī pay less attention to celebrating festivals than do other Muslim peoples in South Asia.

7 RITES OF PASSAGE

The birth of a child is greeted with much rejoicing, music, and singing. Food and sweets are prepared and distributed to commemorate the event. The birth of a male child is cause for greater celebration, and some tribes barely recognize the arrival of a girl. The naming of the child usually takes place on the sixth day after birth. Children may be named after deceased ancestors, days of the week, trees, plants, or animals. Names peculiar to the Balūchī include Lalla, Bijjar, Kannar, and Jihand. Other ceremonies mark occasions such as the circumcision of males, the child beginning to walk, and the first wearing of trousers. This last event, occurring around the age of 15, was traditionally an important stage in a boy's life. It marked his becoming an adult and the time when he took up arms and joined his people in tribal warfare.

Balūchī burial rites follow usual Islamic practices. The corpse is taken to the graveyard, where it is washed and dressed in a shroud. A *mullah* (Muslim priest) reads the prayer for the dead over the body before it is committed to the grave. The body is laid in a north–south direction, with the head turned toward the west, i.e., facing Mecca. Sweets are passed among the congregation, and prayers are offered up before the mourners disperse. For nomads on the move, the body is placed in a pit dug to serve as a grave, rather than in a cemetery. A goat or sheep is killed, and the meat is cooked and distributed instead of sweets. The initial mourning period lasts for three or five days, depending on the sex of the deceased. During this time, normal activities are restricted, and women discard their jewelry and wear black dresses. The end of this period is marked by *asrokh,* a ceremony involving prayers and the distribution of meat. A second period of mourning lasts several months, during which friends come from a distance to offer condolences to the family of the deceased.

8 INTERPERSONAL RELATIONS

When Balūchī greet each other, they normally shake hands. However, if an ordinary tribesperson meets a religious leader, the tribesperson reverently touches the leader's feet. A meeting usually commences with inquiries after health *(durāhī)* and then proceeds to an exchange of news *(hāl).* Not to ask for news of the person one is meeting is considered the height of rudeness.

The Balūchī are guided in their daily lives and social relations by a code of conduct known as *Baluchmayar,* or "the Balūchī way." It is expected that a Balūchī be generous in hospitality to guests, offer refuge to those who seek protection *(bāhot),* and be honest in dealings with others. A Balūchī man should be merciful to women and refrain from killing a man who has sought sanctuary in the shrine of a *pir* (Sufi saint). He

Balūchī leaders of Pakistani opposition parties raise their hands during a demonstration in Quetta, Pakistan. Some 8,000 opposition activists protested in 2006 against the military operation in the restive southwestern Pakistani province of Baluchistan. (Banaras Khan/AFP/Getty Images)

is equally expected to defend his honor *(izzat)* and that of his women and family. Some insults are avenged only by blood, leading to reprisals and blood-feuds that have lasted generations. When both parties involved agree to it, such feuds are settled by the tribal council or *jirgāl*. Invariably blood-money or some form of compensation is required to be paid. Another means of resolving disputes is through *med ,* a informal gathering of tribal leaders and elders who volunteer their services to help reach an end to the conflict.

The Balūchī are organized into territorially based tribes such as the Marri and the Bugti, each under the leadership of a central chief or *Sardār*. The tribes are made up of various kin-groups such as clans, clan sections, and subsections, with the smaller of these groups coinciding with the actual units of settlement found throughout the region.

9 LIVING CONDITIONS

Balūchī nomads live in tents *(gidām)* made of palm matting stretched on poles. Two upright poles are driven into the ground and a third connects them in the form of a crosspiece. The matting is thrown over this, with the corners and sides fastened to the ground with pegs and heavy stones. In winter the matting is replaced by goat-hair blankets. A coarse, goat-hair carpet forms the floor of the tent. Typical contents of the tent include a hand-mill for grinding grain, waterskins, and goat-hair sacks for holding grain, salt, and clothing. Flint and tinder are carried for making fires, and various cooking and eating utensils complete the list of household belongings. Both

the tent and its contents are transported on the backs of pack animals when the camp is on the move.

Permanent settlements are usually occupied during the summer months. They generally consist of small villages comprising a collection of mud huts clustered around the fort of a chief or headman for protection. More recent structures may be made of sun-dried brick, with houses built along narrow, winding village lanes. Both old and newer houses have an open courtyard in front, enclosed by a low mud wall or palm fence.

10 FAMILY LIFE

As in all Muslim societies, women occupy a subservient role among the Balūchī. However, they are less subject to social restrictions than are women among other Muslim peoples in South Asia. Traditionally, *purdah* (seclusion) was not followed, although some upper-class families have now taken up the custom. In addition to household chores, women share in the tending of the family's herds. The gathering of wild plants, water, and firewood are specifically women's work.

Balūchī have strong prohibitions against marrying outside the Balūchī community. Marriages are arranged, with the union of first cousins being common. Such a match has the advantage of strengthening the ties between related families that are already familiar with each other. A bride-price *(lab)* consisting of cash and livestock is customary, although in certain instances an exchange of brides is negotiated. Islamic law permits polygamy, but monogamy is the norm among the Balūchī. Adultery was traditionally punishable by the death of the guilty parties under tribal law. Divorce occurs for reasons such as barrenness but is considered a matter of great disgrace. A widow returns to her father's home on the death of a husband, although she is allowed to remarry if it is acceptable to her family. Inheritance of property passes from father to son, a woman keeping only her personal belongings such as utensils, clothing, and jewelry.

11 CLOTHING

Traditional clothing for the Balūchī man is a long, loose shirt (*jāmag* or *kurtī*) that reaches below the knees, baggy trousers (*salwār*), and a turban (*pāg*) made of a long cloth wound around a turban cap. Shoes of leather or palm-leaf sandals complete the dress. A shawl or wrap (*chāddar*) provides extra warmth in winter but can also be used as a towel, waistband, or headcloth, or to carry objects. In the past, Balūchī wore only white, although this is now changing. An embroidered waistcoat or vest is sometimes worn over the shirt. Balu chi men may wear rings in the ears and on their fingers, but they disdain other jewelry. Hair is worn long, and most Balūchī men sport beards.

Dress for a woman is simpler, consisting of a long shift (*pashk*) reaching to the ankles, and a wrap used to cover the head, shoulders, and upper body. The wearing of trousers under the shift was restricted to women of high status. The clothes of better-class women are often made from silk and are elaborately embroidered. Colors are usually avoided, but widows wear black, and scarlet is popular among girls of marriageable age. Women wear an assortment of rings (nose-rings, earrings, rings on fingers and toes), necklaces, bracelets, and ornaments in the hair. Jewelry is made from gold or silver, depending on one's means.

12 FOOD

The Marri Balūchī take food twice a day, in the morning and evening. The food for the family is cooked together, but men and women eat separately. The most important food-grain is wheat, though millets (*juārī* and *bājra*) and rice are also eaten. They are ground into flour and baked into unleavened bread in mud ovens. Meat is an important part of the Balūchīdiet, *sajjī* being a particular favorite that is often served to honored guests. A sheep is killed, flayed, and carved into joints, with the meat being slashed and sprinkled with salt. The pieces of meat are spitted on green twigs, which are stuck into the ground in front of a blazing log. This dish is eaten with a knife, although Balūchī normally eat with their hands. Milk is drunk and also made into curds, buttermilk, and butter. In summer, a sherbet (*lassī*) is made with milk, molasses, and sugar. Dates and wild fruits and vegetables also form an important part of the Balūchī diet.

13 EDUCATION

With their traditional seminomadic life-style, Balūchī have little access to formal education. Only an estimated 10% to 15% of Balūchī children attend school, mainly in the more-settled areas of the country. As a consequence, illiteracy among the Balūchī is high.

14 CULTURAL HERITAGE

Although they lack a tradition of written literature, the Balūchī are heirs to a rich body of oral literature that extends back at least to the 12th century AD. Poets and minstrels are traditionally held in high regard by Balūchī society. Epic poems, heroic ballads, romances, folk tales, and proverbs all form part of the Balūchī cultural heritage. Many works recount tales of Balūchī heroes and all embody the very essence of *Balūchmayār*, the Balūchī code of honor. Among the more famous and popular of these poems are those relating the legendary exploits of Mir Chakur, a 16th-century Balūchī warrior and chieftain of the Rind tribe. Music plays a role in all ceremonies, except death rituals which are of a more solemn nature. The Lori and Domb castes, though not of Balūchī blood, serve as professional musicians. Dancing accompanies many events such as weddings and other festivals, men and women forming separate dancing circles. Men's dances reflect the warrior traditions of the Balūchī. The drum, the lute, and the shepherd's flute are the most common instruments used to accompany singing and dancing.

15 WORK

The traditional economy of the Balūchī combines dry-crop cereal farming with seminomadic pastoralism based on the herding of sheep, goats, and cattle. Of particular interest in central and southern areas is the cultivation of date palms, irrigated by underground aqueducts (*karez*). Some Balūchī communities along the southern Makran coast derive their living from fishing. Balūchī tend to look down on trade or commerce, these activities being viewed as unworthy occupations. Such business is left largely in the hands of non-Balūchī.

16 SPORTS

Popular games include *chauk*, a type of checkers introduced from Sind and played with wooden pieces on a cloth divided into squares. Moves are governed by six or seven cowrie shells, which are thrown on the ground in the manner of dice. *Ji*, a game of tag, is played by village boys and young men. Games such as wrestling and horse-racing are useful in developing skills in young men for war. Shooting and hunting are favorite pastimes among the upper classes. Card games and gambling are also popular among some groups.

17 ENTERTAINMENT AND RECREATION

Balūchī living in Karachi and other towns of southern Pakistan enjoy all the recreational facilities available to the urban resident. Those who follow a traditional seminomadic way of life in the remote Balūchī heartland have to rely on festivals, music, dancing, and folk culture for their entertainment.

18 FOLK ART, CRAFTS, AND HOBBIES

The Balūchī are not particularly known for their folk art or crafts. However, women are skilled at embroidery and adorn their garments with elaborate geometric and abstract designs. They make felt from sheep's wool, and weave rugs for their own use and for the purposes of exchange.

19 SOCIAL PROBLEMS

The Balūchī have not fared well in modern Pakistan. They form an ethnic and cultural population that has a transnational distribution, and whose natural affinities are more with their fellow Balūchī in Iran and Afghanistan than with other Pakistanis. Indeed, they are viewed as virtual "savages" by the dominant Punjabi and Sindhi majority in the country. It is little wonder that the Baluchī have very little sense of identity with Pakistan. This alienation is intensified by the failure of the national government to promote economic development in Baluchīstan, one of the most underdeveloped areas of the country.

Many see poverty and lack of education as a major hindrance to Baluchī economic and political advancement. Even in major urban centers such as Karachi, Baluchī children are at a disadvantage. Though they speak Baluchī at home, at school they have to struggle with Urdu, Sindhi, English (the language of commerce and higher education), and Arabic or Persian (the languages of Islam). Few advance beyond high school or low-status or menial jobs. The sense that they are viewed as second-class citizens, combined with resentment against their treatment by a central administration seen as heavy-handed and corrupt, has in the past given rise to Baluchī separatist movements. This has occasionally led to armed conflicts such as the Marri insurrection of 1973–77. Though defeated in the 1970s, a resilient Baluchī nationalist movement lingers on, garnering recruits and support from a population disaffected with establishment policies that emphasize resource transfer. In October 1992, ethnic tempers ran high and clashes took place between the Baluchīs and second largest ethnic group, the Pathans in Baluchīstan. After the Chagai nuclear tests by Pakistan in 1998, some Baluchī students hijacked a PIA (Pakistan International Airways) plane to register their disapproval and draw international attention to the prevailing sense of discrimination in Pakistan against Baluch people and Baluchīstan. Baluchī nationalism remains a sensitive issue, especially given the strategic location of Baluchīstan on the shores of the Arabian Sea and the political dynamics of the region. A proposed pipeline will carry natural gas from Turkmenistan to India through Baluchīstan, although the security of the pipeline remains an issue for the Pakistani government, under Prime Minister Yousuf Raza Gilani, in the face of the continuing low level insurgency in Baluchīstan.

Increasing levels of violence in southern Afghanistan since 2005 have been attributed to Al Qaeda and Taliban fighters finding safe haven in the border areas of Baluchīstan along with support from local Baluchīs, with whom the Islamic extremists have cultural affinities. Indeed, from this time, extremists involved in the anti-U.S. conflict in Afghanistan have converted areas of Baluchīstan into an operational rather than a logistical base. Quetta is a hotbed of extremist activities and, though the Pakistani Army is fully aware of this, the Islamabad government under President Musharraf did little to bring the area under government control. It remains to be seen whether the newly elected government will tackle the situation.

In August 2006 Pakistani security forces killed Nawab Akbar Khan Bugti, the 79-year-old chief of the Bugti tribe and former Chief Minister of the province, an incident which was followed by widespread unrest in eastern Baluchīstan. Since early 2005, Bugti, who was seen by locals as a leader, had been fighting the Pakistani Army with a private force of 5,000 loyal tribesmen in the mountains of eastern Baluchīstan. Bugti claimed only to be seeking provincial autonomy for Baluchīstan, a view which, naturally, was not shared by the Pakistani Army and security forces, who saw him as "anti-Pakistani."

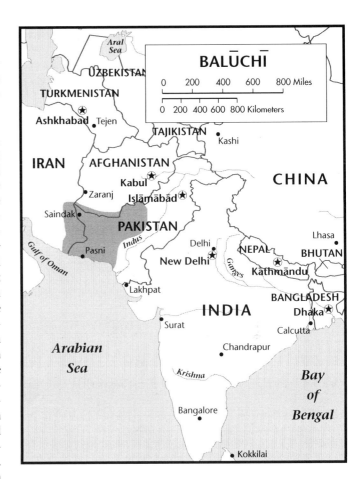

20 GENDER ISSUES

As is to be expected in a Muslim society, Baluchī women are seen as inferior to men and are expected to be obedient to their husbands. However, Baluchī women are less restrained than women among other Muslim peoples in South Asia. As noted earlier, they are not subject to the custom of *purdah* (except in some upper class families). Monogamy is the norm, while divorce is permitted. A Baluchī woman is responsible for household chores, as well as tending the family's herds and the gathering of wild plants, water, and firewood.

"Honor killings," originally common among the Baluchī tribes, is occasionally still faced by Baluchī women who still, even in urban areas, have low literacy and face difficulties in accessing education. Sexual and physical abuse by male family members also remain issues.

Women in Baluchīstan remain extremely poor, illiterate and bound by traditional norms of a tribal society that is patriarchal in nature, but they are nonetheless becoming involved in politics and play an increasingly influential role in society and in determining the future of the province.

21 BIBLIOGRAPHY

Bray, Denys. *Ethnographic Survey of Baluchīstan*. Bombay: The Times Press, 1913.

Janmahmad. *The Baloch Cultural Heritage*. Karachi: Royal Book Company, 1982.

Marri, Mir Khuda Bakhsh. *Searchlights on Baloches and Balochistan*. Lahore : Ferozsons, 1997.

Pehrson, Robert N. *The Social Organization of the Marri Baluch.* Chicago: Aldine Publishing Company, 1966.

Rooman, Anwar. *Balochi Language and Literature.* Quetta: Institute of Writing & Research, Balochistan, 2005.

Salzman, Philip Carl. *Black Tents of Balūchīstan.* Washington, DC: Smithsonian Institution Press, 2000.

—by D. O. Lodrick

BANGLĀDESHĪS

PRONUNCIATION: ban-gla-DESH-eez
LOCATION: Bangladesh
POPULATION: 158 million
LANGUAGE: Bengali (Bangla)
RELIGION: Islam (majority Sunni Muslim)
RELATED ARTICLES: Vol. 3: Chakmas; Vol. 4: Santals; Pakistanis

¹ INTRODUCTION

Banglādeshīs, like Indians and Pakistanis, owe their modern political identity to the events that accompanied the end of the British Empire in South Asia. When British India was partitioned in 1947, areas with a Muslim majority in the population were assigned to Pakistan, the new Muslim state. This included northwestern areas of the Indian subcontinent that were first conquered and settled by Muslim invaders in the 11th century AD. However, Muslim majorities also existed in the east of the subcontinent in Bengal. This area was separated to form the "East Wing" of Pakistan. Residents of the region thus became "Pakistani," members of a Muslim state that was split into two territorial units separated by 1,600 km (1,000 mi) of Indian territory. The link between the two Wings was religion, their populations being followers of Islam. The ties of religion, however, were not strong enough to overcome historical and cultural differences, as the events of the following two and a half decades were to show.

The region in which Bangladesh lies is thought to have been settled around 1000 BC by Dravidian-speaking peoples who came to be called the "Bang." This ancient tribal name is echoed in modern names such as Bangladesh, Bengal, and Bengali. For most of its history, Bengal (as it is convenient to call it) remained on the periphery of the great political events of the Indian subcontinent. At times, it fell under the control of the great pan-Indian empires such as that of the Mauryas (321–181 BC), while at other times it led an independent political existence. In AD 1202, however, Bengal came under the influence of the Muslim Turks who had established themselves in Delhi, and it remained under Muslim rule for the next 550 years. Beginning in the 13th century AD and continuing for several hundred years, Bengal saw the wholesale conversion of its people to Islam. These conversions were generally of the lower-caste Hindus, attracted by the ideals of brotherhood and equality taught by Islam.

Conversion to Islam did not mean adopting the language and culture of Islam. Bengali Muslims spoke the Bengali tongue and displayed a deep-rooted commitment to Bengali culture—something that was never fully understood by the national leaders of Pakistan, who were mainly from West Pakistan. Attempts in 1953 to impose Urdu as a second language in East Pakistan led to riots and several deaths. This day is still celebrated in Bangladesh as "National Mourning Day." Cultural differences, economic pressures, neglect of East Pakistan by the central government, and West Pakistanis' feelings of the superiority of their Islamic heritage, all contributed to deteriorating relations between East Pakistan and West Pakistan.

Popular dissatisfaction among Bengālīs resulted in a growing movement for autonomy in East Pakistan, led by Sheikh Mujibur Rahman (Mujib) of the Awami League. National elec-

Banglādeshī women watch a fair during celebrations of Bengali New Year. (AP Images/Pavel Rahman)

tions held in December 1970 gave Mujib a sweeping victory, and by rights he should have been appointed prime minister of Pakistan. However, General Yahya Khan, President of Pakistan, postponed indefinitely the convening of the National Assembly. When talks between Mujib and Yahya broke down, Yahya decided to solve the problem by force. In March 1971, the Pakistan Army embarked on a terror campaign in East Pakistan aimed at forcing the Bengālīs into submission. They identified and executed students, teachers, writers, members of the intelligentsia—anyone who was deemed a threat to the regime in power. For the next nine months, a bloody civil war was waged, pitting East Pakistan's Mukti Bahini (Liberation Force) against the Pakistani military. One estimate claims that more than a million Bengali civilians died at the hands of the Pakistan Army. The matter was ended when the Indian Army entered the fray, leading to the capitulation of Pakistan's forces on 16 December 1971. The "independent, sovereign republic of Bangladesh," first proclaimed on 26 March 1971, now became a reality.

² LOCATION AND HOMELAND

Bangladesh lies in the eastern part of the Indian subcontinent at the head of the Bay of Bengal. It is a relatively compact country covering an area of 147,570 sq km (56,977 sq mi), roughly the size of the state of Iowa. The Banglādeshī population numbers 158 million people, which ranks the country the seventh most populous in the world.

Except for its southern coastline, Bangladesh is virtually surrounded on all sides by India. Of its 4,246 km (2,638 mi) land border, only some 193 km (120 mi) in the southeast is shared with Burma (Myanmar). Bangladesh extends over 650 km (approximately 400 mi) northwards from the mouth of the Ganges River almost to the foothills of the Himalayas. In the extreme northwest, its border comes so close to Nepal's that less than 40 km (25 mi) of Indian territory separates the two countries. (The vulnerability of this narrow land corridor to Assam and its oil reserves was a strategic factor in India's decision to enter the 1971 war on the side of the insurgent Banglādeshīs.)

Bangladesh lacks the geographical diversity of the other countries of South Asia. The Chittagong Hills in the southeast are the only significant hill system in the country. An extension of the mountain ranges of eastern India and Burma, they form narrow north–south ridges rising to between 600 and 900 m (approximately 1,970–2,950 ft) above sea level. The highest point in Bangladesh (1,046 m or 3,432 ft) lies here in the south east. Roughly 80% of Bangladesh is located on the fertile alluvial lowland of the Gangetic Plain and on the Ganges Delta itself. Soon after it enters Bangladesh, the Ganges River is joined by both the Brahmaputra River (known in Bangladesh as the Jamuna) and the Meghna River to form one of the largest del-

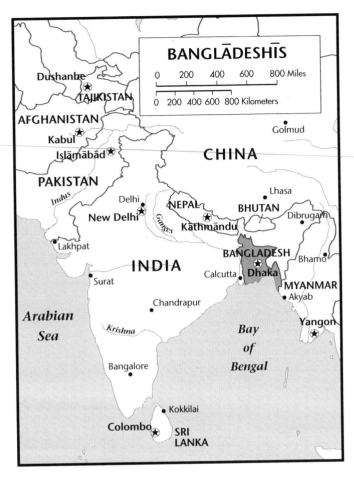

BANGLADESHIS

0   200   400   600   800 Miles

0   200 400 600 800 Kilometers

Dushanbe

TAJIKISTAN

AFGHANISTAN

Kabul

Islamabad

PAKISTAN

Indus

Delhi

New Delhi

Lakhpat

INDIA

Surat

*Arabian
Sea*

Bangalore

CHINA

Golmud

Lhasa

NEPAL

Kathmandu

Ganges

BHUTAN

Dibrugarh

BANGLADESH

Calcutta   Dhaka

Bhamo

MYANMAR

Akyab

Chandrapur

Krishna

*Bay
of
Bengal*

Yangon

Kokkilai

Colombo   SRI
LANKA

tas in the world. The coastal section of the delta is known as the *sundarbans*, a belt of low-lying tidal forests and mangrove trees that is the home of the Royal Bengal tiger.

The rivers of Bangladesh, some 700 in total, are at once its lifeblood and its curse. The annual flooding of the alluvial plain and delta renews the fertile soils of the region and allows it to support some of the highest agricultural population densities in the world. Yet periodically the region is subject to devastating floods with considerable loss of life and economic cost. In 1988, some of the worst flooding in the country's history occurred. Some 83% of the country was affected. Over 1,600 people died, a relatively small number compared to some natural catastrophes in the region, but the cost in terms of lost crops, livestock, and damage to the economic infrastructure was enormous.

Bangladesh experiences a subtropical monsoon climate, with the three distinct seasons typical of South Asia. Cool, dry winters are experienced from October to February. Temperatures rise during the following months to maximums between 32°c and 38°c (approximately 90°f to 100°f) in April, the hottest month. May sees the onset of early monsoon rains, with high humidity making for unpleasant conditions. June to October is the rainy season, with rainfall totals varying from 160 cm (63 in) in the west to 500 cm (approximately 200 in) in the northeast. During the late monsoon season, tropical cyclones periodically sweep in from the Bay of Bengal, often with disastrous consequences. In November 1970, such a storm slammed into the delta with winds exceeding 160 kph (100 mph) and a storm surge of 5.5 m (18 ft). Many of the coastal areas lie be-

tween 4 and 10 feet above sea-level and were completely submerged. Lacking an early warning system and given the poor transportation facilities, an estimated 250,000 people lost their lives in this storm. In November 2007, Bangladesh was struck by cyclone Sidr, which similarly caused enormous damage to the country. This was followed by severe flooding. As the Jamuna, Ganges and Meghna Rivers spilled over their banks, 30 million people were made homeless, 135,000 cattle died and 11,000 kilometers of roads damaged or destroyed. Two-thirds of the country was underwater.

Perhaps more than any other nationality in South Asia, Bangladeshis are characterized by ethnic unity. Over 98% of the population are Bengalis, speaking the Bengali language and identifying with Bengali cultural traditions. Biharis form another element, although a numerically small one, in the Bangladesh population. Biharis are non-Bengali, Urdu-speaking Muslim refugees from Bihar and other parts of northern India. This group stood to lose from Bangladesh's independence and supported the West Pakistanis during the 1971 war. At that time they numbered about 1 million. Many of them were repatriated to Pakistan after the war, however, but their current total is estimated at as many as 500,000 people.

Tribal peoples make up less than 1% of Bangladesh's population but they differ significantly from the rest of the population in their social organization, customs, and rituals. The largest of these groups are the Chakmas who, along with the Marmas, occupy the highland valleys of the Chittagong Hills. The Mros, considered the area's original inhabitants, and the Tiparas are other tribal groups of the Chittagong Hills. These hill tribes are of Sino-Tibetan descent and have distinct Mongoloid features. Other tribal groups, such as the Santal, Khasis, Garos, and Khajons, represent extensions of tribal populations from adjacent areas of India.

³ LANGUAGE

Bengali, or Bangla, is spoken by 98.8% of the population and is also the country's official language. It is a member of the Indo-Aryan branch of the Indo-European family of languages and is written in its own Bengali script. Regional dialects of Bengali include Rajbangshi, Varendra, and Vanga. Dialects such as Sylhetta and Chittagonian show strong Arab-Persian influences. Chakma, the tongue spoken by Chakma tribals, is a dialect of Bengali, although tribal languages such as Magh and Arakanese belong to the Tibeto-Burman branch of the Sino-Tibetan linguistic family. Urdu is the language spoken by Biharis. English remains an important language in Bangladesh.

⁴ FOLKLORE

Bangladeshis identify with the folk traditions of Bengali culture. This includes belief in shamanism and the powers of *fakīrs* (Muslim holy men who are viewed as exorcists and faith healers), *ōjhās* (shamans with magical healing powers), and *Bauls* (religious mendicants and wandering musicians). *Sūfism* is strongly entrenched in Bangladesh, with Shah Jalal and Khan Jahan Ali being among the most celebrated Sufi saints.

Sheikh Mujibur Rahman, leader of the Awami League, and the fighters of the Mukti Bahini are regarded as national heroes of the Bangladeshi independence movement.

⁵ RELIGION

At its creation, Bangladesh was constituted as a secular state. However, a series of constitutional amendments in 1977 and 1978 led to the adoption of Islam as the state religion. Most Banglādeshīs are Muslims, with nearly 90% of the population claiming Islam as their religion (2001 Census). The conversion of local populations to Islam began after AD 1202, when Bengal fell to invading Turkish armies, and continued for several centuries. Conversions were generally collective, with lower-caste Hindus and groups of Buddhists attracted to Islam by its ideals of equality, brotherhood, and social justice. Sufis played a major role in this process, and fakirs and *pirrs* (wandering Muslim holy men) were familiar figures in the villages of the region. Sufism remains an important element in the religious life of the people today. Most Banglādeshīs are Sunnis, although small Shia minorities are found in urban areas. The *Shia* festival of Muharram is widely observed by Sunnis in Bangladesh.

Although many non-Muslims fled Bangladesh in 1947, Hindus still account for 9.2% of the population. Buddhists (0.8%), Christians (0.3%) and tribal groups (0.1%) form other religious minorities in the country.

⁶ MAJOR HOLIDAYS

As an Islamic state, Bangladesh officially celebrates the Muslim festivals of Id-ul-Fitr, Bakr-Id, Muharram, and other Muslim festivals as public holidays. In addition, several Hindu festivals (e.g., Janamashtami, Durga Puja), Christian holy days (Good Friday, Easter Monday, and Christmas), and Buddhist celebrations (Buddha Purnima) are recognized as holidays.

Secular holidays include National Mourning Day (21 February), Independence Day (26 March) National Revolution Day (7 November) and Victory Day (16 December).

⁷ RITES OF PASSAGE

The rites of passage of Banglādeshīs follow normal Muslim patterns. Births are occasions for rejoicing, with male babies preferred over females. Muslim prayers are whispered into the baby's ears, and the naming ceremony is accompanied by the sacrifice of a sheep or goat. Male children undergo the *Sunnat* or circumcision. It is becoming fashionable, especially in urban communities, to celebrate children's birthdays.

Death rituals are performed according to Muslim canonical rules. The corpse is washed, shrouded, and carried to the cemetery where it is interred with the customary prayers for the departed soul. The next forty days are marked by various rituals, ending in the ceremonies held 40 days after death that bring the main period of mourning to a close.

⁸ INTERPERSONAL RELATIONS

Banglādeshīs are a warm, accommodating people and follow the usual traditions of South Asian hospitality. Visitors, even casual ones, are expected to stay for refreshments. Even the poorest host will provide a visitor with a glass of water and a spoonful of molasses, a piece of betel nut (areca nut), or offer a *hukkā* (a pipe used for smoking tobacco).

⁹ LIVING CONDITIONS

Some have described Bangladesh as belonging not to the Third World of developing nations but to the Fourth World, the poorest of the poor. This is reflected in its health statistics and economic indices. Life expectancy at birth in 2001 was 62.5 years—almost 20 years less than in Japan, the world's leading country in terms of life expectancy. Leading causes of death include typhoid fever, tetanus, and respiratory ailments such as tuberculosis. Medical advances have reduced infant mortality rates to around 62 deaths per 1,000 live births. Fertility rates are high, with the average number of births per childbearing woman in the population being 3.11 and the rate of natural increase of population is just over 2% per year.

Banglādeshīs are a rural people, with some 78% living in villages scattered across the country. Rural house types and construction materials depend on local conditions. Reeds are used in the delta, but houses further inland are made of mud, bamboo, and brush wood. Roofs are thatched with palm leaves, though the more prosperous now use corrugated iron. Tribes in the eastern hills build their houses on raised platforms. Villages may also contain the more substantial houses of former landowners *(zamīndārs)* and Hindu moneylenders. Per capita income in 2006 was among the lowest in South Asia, at us$2,300, well below the world average of $10,200 per year. However, the middle classes in cities such as Dhaka (the capital) live very much in the manner of urban elites throughout South Asia.

Land communications in Bangladesh are generally poor, with only 4% of the country's 193,000 km (120,000 mi) of road paved. The numerous rivers of the country make rail transportation difficult (there is an average of six bridges or culverts per kilometer of rail line), but water transport is an important means of communications. Biman Bangladesh Airlines is the country's air carrier, providing both international and domestic services.

¹⁰ FAMILY LIFE

The basic social unit in rural Bangladesh is the family *(paribār or gushtī)*. This consists of an extended family living in a household *(chula)* residing in a homestead *(bārī)*. Individual nuclear families known as *ghar* are often to be found within the extended family. Beyond the circle of immediate relatives is an institution known as "the society" *(samāj)*. This voluntary association concerns itself with issues such as the maintenance of the local mosque, support of a mullah (priest), and settling village disputes.

The extended family is the significant unit of economic endeavor, with jointly held property and household activities under the direction of the father's authority. Banglādeshī society is patrilineal, and married sons and their wives reside in the father's household. Marriage is a civil contract in Islam and is often made for the interests of the family rather than the individual. In Bangladesh, marriages are arranged by parents, although men may have some say in the choice of their spouses. Partners are chosen from families of similar social standing. The custom of paying a bride-price is followed, and some families have adopted the Hindu custom of providing a dowry.

Women remain subordinate to men in Banglādeshī society. Purdah, the seclusion of women from male company after puberty, is practiced to varying degrees. Even among modernized groups that have rejected purdah, segregation of the sexes continues. At public performances or lectures, for instance, it is common for men and women to sit in separate parts of the hall. Purdah also limits women's access to the workplace.

11 CLOTHING

In rural areas, Banglādeshī men wear the *lungi* and a vest or a shirt. The lungi is a piece of cotton cloth, usually checkered, that is wrapped around the waist like a sarong. The better-educated wear a collarless, tunic-length shirt known as a *punjābī*, and *pyjāmās* (loose cotton trousers.) On formal occasions, the sherwani (*śerwānī*), tight trousers known as *chūrīdār*, and a turban are worn. Hindus wear the dhoti or the punjabi-pyjama attire. Women typically wear the sari and blouse, although girls and young women prefer the *salwār-kamīz* tunic and pants combination. Western-style shirts, pants, and jackets are commonly worn by men in urban areas.

12 FOOD

Rice, vegetables, pulses, fish, and meat form the staples of the Banglādeshī diet. The tastes and preferences of Muslims and other groups, however, differ. Beef is popular with Muslims, though taboo for Hindus. At feasts or formal dinners, Muslims often serve Muhgal-style dishes including pilaf and *biryānī* (rice dishes containing meat and vegetables), *kebābs* (barbecued cubes of meat), and *kormās* (meat served in various kinds of sauces). *Ghī* (clarified butter) is commonly served at such meals. Milk forms an important element in the diet, and Bangladesh is known for its milk-based sweets. All communities eat with their hands rather than with utensils.

13 EDUCATION

Nearly 59% of Banglādeshīs 5 years of age and over have no formal schooling, and only 15.3% have completed their secondary education. This is reflected in literacy rates among the lowest in South Asia, with only 43.1% of the population over 15 years old being able to read and write (2001). This figure drops to 32.8% for females. Universal primary education is a goal of government education policy, but high drop-out rates, inadequate resources, and a lack of trained teachers at all levels have hindered education in the country.

The national government has attempted to modernize the curricula of *madrasas,* Islamic religious schools attached to mosques and supported by endowments and public charity but which cater mainly to males.

14 CULTURAL HERITAGE

Banglādeshīs are proud of their Bengali culture, with its traditions of music, dance, and literature. The country shares in the classical and devotional traditions of Hindu and Muslim music but has developed its own regional forms of popular music (e.g., *bātiālī* songs connected with boatmen and life on the river, and *baul,* mystical verse sung by a caste of religious musicians called Bauls). Indigenous dance forms include the *dhali, baul, manipuri,* and snake dances.

The Bengali literary tradition is one of the oldest regional traditions in India, dating to the 11th century AD. Its greatest figure was the poet Rabrindranath Tagore, who was part of the 19th-century revival of Bengali culture. Kazi Azrul Islam is a modern poet and playwright known as the "voice of Bengali nationalism and independence." He forms part of a Muslim literary heritage in Bengali culture that can be traced back to the Sufi devotional compositions of the 13th century. A distinctive regional style of architecture may be seen in mosques and other monuments built by Muslims beginning in the early 15th century.

15 WORK

Bangladesh is primarily an agricultural country, with 60% of the labor force involved in cultivation. Rice is the dominant food crop. Jute is the country's major cash crop and an important export item. The industrial resource base is poor, and the manufacturing sector of the economy is quite small. Since the 1970s, however, Bangladesh has become a major producer of ready-made garments for export to the West (particularly the U.S.). Based on cheap Banglādeshī labor (mostly women), this now accounts for over 80% of export revenues, although the preferential system afforded Banglādeshī-made garments ended in 2005. The export of frozen shrimp and fish has also increased in importance over the last several decades.

Large numbers of Banglādeshīs are working in the Persian Gulf region, and remittances from this population is an important source of foreign exchange for the country.

16 SPORTS

Children in rural areas play games common to all of South Asia, such as hide-and-seek, flying kites, and spinning tops. *Ha-do-do* is a traditional game in which teams send a member into the opponents' territory to tag as many of the opposition as possible while holding his or her breath. Wrestling is a favorite pastime for young men. Soccer is the most popular modern sport, while cricket, field hockey, badminton, and table tennis are also played.

17 ENTERTAINMENT AND RECREATION

In villages, festivals and fairs are occasions for entertainment and relaxation. Dances, music, and song are popular, as are the *jātrās* (village operas based on local myths). Boat races allow young men to display their prowess. In urban centers and those villages that have cinema houses, movies are by far the most popular form of entertainment. Radio and television broadcasts are available, but these are controlled by the government. The press is relatively free, but given the low literacy rates, newspapers in Bangladesh have a low circulation.

18 FOLK ART, CRAFTS, AND HOBBIES

Among the arts and crafts for which Bangladesh is known are *kathas* (finely embroidered quilt-work); hand printed textiles; terracotta dolls, toys, and idols; and *sikhars* (elaborate rope hangings for pots, bottles, etc.). *Alpana* drawings are designs made on floors and courtyards out of rice-paste. They are prepared by Hindu women in connection with certain religious festivals and rites. Copper and brass metalwork, basketry, and mat-weaving are also traditional crafts among Banglādeshī artisans. The region also has an important boat-building industry, and the decoration of boats is a thriving folk art in Bangladesh.

19 SOCIAL PROBLEMS

When Bangladesh became independent in 1971, the country was referred to in some foreign circles as an "international basket case." It suffered from overpopulation, extreme poverty, malnutrition, and lack of resources. It was subject to periodic natural disasters—drought, famine, cyclones, and especially the repeated flooding that plays havoc with peoples' lives and the country's economic infrastructure. Few thought there was much of a future for the country.

A quarter of a century later, little seems to have changed. Bangladesh ranks lowest among the nations of South Asia in many economic indices. Overpopulation and poverty are still a problem, and the country has one of the highest population densities in the world. Daily per capita calorie intake is over 2200 kcal, though 75% of the population is classified as below the poverty line in terms of caloric intake. Natural disasters still devastate the country. Yet the country's very survival is a victory of sorts, and the future looks less bleak than it did in 1971. Slowly, with generous foreign aid provided through the World Bank-led Bangladesh Aid Group in Paris, the economy is struggling upwards. Food production has increased and a nationwide birth control program has succeeded in lowering the rate of population growth. Flood control projects will help limit the incidence of flooding. Diversification of the economy has increased the value of the country's exports.

A major political problem faced by Bangladeshis was that of tribal unrest in the Chittagong Hill Tracts. Chakmas and other tribal groups resorted to armed resistance in support of demands for regional autonomy. Bangladeshi Army operations in the area during the 1980s and 1990s resulted in a flood of refugees into India, and charges of human rights violations against the government. In 1997 a peace agreement was signed between Chakma rebels and the government of Bangladesh, granting a degree of autonomy to the Chakma people. Bangladesh has also survived the imposition of military government and periods of civil unrest. Following rioting in early 2007, a caretaker government (now under Fakhruddin Ahmed, a former World Bank economist) was installed to oversee general elections, which were postponed until the end of 2008.

Concerns exist that Bangladesh is becoming a safe haven for al Qaeda and Taliban extremist terrorist groups.

Bangladesh continues to have major economic, social, and political problems. Despite an expanding economy, it will remain dependent on massive foreign aid for the foreseeable future. Its population remains among the poorest in the world, and its political future is uncertain. But it also has a population united by Bengali culture, the heritage of Islam, the legacy of its struggle for independence from Pakistan, a tradition of democracy and considerable optimism for the future and pride in its nation.

One success story in the development of the Bangladeshi economy has been the widespread propagation of microcredit by Muhammad Yunus (awarded the Nobel peace prize in 2006) through the Grameen Bank. The Grameen Bank currently has nearly 5 million members, many of them poor rural women.

In order to enhance economic growth, the government has set up several export processing zones to attract foreign investment. These are managed by the Bangladesh Export Processing Zone Authority. Exports of garments and agricultural products have helped propel Bangladesh to an annual economic growth rate of around 5% a year—not quite on a par with China and India, but quite impressive in its own right.

20 GENDER ISSUES

The Global Gender Gap Index 2007 ranks Bangladesh 100 out of 128 countries in terms of gender equality. Bangladesh being a predominantly Muslim country, women are viewed as inferior citizens and subject to Shariah law. Despite this, the Bangladesh government is pushing ahead with a new National Women's Development Policy (NWDP). A section of Muslim clerics and some Islamic political parties say equal rights for women in terms of property would violate Sharia law on inheritance, which stipulates that a woman should inherit only half of what her brother would get (in April 2008, there were riots by Muslims protesting women receiving equal rights in terms of inheritance). Only 32.8% of women are literate (compared to 43.1% for men) and only 4% participate in tertiary education. Despite the two most important political parties in Bangladesh (the Bangladesh Nationalist Party and the Awami League) being headed by women (Khalida Zia and Sheik Hasina, respectively), only 15% of parliamentarians are women.

A certain ambiguity exists surrounding the question of violence against women in Bangladeshi society. On the one hand, violence is held in repugnance and may provoke outrage. On the other hand, violence against women is accepted, tolerated and "in certain prescribed forms and given contexts," it is legitimated. Gender inequality, leading to gender violence, is deeply embedded in the Bangladeshi social structure; all Bangladeshi social institutions permit, even encourage the demonstration of unequal power relations between the sexes.

21 BIBLIOGRAPHY

Afsaruddin, Mohammad. *Society and Culture in Bangladesh.* Dhaka: Book House, 1990.

Ahmed, Nazimuddin. *Islamic Heritage of Bangladesh.* Dacca: Department of Films & Publications, Government of the People's Republic of Bangladesh, 1980.

Bangladesh—Country Brief, World Bank, July 2005.

Heitzman, James, and Robert L. Worden, ed. *Bangladesh, a Country Study.* 2nd ed. Washington, D.C.: Federal Research Division, Library of Congress, 1988.

International Crisis Group, *Asia Report* No.121, October 23, 2006.

Johnson, B. L. C. *Bangladesh.* 2nd ed. London: Heinemann Educational Books, 1982.

Mascarenhas, A. Bangladesh: A Legacy of Blood. Hodder & Stoughton, London, 1986.

—by D. O. Lodrick

BANIAS

PRONUNCIATION: BAHN-yuhz
ALTERNATE NAMES: Vania
LOCATION: India (Uttar Pradesh, Rajasthan, Gujarat, and
   Maharashtra states; also sizeable communities in Delhi,
   Bombay, Calcutta and other Indian cities); Singapore;
   Malaysia; Fiji; Hong Kong; elsewhere in the Middle East
POPULATION: 55-65 million
LANGUAGE: Rajasthani, Marwari and other dialects of western
   Hindi or the language of the region from which they
   originate
RELIGION: Hinduism; Jainism
RELATED ARTICLES: Vol. 3: Hindus; Vol 4: People of India

¹ INTRODUCTION

The word *Bania* (also *Vania*) is derived from the Sanskrit
vanij, meaning "a merchant." The term is widely used to identify members of the traditional mercantile or business castes
of India. Thus, Banias are bankers, moneylenders, traders,
and shopkeepers. Though some members of the Bania castes
are cultivators, more Banias than any other caste follow their
traditional caste occupation. Banias are classed as *vaisyas,* the
third of the four great categories of Hindu society, and stand
below *Brahmans* and *Ksatriyas* in caste ranking. They are,
however, considered to belong to the "twice-born" castes of India, they wear the sacred thread, and they adhere strictly to the
rules of behavior that go along with this status. The Aggarw-
als and Oswals are prominent Bania castes of northern India,
while the Chettiar are a mercantile caste of the south.

   Banias believe that the community originated 5000 years
ago when an ancestor Maharaja Agrasen (or Ugarsain) of
Agroha, Haryana divided the Vaisya (third in the Hindu *varna* system) community into 18 clans. Their surnames include
Aggarwal,Gupta, Lala, Seth, Vaish, Mahajan, Sahu and Sahu-
kar. There are six subgroups among the Bania—the Bisa or
Vaish Aggarwal, Dasa or Gata Aggarwal, Saralia, Saraogi or
Jain, Maheshwari or Shaiva and Oswal. The Bisa believe that
they are descendents of the 17 snake daughters of Bashak Nag
(cobra) who married the 17 sons of Ugarsain. The husbands
slept with the handmaidens of the snake daughters resulting
in Dasa offspring. The Bisa ("twenty") consider themselves of
a higher status to the Dasa ("ten") and the Pancha ("five"). The
Saralia are an offshoot of the Bisa who migrated to Saralia,
near Ambala in Haryana State.

² LOCATION AND HOMELAND

Although no recent data are available, the Bania castes make
up an estimated 6% or 7% (or 55 million to 65 million people)
of India's Hindu population. Bania communities are found in
cities, towns, and villages all over India but have their densest concentrations in the northwest in Rajasthan, Gujarat, and
Maharashtra. and in Uttar Pradesh. There is considerable spec-
ulation as to why the trading ethic has been so important in the
western part of the Indian subcontinent. Some scholars have
argued that the harsh desert environment of Rajasthan forced
much of the population to turn to nonagricultural occupations
to support themselves. Others have suggested that proximity
to the overland and maritime trade routes with the Middle

East have played a role in this emphasis on trade and commercial activities. Whatever the facts of the matter, Banias from
the northwest have migrated to all parts of India and beyond.
Much of the commerce of Bombay (Mumbai) is in the hands of
Gujarati Banias. Rajasthani businesspeople, known as "Marwaris" after the region of Rajasthan called Marwar, are found
as far afield as Assam and Tamil Nadu. There is an important,
and also affluent, community of Marwaris in Calcutta.

   The Bania castes, and Gujaratis in particular, also form
an important element in the population of overseas Indians.
They have settled in Singapore, Malaysia, Fiji, Hong Kong, and
elsewhere in Asia where business opportunities present themselves. They are also found in the Middle East and among the
Indian populations of the United Kingdom, Canada, and the
United States.

³ LANGUAGE

Banias speak the language of the region from which they originate. Thus, a Shrimali from Gujarat speaks Gujarati, an Oswal
from Rajasthan speaks Marwari (a Rajasthani dialect), and a
Banajiga Lingayat (a trading subgroup of the Hindu Lingayat
sect) from Karnataka speaks Kannada. Banias who are settled
in regions where other languages are current obviously need
to know the local language in order to do business. But, even
though they are long removed in both distance and time from
their original home, they still use their native tongue among
themselves and at home. Marwari business communities in
Gauhati and other towns in Assam, for example, still keep
their books and converse among themselves in their own Rajasthani language.

⁴ FOLKLORE

The Bania castes share in the mythology and folklore of their
own religious communities and regional cultures. Many Banias, for example, are Jains and are thus brought up in the
traditions of the Jain religion. Vaishnavism is strongly rooted
among the Bania castes of Rajasthan and Gujarat, and for these
Banias the myths and legends of Krishna, the cowherd god of
Hinduism, are of utmost importance. Each caste has its own
lore and folk traditions. The Shrimali caste of Gujarat traces
its origins to Bhinmal, a town in Rajasthan formerly known
as Shrimal. There, they believe, 90,000 Shrimali families were
created by Mahalakshmi, the daughter of the sage Bhrigu, to
maintain 90,000 Shrimali Brahman families. One account says
they came from her thigh; another, from her garland. Some explain the division of the Shrimali castes into two subdivisions
by the fact that the Bisa Shrimalis sprang from the right side of
Mahalakshmi's garland and the Dasa Shrimalis from the left.
Of interest here, Mahalakshmi or Lakshmi is the Hindu goddess of wealth and is of great importance to the Bania castes.
The Shrimali Brahmans are still the family priests for the Shrimali Banias.

⁵ RELIGION

Banias are Hindu or Jain and follow the beliefs and customs
of their respective religions. Some castes, such as the Shrimalis, have both Hindu ("Meshri") and Jain ("Shravak") sections.
Thus, a Dasa Shrimali Shravak is a member of the Dasa section
of the Shrimali caste who follows the Jain religion. Most Jains,
because of religious restrictions on occupations they can follow
without violating the principles of their religion, belong to the

Bania castes. They are split between the *Svetambara* ("white-clad") and *Digambara* ("sky-clad") sects of Jainism. Jains in northern India generally belong to the Svetambara sect. Hindu Banias are almost exclusively Vaishnavas, i.e., they worship the god Vishnu, in his incarnation as Krishna. Most follow the Vallabhacharya sect of Hinduism, in which Krishna is seen as the supreme deity. This sect is also known as *pushti-marga* ("abundance way"), as it calls on its followers to enjoy the good things of life Krishna has provided for their enjoyment.

⁶ MAJOR HOLIDAYS

Banias celebrate the festivals of their religious communities, although some are more significant than others. For example, Divali, the Hindu "Festival of Lights," is kept by all Hindus but it holds particular importance for the Bania castes. It is an occasion for the worship of Lakshmi, the Hindu goddess of wealth, and is also a time when the financial books for the old year are closed and new ones started for the coming year. Houses are painted and all food in the household is thrown out and replaced. It is also a time for card-playing and gambling. The festival of Ganapati or Ganesh, the Hindu god of good fortune, is also important for the Banias. Jains celebrate the usual festivals of Jainism, but they, too, observe Divali, which coincides with their own festival honoring the death of the founder of the religion, Mahavira.

⁷ RITES OF PASSAGE

The life-cycle rituals of the Banias conform in general to Hindu and Jain practices, although they may show variations in their details. In Gujarat, a Hindu Bania woman usually returns to her father's house for her confinement and to give birth. Various rituals such as the Sixth Day worship are performed. Among the objects used in this ceremony are a piece of paper, an inkstand, and a reed pen—items clearly related to the traditional occupation of the Bania caste. Similarly, to mark events such as a betrothal, contributions are made to the caste fund. The caste association is important among Banias, and many castes are still organized into trade guilds or *mahajans*. These are modern survivals of institutions that date to medieval times.

Like all Hindu groups, Banias cremate their dead. But again, some of the death rituals are unique to each caste. On his deathbed, a Hindu Bania in Gujarat traditionally performs Godan ("the gift of a cow") by giving a Brahman a cow or the monetary value of a cow. He also names a sum of money to be given to charity in his name. After death, the body is taken to the cremation ground, bathed, wrapped in a shroud, and burnt on the funeral pyre. The ashes and bones are collected and thrown into a river or the ocean. A cow is milked on the spot where the body was cremated. Various rites are performed during the period of mourning. These include marrying a steer to a heifer, giving food to crows, and feeding dogs. This latter custom is of interest because in Hinduism the dog is usually viewed as an unclean animal. The funeral rites conclude by the giving of a caste dinner.

⁸ INTERPERSONAL RELATIONS

The term *bania* is often used by other castes in a negative sense to mean someone who is greedy, who exploits customers, who resorts to shady deals, and who will do anything to make a profit. There is, perhaps, an element of truth in this stereotype.

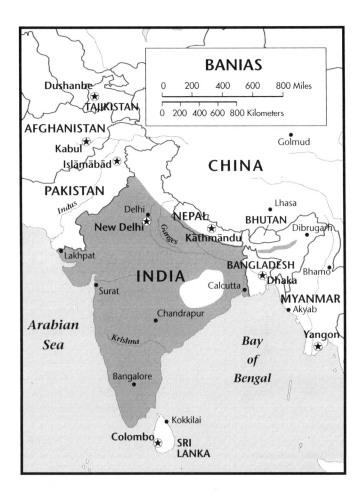

The Bania is the principal moneylender in the villages. Uneducated peasants who borrow money at high rates of interest so that they can grow their crops may never be able to pay off the loan. They eventually end up losing their land, and the Bania is seen as the villain. The same problem in repaying loans applies to the large amounts of money that may be borrowed for marriages and dowries. On the other hand, as bankers, moneylenders, traders, and businesspeople, Banias have played an essential role in the functioning of India's economy. Some scholars argue it was Bania moneylenders who funded British economic development in India. Today, many of the country's important industrialists and capitalists come from the Bania castes.

⁹ LIVING CONDITIONS

Banias are, by and large, prosperous, and this is reflected in their lifestyles and standards of living. However, the specifics of housing, creature comforts, and other aspects of their material culture are determined to a large extent by the place and social context of their lives. The Bania who runs a small shop in a village in Rajasthan lives very much like his or her neighbors. The Bania's house may be bigger and built of better materials, and its furnishings may be more opulent, but in appearance and design it is little different from other houses in the village. On the other hand, the prosperous industrialist in Bombay or Calcutta is likely to live in a luxurious, air-conditioned house, with numerous servants, automobiles, and all the conveniences of modern living.

Traditionally, the Bania are strict vegetarians whose diet consists of wheat, rice, maize, pulses, lentils, vegetables, fruit and dairy products. Many younger men eat meat at social events outside their community. They do not drink alcohol but smoke and chew tobacco and *paan* (betel leaf.)

Literacy levels are high as both boys and girls are encouraged to study further and attain university degrees. Banias visit clinics and hospitals as well as alternative indigenous medicine. Family planning is practiced to limit family size. They have made good use of media and communication and benefited from the government's development programs. They have embraced progress and developments. Agriculturists use fertilizers, pesticides and irrigation to increase crop yields. Loans provided by banks have enabled the Bania to expand or set up new businesses.

¹⁰ FAMILY LIFE

Banias are divided into numerous castes distributed over the Indian subcontinent. As with all Hindu castes or *jati,* they are endogamous social units. The basic unit in which endogamy is practiced, however, may be a subcaste rather than the caste itself. Among the Banias of the northwestern region, the Bisas are considered the most pure and unpolluted section of the original caste. Dasas are ranked lower, perhaps because of intermarriage with local peoples in the past or the taking up of occupations considered demeaning by the caste. The Pancha section is ranked the lowest of the three. These various sections often act as endogamous groups in their own right. For example, the Shrimali caste of Gujarat has all three sections, Bisa, Dasa, and Pancha (known among the Shrimalis as Ladva). These groups do not intermarry, and the Bisa Shrimali does not even dine with the Ladva Shrimali. In this sense, the three sections virtually function as separate castes. The Bisa Shrimalis are exclusively Jain. In northern Gujarat, the Dasa Shrimali Shravaks (Jain Shrimalis) will marry Dasa Shrimali Meshris (Hindu Shrimalis).

Marriage among the Banias reflects the basic differences between North and South India, as well as differing regional customs. In Gujarat, for example, cross-cousin marriage is prohibited, and there is a certain distance of relationship required within the marriage pool defined by the endogamous caste or subcaste. Marriages are arranged and are often seen as business associations between two families as well as unions of a boy and girl. In the past, child marriage was common, although obviously this has changed today. A wedding is an occasion for a display of wealth and may often last as long as eight days. The marriage ceremony follows the Hindu or Jain rites. Residence after marriage is patrilocal, i.e., the newlyweds move into the home of the groom's family. Bania families display the typical joint family structure of Hindu society. The role of women is primarily to deal with domestic matters, with the business affairs of the family left in the hands of the men. Divorce is not socially permitted but does occur rarely. Widow remarriage is allowed and is becoming acceptable except in Karnataka, where it is definitely not permitted. Levirate, i.e. when a women marries a deceased husband's brother, and junior sororate, when a widower marries a deceased wife's younger sister, are permitted by most Bania groups.

¹¹ CLOTHING

Bania clothing reflects regional styles of dress. In Gujarat, this consists of a *dhoti,* over which is worn a jacket, a long-sleeved coat known as an *angarkha,* and a shoulder cloth (*pichodi*). A variety of turbans are worn, depending on locality, but all clearly identify the wearer as a Bania. In northern and central Gujarat, Banias wear a small, tightly folded, cylinder-shaped turban with numerous folds in the front and several coils at the back. Bania women wear the *sari* over a petticoat (*ghaghra*) and bodice (*choli*). Both men and women are fond of ornaments. A wealthy man may wear a silver girdle, a gold armlet above the elbow, earrings, a necklace, and rings on his fingers. A well-to-do Bania woman wears gold hair ornaments, gold or pearl earrings, nose rings, and a variety of necklaces, bangles, anklets, and toe rings.

Although traditional dress is still worn in rural areas and in many towns, the modern businessman in a city such as Calcutta is likely to be dressed in a Western-style business suit, shirt, and tie.

¹² FOOD

Banias observe fairly rigid dietary restrictions. Both Jains and Vaishnavas are strictly vegetarian, out of concern for ritual purity, regard for animal life, and the sanctity of the cow. Liquor and narcotics are prohibited to the Bania castes (although this does not stop many Westernized individuals from drinking alcohol). Actual diet and eating habits tend to reflect regional cuisines. Thus, in Gujarat, where vegetarianism has long been an established tradition, the typical diet consist of breads (*roti*) made from wheat or other grains, eaten with vegetables, condiments, and copious amounts of *ghi* (clarified butter). Jain concern for *ahimsa,* the philosophy of nonviolence to all living things, means that even certain plant foods are taboo. Milk and milk products are an important part of the diet. Even where Banias have migrated to areas such as Bengal or Assam where eating fish is acceptable among the higher castes, they preserve their vegetarian traditions.

¹³ EDUCATION

Banias, as a group, are highly literate because of their need to keep accounts. Young boys receive training in traditional accounting methods, mathematics, and mental arithmetic at an early age. These skills, combined with intelligence, shrewdness, and an ethic of hard work have contributed to the economic success of the community. In the past, they have been employed in positions of responsibility in the administrations of the princely states of northwestern India. The more conservative groups prefer traditional education to Western schooling. However, modern education has come to be seen as a means of success in both personal and business life. Among the Agarwal community of Delhi, for example, a premium is placed on education even for girls. Even though a woman may not use her education, it may be essential for finding her a suitable husband. Among the younger generation who are entering modern industrial or commercial concerns, university and even professional degrees are commonplace.

¹⁴ CULTURAL HERITAGE

The Bania castes have a tradition of patronage and support for culture and the arts and also of giving to charity. They contribute heavily to the support of temples and religious institutions. Many impressive temples in northwestern India, some dating to the 11th century AD, reflect the generosity and piety of the Jain merchant community. The Birlas, a successful, modern bania family, have funded the construction of temples across India. The most recent, the Shri Radhakrishna Temple in Calcutta, with its exquisite Rajasthani carvings, was dedicated in 1996. Banias have supported artists and artisans, as seen in the Jaina school of painting or the magnificent wood and stone work found in the Bania houses and mansions *(havelis)* of Rajasthan and Gujarat. They have built, and still support, hospitals, schools, colleges, and universities throughout India.

Charity is an important part of the Bania ethic. Bania castes have their own charitable funds to help the needy of their caste. They also provide charity to the general public, feeding the poor and supporting hospitals and *dharamsalas* (rest houses for pilgrims). Two unusual institutions of the Banias are the *pinjrapol* and the *goshala*. The former is a Jain home for animals. Sick or injured animals are provided with medical care, and old animals are maintained until they die from natural causes. This institution originates in the Jain concern for *ahimsa* (nonviolence). The goshala, a home for old and useless cows, stems from the Hindu concept of the sanctity of the cow. Both institutions are supported by charitable contributions from Banias.

15 WORK

The Bania castes make up the mercantile classes of Hindu society, and most Banias continue to follow their traditional occupation today. Many remain small entrepreneurs, running stores and shops in villages and towns across India, they are traders of grain, groceries, and spices and also work as money lenders. They have a reputation of being shrewd and mercenary. Money is loaned at very high interest rates with secured collateral, usually against land or gold. They also work in government departments, private enterprise and agriculture, and include administrators, engineers, doctors, advocates, judges, teachers, scholars and stockbrokers among them. Others have emerged as leaders of commerce, trade, and industry in the modern Indian economy. The Birlas, for example, one of the most prominent business families in India, belong to the Marwari community of Calcutta, and the Singhanias, Modis, and Bangurs, also among the top ten business houses in India, are also Marwari. Banias are active in politics at local, regional and national levels and have a powerful presence in India.

16 SPORTS

There are no sports that are distinctively "Bania" in origin or practice.

17 ENTERTAINMENT AND RECREATION

Entertainment and recreation depends on individual circumstances. A conservative village Bania from Gujarat may forgo modern mass media in favor of traditional entertainment associated with religious festivals and local folk traditions. Affluent young Marwaris who belong to Calcutta's business elite are more likely to lead a Westernized lifestyle, turning to golf, horse-racing, and exclusive clubs for their entertainment.

18 FOLK ART, CRAFTS, AND HOBBIES

There are no folk arts, crafts, or hobbies specifically associated with the Bania castes.

19 SOCIAL PROBLEMS

Banias, as a community, are relatively prosperous, and the problems they face are different from those of many other groups in India. As "twice-born" Hindus, they do not face the discrimination met by low-caste and Untouchable communities. As merchants, they are not as dependent as the cultivator on a good monsoon. Many are more concerned with the stability of India's economic policies than with the arrival of the rainy season. Perhaps the most common problem faced by the community is the survival of the stereotype—especially in rural areas—of Banias as greedy moneylenders, traders who adulterate their goods, and shady dealers who make their living by exploiting the common person.

20 GENDER ISSUES

Bania women face the same problems as all women in a male-dominated society. Their families follow local caste customs in terms of arranged marriages, child marriage, dowry demands, widow remarriage, etc., even though child marriages and the giving of dowries have been legally banned by the government of India.

Women among the Bania castes have a low status and are usually confined to their homes though some help their husbands in the family shop and city women work. The women take part in social and religious functions only, although they do have input on financial matters relating to the family. The women sing folksongs and dance at marriages, births and festivals. They are known for their cooking, making rich dishes and sweets on special occasions.

Bania women tend to be better educated than other women in South Asia, though this rarely translates into achievement in the workplace, but rather is a means of obtaining a better match in marriage. The prime role of women is still to bear children, run the household and to complete household chores. Bania women who have migrated to other countries, especially the West, fare better in terms of education and the workplace, if they so choose.

21 BIBLIOGRAPHY

Babb, Lawrence A. *Alchemies of Violence.* New Delhi: Sage Publications, 2004.

Channa, V. C. *Caste: Identity and Continuity.* Delhi: B. R. Publishing, 1979.

Hardgrove, Anne. *Community and Public Culture: The Marwaris in Calcutta, c. 1897–1997.* New Delhi: Oxford University Press, 2004.

Lodrick, Deryck O. *Sacred Cows, Sacred Places: Origins and Survivals of Animal Homes in India.* Berkeley and Los Angeles: University of California Press, 1981.

Saha, Narayan Chandra. *The Marwari Community in Eastern India.* New Delhi: Decent Books, 2003.

Timberg, Thomas A. *The Marwaris: From Traders to Industrialists.* New Delhi: Vikas Publishing House, 1978.

—by D. O. Lodrick

BANJARESE

PRONUNCIATION: BAHN-jar-eez
LOCATION: Indonesia (Borneo)
POPULATION: 3.5 million
LANGUAGE: Banjarese
RELIGION: Islam
RELATED ARTICLES: Vol. 3: Indonesians; Javanese; Vol. 4:
   Malays

¹INTRODUCTION

The modern Banjarese people are the product of the mixing of four Dayak groups (Ma'anyan, Lawangan, Bukit, and Ngaju) with Sumatran Malays, Javanese, Sundanese, Arabs, Chinese, and Buginese. What distinguishes them from their upriver and highland neighbors is their use of the Banjarese language, a dialect of Malay, and their adherence to Islam, both reflecting connections to the maritime world beyond Borneo. Their identity focuses on the now defunct sultanate of Banjarmasin, whose origins go back to the Hinduized kingdom of Negara Dipa. The city of Banjarmasin itself was founded at the end of the 13th century by Ampujatamaka, the son of a merchant from the Coromandel coast of southeastern India. In 1377, a Majapahit prince married the daughter and sole heir of the Negara Dipa king; thus, Banjarmasin became a vassal of the great Javanese realm and experienced strong Javanese influences, still reflected in the language and various local art forms. In 1526, one side in an internal power struggle triumphed, thanks to aid from the north Javanese state of Demak; conversion to Islam was the price for this aid.

The 17th century was the Golden Age of Banjarmasin when it flourished in the pepper trade, enjoyed vigorous commerce with Java and Gujerat in India, and exercised influence along the Borneo coast from Sambas and Sukadana in the west to Kutai and Berau in the east. Dutch attempts at extending its monopoly over Banjarmasin's pepper trade (including once destroying the city and expelling their British East India Company rivals) failed, due largely to competition from Chinese merchants.

From the late 18th to the mid-19th centuries, Banjarese internal struggles encouraged Dutch intervention. In 1817, one sultan with a less-than-solid claim to legitimacy obtained Dutch aid in exchange for ceding the rights to suzerainty over most of Banjarmasin's traditional sphere along the Borneo coast. The Dutch also demanded the right to name the sultan's successor. In 1857, their installation of their own candidate on the throne enraged the Banjarese and started a short but vicious and costly war. The Dutch dissolved the sultanate in 1860 but faced resistance mounted by Pangeran Antasari, a royal descendant, and Sultan Kuning (despite the title, a peasant) until 1864. Islamic leaders were to stage sporadic uprisings until as late as 1905.

With the exploitation of Kalimantan's timber and fossil fuel wealth, as well as the development of the immediate region's agricultural potential, Banjarmasin and South Kalimantan as a whole are developing rapidly. This is accelerating the forces of integration (Malayification and Islamization) through which the Banjarese community has always expanded.

²LOCATION AND HOMELAND

Banjarese are the majority population of the province of South Kalimantan on Indonesian Borneo. The Meratus mountains, a long, broad range with no peak higher than 1,900 m (6,235 ft), run north–south through the province. The great Barito River and the Martapura, a tributary meeting it close to the sea, provide access to the interior of the province and beyond into Central Kalimantan. A vast tidal swamp occupies the coast. Over the last six decades, part of the swamp has been reclaimed for the cultivation of wet-rice and other crops; this area constitutes one of the major rice bowls in the Outer Islands (i.e., outside Java-Bali-Lombok).

According to the 2000 census, Banjarese numbered 3.5 million (Indonesia's tenth largest ethnic group), up from 2,755,000 in 1990. The 1990 figure represented a 55% increase over the 1980 level, the fastest growth rate for an Indonesian linguistic group during that period. As they have become integrated into wider society through conversion to Islam, increased economic activity, and cross-ethnic marriage, speakers of smaller regional languages in South Kalimantan have adopted Banjarese as their primary language in recent years (an acceleration of the process that created the Banjarese identity in the first place). Between 1980 and 1990, the Banjarese-speaking proportion of the province's population rose from 62.8% to 81.7%; in Central Kalimantan, the proportion nearly doubled over the same period, going from 17.5% to 32.3%. By 2000, the Banjarese proportion of the South Kalimantan and Central Kalimantan populations had declined slightly, to 76% and 24% respectively (probably due to the immigration of other ethnic groups, such as the Javanese who accounted for 13% and 18% respectively). At 14%, Banjarese were the third largest ethnic group in East Kalimantan, between the Javanese (30%) and the Bugis (18%), all immigrant groups.

³LANGUAGE

Although popularly regarded as a separate language (and counted as such in Indonesian government usage), the speech of Banjar is essentially a dialect of Malay, although one which differs considerably from other dialects such as standard Bahasa Indonesia. Banjarese itself divides into two dialects: *Banjar Hulu* (upriver or interior) and *Banjar Kuala* (downriver or estuarine). The language is rich in words of Javanese origin, such as *pitu* ("seven"), *banyu* ("water"), and *lawang* ("door"), which correspond to Malay *tujuh*, *air*, and *pintu*. Under the influence of Javanese, a special *bahasa keraton* or "palace language," expressing respect to social superiors, developed and spread to the upper and middle classes. When speaking to someone younger, a person uses *aku* and *ikam* for "I" and "you," respectively. The younger, however, will say to the older, *ulun* and *sampiyan* in the Hulu dialect, and *unda* and *nyawa* in the Kuala dialect.

Banjarese is an oral language: writing (traditionally in the Arabic script) and formal speech-making are in standard Malay. In Islamic rites, Banjarese naturally use Arabic chants. In customary rites, however, incantations are in a mixture of Arabic and Kawi (Old Javanese) or will begin with *"Bismillah..."* ("In the name of Allah..."), go on to express the main content in Malay or Banjarese, and end with *"La ila ha ilallha, Muhammadaddar Rasulullah"* ("There is no God but Allah, and Muhammad is His Prophet").

⁴FOLKLORE

According to the foundation myth of the Banjar kingdom, the first raja's wife emerged from a gigantic mass of white foam (or, alternatively, mud) with the assistance of the vizier Lambung Mangkurat, who would live for three generations to oversee the new realm. Other mythological or historical figures are regularly invoked in traditional rituals, e.g., various sultans, other aristocrats, such as Pangeran Surianata and Puteri Junjung Buih, and the *muwakkal* Datu Baduk a "good" (literally, "Muslim") spirit who came with Sheikh Banjari from Mecca.

Banjarese recognize a variety of spirits or ghosts. One such is the *takau,* which appears as a black cat that can grow to the size of a water buffalo. A woman who has employed black magic to control her husband becomes a *penjadian* after death; smelling of pus, it visits its family to ask for food. *Tabib* (traditional healers) have the power to take spirit form while still alive, transforming themselves into grass or animals or becoming invisible so they can cause mishaps for persons to whom their clients have directed them. A woman who has drunk *minyak kuyang* (a kind of oil) becomes a monster capable of severing its head from its body. With the ears as wings and the heart, lungs, and stomach dangling as a tail, the monster flies about in search of pregnant women whose blood it can suck. The monster leaves the body hidden behind a door and returns to it before daybreak.

One type of amulet is the *jimat tambang liring,* used to enhance beauty and gain popularity. This consists of a paper with Qur'anic verses; a picture of the wayang clown-servants, Semar with his children; and one of the wayang heror Arjuna as Batara Kamajaya, the guardian of the heavenly nymphs *(bidadari),* with seven bidadari. The ink used in the amulet has been mixed with the blood of a killed person, whose spirit must continually be honored.

The Islamic texts *Syair Tajulmuluk* and *Syair Siti Zubaidah* are used to predict the future: one opens such a book to a random page, turns three or seven pages ahead, then interprets the content of the fourth or eighth page. One can diagnose diseases and ascertain cures by turning to the fourth page *before* looking at the random page. A man can similarly employ the surat "Yasin" from the Quran to make a woman fall in love with him or to harm an enemy.

⁵RELIGION

Being Banjarese by definition includes professing Islam. The region has produced Islamic scholars famous throughout the archipelago, the most renowned being Sheikh Muhammad Arsyad Al-Banjari (1710–1812), sent by the sultan to study in Mecca (his book, the *Sabilal Muhtadin,* gives its name to Banjarmasin's great mosque, resplendent with the finest marble and calligraphic decoration). Islamic mystical sects, some of which assert (heretically) the identity of God and self, have long been active. Mystics meditate in large buildings raised in the forest near villages, each man sitting within his own *kelambu* (mosquito net) and leaving only to defecate. In the early 20th century, conflicts arose between conservative and modernizing Muslims (respectively, the "older" and "younger" generations). If a modernizer came to pay respects to an older kinsman of the conservative group, the latter would receive him, but, after the modernizer left, the chair upon which he had sat would be wiped clean as if a leper had been there. Currently, both the conservative Nahdatul Ulama and moderniz-

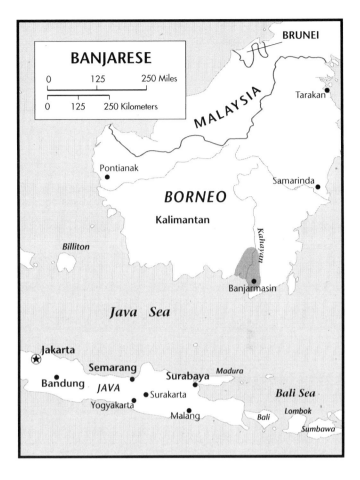

ing Muhammadiyah organizations have strong constituencies among the Banjarese.

Families of *topeng* (masked dance) performers and *dalang* (shadow puppeteers) venerate Hindu gods, respectively Batara Kelana (the *Ramayana*'s Dasamuka) and Batara Kala, chief of the spirits and Lord of Time. A dalang cannot perform without receiving the *bisik wayang* ("whisper of the shadow puppet"), i.e., without being possessed by Arjuna and Semar [*see* **Javanese**].

⁶MAJOR HOLIDAYS

Aruh are ritual celebrations that community tradition obliges a village to hold at regular intervals. Of the various types of aruh, the most elaborate is the *aruh menyanggar banua,* held right before the Islamic New Year, or at any other time deemed appropriate or necessary. Led by older people versed in ritual, this aruh serves to purify the village of the evil of the previous year, ward off disaster in the next, and call on the aid of ancestors and Batara Kala. Prayers are recited and offerings made, including great quantities of uncooked rice, thread, old Chinese coins (*picis),* incense, and 41 kinds of traditional foods prepared by postmenopausal women. Various forms of entertainment complete the celebration: *wayang* (shadow plays); *topeng* (masked dance); *kuda kepang* (hobby-horse dances); and *gamelan* (music).

Another important aruh is the *aruh terbang besar,* celebrating the birth of Muhammad during the month of Maulud. Its

A Banjarese woman sitting at a loom and weaving in a shop in India that sells traditional woven caps.
(© Christine Pemberton/The Image Works)

highlight is the performance of *hadrah,* a combination of Islamic changing and rhythmic movements.

⁷RITES OF PASSAGE

Rites of passage generally resemble those of the Malays. Aspects of the wedding process specific to the Banjarese include the following: parents discuss the choice of a partner for their child with their closest kin and also consult a fortune-teller to learn the fate of the proposed union; and the man's family sends an old woman to make the initial inquiries of the woman's family and chooses a well-spoken and influential person to deliver the proposal. Included in the rites are ceremonial baths of purification. The bride and groom present each other with *palimbaian,* an arrangement of betel leaves and flowers; afterwards these are thrown to the unmarried women among the guests and the ones who catch the palimbaian are believed soon to find a partner. Clans bring out heirloom *naga-naga* (the carved heads of dragon-serpents) to escort the bride and groom in a procession around the village.

⁸INTERPERSONAL RELATIONS

Traditional Banjarese society distinguished two strata: the *tutus* and the *jaba.* Possessing titles such as *pangeran, ratu, gusti, antung, nanang, andin,* and rama, the *tutus* were the aristocrats, descendants of the Banjar rulers. The *jaba* were com-

moners, including various office-holders, such *as kiai adipati, patih, tumenggung, ronggo, demang, mangku,* and *kiai.* While society once divided into aristocrats, *ulama* (Islamic scholars), merchants, and peasants, nowadays the main distinction is between educated people and "ordinary" people, with ulama remaining as a special category.

Etiquette within the family requires that, while eating, older individuals sit with other older folk, and younger sit with younger; older people also sit on a physically higher spot on the floor. Moreover, the younger walk behind the older and assume the heavier tasks.

The only occasion sanctioned by custom for young men and women to meet is during the communal preparation of food for large celebrations.

⁹LIVING CONDITIONS

Villages *(kampung)* usually extend along rivers or roads. Houses line up along a riverside, with their backs facing the water and their fronts facing the road, if there is one. After pacifying the region in 1865, the Dutch forced the inhabitants of scattered interior villages to relocate along a newly built post road. A village includes one or more prayer-halls *(langgar,* or a mosque if the settlement is big enough), a bathing place (usually riverside), and an area for a once- or twice-weekly market.

The most characteristic Banjar house is the *rumah bubungan tinggi,* so called for its "high roof" that rises at a 45o angle, high indeed given the total area of the house. All types of houses are raised on piles. Roofs were once made of dried leaves, but now more often they are made of shingles. Wall materials range from palm leaf to tree bark to bamboo plaiting to wooden planks; beams are of long-lasting ironwood or other hardwoods. The front most section is the *palataran,* an open veranda where the family relaxes in the afternoon and where it receives guests. Deeper into the house on successively higher levels are the chambers *panampik kecil, panampik tengah, panampik besar,* and *palidangan.* The wall between the panampik besar and the palidangan, called the *tawing halat,* is decorated with intricate carvings; in front of it are seated the most esteemed guests during celebrations. On both sides of the palidangan are *anjung,* lofts for sleeping. Behind the palidangan at a lower level is the *panampik dalam.* Behind that and lower still is the *padapuran,* the kitchen; above the door to the kitchen is the *katil,* the sleeping area for the family's unmarried daughters.

South Kalimantan has a Human Development Index (combining measures of income, health, and education) of 67.4 (2005 score), significantly lower than the national HDI of 69.6 and dramatically lower than that of the neighboring provinces, Central Kalimantan (73.2) and East Kalimantan (72.9), which are now attracting Banjarese transmigrants. South Kalimantan's GDP per capita is US $8,644, relatively high for Indonesia (cf. US$9,784 for West Sumatra and US$8,360 for North Sulawesi, but US$6,293 for Central Java and US$6,151 for West Nusa Tenggara), though much lower than that in the contiguous provinces (East Kalimantan's is US$23,253 even minus income from petroleum and gas). In 2000, the rate of infant mortality stood at 69.6 deaths per 1,000 live births, the third highest in the country, surpassed only by North Maluku (74.59) and West Nusa Tenggara (88.55).

10 FAMILY LIFE

The principal productive and property-holding unit is the nuclear family: a man, his wife or wives (polygyny is not uncommon), and their unmarried children.

A newly married couple sometimes remains for a time in the wife's parents' house. This results in parents, their unmarried children, and their married daughters with their husbands and children sharing the same roof (though sleeping in separate annexes and keeping their own kitchens). Married daughters usually, however, move out to a small house they have built themselves or which the parents have given them.

Parents usually choose their children's marriage partners. A young man who already has an eye on a girl other than that selected by his parents may use magic to undermine the arranged engagement. Young women who meet their husbands for the first time only at the wedding ceremony itself often refuse to sleep with their husbands; the family will do everything in their power, including resorting to spells, to persuade the woman to accept her man.

Kin relations are traced through both paternal and maternal sides, but the father or, if he is dead, one of his brothers will represent the bride in the wedding ceremony. Terminology distinguishes a parent's eldest sibling *(julak)* from the second eldest *(gulu),* from the third eldest *(angah),* and from the youngest *(pakacil* for uncles and *makacil* for aunts). Relatives

are almost always addressed with abbreviated kin-terms: *datu* (great-grandparents); *kaye* (grandfather); *ni* (*nini,* grandmother); *bah* (*abah,* father); *ma* (*uma,* mother); *lak* (*julak, eldest uncle or aunt); ngah (angah, middle uncle or aunt); cil (pakacil/ makacil, youngest uncle or aunt); anak* (child); and *cu* (*cucu,* grandchild); or *yut* (*buyut,* grandchild).

11 CLOTHING

Everyday wear for men consists at its most simple of the *salawar culuk,* trousers of unbleached cloth that reach down to the calf; the top of the trousers is folded over and rolled tight at the waist. Shirts and the *laung* head cloth are rarely worn with it. Alternatively, men may wear *salawar panjang* (long trousers), *baju taluk balanga* (an open-collared, long-sleeved tunic), and a *peci* cap. Women wear the *tapih kurung* (sarong), *kebaya* (long-sleeved blouse), and *kakamban* head covers; nowadays, the favored fabrics are from Pekalongan in Java.

Aristocratic styles can still be seen as ceremonial wear. A man will put on a *baju pokok pria,* a white sleeveless undershirt whose sides remain unsewn, secured by ties; and over this a *baju miskat,* a black or red long-sleeved shirt, tapering down to the waist and sporting a wide, stiff collar and buttons (always uneven in number). In addition, he will wear the *salawar pidandang,* trousers that taper towards the bottom to hug the lower leg, and a laung head cloth (differing in style according to rank). Women wear the *baju kurung basisit,* an open-collared, long-sleeved shirt of blue or black satin or silk, extending down to the knees. Ceremonial clothing for both sexes is decorated with motifs (plants, *naga* snakes, etc.), embroidered in gold thread.

12 FOOD

Meals consist of rice and side dishes. The latter could be fish (dried or fried) from rivers or flooded rice-fields, vegetables, and curries (e.g., preparations with squash, jackfruit, or taro). Supplementary foods include cassava, sweet potato, sago, *pati panguning* (a kind of tuber whose plant resembles turmeric), and a variety of bananas. One specialty available throughout Indonesia is *soto Banjar,* a rich soup of chicken meat and duck eggs eaten with *lontong* (rice steamed in banana-leaf wrappers).

Rice provides the basis of local sweets, such as *apam,* which is rice flour, palm or granulated sugar, and coconut milk blended into a batter, poured into molds, and steamed; *dodol,* a taffy made from glutinous rice flour, palm sugar, and lots of coconut milk, which is eaten with coconut meat, durian, or peanuts; and *kalapon,* green-dyed, ping-pong-size balls of rice flour filled with a chunk of brown sugar, steamed, and sprinkled with grated coconut before eating. *Amping* are chips made from newly harvested rice that has been pounded; they are eaten with grated coconut or sugar. One local drink of note is *banyu tipikan,* water in which ginger and brown sugar have been boiled.

13 EDUCATION

In 2005, South Kalimantan's level of literacy stood at 94.47%, relatively high by Indonesian national standards, comparable to provinces with higher HDIs, such as West Java and Jambi (*see* also the article entitled **Indonesians**).

[14] CULTURAL HERITAGE

An accompaniment for celebrations, such as weddings, *hadrah* is a performing art of Arab origin that combines Islamic chanting, the striking of the *rebana* tambourine, the waving of multicolored pennants, and the spinning of decorated umbrellas.

Mumenggung is an elegant step-dance welcoming spectators to all-male *mamada* plays (dramatizing tales from the *Thousand and One Nights*). The Banjarese also perform Javanese-style dances, *topeng* (masked dances), *wayang* (shadow plays), and *gamelan* music.

[15] WORK

Agriculture is the most common occupation among the Banjarese. Since 1939, from the vast tidal swamp between Banjarmasin and the Java Sea, 100,000 hectares (247,100 acres) of land have been reclaimed for wet-rice fields, tangerine and orange groves, and vegetable gardens. Varieties of rice are cultivated that can grow in as much as 2 m (6.5 ft) of water; farmers harvest these from boats. Less and less by the swidden (shifting-cultivation) methods of the past, Banjarese also grow crops in dry-fields: dry rice, oil palm *(kelapa sawit)*, *rosela* (a plant yielding fiber for sacks and ropes), sugarcane, and fruits. Traditionally, pepper was the primary cash crop, but cacao, *illipe* nuts, and especially rubber have taken its place.

Livestock includes water buffalo, horses, cattle, goats, sheep, ducks, and chicken. Some 160,000 people make a living fishing in the province's inland waters, and another 5,000 from the sea; large quantities of dried fish are exported to Java.

Although Banjarese shun work in the local lumber mills that process wood from the Kalimantan interior (leaving it to Javanese migrants), many do work in factories where upriver rattan is transformed into mats and furniture. Another alternative to agriculture is small-scale mining for gems (including diamonds) and panning for gold. Many Banjarese engage in commerce, such as the women of Banjarmasin's *pasar terapung* ("floating market"), who sell vegetables and other produce from boats. The region has long been the source of various "exotica": frog legs, snake and lizard skins, and roots for *jamu* (traditional herbal remedies).

[16] SPORTS

Kite-flying and top-spinning are popular pastimes and form an integral part of post-harvest festivals.

[17] ENTERTAINMENT AND RECREATION

See the article entitled **Indonesians**.

[18] FOLK ART, CRAFTS, AND HOBBIES

Traditional crafts include the weaving of baskets and mats, the carving of house walls and furniture, and the working of metal and gems. One regional specialty is *batik sasirangan*, a tie-dyed cloth of many designs, once believed to ward off evil spirits and cure disease.

[19] SOCIAL PROBLEMS

See the article entitled **Indonesians**.

[20] GENDER ISSUES

South Kalimantan's Gender-Related Development Index (combining measures of women's health, education, and income relative to men's) is 61, slightly above Indonesia's national GDI of 59.2. The province's Gender Empowerment Measure (reflecting women's participation and power in political and economic life relative to men's), however, is 51.8, lower than the national GEM of 54.6.

[21] BIBLIOGRAPHY

Badan Pusat *Statistik: Statistik Indonesia.* http://demografi.bps.go.id (November 9, 2008).

Muller, Kal. *Borneo: Journey into the Tropical Rainforest.* Lincolnwood, IL: Passport Books, 1990.

Profil Propinsi Republik Indonesia. Vol. 11, *Kalimantan Selatan.* Jakarta: Yayasan Bhakti Wawasan Nusantara, 1992.

Rosantini, Triana. "Banjar, suku bangsa." In *Ensiklopedi Nasional Indonesia,* Vol. 3. Jakarta: Cipta Adi Pustaka, 1989.

Steinhauer, Hein. "The Indonesian Language Situation and Linguistics." *Bijdragen tot de Taal, Land en Volkenkunde* 150-IV (1994).

Tobing, Nelly, ed. *Adat Istiadat Daerah Kalimantan Selatan* [Customs of South Kalimantan]. Jakarta: Department of Education and Culture, 1978.

—revised by A. J. Abalahin

BATAK

PRONUNCIATION: BAH-tahk
LOCATION: Indonesia (North Sumatra)
POPULATION: 6.1 million
LANGUAGE: Various Batak dialects
RELIGION: Christianity; Protestant Toba church (Huria Kristen Batak Protestant) and Catholic; Pebegu (indigenous animist religion); Islam
RELATED ARTICLES: Vol. 3: Indonesians

¹INTRODUCTION

The name "Batak," which also applies to a totally different ethnic group on the Philippine island of Palawan, seems to have originated as a derogatory term by which Muslim lowlanders of the archipelago referred to pagan highlanders. In North Sumatra, six related though distinct peoples have come under the blanket classification of "Batak": the Toba, Karo, Simalungun, Dairi (Pakpak), Angkola, and Mandailing. Of these, the heavily Islamized Angkola and Mandailing reject the label; only the largely Christianized Toba, the largest of the groups, has taken this former insult as a badge of pride.

The Batak descend from the earliest Austronesians to have settled on Sumatra, arriving from Borneo perhaps as early as 2500 BC, well in advance of the Malayic peoples whose dialects would come to dominate the coasts and, in the south, even the interior of the island [see **Malays**, **Achnese**, and **Minangkabau**]. Thickly forested mountain ranges and the Batak's own reputation for ferocity deterred coastal states from penetrating the highlands; thus, Batak villages enjoyed not only independence from foreign rule but also the freedom to wage war on each other. Moreover, although from the earliest times trade (most importantly in local benzoinwood, used to make incense) linked the Batak lands to the outside world, the Batak experienced the waves of Indic influence that transformed neighboring societies only as faint ripples, mediated by the island's more modest Hindu-Buddhist statelets or by armed Tamil merchant guilds on the coast. While in general lowlanders or coastal peoples feared highland or interior peoples as headhunters (for instance, the Dayak of Borneo or the Igorots of Luzon), the Batak were also infamous as cannibals. Popular rumor has greatly exaggerated the extent of Batak cannibalism; some Batak groups were only recorded as subjecting a person condemned to die for especially heinous crimes to the additional torture of having fellow villagers slice off and swallow bits of his flesh.

Islamic influence remained similarly superficial until the early 19th century, when the Padri struggle to purge Minangkabau culture of pre-Islamic elements spilled over into the southern Batak lands as a war to force the conversion of the pagan Mandailing and Angkola. Intervening against the Padri, Dutch colonial power followed them into the southern Batak lands; by the 1840s, the coasts below the Batak highlands fell under Dutch control. Despite facing no pan-Batak resistance, the Dutch subdued all the Batak only after several fierce campaigns over the latter half of the 19th century.

In 1862, Ludwig Nommensen of the Rhenish Mission Society (German Lutheran) began working among the Toba. By 1900, most Toba had become Protestants, thanks in great part to Nommensen distancing himself from the Dutch colonial authorities and offering his services as doctor, teacher, and mediator. Most concretely expressed in the 1908 construction of the first road into the highlands (formerly accessible only by footpaths), the Dutch penetration of Batak society, nonetheless, did face resistance: in armed syncretistic and messianic movements; in Karo and Simalungun mistrust of a Christianity viewed as a partner of colonialism; and, in the establishment of a self-governing Batak church, free of European missionary paternalism.

The educational advantages that Batak received from the mission schools enabled them to fill commercial and teaching jobs throughout the Netherlands Indies and, later, to play prominent roles in Indonesia's national leadership from the revolution down to the present day. The Batak lands are undergoing rapid development as the farming hinterland of the oil- and rubber-rich northeast Sumatra coast, of Medan (the metropolis of western Indonesia), and even of Singapore and Malaysia. The Karo and Toba highlands are attracting the greatest number of tourists in all of Indonesia, after Bali and Yogya.

²LOCATION AND HOMELAND

The Batak homeland in North Sumatra province is located on a high rolling plateau (1,000 m or 3,280 ft above sea level) between the two parallel volcanic ranges of the 2,000 m (6,560-ft-high) Bukit Barisan Mountains. The region centers on Lake Toba, a veritable inland sea occupying the crater left by a vol-

A Batak man in Lake Tobo, Indonesia. The Bataks are some of the original inhabitants of Indonesia and are now a remote tribe that lives around Lake Tobo in Northern Sumatra. (AP Images/Horst Faas)

canic explosion 75,000 years ago (2,000 times more powerful than that of Mount Saint Helen's). In this century, overpopulation has forced many Batak to settle in the densely forested piedmont and in the coastal plantation zones to both the east and west. Batak also form a major part of the population of the multiethnic metropolis of Medan and can be found in cities throughout Indonesia.

According to the 2000 census, Batak numbered 6.1 million, Indonesia's fifth largest ethnic group, which is 3% of the population. This was almost twice the 1990 census figure of 3.1 million for speakers of the three Batak languages. A more recent estimate puts the number at 9 million. The relative size of the various Batak sub-groups can be judged from the following estimates from 1991 (or 1989, where noted): 2 million Toba, living around Lake Toba, on Samosir Island, and in the highlands to the south; 600,000 Karo to the northwest of the lake; 1.2 million Simalungun, east of the lake; 1.2 million Dairi, west of the lake; 750,000 Angkola (1991) and 400,000 Mandailing (1989) between the Toba and the Minangkabau; and 800,000 Alas-Kluet (1989) in southern Aceh.

³LANGUAGE

Batak dialects divide into three mutually unintelligible groups: Toba-Angkola-Mandailing, Karo-Dairi, and Simalungun. In the past, intercommunication was possible because many Batak knew Batak languages other than their own and some-

times also Malay (which could also be used with non-Batak). Today, it is a widespread mastery of Bahasa Indonesia that facilitates intercommunication.

Batak religious specialists have long employed a script (ultimately of Indian origin) to record occult knowledge; the letters vary slightly among the six Batak groups.

Children take as surnames the clan *(marga)* names of their father.

⁴FOLKLORE

According to the Toba creation myth, the primordial universe consists of the seven-layered upperworld of the god Mula Jadi Na Bolon, and the watery underworld of the dragon-serpent Naga Padoha. Mula Jadi Na Bolon sired three sons by a blue hen: Batara Guru, Mangalabulan, and Soripada. He also sired three daughters to give to his sons as wives. It is the daughter of Batara Guru, Si Boru Deak Parujar, who created the earth. She married her cousin Boraspati ni Tano, the lizard-shaped son of Mangalabulan, and gave birth to twins of different sexes. In turn, these twins married each other, descended to the earth at the volcano Pusuk Buhit (on the west shore of Lake Toba), and founded a village, Si Anjur Mulamula. From this pair, all humanity descends. From one of their grandchildren, Si Raja Batak, all the Batak descend (the other Batak groups do not widely recognize this genealogy).

⁵RELIGION

The Toba have been predominantly Protestant Christian for over a century, while the Angkola and Mandailing have been Muslim several decades longer. Pebegu, the indigenous animist religion, is strongest among the Karo, claiming 57% as adherents (though many of these describe themselves as "secular," i.e., with a rather uncertain grasp of their religion). Some 12% of Karo profess Islam, while 31% are Christian (converts were few until the 1965 suppression of communism compelled every Indonesian to declare adherence to a universal religion). The self-governing Toba church (Huria Kristen Batak Protestant or HKBP) is the largest Christian body in Indonesia and one of the most powerful. The Simalungun and Karo Protestants have each established their own churches. Finally, about 10% of all Batak are Catholics, missionary work having begun only after independence. To a considerable extent, however, Christian and Muslim Batak maintain beliefs and practices of the traditional religion alongside those of the newer creeds.

The traditional Batak religion recognizes numerous gods but focuses much more upon handling spirits directly associated with human life. One of two deities who do figure prominently is Boru Saniang Naga, goddess of rivers and lakes, who must be honored before fishing, farming, and making or traveling by boats. The other is Boraspati ni Tano, a fertility god whose lizard form appears on house façades; every working of the soil requires that he be appeased.

Tondi (in Toba, *tendi* in Karo) is the life-force present in human beings (as well as in rice and iron). The god Mula Jadi Na Bolon gives each person his or her tondi before birth; the tondi also chooses the person's destiny before birth. The tondi is not bound to the body; it may roam, or a more powerful spirit may capture it. The separation of the tondi from the body causes illness, and, if the tondi cannot be enticed back by offerings or successfully summoned back by mediums, this can lead to death.

Upon death, the tondi disappears, releasing the *begu* or essential soul. The begu remains near its former home or in the vicinity of the cemetery and can contact surviving kin and descendants (for instance, it can express disapproval through a nightmare or a particular mishap). Babies who die before breaking their first tooth; persons who die by accident, murder, or suicide; and young women who die unmarried become begu who protect their families. If their kin group mounts large-scale funerary sacrifices, the begu of powerful individuals attain the higher status of *sumangot,* an ancestor figure around which a new subclan can be formed. Further rituals can promote sumangot to *sombaon,* prominent ancestors of 10 to 12 generations back who dwell in spooky places such as mountains or dense forests. Unelevated begu become resentful and, if not sustained through offerings, can harm rather than help humans. The begu is not immortal but will die seven times before turning at last into a blade of grass.

Religious specialists include *guru sibaso* (female spirit mediums) and *datu* (male priests). The latter acquire a specialized knowledge of the occult through a rigorous apprenticeship. *Pustaha,* folding bark-books in Batak script, record information on magic, divination, and medicine.

⁶MAJOR HOLIDAYS

See the article entitled **Indonesians**.

⁷RITES OF PASSAGE

A wedding links not only two individuals but, more importantly, two kin groups, usually reaffirming longstanding relations. The man's family sends a delegation to deliver an initial proposal to the woman's family. If the latter accepts the proposal, the two sides hold a later discussion to negotiate the bride-price and the gifts to be given by the man's side to the woman's relatives, as well as to fix the date of the wedding. Among Christianized Toba, it is important for the families to announce the wedding formally to the church congregation. The wedding feast is attended by kin of both sides and by all the inhabitants of the village where it takes place. The celebration includes the handing over of the bride-price, the slaughtering of a water buffalo or several pigs, and the distribution of the meat to the relatives.

Should any of the kin object to the wedding, the couple may elope, the man taking the woman to his parents' house. Before one day passes, the man's kin must send a delegation to the woman's side to inform them of the elopement and of the man's intention to marry the woman. After a while, the man's side asks pardon of the woman's side in a formal ceremony, after which a conventional wedding can take place.

Even among Christians, traditional funerary practices continue to be practiced. These include having masked dancers accompany the coffin to the grave. These masks, representing a male, a female, and either a hornbill or a horse, are oversized, as are the wooden hands that go with them; the masks are left on top of the coffin as protection against evil spirits. Proper funerary rites must be performed by a son; therefore, among the Toba, those without sons substitute a *si gal-gale,* a dummy with wooden limbs, for the son never born or earlier deceased.

While the poor are simply wrapped in a mat and interred, the wealthy receive elaborate, often massive, coffins, whose crafting often begins while the person is still alive. These incomplete coffins can be seen under houses. Karo are known for the *pelangkah,* a boat-shaped coffin adorned with a hornbill head at one end. Some Karo and Dairi place the elaborately coffined body of a prestigious notable in a special structure, burning it after a year. More common is for Batak to exhume the bones of the powerful for reburial in a large stone sarcophagus, often with a *singa* (lion) carved in the front. Today, tombs no longer use stone but rather consist of massive concrete structures and statuary.

⁸INTERPERSONAL RELATIONS

In pre-colonial times, political organization above the village level hardly existed. Among the Karo, an *urung,* a confederation of villages, looked to a *raja urung* or *sibayak* for leadership in time of war. The Toba recognized a line of priest-kings of very limited authority, the *si singamangaraja.* Only Simalungun chiefs who had received titles from the Acehnese sultan were said to wield "despotic" power over their districts.

Thus, for the most part, villages were independent and the individual village chief (*raja*) answered to no higher authority. The raja arbitrated disputes, extended hospitality to visitors to the village, and gave permission for people to move in or move out of the village. Although a member of the village's founding (and dominant) clan (in Karo, *merga taneh*), the raja himself was no more than a first among equals, relying on personal charisma to attract loyalty and compliance. He could not exercise authority without consulting with village elders and his family's *anak boru* (wife-takers). The community could remove a *raja* for incompetence, and a wealthy freeman *(anak mata)* could command as much influence as an impoverished raja.

Traditional society distinguished between free persons and slaves (in Toba, *hatoban; in* Karo, *kawan*). The former divided into *biak raja,* the descendants of chiefs and other notables; specialists believed to be mystically potent (iron- and goldsmiths, woodcarvers, musicians, and singers); and ordinary people. Slaves were either debt-pawns or prisoners of war; they worked the lands of the raja and were generally well treated. The Dutch abolished slavery in 1860.

One is careful to speak respectfully to older people and strangers, for instance by prefacing a refusal with words of apology (in Toba, "*sattabi*"; in Karo, "*ula ukurndu litik*"). One touches hands in greeting, giving thanks, and bidding farewell.

Among the Toba, one way young people of different sexes may meet acceptably is *martandang*. In the evening, young men visit the house where young women live, under the supervision of a widow. The young people communicate in riddles. Should a young man find one of the maidens to his liking, he approaches her parents to ask her hand. Among the Mandailing, a young man can communicate with the object of his affection by *markusip*. He enters the space under her house, stands under the spot where she sleeps, and gives a secret signal to announce his arrival; the two whisper through the floorboards.

⁹LIVING CONDITIONS

The traditional Toba village *(huta)* consists of 8 to 10 houses facing each other across a broad central avenue, which serves as a place for drying rice and gathering for ceremonial celebrations. All of the village inhabitants belong to the same clan. Community meetings take place in an open area *(partukhoan)* near the village gate. The Karo *kuta* is much larger, includes families of different clans, and possesses a meeting-house *(balai kerapatan).* Batak villages established in warlike pre-colonial times were ringed by a high wall of earth or sometimes stone blocks, a moat, and thick stands of bamboo.

Most Batak now live in brick or cement houses, and roofs of corrugated metal sheets have replaced thatched ones even on many traditional homes. Traditional Batak houses are rectangular structures raised on piles. The Toba house is home to a single couple, their unmarried children, the eldest son and his family, and the father's widowed sisters. The house has a high saddle roof whose ends project well beyond the walls of the house; the roof juts farther out in the front where there is a veranda; the foot of the entrance staircase is under the veranda.

The much larger Karo dwelling houses eight related families, each family inhabiting 5 sq m (approximately 54 sq ft) of living space and sharing a hearth with one other family. The apartments (which today can be rented by unrelated families) line up, four on either side of a central hall that often has a gutter down the middle for debris. The house has identical verandas and doors at both front and back. One particularly distinctive type of roof, for houses with a square plan, has side surfaces rise evenly to the ridgepole, while the front and back sides stop under the ridgepole and connect to it with a wall. Most impressive were the *rumah anjung-anjung* of rajas whose roofs were topped with a miniature house.

Human Development Indices (combining measures of income, health, and education) in the Batak region vary widely: the HDIs for the residencies of Toba Samosir (74.5) and Karo (73.5) are higher than that for North Sumatra as a whole (72), while those for Simalungun and Dairi residencies are below (71.3 and 70.5 respectively). All are above Indonesia's national HDI of 69.6. One Batak area, Mandailing Natal residency, has one that is slightly below, 68.8. Its GDP per capita is only US$3,677, compared to US$8,035 for Toba Samosir, and its infant mortality rate is 66.61 deaths per 1,000 live births, compared to 25.78 for Karo. The provincial IMR is 43,69.

¹⁰FAMILY LIFE

Batak belong to lineages that trace back to a common ancestor though the male line. These broad patrilineages or clans (in Toba, *marga;* in Karo, *merga*) are numerous and divide further into subclans. A Toba marga is named after a common ancestor who can be traced back 20 or more generations through genealogies *(tarombo).* A Karo merga carries a group name that does not refer to a specific ancestor and does not keep tarombo.

The most important social unit is the group (in Toba, *saompu;* in Karo, *sada nini*) of all the descendants of a common grandfather who live together in the same settlement. Within the saompu/sada nini are numerous nuclear families (in Toba, *ripe;* in Karo, *jabu),* each of which includes a couple, their unmarried children, and their married sons.

The ideal (though now rare) match is between a man and his mother's brother's daughter. Matches between people of the same marga and between a man with his father's sister's daughter are taboo. Members of one kin group customarily take wives from a specific kin group, while giving wives to yet another kin group. Typically, kin group A would give wives to kin group B, which in turn would give wives to kin group C, which would give wives to kin group A, thus forming a circle.

A husband treats his wife's family with great respect, regarding them as *dibata ni idah,* "gods on earth." Only the wealthy have ever been able to take more than one wife. From time to time, a husband takes a second wife but only visits her, as she remains living with her parents (Christians do not practice this).

Along with childlessness and adultery, a wife's inability to get along with even one of her husband's kin is sufficient reason for divorce. The *raja urung* among the Karo or the convened village passes divorce decisions, usually requiring the wife's side to return the bride-price. A Karo wife can have a "temporary divorce" *(ngelandih)* if she goes to stay at her parents' house after a quarrel.

¹¹CLOTHING

Although elements of traditional clothing can still be seen in everyday use, modern Batak dress much as other Indonesians do, wearing international fashions, such as tee-shirts and jeans, or Malay-style *kebaya* blouses. Rectangular, finely patterned cloths called *ulos* (in Toba; *uis* in Karo) continue as an essential part of ceremonial celebrations, both as part of the attire and as gifts exchanged to affirm the bonds between social groups. An ulos can be folded for a broad headcloth, or worn over the back as a shawl or over the shoulder as a sash (also a baby-carrier). In former times, women wore an ulos as a sarong with the breasts exposed, or wore the cloth wrapped around their whole body with only the shoulders bare. Traditional clothing also included jackets and vests.

The colors of traditional ulos were symbolic: white of the upperworld and life; black of the underworld and magical power; and red of the middle world, bravery, and spiritual potency. While Karo tradition preferred cloth of indigo, contemporary Karo prefer dark red, following Simalungun taste. Toba weavers have long produced cloth in Karo patterns for Karo buyers. Machine-woven fabrics imitate the older hand-woven styles and are actually preferred by the younger generation, who also have begun to request that traditional patterns be done in gold or silver thread (Malay-style *songket*).

12 FOOD

Rice is the staple food, supplemented by cassava, taro, maize, beans, and bananas. A common side dish is *bulung gadung tumbuk,* cassava leaves pounded and then stewed as a curry. A popular feast food is *saksan,* roast pig eaten with a ginger-laden spicy sauce that includes the blood of the animal. *Dengke ni ura dohot na margota* is a big lake fish, spiced and mixed with tamarind as a souring agent and kept for two or three nights before eating. *Dengke ni arsik* is carp with cassava leaves, spiced, then cooked until the fish is tender and dry. *Pinadar* is chicken or pig meat grilled until dry, then mixed with hot spices, tamarind, and salt. *Tuak tangkasan* is palm-sap alcohol, flavored with a kind of bark.

13 EDUCATION

In 2005, the Batak region's level of literacy was very high by Indonesian national standards; that of Mandailing Natal, the regency with the lowest HDI of all the Batak region's regencies, 98.53, was even higher than that of the national capital, Jakarta, 98.32. (*See* also the article entitled **Indonesians.**)

14 CULTURAL HERITAGE

Batak are celebrated throughout Indonesia for their love of music-making, often appearing as entertainers in hotels and restaurants. Traditional ensembles divide into two types: one for loud, outdoor ceremonial music and the other for soft, indoor informal music. The former includes *gondang* (a set of long, cylindrical, tuned drums, beat in dynamic rhythms), *sarune* (a penetrating oboe played with circular breathing), and *ogung* (gongs). The latter type of ensemble includes the *hasapi* (a long-necked lute), the *surdam* (a bamboo flute), and the *keteng-keteng* (a bamboo-tube zither, struck with sticks).

Accompanying themselves on guitars (and nowadays also on Yamaha electric organs), Batak sing passionate songs *(lagu Batak),* whose style reflects Portuguese and Spanish influences. This music is widely available on cassette. Churches may have as many as 10 choirs, singing (in unison and improvised four-part harmonies) many hymns that are no longer known in Europe.

Traditional dances served mainly three different functions: to show respect for guests, especially the host's wife-giving kin group; to induce possession by spirits (through orchestral crescendo); and for young people to divert themselves (often with a humorous erotic component). Funerals include the *tortor,* a solemn dance with slow and rigid movements.

Oral literature includes *andung-andung,* laments for the dead, including fixed expressions that can no longer be understood; and *tonggo-tonggo,* poetical prayers recited during offering ceremonies (these include *tabas* incantations).

15 WORK

Most Batak gain a living from agriculture, in some areas cultivating irrigated rice, in others raising maize, cassava, indigo, sugar palm, and other crops in dry-fields, to some extent still with swidden (shifting-cultivation) methods. Karo and Simalungun farmers grow vegetables and fruits for the Medan market, but also for Singapore and Malaysia. Spreading over the Simalungun area since colonial times, and once employing primarily Chinese and Javanese labor, plantations grow rubber, oil palm, cacao, tea, and tobacco. Other cash crops are coffee (especially among the Mandailing and Dairi) and cloves.

Men clear and plow the land as well as set up irrigation systems, while women plant, weed, and harvest; neighbors and close kin cooperate in accomplishing agricultural tasks. Batak keep water buffalo as draft animals and to be sacrificed and consumed at ritual celebrations; pigs are raised both for meat for everyday meals and feasts. Cattle, goats, chickens, and ducks are raised for sale in coastal cities. Fishing is a major occupation on Lake Toba.

Because of a relatively high educational level, Batak fill office (including bureaucratic), teaching, and health service jobs throughout Indonesia.

16 SPORTS

See the article entitled **Indonesians**.

17 ENTERTAINMENT AND RECREATION

See the article entitled **Indonesians**.

18 FOLK ART, CRAFTS, AND HOBBIES

Villages and regions specialize in particular crafts: textile-weaving; mat- and basket weaving; iron-, gold-, and silver working; pottery; and woodcarving (important in decorating the walls of traditional houses).

19 SOCIAL PROBLEMS

See the article entitled **Indonesians**.

20 GENDER ISSUES

In 2002, the Gender-Related Development Indices (combining measures of women's health, education, and income relative to men's) of the regencies of the Batak region were almost all higher than Indonesia's national GDI of 59.2: 69.3 for Toba Samosir, 68.5 for Karo, 66.5 for Dairi, and 61.5 for Simalungun. Only Mandailing Natal was lower, at 58.4, which was also lower than that for North Sumatra as a whole, 61.5. The Batak regencies' Gender Empowerment Measures (reflecting women's participation and power in political and economic life relative to men's), however, were all lower than the national GEM of 54.6, ranging from Dairi's 53.4 to Karo's 46.

21 BIBLIOGRAPHY

Ayatrohaedi, et al. *Tatakrama di Beberapa Daerah di Indonesia* [Etiquette in Some Regions of Indonesia]. Jakarta: Department of Education and Culture, 1989.

Badan Pusat Statistik: DataStatistik Indonesia. http://demografi.bps.go.id (November 2008).

Bangun, Payung. "Kebudayaan Batak." In *Manusia dan Kebudayaan di Indonesia* [Man and Culture in Indonesia], edited by Koentjaraningrat. Jakarta: Djambatan, 1975.

Gordon, Raymond G., Jr. (ed.). *Ethnologue: Languages of the World*, 15th ed. Dallas: Texas: SIL International, http://www.ethnologue.com (November 16, 2008).

LeBar, Frank M., ed. *Ethnic Groups of Insular Southeast Asia.* Vol. 1, *Indonesia, Andaman Islands, and Madagascar.* New Haven, CT: Human Relations Area Files Press, 1972.

Melalatoa, M. Junus. "Batak, suku bangsa." In *Ensiklopedi Nasional Indonesia,* Vol. 3. Jakarta: Cipta Adi Pustaka, 1989.

Oey, Eric. *Sumatra: Island of Adventure.* Lincolnwood, IL: Passport Books, 1991.

Profil Propinsi Republik Indonesia. Vol. 25, *Sumatra Utara.* Jakarta: Yayasan Bhakti Wawasan Nusantara, 1992.

Sibeth, Achim. *Mit den Ahnen Leben: Batak—Menschen in Indonesien* [Living with the Ancestors: Batak—Men in Indonesia]. Stuttgart: Hansjörg Mayer, 1990.

—revised by A. J. Abalahin

BEDU

PRONUNCIATION: BEH-doo
ALTERNATE NAMES: Bedouin
LOCATION: Deserts of Israel, Jordan, Lebanon, Syria, Saudi Arabia, Iraq, Kuwait, Yemen, Oman, Qatar, the United Arab Emirates, Bahrain, and Egypt
POPULATION: 4 million to 5 million
LANGUAGE: Arabic
RELIGION: Islam

¹ INTRODUCTION

The Western term *Bedouin* is actually a double plural; in their own language (Arabic), Bedouin refer to themselves as "Bedu" (also plural, but for simplicity it will be used here as both singular and plural). The definition of who is and is not a Bedu has become somewhat confused in recent times, as circumstances change and the traditional nomadic life of the desert herders had to adapt. Generally speaking, a Bedu is an Arab who lives in one of the desert areas of the Middle East and raises camels, sheep, or goats. The Bedu traditionally believe they are the descendants of Shem, son of Noah, whose ancestor was Adam, the first man. Bedu society is based on complicated lineages that govern the formation of tribes and family clans. Bedu introduce themselves by giving their name, then naming two generations of male ancestors, and then stating their tribe: for example, "Suhail son of Salem son of Muhammad of the Bait Kathir." Women are also known as the daughters of their fathers and grandfathers, and they keep their family names even if they marry into a different tribe.

Genetically speaking, the Bedu are Semitic in origin, of the Caucasian race. The Arabian Peninsula historically has been the crossroads for trade as well as war. Bedu tribes often took strangers into their system as *mawali* and offered them the tribes' full protection and identity, thus intermingling with other peoples. Where the Bedu have had little contact and, therefore, little intermingling with other races, their skin complexion is fair where it is not exposed to the sun. Bedu are considered the "most indigenous" of modern Middle Eastern peoples, meaning they lived there before anyone else. At the time when Arabs were first distinguished from other races, they were desert nomads. The first appearance of nomadic peoples in the Arabian desert can be traced back as far as the third millennium BC.

² LOCATION AND HOMELAND

Bedu territory covers the Arabian deserts of the Middle East, including parts of the Palestinian territories and the modern states of Israel, Jordan, Lebanon, Syria, Saudi Arabia, Iraq, Kuwait, Yemen, Oman, Qatar, the United Arab Emirates, Bahrain, and Egypt. Their entire range extends over 2.5 million sq km (1 million sq mi), which is about the size of western Europe. It is difficult to count the exact number of Bedu living within this huge territory. Most estimates figure that the Bedu population is about 4 million to 5 million, which puts the population density at less than 1 person per sq km (around 2.5 persons per sq mi). It is estimated that approximately 10% of all Bedu continue to live in a purely traditional way: nomadic camel herders who follow the scattered, sporadic rainfall to find grazing for their animals, live off the products of those animals (milk, meat, hair, and skins), and use them as their sole form of transportation. This article primarily focuses on the nomadic Bedu. Life for the other 90% of the Bedu is similar to that of other urbanized Arab peoples.

The desert environment is harsh and does not lend itself easily to the support of human life. Much of the Bedu territory receives only four inches of rain per year, and those four inches are scattered and unpredictable. Temperatures can go as high as 50¡C (122¡F) in the shade during the summer months, and as low as 0¡C (32¡F) during the winter. At night, the temperature drops dramatically, plunging as much as 30¡C (54¡F) from daytime temperatures. The beginning of summer is often heralded by violent sandstorms and scorching winds. The Bedu recognize four or five "seasons" that vary in length depending on the amount of rainfall. In a good, rainy year, spring can last as long as six weeks (during February and March), whereas in a dry year there may be no spring at all, with winter simply shifting right into summer.

Despite these harsh conditions, a great deal of life manages to exist in the desert. Wolves, foxes, wildcats, gazelles, hares, small rodents, reptiles, and many insects and spiders make their homes there, and flocks of migratory birds pass through on their way from summering to wintering grounds (and vice versa). A variety of plant species have also adapted to the extreme temperatures and lack of water, developing long roots and spiny leaves, water storage capacities, and seeds that will last hundreds of years in a dormant stage until conditions become right for sprouting. The Arabian deserts are not all sand, either, although they do boast the highest sand dunes on Earth, with some as high as 600 m (2,000 ft). Within Bedu territory are mountains, rock outcroppings, gravel and stony plains, wadis (dry riverbeds, which can become sudden torrents during a heavy rainfall), and stands of scrubby bushes or trees. A few days or weeks after a rainstorm, the desert floor is transformed into a carpet of grasses and brilliantly colored wildflowers. The Bedu travel in search of these green places in the desert.

³ LANGUAGE

The Bedu speak Arabic, but it is a very rich, stylized Arabic. Bedu Arabic is somewhat comparable to Shakespearean English. As is the case with many indigenous peoples, the Bedu language is filled with words that pertain to the details of their life, making distinctions that are difficult for others to comprehend. Just as the Inuit people have many words for snow, the Bedu have more than one word for desert, and the differences between them are hard to define in English. A *badiya* is something open and uncovered, a country in full view. A *sahra* is a vast open space that is generally level, defined in contrast to a "settled" area. The Bedu also have many words for water, which was historically far more important as a scarce resource in the desert.

⁴ FOLKLORE

The two main types of Bedu folk tales are realistic stories involving the familiar Bedu way of life and fantasies that tell of love and include a woman as a main character. These two types of folk tales generally fall into three categories: raiding stories, which celebrate heroism, strength, and courage; love stories, which revel in the emotional highs and lows of star-crossed lovers and struggles to overcome obstacles to true love; and

stories about thieves of the desert, which tell of robbery, murder, and treachery.

Some Bedu are superstitious, putting great stock in amulets and charms, lucky numbers (odd numbers are usually considered lucky), and spirits. Stones and designs in jewelry have magical qualities. Triangles, which represent hands, called *khamsa*, ward off the evil eye, as do blue stones, such as turquoise or lapis lazuli; red stones will stop bleeding or reduce inflammation. Children, especially boys, are protected by charms hung around their necks or ankles and with ear studs containing magical stones. Many adult Bedu still have the holes in their earlobes from these magic ear studs. Animals that prey on the Bedu herds (e.g., wolves, wildcats) are considered the embodiment of evil, and in southern Arabia the camel is believed to be the direct descendant of the spirits of the desert.

⁵ RELIGION

Bedu are now Muslim. At one time there were Jewish and Christian tribes, but none of them survive today. For the most part, Bedu do not follow Islamic duties and rules strictly. Given the Bedu desert environment and demanding existence, many Islamic rituals are difficult to practice in the same manner as elsewhere. For example, ritual dry washings are utilized when there is insufficient water. The *Hadj* (pilgrimage to Mecca) is an important ritual for the Bedu, and most parents take each of their children on his or her first pilgrimage at the age of seven or eight. Some Bedu construct a place of prayer, called a *masjid* or *mashhad*, shortly after setting up their tents by enclosing a small piece of land with pebbles. The morning and noon prayers are usually considered the most important of the five daily prayers of Islam.

⁶ MAJOR HOLIDAYS

The most highly regarded Islamic festival among Bedu peoples is *Ayd al-Adha*, the "feast of sacrifice," when the Bedu sacrifice a camel or sheep from their herd to commemorate Abraham's willingness to sacrifice his son. (Because Islam uses a lunar calendar, the dates for Muslim holy days change each year on the Gregorian calendar.) Given the strong identification with lineage and kinship in Bedu society, the rite of honoring those who have died is taken very seriously.

Because many Bedu do not fast during the month of *Ramadan* (the ninth month of the Muslim year, during which Muhammad received his first revelations, celebrated by complete fasting from dawn until dusk each day of the entire month), the festival of *Ayd Al-Fitr* (a three-day celebration to break the fast at the end of *Ramadan*) has little meaning. Bedu also do not pay much attention to the celebration of the prophet Muhammad's birthday or his *hegira* (Muhammad's flight from Mecca); in fact, some Bedu do not even know the dates for those holy days in any given year.

⁷ RITES OF PASSAGE

In some tribes, when girls reach puberty they must then cover their hair and wear a mask or veil over their faces when in public (which, in Bedu terms, means whenever anyone but immediate family is present). Girls look forward to wearing these head and face coverings as a sign of maturity, and many design them so as to be alluring and provocative. They use their masks and veils to great effect in flirtations.

8 INTERPERSONAL RELATIONS

Two things shape the interactions of Bedu people: the Arab tradition of hospitality and the Bedu code of honor, or *sharaf*. These things themselves are shaped by the extreme conditions of desert nomadism. Survival as small groups of wanderers in the unforgiving desert required tremendous cooperation. The guest fed in one's own tent today may be the one who can provide food tomorrow. Passersby traditionally exchanged formal greetings with the families in the tents they passed and were asked for any news. The polite reply was to say one has no news or only good news. The passersby were then invited into the men's side of the tent for coffee and tea, served in a ritual way. It is considered polite to drink at least three cups before wobbling your glass to show that you do not want it refilled. Guests were assured of food and shelter for three and one-third days and then protection for another three days after leaving the tent, that being considered the length of time it takes for all traces of the host's food to pass through the guest's body. (Before a guest departed, the host burned incense in a special crucible called a *madran* or *mijmar*, and the guest perfumed his headscarf and beard with the smoke.) Anyone who even exchanged greetings, whether they came into the tent or not, was considered a guest entitled to the host's protection for the customary three days.

Women are inviolate in the Bedu code of honor. No man who is not intimately related to a woman may touch her in any way, not even so much as to brush his fingers against hers while handing her something. To do so is to dishonor her, and the traditional punishment for that was death. Likewise, in some tribes, if a woman brings dishonor to herself, she shames her family, because honor is held not by individuals but by whole families. According to old Bedu custom, if a woman committed any shameful conduct, her father or brother traditionally had the right, and was expected, to kill her immediately. Even in wars or raids, women were not touched. Raiding parties left enough supplies in the raided camp to support the women and children there. The loss of a woman's honor, her *ird*, is extremely serious in the Bedu code.

Long-time warriors, the Bedu have developed a very clear idea of what constitutes a fair fight and have strict rules governing the conduct of wars and raids. Another important element of Bedu honor is *as-sime,* giving up something so that a weaker person will benefit. Children are trained in the code of honor and tradition of hospitality from a very early age. By the time they are seven or eight years old, boys and girls know well what is expected of them and can behave with adult dignity when called upon.

9 LIVING CONDITIONS

The traditional Bedu live either in tents made of woven goat hair, known as a *bait sharar* ("house of hair"), palm-frond shacks called *barasti,* or in the shelter of a few bushes or trees, on which they may drape blankets for more protection from the wind. Bedu adapted to more modern customs live more settled lives in villages or take advantage of technological items such as "portacabins."

Bedu tents vary in size, depending on the number and wealth of the people living in them. The smallest are two-room tents, about 4 to 5 m (12 to 16 ft) long, and the largest can be anywhere up to 45 m (150 ft) or more in length. Most tents are about 2 m (6 ft) high. Larger tents are harder to move, so nomadic Bedu tents tend to fall somewhere between those two extremes. A tent houses an extended family of around 10 people, and it is divided into at least two sections—the men's side, or *al-shigg*; and the women's side, or *al-mahram*. Cooking is done and possessions are stored on the women's side, unless the tent has a third section for those purposes. Guests are entertained on the men's side, and the coffee and tea utensils and a fire for heating the water are located there. The men's and women's sections are divided either by a woven curtain called a *sahah* or *gata'ah*, or by a wooden mat called a *shirb* held together by wool woven around the canes in geometric patterns. These tent dividers are frequently beautiful works of art.

Bedu families stay close to their permanent wells during the dry summer months, then migrate to better grazing areas during the winter. The Bedu can travel as much as 3,000 km (1,600 mi) or more in a year. Traditional Bedu ride camels, which move by lifting both legs on one side at the same time, giving them a seesaw motion that requires a great deal of balance to ride. Some modern Bedu have acquired trucks and other four-wheel-drive vehicles to replace the camel as transportation. Each tribe has its own territory, or *dirah*, but as modernization encroaches on their range, the Bedu have had to cross over each other's territories much more frequently, and now it is commonplace to do so. However, each tribe still knows its *dirah* and the boundaries of those of other tribes.

The life of Bedu in oil-rich Arab nations is not quite as harrowing, as tanker trucks often bring water to outlying areas. Mobile medical units have made Western medicine more available to the Bedu, but most only turn to them when folk medicine fails. Traditional Bedu beliefs held that physical health is related to the actions of spirits and devils. The Bedu traditionally put red-hot coals to their skin to open a door for an evil spirit to exit the body at a place where it was causing trouble (e.g., between the eyes in the case of headaches). Herbal medicine (teas, poultices, etc.) is widely used, as are charms and amulets. Today, herbal treatments are no more considered "magical" among the Bedu than acupuncture is in the West. If all else fails, including folk and Western medicine, the Bedu may turn to *sahar*, practitioners of alternative medicine who have been outlawed by most state governments but who continue to provide their services.

10 FAMILY LIFE

Bedu live in extended families made up of paternal cousins. A group of families who are related to each other make up a *fakhadh* (literally, "thigh"), which means a clan "of the same root" or "part of the whole." A group of fakhadhs constitutes a tribe, called a *kabila* or *ashira*, though these words may also refer to subsections of a larger tribe. A group of tribes is a "confederation." Tribes vary widely in size and are constantly changing through marriage or territorial needs for grazing. A small tribe that has to move into the territory of a larger tribe to feed its herds may become absorbed by the larger tribe. Later, if the original small tribe has gained enough members and/or wealth, it may strike out on its own again.

Every group of Bedu has a *sheikh*, or leader. The sheikh always comes from the same family line within each group, but it is not necessarily the oldest son who takes over when the father dies. The post is given to the male family member most qualified for the job. A sheikh leads by consensus, not by absolute will, so all members of the group must respect the sheikh in order for him to lead them effectively.

Marriage is more of a social contract among the Bedu than a love match, although love often enters into it and sexuality within marriage is greatly enjoyed and celebrated by both men and women. The bride and groom are usually first cousins. Women marry between the ages of 16 and 22, while men marry between the ages of 18 and 30. The wedding is accomplished without much ceremony. It is essentially a process of customary negotiations after which the bride is escorted to the groom's tent. Divorce is just as simple: a man simply states in front of witnesses that he wants a divorce. A woman can initiate a divorce by moving back to her parents' tent. If she refuses to return to her husband's tent with him, he will grant her a divorce. Women give birth without much fuss as well. Siblings are very close to and protective of one another; brothers in particular guard their sisters' honor fiercely. Incest is forbidden and is virtually unknown.

11 CLOTHING

The primary article of clothing for both Bedu men and women is the *dishdasha*, a long gown worn by most Arabs that covers the body from the base of the neck to the wrists and ankles. Men wear the dishdasha as an outer garment with baggy trousers called *sirwal* underneath (some modern Bedu men wear sweatpants now instead), while women wear the dishdasha as an underdress beneath a larger, looser dress called a *thob*, which is almost always black. Women also wear baggy trousers, which are tight at the ankle and embroidered, under their dresses. Bedu men wear some sort of headcloth, the design of which varies from tribe to tribe. Adult women wear veils over their hair and either veils or masks on their faces (in most tribes). Both men and women use *kuhl* (kohl, a black powder made from lustrous antimony) to accent their eyes. It reduces glare from the harsh desert sun and is believed to help repel flies as well. Bedu traditionally walk barefoot.

Women love jewelry and wear a lot of it; they may also wear the family's wealth as jewelry, which will then be completely safe since, according to the code of honor, women cannot be touched. Older women may have tattoos, which were believed to enhance their beauty, but that tradition is dying out, and very few younger women wear them. It is considered effeminate for a man to have a tattoo. Men wear silver or gold belts with elaborate curved daggers called *khanja* strapped to them. Belts designed for carrying bullets are now popular, and nomadic Bedu men are rarely seen without their rifles.

12 FOOD

Bedu cooking emphasizes quantity rather than style. The traditional Bedu diet consisted mainly of camel milk, served cold or hot, boiled with bread, or cooked with rice. Meat, usually goat's meat, was an occasional luxury. Bedu along coastal areas also eat fish. Thin, flat bread is cooked over the fire on a curved metal sheet. The Bedu also hunt for meat to supplement their diet. They traditionally used trained falcons captured in the fall and released in the spring to hunt desert hares and foxes or migratory birds. Many Bedu hunt with a breed of dog called *saluki*, which is somewhat like an elegant greyhound. Although herding dogs are considered unclean and are never allowed to enter the living area, salukis are treated with a great deal of affection and live in the tent with their masters.

13 EDUCATION

Traditional Bedu education consists of training in the skills necessary to live the life of the nomadic desert camel herder. It takes years to learn how to take care of a herd of camels and a family in the harsh desert environment. Although some Bedu parents are beginning to provide a more formal education for their children in schools, this makes it difficult for those children to learn their desert skills. These skills are hunting, rope-weaving, camel-herding, -riding, -milking, and -breeding, tracking, and the rituals of entertaining guests for Bedu boys and weaving of all sorts, embroidery, cooking, cleaning, setting up and taking down camp, tent-making, and herding for Bedu girls. Traditional Bedu society was largely oral, without much need for reading and writing. However, reading the Quran is very important, and there are always some members of the family, including women, who must know how to read and write. Bedu can recite poetry and tell stories by memory, however, and recognize all of the hundreds of *wasm*, the camel brands of their own tribe and neighboring tribes. They can also "read" the signs left on the hard desert ground by people and animals that have passed that way.

14 CULTURAL HERITAGE

Poetry is considered the highest art in Bedu society; it is the outlet for emotional expressions otherwise restricted by the code of honor. The *rabab*, the one-stringed Bedu violin, is often played to accompany the recitation of poetic verse. Other literary genres, all oral, in the Bedu world are the *qissa* (folk tale), *qasid* (ode), riddles and proverbs, the *murafa'a* (pleading one's case before the magistrate), and the discussions of the *majalis* sessions (gatherings of family to pass on wisdom and traditions to the younger members).

Many Arab nations and even many Zionists within the modern nation-state of Israel regard the image of the Bedu as important to their cultural identity. For many, the Bedu shepherd is regarded as a bridge to the past. That link to the past is essential to nations that encompass ancient lands, peoples, and traditions but are relatively new as modern states.

15 WORK

Herding camels during the winter migration is a full-time job for at least two family members and usually requires two others part-time. Men and boys do most of the herding, but if there are not enough sons to do the job, teenage girls will help out. In a family with no sons, daughters take on all the work, including herding, entertaining guests, driving the vehicles (if they have any), and so on. Setting up and taking down camp is the women's job, plus all of the cooking, cleaning, weaving, and sewing. Pregnant women generally work right up to the time of delivery and then go back to work as soon as possible after giving birth. Nomadic Bedu life is a constant round of chores: collecting firewood, filling water drums, obtaining and preparing food, taking camels to pasture in the morning, and bringing them back to camp at night, milking the camels, moving camp, making and repairing tent cloths and clothing, and so on.

Many Bedu have given up full-time nomadic herding to take on wage-earning jobs. In many Middle Eastern countries, Bedu men form important elements in the military and are well compensated. In Jordan and Saudi Arabia, the armed forces are composed almost entirely of Bedu. In Israel, they have also been enlisted as trackers and wardens to protect endangered desert species.

16 SPORTS

Nomadic Bedu do not have much time for sports, but they do enjoy camel racing and spend quite a bit of time and energy breeding fast, light camels and even training them to pick up alternate feet, rather than both feet on the same side at the same time, to make them easier to ride at high speeds. Hunting is done purely for sport by wealthier Bedu, though it is a necessity for poorer families.

17 ENTERTAINMENT AND RECREATION

Winter is a sociable time for the Bedu, with many clans and tribes gathered in good grazing areas, rather than stuck by their isolated wells in the dry summer. At night, they gather to recite stories in verse around the campfire. Other times, the women may sing to the men in an informal performance called a *summejr*. Given the harsh realities of nomadic Bedu life, there is not much time for more recreation than this.

18 FOLK ART, CRAFTS, AND HOBBIES

Textiles woven by Bedu women are the most important product and one of the oldest crafts of Bedu society. The ground loom used by Bedu women is shown in an Egyptian fresco dating to 2200 BC. The women weave sheep's wool, goat or camel hair, or cotton into geometric designs, sometimes including stylized representations of everyday objects such as coffee pots, scissors, or camels. The Bedu traditionally put no border on their designs, instead letting the design go all the way to the edge of the cloth to reflect the infinite horizon of the desert, which leads one's mind to reflect on the infinity of God. Natural dyes were traditionally used, producing muted earth tones, reds, and blues, but they are difficult and time-consuming to make, so many Bedu women now purchase commercial dyes that create brighter colors. Other Bedu crafts are basketry and weaving palm fronds into mats and bags.

19 SOCIAL PROBLEMS

The modern invention of national boundaries and the encroachment of cities and cultivated areas on the desert has reduced the Bedu range and forced many to become only semi-nomadic, settling in villages for part of the year and returning to their herds in the desert for only a few months, or to give up the Bedu way of life altogether. With the advent of trucks and planes, the Bedu services were no longer needed to transport goods and people along the Middle East desert trade route by camel caravan. The Bedu thereby lost their biggest asset and source of much of their wealth and power. Many of the Bedu themselves have purchased trucks and other four-wheel-drive vehicles for their own use or to cater to tourists as "taxis." Once the Bedu succumb to modernization, becoming dependent on motor vehicles and wells, they need cash to maintain this new lifestyle. When men take wage-earning jobs in the villages or cities, it separates them from their families and herds. Bedu parents see that their children will need formal schooling if they are going to succeed in this new modern life, so they settle near villages to take advantage of public education. The children then are divorced from their ancestors' traditional lifestyle and can no longer survive in the desert, so they must take wage-earning jobs. As the Bedu come into more contact with the industrial world, they also see that their *sheikh*s have little authority there, threatening the respect necessary for the sheikh's leadership.

These changes have undermined the traditional Bedu way of life and threaten their very existence as a separate people. Because of assimilation into the settled, technological world and the poverty (even death) of those Bedu who attempt to continue their nomadic ways, the Bedu as an identifiable group may soon become extinct. Yet, the Bedu are a proud people and have fought to retain their way of life. Arab nations and even many Israelis recognize the importance of the Bedu to their cultural heritage and have tried to accommodate the nomadic way of life. Efforts to incorporate the Bedu into modern nations have had varying degrees of success. Israel, for instance, tries to encourage the Bedu to give up their nomadic ways and to settle into modern Israeli society. Many Bedu resist this call because they prefer their nomadic, rural way of life. Other Arab nations such as Jordan have tried to build their national identity on the basis of their leaders' Bedu ties. However, the difference between the settled nature of modern nations and the wandering way of life of the Bedu is difficult to reconcile.

20 GENDER ISSUES

The rise of the modern nation-state has not been beneficial to Bedu women. The nomadic lifestyle was harsh, but it did give women a great deal of independence and authority. Bedu women typically supervised the domestic affairs of their clans. While men dealt with matters of herding, women ensured that the social relationships within a clan functioned. Divorce often was instituted by women who chose to express their displeasure with a spouse by moving back into their natal family's tents. As Bedu were forced to settle into planned communities, women lost a great deal of their autonomy. Their role became one not of supervising movement but of housecleaning and serving the male members of their clans. Many modern Bedu women have rebelled against the constraints that the new way of life imposes upon them and have often left their clans to integrate more fully with modern Arab society.

21 BIBLIOGRAPHY

Berman-Kishony, Talia. "Bedouin Urbanization Legal Policies in Israel and Jordan: Similar Goals, Contrasting Strategies. *Transnational Law & Contemporary Problems,* 17.2 (Spring 2008): 393-413.

Jabbur, Jibrail S. *The Bedouins and the Desert: Aspects of Nomadic Life in the Arab East.* Albany, NY: State University of New York Press, 1995.

Katakura, Motoko. *Bedouin Village: A Study of a Saudi Arabian People in Transition.* Tokyo: University of Tokyo Press, 1977.

Keohane, Alan. *Bedouin: Nomads of the Desert.* London: Kyle Cathie Ltd., 1994.

Queder, Sarab Abu-Rabia. "Permission to rebel: Arab Bedouin women's changing negotiation of social roles," *Feminist Studies* 33.1 (Spring 2007) 161-188.

Zerubavel, Yael. "Memory, the Rebirth of the Native, and the 'Hebrew Bedouin' identity. *Social Research* 75.1 (Spring 2008): 315-353.

—revised by H. Gupta-Carlson

BENGĀLIS

PRONUNCIATION: ben-GAWL-eez
ALTERNATE NAMES: Bangalis
LOCATION: Bangladesh (Bengal region); India (state of West Bengal and other northeastern states)
POPULATION: 380 million (estimate, including expatriates)
LANGUAGE: Bengali
RELIGION: Islam; Hinduism
RELATED ARTICLES: Vol. 3: Hindus; Vol. 4: Muslims

¹ INTRODUCTION

Bengālis are the inhabitants of Bengal in the northeastern part of the South Asian subcontinent. Historically, the area was known as Banga, after local peoples who settled in the region over 1,000 years ago. This ancient term survives in many modern names, e.g., the region of Bengal, the Bengali (or Bangla) language, and the country of Bangladesh (literally, "the land of the Bengali people").

Bengal came under the influence of many political empires that arose in northern India. It was ruled by the Buddhist Pala dynasty from the 8th to the 12th centuries AD. Following this, it had a series of Muslim overlords and by the late 16th century formed part of the Moghal Empire. With the decline of the Moghals, the region was governed by the independent Nawabs of Bengal until they were deposed by the British in the middle of the 18th century (1757–64). In 1757, at the Battle of Plassey, a small village and mango grove near Calcutta (Kolkata), the forces of the East India Company under Robert Clive defeated the army of Siraj-ud-daulah, the Nawab of Bengal, and thus the Company gained the right to administer Bengal, and in 1765 it gained the *Diwani* of Bengal, which virtually conferred upon it the civil authority of the Province in perpetuity.

In 1905, Bengal was divided into the Provinces of Bengal (essentially the modern state of West Bengal and Bihar) and Eastern Bengal and Assam (the modern Bangladesh and the Indian state of Assam). There was considerable opposition to this partition, particularly among Bengālis, and in 1912 Eastern Bengal was reunited with Bengal. Assam was created as a separate province in 1914. At the same time, at the end of 1911, the capital of British India was moved from Calcutta to Delhi, where Lutyens and Baker created an imperial capital that is today New Delhi.

The political events in the region following Independence in 1947, led to another partition of Bengal into East and West, again dividing the peoples of Bengali culture, not only between two administrative units, but between two countries. The eastern parts of Bengal, where Muslims were most numerous, were assigned to Pakistan when India was partitioned in 1947. East Pakistan, as it was known, became the independent nation of Bangladesh in 1971, following a bloody civil war between Bengālis and West Pakistanis.

Calcutta, on the River Hooghly—a tributary of the River Ganges, is the capital of the Indian state of West Bengal and is the "Bengali" city, par excellence. It is a major center of intellectual activity (Bengālis see themselves as the "intellectuals" of India). Today, it has a population of about 5 million and forms an urban conglomeration of approaching 16 million people, ranking third in size in India, after Delhi and Bombay.

Until 1911, Calcutta served as the capital of British India (it is the starting point of the Grand Trunk [GT] Road that links the cities of the Ganges Plain over its 2,500 km length to the North West Frontier) and is said to have rivaled London in its splendor. One only has to see the magnificent, decaying mansions that abound in Calcutta to get a sense of what it must have been like in the 19th century. Unlike Delhi, Calcutta is a colonial creation, being founded by the British in 1690. The city was a hotbed of the Free India movement prior to Independence, but experienced massive Hindu-Muslim riots prior to partition. The 1947 Partition of Bengal affected Calcutta's hinterland. For instance, the city, a major regional center of the jute manufacturing industry, lost access to its jute-growing areas, which fell to East Pakistan.

West Bengal is one of the few states in the world that has had a democratically-elected communist government for several decades. The government led by Chief Minister Buddadeb Bhattacharjee of the Communist Party of India-Marxist (CPI-M), is formed by the Left Alliance, a coalition led by the CPI-M. As of 2008, it had been in power since the 1970s.

² LOCATION AND HOMELAND

The 2001 census puts the population of West Bengal at just over 209.5 million and that of Bangladesh at 131.3 million. This, along with the number of ex-patriots and growth since 2001, makes the 2008 estimate of the numbers of Bengali speaking peoples in the world around 380 million people. The greatest number of Bengālis are found in Bangladesh with the remainder living in the Indian state of West Bengal. Significant communities of Bengali-speaking peoples are distributed throughout other states in northeastern India. Bengālis have also emigrated in large numbers to the United Kingdom, Canada, and the United States.

The lower plains and vast delta of the Ganges and Brahmaputra Rivers lie at the heart of the Bengal region. The rich fertile soils, renewed by periodic deposits of sediment, support some of the highest agricultural population densities found anywhere in the world. Water is constantly present, in rivers, streams, and ponds. The many rivers that cross the landscape provide an important means of transportation, but also hinder land communications. Frequent floods in the region cause extensive damage and loss of life. In the extreme north, a narrow strip of West Bengal State reaches into the foothills of the Himalayas around Darjiling. The climate on the plains is hot and humid, with mean monthly temperatures at Calcutta ranging from 20°c (68°F) in winter to 30°c (86°F) in summer. In May 1991, maximum temperatures in Calcutta rose to 40° (104°F). Heavy rains, most of it falling between May and early October, occur during the monsoon period. Calcutta receives 158 cm (62 in) annually, though this total increases to nearly 400 cm (over 150 in) in some parts of the region.

³ LANGUAGE

The language of the region is Bengali, which is a member of the Indo-Aryan branch of the Indo-European linguistic family. Like most of the other languages of northern India, it is derived from Sanskrit. Dialects of Bengali, such as Radha, that are spoken in the western region are quite different from those in the east, which show strong Arabo-Persian influences. Other regional dialects include Rajbangshi, Varendra, and Vanga. Bengali is written in its own script, which contains 57 letter

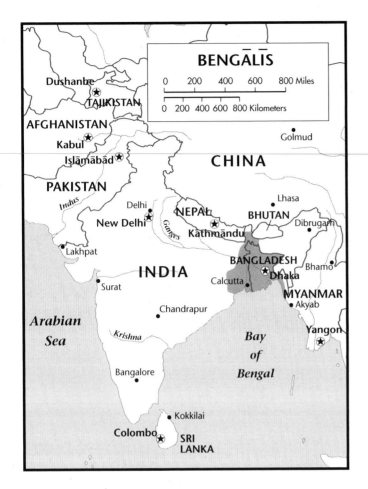

BENGĀLĪS

0   200   400   600   800 Miles

0 200 400 600 800 Kilometers

symbols. Numerous Bengali speakers have migrated into the Indian state of Assam, so much so that Bengali is one of the state's official languages.

⁴ FOLKLORE

The folk traditions of Bengal include folk tales, songs, and riddles that express the values, beliefs, superstitions, and taboos of the common Bengali people. One popular folk tale, known all over the region and even forming the basis for a film, is "Seven Champa Brothers and One Sister Parul." (The Champa and Parul are trees native to the Bengal area.) There once was a king, so the story goes, who was married to seven queens. When the favorite youngest queen gave birth to seven sons and a daughter, the barren elder queens were jealous. They killed the babies, buried them in a garbage heap, and substituted puppies and kittens instead. Fearing witchcraft, the king banished the youngest queen. Seven Champa trees and one Parul tree grew out of the garbage heap where the babies were buried. When the evil queens, and even the king, tried to pluck the flowers from the trees, the flowers moved away. They asked for the banished queen to be brought to them. She plucked the flowers, and a boy emerged from each Champa flower and a girl from the Parul flower. They were reunited with their mother and their father, the king. When the king learned the truth, he had the jealous queens killed and lived happily ever after with his remaining wife and children. The main theme of this tale is that jealousy leads to wrongdoing, but this will eventually be found out and punished.

⁵ RELIGION

Bengālīs, though unified by a common language and culture, are divided by religion. Over 60% of Bengālīs, most living in Bangladesh, are Muslim. Even in Hindu India, more than 20% of West Bengal's population is Muslim. This reflects the historical importance of Islam in Bengal during nearly 800 years of the region's history. Most Muslim Bengālīs are Sunnis, though Sufism also plays a role in their religious lives.

Bengālīs in India are mainly Hindu, with beliefs and customs conforming to the orthodox forms of the religion. West Bengal, however, is also known for some unusual Hindu sects. Vaishnavas are followers of the Hindu god Vishnu. But Bengali Vaishnavas believe that Krishna is the supreme deity, rather than an incarnation of Vishnu. Accordingly, the rituals of this devotional (bhakti) movement focus solely on the forms and images of Krishna. Shaktism is a religious cult based on the worship of the female principle (śakti, literally "energy"). The Bengal form of Shaktism involves the worship of the goddess Kali. Kalighat in Calcutta, where animal sacrifices are carried out in the name of the goddess, is one of the major Shakti centers in the region. Popular religion in Bengal reflects a mixing of Hindu and Muslim folk beliefs, deities, and customs. For example, Hindus as well as Muslims worship at Sufi shrines.

Bengal is known for its itinerant religious musicians such as the Bauls. These, who are both Hindu and Muslim and tend to ignore sectarian differences between the two religions, wander from village to village singing devotional hymns and folk songs for the local people.

⁶ MAJOR HOLIDAYS

Bengālīs celebrate the major holidays of the Muslim and Hindu faiths. For Muslims, these include Id ul-Fitr, Id ul-Adha (Bakr-Id), and even Muharram. Bengali Hindus observe Holi, Divali, and other important festivals on the religious calendar, but Durga Puja is of particular importance to them. Dedicated to the goddess Durga, who is a manifestation of Shakti (female energy), the festivities last for nine days. Months before the festival, special images are made of Durga, showing her mounted on a lion and killing the evil demon Mahishasura. These images are lavishly painted and decorated. They are worshiped on each day of the festival. On the tenth day, the image, garlanded with flowers, is carried through the streets in procession by an excited crowd. The procession makes it way to a river or the ocean, where the image of Durga is thrown into the water to be carried away by the current or tide. Lakshmi, goddess of wealth, and Saraswati, goddess of learning, also have their annual festivals. At the level of folk religion, both Hindus and Muslims worship local deities such as Shitala, the goddess of smallpox.

⁷ RITES OF PASSAGE

Rites of passage followed by Bengālīs are prescribed in outline by Islam or Hinduism but have underlying currents that are specifically "Bengali" in nature. For example, Muslims follow the custom of saying the Call to Prayer (azān) to the newborn, but the umbilical cord is cut by the midwife who is usually a Hindu of the Hari caste. She performs the same task for Hindus, except for those who are of too low a rank to receive her services. Hindus observe the naming ceremony, the initiation ritual known as the "first feeding of rice" (annaprāśana), and—for the higher castes—the sacred thread ceremony (upanaya-

na). Muslim boys undergo the all-important circumcision rite *(sunnat).*

As with other Hindus, Bengālis cremate the dead. The funeral pyre is usually lit on the banks of a river or stream, with the necessary rites normally performed by the deceased's eldest son. Death is followed by a period of mourning (which varies in length according to caste), purification rites, and the *śrāddha* or death feast held at the end of the mourning period. Muslim practice requires that the body be ritually bathed and wrapped in a shroud before being taken to the place of burial. There the body is laid in its grave with the face turned to the west, i.e., in the direction of Mecca. Prayers for the dead and readings from the Quran are part of the funeral rites.

8 INTERPERSONAL RELATIONS

Hindu Bengālis greet each other by saying "Namaskar," placing the hands together in front of the body with the palms touching. This form of greeting is widespread throughout India. Sometimes the phrase "Kamen asso" (How are you?) is added. Muslim Bengālis use "Salaam" or "Salaam alaikum," accompanied by the appropriate gestures.

9 LIVING CONDITIONS

Rural settlement patterns in Bengal vary from the compact, shapeless villages of West Bengal, to the isolated farmsteads of the Ganges Delta, to the hamlet clusters of the northern plains. House types and construction reflect local environmental conditions. In the interior, houses are made of mud, bamboo, and brush wood. Roofs are thatched, though the more-prosperous now use corrugated iron. In Bangladesh, a typical village house consists of several huts around a compound. Facing the compound is the main structure, with a veranda in front that leads into the living quarters. These may consist of one or more bedrooms, a sitting room, and a kitchen. Other huts on the sides of the compound are used for storage and cattle sheds. There is usually no latrine, with villagers using the fields for their daily functions. Such a lifestyle and standard of living are in marked contrast to those of the urban elites, who enjoy all the modern conveniences of city living. Some of the wealthy industrialists and business owners of Calcutta have a style of living that compares favorably with that found among the wealthy in the United States.

10 FAMILY LIFE

Bengālis follow the normal patterns of Hindus and Muslims in South Asia in their social organization. Bengali Hindus belong to castes *(jāti),* and their caste ranking influences many aspects of their economic and social lives. Muslims are, in theory, egalitarian but they also retain traces of a social hierarchy. In both communities, marriages are arranged by the parents. Hindu marriages are governed by rules of caste endogamy (i.e., marriage within the caste) and lineage exogamy (marriage outside one's immediate line of descent). In contrast, Muslims have no caste restrictions, although marriage partners are usually chosen from families of similar social standing. Cousin marriage is common among Bengali Muslims. The actual wedding ceremonies follow standard Hindu or Muslim rites. After marriage, the newlyweds typically take up residence in the household of the husband's father.

The extended family is common among both Hindus and Muslims, though this is changing among the educated, urban

A Bengālī girl with water lilies. The water lily is Bangladesh's national flower. The girl sells them to visitors. (AP Images/Pavel Rahman)

elites. As in most communities in South Asia, women remain subordinate to men. Some Muslims continue the custom of *purdah* (the seclusion of women from males). Divorce and widow remarriage reflect traditional Hindu and Muslim practices.

11 CLOTHING

In rural areas, Muslim men wear the *lunglī,* a piece of (often checkered) cloth that is wrapped around the waist and extends to the ground, covering the legs. Hindus dress in the *dhotlī,* the long piece of white cotton cloth that is wrapped around the waist, then drawn between the legs in the manner of a loincloth. Village men usually go shirtless but on occasion may put on a vest or a long shirt called a *punjāblī* as an upper garment. Wooden sandals are common, and during the rainy season almost everyone sports an umbrella. Women wear the *sari* and blouse, though younger Muslim girls may favor the combination of *salwār* (loose trousers) and *kamlīz* (tunic). Women in the countryside go barefoot. A variety of rings, bangles, and other ornaments and jewelry are worn by women of all classes.

In large metropolitan areas such as Calcutta and other cities and towns, safari suits or Western-style business suits, shirts, and jackets are a common sight. Younger urban women may also dress in Western fashions, although the sari is retained for formal occasions.

12 FOOD

Boiled rice is the staple food in rural Bengal, eaten with vegetables such as onion, garlic, eggplant, and a variety of gourds according to the season. Fish and meat are favorite foods, but their cost places them beyond the reach of most villagers. The vegetables, fish, and meat are prepared as spicy curried dishes. Beef and water-buffalo meat are popular with Muslims. Hindus view the cow as sacred, and so they do not eat beef. Most Bengali Hindus are not vegetarians, however, and will eat goats, ducks, chickens, and eggs, in addition to fish. Cuisine among the more-affluent includes Mughal-style dishes including pilaf and *biryanī* (rice dishes containing meat and vegetables), *kebābs* (barbecued meat), and meat dishes known as *kormā*. Milk forms an important element in the diet, and milk-based sweets are popular throughout the region. Tea may be drunk, as it is throughout India, at any time of the day.

13 EDUCATION

Literacy rates vary among Bengālīs. Those living in Bangladesh, especially in rural areas, are likely to be poorly educated and illiterate. Bangladesh has the lowest overall literacy rate (34.8%) of any South Asian country. By contrast, literacy in West Bengal (57.7% in 1991) is slightly higher than the average for India (52.6%). Education has long been a mark of higher social status among Bengālīs, and this is reflected in the high college enrollment in West Bengal. Vishva-Bharati University, founded by the Bengali writer Rabrindanath Tagore in Shantiniketan, is world-famous as a center for the study of Indian history and culture. The University of Calcutta, with its numerous affiliated colleges, is one of the major academic institutions in India.

14 CULTURAL HERITAGE

Bengālīs are heirs to one of the richest literary traditions in the Indian subcontinent. The earliest known works in Bengali are Buddhist texts that date to the 10th and 11th centuries AD. The influence of the Vaishnava saint and mystic Chaitanya (1485–1534) on the development of medieval Bengali literature was immense. Some of the gems of Bengali poetry at this time were the songs dedicated to Krishna and his consort Radha. Islam, too, contributed to medieval Bengali literature through the devotional works of the Sufis and the writings of other Muslims.

More recently, Bengālīs have created a vibrant modern literature ranging from the novel and short story to poetry and drama. Rabindranath Tagore, the Bengali poet and writer, was awarded the Nobel Prize for Literature in 1913. Bengālīs have also achieved great success in the field of classical Indian music and dance. Satyajit Ray (1921–1992), the only Indian film director of his era to gain international fame and acclaim, was a Bengali. There still exists an important film industry in Calcutta producing Bengali films.

15 WORK

Bengālīs are predominantly rural and agricultural in nature, with over two-thirds of the region's population engaged in cultivation. Bengal's climate allows three crops to be grown in the year, with wet-rice cultivation dominating the economy. Jute, produced mostly in Bangladesh, is the major cash crop of the region. West Bengal, however, is also an industrial area. The cities and towns along the banks of the Hooghly River (an arm of the Ganges) make up one of India's most important manufacturing regions. It is here, 154 km (96 mi) upstream from the Bay of Bengal, that Calcutta is located. Founded in 1690 as a British trading post on the banks of the river, Calcutta is now one of the world's largest cities with a population of over 12 million people. Its industries include jute processing, engineering, textiles, and chemicals. Calcutta is perhaps the most important intellectual and cultural center of India, a fact of which Bengālīs are extremely proud. The city is the birthplace of Indian nationalism, and of modern Indian literary and artistic thought.

16 SPORTS

Bengali children play games common to children all over South Asia. These include tag, hide-and-seek, kite-flying, marbles, and spinning tops. Youths and young adults enjoy wrestling. Cricket, soccer, and field hockey are major spectator sports, and many children play these games at school as well. Sports such as tennis, golf, and horse-racing are popular among the Westernized urban middle classes.

17 ENTERTAINMENT AND RECREATION

Recreational activities among Bengālīs vary to a considerable degree. Villagers in isolated rural areas may derive their greatest pleasure from fairs, religious festivals, and Bengali folk traditions such as *jātrā* (itinerant folk theater), the *bhātiālī* (boater's songs), and the *baul* (mystical songs sung by wandering minstrels). On the other hand, the sophisticated resident of Calcutta has access to radio, television, theater, movies, films, museums, and other cultural activities.

18 FOLK ART, CRAFTS, AND HOBBIES

The folk arts and crafts of Bengal reflect the diversity of its people and the skills of its artisans. Among the items produced are hand printed textiles, embroidered quilt work, terra-cotta dolls, toys, and idols such as those used during Durga Puja. *Alpana* drawings, religious designs prepared by Hindu women, are made on walls, floors, and courtyards out of rice-paste. The decoration of boats is a thriving folk art in the delta region. Copper and brass metalwork, pottery, weaving, basketry, and carpentry are among the many activities pursued by the craftspeople in the region.

19 SOCIAL PROBLEMS

As might be expected in such a large and diverse population, problems vary considerably in their nature and scope. Some problems, such as frequent flooding in Bengal, reflect the region's environmental setting. Others—for example, poverty and illiteracy—result from the fact that the people live in countries that are still developing. Thus, malnutrition among villagers in rural Bangladesh mirror that country's standing as one of the poorest nations in the world. Similarly, the plight of the urban poor in cities like Calcutta and Dhaka is linked to the dynamics of urban growth in the Third World. Still other problems originate in the political volatility of the region. Bangladesh, for example, has experienced civil unrest, suspension of democratic rights, and repressive military governments.

Social tensions in the region often arise from a mix of cultural, historical, and political factors. There are non-Bengali minorities in both West Bengal (the Gorkhas in the north who want a Gorkha homeland) and Bangladesh (e.g., the Chakmas in eastern Bangladesh) who have resorted to violence to fight what they see as Bengali cultural imperialism. Similarly, large numbers of Bengālīs fled Bangladesh during both Partition and the country's 1971 War of Independence. In West Bengal, this refugee problem was largely one of numbers. However, in India's northeastern states such as Assam and Tripura, where the population is non-Bengali, this created ethnic tensions between Bengali refugees and the local peoples. Resentment against these "foreigners" is strong and periodically, as in Assam in the early 1980s, leads to ethnic violence. An armed militant organization namely United Liberation Front of Assam (ULFA) was established in 1979 "with a purpose of liberating Assam from the illegal occupation of India," i.e. limiting the Bengali presence in Assam. Such events, however, are but the most recent chapter in the story of a people that extends back almost 1,000 years. Language, history, and shared traditions give Bengālīs a sense of identity that makes Bengali culture one of the most unique and distinctive in all of South Asia.

20 GENDER ISSUES

Despite the efforts of governments and nongovernmental organizations (NGOs) such as Women for Women to promote gender equality for women among Bengālīs, Bengali women suffer from the constraints of the society in which they live. Thus Hindu women face problems of arranged marriages, exploitation of girl children, child marriage and dowries, while Muslim women face issues of *purdah*, the wearing of the *burqa* and the role of women in Islamic society. Among both Hindus and Muslims, women are regarded as inferior to men and their main role is to take care of the household and bear (male) children. In rural areas, women participate in agricultural activities. Poverty is an issue for many Bengali women (though institutions such as the Grameen Bank in Bangladesh are providing capital for poor women wishing to go into business). Literacy among women in Bangladesh hovers around 40%, over 25 percentage points below the male average, and of course is much higher in urban areas than in the countryside. Fewer than 10% of Bengali women continue with higher education. However, women writers, such as Suchitra Bhattacharya and Bani Basu, have made a considerable name for themselves in the world of Bengali literature, in keeping with a tradition that extends back several centuries.

21 BIBLIOGRAPHY

Afsaruddin, Mohammad. *Society and Culture in Bangladesh.* Dhaka: Book House, 1990.

Ali, A. "Vulnerability of Bangladesh to climate change and sea level rise through tropical cyclones and storm surges." *Water, Air, & Soil Pollution* 92 (1-2): 171-179, 1996.

Halder, Dilip. *Partition's Forgotten Victims: The Dalits of Bengal: a Human Rights Question.* Calcutta, London: Sampark, 2006.

Basu, Tara Krishna. *The Bengal Peasant from Time to Time.* London: Asia Publishing House, 1962.

Baxter, Craig. *Bangladesh: From a Nation to a State.* Boulder, CO: Westview Press, 1997.

Bertocci, Peter. J. "Bengālīs." *In Muslim Peoples: A World Ethnographic Survey*, edited by Richard Weekes. Westport, CT: Greenwood Press, 1984.

Mukherjee, Ramakrishna. *Six Villages of Bengal.* Bombay: Popular Prakashan, 1971.

—by D. O. Lodrick

BHILS

PRONUNCIATION: BEELZ
LOCATION: India (Southern Rajasthan and bordering areas of Gujarat, Madhya Pradesh, and Maharashtra states)
POPULATION: 12,705,753 (2001 census)
LANGUAGE: Bhili
RELIGION: Tribal religions (97%); Hinduism
RELATED ARTICLES: Vol. 4: Minas; People of India; Rajputs

1 INTRODUCTION

The name Bhil identifies various ethnic communities inhabiting the hills and forests of southern Rajasthan and neighboring areas of western India. Some scholars argue that "Bhil" comes from the Dravidian word for bow (*billa* or *billu*) and reflects the popularity of the bow and arrow as a weapon among these groups. The term is also used in a broader sense to refer to the aboriginal peoples of this region. Bhils are divided into numerous tribes and subtribes, including the Barela, Bhilala, Garasia, Gameta, Mina, Tadvi, and Vasave. Many of these groups, however, see themselves as quite distinct from the Bhil community.

The Bhils are mostly tribal in nature. In the past, they acquired a reputation for a fierce sense of independence. Isolated from the rest of Indian society by their rugged environment, Bhil groups have managed to preserve many of their ancient tribal customs. At the same time, close social and economic ties with their neighbors have exposed them to Hindu cultural influences.

Though little is known of their origins, the Bhils appear to be the oldest inhabitants of the area. They are generally dark complexioned and small of stature. Their racial affinities are uncertain, although they have been identified with both the Dravidian and pre-Dravidian peoples of South Asia. Some writers suggest that the wild, hill peoples of the region mentioned in the ancient Sanskrit literature were, in fact, the Bhils. A Sanskrit text dating to the very end of the 6th century AD mentions a Bhil chieftain, mounted on an elephant, opposing the passage of another king through the Vindhya Mountains. By the 7th century, various Rajput clans began to settle in western India and subdue the local peoples of the area. Some Bhils resisted the invaders and fled into the interior to preserve their independence. Other Bhil groups seem to have accepted this conquest peacefully, even intermarrying with the newcomers. One finds other ties linking the Bhils and the Rajputs. Bhils, for example, played a role in Rajput coronations. In some Rajput states, it was customary for a Bhil to place a ceremonial mark (*tika*) made with his own blood on the forehead of a new *raja* (king). Although no longer followed, the ritual has been seen by historians as a sign of Bhil allegiance to the Rajputs as well as of former Bhil power. The figure of a Bhil chief is included on the emblem of Mewar (Udaipur), an important Rajput state in southern Rajasthan.

The Bhils were treated quite differently by the Marathas. This Hindu group, which extended its military power northwards from Maharashtra into the region at the beginning of the 17th century, mercilessly persecuted the Bhils. If a criminal were caught and found to be a Bhil, he or she would often be killed on the spot. Historical accounts tell of entire Bhil

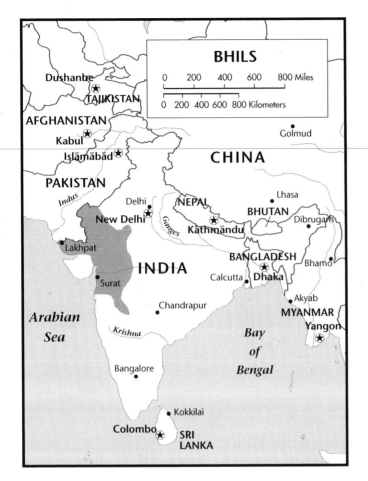

Madhya Pradesh, and Maharashtra states. Bhil populations are concentrated in the southernmost hills of the Aravalli Range, the western uplands of the Vindhya and Satpura ranges, and the northernmost hills of the Western Ghats. Some Bhil groups occupy the nearby river valleys and coastal plains. The Gujarati term "Rewakantha," the basin of the Rewa (Narmada River), is sometimes used to describe the traditional territory of the Bhil peoples.

The environments inhabited by the Bhil are relatively inaccessible and unproductive. The rugged Aravalli hills of southern Rajasthan attain a height of 1,722 m (5,650 ft) at Mount Abu. The region experiences a semiarid climate. Annual rainfall in southern Rajasthan and Gujarat averages around 63.5 cm (25 in) and comes mainly from the summer monsoons. Rainfall is highly variable, however, and droughts are frequent. Maximum temperatures during the summer average over 40°c (104°f), but in winter they can approach freezing. The natural vegetation is thorn scrub forest, dominated by drought-resistant species such as acacias. The vegetation cover has been much degraded through overuse by humans and animals. To the south, in Maharashtra and Madhya Pradesh, rainfall increases and temperatures become less extreme. Scrub forests give way to denser deciduous forests, but here, too, the vegetation has suffered from human and animal activity.

The Bhils numbered 12.7 million people (12,705,753 according to the 2001 Census of India). Assuming population growth rates that approximate those of the rest of India, the current population of Bhils will be close to 14 million people. The Bhils are exceeded in number only by the Gonds among the tribes of India and account for over 10% of the country's total tribal population. The accuracy of the census data, however, is open to debate because of questions concerning exactly which groups should be included under the classification of "Bhil." The Bhils remain, nonetheless, one of the largest tribal groups in South Asia.

³ LANGUAGE

The language of the Bhils is called Bhili, a term that refers to the numerous dialects spoken by Bhils throughout western India. For example, Wagdi, Dungri, and Mavchi are Bhili dialects spoken in Rajasthan, Gujarat, and Maharashtra, respectively. Dialects change within a radius of 32 to 48 km (20 to 30 mi) and Bhils from one area may have difficulty in understanding those in a neighboring area. Bhili dialects show varying degrees of influence of regional languages such as Rajasthani and Marathi, but they all appear to have their origins in Gujarati. Gujarati, the language spoken in Gujarat, belongs to the Indo-Aryan language family. Thus, linguistically, the Bhils are unlike most tribal groups in India whose tongues more commonly are Dravidian or Munda in origin.

⁴ FOLKLORE

Bhil mythology and folklore place great emphasis on the antiquity of the Bhils, as well as the Bhils' traditional place outside the mainstream of Hindu society. At the same time, Bhil traditions demonstrate the longstanding influence of Hinduism on Bhil culture.

One account of the origin of the Bhils holds that Mahadeo (literally, the "great god," an aspect of the Hindu god Shiva) was resting in a forest, sick and unhappy. A beautiful woman appeared before him and, on seeing her, Mahadeo was cured

communities being wiped out. The Bhils retreated to the safety of their strongholds in the hills. From there, they raided villages in the neighboring lowlands and robbed travelers passing through their lands.

Although their reputation for banditry, thievery, and lawlessness has been exaggerated, the unruly Bhils did pose problems for local rulers. The British government in India, which gained control of the region in the early 19th century, even set up special military units to pacify local Bhil populations. The Bhils also took part in local tribal resistance movements during the 19th and early 20th centuries, protesting political and social injustices. However, the Mewar Bhil Corps, a unit of Bhils formed in Mewar in the 1840s with a view to weaning them away from their predatory habits, to give them honorable employment, and to assist the government in preserving order, were the only native troops in Rajasthan to stand by the British during the 1857 Mutiny.

The Indian Constitution (1949) designated the Bhils as a Scheduled Tribe, one of the groups identified as needing special representation and assistance in India after independence from British rule. Today, the Bhils remain a disadvantaged community with high levels of poverty, illiteracy, and other social problems.

² LOCATION AND HOMELAND

The Bhil homeland lies at the western end of India's tribal belt. It includes southern Rajasthan and bordering areas of Gujarat,

of all his ailments. The god was smitten by the woman and together they produced many offspring. One of these children was an ugly and vicious son. Mahadeo, enraged when this son killed his favorite bull, expelled him. All Bhils are said to be descended from this outcast.

Numerous variants of this tale exist, but Bhil myths of origin universally ascribe the beginnings of the Bhil tribes to some similar misdeed, a misfortune, or an incestuous union.

⁵ RELIGION

Bhil religion is essentially animistic in nature. It is the belief in the powers of supernatural forces and the need to order one's relations with these forces that dominate Bhil religious life. The Bhils are highly superstitious. They believe in omens and the evil eye and wear charms and amulets for protection from ghosts, evil spirits, and witches. Individuals, usually women, suspected of witchcraft, sorcery, or magic are identified by a shaman or witch-finder. (This figure is called a *Bhopa* in Rajasthan and *Badava* in eastern Gujarat). Traditionally, the victims were subjected to trial by ordeal, tortured, and even killed. The Bhopa and Badava play an important role in rituals performed to exorcise ghosts. The Bhils recognize gods and goddesses in the natural world, revering various deities of the sky, trees, water, and rain. Fire is held to be sacred, and totemic animals include the horse, tiger, boar, peacock, and sparrow. Animal sacrifice is a common Bhil practice.

The Bhils have long paid homage to Hindu deities such as Mahadeo, viewed as the creator of the universe; his consort Parvati; Hanuman, the monkey-god; and Bhairon. Mataji (Kali) is much respected and propitiated by the sacrifice of goats and male buffaloes. Numerous lesser gods and local godlings are worshiped.

Groups such as the aristocratic Bhilala, the descendants of Bhil-Rajput marriages, and some plains' Bhil have adopted formal Hindu practices. They use Brahman priests, accept the existence of a caste hierarchy, and show a greater degree of integration into Hindu society. Small numbers of Bhils have converted to Islam. Others have adopted Christianity as the result of the efforts of Christian missionaries during the 19th and early 20th centuries. However, census returns show that 97% of the Bhils follow tribal religions.

⁶ MAJOR HOLIDAYS

Although their chief festivals are held to honor the dead, Bhils also observe the Hindu festivals of Holi, Dasahara, and Divali in much the same way as their Hindu neighbors. Holi, the spring festival of India, for example, is marked by the burning of bonfires and throwing of colored water; and Dasahara, the autumn festival honoring the goddess Durga, is accompanied by the sacrifice of goats and buffaloes. There are, however, differences in observances. Holi, in particular, is celebrated with much revelry, with singing, dancing, and drinking lasting for up to 10 days or more. Bhils tend to celebrate the festivals of their region. In Rajasthan, for instance, Gauri is a popular festival.

Bhils, in the new Indian state of Chhattisgarh, celebrate the Bhagoriya Festival, a festival that occurs a week before Holi when lovers are officially given permission to elope. A male applies gulal (colored powder) to the head of a girl he likes and, if she reciprocates, the couple is at complete liberty. The marriage is formally consecrated at a later date. On the occasion of this festival, Bhagoradev or the God of Dancing is worshipped religiously by the people of the Bhil community. The eldest member of the village supervises over the ceremony. Sweets are offered to the god and later these are distributed amongst the members of the tribe. (Chhattisgarh was created out of the southeastern districts of Madhya Pradesh and has a distinctive language and culture. It, along with Jharkhand and Uttarakhand, came into being as states in India in 2000).

⁷ RITES OF PASSAGE

Rites of passage of the hill Bhils tend to differ from those who live in the plains. For both groups, however, the chief ceremonies are associated with the naming of a child, the shaving of the male child's head, marriage, and death.

The birth of a son is announced to the community at large by a particular beat of a drum (*dhol*). Hymns may be sung to propitiate Shitala Mata, the goddess of smallpox who is widely feared by primitive peoples in India, and sweets and liquor are distributed. The male child's head is shaved after a few months and the naming ceremony soon follows. Among some groups, the shaving ceremony may not occur until the child is several years old. It is common for a child to be named for the day of the week on which it is born, or for some characteristic feature. For example, a child may be called Navapuria to denote that it was born on a Saturday, or Kalia (the dark one) because of its dark complexion. Male children are often tattooed on the wrist and forearm.

The ceremonies accompanying death are important in Bhil society. The dead are cremated after a period of mourning, although infants and victims of smallpox are buried. A carved wooden post or a stone tablet is placed at the site of cremation of males, with the deceased often represented on horseback with lance, sword, or shield. After 10 or 12 days, the *kata* (death-feast) is held for the community. Food consumed at this time includes maize, rice, sometimes the flesh of goats or buffaloes, and considerable quantities of liquor. During the feast it is important that a Bhopa be present to give voice to the demands of the spirit of the deceased. These demands are invariably met by the family and, once appeased, the spirit departs the confines of the settlement.

⁸ INTERPERSONAL RELATIONS

Social interaction among the Bhils conforms to local and regional practices. Bhil communities that are more integrated with broader society have greater contact with non-Bhil groups, while those in more isolated areas tend to keep to themselves. The Bhils are hospitable to visitors. No guest goes without food and refreshment, no matter how scarce such supplies may be.

⁹ LIVING CONDITIONS

Traditionally, Bhils live in small, dispersed hamlets known as *phala,* which are occupied by families of the same clan. Each settlement comprises a hut or group of huts standing alone in the middle of an area of cultivated land. Several hamlets may grow together to form a village or *pal*. The village may be a multi-clan community. Each village has a hereditary headman, who is a member of the village's dominant or founding clan. The headman is called *panch, vasavo, tadavi, naik, mukhi,* or other names according to local usage. The presence of the headman is necessary at most social and ritual functions in the village.

Young girls of the Bhil tribe at the Bhagoria fair in Valpur village, India. Bhagoria is an annual tribal festival held a week before Hoki, the Indian festival of colors. (AP Images/Prakash Hatvalne)

Individual huts are often surrounded by a bamboo fence. Their walls are typically built of mud or bamboo, wattled with mud, clay, and cow dung. The roofs are thatched, made from grass or leaves, and supported by rafters of teak or whatever wood is available. Huts are windowless and have a single entrance only. They are often used both as living quarters and for housing cattle. Bedsteads woven from bamboo or sleeping mats are used for sleeping, while household utensils are usually made from clay rather than metal. Earthenware jars and baskets are used for storage. The more affluent farmers may own cattle and possess a bullock-cart and other agricultural implements. Few Bhils attain this level of prosperity, and livestock is more commonly limited to a few goats and poultry.

10 FAMILY LIFE

Kinship among the Bhils reflects regional Gujarati, Rajasthani, and Maharashtrian patterns. Bhil tribes and subtribes are endogamous; that is to say, marriage occurs within the social group. There is, however, little intermarriage between the inhabitants of the hills and the plains. The Bhils also make a distinction between the Ujwala (pure) Bhils and the Kalia (impure) Bhils, groups that also rarely intermarry. The Bhils are divided into numerous clans, and clan exogamy (marriage outside one's own clan) is strictly followed. However, beyond

its name and its role in defining a pool of marriage partners, the clan is of little significance in Bhil society.

In practice, brides come from villages within a limited geographical area—villages that are already linked through institutions such as the Gauri festival, weekly markets, and existing matrimonial ties. Marriage proposals invariably come from the suitor or his family, rather than from the girl's father. The groom's family pays a bride-price to the father of the bride. Marriage among the Bhils occurs much later than among Hindus, occurring between the ages of 16 and 21 years. The eve of the marriage ceremony is marked by singing, dancing, feasting, and drinking. Marriage rituals are similar to Hindu rituals, with the bride and groom walking around the sacred fire, and the giving of presents.

Bhil society is patrilineal, with inheritance passing down the male line. The new bride moves into the home of her husband's family and assumes the burden of household chores. She also participates in the family's agricultural activities. It is customary for a father to provide his son with land and a hut on his marriage, so that among the Bhil the nuclear rather than the extended family is the norm.

Polygamy, the custom of having more than one wife, is acceptable, particularly if the first wife is barren or too ill to keep house. Widow remarriage is permitted, with the deceased husband's younger brother being the most desirable partner. Divorce, though uncommon, is allowed but can only be initiated by the husband.

¹¹ CLOTHING

Though many have now adopted the local dress of loincloth, jacket, and turban, the Bhil formerly went nearly naked, wearing a loincloth and perhaps a blanket during cold weather. As is common throughout India today, some males wear Western-style shirts. The hair is traditionally worn long, either partly plaited and fastened with a wooden comb, or falling freely to the shoulder. Males wear earrings, and some carry guns or swords. The Bhils' traditional weapon, however, is the bow and arrow.

Women's dress consists of a skirt, bodice, and a loose cloth pulled up over the head. Clothes worn for festivals and special occasions are more colorful and made of finer cloth. Women wear head ornaments, usually made of silver or tin, and commonly wear brass rings around the arms. Brass rings may also be worn on the legs, often extending from ankle to knee. Children wear few clothes until close to puberty.

¹² FOOD

The Bhils were originally hunters and gatherers. They subsisted by hunting small game such as rabbits, foxes, deer, wild pigs, birds, and rodents. They fished the local streams and rivers, and gathered edible plants and fruits from the forest. When they turned to agriculture, the Bhils adopted the slash-and-burn techniques of shifting cultivation (*jhum*). Many continued this form of subsistence activity up to the middle decades of the 20th century. Today, however, most Bhils engage in settled agriculture using the plow and draft animals. The staple foods are maize, millet, barley, pulses such as lentils, chickpeas, and vegetables. Food is taken twice a day, normally in mid-morning and then again in the evening. Rice is occasionally eaten, but the Bhils partake of the flesh of the goat or buffalo only on special occasions.

Bhils are strongly addicted to the use of tobacco and alcohol, making liquor from the flower of the mahua tree (*Bassia latifolia*) or from the bark of the babul (*Acacia arabica*). The consumption of alcohol accompanies every feast and celebration.

¹³ EDUCATION

As an economically depressed group, often inhabiting isolated and difficult terrain, the Bhils' access to education is limited. Despite the availability of state-supported schools and government-sponsored programs for the Scheduled Tribes, literacy levels and educational achievement among the Bhils are low, literacy rates being 6.6% (for women it is less than 1%).

¹⁴ CULTURAL HERITAGE

Music, song, and dance are an integral part of Bhil life and accompany all feasts and celebrations. The Ghanna or Gher is a ring dance of Rajasthan. Men carry sticks in their hands and revolve in a circle around the drummers, alternately hitting the sticks of the men ahead and behind them. Other dances are performed to propitiate Mataji and other deities.

An important Bhil institution is the Gauri, a dance-drama with a strong ritual element that presents various episodes from the life of Mahadeo and Parvati. Undertaken by a village once every three or four years, the Gauri festival is held at the end of the rainy season (usually in August). The festival may extend over a period of 40 days or more. Once the bhopa has given permission for the Gauri to take place, the village sends out a troop of male actors to stage performances in neighboring villages. The host villages are expected to provide food and gifts for the visitors, hospitality that is reciprocated when these villages in turn stage their own Gauri celebrations. The Gauri festival serves to tie villages together through ritual exchanges, because the villages visited by the performers are those where there are kinfolk, daughters who have been married, and those with important economic ties to the village that stages the Gauri.

¹⁵ WORK

Most Bhils are farmers. However, the pressures of subsistence agriculture, uneconomic land holdings, the burden of debt, and frequent drought have forced many Bhils to leave the land and turn to other occupations. Many are laborers or earn a living cutting wood, preparing charcoal, and gathering forest products like gum and lac. Bhils in the past have made their living from hunting and other forest activities, and are renowned as trackers. Some Bhils have been employed as watchmen, while others have learned shop-keeping from their encounters with the bania (trading) castes, and a small number of them—perhaps 3%—operate shops, tea stalls and flour mills. Again, largely because of a lack of education, a few Bhils are involved in the service industry, but the vast majority are agricultural laborers.

Despite efforts by the Union and State Governments to promote economic development among the Bhil Adivasis (tribals), especially in the areas of agriculture, sericulture, and education, Bhils in India remain socially and economically disadvantaged.

¹⁶ SPORTS

The Bhils do not engage in any organized sports.

¹⁷ ENTERTAINMENT AND RECREATION

The Bhils, though regarded by outsiders as shy and retiring, have a strong sense of community. Social and cultural occasions are celebrated by singing, dancing, and feasting, with the free consumption of liquor. Hunting and fishing, formerly a means of subsistence, are popular pastimes, although opportunities for such activities today are greatly limited.

¹⁸ FOLK ART, CRAFTS, AND HOBBIES

The Bhils do not possess a tradition of folk art or crafts. They rely on artisan castes to provide clothing, utensils, and other material necessities.

¹⁹ SOCIAL PROBLEMS

During the last 100 years, many attempts have been made to improve the social and economic conditions of the Bhils. Christian missionaries, Hindu reformists, the followers of Mahatma Gandhi, and modern social workers have all worked to eradicate what have been perceived as the evils of Bhil society—the traditions of magic and witchcraft, thievery, alcoholism, meat-eating, and animal sacrifice. Many Bhil groups have abandoned their traditional customs and one community, the

Bhagats, has even adopted the observances and practices of orthodox Hinduism.

The Bhils face many social and economic problems today. Frequently inhabiting isolated and marginally productive environments, they experience widespread poverty and live in depressed economic conditions. Rapid growth of population, land fragmentation, unproductive landholdings, inefficient farming techniques, and constant indebtedness have forced many off the land to seek work as landless laborers.

While some groups have assimilated to a degree into Hindu society, the Bhils remain a people set apart from the mainstream of Indian society. They have yet to share in the wealth and social and economic advances of post-Independence India.

[20] GENDER ISSUE

Generally, women in tribal societies experience more gender equality than their counterparts in Hinduism or Islam, although they still play a subordinate role to men. Bhil women are subject to arranged marriages and their families receive a bride price rather than pay dowries, but marriage remains a loose arrangement, and pre-marital and extra-marital affairs are common. However, once an affair becomes public, disputes are resolved by local panchayats, which tend to favor males and give short shrift to women's rights. In the past, movements existed among the Bhils for the identification and killing of witches.

Bhil women are sometimes subject to many of the restrictions of their Hindu upper caste neighbors. For instance, some Bhil groups have adopted the Hindu custom of veiling their women. Married women have to veil themselves in front of their elder male in-laws. This means that whenever they go out into public places like a market where an elder male in-law might pop up at any time, the married Bhil women have to remain veiled all the time, even though the custom is opposed by the Kansari nu Vadavno, a mass organization of Bhil women formed in 1998 to address women's issues (Kansari is the goddess who symbolizes the life-giving power of jowār (sorghum), the staple of Bhil life).

Kansari nu Vadavno ran a fairly successful campaign against the sale of illicit alcohol during the late 1990s. Their take was that the men under the influence of alcohol not only did not work but also beat them up and demanded excessive sex from them. They contended that the alcoholism of their men added considerably to the overall patriarchal oppression that they suffered.

Domestic violence, poverty, illiteracy, and lack of access to education remain issues for Bhil women.

[21] BIBLIOGRAPHY

Bhuriya, Mahipal. "Tribal Religion in India: A Case Study of the Bhils." *Social Compass* Vol. 33, No. 2-3, 275-283, 1986.

Deliége, Robert. *The Bhils of Western India*. New Delhi: National Publishing House, 1985.

Doshi, S. L. *Processes of Tribal Unification and Integration : A Case Study of the Bhils*. Delhi: Concept, 1978.

Hardiman, David. "The Bhils and Shahukars of Eastern Gujarat." In *Subaltern Studies V: Writings on South Asian History and Society*, edited by Ranajit Guha. Delhi: Oxford University Press, 1987.

Kumar, Baghan. *Bhils: An Ethno-Historic Analysis*. Delhi: Sharada Prakashan, 1997.

Kumar, Pramod. *Folk Icons and Rituals in Tribal Life*. New Delhi: Abhinav Publications, 1984.

Ram, G. *Politics, Development and Modernization in Tribal India*. Delhi: Manak, 2001.

Nath, Y. V. S. *Bhils of Ratanmal: An Analysis of the Social Structure of a Western Indian Community*. Baroda: The Maharaja Sayajirao University of Baroda, 1960.

Vyas, N. N., R. S. Mann, and N.D. Chaudhary, eds. *Rajasthan Bhils*. Udaipur: Manikyalal Verma Tribal Research and Training Institute, Social Welfare Department, Government of Rajasthan, 1978.

—by D. O. Lodrick

BHUTANESE

PRONUNCIATION: BOOT-un-eez
LOCATION: Bhutan
POPULATION: About 800,000–1.8 million (including Nepalese immigrants and other minorities, and Bhutanese in refugee camps in India and Nepal)
LANGUAGE: Dzongkha (official); Nepali; Assamese; Gurung; Tsangla; some Hindi
RELIGION: Mahayana Buddhism (official); Bon (shamanism); mix of Hinduism and Buddhism; Islam
RELATED ARTICLES: Vol. 3: Assamese; Bhutia; Gurung; Vol 4: Nepalis

¹ INTRODUCTION

Bhutanese is the name given to the population of the kingdom of Bhutan, a small, landlocked country situated on the northern mountain rim of South Asia. The name *Bhutan* is derived from a word that means the "borderland" of Bhot, or Tibet. The Bhutanese themselves call their country *Druk-Yul* or the "Land of the Thunder Dragon." The ruling monarch of the country carries the title *Druk Gyalpo* or "Dragon King."

Bhutan's early history remains obscure, although from the beginning of the 9th century AD the region was settled by Tibetans migrating southwards from the upland plateaus of their homeland. Some historians view this migration as an organized invasion, with Tibetan troops seizing the region from the ruling Hindu *maharaja* (princely chief). Bhutan assumed a distinct political identity in the early 17th century, when a Tibetan Buddhist monk established his authority as king, taking the title of *Dharma Raja*. The early Dharma Rajas were both temporal rulers and spiritual leaders, but they gradually left the country's government in the hands of ministers who came to be known as the *Deb Rajas*. The current king, Druk Gyalpo Jigme Khesar Namgyel Wangchuk, is the fifth in a line of rulers descended from a territorial governor who was elected to become the hereditary king in 1907. The Dharma Raja has continued as leader of the Drukpa sect of Tibetan Buddhism, which remains the official monastic order of Bhutan.

The extension of British rule to India's Brahmaputra Valley in the 1820s eventually led to conflict with Bhutan, which lies just to the north of Assam. At various times during the 19th century, Bhutan ceded territory to the British, and in 1910 its external relations were placed under the control of British India. In return, Britain agreed not to interfere in Bhutan's internal affairs.

In 1949, India assumed Britain's role in handling Bhutan's external affairs. The occupation of Tibet by Chinese forces in 1950 further strengthened Bhutan's ties with India, as Bhutan saw the need for foreign support against a potential threat from China. During the 1960s, Bhutan abandoned its historic policy of isolation (foreigners could only enter Bhutan at the invitation of the king) and embarked on a policy of modernization, which led to a coup d'etat against the king at the end of 1964. The political crisis of 1964–1965 compelled the king to forge an alliance between him and the traditionalists and abandon his efforts at modernization. The integration of diverse ethnic and cultural groups into the Bhutanese state was forgotten, and Bhutan became dominated by the Ngalong (Dzongkha-speaking Bhutanese). At this time, the king ruled as a constitutional monarch, although there was a 152-seat national assembly, the Tsongdu, with many of its members elected by popular (though indirect) vote. The king appointed the prime minister, the Cabinet, and a number of delegates to the Tsongdu. Religious groups also appointed a number of representatives to nonelective assembly seats.

Under the king, the state's "Bhutanisation drive" and 1989 promulgation of Driglam Nam Zha (Etiquette and Manners), by which people were required to wear traditional Bhutanese clothes in public, led to ethnic conflict between the Ngalong-dominated state and the people of Nepali origin. As a result, numerous people of Nepali origin were expelled from Bhutan. The majority of them, estimated to be between 100,000 and 135,000 in number, are now living in the refugee camps in eastern Nepal maintained by the UNHCR.

The Bhutanese view the Nepalese as newcomers and fear having them become the most populous ethnic community in the country (they have the model of Sikkim, once an independent country, but now a state in India, in mind). Since 1990, antigovernment extremists among the Nepalese have been waging a terrorist war in Bhutan. Southern Bhutan was placed under Army control, and international human rights agencies have claimed extensive violations of human rights in the Bhutanese security forces' operations against Nepalese dissidents.

In March 2005, King Jigme Singye Wangchuck unveiled the government's new draft constitution—which would introduce major democratic reforms. In December 2006 the King abdicated the throne to his son, Jigme Khesar Namgyel Wangchuck, in order to give him experience as head of state before the democratic transition. In early 2007 India and Bhutan renegotiated their treaty to allow Bhutan greater autonomy in conducting its foreign policy, although Thimphu continues to coordinate policy decisions in this area with New Delhi. In July 2007 seven ministers of Bhutan's 10-member cabinet resigned to join the political process, leaving the remaining cabinet to act as a caretaker regime until the new government assumed power following parliamentary elections. Bhutan completed its transition to full democracy in 2008, when its first fully democratic elections to a new National Assembly were held on 24 March 2008. Two parties contested the election: the Bhutan Peace and Prosperity Party (DPT, for *Druk Phuensum Tshogpa*), which was formed by the merger of the previously established Bhutan People's United Party and All People's Party, which is led by Jigme Y. Thinley, and the People's Democratic Party (PDP), led by Sangay Ngedup. The DPT won over 67% of the vote and 45 of the 47 seats in the new parliament. Thinley's party, which is widely viewed as being the most loyalist of Bhutanese political parties hews closely to the king's vision for Bhutan and seeks to promote the objective of "Gross National Happiness," an all-encompassing political philosophy that seeks to balance material progress with spiritual well-being.

The new government was to adopt the new constitution when it met in May 2008. This was to complete the historic transition from an absolute monarchy to a parliamentary democracy, albeit with considerable power still concentrated in the hands of Bhutan's king.

² LOCATION AND HOMELAND

Population data for Bhutan are unreliable. The Census of Bhutan, 2005, places the total population at 634,982. This figure,

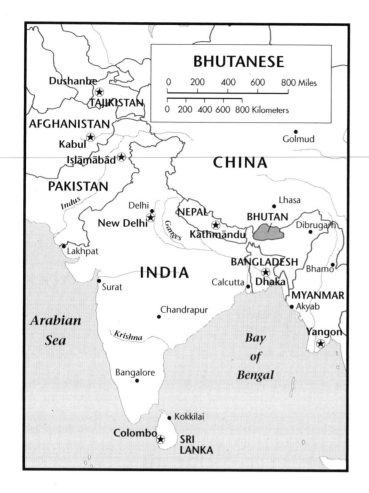

3 LANGUAGE

The official language of Bhutan is Dzongkha, one of the many dialects of Tibetan spoken by the Bhutia people. In its written form, Dzongkha is identical with Tibetan. Some 40% of the Bhutan's population speak Dzongkha. Other languages spoken in Bhutan include Nepali, Assamese, and Gurung. Tsangla is a language of the Mon family spoken in eastern districts of the country. Some Hindi is found in southern areas that border India.

4 FOLKLORE

The Bhutanese possess an extensive lore relating to events and personalities of the region's past. One tradition tells of an Indian prince who settled in Bhutan in the 8th century AD and invited the monk Padmasambhava to his kingdom. Known in Tibet as Guru Rimpoche ("Precious Teacher"), Padmasambhava was primarily responsible for introducing Buddhism into Bhutan. Other stories center on the 15th-century lama Pemalingpa, who is seen as an incarnation of Padmasambhava. Pemalingma is known for composing various dances that are popular among the Bhutanese. Another heroic figure of Bhutan's past is Shabdrung, the lama who assumed the title of Dharma Raja in the 17th century and laid the political foundations of Bhutan State.

5 RELIGION

Approximately 75% of the Bhutanese are Buddhist. Mahayana Buddhism is the official religion of Bhutan. The dominant religious order in the country is the Red-Hat sect (Kargyupa). The Bon religion, which embraces pre-Buddhist shamanistic traditions, is also practiced in Bhutan. Beliefs in sorcerers, spirits, demons, and the need for exorcisms as undertaken in the "devil dances" are thus a part of everyday Bhutanese religious practices. Lamas skilled in rituals are used to perform the necessary religious observances. Animal sacrifice has been replaced in Bhutan by the offering of *torma,* ritual figures made from dough and butter. Hinduism, or the mix of Hinduism and Buddhism that typifies Nepali culture, is the religion of the Nepalese peoples of Bhutan. Some 5% of the population follow Islam.

6 MAJOR HOLIDAYS

Losar, the Tibetan New Year, is one of the most important festivals in Bhutan. It is celebrated in February with feasting and drinking. Folk dances, including masked dances, are performed and archery competitions held. A recent custom is the exchange of greeting cards between friends and relatives. Domcheo and Tsechu are annual religious festivals marked by worship ceremonies and performances of the ritual masked dances by monks. These are held at monasteries and *dzongs,* the forts around which many Bhutanese villages are built. Various other Buddhist and Hindu festivals are observed. The king's birthday (February 22) and the National Day of Bhutan (December 17) are celebrated as public holidays.

7 RITES OF PASSAGE

Birth and marriage in Bhutan are observed with a minimum of ritual, being a social or family event rather than a religious one. Funerals, on the other hand, are elaborate affairs. After a death, a lama is called in to extract the spirit (*sem*) from the

however, excludes a large number of immigrants from Nepal. If the Nepalese and other minorities are included, the population may currently exceed 1.8 million. There are three major ethnic groups in Bhutan: the Bhutia (also Bhotia, or Bhote), Nepalese, and Assamese. Bhutia comprise roughly 50% of Bhutan's population. The Nepalese, who include Rai, Gurung, Limbu, and other peoples, account for another 35%, while the Assamese and tribal groups make up 15% of the country's inhabitants.

Bhutan, with an area of 47,182 sq km (18,217 sq mi), lies in the eastern Himalayan Mountain Range. The country's location between India and Tibet gives it considerable strategic importance. Bhutan falls into three distinct geographic regions. In the south is a narrow strip of lowland known as the Duars Plain. The area receives between 500 cm and 760 cm (200–300 in) of rain a year. It is covered with dense subtropical forest and undergrowth and is hot, humid, and generally unhealthy. North of the Duars is the Inner Himalaya, a region of mountain spurs extending southwards from the main Himalayan Range. Between these spurs lie fertile valleys at elevations between 1,500 m and 2,700 m (5,000–9,000 ft). With a relatively moderate climate, these valleys support agriculture and relatively dense populations. Further to the north, along the Tibetan border, are the main ranges of the Great Himalaya. The highest peaks approach 7,300 m (24,000 ft), with Kula Kangra soaring to 7,554 m (24,784 ft). Below the high peaks are alpine meadows used for grazing yaks in the summer months.

body and speed it on its way. The body is placed in a sitting position before an altar, on which various ritual objects—including *torma* (figurines made of dough and butter)—are placed. A lama leads the service for the dead, reciting passages from various Buddhist texts. Cremation is the usual form of disposal of the corpse, although bodies may be buried or thrown in a river. Rituals are performed for 49 days after death, and during this period an effigy of the deceased is kept in the house. The end of the mourning period is marked by a feast, as is the first anniversary of the death.

8 INTERPERSONAL RELATIONS

A Bhutanese host greets a guest by bowing slightly, extending his or her hands towards the ground with palms facing the visitor, and moving the hand in a gesture inviting the guest into the house. The host may also say, *"Yala! Yala! Kuzu zangpola?"* (Hello! How do you do?). The guest, after responding in an appropriate manner, is then seated in the drawing room where she or he is served tea, beer, or other refreshments. Men and women mix and converse freely, without the restrictions that separate the sexes among other groups in South Asia.

9 LIVING CONDITIONS

Bhutan historically remained isolated from the outside world, and it was only in the 1960s that the country embarked on a path of modernization. As a result, Bhutan ranks among the lowest of the South Asian countries in terms of indices of development. Leading causes of death include respiratory tract infections, diarrhea and dysentery, various skin and parasitic infections, and malaria. Infant mortality rates are extremely high, running at over 70 deaths per 1,000 live births in 2003. The natural increase of population is 2.17% per year (2006 est.).

Bhutan is a predominantly rural country, with nearly 90% of the population living in villages scattered throughout the country. Although there are a handful of small towns in Bhutan, only Thimphu, the capital, exceeds 20,000 inhabitants in size. Domestic architecture in the north is Tibetan in style, while southern areas show Indian influences in house types and construction. Living standards are generally low, with per capita income standing at us$1,400 per year (2006 est.), making Bhutan one of the poorest countries in the world.

Bhutan's mountainous terrain makes for difficult land communications. No railroads exist in the country, and there are only 2,418 km (1,502 mi) of road providing links with India. Bhutan's national airline, Druk Air, links the town of Paro with India, Nepal, Bangladesh, and Thailand.

10 FAMILY LIFE

The various ethnic groups that make up Bhutan's population are endogamous, i.e., they marry within their own community. The age of marriage has been raised by the government to 16 years for women and 21 years for men. Although in the past marriages were arranged, more and more young couples are beginning to select partners for themselves on the basis of mutual attraction. Compared to the elaborate and expensive Hindu marriage ceremonies, Bhutanese marriages are relatively simple. A lama officiates at the religious ceremony. Offerings of *chang* (beer) are made to ghosts and spirits, and betel leaves, areca nuts, and fruits are distributed to those present at the wedding. Guests are provided with food and entertainment.

The Bhutanese are essentially monogamous. Polyandry (multiple husbands) has recently been abolished, and polygamy (multiple wives) has been restricted to a maximum of three wives per man. Bhutan is essentially a matriarchy, and a bride does not necessarily move into her husband's household, as is common throughout much of the Indian subcontinent. The new husband may reside with his wife's family if their need for labor warrants it. Alternatively, the new couple may set up their own household on their own plot of land. Divorce is permitted in Bhutanese society, although compensation is required from the party seeking the separation.

11 CLOTHING

Bhutanese dress consists of a long, loose robe (*ko*) that reaches the ankles. During the day, the robe is hoisted up and fastened at the waist by a woven belt so that it reaches the knees. At night, it is let down to the ankles. The coat fastens at the neck and, generally, during the day is left open. The sleeves are long and loose. Bhutanese men seldom wear a hat, but they sometimes wrap a scarf around the head at night. Shoes are rarely worn, though some men wear sandals, and those of the wealthier class use Tibetan-style woolen boots. Every man carries a long knife slung from his belt. When the ko is tied in the "up" position, it forms a pouch that is used for carrying objects.

Bhutanese women wear the *kira,* a woven dress that is fastened at each shoulder by silver buckles. A woven belt is tied around the waist. Women commonly wear necklaces of coral and turquoise, strung together with silver amulets. The hair is usually cut short.

12 FOOD

Rice is the main food in Bhutan and is eaten with meat whenever this is available. Though most Bhutanese are Buddhists, they are nonvegetarian and eat beef, pork, goat, chicken, and eggs. A typical Bhutanese meal might consist of *thugpa,* a meat soup prepared with herbs, rice (of the round, red variety), and a meat curry or omelet. Sweet rice (white rice cooked in milk and sugar) is served on special occasions. Tea, made with salt and butter, is a Bhutanese staple. Beer (*chang*) is made from cereals and served to guests and friends, as well as being offered to the gods.

At high altitudes where rice is not cultivated, barley and buckwheat are grown. The cereals are ground, then roasted or fried, and stored for future use. Fried corn powder is as popular among the Bhutanese as *tsampa* (roasted ground barley) is among Tibetans. Milk is scarce and of poor quality, although a hard cheese is made from yak milk.

13 EDUCATION

No formal schools existed in Bhutan before the early 1960s, except for those associated with religious institutions. Despite a concerted effort on the part of the government, and especially King Jigme Dorji Wangchuck, to improve education, Bhutan lags behind other South Asian countries in its educational achievements. A modern educational system was introduced into Bhutan only in the 1960s. Although in 2004 education was made compulsory up to the age of 11, only about 73% of primary-school-age children attend school, and this figure drops to 35% at the secondary-school level. Education, however, is a major priority of Bhutan's development programs and there now exist over 350 educational institutions in the country. These include The Royal University of Bhutan, founded in 2003, which was established to consolidate the management of tertiary education in the country. It is a federated university with 10 member colleges spread across the Kingdom. Literacy among adults now stands at about 47%. International organizations such as the World Bank and UNICEF are involved in promoting educational projects in Bhutan.

Bhutanese seeking higher education or professional training have to turn to foreign educational institutions. Most Bhutanese students being educated abroad receive technical training in India, Singapore, Japan, Australia, New Zealand, Britain, the Federal Republic of Germany (West Germany), and the United States. English-speaking countries attracted the majority of Bhutanese students. The vast majority of Bhutanese students return to their homeland.

14 CULTURAL HERITAGE

Bhutan's culture is deeply rooted in Tibetan Buddhism. The country began as a theocracy (i.e., its ruler was a religious leader), and even today lamas are highly influential in the affairs of the country. The *dzongs* (forts) and monasteries remain centers of political, economic, social, and religious life. It is here that festivals are celebrated with religious music and masked dances, and lamas continue the traditions of Buddhist learning. Religion finds architectural expression in numerous *chorten* (relic mounds) and temples, while dzongs are often patterned after the Potala, the Dalai Lama's palace in Lhasa, the capital of Tibet. Religious objects such as the *mandala* (Buddhist Wheel of Life) and *thanka* (a painted religious scroll) are works of art in their own right.

15 WORK

Bhutan is essentially an agrarian country, with 67% of its labor force involved in subsistence agriculture and animal husbandry. Much of the land is mountainous or heavily forested, and less than 3% of the country's area is under permanent cultivation. Rice, wheat, maize, and millet are the main crops grown in the country. Fruit production is important, with apples, peaches, plums, and apricots among the varieties grown. Livestock raised in the region include cattle, sheep, pigs, chickens, and the yak, a bovine adapted to high altitudes.

Although Bhutan restricts the number of tourists allowed into the country in order to limit foreign influences, tourism has great potential. The tourist dollar accounts for about 1.6% of the gross national product, but this figure may be expected to increase in the future. Electricity, timber and wood products, fruits and vegetables, and cement are important export items. India is Bhutan's major trade partner.

16 SPORTS

The Bhutanese are well known for their archery skills, and archery competitions are commonly held at the time of festivals and national holidays.

17 ENTERTAINMENT AND RECREATION

Bhutanese have limited access to modern forms of entertainment. In June 2000 FM radio service became available for western Bhutan with the inauguration of the main FM station at Dobchula and one relay station at Takti in the south. The FM service was extended to central Bhutan in January 2001 and the rest of the country in 2005.

In 1989, in an attempt to preserve Bhutan's culture, the government banned the viewing of foreign television by ordering all TV antennas in the country to be dismantled, but in June 1999 permitted television—and later, the Internet—into the country. The last country in the world to permit television within its borders, Bhutan—which had remained virtually unchanged for centuries—was suddenly bombarded with 46 cable channels. The introduction of television into Bhutan was sparked by the World Cup Soccer Final of France in 1998. The 3-0 victory of the home side over Brazil was watched by thousands on a big screen in Bhutan's National Square. TV in Bhutan was such a success that a year later, on the 25th anniversary of his coronation, King Jigme Singye Wangchuk decided to allow the Bhutan Broadcasting Service (BBS), founded in 1973, to broadcast TV programming. However, the vast majority of Bhutan's population today (some 70%) do not even have electricity, let alone access to television.

Now, both cable TV, the Internet, and cell phone service are available in Bhutan, providing access to the outside world. With its new satellite television service (launched in February 2006), BBS's programming is now received in almost 40 Asian countries—from Turkey in the West to Indonesia in South East Asia.

The impact of access to TV screens has changed Bhutanese society considerably, especially one that, as a matter of policy, attempts to preserve and conserve traditional values. The editor of Bhutan's only regular newspaper, the bi-weekly *Kuensel*, explained that the thinking in the country is that as it will never be a military or economic power, its strength must be its unique society. He believes that television represents a direct threat to this. Some observers have noted an increase in violence among children and a rise in crime, while others note that the more the Bhutanese are exposed to globalization, the more likely they are to lose their own culture. Such concerns have led to the regulation of the industry and control what goes out over the airwaves through acts such as the 2006 Information, Communication, and Media Act, which bans the broadcasting of material (e.g. pornography and the U.S. wrestling series WWE, both of which, it is believed, leads to violence among Bhutanese children) thought to be detrimental to Bhutanese society.

The government publishes a bi-weekly newspaper, *Kuensel, which faces competition from two other private newspapers* the *Bhutan Times* and the *Bhutan Observer*, which began publication in 2006. But with the country's low literacy rate (47% in 2003), the papers have a very small circulation. Religious festivals and folk traditions such as singing and dancing are the primary forms of entertainment and recreation.

18 FOLK ART, CRAFTS, AND HOBBIES

Bhutanese women are skilled at weaving and make their own clothing, bedding, tablecloths, floor coverings, and items for religious use. Embroidery is a favorite art. Much effort goes into making costumes and masks for the ritual dances performed at festivals. Smiths excel in working gold, silver, brass, and other metals.

Bhutanese men, in traditional attire, engage in archery in Thimphu, Bhutan. Archery is one of the few sports to which Bhutan sends a team to the Olympics. (AP Images/Sherwin Crasto)

[19] SOCIAL PROBLEMS

The Bhutanese live in the least-developed country in all of South Asia. Despite efforts at modernization since the 1960s, poverty, lack of potable water, inadequate health care, illiteracy, and difficulties in transportation remain serious problems. Bhutan is heavily dependent on foreign aid in its efforts to improve the life of its people. Recently, ethnic tensions between the Bhutanese and Nepalese minority have created a problem in the country. Mindful of what happened in nearby Sikkim, where Indian immigrants eventually outnumbered the native Sikkimese and voted to accede to India, Bhutan has acted to restrict immigration from Nepal. Despite this, some estimates place the Nepalese population as high as 40% of Bhutan's total. The Nepalese see themselves as second-class citizens, resent government restrictions on them, and demand a greater say in the affairs of the country. They also object to government efforts to develop a Bhutanese "national identity" based on a Bhutia model.

[20] GENDER ISSUES

Women in Bhutan enjoy considerable freedom and equal opportunity both in government and society in general. This is attributed mainly to the strong influence of Buddhism in every aspect of Bhutanese religion, culture, and tradition. In Mahay-
ana Buddhism, male and female are considered equal. Women are treated as equal to men under Bhutan law. The law of inheritance, for example, reserves equal rights for all children, irrespective of sex and age. Both men and women enjoy equal freedom to choose their partners. In contrast to other South Asian countries, parents in Bhutan do not have strong gender preferences for their children and treat girls and boys equally.

However, although officially the government encourages greater participation of women in political and administrative life, male members of the traditional aristocracy dominate the social system. Economic development has increased opportunities for women to participate in fields such as medicine, both as physicians and nurses; teaching; and administration. Reflecting the dominance of males in society, girls were outnumbered three to two in primary and secondary-level schools.

Women play a significant role in the agricultural work force, where they outnumber men, who were leaving for the service sector and other urban industrial and commercial activities. Up to 90% of all Bhutanese women are involved in agricultural work (70% of the land registered in Bhutan is owned by women), although this figure is decreasing as more opportunities become available for women in other sectors of the economy.

The government founded the National Women's Association of Bhutan in 1981 primarily to improve the socioeconomic status of women, particularly those in rural areas. The association, at its inaugural session, declared that it would not push for equal rights for women because the women of Bhutan had already come to "enjoy equal status with men politically, economically, and socially."

21 BIBLIOGRAPHY

Chakravarti, B. *A Cultural History of Bhutan.* Chittraranjan, India: Hilltop Publishers, 1980.

Dimri, Jaiwanti. *The Drukpa Mystique: Bhutan in the 21st Century.* Delhi: Authorspress, 2004.

Karan, P. P. *Bhutan: A Physical and Cultural Geography.* Lexington, KY: University of Kentucky Press, 1967.

Matles, Andrea, ed. *Nepal and Bhutan: Country Studies.* Washington, D.C.: Federal Research Division, Library of Congress, 1993.

Upreti, B. C. *Bhutan (Dilemma of Change in a Himalayan Kingdom).* Delhi: Kalinga Publications, 2004.

Wangchuck, Ashi Dorji Wangmo. *Treasures of the Thunder Dragon: A Portrait of Bhutan.* New Delhi: Viking Books, 2006.

—by D. O. Lodrick

BHUTIA

PRONUNCIATION: BOOT-ee-uh
ALTERNATE NAMES: Bhot; Bhotia; Bhute
LOCATION: Bhutan, Nepal, and India (southern Himalayan region)
POPULATION: Over 1 million
LANGUAGE: Bhutia; Tibetan; Hindi, Nepali
RELIGION: Forms of Buddhism, Hinduism, and animism
RELATED ARTICLES: Vol. 3: Bhutanese; Buddhists; Hindus; Vol. 4: Nepalis; People of India

1 INTRODUCTION

Bhutia (also Bhot, Bhotia, Bhute) is a generic term that identifies several socially unrelated groups of India's northern mountain rim. The name *Bhutia,* thought to be derived from "Bhot" or "Bod," which means "Tibet," reflects the Bhutia's origins. The Bhutia are believed to have emigrated southward from Tibet in the 9th century AD or sometime after and settled in the Himalayan mountain ranges along the Indo-Tibetan border. Although they are Tibetan in origin and retain Tibetan cultural traits, many Bhutia groups have adopted elements of Hindu culture. Bhutia society is transitional, representing a blending of Hindu-dominated South Asian and Buddhist Central Asian cultures. Although the various Bhutia groups of the Himalayas exhibit social, cultural, and religious differences, they do have certain features in common. All live in a mountain habitat and traditionally have been involved in trade across the Himalayas between South Asia and Tibet.

2 LOCATION AND HOMELAND

The Bhutias occupy a narrow belt of mountainous territory that lies along on the southern flanks of the Himalayas. This zone extends from the kingdom of Bhutan in the eastern Himalayas, through Nepal and the northern mountain states of India, to the mountains and plateaus of the Ladakh region of Kashmir. Population data for the Bhutia are unreliable, although their numbers exceed 1 million. They make up approximately 50% of Bhutan's population (approximately 400,000), and form minorities in Nepal (200,000) and India (200,000).

The Bhutia in the Garhwal region of India are the focus of this discussion. They live in three mountain districts known collectively as Uttarakhand (in 2008, the Garhwal and Kumaon regions of Uttar Pradesh became the 27th Indian state, known as Uttarakhand. Raputs form the main element in the state's population). In the north lie the main ranges of the Himalayas, with peaks reaching over 7,600 m (25,000 ft) above sea level. Much of this area is under permanent snow and totally uninhabitable. Bhutia settlements are found at altitudes up to around 4,500 m (15,000 ft) in valleys carved into the mountains by streams flowing in a general southwesterly direction. Winter conditions at these elevations are severe, and the Bhutia spend this time of year in the lower valleys.

3 LANGUAGE

The Bhutia speak various dialects of the Bhutia language, a member of the Tibeto-Burmese branch of the Sino-Tibetan language family. The dialects found in Uttarakhand belong to the Central Bhutia group, and include Rankas, Chaudansi, and Darmi. Some Bhutia communities, such as the Joharis of Pithoragarh District, have forgotten their own dialects and use the language of their southern neighbors. All Bhutia groups are multi-lingual and know Tibetan, local hill (Pahari) dialects, and Hindi as well as their own tongue.

⁴ FOLKLORE

All Bhutia groups in the Himalayas have their own folklore and traditions. In Uttarakhand, both the landscape and folk culture are dominated by Nanda Devi. At 7,817 m (25,645 ft), the mountain Nanda Devi towers over the other peaks in the region. Like many other Himalayan peaks, the mountain is identified with a deity, the Hindu goddess Nanda Devi. For more than 1,000 years, central Himalayan rulers have legitimized their authority by claiming a relationship with Nanda Devi. Nanda Devi, a form of Shiva's consort Parvati, is the focus of a local cult and figures prominently in the life of the Bhutia and other peoples in the region. Folk songs are devoted to Nanda Devi, pilgrimages made in her name, and the goddess is honored at the Nandashtami festival.

⁵ RELIGION

Bhutia religion varies according to the specific Bhutia community involved. In Bhutan, for example, Bhutias are followers of the Tibetan form of Mahayana Buddhism. In the Central Himalayas, however, only the Jad Bhutia profess Buddhism. Other groups are Hindu, or their religion reflects a mixture of Lamaistic Buddhism, Hinduism, and animism. Hinduized groups such as the Johari Bhutia use the services of Brahmans while performing *puja* worship to the Hindu deities. Gabala, the god of trade, is among the most popular deities and is worshiped along with other Hindu deities such as Mahadev (Shiva) and Nanda Devi. Some gods (e.g., Saai and Laandey) are exclusive to the Bhutia, who also have their own clan deities. Ancestor worship is an important part of Bhutia life, and Bhutias also believe in ghosts and spirits. When disease or other misfortune befalls a community, a magician-priest becomes possessed and identifies the cause of the trouble. The villagers then perform the appropriate rites or sacrifices to appease the offended deity or spirit.

⁶ MAJOR HOLIDAYS

All the Hindu festivals are celebrated by the Bhutia of the Central Himalayas. Some have particular significance and are the occasion for religious fairs. An annual fair is held at Bageshwar in mid-January. Bageshwar lies at the confluence of the rivers Gomti and Sarju, and participants take ritual baths at this sacred place and offer water to Shiva in the Bagnath Temple. Bhutia traders and customers from the entire region attend the fair to buy and sell woolen clothing, shawls, carpets, ponies and other livestock, and miscellaneous goods. Some festivals that are exclusively Bhutia in nature center on the community's seasonal migrations. At the Lapsa festival, which falls in October when the Bhutia are leaving their summer quarters, prayers are offered to the goddess Nanda Devi for a safe journey down the mountains. Bikhid and Asadh Shankranti are festivals related to the spring migration to the summer pastures. The Losar, the Tibetan New Year, is also an important festival celebrated by the Bhutia community. Losoong, which

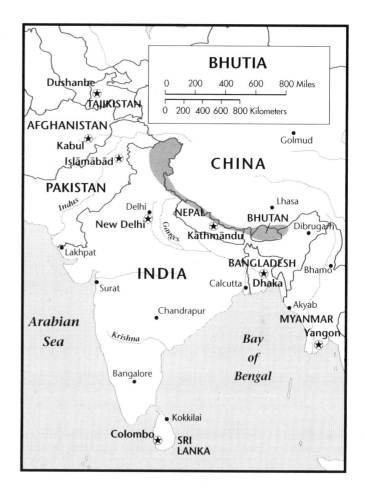

marks Sikkimese New Year, is celebrated in December by Bhutias in Sikkim.

⁷ RITES OF PASSAGE

The Bhutias of Uttarakhand show a considerable degree of Hinduization in their life-cycle rituals. Horoscopes may be drawn up by Brahmans, and a naming ceremony is held about three weeks after birth. Male children undergo the *mundan* (head-shaving) ceremony when they are around three or four years old. Infants are carried around on the backs of their mothers or elder sisters, tied in place with a length of cloth. For the seasonal migrations between winter and summer quarters, infants in arms are usually placed in a cylindrical basket strapped to their mothers' backs. As soon as they reach six or seven years old, however, Bhutia children are expected to assume a role in the annual migration of the family and its herds.

The Bhutia cremate their dead, except for children and those who died of tuberculosis, smallpox, or leprosy. It is customary for the men of the community to each carry a log of wood to the cremation ground for the funeral pyre. The final funeral ceremony, called *dudhung*, is usually performed in the family's summer residence. As traditional customs disappear, the dudhung is giving way to the Hindu forms of *sraddha* rites. The sraddha is an important ceremony involving numerous rituals, a feast, and the giving of gifts to Brahmans in the name of the deceased. It is believed that if the rites are not performed properly, it will adversely affect the soul of the departed.

8 INTERPERSONAL RELATIONS

A traditional institution of the Bhutias is the *Rang-Bang*, a meeting place or dormitory for unmarried youth. Young girls and boys from the village (and surrounding villages) gather in the evenings in a vacant house for dancing, drinking, and music. A considerable degree of sexual license is permitted. Couples pair off and spend the night together, going their own ways in the morning. Such meetings sometimes lead to courtship and marriage. Care is taken not to violate any taboos such as having sexual relations with a member of one's own clan. Today, the Rang-Bang is rapidly disappearing as an institution under the increasing influence of Hinduism and Hindu social values.

9 LIVING CONDITIONS

Bhutias in Uttarakhand typically have two settlements, one for summer and one for winter. The main village is the summer settlement, situated at elevations between 3,500 and 4,500 m (11,500–15,000 ft), where the community lives from May to October. These villages serve as bases for pasturing animals in summer and trade across the mountains into Tibet. Women, children, and livestock are left there while the men travel to the Tibetan market centers. Houses are built with stone walls and slate roofs and set in the middle of a patch of cultivated land. The harsh winters in the highland valleys force the Bhutia to descend to lower elevations for part of the year. They spend November to March in villages situated at altitudes between 1,500 and 2,500 m (5,000–8,000 ft). These winter quarters are not exclusively Bhutia settlements. Bhutia live in villages alongside Brahmans, Rajputs, Shilpkar, and other castes of the area. The more affluent among the Bhutia have both houses fully furnished, but most people must transport all of their household goods between the two residences every time they move.

10 FAMILY LIFE

The Bhutias of Uttarakhand are divided into eight subgroups based on factors such as religion, territory, and dialect. Each subgroup is again divided into clans, lineages, and sublineages, which serve to regulate marriage. The Johari Bhutia, for example, are defined on a territorial basis (they inhabit the Johar Valley). They marry within the Johari community, but are divided into 14 exogamous clans. Being the most Hinduized of the Bhutias in the region, they also have three endogamous social classes (Nitwal, Bharet, and Kunkiya) that function much like Hindu castes. The Kunkiya are regarded as ritually impure by the Nitwal and Bharet groups, who do not interdine or intermarry with them. Cross-cousin (i.e., father's sister's daughter, or mother's brother's daughter) marriages are preferred. Formerly, Bhutias had considerable freedom in selecting partners, but arranged marriages are becoming more common. "Bride-price" is paid and marriages solemnized according to Hindu rites. Women have traditionally had a considerable degree of freedom and equality in Bhutia society. However, as Bhutia communities come more under the influence of Hinduism, women are slipping into the lower status assigned them by Hindu society.

11 CLOTHING

The dress of Bhutias varies throughout the region, although many groups resemble the Tibetans in their appearance. In Bhutan, Bhutia men wear long, loose-sleeved robes (*ko*) tied at the waist. Women wear the *kira,* a woven dress fastened at each shoulder by silver buckles. In Uttarakhand, as elsewhere in Bhutia country, clothes are of wool and usually made at home by Bhutia women. Male dress consists of tight-fitting trousers, a long coat that fastens on one side of the neck, woolen boots, and a white turban. The turban is sometimes replaced by a round "hill" cap or, at higher altitudes, by the warmer Tibetan-style hat. The traditional female dress is the *Chyung-bala.* The *bala* is a skirt, and the *chyunga* is a tunic-like smock that is open down the sides to the waist. A full-sleeved blouse is worn under the chyunga. A pair of embroidered boots and a white sash worn around the waist completes the outfit. A white, hood-like cap, multi-colored at the back and reaching down to the waist, is worn on the head. Jewelry includes earrings, nose rings, and an array of necklaces and chains around the neck.

12 FOOD

The staple food of Bhutias is rice, supplemented by millet, barley, wheat, and, in some areas, potatoes. Bhutias, whether Buddhist or Hindu, are nonvegetarian and eat beef, pork, and mutton. A typical meal in Bhutan might consist of *thugpa*, a meat soup prepared with herbs, red rice, and a meat curry or omelet. The Johari Bhutia of Uttarakhand have abandoned beef-eating, but still relish other meats. Lentils and vegetables, along with chutneys, are commonly taken at meals. The local version of Tibetan tea—made with tea, butter, and salt—is known as *namkin chai*. The butter is derived from the milk of goats, zebu cattle, and the yak. Bhutias can drink alcohol, both liquor distilled from rice and molasses and fermented rice-beer. Chang, a beer made from millet or other grains, is popular. Liquor is also offered when worshiping spirits and local deities.

13 EDUCATION

Education levels and literacy vary among the numerous Bhutia groups of the Himalayan region. Bhutan lags behind India and Nepal in the area of education, literacy among Bhutanese adults in Bhutan standing at 47% (2005). Compared to this, literacy among the Bhutias of Sikkim is 67.9% (according to the 2001 Census of India), above the norm among the Scheduled Tribes of India. In Uttarakhand, where literacy in the state stands at 72% (Census of India, 2001), the attitude of the Bhutias to education is positive, and the literacy rate is higher than the average for tribal groups in India. Nonetheless, the yearly migrations are disruptive to education, and drop-out rates are high, especially among the children of lower-income Bhutias.

14 CULTURAL HERITAGE

Many Bhutia customs reflect the influence of Tibetan culture on Bhutia life. In the days of Tibetan trade, the Bhutias were exposed to *lamas* and their teachings. They would build "Mana Walls," stone walls with the Buddhist mantra *Om Mani Padme Hum* inscribed on the boulders, for the safety of the village and its inhabitants. Bhutias believe that this mantra has great powers to protect against evil spirits and misfortune. The Bhutias are also greatly influenced by the Tibetan dragon symbol, which features as a prominent design in their handicrafts. Like virtually all Himalayan peoples, the Bhutia have a tradition of folk songs in which the mountains figure prominently. Dancing is popular, with both sexes usually participating. Some dances are performed at the time of weddings, and others contribute to the evening's festivities at *Rang-Bang* gatherings.

15 WORK

Bhutias were traditionally engaged in pastoralism and trade across India's northern border. They would carry food grains, *gur* (molasses), utensils, clothing, woolen goods, and assorted manufactured items north into Tibet. There they would barter these goods for salt, wool, borax, musk, and yak-tails. The closing of the Tibetan border in the 1960s destroyed this trade. Bhutias were forced to turn to cultivation, their secondary occupation. In the Uttarakhand region, however, Bhutia land holdings were commonly too small for self-sufficiency, and many people had to seek other employment. Today, about one-third of the area's Bhutias are engaged in agriculture, and a similar number are involved in weaving and embroidery as a cottage industry. Some have turned to manual labor, and only a very small percentage of Bhutia continue in their traditional occupation of trade and commerce.

16 SPORTS

There are no sports that can be identified with the Bhutia community in general. However, certain groups have developed individual skills. The Bhutanese, for example, are well known for their archery skills, and they stage competitions for festivals and national holidays.

17 ENTERTAINMENT AND RECREATION

Living mostly in isolated villages and leading semi-nomadic lives, few Bhutias have access to modern forms of entertainment. However, their lives are enriched by the activities associated with religious fairs and festivals, social events, and folk traditions such as dancing and singing.

18 FOLK ART, CRAFTS, AND HOBBIES

Bhutia women in the Central Himalayas have a reputation as excellent weavers and embroiderers. Not only do they make their own clothes, but in the past they traded their blankets, rugs, and shawls to Tibet. Today, many women continue to produce these items for local markets as part of a thriving cottage industry.

19 SOCIAL PROBLEMS

Bhutia communities are found in the Himalayas from Bhutan to Ladakh. Each group faces problems that reflect its specific social, cultural, economic, and political context. The Bhutia, for example, are well aware of the deforestation and environmental degradation that is rampant in the Himalayan foothills. Bhutia in Uttar Pradesh are deeply involved in the Chipko movement, a popular environmental movement aimed at preventing the cutting down of trees. Historically, all Bhutia groups depended on trade with Tibet. The political events that brought an end to this trade have resulted in profound changes in the life of the Bhutias of Uttarakhand. They do not have the land to support themselves and so must purchase food grains. They have also seen a decline in the numbers of their livestock. The cutting off of wool supplies from Tibet has affected their weaving industry, leading to impoverishment for many. The plight of the Bhutia was recognized by the state government, which designated them a Scheduled Tribe in 1967. Many Bhu-

Monks of the Bhutia community in India blow traditional ceremonial horns during a demonstration in New Delhi, India. (Prakash Singh/AFP/Getty Images)

tia have abandoned their traditional occupations and turned to labor, office work, and government service.

In 2008 Baichung Bhutia, well-known international soccer player from Sikkim and currently captain of India's soccer team, was solicited to run with the Olympic torch in India, but he refused to carry the torch to show support for the Tibetan independence movement. "I sympathize with the Tibetan cause. I'm against violence but I thought I should stand by the Tibetan people in their fight," Bhutia said. His actions won him praise from the Tibetan community and its supporters in India.

20 GENDER ISSUES

Specific issues relating to gender vary considerably among the Bhutia. For example, Buddhism treats women as equal to men, and so Bhutia women in Bhutan, where the official religion is Buddhism, fare differently than their counterparts in the Indian Himalayas, especially among those groups who have adopted Hinduism. In the Indian state of Sikkim, for instance, though agricultural chores are shared by men and women on a relatively equal basis, women are primarily responsible for taking care of poultry, hauling water, cooking, and other household chores. Bhutias are classed as a Scheduled Tribe in most states in India and, as such, are not subject to the Hindu Marriage Act of 1955. Custody of children and of household property is determined by customary law, which relies on elders to resolve custody issues. Child marriage and the dowry system are unknown among the Bhutia, though daughters have no rights of inheritance to their fathers' properties, even when there are no sons. All land is registered in the male's name, Bhutia society being patrilineal in nature. Bhutia women who marry outside of their ethnic group forfeit their rights to any property.

Bhutia women in Sikkim tend to have benefited best from access to education with over 60% of them being classed as literate, whereas in Ladakh, where the status of Bhutia women is generally low, many women have never attended school at all.

21 BIBLIOGRAPHY

Kandari, O. P., and O. P. Gusain, eds. *Garhwal Himalaya: Nature, Culture & Society*. Srinagar, Garhwal: Transmedia, 2001.

Kumar, P. *The Uttarakhand Movement: Construction of a Regional Identity*. New Delhi: Kanishka Publishers, 2000.

Lama, Mahendra P. *Sikkim: Society, Polity, Economy, Environment*. New Delhi: Indus Publishing, 1994.

Prasad, R. R. *Bhutia Tribals of India: Dynamics of Economic Transformation*. New Delhi: Gian Publishing House, 1989.

Shashi S. S. *The Nomads of the Himalayas*. Delhi: Sundeep Prakashan, 1979.

Singh, K. S. ed. *People of India. Vol. 3: The Scheduled Tribes*. Delhi and Oxford: Oxford University Press with the Anthropological Survey of India, 1994.

—by D. O. Lodrick

BRAHMANS

PRONUNCIATION: BRAH-muhns
ALTERNATE NAMES: Brahmin
LOCATION: India; Nepal
POPULATION: 65–70 million
LANGUAGE: The language of their geographic region; Sanskrit for religious purposes
RELIGION: Hinduism
RELATED ARTICLES: Vol. 3: Hindus; Vol. 4: People of India

1 INTRODUCTION

Brahmans are members of the first and highest-ranked of the four *varnas* or classes of traditional Hindu society. The name *Brahman* is frequently spelled " Brahmin" to avoid any confusion between the caste, the supreme being of the Hindus (*Brahma*), and the sacred scriptures known as the *Brahmanas*. In ancient times, Brahmans were above all a priestly caste. Their duties included daily recitation from the *Vedas*, performing religious rituals, conducting sacrifices, and studying and teaching the sacred books of Hinduism. It was almost inevitable, given their control of ritual sacrifice and claim to be the exclusive guardians of sacred knowledge, that Brahmans should rise to a dominant position in the life of the Hindu people. Wherever Hindus went, as during their expansion into Southeast Asia in the 1st and 2nd centuries AD, Brahmans followed. (However, some scholars have argued Brahmans were brought to Southeast Asia by local rulers to help set up the administrative structures of their states). Even today, their former presence in the region can be seen in the Brahmans and caste system found on the Indonesian island of Bali.

Brahmans have faced periodic challenges to their power. The reformist religions of Jainism and Buddhism, for example, were founded on the basis of a society without castes or priests. The conversion of Ashoka (273–232 BC), in particular, to Buddhism was a serious setback to the Brahmans in India. However, the 5th century AD saw the beginnings of a Hindu revival that raised Brahmans to a position of social dominance. This was based on three features of Brahman society: a hostility to all languages not Sanskrit, an intolerance for all religions not Hindu, and a deep prejudice towards all castes not Brahman. From this point on, Brahmans openly claimed superiority in all aspects of life. This state of affairs continued for several centuries, until the Brahmans' dominance was threatened by the introduction of Islam and its egalitarian ideals at the end of the 12th century. Western ideas, introduced by missionaries and social reformers, and ideals of democracy have acted to reduce the power and prestige of the Brahmans in recent times.

2 LOCATION AND HOMELAND

Brahmans make up about 6% of all Hindus, or roughly 65 to 70 (2007 est.) million people. Rather than being a single caste, Brahmans form a bewildering array of subgroups. Each of these can be considered a caste (*jati*) in its own right in that it is endogamous (i.e., marriage occurs within the group) and subject to restrictions on interdining. The orthodox Brahman from Malabar in South India, for example, cannot eat with the orthodox Brahman from Kashmir. Today, there are over 1,800 subdivisions of Brahmans. The Brahman castes are generally divided into two broad divisions: those of northern India (*Pancha Gauda*), and those of the south (*Pancha Dravida*). Each of these divisions is further divided into five categories. The Pancha Gauda categories are the Sarasvata Brahmans of the Sindh, Punjab and Kashmir, the Kanykuba Brahmans of Kanauj, the Gauda Brahmans of Bihar and Bengal, the Utkala Brahmans of northern Orissa, and the Maithila Brahmans of the areas of Bihar and Nepal north of the River Ganges. These groups include both high caste groups (e.g. the Kashmiri Pandits) and those of lower ranking (e.g. the Chithu and Prot [Purohit] Brahmans, also of Kashmir). Although in any given area Brahmans are ranked as the highest caste, there is no relationship between the Brahman castes of different regions. The Brahman castes are even ranked into a hierarchy among themselves, depending on factors such as occupation and descent.

Although Brahmans are found throughout India and Nepal, they are not spread evenly over the subcontinent. Their highest concentration is in Kashmir, where they form 35% of the Hindu population. Around 12% of Hindus in the upper Ganges plains are Brahmans. However, the numbers of Brahmans drop dramatically in areas distant from the Aryan heartland. In Assam, Orissa, and Tamil Nadu, for example, they make up less than 3% of the Hindu population.

³ LANGUAGE

Brahmans speak the language of their geographic region. Thus, the Kashmiri Pandit speaks Kashmiri, the Nambudiri Brahman of Kerala speaks Malayalam, and the Ayyar Brahman from Tamil Nadu speaks Tamil. The sacred language of Hinduism, however, is Sanskrit. Brahmans need to know Sanskrit to carry out their priestly functions. There is, however, considerable variation in the level of the Brahman's knowledge of Sanskrit. A Vedic scholar may have extensive knowledge of Sanskrit and Sanskrit literature. On the other hand, a temple functionary may be illiterate and have learned the Sanskrit passages he needs to perform his duties by rote.

⁴ FOLKLORE

In Vedic legend, Purusha was a giant being, representing the original primeval male. He was thought to be a form of Brahma, who created the universe. The *Rig Veda*, the earliest of the Vedas, tells of the sacrifice of Purusha that served as the model for all future sacrifice. The four castes (*varnas*) of Hinduism were created from Purusha's severed body. The Brahman was created from his mouth for the purposes of teaching humankind. The *khsatriya* came from Purusha's arms, the *vaishya* from his thighs, and the *sudra* from his feet. It is this origin from Purusha's (i.e., Brahma's) mouth that underlies the Brahman's claim to superiority over all other castes in Hindu society.

⁵ RELIGION

Brahmans are Hindu and embrace the fundamental beliefs of Hinduism. These include concepts of the soul (*atman*), the illusion that surrounds one's physical existence (*maya*), the cycle of rebirths (*samsara*), the law of *karma*, the pursuit of righteous behavior (*dharma*), the philosophy of nonviolence (*ahimsa*), and the total release (*mokhsa*) of the soul from the physical world. They also include belief in the authority of the Vedas, in the caste system, and in the superiority of the Brahman caste. Beyond this, however, Brahmans may follow differ-

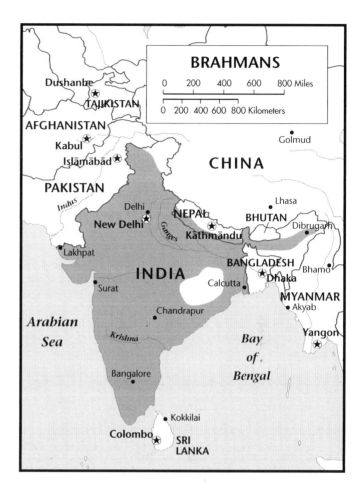

ent philosophical systems. The Smarta Brahmans, for example, are followers of the Smarta sect of Hinduism. They are orthodox, but in their worship ceremonies they invoke five deities (Shiva, Vishnu, Suraj, Ganpati, and Shakti). In contrast, the Shri Vaishnava Brahmans of the Tamil region exclusively worship the Hindu god Vishnu. There are almost as many differences in Brahman religious customs and practices as there are Brahman castes in the country.

⁶ MAJOR HOLIDAYS

Brahmans celebrate all of the major festivals of the Hindu calendar. Of particular importance to Brahmans, however, is the festival of Shravani-purnima, the full moon of the month of Shravana (July-August). Sometimes this is known as "Coconut Day" because people commonly throw coconuts into the ocean and rivers. It is a day on which Brahmans (and other high-caste Hindus) renew the sacred thread. For many Brahmans, this is the beginning of the sacred year, and the rituals they perform on this day serve to purify them of the sins of the past year.

⁷ RITES OF PASSAGE

All periods of transition and change in Hindu life are held to be times of danger and are accompanied by rituals to counteract evil influences. These rituals (*samskara*, in Sanskrit) are set out in the Vedas and other Hindu texts. At one time they numbered over 300, but now have been reduced to around 9 or 16 (there is disagreement among scholars as to the exact number of rites that should be performed). All Hindus perform these rituals, no matter what their caste, although they are often more elaborate for Brahmans. The Maithila Brahmans of northern Bihar, however, observe no pre-birth rituals. Mother and child are viewed as ceremonially unclean until the *Chhatthihar*, the ritual purification undertaken on the sixth day. During infancy, rituals to protect the child from black magic, the first-feeding ceremony, and the head-shaving ceremony (*mundan*) are performed. One of the most important rites for the Maithila Brahman is the *upanayana* ceremony, the donning of the sacred thread. This is a ritualistic rebirth (hence the term "twice-born") by which the male is initiated to the full status of a Brahman.

In theory, soon after the sacred thread ceremony, a boy should enter the first of the four stages (*asramas*) into which a Brahman's life is divided. He lives as a student in the house of his teacher, studying the Vedas and the sacred law. Around the age of 30, he should return to his father's house to marry, raise a family, and become a householder (the second asrama). Then, having raised his children and fulfilled his family obligations, a Brahman is free to seek his own salvation. During the third stage, the Brahman leaves his family for an austere life of discipline and meditation in the forest. Finally, he progresses to the stage of Sannyasa. A *sannyasin* is an ascetic who has given up his possessions and renounced the world. He has no home, begs for his food, and wanders the country awaiting the ultimate release of the soul from the physical body. Few Brahmans follow the ideal of the four asramas today, although individuals who have become sannyasin may be seen today at Hindu pilgrimage centers and holy places across the land.

Maithila Brahman death rituals involve the custom of Godan, or "gift of a cow." When possible, just before death a Brahman worships a cow and gives it away as a gift to a near relative. This is seen as essential, as the cow will carry the dead Brahman across the river of blood and filth (Vaitarani) that separates the earth from the land of the dead (this rite is described in the Vedic literature). The body is placed on a bamboo stretcher and carried out to be cremated. The Maithila Brahmans have no common cremation ground, each family having its own place, usually in a mango garden, for the burning of bodies. Water is sprinkled on the ground to thwart evil spirits. The corpse is bathed, dressed in a white shroud, and placed on the funeral pyre with the head pointing south. The chief mourner, usually the eldest son, places five pieces of wood on the pyre, walks around it three times, and then sets it alight. All the participants in the funeral ceremony take a ritual bath in a river or pond before returning home. Before entering the house, they are required to touch iron, stone, and fire, and then tear a chili into three pieces. Various rituals are performed in the following days, including the gathering up of the bones and ashes and placing them in the sacred Ganges River. A grand feast, at which fish and meat are served and to which a minimum of 11 Brahmans have to be invited, is held on the thirteenth day to complete the *sraddha* (funeral) rites. If the funeral rites are not performed correctly, it is believed the soul of the departed will become a ghost (*preta*) and never obtain salvation.

8 INTERPERSONAL RELATIONS

Brahmans use the standard Hindu greetings, "Namaste" or "Namaskar," accompanied by the joining together of hands in front of the body. Orthodox Brahmans concerned with ritu-

al purity take great care to avoid physical contact with people of lower castes, and, thus, rarely venture into crowded public places or use public transport. Even the shadow of an Untouchable falling on a Brahman is polluting and requires ritual purification.

9 LIVING CONDITIONS

The living conditions of Brahmans reflect factors such as occupation, economic status, and regional culture. The Anavil Brahmans, who are relatively affluent landowners in Gujarat, have a very different lifestyle from the Ganga-patra, a Brahman who guides pilgrims through the sacred city of Varanasi (Banaras). The pilgrim-guide also leads an existence quite different from that of the Vedic scholar who lives and works in Varanasi, the holiest of the Hindus' holy cities. In general, the material culture of Brahmans (e.g., settlement patterns, house type, household belongings, and furniture) conforms to regional cultural patterns.

10 FAMILY LIFE

Brahmans generally follow regional systems of kinship and marriage, although considerable diversity exists in their practices. Among the Nambudiri Brahmans of Kerala, for example, only the eldest son was traditionally allowed to marry. Like all Hindu castes, Brahmans are divided into exogamous *gotras*. One marries outside one's gotra, but there are also complex rules delineating other gotras and degrees of relationship that are taboo. Marriages between persons of the same name is usually prohibited because they are considered to be related. The matter is further complicated by the fact that many Brahmans will not marry outside their own sect. Brahmans have been known to practice hypergamy, i.e., members of a caste will accept daughters from a caste of lower status but will not give their daughters in return. Marriages are, of course, arranged, and the forms of marriage available to the Brahman are clearly set out in the sacred texts. The extended family with patrilocal residence is the norm for Brahman families. Most Brahman groups do not recognize divorce or widow remarriage.

11 CLOTHING

The traditional dress for the Brahman man is the *dhoti*, a single piece of white cotton wrapped around the waist for half its length, and then drawn between the legs and tucked into the waist behind. There are regional variations in the way the dhoti may be tied. The chest is usually left bare. A turban, often red in color, may be worn by the cultivating castes. Any items made of bone or leather are regarded as unclean and are shunned. Women wear the typical Hindu dress of *sari* and *choli* (bodice) and share in their countrywomen's love of jewelry. Orthodox Brahmans continue to wear their traditional clothing, though in many areas the cultivating castes have adopted local styles of dress.

12 FOOD

Geography and ecology set the broad outlines of the Brahmans' diet. In the drier northern and western regions, cereals (wheat, millet, barley) made into flat, unleavened breads (*roti*) are the staple food. This is eaten with spiced vegetable dishes, pulses (*dal*), and fruits. Rice (*chawal*) replaces the cereals in the more humid east and south.

Thai officials prepare for rice planting during royal plowing ceremonies, Bangkok, Thailand. The royal plowing ceremony is an ancient Brahman ritual that was reintroduced by King Bhumibol Adulyadej in 1960. It is considered the official commencement of the rice-growing season. (AP Images/Sakchai Lalit)

The specifics of the Brahman diet are determined by concerns for ritual purity and the need to avoid pollution. Food habits in Hindu society are closely linked to social status and standing in the caste hierarchy. As high-caste Hindus, Brahmans are subject to rigid dietary restrictions. In theory, Brahmans are strict vegetarians, eating no animal flesh and even avoiding eggs. But Kashmiri Brahmans eat mutton, and Brahmans in Bengal eat fish. In South India, however, no orthodox Brahman will eat animal flesh. No Brahman in India will eat beef, either, as this violates the basic Hindu concept of the sanctity of the cow. Milk and milk products are important foods, however. They also have ritual significance, because the five products of the cow are regarded as both sacred and sanctifying. (These five products are milk, curds, *ghi* or clarified butter, dung, and urine—known collectively as *pancha-gavya.*) Some Brahmans even avoid foods such as onions and garlic that grow in the ground and are regarded as unclean. Alcohol is strictly forbidden. Even inadvertent violation of food taboos can lead to serious problems. An incident is recorded among the Maithila Brahmans where an individual accidentally ate a vulture, thinking it was a water-hen. He was cast out of the community for this act, and the priest refused to purify him.

Dietary restrictions extend not only to the foods a Brahman will eat, but also to who can prepare the food and with whom the Brahman can eat. In any given region, rules of commensality, i.e., rules concerning with whom one can eat, are a clear indication of one's standing in the caste hierarchy.

13 EDUCATION

Educational levels vary among Brahman castes across the country. Some, such as the elites among the Pandits of Kashmir, have a long tradition of learning and scholarship. Jawaharlal Nehru, India's first prime minister, was of this caste. By contrast, a Brahman cultivator in a desert village in Rajasthan may have had hardly any schooling at all. There is a tendency among the more conservative groups, such as the Nambudiri Brahmans of Kerala, to shun Western education. This has restricted their opportunities for advancement in modern India.

14 CULTURAL HERITAGE

Brahmans all over India share many common features, e.g., high social status, traditional priestly functions, and restrictive food taboos. However, the cultural heritage of a particular Brahman group is rooted in the group's own regional culture. Each group shares in the language, literature, history, and folk traditions of the regional society of which it forms a part. Thus, the Ayyars of South India are Brahmans by caste but Tamil in culture; the Pandits of Kashmir have helped shape Kashmiri society; and the Maithila Brahmans are an integral part of the peoples and culture of the middle Ganges plains.

15 WORK

The traditional occupation of the Brahman castes is to serve as priests for Hindu society, either in temples or as family priests (*purohit*). In the past, because of their learning and literacy,

Brahmans rose to positions of power in the state administrations, acting as royal advisors and even attaining the rank of "Diwan" (Chief Minister). Textual sources indicate that, in addition to their priestly role, Brahmans have been teachers, soldiers, tillers of the soil, and even traders. Today, there are still Brahman castes (e.g., the Anavil Brahmans, the Bhaghban, and the Bhumihar) who are primarily landowners and cultivators, and who are barred from performing priestly functions. These groups do not, of course, have the ritual status of the priestly castes. Brahmans are also found in occupations such as teacher, scribe, and government clerk.

Of the Brahmans involved in religious occupations, those connected with the actual rituals of temple worship are considered socially inferior. These include the *pujari* who performs the *pujas* (rituals of worship) at temples and shrines, the *ojha* who exorcises demons and evil spirits, and the *jyotisha* or astrologer who casts horoscopes and determines auspicious dates. The Brahmans who act as guides for pilgrims at sacred centers such as Varanasi or Allahabad, as well as those who preside over funeral rites, also fall into this category of "inferior" Brahmans. By contrast, the Sarasvata Brahmans of the northwest are regarded as among the purest of the Brahman castes.

16 SPORTS

There are no games or sports associated specifically with Brahmans, although individual groups have developed certain athletic skills. For example, the Chaturvedis are a Brahman caste of Mathura (in western Uttar Pradesh) who are known for their wrestling ability.

17 ENTERTAINMENT AND RECREATION

There are no forms of entertainment or recreation specifically identified with the Brahman castes.

18 FOLK ART, CRAFTS, AND HOBBIES

Brahmans are not known for any unique folk arts or crafts.

19 SOCIAL PROBLEMS

Given the wide geographical distribution and varied occupations of Brahmans, it is difficult to generalize about their problems. Some problems, such as the violence and political instability in Kashmir or the deteriorating law and order situation in Bihar, are regional in nature and affect all castes. Others, for instance the difficulties faced by struggling Brahman cultivators, are class—rather than caste—related. Perhaps the single greatest problem facing Brahmans in recent years has been the emergence of a secular and democratic India. The modernization of India, especially in economic terms, has eroded the traditional power and prestige of the Brahmans. The adoption of the democratic principle of one person, one vote has given the lower castes, and especially the Untouchables, political power that they could never have possessed in times past. Political movements among the lower castes, such as the Dalit Panthers of Maharashtra State, often are based on a rejection of Brahmanism. Recent government actions, such as the Mandal Commission's recommendations to "reserve" government jobs and university places for the Scheduled Tribes and Scheduled Castes, have further strengthened the position of the lower castes at the expense of the upper castes. It is per-

haps no accident that a militant Hindu nationalism (*Hindutva*), supported in part by Brahmans, has recently emerged as a major force on the Indian political scene.

The Bharatiya Janata Party (BJP) is an example of this. Created in 1980, the BJP is a major center-right Indian political party championing the socio-religious cultural values of the country's Hindus and is supported by members of the set of Hindu nationalist organizations informally known as the Sangh Parivar, in which the Rashtriya Swayamsevak Sangh (RSS) plays a leading role. Currently, the BJP rules in eight states of India (Gujarat, Chhattisgarh, Himachal Pradesh, Madhya Pradesh, Meghalaya, Nagaland, Rajasthan, and Uttarakhand) and while its leaders are not necessarily Brahmans, the party supports the traditional values of Hinduism. Under Atal Bihai Vajpayee, the BJP led the National Democratic Alliance, which formed the Union (central) Government in Delhi between 1998 and 2004. L. K. Advani, Deputy Prime Minister under the Vajpayee administration explained the BJP's unexpected loss to the Congress-led UPA (United Progressive Alliance) in the 2004 general elections in terms of a failure to keep to the tenets of Hindutva.

20 GENDER ISSUES

The Brahman's emphasis on ritual purity has led inevitably to discrimination against women. In the past, Brahman women have been subject to the worst excesses of Hindu society—child marriage, early consummation of marriage, prohibitions against widow remarriage, and demands for dowry. As members of India's highest castes, they were expected to religiously practice the basic tenets of Hindu society. Even though many of these practices have been made illegal in modern India, (viz. the 1984 Dowry Prohibition [Amendment] Bill), they still occur. One only has to read the press, even today, to find instances of "dowry deaths": over 6,700 dowry deaths were reported in India in 2005 and one suspects many more go unreported as such. Brahman women also face problems in accessing education and tend to experience the same discrimination faced by all Hindu women, especially in rural areas where they are expected to perform agricultural labor, as well run the households. Casteism absolutely forbids a Brahman women from having any kind of physical relationship with a man of lower caste and requires marriage (usually arranged) into the Brahman caste.

Brahman women, by virtue of their status, tend to be better educated than other women in South Asia, and many have achieved prominence in public life in India. Indira Gandhi (Nehru's daughter) was a Kashmiri Brahman (Pandit), who was educated at Oxford and continued the Nehru dynasty, ruling India with an iron fist from 1966 until her assassination by Sikhs in 1988 (with an inter-regnum between 1977 and 1980). Brahman women have risen to positions of prominence in science (for instance, Ashima Chaterjree in organic chemistry and Archana Sharma in particle physics) sports, and politics. But in general, they still play a subordinate role to males and their husbands, in particular, and face many of the same issues—access to education, poverty, health awareness, sexual discrimination and abuse, inequality in the workplace, inheritance of property and balancing work and family life—as other women in modern Hindu society.

21 BIBLIOGRAPHY

Ghosh, G. K. and Shukla Ghosh. *Brahmin Women.* Kolkata : Firma KLM, 2003.

Kumar, Raj. *History of the Brahmans: A Research Report.* Delhi: Kalpaz Publications, 2006.

Maitra, Asim. *Religious Life of the Brahman: A Case Study of Maithil Brahmans.* New Delhi: Inter-India Publications, 1986.

Sharma, Rajendra Nath. *Brahmins through the Ages: Their Social, Religious, Cultural, Political, and Economic Life.* Delhi: Ajanta Publications, 1977.

Stevenson, Mrs. Sinclair. *The Rites of the Twice-Born.* London: Oxford University Press, 1920.

Walker, Benjamin. "Brahmin." In *Hindu World: An Encyclopedic Survey of Hinduism.* London: George Allen and Unwin, 1968.

—by D. O. Lodrick

BRAHUI

PRONUNCIATION: brah-HOO-ee
ALTERNATE NAMES: Brohi
LOCATION: Pakistan (Baluchistan Province); a small number live in southern Afghanistan and Iran
POPULATION: 2.3 million
LANGUAGE: Brahui; Sindhi
RELIGION: Islam (Sunni Muslim)
RELATED ARTICLES: Vol. 3: Baluchi

1 INTRODUCTION

Among the rugged hills of South Asia's western borderlands lives a group of tribes known as the Brahui (also Brohi). Various explanations of the name *Brahui* have been suggested, the most likely being that it is a corruption of *Barohi*, meaning "mountain-dweller" or "highlander."

The origins of the Brahui remain unclear. The Brahui language belongs to the Dravidian linguistic family, and this has led some writers to argue that the Brahui are survivors of the peoples who developed the Harappan civilization. Others have argued that the Brahui and the Baluchi are one and the same, and that the term *Brahui* designates status rather than any ethnic differences. If this were true, then the Brahui would have been part of the Baluchi migrations into their present region between the 5th and 7th centuries AD. During the 17th century, the Brahui rose to prominence in Kalat, in Baluchistan, when Mir Ahmed Khan I acceded to the leadership of a confederacy of Brahui tribes in AD 1666. For nearly 300 years from that time, an unbroken line of Brahui rulers held the Khanate of Kalat. British expansion westward from Sind, and their interest in the Afghan border regions, brought them into conflict with the Khans of Kalat in the middle of the 19th century. The British eventually acquired control over the strategically located Kalat, although the state remained nominally independent until it was incorporated into Pakistan in 1948.

2 LOCATION AND HOMELAND

The current estimate of the Brahui population is 2.3 million people. Most of this number is concentrated in Pakistan's Baluchistan Province around Kalat, the historical focus of Brahui territory and power. Brahui-speakers are also found in southern Afghanistan and Iran.

The Brahui homeland lies on the Kalat Plateau, where elevations vary between 2,135 m and 2,440 m (7,000–8,000 ft). Running roughly north–south through the region is the Central Brahui Range. West of these mountains lie the uplands of Jhalawan and Sarawan. To the east, the land descends to the alluvial lowlands of Kacchi. This is an extension of the Indus plain that runs northward towards Sibi and the Bolan Pass. The region is extremely arid, with annual rainfall averaging less than 20 cm (8 in). Strong northwesterly winds prevail through the area, bringing dust from the Iranian deserts and scorching temperatures in summer and bitter cold weather in winter. The plateau consists of extensive areas of barren rock, or hills with a thin cover of drought-resistant vegetation.

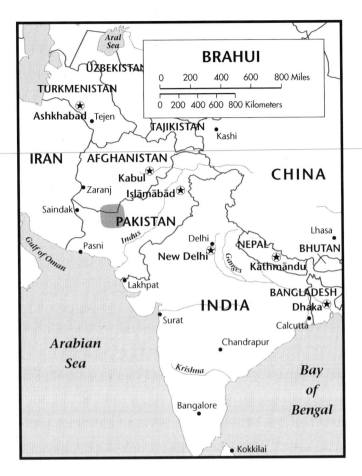

when plans are too complicated or never come to fruition. The story goes that a simple, but foolish, man Balwān (or Balo Khān) was engaged to be married. His greedy father-in-law-to-be asked Balwān to bring him the required bride-price to marry his daughter. So, Balwān went to his relatives and collected the required amount of money. But when he went back to his father–in-law, the latter asked for more money. Balwān returned to his family to obtain the extra funds, and this situation continued for many rounds, so that Balwān never succeeded in marrying and died single. Hence the proverb.

Another Brahui story tells of Mulla Mansur, an orphan who got a job in the house of a *qadi* (a Muslim religious leader). The qadi was an insensitive man. Even though Mansur had served him loyally for seven long years, he beat him over a trifling mistake. Mansur left the qadi and took to traveling the world. He met an old shepherd, fell in love with his daughter, and married her. When Mansur and his wife returned to his home, the beauty of his wife caused such a stir that everyone from the qadi to the king desired to possess her. However, Mansur's wife was steadfast in her fidelity to her husband. When the qadi continued to make advances and tried to seduce her, she exposed him publicly. All the people joined in condemning the qadi, and the king banished him from the Brahui lands. This tale presents the Brahui view of the qualities and strength of character desirable in a wife, as well an element of skepticism toward religious leaders who preach purity to the world but practice otherwise.

5 RELIGION

The Brahui are Muslim, belonging mostly to the Sunni sect of Islam. They follow Islamic religious beliefs and practices as set out in the *Quran* (Koran), though many of their social customs are Indian in origin. Communal worship focuses on the mosque, and *mullahs* (Muslim priests) see to the spiritual and ritual needs of the people. Reverence for saints (*pirs*), a characteristic of Islam in South Asia, is also deeply entrenched in Brahui culture. Every family has its particular saint, and women often keep in their houses some earth (*khwarda*) from the saint's shrine to be used in time of need. For example, a little earth may be fed to a sick person along with prayers to the saint for a cure. Sacrifices of sheep or goats are performed at the shrines as an offering to the pir or in fulfillment of a vow. Many take their children to a shrine for the first shaving of the head or, failing that, place a little bag of the hair in the shrine, where it is hung from a pole. The Brahui believe in sorcery and possession by *jinn* or evil spirits. A mullah or *sayyed* (holy man) is often called in to read from the Quran or provide charms and amulets to exorcise these spirits. Should this fail, a sheikh, who is known for his power over jinn and casts them out by dancing, may be used.

6 MAJOR HOLIDAYS

The Brahui observe the usual holy days of the Muslim calendar. On the eve of most high festivals, respect is paid to the souls of the dead. The holiest of all is the eve of the tenth day of Muharram, which is known as *Imamak*. Women prepare special dishes of meat and rice during the day. The family gathers near sunset in the presence of a *mullah* (Muslim priest), who reads from the Quran and recites prayers for the dead over the food. Dishes of food are then sent to relatives and neighbors, who reciprocate with their own offerings. The following morn-

3 LANGUAGE

The Brahui language is a Dravidian tongue related to the languages spoken in South India. The existence of this isolated pocket of Dravidian speakers almost 1,800 km (1,000 mi) from the main area where Dravidian languages are found is a problem that has long puzzled South Asian linguists. Brahui contains many loanwords acquired from the Indo-Aryan languages (e.g., Baluchi, Sindhi, and Persian) spoken by the peoples of the surrounding region. There is no Brahui script. Many Brahui-speakers are bilingual, speaking Baluchi or other local languages. Those Brahui settled in Sind tend to speak Brahui at home but use Sindhi (or in Karachi, Urdu) in dealings with others.

4 FOLKLORE

The Brahui language is rich in oral literature, the various genres including stories and tales, proverbs and riddles and songs. Brahui folk stories are mostly created by nomads, shepherds and farmers for the entertainment of their children and immediate family members. Mothers, for instance, tell their children legends about the mammā, a large apelike creature known for its physical strength and resemblance to humans, and once thought to be quite numerous. Other stories criticize the sardārs (hereditary tribal chiefs) and landowners from the point of view of the oppressed classes.

In Brahui, as in Baluchi, proverbs tend to have background stories. There is, for instance, the saying Balwān nā barām ("This is like the marriage of Balwān"), which is often used

ing is an occasion for the head of the house to visit the grave-yard to pray at the graves of his dead relatives.

7 RITES OF PASSAGE

The birth of a son is of utmost importance for a Brahui. A daughter is seen as little more than a gift to one's neighbor. Barrenness in a wife is a cause for reproach, and in the past female circumcision is reported to have been secretly practiced to try to remedy this situation. A craving for earth, and earth-eating, among pregnant women is also reported. When a son is born, the father announces it to the community by firing shots in the air. Various rituals are followed to protect the mother and child from the attention of witches and *jinn* (evil spirits). For the mother, the period of postnatal impurity lasts 40 days. Sheep are killed (two for a son and one for a daughter) and a feast held for relatives, friends, and neighbors. The child is then named, sometimes after a worthy ancestor. The head-shaving ritual (*sar-kuti*) is performed by the time the child is 2 years old, often at the shrine of a favored saint. A male child may undergo circumcision (*sunnat*) within 6 months, though the cost associated with the celebrations cause many to postpone it until as late as the age of 10 or 12.

No particular ceremonies accompany the male reaching puberty. An unusual rite is reported to be followed when a girl begins to menstruate for the first time. At sunset, the mother arranges three stones in a triangular pattern on the ground and has her daughter leap over them three times. It is thought that this will ensure that the girl's periods during the rest of her life will last no more than three days. Childhood did not last long in traditional Brahui society. If a girl were not married as a child, she would be soon after puberty.

At death, word is sent to relatives and friends, who gather for the funeral. A shroud is sent for from outside the house, and when the *mullah* (Muslim priest) arrives, the body is carried to a place of washing. It is washed by the mullah and near kinsmen (or the mullah's wife and female relatives, in the case of a woman), then wrapped in the shroud. The body is taken in procession to the graveyard, with the mourners reciting the *kalima,* the profession of faith. At the graveside, the mullah offers the prayer for the dead, and the body is given its burial. The traditional period of mourning was 11 days for a man and 9 for a woman, but this has been reduced in modern times. Women weep and wail, covering their faces in mourning. Other rituals include the singing of dirges (*moda),* and a death feast (*varagh).* Another feast is held on the first anniversary of the death.

8 INTERPERSONAL RELATIONS

The Brahui share their forms of greeting with the Baluchi. On meeting, they stop, shake hands, and embrace each other. The encounter continues with inquiries after each other's health and then proceeds to an exchange of news (*hal*) concerning family, friends, cattle, etc. Brahui are known for their hospitality to their guests.

9 LIVING CONDITIONS

Brahui settlements essentially reflect the economic activities of their inhabitants. Pastoral nomadism was the traditional occupation of many Brahui, and nomadic herders lived in tents and temporary camps, migrating with their herds in search of pasture. By contrast, in the Kacchi plains Brahui live in permanent villages that differ little in form and function from their Baluchi neighbors' settlements. Pastoralism has declined in importance in recent years, and many Brahui in the upland areas have adopted a transhumant economy. Transhumance is based on a seasonal migration to differing elevations. Highland cultivating villages in the Korat Plateau are occupied for nine months of the year. During the winter months, however, the inhabitants drive their herds to the Kacchi lowlands where they live in tent camps. (This pattern is the reverse of transhumance in Europe. There, settlements are at lower elevations, and animals are taken up to alpine pastures during the summer months.)

10 FAMILY LIFE

The Brahui are organized into tribes, each of which has a hereditary chief (*sadar).* These are unlike the clans of the Rajputs with their elaborate genealogies; rather, they are loosely structured units based on patrilineal descent and political allegiance. This allows for a considerable degree of fluidity, with Baluchi and Pathan groups incorporated into the Brahui tribal units, and the movement of sections between Brahui tribes. Some of the more numerous Brahui tribes are the Mengals, Zahris, and Muhammad Hosanis. The Khans of Kalat were of the Ahmedzai tribe. The Brahui tribes are further divided into descending kin-groups down to the level of the immediate lineage.

The favored marriage among the Brahui is with the father's brother's daughter. Marriages are arranged, although the wishes of the couple are taken into consideration. In the past, child marriage was common, though this practice is now banned under Pakistani law. The betrothal and marriage ceremonies are important events in the life of both family and tribe. Disputes within tribes are usually settled at the time of marriages. A bride-price (*lab*) is paid by the groom's family. Although Muslim law allows polygyny (multiple wives), economic realities mean most Brahui marriages are monogamous. Family structure tends to reflect economic systems. The nuclear family predominates among nomadic Brahui, while extended families are common among village inhabitants. Divorce, though simple, is rare. In the past, adultery was punishable by death, although such practices are forbidden by Pakistani law. Widow remarriage is accepted.

11 CLOTHING

A young boy is given his first trousers at about three years of age, and thereafter wears clothes similar to those of adult males—the *kurti* (long shirt), worn over the *salwar,* the loose, baggy trousers found throughout the area. For men, a turban (*pag*) completes the outfit.

Women wear a long shift over trousers, although among Brahui nomads women wear skirts rather than trousers. Among the Brahui of the Jhalawan region, women's shifts are typically black in color. Women's clothes are embroidered with various patterns and designs in colored thread. Women's ornaments include finger rings (*challav),* nose rings (*vat),* and earrings (*panara).* Brahui settled in Sind tend to be indistinguishable from the Sindhi population in their dress.

12 FOOD

The settled Brahui cultivate wheat and millet, which are ground into flour and baked into unleavened breads. Rice is also eaten, but usually only on special occasions. Mutton and goat are important in the diet of the Brahui, with the flesh of animals that are sacrificed at various rituals and festivals distributed to the community at large. The more-affluent farmers in lowland areas may raise cattle. As is common throughout South Asia, food is eaten with one's hands, and often from a communal platter. Milk is drunk and also made into curds, *ghi* (clarified butter), buttermilk, and butter. Dates, wild fruits, and vegetables are also part of the Brahui diet. Tea is drunk at meals and is also taken as part of various social ceremonies. Opium is also used.

13 EDUCATION

In general, levels of literacy among the Brahui are extremely low. The 1972 census for the Kalat Division of Baluchistan Province records an overall literacy rate of only 6.3% in the population over 10 years of age. The Brahui community is essentially rural in nature and lives in areas of Pakistan where the social infrastructure is poorly developed. Nomadic groups have no access to formal schooling, and even where schools do exist, attendance is low. In settled areas such as Sind where Brahui children are more likely to attend school, they are taught in the local language rather than in Brahui.

14 CULTURAL HERITAGE

The Brahuis have an oral tradition of folk songs and heroic poems. These are sung by a class of professional minstrels and musicians called Dombs, who are attached to every Brahui community. Musical instruments include the *rabab* (an Afghan stringed instrument plucked with a piece of wood), the *siroz* (a stringed instrument played with a bow), and the *punzik* (a reed instrument). These have replaced the *dambura* (a three-stringed instrument played with the fingers) that is found in the more isolated areas. Dancing is an important feature at events such as weddings and funerals. The local country dance known as *chap* has largely been abandoned, however.

15 WORK

Historically, the Brahui were pastoral nomads, migrating with their herds of sheep, goats, and cattle from the upland plateaus to the low-lying alluvial plains. Today, however, many Brahui have abandoned their pastoral activities in favor of transhumant or settled agriculture. In the Kacchi lowlands, river and canal irrigation support cultivation, but settlements in other areas of the Brahui region depend on *qanats*. Qanat (or *karez*) irrigation is found over a wide area of Iran and Southwest Asia and even in the Turfan Depression of Xinjiang Province of China. It involves sinking a line of vertical shafts and then tunneling horizontally at the bottom of the shafts to create an underground passageway to carry water from its source to the fields.

16 SPORTS

Horse-racing and target-shooting were traditional sports popular among the more affluent sections of the Brahui community.

17 ENTERTAINMENT AND RECREATION

In the past, the Brahui had to depend on their own resources for entertainment and recreation. They found this in their family celebrations, their traditions of folk song and dance,

and in the festivities accompanying religious observances. This is still true for nomadic Brahui today. Epic poems are performed by specialist poets known as Lorî, who are considered as belonging to the lower-status groups in Brahui society. Their traditional occupation was to serve the Brahui at marriage ceremonies, playing the dhol (drum) at festivities and at funeral ceremonies. Folk songs are most often sung by the Brahui without musical accompaniment, although both men and women play musical instruments such as the sironz (a fiddle) and the dambura (a plucked string instrument). Women play the daira (tambourine). The Brahui settled in Karachi or villages on the plains have access to more modern forms of recreation.

18 FOLK ART, CRAFTS, AND HOBBIES

Like other women of the region, Brahui women embroider their garments with colorful designs. Tents and rugs are made from sheep's wool or goats' hair.

19 SOCIAL PROBLEMS

The Brahui tribes inhabit some of the harshest, most-isolated, and least-productive environments in Pakistan. This is reflected in the relative inefficiency of traditional economic systems and the generally low standards of living of the community. Belated government efforts to bring development to the region have done little for the welfare of the Brahui, who are essentially nomadic and rural in character. The lack of a written literature (what there is dates only from the 1960s) has hindered the development of a tribal consciousness, and matters are made worse by the declining numbers of people speaking Brahui. The Brahui appear to be rapidly assimilating with the surrounding Baluchi populations. Apart from their language, which gives them a sense of cultural identity, the Brahui lack a sense of identification with their country and have very little representation in the political arena. They still tend to function on a tribal basis, dealing with the government through their *sardars* and other tribal leaders. The Brahui remain one of the many tribal peoples of Pakistan who remain "outsiders" in a country dominated by ethnic elites such as the Punjabis and Sindhis.

20 GENDER ISSUES

Brahui women face the same gender discrimination that women do in all Muslim societies. Brahui women, for instance observe *purdah*, i.e. the segregation of women to ensure that family honor is maintained. This means that women live in compounds behind mud walls where they are virtually hidden from view. Women must avoid being seen by strangers, especially strange men. Access to compounds is restricted and a woman's mobility outside the compound is controlled by her husband and male relatives.

Most Brahui women are engaged in agricultural labor. During the productive season from March through mid-November, a woman may spend as much as 60% of her time in her agricultural role. A typical day for a Brahui farmer's wife is seventeen hours long, but her work is sheer drudgery because the labor she performs is merely repetitive and requires no decision-making as to how land and other resources are to be utilized—this is the prerogative of the males in the family. Women are responsible for transplanting, weeding, harvesting, and collecting fuel and water. Official statistics grossly under estimate the contribution of women to the agricultural gross domestic product (GDP) in rural areas of Pakistan. Very few government departments or even projects collect gender disaggregated data, and most development projects are geared towards men.

In addition to the payment of bride-price and the custom of *purdah*, Brahui women are subject to all the ills of women in Pakistan—domestic violence, rape, "honor killings," acid attacks, and trafficking. Proof of rape generally requires the confession of the accused or the testimony of four adult Muslim men who witnessed the assault. If a woman cannot prove her rape allegation she runs a very high risk of being charged with fornication or adultery, the criminal penalty for which is either a long prison sentence and public whipping, or, occasionally, death by stoning.

21 BIBLIOGRAPHY

Ali, Shaheen Sardar Ali and Javaid Rehman. *Indigenous Peoples and Ethnic Minorities of Pakistan: Constitutional and Legal Perspectives.* London: Routledge Curzon, 2001.

Bray, Denys. *The Life-History of a Brahui.* Karachi: Royal Book Company, 1977 [1913].

Irons, William and Neville Dyson-Hudson. *Perspectives on Nomadism.* Leiden: E. J. Brill, 1972.

Mills. Margaret A., Peter J. Claus and Sarah Diamond, ed. *South Asian Folklore: An Encyclopedia: Afghanistan, Bangladesh, India, Nepal, Pakistan, Sri Lanka.* New York: Routledge, 2003.

Rooman, Anwar. *The Brahuis of Quetta-Kalat Region.* Memoir No. 3. Karachi: Pakistan Historical Society, 1960.

Swidler, Nina. "Brahui." In *Muslim Peoples: A World Ethnographic Survey,* edited by Richard Weekes. Westport, CT: Greenwood Press, 1984.

—by D. O. Lodrick

BRUNEIANS

PRONUNCIATION: Bru-NYE-uhns
LOCATION: Brunei
POPULATION: 372,360 (2005 estimate)
LANGUAGE: Malay
RELIGION: Islam

1 INTRODUCTION

The official name of Brunei, a tiny oil-rich Southeast Asian nation, is Negara Brunei Darussalam, which means, "The Country of Brunei, Abode of Peace." According to Chinese and Arab records, Brunei existed as early as the 7th or 8th century AD at the mouth of the Brunei River. In the 9th century, Brunei was conquered by the Srivijaya Empire based in Sumatra. By the 13th century, Islam had spread to Brunei. In the 14th century, it was ruled by the Majapahit Empire based in Java. Brunei then became independent and experienced its golden age from the 15th to the 17th centuries when it was a huge empire and controlled the entire island of Borneo as well as parts of the Philippines. During this period, Brunei's fifth sultan, Bolkiah (1473–1521), was famous for his sea exploits and for capturing Manila, while its ninth sultan, Hassan (1605–1619), was known for developing an elaborate court structure that, in part, still exists today.

Brunei then entered a period of decline due to internal problems over succession, which led to civil war, and to external problems in the form of Western colonialism, which resulted in its loss of territory. Brunei lost much territory to the British in Sarawak and Sabah. In the case of Sarawak, in 1839 a British adventurer, James Brooke, helped the Sultan of Brunei quell a rebellion by local chiefs and in return gained land that became the First Division of Sarawak. Brooke soon gained more land from the Sultan—Sarawak's Second Division in 1852 and its Third Division in 1861. His successor, Charles Brooke, obtained further territory for Sarawak at Brunei's expense. For instance, in 1882 Charles purchased Brunei's Baram district, which became Sarawak's Fourth Division, while in 1890 he took Brunei's Limbang district (without the Sultan's permission) and made it the Fifth Division after some chiefs had asked for his help against the Sultan. In the case of Sabah, in 1865, the Sultan of Brunei gave a ten-year lease to Charles Lee Moses who established the American Trading Company. In 1875 this company was purchased by an Austrian Consul, Baron von Overbeck, and his English partner, John Dent. In 1881, Dent bought Overbeck's share in the company and formed the British North Borneo Chartered Company. The same year, the Sultan of Brunei permitted the Company to rule over Sabah. In 1888 Britain made Brunei, Sabah, and Sarawak British Protectorates to prevent the Brooke family or the Company from taking over Brunei. In 1906 Britain established the Residential System in Brunei, whereby a British Resident was to advise the Sultan in all matters except Malay customs and religion. In the 1920s the British discovered oil and natural gas in Brunei and began the extraction of these resources. During World War II the Japanese invaded and occupied all three areas. After the war, Brunei remained a British protectorate and retained a British Resident until 1959 while Sabah and Sarawak became Crown Colonies.

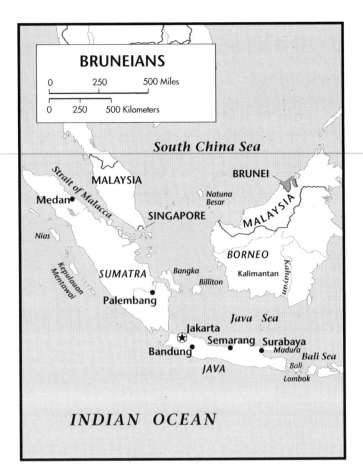

BRUNEIANS

0   250   500 Miles

0   250   500 Kilometers

South China Sea

MALAYSIA

Medan

Strait of Malacca

BRUNEI

Natuna Besar

SINGAPORE

MALAYSIA

Nias

BORNEO

Kepulauan Mentawai

SUMATRA

Bangka

Kalimantan

Billiton

Kahayan

Palembang

Java Sea

Jakarta

Semarang Surabaya

Bandung

Madura

Bali Sea

JAVA

Bali

Lombok

INDIAN OCEAN

In 1959, Sultan Omar Ali Saifuddin introduced the country's first constitution, which made Brunei a self-governing state with Britain still responsible for its foreign affairs and defense. The Sultan was not keen on full independence, preferring instead a British presence. In 1961 he favored federating with the other British territories of Malaya, Singapore, Sabah, and Sarawak, and Brunei to form a larger political unit, the Federation of Malaysia, by 1963. In late 1962, however, he changed his mind about the merger after an armed coup by the Brunei People's Party, led by A.M. Azahari, revealed local opposition to the Federation. The British authorities crushed the armed revolt while the Sultan declared a state of emergency in Brunei. Since then, the Sultan of Brunei has ruled by decree as a non-elected prime minister. In October 1967 Sultan Omar Ali Saifuddin abdicated in favor of his son, Sultan Hassanal Bolkiah. In January 1979 Britain and Brunei signed an agreement declaring that Brunei would become fully independent within five years.

Brunei remained a British protectorate until 1 January 1984 when it attained full independence. On Brunei's Independence Day, Sultan {xe "Bolkiah, Hassanal"} Hassanal Bolkiah proclaimed Brunei's National Philosophy: Melayu Islam Beraja (Malay Islamic Monarchy), which incorporates the Malay language, culture, and customs with Islamic laws and values and with the monarchy system. In 1984 Brunei also joined the Association of Southeast Asian Nations (ASEAN) as the regional body's sixth member. In 1992, when Brunei celebrated the Silver Jubilee of the reign of Sultan Hassanal Bolkiah, the Sultan set up the Sultan Hassanal Bolkiah Foundation as a gift to his people. In 1994 through the Davao Agreement, Brunei

joined Indonesia, Malaysia, and the Philippines to form the East ASEAN Growth Area (BMIP-EAGA) to improve trade between them. In 1998 the Sultan proclaimed his son, Prince Haji Al-Muhtadee Billah, as the Crown Prince.

In 2000 the Sultan began civil proceedings against his brother, Prince Jefri, for misappropriating $16 billion from the Brunei Investment Agency, but the case was later settled out of court. Since 2003 Brunei and Malaysia have held talks over the disputed territory of Limbang, which the Brooke family in Sarawak took from Brunei without permission in 1890. Meanwhile, in September 2004, the Sultan reconvened the 21-member Legislative Council, suspended since 1984, to debate several proposed amendments to the Brunei's Constitution, including the direct election of 15 members to the Legislature. In May 2005 the Sultan reorganized his cabinet, dismissing four prominent ministers and replacing them with new ministers with private sector experience. His other changes included the creation of a new Ministry of Energy and the appointment of the first ethnic Chinese to a cabinet position, Pehin Dato' Lim Jock Seng as Minister of Foreign Affairs II. In September 2005, the Sultan dissolved the existing Legislative Council, which acts as Brunei's Parliament, and appointed 29 new members. As of 2008, no schedule had been established for the holding of elections.

Brunei is an absolute monarchy, with the Sultan serving as Premier, Defense Minister, Finance Minister, and as the religious head of Brunei. The present Sultan is the 29th in a line that dates from Sultan Muhammad, who converted to Islam in 1514. His brother, Prince Mohamed, serves as the Foreign Minister while his son, Prince Haji Al-Muhtadee Billah, serves as the Senior Minister. The Sultan's cabinet is made up of members of his extended family, the Bolkiahs, who control all the government departments and most of the nation's wealth. The Sultan is assisted and advised by his Cabinet, the Religious Council, the Privy Council, and by the Council of Succession.

² LOCATION AND HOMELAND

Brunei is located on the northern coast of the island of Borneo; it lies between the South China Sea and the Malaysian states of Sarawak and Sabah. It is divided by Sarawak into two unconnected parts: a larger western portion and a smaller eastern portion. The western portion contains three of Brunei's four districts—Brunei Muara, with the capital, Bandar Seri Begawan; oil-rich Beliat; and agricultural Tutong—while the eastern portion has the sparsely populated district of Temburong, which is separated from the rest of Brunei by Sarawak's Limbang district.

With a total area of only 2,228 sq mi (5,770 sq km), Brunei is a very small country that is roughly the size of Delaware. Its population centers are mainly along its flat coastal plains. To its west, Brunei has hilly lowlands, and to its east, mountains. Over 70% of Brunei's entire land area is covered by tropical rainforests. The Brunei government has set aside 317 sq mi (820 sq km) as national parks or forest reserves, in part to protect the unique wildlife found in its rainforests, such as the Borneon proboscis monkey, the silvered leaf monkey, and the slow loris, a tree dwelling nocturnal primate. Brunei has an equatorial climate that is hot, humid, and wet all year round. The average daytime temperature is between 79° F and 95° F. Although typhoons, earthquakes, and severe flooding are rare,

Brunei is subject to seasonal haze from forest fires in Indonesia. The country is rich in petroleum, natural gas, and timber.

Brunei has a population of 372,360 (2005 estimate), which is growing by 1.9% annually. Over 75% of the population lives in the urban areas, with 60,000 in Bandar Seri Begawan, the largest city. The Malays, the largest ethnic group, comprise 67% of the population while the Chinese make up 15% and the indigenous groups, including the Ibans, Muruts, Dusuns, and Melayu Tutong, form 6%. The remaining 12% includes European, Asian, and North American expatriates.

³ LANGUAGE

The official language of Brunei is Malay (Bahasa Melayu), which is the primary language of most Bruneians. A common greeting in Malay is *Apa Khabar*? (How are you?). Another typical greeting, particularly among Muslims, is the Arabic *Assalamu alaikum* (May peace be among you), to which the reply is *Wa'alaikum salaam* (And peace be upon you).

English is also widely spoken and used, especially in business settings. Among the Chinese, Mandarin, Hokkien, and other Chinese dialects are commonly used. Each indigenous group in Brunei also has its own language.

⁴ FOLKLORE

One Brunei folktale is the legend of Nakhoda Manis (Sweet Sailor) that tells of how the ship of an unfilial son was turned into a huge rock, known as Jong Batu, in the Brunei River. According to this legend, a widow, Dang Ambon, lived with her son, Nakhoda Manis, in the village of Kampong Ayer until he left home to seek his fortune in the city of Sulu. He eventually gained wealth and success, married a noblewoman, and became the owner of a large ship. He then planned a trip to the Brunei River to visit his mother. Since his mother longed to see him again, she paddled out in a small boat to his ship, shouting that she missed him. However, when the wife of Nakoda Manis saw the mother, she was so disgusted with what she viewed as a very old and poor woman that she demanded that the mother be chased away. Unfortunately, Nakhoda Manis listened to his wife and ordered his crew to push his mother's small boat away. The heartbroken Dang Ambon then cursed her son. Soon thereafter his ship capsized in a storm. After the storm, a huge rock, called Jong Batu, appeared in the Brunei River where Nakhoda Manis had anchored his vessel.

⁵ RELIGION

Brunei's state religion is Islam. The importance of the Islamic religion is clearly seen in Brunei's description of its government as a Malay Islamic Monarchy (Melayu Islam Beraja), with the Sultan serving as the head of the Islamic community. He represents the main ethnic group in the population, the Malays, who are Sunni Muslims and who comprise over two-thirds of the total population. For Muslims in Brunei, Islamic law (Shariah) takes precedence over civil law in a number of areas, including divorce and inheritance. The importance of Islam in Brunei is also seen in the adherence by Muslims to the Five Pillars of Islam: profession of faith that there is no God but Allah and Muhammad is his prophet; prayer five times a day; giving alms to the poor; fasting from dawn until dusk during the holy month of Ramadan; and making a pilgrimage during one's lifetime to Mecca in Saudi Arabia. Under Islamic law, the drinking of alcohol is forbidden as is the eating of pork.

In 1991 the government introduced laws that made the sale of alcohol illegal.

The Sultan encourages the recital of the Holy Quran every morning prior to the start of work to obtain blessing and guidance from God. Every government function and project also incorporates the *Doa*, a very important link to God's blessing. The main mosques in Brunei are the magnificent Omar Ali Saifuddin Mosque, completed in 1958 in classic Islamic style, and the Jame 'Asr Hassanal Bolkiah Mosque, Brunei's largest, built to commemorate the Silver Jubilee of Sultan Hasssanal Bolkiah's reign in 1992.

During the fasting month of Ramadan, all government officers and staff work a six-hour day, instead of the usual seven and a half hour workday, and all entertainment and sports activities are temporarily suspended. Non-Muslims are also encouraged during this period to refrain from eating, drinking, or smoking in public and from wearing clothing that expose their arms or feet.

The other two main religions in Brunei are Buddhism and Christianity, with Buddhists making up 13% of the population and Christians about 10%. Animism is also practiced in Brunei by some of the indigenous groups. The Brunei constitution guarantees religious freedom.

⁶ MAJOR HOLIDAYS

In Brunei, the following are public holidays: New Year's Day on January 1, National Day on February 23, the Royal Brunei Armed Forces Day on May 31, the Sultan's birthday on July 15, Christmas Day on December 25, and Chinese New Year, which follows the lunar cycle. Muslim celebrations, which follow the lunar calendar, are also public holidays. These include Hijrah (Islamic New Year); the Prophet Muhammad's birthday; Hijrah Hari Raya Aidiladha (the Feast of Sacrifice); Isra' Mikraj (the anniversary of Muhammad's ascension); Hari Raya Ed-il-Fitri (the end of Ramadan); Hari Raya Haji (the end of the Haji pilgrimage session); and Nuzul Al-Quran (the anniversary of the revelation of the Holy Quran).

Because the lunar cycle is shorter than the Gregorian calendar year, the Islamic New Year can occur twice in one Gregorian calendar year. For example, in 2008 the Islamic New Year fell on January 10 and on December 29. State-level celebrations accompany the Muslim celebrations.

⁷ RITES OF PASSAGE

One rite of passage is a ceremony called *mandi belawat*, held after a mother gives birth to the couple's first child. During this ceremony the mother and baby wear the *kain jong sarat* (a hand-woven brocade with gold and silver threads) while the guests present the *zikir*, a form of religious chanting, praising the prophet Muhammad. The *zikir* is a traditional welcome used not only for a baby's birth but also to welcome the arrival of a guest of honor at an event or ceremony.

Another rite of passage, a traditional one for Muslim boys, is the circumcision ceremony, which takes place when a boy is between the ages of 9 and 12. Whereas traditional healers used to perform the circumcision, nowadays the circumcision is usually carried out in a hospital. The circumcision is then followed by a family celebration.

Yet another rite of passage is the burial of Muslims after death. According to Muslim tradition, the burial must take place as soon as possible after a person dies. The body is first ritually washed and then wrapped in a white cloth before it is placed in a coffin and transported to the cemetery. For the next three nights, prayers known as *takhil* are offered for the deceased at a family ceremony. In the weeks that follow, these prayers can be repeated by individuals or by groups of mourners. After a death, friends and relatives can offer condolences and money to the deceased's family but never flowers.

There are also rites of passage concerning marriage between Muslims in Brunei. After a Muslim couple decides to marry, several stages precede their wedding ceremony. For example, in the first stage, the members of the prospective groom's family make a formal marriage proposal to the family of the prospective bride. In the second stage, the engagement ceremony (*bertunang*), the groom's mother places the engagement ring on the bride's right hand. In the third stage, as the wedding approaches, the sending of dowries and gifts (*menghantar berian*) takes place. For example, the groom's family gives the bride's family a cash dowry and gifts such as a *kain jong sarat*, shoes, and handbags while the bride's family also gives some gifts in return. In the fourth and final stage before the wedding, the *majlis berbedak* is held separately for the bride and groom where they are given a religious blessing and showered with scented perfume. At this ceremony, family members also place dye on the palms of the bride and groom. The bride wears the *kain jong sarat* and also a floral headdress.

Then the wedding ceremony, or *akad nikah* (the solemnization of marriage vows) is held, usually at the home of the bride. At this ceremony, an *imam* (Muslim religious leader) reads a sermon and officially pronounces the couple as husband and wife. The wedding reception (*bersanding*) follows, with the couple seated on a dais as guests come up to congratulate them. The same evening, the groom's family brings food for the bride's family and the bride and groom feed each other. Three or seven days after the wedding, the groom's family usually brings the couple household items like rice and sugar or appliances like a washing machine or a television. The groom then stays with the bride's family for at least a week before the couple moves out to go to their own place.

8 INTERPERSONAL RELATIONS

When Bruneians meet, they shake hands by lightly touching the hands and then bringing their hands to their chest. Some also shake hands in the Western manner. When meeting with members of the opposite sex, some do not shake hands with them but instead nod, smile, or give a verbal greeting. When a person joins a small group, it is polite to greet each person individually, beginning with the person on the right. In the case of members of the royal family, they are first greeted by a bow and then by a light handshake.

When greeting others, Bruneians usually address them by their given name. In formal situations, however, full names are used. Malay men use their father's name, preceded by their own given name, as in Ahmad bin Ibrahim, with bin denoting "son of". The usual honorific for men is Awang. Malay women also use their father's name preceded by their own name and with a binte in between, to denote "daughter of," as in Fatimah binte Yusof. The usual honorific for women is Dayang.

In formal situations, titles are also used. For example, members of the hereditary nobility have the title *Pengiran* before their name and this title is included when addressing them. Another title is *Pehin*, awarded by the Sultan to commoners

and the equivalent of a life peerage in the United Kingdom. Some men also have the title *Dato*, awarded by the Sultan to male subjects and the equivalent of a knighthood in the United Kingdom. On the other hand, some women have the title *Datin*, awarded by the Sultan to his female subjects and the equivalent of a damehood. For men who have completed the pilgrimage to Mecca, the title *Haji* is used before their name whereas for women who have made the pilgrimage the title *Hajjah* is used before their name.

An important aspect of Bruneian life is visiting friends and neighbors. These visits usually take place without prior notification, although visitors know that they should avoid doing so during the Muslim prayer times. Evening visits usually take place around 8pm after the last prayer for the day. For special occasions like weddings and birthdays, formal invitations are extended. During a visit, guests remove their shoes before entering a home. Among the older generation, male guests often enter before the female guests. The host usually offers a drink of either tea, coffee, or a soft drink, and some snacks in the form of finger sandwiches, cakes, cookies or puddings. When visiting a sick person, gifts are not expected, but some visitors do bring cakes, fruit, or a cash gift for the sick person's family. When receiving food or gifts, only the right hand is used although the left hand may be used for support. When refusing any food that is being offered, it is considered polite to touch the plate lightly with the right hand.

It is considered rude to point with the index finger. Instead, the thumb of the right hand is used, with the four fingers folded beneath it. It is also considered rude to touch another person's head, although an adult may touch a child's head. In conversation, hand gestures are usually not used. However, among close friends and family members, some Bruneians do use some hand gestures.

Before entering a mosque, the shoes must first be removed. In the mosque, the women cover their heads and wear clothing that also covers their knees and arms.

9 LIVING CONDITIONS

Brunei's per capital gross domestic product (GDP), at $33,600 in 2005, is among the highest in Asia. Crude oil and natural gas production account for over half of GDP and more than 90% of exports. Brunei is the third largest oil producer in Southeast Asia and the world's fourth largest producer of liquefied natural gas. The nation has no external debt and the Sultan ranks as one of the wealthiest men in the world. Brunei also has no personal income tax.

Brunei's healthcare system ranks among the best in Asia. Health services are free for Brunei citizens while permanent residents and expatriates pay a nominal charge. The healthcare system is a three-tiered system, with health clinics providing primary care, health centers providing secondary care, and district hospitals providing tertiary and specialized care. Patients requiring very specialized treatment are sent abroad, with expenses for Brunei citizens being borne by the government. Brunei's healthcare system is heavily subsidized by the government and its quality is comparable to any developed country. Private and public hospitals have very modern and up-to-date facilities. Nearly all the villages in Brunei have health centers and children clinics. In remote areas that are not easily accessible, the government provides health care through its Flying Medical Services. The military has its own hospitals to look af-

A young Bruneian girl, wearing a traditional Muslim head-dress, known as a tudong. (AP Images/David Longstreath)

ter the military personnel and their dependents. Since 1970 all major diseases have been eliminated, including malaria, cholera, and smallpox. The Ministry of Health carries out regular immunization programs and has a successful track record in preventative medicine.

Regarding housing, the Brunei government provides its employees with various types of accommodation at a monthly rental that is maintained at a relatively low price. The government also provides its employees with interest-free loans to enable them to build their own home or to buy one that has already been built. There are also national housing schemes of three categories that are open to all eligible citizens: the National Housing Development Program (NHDP), the Landless Indigenous Citizens Housing Scheme (LICHS), and the Land Entitlement and Infill Scheme (LEIS). Under the NHDP, there are five types of houses, each with three to four bedrooms. These houses are located at various housing sites with facilities like schools, community centers, mosques, parks, and playgrounds. The houses cost between $52,000 to $95,000 Brunei dollars, payable within a period of 15 to 30 years. Besides the government housing and the National Housing Schemes, Brunei has private sector housing schemes, such as the Brunei Shell Petroleum Housing Scheme and the Yayasan Sultan Haji Hassanal Bolkiah Scheme.

As for infrastructure, Brunei has two airports—the Brunei International Airport located in Berakas, near Bandar Seri Begawan, and the airport in Anduki, near Seria, used by the Brunei Shell Petroleum Company for its helicopter ser-

vices. The national air carrier is the Royal Brunei Airlines, which operates flights to destinations in Asia, Australia, Europe, and the Middle East. Regarding ports, the main one is Muara, about 28 km from the capital, while other important ones are the smaller Bandar Seri Begawan port and the port at Kuala Belait. There are also ferry services between Brunei and Labuan, Malaysia. There is one railway line, a 19 km railway in Seria operated by the Brunei Shell Petroleum Company. Regarding roads, a major highway is the Muara-Tutong coastal road. There are also several highways linking the districts and the towns and an extensive overland road network that connects Brunei to Sarawak and Sabah. From Brunei, one can also travel, via Sabah and Sarawak, to the Indonesian province of Kalimantan by road, air, or sea.

Brunei has one of the highest rates of car ownership in Southeast Asia, with most families having at least two cars. Drivers drive on the left hand side of the road. Taxis are available and are metered. Water taxis are also available and are unmetered, with fares negotiable. These water taxis are used to get to Kampong Ayer, Temburong District, and to the Malaysian towns of Limbang, Lawas, and Labuan. Bus services operate along selected routes throughout Brunei. Regarding tourist facilities, these are very good but underutilized; there are over 2,500 rooms spread over 30 establishments ranging from guesthouses to the very luxurious Empire Hotel and Country Club.

Most individuals in Brunei own a cellular phone and most households have a landline telephone. Broadband Internet is also widely available. The only local television station is government-owned, but foreign stations are available by satellite. The local television station broadcasts local programs and news as well as programs from the region and from around the world. Brunei has an advanced telecommunications system that offers international direct dialing services to 160 countries through two earth satellite stations. It also has a full range of worldwide telephone, telex, and facsimile facilities.

10 FAMILY LIFE

On the whole, Bruneians have large families. This is especially so among the Malays and the indigenous groups, while the Chinese tend to have smaller families. A generation or so ago, many couples had as many as eight children and relied on help from extended family members to raise their children. Nowadays, however, the trend is towards smaller families as most women now work outside the home. Moreover, although extended families can still be found, in some cases with three generations living together, there are presently many nuclear families as well. Regarding maternity leave, women who work in the public sector receive 56 days of paid maternity leave. Women continue to be mainly responsible for looking after the children and for managing the household. For families who can afford the expense, they employ live-in domestic helpers, mainly from the Philippines or Indonesia, to help with childcare and with the tasks of cooking and cleaning. These live-in domestic helpers are usually given a separate room in the family home.

The family home, in olden days, was a traditional wooden house built on stilts. Now the usual family home is a modern Western style brick house with three to four bedrooms, a living room, and a kitchen. However, some traditional wooden homes can still be found in the rural areas, but with metal roofs, and in Kampong Ayer (Water Village), a residential area of Bandar Seri Begawan, where homes are built on stilts over the Brunei River. Kampong Ayer has been called the world's largest water village on stilts. In fact, about 10% of Brunei's population lives in Kampong Ayer but the wooden houses are now equipped with modern appliances, satellite television dishes, and the latest amenities. Kampong Ayer is almost self-contained, with its own shops, mosques, schools, clinics, and a police station. To get to the mainland, the residents of Kampong Ayer use speedboats. In some parts of Brunei, one can also find many traditional longhouse communities where several families still live in one longhouse.

While family homes among the indigenous, the Malay, and the Chinese may differ in structure, the people of Brunei are one when it comes to their attitudes toward the elderly. They all tend to respect their elders and to care for them when they grow old. Because of this traditional respect for elders, Brunei has very few old folks homes or retirement homes. Many young adults also live with their parents, even after marriage. Arranged marriages have become less common as most of the young people prefer to choose their own spouse. Under Muslim law, unmarried couples are forbidden to date in secluded areas or to be by themselves in empty rooms or houses. Those caught violating these rules are fined by religious officials.

[11] CLOTHING

The people of Brunei wear either traditional clothing or Western-style outfits and are usually smartly dressed. The traditional clothing for women is the *baju kurung*, a loose-fitting outfit consisting of a long blouse and a long skirt. The material used is either cotton, satin, or silk. This outfit is in keeping with the requirement under Muslim law that women wear conservative clothing, with the body to be covered except for the face and hands. Clothing that is revealing is considered immodest and thus socially unacceptable. Most Muslim women also wear a *tudong*, a headscarf that covers their hair.

For men, the traditional clothing consists of a *baju*, a loose shirt with long sleeves, trousers, and a *kain samping*, or short sarong. The *baju* and the trousers are of the same material and color. The *kain samping* is worn over the *baju* and trousers, covering the waist to the knees. The material used for the *kain samping* can vary in quality, with some made from brocade. Some men also wear the traditional Malay headdress, the *songkok*, a brimless hat made of black or blue velvet. For men who have performed the *Haj*, the pilgrimage to Mecca, they wear a white skull cap instead of the *songkok*.

Westernization has impacted traditional dress and costumes in Brunei as Western clothing and other fashions from abroad are popular. For instance, professional women like bankers and lawyers often wear dress suits and other Western business attire while professional men are usually seen dressed in business suits and ties. Moreover, Western clothing like jeans and sports jackets are commonly worn by the young people.

[12] FOOD

For breakfast, along with tea or coffee, Bruneians usually have fried rice, noodles, *soto* (noodle soup), *cucur* (fritters) or sandwiches. For lunch and dinner, the meal revolves around rice, the main staple, which is eaten with chicken, beef, lamb, seafood, or vegetables. Lunch is traditionally the main meal of the day but, with family members having different work and school schedules, they usually sit down to a family meal at dinner time.

For most Bruneians, the traditional way of eating is with the fingers of the right hand although some do use utensils. Popular dishes at mealtime include *pais lauk* (grilled fish), *pais daging* (grilled meat), *lauk rabus* (a sour and spicy fish soup), and *nasi katok* (spiced chicken or beef with rice). These dishes, heavily spiced with garlic, chilies, ginger, and tumeric, are usually accompanied by *sambal belachan* (a spicy shrimp paste). Locals are also fond of *satay*, pieces of marinated meat cooked on skewers, and eaten with a tangy peanut sauce, fresh slices of cucumber and onions, and with *ketupat*, rice filled in pouches made of coconut leaves. A special dish, often referred to as Brunei's national dish, is *ambuyat*, made from the pith of the sago palm. This pith is grated, dried, and emulsified into a starchy paste that is then boiled with water to form *ambuyat*. To eat the *ambuyat*, special joined chopsticks called *chandas* are used to twirl the *ambuyat* like spaghetti around it. The *ambuyat*-coated *chandas* are then dipped into a special *ambuyat* sauce made from salted durian, lemon juice, shrimp paste, and binjai, a mango-like Bruneian fruit. Other side-dishes that traditionally accompany a meal of *ambuyat* include salads, boiled fish in a very hot sauce made from small chilies, and a preparation of ferns, or *pakis*, sautéed with ginger and garlic. One very popular salad is *rojak sotong*, which includes sweet turnip, cucumber, pineapple, and calamari.

Desserts are either fried or steamed and are made from glutinous flour, sugar, coconut and *pandan* (pandanus leaves). The desserts include *kuih talam*, made from sticky rice and *pandan* leaf jelly, and *kuih tako*, made from coconut and *pandan* leaf. A favorite drink is *teh tarik*, a frothy tea prepared from powered local tea-leaves. Other favorite drinks are cool, sweet drinks made from local fruits and spiced with cinnamon and anise. During Ramadan, drinks made from sugar and pandan, like *air selasih* and *air cincau*, are very popular. Local fruits include the durian, the rambutan, and the langsat.

[13] EDUCATION

In Brunei, education begins with preschool, followed by six years of primary education and up to seven years of secondary education. For citizens, education is provided free from the age of five years and is mandatory for nine years. Muslim students who live more than eight kilometers (five miles) from their school are entitled to free accommodation in hostels, free transportation to school, or a subsistence allowance.

The schools are either Malay, English, or Chinese schools as they are classified according to the language of instruction. The Malay schools are public schools. While Malay is the medium of instruction in these schools, English and Arabic are used for certain subjects and Islamic studies form an important part of the curriculum. Students usually attend Islamic classes in the mornings or afternoons. Those who pass the sixth year of religious instruction can enter an Arabic course of study and many choose to go overseas, especially to the Al-Azhar University in Cairo. The private schools mainly use English or Chinese as the medium of instruction. The families of government employees receive educational allowances for sending their children to private schools.

The literacy rate in 2006 was 94.7%. In 1985 the Brunei government established the University of Brunei Darussalam on a sprawling campus overlooking the South China Sea. By 2005 the university had about 3,674 students and over 300 instructors. Another institute of higher learning in Brunei is the Brunei Institute of Technology. However, most of Brunei's college students attend universities abroad and on government scholarships, especially when the fields of study sought are unavailable locally. The most popular destination abroad for higher studies is the United Kingdom although many students also go to the United States, Australia, Malaysia, and Singapore.

14 CULTURAL HERITAGE

Brunei's cultural heritage is derived from the Old Malay World, a region that encompasses the Malay Archipelago. The Malay origins of Brunei's culture are reflected in the country's language, architecture, customs, and ceremonies. Brunei's Malay culture has been impacted by animism, Hinduism, Islam, and by Western influences in the form of colonialism, legal systems, and trade. The most important impact, however, has been Islam, as clearly seen in Brunei's national ideology and philosophy of a Malay Islamic Monarchy, which incorporates Malay culture and the Islamic religion. This national ideology and philosophy is aimed at forging a stronger sense of identity and at fostering unity and stability.

The Brunei government is committed to the preservation of its people's culture, especially the core ethnic Malay and Islamic elements of that culture. In 1975 the government set up the Arts and Handicraft Center as a living testimony to the preservation of Brunei's traditional arts and crafts, such as boat making, bronze tooling, cloth weaving, silver-smithing, wood carving, and basket and mat weaving. Also on display at the Center are Malay weaponry, the Malay art of self defense (*silat*), traditional games, and traditional musical instruments. Some of these cultural artifacts can also be found in the Brunei Museum and in the country's Malay Technology Museum.

At handicraft centers and shops, traditional cloths can be purchased. These cloths include the beautiful gold or silver-threaded material known as *kain jong sarat* and collector textiles called *kain tenunan*. *Jong sarat* is usually worn during weddings and formal occasions. Also on sale are brassware, silverware, bronze items, gongs, and the traditional Malay dagger known as the *kris*. Some of the brassware, silverware, and bronze have been hammered and crafted by hand into attractive trays, jugs, spoons, jewelry boxes, bracelets, and napkin rings.

Brunei's cultural heritage includes its fine collection of Islamic art outside of the Arab world, such as its gilded Holy Qurans, its ceremonial items, and its intricate mosaics that adorn several of its religious monuments.

15 WORK

The government is the largest employer in Brunei, employing more than half of the total labor force, which totaled 180,400 in 2006. About 10% of the labor force is employed in the oil and gas industries. The major sectors in Brunei's economy are oil, natural gas, government, construction, services, retail, and some light manufacturing industries. The light industries include textiles, foodstuffs, mineral water, soft drinks, and cement. In 2003 around 2.9% of the labor force was employed in agriculture, 61.1% in industry, and 36% in services. In 2006 the unemployment rate was 4%.

Because Brunei's small population is insufficient to provide all its manpower needs, the government relies on foreign workers from Malaysia, Thailand, Indonesia, Singapore, Bangladesh, India, and the Philippines. They work mainly in the construction industry. The government carefully regulates the flow of overseas workers into Brunei. Work permits for foreigners are issued for short periods and must be continually renewed. Despite these restrictions, foreigners make up a significant portion of the work force, numbering 60,000 in 1995. The government is trying to reduce the country's reliance on foreign workers and is training more locals in technical and professional fields.

The economy's dependence on oil has made Brunei vulnerable to swings in world oil prices. Since oil reserves are expected to run out in the next 50 years, the government is doing its best to diversify the economy by developing tourism and other industries. Agriculture and fisheries are among the industrial sectors that the government has selected for highest priority in its efforts to diversify the economy as only about 15% of Brunei's land area is cultivated while roughly 80% of its food is imported. The government owns a cattle ranch in Australia and most of its beef supply comes from that ranch, which is larger in size than Brunei itself. The government is also encouraging foreign investments and developing education and human resources.

16 SPORTS

Traditional sports include *silat*, a self-defense sport, and *sepak takraw*, a court game in which players pass a rattan ball using only the head, shoulders, or legs.

Brunei's most popular sport is soccer, which is both widely played and a spectator sport. Another very popular game that is also a spectator sport and widely played is badminton. Other popular sports are indoor soccer (*futsal*), cycling, golf, volleyball, softball, basketball, netball, cricket, and rugby.

Water sports include swimming, sailing, water-skiing, windsurfing, and snorkeling. Swimming pools are found throughout Brunei, for private and public use. Brunei also has several fitness and sports centers and a water sports marina. Other sports include athletics, squash, and horseback riding. Brunei has an assortment of world-class championship-quality golf courses, with some offering floodlit night golfing for cooler play. The Trijaya Equestrian Park has first-class facilities, including horses imported from Argentina, and is the world's largest indoor arena that can accommodate up to 50 horses at a time. It offers classes to all ages and abilities, including polo lessons for adults.

17 ENTERTAINMENT AND RECREATION

For entertainment and recreation, families with young children go to the cinema or theater, or they go on hikes, jogs, or walks through a national park or a forest reserve. One of Brunei's best known attractions is Jerudong Park and Playground, a 57-hectare amusement park in Brunei's capital, with facilities that include an outdoor amphitheatre, a Sky Tower, a roller coaster, a skating rink, a go-kart track, a video arcade, a shooting gallery, and a French carousel for children. Another very popular family-oriented attraction is the Oil and Gas Discovery Center (OGDC), which is in Seria, outside the capital. With its seven galleries that showcase over 100 interactive exhibits, the Center attracts many visitors and is both an educational and recreational landmark.

On weekends, some families enjoy picnics at a swimming pool or at a beach. Karaoke is popular at restaurants and at home, as most families have karaoke machines. Other recreation activities in Brunei include kite-flying, snooker, and bowling. In the case of the young people, many of them enjoy socializing at sidewalk cafes and at shopping malls. For some, going shopping is also a favorite leisure time activity. Shoppers can be found at traditional markets, at tiny boutique shops, or in large shopping malls. The malls include the Yayasan Shopping Complex, the Hua Ho Mall, The Mall, and the Seria Plaza.

18 FOLK ARTS, CRAFTS, AND HOBBIES

In general, Bruneians enjoy music and dance. The government's Ministry of Culture, Youth and Sports sponsors musicians and dancers who perform locally and abroad. Folk arts include traditional Bruneian performances like *Adai-adai*, a song and dance performed by men in fishermen attire, and *Puteri Lela Menchanai*, a musical tragedy about the accidental death of Brunei's fifth Sultan at the hands of his queen.

Among traditional crafts are weaving, silverwork, wood carving, and metalwork. Some of these crafts are taught to the young people in Brunei at a government-sponsored center aimed at preserving Brunei's national heritage.

Hobbies include the playing of traditional musical instruments, such as the gong, the small gongs or *tawak-tawak*, and a type of xylophone known as the *gulingtangan*. These musical instruments are played at wedding ceremonies and family gatherings. Among youth, their hobbies also include contemporary music and dance; these are taught at private studios.

19 SOCIAL PROBLEMS

The Brunei government is concerned about the increase in domestic violence and abuse against women and currently has several pieces of legislation in place to protect women. The government is also concerned about the sexual exploitation and trafficking of women and children and has legislation to deal with these crimes.

There is also some concern about drug use but this is not a major problem. On the whole, Brunei has a very low crime rate, due to government stability and economic prosperity. It also has a very low prevalence of HIV/AIDS (less than 0.1% in 2003) as health care services are very good. Homosexuality is illegal in Brunei.

While race relations between the Malays and the Chinese remain cordial, it needs to be pointed out that it is not easy for the Chinese in Brunei to become citizens. The 1961 Citizenship Law raised the residency requirement for non-indigenous peoples (mainly Chinese) to 25 years, of which 20 years had to be continuous. In 1984, another Citizenship Law raised the residency requirement for non-indigenous peoples to 30 years, of which 25 years had to be continuous. As a result, many Chinese are stateless. Under the country's law, birth in Brunei does not automatically confer citizenship. All seeking citizenship in Brunei have to pass tests on Malay culture, customs, and language.

20 GENDER ISSUES

Males outnumber females in population figures. Males also comprise the majority of scholarship holders and dominate the upper levels of the government echelon although more women have achieved high government positions, including the posts of ministers. Moreover, of the 60 local pilots in the Royal Brunei Airline, only 4 are women. In addition, under Muslim law, women are left less inheritance money compared to men. However, in a marriage, a husband is required to share his earnings with his wife but is forbidden to touch his wife's money.

Females outnumber males at the university level, with nearly two thirds of Brunei University's entering class in the late 1990s being women students. Brunei also has more female than male teachers. Women serve in the armed forces and they have equal opportunities to land and house ownership. The government also emphasizes affordable and equal access to healthcare. In general, women have fair access to jobs across the Sultanate and Brunei does not have gender wage bias issues. In Brunei's public sector, the gender wage gap hardly exists due to the uniform pay scale for men and women. In the private sector, however, men on average earn 28% more than women in all occupations.

The percentage of women in the Bruneian workforce has grown significantly, from 20 % in 1971 to 59 % in 2006. Under Brunei law, women under the age of 18 are not allowed to work at night or on offshore oil platforms. The employment of children below the age of 16 is also prohibited. In the business sector the government's supportive measures for women include the financial assistance schemes through commercial banks, such as the Enterprise Facilitation Scheme, the Micro-Credit Financing Scheme, and the Working Capital Credit Fund. Nearly two-thirds of the beneficiaries of these schemes are women. The main government agency for women's affairs is the Department of Community Development, in the Ministry of Culture, Youth and Sports. This Department is responsible for the protection of women and girls and provides counseling services, welfare allowances, and emergency relief when needed. The Department's programs are strongly supported by the Women's Council of Brunei Darussalam, a non-governmental organization affiliated to the ASEAN Council of Women's Organizations, and by other government agencies and the private sector. Brunei has acceded into the Convention on the Elimination of All Discrimination against Women and is committed to the Beijing Declaration and Platform for Action and other regional and international declarations on gender issues. Brunei's National Registration and Immigration Act allows children of female citizens married to foreign nationals to be accorded Brunei citizenship upon application.

Regarding homosexuality in Brunei, it is frowned upon and considered illegal. As Brunei is a Muslim country, homosexuality can be punished by up to 10 years imprisonment or a fine of 30,000 Brunei dollars.

21 BIBLIOGRAPHY

"Brunei." *Culture Grams World Edition 2008*. Ann Arbor: ProQuest CSA, 2007.

Embassy of Brunei Darussalam. Washington, D.C. www.bruneiembassy.org (June 2008).

Saunders, Graham. *A History of Brunei*. Kuala Lumpur: Oxford University Press, 1994.

U.S. Department of State. "Background Note: Brunei Darussalam." http://www.state.gov/r/pa/ei/bgn/2700.htm (June 2008).

—by P. Sodhy

BUDDHISTS IN SOUTH ASIA

PRONUNCIATION: BOO-dists
LOCATION: Sri Lanka; India; Nepal; Bhutan; Myanmar; all other countries of South Asia; East Asia
POPULATION: 30 million
LANGUAGE: Language of community or region in which they reside
RELIGION: Various sects include Theravāda (Hīnayāna), Mahāyāna, Tantric; also Tibetan Buddhism (Lāmāism)
RELATED ARTICLES: Vol. 4: People of India

¹ INTRODUCTION

Buddhists are believers in the teachings of Gautama Buddha, who was born in the 6th century BC in what is now Nepal. Although his views represented a system of morality or ethics more than a religion, the Buddha founded what was to become one of the world's great religions. Today, there are an estimated 325 million Buddhists in the world. Buddhism is the dominant religion in the countries of mainland Southeast Asia and has a strong presence in East Asia. In South Asia, however, although it is of considerable historical importance, Buddhism has relatively few followers.

The birthplace of Buddhism lies on the Ganges plains in the modern Indian state of Bihar and adjacent areas of Nepal. This is where Buddha lived and died, leaving behind the Sangha ("Order") to continue his work. Buddhism remained a minor sect until the Mauryan Emperor Ashoka was converted in the 3rd century BC. This marked the beginnings of Buddhism as a world religion. Ashoka sent missionaries to the island of Ceylon (Sri Lanka) and converted the entire island to Buddhism. The southern form of Buddhism (Theravada or Hinayana) eventually spread from Ceylon to mainland Southeast Asia and Indonesia. Buddhism also spread northward into Central Asia and from there to China and Japan.

By AD 700, Buddhism had entered a period of decline in much of India, mostly as a result of the revival of Hinduism. The arrival of the Muslims after the 12th century was the death knell for Buddhism in India. Monasteries were destroyed, Buddhist monks were slaughtered, and the survivors fled to safety outside the country. It is one of the great ironies of South Asian history that Buddhism is virtually absent from the land of its birth.

Buddhism in India saw a revival in the late 19th century, with an increased interest in the religion on the part of both Western and Indian scholarship. Buddhists from outside India have campaigned to restore Buddhist sites in India, and post-1947 Indian governments have participated in efforts to preserve that part of the country's cultural heritage. The conversion to Buddhism of "untouchables" seeking to escape the inequalities of the Hindu caste system has swelled the ranks of Buddhists in India in recent years.

² LOCATION AND HOMELAND

Buddhists in South Asia number approximately 30 million people. They are present in all countries in the region, although their greatest concentration is in Sri Lanka. Buddhism is the religion of the Sinhalese people and accounts for 69% (c.14 million people) of the island nation's population. They are distributed throughout the country except in the north, where Hindu Tamils are in the majority.

There are some 11 and a half million Buddhists in India, amounting to a mere 1.1% of the population (Census of India, 2001). Found mainly in central India, many are recent converts to the religion and have been named "neo-Buddhists." Buddhists are also present in the northern mountains that fringe the Indian subcontinent. These are mostly followers of the Tibetan form of the religion, which is also known as Lamaism. Nearly 10% (about 4 million people) of Nepal's population are Buddhists, living mainly in the Kathmandu Valley and the northern mountain areas. Some 75% of the mountain kingdom of Bhutan's over 800,000 people are Buddhists. Buddhists are found in the Indian state of Sikkim and among the Bhutia population of eastern Kashmir. Small Buddhist communities are also found in Bangladesh and the Andaman and Nicobar Islands.

³ LANGUAGE

There is no language specifically identified with Buddhists. Buddha himself used the language of the common people, and the sacred literature of southern Buddhism is written in Pali, a literary language closely related to the language of Buddha's homeland. The scriptures of Mahayana Buddhism, however, use Sanskrit, the classical language of northern India.

Buddhists today use the language of their community or region. Sri Lankan Buddhists speak Sinhala, the language of the Sinhalese people. This is an Aryan language of the Indo-European language family and is closely related to the languages of northern India. Buddhists in Maharashtra speak various Marathi dialects. In the northern mountain belt, however, Buddhists speak languages of the Tibeto-Burmese branch of the Sino-Tibetan language family. They include Lepcha and dialects of Bhutia such as Dukpa in the eastern Himalayas and Ladakhi in Kashmir.

⁴ FOLKLORE

Numerous legends are told about the birth and life of Buddha. Before his birth, Buddha's mother Maya dreamed that four kings raised her to the Himalayas where their wives bathed her and dressed her in heavenly robes. Buddha appeared in the form of a white elephant carrying a silver lotus in his trunk. He circled the queen's bed three times, struck her right side, and entered her womb. Tradition has it that at the birth of the Buddha, the udambara tree (*Ficus glomerata*), which is said to blossom only when a Buddha is born, burst into flower.

Another story tells how the Buddha came to renounce his normal life and begin his search for the truth. Born into a noble family, the Buddha was kept protected from the outside world. However, one day while driving in his chariot, the young prince saw an old man bent with age stumbling down the road. He was struck with sorrow that all things must grow old. At another time, he saw a sick man and felt sad at the thought of the suffering brought on by disease. On a third occasion, he saw a corpse. On a fourth journey, Buddha saw an ascetic, totally at peace with himself, setting out with a begging bowl in search for wisdom. After pondering these signs, the prince left his family, newborn son, home, and possessions to pursue his search for enlightenment.

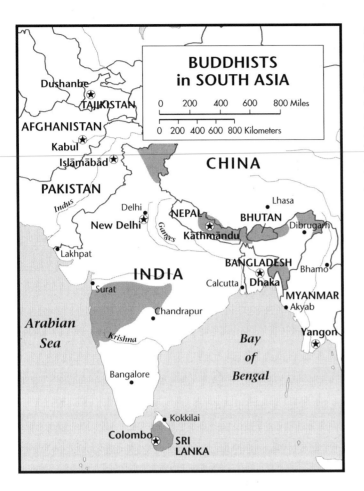

Over the centuries, the relatively simple mythology surrounding the life of Buddha became much more complex. Buddha came to be seen as the seventh in a series of Buddhas, and a popular mythology soon developed around his previous lives. These stories were later gathered in the *Jātakas,* a collection of 550 tales, riddles, and legends about his acts and teachings in past incarnations. In each tale, Buddha appears as a king, or a peasant, an animal, a bird; each story has a moral that elaborates on some Buddhist virtue. Westerners may be indirectly familiar with these stories through Aesop's Fables, which appear to incorporate some of the Buddhist tales.

5 RELIGION

Buddha was born Siddhartha, son of a king and member of the Gautama clan of the Sakya tribe, around 563 BC. His birth place was Lumbini, close to Nepal's border with India. The young prince led a pampered and secluded life, but in his 29th year he left his home to seek enlightenment. He became the student of a number of renowned teachers before rejecting asceticism as the path to salvation. He ultimately found Enlightenment (*Bodhi*) under a pipal tree (*Ficus religiosa*) at Bodh Gaya at the age of 35. From that time, he was honored as the "Buddha" (the Enlightened One). He preached his first sermon in the Deer Park at Sarnath, near Varanasi (Banaras). Buddha died at Kusinagar in Bihar at the age of 80.

There is little evidence to suggest Buddha set out to reform Hinduism, but many of his teachings were in direct contrast to the practices and customs of the Hindus. He rejected the authority of the *Vedas* (the sacred books of the Hindus), the superiority of the Brahmans, and the whole idea of the caste system. He was strongly opposed to ritual, the worship of idols, and particularly the sacrifice of animals. Nonetheless, Buddha's teachings embraced many of the philosophical concepts current in the religions of the time. Although they may be interpreted differently, concepts such as dharma, samsārara, karma, and ahimsā are common to Hinduism and Jainism as well as to Buddhism. In Buddhism, dharma has come to mean the Law, i.e., the teachings of Buddha. Samsara is the cycle of birth–death–rebirth in which we are all caught. Karma relates to the effect of good or bad deeds in life determining the nature of one's rebirths. Ahimsa is the doctrine of noninjury to living things that underlies much of Buddhist behavior.

Buddha taught that people are bound to the Wheel of Existence, an endless cycle of rebirths full of suffering and misery. The only way to obtain total release (*nirvāna*) from this cycle of existence is through the teachings of Buddha. In order to fully appreciate these teachings, certain basic truths have to be understood. These are the Four Noble Truths of Buddhism: 1) life is full of suffering; 2) the cause of suffering, which leads to endless rebirths, is desire; 3) release from suffering can only be achieved by abandoning desire; and 4) the way to stop suffering includes right views and right conduct—honesty, noninjury to living creatures (ahimsa), and forgiveness of enemies. A set of rules known as the Eightfold Path guides the pilgrim on the road to Nirvana, which is the ultimate goal of the Buddhist.

At his death, Buddha left behind the Sangha, the community of monks (*bhikku or bhikshu*), nuns, and laity who had accepted his teachings. The Order grew rapidly in numbers, but Buddhism remained a minor religion until the conversion of Ashoka, the third Mauryan Emperor, around 260 BC. Under his patronage, Buddhism spread throughout the Mauryan Empire, which included nearly the entire Indian subcontinent. Ashoka's newfound beliefs can be seen in the inscriptions he had carved on rocks and pillars throughout his empire. These Edicts of Ashoka were in effect statements of public policy. Their pronouncements included strong support for ahimsa and banned animal sacrifice, regulated the slaughter of animals for food, and even encouraged the creation of hospitals for animals. Ashoka was also responsible for sending Buddhist missionaries to Egypt, Greece, Syria, Malaya, and other countries outside of India. His own son and daughter went to Ceylon, where they converted the island's ruler to the Buddhist faith.

Following Buddha's death, Buddhism soon splintered into numerous sects. A major division is that between *Theravada* and *Mahāyāna* Buddhism. Theravada Buddhism, defined by the *Thera* (Elders) at the First Buddhist Council held c. 483 BC, remains true to the original teachings of Buddha. According to its teachings, there is no God, Buddha was an ordinary mortal who should be revered but not worshipped, and everyone is responsible for working out his or her own salvation. This form of Buddhism, sometimes called "southern" Buddhism, was introduced into Ceylon, and from there spread into Southeast Asia. It is also called *Hīnayāna* Buddhism, the "Lesser Vehicle." Mahayana Buddhism, on the other hand, is derived from a sect that broke away from orthodox Buddhism at the beginning of the 4th century BC. Mahayana, literally the "Greater Vehicle" because it holds that salvation is open to greater numbers, made Buddha divine, surrounded him with angels and spiritual beings, and developed elaborate rituals for worship.

Buddhist monks attend morning prayers at the Kopan Buddhist Monaastery in Kathmandu, Nepal. Kopan Monastery hosts 360 Buddhist monks. (AP Images/David Longstreath)

Mahayana Buddhism also contains the central concept of the *bodhisattva*, the "Savior Buddha," who appears on earth at intervals to guide people on the path to salvation. It was Mahayana Buddhism that was carried northwards over the mountains and along the trade routes of Central Asia to China and Japan.

Two other forms of Buddhism have a presence in South Asia. *Tantrism* is of unknown origins, but it came to influence certain Buddhist (and Hindu) sects, especially in the east of the region. Tantrism is generally associated with occultism, black magic, and perverse sexuality. Tantric Buddhism gives tantric interpretations to Mahayana concepts. Thus "Buddhas" are demoniacal figures, each with their consorts, and forever involved in acts of sexual debauchery with female beings. Elements of Tantric Buddhism have been absorbed into the religion as practiced by the Buddhist peoples of the eastern hills of the Indian subcontinent.

It was a Tantric master that gave form to Buddhism in Tibet, the country located immediately to the north of India and Nepal. Buddhism had reached Tibet in the mid-7th century AD, most likely from Central Asia and China. Towards the end of the 8th century, however, a celebrated Indian Tantric monk was invited to Tibet. He was reputed to have miraculous powers and is credited with subduing the demons and spirits associated with Bon, the indigenous religion of the area. Despite the existing influence of Chinese Buddhism, a council decided that the Indian form of Buddhism should prevail. Tibetan Buddhism represents an intermingling of the sexual-magical Tantric Buddhist cult with Tibetan shamanism. Abandoning the traditional nonviolence of the Buddha, it holds that evil gods and spirits are to be overcome by the superior force of benign powers. The most important rituals are religious dances in which the performers, wearing fearsome and grotesque masks, impersonate the gods and demons. The masks of the gods are intended to strike fear into the hearts of the evil spirits. These so-called "devil dances" form part of all festivals of the Tibetan Buddhists. Tibetan Buddhism is also called Lamaism because of the important of the *lāmās* or spiritual leaders in the religion. It is the form of Buddhism prevalent among groups such as the Lepchas, Bhutia, Sherpas, Tamangs, and other peoples of the Himalayan region.

Although Buddhism spread around the world from its place of origin in South Asia, it did not fare so well in its homeland. At times, under imperial patronage, Buddhism flourished throughout the subcontinent. But by the beginning of the 8th century, Buddhism in India was coming under increasing pressure from a revitalized Hinduism. Although it survived and flourished in northeastern India under the Pala kings, the death-blow came with the Islamic conquest of India following the 12th century. Muslims killed Buddhist monks, burnt their books, and destroyed their monasteries and centers of learning. Although Buddhism survived in Ceylon and in the mountain periphery, it was virtually annihilated in the heartland of the Indian subcontinent.

It is unlikely that Buddhism will ever again achieve its position of former prominence in India. However, two separate events have stimulated the expansion of Buddhism in the country since the mid-20th century. Dr. B. R. Ambedkar, author of the Indian Constitution and himself a member of an untouchable Hindu caste, announced his conversion to Buddhism in 1956. He recommended this as a means for the entire community of "untouchables" in India to escape the social and economic inferiority imposed on the lower castes by the Hindu caste system. Mass conversions occurred largely among two low-caste groups, the Mahars of eastern Maharashtra, and the Jadavs of Uttar Pradesh.

The second event that contributed to the modern Buddhist revival in India occurred in Tibet. From the mid-17th century, Tibet had been a theocracy, that is, its political ruler was also its religious leader. This figure was the Dalai Lama, the spiritual leader of the Tibetan Buddhists. For centuries, Tibet was in effect an independent country. In 1950, however, China invaded Tibet in support of its historical claim to the region. Resentment at Chinese attempts to undermine Buddhism led to an unsuccessful uprising by the Tibetan people. This was suppressed with considerable brutality by the Chinese Army, and in 1959 the Dalai Lama and some 100,000 of his followers fled to India. The Dalai Lama remains in exile in India. His presence, along with the Tibetans who have settled at Dharmsala, Kalimpong, Delhi, and other locations, has given added impetus to Buddhism in northern India.

The "Tibetan" issue has continued to fester since 1959. In 1995, for instance, the Dalai Lama in exile in India, with the help of Chatrel Rimpoche, the abbot of Tashilhumpo monastery (Xigaze, Tibet), named Gedhun Choekyi Nyima, aged six, as the new Panchen Lama. The Panchen Lama is the second highest ranking Lama after the Dalai Lama in the Gelugpa sect (also known as the Yellow Hat sect) of Tibetan Buddhism (the sect that controlled Tibet from the 16th century until the Seventeen Point Agreement established Chinese hegemony over Tibet in 1951). The successive Panchen Lamas form a tulku (reincarnation lineage) and are said to be incarnations of Amitabha Buddha. The name, Panchen Lama, meaning "great scholar," is a Tibetan contraction of the Sanskrit pandita (scholar) and the Tibetan chenpo (great). In November of the same year, the Religious Affairs Office of China, in a bid to weaken the authority of the Dalai Lama, chose another six-year-old boy, Gyaincain Norbu, citing special ritual reasons. After this recognition, the little Gedhun Choekyi Nyima was apparently kidnapped by police and disappeared and has not been seen since. The Chinese authorities say "he is well, living with his family and does not want to be disturbed." In March 2008, prior to the Olympic Games in Beijing, and coinciding with the 49th anniversary of the 1959 uprising in Tibet against China, violence erupted again in Tibet. Activists claimed over 100 protestors, mainly Buddhist monks, were killed and 1,000 arrested by the Chinese authorities. They sought to use the occasion of the Olympics to protest China's "occupation" of Tibet. Protests and violence marred the carrying of the Olympic torch through the streets of London, Paris, and San Francisco, as supporters of Tibet rioted, and calls were made for world political leaders to boycott the Opening Ceremonies of the Games in Beijing in August 2008. In April 2008, however, the Dalai Lama announced his envoys would be willing to meet with the Chinese authorities to discuss Chinese-Tibetan relations and the meetings commenced at the beginning of May.

Popular forms of worship reflect differing Buddhist traditions as well as regional cultures, but there are two practices common to Buddhism wherever it is found. The first is veneration of the Buddha, or Buddha-like figures such as the bodhisattvas. The second is the support of monks by the lay Buddhist community. Other than this, Buddhists in different areas of South Asia have their own forms of religious practice. Tibetan Buddhism, with its distinctive monasteries, use of prayer wheels and prayer flags, mantras, and colorful festivals has quite a different feel from the more austere Theravada Buddhism of Sri Lanka, and both differ from the Buddhism of the hill tribes of eastern India or the neo-Buddhists of central India.

If religious customs vary among lay Buddhists in South Asia, the life of the monk is much more structured. The rules and responsibilities of life in the monastery are clearly defined. Initiation ceremonies for novices, the rites for ordination of monks, the custom of retreat during the rainy season, and other monastic practices are all set down in the Buddhist texts.

Pilgrimage is an important part of Buddhist religious life in South Asia. A pilgrimage may be undertaken for any number of reasons ranging from a desire for spiritual fulfillment to redeeming a pledge made at a time of sickness or misfortune. Lumbini, Bodh Gaya, the Deer Park at Sarnath, and Kusinagar—the places where the four great events in the Buddha's life occurred—are the most sacred pilgrimage centers. Buddhists from around the world make the journey to visit these sites. Many Buddhist groups from outside South Asia have built temples and established educational centers at these locations. There are many Buddhist holy places in Sri Lanka, the most important being Kandy, where the Tooth Relic of the Buddha is kept, and Anuradhapura, where an offshoot of the original *bo* tree under which Buddha found Enlightenment still grows.

⁶ MAJOR HOLIDAYS

For Buddhists, Buddha Purnima (the full moon day that falls in the month of Vaisakha [May]) is a thrice sacred day. It is celebrated as the anniversary of Gautama Buddha's birth; it is on this day that Buddha received Enlightenment under the pipal tree at Bodh Gaya; and it is also the day on which Buddha attained Nirvana. The festival is described by the Chinese traveler Fa-hsien, who visited India in the 5th century AD, and it has changed little from ancient times. It is marked by continuous recitation from the Buddhist scriptures and the worship of the statue of Buddha, with offerings of incense, candles, flowers, and fruits. Fruits and clothes are distributed to the sick. The Bodhi tree, the tree under which Buddha attained Enlightenment, is also worshipped and its branches decorated with garlands and colored flags. Oil lamps are placed around the tree, and milk and scented water are sprinkled on its roots. Large numbers of pilgrims gather at the four sites where the great events of Buddha's life occurred to participate in the celebrations.

Other festivals commemorate Buddha's sermon in the Deer Park (Wheel of Law Day), the end of the Bhikshu Vassa (the three-month period during the rainy season when monks are confined to their monasteries), and Magha Purnima, the full moon day in February when Buddha announced the time of his impending death. Madhu Purnima is observed by offering honey (*madhu*) to Buddha and to monks in the monasteries. This celebrates the occasion when, according to the Buddhist scriptures, Buddha was presented with honey by a monkey while staying in a forest.

Every June a major festival is held at Hemis Gompa (monastery) near Leh, the capital of Ladakh in India, to honor the birthday of the monk who founded Lamaism in the 8th century AD.

⁷ RITES OF PASSAGE

Buddhists follow the practices of local cultures in their birth rituals. It is customary among some Buddhist groups for boys to enter a monastery for a short time on reaching puberty. They shave their heads, don the saffron robes, and lead the life of a novice before returning to normal life.

Buddhists in South Asia follow the basic customs of the region in their death rites, with bodies being cremated on a funeral pyre. The Buddhist scriptures tell how the Buddha's ashes were dispersed and entombed in *stūpas* across the land. In the northern mountains, however, where wood is scarce, it is the custom to expose bodies to be consumed by vultures and wild animals. Important figures in Lamaistic Buddhism, such as the Dalai and Panchen Lamas, are entombed in stupas in attitudes of meditation. In Tibetan monasteries, a sacred text known as *The Tibetan Book of the Dead* is sometimes read to dying monks. It is believed that the last thoughts in one's mind before death are of significance.

⁸ INTERPERSONAL RELATIONS

Buddhists follow local forms of greetings and visiting customs.

⁹ LIVING CONDITIONS

The living conditions of lay Buddhists reflect those of the culture and society to which they belong. Monks and nuns reside in monastic communities known as *vihāras* in India or *gompas* in Tibetan Buddhism.

¹⁰ FAMILY LIFE

Buddhist society reflects the kin system, family structure, and marriage customs of specific ethnic communities or of the dominant regional culture.

¹¹ CLOTHING

Buddhist monks and nuns shave their heads and dress in simple saffron (yellow) robes when they join the monastic order. Tibetan Buddhist monks wear a coarse red outer robe, and on ceremonial occasions they wear elaborate headdresses. In lay society, Buddhists adopt local forms of dress.

¹² FOOD

Food habits of Buddhists in South Asia reflect regional dietary patterns, subject to the specific restrictions imposed by their religion. However, Buddhist dietary laws and practices lack unity and show considerable variation from place to place. Many Buddhists are strict vegetarians out of respect for the ahimsa principle and reluctance to take animal life. But even Buddha himself taught that fish and meat could be eaten if the animal were not killed specifically for one's consumption (Buddha

is thought to have died after eating tainted pork). Thus in Sri Lanka, the Sinhalese Buddhists object to the slaughter of animals or the raising of livestock for food, yet many eat beef. By contrast, tribes in the eastern hills of India, though nominally Buddhist, make offerings of chickens, goats, and even pigs to deities and local spirits and eat the flesh of the sacrificed animals. Similarly, Buddhists in the western Himalayas avoid fish and even view fishing as sinful, while Buddhists elsewhere have no prejudices against eating fish.

¹³ EDUCATION

Education is important in Buddhism, and monasteries have always been centers of learning and religious education. In lay society, Buddhists mirror the educational standards of their specific communities. Thus, literacy rates vary from among the highest in South Asia (over 90% in Sri Lanka) to the lowest (15%) among the Chakmas of Bangladesh and other hill tribes of eastern India.

¹⁴ CULTURAL HERITAGE

Buddhists have a rich heritage of literature and art in South Asia. The Pali canon, the sacred literature of Theravada Buddhism, was set down between 350–90 BC. In addition to discussions of philosophy, it covers subjects ranging from the rules of monastic discipline to the ethical teachings of the Jataka stories. The best known of this collection of texts is the Dhammapada, the "Law-Path." The Dīpavamsa and the Mahāvamsa are later Pali works chronicling the history of Buddhism in Sri Lanka. Mahayana scriptures are presented as a series of dialogues and sermons (*sūtras*) delivered by Buddha himself. There are many hundred sū⁻tras, most originally written in Sanskrit and translated into Tibetan, Chinese, and other Asian languages.

Buddhist architecture flourished centuries before the oldest known Hindu temples were built. The first Buddhist monuments were stupas–massive, hemispherical funeral mounds built to hold the relics of the Buddha. Stupas, though of a later date, are found today at Sarnath, Sanchi, and other Buddhist sites. The Buddhist sculptures at Bharhut, Sanchi, and Bodh Gaya (all dated c.185–80 BC) are among the earliest in South Asian art. Buddhist frescoes at the Ajanta caves, along with the rock art at Sigiriya in Sri Lanka, are regarded as outstanding examples of early South Asian painting. The unique sculptures of Gandharan art represent a blending of Western influences with Buddhist traditions. In Sri Lanka, a Buddhist heritage extending unbroken for over two millennia is seen in the island's numerous monasteries, temples, and sculptures. The huge statue of the reclining Buddha (14 m or 46 ft long) at Polonnaruwa is one of the highest achievements of Sri Lankan art.

Buddhism has influenced many other aspects of life in the region. Buddhists kept the first systematic historical records in India. Three of India's greatest rulers (Ashoka, Kanishka, and Harsha) were Buddhist, and many early political and administrative systems have their origins in Buddhist democratic assemblies. The Buddhist universities at Nalanda and Taxila were ancient centers of learning in India. Buddhism has also had a profound influence on Hinduism, which adopted Buddhist practices in a struggle for the allegiance of the common people. Concepts such as nonviolence (ahimsa) and prohibitions against meat-eating and drinking liquor are Buddhist rather than Hindu in origin. Although Buddhism is virtually absent from South Asia today, South Asian civilization cannot be fully understood without an appreciation of the contributions of Buddhism and the Buddhists.

15 WORK

Belief in ahimsa, though not carried to the same extreme as in Jainism, prohibits Buddhists from occupations related to the killing of animals for food. Thus Buddhists do not become butchers, and some even object to the raising of livestock for slaughter. Beyond this, and some restrictions relating to anti-fishing sentiments among some groups, Buddhist laity are free to engage in the full range of activities offered by the economies of South Asia.

16 SPORTS

There are no sports unique to Buddhists.

17 ENTERTAINMENT AND RECREATION

There are no forms of entertainment or recreation associated specifically with the Buddhist community.

18 FOLK ART, CRAFTS, AND HOBBIES

While there are no folk arts that can be termed "Buddhist," there are Buddhist (and non-Buddhist) artisans who produce items having religious symbolism for sale. These include the thankas (painted scrolls) and prayer wheels of Tibetan Buddhism, masks used for "devil-dancing," and metal and stone statues of the Buddha.

19 SOCIAL PROBLEMS

Given the nature of Buddhism in South Asia today, it makes more sense to talk about individual Buddhist communities rather than Buddhists in general. Each community exists in its own cultural setting and each has its own set of problems. For the most part, these are political and social in nature rather than stemming directly from religion. In Sri Lanka, for example, Buddhism is symbolic of the island's Sinhalese majority. It is fear and resentment of the cultural dominance of this group that has led to the Hindu Tamil uprising in the north of the island. The problems of the Chakmas of eastern Bangladesh exist not because they are Buddhists, but largely because they are a non-Muslim tribal minority that is fighting to retain its identity and some of its traditional freedoms. The Tibetan refugees in northern India fled what was a concerted attempt on the part of the Chinese to stamp out the authority of Buddhism in Tibet. Although accepted by India, they remain exiles in a foreign land.

Dr. Ambedkar, a member of the Mahar community (a Hindu Untouchable group), converted to Buddhism in 1946 and gave rise to what have been called "neo-Buddhists" i.e. low caste Hindus who converted to Buddhism to escape the strictures of the Hindu caste system. On the occasion of his conversion, Ambedkar repeated what he had been saying for years: that only conversion could really change the social status of the lowest castes. However, unlike many of his followers, Ambedkar did not convert to Buddhism merely because he found it socially useful. He had studied Buddhism and did believe that it was the most rational and humane religious tradition, the best for all human beings, untouchables and touchables alike. He consequently rejected "opportunistic" conversions to Islam and Christianity, not merely because he considered these religions a threat to India (on this point, he is supported by the Hindutva spokesmen), but because he considered these religions inferior to the humanism and rationalism of Buddhism. An additional reason for his choice of Buddhism was his highly unlikely belief that Buddhism, an elite religion thriving on patronage, had been the original religion of the Dalits. In Ambedkar's view, the Dalits should not seek a new religion but return to their original religion.

Today, there are about 10 million neo-Buddhists in India, most of them from Ambedkar's own Mahar caste and related Scheduled Castes. Occasionally, local mass conversions to Buddhism still occur in these communities. Buddhist sources claim that, in 2006, over 300,000 Dalits in central India converted to Buddhism on the occasion of the 50th anniversary of Ambedker embracing the religion, though one suspects this number is exaggerated. Unlike the Dalai Lama, who emphasizes the close tied between Hinduism and Buddhism before his Indian hosts, the Ambedkarite tendency in Buddhism is overtly anti-Hindu and tries to maximize the separateness of the religion.

The problems of the neo-Buddhists are of a different nature than those of other Buddhists in India. With no local historical roots, and isolated from contact with the broader Buddhist community, they lack the traditional structures of Buddhist society. There is, for example, a scarcity of Buddhist monks to perform religious functions. As a result, it is common for leading members of the community to officiate at marriages and other ceremonies. One might reasonably expect neo-Buddhist society to develop along slightly different lines, with monks playing a less important role than in other Buddhist communities. This will only add to the diversity that characterizes Buddhism in South Asia today.

20 GENDER ISSUES

Theoretically, in Buddhism, women are treated as equal to men and so gender issues should be absent from Buddhist societies, as claimed by women's groups in Bhutan. There are, for example, Buddhist nuns, but in Sri Lanka there is strong opposition to the idea of full ordination for women from conservative monks. Indeed, after the schism of Buddhism between Māhāyāna and Hīnayāna Buddhism, discrimination against women became entrenched in the latter. For instance, in Hinayana Buddhism, a woman cannot attain full Buddhahood. Such attitudes originate essentially in the views of Hinduism towards women.

Thus, the place of Buddhist women in society varies considerably throughout South Asia and is determined largely by the individual group among which a woman lives. Women in Hinayana societies, such as that prevalent in Sri Lanka, are seen as somewhat inferior to men, whereas in the Mahayana Buddhism prevalent in the north, such discrimination is not so overt. Women in Buddhist societies in India, such as newly converted low-caste groups, are strongly affected by traditional Hindi attitudes towards women and tend to occupy the role of inferior citizens so typical of Hindu societies. Poverty and lack of education remains the key to the role of Buddhist women in society.

Several states governed by the Hindu nationalist party, the Bharatiya Janata Party (BJP), have introduced laws to make conversions of low caste Hindus to Buddhism difficult. The states of Rajasthan, Madhya Pradesh, and Tamil Nadu have all passed laws restricting conversions. Gujarat has reclassified Buddhism and Jainism as branches of the Hindu religion, in an attempt to prevent conversions away from Hinduism eroding the BJP's bedrock support. Officially, caste discrimination was outlawed when India gained independence in 1947, but many of the country's Dalits say that people's attitudes towards them remain the same.

21 BIBLIOGRAPHY

Bailey, Greg and Ian Mabbett. *The Sociology of Early Buddhism.* Cambridge: Cambridge University Press, 2004.

Basham, A. L. *The Wonder That Was India: A Survey of the Culture of the Indian Subcontinent Before the Coming of the Muslims.* London: Sidgewick & Jackson, 1963.

Conze, Edward. *Buddhist Thought in India: Three Phases of Buddhist Philosophy.* Ann Arbor, MI: University of Michigan Press, 1962.

Gengnagel, Jörg, Ute Hüsken and Srilata Raman. eds. *Words and Deeds: Hindu and Buddhist Rituals in South Asia.* Wiesbaden, Germany: Harrassowitz, 2005.

LaFleur, William R. *Buddhism: A Cultural Perspective.* Englewood Cliffs, N.J.: Prentice-Hall, 1988.

Lamotte, Etienne. *History of Indian Buddhism: From the Origins to the Saka Era.* Trans. Sara Webb-Boin. Louvain (Belgium): Catholic University of Louvain, 1988.

Ling, Trevor. *Buddhist Revival in India: Aspects of the Sociology of Buddhism.* New York: St. Martin's Press, 1980

Ray, Himanshu Prabha. *The Winds of Change: Buddhism and the Maritime Links of Early South Asia.* Delhi: Oxford University Press, 1994.

Uekii, Masatoshi. *Gender Equality in Buddhism.* New York: Peter Lang, 2001.

—by D. O. Lodrick.

BUGIS, MAKASSARESE, AND MANDARESE

PRONUNCIATION: BOO-gheez, muh-KAHSS-uh-reez, and MAHN-duh-reez
ALTERNATE NAMES: Buginese, Bugis-Makassarese, Mandar
LOCATION: Indonesia (Sulawesi)
POPULATION: Bugis (5 million); Makassarese (2 million); Mandarese (0.5 million).
LANGUAGE: Buginese; Makassarese; Mandarese; Makassar Malay
RELIGION: Islam (Sunni Muslim)
RELATED ARTICLES: Vol. 3: Indonesians

1 INTRODUCTION

Although the majority gains their livelihood from wet-rice cultivation, the Muslim peoples of Sulawesi's southwestern peninsula have long been renowned throughout the Indonesian archipelago as seafarers, whether as shipbuilders, traders, pirates, mercenaries, or migrants. While the Bugis, Makassarese, and Mandarese speak mutually unintelligible languages, they otherwise share so much in common that Indonesians often speak of one "Bugis-Makassar" ethnic group.

Austronesian-speaking agriculturalists entered Sulawesi from the Philippines about 4,000 years ago. In comparison with regions farther west, Indian civilization made little impact on early Sulawesi cultures, although pre-Islamic graves full of Chinese, Siamese, and Annamite porcelain attest to a bustling trade at this stopover on the route to the spice-rich Moluccas. First referred to in 14th century Javanese writings, the first kingdoms were founded on control of iron mines in eastern Luwu. Over the next three centuries, local rulers transformed village confederations into monarchies, basing claims to divine ancestry on possession of *arajang*, regalia believed to have descended from heaven.

Two of these kingdoms, Makassarese Gowa and Tallo, joined to form a power whose hegemony in the early 17th century extended far beyond the peninsula to coastal states in eastern Kalimantan, eastern Sulawesi, and the Lesser Sundas. Its capital, the fortified port city of Makassar, attracted Portuguese, Spanish, English, and Danes as well as Malays, Gujeratis, and Chinese eager to circumvent the monopoly that the Dutch East India Company (VOC) was then attempting to impose on the Moluccan spice trade. These widened contacts introduced South Sulawesi to Islam; Luwu converted in 1603, Gowa-Tallo two years later, and the other Bugis kingdoms shortly thereafter, upon being defeated by the Makassarese.

In 1615, Sultan Alauddin of Gowa replied thus to VOC envoys: "God made the land and the sea: the land He divided among men and the sea He gave in common. It has never been heard that anyone should be forbidden to sail the seas." The VOC succeeded in crushing this greatest obstacle to its monopoly only in alliance with Arung Palakka, a nobleman from the Bugis kingdom of Bone, who was able to gather a great army of Bugis resentful of Gowa dominance. As a VOC city rose on the ruins of Sultan Hasanuddin's capital, and power in the peninsula shifted to Bone, many Makassarese and Wajo Bugis found refuge elsewhere in the archipelago, the former fighting along-

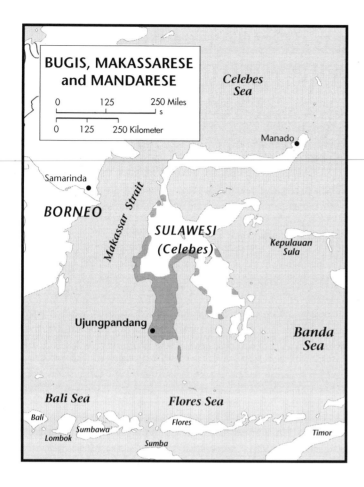

BUGIS, MAKASSARESE
and MANDARESE

0	125	250 Miles

0	125	250 Kilometer

*Celebes
Sea*

Manado

Samarinda

BORNEO

Makassar Strait

*SULAWESI
(Celebes)*

*Kepulauan
Sula*

Ujungpandang

*Banda
Sea*

Bali Sea

Flores Sea

Bali

Sumbawa

Flores

Lombok

Sumba

Timor

try with comparably dense populations and high incidences of poverty, such as Java and Bali. South Sulawesi has experienced a disproportionate amount of the collective violence occurring in Indonesia during the final years of the Suharto regime and immediately after and ranked third in number of incidents of inter-group or village brawls (132 in 1990-2003, compared to 193 for Central Java), as well as high in incidents of vigilante "popular justice" violence. The rioting that destroyed much of the Chinese section of Ujungpandang/Makassar in September 1997 as the Asian/global emerging markets financial crisis was making itself felt in Indonesia is only the most infamous example.

² LOCATION AND HOMELAND

The topography of Sulawesi's southwestern peninsula ranges from the precipitously rising limestone mountains of the north to a broad plain in the center (its lakes are the remnants of a shallow sea) to a volcanic range in the south. December and January bring the heaviest monsoon rains, while the hottest and driest season runs from June to August. The 1.5 million Makassarese (Indonesia's thirteenth largest ethnic group) reside along the mountainous southernmost coast of the peninsula, on Selayar and other offshore islands, and on a bit of fertile lowland north of Makassar city. The 5 million Bugis (the country's eighth largest ethnic group) live to their north, stretching as far as the northern highlands and farming the peninsula's lowland midriff, eastern Indonesia's greatest rice-bowl (while linguistically closer to the Sa'dan Toraja, the Massenrempulu of the northern highlands and the Luwu at the head of the Gulf of Bone are usually classified as Bugis due to their adherence to Islam). The Mandarese (500,000) occupy the mountainous westward bulge of the island, comprising half of the population of the new province of West Sulawesi (separated from South Sulawesi in 2004).

In addition, Bugis communities (and to a lesser extent Makassarese) can be found scattered along the shores of eastern Indonesia's islands; they have traveled as far as the Philippines, Sri Lanka, and northern Australia and have settled in Sumatra, Malaya, and in the cities of Java. According to the 2000 census, Bugis, 42% of their ancestral province of South Sulawesi constitute the second largest ethnic group in the following provinces: 19% in Southeast Sulawesi; 14% in Central Sulawesi Tengah; and 18% in East Kalimantan Timur. An opposite movement has recently affected Luwu and Polewali Mamasa (directly east of the Mandar region): transmigrants from Java, Bali, and Lombok have compounded ethnic diversity in those areas. Makassar has long been a multiethnic city (the city's official name from 1971 to 1999, "Ujungpandang," recognized this reality); in addition to Makassarese, Bugis, Mandar, and Toraja, its population includes Chinese, Javanese, Minahasans, Ambonese, and representatives of virtually every group in eastern Indonesia.

³ LANGUAGE

Buginese, Makassarese, Mandarese, and Sa'dan Toraja constitute a discrete group of closely related Austronesian languages. Regionally prestigious, Bugis has over 500,000 second-language speakers, and Makassarese has over 400,000 (this does not include the many ethnic Chinese in Makassar for whom Makassarese is the first language). As its lingua franca, the multiethnic city of Makassar has long had its own dialect of

side other enemies of the Dutch and the latter founding dynasties as far away as Johor and Selangor on the Malay peninsula.

Outside of the VOC strongholds at Makassar and along the south coast, Dutch colonial rule came to South Sulawesi only in the first decades of the 20th century after a series of hard-fought wars from 1824 to 1906 (the last Mandar resistance ended in 1916). After 30 years of stability, Sulawesi again changed hands, falling under the administration of the Japanese Navy from 1942 to 1945. Although the nationalist movement had only the shallowest of roots there, a very effective guerrilla movement sprang up to fight the bloodiest Dutch counter-revolutionary campaign in the whole archipelago. However, even after the Dutch puppet-state of "East Indonesia," based in Makassar, dissolved itself on 17 August 1950, local strongmen who had seized power in the previous years of chaos were reluctant to move aside for the central government, and the central government in turn alienated much of the population by deflating hopes for an Islamic state and local autonomy. In July 1950, Kahar Muzakkar, a modernist Muslim leader and a revolutionary activist, launched a rebellion against the Jakarta government that only ended upon his death in 1965.

Under Suharto's New Order regime (1965–1998), economic development resumed in South Sulawesi, and a new commercial elite emerged to join bureaucrats, military officers, university graduates, and Islamic religious leaders in replacing the aristocracy that had lost power with the coming of the Indonesian independence. Despite the real progress made, South and West Sulawesi continue to lag behind parts of the coun-

Malay, distinguishable from the now-common Bahasa Indonesia by, among other features, its use of Makassarese sentence-final particles (e.g., for "One only," "*Satu ji*" instead of the standard "*Satu saja*").

Reflecting Islam, personal names generally are Arabic in origin. Family names are not used.

⁴ FOLKLORE

Running to thousands of pages, the Bugis epic *I La Galigo,* the greatest repository of the pre-Islamic mythology common to all the peoples of South Sulawesi (including the Sa'dan Toraja), recounts the adventures of the *Tomanurung,* beings descended from heaven whom South Sulawesi's kings claimed as ancestors. The epic begins with Batara Guru, the eldest son of the principal god of the upperworld, descending through a bamboo tube to eastern Luwu, then creating the earth's flora and fauna. After he completes a 15-day fast, other heavenly beings join him to cultivate the earth, and his cousin, a princess of the underworld, emerges from the sea to marry him. The rest of the epic focuses on six generations of his descendants, beginning with his son Sawerigading who, unable to consummate his love for his twin sister, embarks on adventures in the upper, middle, and lower worlds, finally gaining the hand of the princess We Cudai'. They have a son, La Galigo, whose exploits in love and war occupy most of the remaining narrative.

⁵ RELIGION

Virtually all Makassarese, Bugis, and Mandarese adhere to Sunni Islam. These peoples are considered among the strongest believers of any in the archipelago, comparable in devotion to the Acehnese and the Minangkabau. Although Muslim Malay traders had sojourned in the peninsula's port since at least the 15th century, tradition attributes Islam's initial propagation to Minangkabau holy men arriving at the beginning of the 17th century.

Islam as practiced in South Sulawesi often includes elements of the pre-Islamic religion: offerings to ancestors and spirits of the sea, earth, and rice (an homage rendered also to Muslim saints); healing, agricultural, house-, and boatbuilding rituals; the care of *saukang* (supernaturally charged places); even a (now almost entirely vanished) transvestite priesthood *(bissu)* to care for the *arajang* regalia and perform oracles. In the 20th century, modernist Muslims, who considered many of the local traditions idolatrous, have worked with considerable success to eliminate them. However, pre-Islamic religious traditions are still observed by the To Lotang of Sidenreng (the government has classified their beliefs as Hinduism) and the Amma Towa of Bulukumba (who defend their identity as Muslims).

⁶ MAJOR HOLIDAYS

See the article entitled **Indonesians**.

⁷ RITES OF PASSAGE

Getting married among the Bugis and Makassarese entails the following steps. The man's family pays a formal visit to the woman's family to sound out the possibility of a union. If a proposal can be made, the man's family sends a representative to negotiate the bride-price, a wedding date, wedding expenses, and feast arrangements. After this, the wedding can be announced to all the kin of both sides. On the wedding day

itself, the groom with a procession of kin, young and old, male and female, arrives at the bride's house bearing the bride-price, women's clothing, and different kinds of food. Then, the wedding ceremony itself follows. For the reception, guests are invited inside the house; they give presents or money (formerly, paddy fields, gardens, or livestock) as a kind of competition between the bride's and groom's sides. A few days after the wedding, the new couple visits first the groom's family and then the bride's, giving out presents to all family members. The couple stays with the bride's parents before setting up their own household.

If the woman's family refuses the man's proposal or sets the wedding expenses too high (a kind of subtle refusal), the couple may elope. The elopement causes the woman's family to lose face, and her male kin might pursue and kill the man, if they catch him. The man seeks the protection of a powerful person who will try to assuage the anger of the woman's side. If the woman's family shows signs of accepting the union after all, the man's family takes the initiative to make a reconciliation meeting.

For additional information on rites of passage, *see* the article on **Indonesians**.

⁸ INTERPERSONAL RELATIONS

The central value governing interpersonal relations is *siri',* a powerful sense of face that demands that the individual or the group strive as hard as possible to win prestige as well as uphold honor at all costs, even going as far as dying in the attempt to kill offending parties.

Traditional society distinguished three classes: nobility ("descendants of kings"); commoners ("freemen"); and slaves (war captives, violators of custom, and those selling themselves to pay debts). In the 20th century, the category of slave has disappeared. Noble titles (*Karaenta, Puatta, Andi, Daeng, Puang*) are still used, but, since World War II, education and bureaucratic position earn as much or more deference than ancestry alone.

Although linguistic etiquette is far simpler than in Java or Bali, one does modify one's speech according to whether the addressee is one's social superior, equal, or inferior: e.g., "Where are you coming from?" can be rendered in Bugis as *Pole tegai petta?* (deferential), *Pole tegaki?* (polite), or *Pole tegako?* (brusk, appropriate towards children or people of greatly inferior status). To show greater respect, euphemistic or indirect expressions can be employed: e.g., *Leccekki yolo mabbura,* "Please transfer there and take the remedy," rather than *Lokkakki yolo manre,* "Please go eat." To persons of the highest status, such as religious teachers or royalty, an appropriate greeting is to bow and kiss the person's hand.

Contact between unrelated members of the opposite sex outside the surveillance of older family members is still strongly discouraged, although modern education and work provide some opportunities for this. For a young man to show interest in a girl, one strategy acceptable to custom is for him to steal her underwear while she (covered in a sarong) is bathing by a river. He then returns the underwear to her without telling anyone else about it. If the theft does become known to others, the girl's family loses face and may harm the young man.

⁹ LIVING CONDITIONS

Villages consist of 10 to 200 houses facing either south or west or backing onto a river if there is one; a banyan tree and a mosque or prayer house lies at the town center. .

Traditional wooden-frame houses are raised on 1.5-m to 2-m (5–7 ft) stilts. For floors and walls, richer houses use wood with zinc roofing, while poorer ones use bamboo with leaf-fiber roofing. The house is divided vertically into three parts: the spirit-inhabited area immediately under the roof; the middle area for human living; and the area under the house floor for storing tools and keeping animals. Horizontally, beginning in front facing the road, the house is partitioned into: an unroofed veranda; a vestibule where the family relaxes and guests wait before being invited in; a second room where the family eats, containing heirloom weapons and the house's central pillar (the place of the house's protective spirit); and a sleeping room, further divided into a front section for the parents and a back section for the daughters (sons sleep on the front veranda or at the village mosque). Commoner houses will have one lower roof over the vestibule and another higher one over the rest of the house; aristocratic houses may have as many as five further roofs. Cooking takes place at the back or behind the house.

South Sulawesi, comprising the ancestral homelands of the Bugis and Makassarese, has a Human Development Index (combining measures of income, health, and education) of 68.1 (2005 score), while that of West Sulawesi, the homeland of the Mandar, is 65.7, both figures considerably lower than the national HDI of 69.6. South Sulawesi's GDP per capita is US$6,913, relatively low for Indonesia (US$9,784 for West Sumatra, US$8,360 for North Sulawesi, but US$6,293 for Central Java and US$6,151 for West Nusa Tenggara).

¹⁰ FAMILY LIFE

Ideal (but not obligatory) marriage partners are cousins of the first, second, and third degrees; marriage with a sibling, a child of a sibling, or a grandchild, however, is taboo.

A household consists of one nuclear family, including grandparents and unmarried adult children. In wealthier urban households, relatives from the countryside may stay for considerable lengths of time, joining in household chores. Traditionally, husbands and wives address each other respectively as "Father of [child's name]" or "Mother of [child's name]," e.g., in Bugis, *"Ambonna/Ambenna Beddu"* or *"Indonna/Emmakna Beddu"* (Beddu being the child). Parents call sons *"Baco"* and call girls *"Becce."* Children address fathers with a variety of titles (*Ambo, Abba, Puang, Petta,* and others) and mothers with *Indo, Emmak, Ummi/Mi* or a shortened form of the mother's name (e.g., "Lima" for "Halimah"). Older siblings call younger ones by their name or with *Anri;* younger siblings address older ones with *Kaka, Daeng,* or sometimes with their name.

¹¹ CLOTHING

House clothes are shorts with or without a shirt for boys, and a shirt and a skirt down to the knees for girls. Adult men wear a plaid-patterned sarong with or without a sleeveless undershirt, while adult women wear a batik sarong with a *kebaya* blouse or a shirt with sleeves down to the elbow. In contrast to the practice elsewhere in Indonesia, men and women both wear the same type of tubular sarong, the only difference being that

traditionally men kept the sarong in place with a knot while women draped the edge over their right forearm.

For male street wear, although Western-style trousers and shirts are common, so too is the sarong with a long- or short-sleeved shirt. It is impolite to go out in public without a head-covering (a black velvet cap, a white *hajji* cap, or, now rarely, the *sangkok rucca,* a traditional brimless, flat-topped cap woven of palm-leaf fibers). For traditional ceremonies, a man adds a buttoned-up jacket to the shirt and sarong (often silk).

Female street wear consists of the sarong-blouse combination or modest Western dress. Traditional clothing, now largely ceremonial, is a silk sarong with a *baju bodo,* a blouse with wide, short sleeves (now over an undershirt). Before Indonesian independence (much less so now), the color of the baju bodo had to fit age and status: light reds for teenage girls and still-childless married women; dark reds for married women with children; green for the daughters of aristocratic families; purple for widows; white for nursemaids; and black for the elderly.

¹² FOOD

Daily food consists of rice with fish, soupy vegetables, pickles, and chili sauce. Grilled fish, shrimp, and other seafood eaten with dipping sauces are popular, as are curries and meats stewed in coconut milk. Nationally famous are the region's sweets and cakes, *konro Makassar* (a beef-rib soup), and *coto Makassar* (a soup of water-buffalo lungs, intestines, liver, and tripe eaten with rice steamed in palm leaf packets).

Men eat first in the front room of the house, while women eat later there or in the kitchen. According to folk belief, one should close windows and doors before eating.

¹³ EDUCATION

In 2005, South Sulawesi's level of literacy stood at 84.6%, low by Indonesian national standards and even below other densely populated provinces with large numbers of poor, such as East Java and Bali. (*See* also the article entitled **INDONESIANS**.)

¹⁴ CULTURAL HERITAGE

Played solo or in small ensembles, traditional musical instruments include the drum, gong, *kesokeso* (a two-string vertical fiddle with a pot-bellied soundbox), a boat-shaped zither (*kecape* in Bugis or *kacaping* in Makassarese), the *pui-pui* (a high-pitched oboe-like instrument), and the Mandarese *jarumbing* (a pronged bamboo cane). Popular songs following national or international models are sung in the local languages, such as in the genre *lagu Makassar.*

Traditional dances divide into court and folk dances. Among the former are the Bugis *Pajaga* (danced by 12 aristocratic girls), the Makassarese *Pakarena* (12 girls and 12 boys), and the Mandarese *Pattudu* (6 to 8 girls); these contrast the restrained movements of the dancers with dynamic drumming. A similar aesthetic governs a wedding dance in which the bride remains impassive while being taunted by a pair of older male dancers. Folk dances include martial dances accompanied by the *rebana* flat drum, the *Pattenung* depicting weaving, the *Mappuka,* which imitates fishing, the Bugis *Mappadendang* harvest dance (an occasion for much horseplay among young man), and the Makassarese *Ganrang Bulo,* a highly syncopated dance with young boys beating time with bamboo rods.

The Bugis and Makassarese have written extensive literatures in their own script called *aksara lontara'*, after the lontar palm leaves used as paper (the Gowa king Daeng Pamatte standardized the letters in the 16th century). This literature encompasses customary regulations, augury books (especially for planting and harvesting times), genealogies, dynastic origin myths, factual chronicles, and court diaries (the last two genres are unique in Indonesia).

There is also a religious literature written in Arabic-derived letters called *aksara serang*, presumably introduced via Seram in the Moluccas. Local literary works were also composed in Malay, the most famous being the *Sya'ir Perang Mangkasara* about the defense of Makassar against the Dutch.

15 WORK

In earlier times, South Sulawesi exported rice, livestock, and dried fish to the food-deficient Eastern Kalimantan, Southeast Sulawesi, and the Moluccas. Decades of warfare ending only in the mid-1960s left the province among the poorest in Indonesia, and income remains below the national average, though it is rising rapidly as the region begins to fulfill its potential as eastern Indonesia's service and production center. In the past, the Bugis in particular have been dependent on rice cultivation for a livelihood but now are diversifying into coconuts, coffee, cloves, kapok, candlenut, and tobacco. Erosion caused by deforestation, however, threatens agricultural expansion. Fishing, and the collection of sea products such as sea cucumber for the Chinese market, is also an important occupation, particularly among the Makassarese and Mandarese.

Unlike certain other groups such as the Javanese, there is no prejudice against manual labor; what is important in a job is the extent to which one is free of other's commands.

16 SPORTS

One traditional sport is *paraga* in which boys or young men attempt to keep a rattan-work ball in the air with their feet to the sound of the drum and *pui-pui* playing.

17 ENTERTAINMENT AND RECREATION

See the article entitled **Indonesians**.

18 FOLK ART, CRAFTS, AND HOBBIES

The first European travelers admired the region's boat builders, the premier center being Bira at the southwestern tip of the peninsula with its access to the ironwood of Bulukumba and Selayar. Bira boatbuilding teams travel all over the peninsula and even to Kalimantan and Java in order to sell their skills. The boats are built from memory without written designs and with the simplest tools: a vertical saw, hand drill, adze, and a plane, and *no* nails. Only bolts are used to secure ribs to the hull. Traditional boat-types include the large, elegant *pinisi* and smaller outriggered *lepa-lepa* and *sande*. Today, the biggest boats are motorized and reach 500 tons.

Until the early 20th century, South Sulawesi exported silk and cotton; weaving still provides supplementary income for village women. Two styles are best known: *sarong Mandar*, cloth of very fine weave with checkered patterns in sober colors, widely traded in the archipelago; and *sarong Bugis*, brilliantly colored silk cloth with large patterns reminiscent of Thai fabrics.

Other highly developed crafts are blacksmithing (now using scrap metal rather than freshly mined ore), gold- and silver smithing (a specialty being fine filigree work), and mat- and basket-weaving.

19 SOCIAL PROBLEMS

See the article entitled **Indonesians**.

20 GENDER ISSUES

South Sulawesi's Gender-Related Development Index (combining measures of women's health, education, and income relative to men's) is 56.9, significantly below Indonesia's national GDI of 59.2. The province's Gender Empowerment Measure (reflecting women's participation and power in political and economic life relative to men's) is 45.6, also lower than the national GEM of 54.6.

According to anthropologist Christian Pelras, Bugis culture overall emphasizes the equality and complementarities of the two genders, despite Islamic influence often appearing to put men in the foreground and women in the background. The freedom and power of women in Bugis society struck early European observers; many instances are known of woman rulers (even one ruling her kingdom without interference from her husband, the ruler of another kingdom!) and woman warriors (female fighters participated in the Indonesian struggle for independence and female squads fought in the rebellions of the early post-colonial years). The strict barriers between classes in traditional Bugis society actually permitted a woman ruler to have men of lower rank, men who could never marry her, as her vassals or retainers. Although village leadership tends to be male, these male leaders are called "mothers of the people," another indication that political power and womanhood are not considered incompatible.

Women are not regarded as inherently weaker or more delicate than men (one type of "women's work," pounding rice, is very physically demanding). In the first years of his marriage, a man generally moves into his wife's parents' house and for that reason is not likely to be domineering towards his wife. The home is the domain of the wife, but this does not mean that the wife does not contribute to the family's economic livelihood; on the contrary, she, in addition to helping out with farming, engages in weaving, petty trade, or other activities to bring in income (in the case of fishing families, it is the wife who supports the family while the husband goes to sea, his earnings going largely to sustain him while he is away from home with the surplus he brings back serving as a mere supplement to family resources).

21 BIBLIOGRAPHY

Ayatrohaedi, et al. *Tatakrama di Beberapa Daerah di Indonesia* [Etiquette in Some Regions of Indonesia]. Jakarta: Department of Education and Culture, 1989.

Data Statistik Indonesia. http://demografi.bps.go.id/ (November 9, 2008).

Harsrinuksmo, Bambang. "Adat Perkawinan" [Wedding Customs]. In *Ensiklopedi Nasional Indonesia [ENI]*, Vol. 2. Jakarta: Cipta Adi Pustaka, 1988.

Karman, Ummy, and Anin Suhardan. "Bugis, Arsitektur." In *ENI*, Vol. 3. (1989).

LeBar, Frank M., ed. *Ethnic Groups of Insular Southeast Asia.* Vol, 1, *Indonesia, Andaman Islands, and Madagascar.* New Haven, CT: Human Relations Area Files Press, 1972.

Mattulada. "Kebudayaan Bugis-Makassar" [Bugis-Makassar Culture]. In *Manusia dan Kebudayaan di Indonesia* [Man and Culture in Indonesia], edited by Koentjaraningrat. Jakarta: Djambatan, 1975.

Melalatoa, M. Junus. "Mandar, Suku Bangsa." In *ENI,* Vol. 10 (1990).

Partrijunianti, Endang. "Makasar, Suku Bangsa." In *ENI,* Vol. 10 (1990).

Profil Propinsi Republik Indonesia: Sulawesi Selatan. Jakarta: Yayasan Bhakti Wawasan Nusantara, 1992.

Pelras, Christian. *The Bugis.* Oxford, UK: Blackwell, 1996.

Reid, Heken, and Anthony Reid. *South Sulawesi.* Berkeley: Periplus, 1988.

Rosantini, Triana. "Bugis, Suku Bangsa." In *ENI,* Vol. 3 (1989).

Suwondo, H. Bambang, et al. *Permainan Rakyat Suku Bangsa Bugis Makassar di Sulawesi Selatan* [Folk Games of the Bugis-Makassar Ethnic Group in South Sulawesi]. Ujungpandang: Department of Education and Culture, 1984.

Varshney, Ashutosh, Rizal Panggabean, and Mohammad Zulfan Tadjoeddin. "Patterns of Collective Violence in Indonesia (1990-2004)." Jakarta: United Nations Support Facility for Indonesian Recovery, 2004.

Volkman, Toby Alice, and Ian Caldwell, ed. *Sulawesi: Island Crossroads of Indonesia.* Lincolnwood, IL: Passport Books, 1990.

—revised by A. J. Abalahin

BURMAN

PRONUNCIATION: BUR-muhn
ALTERNATE NAMES: Burmese, Myanmar
LOCATION: Myanmar (Burma)
POPULATION: 30 million, estimated.
LANGUAGE: Burmese (also called Myanmar)
RELIGION: Theravada Buddhism

[1] INTRODUCTION

The country known today as Myanmar or Burma is a multi-ethnic entity, formed in colonial times from Burman, Rakhine, and Mon kingdoms; Karenni and Shan principalities; Chin, Kachin, Naga, and Wa chiefdoms; as well as Karen and other communities. Burmans are the largest ethnic group, with an estimated 68% of the population. Myanmar is an ancient name for the land of the Burmans, Burma (or Bama) is a less formal name. Burma was used as the name of the entire nation during the British colonial period and following independence, but the military government officially renamed the country Myanmar in 1989. The Burmese democracy movement, U.S. government, and BBC News continue to use Burma while the United Nations uses Myanmar. The Burman people are also called Bamar or Burmese.

Like many other peoples of Myanmar, the ethnic Burmans descended from western China. During the 7th century, they migrated to the dry areas in the valleys of the Irrawaddy River and the Chindwin River. Originally a hill tribe, they learned the art of wet rice cultivation from the indigenous Pyus and converted themselves to Buddhism, which flourished then among the Pyus. From the dry zone of Burma, the Burmans migrated to what is now lower Burma. In British colonial times, many Burmans moved to lower Burma, outnumbering the Mons in their own land. In the country's largest city, Rangoon (also spelled Yangon), much of the population is of mixed descent from China, India, and Europe.

King Anawrahta founded the first Burman kingdom in 1044 at Pagan. There were three Burman dynasties: the Pagan, Ava, and Konbong. Most Burman kings were aggressive towards their neighbors and attacked Arakan, Mon, Thai, Manipur, Shan, and Assam kingdoms whenever they were confident and militarily strong enough. Loot, slaves, and white elephants were the main attractions.

Burma's sovereignty ended in 1885 when the British annexed Burma for the final time and colonized the region. During World War II the Japanese invasion force was initially backed by ethnic Burman leaders and most of the Burman population, while other ethnic groups supported British and American forces. Although the Burman leadership under General Aung San switched sides later in the war, the wartime ethnic conflict continued after the war was over. The Burmans and other ethnic groups had grown to distrust each other.

In 1947 the Burman leader General Aung San negotiated with the British for Burma's independence. In the course of the negotiations, Aung San met with the leaders of the people bordering the land of the ethnic Burmans. The Chin, Kachin, and Shan agreed to join the Burman union. In 1948 Burma gained independence together with the Chin, Kachin, and Shan. General Aung San and his cabinet were assassinated right after independence. Since gaining independence the ethnic Burmans have built the governments that have ruled Burma, first replacing the British with the democratic government of the Union of Burma. Burma remained democratic until 1962, when the head of the military, General Ne Win, took over in a coup d'état, in order to crush ethnic and Communist insurgency. Ne Win's military dictatorship introduced "The Burmese Way to Socialism" and the Burma Socialist Program Party (BSPP), which ran the affairs of the country. A prosperous country under the British, Burma became one of the 10 poorest countries in the world. General Ne Win dissolved the BSPP in response to a mass civil disobedience uprising led by students against the government in 1988. After killing several thousand peaceful demonstrators, another military government—the State Law and Order Restoration Council (SLORC)—took over in September 1988 and was still in power as of 2008, although its name was changed to the State Peace and Development Council (SPDC). The most powerful of the generals is the SPDC junta's head, Gen. Than Shwe.

Rebellion by non-Burman ethnic groups continued on a small scale into the 21st century and the regime was notorious for its human rights violations against civilians in the non-Burman areas, including Karen and Shan States. Repression also extended to the Burman population, with Gen. Aung San's daughter, Aung San Suu Kyi, an extremely popular democracy movement leader and Nobel Peace Prize Laureate, held under house arrest for many years. Her party, the National League for Democracy won 1990 elections in a landslide, but was never allowed to take office. In 2007 Buddhist monks led tens of thousands of demonstrators in the streets of cities and towns, peacefully calling for change, but the "Saffron Revolution" was violently suppressed by the regime. On 2 May 2008 Cyclone Nargis devastated Burma's Irrawaddy Delta region, killing at least 80,000 people in Myanmar's worst recorded disaster, and leaving millions with their homes and farms destroyed. The Delta's population is mostly Burman and Karen and had been the major rice producer for the nation. The military regime was strongly criticized by the international community for rejecting immediate relief efforts from the outside world.

² LOCATION AND HOMELAND

The population of ethnic Burmans is estimated at around 30 million, but a true census has not been taken since the 1930s. Burma is bordered by India, Bangladesh, China, Tibet, Laos, Thailand, and the Indian Ocean and it is the largest country in mainland Southeast Asia. Most of the Burman people live in central and southern areas, including the cities of Rangoon (Yangon), and the former royal capital, Mandalay, which is considered the cultural center for the Burman people. There are also many Burman refugees and emigrants in many other countries, although the bulk of overseas populations from Myanmar are of other ethnic groups.

³ LANGUAGE

The Burmese language (also called Bamar) belongs to the Tibeto-Burman subgroup of the Tai-Chinese group of languages. The Burmese language has affinity to Tibetan and the Lolo tribes in China. The Burmese script was taken from Sanskrit and is similar in that way to Urdu, Hindi, Thai, and Cambodian, although its rounded letters are very distinctive. Because of the colonial influence, English is widely spoken as the

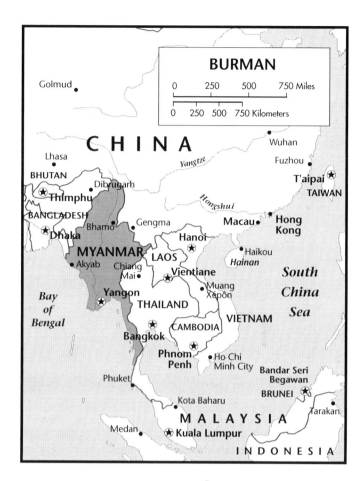

second language of the Burmans, especially among the older generation.

Burman names are equivalent only to a first or personal name. The Burmans usually have no family names. Burman names have meanings. For example, "U Nu" (former Prime Minister) means "uncle young," or "uncle tender." "U" means "uncle" but is used in the same way as "Mr." in English. "Ma" is equivalent to "Miss" and "Daw" (aunt) for women. The Burmans stress age in social and human relations. An elder must be addressed as "uncle" or "aunt" or, if the ages are not far apart, as elder brother ("ako") or elder sister ("ama"). Most Burmese names consist of two or three words (e.g., Ne Win or Khin Maung Gyi.) Infrequently, a Burmese person will add a family name to their own, most notably Aung San Suu Kyi, whose name contains the name of her father, Burma independence hero Gen. Aung San.

⁴ FOLKLORE

The Burmans fear and respect spiritual beings called the Nats, which they celebrate in their ritual plays, prayers, sacrifices, and dances. These beliefs coexist with Buddhism in Myanmar, but are not part of the Buddhist religion. The Nats are believed to be very clever and possess immense power. They have human bodies and can exist in the trees, on top of mountains, in the ocean, and anywhere else. The 37 major Nats have distinct personalities, usually based on real people who died terrible deaths. The people give offerings to the Nats out of fear, so that they will protect them. Thagyamin, considered to be

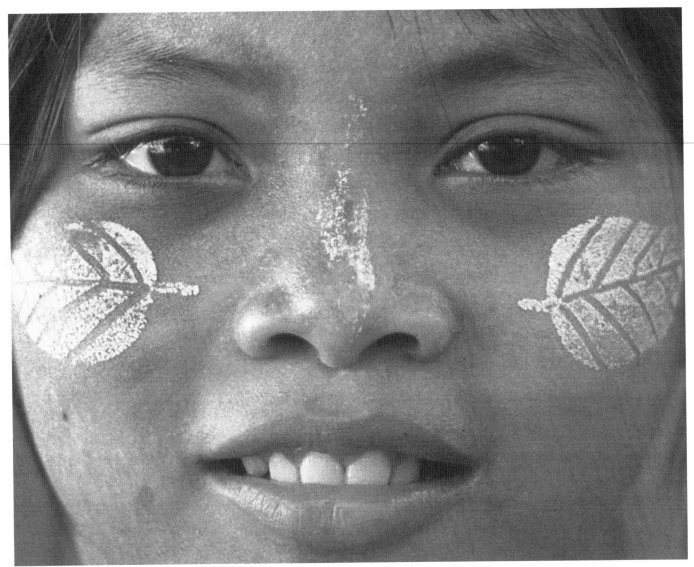

A Burman girl with a decorated face from a local cosmetic, called Tanaka, is photographed while selling souvenirs to tourists at a temple in Mandalay, Myanmar. Mandalay's Buddhist monasteries are among the most important in the country. (AP Images/Apichart Weerawong)

a god, hears all and knows all, and is usually honored during the New Year Festival. The Burmans also honor the Naga, divine serpents that live at the bottom of rivers, seas, and oceans in palaces built from precious stones and pearls. They are the protectors of the water and land. The Naga serpents have the advantage of being able to take the form of human beings, whereby the female Naga can become beautiful women and marry powerful men in order to influence them. The Burmans also believe in Bilus, monsters who live in hidden places.

5 RELIGION

The Burman people are close to 100% Buddhists of the Theravada type, which originated in Sri Lanka and emphasizes the wisdom of ancient scriptures to show how humans may overcome suffering. Before the Burmans came to Burma, the Pyu and Mon people were influenced by the Buddhism of India and Ceylon (Sri Lanka.) Burman kings invaded their neighboring countries and brought back slaves and artisans to build

pagodas or temples and captured religious teachers, such as the Mons. Burma has over one million Buddhist temples. Old Burman cities, such as Pagan, Ava, Sagaing, and Mandalay, remember past Burman glories with their numerous pagodas. Rangoon is the site of the magnificent gold leaf covered Shwe Dagon Pagoda. In cities, towns and villages, Buddhist monasteries are centers of community life, culture, and learning. In the morning, lines of monks walk along the streets, accepting offerings of food and blessing the households. Many Burmans practice meditation every day, as a way to gain insight into life and achieve a calm state of mind.

Although Buddhism is supposed to be tolerant, Myanmar's military regime has been accused of trying to impose the majority religion on non-Burman, non-Buddhist ethnic groups. Buddhist monks have often been a political force in Burma and marched against military rule in 2007's Saffron Revolution. They are highly respected by the Burmans, but many were beaten, arrested, and even killed by the military at that time.

After Cyclone Nargis in 2008 Buddhist monasteries provided sanctuary for storm victims and organized local relief efforts.

6 MAJOR HOLIDAYS

The Burmans have two major holidays. The New Year, combined with the Thingyan (or "Water Festival"), takes place April 13–16; April 17 is the New Year. During the Water Festival, at the height of Myanmar's hottest season, everyone sprays each other with water from cups, buckets, or water-pumps. Respect is shown to elders, who have water poured gently on their hands, but everyone else (including foreign tourists) is fair game for getting completely soaked by the water splashing. Young Burmans take this opportunity to express their secret love to girls or boys by throwing water on them. Song and dance performances and satirical skits also take place at this festive time. The other major Burman holiday takes place on the full moon of Tasonmon in November and is called the Light Festival. Like Christmas in the Western world, at that time the Burmans decorate their houses with lights, mostly candles. Wearing their best outfits, young men and women walk the town streets, which are filled with people.

Myanmar's national holiday commemorates independence from Britain on the fourth of January with military parades, speeches, and gun salutes. Union Day, observed on February 12, celebrates the signing of the Panglong agreement, in which the Shan, Kachin, and Chin agreed to join the Burmans to form the Union of Burma in 1947. Martyr's day (August 12), the day Aung San, the founding father of the Union of Burma, was assassinated, is also observed.

7 RITES OF PASSAGE

As soon as a baby is born, the mother avoids eating meat, especially fish. From birth, boys and girls are treated differently. Names are usually given immediately after birth, but it is not unusual for the baby to be unnamed for many months. The initials of the names reflect the day of the week on which the baby was born, and that day is important in Burmese astrology, with an animal or symbol for each day of the week. For a girl, ear-piercing is an important event, meant to beautify her. When a boy is born, a learned man is invited to wash the baby's hair. The learned man places gold and silver coins in a cup, which is used to wash the baby's hair so that he will grow up rich.

One of the most important duties of the parents of a boy is to send him to the Buddhist temple to train as a novice monk. The boy can be anywhere between 9 to 13 years old, depending on whether the boy believes he is able to survive without food from noon until night, when the monks fast. The celebration starts with the boy's dressing up as a prince and being carried on a platform to the temple. He is not supposed to touch the ground. On reaching the temple, the parents bring out a special cloth, on which the hair of the boy is to drop without falling on the ground. After the boy's hair is shaved, he officially becomes a novice monk with prayers and Buddhist chanting. The duration of the monkhood can last from three days to a week. Some novices stay on to become monks, in which case the monkhood lasts a lifetime. Grown men sometimes go back to the monastery as monks for a limited period. Girls and women may become Buddhist nuns, sometimes in later life if they are widowed. In Myanmar, Buddhist monks wear robes of a dark red color, and Buddhist nuns wear pink robes. Their vocation is to know and teach the Buddhist scriptures, but the monks and nuns provide support to their communities in many other ways.

A deceased person may be buried or cremated with a coin in their mouth so that the deceased can pay for boat and bus fares in the afterlife. The family brings leaves from the funeral ground back home so that the dead relative will know the way home. Seven days after death, a monk is called to tell the deceased that he can go anyplace he or she wishes to go from that day on. Most Burmans believe in ghosts and haunted houses.

8 INTERPERSONAL RELATIONS

Burmans greet each other by asking "Have you eaten?"—they do not have a specific "good morning" or "good evening" greeting. If the person is visiting and replies in the negative, the host is obligated to serve food. If the answer is in the positive, then the next question will be, "What did you have for your meal?" Meeting on the street, they tend to ask, "Where did you go?" or "From where did you come?" These greetings are more a formality than an actual question. In the morning they may say to each other, "Are you up already?" There is also an expression, "Mingalaba," which means "Welcome" or "Hello."

Burman men and women hold hands in public only if they are already engaged or married. However, men often hold hands with each other, and women may hold hands with each other, just as friends. Kissing is still regarded as a Western custom, and kissing in public places is regarded as uncultured. As would be expected, nodding the head means "yes," and shaking the head means "no."

Because telephones are very expensive, people visit each other at home whenever they have time. They visit each other in the very early morning or at night, usually unannounced. The Burmans are very friendly and are always open to visitors.

Parents often play a role arranging their children's marriages. Astrologers match their birth day of the week for a man and woman; for example, two people are a good match if they are born on a Wednesday and a Saturday. Nowadays, a boy and a girl might meet more casually and go to see a movie or have dinner together. If a boy likes a girl, he may walk in front of the girl's house a thousand times until the girl and her family notice him. He may also give her a love letter, which she might refuse or reluctantly accept, which does not mean complete rejection. In traditional Burman society, a girl's acceptance of admiration is a serious commitment and indicates that a wedding is not far off. More casual relationships have become normal in urban areas and universities, however.

9 LIVING CONDITIONS

Myanmar's health care system has gotten worse and worse under military rule, and malaria, diarrhea, dysentery, tuberculosis, hepatitis, and HIV/AIDS are among the common diseases. Malnutrition is also widespread, particularly among children. Most people live on one dollar a day or less, and own very few possessions. They have only necessities, such as two or three cooking pots, a few plates, wooden spoons, and some articles of clothing. Radios and books are cherished possessions, and only the elite own cars, telephones, computers, or TV sets. Even for well-off people in the cities, electricity is unreliable, so they must use generators to keep lights and appliances running.

Burma is an agricultural country and therefore about 80% of the population lives in the countryside. Most Burman farmers have a pair of oxen or water buffalo for wet rice cultivation, a hoe, and a cart. Chickens, goats, and pigs are raised for food. Burman farmers do not own horses, but some towns still have horse carriages for transportation. Houses of the Burman rural people are made mostly from bamboo and have two partitions; one side is for cooking and storage, and the other half is used for sitting and sleeping. In urban areas, brick and concrete buildings, often dating back to colonial times, contain small apartment spaces.

Burmans' means of transportation include ox carts, bicycles and motorbikes. Trucks and jeeps take passengers between towns. River ferries, buses, and trains link towns and cities, and are usually very crowded and slow. There are also domestic airlines, which fly between Rangoon (Yangon), Mandalay, and a few other airports, but they are used mainly by government officials and tourists.

10 FAMILY LIFE

Usually a Burman family has at least five children. The family also includes grandparents and the extended family members. When a Burman man marries a woman, it is most likely that he will live with the woman's family. The grandparents of his wife and possibly the parents of his mother-in-law all live in the household. The brothers and sisters of his wife might also live in the house. The man goes to live with his in-laws because he is expected to go to work all day and be absent from the home. He has very little contact with his mother-in-law. On the other hand, if the wife went to live with his family, she would be in constant contact with her mother-in-law, and they may experience difficulties. Young couples also live together with their parents because the babies can be better taken care of by aunts and grandmothers. Burmans are expected to look after their elderly, so it possible that parents may stay with their children their whole lives.

Dogs are the most common pets, but are kept outside to guard the house. Cats are also a common pet. Many Burman farmers keep cows and water buffalo for plowing their fields and pulling carts.

11 CLOTHING

Both Burman women and men wear sarongs, called htami for women and longyi for men. The sarong is a long tube of cloth that is wrapped and tucked in at the waist for women, knotted at the waist for men. The designs on the longyi and htami are different according to regions and fashions. Men traditionally wear collarless shirts with their longyis and women wear short, fitted blouses and jackets. The traditional clothes are made of cotton, but for special occasions they are woven of silk. Wealthy people adorn themselves with gold jewelry and the gems produced in Myanmar: rubies, sapphires, pearls, and jade. Farmers wear big conical hats as sunshades, and people often carry umbrellas as shelter from sun or rain. Burman women and children use a fragrant wood paste called thanaka as a cooling sunscreen on their faces and women also pin flowers in their hair.

Because the sarongs don't have pockets, a cloth shoulder bag is an essential accessory for men and women. Among younger Burmans, jeans have become popular. Sometimes jean jackets or t-shirts are worn with sarongs by younger people. The Myanmar school uniform is a green sarong and a white shirt for boys and girls, with a cloth shoulder bag for carrying books. Everybody wears flip-flops outdoors and goes barefoot inside the house.

12 FOOD

The staple item of Burman food is white rice, eaten with a curry of fish, pork, beef, or chicken, plus vegetables, garlic, and ginger. Fish sauce, chili, and dried shrimp are used for flavor. Ngapi, a pungent fish paste, is eaten at almost every meal. Burmans do not eat meat in large quantities. Meat is usually cut into small pieces, about one-half inch on all sides, and fried with lots of oil. The two most common Burman noodle dishes are Mohinga and Ohnokhaukswe. Mohinga is rice noodles mixed in a thick fish soup. Ohnokhaukswe is a chicken stew cooked in coconut milk, also served with noodles. Burmans love to eat sour, sweet, salty, bitter, and spicy snacks. Unripe mangoes and limes are a must for the meal to be properly served. Fruit is usually served for dessert or a snack and may include ripe mango, pineapple, watermelon, or mandarin oranges. Tea, either plain or with milk and sugar, is the most common beverage. A salad called laphet thoke is made of pickled tea leaves with garlic and peanuts. Beer and soda pop are produced in Myanmar and imported beverages are very expensive.

Burmans eat rice and curry with their fingers and soup is eaten with a spoon from a shared bowl. Most restaurants in Burman areas are run by Chinese or Indian ethnic people; Burman food is normally available in homes or at temple fairs. Burmans normally eat two times a day, once in the morning, which could be considered brunch, and the other meal in the afternoon. They may start and end the day with tea or coffee and a few cookies. As the country has become more impoverished, many Burmans subsist only on watered-down rice soup, instead of rice and curry.

13 EDUCATION

The literacy rate among the Burmans was traditionally quite high because Buddhist monasteries served as the center of learning, where the monks functioned as teachers. After independence, with public schooling, Burma had one of the highest literacy rates in Asia. However, education steadily lost funding and declined under military rule. Because university students led the 1988 pro-democracy uprising, the regime closed down educational institutions nationwide for several years. Myanmar's educational system is highly controlled, with university students assigned their major fields of study instead of choosing for themselves. Teachers are underpaid and often work second jobs. Access to books and computers is very limited. In spite of the many problems, Burmans seek educational opportunities for their children (girls as well as boys) as their highest personal priority. Many overseas Burmans have advanced degrees and are medical doctors or university professors.

14 CULTURAL HERITAGE

Burmese classical music is performed by orchestras at Pwes or concerts, usually in open-air theaters. It uses a gong and drum percussion ensemble for complex rhythms, accompanied by stringed instruments and horns. Some Burmese music has also been adapted for the piano, an instrument imported by the British. Vocal music uses the orchestral compositions or a harp as background.

Burmese dances are very graceful movements of the whole body and feature hand gestures combined with fast, skilled footwork. The classical dances are performed by learned professionals with years of strict training. Burmese dance dramas, with an orchestral score, mostly are romantic love stories and are accompanied by an orchestra.

"The Glass Palace Chronicle," written in the 19th century, recounts the history and mythology of the Burman monarchy. Although the Burmans have a rich literary history, often with Buddhist themes, literature has been very limited under military rule by strict censorship. It is extremely hard to get serious fiction or any nonfiction published, but popular magazines feature romantic stories and poetry. Books in Burmese and English are considered very valuable and are shared by many readers.

15 WORK

Most Burmans are farmers, going to work in their rice and vegetable fields very early in the morning, before dawn. When the sun becomes hot they go home to rest and eat. They go back to the fields when it cools down until darkness. Part of the rice crop is often confiscated by the military.

People with education often work as civil servants. Office hours are from 9:30 in the morning to 3:00 in the afternoon. In 2005 the SPDC moved the capitol of the country from Rangoon to Naypyidaw, in a remote area 200 miles to the north. Government workers were compelled to move there and a new complex of office buildings was built for them. Many government workers, and even teachers and doctors, must take second jobs to support their families.

Myanmar has some manufacturing of goods for local use and garments for export, although factory wages are low. Many Burmans work in small craft workshops, making lacquer ware, baskets, pottery, and tobacco cheroots. Burman men and women run shops, market stalls and street carts, selling a great variety of goods in rural and urban areas. Extra farm produce is brought to markets for sale, usually early in the morning. Children work on farms and in other occupations, including manufacturing and construction.

The army in Myanmar is very large, with almost half a million mostly Burman troops. Most soldiers join voluntarily in hopes of a better living standard; however, many are forced to join, and Myanmar's army is known for its thousands of child soldiers, who are raised with the military as their parents.

Burman refugees have tried to continue their education in exile, although most take any work available so they can survive in a new land. Some have careers in journalism or work for human rights organizations. Other exiles are professionals in the arts and sciences and Burman doctors can be found around the world.

16 SPORTS

Chinlon, a typical Burman sport, resembles hacky sack. A cane ball about 6 inches in diameter is kicked by people standing in a circle, passing the ball from one to the other. This sport can be played by two or more people, on flat ground anywhere. Soccer is the favorite spectator sport of the Burmans, attracting large crowds. Other popular sports include volleyball, badminton, and Burmese kickboxing.

17 ENTERTAINMENT AND RECREATION

The most common live entertainment for the Burmans is the Pwe, in which music and dance dramas are played along with comedy skits, usually outdoors and lasting all night as part of a temple fair. Traditional puppet shows use a set of characters portrayed by large wooden marionettes.

Myanmar's television stations, like newspapers and other media, are completely controlled by the military regime, so satellite TV is a popular alternative. Burmans watch local or foreign movies in theaters, or on disc at video parlors. Hollywood movies set in Myanmar include *Beyond Rangoon* and *John Rambo*, both of which are banned by the regime.

Satirical comedy performances are a Burman tradition but often land the performers in trouble with the regime. Myanmar has an underground hip hop culture, whose rappers have ended up in prison as politically suspect. The SPDC controls the Internet servers, but young Burmans find ways to communicate with the outside world through Internet cafes. Burmans also enjoy karaoke singing and video games.

18 FOLK ART, CRAFTS, AND HOBBIES

Myanmar's Burman areas are replete with pagodas and monasteries. The prayer pavilions of the pagodas are decorated with elaborate wood carvings. Most Burman homes have a Buddhist shrine with Buddha images set on wood carvings resembling the thrones of Burman kings. Painted wooden statues of the various Nats are also made by the Burmans. Lacquer ware, in which layers of shiny shellac form a colorful coating on a bowl, tray, or box, is a popular Burman craft. The lacquer items often are carved with scenes or painted in gold. Burmans are also known for their silk weaving and for kalaga tapestries of royal or mythical scenes, which are embroidered with velvet and sequins. Charming toy tigers, elephants, and owls, handmade of paper maché or wood are still sold in the markets of Myanmar.

19 SOCIAL PROBLEMS

Myanmar is one of the world's poorest countries despite many natural resources. Corruption is pervasive, usually involving military officials and rich business owners. Narcotics are easily available, and drug abuse affects a large section of the population, especially young people. Many people are unemployed and seek sanctuary in the power of drugs to forget their daily miseries.

In Burman areas the regime often demands that each household or family must supply laborers to work in the construction of railroads, roads, government buildings, etc., calling it voluntary work. However, these people are never paid and must bring their own food for the duration of their assignment. If a household is unable to supply a laborer, the household is fined a large sum of money.

While human rights violations are most severe in non-Burman areas of Myanmar, repression is also pervasive in Burman regions. People are often arrested without any reason given and jailed without trial for many years. Family members may be imprisoned if a dissident relative has escaped from arrest. Freedom of expression is almost completely nonexistent in Myanmar, although ties to the outside world through underground Internet and cell phone networks are increasing. Overnight house guests must register with the authorities and travel is highly restricted. Decades of repression and poverty for the Burmans and other people of Myanmar have led to a psychology of fear, depression, and resignation, which Aung San Suu

Kyi, the Buddhist monks, and student activists try to overcome with messages of hope and by examples of courage.

[20] GENDER ISSUES

Traditional Burman society was distinguished by rights for women in property ownership, marriage, and divorce. While women are considered to have less status than men in Theravada Buddhism, they have always played an active role in Burman society. Women are vital participants in health care and education. Burman women sell goods in markets and shops and own small businesses. In the family, the wife has the duty to look after what her husband earns. The husband delivers his total paycheck to the wife, and the wife administers the household budget. Burmans are usually as eager to educate their daughters as their sons.

Contradicting the social and economic status of Burman women is Myanmar's military rule, which is entirely male-administered, with no women holding important office, although the main opposition party is headed by a woman, Aung San Suu Kyi, who is greatly respected throughout Myanmar and around the world. Burman folk beliefs also express a suspicion of women, who are thought to have powers that can weaken men. Many Burmans believe that these powers can contaminate men if they come into contact with women's sarongs or undergarments. Women and transgender people can become mediums to the world of the Nat spirits, a respected role in Burman society. Although its emphasis is on male/female marriage, Burman society is usually very tolerant of gay, lesbian and transgender people.

[21] BIBLIOGRAPHY

Abbott, Gerry. *The Traveller's History of Burma*. Bangkok: Orchid Press, 1998.

Alford, Jeffrey, and Naomi Duguid. *Hot, Sour, Salty, Sweet: A Culinary Journey Through Southeast Asia*. New York: Artisan, 2000.

Allen, Louis. *Burma, the Longest War, 1941–45*. New York: St. Martin's Press, 1984.

Aung San Suu Kyi, and Michael Aris. *Freedom from Fear: And Other Writings*. New York: Penguin Books, 1991.

Aung San Suu Kyi. *Letters from Burma*. London: Penguin Books, 1997.

Cady, John Frank. *A History of Modern Burma*. Ithaca, N.Y.: Cornell University Press, 1958.

Chit, Khin Myo. *A Wonderland of Burmese Legends*. Bangkok: The Tamarind Press, 1984.

Esche, Annemarie. *Burmesische Märchen*. Leipzig, Germany: Insel Verlag, 1993.

Falconer, John, Luca Invernizzi, and Kim Inglis. *Myanmar Style: Art, Architecture and Design of Burma*. Hong Kong: Periplus, 1998.

Fink, Christina. *Living Silence: Burma Under Military Rule*. London: Zed Books, 2001.

Fraser-Lu, Sylvia. *Burmese Lacquerware*. Bangkok: Orchid Press, 2000.

Fraser-Lu, Sylvia. *Splendour in Wood: The Buddhist Monasteries of Burma*. Bangkok: Orchid Press, 2001.

Hla, Ludu U. *The Caged Ones*. Bangkok: Tamarind Press, 1986.

The Irrawaddy Magazine. www.irrawaddy.org (1 July 2008)

Larkin, Emma. *Finding George Orwell in Burma*. New York: Penguin Press, 2005.

Lintner, Bertil. *Outrage: Burma's Struggle for Democracy*. London: White Lotus, 1990.

Marshall, Andrew. *The Trouser People: A Story of Burma in the Shadow of the Empire*. Washington, D.C.: Counterpoint, 2002.

Nash, Manning. *The Golden Road to Modernity; Village Life in Contemporary Burma*. New York: Wiley, 1965.

National Coalition of the Union of Burma: *Human Rights Year Book 1993–1996*. Bangkok: Human Rights Documentation Unit (NCGUB).

Schramm-Evans, Zoe. *Dark Ruby: Travels in a Troubled Land*. London: HarperCollins, 1997.

Sell, Julie. *Whispers at the Pagoda: Portraits of Modern Burma*. Bangkok: Orchid Press, 1999.

Silverstein, Josef. *Independent Burma at Forty Years: Six Assessments*. Ithaca, N.Y.: Southeast Asia Program, 1989.

Thant Myint-U. *The River of Lost Footsteps: Histories of Burma*. New York: Farrar, Straus and Giroux, 2006.

Tucker, Shelby. *Burma: The Curse of Independence*. London: Pluto Press, 2001.

U.S. Campaign for Burma. www.uscampaignforburma.org (1 July 2008)

—revised by E. Mirante)

BUYI

PRONUNCIATION: BOO-yee
ALTERNATE NAMES: Buyue, Bunong, Buyai, Buzhang, Burao, and Buman
LOCATION: China
POPULATION: 2.5 million
LANGUAGE: Buyi
RELIGION: Ancestor worship; some Catholicism and Protestantism
RELATED ARTICLES: Vol. 3: China and Her National Minorities

¹INTRODUCTION

The Buyi represent one of the most ancient nationalities of China. They formed a branch of the ancient Yue of southern China, called Liao in ancient Chinese books. Around 200 bc, the state of Yuelang was established in an area long inhabited by the Buyi; thus, there may be a historical link between the Yuelang and the Buyi people. This area was later incorporated by the Western Han Dynasty (206 bc—ad 8). During the Tang Dynasty (ad 618—907), it was ruled by native officials following an agreement with the central government. In the 18th century, the native officials were replaced by Manchu or Chinese officials appointed directly by the Qing Dynasty (1644—1911). This reform evoked strong opposition from the Buyi and led to uprisings. Although their rebellion was short-lived, the names and heroic deeds of their leaders are still frequently on the lips of Buyi people.

²LOCATION AND HOMELAND

The Buyi are mainly distributed in Guizhou, Sichuan, and Yunnan provinces, with dense concentrations in the city of Guiyang, the district of Anshun, and two autonomous prefectures in Guizhou. The famous scenic spots of Huangguoshu Waterfall and Huaxi are located in Buyi territory. On the whole, the Buyi inhabit fertile lands with smooth terrain, mild climate, and abundant rainfall, very suitable for farming. Their population was over 2.9 million in 2000.

³LANGUAGE

Buyi language belongs to the Sino-Tibetan family, Zhuang-Dong group, Zhuang-Dai branch, and is closely related to the Zhuang language. The Buyi did not develop their own writing system, but use Chinese characters. In the 1950s, a written language based on Latin was created, and is very useful and convenient for the Buyi people.

Buyi is a self-given name. Other designations include Buyue, Bunong, Buyai, Buzhang, Burao, and Buman, reflecting a historic era when each clan had its own name. The ancient Chinese books called them Liao, Man, Li, Zhongjia, Yijia, etc. Buyi is the most commonly used designation nowadays.

⁴FOLKLORE

Buyi folklore was transmitted orally from generation to generation for many centuries. Their myths were deeply influenced by those of the Chinese and other nationalities, so that we find many similarities among them. A myth called *Buji* describes the creation of the universe by Pangu, a creator god. Buji was the man who successfully mastered the flood but died a heroic death. His son and daughter escaped from danger by hiding in a calabash. (They rolled down from the mountain top two millstones that laid one on top of the other when they came to rest, a heavenly-sent sign that they must marry.) After marriage, the girl gave birth to a fleshy lump. Her husband cut it into 99 pieces and threw them in all directions. They turned into 99 villages, each having its own name. Another myth called "Nian Wang shoots suns" says that there were originally 12 suns in the sky and the people suffered a great deal from their fierce irradiation. Nian Wang shot down 11 of the 12 suns to save the people.

The Buyi revere their heroes. Wei Chaoyuan and Wang Achong were leaders of an insurrectionary army against the Qing Dynasty. The Buyi erected statues in their honor and worshipped them (in Anlong County and Dangzhang village). This is rarely seen among other national minorities.

⁵RELIGION

The Buyi believe in ghosts and worship their ancestors. The shaman, called *laomo* by the Buyi, acts as an intermediary between ghosts and human beings. Illness is considered mischief caused by a ghost, so a shaman is invited to perform rituals in which poultry or livestock is sacrificed. The importance of the sacrificial offerings depends upon the virulence of the ghost, which can only be assessed by the shaman. The Buyi also believe in chicken divination; whatever they want to do must be decided beforehand by divination, especially in the case of marriage, funerals, and house building. The Buyi regard their ancestors as gods of protection and blessing.

Since the beginning of this century, a sizable number of Buyi have converted to Catholicism and Protestantism.

⁶MAJOR HOLIDAYS

In addition to the Spring Festival and Mid-Autumn Festival, which they share with the other nationalities and with the Chinese, there are other major spring holidays. April 8 (lunar calendar; Western calendar, between May 2 and May 30) is called the Buffalo King Festival, held after the fields are plowed in the spring. Every household makes Buffalo King cakes and steams multicolored rice. People first offer them to the ancestors, then call back the spirit of the buffalo, and finally give half of the food to the buffalo and let it rest for one day. Today, all national minorities in Guizhou participate in this festival. There are spectacular performances, sporting games, and *sheng* (a reed-pipe wind instrument) competitions. The sixth of June (lunar calendar; Western calendar, between June 27 and July 27), called Genjiang or "lesser New Year" is second in importance only to the Spring Festival. Every village kills pigs and cows as sacrificial offerings to the gods of the mountain, of the land, and of the cooking stove. The Buyi of Zhenfeng County in Guizhou take a chicken, a piece of pork, and a cardboard paper horse to the limit of their field. They kill the chicken, splatter the blood onto the paper horse, which is then planted into the field. All of these rituals aim to avert misfortune and obtain a good harvest.

⁷RITES OF PASSAGE

The Buyi pay much attention to their newborn children. Besides celebrating the birth, they try to find a god to bless the baby and protect him or her from disease and danger. In the

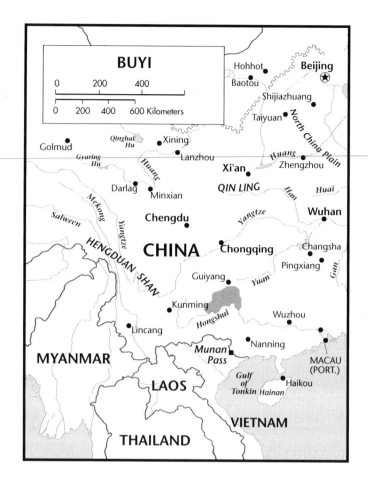

BUYI

past, the Buyi had a custom called *Qiangbaohun* (marriage in swaddling bands), that is, matrimonial engagement shortly after the baby's birth. When the boy grew to teenage years, he would ask somebody to put a hat called *jiake* on his fiancée's head. This meant that she was caught by her fiancé, indicating his request for a wedding. If she did not want to marry yet, she should beware lest anyone put the *jiake* hat on her head.

The Buyi make offerings to the spirit of the dead during funerals. The family will kill a buffalo as sacrifice to release the soul of the dead from purgatory. According to traditional custom, the Buyi bury the dead underground.

8 INTERPERSONAL RELATIONS

The Buyi are hospitable. A village is usually composed of 10 or more families belonging to a few clans. They are on intimate terms with each other. If something happens, the whole village will come to help. Guests will be treated cordially with wine and dishes. Song will never cease. Duck is often offered—first the head followed by the body—and presented politely. This indicates the hospitality of the host: the duck is all for the guest, from top to toe. The guest should never beg to be excused. Otherwise, it might seem that he thinks the food is unclean.

The Buyi youngsters practice group dating called *ganbiao*. They take advantage of festivals (or going to fairs) to get together. If a girl takes a fancy to a boy through antiphonal singing, she will throw an embroidered ball to him. If he is glad to receive it, they will move to a place close to the other youngsters and sing love songs to each other. After several dates, they

may be deeply in love, but their marriage must be approved by their parents. If disapproved, they usually cannot get married.

9 LIVING CONDITIONS

Most of the Buyi dwell at the foot of a hill and beside a stream. They live in houses of one or two stories. Some are combinations of one-story and two-story houses, that is, houses built on the slope, two-story on one side and one-story on the other. The family lives upstairs, while the bottom is for livestock and fowl. The frame of the house is made of wood, and the roof of tile, flagstone, or straw. Buyi in the Biandan Mountain district (in Guizhou) live in houses made of stone with stone tables and stools.

Most traditional infectious diseases have been eliminated or brought under control. By the time babies are one year old the majority have been inoculated against diphtheria, pertussis, infantile polio, and measles.

10 FAMILY LIFE

Patrilineal extended families of three and more generations are prevalent among the Buyi. A large family means that the parents live with several married sons and daughters-in-law. In the family, men are persons of authority, while women are in a subordinate position. Buyi families are monogamous. Although close relatives are not allowed to marry, marriage between cousins is prevalent. Furthermore, a woman should marry her husband's younger brother after her husband's death. In the old days, the Buyi married very early. The bride went back to her parents' home right after the ceremony and only returned to live with her husband for a few days at a time during festivals or the busy season. She moved to her husband's house if she got pregnant. After childbirth, she changed her hairstyle from pigtails to combing it plainly, as a nun, and fixing it with hairpins made of silver or horn.

Common pets include dogs, cats, and birds.

11 CLOTHING

Men usually wear long-sleeve shirts and long robes covering their pants down to the ankle. Solid navy or white-navy checked scarves are used on their heads. Women wear Mandarin-style blouses and trousers. Sometimes, they wear lace-trimmed blouses over multi-pleated and wax-printed long skirts. A beautiful embroidered cotton apron covers the skirt. During the holidays, Buyi women also like to use silver ornaments to decorate their costumes.

12 FOOD

The Buyi are agriculturists. Their staple food is rice, supplemented by wheat, millet, corn, buckwheat, and yams. They love glutinous rice most. They eat Chinese cabbage, radishes, hot peppers, melons, and beans. Protein comes from pork, beef, mutton, chicken, duck, goose, fish, and eggs. A favorite drink of the Buyi is sweet wine fermented from glutinous rice. Mixed with spring water, it makes for a cool beverage in summer. The Buyi take breakfast as early as five o'clock in the morning, then go right away to work in the fields. They return home for lunch at noon, although they sometimes bring a simple meal, which they eat at the edge of the fields. They leave work at five or six o'clock, then do the cooking at home, and take dinner at six or seven o'clock.

Buyi people eating beside a tree in China. (© Panorama/The Image Works)

¹³EDUCATION

There are primary schools in large villages of Buyi districts. All children over seven are able to receive a formal education. Middle schools, vocational schools, and normal schools were established in counties and some small towns. There are colleges in the cities. As a result, the number of professors and teachers, as well as professionals and technicians, has been increasing rapidly. However, rural families pay little attention to girls' education. The rate of illiteracy is very high among Buyi women.

¹⁴CULTURAL HERITAGE

Buyi songs include historic songs, love songs, labor songs, "weep songs," and lyrics. They can be divided into songs in the major mode and those in minor mode. The former are sung with inspiring strains on ceremonial occasions, such as marriages and funerals. The latter are sung tenderly in dating. *Yueqin*, a four-stringed plucked instrument with a full-moon-shaped sound box, and *Dongxiao* (or *Duanxiao*), a vertical bamboo flute, are their favorite instruments. An age-old traditional percussion instrument, the bronze drum with various figures and geometrical patterns, is available in almost every village. It is used as accompaniment for bronze drum dances in grand festivals, or beat by the shaman on funeral or sacrificial offering rites. Famous dances include "Sewing Dance," "Chaff Packet Dance," and "Lion Dance."

The Buyi culture is rich in folk tales, myths, stories, fairy tales, fables, proverbs, and poems.

¹⁵WORK

The Buyi engage in self-sufficient agriculture. Sometimes the males go hunting in the slack season of farming, and the females gather edible wild herbs. Some peasant households grow apples and medicinal herbs. The double-cropping of rice requires intensive labor. Besides crop-growing labor, the household chores are women's burdens. The ready-made clothes now available in the market greatly lighten their load.

¹⁶SPORTS

Horse racing on festive occasions is a traditional sport. We find in Guizhou a kind of horse with short legs but great galloping speed and stamina. Dragon boat regattas held in broad rivers also attract a large number of spectators. The youngsters like to play a game called "throwing the chaff packet." Boys stand in line on one side and girls on the other. They throw small cloth packets filled with chaff to the opposite line, generally to the individual he or she likes.

[17] ENTERTAINMENT AND RECREATION

Singing competitions are often held on festivals as entertainment. Dozens of singers of both sexes sing musical dialogues in antiphonal style. The songs are not allowed to cease and the words of the songs may not be repeated. There are two kinds of plays that are bound to appear on festive occasions. One is called *Dixi*, performed with masks and stage costumes, the songs being folk melodies. The other, a festive lantern play, is performed with a distinctive tune. The Buyi also like gamecock and buffalo fighting on festivals for recreation. Buffalo fighting is held among villages. Each side chooses buffalo of extreme sturdiness and prompts them to fight along the river bank. A rosette will be placed on the winning animal with pride and joy by the owner.

[18] FOLK ART, CRAFTS, AND HOBBIES

The *ko-hemp* cloth, a typical Buyi craft, was traditionally sent as a tribute to the emperor. Wax printing cloth is one of the most famous crafts of the Miao and Buyi. They draw figures of wax on the white cloth, which is then dyed and dewaxed. A white decorative pattern in a blue background thus manifests itself at once. After a series of improvements in the technological process, multicolored wax printing cloth (*batik*) was developed and greatly welcomed in the market. Embroidery is a tradition of Buyi women. A pyramid-shaped bamboo hat with a variety of figures is not only beautiful and durable, but also useful as an umbrella for rain and sun.

[19] SOCIAL PROBLEMS

Poverty and isolation are still the most important socio-economic problems of the Buyi. Modernization through reform and opening to the outside world has brought social and economic development to the coastal areas, border areas, and areas along the Yangtze River. The Buyi districts share, to a limited degree, in this new-found wealth.

[20] GENDER ISSUES

The Chinese constitution states that women have equal rights with men in all areas of life, and most legislation is gender neutral. However, there are continued reports of discrimination, sexual harassment, wage discrepancies, and other gender related problems. The gap in educational levels between women and men is narrowing with women making up 47.1% of college students in 2005, but only 32.6% of doctoral students. China has strict family planning laws. It is illegal for women to marry before 20 years of age (22 for men), and it is illegal for single women to give birth. The Family Planning Bureau can require women to take periodic pregnancy tests and enforce laws that often leave women with no real options other than abortion or sterilization. Prostitution and the sex trade is a significant problem in China involving between 1.7 and 5 million women. It involved organized crime, businessmen, the police, and government workers, so prosecution against prostitution has limited success. In 2002, the nation removed homosexuality from its official list of mental illnesses, and though it is still a taboo topic, homosexuality is increasingly accepted, especially in large, international cities.

[21] BIBLIOGRAPHY

Chiao, Chien, Nicholas Tapp, and Kam-yin Ho, ed. "Special Issue on Ethnic Groups in China." *New Asia Bulletin* no 8 (1989).

Dreyer, June Teufel. *China's Forty Millions.* Cambridge: Harvard University Press, 1976.

Eberhard, Wolfram. *China's Minorities: Yesterday and Today.* Belmont: Wadsworth Publishing Company, 1982.

Heberer, Thomas. *China and Its National Minorities: Autonomy or Assimilation?* Armonk, NY: M. E. Sharpe, 1989.

Lebar, Frank, et al. *Ethnic Groups of Mainland Southeast Asia.* New Haven: Human Relations Area Files Press, 1964.

Lemoine, Jacques. "Les Pou Yi." In *Ethnologie régionale II* (Encyclopédie de la Pléiade). Paris: Gallimard, 1978.

Ma Yin, ed. *China's Minority Nationalities.* Beijing: Foreign Languages Press, 1989.

Miller, Lucien, ed. *South of the Clouds: Tales from Yunnan.* Seattle: University of Washington Press, 1994.

Ramsey, S. Robert. *The Languages of China.* Princeton: Princeton University Press, 1987.

Wiens, Harold J. *Han Chinese Expansion in South China.* New Haven: The Shoestring Press, 1967.

—by C. Le Blanc

CHĀKMĀS

PRONUNCIATION: chahk-MAHZ
ALTERNATE NAMES: Changma; Sawngma
LOCATION: Bangladesh; India; Myanmar (Burma)
POPULATION: around 700,000 (est.)
LANGUAGE: Dialect of Bengali (Bangla)
RELIGION: Theravada (Southern) Buddhism
RELATED ARTICLES: Vol. 3: Buddhists

¹ INTRODUCTION

Chākmā is the name given to the most numerous tribe found in the hilly area of eastern Bangladesh known as the Chittagong Hill Tract (CHT). The name Chākmā was first used by British census-takers in Burma to describe the hill peoples of the Arakan. The tribe call themselves Changma or Sawngma. The derivation of this is unclear, though one author suggests it means "people of the Thek clan," Thek being a Burmese name for the Chākmās.

Little is known about the origins and early history of the Chākmās. According to Chākmā tradition, the tribe is linked in some way to a mountain kingdom in the Himalayas and the Sakya clan (the clan to which Buddha belonged). Sakyas entered Burma and established kingdoms in northern Arakan and upper Burma at an early date, but the exact link with the Chākmās is unclear. Similarly, the Chākmās believe their ancestral homeland to be Champaknagar. The location of this is uncertain, though many place it in the modern Bihar.

More recent events are easier to outline. Chākmā oral history holds that the tribe migrated from Champaknagar to Arakan, the western hill region of Burma, where they lived for about 100 years. Around the 16th century, they moved northwards into Bangladesh and were granted permission by the ruling Nawab of Bengal to settle in the hill region of Chittagong. When political power in Bengal passed to the East India Company in AD 1760, the British formally defined Chākmā territory and recognized the powers of the Chākmā Raja—subject to payment of tribute. The exact amount of this tribute was a matter for dispute and resulted in a long drawn out war fought by the Chākmā Rajas against the British. The issue was settled by the peace treaty signed in 1787 between Raja Janbux Khan and the British government.

By and large, the Chākmā rajas and the British colonial administration remained on good terms. At first, the British followed a policy of noninterference with the Chākmā hill tribes. But unrest in the hill areas ultimately led to Chākmā territory being brought under direct British control. In 1860 and 1900, various rules and regulations were set in place for the administration of the Chittagong Hill Tracts.

At the partition of India in 1947, the Chittagong Hill Tracts were awarded to Pakistan rather than to India. This caused considerable resentment among the predominantly Buddhist Chākmā population, who saw their cultural affinities to be with the Hindu peoples of India rather than with the Muslims of East Pakistan. This resentment increased with the removal of the old British "Excluded Area" status that provided some protection for tribal areas. One result of this was an influx of Muslim settlers into the region. The seeds were thus sown for a tribal movement that came into focus in the early 1970s, when

it became clear that the policies of the new Bangladeshi government would differ little from those of the Pakistanis. The year 1973 saw the beginnings of an armed insurgency by the Shanti Bahini ("Peace Force"), aimed at gaining autonomy for the Chittagong Hill Tracts.

The problems in the Chittagong Hill tracts can be traced back to the completion of a dam at Kaptai near Rangamati between 1957 and 1963 when the area was a part of East Pakistan. At least 54,000 acres of settled cultivable land, mostly farmed by the Chākmā tribe, were lost in 1957 when the government began the construction of the Karnaphuli hydroelectric project. Over 400 square miles of land were submerged with far-reaching effects on the economy and life-style of the tribal people there. Some 100,000 people lost their homes and prime agricultural lands. Compensation for lost land was inadequate and over 40,000 Chākmā tribals crossed the border into India where the majority have sought Indian citizenship. At the same time, the Pakistan Government announced its intention to open up the area for economic development and encouraged poor Bengali families to settle there. This policy was even more vigorously pursued by the Bangladeshi government. Conflict over land together with the threat of assimilation into the majority culture of Bangladesh, provide the background to the armed conflict between Chākmās and Bangladeshis.

The Shanti Bahini was the name of the military wing of the Parbatya Chattagram Jana Sanghati Samiti (PCJSS)—the United People's Party of the Chittagong Hill Tracts. It was formed in 1972, shortly after the creation of Bangladesh following the 1971 war between India and Pakistan, to preserve the rights of the tribal people in south-eastern Bangladesh, and fought for many years against the central government. In February 1972, a tribal delegation called on Prime Minister Sheikh Mujibur Rahman to put forward four basic demands: autonomy for the Chittagong Hill Tracts, together with provisions for a separate legislative body; retention of the provision of the 1900 Regulation that allowed a form of self government; the continuation of the offices of the traditional tribal chiefs; a constitutional provision restricting amendment of the 1900 Regulation; and the imposition of a ban on the influx of non-tribals into the area. All the demands were rejected and the 1972 Constitution of Bangladesh made no provision for any special status for the Chittagong Hill Tracts.

The Shanti Bahini did not become militarily active until the mid-1970s when it began to attack military and paramilitary personnel and their bases in the Chittagong Hill Tracts, as well as non-tribal settlers, resulting in hundreds of deaths and the abduction of foreign nationals for ransom money. Violent army operations in the Chittagong Hill Tracts began in March 1980 when it was reported that 22 soldiers were ambushed by the Shanti Bahini in the village of Kaukhali west of Rangamati where Bengali families were being resettled. The army retaliated by deliberately firing on two groups of unarmed tribal people killing a number of villagers after they were ordered to line up. From then on, Bengali settlers began to attack the tribal people apparently at the instigation of the army or in conjunction with the operations of army personnel. The army reportedly recruited armed groups known as Village Defense Parties (VDP—also called village defense police) from the new settlers and provided them with firearms to resist the Shanti Bahini. Official figures indicate that more than 8,500 rebels, soldiers and civilians were killed during two decades of insurgency. The

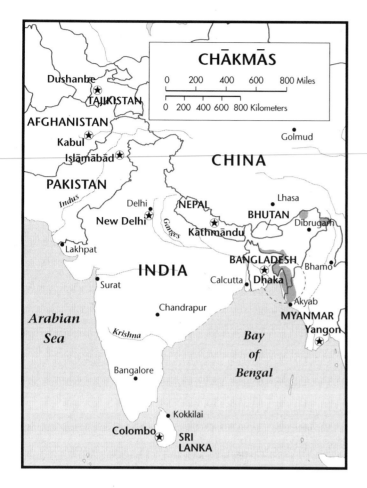

CHĀKMĀS

0   200   400   600   800 Miles

0 200 400 600 800 Kilometers

number of civilians killed is estimated at 2,500, with Amnesty International, the human rights organization, reporting serious violations of human rights in the Chittagong Hill Tracts by Bangladeshi military personnel, including rape, torture, indiscriminate shooting, assaults on women, capture of farmland by Muslim settlers, and the killing of Chākmā.

Rebels and Bangladeshi security officials say that, after the assassination in 1976 of Sheikh Mujabir Rahman, India secretly provided arms and money to the tribal insurgents fighting in the area. The rebels, who were mostly Buddhists, say they were being persecuted and pushed off their fertile lands by an influx of ethnic Bengali Bangladeshis, who are overwhelmingly Muslim. "We are not separatists and we do not want armed intervention by India," said Mr. Chākmā, a rebel spokesman. He said they wanted a stop to Muslim settlers, protection of the region's (Chittagong Hill Tract's) demographic character, free elections, and extensive economic and political powers.

In August 1992, the Parbatya Chattagram Jana Sanghati Samiti declared a unilateral cease-fire for three months, which remained in force indefinitely until the signing of the peace accord with the Bangladeshi government on 2 December 1997, although some organizations such as the Hill Students Council, Hill Peoples Council, and Hill Women's Federation opposed the peace deal and formed the United Peoples Democratic Front (UPDF), a dissident political party. The main provisions of the Peace Accord included the establishment of a Chittagong Hill Tracts Regional Council with its Chairman, who would be a tribal, having the status of a state minister.

Any new laws in connection with the Chittagong Hill Tracts were to be enacted in consultation with and on the advice of the Regional Council. No amnesty was to be provided to the army and police personnel for past human rights violations, but there was no commitment in the Accord that past human rights violations by the law enforcement personnel or the Bengali settler groups close to the army would be addressed. However, a general amnesty was to be extended in the accord to the former members of the Shanti Bahini who surrendered their weapons. The Accord committed both sides to "uphold the characteristics of tribal creed and culture."

Although the government has amended some existing laws to provide for the implementation of the Peace Accord, the Accord is currently in tatters. It was opposed by opposition groups at the time of signing and the current unstable political situation in Bangladesh has not helped matters (a caretaker government is in power to oversee general elections scheduled for the end of 2008). In August 2007 the High Court directed the government of Bangladesh to explain why the Accord should not be declared "illegal," and it has already set aside certain provisions of the Accord by directing the authorities to allow the illegal plains settlers who were implanted into the Chittagong Hill Tracts to register themselves in the voters' list. Few instances of past human rights violations have been investigated, and the main provisions of the Peace Accord have yet to be implemented.

2 LOCATION AND HOMELAND

The Chākmā population today is estimated to be around 700,000 people, but it is spread over three different countries. The majority (approximately 450,000 people) are located in the Chittagong Hill Tracts of Bangladesh. This population spills over into neighboring areas of southwest Mizoram State in India, where another 100,000 Chākmās live, and Burma (Myanmar), which has around 30,000 Chākmās. In addition, Tripura State in India had some 50,000 Chākmā refugees who fled Bangladeshi Army operations against their villages in the Chittagong Hills in 1988. By 2000, most of these refugees had been repatriated to their homeland. Another group of Chākmās, numbering around 100,000 people, is found in the foothills of the Himalayas in northeastern India. These refugees fled from Bangladesh to adjacent areas of India in the 1960s and were later relocated to Arunachal Pradesh state by the Indian government. The Chākmā refugees are often stateless, despite petitioning the Indian government for citizenship, although some have recently been granted voting rights in India over the protests of local populations.

Ethnically, the Chākmās are a Mongoloid people related to the Arakanese of southwestern Burma. The Chittagong Hills, the homeland of the Chākmās, are a northerly extension of the Arakan Hills and form part of the western fringe of the mountain systems of Burma and eastern India. They are formed by narrow, steep-sided ridges running north–south at elevations between 600 and 900 m (approximately 1,970 to 2,950 ft) and rising to the highest point in Bangladesh (1,046 m or 3,432 ft) in the southeast. The ridges are separated by lush valleys drained by numerous small rivers. On the west, the hills are bordered by a broad, fertile plain that extends to the Bay of Bengal. The climate of the region is subtropical monsoon, with warm temperatures, monsoonal rainfall patterns, and high humidity.

³ LANGUAGE

The Chākmās speak a dialect of Bengali (Bangla) and nowadays write in the standard Bengali script. This language of the Indo-Aryan branch of the Indo-European family of languages has clearly been adopted by the Chākmās through contact with their Bengali neighbors. At one time, however, it seems that the Chākmās spoke a Tibeto-Burman tongue, which today is called Changma Vaj or Changma Kodha. Changma Vaj is written in its own script, known as Ojhapatt, which uses a cursive script similar to those found in Burma and Cambodia, which in turn are derived from the scripts of southern India. Some authors suggest that the Chākmās common language is so distant from Bengali that its classification as a Bengali dialect is questionable.

⁴ FOLKLORE

The Chākmā myth of origin traces the tribe to the ancient kingdom of Champaknagar. One of the king's sons, so the story goes, marched east with a large army in the hope of conquering new lands. He crossed the "sea" of the Meghna River and captured the kingdom of Arakan in Burma, where he settled. His people intermarried with the Burmese and gradually adopted the Buddhist religion. The last of the Champaknagar dynasty was a ruler named Sher Daulat (contact with the Muslims led to the Chākmā rulers adopting Muslim names). He was credited with supernatural powers and was supposed to purify himself from sin by bringing out his intestines to wash them in the river. His wife, out of curiosity, hid herself and watched him do this one day. Sher Daulat found her spying on him and, in a fit of rage, killed her and all his family. His eccentricities and tyranny grew so great that finally his people tired of them and killed him. Fearing the consequences of this, the people left the Arakan, moving north into the area of the Chittagong Hills they occupy today.

⁵ RELIGION

The Chākmās are Buddhists and officially follow the Southern, or Theravada, form of the religion. Theravada Buddhism was introduced into Southeast Asia from Sri Lanka, but in Burma there appears to have been a mixing with elements of northern Tantric Buddhism. Exposure to Hinduism in the 19th century brought Hindu influences to Chākmā society. Likewise, Buddhism in the region has absorbed rather than displaced existing pre-Buddhist beliefs. Buddhism, as practiced by the Chākmās, is thus a mixture of the southern and northern forms, with a touch of Hinduism and aspects of shamanism and animism thrown into the mix.

Almost every Chākmā village has its Buddhist temple (*kaang*). Buddhist priests or monks are called *Bhikhus* and preside at religious festivals and ceremonies. The villagers support the monks with food, gifts, and offerings to Buddha. In the past it was customary for boys, usually around the age of puberty, to take Buddhist vows, even if only for a few days. The novice would shave his head, don the saffron robe, and live the life of a monk until his return to lay society.

The Chākmās also worship Hindu deities. Lakshmi, for example, is revered as the Goddess of the Harvest, and offerings of pigs and chickens are made to her. Similarly, *pūjās* (worship ceremonies) are performed for spirits of the hill, the wood, and the stream, with offerings of rice, fruit, and flowers. Spirits that bring fevers and disease are propitiated by the sacrifice of goats, chickens, or ducks. Animal sacrifice is, of course, totally against Buddhist beliefs, but the Buddhist priests turn a blind eye to the practice. Exorcists (*ōjhās*) and spirit doctors (*baidyo*) are called in to deal with harmful spirits. The Chākmās believe in witchcraft and the casting of spells for both good and evil purposes. It is considered a very bad omen if vultures, kites, or owls settle on the roofs of Chākmā houses, and pūjās are immediately performed to counter this misfortune.

⁶ MAJOR HOLIDAYS

Chākmās celebrate various Buddhist festivals, the most important being Buddha Purnima. This is the anniversary of three important events in Buddha's life—his birth, his attainment of enlightenment, and his death. It is observed on the full moon day of the month of Vaisakh (usually in May). On this and other festival days, the Chākmā put on their best clothes and visit the temple. There, they offer flowers to the image of Buddha, light candles, and listen to sermons from the priests. Alms are given to the poor, and feasts are held for the priests. The three-day festival known as Bishu, which coincides with the Bengali New Year's Day, is celebrated with much enthusiasm. Houses are decorated with flowers, young children pay special attention to the elderly to attain their blessings, and festive dishes are prepared for guests. The Mahamuni fair, held at Rangunia at the time of Bishu, is a favorite with all the hill tribes, who attend in great numbers.

⁷ RITES OF PASSAGE

A Chākmā woman is subject to no particular restrictions during pregnancy. After the birth of a child, the father of the child places some earth near the bed and lights a fire on it. This is kept alight for five days, after which the earth is thrown away, and the mother and child are bathed. A woman is considered polluted for a month after childbirth and is not allowed to cook food during this period. Children are suckled to a considerable age by their mothers.

Chākmās cremate their dead. Sometimes, if death occurs during times of hardship when the proper funeral rites cannot be performed, the corpse may be buried and disinterred after the harvest for cremation. The body is bathed, dressed, and laid out on a bamboo bier. Relatives and villagers visit the body, and a drum used only at this time is beaten at intervals. Cremation usually occurs in the afternoon, and the ritual is presided over by a priest. The rich are carried ceremoniously to the cremation ground in a decorated chariot. The morning after the cremation, relatives of the deceased will visit the cremation ground to search for footprints, believing the departed will have left some mark of his or her new incarnation. Some remains of bones are collected, placed in an earthen pot, and placed in a nearby river. The mourning period for the family lasts for seven days, during which no fish or animal flesh is eaten. On the seventh day, the final ritual (*Sātdinya*) is held. At this time the family offers food to their ancestors, Buddhist monks deliver religious discourses, offerings are made to the monks, and the entire village participates in a communal feast.

⁸ INTERPERSONAL RELATIONS

Chākmā hospitality is a byword in the region, with guests plied with home-brewed liquor and the *hukkā* pipe. In the hills, Chākmās hail each other with the traditional hill-cry

"Hoya." This exuberant shout is also used to express pleasure at victory in sports such as tug-of-war that accompany the numerous hill festivals held throughout the year. The influence of Muslim contacts is seen in the use of the "Salaam" greeting by some Chākmās.

9 LIVING CONDITIONS

Chākmās build their houses on slopes near the banks of a river or a stream. A few related families may build on the same plot of land, creating a homestead (bārī). Baris cluster together to form hamlets (parā), and a number of hamlets make up a village (grām).

The traditional Chākmā house is made of bamboo. It is constructed on a bamboo or wooden platform roughly 2 m (6 ft) above the ground, with access by means of a crude wooden ladder. The front area of the platform is bare, providing space for household activities. It is usually enclosed by a low fence for the safety of young children. The house is built on the rear of the platform. Mat walls divide the house into separate compartments, the exact number depending on the needs of the household. A veranda in the front of the house is divided in two by a mat partition, one area being used by males and the other by females. Small compartments may be built for storage of grain and other possessions. Household objects ranging from baskets to pipes for smoking tobacco are made out of bamboo.

10 FAMILY LIFE

Chākmās are divided into about 150 clans (gojas), which are further subdivided into subclans (guttīs). Chākmā rules of exogamy forbid marriage between members of the same subclan, although this practice is not always strictly observed. Adult marriage is the norm in Chākmā society. Parents arrange marriages, although the wishes of sons and daughters are taken into account. A bride-price is fixed during the course of negotiations. The marriage ceremony is known as Chumulong and is performed by Buddhist priests. If young people elope, the marriage can be formalized on payment of the appropriate fines. Chākmā society is patrilineal and patrilocal. Polygamy, i.e., marriage to more than one wife, is acceptable but rare. Divorce is allowed, as is widow remarriage.

11 CLOTHING

Chākmā men have given up their dress of dhotī, kurtā, and white turban in favor of Western-style shirts and trousers. It is the women who maintain the traditional Chākmā style of clothing. This consists of two pieces of cloth. One is worn as a skirt, wrapped around the lower part of the body and extending from waist to ankle. Its traditional color is black or blue, with a red border at top and bottom. The second piece of cloth is a breastband, woven with colored designs, that is tightly wrapped around the upper body. This is worn with a variety of necklaces, bracelets, anklets, rings, and other ornaments. Chākmā women are skilled weavers and make their own cloth. The sārī is becoming increasingly common.

12 FOOD

The staple food of the Chākmās is rice, supplemented by millet, corn (maize), vegetables, and mustard. Vegetables include yams, pumpkins, melons, and cucumbers and are supplement-ed by produce gathered from the forest. Fish, poultry, and meat, even pork, is eaten, despite the Buddhist taboo on consuming animal flesh. Traditional diets have slowly been abandoned, as the Chākmās have been forced to flee their homeland and/or come into contact with nontribal populations. Some typical Chākmā dishes include fish, vegetables and spices stuffed into a length of bamboo and cooked in a low fire; foods wrapped in banana leaves and placed beside a fire; and eggs that are aged until they are rotten. Like most hill tribes, Chākmās view milk with distaste. Chākmās are hard drinkers, and every household distills its own rice-liquor. Alcohol is consumed freely at all festivals and social occasions.

Food is customarily served on a low table, roughly 15 cm (6 in) high. This is made of bamboo or, among the higher classes, copper. Diners sit cross-legged on a mat on the floor.

13 EDUCATION

As might be expected in a non-Muslim minority population in one of the more isolated parts of Bangladesh, Chākmās do not score highly in terms of educational achievements. Individual figures for Chākmās are not available, but overall literacy among the hill tribes stands at 14.8%. This figure drops to 7.2% for women. Literacy rates are much higher in the states of India. Mizoram, for instance, ranks second behind Kerala among the states of India for literacy, but even here the figures for Chākmā are only 45.3% for men and 36.6% for women. In Bangladesh, however, literacy in a second language (usually Bengali) stands at over 70%, which provides some indication of the extent to which the Bengali language is replacing Chākmā.

14 CULTURAL HERITAGE

The Chākmās possess a literary tradition of sorts, with a variety of works written in the Chākmā language. Buddhists texts, translated into Chākmā and written on palm leaves, are known as Aghartara. The Tallik is a detailed account of medicinal plants, methods of their preparation, and their use in the treatment of disease.

Folk music is a major aspect of Chākmā tribal culture. It includes romantic love songs known as Ubageet, the Genkhuli ballads relating some incident from the past, and epic poems like Radhamon and Dhanapati. This last work recalls the period when the Nawab of Bengal first gave shelter to the Chākmā Raja when the tribe entered southern Chittagong during the 15th century. Traditional musical instruments include a bugle made from buffalo horn, a circular piece of iron with a string stretched across it that vibrates to produce sound, and the drum. The bamboo flute is played by almost all Chākmā youth. Unlike other tribal groups of the eastern hills, dancing is not an important part of Chākmā life.

15 WORK

The Chākmās are agriculturalists, traditionally practicing shifting cultivation known by the local term jhum. This is common in the hill areas, where the slope of the land may be quite steep. Each year, land is selected for cultivation. There is no ownership of land, but Chākmā custom holds that no one should encroach or interfere with jhum fields that bear the mark of another person. Land is cleared of trees and bushes, and any remaining vegetation is burned during the dry season in April. Crops are planted after the first heavy rains, and harvesting usually takes place in October and November. All

A Chākmā woman with her children in the Bijoypur Chākmā refugee village. Several thousand Chākmās were displaced during the 1960s following atrocities allegedly committed by the majority Muslims and the construction of a hydro-electric dam in the Chittagong Hill Tracts of Bangladesh. The Chākmās sought refuge in India. (Parthajit Datta/AFP/Getty Images)

agricultural work on the fields is done by hand, or with a hoe. The fields are fenced to protect the crops from animals. Crops raised include dry paddy rice, root crops such as taro and ginger, vegetables, pulses, chilies, and garlic. Cotton is also grown, with Chākmā women using this for spinning and weaving cloth. Many of the tribes have now adopted permanent cultivation and use ploughs and cattle to till fields in the flatlands along the valley floors. Irrigated rice cultivation dominates in these lowland areas, with conditions favoring two harvests a year.

Some Chākmās have given up their farming lifestyle and entered the local labor market. Those fortunate enough to have the necessary education have gone on to clerical and other white collar jobs. Many, however, work as laborers in the factories and industrial projects that have grown up along the valley of the Karnafuli River.

16 SPORTS

Ha-do-do is a game played throughout Bengal. Two teams of equal numbers stand on either side of a central line within a defined playing area. They take turns sending a player into opposing territory to touch as many people as he or she can during the space of one breath, while at the same time saying "Ha-do-do." If the player runs out of breath or is caught by his

or her opponents, he or she goes out. On the other hand, if the player successfully returns to his or her own territory, the players he or she has tagged must leave the game. Other pastimes include *Gila Khela,* a type of marbles game in which small wooden disks are used in place of marbles; *Nadeng Khela,* played with a spinning top; and various wrestling games. Girls do not have dolls or play at being "mother."

17 ENTERTAINMENT AND RECREATION

Because Chākmās live in the more remote, hilly areas of Bangladesh and neighboring countries, their access to modern forms of entertainment is limited. Traditional forms of recreation include popular folk songs and music, and *jātrā,* the village opera. Wrestling and other sports held at fairs are popular. In the past, hunting and fishing were favorite pastimes, although they are less so today.

18 FOLK ART, CRAFTS, AND HOBBIES

The Chākmā are adept at making a variety of household goods from bamboo, often with nothing more than a hill-knife (*dao*) at their disposal. Women are expert weavers and dyers and make their own cloth called "Alam." They are skilled in the art of making baskets from bamboo.

¹⁹ SOCIAL PROBLEMS

The Chākmā people face an unenviable situation today. Numerically, their population is larger than that of over 60 independent nations in the world, yet the tribe is fragmented and scattered over three countries. In each country, Chākmās form a minority and many are refugees from their homeland, living in conditions of squalor. One group of Chākmā has been transplanted over 500 km (approximately 300 mi) from their traditional home to Arunachal Pradesh in northeastern India. Chākmā refugees face resentment from local populations. A recent Indian Supreme Court ruling that Chākmās in Arunachal Pradesh be granted Indian citizenship is being strongly opposed by local politicians and other peoples of the area.

The most serious problem faced by the Chākmās is in Bangladesh, where charges of genocide have been leveled against the Bangladeshi government. Facing increasing numbers of Muslim migrants in the Chittagong Hill Tracts and erosion of tribal identity as the area was opened to economic development, tribal groups formed a political party (PSJSS or Parbatya Chattagram Jana Samhati Samiti) to fight for their rights. (The tribal peoples of the area now refer to themselves collectively as the Jumma people or the Jumma nation.) Some Chākmās and other tribal peoples have resorted to armed resistance, and since 1973 they have been involved in guerrilla warfare against the government. This, in turn, has led to reprisals by the police and Bangladeshi Army. Both Amnesty International and the U.S. State Department have reported human rights violations against civilians in the tribal area. The 1997 Peace Accord, signed with the Bangladeshi government, has yet to be fully implemented, and, given the general political situation in Bangladesh, may never be so.

²⁰ GENDER ISSUES

Chākmā women, despite being Buddhist and therefore viewed as theoretically equal to men in their own society and facing none of the discrimination that characterizes their Hindu and Muslim neighbors, have fared badly in the conflict with Bangladeshi Muslims. Women have been subject to rape, violence, and other sexual abuses during the Chākmā insurgency. In 2002, for example, after the death of a local Muslim, which was blamed on local Chākmā, all the menfolk of the community of Madarbania, a remote village in the hill-tract Ukhia subdistrict of Cox's Bazaar, fled the village. With the menfolk gone, brutalities were heaped on the remaining Chākmā women. Many of them were raped or molested and several badly beaten up by the local attackers, who subsequently carried away all the livestock that the Chākmās had and prevented any women from getting out of the village. Occasional attacks on Chākmā women by the illegal plains settlers and security forces are still reported in the press.

Some women have banded together to form the Hill Women's Federation (HWF) to raise consciousness among the tribal women about their rights and duties as the most repressed section of Bangladeshi society in the Chittagong Hill Tracts. HWF is highly vocal against military repression on women and organizes protest demonstrations against every incident of human rights violations against tribal women. In 1996, HWF came into the national and international limelight when its organizing secretary Kalpana Chākmā was abducted by the Bangladeshi military, but, so far, the government has failed to bring the culprits responsible for her abduction to justice.

²¹ BIBLIOGRAPHY

Bessaignet, Pierre. *Tribesmen of the Chittagong Hill Tract*. Dacca: Asiatic Society of Pakistan, Publication No. 1, 1958.

Chakma, Sugata. "Chakma Culture." *Folklore (The Journal of the Folklore Research Institute, Bangladesh)* 7 (January): 58–75, 1982.

Hutchinson, R. H. S. *An Account of the Chittagong Hill Tracts*. Calcutta: The Bengal Secretariat Book Depot, 1906.

Maitra, S. R. *Ethnographic study of the Chakma of Tripura*. Kolkata: Anthropological Survey of India, Ministry of Tourism and Culture, Dept. of Culture, 2002.

Majumdar, Chandrika Basu. *Genesis of Chakma Movement in Chittagong Hill Tracts*. Kolkata: Progressive Publishers, 2003.

Talukdar, S. P. *Chakmas: An Embattled Tribe*. New Delhi: Uppal Publishing House, 1994

———. *The Chakmas, Life and Struggle*. Delhi: Gian Publishing House, 1988.

—by D. O. Lodrick.

CHAM

PRONUNCIATION: CHAHM
LOCATION: Cambodia; Malaysia; Vietnam
POPULATION: About 250,000
LANGUAGE: Cham; Cambodian
RELIGION: Islam; orthodox Cham; Hinduism
RELATED ARTICLES: Vol. 4: Muslims

¹ INTRODUCTION

The Cham of Vietnam and Cambodia are descendants of refugees from the ancient kingdom of Champa, who fled central Vietnam 500 years ago. The Cham may have originally come from Java before migrating to the mainland peninsula of Southeast Asia—certainly their Kings and ruling class incorporated many Javanese traditions. They are one of several groups of Malayan stock, which also includes the Jarai and Rhade of Vietnam, the Dayak of Borneo, and the Igorot of the Philippines. The Cham of Cambodia, in current statistics, also includes more recent Malay immigrants.

The ancient Cham were heavily influenced by Java, which in turn was influenced by India, as seen in borrowed cultural elements, such as religion and art. Cham were fishermen, seagoers, rice-cultivators, and masters at temple construction. The remains of their religious monuments dot the landscape of Vietnam and Cambodia today and were imitated by others who came after them.

The Kingdom of Champa ruled much of what is now central Vietnam from the 2nd to the 15th centuries. From the 2nd to the 10th centuries, the Cham were usually at war with China to the north. From the 10th to the 15th centuries, Champa was frequently at war with the Khmers to the west, and the Vietnamese, also to the north.

By 1213 the Vietnamese had reduced Champa to a feudal state but Champa again gained its independence in 1326. Under a Cham hero named Che Bong Nga, Champa repeatedly attacked Vietnam throughout the 1300s. After this hero's death, Vietnam again continued its incursions into Cham land. By 1471 the Vietnamese ruler Thanh Ton had completely subdued Champa.

Over the next years, the Cham attempted but failed to end Vietnamese rule. From the 16th century on, the great Champa kingdom had been extinguished with the Cham. Numerous Cham fled central Vietnam for Cambodia, including a number of nobles and other dignitaries. The last royal descendent died in the early 1900s.

Since the 16th century, Cham have continued to live in Vietnam and Cambodia, minority neighbors to the majority ethnic Vietnamese and Cambodian population around them. Cambodian Cham today remember themselves as the survivors of the massacre of their people by the Vietnamese and the fighting in 1841 against the Cambodian armies of King Ang Duang.

Those who settled in Cambodia were well-treated by the French. From the first elections in 1946, they supported the Liberal Party of Prince Norindeth, and then, from 1955, the Sangkum movement of Prince Norodom Sihanouk. One prominent politician of Cham ancestry, Eng Meas, worked in the police, and his daughter Eng Marie, married Sihanouk's

second son Prince Norodom Ranariddh. Many Cham served in the Royal Cambodian Army and after the 1970 takeover by Lon Nol, a large number continued to serve him and also the pro-U.S. FULRO organization (United Front for the Liberation of Oppressed Races), which also heavily recruited from the Mountain Khmers. A Cham, Yisales Yasya, also served as a senator from 1972 until 1975.

In 20th century Cambodia, the Cham were again the victims of massacres by the neighboring majority population. From 1975 to 1979 Cambodia was ruled by the Khmer Rouge, Communist extremists determined to erase all non-Khmer characteristics from the population. The Cham were special targets of the Khmer Rouge for a number of reasons. In fact, it was a surprise to many surviving Cham and to observers that any remained in 1979. Many of those who managed to flee Cambodia during the 1980s supported the Khmer People's National Liberation Front or their allies, the Royalist FUNCINPEC movement (National United Front for an Independent, Neutral, Peaceful, and Cooperative Cambodia); although several, such as Abdul Koyom and Mat Ly (son of Sos Man, a longtime Communist), held senior positions in the pro-Vietnamese Communist party of Hun Sen.

The Cham were forced to adopt Cambodian language and customs and to abandon their own. Their communities, which had traditionally been separate from Buddhist Cambodians, were broken up and the people dispersed to other villages. Fishermen were forced to grow rice and dig canals, and religious leaders were stripped of their authority. Many were killed. In just two districts of Kompong Cham alone, over 40,000 Cham were killed by Khmer Rouge soldiers in the late 1970s.

The Cham claim that 132 of their mosques were destroyed during the Khmer Rouge period, and the Cham were not allowed to practice their religious rituals. Only 20 of the 113 most prominent clergy survived the Khmer Rouge period. This loss of leadership, as well as the destruction of mosques, dispersion of the population, and poverty, has slowed the re-establishment of mosques, services, and schools. Despite the losses, however, the number of mosques in Cambodia is roughly what it was before the Khmer Rouge era.

In Vietnam, the Cham have fared much better, but have also been subject to discrimination, pressure to assimilate to Vietnamese society, and ridicule for retaining their customs.

² LOCATION AND HOMELAND

By the late 1800s, according to some reports, not many Cham were left—maybe as few as 15,000 in both Vietnam and Cambodia. By 1910, in other reports, there were approximately 45,000 Cham in both countries, half as many in Vietnam as in Cambodia. Their numbers then increased rapidly. In 1936 the census for Indochina listed the Chams as being 73,000, with 29,786 listed on the electoral roll (males over the age of 21), with a population of about 250,000 in 1975 when the Khmer Rouge Communists came to power.

From 1975 until 1978, the Cham were a particular target of the Communist Democratic Kampuchean government. Many died and others fled Cambodia entirely. By the late 1980s, though, their numbers were increasing. Some observers suggest their numbers still do not approach the figures of the 1970s; others conclude that the Cham population at least equals its number prior to 1975, although exact numbers remain elusive.

In Vietnam, most Cham continue to live in the south central area of the country. In Cambodia, the Cham have settled along the Tonle Sap and Mekong rivers and in western, southern, and central Cambodia. They have fared relatively well with their much more populous Khmer neighbors (with the exception of the late 1970s), despite their differences in religion, language, schooling, and even subsistence patterns.

Following the violence and massacre of late 1970s Cambodia, some Cham, along with other Cambodians, fled their homeland for Thailand. After some time in refugee camps, most were resettled in Malaysia, and also Western countries, where they continue to live.

Many resettled Cham live in communities separated from their fellow Cambodian and Vietnamese countrymen. Some have migrated thousands of miles in their new lands to join fellow Cham, even if they were strangers. Those in Malaysia have been welcomed by the majority Malay community. Other Cham attended the local mosque and found themselves having more in common with black American Muslims and immigrants from the Middle East, Africa, and Asia, than they did with other migrants from Cambodia.

3 LANGUAGE

Cham is an Austronesian language, and thus Cham is related to languages spread over much of Asia and the Pacific. Cham is also related to Jarai and Rade, languages spoken by Mountain Khmer hill tribespeople in northeastern Cambodia, and to Malay, a language also spoken in Cambodia.

Most Cham in Cambodia are bilingual, speaking both Cham and Cambodian (Khmer). Cambodian Cham speak a dialect called Western Cham, which is also spoken by some Cham in Vietnam. Western Cham is distinguished from Eastern Cham, which is spoken by Cham in coastal central Vietnam. Western Cham has borrowed numerous words from Khmer, Arabic, and Malay, and has borrowed also from Vietnamese, Chinese, Southeast Asian, and Malayo-Polynesian languages. The Cham language is atonal, with words containing up to three syllables.

The Cham language has its own writing system. Western Cham speakers, however, no longer use the traditional Cham script originally based on Indian Pali script, although it has been retained by Eastern Cham in Vietnam. Instead, Cambodian Cham is written in Arabic script. Protestant missionaries also developed a romanized script in the 1960s, which has been used occasionally.

4 FOLKLORE

Many ancient Cham are remembered as great heroes. The most famous was the king named Che Bong Nga, who ascended the Cham throne of central Vietnam in 1360. He led his armies against the Vietnamese and reoccupied Cham land to the north. While his victories were temporary, with the Vietnamese eventually overtaking the Cham empire, his triumphs over the Vietnamese are remembered.

The most renowned king of all, Po Rome, ruled Champa from 1627 to 1651. But his rule, remembered as glorious by present-day Cham, was overshadowed by a Vietnamese invasion. When Po Rome was killed by his Vietnamese enemies, his Vietnamese wife threw herself on his burning funeral pyre in grief.

5 RELIGION

Although numbers of Cham were already Muslim, the Cham who fled the Champa kingdom of central Vietnam in the 15th century apparently converted to Islam sometime before the 17th century, influenced by contacts with Malay kinfolk, who had been Muslims for some centuries.

Cambodian Cham are all Muslim, with Islam being their defining characteristic, and Cham adherence to their religion has undoubtedly helped their survival as a separate ethnic group. The Cham worship in their own mosques. Their holy book is the Quran, and each Cham community has a community and religious leader, called the *hakem*. There is also a *bilal* who calls the faithful to prayer and an *imam* who leads them in their prayers. Influenced by Hinduism from India, Cham continue to practice some Hindu beliefs along with their Muslim faith.

The spiritual center for Cham within Cambodia is Chrouy Changvar, a market town near Phnom Penh. There they go to consult the high Muslim officials in residence, to celebrate special occasions, and to visit with Cham throughout the country. Some young male Cham go each year to study the Quran in Malaysia or in Mecca. The greatest wish of every Muslim throughout the world, including Cambodia, is to make a *haj*, a pilgrimage to Mecca. In the 1950s, about 7% of the Cham population made the trip, and today, many more long to go.

Many Cambodian Cham are Sunni Muslim of the Shafii school, although there are traditionalist and orthodox branches. Traditional Cambodian Cham, numbering about two-thirds of the population, have kept many ancient traditions and rituals. Although they consider Allah the single, all-powerful God, they also recognize other non-Islamic deities. In this respect they resemble the Cham of coastal Vietnam more than Muslims of other countries. Traditional Cham believe in spirits and practice magic to avoid illness and death. Less concerned with making a pilgrimage to Mecca or praying daily, they do nonetheless celebrate many Muslim festivals.

The remaining one-third of Cambodian Cham are orthodox Cham, who retain religious beliefs and practices much closer to Muslims from other countries. They do so in part because of their close ties to the Malay migrant community in Cambodia. Many orthodox Cham have adopted Malay customs and many speak the Malay language in addition to Cham and Cambodian. They are much more integrated into the worldwide community of Islam believers, making the pilgrimage to Mecca and attending conferences, visiting mosques, and studying in other countries.

Most traditional Cham are scattered throughout central Cambodia, while orthodox Cham are located primarily around the capital of Phnom Penh, the former capital of Udong (formerly Oudong), and in provinces to the south.

Most Cham in Vietnam are Hindus who practice a form of Shaioita Brahmanism. The most important Hindu officials among the Vietnamese Cham are the priests, who are chosen for life. These men belong to the *basaih* caste. Some members of the basaih caste are taught sacerdotal rituals as young as 10 or 11 years of age. Other Hindu Cham officials include the priestess, who must remain celibate.

Members of the *camenei* caste, considered inferior to the basaih caste, maintain the temples. Musicians sing and play instruments in accompaniment to religious ceremonies. Another category of people gives offerings to higher officials and

A tourist looks at Cham artifacts in one of the temples at My Son in Quan Nam province, Vietnam. My Son was an important spiritual center for the ancient Hindu kingdom of Champa from the 4th to the 13th century. (AP Images/Richard Vogel)

performs ceremonial dances. Other officials, such as family priestesses, preside over family magical and religious rituals.

6 MAJOR HOLIDAYS

Both Hindu and Muslim Cham observe a number of religious and magic ceremonies. Most religious and magical ceremonies contain rituals that originate in Islam, Hinduism, and traditional religions of the area.

The two most important festivals of the Hindu Cham are the *Bon Kate* and *Bon Cabur*. Bon Kate is held during the lunar month, which corresponds to late September/early October, preferably on the fifth day of the fifth lunar month. Bon Kate is celebrated over a period of five days if possible, during which time Hindu Cham make religious offerings of a goat, two cups and one box of cooked rice, a tray of ground rice cakes, five cups of sticky rice, lemon juice, and 10 pieces of betel to the statue of their god. This ceremony continues to be celebrated by non-Muslim Cham in Paris, France.

The other important ceremony is Bon Cabur, held during the lunar month corresponding to late January/early February. Both ceremonies honor the spirits of the dead: similar festivals are also held by both the Vietnamese and Cambodian neighbors of the Cham. The people gather to share an elaborate feast and to celebrate for a period of five days.

Another major holiday is *Eidul-Fitr*, which celebrates the breaking of the 30-day fast observed by Muslims throughout the world. For the entire month of *Ramadan*, Muslim Cham refrain from eating from sunrise to sunset. A typical holiday feast includes lamb, chicken curry, and fish with the standard rice and vegetables.

7 RITES OF PASSAGE

As with their fellow Cambodians, the birth of a Cham child is considered a blessed event and is greeted by the family and community with great joy.

Toddlers are nursed until two to four years of age and are treated with considerable lenience. At age four, children are expected to feed, bathe, and control themselves, and shortly thereafter, to care for their younger siblings as many Cham have large families.

Most parents continue to exert almost complete control over their children until they are married. Even then, the influence of their parents is heavy. Children are expected to show great respect to their parents and elders and are severely punished for any lapse.

While the Khmer Rouge loosened the traditional control of parents over their children and modernization in urban areas continues to threaten traditional respect and obedience toward parents, most Cham continue to observe traditional family behavior. Cham express pride in the fact that their children have suffered less rebellion and their families less conflict than many other Cambodian families. Children become full adults when they have jobs, their own households, spouses, and children. Even then, they are expected to follow the advice of their elders.

The Cham bury their dead after the funeral service. In the year following the funeral, several more ceremonies are held, each honoring the deceased person. At the end of the year, the bones of the deceased are exhumed and reburied in one final ceremony. The bones are then carried to the final permanent cemetery and are buried with the rings of the deceased person.

8 INTERPERSONAL RELATIONS

The Cham often exchange the traditional Muslim greeting, giving one another a blessing. One person begins by saying *"Salamu alaikum,"* to which another responds *"Alaikum salam."*

Cham in Cambodia also greet each other with the traditional Khmer greeting, the *sampeah*, joining their palms together, their fingers pointing up or slightly tilted toward the other person, then bringing their hands up to their chest or forehead.

The Cham, like their fellow Cambodians and Vietnamese, place importance on hierarchy and proper behavior, influenced by Confucian ideas. Women must respect men, children must respect their elders, and everyone must respect their superiors, which includes anyone with higher status, greater wealth, or a more important job. Inferiors greet their superiors with greater respect, a deeper bow, or greater stoop when offering food or passing by. Visitors, both familiar and strange, are treated to the best the household has to offer.

Few young people date, and virginity remains highly valued for brides. Girls and boys have the opportunity to talk and flirt only on special occasions and during these times are surrounded by relatives and neighbors.

Most men marry between 19 and 25 years of age; women are slightly younger, usually between 16 and 22. Most young people continue to court as their parents did. It remains much more common for a young man to ask his parents' permission and assistance in obtaining a wife than to do so on his own. His parents or a matchmaker approach the young woman's family to see if they are interested in a match. If the response is positive, the families negotiate the terms and time of the marriage.

After an exchange of gifts, the young couple marries. It is still common for many young couples to spend the first year of marriage living in the home of the woman's parents. After the parents are assured of their son-in-law's stability, or after the birth of the first child, the young couple commonly moves into a new house built for them by their families.

9 LIVING CONDITIONS

Health care in Cambodia and Vietnam has been devastated by the events of the past decades. The subsequent isolation of both countries from much of the international community and the embargo against most imports and aid meant that inhabitants went another decade without even the minimum of modern health care.

International health assistance has improved services to many people. But the Cham continue to patronize local spiritual leaders for most health needs. Modern medicine is expensive, with patients having to pay before being seen for services and medicines supposedly offered without fee.

Cham villages are usually comprised of only Cham. Most are located on or near the banks of rivers or lakes, although some are located inland. Villages remain small, with between 200 and 300 people.

Like the houses of the Vietnamese and Cambodians around them, their homes are made of split bamboo and thatch. Most houses are built on stilts to protect them from seasonal flooding; thus most stand 4–12 feet off the ground. The area beneath the house is used for housing domestic animals, such as chickens, ducks, and oxen, and is shelter for the family during the heat of the day. Families often gather there during the day to do chores, look after the children at play, and visit with neighbors and passersby. In the evening, most Cham retreat upstairs to their homes, where they eat, chat, and rest. Visiting is a traditional activity and occurs frequently.

The upstairs portion of the house may be an open room or may be divided into several rooms: a private room for keeping possessions and a public room for entertaining guests, eating, and visiting. A lean-to kitchen may be attached to the house, also on stilts.

Because of their isolation, most Cham do not have electricity, running water, sewage systems, or appliances, although in recent years some have installed small generators. Houses usually contain little furniture, decoration, or utensils. Most Cham continue to own few objects that they have not made themselves. A few books, a pad of paper, and a pencil or two may be wrapped in plastic and placed in the rafters for safe-keeping. The package is out of the way but can be easily reached. Other possessions are placed similarly or hang on pegs on the walls. People sleep on mats, which are rolled up and leaned against the wall or stored overhead during the day.

The most common piece of furniture for many Cham, especially in Cambodia, is a low platform bed. Bedding materials include mats made of rush or plastic, which people place on the wooden platform, and cotton and synthetic blankets.

Rather than using modern electric appliances in their kitchens, Cham use simpler, less expensive, often handmade items. They cook over an earthenware stand placed over a fire. Because most Cham do not have refrigeration, women use preserved, salted, or fresh food. Kitchen utensils include pots, bowls, cooking ladles, and spoons made of coconut shells, although plastic plates and utensils have started to be used by some communities. Basic work tools of Cham women include looms, spinning wheels, mortars for pounding rice, baskets, jars, and trays. The Cham also make rope, mats, wooden implements, and some iron tools.

Like many of their fellow countrymen, the vast majority of Cham have never ridden in an airplane, car, or motorized boat, although most have been in buses. Most have paddled a boat and those who own a bicycle consider themselves lucky, and the dream of most youth and adults is to be able to purchase a motorbike. For most Cham, the most common form of transportation continues to be by foot.

10 FAMILY LIFE

Women are viewed as important members of society, contributing materials and skills without which the group could not live. The Cham observe a fairly strict division of labor, with women caring for children and the household, and men representing the family in public and bearing the brunt of responsibility for supporting the family.

Men remain responsible for rice cultivation and the heavier chores of construction, tool craft, and repair. Men have the responsibility of gathering information from others, the government, and knowledgeable leaders. Both women and men are engaged in planning family subsistence activities and carrying them out. Men and women share much of the labor involved in supporting the family. Women tend to manage the household affairs and do most of the textile manufacture, such as carding, spinning, and weaving cotton. They are also generally responsible for the family vegetable and fruit gardens and for threshing, husking, and milling the grain. Women carry most of the family's water from the nearest lake, river, or pond to the family house.

The vast majority of Cham marry within their own group and religion. Those who do not often have difficulty adjusting to village schedules, diets, language, clothing, and ways of making a living. When Cham do intermarry, it is usually with members of other minority groups such as Vietnamese, Burmese, Malay, or Chinese in Cambodia, with Chinese or Cambodian in Vietnam.

Both young men and women are given considerable freedom in choosing a spouse, with preference going to other Cham. When a girl and her parents agree on a selection, her parents approach the parents of the young man.

Cham marriages are simple, involving little expense or ceremony. In the presence of an imam who acts as the witness, the parents of the young woman ask the groom if he will accept their daughter as his bride. After he agrees, the marriage is concluded and is then celebrated with a feast. Polygynous marriages are allowed (up to four wives), although the first wife must approve the selection of any subsequent wives. Divorce is also permitted. Most polygamy and divorce occurs in families with more resources.

Cham families are matriarchal and matrilineal. Cambodian Cham trace their descent and pass inheritance through the maternal line. Residence is also matrilocal, so that young couples go to live with the wife's family.

In the past, the Cham said they had a matrilineal clan system with two clans struggling for dominance: the areca nut tree clan and the coconut tree clan. Royal succession, however, was patrilineal, with the king's son inheriting the throne in the kingdom of Champa.

Cham villages are often divided into hamlets and are governed by elected officials. The religious leaders of the community often have considerable political influence.

Animals are kept to support the family, and an animal that does not contribute to the family's income or diet is a luxury that most families cannot afford. This is not to say that children do not occasionally get close to a dog or cat, but pet relationships as they exist in the United States are rare.

11 CLOTHING

The Cham wear distinctive clothing. Both men and women wear a *batik*, a garment much like a sarong, which is worn knotted around the waist. Men wear a shirt over their batik, while women wear close-fitting blouses with tight sleeves over theirs. Men and women usually wear a turban or a scarf.

On religious days, both men and women don their best clothing. Their leaders dress completely in white and shave their heads and beards. On other days they wear clothing similar to other Cambodians: a *sambot* and blouse for women, a sarong or trousers and shirt for men. Children usually wear shorts, girls add a blouse, and both go barefoot or wear rubber thongs.

12 FOOD

With several important exceptions, the Cham of Cambodia and Vietnam eat much as their fellow countrymen. Rice is the most important food; eaten at virtually every meal, it forms the basis of most dishes.

Fish is almost as important and is eaten fresh, dried, and salted. Vegetables are also a vital part of their diet. The Cham grow a number of crops in their gardens, including onions, peppers, eggplant, tomatoes, and potatoes. Many homes are surrounded by coconut and banana trees and numerous other plants. Other fruits include mangoes, papayas, jack fruit, durian, and palm fruit. The sugar palm also yields syrup, which is used in cooking.

A traditional meal is a bowl of steamed rice eaten with a sauce containing bits of fish, fowl, or meat, eggs, vegetables, and spices such as onions, chilies, garlic, mint, ginger, or lemon grass.

The two important exceptions are pork and alcohol, consumed by many of their fellow Cambodians but forbidden to the Cham on religious grounds. Their refusal to eat pork is so great that many lost their lives during the Khmer Rouge period for refusing to do so.

The Cham usually eat an early meal of left-over rice, cakes, or fruit either at home or in the field. The big meal of the day is lunch around midday, followed by supper at twilight.

Cham men usually eat together, women and children later. Each has a bowl of rice and all take bites of food from several dishes sitting in the middle of the group. When eating on the job, away from the house, or under the house, Cham may eat sitting in a squatting position, their feet flat on the ground, their knees bent sharply, and their bottoms hanging almost to the ground. Whether squatting or sitting on the ground, the men cross-legged or, like the women, with their legs folding back to one side, they can sit for hours in positions that are uncomfortable for Westerners after just a few minutes.

In Vietnam most Cham use chopsticks to eat, while in Cambodia most use spoons like other Cambodians.

13 EDUCATION

A higher than average number of Cham are literate, for literacy is greatly valued and parents and religious leaders go to great lengths to teach reading and writing to their children. Cham children attend their own schools, where they learn Cham language and writing, religious instruction, and Cham history and traditions. Some children also attend Cambodian or Vietnamese public schools, their parents wanting them to have the benefits not only of Cham heritage but the economic opportunities available in the surrounding society.

14 CULTURAL HERITAGE

Literature is extremely important to the Cham, and they highly value their books and religious texts. The greatest cultural heritage of the Cham is their religion. Without it, they say, they could not sustain life, nor would they wish to. However, many of the holy books were destroyed by the Khmer Rouge in 1975.

[15] WORK

Most Cham are involved in agricultural subsistence activities but are also engaged in domesticating animals, hunting, and fishing. Hunting is done with bows and arrows (and now guns), nets, beaters, dogs, and traps. Fishing is done primarily with nets.

Most agriculture involves the cultivation of rice, both wet and dry. The Cham also grow maize, manioc, peanuts, ferns, and vegetables. Other non-food plants include cotton, tobacco, and plants that yield castor oil. The Cham domesticate buffalo, goats, dogs, and fowl. They use animals not only for food but for making tools and in religious ceremonies.

The inhabitants of river villages are primarily engaged in fishing, cultivating rice, and growing vegetables. Many grow onions. Fishermen who do not cultivate rice or who need extra amounts exchange their fish for it with neighboring Cambodians. Women may make extra money by weaving. Other cash crops include tobacco and mangrove tree cultivation.

The residents of inland villages support themselves by fishing, cultivating rice, and numerous other activities, depending on their location. Some villages specialize in raising fruit or vegetables. Others concentrate on metal working.

Some Cham cultivate rice by swidden cultivation, which involves the slash-and-burn technique, whereby they cut down trees and underbrush, burn the material, and then cultivate the cleared area. The ash benefits the soil and crops can be cultivated there for several years before the process must be repeated in another area.

Many Cham are butchers, since Buddhists hesitate to do so because their religion teaches not to kill animals. Cham also have a reputation for breeding water buffalo.

[16] SPORTS

Most Cham children spend only a few years in the classroom. The rest of their time is spent helping their families make a living. Even the smallest children help their parents fish, cook, gather firewood, and do a variety of chores. Both boys and girls help with younger children, and it is not uncommon to see boys carrying a baby sister for hours at a time.

Children are often responsible for caring for the animals. Boys herd the water buffalo and oxen when they are not being used for plowing, and girls feed the pigs and chickens. Boys climb up sugar palm or coconut trees seeking syrup or coconuts.

Children usually turn these subsistence activities into play and games. In addition, they enjoy swimming and running. A popular village game is played with rubber thongs. The boys draw a line in the dirt, then stand back and throw their sandals at the line. The boy who gets the closest is the winner. Girls and smaller children play a similar game with rubber bands, and the winner wears his captured bands around his wrist. Girls also play hopscotch.

The most popular spectator and participant sport is soccer. Volleyball is also a favorite, and both are seen frequently in Cham villages.

[17] ENTERTAINMENT AND RECREATION

In Cham villages, local festivals remain the most common and popular leisure activity. Playing, games, visiting, and gossiping are everyday pleasures. Modern leisure activities, such as television, movies, and videos are still rare in most Cham villages and homes.

[18] FOLK ART, CRAFTS, AND HOBBIES

Like all Muslims, Cambodian Cham do not focus on visual arts, one reason being that Muslims believe it is improper to visually portray an image of God or of his prophets. Music, however, is exceedingly important. Cham musical instruments are similar to Cambodian and Vietnamese musical instruments and range from guitars to gongs, drums, and xylophones.

[19] SOCIAL PROBLEMS

The Cham are proud of never having completely assimilated to either Cambodian or Vietnamese culture. A few Cham hope that one day the international community will force the Vietnamese to abandon Vietnam. When that happens, some Cham say their dream will come true and Champa, their great and ancient nation, will be reestablished and reoccupied by the Cham. But most Cham—in Cambodia, Vietnam, and overseas—are content to raise their families, practice their religion, and hope for a somewhat better life for their children.

[20] GENDER ISSUES

Until the 1970s most Cham women remained home-makers, performing traditional roles in the house and in villages. The dislocation from the Civil War from 1970, and the Communist Khmer Rouge rule from 1975–1978, led to the deaths of many Chams, including large numbers of men, forcing many women to be involved in working in the rice fields and even in hunting. As the population has stabilized, women have returned to the traditional roles in the villages.

[21] BIBLIOGRAPHY

Cabaton, Antoine. *Nouvelles recherches sur les Chams.* Paris: E. Leroux, 1901.

Hickey, Gerald C. "Cham" In *Ethnic Groups of Mainland Southeast Asia*, Frank M. LeBar, G. Hickey, and J. K. Musgrave, eds. New Haven, CT: Human Relations Area Files Press, 1964.

Kiernan, Ben. *The Pol Pot Regime.* New Haven: Yale University Press, 1996.

Manguin, Pierre-Yves. "The Introduction of Islam into Champa." *Journal of the Malaysian Branch of the Royal Asiatic Society* Vol. 58/1 (1985), pp. 1-28.

Marrison, Geoffrey E. "The Chams and Their Literature." *Journal of the Malaysian Branch of the Royal Asiatic Society* Vol. 58/2 (1985), pp. 45-70.

Maspero, Georges. *Le royaume de Champa.* Paris: G. Van Oest, 1928.

—revised by J Corfield

CHAMĀRS

PRONUNCIATION: chah-MAHRS
ALTERNATE NAMES: Untouchables; Scheduled Caste
LOCATION: Northern India (mainly Uttar Pradesh state)
POPULATION: About 90 million (est.)
LANGUAGE: Local dialects of the region in which they live
RELIGION: Hinduism; traditional animism, nature-worship, and superstition
RELATED ARTICLES: Vol. 3: Hindus; Vol. 4: People of India

1 INTRODUCTION

Chamārs form one of the major occupational castes of India. Although known by different names in different areas, they are traditionally associated with the working of leather. Their name is derived from the Sanskrit word for a shoemaker or tanner (*charmakāra*). Chamārs include groups that skin and dispose of animal carcasses, tanners, and makers of shoes and other leather goods. Found throughout the country, Chamārs are most numerous in northern India.

Chamārs may be traced back to very early times in the Indian subcontinent. They are mentioned in the *Rg Veda*, the earliest of the *Vedas* that probably was composed some time before 900 BC. There are numerous references in the Vedic literature to leather goods (e.g., leather bags, clothing, bowstrings, reins, leather shields, etc.), and even instructions for the preparing of skins for manufacture. Tanners and leatherworkers were clearly an important occupational group in early Aryan society. But even at this time, it is likely that they were of inferior social standing. The Aryan village community must have been organized very much along the lines of villages in India today. The cultivators residing in the villagers were Aryans, but on the outskirts of the village there would be laborers whose occupations made them unclean. These were often the conquered inhabitants of the country, or peoples of mixed descent who lived outside the Aryan community. It was to this non-Aryan segment of Vedic society that the Chamārs belonged.

The sheer number of Chamār castes and their widespread distribution in India today suggest that the Chamārs have originated from numerous sources. Some groups were tribal peoples who were assimilated into the lowest strata of Hindu society. Others appear to have been of higher social standing who were conquered or otherwise degraded to their present status. Still others may have their origins in illicit sexual relations between peoples of different castes. Yet there are certain characteristics common to all Chamār groups. Their traditional occupation handling carcasses, hides, and leather makes them "unclean." This is reinforced by certain common practices, such as eating meat, that are usually identified with the lowest classes. Their touch is polluting to caste Hindus, and so they are regarded as "untouchables." As such, even if they no longer follow their traditional occupation, Chamārs occupy the lowest rungs of Hindu society.

Chamārs are fighting for political representation in India, claiming they have been ignored for too long. Chamār and Madiga (leather workers from Andhra Pradesh) leaders from the south claim that they were not given a single position on the All India Congress Committee (AICC) or the Congress Working Committee (CWC), with the Chamār representation on the latter coming from Uttar Pradesh and Maharashtra. Their claim is that there is poor representation of the "Chamārs" from the south despite Chamārs making up over 50% of the Dalit population in the country.

Chamārs and Dalits in the north have banded together to form a political outlet for Bahujans (the Other Backward Castes [OBCs], Scheduled Castes [SCs], Scheduled Tribes [STs]) who are viewed as being at the bottom of the Indian caste system. The Bahujan Samaj (*Bahujān Samāj*) Party (BSP) is a national political party with socialist leanings that claims to be inspired by the philosophy of Dr B. R. Ambedkar. The BSP was founded by the high-profile charismatic leader Kanshi Ram in 1984. The BSP is one of the most powerful political parties in north India, has 19 members in the lower House of Parliament (the Lok Sabha), supports the Congress-led United Progressive Alliance (UPA) coalition, which forms India's current government in New Delhi, and is led today by Ms. Mayawati Kumari, herself a Chamār. The BSP was created and is dominated by Chamārs but nowadays also includes Brahmans and other high caste Hindus. At present, the BSP forms the state government of Uttar Pradesh with Ms. Kumari as Chief Minister (in fact, this is the third time Ms. Kumari has been Chief Minister. She occupied that position for a short time in 1995 and also in 1997 as part of a coalition with the Bharatiya Janata Party [BJP]).

2 LOCATION AND HOMELAND

The number of Chamār castes and subcastes, the diversity of names by which they are known, and the sometimes arbitrary identification of groups as Chamārs by census-takers makes it difficult to provide an accurate count of the Chamār population in India today. An acceptable estimate would place their total number at around 90 million people, although this number is a crude estimate, because of the problem of enumerating Chamār communities in census figures. It is based on Chamārs making up 50% of the Dalit (Untouchable) community, which is approximately 16% of India's total population. Though Chamārs are found in small numbers throughout India, their main concentrations lie on the plains of the upper and middle Ganges Valley. By far the largest Chamār population—perhaps close to 50% of the total—is found in Uttar Pradesh. The neighboring states of Bihar, Madhya Pradesh, Rajasthan, Haryana, and Punjab all have significant numbers of Chamārs in their populations, as do areas of Nepal close to the border with India.

The explanation for this pattern is not immediately clear and may reflect a number of factors. In its broad outlines, Chamār distributions fall within the drier areas of India where cattle-breeding is an important economic activity. The role played by Chamārs in this context would be of more significance than in the wetter, rice-growing areas of the south and east. But perhaps of greater importance is the fact that the upper and middle Ganges Valley were among the first areas to be colonized by the Aryans as they expanded out of their original heartland in the Punjab. One might expect to find the structures of traditional Aryan society more developed here than in the non-Aryan parts of the country.

Many Chamār groups go by other names, and some such as the Jadav, Mochi, Satnami, and Raidas claim an identity distinct from the Chamār. This may be because they have separate origins, different myths, different religious and social practices, or even occupational differences. In Uttar Pradesh, the

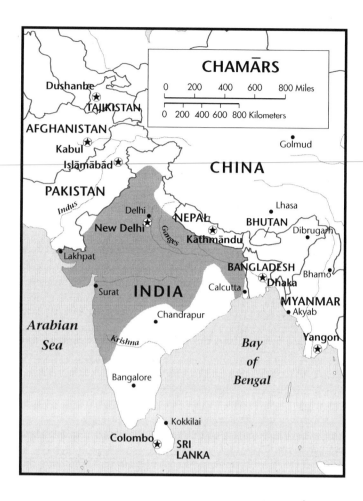

Jadav and the Raidas are the main Chamār groups. Chamārs in Rajasthan are called Regar. Bhambi is a name used in Maharashtra. In the Punjab State, many Chamārs have converted to Sikhism and are known as Ramdasias (after Guru Ramdas). Mochis are a subgroup of Chamārs found in Madhya Pradesh, Orissa, and West Bengal. In Andhra Pradesh, the leather workers, equivalent of Chamārs elsewhere, belong to the Madiga caste. Chamārs are also referred to as Untouchables, for reasons already explained, and as a Scheduled Caste, because they are identified in special government schedules (lists) as a disadvantaged caste. Mahatma Gandhi called Chamārs *Harijans* ("Children of God") in an attempt to improve their social standing. Today, many Chamārs consider themselves "Dalits," another name for unclean, lower-caste Hindus.

³ LANGUAGE

Chamārs speak the local dialects of the region of India in which they live. Thus the language of Jadavs living around Mathura in Uttar Pradesh is called Braj Basha. Literally the "language of Braj," the local name for the region, this is the dialect of Hindi spoken in the area. Similarly, a Chamār living in central Rajasthan speaks Marwari, the dialect of Rajasthani current in the region. Ramdasias in the Punjab are likely to speak Punjabi and write in the Gurmukhi script (the Sikh script). Hindi, Rajasthani, Punjabi, and the other languages of northern India commonly spoken by Chamārs belong to the Indo-Aryan branch of the Indo-European language family.

The leatherworking castes in southern India speak languages belonging to the Dravidian family. The Chakalliyans of Tamil Nadu, for example, speak Tamil, while the Madigas of Andra Pradesh speak Telugu.

⁴ FOLKLORE

Chamārs are mostly Hindus and share in the mythological traditions of the Hindu religion. However, many Chamār groups have their own myths of origin. One account traces the Chamārs to a union between a lowly boatman and a despised Chandal (i.e., of non-Aryan or mixed descent) woman, but others assign them a respectable lineage. According to one legend, in the beginning there was only one family of men of the highest caste. In this family, there were four brothers. One day, a cow died. Since no one could be found to remove the carcass, the three older brothers decided the youngest should dispose of the animal. They agreed that they would accept him back on an equal footing after he had bathed. With much effort, the youngest brother dragged the carcass into the jungle, but his brothers refused to accept him back on his return. They made him live some distance away and told him that he was to skin carcasses and work with leather. So the Chamārs were born. On another day, the story continues, a buffalo died. The Chamār told his brothers that he was not strong enough to remove it, so the carcass just lay there. The three brothers complained of this to the god Shiva, who happened to be passing. Shiva suggested that one of the brothers help, but they protested at this. So Shiva told the Chamār to make a pile of refuse (kūrā) and urinate on it. When he did this, a strong man rose from the refuse, and from this man the Kuril subcaste of Chamārs arose.

⁵ RELIGION

In general, Chamārs are Hindus. They accept fundamental Hindu doctrines such as karma (the law of cause and effect) and samsāra (transmigration), follow Hindu rituals, and worship many Hindu deities. However, they do reject the Hindu teachings that make them Untouchables and the Brahman priests who proclaim these teachings. This does not affect the inferior status assigned to Chamārs by other Hindus. In the past, they were barred from entering many Hindu temples, and some Brahman priests still refuse to serve them. They are allowed to make offerings at temples dedicated to Devi, Bhairon, to various mother-goddesses, and at some Shiva temples. In many places, Chamārs have their own temples.

Underlying this layer of Hinduism is a widespread and deep-rooted belief in animism, nature-worship, and superstition. The worship of stones is universal. The stones represent village godlings and are anointed with vermilion (a red coloring), possibly a survival of an ancient blood-sacrifice. Many trees are worshipped, in particular the pipal tree (*Ficus religiosa*) and the nim (*nīm*) tree (*Azadirachta indica*). The nim is considered to be the home of Shitala Mata, the goddess of smallpox. The snake, the tiger, the elephant, and various other animals and birds are revered and worshipped. The Chamār have numerous superstitions about evil demons, spirits (*bhūts*), and ghosts who have to be driven away or appeased through blood-sacrifice. Various diseases or epidemics are thought to be brought on by deities such as Shitala Mata or Mari, the goddess of cholera. Goats, pigs, chickens, and eggs are among the sacrificial offerings made to appease demons and gods. Chamārs strongly believe in the dangers of witchcraft and of the evil eye.

Chamārs have a number of resources they can turn to for protection from evil spirits. There are numerous godlings—spiritual beings and local saints who are seen to have special powers over the forces of evil. Guga Pīr, for example, is worshipped in the Punjab to prevent snake-bite. He was born a Hindu, so his legend tells, but became a Muslim so he could enter the earth and bring the snake-kingdom under his control (a *pīr* is a Muslim saint). He is also worshipped on behalf of sickly children, to cure various diseases, and to remove barrenness. In addition, there are various practitioners skilled in dealing with the spirit world. These include sorcerers, magicians, witch-doctors, shamans, and the like known by names such as *ōjhā*, *sayānā*, *baigā*, and *bhagat*.

Given their low status in traditional Hindu society, it is not surprising that Chamārs have been attracted to religions that downplay or reject notions of untouchability. Many are followers of devotional *(bhaktī)* Hindu sects such as the Kabir Panth. One such group is the Satnami Chamār of Madhya Pradesh. Some Chamārs have accepted the teachings of the Sikh Gurus, while other Chamār castes such as the Julahas are Muslims. Christianity has made some headway among the Chamārs. More recently, some groups such as the Jadavs in Uttar Pradesh have converted to Buddhism. They were motivated in this by Dr. B. R. Ambedkar, an Untouchable and India's first minister of law, who became a Buddhist in 1956.

6 MAJOR HOLIDAYS

Chamārs observe the normal festival cycle of their religions and their regional cultural traditions. The spring festival of *Holi* is an important celebration among Hindu Chamārs and is marked with the customary bonfires and throwing of red colored powder. It is a time of drunkenness and sexual license that can last for days. *Nagpanchami* is held in the middle of the rainy season to honor snakes. Women make images of snakes out of cow dung and worship them. Saucers of milk are placed outside the house as offerings to snakes, and milk and dried rice are poured down snake holes. *Divali*, the festival of lights, is a time when the ancestral spirits visit their old homes. *Govardhan Puja*, a festival honoring Krishna and cattle, is accompanied by excessive drinking and gambling.

7 RITES OF PASSAGE

The bearing of children, especially sons, is of utmost importance to Chamār women. Barren women visit shrines and perform various rituals to ensure they conceive, and pregnant women employ ritual and magical devices to obtain sons. Chamārs take elaborate precautions to protect the expectant mother from witchcraft and the influence of evil spirits. After a birth, the local women gather and sing songs to Shitala Mata. The singing continues day and night for six days, and during this period, mother and child are never left alone. Purification rites are performed on the sixth day and again (usually) on the 12th day after birth. A black goat is frequently sacrificed to Kali Devi (the local form of the goddess Kali, the consort of Shiva) on the twelfth day. Childhood rituals include the first "rice-feeding" ceremony, held at about 6 months of age.

No special rites mark the onset of puberty, so there is no formal initiation ceremony such as the sacred thread ritual of the higher castes. However, a girl is carefully watched for the first signs of menstruation and at its onset is kept in seclusion for four days. She must be kept out of the sight of men, and no one is allowed to touch her during this period. This results from a superstitious fear of menstrual blood. The menstruating girl has to avoid food containing sugar, salt, yogurt, and tamarind. She must not look up into the sky, nor see the sun, a cat, or a crow.

Chamārs both burn and bury their dead. The poor, who often cannot afford the wood necessary for a cremation, may scorch the face of the corpse and then dispose of it in a nearby river. Members of the Shiv Narayan sect practice burial. Death rituals include emptying all the water containers in the house, and breaking any earthenware utensils touched by the deceased just before the time of death. Chamārs believe that the dead return to visit the house, so for 10 days food is set out for the departed spirit. On the tenth day, a feast is held for relatives and friends to conclude the funeral rites. Portions of the food may be set aside as offerings to Brahmans and to local godlings. Food is also placed out for crows, in the belief that it will reach the ancestral spirits.

8 INTERPERSONAL RELATIONS

Chamārs follow the general customs of their region and religious community in their interpersonal relations.

9 LIVING CONDITIONS

Chamārs are among the most economically disadvantaged castes of India and, in general, live in poverty and squalor. Most live in villages, but as Untouchables they are required to remain separate from the other Hindus in the community. They are not even allowed to use the same wells as caste Hindus, as their presence is polluting. Small clusters of Chamār houses are found on the outskirts of virtually all Indian villages. These are usually simple, one-room structures made of mud and clay, and plastered with a mixture of mud and cow dung. Houses are sparsely furnished, according to the means of their occupants. In villages, there are no latrines and the people relieve themselves in nearby fields. Chamārs who live in cities may have better standards of living. Their houses may be of brick, have two stories, and possess some basic sanitary facilities. Chamārs in urban areas still live in segregated neighborhoods.

10 FAMILY LIFE

With the wide geographical distribution and diversity of religions found among the Chamārs, variations are to be expected in Chamār social organization and kinship systems. However, they tend to follow general regional practices. Castes and subcastes *(jāti)* are endogamous units, i.e., one marries within the caste community. These are subdivided into patrilineal clans *(got)* and lineages that are exogamous. Chamārs usually practice village exogamy, seeking marriage partners from outside the village in which they live.

Marriages among the Chamārs are arranged. In the past, it was customary for the first step, the betrothal *(mamgnī),* to take place during infancy. The actual wedding ceremony *(śadī)* would be performed in childhood, when the bride was around 8 years. In its outline, this ceremony follows Hindu marriage rituals—various ceremonies are performed in the homes of the bride and groom, the marriage procession *(barāt)* makes its way to the bride's home, and the wedding includes the ritual

Some of India's poorest people, known as Chamārs, or untouchables, participate in a march where they are demanding the government give back their land. The marchers say they aim to shame the government into keeping its promise to redistribute land. (Tauseef Mustafa/AFP/Getty Images)

walk around the sacred fire (*pherā*). Some customs, however, reflect the Chamārs' lowly origins. Among castes not served by Brahman priests, a senior relative has to officiate at the ceremony. Some groups sacrifice a goat or a ram as part of the wedding ritual. Bride and groom return to the groom's home for further ceremonies. If the bride is not of an age when the marriage can be consummated, she returns to her parents' house. The final step in marriage, the consummation or *gaunā*, occurs at puberty. A dowry is usually paid to the groom's family.

The role of a Chamār woman in family life is typical of all South Asian groups. She marries at an early age but does not achieve full respectability until she bears male children. She manages the household, cooks for her family, and performs all the household chores. A Chamār woman also contributes to the family income, working at menial labor, and even skinning animal carcasses.

11 CLOTHING

In their clothing, Chamārs are usually indistinguishable from the lower classes of their region. In Andhra Pradesh, for ex-

ample, the dress of Mochi males consists of a shirt and a *dhotī*, the typical Indian lower garment. They also wear a cloth on the shoulders, draped from the right to the left side. They tie their hair in a knot at the back of the head. Mochi women wear the sāri and blouse, with the usual array of ornaments, nose studs, and bangles.

12 FOOD

The staple diet of the Chamārs consists of breads (*roti*) made from cereals such as wheat, maize, barley, and millet (rice replaces rotī in the wetter areas). Their main meal is consumed at night, when pulses (*dāl*) and vegetables supplement the breads. Chamārs also eat meat, even carrion meat (flesh from carcasses), which is a practice that contributes to their low-caste status in Hindu society. However, individual Chamār groups vary considerably in their attitudes towards meat-eating. For instance, the Bhambi, the leatherworkers of Maharashtra, are nonvegetarian, eating goat, pork, chicken, deer, and hare. The Bhambi of Karnataka will eat beef, but not pork. In Gujarat, however, Bhambis will eat fish and mutton, but not beef. Some Chamār groups have abandoned meat-eating in an effort to raise their caste status.

Food in India has important ritual and social dimensions as well as its basic nutritional function. This is true of Chamār society. The specific ranking of Chamār castes and subcastes in any region, who will accept food from whom, who can provide acceptable marriage partners, and many other social attributes are linked to the dietary patterns of specific Chamār groups.

13 EDUCATION

Historically, poverty and discrimination barred Chamārs from access to education. After independence, India legally abolished the practice of untouchability. The government set in place policies providing increased educational opportunities for disadvantaged communities such as the Chamārs. Many Chamār groups favor education, especially for boys, but educational levels vary from place to place. Literacy among the Chamārs of Goa, who are called Chambhars, is 58.02%, which is far above the average for the Scheduled Castes. By contrast, Chamārs in Bihar show a literacy rate of only 11.52%, with female literacy falling as low as 2.36%.

14 CULTURAL HERITAGE

Although they can hardly be said to possess a distinctive cultural heritage, Chamārs share in traditions of regional folk culture. Thus, legends of Guga Pīr (also known as Zahra Pīr) are widely known and popular among Chamārs and other low castes throughout northwestern India. In addition, specific groups have developed their own cultural traditions. The Chamārs of Gujarat, for example, express their art and culture in their leather goods, floor designs, tattooing, Garba folk dance, and folk songs sung at the time of birth and marriage. As with most nonliterate groups, Chamār culture is largely oral in nature, focusing on folk tales, song, music, and dance.

15 WORK

In the past, Chamārs carried out their occupation as tanners and leatherworkers in the context of the traditional Hindu economic system, the *jajmānī* system. In this, Chamārs had a hereditary relationship with a *jajmān* or patron, usually a landowner in the village. They provided their services to the jajmān and in return received a portion of the landowners harvest. With the emergence of the cash economy, the mutual responsibilities of such a relationship no longer have meaning. Furthermore, historically Chamārs could not own land. While this is no longer true in independent India, few Chamārs have the resources to buy land. As a result, although some Chamār castes follow their traditional occupation as tanners, leatherworkers, and shoemakers, many Chamārs in rural areas live as landless agricultural laborers.

Those Chamār individuals who have managed to obtain the necessary education have been able to pursue white-collar jobs and enter the professions. A few successful Jadavs in cities in Uttar Pradesh, for example, own their own factories. Social policies that "reserve" jobs and legislative seats for the Scheduled Castes have allowed some of the more educated generation to enter government employment and politics.

16 SPORTS

There are no sports associated specifically with the Chamār community. Children play games common to the young throughout the country.

17 ENTERTAINMENT AND RECREATION

Chamārs enjoy gambling, while country liquor is consumed at most social events. In rural areas, entertainment is essentially limited to activities related to fairs and festivals. Chamārs living in towns and cities have access to movies and other urban entertainment.

18 FOLK ART, CRAFTS, AND HOBBIES

Not all Chamārs follow their traditional occupation today. Many of those who do, however, are known for their leatherworking skills. Chamārs have a strong tradition of folk songs and music.

19 SOCIAL PROBLEMS

The Chamārs are an economically depressed and socially disadvantaged community in India. They face problems of landlessness, poverty, debt, and lack of education. Gambling and excessive drinking is common among some Chamār groups. Population growth has resulted in increasing pressure on limited resources. The traditional occupation of Chamārs makes them polluted and polluting to caste Hindus. Even though they might no longer handle hides and carcasses, they are despised by most upper-caste Hindus. Recent attempts by Chamārs to claim some of their newfound rights in an independent, democratic India have led to conflict with upper castes in villages and towns across India. For example, serious rioting involving Jadavs and upper-caste Hindus occurred in Agra in 1978. As lawmakers in the United States have discovered, social equality can be proclaimed by the stroke of a pen. But it takes much longer to change social and cultural attitudes that have been in place for centuries—for the Chamārs, attitudes that have been in place for millennia.

20 GENDER ISSUES

In most states of India, Chamārs are classified as belonging to the Scheduled Castes, i.e. castes identified by governments as needing special help in terms of education and development.

Scheduled Castes also have "reservations," i.e. a certain number of places in colleges and positions in the government are allocated to them in a type of affirmative action program. Because of their traditional occupation as leather workers and handlers of animal carcasses, however, Chamārs are considered as "untouchable" and polluting to caste Hindus. Chamār women are thus alienated from society on the basis of class, caste and gender. They tend to be poor and illiterate—in Tripura, only 54.4% of Chamār women were classed as literate in the 2001 Census of India, compared to 63.4% for Chamārs as a group—whereas in Bihar, the literacy rate among female Chamārs falls below 14%. Even though many Chamārs have changed their occupations (in the terai of Nepal, for example, they act as midwives), poverty and illiteracy have limited their upward social mobility. Other Hindu castes tend to treat Chamārs as traditional "untouchables," no matter what their current occupation. One writer indicates that Chamār women are not very "shapely" and their lot remains "poverty and disease." Chamār women experience the same travails as all women in Hindu society—arranged marriages, child marriage, dowry-giving (despite the giving of dowries being made illegal by the Union Government in 1961), limited access to education and health facilities, and lack of property rights.

Despite India being a signatory to the United Nations Convention on the Elimination of All Discrimination Against Women (CEDAW), which came into force in 1982, cultural oppression and social subjugation remains an issue with Chamār women, who are often subjected to domestic violence, physical assault, verbal abuse, sexual exploitation, rape, abduction, forced prostitution, and murder etc., which are usually inflicted by the men belonging to caste Hindus.

Nonetheless, some Chamār women have risen to a position of prominence in the political sphere. Ms. Mayawati Kumari, for instance, is leader of the Bahujan Samaj Party that forms the government of Uttar Pradesh State and she is, in fact, the State's Chief Minister. She remains a national emblem for Chamār women.

21 BIBLIOGRAPHY

Briggs, George W. The Chamārs. Calcutta: Association Press, 1920.

Mukerji., A. B. The Chamārs of Uttar Pradesh. Delhi: Inter-India Publications, 1980.

Sharma, Satish Kumar. The Chamar Artisans : Industrialization, Skills, and Social Mobility. New Delhi: B.R. Publishing Corporation, 1986.

Showeb, M. Education and Mobility among Harijans: A Study Based on Students, Government Employees, and Traditionally Employed Chamars of Varanasi. Allahabad, India: Vohra Publishers, 1986.

Singh, K. S., ed. "Chamār/Chambhar/Chamār or Ramdasia." In People of India. Vol. 2. The Scheduled Castes. Delhi and Oxford: Oxford University Press with the Anthropological Survey of India, 1993.

Snodgrass, Jeffrey G. Casting Kings: Bards and Indian Modernity. Oxford: Oxford University Press, 2006.

—by D. O. Lodrick

CHIN

PRONUNCIATION: CHIN
ALTERNATE NAMES: Sho, Asho, Zo, Mizo, Lai, Yaw, Zomi
LOCATION: Myanmar (Burma); India; Bangladesh
POPULATION: About 2 million in Myanmar, over 1 million in India
LANGUAGE: Chin
RELIGION: Christianity

¹ INTRODUCTION

The Chins are a Tibeto-Burman people. Although they are collectively known as Chin by outsiders, they call themselves names such as Sho, Asho, Zo, Mizo, Lai, Yaw, Laizo, Zotung, Zophei, and Zomi. Whether their original name is Chin, Lai, Zo, or Sho is debatable, but it can be concluded that most of their clan names are similar sounding. Based on old Burmese inscriptions from the Pagan period, some contend that Chin is the original name. In history books written by British colonial officers, the people were referred to as Kuki, Lushai, and Chin because the British came in contact with Bengalis, Thado, and Burmese. The Bengalis called them Kuki, and the Thado, who the Bengalis gave the name Kuki, called the other clan living next to them Lusei, which was corrupted by the British to become Lushai. The British adopted the Burmese term "Chin" when they came to Burma (which was renamed Myanmar by its military government in 1989). The name Chin is commonly used in Myanmar and Zo or Mizo in India.

The Chin people originated from somewhere in Western China (possibly where the Lolo people, a Tibeto-Burman ethnic group, still live today) or Tibet. They reached the Chindwin Valley, northeast Burma, in the first millennium AD. After living in the Chindwin Valley they gradually moved into the Kale-Kabaw, Yaw, and Myittha valleys. During the 12th and 13th centuries they came in contact with the Burmese (Burman) ethnic group, Burma's largest. Some, known today as the Asho, wandered to the south to live in the plains of Burma. The majority of them moved to the Indo-Burman ranges, where they have made their home for the last 500–600 years. Because fertile land was scarce in these Indo-Burman ranges, each clan either had to protect its own territories or find new ones, which created clan-oriented societies whose acquired territories were guarded by means of warfare. Through these skirmishes the people were pushed toward the north, south, and west, resulting in the formation of many different dialects and customs among the same people. The mountainous terrain further isolated different dialect groups. Each clan was ruled by its own chief. Some clans would attack others to widen their influence. Just before the British annexation, the Falam clan had control of almost the whole people. During the early 1800s, the British annexed the Chin country in the west at the Bengali/Chin border. They completed colonization of the Chin people in the 1890s. Even today, Chin society is often divided by clan-based regional rivalry.

² LOCATION AND HOMELAND

The Chin people as a whole number over 3 million, with around 2 million in Myanmar (Burma). In India, at least 800,000 live in Mizoram state. The Chin population in Bangladesh is about 50,000.

The Chins live mostly in the Indo-Burman ranges stretching from the Letha range in the north to the Arakan mountains and neighboring plains. Some also live in the Pegu and Popa hills of Myanmar, in the midst of the Burmese people. The British colonial administration divided the people into many administrative districts. The borders drawn by the British that divide the Chin exist still today. There is great contrast in living standards between the impoverished Chin areas of Myanmar and Mizoram, a modern, Mizo-governed state of India. In Myanmar, the Chins reside mainly in the Chin state and surrounding areas, in the State of Arakan, in the Prome-Thayetmyo area, in the Yaw Valley, in the Kale-Kabaw-Myittha valleys, in the Tamu-Hkamti area, and in the Popa and Pegu hills; in India, they reside in the Mizoram, Manipur, Tripura, and Assam states; and in Bangladesh, they reside in the Chittagong-Bandarban Hill tracts. Uneasy relations between the Kuki (Chin) people in Manipur, India and the non-Chin ethnic groups of that state have sometimes resulted in violent conflict.

Tens of thousands of Chins from Myanmar have fled the ruling military regime, taking refuge in neighboring Mizoram, where relations with the related Mizo people are often difficult, with the Mizos accusing the Chin refugees of being criminals. There are also thousands of Chin refugees in Indian cities such as New Delhi, in Malaysia, and other countries. Chin refugees have been settled in the United States in increasing numbers since 2006. Battle Creek, Michigan, is one place where many of those new immigrants have found a new life.

³ LANGUAGE

The Chin language belongs to the Tibeto-Burman family of languages. Dozens of regional dialects exist among the Chin. The major dialects are the Duhlian, Lai, Paite, Khumi (Mru), Cho, and Asho.

The Chins have family or clan names. With their clan names, they can recognize each other as relatives and friends. Whole communities can have a single name, such as Sizang, for example. The Sizang have a population of about 5,000 people living in five neighboring villages; all of them have the same clan name of "Suantak." Because villages commonly carry the name of their founder, and all the village members stem from the same clan, they all have the same family name. Consequently, among their own people, the Chins usually do not use their family name, unless they come in contact with the outside world. Many of their names usually consist of two or three words. Every name has a meaning and describes the status of the person giving the name, as explained below.

The paternal grandfather has the prerogative of naming the male children. In the Tedim (Zomi) district, the grandson's name begins with the last name of the grandfather's first name (since names consist of more than one name). For example, if a grandfather's name was En Vum, the grandson would receive the name "Vum Son." The name "Son" means "to tell." In other words, the name given to the baby means he should tell of the deeds of his grandfather. While the naming practice is similar in other Chin, they do not necessarily begin their names with the names of relatives. Conversely, the paternal grandmother has the prerogative of naming her granddaughters. Next in line are the maternal grandfather and grandmother. After them, uncles or aunts may name the children. The people of northern Mizoram and Hualngo differentiate male and female by ending male names with the "a" sound and female names with the "e" sound. Chin people often have a Christian name from the Bible or an English nickname, as well as their traditional Chin name.

⁴ FOLKLORE

The Chins say that they had their own writing at one time, which was kept written on leather. A myth tells that a dog ate the leather, and the writing was lost. Although they had no trace of that writing, the Chins have a long oral history, tracing back their history through songs. Every successful man had his own song. When Chins gather in mourning or in celebration they sing the songs of their forefathers, in which are composed the deeds of the ancestors. These songs have kept their history alive. However, because most Chins have converted to Christianity and these songs may be perceived as unchristian, their people's oral history has been neglected.

The Chin heroes are those ancestors who were successful and whose lifetime deeds are recorded in the songs sung by their descendants. Many Chin clans have a myth that their originator came out of a hole in the earth, a cave named Sinlung.

⁵ RELIGION

The Chin people were once animists. They believed in evil spirits who lived in trees, caves, high mountains, water springs, and everywhere else—even in human bodies. They could be two-legged or one-legged beings, and were always ready to bite or punish human beings. They were the source of all human suffering. The people therefore gave offerings to the evil spirits when they fell ill or when their crops failed. At funerals they sacrificed chickens, dogs, pigs, cows, and mithuns, a huge domesticated gaur (wild ox) so that the deceased could arrive in heaven as a rich person. Many families would keep a mithun as a family pet, letting it graze in the forest by day and calling it by name to come home at night. The mithun is the rarest of the large animals domesticated by humans. While they ate most of the meat of the sacrificed animals, they laid the rest of the meat, such as the legs or parts of the animal not suitable for human consumption, on altars for the evil spirits.

The Chins also believed in a powerful god, called Pathian, who was good to them. They did not give offerings to Pathian because he did not harm them. They also believed in going to another place after they died. They believed that they could take along their possessions. Thus, when someone died, the families had extravagant funerals at which they might slaughter a number of animals, especially the mithun. Long ago, when a powerful chief died, they went out to hunt for heads so that he could take slaves to his next life.

Christian missionaries arrived in the land of the Chins during Burma's British colonial period. The first were American Baptist missionaries who came to the Hakka area in 1899. They were followed by other missionaries, who did medical work among the Chins and preached to them. Eventually, the majority of Chin people (estimated 90%) joined Christian churches, including Presbyterian, Baptist, Methodist, Catholic, Anglican, and other denominations. The Chins are known for a diversity of Christian sects, with a number of different churches even in small villages. There are also "new religions," indigenous varieties of Christianity, and some Chins in Myanmar and Mizoram who became Jewish, following the Old Testament and considering themselves a Lost Tribe of Israel. Some of the Jewish Chin/Mizo population has emigrated to Israel in the 21st century.

Most of the Chins' animist beliefs gave way to Christianity, but some survive, such as the use of mithuns for feasting. Many of the churches discourage the use of traditional fermented beverages like Zu. The Chins in Myanmar have experienced pressure from the military regime to convert to Buddhism, the country's majority religion. Some Chin children have been taken to Buddhist boarding schools, and crosses erected by Chins on hilltops have been torn down and replaced by Buddhist pagodas by Burmese soldiers. It is very difficult for Chin congregations to get permission from the regime to repair or rebuild church buildings. Pastors and other church workers have been arrested and even killed by the Myanmar military, according to reports by the U.S. government and international human rights groups.

⁶ MAJOR HOLIDAYS

The traditional Chin/Mizo holiday is the Harvest Festival during November/December at the end of the harvest season. The Harvest Festival is named according to the dialect of the people, such as Khuado, Khuangcawi, etc. The Harvest Festival begins with the slaughter of family-reared pigs, which must be large enough to produce some amount of pork fat. This time is the opportunity to eat plenty of food, when every household shares their cooking with relatives, friends, and the community. The women prepare plenty of *Zu*, a fermented rice, maize, and millet alcoholic beverage that is the Chin national drink. Everyone joins in the drinking, singing, and dancing in the evenings that could go on for the whole night and up to four days. There is also a corn harvest festival in Mizoram in August.

Christian holidays including Christmas and Easter are celebrated by the Chins with church services, singing, and feasts. Young people go from house to house with candles and torch lights, singing Christmas carols. The Chins in Myanmar also commemorate the arrival of the missionaries and founding of churches in their land. A Chin National Day is commemorated early in the year by exiles from Myanmar.

⁷ RITES OF PASSAGE

The birth of a child is traditionally celebrated with the drinking of Zu by the neighbors and relatives. Friends or relatives kill a chicken, cook it at home, and bring it to the family. The chicken soup is for the mother, so that she has plenty of milk to breast feed the baby. A few days, weeks, or even months go by before the Chins give a name to the newborn. The giving of a name is celebrated by inviting relatives. The person naming the child contributes Zu and the meat, usually a pig or a cow.

A child joins his or her parents in the fields as soon as he or she can walk the distance. Most teenage boys and girls do the same work as their parents. Boys have fewer duties than their sisters. As soon as a girl is able, at the age of six or so, she is expected to help her mother in preparing food or other chores. Because many villages are built on the tops of hills, one of the usual duties of the girls is to carry water from the springs or streams to the house. They are also expected to carry firewood and to pound rice and corn. Boys are expected to look after the livestock, to hunt, and to make traps to catch wild animals. In the villages, teenage boys used to sleep in a designated house; for example, the Mizo had the Zawlbuk (bachelor's house), where all young men of the village would sleep.

Life expectancy for the Chin in Myanmar is short, due to a high child mortality rate, and access to health care is very limited, so many people rely on traditional herbal medicine. The Mizos in India enjoy better access to hospitals, clinics, and health workers. Before the influx of Christianity, the dead were kept at home until the family could afford a proper burial. A proper burial included killing several animals and drinking a large number of Zu pots. Before the corpse was buried, the family would recreate the likeness of the person, wrapping his clothes around the skeleton. The people sang the songs of their ancestors, most importantly the song of the deceased. On wooden posts they would hang the skulls of the animals killed at the funeral. For an important person, relatives still erect a monument, usually a stone platform or tablet on the main road or trail. The monument carries inscriptions and animal figures that show how many animals the deceased hunted.

8 INTERPERSONAL RELATIONS

Before the British came the Chins normally did not shake hands, but today it is common practice. Their greetings are very personal, such as "Have you had your meal?," "Where are you going?," or "What are you doing?" If someone comes by to visit, they may say, "Are you coming to visit me?" Or if somebody is eating, the greeting will be, "Are you eating?" Then the person eating will say, "Please join me and have food." Should there be a guest when the family is eating (breakfast, lunch, or dinner), the guest is invited to join in the meal. The duration of the visit has no limits. It is very impolite to tell someone to go home. People visit each other early in the morning or any time of the day. If the host is busy the guest might help with the work while they chat.

In the traditional Chin society, when a young man was of age, which could be as young as 16, a marriage could be arranged. Because the Chins trace their ancestries over many generations, each person's lineage was known. A young man was expected to marry a girl from the mother's lineage. A man of good standing in the family, either the father, an uncle, or a close relative, was chosen as the ambassador to go to the house of the prospective girl to meet with her parents or guardians. The ambassador would take a chicken or a pot of Zu with him. In more recent times, he might take a small bag of sugar. The ambassador announces his mission in a cordial and very humble manner. For example, he may say, "The good-for-nothing boy of mine, Zam Tual, has come of age, and in life a man needs a woman to fulfill his life's obligations. I am here to ask your kindness in agreeing to match your daughter and my son." The parents of the girl, whether they mean it or not, will appear unwilling to give their daughter—not because they think the boy is not good enough for their daughter, but because their daughter is unfit for the boy. They may say, "The girl is lazy. She does not know how to work. She has a bad character, and you would not like her at all as your daughter-in-law." Now the ambassador would insist, explaining to the girl how bad the boy is but how much the boy needs a wife. He also must explain that because of the family ties, there is the need for the union of the two families. The girl's parents then explain the impossibility of giving away such a useless girl in

marriage. They then part cordially. The admirer and his family must wait about a month for the girl's reply. If the family does not return the presents, they have accepted the request. The ambassador once again goes to the girl's house to discuss the terms of the marriage, such as how many cows or mithuns are to be slaughtered at the wedding, what kind of bride-price the groom must pay, and the timing of the wedding. If the families had been at odds before, then a solution has to be found—usually an expensive bride-price or an elaborate wedding. The bride-price may depend also on the community's tradition, or on the physical appearance of the bride.

These days, young people are likely to meet at church activities and decide for themselves who they want to marry, but parental blessings are still important. In addition to a church marriage ceremony, weddings are celebrated by killing a cow or mithun at the bride's house. On that day, the main bride-price, given to the parents, is settled upon. There are also prices to be paid to the aunt, who took care of the bride when she was a baby, when the mother was working in the fields. After dinner is served, the bride is taken to the groom, where the friends will sing and play games the whole night. The actual wedding celebration is the next day when more cows or mithuns are slaughtered and the whole village and neighboring villagers are invited.

9 LIVING CONDITIONS

The land where most Chin people live is very rugged. Fertile land is scarce, and therefore living conditions for most Chins are very basic, although there is a much higher standard of living for the Mizo/Chin people in India than for Chins in Myanmar. The capital of Mizoram state, Aizawl, has a population of 340,000. The city's houses are mostly wood and bamboo, built on a series of hills connected by roads, paths, and stairs. Roads and an airport connect Aizawl with the rest of India. In Myanmar raids by soldiers and forced labor contribute to living difficulties for the Chins and cause many to look for refuge and work in other countries.

Chins in rural areas build their own houses with lumber and bamboo they cut themselves. Every homeowner yearns for two things: a wooden platform in front of the house and a corrugated zinc roof. Most Chin houses are divided into two parts. One part, the larger part of the house, stores grain. The other part of the house is used for eating and sleeping around a big fireplace. The front of the house is usually only partially enclosed and stores firewood and utensils for corn and rice husking. Most of the household chores are done in this part of the house, including pounding the rice or corn. As decoration, skulls of wild animals may hang on the walls. Family photographs, calendars, and Christian posters decorate the rooms.

Most Chins have very few consumer goods, weaving their own clothing and making all their utensils themselves, mostly using bamboo. There is hardly any furniture in the houses, except for cane or bamboo stools or benches for sitting. The only luxury in the house is the fireplace, used for cooking and warmth. Family members and visitors sit around the fireplace every day when it is cold. People use their blankets to keep warm when they go out in the cold mountain mornings or evenings.

In the Chin Hills of Myanmar, transportation of goods is mostly on people's shoulders and backs. Few people own horses, and carts cannot be used in the hills since there are few roads. People carry grain from the field to the house. Fire-

A little Chin girl holds her mother's hand during the Kut festival in Churachandpur, India. The skirt of her mother and the pattern in the girl's sweater reflect traditional motifs. (© Lindsay Hebberd/Corbis)

wood and drinking water are also carried the same way, but some villages may have bamboo flumes to guide water to their houses. In Myanmar only the towns and cities have electricity but even there the service is sporadic. In Mizoram roads good enough for four-wheel drive vehicles have been built to reach all but the most remote villages.

Most Chin households keep cats and dogs. The cat's purpose is to catch rats and mice, which eat the grain stored in the house, and the dogs are used for rat catching, guarding the village, and hunting.

10 FAMILY LIFE

Most Chin families are large, averaging about five children per family. Girls marry and go to live with their husbands. The families in rural areas work together on their farms and older and younger generations live in the same house. Chin customs differ on who inherits the parent's house. The child inheriting the parents' house is expected to care for the parents in their old age. When the oldest son inherits the parent's property, he remains in the house. His brothers must move out soon after they marry. When the youngest son inherits the house, the older brothers move out after they get married. This makes sure that there is constantly a daughter-in-law who cares for the parents.

11 CLOTHING

Men's traditional daily wear was the loincloth and, when the days were cold, men used the same blanket they slept under at night and wrapped it around them for warmth. For the women, traditional dress was a woven short skirt and, to keep out

the cold, they also wrapped their blankets around themselves. A jacket, longer skirt, and a headdress of porcupine quills are worn as dance costumes by Chin/Mizo women today. At present the Chin men wear trousers, jeans or shorts with t-shirts or other shirts, and jackets, while the women wear sarongs and blouses in Myanmar and skirts, dresses, or jeans in Mizoram, with sweaters or jackets for the cold. Even with those changes, traditional woven blankets are still used as cloaks and as ceremonial gifts, and traditional embroidery is used on sarongs, blouses, jackets, and even neckties. Chin men and women both carry woven and embroidered cloth shoulder bags. Weaving patterns, colors, and embroidery are very regionally distinctive, so one call tell where a person comes from by the clothes they wear. Christian symbols, such as crosses, are often included in the weaving or embroidery. Necklaces made out of Pumtek (petrified wood) or carnelian beads and silver bracelets are favorites among the women. Some older women still have traditional tattoo patterns on their faces.

12 FOOD

Although the Chins work daily in the fields, they may not harvest enough food for the year. The Chin seldom eat meat. They usually eat two to three times a day. Their breakfast, lunch, and dinner may be very similar. Corn and millet are the staple foods for people living in higher elevations. Potatoes and sweet potatoes are commonly served for dinner. Dry corn grains are pounded to get rid of the skin, then cooked for four to six hours. Rice is the staple food for people who live in more fertile areas where rice can be grown in hillside fields. Meat usually is boiled for a long time. The Chin were only introduced to spices by the Burmese and Indians, so they are not prevalent.

Chin farming tools are basically a hoe, a long knife, and an ax. The use of spades, breaker bars, and shovels was introduced by the British and they become very popular. Cooking pots and dishes made in China, India, or other parts of Myanmar are traded to the Chins; however, locally made pottery is also important because it is used for boiling corn soup, the staple food of the Chin. Every 48 years, a common type of bamboo that grows thickly in Chin/Mizo regions flowers, produces fruit, and then dies off. A huge population explosion of rats accompanies the bamboo flowering, as the rats eat the bamboo fruit. When the bamboo fruit is gone the rats raid the people's grain storehouses and devour everything. This phenomenon, known as *Mautam,* caused severe famines in the region in 1911 and 1959. While Mizoram prepared for the 2008 bamboo flowering by building roads and helicopter landing pads for food relief shipments, reports of starvation in Chin areas of Myanmar began emerging in early 2008. With a worldwide rice shortage and severe increases in the price of rice in Myanmar following Cyclone Nargis in May 2008, this was considered a particularly dangerous situation for the Chins.

13 EDUCATION

Prior to the British invasion in the later part of the 19th century, there were no schools for the Chin people. The only education they received was how to survive on rugged land. Although a writing system invented by Paucinhau (1859–1948) became popular in the Chin Hills in the 1930s, Christian missionaries taught the people to write their language with the Roman alphabet. The missionaries then translated the Bible into the Chin language with the Roman alphabet, so the Chin writing was lost. Today, the Chins are not allowed to teach their own language in the schools in Myanmar. Many young people cannot read or write in their language.

Although the British colonial administration offered very few schools, the missionaries started many schools. Today, Mizoram (in India) has a high literacy rate. However, the overall level of education in the Chin area of Myanmar is very low, due to lack of education by Myanmar's regime. Rules and regulations introduced by the military regime have prevented entry into the medical and engineering professions for Chin students. Because of the hardships faced by the people to simply survive, parents try to encourage children to go to school and learn so that they may gain employment, but it is hard for even the most educated Chins to find jobs in Myanmar.

14 CULTURAL HERITAGE

Because of the conversion of the people to Christianity, much of the traditional culture has disappeared. Instead of traditional songs, people are versed in Christian songs. It was the duty of important chiefs and personalities to compose their own songs, which would be remembered and sung during social gatherings. Today, these traditions are sometimes regarded as unchristian because of the missionaries' message that old forms of traditions were evil influences. Most young people do not know how to sing traditional songs, although there has been a revival of traditional dances for men and women, especially in Mizoram. Flute and stringed instrument music accompanies the dancers. Contemporary Chin/Mizo culture combines Christian influences with some of the old traditions.

Myanmar's military regime is dominated by the Burmese (Burman) ethnic group and suppresses cultural expression by other ethnic groups, including the Chins, but there are some performances by Chin cultural groups on national holidays in Myanmar. In contrast, the Chin/Mizo culture is very much encouraged in India's Mizoram and Manipur states, with literary journals, dance, music, martial arts performances, and a revival of textile arts.

15 WORK

Most Chins are hillside farmers using swidden cultivation, in which fields are cleared with fire and planted on a rotating basis. The farmers move from one location to another every year, returning to the same field in four to nine years, depending on the size of the village land. The whole household pulls together to cultivate the fields they own. Work begins at first light and ends at sundown, usually six days of the week with Sunday as a day of rest and churchgoing. Clearing of the fields starts during winter, sometime in December, and has to be finished before the end of February. The wood and grass are left to be dried by the summer sun, being burned at the end of March or beginning of April. A good burn is the key to good grain production. Surrounding forest is relied on for hunting and foraging but has been increasingly logged for the timber trade by Myanmar's military.

During Britain's colonial rule over Burma, many Chins were soldiers in the British Chin Rifles. Even after Burma's independence, Chins joined the national army, but that trend decreased after 1988, when the military was widely perceived as repressive, especially in ethnic minority areas, like the Chin state. After 1988, Chin students formed an armed resistance group, the Chin National Front, which is one of the few rebel armies in Myanmar that has not made a cease-fire deal with the regime. The Chin National Front occasionally stages guerrilla raids on Myanmar military units stationed in Chin areas. Exiled Chin student leaders founded human rights and refugee advocacy organizations and often present the plight of the Chin people to international conferences and groups of indigenous peoples. In Mizoram, a group that had fought the Indian government negotiated a settlement, and the former rebel leaders are now prominent politicians in the state's government.

Chin and Mizo people who live in towns and cities engage in a variety of occupations and professions, operating small shops and businesses. Not only Chin farmers, but the most educated young people have fled Myanmar as refugees, creating a "brain drain" to other countries. Chins who find work in India, Malaysia, or elsewhere usually try to send money home to their families through underground currency transfer networks. Chins in exile have established news agencies and web-based magazines, including *Khonumthung News Group* and *Chinland Guardian.*

16 SPORTS

Traditional sports included wrestling, martial arts, and the high jump. The British introduced soccer to the Chins, and it is now the most popular sport by far. Other sports such as tennis, badminton, volleyball, and basketball are played in the towns, but are very rarely played in the rural areas because of a lack of flat ground and the cost of equipment.

¹⁷ ENTERTAINMENT AND RECREATION

Church activities, like singing groups, are a primary source of entertainment for many Chin/Mizo people. Those who can afford it watch movies on disc or satellite TV. Mizoram and Manipur have rock and pop music scenes with numerous bands recording and giving concerts, as do the Chin refugee communities overseas. Some Chin pop singers have become well-known in Myanmar.

18 FOLK ART, CRAFTS, AND HOBBIES

The Chin/Mizo people are known for their traditional weaving and embroidery, including blankets, skirts, and bags. Their distinctive textiles have been exhibited in museums in the United States. They also make baskets and stools from bamboo and cane.

¹⁹ SOCIAL PROBLEMS

Severe narcotics problems affect young people on both sides of the Myanmar/India border. The northeast Indian states of Manipur and Mizoram have some of the highest HIV/AIDS infection rates in India, due to injection of narcotics. Drugs used intravenously include heroin refined from cheap opium produced in Burma, amphetamines, tranquilizers, and other pharmaceuticals. There are few options for drug rehabilitation or HIV/AIDS treatment, particularly in Myanmar.

Myanmar stationed increasing numbers of its troops in Chin areas during the 1990s and early 21st century. As in other regions of Myanmar, this military presence was characterized by human rights violations against the local civilians, including rape, torture, summary execution, imprisonment, forced labor, and forced relocation, a pattern that led to the outflow of refugees. Food shortages in 2008 may cause even more people to flee Myanmar's Chin areas

²⁰ GENDER ISSUES

Traditional Chin/Mizo society was patriarchal, with the man regarded as the head of the household. Men rarely participated in the preparation of food and chores in the house; instead, they built and maintained the house itself and took care of the domestic animals. However, there was very little difference between what the women and men could do. The society as a whole was generally quite gender egalitarian.

In agriculture, the women are the main work force. Although the men work with the women and cut down the bigger trees, the women organize and lead the work. After working the entire day in the field and carrying firewood on their backs, the women are still expected to pound rice and corn when they come home. Cooking may be done by the children, supervised by the women. The men may walk around the village, visiting friends and relatives while the women cook, feed the children, and do household chores.

In the towns and cities of Chin/Mizo areas of Myanmar and India, women are often teachers, market vendors, shopkeepers, or owners of other small businesses. In recent years they are playing an increasing role in village administration and church activities, with female pastors leading some congregations. Chin women in exile from Myanmar have founded self-help economic groups and schools for refugee children. Cheery Zahau, an activist of the Chin Women's Organization in exile in India, presented documentation to the international community in 2008, which stated that Myanmar's soldiers were raping Chin girls and women as a strategy to terrorize the ethnic minority people. Chin women participate in an underground movement resisting military rule and smuggling human rights information to the outside world.

Traditional Chin/Mizo society and evangelical Christianity in the region are not particularly tolerant of homosexuality, as the emphasis is on male-female marriage, but gay and transgender individuals are not usually harassed. Mizoram has gay and lesbian networking and support groups.

²¹ BIBLIOGRAPHY

Carey, Bertam S. and Tuck, H. N. *The Chin Hills.* Calcutta: Firma KLM reprint, 1976.

Chin Human Rights Organization. http://www.chro.org/ (29 June 2008).

Chinland Guardian. http://www.chinlandguardian.com (29 June 2008).

Christian Solidarity Worldwide. *Carrying the Cross: Burma's Military Regime's Restriction, Discrimination and Persecution of Christians in Burma.* London: Christian Solidarity Worldwide, 2007.

Diran, Robert K. *The Vanishing Tribes of Burma.* New York: Amphoto Art, 1997.

Fraser, David W. and Fraser, Barbara G. *Mantles of Merit: Chin Textiles from Myanmar, India, and Bangladesh.* Bangkok: River Books, 2005.

Khonumthung News Group. http://www.khonumthung.com/ (29 June 2008).

Lehman, F.K. *The Structure of Chin Society.* Urbana IL: University of Illinois Press, 1963.

McCall, A.G. *Lushai Chrysalis.* London: Luzac, 1949.

Meo, Nick "Plague of Rats Devastates Burma Villages." Sunday Telegraph, 23 June 2008.

Mirante, Edith. *Down the Rat Hole: Adventures Underground on Burma's Frontiers.* Bangkok: Orchid Press, 2005.

Mizoram Tourism. http://mizotourism.nic.in/home.htm (29 June 2008).

Project Maje. *A Chin Compendium.* 1997. http://www.projectmaje.org/docs.htm (29 June 2008).

———. *Ashes and Tears: Interviews with Refugees from Burma on Guam.* 2001. http://www.projectmaje.org/docs.htm (29 June 2008).

———. *Razor's Edge: Survival Crisis for Refugees from Burma in Delhi, India.* 2004. http://www.projectmaje.org/docs.htm (29 June 2008).

Shoumatoff, Alex. "Waiting for the Plague." *Vanity Fair,* December 2007. http://www.vanityfair.com/politics/features/2007/12/famine200712 (29 June 2008).

U.S. Department of State. "International Religious Freedom Report 2007." Washington D.C.:

Bureau of Democracy, Human Rights, and Labor, U.S. Department of State, 2007

http://www.state.gov/g/drl/rls/irf/2007/90131.htm (30 June 2008).

Vumson. Zo History. Aizawl, Mizoram, India: Published by author, 1986.

—revised by E. Mirante

CHINA AND HER NATIONAL MINORITIES

ALTERNATE NAMES: Han (Chinese), Mandchus, Mongols, Hui, and Tibetans
LOCATION: China
POPULATION: 1.33 billion
LANGUAGE: Austronasian, Gan, Hakka, Iranian, Korean, Mandarin, Miao-Yao, Min, Mongolian, Russian, Tibeto-Burman, Tungus, Turkish, Wu, Xiang, Yue, Zhuang
RELIGION: Taoism, Confucianism, and Buddhism
RELATED ARTICLES: Vol. 2: Chinese Americans; Immigrant Americans. Vol. 3: Bai; Buyi; Dai; Derong; Dong; Ewenki; Gaoshan; Han; Hani; Hui; Kazakh-Chinese; Korean-Chinese; Vol. 4: Li; Man; Miao; Mongols; Naxi; Tibetans; Tujia; Uighurs; Yao; Yi; Zhuang.

¹INTRODUCTION

The apparent uniformity of the Chinese population is a die-hard stereotype. The image of an ethnic mosaic better fits the real situation. From time immemorial, the territory comprised within the frontiers of the People's Republic of China has been, and continues to be, the homeland to a wide variety of nationalities.

Chinese historical records dating from the early Zhou Dynasty (1121–222 BC) already speak of the "Four Barbarians," a blanket term covering a large number of tribes or ethnic groups surrounding the Chinese Middle Kingdoms of the Yellow River Valley. In many cases, the nationalities exercised full sovereignty over their land and were considered by the Chinese themselves as kingdoms or principalities.

All through Chinese dynastic history, the relationship between the Chinese (Huaxia in ancient times, Han since the 3rd century AD) and the Barbarians oscillated between hostility and friendly cooperation. There has been uninterrupted intermarriage between the Han and the other ethnic groups, as well as among these ethnic groups themselves, so that there are no pure ethnicities in China.

When Sun Yatsen established the Republic of China in 1912, he defined it as "The Republic of The Five Nationalities": the Han (Chinese), Mandchus, Mongols, Hui, and Tibetans. In his speech of October 1, 1949, announcing the foundation of the People's Republic of China, Mao Zedong characterized China as a "multi-ethnic unitary State." The various ethnic groups were invited to manifest themselves so as to enjoy their newly won equal rights.

By 1955, more than 400 groups had come forward and were registered by the state authorities. After years of research by Chinese ethnologists, this number was reduced to 56; the Han formed the national majority (now more than 1.2 billion people, by far the largest ethnic group on earth), and the other 55 ethnic groups formed the national minorities (now accounting for 113 million people or 8.5% of the total Chinese population).

According to China's constitution, all nationalities are equal under the law. National minorities were granted the right to govern themselves (*zizhi*) under the leadership and the author-

ity of the Chinese State and of the Chinese Communist Party. Five large "autonomous regions" were created for the most compact, populous, or historically important national minorities (Tibetans, Mongols, Uighur, Hui, Zhuang), while 29 autonomous districts, 72 counties, and 3 banners were established within provinces for the other national minorities.

Special laws were enacted by the Chinese State to preserve the culture of the diverse national minorities and to promote their economic and educational development. In order to stimulate their demographic growth, national minorities were exempted from the "one-child" policy; their percentage of the total Chinese population passed from 5.7% in 1964 to 8.5% in 2000.

²LOCATION AND HOMELAND

One of the most striking features of the national minorities is the tremendous size and strategic importance of the land they occupy compared to their small population. Actually two-thirds of China's territory is inhabited by national minorities.

If one looks at a map of China, one realizes that the northern frontier is formed by the Inner Mongolia Autonomous Region (500,000 sq mi), the northwestern frontier by the Uighur Autonomous Region (617,000 sq mi), and the southwestern frontier by the Tibet Autonomous Region (471,000 sq mi) and by Yunnan Province (168,000 sq mi), whose population is composed of no less than 22 national minorities.

One can say in general that the totality of the Chinese continental borders (with North Korea, the People's Republic of Mongolia, Russia [and many former Soviet Republics], Afghanistan, Pakistan, India, Nepal, Sikkim, Bhutan, Burma, Laos, and Vietnam) lie in territories inhabited and governed by national minorities. This creates many sensitive situations; for instance, the same ethnic group may occupy both sides of the border.

The immense territories occupied by the national minorities also pose an acute economic problem: in many cases, the most important timber, hydroelectric, petroleum, and mineral resources needed for China's economic development lie in national minorities' territory. Besides the difficulty of access to these resources because of distance, weather, altitude, and lack of infrastructure (roads, railway, airports, bridges, towns), the reticence of the local populations adds a further obstacle to the development of these resources by the Han Chinese.

³LANGUAGE

Obviously one of the most important factors—but not the only one—to identify distinct nationalities is the language spoken. One may distinguish the following linguistic families in China (figures are 1990 census estimates):

HAN DIALECTS (SPOKEN BY 1.04 BILLION HAN)
Mandarin (all of north and part of southwest: more than 750 million)
Wu (Shanghai region: 90 million)
Gan (Jiangxi: 25 million)
Xiang (Hunan: 48 million)
Hakka (scattered in southern China: 37 million)
Yue (mainly Guangdong, but also Guangxi: 50 million)
Min (mainly Fujian; excluding Taiwan: 40 million)

ALTAIC DIALECTS

Turkish (Uighur, Kazakh, Salar, Tatar, Uzbek, Yugur, Kirghiz: 8.6 million)

Mongolian (Mongols, Bao'an, Dagur, Santa, Tu: 5.6 million)

Tungus (Mandchus, Ewenki, Hezhen, Oroqen, Xibo: 10 million)

Korean (1.9 million)

SOUTHWEST DIALECTS

Zhuang (Zhuang, Buyi, Dai, Dong, Gelao, Li, Maonan, Shui, Tai: 22.4 million)

Tibeto-Burman (Tibetans, Achang, Bai, Derong [Dulong], Hani, Jingpo, Jino, Lahu, Lhopa, Lolo, Menba, Naxi, Nu, Pumi, Qiang: 13 million)

Miao-Yao (Miao, Yao, Mulao [Mulam], She, Tujia: 16 million)

Austronasian (Benlong, Gaoshan [excluding Taiwan], Bulang, Wa: 452,000)

INDO-EUROPEAN

Russian (13,000)

Iranian (Tajik: 34,000)

Many of these linguistic groups show wide dialectical variations; for instance, Mandarin varies significantly according to regions: northern, western, southwestern, and eastern. These regional dialects are mutually intelligible.

Yue (Cantonese) also falls into various regional dialects: Yuehai, Siyi, Gao-Lei, and Qin-Lian, some of which are mutually *un*intelligible. Important dialectical variations also occur within the language family of given national minorities, often due to the isolation of subgroups. On the other hand, Mandarin Chinese is spoken more and more as a second language by the various national minorities.

⁴FOLKLORE

Each national group in China has its own mythological tradition. Myths are usually shared by nationalities belonging to the same linguistic family. Thus, to have a complete view of Chinese mythology, one has to study the myths and heroes of the various peoples inhabiting China.

In most cases, myths and the rituals to which they were attached were handed down from ancient times to the present by an uninterrupted oral tradition. During the course of history, there were many cultural borrowings among the various ethnic groups. With a few exceptions, only the Han recorded their myths in writing.

One of the most common and ancient mythological traditions in China regards the beginning of humanity and society. According to this tradition, in remote antiquity humans and gods lived in harmony in Heaven and on earth. However, due to a conflict among the gods, the earth was flooded, and humanity was destroyed, except for a brother and sister who escaped by hiding in a huge pumpkin that floated on the waters. When the brother and sister came out of the pumpkin, they realized they were alone in the world. They were confronted with the problem of incest—if they did not marry, it would be the end of humanity, but if they married, they would break the taboo of incest.

So, the brother devised a ritual to know the will of Heaven: he and his sister would each let a millstone roll down a hill. If the two millstones laid one on top of the other at the end of their run, it meant Heaven favored marriage; if the two millstones went separate ways, it meant Heaven wanted them to respect the incest taboo.

However, the brother surreptitiously placed two millstones one on top of the other in a hidden place down the hill. Later, he and his sister let two other millstones roll down the hill. Then, the brother led his sister to the two millstones he had hidden down the hill. After they married, the sister gave birth to a formless lump of flesh; the brother cut it into twelve pieces, which he threw in different directions. These became the twelve peoples of ancient China.

This myth seems to have originated with the Miao, who, around 1000 bc, lived in the Yellow River Valley. The Miao often clashed with the Chinese and were eventually forced to flee to southwest China. Their myth of origins spread widely, both among the Chinese and the nationalities of southern and southwest China.

Around the second century bc, the myth, profoundly transformed, was put into writing in Chinese. The brother and sister, called Fuxi and Nüwa, were represented as divine beings with human bodies and reptilian tails and as symbols of *yin* and *yang*.

In the north, the Tibetan, Mongolian, Uighur, Mandchu, and Korean peoples each has its own mythological tradition about the origin of mankind.

Another important myth widely spread in China is that of Huangdi, the Yellow Emperor. This myth, of Chinese origin, deals mainly with the origin of various cultural patterns (esoteric arts), socio-political institutions (marriage, emperorship), and technological inventions (chariot, medicine).

Among other well-known myths, one may mention the myth of Yu the Great, who tamed the great rivers of China and made the land inhabitable and productive, and Pangu, a primitive hero god, whose body, when he died, gave birth to the world.

⁵RELIGION

Three major religious traditions contended for the hearts and minds of the peoples of China: Taoism, Confucianism, and Buddhism. Although many national minorities have preserved their own native religious traditions, they have primarily been influenced by the three major religions of China.

To have a full picture of the religious complexity of China, one would have to treat systematically the specific beliefs and practices of the 56 nationalities of China. Even within one single nationality, one may find important religious variations that demand to be studied on their own. Here, this entry will limit itself to the three great traditions mentioned above.

TAOISM

The origins of Taoism are lost. It seems Taoism derived from ancient popular religions linked to shamanism and nature worship. Around the 6th century bc, a philosophical wing developed whose main ideas were condensed in the *Daode jing* (Classic of the way and its power), attributed to the sage Lao zi, a senior contemporary of Confucius (551–479 bc).

The central idea of Lao zi is that of *Dao*, conceived as the ineffable source of creativity and harmony that animates the universe. The sage and saintly person is one who, being united to the *Dao*, partakes of its creativity and harmony. Such a person lives in bliss, serenity, and inaction, being carried by the Power of the Dao: "doing nothing, nothing is left undone."

When one is united to the *Dao*, all the other beings of the universe, as well as our perceptions and feelings, reveal their relativity. Between the 6th and the 2nd centuries BC, many important Chinese thinkers developed the ideas of Lao zi and formed a "Taoist School of Philosophy."

Among the most important works issuing from the Taoist School of Philosophy, one may single out the *Zhuangzi* (Writings of Master Zhuang, 4th century BC), the *Liezi* (Writings of Master Lie, 4th century BC), and the *Huainanzi* (Writings of Master Huainan, 2nd century BC). These works exerted a deep influence on the Chinese view of life and of the world.

In the 2nd century AD, a Taoist preacher called Zhang Daoling established a formal Taoist Church (perhaps in response to the coming of Buddhism to China in the 1st century AD). Zhang Daoling claimed that the blueprint for his church was revealed to him directly by the divinized Lao zi, who became the god of his church, called the "Heavenly Masters."

The Taoist Church, closely linked to the ancient cults, beliefs, and magical practices of popular religion, developed at a rapid pace, and by the 8th century AD had spread all over China. Despite severe constraints imposed by the government of the People's Republic of China in the 1960s and '70s, the Taoist religion has started to make a comeback in that country. Because of its ancient indigenous roots, it may be called the unofficial national religion of the Chinese people.

CONFUCIANISM

While Taoism refers to an ineffable being, Confucianism refers to the teachings of a human being, Confucius. Confucius was rather reserved about religious beliefs and practices. He said: "One must respect divine beings, but keep them at a distance." He thought human beings had within themselves the power to be wise and good and did not need to seek wisdom and goodness from outside, even from a divine being.

Confucius's main idea was that human beings are naturally inclined to do good to others. His conceptions of education, social relations, and government were based on this premise. Confucius recognized the value of certain religious attitudes, such as respect, earnestness, sincerity, devotion, decorum, etc. But, according to him, these values should foremostly inform human relations and not simply the man-god relation.

Confucius insisted that the quality of human relations within the family circle was the foundation of an orderly society and of a prosperous state. Confucius, the "father of Chinese philosophy," may be viewed as a profound reformer who tactfully demythologized ancient Chinese religious beliefs and practices and sought to establish universal humanistic values based on reason and human nature.

Confucius was never considered a divine being by his contemporaries or by his disciples; he never made claims of divine ancestry or attributions. It was only about five centuries after his death, with the victory of Confucianism as the state ideology of the imperial Han dynasty (206 BC–AD 220), and with the emergence of many religious movements (among them Buddhism and Taoism), that a cult to Confucius as a god was established around the 2nd century AD. But, contrary to Taoism and Buddhism, religious Confucianism was mainly restricted to the literate elite of China, who looked on Confucius as their patron saint and never spread, as a distinct church, among the masses—although many village temples regularly performed rituals at an altar dedicated to Confucius.

BUDDHISM

In contrast to Taoism and Confucianism, which were both indigenous religious traditions, Buddhism came from abroad, mainly from its birthplace, India. Buddhism was established by an Indian prince, Siddharta Gautama of the Sakyamuni clan, on the border between India and Nepal in the 6th century BC.

The term Buddhism comes from an ancient Sanskrit word meaning "enlightened." Buddhism, which laid stress on meditation rather than ritual in reaction against Hinduism, spread rapidly in the Indian subcontinent and in Southeast Asia (mainly Burma and Thailand).

Two main churches developed: that of the "Small Vehicle" (*Hinayana*), which stressed monastic life and celibacy, and that of the "Great Vehicle" (*Mahayana*), which was opened to the laity. Mahayana Buddhism came to China through the Northern Silk Road in the 1st century AD.

Buddhism had been significantly modified by its passage through the Indo-Greek kingdoms established north of India following Alexander's conquests, but the essential teaching remained the "Four Holy Truths" discovered by the Buddha: 1) Life is suffering; 2) suffering comes from desire; 3) to overcome suffering, one must extinguish desire; 4) to extinguish desire, one must follow the "Eightfold Path" (right views, intentions, speech, conduct, livelihood, effort, mindfulness, concentration) and attain the state of perfect bliss (*nirvana*).

Mahayana Buddhism developed rapidly in China, especially during the long period of disunity that followed the fall of the Han dynasty in AD 220. By the time the Tang dynasty (618–907) was established, the Buddhist conquest of China was complete, but it was a Buddhism with very strong Chinese characteristics.

The glory of Buddhism under the Tang was probably unparalleled in any other country to this day. Thousands of sutras and other Buddhist writings, written in Pali, Sanskrit, Persian, and many vernacular languages, were inspiringly translated into Chinese (in many cases, only the Chinese version is still extant); tens of thousands of monasteries, convents, temples, and sanctuaries spread in cities, suburbs, villages, and mountains throughout China. Under the Tang, the Buddhist Church was composed of some ten schools or patriarchates (*zong*). Each school recognized one patriarch as its founder and one sutra as representing its specific teaching and ritual.

Among the most famous schools one may mention *Chan*, whose first patriarch, Boddhidharma, came to China around AD 520; the Chan school was based on the *Lankavatara Sutra* (Sutra of the Transmission of the Lamp), which emphasized the importance of meditation (the Sanskrit *dhyana* was rendered *chan* in Chinese) to attain enlightenment.

Chan was transmitted to Japan around 1200, where it was known as *Zen* Buddhism, Zen being the Japanese pronunciation of the Chinese character for Chan. Because of the richness of its teaching and of its well-organized ritual and monastic life, Buddhism exerted a deep influence on all classes and nationalities of Chinese society.

For almost 2,000 years Taoism, Confucianism, and Buddhism coexisted as the three main religions of China. Their mutual tolerance may be explained, in part, by the fact that

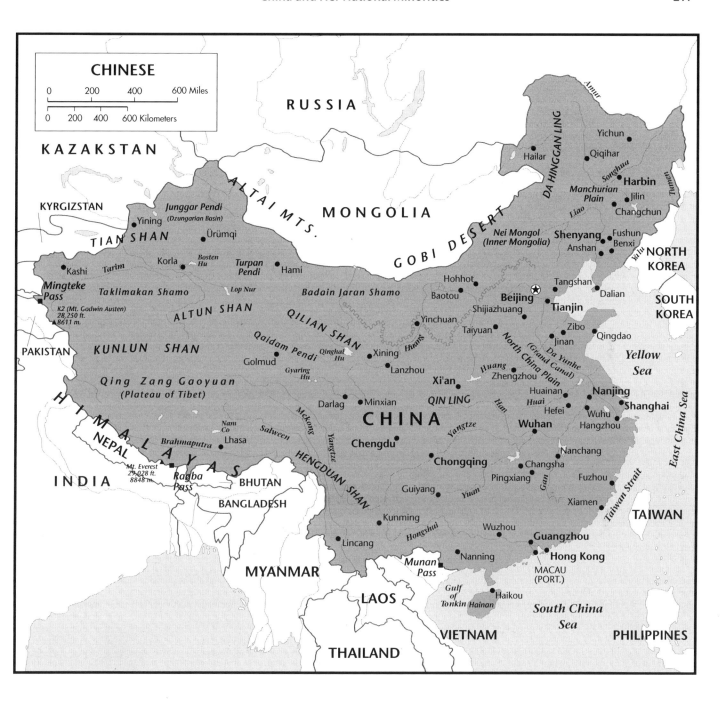

6 MAJOR HOLIDAYS

each emphasized one aspect of three important concerns of religious consciousness: man's relation to nature (Taoism), to society (Confucianism), and to the absolute (Buddhism).

Although most of the numerous feasts and festivals celebrated in China originated with the Chinese, many are shared by the other nationalities. Practically every month there is at least one major celebration. The celebrations are usually held in accordance with the lunar calendar and are based on the yearly solstices and equinoxes. Among the most important, one may single out the following:

The Spring Festival (so called to distinguish the Chinese New Year from its Western counterpart), lasts about a week between January 21 and February 20. The New Year begins with a midnight banquet starting on New Year's Eve; at dawn, the house is lighted and sacrificial offerings of thanksgiving are made to the ancestors and to the gods. Friends and relatives visit each other and share sumptuous banquets, where the main dish is Chinese dumplings (jiaozi). Children receive gifts—traditionally, money in a red envelope (hongbao).

The Lantern Festival (Dengjie), held around March 5, was originally a ritual in honor of the divine Supreme Unity. Recently, it has become a folkloric feast for children. Houses are lighted and large paper lanterns of every shape and color are hung in public places. A special

Performers on the eve of the Chinese New Year celebrate at a park in Beijing, China. The Chinese New Year is based on the lunar calendar.
(AP Images)

cake (yanxiao) made of glutinous rice is eaten on this occasion.

The Qingming ("pure brilliance") is a feast of the dead, which falls at the beginning of April. On this day, families pay a visit to the tombs of their ancestors, tidy up the burial ground, and offer incense, flowers, fruits, and cakes to the departed. On that day, the hearth fire is put out and only cold dishes (hanshi) are served.

The Mid-Autumn Festival (also called the Moon Festival) is both a harvest and a nature celebration (gazing at the full moon), held at the beginning of October. The main dish is "moon cakes." It is said that in the last years of the Mongolian Yuan Dynasty (1279–1368), the Chinese hid a small piece of paper in the moon cakes inviting the population to revolt, and thereby succeeded in overthrowing the Mongolian rulers. The Mid-Autumn Festival is one of the most colorful and joyous celebrations in China. The Dragon-Boat Festival is usually held in conjunction with this festival.

The National Day of China is October 1, marking the founding of the People's Republic of China. It is celebrated lavishly with all the main buildings and streets of cities illuminated.

[7] RITES OF PASSAGE

Because of the restrictive one child policy of the Chinese government, the birth of a child, especially a boy, is considered an important and most joyous event in China. The traditional rituals surrounding courtship have given place to a freer, haphazard, and democratic choosing of partners—at school, at work, or in community activities, such as collective dances organized by the local authorities.

Under the Communist government, marriage has become a rather sober ceremony involving the spouses, some witnesses, and the State authorities. Private celebrations are held with friends and relatives. However, the traditional rituals are still alive in the rural and national minorities' areas. In major cities, such as Shanghai, Beijing, and Guangzhou, well-to-do families tend to adopt Western-style marriages.

Because of demographic pressure, cremation has become the most widely used method of burying the dead. Private ceremonies for the deceased are held within the family circle and with close friends.

[8] INTERPERSONAL RELATIONS

Strong interpersonal relations (*guanxi*) characterize Chinese society, not only within the family, but also among friends and in corporate groups (school, work, sports, entertainment, etc.). Besides daily social intercourse, the numerous feasts and festivals that punctuate the year are special occasions to strengthen individual and community ties. Visiting friends and relatives is an important social ritual; the guests bring gifts, such as fruits, candies, cigarettes, or wine, while the host usually offers a specially prepared meal in tune with the spirit of the feast.

Although most young people think that the best way to find a partner is through their own efforts, there are still a number of them who are helped by their parents, relatives, or friends. The role of the "go-between" is still important in China. On most occasions, the males take the initiative. The response of a girl invited for the first time in her life for a date is usually to postpone it until later, unless she is well acquainted with the inviter. Mutual attraction is of utmost importance in selecting a partner. Position and wealth are also important considerations.

[9] LIVING CONDITIONS

Traditional household architecture varies a great deal according to regions in China. From the 1950s to the late '70s, socialist style architecture has dominated both in the rural areas and the cities, replacing, in part, the ancient structures. On account of their isolation and their attachment to their way of life, the national minorities have, by and large, escaped the destruction of their architectural heritage.

Since the mid 1980s, one witnesses the appearance of modern and even post-modern style, especially in large cities, such as Shanghai and Beijing. In the countryside, many communal apartment buildings have been replaced by two-story individual households with all the modern commodities. This is especially true in the farming villages surrounding large cities, where a class of wealthy peasants has arisen.

Lodging is still a problem in booming cities, such as Beijing, Shanghai, Tianjin, and Guangzhou, where the space available per capita is below the minimum defined by the United Nations. By curbing the influx of newcomers (mainly peasants) into the cities and by developing accelerated programs of apartment building, available space is increasing in urban areas and should reach 8 sq miles of living space per capita by the year 2000.

Transportation systems in and between cities have developed at a dramatic pace over the last decade. These include railways, subways, paved throughways, and air links. It is surely air transport that has known the most rapid development, on account of the relatively small investment in physical infrastructure.

One of the major rail developments is the new electrified line under construction between Beijing and Hong Kong. Rapid throughways already exist between Beijing and Tianjin, around Dalien, while others are under construction in the Shanghai-Nanjing axis and in the Guangzhou-Hong Kong axis. Local roads in the countryside have improved significantly in order to facilitate the exchange of goods.

It is estimated that more than 100 million Chinese travel by train to visit friends and relatives during the first days of the Spring Festival.

On account of China's traditional medicine, it is very difficult for a Westerner to understand the question of health in China. While China represents 20% of the world population, it spends only 3.5% of its gross national product (GNP) on health (world average: 8%); China's health expenditure per capita is only $11/year (world average: $329/year).

Medicine is primarily a family and community affair, at least one person in the extended family having some knowledge of herbal medicine, acupuncture, etc. The Chinese only resort to state clinics and hospitals for major ailments and accidents. Medical knowledge spread in rural areas and national minorities' areas in the 1960s and '70s, thanks to "bare-foot doctors." At present, there is on average one doctor per 1,000 inhabitants in China. The peoples of China have a life expectancy of about 70 years (first among the developing countries).

[10] FAMILY LIFE

Except for a few national groups, such as the Naxi in Yunnan, the various national minorities of China have traditionally adopted a patriarchal family structure. The social status of women was, therefore, rather low. One of the avowed goals of the Chinese Revolution and of the People's Republic of China was to overthrow the patriarchal system, linked to feudalism, and to establish a functional equality between men and women.

There is no doubt that the position of women in China has improved significantly since 1949, especially in the family, in the education system, and in the work place. However, there is still a gap to be bridged in the political sphere.

Mao Zedong advocated large families; from 1949 to 1980, the population of China increased from about 500 million to more than 800 million. Since the 1980s, China has adopted a stringent natality policy, the so-called "one child per family" policy. This policy has been successful (mainly in urban areas, not so much in rural areas) in drastically diminishing demographic growth, but at a significant human cost (forced abortions, female infanticide, international adoption, etc.).

National minorities, which only represent 8% of the population of China, have been exempted from the "one child per family" policy and their demographic growth is double that of the Han Chinese.

[11] CLOTHING

In the 1970s and 1980s, city streets were uniformly grey and dark; men and women, young and old, wore clothes of the same style and the same color. Today, in the frozen north, down jackets, woolens, and fur overcoats in red, yellow, orange, and other bright colors liven the bleak winter scene.

In the south, where the climate is milder, people choose smart Western suits, jeans, sporty jackets, sweaters, and other fashionable clothing to wear year-round. Famous brand names and fashions are a common sight in large cities, and they sell quite well. Cheaper and more practical clothing is also available.

Similar changes have also occurred in the rural areas, especially among the new class of well-to-do farmers, as well as among the national minorities living near the Han Chinese. However, in isolated rural areas, peasants still wear their "Mao suits," while most national minorities have kept their traditional style of clothing.

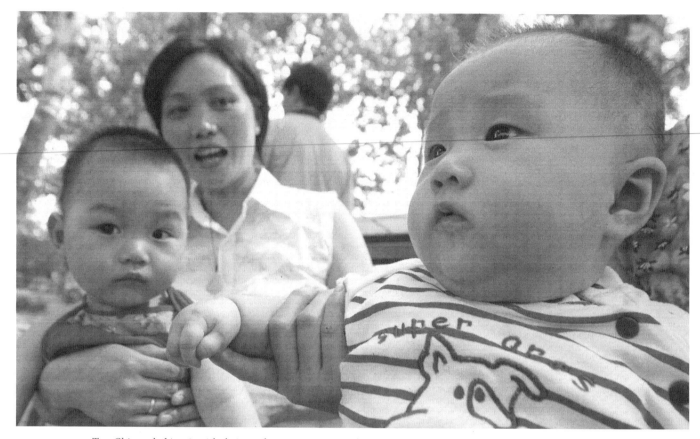

Two Chinese babies sit with their mothers in a Beijing park. As a result of its strict one child policy, China has kept its growth rate from 1990-2000 at a low 1.5 percent.
(AP Images/Greg Baker)

¹²FOOD

There are important differences in the diets and food preparations of the various national minorities of China. The most widespread staple foods in China are rice, flour, vegetables, pork, eggs, and freshwater fish.

The Han Chinese have always laid much stress on cooking skills, making the Chinese cuisine (basically Han) well known throughout the world. Dumplings, wonton, spring rolls, rice, noodles, and roast Peking duck are examples of traditional foods.

¹³EDUCATION

The Han Chinese, who invented an original system of writing more than 3,000 years ago, and the university more than 2,000 years ago, have always prized education and literacy. The imperial government was based for more than 2,000 years on superior literary competence and skills tested by the civil examinations.

The rate of illiteracy and semi-illiteracy among the Han Chinese is only about ten percent. Some 98% of children enroll in school when they reach school age. More than 80% of the students who graduate from primary school and 45% of those who graduate from junior middle school continue to higher levels.

There are more than 1,000 universities and colleges and 800,000 primary and middle schools at different levels, with a total enrolment of 180 million, including 2.6 million college students and graduate students. In addition, 800,000 students are now taking undergraduate training courses at home, while 14 million adult students attend classes of different levels in adult schools.

Although education is in progress, still about five million school age children do not enter school or have dropped out, and the college entrance rate is only 1.8%, below the average of developing countries. Deficiencies in education mainly result from underfunding.

Among the national minorities, the level of education varies significantly and depends on various factors: tradition, way of life, proximity of cities, etc. Some national minorities, such as the Koreans, have the highest level of education of any ethnic group in China, the Han included.

In general, advanced education in China supposes the knowledge of the Chinese language and writing system.

¹⁴CULTURAL HERITAGE

The variety of traditional musical instruments used in China is sufficient to form a full-fledged orchestra. The most popular instruments include the two-string violin (*erhu*), the lute (*zheng*), and the *pipa*.

Institutions of traditional music and dance were established throughout China early in the 1950s in order to promote traditional Chinese music. The rich musical heritage of many nationalities was thus preserved.

Most nationalities in China only have oral literary traditions. Since the 1950s, many important literary works of the nationalities (epics, poems, songs, short stories, novels) have been translated into Chinese and published. Some have now been translated from the Chinese into Western languages.

The Tibetans, Mongols, Manchus, Koreans, and Uighur have rich written traditions and some of their major works have been translated in English and other Western languages. However, it is the Han Chinese who have produced one of the longest and richest written traditions of the world: there is practically no genre in which they have not created world masterpieces.

The traditional literature of the Han Chinese—extending over a continuum of more than 3,000 years and written with the same Chinese writing system—includes poems, drama, novels, short stories, history, philosophy, religion, rituals, letters, and administrative documents. Many works have been translated into many languages and introduced into many countries; however, these translations represent but a tiny fraction of the immense Chinese literary output.

A single anthology of the Tang dynasty (618–907) contains more than 40,000 poems, including those written by the world class poets Li Bai and Du Fu. The monumental Chinese novels, starting in the 14th century with the epic *Water Margin*, also include *Pilgrim to the West*, *Golden Lotus*, and *Dream of the Red Chamber*. One should also mention philosophic masterpieces written around the 5th century BC, namely Confucius' *Analects* and Lao zi's *The Way and Its Power*.

The Han Chinese have also contributed greatly to world civilization by inventing paper and noodles (2nd century BC), ceramics (7th century), gunpowder (10th century), porcelain and movable printing (11th century), and the compass (12th century).

15 WORK

China is a developing country, but the rate of development varies considerably from region to region. The coastal area, open to international commerce, has known a real economic and technological explosion since the early 1980s.

While the hinterland has also developed at a rapid pace, the gap between the seaboard and inland China has widened significantly, producing a socially disruptive disequilibrium. The unbalance is not only *territorial*, it is also *technological*. For instance, in Gansu Province in northwest China, one sees both scientists engaged in highly technical research in nuclear power plants and peasants cultivating the land with centuries-old farming techniques and implements.

In general, the land inhabited by the national minorities, for various social, political, cultural, and logistical reasons, has remained rather undeveloped as compared to the Han Chinese regions. This explains the growing numbers of poor farmers who attempt to migrate to cities and to the eastern coastline in order to improve their lot. This has given rise to the phenomenon of unemployment in urban areas.

About 70% of China's population is rural and engages overwhelmingly in farming; for them, it is very difficult to change their income and lifestyle.

16 SPORTS

Sports do not play the same role in China as they do in the West. This is particularly true for competitive sports. Many sports in China are held only during seasonal festivals or in certain regions (especially among the national minorities).

Of course, the universal sport in China is ping-pong. Other widely practiced sports include traditional shadow boxing (both *wushu* and *taijiquan*). More recently, some Western sports, especially soccer, but also swimming, badminton, basketball, tennis, and baseball, have gained some popularity in China and are practiced mainly in schools, colleges, and universities.

The Chinese government has set up a Federation of Chinese Sports to train Chinese athletes for the international Olympics and for the Asian Olympics. Athletes from China have performed brilliantly in many sports, especially swimming, diving, gymnastics, ping-pong, and volleyball.

In the 2008 Summer Olympics held in Beijing, Chinese athletes earned 100 medals overall, ranking the country second after the United States (with 110). China ranked first in gold medals won, with 51 (to the United States' total of 36 gold medals).

17 ENTERTAINMENT AND RECREATION

Watching television has become a major daily evening entertainment for a majority of families in China. In addition, video cassette recorders and DVD players are now very popular in urban areas. Although movie theaters are usually full, they are scarce and can only accommodate a small percentage of the population.

Young people are often enthusiastic about dancing, karaoke, and rock music, while older people are likely to spend their leisure time attending the Peking opera, local drama, engaging in humorous dialogues, listening to classical music, or playing cards or mahjong.

Travel is quickly becoming a new way to spend one's free time, especially since the five-day work week was introduced in 1995. Storytelling is still a popular form of entertainment among many national minorities, who do not have ready access to television.

18 FOLK ART, CRAFTS AND HOBBIES

Each of China's 56 nationalities has its own tradition of folk art and crafts. The rich heritage of the Han Chinese is, however, the only tradition that has spread widely and is shared by many of China's nationalities. It goes without saying that many motifs and art forms of the Han Chinese were borrowed in ancient times from non-Chinese peoples and progressively "sinicized."

Calligraphy and traditional painting are the most popular folk arts of the Han Chinese. Paper-cutting, embroidery, brocade, cloisonné, colored glaze, jade ware, clay sculpture, and dough figurines, meticulously wrought by craftsmen, are famous around the world.

Chess, kite flying, gardening, and landscaping are hobbies among people of various ages.

19 SOCIAL PROBLEMS

China is in a period of transition, moving from a traditional to a modern society. The coexistence of the old social structure

A Chinese military band playing in Harbin. (E. Gall/EPD Photos)

and the new, immature social system produces a number of contradictions. The widening gap of living standards between rural and urban areas draws a surplus rural labor force of more than 100 million into the coastal areas looking for jobs. This situation, which favors mobility and exchange, entails serious social disturbances.

The disequilibrium of the economic development between the coastal areas and the inland, the irrational income for different occupations, the widening gap between the rich and the poor, the growing inflation, the spread of greed and bribery, and the reappearance of other ugly phenomena, such as gambling, drugs, prostitution, and abduction of women, create serious problems for the people and for the government.

20 GENDER ISSUES

The Chinese government states that men and women have equal rights in all areas of life and most legislation is gender neutral. However, there are continued reports of discrimination, sexual harassment, wage discrepancies, and other gender-related problems. The gap in educational level between women and men was narrowing in the early years of the 21st century,

with women making up 47.1% of college students in 2005 (but only 32.6% of doctoral students).

One area of legislation that affects women involves marriage and family planning. China has strict family planning laws. It is illegal for a woman to marry before age 20 and for a man to marry before age 22. It is also illegal for single women to give birth. The Family Planning Bureau can require women to take periodic pregnancy tests to enforce this law. Single women face few options. They may be forced to undergo abortion or sterilization.

Prostitution and the sex trade is a significant problem in China involving between 1.7 and 5 million women. Because prostitution may involve organized crime, businessmen, the police, and government workers, prosecution of laws against prostitution has limited success.

In 2002, China removed homosexuality from its official list of mental illnesses. Although homosexuality is still a taboo topic, gay men and lesbians are increasingly accepted, especially in large, international cities.

21 BIBLIOGRAPHY

Cambridge Encyclopedia of China. Brian Hook, ed. Cambridge: Cambridge University Press, 1982.

Chiao, Chien, Nicholas Tapp, and Kam-yin Ho, ed. "Special Issue on Ethnic Groups in China." *New Asia Bulletin,* no. 8, 1989.

China Facts and Figures Annual Handbook. Vol. 1–18. Gulf Breeze, Fla.: Academic International Press, 1978–1996.

Dreyer, June Teufel. *China's Forty Millions.* Cambridge: Harvard University Press, 1976.

Eberhard, Wolfram. *China's Minorities: Yesterday and Today.* Belmont: Wadsworth Publishers, 1982.

Fairbank, John King. *China: A New History.* Cambridge, Mass.: Cambridge University Press, 1992.

Gentelle, Pierre, ed. *L'État de la Chine.* Paris: La Découverte, 1989.

Gernet, Jacques. *A History of Chinese Civilisation.* transl. from the French, Cambridge: Cambridge University Press, 1985.

Greenhalgh, Susan. *Just One Child: Science and Policy in Deng's China.* Berkeley: University of California Press, c008.

Gustafsson, Bjorn A., Shi, Li, and Sicular, Terry, eds. *Inequality and Public Policy in China.* New York: Cambridge University Press, 2008.

Harrell, Stevan. *Cultural Encounters on China's Ethnic Frontiers.* Seattle: University of Washington Press, 1994.

Heberer, Thomas. *China and Its National Minorities: Autonomy or Assimilation?* Armonk, N.Y.: M. E. Sharpe, 1989.

———. *Doing Business in Rural China: Liangshan's New Ethnic Entrepreneurs.* Seattle: University of Washington Press, 2007.

Keightley, David N. "Early Civilization in China: Reflections on How It Became Chinese." In *Heritage of China. Contemporary Perspectives on Chinese Civilization.* Berkeley: University of California Press, 1990.

Lebar, Frank, et al. *Ethnic Groups of Mainland Southeast Asia.* New Haven: Human Relations Area Files Press, 1964.

Lemoine, Jacques. "L'Asie Orientale." In *Ethnologie régionale II* (Encyclopédie de la Pléiade). Paris: Gallimard, 1978.

Ma Yin, ed. *China's Minority Nationalities.* Beijing: Foreign Languages Press, 1989.

Pulleyblank, Edwin G. "The Chinese and their Neighbors in Prehistoric and Early Historic Times." In David N. Keightley, ed. *The Origins of Early Chinese Civilization.* Berkeley: University of California Press, 1983.

Ramsey, S. Robert. *The Languages of China.* Princeton: Princeton University Press, 1987.

Wiens, Harold J. *Han Chinese Expansion in South China.* New Haven: The Shoestring Press, 1967.

—by C. Le Blanc

DAI

PRONUNCIATION: DYE
ALTERNATE NAMES: Daile, Daina, Daiya, Daibengm, Dianyue, Dan, Liao, Gold Teeth, Silver Teeth, Black Teeth, Baiyi
LOCATION: China
POPULATION: Over 1 million
LANGUAGE: Dai
RELIGION: Polytheism; ancestor worship; some Buddhism
RELATED ARTICLES: Vol. 3: China and Her National Minorities

1 INTRODUCTION

From ancient times, the Dai inhabited a region at the southern tip of Yunnan Province, which was set up under the name of Yizhou Prefecture in 109 BC by the Western Han Dynasty (206 BC—AD 8). In the 1st century AD, the Dai chief, Yongyoudiao, sent emissaries thrice to Luoyang, the capital of the Eastern Han Dynasty (25—220). Yongyoudiao was subsequently appointed to a high post by the central government, thus establishing formal political relations between the Dai and the Chinese authorities. Later on, the name of Yizhou Prefecture was changed to Yongchang. From the 8th to 13th century, the prefecture was successively under the jurisdiction of the Nanzhao Kingdom and then of the Dali Kingdom of Yunnan.

As early as the 9th century, the ancestors of the Dai planted rice extensively in south and southwest Yunnan. Plowing was done by elephants and buffalo. Extensive water conservation works and irrigation systems were set up to increase rice and other grain production. Dai women wove a special cloth called "silver cotton cloth." The Dai decorated their teeth by covering them with a thin sheath of gold or silver; thus, different Dai tribes were named "Gold Teeth," "Silver Teeth," "Black Teeth," etc. A chief of the Dai in Xishuangbanna, Bazhen, unified all the tribes in the 12th century. Making Jinghong the capital, he founded the State of Jinglong. Paying homage to the emperor of China as his sovereign, he was granted an official title by the central government; the title passed on to his son. From the Yuan Dynasty (1271—1368) onward, the custom of appointing Dai hereditary chiefs became official. It was only in the 18th century, under the Manchu Qing Dynasty (1644—1911), that the Dai chiefs were replaced by officials of Manchu or Chinese nationality. From then on the Dai districts were directly administered by the central government.

2 LOCATION AND HOMELAND

The Dai population amounted to just over one million in 1990. They are mainly concentrated in Xishuangbanna Dai Autonomous Prefecture (South Yunnan) and in three western Yunnan "mixed administrations," namely Dai and Jingpo Autonomous Prefecture of Dehong; Dai and Wa Autonomous County of Gengma; and Dai and Lahu Autonomous County of Menglian. The rest of the Dai are scattered into more than 30 counties of Yunnan Province. They live mostly in the plain and valley areas at the foot of the mountains, a region of the subtropics with abundant rainfall and rich soil.

3 LANGUAGE

Dai is classified as belonging to the Sino-Tibetan family, Zhuang-Dong group, Zhuang-Dai branch. There are three dia-

A young Dai woman performs a traditional dance in Manyangguang village, China. Young girls of the Dai ethic group wear silk dresses to perform the umbrella dance to celebrate Datum, or the "Sending the Buddhist Scripture" festival. (AP Images/Eugene Hoshiko)

lects (mutually unintelligible). The Dai have devised several alphabetic writing systems of their own in various regions, but these systems are mutually incompatible. The main systems are Daina (Dehong dialect), Daile (Xishuangbanna dialect), Daibeng (around Ruijiang), and Dairui (Quanping dialect).

Dai is a self-given name meaning "people who love peace and freedom." The Dai also call themselves by other names, such as "Daile," "Daina," "Daiya," "Daibeng," and so on. Other designations were given by the Chinese or by other nationalities, such as, "Dianyue," "Dan," "Liao," "Gold Teeth," "Silver Teeth," "Black Teeth," "Baiyi," etc. Dai was chosen as a unified designation since 1949.

⁴FOLKLORE

One of the most stirring stories in the rich Dai mythology is the long poem "Princess Peacock and Prince Zhaoshutun." One day, Prince Zhaoshutun of Mengbanjia Kingdom went hunting. He saw seven princesses in peacock clothes bathing in the Golden Lake. Helped by the Dragon God, he stole the peacock clothes of the youngest princess, Nannuona. She could

not fly back to her Peacock Kingdom without those clothes. Besides, she loved the prince at first sight. They married and led a happy life. However, King Peacock was so angry about their marriage that he sent troops to attack the Mengbanjia Kingdom. Prince Zhaoshutun had to leave his beloved wife and lead his army to battle. Unsure about the length and the outcome of the war, King Peacock ordered a shaman to perform divination; he falsely accused Nannuona of being a demon and advised that she should be killed. She asked for remission, but it was refused. She then asked to dance one last time in her peacock clothes before her execution, to which he agreed. As soon as she put on her peacock clothes, she swiftly flew upward and returned to her Peacock Kingdom. Prince Zhaoshutun defeated his enemies and returned in triumph. Overcome with grief and regret, his father told him the story. He went back to the Golden Lake, where he was helped again by the Dragon God to stride over thousands of crags and torrents and ultimately arrived in the Peacock Kingdom. Surmounting all sorts of obstacles put up by the Peacock King, he was finally reunited with Princess Peacock, Nannuona.

According to the myths entitled "The Origin of Yingba" and "The Creation of Yingba," Yingba was the ancestor of all gods. The many stories attached to this mythological figure form an important part of the traditional beliefs of the Dai.

⁵RELIGION

The Dai are polytheistic. They offer sacrifices to "Diula" (a divinized ancestor) on an annual, three-year, and even nine-year cycle. The rite is called "Diula Meng." "Meng" means an area where many villages are bound by blood ties. Therefore, many villages attend the rite, which may last from 1 day to as many as 10 days. The participants wear uniform ceremonial clothes. Oxen and pigs are butchered as offerings. The road leading to the ceremonial place should be sealed off and no outsiders allowed.

The Dai also offer a sacrifice to the Paddy Field Ghost before they transplant the rice shoots and after harvest. A makeshift shed is set up in the paddy field to perform the ritual. Four pairs of candles, a certain amount of areca leaves and one rice roll are used.

Each village may have a few "village gods" of its own; these are actually ancestors who made important contributions to the village in the past. Villagers offer them sacrifices at regular intervals.

Hinayana Buddhism came to the Dai in the 7th century (according to another version, in the 14th century). Sakyamuni receives special homage as the founder of Buddhism. The religion advocates as the highest ideal that the Buddhist believer become a monk or a nun, lead an ascetic life, free oneself from worldly preoccupations and, in the end, reach nirvana (a state of perfect bliss), equally detached from life and death. For this reason, people are asked to offer donations to the monks, the nuns, and their temples. In Dai areas, each village has its own temple and monks are very common. In Xishuangbanna, boys are expected to lead the life of a monk for a certain period of their life. They learn to read and to chant scriptures, then resume their secular life; some of them choose to remain monks all their lives.

⁶MAJOR HOLIDAYS

Most Dai festivals are related to Buddhism, such as the Haolunwa Festival, Danpa Festival, Dangang Festival, Shanghan Festival, Danpopazhao Festival, Aowasa Festival, Danmuohaban Festival, Dandanmu Festival, the Haowasa Festival, etc. One of the goals of festivals is to offer donations to the temples.

Besides these temple festivals, traditional Dai holidays include the Spring Festival, the Multicolored Egg Festival, the Water-Splashing Festival, the Moon Worship Festival, the Opened-Door Festival, the Closed-Door Festival, and Huanglu Festival, and so on. Among them, the Water-Splashing Festival is the most elaborate and the best known. It is comparable to the Spring Festival of the Chinese, but is held June 24—26 (Dai calendar). The first thing the Dai do after dawn on the Festival day is to prostrate themselves before the Buddha and give alms to the monks. They splash clean water on the Buddha image to wash off the dust. Thus, they perform the "Bathe-Buddha Ceremony." Then, they splash water on each other. It is said that a fire demon had occupied Xishuangbanna. One day, it kidnapped seven beautiful girls. The youngest of them, Nongxiang, coaxed a secret out of the demon: a long hair put around its neck would cut its head off. She did a good job with her hair, but the demon's head turned into a fire ball. Wherever it went, it burned. The seven girls splashed a lot of water and finally put out the fire. They rid the people of a fierce scourge. In memory of their contribution, the Dai have performed water-splashing activities annually since then and ultimately turned the ritual into a festival. Water-splashing on each other is considered very auspicious. Many recreational activities, performances, and competitions are held on the same day. It is, of course, a great opportunity for the young people to date. If it happens to be raining, this is regarded as an omen of a bumper crop.

The Closed-Door Festival is a festival in which the door of love and marriage is closed and a grand donation activity is held in the temple. The Opened-Door Festival is held right after the Closed-Door Festival; it is a feast dedicated to young people, where dating and marriage are encouraged.

The Huanglu Festival is both a fair and a parade held at harvest time, fostering the exchange of commodities in the context of festive recreation; it follows the Opened-Door Festival. The central figure of the parade is the image of an elephant, woven with bamboo strips and covered with multicolored papers. It is operated by a man lying beneath the elephant belly. The base of the image is carried on the shoulders of four or eight strong men.

⁷RITES OF PASSAGE

In the past, the education of Dai children was restricted to the temple. Only monks acquired a certain amount of knowledge through religious education. In Xishuangbanna, there has been a tradition that every boy should be a monk from the time when he was seven or eight years old. He only left the temple when he reached adulthood. Most of them then resumed their secular life and soon married. A select few chose the monastic life and remained in the temple for the rest of their lives.

In general, the Dai bury their dead in the ground, but the monks practice cremation. The ash of the dead monk is put into a pot and buried in the rear of the temple. A rite should be held for a widow or widower to cut off her or his relation with the dead. A thread is bound to the body of the widow or widower and its other end is attached to the coffin or to the straw mat wrapping of the dead. A senior person cuts the thread, then the deceased is no longer related to the surviving spouse. This ritual is probably linked to the wedding ceremony, in which a thread-tying ritual is performed.

⁸INTERPERSONAL RELATIONS

Taboos among the Dai often bear profound religious meanings. For example, to stroke a young monk's head is strictly prohibited. When calling on a family, the guest is not allowed to stride over the firepool, sit behind the fire while facing the door, sit on the threshold of the door, lean against a column, or enter the inner rooms. In spite of such formalities, the Dai are very hospitable. Tea, tobacco, and wine are offered as soon as the guests arrive. The family prepares special dishes to honor the guests, including fish, chicken, pork, vegetables, sweet bamboo shoots, peanuts, and fruits after a meal. When a guest is to leave, the host will see him off to the gate.

Dai youngsters enjoy full freedom in dating. The sure way of knowing whether a girl is married or single is to look at her silver waistband. According to Dai custom, a married girl will hang the keys of her household on her waistband, thus indicating that she refuses any advance. "Tossing an embroidered ball" is a sport and also a ritual of social intercourse between boys and girls. The ball is a 4 in square bag padded with cottonseed, with a 1 m-long brocade band attached at one of its corners. Boys and girls are separated into two teams and stand in lines about 10 m apart facing each other. One member of a team—a girl, for instance—holds the band and rotates the ball, then lets the ball fly toward the opposite team; the ball should be caught by a young man. However, if the ball is tossed by a girl he likes, he might purposely "miss" the ball and let it drop; according to the rules, he must then walk to the girl, present a bouquet of flowers, and say something (in this case, of course, words expressing his innermost feelings). The girl should receive the flowers and listen to his confession of love.

⁹LIVING CONDITIONS

The Dai live in stilt-supported storied houses made of bamboo. They use 24 to 40 bamboos as stilts. A wooden floor is laid on the stilts, 2-3 m above the earth. The house is cubic in shape. Rows of straw cover the double slopes of the roof. A bamboo ladder leads to the door. There is a corridor and a balcony for relaxation and cooling off in the evening and for hanging the wash out to dry. Livestock and miscellany are placed on the ground floor. The central room, covered with a large bamboo-strip mat, serves for eating, for resting, and for receiving guests. There is a firepool in the center, with a triangular iron framework for cooking or boiling tea. The inner room, separated by planks or a mat woven with bamboo strips, is the main bedroom; there are also bedrooms on each side of the central room. People should take off their shoes before they enter. Some houses are built with bricks and tiles. In Delong District, most houses are one-story. The wall is built by adobe or bamboo, the roof covered with straw.

Transportation in the Dai districts is very convenient. There are highways connecting almost all the townships and even the villages. A reinforced concrete bridge crosses the Lanchang River. A land and water communication network is already operative around Jinghong. There are airlines connecting Simao and Baoshan with Kunming, capital of Yunnan Province.

[10] FAMILY LIFE

Dai families are patrilineal and small. The parents live with the unmarried children. In case a couple has no son, the man is welcome to live with his bride's family. This situation is quite common. There are quite a few marriage rites. For instance, the bride's side and bridegroom's side set up tables exhibiting their respective wedding gifts. The gifts from the bridegroom's side usually include wine, two rolls of white threads, straight skirts, garments, two silver waistbands, a silver bracelet, a long sword, glutinous rice, eggs, and cooked chickens; the gifts from the bride's side usually include wine, a hat made of banana leaves, a piece of white cloth, a piece of black cloth, five strings of areca, two strings of banana, brown sugar, and salt. These traditional gifts are symbolic and express the wish that the new couple will lead a sweet and tasteful life.

During the wedding ceremony, the bride and the bridegroom sit on a felt mat, side by side. The master of ceremonies ties a white thread on their wrists. Then a senior person among the relatives binds the bridegroom's left shoulder, crosses their backs, and binds the bride's right shoulder. The thread is finally tied by a guest. "White" means pure love. "Tying the thread" means binding the couple together, never to separate.

In some districts, the bridegroom should work for the bride's family for three years. Then, the couple is allowed to move to his family's home.

[11] CLOTHING

Dai men wear collarless, edge to edge tops and long trousers. They usually wrap their heads with white or dark blue cloth. In the winter, they have felt draped over their shoulders. Tattoos are very common. As early as 11 years old, boys are tattooed over the chest, back, belly, loin, and extremities with the figures of animals and flowers, as well as with symbolic designs and even with Dai writing. Quite a number of the aged and middle-aged men are tattooed with Buddhist scriptures over their thighs. It was a custom in the past: anybody whose thigh was not tattooed with scriptures would be looked down upon.

The traditional clothes of women include short garments with tight sleeves and long straight skirts reaching to their feet. In areas around Mangshi, girls wear long trousers and a small waistband. Dai women usually comb their hair into a bun with a multicolored wooden comb stuck into it. They like to wear a silver waistband, a bracelet, and other ornaments.

[12] FOOD

Rice is the staple food of the Dai. They prefer pork to beef. Sweet wine is welcome by all of them, including the children. They usually take two meals a day. Chopsticks and bowls are used. In the case of glutinous rice, they take it with their hand. Their traditional foods include rice in a bamboo tube, sour bamboo shoots, roasted fish, sour vegetables, thick sauce made from shrimp, fish, crab, cicada, ant's eggs, or cricket, as well as fried ant's eggs, fried crickets, roasted spiders, and raw worms in the bamboo. They like to chew areca leaves (tropical Asian palms).

[13] EDUCATION

Primary schools, middle schools (junior and senior), and technical schools are set up in all Dai areas. The vast majority of students receive primary school education. Many Chinese teachers, who learned the Dai language and writing, work as teachers. Newspapers and books written in Dai are published. Programs in the Dai language are broadcasted. Traditional temple education is gradually being transformed; however, the cultural and educational level of the Dai is still lower than the average for the national minorities of China.

[14] CULTURAL HERITAGE

Dai folk singers are called *zhuanha*. Their performances are well received. The Peacock Dance is usually performed on festivals by one or two dancers. They wear white masks and ornaments simulating peacock wings. Their movements imitate those of a peacock, such as leaving the nest, sliding down the slope, taking off, finding the water, looking at their image in the water, drinking, bathing, and flying. The performance is accompanied by musical instruments, such as the elephant foot drum, gongs, and cymbals.

[15] WORK

The Dai have acquired more than 1,000 years of experience in rice cultivation. They have well-integrated systems of cultivation, of water conservation, and of irrigation. This is the basis of their economy. Handicraft, trade, livestock husbandry, light industry, and mining are all making progress. There are nearly 100 small-scale power stations in Xishuangbanna Prefecture. Their Pu'er tea is famous throughout the country. The success of rubber tree plantations promises important developments in the rubber industry in the near future.

[16] SPORTS

Basketball, soccer, and volleyball are very popular with the youngsters. The Dai have also developed a distinct style of shadow-boxing based on the Peacock Dance.

[17] ENTERTAINMENT AND RECREATION

Besides movies and television, which are already popularized, karaoke halls have recently been set up in almost all townships. This is due to the influence of tourists who visit the Dai areas in increasing numbers. But, traditional forms of entertainment remain very much alive—in particular, song competitions and festival entertainment. For instance, during the New Year celebrations, groups of young people sing and dance in front of each household in the village. New Dai theater has developed from traditional themes.

[18] FOLK ART, CRAFTS, AND HOBBIES

The artistic sense of the Dai is best seen in the architecture and design of Buddhist buildings, especially the Manfeilong White Pagoda in Jinghong County, the Mangmengding Pagoda in Yingjiang County, and the Octagonal Pagoda in Jingzhen County. These are not only admired for their architectural sophistication, but also their exquisite carvings and paintings. Among handicrafts, Dai brocade items have a special attraction for the tourists.

[19] SOCIAL PROBLEMS

The Dai have their own calendar, writing system, and a well-developed agriculture. Their educational inadequacy, however, is quite marked among the minorities. This is related to their traditional form of education and inhibits their economic development in the future.

²⁰ GENDER ISSUES

The Chinese constitution states that women have equal rights with men in all areas of life, and most legislation is gender neutral. However, there are continued reports of discrimination, sexual harassment, wage discrepancies, and other gender related problems. The gap in educational level between women and men is narrowing with women making up 47.1% of college students in 2005, but only 32.6% of doctoral students.

China has strict family planning laws. It is illegal for women to marry before 20 years of age (22 for men), and it is illegal for single women to give birth. The Family Planning Bureau can require women to take periodic pregnancy tests and enforce laws that often leave women with no real options other than abortion or sterilization. Though minority populations were previously exempt from family planning regulations, policy has changed in recent years to limit minority population growth. Today, urban minority couples may have two children while rural couples may have three or four.

Prostitution and the sex trade is a significant problem in China involving between 1.7 and 5 million women. It involves organized crime, businessmen, the police, and government workers, so prosecution against prostitution has limited success. In 2002, the nation removed homosexuality from its official list of mental illnesses, and though it is still a taboo topic, homosexuality is increasingly accepted, especially in large, international cities.

²¹ BIBLIOGRAPHY

Chiao, Chien, Nicholas Tapp, and Kam-yin Ho, ed. "Special Issue on Ethnic Groups in China." *New Asia Bulletin*, no. 8, 1989.

Dreyer, June Teufel. *China's Forty Millions*. Cambridge: Harvard University Press, 1976.

Eberhard, Wolfram. *China's Minorities: Yesterday and Today*. Belmont: Wadsworth Publishing Company, 1982.

Heberer, Thomas. *China and Its National Minorities: Autonomy or Assimilation?* Armonk, NY: M. E. Sharpe, 1989.

Hsieh, Shih-chung. "On the Dynamics of Tai/Dai-Lue Ethnicity: An Ethnohistorical Analysis." In *Cultural Encounters on China's Ethnic Frontiers,* edited by Stevan Harrell, 301—328. Seattle: University of Washington Press, 1994.

Lebar, Frank, et al. *Ethnic Groups of Mainland Southeast Asia*. New Haven: Human Relations Area Files Press, 1964.

Lemoine, Jacques. "Les Tai." In *Ethnologie régionale II* (Encyclopédie de la Pléiade). Paris: Gallimard, 1978.

Ma Yin, ed. *China's Minority Nationalities*. Beijing: Foreign Languages Press, 1989.

Miller, Lucien, ed. *South of the Clouds: Tales from Yunnan*. Seattle: University of Washington Press, 1994.

Ramsey, S. Robert. *The Languages of China*. Princeton: Princeton University Press, 1987.

Wiens, Harold J. *Han Chinese Expansion in South China*. New Haven: The Shoestring Press, 1967.

—by C. Le Blanc

DANI

LOCATION: Indonesian province of Papua on island of New Guinea
POPULATION: 270,000
LANGUAGE: Dani
RELIGION: Native Dani, Dani Church, various sects of Christianity

¹ INTRODUCTION

The Dani are a well-known tribal group from the province of Papua, Indonesia. Papua is the largest of the 33 provinces of Indonesia and was formed out of the former province of Irian Jaya in 2003. The province occupies a large portion of the western half of the island of New Guinea and is a disputed territory with the neighboring independent nation of Papua New Guinea. Indonesian encroachment into the highlands rapidly thrust the Dani into the 20th century. The Dani were contacted by expeditions prior to World War II, but wasn't until the 1950s that permanent contact was made by Christian missionaries working and living in the area. Former stone tool users, the Dani are now metal tool-using cash crop growers.

² LOCATION AND HOMELAND

The Dani live in and around the Balim River Valley in the central highlands of Papua. While a significant number (approximately 90,000) of Dani live in the Grand Valley of the Balim drainage, there are an even larger number living west of the Balim River Valley (approximately 180,000). There are about 90,000 Dani in this area alone. The other 50,000 Dani live scattered throughout the highland region at altitudes ranging from 1,000 to 1,800 m (3,300 to 5,900 ft). The Grand Valley is a grassy region with rainfall averaging around 200 cm (79 in) per year. The nights can be very cool at this high altitude. The largest city in Papua, Wamena, is located at the south end of the valley. The best estimate of the population of Wamena is approximately 40,000. Included in this estimate is a significant number of non-Dani living and working there. Wamena has also been developing as a tourist hub with guest houses and hotels for tourists who want to experience Dani culture in the Balim Valley. Relocation of the Dani from their highland valley to the lowlands to allow non-Dani to establish farms continues to be a civil and land rights problem.

³ LANGUAGE

Dani is spoken in several mutually intelligible dialects in the central highlands. The Dani language family, which contains Dani and six other Papuan languages, is part of the larger Trans-New Guinea phylum, which includes most of the languages spoken along the highland ranges on both sides of the border between Indonesia and Papua New Guinea. The Dani have a special form of their language that they call "Police Talk," which was used with the early Dutch colonial officials and is still used with any outsiders who want to learn their language. The language is a simplified form of the everyday form of Dani that they speak to each other. One particularly intriguing aspect of Dani grammar is the fact that the language has only two basic color terms (dark and light), while English, for example, has 11 basic terms. This fact has been explored by linguists and psychologists since the mid-1960s to provide evidence for the universality or specificity of color cognition.

4 FOLKLORE

Myths are not very prevalent in Dani culture. There are myths that are told among the Dani that describe relationships between humans and birds. Each kinship group has a mythical relationship with a particular species of bird, and the group is prohibited from eating this bird. This kind of relationship is called "totemism" by anthropologists. Birds are very clearly identified with human beings; in fact, enemies killed in battle are called "dead birds" in some Dani groups. Dead Birds is the title of a renowned ethnographic documentary about the Dani that was filmed by Robert Gardner and the late Michael Rockefeller between 1961 and 1965.

5 RELIGION

An important part of Dani indigenous religious belief is founded on the concept of *mogat*. Mogat is what leaves a person's body when he or she dies and tends to stay near the place where the person lived. The Dani concept of mogat corresponds very closely to the concept of a ghost. Ghosts are found everywhere, and most Dani have stories about either direct or indirect contact with ghosts. Ghosts are found especially at night and adults generally do not like to venture out after dark. Ghosts in Dani culture do not harm children because they are said to feel sorry for them. The Dani also believe in a vital essence called *edai-egen*. This substance is found in the chest, just below the sternum of adults. Children are born with this substance that grows and settles as they learn to walk and talk and become more social beings. Ghosts can affect the edai-egen and cause it to twist, which causes a person to become weak and susceptible to illness and disease.

In Dani traditional religion, it is only men who perform the ceremonies and rituals. Christianity has made a major impact in Dani territory and is steadily eroding adherence to the traditional ceremonies and rituals.

6 MAJOR HOLIDAYS

The Dani culture does not recognize or celebrate holidays. As one of the populations of Indonesia, the Dani are exposed to Indonesian holidays that are celebrated by the local Indonesian population. Christian Dani celebrate the major holidays in the Christian calendar. An extremely important event for the Dani was the Pig Feast, which is celebrated by an entire alliance every five years. During the two-and-a-half weeks of the Pig Feast, all of the important celebrations since the last feast take place: weddings, funerals, initiations, and ritual affirmations of leadership and authority. The feast involves the killing and cooking of many pigs. Prior to the Pig Feast, the leader of the alliance will install a prohibition on the killing of any pigs. This typically lasts from two to three months before the Feast begins. The Pig Feast also allows people to pay debts they have incurred to others through the exchange of valuables and pig meat.

7 RITES OF PASSAGE

Girls are permitted to marry at the first Pig Feast following puberty. The wedding begins at the bride's home. She is given items to indicate her passage into the world of adult women: a digging stick, carrying nets, and a woman's skirt. The woman's skirt is wrapped around her waist by the older women. The skirt can measure up to 27 m (30 yd) in length and will be decorated with orchid fibers. The skirt is held on by pressure alone. There is a true art to winding and wrapping the skirt so that it does not fall off. A woman will essentially wear the skirt she receives at her wedding for life, only taking it off or replacing it on rare occasions. Since weddings take place only every five years, they are group affairs involving several couples. The ceremony culminates after four days when the new bride is delivered to the home of the groom's family. The groom plays no role in the ceremony at all. The couple will live in his father's house for at least a couple of years, and it is not until they move out that they will begin to have a sexual relationship.

The Pig Feast is also a time for male initiation. The ceremony is not as brutal as those of other groups in New Guinea. The initiation includes a brief period of seclusion, a mock battle, and a final immersion in fire to purify and restore the warmth of the boys at the end of the seclusion. Observers confirm that the boys are not burned because the fire is covered with damp leaves that contain the flames.

Upon the murder of a person, young girls who were particularly close to the individual would have had one or two fingers cut off. The process was performed by a specialist who would take off the first joint of the fingers with a stone adze. The purpose of this practice was to appease the ghosts since a murder had taken place. The Dani discontinued this practice in the mid-1960s.

8 INTERPERSONAL RELATIONS

The traditional Dani greeting among men is to touch each other and to say *"halao,"* which is the shortened version of *halloak-nak*, which translates as "Let me eat your feces." This is a friendly greeting and no one takes the stock phrase literally.

In traditional Dani society, visiting, working in the gardens, tending the pigs, and virtually every activity was constrained by the constant threat of war. War was endemic to Dani culture. Communities located near the frontier between two groups not united by an alliance could see and hear battles every day. These communities had to be on the alert for raids, especially when traveling to the gardens or tending the pigs away from the compound. Groups were separated by areas of fallow fields known as "no man's lands," where formal battles usually took place. Hundreds of men participated in these battles armed with bows, arrows, and spears. Men who carry the long jabbing spears and short throwing spears do not use bows and arrows. Bowmen do not carry spears. The tips of arrows were often smeared with dirt or grease to cause infection when they entered the body. Since the Dutch took control of the area in 1958, efforts have been made to put an end to the warfare in the Grand Valley. Except for a few relapses, warfare has ceased to be a part of Dani social life. The Indonesian government does permit and even at times encourage reenactments at ceremonies and for tourists who visit the area.

9 LIVING CONDITIONS

The basic unit of Dani social life is the compound. The compound consists of a round men's house, a round women's house, a rectangular shared cooking house, and a rectangular pigsty. Large compounds may have as many as a dozen women's houses. All of these traditional houses are built of wood

Dani tribes people wait for their turn to vote outside balloting booths at Pike Village near Wamena Irian Jaya, Indonesia. (AP Images/Mark Fallander)

and have thatched roofs. A few Dani now live in government-built houses made from timber with corrugated roofs.

Health in the Balim Valley was relatively good until the recent introductions of malaria and different types of venereal diseases. Malaria was the byproduct of an agricultural scheme initiated by the Indonesian government to grow rice in Dani territory. Traditional medicine among the Dani was not highly developed, although there were certain botanical and herbal remedies for ailments. Some men were well known for their curing abilities.

10 FAMILY LIFE

Marriage is regulated through membership in moieties. The term moiety comes from French, in which it means "half." In the Dani system, a person is born into the moiety of his or her father and must then choose a spouse from the other moiety. The choice of a spouse may occur either through an arrangement between families of different compounds or through love matches arranged by individuals. The families begin a series of equal exchanges that occur over a generation. The purpose of these is to continue to bind the two families together in an alliance. This was extremely important before pacification took place in the Dani region. Polygyny, having more than one

wife at a time, took place in Dani culture but has now all but disappeared.

After a couple is married, they take up residence in the groom's father's house. Within a few years, the couple will relocate to their own place of residence within the compound. Families are rather small, with most women having only one or two children. Although divorce among the Dani is fairly easy, long-term separation is more likely to be the result of incompatibility.

11 CLOTHING

On most occasions the Dani now wear Western-style clothing. In the not-so-distant past, however, Dani traditional clothing was far from Western standards of modesty. Men wore the obligatory penis sheath made from the gourd of a vine that grows in the area. Women wore a braided cord fiber skirt and a large woven bag draped over their backs and buttocks. This bag would protect them from ghosts that might try to enter their bodies.

Prior to contact with Christian missionaries, Dani men wore their hair long and greased it with pig fat and soot. Men's hair was a source of pride. Following contact and the subsequent conversion of many Dani to Christianity, men began to wear their hair short and washed it regularly. Bathing and washing was seen as a means to finding eternal life. However, as Christianity became better understood by the newly converted Dani, bathing and washing was continued as a habit no longer associated with spirituality.

¹² FOOD

The major foodstuff in the Dani diet is sweet potatoes. They also grow other crops such as corn, taro, yams, sugar cane, bananas, cucumbers, ginger, and tobacco. Domesticated pigs are also part of the Dani diet, but they are not eaten on a daily basis; instead, they are only killed and eaten on ceremonial occasions. Pigs are also an extremely important medium of exchange among the Dani. The Balim Valley has been virtually decimated of all indigenous wildlife and any hunting for wild game must take place in the surrounding montane tropical rain forest. Western foods have not taken hold among the Dani.

¹³ EDUCATION

Formalized instruction of children in traditional Dani society was rare; however, the building of state-sponsored and missionary-sponsored schools in the Dani area has meant that Western-style education is more prevalent among the Dani. A growing number of Dani children are being taught to read and write Bahasa Indonesia, the national language of Indonesia. Child- rearing in general is very permissive and there are few expectations on the part of parents concerning their children.

¹⁴ CULTURAL HERITAGE

Artistic expression is limited among the Dani. Music consists mostly of songs, which include funeral dirges, victory songs after battles, and boy's songs that often have lewd lyrics.

¹⁵ WORK

In sweet potato production, men prepare the fields for planting with wooden digging sticks. Women do the planting, weeding, and harvesting of the crop. Dani men and women make their own fiber string for net bags, though only women weave the bags. There are no full-time specialists for any skill or activity. Dani society is what anthropologists refer to as an egalitarian society; egalitarian societies do not have inherent differences in status among different members of the group.

Dani children are given the responsibly of tending to the herds of pigs as they wander through the fields and nearby forests. Pig theft and loss are problems for the Dani.

¹⁶ SPORTS

Traditional Dani society does not have sports. There are mock battles and children play at the bow and arrow wars that were part of precontact Dani life. Wamena is the home of the Persiwa Wamena soccer team, one of only two such clubs on the Indonesian half of the island of New Guinea. The Persiwa Wamena club competes in the Liga Indonesia league competition that includes only the teams at the top of the Indonesian league system.

¹⁷ ENTERTAINMENT/RECREATION

The Dani have been described by anthropologists as one of the few cultures in the world that lack games. Competition is lacking among the Dani, which is usually given as a rationale for the absence of games as Americans know them.

¹⁸ FOLK ART, CRAFTS, AND HOBBIES

The Dani produce little art of any kind. Body decoration is the most elaborated art form in Dani culture. The Dani do not produce masks, sculptures, or paintings, as do groups from the lowlands of Papua New Guinea. The Dani, like other highland cultures, focus on the body as an art form. Men decorate themselves more elaborately than do women.

¹⁹ SOCIAL PROBLEMS

Maintenance of cultural institutions and the right to self-determination are immense problems for the present-day Dani. The loss of land rights is also a major problem besetting the Dani. Encroachment onto traditional Dani territory by Indonesian transmigrants causes tension. The need for money and the lack of reliable ways to earn it are also problems for the modern Dani.

²⁰ GENDER ISSUES

Like so many other highland societies of the island of New Guinea, the Dani exhibit a pattern of gender antagonism. Males and females are segregated beginning with the incorporation of boys into the men's houses. A group of boys will undergo introduction into the cult of adult men, and there is no corresponding cult for females. Sexual differences are elaborated and developed into a general fear of female sexuality, menstruation, childbirth, and female bodily substances.

Dani men are responsible for the construction of both wood and traditional grass houses. Men also prepare the fields for planting. Dani men weave the fiber skirts worn by women, and they also weave bark and shell bands. Dani women, however, are responsible for weaving the important net carrying bags that form part of their attire.

²¹ BIBLIOGRAPHY

Bensley, Jennifer. *The Dani Church of Irian Jaya and the Challenges it is Facing Today.* MA Thesis, Monash Asia Institute, Monash University, 1994.

Brown, Paula. *Highland Peoples of New Guinea.* Cambridge: Cambridge University Press, 1978.

Heider, Karl. *Grand Valley Dani: Peaceful Warriors.* 2nd ed. Fort Worth: Holt, Rinehart & Winston, 1991.

—by J. Williams

DERONG

ALTERNATE NAMES: Qiao, Qiu men
LOCATION: China (Derong River Valley)
POPULATION: About 7,500
LANGUAGE: Derong
RELIGION: Polytheism
RELATED ARTICLES: Vol. 3: China and Her National Minorities

¹INTRODUCTION

The Derong is a nationality of limited population, amounting to less than 7,500 people. Their history has been overshadowed by several larger nationalities that exerted a marked influence on them. They lived for centuries in a canyon surrounded by great mountains, isolated from the rest of the world. Nobody was aware of their existence until the 13th century, when an ancient Chinese book recorded their presence and called them "Qiao." They were called "Qiu men" in the Yuan (1271–1368), Ming (1368–1644), and Qing (1644–1911) dynasties. Administered by local officials, headmen of the "Mu" clan, of Naxi nationality, they led a primitive life up to this century.

They still preserve many remnants of the primitive commune. There are 15 clans (*nile*) consisting of 54 family groups (*ke'en*). Each family group constitutes a village. There are two, three, or more "extended family houses" in a village, in each of which dwell three to four generations of family members, altogether 20 to 30 people. Collective cultivated land, granary, hunting, fishing, and gathering areas are owned and used by the whole village community. The Derong practice collective labor and egalitarian distribution of goods and commodities. Another form of collective labor is limited to a small portion of people. Small collectives of two to four individual families (mostly brothers, uncles and nephews of the patrilineal line) have their own land, cultivated collectively. All of these collectives are now splitting into smaller ones, mainly into individual farms.

Members of a family group (*ke'en*) belong to a common pedigree, acknowledge a common ancestor, and keep a joint name system. Every family group selects a head, generally of a senior position in the family hierarchy, and having a glib tongue. He takes charge of both internal and external matters of his village, including command of the collective labor, organization of sacrifice offering rituals, arbitration of quarrels, and negotiation of treaties with other villages, as well as participation in collective labor. Although members of a clan (*nile*) may share a bitter hatred of the enemy ("blood feud") when any one of them is treated unjustly or murdered, there is no unified organization of the Derong nationality, even to administer justice.

²LOCATION AND HOMELAND

The population of the Derong amounts to about 7,430 living around the reaches of the Derong River Valley in 2000. The valley extends about 161 km (100 mi), walled in to the east by the Gaoligong Mountains and to the west by the Dandangli Mountains, both chains reaching more than 13,000 ft. Influenced by a maritime current from the Indian Ocean, the rainfall exceeds 100 in per year. There is a great disparity in the temperature at the peak and at the foot of the mountains. The snow cap on peaks over 13,000 ft lasts more than seven months

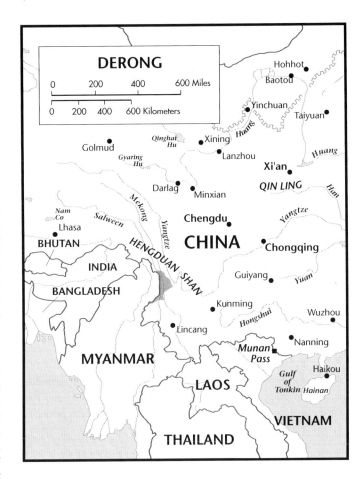

a year, while the annual average temperature in the river valley reaches 74°F. Vast areas of the mountains are covered by a thick primeval forest.

³LANGUAGE

The Derong language is classified as belonging to the Sino-Tibetan family, Tibeto-Burman group, branch undecided. They can communicate with the people of the Nu nationality. They have no writing system.

⁴FOLKLORE

The Derong have myths concerning human origins and the flood. A long, long time ago, there was no human being on earth. One day, two gods, Gamei and Gasha, descended on a big rock. They scraped some soil from the rock and kneaded the soil into a man, Pu, and a woman, Mu. Gamei and Gasha blew air into their bodies and the man and the woman began to breathe. The gods taught them how to work and how to have children. Mu was more clever than Pu, because the gods put more soil into her ribs. Human beings grew in number day by day. When they died, they were buried underground, for they should return to the soil from which they were created.

Another myth relates how human beings lived with ghosts in ancient times. They were friends, so close that they brought up each other's children as a kind of exchange of their friendly feelings. The children of ghosts were brought up nicely by the humans, while the human children were all eaten up by the ghosts. Thereafter, they became enemies. The humans chased ghosts away by means of tree branches. Vengeful, the ghost king attempted to destroy mankind by throwing a large red-hot iron ball into the river, creating a catastrophic flood. All the humans drowned except for a brother and a sister who made a narrow escape to a high mountain. Two snakes that climbed on the same mountain were also spared. That is why snakes are so numerous nowadays. Later, the brother and sister married. Nine sons and nine daughters were born. They married each other and lived on the shores of nine different rivers. They are the ancestors of the Derong, the Nu, the Tibetans, and other nationalities.

⁵RELIGION

The Derong believe in a spiritual world. They ascribe spirits to animals, plants, and many other objects. They call ghosts *bulan,* which means "endowed with a supernatural force." The shaman is not a professional, but usually holds a concurrent post as family group head. The Derong offer sacrifice to the Mountain God at regular intervals each year. This is a group affair, each household offering its own cake, meat, and dough figurines of humans and animals on the slope of the mountain by the village. The villagers are arranged in such an order that the men stand in front while the women are in the rear. Everybody prays to the god for safe and successful hunting. Then they sing and dance around a bonfire. The Harvest God is also revered. Each family offers some of the crops, a chicken, and several cakes to the field after harvest. Illness is always ascribed to the Mountain Ghost. When someone falls ill, the family hangs two bottles of wine and two chickens on a tree as propitiatory offerings. If this does not work, one offers a pig or an ox. The patient should be moved outdoors while the shaman recites the scripture for the diseased. Then, the animal is butchered.

⁶MAJOR HOLIDAYS

The only holiday of the Derong is the Kaqueqi Festival, their New Year. The date is not fixed, but usually falls around November or December on the lunar calendar. Each family group used to choose a lucky day by divination for the New Year. The duration also varies, usually depending upon the amount of food prepared beforehand. For the occasion, they butcher pigs and chickens, invite each other to celebrate, and give a banquet for the guests. The invitation is unique. It takes the form of a piece of wood. The number of notches carved on the wood represents the number of days before the feast. The banqueters usually bring some foods to the host. A rite of "Offering to Heaven" is held on this day. Led by the head of the family group, the villagers tie an ox to a wooden pole. A butcher kills it with a single stab. Then, the crowd of villagers wields their swords and dance, praying to Heaven to bestow good fortune.

⁷RITES OF PASSAGE

Ground burial is practiced. The coffin is carved out of a tree trunk. After the burial, wine and meat are offered to the dead; no tumulus (an artificial hill or mound) marks the grave location. The bereaved family receives grain, chicken, and wine from relatives as condolences for the deceased. Those who died a violent death or from a foul disease undergo fire or water burial.

⁸INTERPERSONAL RELATIONS

The Derong like to share their own food with members of their community. Whoever bags an animal in a hunt or butchers a pig or an ox will naturally give a banquet to his relatives and friends. The host usually presents a gift to the guests upon their leaving. Moreover, it is a custom to entertain a stranger passing by. Quite a few households have an extra firepool ready at any time to accommodate a guest. The firepool keeps the room warm and serves for cooking. Passersby are allowed to stop on the way for a rest at their house.

In the busy season, the Derong usually move to a place by the field. On these occasions, the house door is only fastened with a small wooden rod. A tender twig tied on it tells the guest that the host is not at home and feels sorry about it. When heavy snow seals the mountains, food and tools are hung on the trees; they are never taken by other people.

A small bamboo-strip basket is usually used as a token in relations between young men and women. Young Derong men make these small baskets about 7 inches in diameter. If a young man likes a girl, he will hang a basket on her house door around midnight. The girl can usually surmise who the maker is from the style of the basket. If she likes him too, she will carry it on her arm, to show the basket-maker that she is willing to have a friendly relationship with him and to show the community and especially other young men that she has a young man of her heart.

⁹LIVING CONDITIONS

There are two kinds of storied buildings. One is made of bamboo, usually built on a slope. Doors open to the front and the rear. One comes in and goes out by wooden ladders. The main entrance opens onto two rows of small rooms, each of which can accommodate a couple and their children. In some cases families break away from the collective houses and build their own houses and granaries. These storied houses of individual families are made of logs, usually small and low, the ground floor being dug well below the surface of the earth. The floor of the upstairs room is only 2—3 ft from the surface of the earth. The door is so low that one can enter only by bending. Most of these houses are windowless. There are usually two or more firepools in a house. One firepool symbolizes the family. A married son usually lives with his parents as well as his brothers and sisters, but he and his own family must use the second firepool. If another son gets married, he should build a new house attached to the old one.

Because of the craggy, mountainous terrain and the inclement weather, transportation is extremely inconvenient. From November to May, the mountains are sealed off and transportation is completely interrupted. After the bitter seasons, the only means of communicating with the outside world are sliding ropes and suspension bridges made of rattan or steel rope. The sliding ropes are made of steel wires, usually set up over a narrow river, between two mountains facing each other. Besides the sliding rope itself, a pulley with a few cords (sometimes a bamboo basket) is the only means available to cross the river. To see the Derong use the sliding rope and rattan suspension bridge across the turbulent waves of the Nu River is nothing less than breathtaking.

¹⁰FAMILY LIFE

The Derong families are patrilineal and small. The first married son lives with his parents, although he must use the second firepool. The other sons build their own houses after marriage. These houses are adjacent to the old parental home. This is one of the remnants of the patriarchal clan commune. All Derong women participate in field work, but their position is lower than the men's. They are not allowed to bear children inside the family house: otherwise, the farming and hunting of the family, so they believe, will be seriously affected. Thus, a makeshift shed is set up for childbearing.

The Derong still preserve vestiges of the "pairing marriage." For instance, several sisters may marry one husband without disturbing the family hierarchy. Intra-clan endogamy (marriage within the clan) is strictly prohibited. The systematic practice of exogamy (marriage outside the clan) has led to the formation of a fixed circle of inter-clan marriage. For example, a girl of the Rendang clan is married off to a young man of the Bukawang clan, whose daughter is married off to the Lapian clan. A girl of the Lapian clan is married off to the Bingdang clan, whose girl is married to the Muqiantu clan. The girl of the Muqiantu clan is married off to the Rendang clan. These seven clans form a circle related by marriage, allowing for the continuation of the exogamic rule.

In general, the Derong are monogamous, although polygamy does exist as a result of the sororate and levirate customs (marriage to the brother or sister of a deceased spouse).

¹¹CLOTHING

The only traditional clothing preserved by the Derong and worn by both men and women is a black-and-white or multicolored striped linen wrapping the body and tied over the right shoulder. Otherwise, their garments and trousers are the same as those of the Chinese—polo and ordinary shirts, long trousers, women's skirts, and so on. The aged and middle-aged women usually have tattoos over their faces; formerly, girls were tattooed when they were 12 or 13 years of age. Although the figures and designs were different in different clans, the girls' forebrows usually remained untattooed. Tattooing is now rare among the youngsters.

¹²FOOD

The staple foods of the Derong include millet, corn, and buckwheat. Rice is rare. For six months a year, their food is supplemented by gathering, fishing, and hunting. They gather mainly the stem tuber of some wild plants that contain starch, such as wild yams and wild lily. They like homemade wine, tea, and tobacco; the latter is smoked in a long-stemmed pipe. They prefer roast meat to other cooking. Food and wine are divided equally by the hostess. A guest might have his share. A new firepool is added for a newly married son. Each firepool takes turns cooking for the extended family.

¹³EDUCATION

Nobody in the Derong communities received a formal education in the past. They knew only how to keep records by notching wood or tying knots. In recent decades, more than 20 primary schools have been set up. Half of the teachers are Derong. College students and intellectuals have emerged.

¹⁴CULTURAL HERITAGE

On occasions of productive labor, harvest, hunting, house building, marriage proposal, or festive activities, the Derong all sing and dance to express their thoughts and feelings. There are traditional melodies, while their lyrics are improvised for the occasion. They have only one percussion instrument, the *mangluo,* composed of three gongs fixed on a frame. There is a traditional group dance, *niuguozhuang,* accompanied by songs.

¹⁵WORK

Derong agriculture is based on the slash-and-burn method, yielding very poor results. Because of grass burning and rotation farming, only half of the arable land is available for production in a given year. Rice has been introduced and some terraced fields have been built up. Unfortunately, the cold weather severely affects rice production. Hunting, gathering, and fishing are the main sources of food. Recently, livestock husbandry has been developed. Pigs, sheep, and oxen raised either by family groups or by individual families have proved beneficial to their quality of life. Hunting, fishing, and the manufacture of farm tools and of daily necessities made of wood and bamboo are specific male activities; gathering is left to the women. The Derong River, from which the nationality gets its name, has been its traditional fishing ground. Because of the swift current, small fishnets must be used, resulting in limited production. Thus, the fishing potential of the Derong is not expected to expand significantly.

¹⁶SPORTS

Arrow shooting with bows or crossbows is one of the skills in which the Derong excel; it is the main means of hunting and is very popular as a competitive spectator sport during festivals. Unique skills of the Derong are vigorous and nimble movement on the sliding rope and balanced, swift steps on the rocking and undulating suspension bridge made of rattan—skills that few athletes could perform with such consummate art.

¹⁷ENTERTAINMENT AND RECREATION

Only fearless emissaries of culture—in this case a film projection team—have accepted the challenge of striding across turbulent rivers and steep mountains 12,000 ft above sea level to bring the Derong the benefits of the seventh art in the guise of several long feature films.

¹⁸FOLK ART, CRAFTS, AND HOBBIES

Although the Derong are not known for handicrafts, the small and delicate bamboo-strip baskets usually used as love tokens and the small fishnet devised by the fishermen are exquisite objects of art.

¹⁹SOCIAL PROBLEMS

It is difficult to see how the Derong can overcome their poverty and illiteracy to improve their lifestyle as long as their isolation persists. It seems that the only way would be to leave their valley and accept resettlement. As of now, there is no movement in this direction.

[20] GENDER ISSUES

The Chinese constitution states that women have equal rights with men in all areas of life, and most legislation is gender neutral. However, there are continued reports of discrimination, sexual harassment, wage discrepancies, and other gender related problems. The gap in educational level between women and men is narrowing with women making up 47.1% of college students in 2005, but only 32.6% of doctoral students.

China has strict family planning laws. It is illegal for women to marry before 20 years of age (22 for men), and it is illegal for single women to give birth. The Family Planning Bureau can require women to take periodic pregnancy tests and enforce laws that often leave women with no real options other than abortion or sterilization. While minority populations were previously exempt from family planning regulations, policy has changed in recent years to limit minority population growth. Today, urban minority couples may have two children while rural couples may have three or four.

Prostitution and the sex trade is a significant problem in China involving between 1.7 and 5 million women. It involved organized crime, businessmen, the police, and government workers, so prosecution against prostitution has limited success. In 2002, the nation removed homosexuality from its official list of mental illnesses, and though it is still a taboo topic, homosexuality is increasingly accepted, especially in large, international cities.

[21] BIBLIOGRAPHY

Chiao, Chien, Nicholas Tapp, and Kam-yin Ho, ed. "Special Issue on Ethnic Groups in China." *New Asia Bulletin* no 8 (1989).

Dreyer, June Teufel. *China's Forty Millions.* Cambridge: Harvard University Press, 1976.

Eberhard, Wolfram. *China's Minorities: Yesterday and Today.* Belmont: Wadsworth Publishing Company, 1982.

Heberer, Thomas. *China and Its National Minorities: Autonomy or Assimilation?* Armonk, NY: M. E. Sharpe, 1989.

Ma Yin, ed. *China's Minority Nationalities.* Beijing: Foreign Languages Press, 1989.

Ramsey, S. Robert. *The Languages of China.* Princeton: Princeton University Press, 1987.

Shin, Leo Kwok-yueh. *The Making of the Chinese State: Ethnicity and Expansion on the Ming Borderlands.* New York: Cambridge University Press, 2006.

Schwarz, Henry G. *The Minorities of Northern China: A Survey.* Bellingham, WA: Western Washington University Press, 1989.

—by C. Le Blanc

DONG

PRONUNCIATION: DAWNG
ALTERNATE NAMES: Liao; Geling
LOCATION: China
POPULATION: 3 million
LANGUAGE: Dong; Chinese
RELIGION: Polytheism
RELATED ARTICLES: Vol. 3: China and Her National Minorities

[1] INTRODUCTION

The Dong are a nationality whose origin can be traced through a branch of the Xiou tribe during the Qin (221–206 BC) and Han (206 BC–AD 220) dynasties more than 2,000 years ago. They were also called Liao, Geling, and other names in ancient Chinese works. It was said that some of the Dong ancestors went upstream through the Xun River and the Duliu River and arrived in the area now inhabited by the Dong. The Dong have lived in areas surrounded by the Miao, Zhuang, and Yao; these were ruled by the central government of successive Chinese dynasties. The Dong had their own social and administrative organization. The families of a given Dong village all bore the same surname. Public order was maintained by customary laws, which were decided through consultation among the heads of the villages. As a member of the village organization, every adult male participated in the general membership meeting to discuss matters concerned. This organization has been markedly weakened since the 1950s, but some of the customary laws are still effective to a certain extent.

[2] LOCATION AND HOMELAND

The Dong are mainly concentrated in a mountainous area at the junction of three provinces, Guizhou, Guangxi, and Hunan, with warm climate, abundant rainfall, and criss-crossed by rivers running in all directions. The villages, located at the foot of hills and bordered by streams, are adorned by a drumtower of exquisite beauty at the center with an ancient banyan tree on the side. Dong population was 3 million in 2000.

[3] LANGUAGE

Dong language belongs to the Sino-Tibetan family, Zhuang-Dong group, Dong-Shui branch. There are southern and northern dialects, each having three regional idioms. Most of the Dong know the Chinese language, both spoken and written. An alphabetic system of writing based on Latin was created in 1958, and proved very helpful to those who did not know the Chinese language.

[4] FOLKLORE

The rich mythology of Dong has been transmitted orally from one generation to the next without written records. An epic described the achievements of the Goddess Sasui and her offspring, including the creation, the flood, and the marriage of the brother and sister. This myth of origins is common (with many variants) to many national minorities of southwest China.

Another story described four tortoises incubating four eggs. Three eggs went bad. Only one egg hatched a boy. They tried again. This time, also only one egg hatched, giving birth to a girl. The offspring married and gave birth to 12 sons and daughters. Among them were a brother, Jiangliang, and his sister, Jiangmei, who were naughty. The boy cut a tree with a saw, leading to a fire that hurt the Thunder Goddess. She got angry, so it rained continuously for nine months. Fortunately, Jiangliang and Jiangmei hid in a huge melon when the flood came. The Thunder Goddess raised 12 suns to dry up the flood, but they scorched the earth and the trees. Helped by bees, Jiangliang and Jiangmei shot down 10 suns out of 12. They left one sun for the daytime and the other for the night. An eagle tried to persuade them to marry. They rolled two millstones from the mountain top, which laid one on top of the other, a Heaven-given sign that they should marry. They married and their progeny formed various peoples, the Han, Miao, Yao, Dong, etc.

⁵RELIGION

The Dong are polytheistic. They regard the almighty Goddess Sasui, the most lofty of all gods, as their protector. Each village has a temple in which there is a round altar made of stone, 4 ft in height, more than 10 ft in diameter, surrounded by banana trees and brambles. On February 7 or 8 (lunar calendar; Western calendar, between February 28 and March 27) the Dong will bring chicken, duck, fish, and a gruel of sweetened fried flour, as offerings to the goddess. They also revere huge stones, large trees, wells, and bridges. Divination by means of chicken, grass, eggs, snails, rice, or divinatory symbols is prevalent among the Dong.

⁶MAJOR HOLIDAYS

The Spring Festival (lunar New Year; Western calendar, between January 21 and February 20) is the most important holiday of the year. In some districts, however, they choose one day in October or November (lunar calendar; Western calendar, between October 24 and January 18) as the Dong's New Year. Before the feast, every family member will take a bowl of rice gruel symbolizing a watery field to be ploughed in the future.

On the first of January (lunar calendar; Western calendar, between January 21 and February 20), right after the first cockcrow appears, girls will scramble to draw water from the well. The luckiest sign is to draw a bucket of water with white bubbles. Festival activities include buffalo fighting, mountain climbing, and bronze drum percussions. April 8 (lunar calendar; Western calendar, between May 1 and May 30) is the Festival of the Birth of the Buffalo God. Every household will clean the buffalo pen, feed it with black glutinous rice, give the animal a day off, and kill a chicken or duck as a sacrificial offering. In addition, this is also the day when a heroine boldly delivered a meal of black glutinous rice to her brother (imprisoned for having led an insurrectionary army to occupy Liuzhou City) and rescued him from jail. Commemorating that day, married women gather to sing and dance and to make black glutinous rice cakes that are carried to their parents' homes and offered as gifts to their relatives.

⁷RITES OF PASSAGE

Three days (or one week) after childbirth, relatives bring glutinous rice, eggs, and chickens, as well as a hat, for congratulations. Gifts also include 3—5 ft of yellow cloth for the baby's clothing. According to Dong custom, one is not allowed to

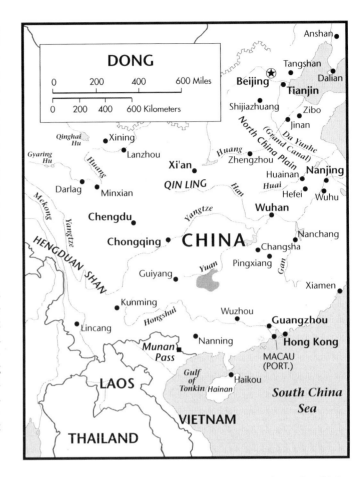

make baby clothes before childbirth. The infant should be draped with used cloths right after its birth. The new clothing should be made of the yellow cloth given by the relatives. The maternal grandmother chooses a name for the baby while sewing the baby's clothes. Girls gather to sing blessing songs until late in the evening. When the baby is one month old, the mother paints the baby's brow with a little tang oil and soot from the bottom of a pan. Accompanied by her mother-in-law, the new mother will bring gifts to her own mother's house, where she will be received warmly. Next day, her mother will send a large glutinous rice cake to her house, indicating that the mother is allowed to call on relatives to present the baby.

The Dong bury the dead underground after shaving the hair and washing the body. It is taboo to have any copper or iron touch the body.

⁸INTERPERSONAL RELATIONS

The Dong are hospitable. Bowls of gruel of sweetened fried flour will be repeatedly offered to the guest. Each bowl is offered with different refreshments. This ritual usually takes one hour or more. The wine before meal is sweet, but bitter wine is offered during the meal. All dishes taste sour: pork, fish, chicken, duck, cucumber, and hot pepper; it is a "sour feast." There is a Dong custom in Guizhou to receive a guest from each family. A man, representing his family, will bring his family's dishes to the dinner party. Thus, a great variety of dishes will be offered to the guests. A grand occasion of Dong celebration is when all the members of a village call on a neighboring village, usually after autumn harvest. There is a deafening sound of gongs and

A Dong child wearing traditional clothing in Congjiang, China.
(© Keren Su/Corbis)

drums, reinforced by songs and reed-pipe wind music. Dating is common and dates last late into the night.

9 LIVING CONDITIONS

Most Dong houses have two or three stories, sometimes more, made of wood. The roof is covered with tiles or bark of China fir. Houses occupied by branches of the same family are sometimes connected by verandas and open into each other. Buildings at the foot of a hill or beside a river are built on stilts, sometimes 20–30 ft high. The family lives upstairs. Firewood and livestock are placed on the ground. A shrine for idols or ancestral tablets is set up in the central room. The "windswept rooms" on both sides are used as bedrooms and firepools. A Dong village is usually made up of row upon row of wooden houses. The pathways are paved with flagstones or crushed stones. The Dong live on self-sufficient agriculture. City dwellers have a standard of living similar to that of other residents.

10 FAMILY LIFE

Dong families are patrilineal. The position of women is much lower than that of men. They are not allowed to touch the bronze drum or to go upstairs if the men stay downstairs. They have a limited right of succession from their parents ("girl's field") only after their marriage—while the man inherits the property. Women participate in heavy labor in the fields and bear the responsibility of all household chores.

The Dong are monogamous. They have freedom to choose their spouse. Arranged marriages are very rare. Youngsters of the same family branch or of different generations are not allowed to marry. The children of brothers are allowed to marry the children of sisters and vice versa, but the children of two sisters are not allowed to marry. The bride, holding an umbrella, accompanied by six women, walks directly to the bridegroom's house. On certain occasions, girls of the whole branch are the bridesmaids. They are received by boys of the bridegroom's branch, who see the bride to her family's door right after the wedding ceremony. She will return to live with her husband for a few days only during festivals or after the busy season.

If she gets pregnant, she will then move to her husband's house. If she does not get pregnant, she is expected to move three to five years after her wedding.

11 CLOTHING

The rural people like to use self-made yarn to dye and knit their traditional clothes, which are in dark navy, purple, white and blue colors. Men wear cotton shirts and pants and always wrap their heads. Women's wear varies in the different districts; most of them wear nice trimmed short tops and multi-pleated skirts. They use dark navy cotton fabric to wrap their legs from knee to ankle and wear sandals. They usually comb their hair into a bun with colorful flowers. This is the typical style of most Dong women. Some women like to use a floral cotton patch to cover their shoulders and sew large pure silver buttons on their costumes for decoration. Others wear long shirts going down to the knee and loose pants. Their sleeve openings and the cuffs of pants are all piped and lace-trimmed. They even make dragon and phoenix embroidery on their clothes. However, Dong people living in urban areas usually wear the same basic clothes as the Chinese.

12 FOOD

The staple food is rice. The Dong like hot and sour dishes. One of their traditional meals is salted fish or meat. Raw fish or meat is salted for three days, seasoned with spicy pepper powder, ginger, Chinese prickly ash, and glutinous rice, and then put in hermetically sealed pots or wooden barrels. The preparation may be served after three months, but only reaches full flavor after many years. The salted fish or meat can be steamed, but the Dong prefer to eat it raw. A gruel of sweetened, fried flour is a favorite dish. Rice is stir-fried with tea leaves, then cooked in water; when it is done, the tea leaves are discarded. To serve, one puts fried glutinous rice, peanuts, walnuts, soybeans, sausages, or pork liver selectively in a bowl, then adds the hot gruel, sweetened or salted.

13 EDUCATION

Primary schools have been established in every village, and middle schools in every district. The number of college students is increasing. More and more teachers, engineers, scholars, and medical doctors are being trained. However, illiteracy is still present in remote mountainous areas, especially among women. Parents support the education of their children. However, boys form the greater majority of middle school and, especially, university students.

¹⁴CULTURAL HERITAGE

One of the striking cultural accomplishments of the Dong in recent years is the creation of the Great Song of Dong, a women's chorus unaccompanied by musical instruments, which, under the leadership of a woman, has developed a unique style, free in tempo and full of power and grandeur.

The Pipa Song is also typical of the Dong musical tradition. The *pipa* is a plucked string instrument with a fretted fingerboard. The song borrows the name of the accompanying instrument.

Dong plays were developed in the last century from a genre of popular entertainment consisting of talking and thinking. The gait and movement are rather simple, but the music for voices is manifold. The actors wear Dong dress, but use no facial makeup. Songs are accompanied by a two-stringed bowed instrument, the *huqin*.

The Dong practice group dancing in a circle, boys and girls holding hands and singing while dancing. A musician-dancer blows the reed-pipe wind instrument *(lüshen)* while going through various dance movements.

The Dong area is the "land of poems and sea of songs." The rhyme scheme of their poems is rather loose. The Dong Song is a chanted rhymed poem, marked by an abundance of striking metaphors. The content includes themes of creation, flood, the origin of human beings, the migration of the Dong, customary law, as well as the exploits and the loves of heroes. Chinese stories also appear in Dong songs and plays.

¹⁵WORK

In addition to farming, men are adept at carpentry and in building Dong-style wooden structures. Today there is a trend among young people to move to coastal areas and to engage in trade.

¹⁶SPORTS

Wrestling is a favorite sport among the youth, while whipping a top is a popular game with children. Other sports widely practiced are basketball, table tennis, volleyball, and chess.

¹⁷ENTERTAINMENT AND RECREATION

Some movies have been dubbed into the Dong language. Many Dong families now have black-and-white television. Recreation for youngsters is almost always related to dating. Singing is one of the favorite pastimes in Dong areas; the aged teach songs, the youth sing songs, and the children learn songs. Singers take much pleasure in performing. The Lion Dance and the Dragon Dance are performed on the Spring Festival.

¹⁸FOLK ART, CRAFTS, AND HOBBIES

Dong crafts include embroidery, cross-stitching, rattan artifacts, bamboo articles, silver ornaments, brocade, and Dong garments. The Dong's wooden buildings are renowned for their exquisite architecture. The Drum Tower, all made of wood, is held by tenon and mortise, without a single iron nail; numbering 3–15 stories, it may reach 40–50 ft in height. It is the symbol of the family branch and a place of rally. The magnificent "Wind and Rain Bridge" is a wooden bridge built on stone piers, with three to five pavilions raised on top of the piers.

¹⁹SOCIAL PROBLEMS

Poverty and slow development are still the most important social problems. Changes are slow and the way to modernization and wealth is long and difficult.

²⁰ GENDER ISSUES

The Chinese constitution states that women have equal rights with men in all areas of life, and most legislation is gender neutral. However, there are continued reports of discrimination, sexual harassment, wage discrepancies, and other gender related problems. The gap in educational level between women and men is narrowing with women making up 47.1% of college students in 2005, but only 32.6% of doctoral students.

China has strict family planning laws. It is illegal for women to marry before 20 years of age (22 for men), and it is illegal for single women to give birth. The Family Planning Bureau can require women to take periodic pregnancy tests and enforce laws that often leave women with no real options other than abortion or sterilization. While minority populations were previously exempt from family planning regulations, policy has changed in recent years to limit minority population growth. Today, urban minority couples may have two children while rural couples may have three or four.

Prostitution and the sex trade is a significant problem in China involving between 1.7 and 5 million women. It involved organized crime, businessmen, the police, and government workers, so prosecution against prostitution has limited success. In 2002, the nation removed homosexuality from its official list of mental illnesses, and though it is still a taboo topic, homosexuality is increasingly accepted, especially in large, international cities.

²¹ BIBLIOGRAPHY

Chiao, Chien, Nicholas Tapp, and Kam-yin Ho, ed. "Special Issue on Ethnic Groups in China." *New Asia Bulletin* no 8 (1989).

Dreyer, June Teufel. *China's Forty Millions.* Cambridge: Harvard University Press, 1976.

Eberhard, Wolfram. *China's Minorities: Yesterday and Today.* Belmont: Wadsworth Publishing Company, 1982.

Gustafsson, Bjorn A., Shi, Li, and Sicular, Terry , eds. *Inequality and Public Policy in China.* New York: Cambridge University Press, 2008.

Heberer, Thomas. *China and Its National Minorities: Autonomy or Assimilation?* Armonk, NY: M. E. Sharpe, 1989.

Lebar, Frank, et al. *Ethnic Groups of Mainland Southeast Asia.* New Haven: Human Relations Area Files Press, 1964.

Lemoine, Jacques. "Les Tong." In *Ethnologie régionale II* (Encyclopédie de la Pléiade). Paris: Gallimard, 1978.

Ma Yin, ed. *China's Minority Nationalities.* Beijing: Foreign Languages Press, 1989.

Miller, Lucien, ed. *South of the Clouds: Tales from Yunnan.* Seattle: University of Washington Press, 1994.

Ou, Chaoquan. *Life in a Kam Village in Southwest China, 1930–1949.* Boston: Brill, 2007.

Ramsey, S. Robert. *The Languages of China.* Princeton: Princeton University Press, 1987.

Wiens, Harold J. *Han Chinese Expansion in South China.* New Haven: The Shoestring Press, 1967.

—by C. Le Blanc

DRUZE

PRONUNCIATION: DROOZ
LOCATION: Lebanon; Syria; Israel; Jordan
POPULATION: 1 to 1.5 million (2007)
LANGUAGE: Arabic
RELIGION: Secret Druze faith (Muhwahhidun)

¹ INTRODUCTION

The Druze are both a unique religious and a unique ethnic group whose history dates back to the 11th century AD. Originating in Cairo, Egypt, in 1009–1010, they then spread to the mountains of southern Lebanon and beyond. The Druze faith grew out of the Isma'ili sect of Shia Islam, but from its beginnings it has been an entirely new religion. Disillusioned with the Isma'ilis in 1009–1010, the Druze turned to caliph al-Hakim, of the Fatamid dynasty based in Cairo, Egypt, as their deliverer. In 1017 he declared himself to be the incarnation of God, and the prophet Hamza ibn 'Ali took over al-Hakim's mortal duties as *imam* (spiritual and political leader). Hamza is considered the leader of the Druze movement. One of his disciples was named Muhammad al-Darazi, who quickly came into conflict with Hamza and was rebuked publicly by him. On the last day of 1019, al-Darazi was assassinated and then proclaimed a heretic. It is commonly believed that the Druze get their name from this heretic; it was probably given to them by their detractors.

Caliph al-Hakim disappeared in 1021 (he was most likely murdered, though no one knows for sure), and Hamza went into hiding. The new caliph, al-Zahir, denounced Druzism and persecuted its followers mercilessly. The Druze in Cairo and north to Aleppo were wiped out. The survivors in southern Lebanon and Syria continued to follow their faith, becoming secretive and highly protective of their survival. Hamza (still in hiding) appointed a new imam named Baha' al-Din after the persecution eased off. Baha' al-Din collected and organized 111 letters and directives written by al-Hakim, Hamza, and Baha' al-Din himself into six books called *al-Hikmat al-Sharifa* (The Noble Knowledge), the Druze bible. In 1043, the call for converts was closed, and since then it is said that no new converts have been accepted, although a few infusions of new blood have occurred over the centuries. Technically, though, one must be born a Druze; one cannot become one by choice.

The Syrian Druze community grew rapidly in the 1980s and 1990s as many fled war-torn Lebanon. The Druze leader Kamal Jumblatt was murdered in 1977 in the Lebanese civil war, triggering an increase in Druze aggressions there. Compared to the Arab Muslims and Christians in Israel, the Arab Druze community is relatively well off because of their unqualified support for Israel. This is in marked contrast to the political position of the Druze in Lebanon, which supports traditional Arab nationalist principles favoring Palestinian independence. It is the only Arab community in Israel, besides a small group of Bedu, allowed to serve in the Israeli armed forces.

² LOCATION AND HOMELAND

The total Druze population throughout the world is difficult to estimate because of the secrecy of the sect and because, for example, Syria's government demographic information is unreli-

able. Some estimates put their numbers as high as 2 million, but it is generally thought there are between 1 and 1.5 million. The vast majority of them live in Lebanon, Syria, Israel, and Jordan. Good estimates as to their dispersion are: Lebanon, 400,000–600,000; Syria, 600,000–800,000; Israel; 85,000 (including 15,000 Syrian Druze living in the Golan Heights); Jordan, 15,000; and at most 80,000 elsewhere in the world. The oldest and largest concentration of Druze is found in Lebanon. The largest communities outside the Middle East are in North and South America, with smaller groups in Australia, West Africa, and Western Europe. All are immigrants from Middle Eastern communities, especially from Lebanon. The Druze population in the United States is estimated at 20,000–27,000. Most US Druze settled in small towns and kept a low profile, joining Protestant churches (usually Presbyterian or Methodist) and often Americanizing their names. However, they continued to send money back to their families in the Middle East and even arranged marriages with persons from their home villages. They have now formed Druze associations in the US to develop community relations in their new homes.

The racial background of the Druze is obscure. They are definitely Arab, with Persian, Kurdish, Turkish, Byzantine, and probably European (from the time of the Crusades) physical traits mixed in. This has led to a great variety in physical characteristics among the Druze, despite centuries of marrying within their own group. Most Druze are still hardy, independent farmers living in mountain villages of less than 10,000. Some, however, have moved to larger urban centers and taken on other sorts of jobs. All Druze villages are located on the tops or sides of hills and mountains for a number of reasons, the first and foremost being defense. This position also puts them closer to their holy shrines, which are also always built on the tops or sides of hills and mountains. For farming purposes, it makes it easy to fertilize their fields: they simply collect dung from their livestock, pile it on the hill outside the village, and let the rains carry it down to the fields below. In Lebanon, most Druze have olive groves and fruit orchards. In southern Syria, they are more likely to be wheat farmers.

³ LANGUAGE

The Druze speak Arabic, with slight distinctive differences. For example, they have kept the *qaf*, the strong guttural *k* sound of classical Arabic that has been dropped or changed to a *j* or hard *g* sound in other Arabic dialects, and they have retained the *dad*, a soft, tongued *d* sound that is close to classical Arabic, which has lost its unique sound in other dialects.

Traditional, religiously significant names used to be common for both boys and girls: *Mohammed, Husayn,* and *'Ali* for boys, and *'A'isha* and *Fatima* for girls. But now most Druze children are given neutral names that are common to Christians and Muslims, such as *Samir, Salim, Fu'*AD, or *Fawzi* for boys.

⁴ FOLKLORE

See the following section entitled **Religion** in this article.

⁵ RELIGION

The Druze believe that Sunni Muslims follow the First Course of literal interpretation of scriptures, Shia Muslims follow the Second Course of allegorical interpretation, and they themselves follow the Third Course (*al-maslak ath-thalith),* or

Tawhid, of real knowledge of the unity of God and the unity of Being in God. They call themselves *Muhwahhidun* (rather than Druze), which means, essentially, Unitarian—they believe in absolute monotheism. Their beliefs have been held in secret since the closing of the call for converts in AD 1043. Since then, only a few people from each community in each generation are initiated into the details of the faith. The rest are called the *juhhal*, which means "noninitiated" but also has an implied meaning of "ignorant" or "uninformed." The juhhal are given a simple outline of the faith to follow.

The initiated are called ʿuqqal (ʿaqil—masculine singular, and ʿaqila—feminine singular), or "enlightened," and are put through rigorous tests to determine if they are able to handle the responsibility of enlightenment. Women have been included in the ʿuqqal since the beginning of the Druze movement. Those who pass the tests then go through a secret initiation ceremony, after which they wear a heavy white turban and never wear bright colors, swear or use obscene language, drink alcohol, or smoke. The ʿuqqal are then divided into two further classes: those who know some of the elementary aspects of the faith, and those who study for years to gain an in-depth knowledge of the mysteries of the religion. This most advanced class of Druze is called the *al-ajawid*, or "the righteous." At the weekly Thursday-evening worship service, held at a place for seclusion and prayer called a *khalwa* or *majlis*, the juhhal attend the first part of the service, where community affairs are discussed, then they leave so the ʿuqqal can engage in prayer, study, and meditation.

Because the Druze faith is held in secret, few of their beliefs are known to the wider world. What is known is that they believe that God is One and All is God; God has had many incarnations in this world, including Jesus, but Jesus is not "God's Son" as Christians believe. According to the Druze faith, the caliph al-Hakim was the final incarnation of God in this world. The Druze believe that prayer and ritual are unnecessary when true knowledge of God's unity is gained (prayer is the association of the soul with the oneness of God and is a constant state of being, rather than something one does at certain times of day). The number of souls of believers and nonbelievers is believed to have been fixed at Creation, so every time a Druze dies, another Druze is born, and the soul of the deceased immediately enters the body of the newborn. This belief in the immediate reincarnation of souls leads the Druze to be fierce and fearless warriors, because death simply means they will leave one body and enter another.

6 MAJOR HOLIDAYS

The Druze believe that they have been freed from ritual on their Third Course, so holy days are not important as religious duties. They do have shrines, called *mazar* or *maqam*, located on the tops or sides of hills and mountains they visit frequently. At the tomb of the holy man or woman to whom the shrine is dedicated, the Druze pray quietly, leave small gifts of food and money, and take away small pieces of colored cloth as tokens of divine blessing to be kept in their homes or in the family car. Some families come for extended stays to sacrifice animals in the fulfillment of a vow. Others just have picnics or spend a quiet weekend there. Annual religious festivals attract thousands of Druze to some shrines, such as al-Nabi Shu'ayb. There is also an annual pilgrimage to the alleged burial place of Jethro, Moses' father-in-law, near Horns of Hittim in Galilee.

7 RITES OF PASSAGE

The circumcision of males is not practiced as a ritual rite of passage among the Druze, as it is among Muslims and Jews. Weddings are small gatherings, though they can be extravagant, depending on the wealth of the family. Funerals are huge community events; people from all around attend. Every Druze village has a *mawqaf*, or "stopping place"—a small cement or stone amphitheater with rows of seats where hundreds, even thousands, can gather to honor and remember the deceased and give condolences to the family. When a respected community or religious leader dies, everyone who knew of the person, whether or not they had ever met, is expected to attend the funeral, either in person or by representative. Funeral arrangements are made immediately after death, and the ceremony is held the next day at the latest. Announcements are made, formerly by a town crier but now usually by loudspeaker, in the deceased's village and other villages where he or she was known. The body is washed, dressed in the finest clothes available, and buried above ground-level just outside the village. Women lament in the traditional Lebanese Muslim way, although not as excessively, and acquaintances tell of the deceased's virtues.

8 INTERPERSONAL RELATIONS

With the habit of secrecy and defensive privacy that the Druze have developed over their persecuted history, the average Druze has little contact with non-Druze, even in the same small village. Among themselves (and others they feel they can trust), however, the Druze are extremely hospitable and generous. There is a strict code of honor that all Druze are committed to maintaining. For example, Druze men, including soldiers, will never touch a woman in any harmful way, even if she is one of the "enemy" during combat. The Druze look after their own community's orphans, widows, and poor people. There is no such thing as a Druze beggar. If an extended family cannot support one of their members for some reason, the rest of the community will help out. Almost all Druze villages have one or more *mudafat* (singular, *mudafa*), guest houses where visitors can stay. There is an extensive system of *awqaf* (singular, *waqf*), endowed properties for religious or charitable use given in wills for the purpose of establishing and maintaining *khalwa* (prayer-houses) or *mazar* (shrines).

9 LIVING CONDITIONS

It has been said by many throughout the ages that the Druze are a healthy and handsome lot. Most Druze still live in small villages. Some villages have electricity and telephone service; others do not. Almost all villages now have regular bus and taxi service to major nearby cities.

The quality of Druze life depends greatly on the country in which they live. Those in Israel, for example, generally have a higher quality of life than do those in small villages in Syria or Lebanon. The Diaspora, which accounts for a large number of Druze, live very comfortably in the West.

10 FAMILY LIFE

The family is central to Druze life, and the Druze make frequent formalized visits to their family members. Even those who have emigrated to other continents maintain their family ties as closely as possible. The most important factor in

Druze sheikhs cross the Quneitra checkpoint between Syria and the Israeli-occupied Golan Heights. Israel seized the strategic plateau in 1967 and annexed it in 1981. Some 18,000 Syrians, most from the Druze community, still live there. (Louai Beshara/AFP/Getty Images)

Druze family life is a woman's honor *(ird),* and her dishonor is the family's worst humiliation. For this reason, even though women have equal rights politically and religiously, they are socially very restricted (to minimize the possibility of dishonor). Women are expected to marry at a fairly early age (17 to 20) and become stay-at-home homemakers. The minimum age for marriage is 17 for women and 18 for men, but most men do not marry until age 21 to 23. Marriage partners usually come from the same village and frequently from the same extended family (including first cousins). These close family marriages are preferred in order to preserve property and maintain the knowledge of family background and heritage. Marriages are almost always arranged by the family, and the groom pays the bride's family a dowry. Polygamy, and the Islamic custom of *mut'a,* or temporary marriage, are forbidden, as is marriage to a non-Druze. *Shaykhs* and *masha'ik al-Din* (community and religious leaders) administer the law in matters of marriage, divorce, and inheritance.

The Druze prefer sons to daughters, particularly for the first-born child, and they will continue to have children until a son is born. The average family has 5 or 6 children, but Druze families can be as large as 10 to 12 children. The failure of a woman to bear children (particularly sons) is a frequent cause for divorce.

¹¹ CLOTHING

Druze living in small villages still wear traditional clothing. Women wear a blue or black peasant dress with a gauzy white head covering called a *mandil,* and red slipper-like shoes that are their only spot of bright color. Most *juhhal* (uninitiated) no longer wear *shirwal,* the baggy pants that are tight at the ankle, worn by the `uqqal* (initiated). Juhhal men wear the common Arab headscarf, the *keffiyeh,* and the `uqqal wear heavy white turbans. Most Druze men sport large moustaches with waxed tips. Westernized Druze dress in modern clothing.

¹² FOOD

Most Druze families grow their own fruit and vegetables and bake their own bread. They eat a mostly vegetarian diet with meat only on special occasions. Typical village meals include olives; mountain bread (paper-thin, round, unleavened bread); eggplant; cauliflower; chickpeas flavored with onions, garlic, and *tahini* (sesame paste); rice; bulghur (cracked wheat); potatoes; salad (made of tomatoes, cucumber, parsley, and other herbs, dressed with olive oil and lemon juice); yogurt; and seasonal fruit. Lamb (or kid—young goat's meat) is the favorite meat, with chicken second, and then beef. Eating pork is not forbidden, but it is not encouraged, either. Some Druze do occasionally eat pork.

¹³ EDUCATION

Among the younger generation of Druze (under age 25), literacy is almost universal. No literacy statistics are available for the general population, but the literacy rate is believed to be fairly high. Most girls traditionally stopped their formal schooling after six years of basic elementary education, but more are now beginning to attend secondary school, and some even go on to university or professional training (as nurses or teachers, for example). Druze women are found on the faculties of universities in Lebanon, Syria, and Israel, but it is still very rare for a rural Druze girl to be allowed to leave home to study abroad. The urbanized Druze communities are far less conservative and Druze girls from these areas regularly attend university.

14 CULTURAL HERITAGE

Druze poetry does not have any love songs, focusing instead on themes such as the love of God and of one's native countryside. Druze poets and writers include Samih al-Qasim, a poet from the town of al-Rama in Galilee; and Shaqib Arslan, a Druze prince known as "the prince of eloquence" (amir al-bayan), who was chosen in 1938 to be president of the Arab Academy in Damascus. Druze musicians have become known in both Western classical music (e.g., pianist Diana Taqi al-Din) and traditional Middle Eastern music (e.g., lute (oud) player, singer, and composer Farid al-Atrash [1916–1976]).

15 WORK

Although they were traditionally farmers, Druze can now be found in all areas of business, including banking, trade, retailing, and transportation services. The former president and principal shareholder of Middle East Airlines, Najib 'Alam al-Dim, was a Druze, and a large percentage of the airline's personnel, including pilots, have been Druze throughout most of the company's existence.

Druze who leave rural communities are often successful businessmen and there are large numbers of Druze working in the oil rich Gulf countries, where they have earned a reputation as hard working and reliable. Druze women rarely work outside the home in rural communities, but in the West and even in the Gulf, Druze women do work in modern jobs.

16 SPORTS

The Druze enjoy most popular sports including hunting, fishing, soccer, basketball, tennis, volleyball, water skiing, and water polo.

17 ENTERTAINMENT AND RECREATION

Traditionally situated rural Druze in the Middle East lead traditional lives. Men dominate the social space and can be seen most days drinking tea in small tea shops. In cities, Druze engage in the sorts of activities typical to the country in which they live. They meet in restaurants, attend and play sporting events, and shop at malls.

18 FOLK ART, CRAFTS, AND HOBBIES

The Druze are known for their weaving, carpet-making, and basketry.

19 SOCIAL PROBLEMS

Because they are such a small, close-knit, protective society, the Druze have very few social problems within their own community. Their protective secrecy, however, has grown out of almost constant persecution from outsiders since their inception. Relegated to small mountain villages, the Druze have learned to take care of their own and to be suspicious of strangers. This same protectiveness has led them to be misinterpreted and misunderstood for centuries, accused of everything from communism to fanatical aggression.

Modernity and the Diaspora have somewhat altered the lives of the Druze. As they have moved around the world, changes have slowly emerged. The tradition of dowry, or bride price, has caused some Druze to actually marry outside the community due to lack of financial resources. In Israel and in the Western Diaspora, women regularly take jobs outside of the community, and this has led to changes in Druze traditions.

20 GENDER ISSUES

Druze women have high status in terms of religion. There are by some accounts, more female uqqal than male, because of teachings that women are more spiritual. Socially, however, women face fairly strict restrictions. It was only in the 1970s that Israeli Druze were allowed to obtain drivers licenses. In most rural Druze communities, women are forbidden to work outside of their home village, go to the cinema, or be photographed—a restriction that has to be overlooked for identity documents in most developed countries. It is forbidden to perform autopsies on Druze women and women are forbidden to give birth in hospitals without female physicians.

Though marriages are generally arranged, the woman has the right to refuse a spouse. Divorce is difficult to obtain, but women as well as men can initiate the proceedings. A man can obtain a divorce on grounds of: failure to bear children, or sons; disobedience; immodest behavior (proven adultery is an automatic, guaranteed ground for divorce); and mental or other chronic illness that makes regular sexual intercourse impossible. A woman can also obtain a divorce on those last grounds, as well as on grounds of impotence, nonsupport, and desertion or prolonged absence. A divorce is irrevocable—once divorced, always divorced. Ex-spouses cannot remarry each other or even be under the same roof ever again. In a divorce, women are almost always given financial compensation because it is difficult for a divorced woman to remarry and thereby be supported.

21 BIBLIOGRAPHY

Betts, Robert Brenton. The Druze. New Haven, Conn.: Yale University Press, 1988.

Dana, Nissam. The Druze in the Middle East: Their Faith, Leadership, Identity and Status. Sussex, UK: Sussex Academic Press, 2003.

Makarem, Sami Nasib. The Druze Faith. Delmar, N.Y.: Caravan Books, 1974.

Melrod, George, ed. Insight Guides: Israel, including the West Bank and Gaza Strip. Boston: Houghton Mifflin, 1994.

Moss, Joyce, and George Wilson. Peoples of the World: The Middle East and North Africa. Detroit: Gale Research, 1992.

Obaid, Anis I. The Druze and Their Faith in Tawhid. Syracuse, NY: Syracuse University Press, 2006.

Westheimer, Ruth K and Gil Sedan. The Olive and the Tree: The Secret Strength of the Druze. Brooklyn, NY: Lantern Books, 2007.

—revised by J. Henry

EMIRIANS (UNITED ARAB EMIRATES)

PRONUNCIATION: em-EE-ree-uhns
LOCATION: United Arab Emirates (UAE)
POPULATION: 4,621,399 (2005 estimate/less than 20% are UAE citizens)
LANGUAGE: Arabic
RELIGION: Islam (majority Sunni)

¹ INTRODUCTION

The United Arab Emirates is a confederation of seven sheikhdoms, or emirates, located on the shore of the Arabian (or Persian) Gulf. Each emirate is named after the main city within its boundaries. The largest is Abu Dhabi, the capital. Dubai is known as the confederation's business center. The other emirates are Sharjah, Ras al-Khaimah, Ajman, Umm al-Qaiwain, and Fujairah.

The nomadic and settled Bedu (or bedouin—*see Bedu*) tribes were converted to Islam during the 7th century AD. The following centuries were marked by continual wars and violence between rival dynasties. The emirates also became known as the Pirate Coast, because their peoples resented foreign ships in the Gulf and raided them constantly. After suffering these raids for many years, Britain launched an attack on the emirates, after which the emirates signed a peace treaty with Britain (1820). However, the raids continued to occur off and on until the emirates and Britain signed a "perpetual maritime truce" in 1853. The emirates then became known as the Trucial States. This arrangement lasted for over 100 years, until 1971.

When the truce ended, Bahrain and Qatar became independent states, and six of the other emirates decided to join forces. On 2 December 1971, Abu Dhabi, Dubai, Sharjah, Ajman, Umm al-Qaiwain, and Fujairah became the United Arab Emirates (UAE). In February 1972 the emirate of Ras al-Khaimah united with them as well. The provisional constitution drawn up at their union was made permanent in 1996. Because Abu Dhabi is the largest and most powerful of the seven emirates, its emir is designated the president of the UAE. The vice president and prime minister is the emir of Dubai, the second-largest emirate.

In 1962 oil was discovered in Abu Dhabi. Until then, the emirates had been poor, with pearling, fishing, and sheep and goat herding being the main forms of livelihood. The discovery and production of oil brought new wealth into the area, turning the Emirians from among the poorest people of the world into some of the wealthiest. Dubai began producing oil in 1969 and Sharjah in 1974. The other emirates have yet to discover oil on their land and depend on Abu Dhabi and Dubai for financial support. Proven oil reserves in Abu Dhabi are estimated to last for another 200 years, based on production rates in 2008. Dubai's oil reserves were projected in the late 1990s to run out in about 30 years, but the UAE has been decreasing its oil production and estimated in 2008 that overall reserves could last more than 90 years. Dubai has become a world trading center and will continue to have international significance and a source of income after its oil runs out.

Sheikh Zayid bin Sultan al- Nuhayyan, ruler of Abu Dhabi, served as president of the UAE from 1971 until his death in 2004. His successor was his son, Sheikh Khalifa bin Zayid al-Nuhayyan. Al-Nuhayyan took office on 3 November 2004 and organized the first elections in the UAE in December 2006. A group of 6,700 electors participated in the historic election.

² LOCATION AND HOMELAND

The UAE is located on the southern coast of the Arabian (or Persian) Gulf and the northwestern coast of the Gulf of Oman. The total area of the UAE is 83,900 sq km (32,400 sq mi), which is about the size of the U.S. state of Maine. The UAE has 621 km (386 mi) of coastline on the Arabian Gulf and Gulf of Oman. Abu Dhabi is by far the largest emirate, with an area of 67,340 sq km (26,000 sq mi). Dubai is the second largest, at 3,885 sq km (1,500 sq mi). The areas of the rest of the emirates are as follows:

EMIRATE	SQUARE KILOMETERS	SQUARE MILES
Sharjah	2,590.0	1,000
Ras al-Khaimah	1683.5	650
Fujairah	1165.5	450
Umm al-Qaiwain	777.0	300
Ajman	259.0	100

The land is mostly desert with a mountain range in the north and oases scattered across the sands. The only other variation in the terrain, except for Ras al-Khaimah, is a few salt marshes. The emirate of Ras al-Khaimah is called the "garden spot" of the UAE because, unlike the rest of the emirates, the land there is very fertile. Almost all of the people in Ras al-Khaimah are farmers. The humidity is high on the coast, where all but one of the major cities and towns are located. The summer months, May through October, are extremely hot, with temperatures reaching 50°C (122°F) in the shade. Winters are much cooler, with temperatures dropping to 10°C (50°F). Humidity can rise as high as 100% in the summer and winters are also damp, but there is little rainfall during the year. Hot desert winds kick up occasional sand and dust storms.

Flamingoes are year-round residents of the coast, and many other birds pass through on their migration routes. As many as 25,000 migratory birds can be counted in August. Desert wildlife includes foxes, rabbits, gazelles, lizards, snakes, and eagles.

The human population of the UAE is estimated at 4.6 million. Only about 20% of these residents are Emirate citizens, or muwatiniii (locals). The rest are foreign workers who come mostly from other Arab countries, Pakistan, India, the Philippines, Western European countries, the United States, and Canada. The foreign workers hold no political power or privileges of citizenship. About two-thirds of the population is male because many of the foreign workers are men who leave their families behind in their home countries, or they are young men who have not married yet. The most densely populated city is the capital, Abu Dhabi, with about 1.7 million residents. Dubai, with 1.3 million residents, is the second most densely populated city.

³ LANGUAGE

The official language and native language of UAE citizens is Arabic. English is widely used in the business and public sectors because of the large presence of foreign workers. Other languages spoken by UAE residents are Hindi, Urdu, Persian, Malayalam, and Tagalog.

Arabic, spoken by 100 million people worldwide, has many distinct dialects, so that people living as few as 500 km (310 mi) apart may not be able to understand one another. The written form of Arabic is called Classical Arabic or, for today's literature and press, Modern Standard Arabic. It is the same for all literate Arabs, regardless of how different their spoken dialects are. Arabic is written from right to left in a unique alphabet, which makes no distinction between capital and lower-case letters. It is not necessary for the letters to be written in a straight line, as English letters must be. Punctuation rules are also quite different from those of English.

"Hello" in Arabic is *marhaba* or *ahlan,* to which one replies, *marhabtayn* or *ahlayn.* Other common greetings are *As-salam `alaykum,* "Peace be with you," with the reply of *Wa `alaykum as-salam,* "and to you peace." *Ma'assalama means* "Goodbye." "Thank you" is *Shukran,* and "You're welcome" is *`Afwan;* "yes" is *na'am* and "no" is *la'a.* The numbers one to ten in Arabic are *wahad, ithnayn, thalatha, arba'a, khamsa, sitta, saba'a, thamanya, tisa'a,* and *`ashara.*

Arabs' names consist of their first name, their father's name, and their paternal grandfather's name. Women do not take their husband's name when they marry but rather keep their father's family name as a sign of respect for their family of origin. First names usually indicate an Arab's religious affiliation: Muslims use names with Islamic religious significance, such as Muhammad and Fatima, while Christians often use Western names, as well as Arabic Christian names, such as Elias and Butrus.

⁴ FOLKLORE

Before the discovery of oil, pearling was a major source of income for the people of the Emirates. Pearl divers made up 85% of Abu Dhabi's male population. The pearl diving season lasted for four months, from May to September, after which husbands, fathers, and sons returned to their homes. The patience and hope of Emirian women for the safe return of their loved ones were beautifully depicted in the following folk song:

Neighbor of mine, my adventurous sailor shall return.
Neighbor of mine, he shall return from the world of dangers.
With perfumes, precious stones, rosewater and incense he shall return.
He shall return, and to see him again will be like seeing the moon.

⁵ RELIGION

Native-born Emirians are all Muslims. Most of the foreign workers are also Muslims, although there are also Hindus and Christians. The majority of Emirians are Sunni Muslims, with a small Shi'ite minority.

Islam is the youngest of the world's Abrahamic religions, having begun in the early 7th century AD when the Prophet Muhammad received his revelations from Allah (God). Within just a few years of Muhammad's death in AD 632, Islam had spread through the entire Middle East, gaining converts at a dynamic rate.

Born into the Koreish tribe of Mecca (c. AD 570), in what is now Saudi Arabia, Muhammad was later driven from the city because of his vigorous denunciation of the pagan idols worshiped there (idols that attracted a profitable pilgrim trade). The year of Muhammad's flight from Mecca, AD 622 (16 July), called the *Hijra,* is counted as the year one in the Muslim calendar. Muhammad fled to the city now known as Medina, another of the holy sites of modern-day Saudi Arabia. Eventually, Muhammad returned to Mecca as a triumphant religious and political leader, destroyed the idols (saving the Black Stone, an ancient meteorite housed in the *Ka`aba,* or Cube, building, which has become a focal point of Muslim worship) and established Mecca as the spiritual center of Islam.

The Islamic religion has five so-called "pillars": 1) Muslims must pray five times a day; 2) Muslims must give alms, or *zakat,* to the poor; 3) Muslims must fast during the month of Ramadan; 4) Muslims must make the pilgrimage, or hajj, to Mecca; and 5) each Muslim must recite the *shahada:* "ashhadu an la illah ila Allah wa ashhadu an Muhammadu rasul Allah," which means, "I witness that there is no god but Allah and that Muhammad is the prophet of Allah." Arabs say all their prayers facing in the direction of Mecca. Both men and women are expected, and greatly desire, to make the pilgrimage at least once in their lifetime. Ramadan, the ninth month of the Muslim year, during which Muhammad received his first revelations, is observed by complete fasting from dawn until dusk each day of the entire month.

Islam is a simple, straightforward faith with clear rules for correct living; it is a total way of life, inseparable from the rest of one's daily concerns. Therefore, religion and politics, faith and culture, are one and the same for Muslims. There is no such thing as the "separation of church and state." In theory, there should be no distinction between private religious values and public cultural norms in an Islamic country; in actuality, history, geography, and daily life have influenced the cultures of Islamic countries, resulting in standards of social behavior and interaction that are not always in agreement with religious codes of conduct.

The difference between the Sunni and Shi'ite Muslims, which has played such an important part in Arab history, has to do with the early history of the religion. After Muhammad's death, the entire Muslim community recognized the legitimacy of the next three successors, or caliphs. The fourth caliph was Ali, Muhammad's cousin and son-in-law. His legitimacy was challenged by Mu'awiyah, the governor of Syria, and after the Battle of Siffin, in 657, Ali was forced to withdraw. He moved his capital to Iraq and was murdered shortly thereafter. His followers refused to recognize the legitimacy of Mu'awiyah's caliphate and established the Shi'ite sect. Although there are doctrinal differences, the fundamental difference between the sects, therefore, is an argument about authority, not doctrine: the Shi'ites believe that caliphs must be direct descendants of Muhammad and that Ali was the legitimate fourth successor, while the Sunnis believe that caliphs should be elected by the people and therefore that Mu'awiyah and his successors were legitimate. Because there are more Sunnis than Shi'ites worldwide, the Sunnis refer to themselves as the "orthodox" sect.

The official religion of the UAE is Islam and the laws of the emirates are made in accordance with Islamic principles. For instance, Emirians and Muslim foreign workers are prohibited from consuming alcohol. However, the UAE exempts

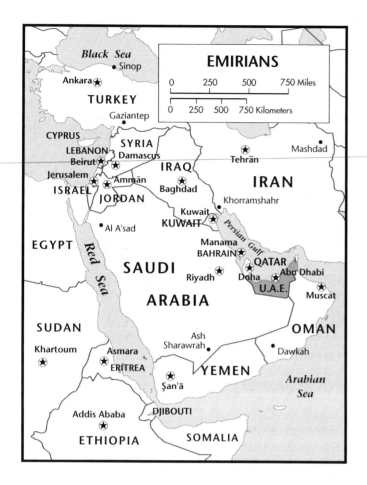

Births, especially the births of boys, are celebrated by Emirians, as they are among Arab Muslims generally. The first word spoken to a baby is "Allah." After birth, the next important event in a boy's life is circumcision, which, performed at the age of seven, formally makes him a member of the religious community. Children and adolescents are prepared for adulthood by being given adult responsibilities, sharply differentiated by gender. In adolescence, the sexes are strictly segregated while outside of their immediate family, and girls are monitored to assure their chastity.

Dating remains unacceptable among Emirians. Marriages are still arranged and often occur within extended families. Young men and women, however, do have the right to reject a proposed mate. Most men marry around age 26 while women marry between the ages of 22 and 24. In the traditional arranged marriage, the groom pays the bride a dowry, or *mahr*, which becomes her property no matter what happens. The mahr consists of two stages. The first stage is the *muqaddam*, which is a dowry given preceding the wedding to allow the bride to buy things for herself and her new home. The second stage, the *muta'akhir*, is a form of insurance for the woman in the event of divorce; the groom pledges in a contract that he will pay the bride an agreed-upon amount if he should divorce her.

Marriages traditionally involved spending a great deal of money on festivities and dowries, which led some Emirian men to seek non-Emirians as wives. The government has tried to encourage Emirians to marry each other and has set a limit on the dowry a groom must pay to his future wife. The government also pays for some wedding expenses and provides free housing to Emirian newlyweds.

8 INTERPERSONAL RELATIONS

Arab hospitality reigns in UAE. When talking, Arabs touch each other much more often and stand much closer together than Westerners do. People of the same sex will often hold hands while talking or walking. (In earlier days, members of the opposite sex, even married couples, never touched in public.) Arabs talk a great deal, talk loudly, repeat themselves often, and interrupt each other constantly. Conversations are highly emotional and full of gestures.

9 LIVING CONDITIONS

Before the discovery and production of oil, conditions were very primitive in what is now the UAE. Emirians had no electricity, running water, or sewage disposal system; there were no paved roads or telephones; public education and health care did not exist; and housing consisted of the bare minimum needs for shelter.

Since oil production began in 1962, conditions have rapidly improved, so that almost all Emirians now live in thoroughly modern homes in ultramodern cities. The government allots land to Emirian families so they can build their own homes and provides no-interest loans for housing.

Roads are paved and well maintained; multilane divided highways connect the major cities and link the UAE with neighboring countries. Automobiles and trucks crowd the streets, and four-wheel-drive vehicles race across the desert sands. A railway system is being planned to relieve some of the traffic congestion, particularly that caused by cargo trucks.

non-Muslims from some rules of Islamic law and allows non-Muslims to practice their religion. Several Christian churches have been formed in UAE cities, and good relationships generally exist between the various religious groups. Despite the influence of Islam, many Emirians continue to identify themselves on the basis of their tribal affiliations. These affiliations influence their political, social, and financial decisions.

6 MAJOR HOLIDAYS

Secular national holidays include National Day, which is celebrated on December 2, and New Year's Day on January 1. Each emirate may also celebrate its own holiday. For example, August 6 is a holiday in Abu Dhabi marking the accession of Sheikh Zayid. Other official holidays are Muslim ones. Muslim holidays follow the lunar calendar, moving back by 11 days each Western year, so their dates are not fixed on the standard Gregorian calendar. The main Muslim holidays are *Eid Al-Fitr,* a three-day festival at the end of Ramadan; *Eid Al-Adha,* a three-day feast of sacrifice at the end of the month of pilgrimage to Mecca, when families who can afford it slaughter a lamb and share the meat with poorer Muslims; the First of *Muharram,* or the Muslim New Year; *al-Mawlid An-Nabi,* the prophet Muhammad's birthday; and *Eid Al-Isra' wa Al-Mi`raj,* a feast celebrating Muhammad's nocturnal visit to heaven. Friday is the Islamic day of rest, so most businesses and services are closed on Fridays. All government offices, private businesses, and schools are closed also during Eid Al-Fitr and Eid Al-Adha.

Five of the emirates have international airports, and there are radio and television broadcasts in Arabic and other languages, and broadcasts from other countries can be picked up on the many satellite dishes on apartment buildings and private homes. Telephone service is state-of-the-art; fax machines are very common.

Traditional *souks,* or street markets, exist right alongside huge new shopping malls. There is almost no crime in the UAE. Medical care is still not up to Western standards, but it is improving. Health care is provided free of charge at hospitals and clinics staffed mostly by foreigners. The average life expectancy of Emirians is 76 years.

10 FAMILY LIFE

Emirians are a tribal people, and family is the center of their life. Marriages are traditionally arranged by parents, with first cousins being the preferred match. Polygamy is legal—a man may have up to four wives, if he guarantees that all will be equally loved and cared for—but it is very rarely practiced. Divorce is a fairly simple procedure, but it does not occur very often. In a divorce, the father is given custody of all children over the age of five, and the mother takes the younger ones with her back to her parents' house, where she will live until she remarries.

Although the UAE is a conservative country by Western standards, it is still one of the most liberal in the Gulf. Women are much less restricted in the UAE than in other Arab countries. Over the past few years, women have made remarkable progress in obtaining education and joining the work force. As of 2008, about 98% of the female population of school age was attending primary or intermediate school. Women form 70% of the student body at the Higher Colleges of Technology and over 60% at the UAE University. The number of employed women almost quadrupled from 1980 to 1990, increasing from 5.3% to 16.3% of the total work force. Emirian women have also joined the armed forces and the police.

11 CLOTHING

Emirians wear traditional Arab clothing. For men, this consists of an ankle-length robe called a *dishdasha,* or *kandura.* The dishdasha is often made of white or off-white cotton cloth and sometimes in a dark color. A large piece of cloth, called a *ghutra,* is worn on the head, held in place with a piece of woven rope called an ʿ*aqal,* which is a thick black circular band made of twisted wool. On formal occasions, a *bisht,* a full-length cloak embroidered with a golden thread edge, is worn on top of the dishdasha. Women's fashions vary and, with the new flow of wealth, some women import the latest fashions from the West. A traditional UAE woman's costume, however, is the ʿ*abaya,* a full-length, black cloak-like garment that covers her from head to toe when she is in a public place.

12 FOOD

The Emirian cuisine includes a variety of dishes that are prepared and served on various occasions. Rice, meat, and fish are staple foods. They are cooked in various ways in varying combinations. Spices are an essential part of the Emirian cuisine. Among the most commonly used spices are coriander, cardamom, saffron, and turmeric.

A favorite dish in the UAE as well as in other Gulf countries is *machbous,* or rice and meat seasoned with spices, on-ions, tomatoes, and dried lemon. During Ramadan, the month of fasting, *harees* is usually served. Harees is a dish consisting of small pieces of shredded meat with wheat and water, mixed together and thoroughly beaten over and over again to the consistency of porridge. Favorite desserts include *al-halwa,* a sweet made from sugar, eggs, starch, water, and oil; *al-Jibeet,* a sweet made from date syrup and sesame seeds; and *Kul Wis-kut,* a dessert made from a mixture of peanuts and sugar.

Coffee and tea are the most popular beverages and are often mixed with spices, coffee with cardamom and tea with saffron or mint.

13 EDUCATION

As a newly developing state, the UAE focuses much of its resources on education to give its young citizens the tools they need to compete in the modern world. Education is compulsory from age 6 to age 12, and it is free through the university level.

The government also provides full scholarships for study abroad if the course of study is not offered at United Arab Emirates University, which opened in Al Ain in 1977. In 2006, UAE University had about 14,500 students, with women making up 79% of the student body. The UAE established a second university, Zayed University, for women in 1998, with campuses in Dubai and Abu Dhabi. As of 2008, 3,400 students were enrolled.

Although public schooling was virtually nonexistent before the late 1950s, enrollment at public primary schools is now almost 100% and the literacy rate has risen to 89% for men and 88% for women, compared with an overall figure of 24.9% in 1980. Most teachers in the public school system are Arabs from other countries. Outside the public school system, there are also schools for foreigners run by their home countries.

14 CULTURAL HERITAGE

The only native Emirian artistic traditions are those passed down from the Bedu (or bedouin) nomads [see Bedu]. These include traditional Arab music, storytelling, dances, and the strong passion for poetry. Traditional Emirian music is characterized by a marked drumbeat accompanied by the sounds of various percussion and stringed instruments. The *tubool,* or drums, which come in various sizes, are beaten with a stick or with the fingers. The *oud,* a popular instrument, is an ancient stringed instrument that is the ancestor of the European lute. The percussion instruments include the soft sad tone of the Arabian flute or *nai,* and the *mizmar,* a long open-ended instrument which produces a loud, nasal sound. Another traditional instrument is the *rebaba,* a one-stringed instrument.

A famous dance which marks the UAE traditions and customs and is performed on almost every occasion is the *ayyala.* Men form two rows, shoulder to shoulder, facing each other at a distance. This is meant to resemble the scene of a battle, where one row represents the line of attack and the other row represents the cannons, reflecting the Arabs' love of expressions of courage and chivalry.

15 WORK

About 90% of the work force in the UAE is foreign. During the early part of 1995, the UAE launched a nationwide campaign aimed at bringing more Emirians into the work force. The largest industry in the UAE is the Dubai Aluminum Company,

Emirati men greeting each other. (arabianEye/Getty Images)

which opened in 1979, but most of the UAE's income (about 40%) comes from the oil industry. Most of the oil wealth comes from the emirate of Abu Dhabi. In the smaller emirates, sheep and goat herding, fishing, and farming are the main occupations along with boat-building, handicrafts, and jewelry. Business and industrial workers in the cities often take a two- to three-hour lunch break and then return to work and stay until 7:00 pm or later.

16 SPORTS

The traditional sports of camel and horse racing still attract great crowds. Nowadays, however, owners and fans often speed alongside the race course in four-wheel-drive vehicles, shouting instructions and cheering. No betting is allowed at camel races. The UAE boasts three ice-skating rinks and some Emirians and visitors enjoy sand skiing in the desert. Water sports are also popular throughout the UAE. The Dubai Desert Classic Golf Tournament is an annual event, drawing top international golfers. It is held at the Emirates Golf Club in Dubai, the first 18-hole grass course in the Gulf region; it opened in 1988.

Dubai also hosts world-class tournaments in tennis, rugby, snooker (or pool), soccer, cricket, volleyball, and chess. The Dubai World Cup is one of the richest horse racing competitions in the world.

17 ENTERTAINMENT AND RECREATION

Movie theaters showing movies in Hindi, Urdu, Persian, Arabic, and English are very popular with Emirians. Videos can be rented, but they are censored. Several satellite channels, over eight TV stations, and numerous radio frequencies from all over the Gulf can be received in the UAE. Camping in the desert, family outings at parks, and listening to music are among Emirians' favorite pastimes.

18 FOLK ART, CRAFTS, AND HOBBIES

Most of the folk art sold in UAE markets is imported. The UAE's Women's Association runs a Handicrafts Center in Abu Dhabi that produces some local basketry and weaving. Baskets are made of palm tree fronds, called *al Khoos*. Wool from sheep is woven into colorful fabrics, to be used for pillowcases, covers, blankets, carpets, and bags.

19 SOCIAL PROBLEMS

The emirates have a long history of intertribal wars and violence, and although they are now united in an attempt at cooperation, old conflicts continually erupt. The financial and political structure also causes problems. Because Abu Dhabi is the largest emirate and has the largest oil reserves (and therefore makes the most money), it makes all the decisions in the UAE. Abu Dhabi's emir is the president of the union. Dubai is the only emirate large and wealthy enough to challenge Abu Dhabi's decisions. The other emirates are all too small and too dependent on financial support from Abu Dhabi to risk speaking out against the Abu Dhabi-dominated government. This creates resentment among the smaller emirates. Dubai occasionally acts on its own, going against decisions handed down by the Abu Dhabi leaders. The union of the emirates is too young, and the new oil wealth and resulting development too recent, to determine if the UAE will be able to maintain its unity and function as a stable federation of states.

The fact that the UAE is a young federation also creates some tensions between the traditional nomadic life of the Bedu and a more modern, sedentary world. Roles of men and women remain primarily traditional, with males expected to provide for their families and women expected to maintain control over the running of domestic affairs.

The UAE also faces some international disputes. Its reliance on foreign workers remains a pressing problem, partly because the government is unwilling to grant citizenship privileges to non-Emirians. Policies approved in 2007 allowed for companies to regulate the activities of foreign workers but gave the workers no additional rights. A longtime boundary dispute with Oman was ratified in 2003, but the agreement had not been published as of 2008. In addition, drug traffickers use the UAE ports as a transfer point in the exchange of illegal drugs. The country's great wealth also poses a possible problem. As a major financial center, the UAE is vulnerable to money laundering. Although the government has imposed some controls, its informal banking sector is largely unregulated.

20 GENDER ISSUES

Emirian women have enjoyed more educational opportunities with the opening of Zayed University, an all-women's university that emphasizes the enrollment of Emirians first. As such opportunities have opened up, women have consistently outperformed men in schooling. However, university opportunities have not been viewed by Emirian women or their families as career choices. Instead, a college degree is seen as improving the value of a young Emirian woman whose family wants her to marry well. Few Zayed attendees intend to pursue careers; most are interested in retaining the traditional social structure.

Women in many Arab nations have begun to press for more equality between the genders in the public sphere. Such a movement has not yet occurred among Emirian women because of the UAE's wealth and because of Emirian beliefs in the value that Islam places on women in traditional, more domestic roles. Many women, even those who attend universities, see a future as a wife and mother as one that their society values. The equality sought in the workplace and political sphere by women in other Arab nations means little to Emirians.

21 BIBLIOGRAPHY

Amnesty International Report 2008: State of the World's Human Rights. http://thereport.amnesty.org/eng/Homepage

Background Notes: United Arab Emirates. Washington, D.C.: US Department of State, Bureau of Public Affairs, Office of Public Communication, July 1991.

Berger, Gilda. *Kuwait and the Rim of Arabia.* New York and London: Franklin Watts, 1978.

Chandler, Patricia M. "Dubai: An Oasis of Modern Commerce." *Transportation & Distribution* 37, no. 2 (February 1996): 88–93.

Crabtree, Sara Ashencaen. "Culture, Gender, and the Influence of Social Change Amongst Emirati Families in the United Arab Emirates." *Journal of Comparative Family Studies* 38:4 (2007): 575 (13).

General Information on the United Arab Emirates, The Emirates Center for Strategic and Research Homepage, http://www.ecssr.ac.ae

Harrison, Marcia S. "Dubai: At the Crossroads of Continents." *Travel Weekly* 52, no. 2 (11 January 1993): 16–17.

Hunt, Carla. "Dubai Leads Emirates in Opening Up to International Visitors." *Travel Weekly* 54, no. 80 (9 October 1995): 24–25.

"New York Firm Has Vacationers Warming Up to Dubai." *Travel Weekly* 55, no. 16 (26 February 1996): 80.

Post Report: United Arab Emirates. Washington, D.C.: US Department of State, 1994.

Sluglett, Peter, and Marion Farouk-Sluglett. *Tuttle Guide to the Middle East.* Boston: Charles E. Tuttle Co., 1992.

United Arab Emirates. CultureGrams: World Edition. Ann Arbor, Mich.: ProQuest LLC, 2008.

—revised by H. G. Carlson

EWENKI

ALTERNATE NAMES: Kamonikan; Suolun; Tongusi; Yakute
LOCATION: China; Mongolia
POPULATION: 30,200
LANGUAGE: Ewenki and Chinese
RELIGION: Traditional beliefs, Lamaism, and Christianity
RELATED ARTICLES: Vol. 3: China and Her National Minorities

1 INTRODUCTION

The ancestors of the Ewenki dwelled northeast of Lake Baikal and in the forest bordering on the Shilka River. They lived from hunting, fishing, and raising reindeer. The Ewenki are historically linked to the Shiwei (especially the Bei Shiwei and the Bo Shiwei), as recorded in the ancient books in the Northern Wei Dynasty (386–534). In 544, the Shiwei began to pay tribute to the Eastern Wei Dynasty (534–550). The imperial Tang Dynasty (618–907) set up a government office in the area where the ancestors of Ewenki dwelled. Later on, they moved eastward. A branch moved as far as the middle reaches of the Heilongjiang River. The ancient books in the Yuan Dynasty (1271–1368) called them "the forest people." Under the Ming (1368–1644) and the Qing (1644–1911) dynasties they were called "the northern mountains deer riding people." From 1633 to 1640, the Manchus of northeast China conquered the Ewenki (at that time called "Kamonikan" and "Suolun"), who had to pay tribute to the Qing imperial government. After the mid-17th century, because of the invasion of Manchu territory by czarist Russia, the Qing moved the Ewenki to the Nen River Valley, close to the Greater Xing'an Mountains. In 1732, the imperial Qing placed more than 1,600 "Kamonikan" soldiers in garrison in the Hulunbeir grassland. They were allowed to bring their wives and children along. They finally settled there and became the direct ancestors of the present-day Ewenki.

2 LOCATION AND HOMELAND

The Ewenki amount to more than 30,200 people in 2000. They are mainly scattered in Inner Mongolia, living together with the Mongols, Daur, Chinese, and Oroqen. The region where they live in compact communities is called Ewenki Autonomous Qi County, a hilly grassland with more than 600 lakes as well as a large number of rivers flowing in all directions. Ewenki villages are also found in Nehe District in Heilongjiang Province.

3 LANGUAGE

Ewenki belongs to the Altaic linguistic family, Manchu-Tungusic group, Tungusic branch. There are three dialects but no writing system. Ewenki children are educated in schools set up in pastoral areas using Mongolian language, both oral and written. In agricultural and mountainous areas, however, Chinese language and characters are widely used.

Until the mid-20th century, the Ewenki living in different areas were called by various names: Suolun, Tongusi, Yakute, and so on. In 1957, according to their will, a unified name was adopted: Ewenki, which means "people living in the wooded mountains."

4 FOLKLORE

The origin of mankind is explained as follows in an Ewenki myth: After the creation of the sky and the earth, the god Enduli made 10 men and 10 women from the skeletons of birds. Encouraged by his success, he planned to make more men and women, 100 of each. He made men first, but in the process of his great work, he nearly ran out of bird skeletons. He had to use soil as a supplement to fashion the women. As a result, the women were weaker, a part of their body being made of soil.

The Ewenki have a special reverence for fire. This may be related to their tough Nordic environment and is reflected in one of their main myths. A woman was injured by a shower of sparks from the household hearth. Angered by her pain, she drew her sword and stabbed violently at the hearth until the fire died out. The following day, she tried in vain to light a fire. She had to ask for a burning charcoal from her neighbor. Leaving her house, she found an old woman crying miserably, with a bleeding eye. Replying to her queries, the old woman said: "It was you who stabbed me blind yesterday." The woman, suddenly realizing what had happened, kowtowed to the Fire God and asked for her forgiveness. The Fire God finally pardoned her. From then on, she never failed in lighting a fire. Up to the present, the Ewenki throw a piece of food or a small cup of wine into the fire as an offering before meals. However, sprinkling water on a fire or poking a fire with a sword during meat roasting is taboo.

5 RELIGION

The traditional beliefs of the Ewenki are rooted in shamanism and totemism, stressing worship of ancestors, animals, and nature. Special rituals are performed for Jiya (the livestock god) and fire. Fire should never be allowed to die out, even when Ewenki families migrate. Among the hunters, a number of rites and taboos demonstrate their reverence for the bear. When a bear is killed in hunting, they wrap its head, bones, and internal organs in birch bark or straw, then hang them in a tree. They kowtow, pretend to cry, and offer tobacco. In some areas, all the clans of the Ewenki have a bird totem, such as the eagle, swan, or duck. Whenever a bird flies overhead, they sprinkle a little milk in the air. Killing or doing harm to a bird is considered taboo, especially if the bird is one's own totem. Almost every clan has a shaman. He is not a professional, often playing the role of headman of a clan or a tribe and enjoying high status. The shaman explains the cause of disease, divines fortune and misfortune, exorcizes ghosts, and dances in a trance. He expects no reward.

In some pastoral areas, the Ewenki believe in Lamaism, the Tibetan form of Buddhism adopted by the majority of Mongols. In some areas, one finds communities belonging to the Eastern Orthodox Church, a remnant of czarist Russia's influence from the 17th to the 19th century.

6 MAJOR HOLIDAYS

In agricultural areas, the festivals of the Ewenki are not different from those of the Chinese. In pastoral areas, their festivals include Aobao Gathering and the Mikuole Festival. Aobao is a Mongolian term meaning "a pile"; it consists of a pyramidal pile of stones and adobes, flanked by a certain number of poles from which float multicolored silk streamers. Some streamers are covered with sacred Buddhist inscriptions. The Aobao is regarded as the dwelling of God in shamanism. In some ar-

eas, the Aoboa is a large tree, called the Aobao tree. The Aobao Gathering, one of the most important festivals of the Ewenki, is held around June or July on the lunar calendar (Western calendar, between June 22 and August 21). Oxen and sheep are slaughtered as sacrificial offerings. The festival includes popular sporting events, such as horse racing and wrestling. The Mikuole Festival is essentially a fair of the stock raisers. It is held in the last ten days of lunar May (Western calendar, between June 11 and July 21). Horses are branded and their overlong manes are shaved; the sheep's ears are incised with the owner's mark. This is a special occasion for villagers to call on each other and to gather in dinner parties. The Ewenki also celebrate the Spring Festival (lunar New Year; Western calendar between January 21 and February 20), which is a common holiday for all the nationalities of China.

7 RITES OF PASSAGE

Regardless of gender, the young pastoral Ewenki start to look after calves at six or seven. Boys learn to ride a horse at seven and lasso and break in a horse shortly afterwards. Girls learn to milk cows at 10. The children pay due respect to their elders. Meeting them, the youngsters always salute by bending at the knee and cupping the hands in front of the chest. The seats and beds in the room are assigned on the basis of generation. Traditionally, the Ewenki practiced tree burial (or wind burial). The corpse was placed in a coffin or wrapped with bark or willow twigs and then hung high in a tree. The blowing of the wind, drenching of the rain, scorching of the sun, and beaming of the moon were regarded as effective in transforming the dead into a star. Ground burial is now more and more prevalent under the influence of the neighboring nationalities.

8 INTERPERSONAL RELATIONS

"People coming from afar," the Ewenki say, "cannot carry their own house on their back; nor can we when we go out." The visit of a guest is always a happy event. A fur cushion will be offered by the host. The guest sits on the cushion wherever it is; any shift of its place is considered impolite behavior. The hostess will carry a birch wood tray and serve deer milk, deer meat, toasted cake, and homemade wild fruit wine. The host will pour a few drops of wine on the fire first, then takes a sip for himself and finally hands the cup over to the guest.

The huntsmen store their food, clothes, and tools in their storehouse in the forest, which is never locked. Any huntsman is allowed to take food from the storehouse as needed without prior agreement with the owner. He should, however, return the amount of food taken when he meets the owner.

Arranged marriages are now abandoned. The youngsters will not lose any opportunity to choose a partner. Unfortunately, opportunities are rather limited in the pastoral areas on account of the great distance between villages and of the clan structure of individual villages.

9 LIVING CONDITIONS

The traditional Ewenki house resembles an umbrella, more than 10 ft in height and 13 ft in diameter, framed by 25–30 poles covered with birch bark and roe or deer skin. One side, provided with a door, is used as the living room. The other three sides are all platforms for sleeping. A fiery pit is in the center, with a pan hanging over it. There is an opening at the top for ventilation. The tablet of the ancestors is attached to the top of the central wooden column.

In hunting areas, the house is a wooden cube. The walls are built by piling up logs. The roof is made of birch bark. In some areas, they live in Mongolian-style *yurt*.

Bicycles, horses, and cars are the main modes of transport of the Ewenki. The epidemic and endemic diseases of bygone days have now been controlled. Hospitals have been set up in various localities of the Ewenki Autonomous Qi County.

10 FAMILY LIFE

The Ewenki live in small patrilineal families. Since they need mutual help in hunting and in searching pastures, they form nomadic villages. Villages, whether nomadic or sedentary (agricultural), have a clan structure in which each family has blood ties with the other families.

Ewenki families are monogamous. Marriage practices retain remnants of clan society, such as the marriage of cousins and inter-clan marriage. In bygone days, arranged marriage was prevalent. The parents of two families "engaged" their children when they were just a few years old or even before they were born. This led to precocious marriage. As an alternative, the custom of "elopement marriage" emerged. The date of elopement is agreed upon by the young man and woman who are passionately in love. The parents of the male side prepare a new house beforehand and an old woman is waiting there for the eloping girl. After dark, the girl escapes from her family. Riding on horseback, she comes directly to the new house. The old woman unties the girl's eight braids and combs her hair into two large ones. This is a symbol that the marriage is now "legal." Before dawn, the couple goes to the man's paternal house and kowtows to the fire and to the tablet of his ancestors. Then, two persons are sent to the bride's family, first to offer *hada* (a ceremonial silk scarf) to her ancestors and then to kowtow. They explain their purpose in coming, ask forgiveness and promise obedience. After long hours of persuasion, the bride's parents finally agree. Consequently, all members of the clan congratulate the couple, who kowtow to the clan's ancestors, to the village Fire God, and to the bridegroom's parents. A sumptuous banquet follows, guests and relatives dancing and singing with utter delight.

There has been no inhibition of intermarriage between the Ewenki and other nationalities. The intermarriage with the Daur has a long history and is very popular. Some families and clans intermarried for generations. Thus, the Ewenki and the Daur are called two "familial nationalities."

11 CLOTHING

In former times, both sexes donned a long fur robe covering the ankles and a long coat down to the knees. The cuffs and the bottom of the women's robes were embroidered with multicolored figures and designs. They all wore fur hats. Today, they mostly wear cloth robes and cotton padded garments in winter. Urban Ewenki dress is similar to that of the Chinese.

12 FOOD

The Ewenki's staple food is animal meat, including deer meat, mutton, beef, and pork of wild hog, supplemented by grains, such as Chinese sorghum, corn, millet, oats, and buckwheat. On account of the Nordic climate, vegetables are scarce. They like roasted meat. "Cooked meat held in hand" is very popular

during festivals. The meat, attached to the bone, is chopped in big pieces and is half-cooked with a little salt. They hold the big piece with their hand while eating. They like gruel with milk, which is also a sacrificial offering to the gods. The diet of Ewenki farmers is not much different from that of the local Chinese or Manchus.

13 EDUCATION

Most of the Ewenki were illiterate in the past. Today, primary school education in the Ewenki Autonomous Qi County has become popular. Eighteen middle schools (junior and senior) have been set up. Quite a number of youngsters enroll in the university. Compared to other nationalities, however, their education is at a low level.

14 CULTURAL HERITAGE

Ewenki folk songs, slow and unconstrained, evoke the vast expanses of the grassland. Dancing styles vary according to region and to occasions. A dance called Ahanba is performed by women at wedding ceremonies. There are no accompanying instruments; the tempo is set by the singers' voices. Each group consists of two to four dancers. In the beginning, they cry softly, "A-Han-Ba, A-Han-Ba," while swinging their arms. Then they turn face to face and bend their knees. The tempo is gradually hastened and the rhythm is intensified by the movement of their feet. Ultimately, the dance bustles in full swing. Another dance is performed by two young men. One of them is a hunter, the other dresses up as a wild hog. With their hands behind their back, they hit each other with their shoulders while roaring. A group led by a singer encircles the two actors, moves around a bonfire, and dances while singing.

Ewenki literature has been handed down orally; it includes myths, tales, folk songs, and riddles.

15 WORK

The frequent migrations of the Ewenki in the course of history have resulted in scattered communities. Because of the significant difference of natural environments in which they dwelled, their mode of production and lifestyle varied a great deal. Those living in Ewenki Autonomous Qi County and in Chen Barag Qi practice livestock husbandry; those dwelling in Butha Qi, Arun Qi, and Morin Dawa Qi have a mixed economy, half farming and half hunting; those inhabiting Nehe in Heilongjiang Province are farmers; those inhabiting Ergun Zuo Qi are huntsmen, riding deer while hunting, and are thus called "Deer back riding Ewenki."

16 SPORTS

The Ewenki start to ride, lasso, and break in horses early in their childhood. Later, they frequently gather to learn arrow shooting, high jumping, pole vaulting, long jumping, and skiing. Brave hunters and capable herdsmen have mastered these skills by the time they are adults. Horse lassoing is a popular competition mostly held on festivals.

As early as 1,300 years ago, the ancestors of the Ewenki, called Shiwei, fashioned a primitive form of skis. The skis used today by the Ewenki for hunting are but an improved version of the Shiwei "snow-sliding boards."

A cuoluzi (a tepee like structure) used by the Ewenki nomadic tribe in Da Hinggan Ling Mountains, China.
(© Earl and Nazima Kowall/Corbis)

[17] ENTERTAINMENT AND RECREATION

Most of the Ewenki areas are provided with a movie theater and a television station. Film studios and television broadcasting stations have been set up in Inner Mongolia and Heilongjiang Province. Therefore, most of the Ewenki can enjoy watching television as daily entertainment. In hunting areas, old hunters are master storytellers, spinning tales about ancient and modern heroes in their fight against the harsh environment and wild animals; this is still the preferred form of entertainment.

[18] FOLK ART, CRAFTS, AND HOBBIES

The Ewenki excel in designing and producing implements for daily necessities as well as toys from birch bark. Painting on the birch bark is a hallmark of the Ewenki. Canoes made of birch bark, besides their unique design, provide swift and easy transport on the many lakes and rivers of the Ewenki land.

[19] SOCIAL PROBLEMS

Poverty and isolation are serious problems confronting the Ewenki. Community fragmentation, harsh environment, illiteracy, and the absence of a market economy, make it difficult to implement a short-term, global solution for the whole population. It seems the situation can only be improved gradually in the long run.

[20] GENDER ISSUES

The Chinese constitution states that women have equal rights with men in all areas of life, and most legislation is gender neutral. However, there are continued reports of discrimination, sexual harassment, wage discrepancies, and other gender related problems. The gap in educational level between women and men is narrowing with women making up 47.1% of college students in 2005, but only 32.6% of doctoral students.

China has strict family planning laws. It is illegal for women to marry before 20 years of age (22 for men), and it is illegal for single women to give birth. The Family Planning Bureau can require women to take periodic pregnancy tests and enforce laws that often leave women with no real options other than abortion or sterilization. While minority populations were previously exempt from family planning regulations, policy has changed in recent years to limit minority population growth. Today, urban couples may have two children while rural couples may have three or four.

Prostitution and the sex trade is a significant problem in China involving between 1.7 and 5 million women. It involved organized crime, businessmen, the police, and government workers, so prosecution against prostitution has limited success. In 2002, the nation removed homosexuality from its official list of mental illnesses, and though it is still a taboo topic, homosexuality is increasingly accepted, especially in large, international cities.

21 BIBLIOGRAPHY

Chiao, Chien, Nicholas Tapp, and Kam-yin Ho, ed. "Special Issue on Ethnic Groups in China." *New Asia Bulletin* no 8 (1989).

Dreyer, June Teufel. *China's Forty Millions.* Cambridge: Harvard University Press, 1976.

Eberhard, Wolfram. *China's Minorities: Yesterday and Today.* Belmont: Wadsworth Publishing Company, 1982.

Gustafsson, Bjorn A., Shi, Li, and Sicular, Terry , eds. *Inequality and Public Policy in China.* New York: Cambridge University Press, 2008.

Heberer, Thomas. *China and Its National Minorities: Autonomy or Assimilation?* Armonk, NY: M. E. Sharpe, 1989.

Ma Yin, ed. *China's Minority Nationalities.* Beijing: Foreign Languages Press, 1989.

Ramsey, S. Robert. *The Languages of China.* Princeton: Princeton University Press, 1987.

Shin, Leo Kwok-yueh. The Making of the Chinese State: Ethnicity and Expansion on the Ming Borderlands. New York: Cambridge University Press, 2006.

—by C. Le Blanc

FIJIANS

PRONUNCIATION: FEE-gee-uhns
ALTERNATE NAMES: Taukei (indigenous Fijians)
LOCATION: Fiji
POPULATION: Approximately 828,000 (57% or 471,960 ethnic Fijians)
LANGUAGE: English; Fijian; Hindi are official languages of the Republic of Fiji
RELIGION: Christianity (Methodist)

1 INTRODUCTION

The term "Fijians" refers to any of the inhabitants of the chain of islands in the Pacific Ocean called the Republic of Fiji. The islands claimed independence from Great Britain in 1970 but remained part of the Commonwealth until October 1987, when they became the Republic of Fiji. Although there are a great number of ethnic groups indigenous to the Fiji Islands, they all share a number of cultural traits. Here the term "Fijian" is used to refer to the descendants of the indigenous population of this chain of islands. The Fijian word *Taukei* is now being used to refer to this group as opposed to other ethnic groups that inhabit the islands. In Fijian the word translates as "owner" or "original inhabitant." This term and the concept behind it have become more important recently as indigenous Fijians have sought to reestablish their claims to the land, resources, and political authority in Fiji.

2 LOCATION AND HOMELAND

The Fijian archipelago lies in the western Pacific Ocean, southwest of Hawaii. There are more than 300 islands within the Fijian group, the two largest being Viti Levu and Vanua Levu. These two islands account for around 86% of the total 18,272 sq km (7,055 sq mi) of land that makes up the island group. Of the approximately 300 islands, only about 100 are either inhabited or capable of human habitation. Most of the larger islands are referred to as "high islands." High islands are volcanic in nature and have high, rugged mountain peaks with deep, winding valleys and quick flowing streams and rivers. The deltas that have been created by the networks of waterways are very fertile and have been the primary areas of human settlement and farming from the earliest times. The archaeological record of Fiji indicates that the first human habitation of the archipelago was approximately 3,500 years ago. The first inhabitants were likely migrants from nearby Vanuatu and New Caledonia. Fiji was a crossroads of the Pacific in prehistoric times. The distinctive cultures and physical features of the Fijian groups are evidence of that fact.

3 LANGUAGE

The Fijian language belongs to the Oceanic branch of the Austronesian language family. Linguists usually refer to the Fijian language as a composite of approximately 300 dialects defined by village membership—that is to say, people from different villages speak different dialects of Fijian. Standard Fijian is based on the dialect spoken by the Bau. This dialect had also formed the basis for an earlier form of Fijian that was used to communicate more easily across dialect boundaries in the time before the arrival of Europeans. Missionaries to the islands chose this

Fijians in traditional dress prepare a drink of Kava during a welcoming ceremony for Chinese Premier Wen Jiabao in Nadi, Fiji. (AP Images/Rob Griffith)

dialect as their standard for translation of the Bible. Wesleyan Missionaries developed a written form of Fijian in 1850, which has contributed to the high degree of literacy in the islands. English is the official language of the country.

4 FOLKLORE

Fiji has a large body of folklore, mythology, and oral history. Many stories revolve around the feats of cultural heroes and gods. One myth details the protection of the island of Kadavu by the Shark God and explains why the inhabitants of the island today have no fear of the sharks which populate their island's reefs. There is also a series of myths which account for the Fiji practice of "fire walking," which has now become an important tourist event. Traditional fire walking was a ceremonial occasion accompanied by symbolic acts and the reenactment of the myth concerning fire walking. Before the fire walking ceremony, men would separate from any contact with women for a period of three days. Men would also refrain from eating coconut during this time. A large pit would be dug and filled with large river stones. A fire would be built on top of the stones about six hours before the event. The coals would be raked over the stones, eventually making the stones become white hot. Then the men would walk the circumference of the pit without any protection for their feet and without any apparent ill effects.

5 RELIGION

The overwhelming majority of indigenous Fijians, nearly 90%, are Methodist. Both Methodist and Catholic missionaries established churches, schools, and missions in Fiji in the 1800s. The Fijians were quick converts to the Wesleyan Methodist Church, probably due, in part, to the Methodists' use of Fijian in services and their early translation of the Bible into Standard Fijian. The Catholic Church still used Latin in mass at that time, and Fijians were not interested in listening to a language that they could not understand.

6 MAJOR HOLIDAYS

Major holidays for Fijians include the annual Hibiscus Festival, a celebration of things Fijian; Queen of England's Birthday in June; Fiji Day, October 13; Constitution Day, June 28; and Christmas Day and Boxing Day, December 26.

7 RITES OF PASSAGE

Children are socialized to recognize the social hierarchy of the extended family and the society as a whole. From the time they can understand, children take orders from the senior males in the family, especially their fathers. Respect and strict obedience are expected of their children by fathers. Discipline and punishment is the domain of the father. Mothers are more indulgent with their children.

In traditional Fiji society, women are expected to be virgins at the time of marriage. Premarital sexual relationships were not advocated within the society.

Disease and death were attributable to malevolent spirits in traditional Fijian culture. The mortuary ceremony was once very elaborate, especially for men of status. Groups with relationships to the deceased would visit the village and pay homage to the corpse. A set of taboos were enforced after the death and they remained in effect for up to 100 nights. In the past, wives were strangled to accompany their dead husbands into the spirit world. It was believed that the god Ruvuyalo would kill the spirit of any man who did not have his spouse accompanying him.

8 INTERPERSONAL RELATIONS

The standard Fijian greeting is *ni sa bula,* or the informal *bula.* Visiting a person's house always entails removing the shoes before entering.

9 LIVING CONDITIONS

The majority of houses on Viti Levu are made of wood and concrete breeze blocks. Almost all homes have electricity and a piped water supply. On the smaller islands, houses are often constructed of local materials and have either thatched or corrugated iron roofs. Western-style houses are a sign of prosperity. Electricity is available in many rural areas. In very remote regions, people still use kerosene or benzene lanterns.

Villages in rural areas are centered on a village green, called *rara* in Fijian. At either end of the rara, each village has a church and a village hall. People who have left traditional villages to live in cities and towns often return for the Christmas season. In the 18th century, Fijians developed a new type of ocean-going double-hulled canoe. This type of canoe had a large mast set in the middle of the larger hulled vessel, and there was no significant difference between the head and stern. These ships were more maneuverable and faster than the other style of double-hulled canoes that were being used in other Oceanic societies. It permitted the Fijians of the time to move more quickly between islands and to escape quickly after raids. These canoes were elaborately carved and decorated.

10 FAMILY LIFE

In traditional Fijian society, the preferred marriage was between cross-cousins. Men were permitted to have more than one wife at a time, and the more wives a man had, the higher his social status. Chiefs especially had many wives and created a number of political alliances in the process. After a couple was married, they would typically reside in the house of the groom's father. Each household was composed of an extended family. Each extended family was under the leadership of one senior male. Divorce was easily accomplished by either the husband or the wife.

Family structure is very hierarchical. This reflects the larger pattern of hierarchy and position in Fijian society. The senior male of the family is equivalent to the chief of the family line. The higher the social position in the family, the more respect that has to be given to the person. Any food that is not eaten by the senior male cannot be eaten by anyone else. A woman's social position within an extended family is traditionally based on that of her husband, unless her family is of higher status than his.

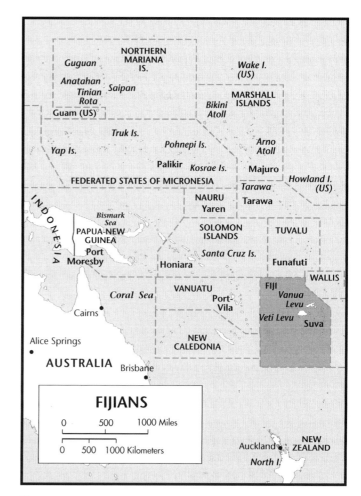

FIJIANS

0   500   1000 Miles

0   500   1000 Kilometers

11 CLOTHING

Traditional Fijian clothing for men is a native kilt called a *sulu.* Men also wear Western-style clothing, as do many women. The sulu is always worn during ceremonial occasions and has seen a renaissance due to social and political developments since the coup of 1987.

12 FOOD

The main staples of the traditional Fijian diet are taro root and cassava. Although sago palms are found on some of the Fijian Islands, this plant was never a staple foodstuff as it was in other nearby islands of the Pacific. Fish and shellfish are still important foods in the current diet, as they were in the past. Western foodstuffs and cooking techniques have become prominent in Fijian society.

13 EDUCATION

The literacy rate for the Republic of Fiji is estimated at 93%. Western education has been available in Fiji since European missionaries became established in the islands. Mission schools were built for the indigenous Fijians by Methodist and Catholic missionaries. Nowadays, primary education is free and compulsory. Villages in rural areas often share a common school. Adolescents between the ages of 12 and 16 attend junior secondary school, which is not free. High school education can only be obtained in towns and cities. The University of the South Pacific is located in the capital city of Suva.

A Fijian throws a casting net to catch live bait in Suva, Fiji. Many Fijians still fish daily to provide food for themselves and to sell in the market place. (AP Images/Rob Griffith)

14 CULTURAL HERITAGE

Dancing is an important part of traditional Fijian culture. Men and women danced separately. Women's dances often utilized intricate and delicate hand gestures. Many of the men's dances related to military exploits and involved aggressive posing with weapons. Both men and women had "sitting" dances. Singing was also important in traditional society. In the present day, Western-style instruments and singing styles have become popular.

15 WORK

Traditional Fijians engaged in subsistence horticulture, and some continue to do so into the present time. They raised taro root and cassava as well as fished and collected marine resources. Agriculture was the traditional domain of men. Fishing and the collecting of marine resources were tasks allocated to women. Now, although around 60% of Fijians are still rural, the loss of labor due to urban migration is a problem for village organization. Many younger Fijians seek wage labor opportunities in the towns and cities. Tobacco and sugar are important cash crops in the Fijian economy.

16 SPORTS

Rugby is an important spectator and participant sport for Fijians. Rugby Union is considered the national sport of Fiji. The Fijian team qualified for the Rugby World Cup in 2003. Soccer is another important sport for Fijians. Fiji sent participants to the 1996 Summer Olympic Games in Atlanta and had very good performances from the athletes who competed in judo and swimming. Cricket is also popular in Fiji, but more so with the Indo-Fijian population there.

17 ENTERTAINMENT AND RECREATION

One form of social intercourse among adult Fijian men is the consumption of *yaqona,* known as "kava." Kava is an intoxicating beverage made through the pounding, grating, or chewing of the root of the shrub Piper methysticum. Kava drinking has a definite set of social rules. The sharing of kava accompanied the performance of pre-Christian religious events, political discussions, the curing of illness, and restricted social interaction of adult, "high status" men in Fijian villages. Kava drinking has become an important attraction for tourists who visit Fiji, although the event does not carry any of the ceremonial importance that it did in traditional contexts.

Electricity has made television, radio, video, and movies all popular forms of entertainment in Fijian cities, towns, and villages.

18 FOLK ART, CRAFTS, AND HOBBIES

Traditional crafts made by Fijian women include pottery, woven mats, and bark cloth. Men did a great deal of carving and sculpting in wood; creating beautiful spears, clubs, ceremonial bowls for kava drinking; and elaborately decorated double-hulled seagoing canoes. In precontact times, the Fijians were well-known for their armory and especially their war clubs. The Fijians had several types of war clubs, each designed to perform a special function in battle. "Throwers" were constructed to be thrown at an enemy and strike with the wide, knobbed butt. "Penetrators" had a spike with a weighted head. They were made of the heaviest wood available and were used only by the most skilled warriors. The club would make a single, fatal hole in the skull of the victim. According to tradition, a person killed in this manner was the most desired for cannibalism and the killer received much prestige.

19 SOCIAL PROBLEMS

With the coup of 1987 and the constitution of 1990, Fijians have made it clear that they want to reclaim the resources and rights to self-determination that have gradually slipped away from them. This has heightened tensions between the Fijians and the other ethnic groups of the island, especially the Indo-Fijians.

20 GENDER ISSUES

Recent statistics for the Republic of Fiji indicate that females and males are now equally educated. There are no gender-based differences in literacy, and in fact, females at all levels have a somewhat higher literacy percentage. School enrollments for males and females are equal. In fact 1995 enrolment figures show girls comprising 48.6% of all primary level enrolments and a little over 50% of total enrollments at secondary level. Female attendance at tertiary level institutions has also significantly increased. However, women still tend to dominate in the courses traditionally considered for females (nurses, secretaries, teachers etc.) while males still dominate course such as engineering and marine studies. Enrolments at the Fiji Institute of Technology in 1996 for example, for these male dominated fields showed less than 3% were females. On the other hand the enrolments for secretarial studies and for office administration were over 98% females. These statistics reflect the prevailing attitudes on gender roles which will take considerable time to change.

The Fiji Women's Crisis Center (FWCC) is a feminist non-government organization that was established in 1984 to deal with the social problem of violence against women and children. FWCC is the first organization of its kind in the Pacific region.

21 BIBLIOGRAPHY

Crocombe, Ron. *The South Pacific: An Introduction.* New Zealand: Longman Paul Limited, 1987.

Fiji Times Online. http://www.fijitimes.com/ (10 June 2008).

Mayer, Adrian. *Indians in Fiji.* London: Oxford University Press, 1963

Siegel, Jeff. *Language Contact in a Plantation Environment: A Sociolinguistic History of Fiji.* New York: Cambridge University Press, 1987.

—by J. Williams

FILIPINOS

PRONUNCIATION: fih-lih-PEE-nohz
LOCATION: Philippines
POPULATION: 93 million
LANGUAGE: Tagalog (national language); Cebuano; Ilocano; Hiligaynon (Ilongo); Bicolano; Waray-Waray; Pampango, and Pangasinan
RELIGION: Roman Catholicism (85%); Philippine Independent Church; Iglesia ni Kristo (Church of Christ); Protestantism; Islam; animism
RELATED ARTICLES: Vol. 2: Filipino Americans. Vol. 3: Bajau; Hiligaynon; Ifugao; Ilocano; Ilongot; Kalinga; Vol. 4: Mangyan; Maranao; Negrito; Tagbanua; Tausug; T'boli.

1 INTRODUCTION

Distributed among thousands of islands, themselves divided by barriers of mountain and jungle, the territory of the Philippines by its very nature has encouraged the proliferation of distinct local cultures. However, three centuries of Spanish colonialism provided most Filipinos with a single framework within which to develop a common, eventually national, culture. Despite speaking several mutually unintelligible mother tongues, the 90% of the population classified as "lowland Christian" share essentially the same civilization. The remaining 10% consist of numerous non-Christian peoples, who differ greatly from the Christian majority as well as among themselves.

As early as 40,000 years ago, the first modern humans, Australo-Melanesian hunter-gatherers ancestral to the modern Negritos, roamed the Philippines, which was at that time virtually linked to Asia by land bridges exposed during the Ice Age. The ancestors of most Filipinos, however, were groups of Austronesian-speaking, Southern Mongoloid agriculturalists who arrived from Taiwan beginning between 3000 and 2000 BC (some of their descendants would migrate further to colonize Indonesia, Madagascar, and the Pacific Islands).

With the opening of a direct passage between China and the Spice Islands through the Philippines in the early 2nd millennium AD, small trading-and-raiding chiefdoms begin to appear in Chinese records. By the 15th century, items of the wider Asiatic civilization, such as Chinese porcelain, the Malay lingua franca, and the Islamic religion, had reached the archipelago. The first natives of the Philippines to be found in European documents are the Luzones (Tagalogs affiliated with the north Bornean kingdom of Brunei) whom Tomé Pires, a Portuguese, described in 1512 as settling in the Malay city-state of Malacca at the crossroads of international trade.

Looking on the archipelago as a base from which to capture the Spice Islands and to evangelize China, Spain sent several expeditions to follow up on Ferdinand Magellan's 1521 "discovery" of the islands (which eventually received the name "Filipinas" after the Habsburg Philip II). Only in 1571 did Miguel López de Legaspi succeed in establishing a viable colony at Manila. Aside from the lucrative galleon trade between China and Spanish Mexico that ran through Manila, there was little to attract Spanish settlers with the exception of Catholic missionary orders, whose friars became the only representatives of the colonial power that most natives ever regularly encountered. The Spanish not only imposed the Catholic religion, but

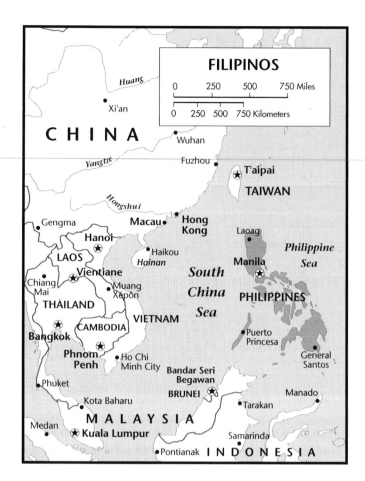

FILIPINOS

0   250   500   750 Miles

0   250   500   750 Kilometers

also introduced forms of political and economic organization, as well as arts and technologies, which transformed native life both for good and for ill. Colonial annals record frequent local revolts against Spanish abuses, but on numerous occasions Catholic Filipinos stood with the Spanish against invaders and their own rebellious brethren.

The opening of the colony to non-Spanish commerce and capital in the 19th century promoted the growth of an economy heavily dependent on plantation-grown cash crops, and the rise of landed elite of largely mixed European-Chinese-native blood. While economic changes exposed most natives to novel forms of exploitation, an unprecedented affluence permitted some Filipino families to send their sons to Europe for an education. The native intelligentsia that was thus created, the *ilustrados* (literally, the "enlightened ones"), at first hoped only to gain for Filipinos equal rights as Spanish citizens but, facing no Spanish response other than repression, began to long for independence.

In 1896, secular ilustrado ideals and folk Catholic notions of justice impelled the Katipunan, a Manilan secret society, to launch a revolution to end Spanish rule. The leadership of the struggle soon shifted to the provincial Filipino elite who were able to raise impromptu militias. Although on 12 June 1898 Filipinos proclaimed their independence, the United States, which had initially collaborated with the Filipinos in defeating the Spanish, moved to take possession of the islands for their strategic value. The ensuing war, which eventually established American dominance, dragged on for years, and caused directly or indirectly the death of a million Filipinos.

American rule introduced mass education in the English language and improvements in public health and communications. Although the United States early on decided to prepare the Filipinos for eventual self-rule, it sought to retain ultimate control by favoring the landed elite whose interests would be bound to its own. Because of this, American-introduced democratic institutions became little more than arenas for competition among powerful families, while the welfare of the laboring masses continued to decline.

Japanese invasion and occupation and American liberation during World War II devastated the country to which the United States was to grant independence in 1946. Desperate for U.S. reconstruction funds, Filipino leaders submitted to treaties that gave Americans privileged access to the Filipino economy, as well as to lands for military bases. Cold War-era American pressure on the Filipino government to exclude leftist parties from legitimate political participation left disaffected peasants no other recourse but armed rebellion. Elite resistance to land reform perpetuated conditions hospitable to Communist insurgency. It was ostensibly to overcome Communist and Muslim rebellions, the breakdown of law and order, and an economic crisis that President Ferdinand Marcos declared martial law in 1972. Marcos, however, accomplished little more than exchanging the old oligarchs for his own cronies, whose corruption and incompetence plunged the economy into a tailspin by the 1980s.

Finally, during snap elections in 1986, masses of unarmed ordinary people mobilized first to thwart government attempts at electoral fraud and then to block government troops from capturing Corazon Aquino, the genuine president-elect, and the generals who had defected to her. In the end, this peaceful revolution, the first to be internationally televised, left Marcos no other option than to flee in an American helicopter to Hawaii. Aquino restored democracy but, belonging to one of the country's biggest land-owning families, restored the pre-1972 oligarchy to power. A series of army coups and natural disasters destabilized her regime and retarded economic recovery. However, with the election of Fidel Ramos in 1992, the country at last began to enjoy stability and embark on a consistent rate of economic growth closer to those set by the Philippine's Asian neighbors.

The Asian/global emerging markets financial crisis of 1997–1998 affected the Philippines less traumatically than neighboring countries like Thailand and Indonesia; growth slowed to a minimal contraction but resumed by 1999 despite the instability under the presidency of former actor Joseph Estrada, who was later impeached on corruption charges in 2001. His successor, Gloria Macapagal Arroyo, has pursued policies that have made the Philippines one of the fastest growing countries in Southeast Asia, as reflected in the blossoming of Manila's skyline and Cebu's malls, though this has yet to translate into substantial alleviation of poverty, as seen in the continuing growth of slums. Many problems persist from earlier decades, including not only communist and Muslim separatist insurgencies but also massive corruption.

² LOCATION AND HOMELAND

The 7,000 islands (1,000 inhabited) of the Philippines comprise a land area equal to that of Italy and a little larger than that of Arizona. If superimposed on the eastern United States, they would stretch east to west from New York City to Chicago and north to south from Massachusetts to Florida. There are 11 major islands: Luzon (more than one-third of the total land area); Mindoro; Palawan; Masbate; Panay; Negros; Cebu; Bohol; Leyte; Samar; and Mindanao (another one-third of the land area).

Mountains separated by narrow valleys dominate the topography on all islands, although Luzon, Panay, and Mindanao have wider interior plains. The source of the fertility of much of the country's soils, the archipelago's volcanoes form a link in the circum-Pacific "Ring of Fire." Throughout the country, deforestation has reduced the once-thick rainforest cover, replacing it with cogon grass; in turn, this has encouraged erosion that ultimately silts up coastal waters and chokes coral reefs, already damaged by dynamite fishing and other harmful practices.

The tropical climate is dominated by the monsoon cycle: (1) from June to October the southwest monsoon carries torrential rains to most of the country; (2) from November through February the northeast monsoon brings warm, dry weather; and (3) from March to May easterly North Pacific trade winds afflict the islands with a period of extreme heat and drought. From 20 to 30 typhoons wreak havoc on sections of the country every year.

Though estimates vary rather widely, in 2008, over 90 million people inhabited the Philippines, making it the 12th most populous country on earth (after Mexico and before Vietnam); this represents a more than thirteen-fold increase since the beginning of the 20th century. Population density stands at a high of 320 persons per sq km. More than one in three of Filipinos (36.2% to be exact) are under the age of 14, constituting a heavy burden on the employed portion of the population and demanding in future years a continual expansion of education and labor opportunities; only 3.8% are 65 years or older (2005). The annual growth rate declined to 1.8% in 2005 from 2.3–2.4% in 1990, 2.6–2.75 in 1980, and 3.08 in 1970; in the period 2000–2005, 3.5 children were born for every woman of childbearing age, down from 6.0 in 1970–1975. However, because of the opposition of the Roman Catholic Church to birth control and to inconsistent government support for family planning, reductions in the population growth rate have not been as dramatic as in the neighboring countries of Thailand and Indonesia.

Between the 1950s and early 1980s, the ratio of land per agricultural worker fell by half, from 1.0 hectare (2.47 acres) per worker to 0.5 hectares (1.24 acres), meaning that even vigorously pursued land reform could not provide each farmer with sufficient land. Land scarcity has forced people to move from more- to less-densely populated regions. More significantly, Filipino cities are growing rapidly, receiving a continual influx of migrants from the countryside: in 2005, 62.7% of the population was urban, compared to 48.6% in 1990 and 31.8% in 1990. Migration within the country has in a sense spilled over the borders, creating one of the great diasporas in modern history. In 2004, 8.1 million Filipinos were estimated to be working temporarily or residing permanently abroad, in countries as diverse as the Hong Kong, Saudi Arabia, Italy, and the United States.

³ LANGUAGE

Some 70 languages are spoken as mother tongues in the Philippines, virtually all belonging to three branches (Northern, Central, and Southern Philippine) of the Austronesian family, which includes the languages of Indonesia, Madagascar, Oceania, and aboriginal Taiwan. The eight languages with the greatest number of speakers are:

Tagalog, the basis of Pilipino/Filipino, the national language, spoken natively by 28% of the total Filipino population (2000 census), concentrated in Manila and the immediately contiguous provinces and extending to coastal settlements on Mindoro and Palawan;

Cebuano, whose native speakers include 21% of the population inhabiting the islands of Cebu, Bohol, southern Leyte, eastern Negros, and the northern and eastern coasts of Mindanao (speakers of the language not from Cebu or eastern Negros prefer to refer to their dialects as "Bisaya" or "Binisaya");

Ilocano, whose speakers (approximately 9% of the population) originated along a narrow coastal strip of northwestern Luzon, but who can now be found throughout northern Luzon;

Hiligaynon (or Ilongo), natively spoken (7.6% of the population) on Panay, western Negros, and southern Mindoro;

Bicolano, whose speakers (almost 6% of the population) inhabit the long southeastern "tail" of Luzon;

Waray-Warray, spoken (nearly 3.4%) on the island of Samar and on northern Leyte; and

Pampango and **Pangasinan,** whose speakers live respectively at the southern and northern ends the Luzon's Central Plain.

Along with a number of smaller language groups, these eight ethnolinguistic groups constitute the "lowland Christian" majority of the country. Outside this lowland Christian majority there is a great diversity of **non-Christian ethnolinguistic groups,** constituting fewer than 10% of the population and falling into four broad categories:

Muslim peoples of Mindanao, the Sulu Archipelago, and Palawan—Maranao, Maguindanao, Tausug (each over 500,000 people), Samal (272,000), Yakan, Bajau, and others.

Animist highlanders of Mindanao, Palawan, and Mindoro—Mangyan (on Mindoro), Tagbanua and Palawan (on Palawan), Subanon, Bukidnon, Bagobo, Manobo, T'boli, and others (on Mindanao).

Animist highlanders of northern Luzon—Ifugao, Bontoc, Ibaloi, Kalinga, Isneg, Ilongot, and others.

Negritos—dark-complexioned, hunter-gatherers of extremely short stature, known to have lived in uplands throughout the archipelago but now confined to the northern Luzon highlands.

Among groups that have settled in the Philippines in historical times, the numerically most significant are the Chinese (mostly speakers of Hokkien), now numbering around 2.2 million people, or over 2% of the population.

Filipino children peek through curtain slots of a passenger jeepney after a rainstorm in Manila, Philippines. The Philippines is slashed by typhoons and tropical storms each year with the heaviest rains falling from July to November. (AP Images/Aaron Favila)

As the Spanish friars who administered most of the country chose to learn the local languages, only a small fraction of the population speak Spanish (Castilian), although numerous Castilian words became part of the native languages. Filipinos refer to Spaniards as "*Kastila.*" In some parts of the Philippines, a creolized form of Spanish, called Chabacano, is spoken as a mother tongue, with the most important concentration of speakers, 600,000, in Zamboanga on the former Spanish frontier on Mindanao.

After conquering the country, the Americans replaced Spanish with English as the language of government and education. In 1937, the Commonwealth government decided to promote the use of Tagalog, the most prestigious of the indigenous languages, as the national language, now called "Filipino/Pilipino," though not without continuing resistance from non-Tagalogs, particularly Cebuanos. Taught in schools and heard in pop music, television programs, and movies, Tagalog-Pilipino has rapidly gained currency throughout the country, although people continue to use their local languages for most everyday purposes. Although competence in English seems to be declining (46.98% of the population, down from 63.71% in 2000), a mastery of English remains the key to professional, academic, government, and business careers. In the media, English-language publications and programming continue to command an audience; the Philippines, by one estimate is the country with the largest number of speakers of English as

an additional language, ahead of more populous Nigeria and Pakistan. It has often been remarked that the true national language is "Taglish," a free mixture of the two languages.

Among Christians, names of Spanish origin predominate, although names from indigenous languages are common enough. While Catholicism requires Spanish baptismal names, a 19th-century Spanish decree directed Filipinos to choose Spanish surnames for taxation purposes (inhabitants of the same locality had to select surnames beginning with the same letter). Filipinos generally have three names in the following order: (1) one's personal name, (2) one's mother's surname (usually appearing only as an initial), and (3) one's father's surname. Upon marriage, a woman's name changes to the pattern: (1) her personal name, (2) her father's surname, and (3) her husband's surname.

Names vary among non-Christian Filipinos according to their ethnic group.

⁴ FOLKLORE

Mounds of earth (including termite nests and backyard garbage heaps), particularly spooky old trees, and mist-shrouded mountains are said to be home to beings that can influence human lives for good or ill. In appearance, they range from beautiful goddess-like figures, such as Mariang Makiling, who is mistress of a Luzon mountain, to monsters, such as the *kapre,* a black-skinned giant, to dwarves and elves (often pictured dressed in medieval European fashions). By far the most widely feared of supernatural creatures is the *asuwang*, a being who appears as an attractive woman by day but who at night leaves behind the lower portion of its body in a hiding place and flies about in search of human victims, usually the sick, from whom it sucks the entrails with the aid of a long, tubular tongue. Inexplicable deaths in sleep are often ascribed to attacks by asuwang, although they are frequently also credited to *bangungot*, a fatal nightmare induced by witchcraft. Filipinos expect recently deceased kin to return in some form, as a moth, a strange breeze, or, if resentful of the living, as a wail heard in the night.

The legendary Juan Tamad ("John Lazy") appears in a great many folk tales; his extraordinary indolence and stupidity embroil him in all sorts of misadventures, usually ending in him being beaten up by his fellow villagers or scolded by his mother. In popular imagination, the opposite of Juan Tamad is Jose Rizal (1861–1896), the national hero, a European-educated doctor, scholar, and novelist. With his execution by the Spaniards during the Revolution (despite his disinclination for a complete break with Spain), Rizal became the supreme martyr; there is even a 250,000-strong sect, the Iglesia Watawat ng Lahi ("Church of the Banner of the Race"), which venerates him as a reincarnation of Christ and anticipates his return to earth to deliver his people from suffering.

5 RELIGION

As a result of Spanish evangelization, 81–83% of the population is Roman Catholic, making it the world's third largest Catholic majority nation (after Brazil and Mexico). This gives the Roman Catholic Church a powerful influence on national life, despite the separation of church and state introduced by the American colonialists. Power within the Church was monopolized by Spanish friars, so that native priests being granted control of parishes became a key reform that was sought by the nationalist movement in the late 19th century, ultimately resulting in the founding of the Philippine Independent Church (also called Aglipayan after Gregorio Aglipay who established it in 1902). Claiming 3.9% of the population, the Philippine Independent Church maintains essentially Catholic practices but does not recognize the pope. Another 1.3% of Filipinos adhere to another indigenous church, the evangelical Iglesia ni Kristo (Church of Christ), founded in 1914, known for its tight hold on its members' lives, demanding a temperate lifestyle, claiming a large portion of personal income (but also providing them with hardship support), and even dictating voting choices. The Church of Christ's well-kept places of worship, noted for their tall, vaguely "Oriental" spires, can now be seen in every town. In addition to these, American missionaries since the beginning of the century have proselytized for various Protestant sects, such as Baptist or Methodist, which now count about 2% of the population among their followers.

First arriving in the 15th century, Islam, the majority religion in neighboring Indonesia and Malaysia, claims about 5% of the population, concentrated in the south of the country. The 3% of Filipinos classified as "tribal" highlanders still follow ancestral animist traditions to varying degrees. The country's Chinese practice elements of Taoism and Buddhism, though many have converted to Christianity.

Belief in supernatural forces unrecognized by official Catholicism persists throughout the population. Faith healers and spirit mediums, often employing exorcistic strategies in addition to the usual herbals and massage, continue in popularity. To a greater extent than in contemporary Europe or North America, Catholicism in the Philippines stresses the veneration of intercessor figures, such as patron saints and the Virgin Mary (who is invoked in frequent group recitations of the rosary). Filipinos concentrate on the more human face of the Christian God, as in the cults of Santo Niño (the Child Jesus, conventionally dressed as prince), especially popular in the Visayas, and of the Dead Christ, characteristic of the Bicol region. Although some do not regularly practice their faith (for instance, adult men tend to avoid weekly mass) or are skeptical of organized religion, many others express an intense personal devotion, subjecting themselves to acts of self-mortification such as the world-famous flagellations and (nonfatal) crucifixions, or joining Catholic lay organizations such as the Cursillo, the ultraconservative Opus Dei, or the charismatic El Shaddai.

6 MAJOR HOLIDAYS

As the majority of the population is Christian, Christian holidays are the most widely celebrated holidays in the Philippines. Christmas festivities begin on December 16 with the first of the *simbang gabi* or *misa de gallo,* masses held before sunrise every morning before Christmas itself. After Midnight Mass on Christmas Eve, kindred families gather at one of their homes for a feast, the *Noche Buena*. On Christmas Day itself, further parties are held, with children making the rounds of relatives and godparents to pay respect to them and receive presents.

The other highlight of the year is Holy Week in March or April, celebrated by spectacles differing from locality to locality. Many towns hold a *sinakulo,* a traditional sung drama, staged over several nights and occupying many hours per segment, focusing on the sufferings of Christ but often including scenes from the Old Testament, all the way back to Genesis. Mass on the night before Easter is followed by the reenactment of the meeting of the resurrected Christ and his grieving mother, represented by life-sized statues carried in procession.

Another important nationwide festival is the Santacruzan in May, commemorating the discovery of Christ's cross by Helen, mother of Constantine the Great, the first Christian Roman emperor. These celebrations feature processions in which the daughters of prominent families are splendidly dressed as Reina Elena (Queen Helen) and accompanied by a male escort and a cortege of other couples. On All Souls' Day (November 2), people gather at the graves of family members for a 24-hour vigil during which, in addition to praying, they clean the graves, decorate them with candles and wreaths, eat, drink, and play cards.

Each town has an annual fiesta in honor of its patron saint. In addition to religious rituals, fiestas include public feasting, fairs, brass-band playing, performing arts, social dancing, sporting events (especially cockfights), and beauty contests.

7 RITES OF PASSAGE

Taking care to bury the placenta in a place where it will not be stepped on is one the many folk customs that to some extent still ensures the well-being and good fortune of a newborn child. For Christians, baptism offers an occasion for the parents to make alliances with kin and non-kin through the godparent relationship.

Around the onset of puberty, Christian boys undergo circumcision, without religious connotations; a simple lecture on hygiene by older female relatives accompanies a girl's first menstruation. Graduations from elementary, high school, and college require major celebrations. Elite families give their daughters debuts on their 18th birthday; the girl, her close female relatives, and male partners rehearse set pieces of ballroom dancing to perform in front of the guests.

Catholic weddings in the Philippines consist of the standard nuptial mass, but also include a section during which a white veil and a cord are draped over the couple's shoulder and an *arias,* an object made of coins, is presented to them, all symbols of unity and prosperity. A couple will have several sponsors ("wedding godparents"). A reception follows, to which everyone even remotely connected to the couple and their families is invited.

Funerals are extended affairs, usually postponed several days, waiting for relatives of the deceased to arrive from as far away as the United States. The body remains in the house, and there are always people keeping vigil over it, usually by playing cards or mah-jong through the night. A procession accompanied by somber music from a brass band brings the body to church for the funeral mass and takes it from there to the cemetery amid dramatic weeping from older kinswomen. Afterwards, mourners gather for nine nights to pray for the departed, and then again at longer intervals such as the first anniversary of the death. Surviving kin will avoid brightly colored outfits for some time, often attaching a black ribbon to their clothes; a widow will wear only black for a full year.

8 INTERPERSONAL RELATIONS

Filipino values aim to promote group solidarity and to underline individuals' mutual dependence. A person must have *hiya,* a sense of "shame," which prevents him or her from violating social norms. Behavior unacceptable to the wider society will damage the reputation of the groups to which one belongs, particularly the immediate family. Moreover, an individual should strive to earn and keep the esteem of others (in other words, protect his or her good name), a value called *amor-propio,* Spanish for "loving oneself"; those who do not care about their own "face" will not be sufficiently sensitive to the dignity of others.

Filipinos are careful to show deference to those of superior status (greater age, educational attainment, organizational rank, perceived wealth, etc.). For instance, when speaking in Tagalog-Pilipino to an elder, a social superior, or a stranger, a person inserts the particle *po* or *ho* ("sir" or "ma'am") into virtually every utterance. In order to save face, both one's own and that of others, one avoids making direct demands of others by either resorting to "beating around the bush" or enlisting a go-between. A person should show proper gratitude for the good others have done him or her and be eager to reciprocate in whatever way he or she can. Some *utang na loob* ("inner debts") can never be repaid, e.g. a child's debt to its mother for the gift of life.

In addition to the Spanish-derived *"Kumusta?"* ("How are you?"), the most common greetings translate as "Where have you just come from?" and "Where are you off to now?" In reply, no one expects to hear more than "Just over there."

It is customary to greet older relatives with a kiss on the cheek or forehead or, more traditionally, to bow in front of them, take their hand, and press it to the forehead to receive a "blessing." While passing in front of older or higher-status people, etiquette dictates that one walk slowly, bowing the head and either clasping the hands together in front or extending one of the open palms in the direction one is going. One beckons another to come closer with a downward motion of the open palm. Pointing with the fingers is offensive; people point pursed lips in the direction they wish to indicate. When catching sight of acquaintances, quickly raising and lowering the eyebrows is sufficient sign of recognition and may substitute for small talk if one is in a hurry. Prolonged staring, however, is considered aggressive, as is holding the arms akimbo. With merely a sharp, clipped hiss, mothers can show displeasure to their children; anyone can use a softer, somewhat more prolonged hiss as a very informal means of catching someone's attention. Physical contact between members of the same sex is a common sign of affection without homosexual connotation. In embarrassing situations, the reflex is to smile to cover over the natural emotion, or sometimes also to lower the head and rub the back of the neck.

Before entering a house, a visitor announces his or her presence by saying *Tao po* ("A person is here, sir/ma'am") and waits to be invited in. Even unexpected guests are always served drinks and whatever snacks are available. It is polite to appear shy to accept what is offered, but the host will vigorously insist that the guest partake. The guest leaves a little on the plate to show that the host has provided more than enough. Taking formal leave of the hosts and any older or distinguished people is a must; this is usually a lengthy operation as there tends to be a line of people waiting to say goodbye, and farewells tend to ramble. Party hosts always wrap leftovers for the departing guests to take home. Similarly, those returning from long-distance trips are expected to bring back presents *(pasalubong)* for those remaining at home.

In the past, a suitor stood below the door of his interest's raised house and serenaded her, often with companions at his side literally to provide accompaniment. If the girl liked him, she could invite him in to chat with her and her family. Contact between the sexes unmonitored by elders is increasingly common (such as in discos), but same-age chaperones and group dates continue to make "courting" a public affair. This is becoming more so as Filipinos introduce their relatives and friends to likely partners or approach their interests by asking the help of a common friend. Public displays of affection, though no longer taboo, are still subject to social disapproval; girls, in particular, are careful not to appear too free with boys. In urban areas today, though usually only after much dating, many young people engage in discreet premarital sex, often going to "love motels" because of lack of privacy at home. Many young men have their first sexual experience with a prostitute.

According to survey data plotted on the Inglehart-Welzel World Values Map, Filipinos are moderately more tradition-oriented than secular-rational-oriented and slightly more survival-oriented than self-expression-oriented (most resembling Peruvians, who are slightly more tradition-oriented, South Africans and Iranians who are slightly more tradition- and survival oriented, and Indonesians, who are both somewhat less traditional- and less self-expression-oriented).

Children throw confetti to dancing women wearing traditional dress during a celebration of the feast of Sto. Nino, Manila, Philippines. (AP Images/Pat Roque)

⁹ LIVING CONDITIONS

In 2005, per capita GDP, adjusted for Purchasing Power Parity, stood at US $5,137 a year, placing the Philippines in the category of lower middle-income nations. Its ranking in the United Nations Human Development Index is 90 (out of 177 countries ranked). Countries with similar HDI's are Peru, Lebanon, Tunisia, Fiji, and Iran. Its HDI ranking is eleven places higher than its ranking according to GNP per capita (PPP), indicating that its population is somewhat better off in terms of health and education than per capita income alone would provide for (Tunisia's per capita GDP, adjusted for PPP, is 60% higher than the Philippines, but its HDI is slightly lower).

Some 30% of the population lives below the government-set poverty line (although the sharing of resources by more affluent family members and relatives working overseas mitigates somewhat the hardship of many of the poor). While recent economic growth has benefited a growing portion of the population, most of the nation's wealth remains in the hands of a small fraction of the population—elite families (some Spanish mestizo but mostly Chinese mestizo and Chinese-Filipino) who own plantations and other large enterprises. Nearly half the population (43%) lives on less than two dollars' equivalent a day, and 14.8% on less than a dollar a day. The proportion of the population living below the national poverty line (earning less than the amount needed to provide themselves a daily intake of 2,100 calories and other basic needs) has declined dramatically over the years, from 40.1% in 1976 to 16.58% in 2007. This last figure, however, represents a recovery from the situation in the aftermath of the economic collapse of 1997–1998; in 1990 the figure was 15% while the average for the years 1990–2004 was 27.1%. As measured by its Gini coefficient of 44.5, income inequality in the Philippines is severe by world standards (it is greater than in Japan, 29.9; Indonesia, 34.3; and the United States 40.8; though far less than in Brazil, 57). The richest 20% earns 9.4 times as much as the poorest 20%. Moreover, there is wide variation in the standard of living from region to region and between urban and rural areas.

Spanish colonialism dictated a settlement pattern that had at its core a *población,* a town laid out in a grid plan focused on a church plaza. The *población* was in turn the center for a number of *barrios,* villages surrounded by fields. Finally, the *barrios* themselves had often remote satellite hamlets, *sitios* with a small chapel visited only intermittently by the priest permanently resident in the *población.*

The *bahay kubo* or nipa hut, a two- or three-room structure with bamboo walls and floors and a cogon-grass or palm-leaf roof raised on wooden pillars, has provided housing for the peasants, who make up the vast majority of Filipinos, until recent times. Animals, primarily pigs, chickens, and a water buffalo, are kept below the house. . In less-developed parts of the country, this remains the most common type of house. In Sulu, 1990 census figures count nearly 90% of houses as having neither solid roofs nor solid outer walls; the national average is 44.4% and 39.1%, respectively.

In contemporary towns, houses typically have two stories with wooden walls, corrugated iron roofs, and cement foundations. Wealthier residences adopt Spanish elements, such as tiled roofs and floors, walls of brick or stone, and iron grillwork on windows, fences, and gates. Whereas traditional neighborhoods juxtaposed rich and poor houses, modern urban development has favored: the growth of upper-class residential areas surrounded by walls, with entrances guarded by security personnel; middle-class subdivisions (including gated condominium complexes); and squatter settlements whose houses are improvised from scrap materials and lack utilities. About 25% of the Manila population was squatters in the early 1980s.

In 2004, 80.2% of households had access to safe drinking water within their residence, 86.2% to a sanitary toilet, and 79.7% to electricity. About 64.4% of households owned their residence, and for 70.5% of households that residence was a "strong housing unit," defined as one with roof and outer walls of galvanized iron/aluminum, tile, concrete, brick, stone, and asbestos. In 2000, 1 in 3 households had a refrigerator, up from 1 in 5 in 1990 and 1 in 20 in 1970. About 46.1% of households in 2000 still disposed of garbage by burning it in their backyards, although the percentage of households that had their garbage picked up by a truck rose to 32.5% from just 15.8% in 1990.

Life expectancy has risen dramatically over the last generation: standing at 51.2 years for both sexes in 1960 and 58.1 in 1970–1975, figures for 1990 reached 69 years for women and 63 years for men, and for 2005 it increased to 73.3 and 68.9 respectively. Infant mortality was halved between 1950 (101 deaths per 1,000 live births) and 1989 (51.6 deaths); it was halved yet again by 2005 when it ran to only 25 per 1,000 live births. Still, 1 in 5 infants were underweight at birth and around 1 in 3 children under 5 years old were underweight and under height; 18% of the general population was undernourished (1996–2005 averages, down from 26% in 1990–1992). In 2005, 13.78% of deaths were due to intestinal tract infections. Communicable diseases were the cause of 25% in 1980 and 75% in 1923. About 41.8% of households included a member enrolled in the government health care plan; access to physicians and hospitals remains limited in rural areas, where there were only 58 physicians per 100,000 people. Individuals still consult traditional healers and employ herbal remedies.

Telephone access is spreading rapidly. Although the number of telephone landlines per 1,000 people only rose from 10 in 1990 to 41 in 2005, there were 419 cell phone subscribers for every 1000 people in that year. The number of internet users has reached 54 per 1000 people.

In 1990, only 7.9% of households owned a motor vehicle; by 2000, the figure had risen to 12.2%. Within urban neighborhoods or in the countryside (where *kalesas,* horse drawn carts, can still be seen), people take tricycles (motorcycles with a passenger car on the side). Brightly painted *jeepneys* (originally U.S. military surplus jeeps with back sections lengthened to accommodate passengers) are the cheapest way to get around cities and between towns. Buses, some air-conditioned, also carry passengers within cities and between more distant locations. Commuting to and within cities, metropolitan Manila above all, consumes much time due to extreme traffic congestion. Interisland travel is by large ferries or passenger ships or,

more expensively, by airplane; the traditional *bangka,* an outrigger canoe, is still in common use for fishing and local transport. Overall, per capita carbon dioxide emissions are still low, at 1.0 tons in 2004 (up from 0.7 in 1990).

¹⁰ FAMILY LIFE

The family is Filipino society's central institution; to it individuals subordinate their own interests and frequently their obligations to other social groups, their workplace, or the government. The typical household consists of a married couple, children, grandparents, and sometimes servants, who are common in middle-class households. Children generally live at home until marriage, and often newlywed couples stay with either set of parents for some time. Older children, as well as grandparents and other relatives, aid the mother in caring for younger children; it is common for older children to sacrifice for the younger, such as by working to put them through school.

Great respect is shown for elders. Older siblings are addressed with special terms. In Tagalog-Pilipino, "Ate" is used for an older sister and "Kuya" for an older brother. Older cousins (as well as friends and associates) are also addressed with these titles. Traditionally, a person would address a younger cousin as "older sibling" if the cousin's parents were older than his or her own parents. Filipinos have a bilateral kinship system that bonds them equally to relatives from both the mother's and father's sides. Relations between cousins of as far as the second and even third degree are close. Married couples are expected to maintain equal closeness with both spouses' kin groups, though this is not always achieved. Inheritances are divided equally among the children of the deceased.

The Catholic sacraments of baptism, confirmation, and marriage give Filipinos opportunities to establish or reinforce relationships with non-kin through asking non-kin to become godparents to one's children; these godparents can be old friends or individuals one wishes to make alliances with or seek the patronage of, though very often they are actually one's own relatives. The godfather and godmother of one's child are called one's *kumpare* and *kumare* (from Spanish *compadre* and *comadre*), and one's own godfather and godmother are called *ninong, ninang* (from Spanish *padrino* and *padrina*).

Individuals are free to choose their marriage partners, but family approval is an important consideration, often a decisive one. In agreement with Catholic doctrine, divorce (though not separation) is illegal except among Muslims and other non-Christians. Often, a man takes a mistress (*querida*), with whom he may have a second family. The need to work away from home or even outside the country has produced numerous "incomplete" households, which can be where one parent (often the father) must raise the family with only the occasional presence of the other, where grandparents must care for their grandchildren, or where elder siblings must care for their younger siblings. Illegitimate births have become common and do not always lead to marriage as was the case in the past because today there are fewer stigmas around this situation.

Filipinos are relatively tolerant of homosexuality. Though often the object of good-natured teasing, the *bakla*, the effeminate man with a "woman's heart" (*pusong babae*) has an established place in society (*bakla* beauty contests are popular entertainment for the general public).

11 CLOTHING

The Spanish pressured Christianized Filipinos into abandoning the more "immodest" Southeast Asian articles of dress such as the G-string, but prohibited them from fully adopting European fashions. *Indio* (native) men wore collarless, long-sleeved, untucked shirts *(baro)* and loose pants that could be rolled up easily for heavy work. Indio women wore wide-necked, wide-sleeved short blouses and ankle-length skirts; in public, they draped a shawl over their shoulders and wrapped a *tapis,* a small piece of cloth, over the skirt (the tapis was in fact the skirt of pre-Christian times). The wealthier *mestizo* (mixed-blood) men added collars and cuffs to the baro, thus creating what would become the male national costume, the *barong tagalog,* finely embroidered and woven of pineapple leaf fibers. Mestizo women preferred fuller skirts (or sometimes ones ending in a long train) and butterfly sleeves, developing the *terno,* the later female national costume.

Nowadays, for formal occasions men wear either the barong tagalog or Western-style suits, and women wear either a modified terno or Western-style dresses. Suitable home attire very often consists of no more than shorts with or without a tank top for men, and a *maong,* a loose one-piece dress with wide sleeves and open neck for women. For younger people, t-shirts and jeans are common streetwear.

12 FOOD

Except for the 20% of the population (in the central Visayas) for whom maize is the staple, boiled rice is the indispensable component of a full meal, with all other foods being termed *ulam* (accompaniments). For peasants, the ulam may consist of no more than dried fish and some sliced tomato or onion. Only for the comparatively well to do is meat a regular part of the diet; most consume meat only at special celebrations (often in the form of *lechon,* roast whole pig). Common preparations include soups heavy with vegetables and meat or seafood (such as *sinigang* and *tinola*), meat or seafood simmered in coconut milk *(ginataan),* Chinese-derived noodle dishes (such as *pansit*), stewed meat dishes of Spanish origin (such as *adobo* or *kaldereta*), or, most simply, freshly grilled fish. Party menus emphasize dishes inspired by Chinese or Spanish cuisine, such as *lumpia* (spring rolls) and *paella* (a dish of meat, seafood, and rice cooked together).

Seasonings tend to be simpler than elsewhere in Southeast Asia, with ordinary dishes rarely employing more than garlic, ginger, peppercorns, soy sauce, fish sauce, and shrimp paste. Although Muslim peoples and Christian Bicolanos cook with hot chilies as much as Indonesians or Thai, elsewhere in the country one regularly encounters chili only as a flavoring for vinegar.

Aside from a Spanish custard, *letseplan,* and rich American-style baked goods, desserts consist of a variety of rice- or cassava-based cakes. A wide selection of fruits is available, such as numerous types of bananas (bananas are sometimes even eaten alongside the main meal).

Associated with peasant ways, the traditional mode of eating has been to scoop up food from flat dishes with the fingers of the right hand (the left hand being reserved exclusively for washing oneself after defecation). It is considered more refined to eat with a spoon and fork (using the fork in the left hand to push food on to a spoon in the right hand). Individual portions are not separated; rather, everyone takes from common dishes laid out in the center of the table.

Breakfast usually consists of leftovers from the previous evening's dinner (the remaining rice is often fried with garlic) or, alternatively of bread bought fresh from bakeries and eaten with coffee. Other common breakfast dishes consist of fried rice, fried eggs, and a meat product (longanisa sausage, tosino bacon, beef tapa, or spam). The heaviest meal of the day is lunch for country people (to satisfy hunger built up working in the morning, the coolest part of the day) and dinner for city people (when the entire family can gather together). Taking an afternoon snack, called the *merienda,* often virtually a meal in itself, is common for those who can afford it.

Smoking is common among men, but women smokers are rare. For a mild stimulant, some (far fewer than in the past) chew betel nut. Wines, made from palm sap, sugarcane, or rice, are the traditional alcoholic beverages, but today beer predominates. Small groups of men often gather at night on the porch of a house to chat and drink beer with *pulutan,* snacks ranging from peanuts or the eggs of quail or duck (the last often a fully formed chick in the shell, called *balut*) to grilled fish or shrimp.

13 EDUCATION

In 2003, literacy stood at 93.4%, a 10% increase over the 1970 level, though a minimal change from 1990. Elementary school lasts for six years beginning at age seven, and high school lasts for four years (seven years of education is compulsory). While 94% of the relevant age group was enrolled in elementary school, which is free, in 2005, only 61% of the relevant age group attended high school that year because poorer families cannot spare the money for fees, as well as travel costs to the often distant high schools, and need teenagers to help in the fields or otherwise earn income for the family. Of high school graduates, a large percentage go on to college, ranging from low-quality "diploma mills" to excellent universities, the most prestigious being the state-run University of the Philippines, the Jesuit-run Ateneo de Manila, and the Dominican-run University of Santo Tomas, which has been in existence longer than Harvard. About 31.2% of the relevant age cohort is enrolled in a tertiary educational institution. In 1990, 12.9% of the population held an academic degree. In addition to the public school system, private schools abound at all levels, teaching 7.3% of students at the primary level and 30.8% at the secondary, usually run by the Catholic Church or other Christian sects; Chinese and Muslim communities also have their own schools.

American policy promoted mass public education, the beginnings of which date back to 1863 under the Spanish. Since then, Filipinos have held a deep reverence for education, seeing it as a means of freeing oneself from manual labor by entering more prestigious occupations as doctors, lawyers, or, at least, schoolteachers. Families are willing to sacrifice a great deal to send a child to college. A major national problem has been providing the great number of college-educated people with jobs commensurate with their qualifications; many emigrate to attain the living standard proper to their educational attainments.

14 CULTURAL HERITAGE

The most prominent types of traditional group music making are the *rondalla, which is* an ensemble of Hispanic plucked and bowed string instruments to accompany social dancing and suitors' serenades, and the municipal brass band, whose repertoire includes Italian opera overtures and other orchestral music to contribute to the gaiety of fiestas. Traditional songs (for instance the *kundiman*, a melancholy love song) are generally reminiscent of Spanish forms; certain types demand operatic vocal delivery. Similarly, modern vocal music follows American pop models with a preference for the sentimental and the Broadway-style dramatic (although rap in Tagalog-Pilipino does exist).

Folk dances include those that have analogues elsewhere in Southeast Asia, such as the *tinikling*, where a couple executes intricate figures while skipping through two bamboo poles being clapped together at an accelerating pace. Others are adaptations of European couple dances such the waltz, polka, and mazurka. Both disco and ballroom dancing have long been popular (especially Latin American styles such as the cha-cha).

At the time of the Spanish arrival, Filipinos were using their own alphabet (one derived via Javano-Malay or Cham scripts that in turn derived from Indian ones), incising messages (though not literature, which remained oral) on palm leaves or bamboo. Word play ranged from riddles (*bugtong*) to extended poetical debates (*balagtasan*), an integral part of courtship; formal declamation remains an important art. Long verse narratives, from retellings of Christ's Passion to heroic tales set in mythical lands, came to be composed in native languages; the culmination of this tradition was the Tagalog classic *Florante at Laura*, composed by Francisco Baltazar in the 1830s. By the last decades of the 19th century, Filipinos were producing poetry and novels in Spanish. Jose Rizal's patriotic poem "*Mi ultimo adiós*" and his anti-colonial novels *Noli Me Tangere* and *El filibusterismo* are the most famous examples. Under the Americans, writers switched to English, a tradition that continues today. Nick Joaquin is one of its most renowned heirs. Meanwhile, poetry, prose, and drama continue to be written in Tagalog-Pilipino and the other indigenous languages, although Filipino novels face strong competition from imported English-language books. For most people, consumption of literature in native languages is confined to stories (*nobela*) appearing serially in comics.

15 WORK

In 2004, over one in three Filipino workers (37%) was employed in agriculture, a dramatic reduction from the 1980 figures of one in two (49.2%). Some 70% of agricultural workers do not own the land they work, working either as tenant farmers or plantation laborers. The staple crops are rice, maize, and sweet potatoes. Wet-rice fields dominate the rural landscape, in some places as terraces climbing steep mountainsides. The principal cash crops are coconuts, bananas, pineapples, sugar, tobacco, and abaca (hemp). Livestock includes pigs, chickens, ducks, and goats. Raising cattle is limited to the few areas with suitable grazing lands; *carabao* (water buffalo) pull plows and carts and also provide meat and milk. Fishing provides many rural families with a livelihood or at least supplementary income. Complex networks of bamboo traps cover lakes and other bodies of water.

Manufacturing and construction employ 15% of the working population. Traditionally, industry has focused on producing consumer goods for the domestic market and the processing of exported primary agricultural products. Recent years, however, have seen the growth of export-oriented manufacture, such as computer components assembly; though to a lesser extent than in neighboring Asian countries, Japanese and South Korean firms have outsourced many of their production operations to factories in government-established special economic zones in the Philippines, such as the one on the territory of the former U.S. naval base at Subic Bay.

Services accounted for 48% of all workers. Considerable stigma was traditionally attached to manual labor and mercantile occupations, though careers in business and technical professions, such as engineering, have recently gained greatly in respectability. Thanks to having one of the largest populations of young highly educated English-speakers in the world and low labor costs (in this respect resembling India, the world leader), the Philippines has become a major center of the call center industry; in 2004, it employed over a million people (largely in the Metro Manila region) and contributed to 12% of GDP.

Unemployment is high, estimated at 7.9% in 2007 (the 2004 figure reached 10.9%). Over 45% of the working population was employed in the informal sector.

Finally, the country's economic difficulties have pushed many people to emigrate in search of work. Although Filipinos already sought education and employment abroad in late Spanish times and Filipino migration to the United States began with the U.S. conquest of the Philippines at the very end of the 19th century, large-scale migration there and to elsewhere in the world only began in the 1970s. A command of English and a high level of education giving them a competitive in the world labor market, Filipinos can now be found in every region of the world, in over 200 countries and territories. In 2004, 8.1 million Filipinos, equivalent to nearly 10% of the population, were estimated to be abroad, mainly in the Middle East, Pacific Asia, North America, and Europe. These are divided into three categories: 3.6 million legally working abroad (termed "OFWs"/"Overseas Filipino Workers"); 1.3 million working illegally (mainly in the United States and Malaysia); and 3.2 million residing permanently abroad (termed "balikbayan," "returnees to the homeland"). About 1.4 million had settled in the United States, where they constituted the second-largest group among the foreign-born, after Mexicans.

About 20% of all Filipino OFWs work as shipmen, and 25% of all shipmen worldwide are Filipinos. Filipinos are also particularly prominent in health care, (women) domestic service, and (men) construction work. Since 1992, women have outnumbered men among labor emigrants. Estimated at US$8.5 billion in 2004 and expected to surpass US$10 billion in 2005, remittances are essential to the economy as a source of hard currency, even surpassing the value of foreign direct investment; the Philippines is the world's fifth largest recipient of remittances (after India, China, Mexico, and France). Establishing a whole agency for the purpose, the government has institutionalized its management of labor migration/labor export, aiming to deploy 1 million OFWs annually. The country has developed a "culture of migration" under which true "ambition" is equated with the willingness to work abroad and 1 in 5 adults and 1 in 2 children 10–12 years of age express the desire to do so.

¹⁶ SPORTS

Sipa is an indigenous game in which two teams of one to four players each hit a wickerwork ball with their knees, legs, or feet over a net or across a circle. Introduced by the Americans, baseball and basketball are popular. The avidly followed professional basketball league pits teams identified by the companies that own them, rather than with cities as in the United States. Fond of watching boxing, many Filipinos also practice *arnis,* an indigenous martial art employing bamboo rods 1 m (3 ft) long. Cockfighting commands a fanatical following. Held during Sundays, public holidays, and fiestas in mini-stadiums, cockfights are the occasion for intense gambling.

¹⁷ ENTERTAINMENT AND RECREATION

In 2000, three in four households had a radio, and one in two had a television (up from two in three households and one in three respectively in 1990). Domestically produced programming is strong on talent shows, comedies, fantasy series, and tearjerker family dramas and romance stories.

Traditional theater consisted of the *comedia* or *moro-moro,* which are verse-plays depicting warfare between Christians and Muslims, usually ending in the conversion of the former. From the end of the 19th century, the *zarzuela,* a Spanish-derived operetta sung in local languages, has become popular. Film tickets are comparatively cheap, and cinema attendance rates are among the world's highest. The Philippines possesses one of the world's most prolific film industries, which turns out mainly comedies, action films (frequently punctuated with shoot-outs and kung fu), and melodramas (for which typical plots would be an ill-fated romance or the reunion of a dispersed family or the reconciliation of a divided one). For both television and cinema viewing, American imports attract a wide audience who generally can understand the dialogue. In recent years, foreign programs dubbed into Tagalog, such as Japanese anime and Korean and Latin American soap operas, have become more and more popular, not least because they express cultural values much closer to those of Filipinos than American shows do.

Children commonly play *sungka,* a game of skill in which players move cowrie shells around a course of two rows of seven holes carved in a wooden board. Every neighborhood will have chess enthusiasts, and the Philippines has produced many world-class players. Card games and *mah-jong,* a rummy-like Chinese game played with ivory tiles, regularly involve the gambling of large sums of money. There are 4 personal computers for every 100,000 people, but internet cafes are common not only in cities but also in provincial towns, where the clientele consists largely of young people playing computer games.

¹⁸ FOLK ART, CRAFTS, HOBBIES

A variety of crafts are practiced by individual Filipino ethnic groups, including woodcarving, weaving textiles, baskets, and mats, and tie dying.

¹⁹ SOCIAL PROBLEMS

Under the civil war conditions during the Marcos and Aquino regimes, human rights abuses were common, with government forces, insurgents, and anti-insurgent vigilantes victimizing noncombatant civilians as a matter of course. Under the Ramos and later regimes, the more prominent problem was violence by criminal elements, and by supposedly noncriminal elements such as corrupt law-enforcers and elected officials. Filipinos have little faith in their justice system since the wealthy and powerful are able to buy the verdicts they want. Gambling (most notoriously the hugely popular jueteng numbers game), drug abuse, and the violence, criminality, and government corruption associated with them are major problems. Population growth has slowed but continues to overwhelm the country's economic, educational, ecological, and other systems. In 2008 a reproductive health bill mandating government funding for contraception and sex education was being hotly debated. Opponents, in addition to invoking Catholic moral principles, argue the economic benefits of a large, young population and the negative practical consequences of a shrinking, aging population as well as assert that calling for population control is a substitute for seeking genuine structural social reforms.

²⁰ GENDER ISSUES

Filipino women have approached equality with men more closely than in most Asian countries. The country's Gender-Related Development Index is 0.768, slightly less than its HDI of 0.771. Although Filipino men often project machismo, women wield considerable power. Filipino wives manage family finances, dispensing pocket money to their husbands just as to their children. In terms of literacy and primary, secondary, and tertiary enrollment, rates for Filipino women (which are high) have surpassed those for men (most dramatically, a fourth more women are in tertiary education than men). Because of the gender preferences of jobs such as factory work and domestic service (as well as, unfortunately, prostitution and nightclub work), rural women are freer than men to find urban employment to support their families. Women are well represented in the professions, business, and the government, although women are still in the minority among the holders of top positions (women hold 22.1% of the seats in the national legislature and 25% of ministerial level positions). The country has had two woman presidents, Corazon Aquino and Gloria Arroyo, and Imelda Marcos, in addition to being first lady, served as governor of Metro-Manila, minister of human settlements, and special envoy to foreign leaders.

Reflecting the pervasive influence of Catholicism, both abortion and divorce are prohibited (Muslims, however, may divorce as permitted by their religion). In 2000–2005, the fertility rate stood at 3.5 births per woman. 92% of women from the richest 20% of society were attended by a skilled health professional while giving birth; the proportion was only 25% for the poorest 20% of society. About 170 women died in childbirth for every 100,000 live births during the period 1990–2004. For the richest 20% of society, infant mortality ran to 19 per 1,000 live births and under-five mortality to 21 per 1,000 live births; for the poorest 20 % of society, the figures were respectively 42 and 66.

Despite enjoying empowerment in many contexts, in others many Filipino women continue to face exploitation and abuse. In export-processing zones where young women form the major component of the labor force in factories owned by multinational corporations, the government does not enforce laws protecting workers' rights. Filipino women working abroad as domestic servants often suffer inferior working and living conditions as well as physical brutality and sexual harassment from employers. Coerced prostitution, human trafficking, and domestic violence are significant problems.

21 BIBLIOGRAPHY

Abinales, Patricio, N. and Donna J. Amoroso. *State and Society in the Philippines*. Lanham, MD: Rowman and Littlefield, 2005.

de Leon, Felipe M., Jr. *The Filipino Nation. Vol. 3, Philippines Art and Literature*. N.p.: Grolier International, 1982.

Euromonitor International. "Philippines Statistics." http://www.euromonitor.com/factfile.aspx?country=PH (November 3, 2008.

Federal Research Division. *Philippines: A Country Study*. Washington, D.C.: Library of Congress, 1993.

Gochenour, Theodore. *Considering Filipinos*. Yarmouth, ME: Intercultural Press, 1990.

Gordon, Raymond G., Jr. (ed.). *Ethnologue: Languages of the World*, 15th edition. Dallas, Tex.: SIL International. http://www.ethnologue.com.

Harper, Peter, and Evelyn Peplow. *Philippines Handbook*. Chico, CA: Moon Publications, 1991.

Human Rights Watch. "Regional Overview of Women's Rights in Asia." http://www.hrw.org/women/overview-asia.html (November 3, 2008)

Migration Policy Institute. http://www.icmc.net/pdf/traffreport_en.pdf (November 3, 2008).

National Statistics Office (Philippines). http://www.census.gov.ph.

Tarling, Nicolas, ed. *The Cambridge History of Southeast Asia*. Vols. 1 and 2. Singapore: Cambridge University Press, 1992.

United Nations Development Programme. Human Development Reports, "2007–2008 Report: Indonesia." http://hdrstats.undp.org/countries/data_sheets/cty_ds_IDN.html (November 3, 2008).

United Nations Children's Fund. "At a Glance: Philippines—Statistics." http://www.unicef.org/infobycountry/philippines_statistics.html (September 7, 2008).

World Values Survey. "Inglehart-Welzel Cultural Map of the World." http://www.worldvaluessurvey.org (November 5, 2008).

—revised by A. J. Abalahin

GAOSHAN

ALTERNATE NAMES: Milin; Sanmei; Liuqiu; Amei; Taiyar; Paiwan; Bunong; Lukai; Beinan; Zou; Saixia; Yamei and Pingpu

LOCATION: China; Taiwan

POPULATION: 500,000

LANGUAGE: Taiyer, Saide, Zou, Sha, Ka, Paiwan, Ameisi, Bunong, Lukai, Saixiate, Beinan, Shao, Chinese

RELIGION: Traditional beliefs

RELATED ARTICLES: Vol. 3: China and Her National Minorities

1 INTRODUCTION

The ancestors of the Gaoshan belonged to the Min-Yue people (inhabiting part of present-day Fujian and Guangdong provinces) and, more remotely, to the Baiyue of ancient China. The history of the Gaoshan is closely related to that of Taiwan, because the Gaoshan are the aboriginals of that island. According to historical documents of the Three Kingdoms (220–265), their ancestors were divided into tribes, the members of which were called "Milin." Public affairs were administered by the tribe members themselves. Agriculture and livestock husbandry appeared in the 7th century, complementing hunting and fishing.

The historical records of the Ming Dynasty (1368–1644) describe their trade with the coastal inhabitants of mainland China. Between 1563 and 1603, the Japanese army invaded Taiwan several times, but it finally was defeated by the military forces of the imperial Ming. In 1624, the Netherlands' army intruded into southwest Taiwan, where it established fortresses and occupied the land. The Spanish army made incursions into the northern part of the island in 1626; however, the Dutch vanquished the Spaniards in 1642 and replaced them in northern Taiwan. An uprising led by Guo Huaiyi against Dutch domination in 1652 failed. In 1661, a former general of the imperial Ming, Zheng Chenggong, better known as Koxinga (1624–1662), setting out from Xiamen and Jinmen on the mainland, succeeded in landing his army on Taiwan. After nine months of fierce fighting, the Dutch invaders were compelled to lay down their arms.

In 1683, the Qing Dynasty (1644–1911) unified Taiwan. At that time, there were approximately 300 villages of Gaoshan people who had preserved important aspects of their primitive family type, clan organization, and religious beliefs. From the 17th century onward, there was a continuous flow of Chinese migrants to Taiwan, mainly Minnan from southern Fujian Province and Hakka (or Kejia) from Guangdong Province. In 1786, an armed conflict between the Gaoshan and the Chinese erupted and continued for more than one year but ended in a stalemate. Japan occupied Taiwan after the Sino-Japanese War of 1895. The Gaoshan and the Chinese united in opposing Japanese domination, uprisings flaring up every other year. An uprising in 1930 wiped out more than 4,000 Japanese soldiers. Following the end of the Second World War (1939–45), Taiwan returned to China in 1945.

2 LOCATION AND HOMELAND

The Gaoshan people number about 500,000, living mainly in mountainous areas, in the eastern coast plains of Taiwan, and on Lanyu Island; they are also found in Beijing, Shanghai, Wuhan, and Fujian. They form a small portion of Taiwan's overall population of 24 million. The Taiwan Mountain chain extends from north to south, exerting a strong influence on the weather. Large areas of Taiwan, especially in the center and in the south, boast spring-like weather year-round. The abundant rainfall and rich soil make it possible to reap two rice crops a year and even three in the central and southern parts of the island. Taiwan is famous for its abundant production of sugarcane, tea, and fruits. There are vast forested areas; the production of camphor accounts for 70% of the world's output. The fishing industry, especially on the Pacific coast, is thriving. Mining is also an important economic activity. Since the 1970s Taiwan has become a leader in the productivity of its manufacturing sector, including both light and heavy industries. It is obvious that the Gaoshan have not benefited as much as could have been desired from this economic boom.

³LANGUAGE

Gaoshan languages are classified as belonging to the Austronesian family, Indonesia group. They have no writing system. The Gaoshan who have different names speak different languages. More than 20 languages have been identified, of which 13 are still in use. These languages can be divided into three groups: the Taiyar group, including Taiyer and Saide languages; the Zou group, including Zou, Sha, and Ka languages; and the Paiwan group, including Paiwan, Ameisi, Bunong, Lukai, Saixiate, Beinan, and Shao languages. In addition, there is a Yamei language on Lanyu Island. Most of these language groups are mutually unintelligible. The Pingpu branch of the Gaoshan now speaks Chinese.

Chinese historical documents recorded some of the ancient names of the early inhabitants of Taiwan: Sanmei during the Three Kingdoms, Liuqiu in the Sui Dynasty (581–618), etc. After the Tang Dynasty (618–907), Malays and other nationalities migrated to Taiwan successively and assimilated with the aboriginals. They were called Dongfan and Yi in the Ming Dynasty and Fanzhu and Tufan in the Qing Dynasty. During the Japanese occupation, they were called Fanzhu and Gaobushaozhu. The inhabitants of Taiwan other than Gaoshan usually call them Shandiren or Shanbao, which means "mountain people." Because of their different languages and locations, they were divided into the Amei, Taiyar, Paiwan, Bunong, Lukai, Beinan, Zou, Saixia, Yamei, and Pingpu.

⁴FOLKLORE

The Gaoshan have a rich mythology. On Lanyu Island, it is said that the Yami are the offspring of two male gods, one of whom appeared from the splitting of a rock, the other from a bamboo rent in two by a seismic sea wave. When the gods' knees bumped against each other, there emerged a man and a woman, the remote ancestors of the Yami. According to the legend of the Saixia, a long time ago the almighty God created a number of men and women who led peaceful lives in the mountains. One day, a violent typhoon attacked them. Torrential rains poured down for days. Suddenly, an avalanche of water and mudflow rushed down the mountain. People, engulfed, disappeared in an instant. Only one man was lucky enough to escape. Viewing the bodies of the people, the almighty God was very sad. When he saw the only man alive, an aspiration to recreate mankind welled up in his heart. He put the man's skin

and flesh into the sea, and these became a multitude of people swimming to the land, setting up villages and settling down. God called them "Sasite," the ancestors of the Saixia. He then put the intestine of that man into the sea. Another group of people appeared. They were the ancestors of the Chinese who dwell in Taiwan. They lived a long (chang) life because they came from the intestine (chang) of that man.

There is also in the legends of the Gaoshan a hero called Ali. He was a brave and good-natured hunter. One day, he saw two girls attacked by a tiger. He saved them from its jaws. Then came an old man, who seized the girls. When Ali drove him away, the sky turned dark all around, with lightning accompanied by peals of thunder. The girls told him that they were fairy maidens. Since they had stayed too long in the world, they would suffer a cruel punishment; his rescue had only made matters worse. Subsequently, the Jade Emperor ordered the Thunder God to kill all the people as well as the plants and animals in the area where Ali had saved the girls. The girls sought to draw the thunder against themselves at a barren mountain not far away, where the fire could not spread. Thinking that it was he who stirred up all the trouble, Ali ran to the barren mountain. He cried loudly to the Thunder God: "It is all my fault, so punish me if you want!" A deafening thunderclap smashed the body of Ali to pieces. Since there were no trees or bushes on the barren mountain, the fire died out quickly. After his death, the barren mountain was covered by a thick forest. Deeply moved by his heroic behavior, the two fairy maidens turned themselves into grass and flowers. In memory of this nice young man, the mountain has been called "Alishan" since then. It is now a very famous tourist resort.

⁵RELIGION

The Gaoshan have preserved many primitive beliefs and rituals. They believe the spirits are in all things around them and revere a great many gods, such as the gods of the universe, of Heaven, of nature, as well as a variety of spirits and goblins. However, the gods they worship are not the same from one district to the next. Witchcraft is widespread. There are various talismanic scriptures. Methods of divination include birds, dreams, water, bamboo, rice, and the wooden dipper.

⁶MAJOR HOLIDAYS

Gaoshan holidays, based on the lunar calendar, are closely related to their work and to their religion. On lunar New Year's Eve (Western calendar, between January 20 and February 19), members of each household are reunited for a dinner party held around a large table, on which a chafing dish is the central dish. People are entertained with drama in the temple. It is humorously called "creditor avoiding drama," because some people hide themselves among the spectators to dodge the creditors at the end of the year—the time for settling accounts. On the Spring Festival (Western calendar, between January 21 and February 20), they call on each other's family, saying a few auspicious words, and participate in recreational activities. The Good Year Festival coincides with traditional holidays in August, lasting for about 10 days. They offer sacrifice to ancestors. Many centuries ago, the sacrifice included a human head. Later on, it was replaced by a half-year pig. Actually, a series of sacrificial rituals are held, including the family ritual, the village ritual, the road ritual, the rally ritual, the moon watching ritual, the god touring ritual, the god greeting ritual, the sing-

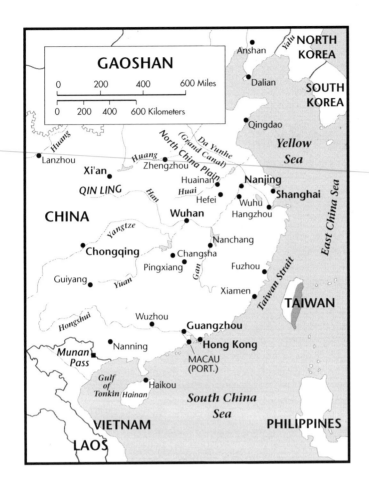

length or a deer skin. In other districts, the box is made of stone slabs, cubic in shape, and the body is put in a sitting posture with the knees flexed. In certain districts, they practice naked burial. The clothes are completely taken off and the body is wrapped with deer skin. Four relatives carry it to the mountain. They open the deer skin, put the body inside a cavern, wrap it with a few pieces of the dead person's clothes, and finally cover it with earth. They consider that the dead body does not need clothes any more, which should be offered to the soul.

⁸INTERPERSONAL RELATIONS

The Gaoshan are very hospitable. Guests are received by the host and offered not only a cup of tea, but also some bread or biscuits.

Every youngster is free to express his or her affections. For instance, the Taiyar young man conveys his feeling through whistles. Some Amei girls go to a young man's family to present a gift and to express their love-sickness. In some districts, a girl's parents build up a room for their daughter when she reaches adulthood, where she may live by herself. The young men will come to play musical instruments to express their passions. One of them will be invited to her room to talk about love. Before long, they will go hand in hand to her parents, announcing that they have decided to be life-long companions. A wedding ceremony will be held.

⁹LIVING CONDITIONS

Most Gaoshan houses have wooden structures, thatched roofs, and small square windows. The beds encircle the room. Some houses are built of stone, roofed with flags and floored with slab stones. Coastal Gaoshan double the wall thickness of their house with planks inside and cobbles on the exterior. The floor is two-to-three meters (about two-to-three yards) below the ground. This is an ingenious means devised by the Gaoshan to withstand the typhoons, which yearly hit the east coast with formidable strength.

Communications and transport are very difficult for Gaoshan inhabiting the high mountains. They throw sliding ropes, suspension bridges made of rattan and bamboo, and arch bridges, across the canyons. They live in compact communities, each consisting of 60–70 families. A large village community may accommodate 600–700 households. There is public land, a part of which may be used freely by the community members. There are also collective activities, such as sacrificial rites, hunting, fishing, and farming. Therefore, one notices hardly any difference in the living standards of the villagers of a given community.

ing and dancing ritual, etc. The ceremonies are presided over, in turn, by the headmen of the clans. On the first day of the festival, matches should not be used for lighting the stove; they are replaced by drilling wood to make a fire. Grand performances of dancing and singing are held for entertainment. The Bumper Harvest Festival is held in October, lasting for three or four days. More than 100 wine jars are placed in an open space. The ceremony is presided over by the headman of the tribe, who dips his fingers in the wine and sprinkles it to his left and right, in the air and on the earth. This is the libation for the gods and ancestors. Then all of the participants dance hand in hand while singing and drinking. The Fifth Year Festival is so named because it is held only once every five years on a selected date after the autumn harvest. For the occasion, a sacrificial rite for the ancestors is held. Participants celebrate the bumper harvest and enjoy the entertainment.

⁷RITES OF PASSAGE

A tradition handed down from the ancient Yue on the mainland requires that youngsters reaching adulthood should have one or two canine teeth extracted. This rite of passage, which also includes tattooing, is still practiced in some districts today. In other areas, lovers will each extract two incisors and exchange them as a token of their lasting affection.

The Gaoshan generally practice ground burial. In some areas, however, the body is buried inside the house beneath the bed of the deceased. They put the body inside a box made of wooden planks, which also contains half of the deceased's clothes, a dark blue cloth three meters (about one yard) in

¹⁰FAMILY LIFE

One finds patrilineal, matrilineal, and bilateral families among the Gaoshan. The Bunong and the Zou belong to a patrilineal family structure, with a man as the patriarch and only men have the right of inheritance. The Amei and the Beinan are matrilineal, with a woman as the head of the family. The pedigree follows the matrilineal line, the eldest daughter inheriting the family property and married men live with their wife's family. Families of the Paiwan are bilateral: the family property is inherited by the eldest son or eldest daughter. Therefore, the size of the family varies, 6–7 members on average, 30–40 in some cases.

The Gaoshan are monogamous. The youngsters select their spouses, but marriage of close relatives is prohibited. Young men of the Amei and a part of the Paiwan live in a public meeting place for a period of time before their marriage—until they reach adulthood.

11 CLOTHING

Gaoshan clothes are mostly made of linen and cloth. They vary in style in different areas. The men usually wear capes, vests, short garments, shorts, head wrappings, and puttees (leggings). Some of their vests are made of rind of rattan or willow. The women usually wear a short garment (with or without sleeves), trousers or skirts, an apron, and a cloth (or linen) wrapping the body and tied over the shoulder. The cloth or linen is woven and dyed by women. They like to do embroidery on their scarf, apron, sleeves, and garments. The Taiyar sew strings of shells in transverse rows on their clothes. Some of them sew strings of pearls or shells on a cloth and sell it as "pearl cloth" or "shell cloth." Women like to wear ornaments made of shell or animal bone. Men carry a bag containing a smoking set and areca for chewing. Some of them like to decorate their hair with eagle feathers. Tattooing is practiced in some districts. As for the Gaoshan living in cities, their lifestyle is hardly different from that of the Chinese.

12 FOOD

The staple foods of the Gaoshan include rice, millet, and taro. They take three meals a day, some only two. Rice is taken at breakfast and dinner. They like glutinous millet cakes. Some of them add peanuts and animal meat in glutinous millet, rolled up in leaves and steamed. The diet proteins come from pork, beef, and chicken, sometimes from wild game, which is taboo for pregnant women. The Gaoshan take roasted meat and rice in bamboo tubes and chafing dishes on festivals. They produce their own utensils, mostly potteries. Drinking and smoking are prevalent.

13 EDUCATION

Urban Gaoshan have a high level of education, while peasants in the mountainous regions have a rather low one. The Pingpu receive the same formal education as the Chinese do.

14 CULTURAL HERITAGE

The Gaoshan gather to sing and dance on festivals. Their folk songs include ancestors' songs, hunting songs, cultivating songs, and elegies. The "Pestling Song" of Gaoshan women is unique. They gather around a stone mortar while pestling the rice. The regular rhythm of their pestling sound creates a tempo of percussion, which accompanies their melodious songs.

Besides the "Drinking Dance" performed by a few dancers, the "Sacrificial Rite Dance" of both sexes and the "Hair Swinging Dance" of the girls are group dances. The "Hair Swinging Dance" is popular on Lanyu Island. Girls in rows sing a traditional song while dancing. They swing their long hair slowly in the beginning. Following the acceleration of tempo, they bend their body to touch the ground with their hair, then swiftly stretch their body to swing their hair behind their head. They dance in this way until they are exhausted.

Myths, legends, and folk songs form the main body of their literature, which was handed down orally.

15 WORK

Generally speaking, the Gaoshan mainly engage in agriculture. Those dwelling in the mountainous areas hunt as a sideline. The Amei and the Beinan hold large-scale hunting expeditions once or twice a year. Guns, arrows and crossbows, nets, and pitfalls are used. The Yamei of Lanyu Island fish and raise chickens and pigs. The main economic activity of the Paiwan is ox-raising. The Zou and Bunong, living in mountainous areas, are good at tanning hides. The Amei and the Beinan build canoes out of tree trunks, while the Yamei of Lanyu Island make a unique fishing boat with both ends rising high above the water. The Taiyar are adept at fishnet and string bag weaving, as well as at wood carving of mortar and pestle.

16 SPORTS

Spectator sports are usually held on festivals. The sports include wrestling, tug-of-war, arrow shooting, and a series of competitions related to their daily life, such as rice pestling, thatched cottage building, and weight lifting. In the rice pestling competition, a young man and girl representing the village pestle an equal amount of paddy. Those who attain the best quality in the shortest time win the match. Thatched cottages as shelter are necessary in hunting; therefore, cottage-building competitions are meaningful for young men. It begins with bamboo-strip paring and concludes when a thatched cottage is built. Time, quality, and external appearance are the main standards of evaluation. The weight lifting competition, held right after harvest, is quite exhausting. The ears of rice are tied up into two bundles (altogether 450–550 lbs) and put on the two ends of a bamboo pole. Several young men lift the pole to one shoulder of a contestant, who marches on at once. The distance the contestant can carry the load is the main criteria for determining the winner.

17 ENTERTAINMENT AND RECREATION

Movies and television are already popular and easily accessible for the Gaoshan in Taiwan. But most Gaoshan still prefer their rich fount of traditional songs and dances, in which they excel and which plays an important social function, especially on festive occasions. There are quite a few "social" games that retain their appeal for the community at large. For instance, a girl carries a basket on her back and runs ahead in twists and turns while a young man, chasing her, tries to throw areca or oranges into her basket. He who has placed the largest number of areca or oranges inside the basket within the prescribed time is declared the winner. Flower crown weaving is a game for girls. They must weave the most beautiful flower crowns during a given time. The crowns are offered as gifts to the spectators.

18 FOLK ART, CRAFTS, AND HOBBIES

The Gaoshan, especially the Paiwan, excel at painting and carving. The columns, thresholds, wall planks, and lintels of their house, daily-used artifacts and ornaments, implements and canoes, are frequently adorned with painting or carving of personages, animals, flowers, figurines, and geometric designs. They like to engrave the image of snakes with human heads. Articles made of bamboo and rattan, such as baskets, hats, vests, or suits of armor, are solid and artistically made.

Chiu Ku and A Pei-lung of the Gaoshan tribe play together as they wear traditional Gaoshan costumes and crowns made of millet and leaves during an aborigines harvest festival, Taipei, Taiwan. Taiwan's aborigines represent nearly 2% of the population and are divided in ten main tribes. (AP Images/Jerome Favre)

¹⁹ SOCIAL PROBLEMS

The different Gaoshan groups have profited in a very unequal manner from the tremendous economic development of Taiwan: Those residing in the plains near the cities (Suao, Hua-Lien, Pingtung, Kaohsiung, Taichung, etc.) have experienced unprecedented economic development, while those inhabiting high mountainous areas or barren coastal areas have become relatively poor (in terms of purchasing power). Although attempts have been made to improve the education of the Gaoshan, no effective school system has been set up, especially for the poorer and more disadvantaged Gaoshan groups.

²⁰ GENDER ISSUES

The Chinese constitution states that women have equal rights with men in all areas of life, and most legislation is gender neutral. However, there are continued reports of discrimination, sexual harassment, wage discrepancies, and other gender related problems. While the nationwide gap in educational level between women and men is narrowing (with women making up 47.1% of college students in 2005, but only 32.6% of doctoral students), the Gaoshan have not participated significantly in higher education.

China has strict family planning laws. It is illegal for women to marry before 20 years of age (22 for men), and it is illegal for single women to give birth. The Family Planning Bureau can require women to take periodic pregnancy tests and enforce laws that often leave women with no real options other than abortion or sterilization. While minority populations were previously exempt from family planning regulations, policy has changed in recent years to limit minority population growth. As of 2008 minority couples living in urban areas may have two children, while minority couples living in rural areas are permitted three or four children.

²¹ BIBLIOGRAPHY

Alvarez, Jose Maria. *The Aboriginal Inhabitants of Formosa*. St. Gabriel-Modling bei Wien: Anthropos, 1927.

Chiao, Chien, Nicholas Tapp, and Kam-yin Ho, ed. "Special Issue on Ethnic Groups in China." *New Asia Bulletin* no 8 (1989).

Dreyer, June Teufel. *China's Forty Millions*. Cambridge: Harvard University Press, 1976.

Eberhard, Wolfram. *China's Minorities: Yesterday and Today*. Belmont: Wadsworth Publishing Company, 1982.

Ferrell, Raleigh. *Taiwan Aboriginal Groups: Problems in Cultural and Linguistic Classification*. Nakang, Taipei: Institute of Ethnology, Academia Sinica, 1969.

Gustafsson, Bjorn A., Shi, Li, and Sicular, Terry, eds. *Inequality and Public Policy in China*. New York: Cambridge University Press, 2008.

Heberer, Thomas. *China and Its National Minorities: Autonomy or Assimilation?* Armonk, N.Y.: M. E. Sharpe, 1989.

Lebar, Frank, et al. *Ethnic Groups of Mainland Southeast Asia.* New Haven: Human Relations Area Files Press, 1964.

Ramsey, S. Robert. *The Languages of China.* Princeton: Princeton University Press, 1987.

Ruey, Yifu. "The Ethnic Groups of Taiwan." In *China: The Nation and Some Aspects of Its Culture,* vol. II. Taipei: Yi Wen, 1972.

Schwarz, Henry G. *The Minorities of Northern China: A Survey.* Bellingham, Wash.: Western Washington University Press, 1989.

Shepherd, John R. "Plains Aborigines and Chinese Settlers on the Taiwan Frontier in the Seventeenth and Eighteenth Centuries." Thesis (Ph. D.)—Stanford University.

Shin, Leo Kwok-yueh. The Making of the Chinese State: Ethnicity and Expansion on the Ming Borderlands. New York: Cambridge University Press, 2006.

Wiens, Harold J. *Han Chinese Expansion in South China.* New Haven: The Shoestring Press, 1967.

Xu, Muzhu. *Culture, Self, and Adaptation: the Psychological Anthropology of Two Malayo-Polynesian Groups in Taiwan.* Taipei: Institute of Ethnology, Academia Sinica, 1991.

Zhai, Zhengang. *Taiwan Aborigines: A Genetic Study of Tribal Variations.* Cambridge: Harvard University Press, 1967.

—by C. Le Blanc

GOANS

PRONUNCIATION: GO-uhns
LOCATION: India (Goa state)
POPULATION: 1,343,998 (Census of India, 2001)
LANGUAGE: Konkani; Marathi; some English and Portuguese
RELIGION: Hindu; Christian; small numbers of Muslims
RELATED ARTICLES: Vol. 4: People of India

¹ INTRODUCTION

Goans are the inhabitants of the former Portuguese territory of Goa, which is located on the west coast of India some 400 km (250 mi) south of Bombay (Mumbai). Although Goa is now an Indian state, Goan culture and religion reflect nearly five hundred years of Portuguese influence.

Goa is mentioned in the *Mahâbhârata* epic, and the *Purânas* refer to it as Govapuri, "the Paradise of India." During the third century BC, Goa formed part of the Mauryan Empire. After the decline of the Mauryans, the area was ruled by a series of Hindu dynasties that arose in west central India. The most notable of these were the Satvahanas, the Chalukyas, and the Kadambas. Goa was held briefly by the Muslims during the fourteenth century before it was incorporated into the Vijayanagara Kingdom. The Muslims reconquered Goa in 1469, but in turn they were ousted by the Portuguese under Afonso de Albuquerque in 1510. Goa was the first Portuguese territory in Asia and remained under Portuguese control for the next four and a half centuries. Its natural harbors and location on the shipping routes to the Far East gave it great strategic significance for the Portuguese. Goa eventually became the capital of all the Portuguese territories in Asia.

After Britain's departure from India in 1947, Portugal came under increasing pressure to cede Goa and its other territories on the subcontinent to India. The matter was resolved in 1961, when India's armed forces invaded and "liberated" Goa, Daman, and Diu. Goa was a Union Territory administered by the central government until 1987, when it became a state of the Indian Union.

² LOCATION AND HOMELAND

Goa's population is currently estimated to be just under 1.5 million persons (the 2001 census reported a population of 1.34 million). Sizable emigrant populations of Goans are found in Bombay and also overseas in the Gulf States, Britain, and North America (particularly in Toronto, Canada).

The ethnic makeup of Goans reflects the many peoples that have contributed to the population of the Konkan (the coastal region between Bombay and Mangalore). These include Proto-Australoid tribal groups, Dravidian speakers, and, later, Indo-Aryan peoples. Of particular significance over the last 500 years has been the Portuguese presence in the region. The Portuguese encouraged intermarriage of settlers with local women, and today Fernandes, Pereira, Gomes, and de Souza are common family names in Goa.

Goa is one of India's smallest states with an area, of only 3,702 sq km (1,429 sq mi) and ranks as 4th smallest in terms of population, behind Sikkim, Mizoram, and Arunachal Pradesh. The original Portuguese colony was centered on the estuaries of the Mandavi and Juari Rivers, and today Goa's capital, Panaji, is located on the south bank of the Mandavi. The modern state has 100 km (62 mi) of coast, lined with coconut palms and sandy beaches, along the Arabian Sea. Inland, the coastal plain gives way to rolling hills before rising to the peaks of the Western Ghats. These mountains reach an elevation of 1,034 m (3,393 ft) in the area of the Sahyadri Hills.

The climate is hot and humid. Annual rainfall varies from 240 cm (about 94 in) on the coast to over 400 cm (157 in) in the Ghats, which receive the full force of the summer monsoon. Temperatures average close to 26°C (79°F) through much of the year.

3 LANGUAGE

Hindus and the majority of Goan Christians speak Konkani, the language of the Konkan region. Many also know Marathi, which is commonly used for correspondence. Although Konkani is the state's only official language, Marathi can also be used for any official purpose. Both Konkani (which has borrowed words from Portuguese) and Marathi belong to the Indo-Aryan language family and are written in the Devanagari script. When Christians write Konkani, however, they use the Roman alphabet. Many Goan Christians speak English, and members of the older generation of Goans may also speak Portuguese.

4 FOLKLORE

Goan proverbs, songs, dance-music and folktales hold the key to the social history of pre-Portuguese Goa. Perhaps the most honored of all artisans in Goa are the goldsmiths. The belief in Goa was that the metal was a representation of the Sun and that the yellow metal also had therapeutic properties. In pre-Portuguese Goa, Brahmans, goldsmiths, and merchants were exempted from being flogged even if they had committed heinous crimes. It is small wonder then that the goldsmiths of Goa became the butt of jokes in Goan folklore. Despite the honor and the ridicule accorded to the village goldsmith, it was simple jasmine flowers that came to be seen as a Goan girl's best friend. Mardol village in North Goa is supposed to be famed for its supply of fresh jasmines. In a folk song from this region a dancer says to her Lord, "I shall buy flowers in profusion, I shall deck my hair with them. I shall sit in front of my Lord. Yes, I shall sit."

In another story titled *The Girl in the Straw Hat*, a poor girl is on her way from her wealthy husband's house to her grandmother's when she is accosted by three water nymphs who give her a grain of rice each. "Throw this grain of rice on your grandmother's hut and it will turn into a palace," says the forest water nymph. "Throw this grain into your grandmother's room and it will be filled with riches," says the second water nymph. "Throw this grain of rice in the kitchen and it will be filled with a hundred servants," says the third. This is a symbolic illustration demonstrating to the young girls of pre-Portuguese Goa that a good harvest is the only key to a wealthy and prosperous home.

Although Goa has its own folk traditions, it is better known throughout the Roman Catholic world for a historical personage who has attained almost legendary status, St. Francis Xavier. His tomb is in the Basilica of Bom Jesus in Old Goa. A pupil of Ignatius Loyola, who founded the Jesuit Order, Francis Xavier arrived in Goa in 1542 to begin his missionary work in Asia. After several years in India, he traveled to the Moluccas (now in Indonesia) and to Japan to spread the Christian faith.

He fell ill and died on the return journey and was buried in the Moluccas. Later, when his successor opened the grave to pay his respects, the body was still fresh and lifelike. Francis Xavier's remains were sent to Goa, where he was elevated to sainthood, and the body was placed in the Basilica of Bom Jesus. Parts of the body have been removed and sent to Rome and other places for use as relics. It is said that a Portuguese woman who wanted a relic of the saint bit off one toe in 1554. The body of St. Francis is taken out in procession every ten years, the last time being in 2004. An annual festival is also held in Old Goa every December 3, the anniversary of St. Francis's death in 1552.

5 RELIGION

Goans are mostly Hindu (about 66% of the population) and Christian (27%) and there are a small number of Muslims (under 7%). Whatever their religion, Goans tend to be orthodox in their beliefs.

Goan Christians are Roman Catholics, like their Portuguese conquerors. The Inquisition vigorously stamped out any of the older "heathen" customs that converts tried to bring into their new religion. Like all Catholics, Goans believe in the divinity of Jesus Christ, worship Mary as the mother of God, and revere the Christian saints. They worship in churches and attend confession and Mass. The many churches and cathedrals of Goa, some active today but many now abandoned, bear witness to the piety of the Portuguese and their subjects in the past.

The Hindus are largely followers of Shiva, although they show the characteristic diversity of beliefs and practices identified with Hindu peoples.

6 MAJOR HOLIDAYS

Goan Hindus observe all the major Hindu festivals, but perhaps the most important for them is Ganesha Chaturthi, the birthday of the god Ganesha. Known in Goa as Chovoth, this festival can last up to nine days, and it is a time for worshipping Ganapati (Ganesha) and his parents Mahadev (Shiva) and Gauri (Parvati). Shigmo is the Goan counterpart of the Holi festival.

The Christian community celebrates Christmas, Good Friday and Easter, and the feast days of various saints. Carnival (the equivalent of Mardi Gras) is an important Christian festival held just before Lent. The first day, Sabado Gordo or Fat Saturday, is marked by a parade of floats in Panaji, headed by the character King Momo. People dress in costumes, wear masks, and indulge in three days of revelry and excitement. The Procession of the Saints, when images of twenty-six saints are carried through the streets, is held in Old Goa on the first Monday of Easter week. The Feast of St. Francis Xavier, the patron saint of Goa, is celebrated every year on December 3.

Muslims, as elsewhere in India, keep the festivals of Muharram, 'Id ul-Fitr, and 'Id ul-'Adha'.

7 RITES OF PASSAGE

Certain social customs appear to be observed by all Goans, whatever their religious community. It is not unusual, for example, for a Christian woman to be sent to her mother's home for the delivery of her first child. This practice is widespread among Hindus in India. Similarly, Christians announce the birth of a child with firecrackers—two for a girl, three for a boy—as do Hindus. In their rites of passage, however, Goans follow the rituals prescribed by their respective religions. These include baptism, the first Holy Communion, and confirmation for Christians; various *samskaras* (e.g. the naming ceremony, the head-shaving ceremony) for Hindus; and birth ceremonies and circumcision for Muslims.

At the time of death, Christians are given the last rites, a funeral service is held in the local church, and the deceased is buried in the cemetery. Masses are held periodically for the soul of the departed. Hindus cremate their dead, except for the Gavli (milkman) caste, who claim to be Lingayats and bury their dead in a sitting position. Their funeral customs conform to those of other Konkani Hindus, with a period of mourning, a *sraddha* ceremony, and the offering of food and gifts to Brahman priests. Muslims bury their dead with rites similar to those of other Muslims in South Asia.

8 INTERPERSONAL RELATIONS

Hindus use the "*Namaste*" to greet each other while Christians, especially in the better-educated upper castes, follow the custom of shaking hands when meeting. In general, social relations are determined by caste status. Even among Christians, who are more flexible in such matters, the upper castes tend to keep the lower castes at a distance.

9 LIVING CONDITIONS

Living conditions in Goa vary according to locale, caste, and economic status. The old parts of towns such as Panaji preserve much of their Portuguese character, with narrow winding streets, white-washed houses with overhanging balconies, and red-tiled roofs. Wealthy Christian landlords of upper-caste standing have spacious one-story mansions, with antique furniture, mirrors, and European-style chandeliers, and sometimes even a private chapel. The walls of their houses are often tiled, a typically Portuguese custom. By contrast, houses of lower-caste villagers, whether Hindu or Christian, are likely to be much more modest, built of mud with thatched roofs, and more sparsely furnished.

10 FAMILY LIFE

Goan Christian society has a caste system very much like its Hindu counterpart. The high-caste Christians are the *Bamonn* (converts originally from the *Brahmans*), the *Chaddhe* (*Ksatriyas*), and the *Gaude* (*banias*). The Christian equivalent of the *sudras* or artisan castes are the *Sudir*, while Christians of aboriginal heritage are called *Kunbis* or *Gaudas*. Christians, just like Hindus, are required to marry within their own caste. A *Bamonn* will marry another *Bamonn*, a *Chaddho* (singular of *Chaddhe*) will marry another *Chaddho*, and so on. Marriages are not arranged; most young men and women select their own partners. Once a suitable match has been found, however, details of the marriage proposal, acceptance of the proposal, negotiation of the dowry, and so forth are left to the families. Marriages are performed in church according to the Catholic rites. The ceremony is usually followed by a Western-style reception and dance. Newlywed couples may live with the groom's father although the joint family is increasingly giving way to the nuclear family structure.

Goan Hindus and Muslims follow the traditions of their own communities.

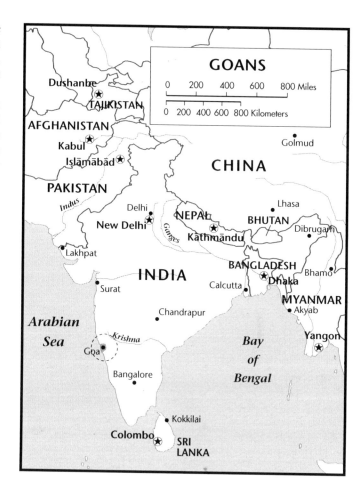

11 CLOTHING

Christians dress in Western clothes, with men donning pants and shirts for everyday wear and dark suits and ties for formal occasions. Women wear blouses and skirts or dresses, but for special occasions they use the elegant Indian *sari* or long formal gowns. Young girls keep up with the latest in Western fashion. Only Christian women of the laboring classes wear the sari as their usual clothing. Hindus wear clothes similar to those of their neighbors in Maharashtra. For men, this is the *dhoti*, or loincloth and shirt. Most men do not wear hats, but some members of the older generation still wear "Gandhi caps," the type of folding cap that Mahatma Gandhi made popular earlier in this century. Many men have adopted the Western-style pants and shirt. Hindu women wear the typical dress of the Konkan—the short-sleeved bodice or blouse (*choli*) and a sari tied in the Maharashtrian fashion (pleats tucked in at the back of the waist, and the end of the cloth drawn under the right arm, across the chest, and over the shoulder). Both men and women seem to enjoy wearing jewelry and ornaments.

12 FOOD

The staple food of Goans, both Catholics and Hindus, is fish. A typical lunch consists of a prawn or fish curry eaten with rice. The meal is often accompanied by fried fish or shrimp and green vegetables. However, the similarities end there. The Hindu diet appears to have been little influenced by the European tastes, while the food of Catholics shows a strong Portuguese influence. Catholics eat both beef and pork, which are taboo

Dancers from Goa perform during the annual Goa carnival celebrations in Panaji, India. (AP Images/Str)

in most Hindu households. Pork *vindalho* (a type of spicy pork curry) is a typical Christian Goan dish and *sarapatel* is considered a Goan classic. It is thought to be derived from two Portuguese dishes, *sarrabulhada* (a pork stew) and *cabidel* (pork giblets). Another Goan specialty is *chouriço,* or pork sausage. *Sanna* are rice cakes that are soaked in palm toddy (liquor made from the fermented sap of palm trees) before cooking. Prawn *balchao* is a type of spicy prawn condiment that may have originated in Southeast Asia. Goans brew a liquor called *feni* from cashew nuts or coconuts. Christians drink alcohol at their social gatherings.

13 EDUCATION

The literacy rate among Goans seven years and older stands at 82% (as of 2001). The figures for males and females are 88% and 76%, respectively. This rate is second only to Kerala and Mizoram among all the Indian states. There are many private schools in Goa, many of them affiliated with the Catholic Church. Most of them hold their classes in the English language. The benefits of education are apparent to even the lower-caste villagers, who enroll their children in free, government-run primary schools. English and Konkani are the languages of instruction, and Marathi is sometimes being taught as a third language. Most students in Goa, however, complete their high school using English as the medium of instruction. Primary schools, on the other hand are largely run in Konkani. As is the case in most of India, enrollment for vernacular media has seen a fall in numbers in favor of English medium education.

Goa University is the sole university in the state located in Taleigao and all Goan colleges are affiliated with it The state of Goa contains four engineering colleges and one medical college. In 2004 BITS Pilani university (the Birla Institute of Technology and Science is located in Pilani in Rajasthan and consistently ranks among the top 5 engineering schools in the country) started its first Indian satellite, BITS Pilani Goa Campus near Dabolim. Unlike other Goan institutes, BITS Goa admits students through a nation-wide aptitude test that it shares with its parent institute. Because of this BITS Pilani Goa Campus is the only college in the state to have a regionally mixed student body.

There are also two national oceanographic science-related centers in Goa, the National Centre for Antarctic and Ocean Research (NCAOR) and the National Institute of Oceanography (NIO), located in Vasco and Punjim, respectively.

14 CULTURAL HERITAGE

Portuguese heritage is seen in religion, architecture, place names, language, food, and many other aspects of Goan life and culture. There is often a blending of the European and the Indian in Goa. Christians, for example, have borrowed the caste structure of Hindu society. On the other hand, Carnival has become a Goan celebration rather than a specifically Christian religious festival. There is a body of historical literature in Konkani, the local Indian language, but it is mainly of Christian inspiration and is written in the Roman alphabet—a practice introduced by the Portuguese. Even though Konkani is not one of the languages recognized in the Indian constitution, it has the status of a modern literary language in India. Although Goans never developed any classical forms of dance or music, there are many local traditions of folk music and dance-drama. *Mando*—not quite a waltz and not quite a Portuguese *fado* (popular romantic song) but with elements of both—is a dance popular among Goan Christians. The *Khel* is a form of folk-drama that entertains villagers through criticism and caricature of socially prominent people such as the village landlord. Hindus have their own repertoire of Konkani folk songs and dances.

15 WORK

Agriculture continues to be the main activity of Goans. Christians are involved in cultivation, but they are also found in a wide range of other occupations: office workers, government employees, accountants, hotel workers, and the tourist industry. Some Goans are engaged as cooks and crewmen on ships. Many Goans work abroad, and the money they send back to their families helps to raise the standard of living of many people.

In addition to the tourist industry, Goa is developing as a center of the high-tech industry. It has been selected by the Union government to be the location of a high-tech park, no doubt based on making use of the educational facilities found in the state. The Info Tech Corporation of Goa Ltd. is setting up the software park on 75 acres of land at Dona Paula, about 30 kilometers from the Goa Airport and about 8 kilometers from the capital, Panaji. The Hi-Tech Habitat is proposed to be a modern, state-of-the-art and high quality IT software park and services unit with necessary infrastructure including roads, services, satellite connectivity, captive power supply, "plug and play" facilities, Internet cafeteria, health and recreational center, and landscaping. It will also have a conference center.

16 SPORTS

Young boys play with toys such as rattles, pipes, and whistles, while girls have their dolls. As they grow up, children play tag, hide-and-seek, and similar games. *Kaji* is a popular game in which boys line up cashew nuts (*kaju*) and try and hit them from a distance with a heavier cashew nut. Team games include *kabaddi* (wrestling) and *khokho* (team tag). Modern sports such as cricket, field hockey, and basketball are played, but soccer is by far the most popular sport.

17 ENTERTAINMENT AND RECREATION

Modern entertainment in Goa includes movies, radio, and television. Goan Christians have followed Western trends in music, and some have their own rock bands. Many of the hotels have modern discos for tourists. In the villages, however, recreation still centers around festivals and folk traditions.

18 FOLK ARTS, CRAFTS, AND HOBBIES

The main handicrafts of Goa are pottery making, wood carving, and making lacquer ware and brass articles. Goan artisans are also skilled in ivory carving and silver work. A government-run store has been set up in Panaji to promote the sale of local handicrafts.

19 SOCIAL PROBLEMS

With its blend of Portuguese and Indian culture, Goa is unique among the states of India. While many Goans would have preferred to remain independent in the post-colonial era, it was always likely that India would eventually annex Goa. Liberation in 1961 brought many Hindus to Goa from nearby areas. Goa's relatively small size and population help keep to a minimum some of the social and economic problems that are found in other parts of India. Many Goans have left to pursue opportunities in other places, but they continue to send money back to their families. Goa is an important tourist center, and this not only brings in the tourist dollar, but also provides jobs for the local people. During the 1960s Goa's magnificent beaches were a magnet for the hippie generation from the West. While this era is long gone, drugs (although illegal) are still readily available and something of a problem.

Tourism is still a big part of Goa's economy, but often brings increased levels of crime, prostitution, and drug use into local communities, negatively influencing local cultural norms. For instance, in March 2008 the Minister of Tourism in Goa accused local Indian police of trying to cover up the murder of a British girl. Scarlett Keeling was found dead on a beach in Goa in February 2008. Police initially said she had died after drinking too much and a local man, Samson D'Souza, was charged with rape but not with murder. The statement by the government official was made after the dead girl's mother pressed the issue, the cover-up clearly being an attempt not to impact tourism negatively. Goa's indigenous culture is deeply conservative. But many Westerners think India's poverty and tolerance of outsiders frees them to behave in a way that would be tasteless in London, let alone elsewhere in the developing world. The Times of India said 126 foreigners have died in Goa over the last two years—many from drug overdoses—while Western women have been attacked, sexually assaulted, and even murdered. Goa is also a Mecca for pedophiles with an emerging, though unwelcome, reputation as a center for child sex tourism.

Goa's BJP government is said to be the most corrupt in a long time—corrupt but effective. "Better to have a corrupt government that gets things done than a corrupt one which does nothing," was a philosophical Goan's observation. Talk has it that key figures in the opposition Congress party, too, have been bought off. A construction boom is underway in Goa and where there is construction and developers, payoffs are inevitable, at least in India. Apparently, the amount that developers have to pay to the concerned ministry has also been fine-tuned. India's National Security Council also claims that the Russian mafia, which is heavily involved in drugs and prostitution, is laundering money by investing in real estate in Goa.

20 GENDER ISSUES

The Christian Anglo-Indians of Goa are regarded as "loose" by many Indians, largely because of their Westernized lifestyle However, ever since the neighboring state of Maharashtra closed its "dance-bars" in early 2005 because they were viewed as a breeding ground for crime and prostitution, there has been a migration of women (mostly Hindu) from Bombay (Mumbai) to Goa where they work in the vice trade.

In May 2005 a national conference on women's issues was held in Goa attended by some 400 registered participants. This reported that rather than being "victims" of the technological development that has focused on fisheries, many Goan Catholic fisherwomen, in contrast to their Hindu counterparts, have made an economically successful transition from "barefoot, headload peddlers" in the villages to market entrepreneurs. However, the Kharvi caste of fishers (the women do the fishing) have not made the transition so successfully. Though their average working hours are very high, the returns are insignificant. They lament that they "have lost their hold over their traditional occupation." Surprisingly, this closely knit and vociferous community of fisherwomen has neither institutionalized itself nor claimed minority rights, although the Kharvi are classed as a "backward" Hindu caste.

Christian Goanese women are generally freer than their non-Christian counter-parts, Hindus and Muslims usually being subject to the restraints of their religions. Given the relatively high rates of literacy and excellent educational system, the main issues for women in Goa arise out of poverty, limited access to health care and traditional cultural values.

21 BIBLIOGRAPHY

Gomes, Olivinho J. F. *Goa*. New Delhi: National Book Trust, 2004.

———. *Village Goa: A Study of Goan Social Structure and Change*. New Delhi: S. Chand, 1987.

Gune, V. T., ed. *Gazetteer of the Union Territory: Goa, Daman and Diu. District Gazetteer Part 1: Goa*. Panaji, Goa: Gazetteer Department, Government of the Union Territory of Goa, Daman and Diu, 1979.

Richards, James Maude. *Goa*. New Delhi: Vikas, 1982.

Phal, S. S. *Society in Goa: Some Aspects of Tradition and Modern Trends*. Delhi: B. R. Publishing, 1982.

Rodrigues, Maria de Lourdes Bravo da Costa. *Feasts, Festivals, and Observance of Goa*. Tiswadi, Goa: L. & L Publications, 2004.

School Education in Goa: Status, Issues, and Future Perspectives. New Delhi: National Council of Educational Research and Training, 2004.

—by D. O. Lodrick

GONDS

PRONUNCIATION: GAHNDS
ALTERNATE NAMES: Koi; Koitur
LOCATION: India
POPULATION: About 14 million
LANGUAGE: Gondi
RELIGION: Cult of the Persa Pen (clan deities); ancestor spirit worship
RELATED ARTICLES: Vol. 4: People of India

1 INTRODUCTION

The Gonds are numerically the most important tribe in South Asia. Strictly speaking, the term Gond is a generic one that refers to numerous tribal peoples who are found over wide areas of the interior of the Deccan peninsula of India. While they are by no means all alike, there is a limited measure of cultural uniformity among these groups. Most significantly, they all describe themselves as Gonds or, in the local Gondi dialects, as Koi or Koitur. The meaning of the latter names is uncertain. It was the Mughals who first used the name "Gond" (hill people) to describe the peoples of the area. Gonds have lent their name to Gondwana ("the Land of the Gonds"), the part of India in which they live. They are found over almost all of India except the northwestern states (Rajasthan, Haryana, Punjab and Jammu and Kashmir) and the extreme south, but have their greatest concentrations in the rugged hill country of central India.

Little is known about the origins of the Gonds. They belong to the strata of aboriginal peoples of India who pre-date the Aryan and Dravidian speakers of the country. They are usually classified as Proto-Australoids by race. As their language is Dravidian, the Gonds may have passed through lands to the south where the Dravidian languages are found. DNA evidence suggests they might have branched off from early Proto-Australoids who apparently traveled from Africa to Australia along the coastal margins of India. But Gond migrations before they reached their present homeland remain shrouded in the mists of time. Scholars believe that the Gonds settled in Gondwana between the 9th and 13th centuries AD. The core region of Gondwana can be considered to be the eastern part of the Vidarbha region of Maharashtra, the parts of Madhya Pradesh immediately to the north of it, and parts of the west of Chhattisgar. From the 14th century onwards, Gond history comes into focus with Muslim writers describing the rise of Gond states in the region. Between the 16th and mid-18th centuries, when Gonds were at the height of their power, Gond dynasties ruled in four kingdoms (Garha-Mandla, Deogarh, Chanda, and Kherla) in central India.

Following the 1740s, the rising tide of Maratha power swept over the Gonds. The Gond *rajas* were overthrown and their territory annexed, except for some of the more remote hill areas that held out against the invaders. Local Gond *zamindaris* or estates survived in the region until relatively recent times.

The recent creation of two new states in central India, Chhattisgarh and Jharkhand, has increased the relative proportions of Gonds, who are classified as Scheduled Tribes in both states, in the population. Thus, in Chhattisgarh, which was formed in 2000 from sixteen Chhattisgarhi-speaking districts in southeastern Madhya Pradesh, Gonds number over 4 million people, of the current estimated state total population of c. 24 million people. They are concentrated in the south, especially in Bastar district, where they account for more than 20% of the district's total population. Jharkhand, created in 2000 from the southern areas of Bihar largely to fulfill the aspirations of its tribal populations (c. 89% of the total state's population), also contains a considerable number of Gonds among its estimated 40 million people.

2 LOCATION AND HOMELAND

The Gonds form the largest tribal group in the Indian subcontinent and perhaps even in the entire world. The Census of India 2001 did not enumerate caste, so the population figure should be regarded as approximate, since many Gond communities have become Hinduized and are no longer counted as Gonds. Nonetheless, even using conservative estimates of growth rates, the Gond population in India must exceed14 million today.

Gonds are found over a wide area of central India. Gondwana, their traditional homeland, lies in the eastern part of the state of Madhya Pradesh and western Chhattisgarh, though large Gond populations are also found in Maharashtra and Orissa States. Gond territory lies south and east of the upper reaches of the Narmada and Son rivers and extends to the Godavari River and the Madhya Pradesh–Orissa border. Within this area, there are numerous tribal communities who are designated as Gonds. Madhya Pradesh classifies over 50 Gond groups as belonging to the Scheduled Tribes (communities in India identified as needing special social and economic assistance). A similar number of Gond groups in Maharashtra are designated as Scheduled Tribes. By contrast, there are Gond groups such as the Raj Gonds and the Katholias who claim high social standing and have substantial land holdings. The Dhur Gond, Bisonhorn Maria (so-called because of their distinctive horned headdress worn for dancing), the Muria Gond, and the Paharia Gonds are some of the Gond groups found in the region.

As might be expected with Gond tribes dispersed over so wide an area, the environmental setting in which they live varies greatly. Yet their characterization as "hill people" identifies one of their underlying traits, namely their traditional association with the hills and uplands of the Peninsula's interior. The densest concentrations of Gonds are found in the eastern ranges of the Satpura Hills, the Maikala Range, and the Son-Deogarh uplands. South of this line of hills, the Gond population thins out in the Waiganga Valley and the Chhattisgarh plain. As one continues south, however, the highly dissected plateau of Bastar forms another stronghold of the Gond tribes. A distinct cluster of Gond tribes, somewhat isolated from the main Gond distributions, occurs in the Garhjat Hills of northern Orissa. The upland areas generally lie between 600 and 900 m (roughly 2,000-3,000 ft), with isolated peaks occasionally exceeding 1,200 m (approximately 4,000 ft). The region is drained by the headwaters of many of India's major rivers (e.g., the Narmada, Tapti, Son, Mahanadi, and Godavari). Forest cover is dense in places, and communications are generally difficult. The climate is typical of the northern interior Deccan. February sees the start of the hot season, with temperatures rising to over 40°c (104°f) in early June. The summer brings the monsoon rains, with precipitation amounts varying from 120 cm (47 in) to over 160 cm (63 in) in the more southeaster-

ly locations. Late September marks the return of the cool, dry weather of winter.

3 LANGUAGE

Gondi is the mother tongue of the Gonds. It belongs to the Dravidian family of languages and is closely related to Tamil and Kannada. Clearly, the Gonds are not physically related to the Dravidian-speaking peoples of India, thus at some time they must have abandoned an earlier language in favor of Gondi. There is, however, no evidence of what this language might have been. It is the Gondi language, as much as anything else, that lends a sense of cultural uniformity to the diverse tribal groups that make up the Gonds. Even so, many Gonds are bilingual or trilingual, speaking Hindi, Marathi, or Telegu as well as their mother tongue. Some Gond groups have totally abandoned Gondi and speak the language or dialect common in their locality.

4 FOLKLORE

Gond myths and legends are preserved by hereditary bards and professional storytellers called Pardhans. All Gond traditions are oral and, consequently, numerous variations of the same tales are recounted. Yet it is in mythology and the deeds of Gond heroes that the social norms of Gond society are rooted.

According to the Gond creation myth, when the Gond gods were born they were abandoned by their mother. The goddess Parvati rescued them, but her consort Sri Shambhu Mahadeo (Shiva) imprisoned them in a primeval cave. They were rescued from the cave by the Gond culture hero Pahandi Kapar Lingal, with the assistance of the goddess Jangu Bai. When released from captivity, they came out of the cave in four groups, thus laying the foundations of the basic fourfold division of Gond society. Lingal is also held to be responsible for the creation of the Gond kinship system, as well as the establishment of the great gods (Persa Pen) who were to be worshiped by the Gonds.

5 RELIGION

The most distinctive feature of Gond religion is the cult of the Persa Pen, or the clan deities. Like many other tribes in the region, Gonds worship a high god known as Baradeo, or Bhagavan, or Sri Shambu Mahadeo (known sometimes, rather confusingly, as Persa Pen). Baradeo is the Supreme Being, creator of the universe and giver of life and death, but he is rather remote. He oversees the activities of the lesser gods and he is to be respected and worshiped, but he does not receive the fervent devotion reserved for the clan deities. Each Gond clan has its Persa Pen, who extends its protection to all clan members in return for their ritual offerings and worship. The Persa Pen is essentially good but can be dangerous and violent. Many Gonds believe that the play of the Pardhan bard on his fiddle is necessary to control the deity's fierce powers.

In addition to Baradeo and the clan deities, the Gond world is populated by numerous other deities and spirits that are to be worshiped at the appropriate time. Each village has its Village-Guardian and Village-Mother who must be worshiped whenever the village community embarks on ritual activities, such as a seasonal celebration or a sacrifice. There are family gods and household gods to be propitiated. Gods of the field and gods of cattle must receive their offerings to ensure a productive harvest. Disease must be warded off by appeasing dei-

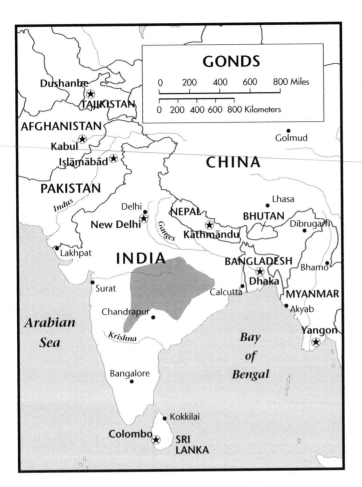

GONDS

0   200   400   600   800 Miles

0 200 400 600 800 Kilometers

Dushanbe

TAJIKISTAN

AFGHANISTAN

Kabul

Islamabad

PAKISTAN

Golmud

CHINA

Indus

Delhi

New Delhi

NEPAL

Lhasa

Kathmandu

BHUTAN

Dibrugarh

Lakhpat

INDIA

Ganges

Surat

BANGLADESH

Dhaka

Bhamo

Chandrapur

Calcutta

MYANMAR

Arabian
Sea

Krishna

Akyab

Bay
of
Bengal

Yangon

Bangalore

Kokkilai

Colombo

SRI
LANKA

While the village and clan priests perform sacrifices, diviners and magicians deal with the supernatural in another way. Gonds believe that most diseases and misfortunes in life are caused by evil spirits and the displeasure of the gods. They turn to soothsayers and diviners to find out the cause of their problems and the appropriate remedies to be taken. If these practitioners cannot help, the services of magicians and shamans must be sought. Magicians believe that through magic formulas they can control the actions of the deity or spirit who is the cause of a particular affliction. Shamans are individuals who fall into a trance and give voice to the demands of the offended god or spirit. Like many tribes in the area, Gonds believe in the evil eye, black magic, and witchcraft. Witches, usually women, are held to bring sickness and misfortune to the community. They are widely feared and, when discovered, are driven from the village or even killed.

6 MAJOR HOLIDAYS

The details of the Gond festival calendar varies from region to region but, as might be expected of agricultural peoples, many of the important celebrations are connected with the agricultural seasons. Some Hindu festivals, such as Holi, Dasahara, and Divali, are celebrated, though often the Gonds have no real understanding of the significance of these feasts. The Gonds, however, have their own explanation for their observance and celebrate the feasts in the Gond manner, complete with sacrifices. Pola, a cattle festival, and Nagpanchami, the snake festival, are celebrated by the Gonds along with the other peoples of the area.

Some festivals, such as the feasts of village or clan deities, are specifically Gond celebrations. One particular custom is the Dandari stick dancing undertaken by young people in the two or three weeks following Dasahara. Bands of young people, dressed in their newest and best attire, travel from village to village entertaining the inhabitants with dancing, music, and singing. In doing so, they are perpetuating a custom initiated by the legendary heroes of the Gond epics. The dancing is seen as a religious duty as much as an occasion for fun and entertainment.

7 RITES OF PASSAGE

Pregnant women are subject to certain taboos as a protection against magic spells and evil influences. Various rituals, including sacrifice to the household gods, are performed after birth. The baby is named after three to four weeks, with the name-giver usually being the mother's brother for a boy, or the father's sister for a girl. Although sons are preferred, daughters are equally welcomed. There is little to mark the passage from childhood to maturity. Children grow up as part of a family, clan, phratry (one of the four main divisions of Gond society), and village community and gradually learn the ways of their people. At a certain age, they begin to assume some responsibility for household and agricultural chores. Both boys and girls help guard their family's crops from birds and monkeys. Males undergo a ritual shaving of the beard, mustache, and eyebrows as a sign of adulthood, although many boys undergo the rite long before they reach puberty. There is no comparable rite for girls, but a girl is considered full-grown at her first menstruation. Only the Muria Gonds of Bastar have youth dormitories (ghotul) that are used for the education of youth in married and civic life.

ties such as Shitala Mata, Goddess of Smallpox. Every hill, every river, every lake, every tree is inhabited by a spirit who may be benevolent but may also be unpredictable and harmful. The ancestor spirits, who reside with the clan deities, are also to be worshiped.

Gond relations with the gods and the spirits lie mainly in the hands of priests and individuals with special supernatural powers. The village priest (devari), whose office is usually a hereditary one, performs the sacrifices and rituals for village festivals. Family ceremonies and sacrifices are carried out by the head of the household. The clan priest (katora) has the responsibility of tending the shrine and ritual objects of the clan's Persa Pen. He is the guardian of the sacred spear point, which is never kept in the shrine but rather is hidden in a location known only to himself and a few close kinsmen. He also organizes and officiates at the annual clan festivals.

Virtually all aspects of Gond ritual life, from the greatest festivals to the building of a new cattle shed, are accompanied by sacrifice. The offering depends on the particular deity involved. Certain deities, especially female ones, demand blood-sacrifice. Chickens, goats, and sometimes male buffaloes (and reputedly in the past, humans) are the sacrificial victims. Periodically (every 9 or 12 years), the Gonds sacrifice a pig to the god Narayan Deo in an important ceremony known as the Laru Kaj ("Pig's Wedding"). Not all Gond ritual requires animal sacrifice; offerings sometimes include fruits, coconuts, flowers, colored powder, and strings.

Gonds cremate or bury their dead, depending on status and the circumstance of death. Children, unmarried persons, and individuals dying an inauspicious death (e.g., in an epidemic) are buried without much ceremony. Elaborate and costly ceremonies, including sacrifice, are performed at funerals by those who can afford it. The Gonds believe that a human being has a life-force and a spirit. On death, the life-force is reincarnated into another earthly existence, but the spirit remains in the other world. All Gond death rituals are undertaken for the welfare of the spirit, performed to ensure its smooth passage through the spirit world and its acceptance by the ancestral spirits of the clan. In times of economic stress, the important *karun* rite may be postponed for up to three years but it has to be completed in order for an heir's obligation to the deceased to be fulfilled. Memorial pillars are erected to honor the dead. Gonds believe the ancestral spirits watch over the moral behavior of the living and punish offenders of tribal law. In this sense, they are the guardians of the Gond community.

8 INTERPERSONAL RELATIONS

Visiting customs vary throughout the region, though Gonds are normally a hospitable people. The visitor is welcomed and presented with small gifts, perhaps some dried tobacco leaves or fruits from the forest. Many villages and homesteads have guest huts where the visitor may stay with some degree of privacy.

9 LIVING CONDITIONS

Gonds live in villages scattered throughout central India. Each village has a headman (known by local names such as *mukhia, mahji, or patel*) and a village council (*panchayat*) chosen by the villagers. The council, made up of the headman, the priest, the village watchman, and four or five elders, is responsible for the smooth running of the village and upholding Gond customs and traditions. More important affairs are discussed and decided upon by all the men of the community. In addition to its Gond inhabitants, a village has its service castes such as the Ahir (cowherds), Agaria (blacksmiths), Dhulia (drummers), and Pardhan (bards and singers).

A typical Gond village is made up of several hamlets, each consisting of the homesteads of a group of closely related kinfolk. The homestead (which contains dwellings, stables, and sheds) houses a family, often a joint family, consisting of the parents, married sons, and their families. Houses are usually rectangular, built of mud and thatch. They consist of a living room, a kitchen, a veranda, and a special room to which women retire while they are menstruating. Among many South Asian societies, women in this condition are regarded as ritually polluted and are segregated from the rest of the family. In one corner of the house is the shrine to the clan gods.

Standards of living among the Gonds reflect socioeconomic status. Many Gonds are relatively poor farmers or agricultural laborers, and this is seen in their lack of material possessions. Gond houses contain little furniture, perhaps some cots and a few wooden stools, with mats used for sitting and sleeping. The kitchen contains an assortment of cooking utensils, brass and earthenware pots, and baskets for storage. Today, wealthier Gonds build their houses out of stone and furnish them more lavishly.

10 FAMILY LIFE

Gond society is divided into four exogamous, patrilineal descent groups known in anthropological terminology as phratries. Each phratry (*saga* in Gondi) traces its descent to one of the four groups of gods who emerged from the primeval cave after their release by the hero Lingal. The phratry is divided into a number of exogamous clans (*pari*). A clan consists of a group of people who believe that they are descended in the male line from a common ancestor. Thus, no one can marry a partner belonging to the same phratry or clan. Violation of the rule of exogamy is considered to be incest. Not only would offenders expect to be punished by the gods, but they are also excluded from the tribal community. Many of the Gond clans bear the names of animals or plants, which suggests a totemic origin. Some Gond clans still observe totemic taboos and avoid eating the flesh of certain animals.

Kinship and marriage customs among the Gonds reflect broader regional patterns. The norm is the cross-cousin marriage (e.g., marriage with one's mother's brother's daughter) so typical of South Indian society. Groups that have been influenced by northern peoples such as the Marathas, however, follow northern customs in determining marriage partners. Similarly, northern Gonds allow what are called "levirate" marriages, that is, a widow remarries a brother of the deceased husband. This is not allowed in southern India, and the southern Gonds conform to this prohibition.

Gonds traditionally married on reaching physical maturity, with the selection of mates based on mutual choice, subject to the approval of the tribal council. Nowadays the Gonds increasingly follow the Hindu custom of arranged marriages when the children are still young. A bride-price is paid by the father of the groom. A Gond wedding is accompanied by many significant ceremonies, although, in general, rites conform to the marriage customs of the locality. The central rite of the Gond wedding consists of the groom walking with his bride seven times around a wedding post erected in the center of the wedding booth. Gond society is patrilocal and the newlyweds reside with the groom's family until such time as they move into a house of their own. Although the extended family is traditional among the Gonds, the nuclear family is becoming more common. Inheritance passes down the male line, with all sons receiving equal shares.

In addition to the negotiated marriage, other forms of marriage among the Gonds include elopement of an unmarried girl with a boy, or the capture of a girl and her forced marriage to her captor. Such marriages must later be legalized by the relatives and village councils of the partners. Similarly, divorce is permissible among the Gonds and is relatively easily obtained, but it must be obtained from the panchayat.

11 CLOTHING

Gonds differ little from the other cultivating castes of their locality in the area of dress. Men typically wore a small loincloth, but many have now adopted the *dhoti*. This is a long piece of white cotton cloth that is wrapped around the body, with its end drawn between the legs and tucked into the waistband at the back. In the past, the torso remained bare, but today cotton shirts are worn with the dhoti. White or colored turbans complete the outfit. In winter, waistcoats or woolen pullovers are worn for warmth, and sometimes a coarse woolen blanket is used for extra protection. Women and girls wear the

A ruined palace that was built by the Gond kings sits on the Narmada River, Ramnagar, India. (© Brian A. Vikander/Corbis)

cotton *sari*. This is wrapped around the waist, with one end drawn between the legs and tucked in at the back and the other thrown over the right shoulder covering the breasts and stomach, which are left bare. More and more Gonds are wearing the bodice *(choli)* along with the sari, in the manner of Hindu women.

Both men and women wear heavy silver ornaments bought from professional silversmiths. Women also wear colored glass bangles, as well as several types of beads, including their marriage necklaces made of small black beads. They often tattoo their bodies.

12 FOOD

The staples of the Gond diet are two millets known locally as *kodo* and *kutki*. These are prepared either boiled to a broth or cooked until all the water has evaporated. Sometimes it is ground and baked into a flat cake. Millet is eaten three times a day, with the broth being preferred for the first two meals and the dry cereal taken with some vegetables in the evening. Vegetables are either grown in the garden or collected from the forest along with roots and tubers. Honey is also gathered from the forest.

Rice is preferred by many Gonds, but for most it is too expensive to purchase and their land is too poor to cultivate it. Rice remains a dish reserved for feasts or festival days. Most Gonds, except for those who have adopted Hindu dietary taboos, like meat. Animals sacrificed at ceremonies are eagerly consumed, and the diet is supplemented by animals hunted in

the forest. Gonds must abstain from the flesh of certain animals, e.g., the tortoise, that are their clan totems.

Gonds are passionate smokers and grow tobacco for their own consumption. They also consume large amounts of liquor distilled from the *mahua* tree *(Bassia latifolia)* as a part of both religious and social celebrations.

13 EDUCATION

Education and literacy levels among the Gonds vary but are generally low. Literacy varies from 62.5% in Maharashtra to 50.3% in Madhya Pradesh. Among females in Madhya Pradesh, it drops to only 30.4%. Few children attend school regularly, and girls rarely continue past primary school. Only 1.5% of the population, mainly males, continues on to graduate level studies.

14 CULTURAL HERITAGE

Music, song, and dance play an important role in Gond society. Gonds are ardent dancers and all festive occasions are celebrated by song and dance. In some instances, such as with the Dandari dancers, dances celebrate the dramatic retelling of events from Gond mythology. However, dances are not necessarily associated with any particular event or festival and may be performed just for enjoyment. Many of the songs that accompany dances tend to be of a suggestive nature. The Dhulia is the professional musician caste serving the Gonds. Pardhan bards preserve the legends, myths, and history of the Gonds, passing these traditions on from generation to generation. Among the numerous myths of the Gonds, perhaps the most important is the great epic that celebrates the origins and exploits of the culture hero Pahandi Kapar Lingal.

15 WORK

The Gonds' ties with the forest suggest that, in the past, they were nomadic hunters or food gatherers who took up shifting cultivation. Today they are mainly plough-cultivators whose agriculture differs little from other farming castes in their region. Although some Gond communities have risen to the status of landowners, increasing pressure on land is reflected in large numbers of landless laborers among the Gonds.

16 SPORTS

There are no sporting activities associated with traditional Gond society.

17 ENTERTAINMENT AND RECREATION

Leisure time is passed with the family or visiting friends and neighbors. Gonds like to assemble on feast days or full-moon nights to sing and dance. Cock-fighting is a favorite pastime of some Gond groups.

18 FOLK ART, CRAFTS, AND HOBBIES

Gonds have a rich tradition of tribal arts and crafts that includes pottery, basket-making, body-tattooing, and floor-painting. They are artistically gifted, painting designs on their house walls in red and black on a white background. The drawings are often done to celebrate festivals and include animals and birds, human figures, the hunt, and the dance. The Gonds make musical instruments, and they carve memorial pillars in wood and stone for their dead. They often carve doors and panels to decorate their houses.

19 SOCIAL PROBLEMS

The Gonds face problems typical of tribal peoples throughout South Asia. As a less sophisticated group, they have faced exploitation and discrimination from their culturally more advanced neighbors. They occupy less productive lands in some of the more remote areas of the country. They are experiencing increasing pressure on their land, a rise in the number of landless laborers, and high levels of poverty. Lack of education and low levels of literacy further reduce economic opportunity.

Beyond this, the very nature of the Gond community is in itself a problem. Despite their numbers, the Gonds are an assemblage of diverse tribal groups. Although they all see themselves as Gonds, there is little to unite them into a cohesive political force. Their wide geographical distribution and degree of tribal fragmentation works against the creation of a Gond political identity. Even if this were not so, the leadership to achieve this is sorely lacking. This places the Gond community at a major disadvantage in India today, where access to resources for socioeconomic advancement is often subject to political patronage.

For instance, some non-tribals, through political jockeying, have managed to gain legal tribal status, that is, to be listed as a Scheduled Tribe. The Gonds of Andhra Pradesh effectively lost their only advantage in trying to protect their lands when the Banjaras, a group that had been settling in Gond territory, managed to get classified in the state as a Scheduled Tribe in 1977. Their newly acquired tribal status made the Banjaras

eligible to acquire Gond land "legally" and to compete with Gonds for reserved political seats, places in education institutions, and other benefits reserved for Scheduled Tribes. Because the Banjaras are not scheduled in neighboring Maharashtra, there has been an influx of Banjara emigrants from that state into Andhra Pradesh in search of better opportunities.

20 GENDER ISSUES

The status of women is markedly better among Gonds than in Hindu caste society. Women play an important role in the domestic economy of Gond societies, they are usually allowed to move freely, and have the right to choose their marriage partners or at least have a large say in this (it is always, at the very least, a family affair). Divorce is possible and much easier to obtain than in Hindu societies, and tribal widows—unlike their Hindu sisters—have no problem in remarrying. But, again, these are generalizations and there are indigenous societies in which child and forced marriages are common. In many tribal societies, paying a bride price is part of the marriage arrangement. This stands in contrast to the dowry practice in Hindu society, which means that the birth of a baby girl represents a heavy economic burden for poorer Hindu families, with enormous repercussions on the status of women, and on the sex ratio in the population. Studies have shown that baby girls are less well-looked after than boys in Hindu society, leading to a higher infant mortality rate among Hindu children. The possibility of pre-natal sex identification has led to a rapid drop in the births of baby girls. But the sex ratio of Gonds is higher than the national average, suggesting that discrimination against female children is totally lacking, or at least less than in other groups.

In hardly any indigenous society do women participate in formal political decision-making and this, too, is true of the Gonds, though women are often consulted, by their husbands or in community meetings. But they are not members of village councils and cannot become the village chief. Women also hardly ever play an important role in religion, although they may be spirit mediums or healers. Generally, Gond women are valued mostly for their productive and reproductive functions.

With the exception of a few matrilineal societies (such as the Garo and Khasi of Meghalaya in the north-east of India), women in the country do not inherit land. And even among the matrilineal societies, the land is in reality managed and controlled by men. But it is very important for unmarried women and widows. Ownership normally rests with their fathers, brothers or husbands. Men therefore tend to have greater control over agricultural production and products. However, Gond women do enjoy spheres in which they retain some control. In India, in particular, the gathering of forest products—which has been very much a female activity—is crucial for women to maintain at least some degree of autonomy since they have control over these products, i.e. they sell them themselves. However, poverty and lack of access to educational and health facilities remain major stumbling blocks in the way of Gond women bettering themselves.

Some Gond women have banded together to help alleviate poverty and promote female empowerment. For instance, in Orissa's Kalahandi and Nuapada districts, life is an endless nightmare of deprivation and hunger for Gonds. The men leave their homes in search of employment, often ending up as bonded labor in distant places. Left to fend for themselves, the women, the elderly and children have to eke out an existence or starve. Now, thousands of tribal women have, quite literally, spun themselves out of the web of despair in which they were trapped, thanks largely to a local livelihood initiative that employs Gond women to make handmade cotton fabric. Aptly called "Nuakala," which means "new craft," the name also incorporates the first two syllables of the districts Nuapada and Kalahandi where the program is based.

²¹ BIBLIOGRAPHY

Banerjee, B. G., and Kiran Bhatia. *Tribal Demography of Gonds*. Delhi: Gian Pub. House, 1988.

Elwin, Verrier. *Leaves from the Jungle: Life in a Gond Village*. Oxford: Oxford University Press, 1991.

Fuchs, Stephen. *The Gond and Bhumia of Eastern Mandla*. Bombay: Asia Publishing House, 1960.

Fürer-Haimendorf, Christoph von, and Elizabeth von Fürer-Haimendorf. *The Gonds of Andhra Pradesh: Tradition and Change in an Indian Tribe*. New Delhi: Vikas Publishing House, 1979.

Grigson, Wilfred. *The Maria Gonds of Bastar*. London: Oxford University Press, 1949.

Sharma, Anima. *Tribe in Transition: A Study of Thakur Gonds*. India: Mittal Publications, 2005.

Singh, K. S., ed. "Gond." In *People of India. Vol.3: The Scheduled Tribes*. Delhi and Oxford: Oxford University Press with the Anthropological Survey of India, 1994.

—by D. O. Lodrick

GREEK CYPRIOTS

LOCATION: Cyprus
POPULATION: 786,800 (2007)
LANGUAGE: Greek and English
RELIGION: Church of Cyprus (Greek Orthodox)
RELATED ARTICLES: Vol. 5: Greeks

¹ INTRODUCTION

The name "Cyprus" comes from the Greek word for "copper" (*kypros*). It was the island's lucrative deposits in copper, discovered around 3000 BC on the slopes of the Troodos Mountains, which first appealed to many foreign powers along the eastern Mediterranean coast. The conflicts among these rival groups and their rise and fall in power form the turbulent history of Cyprus, which is the third largest island in the Mediterranean and neighbors Syria to the w (100 km/60 mi), Turkey to the s (68 km/40 mi), and the Egyptian coast to the N (343 km/203 mi).

The first inhabitants of Cyprus, who resided in the Khirokitia region and are traceable to the peoples of Asia Minor (modern-day Turkey), date from the 8th to the 6th millennium BC, as evidenced from samples of obsidian rock which identify these Cypriots of the Neolithic Age as rather impressive Indo-European peoples who possessed a written language. The Greek heritage of the island was introduced through the settlement of Achaean Greeks from 2000 to 1600 BC, as well as Arcadian commercial traders who arrived from the northeastern Peloponnesus region of the Greek mainland after 1400 BC. These settlements and a distinctly Hellenic culture were reinforced by the subsequent arrival of Trojan War heroes in 1184 BC.

In contrast to the distinct Hellenic ethnicity of Cyprus's early peoples, the conquest of the island by the Egyptian leader Thutmose III around 1450 BC preceded a varied line of eastern and western invaders who seized the island until their defeat by another foreign power. Thus, Egypt lost power to the Assyrians in 800 BC, who then fell to the Egyptians in 550, who in turn were usurped by the Persians in 525. Until Turkey finally dominated the island from AD 1571 to 1878, Cyprus had been claimed and controlled by peoples and leaders as diverse as Alexander the Great (333 BC), the Egyptian Ptolemies (323 BC), Rome (58 BC), and England's Richard I (AD 1191), who passed Cyprus to the titular king of Jerusalem and Frankish ruler Guy of Lusignan.

Turkey finally claimed Cyprus from its Venetian–Lusignan possessors of AD 1489–1571 and held firm to the island until its own collapse in the Russo–Turkish Wars of 1877–1888. For an annual "lease" of $500,000, through which Turkey retained formal possession of Cyprus, Britain accepted administration of the island at Turkey's request in order to curtail the spread of Russian power. However, the annual fee was never received by Turkey, but instead deposited in the Bank of England to compensate for Turkey's defaulted Crimean War loans; this disturbed Cypriots as well as the Turks. After World War I (1914–1918), the 1923 Treaty of Lausanne was imposed on the Turks as a peace settlement, through which Britain gained formal possession of the island.

GREEK CYPRIOTS

0   100   200 Miles

0   100   200 Kilometers

Black Sea

İzmit Adapazari

Bursa *Sakarya*   Ankara ⊛
                                     Kirikkale
Balikesir   Eskişehir   Sivas
                              Kizilirmak

T U R K E Y   *Tuz*   Kayseri
                         Gölü

                   Konya
Denizli   *Beyşehir*
               Gölü   T O R O S   D A Ğ L A R I   *Seyhan*

Antalya   Tarsus Adana
                               Mersin
      Antalya   Alanya   İskenderun
      Körfezi

                                 Al Lādhiqīyah

                    ⊛ Nicosia
      CYPRUS   S Y R I A

Mediterranean   LEBANON
Sea

Despite Britain's dominance and perceived control over Cyprus, riots erupted in 1931 from the Greek community's petition for and denial of *enosis,* the political union of Cyprus with its Greek mainland. Britain responded by suppressing the island's political parties and activities, as well as dismantling the Cypriot legislative council. Following World War II Britain offered the Cypriots the potential for self-rule; however, enosis was a priority to the islanders and both the AKEL party (*Anorthotikon Komman Ergazomenou Laou*—Progressive Party of Working People) and the EOKA party (*Ethniki Organosis Kypriakou Agonos*—National Organization of Cypriot Struggle) were formed as separate efforts to secure enosis, the spokesman of which was Makarios III. In response to heightened riots, Archbishop Makarios was elected president on 13 December 1959, while a Turkish Cypriot, Fazil Kuchuk, was elected vice president.

The Greek Cypriot cries for enosis were only countered by the Turkish Cypriot movement toward partition (*taksim*). What had optimistically become the independent Republic of Cyprus in 1960, represented by both Greek and Turkish leaders, collapsed only three years later through the dysfunction of bicommunal provisions which were intended to provide equal treatment and representation to both Greeks and Turks. By the close of 1963, the Turks had fully abandoned their political positions and, as the ability to share government power further declined and intercommunal violence increased. United Nations (UN) peacekeepers were sent to the island in 1964.

The peace process fully faltered in 1974 after a Greek coup displaced Makarios and installed Nicos Sampson, formerly an EOKA terrorist, as a more aggressive move toward enosis. This only prompted the response of taksim and a Turkish invasion that left 180,000 Cypriot refugees and divided the island at the "Green Line," which spans the area from Morphou through Nicosia to Famagusta. In 1983 the Turkish Cypriots declared independence as the Turkish Republic of Northern Cyprus. This independent status, however, has only been officially recognized by the government of Turkey. UN peacekeeping forces have continued to protect a buffer zone between the north and south. On 1 May 2004 the Republic of Cyprus became a member of the European Union (EU), and adopted the euro on 1 January 2008. In March 2007 the Greek Cypriot authorities demolished a wall that for decades had stood at the boundary between the Greek Cypriot controlled side and the UN buffer zone. The wall had cut across Ledra Street in the heart of Nicosia and was seen as a strong symbol of the island's division. In 2008 Ledra Street was reopened in the presence of Greek and Turkish Cypriot officials.

² LOCATION AND HOMELAND

Following Sicily and Sardinia, Cyprus is the third largest island of the east Mediterranean basin. Geologically part of Asia Minor, it measures 9,251 sq km (3,572 sq mi) and stretches 206 km (128 mi) w to E, and 97 km (60 mi) from Cape Gata in the s to Cape Kormakiti in the N. Comparable to the state divisions which comprise the United States, Cyprus is divided into six districts: Famagusta, Kyrenia, Larnaca, Limassol, Paphos, and Nicosia. Nicosia has remained the capital of the island despite the 1974 Turkish invasion and partition of the island.

The topography of Cyprus, flat and largely deprived of forestation, is sculpted by the Troodos Mountains, an igneous rock formation in the southern and western regions of the island which ranges from Pomos Point in the northwest almost to Larnaca Bay. Mt. Olympus, the highest point on the island, which is a haven for skiers in the winter and hikers in the summer, rises to 6,505 feet and is called by islanders Mt. Chionistra (*chioni* meaning "snow"), for its accumulation of snow during the winter. The jagged, steep limestone slopes of the Kyrenia Range, perhaps the most dramatic, spectacular aspect of the topography, extend from Cape Kormakiti to Cape Andreas. These mountainous regions dramatically surround the flatland of Cyprus, the Mesaoria, which receives less rain than regions of higher altitudes. Cypriots endure hot, dry summers from June through September (mid-summer temperatures swelter to 112° F), and they likewise enjoy mild, though rainy winters from October through March (averaging 22° F).

In 2007 the population of the Greek Cypriot controlled area of southern Cyprus was estimated at 786,800 inhabitants. After the 1974 Turkish invasion, thousands of Greek Cypriots were displaced from their homes in northern Cyprus. At the end of 2006 the estimated number of displaced Greek Cypriots and their descendents was 238,000. The same year there were approximately 369 Greek Cypriots living in the Turkish controlled north.

³ LANGUAGE

While Greek, Turkish, and English are all official languages of Cyprus, Greek is the primary language spoken by Greek Cypriots. The Greek spoken by Cypriots, however, resembles ancient rather than modern Greek dialects. Greeks from Cyprus therefore seem to speak a different language than those from the mainland, who, for example, say *ti kanete* ("how are you?") in contrast to the Cypriot pronunciation of *tambu ka-nete*; likewise, the commonplace conjunction *che* ("and") is the Cypriot pronunciation for the standard Greek *ke*. Greek Cypriots strongly maintain English as a second language, largely because the island was a British colony until 1960. In contrast, Greek Cypriots typically have no fluency in Turkish as a result of the political and physical boundaries imposed between the two peoples after the 1974 Turkish invasion and partition of the island.

Despite differences in pronunciation, the Greek Cypriots share the 24-letter alphabet of the Greek mainland, which is pronounced and appears as follows:

Αα	alfa	a as in alfalfa
Bb	veeta	v as in victory
Γγ	gamma	g as in language
Dd	thelta	th as in the
Εε	epsilon	e as in eatible
Ζζ	zeeta	z as in zebra
Ηη	eeta	e as in eat
Θθ	theeta	th as in thread
Ιι	yota	y as in yoke
Κκ	kapa	k as in kitchen
Λλ	lambda	l as in lamb
Μμ	me	m as in meat
Νν	knee	n as in neat
Ξξ	xee	x as in extra
Oo	oh	o as in only
Ππ	pea	p as in pear
Ρρ	row	r as in rodeo
Σσ	sigma	s as in seat
Ττ	taf	t as in tax
Υυ	epsilon	e as in bee
Φφ	fee	f as in find
Χχ	hee	h as in hair'
Ψψ	psi	psi sound as in *pepsi*
Ωω	omega	o as in oat

4 FOLKLORE

Populated by some 30,000 Cypriots on the west coast of the island, Paphos pays tribute to Greek mythology as a landmark for the birth of Aphrodite, the erotic goddess of love and desire who, according to myth, emerged from the foam of the Cypriot waves, as captured in Botticelli's famous *The Birth of Venus* painting. Paphos shares its name with the mythical daughter born of Venus (Aphrodite's Roman name) and Pygmalion, and features of its western landscape symbolically reinforce the myth of Aphrodite's birth: the jagged rocks scattered to the south of Paphos are regarded as Aphrodite's Rocks (*Petra tou Romiou*); the sanctuary of Aphrodite and onetime shrine is located at Kouklia Village within Paphos; the Baths of Aphrodite, a celebrated site of fertility where the goddess of love bathed before her marriage, are found at Polis; and the Fontana Amorosa, the Fountain of Love spring which enamors its drinkers, is likewise in Paphos.

Digenis Akritas also colors the folklore of Cyprus as a figure of an anonymous epic poem who often battled the deathly grip of Charon, the ferryman of death, before succumbing to his mortality. He is also credited with the creation of *Pentadakty-los* (five-fingered), another name for the mountainous Kyrenia Range in northeastern Cyprus, which resembles five fingers

and which resulted from the drowning Digenis' gripping the range from the Mediterranean Sea, leaving the imprints of his one hand in the mountain range.

Folklore which enters the modern-day beliefs and practices of the Greek Cypriots include the existence of *kalikanzari* (little monsters), who, until Christmas, devour the trunks which were believed to hold the earth in place. During Christmas, their respite from this habit allows the earth to heal, as they rise from the depths beneath the earth to participate in and sabotage Christmas festivities. Epiphany, celebrated by Cypriots on January 6, carries this pagan overtone into the common practice of throwing *lokmades* (little doughnuts) atop the roofs of their homes to appease the little monsters and to return them to the depths, where, unfortunately, they continue to devour the trunks of the earth until the Christmas season returns.

5 RELIGION

Nearly all Greek Cypriots belong to the Orthodox Church of Cyprus, which is an independent church of the Eastern Orthodox tradition. Greek Cypriots are proud of their Christian heritage. Universally, Christians recognize Cyprus as the sacred site at which the first pagan political authority, the proconsul Sergius Paulus, was converted to Christianity by the apostles Paul and Barnabas, who arrived in Salamis and journeyed to Paphos in AD 45. Apart from the impact of these apostles, whose missionary work in Cyprus is documented in the New Testament (Acts 13), Christianity subsisted until the rule of Constantine the Great in AD 313, which resulted in an increased number of dioceses. The 5th century was not only a period of grand basilica construction, as can be seen today in Kourion and Cape Drepanum, but also the time at which the Church of Cyprus earned its privileged status as an autocephalous church free from other patriarchates, a status it powerfully retains today. Cyprus attained this unusual, privileged status through the Archbishop Anthemius of Constantia (Salamis), whose unique vision led him to the tomb of St. Barnabas, where he discovered the Gospel of St. Mark. Thereafter, as endorsed by the emperor Zeno (the recipient of the Gospel), the archbishop functioned as an imperial power, carrying a scepter rather than a pastoral staff, wearing purple robes, and signing his name in purple ink.

Still, during the Byzantine Empire, Cyprus was subject to the Eastern Empire at Constantinople, under which Orthodoxy and its distinctions evolved until the period of Lusignan and Venetian rule (1192–1489). The Church of Cyprus, then acknowledged as different and separate from the precepts of the Catholic faith, was compelled to uphold the Roman pope as a religious authority. When Cyprus was then usurped and controlled by the Ottoman Empire (1571–1878), the Cypriots' religion was overlooked by these Muslim conquerors, whose rule through "millets" or religious communities enabled the Church of Cyprus to gain sovereignty; positions within the church were therefore upheld for their spiritual as well as secular authority. This duality of church and state is embodied in the figure of Mihail Mouskos, later dubbed Archbishop Makarios III, a young monk who was elected president of the republic in 1959 and held the position until his death in 1977. As president, Mouskos heightened the quality and training of priests at the Cypriot seminary in Nicosia, and served as a political activist for the cause of *enosis* (union with the Greek mainland). His status as both a religious and political authority was succeeded by the conservative Archbishop Chysostomos, who led the Church of Cyprus until illness led to his removal from office. He was succeeded in 2006 by Archbishop Chysostomos II.

The constitution allows the Orthodox Church of Cyprus to have full authority over the administration of its own internal affairs and property. The Church is one of the largest landowners in the country and holds significant investment properties in banking, construction, and hotels.

Unlike most Greek Orthodox churches in the United States, the Cypriot Orthodox service doesn't feature a choir, and the balcony area found in most churches is reserved for women (termed *ginekonitis*, which literally translates to mean "women's section"). Segregation likewise exists on the ground level of the church, as men usually sit on one side and women on the other, an observed separation which will even split married couples apart for the duration of the service, though this practice is more common among rural, village churches than in urban ones.

6 MAJOR HOLIDAYS

Most Cypriot holidays revolve around the Orthodox religion, with the celebration of Easter serving as a central event. Religious holidays in the Orthodox churches are celebrated following the Julian calendar, rather than the Gregorian calendar used by Western Christians, therefore the dates of such holidays as Easter and Pentecost are often different than those celebrated in the Western world.

Like the American Mardi Gras, Carnival, most notably that of Limassol, is upheld as a time to feast extravagantly before the fast of Lent. It is celebrated with colorful parades and an abundance of specialties, including *bourekia* (a minty-cheese pastry) as well as the sweetmeats *daktyla* and *kandaifi*. The first week of Carnival is known as Kreatini, or Meat Week. The second and final week of Carnival is known as *Tyrini* (cheese week) and extends to Green Monday.

Green Monday, 50 days before the Orthodox Easter, is the first official day of Lent. It is a legal holiday celebrated as a day for picnics and kite flying, when Cypriots head for the hillside or the mountains with a basket of "greens," or a vegetarian meal, to be enjoyed by family and relatives. Freed from work responsibilities, Cypriots optimistically greet this dawning of the Lenten season with the phrase *Tha pame na kopsume ti miti tis Sarakostis* ("We're going to cut the nose of the first forty days") and do so with a Lenten feast which includes fresh vegetables, baked potatoes, pickles, fresh bread, and a sweet called *halva*. Only the most devout Cypriots continue this fast from meat, milk, eggs, and olive oil for the entire 40 days of Lent (Sundays are not counted as fasting days during Lent since the Lord's day is always meant to be a celebration). Most Cypriots will not observe these eating restrictions again until Holy Week.

Holy Week features many lengthy, elaborate services and ceremonies that bring most Cypriots to church each evening. The betrayal of Jesus is observed on Holy Thursday through a lengthy three-hour service which requires Cypriots to stand and listen to the solemn reading of the gospels; with each reading by the priest, a candle is lit. School children also participate in the service through their adorning of the *epitaphion*—a large, ornately carved, free-standing structure which sym-

bolizes Christ's tomb—with flowers they have gathered from the village. The crucifixion is then observed on Good Friday, when the epitaphion is carried by laymen of the church in a funeral-style procession. On this day the women of the village prepare rich pastries called *flaouna*, which are made with a special cheese and which prompt ceaseless discussion among housewives in defense of their special recipe. The resurrection, the climax of Holy Week, is celebrated on Holy Saturday in a midnight candle-light service which closes with the repeated singing of *Christos Anesti* (Christ is Risen), a phrase which is repeated by devout Cypriots in passing 50 days thereafter. After the midnight service, families and relatives return to their homes to feast on an Easter "breakfast," which consists of a lemon-based chicken and rice soup (*avogolemono*), along with boiled eggs dyed red to commemorate the gloriously shed blood of Christ. As among the Greek-Americans in the United States, the eggs are used in a tableside game in which one person holds an egg steady between forefinger and thumb while his "competitor" hits the stationary egg with his own egg; the champion possesses the egg which remains free of cracks.

During the Easter day, the midday meal—which usually consists of a whole lamb, a goat, or other skewered meat—is grilled outside and shared by relatives who visit for the day. The Easter Sunday meal is enjoyed among family and acquaintances, and children often receive a chocolate egg and, more recently, gifts. The festivities and visits of Easter Sunday extend into the week, as many Cypriots are relieved of their work responsibilities on the Monday and Tuesday which follow Easter.

The Day of Ascension, 40 days after Easter, is observed as a holiday of fasting, prayer, and mediation. Pentecost, the Day of the Holy Spirit, is celebrated 50 days after Easter. In Cyprus a holiday known as Kataklysmos (which means "flood" is celebrated on the same day as Pentecost. Originally celebrated as a water festival to commemorate Aphrodite, its water theme has evolved into a Christian celebration of the flood story of Noah from the Old Testament and involves music, dancing, and poetry readings in a fair-like setting. The Feast of the Assumption of Mary on August 15 is a public holiday, as are Christmas and Epiphany (celebrated as the Baptism of the Lord).

Secular, more politically inspired holidays include Greek Independence Day (March 25), Independence Day (October 1), and Greek National Day (October 28).

7 RITES OF PASSAGE

Engagement, marriage and childbirth are events which herald a child's arrival to adulthood. As premarital sex is strongly condemned, girls formally become women and mothers through the vow of marriage and it is only when they have children that they learn how to care for them. Unlike in the United States, grandmothers attend to children and act as babysitters, rather than teenagers.

For men, military service is a rite of passage and is demanded of all males 18 years of age for a period of 26 months. Prior to their service and immediately following their graduation, boys will devote many hours to friends—either making commitments to girlfriends or spending hours with other boys at discos and listening to music which dramatizes their sentiments at this crucial maturation point in their lives. A few weeks following high school graduation, boys begin basic training and learn their location site, the most desired being air artillery and communication units, the worst being the infantry.

A Cyprus farmer stands in a field with his goats and sheep. (Hugh Sitton/Getty Images)

8 INTERPERSONAL RELATIONS

To maintain a tourism industry, Cypriots have acquired a national reputation as very hospitable, pleasant people. The islanders themselves, particularly in the 300 remaining villages, sustain close same-sex relations: men often gather together at cafés to play an intense game of *tavali* (backgammon) and to talk politics, though women, except for tourists, are strictly excluded from the café. Male bonding also endures between a groom and his *koumbaro,* the best man at his wedding who also baptizes the first child; women also maintain close relations with their *koumbara.*

9 LIVING CONDITIONS

The shift of Greek Cypriot living from the village to the city peaked in 1974, when the Turkish government seized the most fertile, productive agricultural regions of the island. The houses and apartments of urban Cyprus are equipped with the amenities found in any modern city. Families are typically situated close to each other within the city and maintain a village house as well.

Despite movements toward a more urban society, a connection between the villages and the cities was made through advancements in transportation; British annexation of the island in the early 1900s introduced isolated villages to the cities through a system of roads. An estimated 10,448 km of highway stretch across the Republic of Cyprus, roughly half of which are paved. The cars which travel those highways—the most popular being Japanese models as well as Mercedes and BMW—cost Cypriots double what Americans pay; car maintenance and even gasoline are also highly priced. Since the shutdown of the Nicosia International Airport after the 1974 Turkish invasion, the only legal means of entry into the country has been through the Larnaca International and Paphos International Airports, as well as the ports of Limassol, Larnaca, and Paphos.

Despite the 75-year life expectancy for males and the 80-year life expectancy for females, most Cypriots are aged between 15 and 64; a mere 12% are over the age of 65. In 2008 the birth rate averaged 12.5 births/1,000 population, while the death rate averaged 7.8 deaths/1,000 population, with a national population growth rate of 0.52%. As in the United States, good health is maintained through athletic clubs, which largely appeal to young male and female professionals, who will pay a monthly membership to reap both the social and physical benefits of industrialized fitness. Women usually participate in same-sex aerobics classes and perform some weightlifting, which is more common among men, in addition to running and using a punching bag. Older people become members only at the recommendation of a doctor and many heart patients will opt for a morning walk rather than the more modern gym.

¹⁰ FAMILY LIFE

Traditionally, Greek Cypriots define themselves through their family. A Cypriot household will typically house a husband, wife, and unmarried children. Grandparents usually live nearby or within the home of an adult child (usually the daughter) in the event of declining health. Nursing home facilities are seldom used and only when the aged parent is beyond home care. Grandparents in otherwise good health retain a functional, respected role in Greek Cypriot families and are revered in the eyes of their grandchildren. Grandfathers will often take their grandchildren to and from school and grandmothers perform most child-rearing responsibilities while mothers work. Until the 1950s marriages were accompanied by oral promises in which parents contributed to the new lives of the couple through traditional gifts: the bridegroom's family would provide a home which the bride's family would furnish. In some cases a written dowry contract is signed by the couple and their parents and then authorized by a religious party.

The Old World attitudes toward marriage failed to consider love as a viable motivation, as romantic love was disparaged in Cypriot society and marriages were often mediated by a third matchmaking party whose intimate knowledge of the family qualified them and endorsed the match. In modern culture, men and women typically select a mate of their own accord and interests and are largely swayed by feelings of romance. In the past, heterosexual contact was only permitted with parental supervision and within the physical boundaries of the village fountain and the church. Modern-day Cypriot society encourages earlier heterosexual contact within academic settings and the work force. While sexual promiscuity and a relaxing of morals is evident among adolescents and unmarried couples, it is still considered taboo for an adolescent couple to be home or out alone and relationships in general are platonic. Adolescents congregate in groups, though there is virtually no pressure to enter a relationship during adolescence, and boyfriends and girlfriends who are present among teen groups seldom stray off by themselves. Though parents might be aware of their son or daughter's relationship, they usually make no effort to meet the beau, who would not be invited to dinner and whom the adolescent would keep to himself or herself anyway.

Once a Cypriot has completed his or her education, possible university studies, and has secured a job, engagement is the necessary course of action for the bulk of the Cypriot population. Couples may discover each other through the friends and co-workers encountered at their places of employment. For example, a woman who is introduced to a co-worker's brother and considers him a prospect for marriage will ask her co-worker about the bachelor's "eligibility" and potential as a husband. If the woman receives an endorsement from the co-worker, the two families will work together at arranging meetings to determine the viability of the match and to make plans for engagement, which has the same weight and formality as the actual wedding.

Greek Cypriot weddings of the past, in the Orthodox tradition, encompassed an entire week of festivities; modern weddings are performed in only half a day and begin with the elaborate dressing of the bride and groom, who proceed to the church service. The equivalent of the American wedding reception usually begins at 8 pm and includes traditional Cypriot fare (*kleftiko, pastitsio, resi,* and *kourabiedes*), and is accompanied by traditional music otherwise not usually heard in modern Cyprus. *Bouzoukia,* the electric guitar, drums, and the violin are harmonized together for dances such as the *tsifteteli* belly dance and the historic *remetiko,* performed by a sole dancer within a circle of clapping acquaintances. The final dance of the evening is the *choros tou androjinou,* which finds the married couple alone on the dance floor strewn with banknotes. Separation and divorce, usually caused by extramarital affairs and abuse, are more common and legally permissible in modern culture than in the past.

¹¹ CLOTHING

Traditional Cypriot dress, reserved for some weddings and festivals, finds men in loose, black *vrakas* (knicker-like pants), dark vests embellished with bright designs, and tall black boots. However, styles in Cyprus reflect the modern fashion industry in Europe and America. Jeans and casual shirts are often worn at home and at leisure. Business attire and formal wear are similar to that found across Europe.

¹² FOOD

The rich food of Cyprus, while largely Greek in flavor, traces its origins to the palates of the island's diverse invaders and settlers, featuring Greek, Turkish, Arabic, and even some British influences. Therefore, one who sits down to a challenging table of *Meze,* which translates as "mixture" and which forms the common fare *Mezedhes* ("little delicacies"), could encounter up to 30 sample cuisines. A common table of Mezedhes will include the Cypriot specialties of *halumi,* cheese exclusive to Cyprus and produced from thyme-fed goats; *taramosalata,* a dip of smoked cod's roe; *kleftiko,* slow-roasted lamb; and *moussaka,* a minced lamb and potato casserole which is flavored with bechamel sauce. *Koupepia,* or grape leaves, are a favorite of the village as well as the city:

Koupepia

Koupepia are basically made in two steps: the first prepares the leaves, the second prepares the filling for the leaves.

Leaves
Blanch and rinse in cold water 30 vine leaves (which can be picked from grape vines in June); put them aside.

Filling
1 tablespoon finely minced peppermint, parsley, and onion
½ pound diced tomatoes
1 egg white
½ pound ground meat, browned.
Salt and pepper to taste

Mix together the peppermint, parsley, onion, tomatoes, egg white, and ground meat. Add salt and pepper to taste.

Sprinkle lemon juice over 2 tablespoons rice; let stand for five minutes, then add to meat mixture.

Carefully place a blanched and rinsed grape leaf on your work area, and place 1 tablespoon meat filling in the center. Fold the edges of the leaf together so they meet, and then roll the leave up to resemble a small sausage.

Place all the filled vine leaves in a pot; cover with meat broth, and simmer for 40 minutes.

Common morning fare for Cypriots includes toast topped with a slice of cheese and perhaps honey. Similarly, the older generation awakens to bread with tomatoes, olives, and *halloumi*, a cheese only made in Cyprus. This is accompanied for most with instant coffee made with milk and served either cold or hot. Children drink Nesquick, while their grandparents usually drink warm, sweetened milk.

In accordance with the fasting of meat, eggs, and dairy products which is observed under the Greek Orthodox religion, lunch for devout Cypriots consists of dried or fresh beans three days a week. The vegetarian victuals are either dressed in olive oil and lemon juice and eaten with plenty of fresh bread and tomatoes, or cooked with a tomato sauce stew of celery, carrots, and onions. Those who choose not to fast enjoy both traditional fare, which can be sampled at a table of Meze, as well as more British entrees such as steak and french fries, as meat is enjoyed by most Cypriots on a daily basis.

13 EDUCATION

While Cyprus bitterly endured British control of the island, it was the presence and initiative of the English, through the Education Law of 1895, which empowered the local government to raise taxes to develop primary schools. The number of schools created through this legislation more than doubled from the 76 that existed in 1897 to 179 only 20 years later. In addition, the British diminished illiteracy on the island. In 2003 the literacy rate was at estimated at 97%.

Like children in America, Cypriot children begin their educational careers at the age of about 5½; unlike American children, they are required to attend school only to the age of 15. The Greek Cypriot school system, which is rigidly governed by the Ministry of Education, potentially spans four levels. Pre-primary education for children aged from 2 to 5½ emerged only after the 1974 Turkish invasion of the island and more than half of the eligible Greek Cypriot students are estimated to attend preschools. Primary school is required and begins for students aged 5½; it covers a six-year, general curriculum program in which English is a required course for the final two years. Students continue their education in secondary school, the first level of which is required, free, and termed "Gymnasium"; the final three years of secondary school, which are optional, is termed the "Lyceum," and it offers five fields of concentration: classical, science, economics, commercial/secretarial, and foreign languages.

Higher education and specialized training for professionals such as teachers, technicians, engineers, hoteliers/caterers, foresters, nurses, and health inspectors is furnished by technical and vocational colleges. The University of Cyprus located in the capital city of Nicosia, was founded in 1989 and enrolled its first students in September 1992. The cost is free for Cypriots who maintain a twelve-credit course load. Most Greek Cypriots seeking a college education will attend schools in Greece, the United Kingdom, or the United States.

14 CULTURAL HERITAGE

The Ministry of Education is charged with the cultural enhancement as well as the educational advancement of Cypriots. Cultural Services, established by the Ministry of Education in March 1968, is the branch of government which ensures the preservation of Cypriot culture by financing and promot-

ing such groups as the Cyprus State Chamber Orchestra; the Cyprus State Youth Orchestra; the Establishment of Cultural Centers; the Development of Refugee Settlements; archives for writers, painters, and sculptors; the National Struggle Museum; the National Gallery; and Folklore Culture. Cultural Services also issues state awards for literature, donates Cypriot books abroad, and purchases publications within Cyprus as well as work from Cypriot artists.

The Cyprus Department of Antiquities is another government organization whose excavation and preservation of historic sites and artifacts—including theatres, sanctuaries, castles and churches—allows Cypriot culture to flourish.

As the ancient theatres of Salamis, Soli, Kourion, and Paphos were cultural centers since the Middle Ages, so they have been excavated by the Cyprus Department of Antiquities, and are the modern sites of both classical and contemporary plays from around the world. The Cyprus Theatre Organization (THOC) was organized in 1971, consists of a nine-member panel, and promotes theatrical arts both on the island as well as international exchanges outside Cyprus.

15 WORK

The Greek Cypriot labor force numbered about 373,000 in 2006. Jobs commanding the highest respect are "professional" positions: doctors, lawyers, civil servants, teachers, dentists, and business men. Wealthy "upper class" professionals—typically educated in elite institutions in the United Kingdom, Western Europe, or the United States—enter such professional positions. They typically own manufacturing, construction, and consumer goods companies. As in the United States and other countries, the upper class enjoys increased upward mobility in banks and semi-governmental organizations because of contacts, which are virtually necessary for professional success in Cyprus. The middle class are either educated in the United States and Europe, where exclusive college scholarship opportunities are offered to Cypriots, or in Greece, where free education is available for students who perform well on placement exams. Jobs taken by scholarship-educated, middle class Cypriots are in areas of government, teaching, banking, insurance, and semi-governmental organizations, as well as management within the retail sector. These positions still command adequate respect, unlike the lower class vocations of manual laborers, skilled craftsmen, and manufacturing and construction workers; the sheer scarcity of these workers has actually allowed them to earn high wages, as do many farmers. While considered low class, farmers are usually wealthy because land in Cyprus is valuable, especially if near the sea and zoned for hotels.

In 2006 about 71% of the labor force was employed in service-related industries. About 21% of the work force was employed in industry and 8% in agriculture. Unemployment in 2007 was estimated at 3.8%.

16 SPORTS

Though Cypriots were allegedly numbered among the first Olympians and ancient gymnasiums have been preserved on the island, sports only recently commanded government attention through the creation of the Cyprus Sports Organization (CSO) in 1969. This non-profit, government organization successfully administered its first Five-Year Development Plan from 1978 to 1982, initiating the construction of stadiums, swimming pools, and sports halls throughout the island. Successive Five-Year Development Plans continued the construction and maintenance of sports facilities and channeled grants to various sports organizations. In addition, the CSO extended its interest in sports to the international level, creating protocols and developing sports relations with the Commonwealth of Independent States, Bulgaria, Czechoslovakia, Austria, and Germany. Cyprus also shares sports-related technical and financial interests with Greece. The third Five-Year Development Plan aimed to enhance the performance and competitive aspect of individual sports; consequently, 35 sports federations and 4 cofederations are present on the island and are acknowledged by parallel international organizations, as well as by the International Olympic Committee.

Greek Cypriot men, reflecting the recreational tastes of so many European countries, are most strongly drawn to football (soccer in America) as both spectators and players. Three league divisions composed of 36 teams currently exist under the Cyprus Football Association, and the island has been a participant in World Cup matches. The hunting season likewise attracts a throng of Cypriots, as the countryside will host as many as 40,000 male hunters on Wednesdays or Sundays.

Apart from ballet, dancing, and karate, which are strongly affiliated with the performing and cultural arts, sports are not introduced to young Cypriots by way of arduous training which underlies the development of stellar athletes. Still, many Cypriot children have increasingly participated in sports through the CSO's Sports For All and other programs targeted at children. The natural resources of the island offer Cypriots of all ages diverse sports activities in a variety of seasons. The installment of three ski runs on Mt. Olympus has drawn skiers to the Troodos Mountains from the months of January through mid-March. During the warmer seasons, swimming can be enjoyed throughout the many beaches.

17 ENTERTAINMENT AND RECREATION

Like many tourists, Cypriots enjoy packing the car with family, relatives, and ample foods, and heading for the mountains. While nightclubs, restaurants, and movie theaters are popular for many, most Greek Cypriots enjoy entertaining family and friends in the home.

18 FOLK ART, CRAFTS, AND HOBBIES

For more than a century, *lefkaritiki* embroidery and linen has been marketed throughout the world, and it takes its name from the city of its origin, Pano Lefkara. Crafted from Irish linen, each piece is unique, requires several weeks of work, and can be quite costly. The art has been somewhat industrialized, however, by four manufacturing companies within Lefkara who together employ more than 600 workers, and have brought much prosperity to the city through this art.

Official Handicraft Centers have been established in Limassol, Larnaca, Paphos, and Nicosia for the purpose of maintaining folk art, which has recently suffered from the cheap reproductions of authentic Cypriot pieces that have been mass-produced and imported from Hong Kong and Greece.

19 SOCIAL PROBLEMS

Social and political tensions between the Greek Cypriots and Turkish Cypriots have led to discrimination between the groups, but incidences of major violence have been rare as UN-sponsored negotiations continue. Harassment and acts of vandalism have been reported as effects of discrimination from both sides. Greek Cypriots are particularly interested in resolutions that would insure property and settlement rights and a return of territory under a single integrated government structure. The Turkish Cypriots, however, are in favor of maintaining two autonomous societies with limited contact between the governments and political equality in the eyes of the world. While travel between the two communities is allowed, each side places certain restrictions and regulations on border crossing. For example, Greek Cypriots must have automobile insurance from a company within the Turkish Cypriot administered area in order to drive into the area. The Greek Cypriots place a similar regulation on Turkish Cypriot motorists. At the end of 2006 there were approximately 238,000 Greek Cypriots listed as internally displaced persons as a result of the political conflict. Many of these individuals rely on government financial assistance. The entrance of Cyprus into the European Union in 2004 caused a great deal of tension between the Greek and Turkish Communities, since the Turkish Cypriot administered area is not recognized as an independent government within the European Union. Though the recognized Cypriot government has switched its currency to the euro as of January 2008, the northern Turkish Cypriot controlled government continues to use the new Turkish lira.

There have been some reports of discrimination against other minority ethnic groups within the country, such as the Roma. Homosexuals also face social discrimination despite antidiscrimination laws. While Cyprus was once believed to be a narcotics brokering center for drugs shipped to Europe, Cypriot police have joined with other European centers of justice to curtail drug trafficking and have developed no tolerance policies on drug trafficking issues.

20 GENDER ISSUES

While women have been granted the same legal status as men and are generally able to find positions in the workforce, there is still a strong belief in society that a woman's primary roles are those of wife and mother. Sexual harassment in the workplace is widespread, even though a majority of specific cases go unreported by women who may fear losing their jobs or simply enduring an increase in harassment. Domestic abuse of women is also widespread, again with many incidences left unreported. While the law requires that men and women receive equal pay for equal work, most women in blue-collar jobs earn about 25% to 30% less than their male counterparts. The percentage is less in white collar professions, but there is still no pay equity.

21 BIBLIOGRAPHY

Boroweic, Andrew. *Cyprus: A Troubled Island.* Westport, CT: Praegar, 2000.

Brey, Hansjorg, and Claudia Muller, ed. *Insights Guides. Cyprus.* Boston: Houghton Mifflin Company, 1993.

Cyprus. Published by the Press and Information Office, Republic of Cyprus.

Hannay, David. *Cyprus: The Search for a Solution.* New York: Palgrave Macmillan, 2005.

Papdakis, Yiannis, et al. *Divided Cyprus: Modernity, History, and an Island in Conflict.* Bloomington, IN: Indiana University Press, 2006.

Solsten, Eric, ed. *Cyprus: A Country Study.* 4th ed. Federal Research Division, Library of Congress, 1993.

—revised by K. Ellicott

GUJARATIS

PRONUNCIATION: goo-juh-RAH-teez
LOCATION: India (Gujarat state)
POPULATION: 50,596,992 (2001 Census of India)
LANGUAGE: Gujarati
RELIGION: Hindu; small populations of Muslims, Jains, Parsis
RELATED ARTICLES: Vol. 4: People of India

¹ INTRODUCTION

Gujaratis are the inhabitants of Gujarat, one of the western states of the Republic of India. The names of both the state and its people are derived from the "Gujara," a people identified by some as a branch of the White Huns, who ruled the area during the 8th and 9th centuries. The name "Gujarat" has also been linked to the Gujaras, a pastoral caste found throughout northwestern India.

Gujarati history goes back much farther than the Gujaras. Archaeological evidence reveals that the region was settled during prehistoric times. The remains of cities in Gujarat dating from around 2000 BC indicate that the people shared in the cultural achievements of the Harappan civilization. The known history of Gujarat, however, begins around 250 BC. Carved rock edicts in the Girnar Hills in Saurashtra show that Gujarat formed part of Ashoka Maurya's Empire at this time. In succeeding centuries, the region came under the rule of most of the great dynasties (e.g. the Sakas, Guptas, Gujaras) that arose in western India. The end of the thirteenth century, however, saw Gujarat conquered by the Muslims.

For the next 450 years, Gujarat was ruled by Muslims, either independent sultans or the vassals of the Mughal emperors. Gujarat was overrun by the Marathas in the mid-eighteenth century, but its control passed to the British East India Company in 1818. In the following decades, the Gujarat area was administered variously as a part of Bombay Province, as a province in its own right, and as a States Agency (the region contained many princely states paying tribute to the British). Following India's independence in 1947, Gujarat was incorporated into Bombay State. In 1960, the Gujarati-speaking areas of Bombay were split off to form the present-day state of Gujarat.

In the years following 1960, the state government of Gujarat was formed by the Indian National Congress, interspersed with rule by the Janata party in its various incarnations (1975–76, 1977–80, 1990–94, 1996–98), but in 1995 the Bharatiya Janata Party (BJP), a Hindu nationalist party, took power (the Rashtriya Janata Party ran the state government from 1996–98). In 2008 the Chief Minister, Narendra Modi was serving his third term as Chief Minister—he and his government belong to the BJP—and assumed his office in 2002. Modi has been accused of presiding over what the Indian press has termed the "Gujarat Holocaust." The story begins with the destruction of the Babri Mosque in 1992 by Hindu nationalists, supported by the opposition (at the national level) BJP. The mosque was believed by Hindus to have been built on the site of Ram's birthplace (Ram Janmabhoomi—Ram was a king in ancient India and is held to be an incarnation of Vishnu, an important Hindu deity) in Ayodhya in the Indian state of Uttar Pradesh. Despite a commitment by India's Supreme Court that the mosque would not be harmed, the mosque was stormed and destroyed by Hindu nationalists, who saw its presence as a sacrilege. They were believers in "Hindutva" (Hinduness), a word first coined in 1923 and used to describe movements devoted to Hindu nationalism. Ever since, the site has been a center of pilgrimage for devout Hindus, and trainloads of Hindus, volunteers for the Vishva Hindu Parishad (VHP), an organization dedicated to serving the interests of Hinduism worldwide, have been making the journey by train from Ahmedabad in Gujarat to Ayodhya for pilgrimage and "*kar seva*" (technically, kar seva means "construction of or cleaning of religious sites").

On 27 February 2002, a train carrying Gujarati kar sevaks was returning to Ahmedabad from Ayodhya, where they were helping build a temple to Ram on the site of the former *masjid* (mosque), when it was stopped by a mob near Godhra Junction railway station, east of Ahmedabad in Gujarat State: the train was set alight, one car was completely gutted, and 59 people, all Hindus, died in the conflagration. A *bandh* (general strike) was called by the VHP for the next day, even though bandhs are generally accompanied by violence and have been made illegal by the central government. The bandh was supported by the Modi administration. The next day turned into an anti-Muslim orgy of mass slaughter, arson, and the complete breakdown of law and order in the state. Over the next three months, Muslim shops and homes were destroyed and in Ahmedabad and Vadodra (Baroda) several Muslims, including a former Congress MP for Ahmedabad, were burnt alive. The communal violence between Hindus and Muslims continued until May 2002 and Modi was accused of at best standing by and doing nothing to stop the carnage and at worst of being complicit in the violence.

In September 2004 the Banerjee Committee, a panel appointed by the central government and headed by former Supreme Court judge UC Banerjee to probe the Godhra train fire concluded that the fire was accidental. Its findings, however, were challenged by the BJP and the Gujarat inspector-general of police. A Citizens Tribunal headed by retired Supreme Court justice Krishna Iyer collected evidence and testimony from more than 2,000 riot victims, witnesses, and others. In its report, the tribunal accuses the state government and Chief Minister Modi of complicity in the violence. International organizations estimate over 2,000 people, mostly Muslims, were killed during this period.

2 LOCATION AND HOMELAND

The 2001 census reported Gujarat's population as 50.6 million persons. Assuming population growth rates similar to those of the 1991–2001 decade, the current population is estimated to be close to 59 million. This figure does not include the sizable community of overseas Gujaratis, mainly pursuing business activities, in Asia and the Pacific, the Middle East, Africa, and the West.

Gujarat lies on India's west coast, and part of its western boundary is also India's international border with Pakistan. Its coastline runs from just east of the mouth of the Indus River, curves around the great peninsula of Saurashtra that juts out into the Arabian Sea, then swings south to a point roughly 160 km (100 mi) north of Bombay. Geographically, Gujarat falls into three broad divisions, mainland Gujarat, the Saurash-

tra Peninsula, and Kachch. Mainland Gujarat consists of the broad coastal plains east of the Gulf of Cambay. These merge to the north with the lowlands around Ahmedabad and northern Gujarat. Fringing this area on the north and east are the uplands of the southern Aravallis, the western Vindhya and Satpura Ranges, and the Western Ghats. The Narmada and the Tapti are major rivers that flow across the southern lowlands to enter the Gulf of Cambay. Southern areas receive 160 cm (63 in) of rain a year, which, combined with fertile soil, makes them a productive agricultural region. The amount of rainfall declines rapidly to the north and west, however, and most of Gujarat is semiarid or arid.

Saurashtra (also known as Kathiawar) is an important historical and cultural region of Gujarat. It consists of a peninsula bounded by the Gulf of Cambay, the Arabian Sea, and the Gulf of Kachch. Broad coastal plains surround a series of low plateaus and hills in the interior. One of these, the Gir Range (about 640 m or 2,100 ft), is home to a wildlife sanctuary for the last Asian lion population in the world. Kachch, in the far west, is another historical and cultural region. Much of its area is taken up by the Rann of Kachch, a vast expanse of tidal mud flats and salt marshes that merges almost imperceptibly with the Thar Desert to the north. Rainfall in the Rann averages around 30 cm (about 12 in). Maximum temperatures in the hot season average over 43°C (110°F) in northern Gujarat.

In the early hours of 26 January 2001, Gujarat experienced a devastating earthquake. Resulting from the release of pressure as two of the earth's major tectonic plates (the Indian and the Eurasian plates) collided, and measuring 8.1 on the Richter scale, the quake had its epicenter near Bhuj, in Kachch, and resulted in the death of at least 20,000 people with more than 150,000 people injured and over 1 million homes destroyed. National and international aid in the form of specialized rescue assistance, medical aid, food and clothes poured in, but the distribution of this aid offered an insight into the partisan nature of both state and society in Gujarat and provided a portent of events to come in early 2002 (the Godhra communal violence). There was discrimination against Muslims in the distribution of aid by both the state government and the Sangh Parivar, the loose association of Hindu organizations in the state, through which much of the aid was administered.

3 LANGUAGE

Gujarati, the language of Gujarat, is an Indo-Aryan language derived partly from Sanskrit and partly from Prakit (an ancient language spoken by the common people of India rather than by Brahmans and scholars). There are several dialects of Gujarati. These include Kachchi, spoken in Kachch, the Kathiawadi of Saurashtra, and the Surati dialect of the southern region around Surat. Bhili, the tongue of the tribal Bhils in the northern and eastern areas of the state, is very similar to Gujarati. An ancient form, Old Gujarati was once spoken in neighboring areas of Rajasthan, and dialects in these areas still show strong connections with Gujarati. Gujarati is written in a cursive script modified from Devanagari.

4 FOLKLORE

According to Hindu legend, the hero-god Krishna was forced to abandon his ancestral home of Mathura and moved his capital to Dvaraka (the modern Dwarka) at the western tip of the

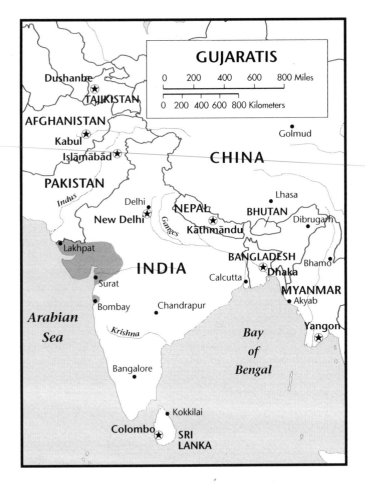

GUJARATIS

0   200   400   600   800 Miles

0 200 400 600 800 Kilometers

jarati Hindus accept the fundamental beliefs and philosophy of the Hindu religion.

Muslims make up some 8.73% of Gujarat's population. Sunnis predominate, although the Khoja and Bohra form a significant Shiite minority. Jains, although comparatively few in number, have played a major role in the shaping of Gujarati culture. They are mainly of the Svetambara ("white-clad") sect of the religion. Girnar and Satrunjaya Hill, near Palitana, are major centers of Jain pilgrimage. There are small Parsi communities in Surat and Navsari.

⁶ MAJOR HOLIDAYS

The various communities of Gujarat celebrate their own religious festivals. Thus Muslims observe Muharram and the "Ids," Jains celebrate Mahavira's birthday, and Parsis keep their Gahambars (six seasonal festivals). Hindus observe the major festivals of the Hindu calendar, but Navratri is a special holiday of the Gujaratis. Navratri, literally "nine nights," is celebrated on the nine nights leading up to Dasahara day. It is a time of gaiety, when men and women gather in village squares and temple compounds to sing and dance. The festival ends on Dasahara day, when artisans worship their tools, farmers their ploughs, and students their books.

Janamashtami (Krishna's birthday) and other Krishna festivals are important for Vaishnavas. Of particular significance in Gujarat is the national holiday that marks M. K. Gandhi's birthday. Mahatma Gandhi, one of the great men of the twentieth century, and universally regarded as the father of the modern Indian nation, was born in Porbandar in Saurashtra on 2 October 1869.

⁷ RITES OF PASSAGE

Gujaratis follow the life-cycle rituals prescribed by their communities. Thus, although the details of the ceremonies may differ according to caste, Hindus observe the rituals (*samskaras*) set out in the Vedas and other Hindu texts. These include ritual purification after childbirth, the name-giving ceremony, the first-feeding ceremony, and the head-shaving ceremony.

One of the most important rites for the higher castes is the *upanayana* ceremony, the donning of the sacred thread. Virtually all groups have some sort of period of seclusion followed by purification rites for girls at their first menstruation. Jain rituals in general follow Hindu patterns. Muslim practices include whispering the Call to Prayer (*azan*) in a newborn baby's ear, head-shaving and naming ceremonies, and the all-important circumcision (*sunnat*) for males.

Most Gujarati Hindus cremate their dead, although some lower-caste groups bury them. Again, death rites follow procedures set out in the Hindu sacred texts, with Brahman priests officiating at the funeral ceremony. Ashes and bone are collected from the funeral pyre to be scattered, if at all possible, in the sacred Ganges River. Hindus carry out rituals to remove pollution after the funeral, observe a period of mourning, and hold the important death feast (*sraddha*). Jain funeral customs tend to follow the Hindu pattern, while Muslims bury their dead.

⁸ INTERPERSONAL RELATIONS

Gujarati Hindus greet each other with the *namaskara*, which consists of the gesture of joining hands (*anjali*) accompanied

Saurashtra Peninsula. Following the events related in the epic known as the *Mahabharata*, Krishna returned to a city beset by ominous signs. The Yadava chiefs, Krishna's relatives, began to quarrel and became engaged in a drunken brawl that had the entire city in an uproar. Soon, nearly all the Yadava chiefs were dead. Krishna's own son was killed, and his brother was mortally wounded. Disheartened by these events, Krishna retired to the forest near the city to ponder the situation. He was mistaken for a deer and killed by a hunter. The city of Dvaraka was then engulfed by the sea.

Writers note that the events of Krishna's later life are quite "un-Indian" in their tragic nature. The drunken brawl, the slaughter of so many people, the slain hero, the city engulfed by the sea—all are themes found in early European literature, but nowhere else in Hindu mythology.

⁵ RELIGION

Gujaratis are overwhelmingly Hindu; about 90% of the population follows Hinduism. The Vallabhacharya sect of Krishna worshipers has a particularly strong following among the Gujarati *bania* (trading) castes. Dwarka, Krishna's famed capital in Saurashtra, is an important place of pilgrimage for this sect, and is regarded as one of India's seven sacred cities. Shiva also has his following among Gujaratis. The Somnath Temple, on Saurashtra's southern coast, is an important Shaivite shrine. Although their religious practices may differ in details, all Guby the words "Namas" or "Namaste" (an exclamation of homage for the deity). Muslims use the "Salaam" when they meet. A handshake or a casual wave of the hand is a common greeting in urban areas.

9 LIVING CONDITIONS

A typical Gujarati village consists of a cluster of one- or two-story houses arranged along a central street. A temple, a village square, a few shops, and the well used by higher castes are found in the village center. Around this central area, where the agricultural and trading castes live, are the houses of the artisan castes. In the past, villages were surrounded by mud walls for protection against robbers. The untouchable castes, the Dheds (road sweepers) and Bhangis (cleaners), live outside the boundaries of the village.

The houses of the cultivators are generally roomy, and built of mud or brick, according to the wealth of the owner. Furniture consists of a couple of strong wooden boxes to hold valuables, wooden bed and coverings, and copper and earthenware cooking utensils. There is usually no stable for livestock, so cattle and goats are kept in the house. Living conditions in a village setting are quite different from those of the affluent business castes in cities such as Ahmedabad, Vadodara (Baroda), and Surat.

10 FAMILY LIFE

In general, Gujaratis conform to northern Indian patterns of kinship, marriage practices, and family structure. The norm is to marry within one's caste, but outside one's clan. Caste divisions and subdivisions among the *Banias* can be quite complex. Descent is determined through the father's line, and newlyweds live with the father's family. Marriages are arranged, and marriage rituals follow the customs and traditions of each individual caste or religious community. The joint family is typical among Gujaratis, with a household consisting of two or three generations of men and their dependents. A woman's main responsibility is the bearing and raising of children, preferably sons. Among the higher castes, women are mostly housewives. Lower caste women are expected to work in the fields or otherwise contribute to the family income.

11 CLOTHING

The traditional dress of a well-to-do Hindu man in Gujarat consists of a loincloth (*dhoti*), over which he wears a shirt (*badan*) and a coat (*angharko*) closed with strings instead of buttons. A length of cloth (*picchodi* or *dupatto*) is worn as a scarf over the shoulders or sometimes tied around the waist. The turban (*paghdi*), often fringed with gold brocade at each end, is tied in a manner that identifies the wearer's caste. Country-made shoes complete the outfit. A woman of high status typically wears the *sadi* or *sallo* (types of *saris*) with the *choli* (blouse). Gujarati women share their fellow Indians' love of jewelry.

As in the rest of India, dress styles vary according to caste and region. A *Bania* merchant from Ahmedabad dresses differently from a *Kunbi* farmer in Saurashtra, who in turn dresses differently from a member of the Bhil tribe of eastern Gujarat. There are also distinct regional patterns of dress. A man from Kachch, for example has clothes and a style of tying his turban that set him apart from someone from Junagadh or Bhavnagar.

A Gujarat woman. (Anthony Cassidy/Getty Images)

While traditional dress is still seen in rural areas, many urban dwellers (particularly men) have followed the modern trend toward Western-style clothes.

12 FOOD

Gujarati cuisine is strictly vegetarian, reflecting the strong influence of Jains and the Vaishnavas in the region. Wheat and the two kinds of millet (*jowar, bajri*) are the main staples. Flour is made into unleavened bread called "roti." This is eaten with a variety of vegetable dishes. The villager takes a light breakfast of roti and milk or curds before setting out for the fields. Lunch is usually roti and buttermilk.

The main meal is eaten in the evening and consists of rice, split peas (*dal-bhat*), and vegetables. More substantial meals are served on the *thali*, a metal tray on which roti, rice, and small round bowls containing various dishes are placed. The bowls may hold vegetables such as eggplant, potatoes, beans, *dal* (lentils), and *dahi* (curds). *Kadhi*, a savory curry of curds and fried cakes made from pulses, is a popular dish. And no Gujarati would eat a meal without generous helpings of *ghi* (clarified butter). Milk-based desserts are common. *Srikhand* is a rich dessert made with curds and spiced with saffron, cardamom, nuts, and fruit. Gujarat is also known for its delicious ice cream. There is strong religious-based sentiment against alcohol, and Gujarat has been under prohibition since 1947.

13 EDUCATION

The Gujarati emphasis on business activities provides a strong motivation for literacy. Among the *Bania* castes, education in reading, writing, mathematics, and accounting begins early in life. Literacy among males approaches 100%. However, when tribal people and the lower castes are figured into the equation, literacy in Gujarat State drops to 69.97% (80.5% for males and 58.6% for females). These figures were reported in the 2001 census.

14 CULTURAL HERITAGE

Gujaratis have a cultural heritage that can be traced back to the Harappan civilization of three thousand years ago. While the exact nature and extent of Harappan contributions to Gujarati culture are unclear, it is likely that some elements survive in modern folk traditions. The beadwork of Saurashtra, for instance, may well have had Harappan origins. A substantial bead factory was uncovered at the archaeological site at Lothal. Gujaratis have a literature that dates to the twelfth century.

Many other groups have contributed to Gujarati culture. From the Vaishnavas come the legends and mythology of Krishna, to whom are ascribed the popular *Ras* and *Garba* folk dances. Jains influenced temple architecture and developed a distinctive style of painting. The Jain commitment to nonviolence (*ahimsa*) is seen not only in Gujarat's vegetarian cuisine, but in institutions such as animal homes (*pinjrapols*). Muslim architecture in Gujarat combined Hindu elements with its own styles.

15 WORK

The trading (*bania*) castes are very important among the Gujaratis. They make up a significantly higher proportion of the population than elsewhere in India. Gujaratis have traveled to Bombay, to other cities in India, and around the world in search of business opportunities. Gujarat is also a leading industrial state. Ahmedabad, often referred to as the "Manchester of India," is a major center of textile manufacturing. Vadodara and Surat are also important industrial towns. Agriculture is more commercial than in many other parts of India; cotton, sugarcane, oilseeds, and peanuts are major cash crops.

16 SPORTS

Children in Gujarat are relatively free of responsibilities until about nine or ten years of age and spend their leisure time in a variety of ways. Girls play "house," dress their dolls, and hold mock wedding ceremonies for them. Boys" activities center on playing marbles, spinning tops, and flying kites, and games such as *kabaddi* (team wrestling). *Khokho*, a kind of team tag game, is another popular local pastime. Modern sports such as soccer, cricket, field hockey, and basketball are played throughout the Gujarat region.

17 ENTERTAINMENT AND RECREATION

Especially in the cities, Gujaratis have access to movies, radio, and television. In the more isolated villages, however, traditional forms of entertainment remain a part of community life. These may be linked to religious fairs and festivals or provided by traveling bands of professional entertainers. A folk drama known as *Bhavai* is performed by Targalas and other castes whose ancestral profession is music and the theatrical arts. The Bhats and Charans are bards and genealogists in Gujarat who have preserved much of the region's folk culture and traditions.

18 FOLK ARTS, CRAFTS, AND HOBBIES

Gujarat is well known for its traditional handcrafted textiles. Fine silk saris are made in Patan, and attractive block prints are produced in Ahmedabad. Surat is famous for its *zari*, embroidery using gold or silver thread. Jumnagar is a center of colorful tie-dyed work, while peasant women in Saurashtra and Kachch produce embroidery containing tiny mirrors as well as beadwork items. The making of jewelry and cutting of precious stones is a traditional handicraft of Gujarat. The artisans of Kachch are known in particular for their silver work. Woodcarving is an ancient skill in Gujarat, as can be seen in the fine carvings found in houses and temples throughout the region. Wooden furniture is also produced in a distinctive Gujarati style.

19 SOCIAL PROBLEMS

Although Gujaratis have made great strides in improving the living conditions of their state's population, problems of poverty, malnutrition, and a lack of basic amenities such as drinking water and health facilities remain in some areas. An outbreak of pneumonic plague in Surat in 1994 caused panic among the population and also drastically reduced tourism in India at that time. The Gujarat government is deeply involved in the massive Sardar Sarovar Dam which has been built on the Narmada River. Although it was planned to help provide irrigation and power to the state, a lack of resources combined with squabbling among the partner states (Gujarat, Maharashtra, Madhya Pradesh, and Rajasthan) has delayed the project. An anti-dam environmental movement has reached a national and even international audience.

As Gandhi's home state, Gujarat has been identified with the nonviolence movement. However, communal violence erupts from time to time across the normally peaceful state. In December 1992, for example, riots that cost both Muslim and Hindu lives swept Ahmedabad, Vadodara, and Surat. They were triggered by the destruction of the Babri Masjid mosque in Ayodhya in Uttar Pradesh by Hindu fundamentalists. On the positive side, Gujaratis have taken full advantage of the recent liberalization of India's economic policies to attract foreign business and investment to the state.

A major, ongoing issue in Gujarat is the displacement of population from the countryside by the construction of the Sardar Sarovar Dam on the Narmada River, in south-eastern Gujarat. The Dam is part of a network of more than 3,000 dams that will make up one of the world's largest water projects with an extensive canal and irrigation system providing water to, according to government estimates, over 1.8 million hectares (over 700,00 acres) of the states of Rajasthan, Madhya Pradesh, Maharashtra and (mainly) Gujarat. However, over 25,000 families will be displaced by the dam, their villages and lands submerged under water, and the construction is opposed by organizations such as the Narmada Bachao Andolan (NBA). Protests against the dam's construction, such as those organized by NBA, played a major role in convincing the World Bank to pull funding from the project in 1993. The displaced families claim that the compensation and land they are due to receive is inadequate, but in 2000, despite this opposition, the Supreme Court of India gave permission for the construction of the dam to proceed.

20 GENDER ISSUES

Hindu women, especially those of lower caste experience the constraints of their religion and, like their Muslim counterparts, suffer from poverty and illiteracy. Gujarat, despite being considered an industrialized, developed, wealthy and cultured state, ranks 21st amongst India's states in the sphere of women's literacy. The Census of India 2001 shows female literacy in Dahod, a town in eastern Gujarat on the borders of Rajasthan and Madhya Pradesh to be only 31.87%. The difference between literacy rate of male and female is over 20%, a difference which the Government of Gujarat and the people of Gujarat cannot ignore. This issue is being addressed as part of the government's Continuing Education Scheme which involves the setting up of Continuing Education Centers (CECs) and Nodal Continuing Education Centers.

According to the 2001 Census of India, Muslims form the largest minority group in Gujarat, numbering over 50 million people and accounting for nearly 8.73% of the population (89.48% of Gujaratis are Hindu). Women in the Muslim community suffer the restrictions of their religion, from *purdah* and wearing the *burqa* to child marriages and "honor killings." In addition to illiteracy and poverty, Muslim women were subjected to "unimaginable inhuman and barbaric" sexual violence during the 2002 Godhra carnage, and some still live in refugee camps, being too afraid to return to their homes.

Fetching and carrying water is women's work in rural India. In the villages of the desert district of Banaskantha, in northern Gujarat, women spend up to six hours a day bringing water from distant sources to their homes. They carry up to 15 liters on their heads on each trip, often walking barefoot. Banaskantha receives less than 7 inches of rainfall each year. The water table has dropped by 6.5 feet a year, as withdrawals exceed natural replenishment. Over 75% of the district's villages no longer have reliable, year-round sources of fresh water. It was not until the end of the 20th century that the government formally recognized the need to involve rural communities in managing water resources, and only in 1999 did it establish guidelines for involving women. However, the women of Gujarat began taking their first steps toward self-governance in water issues long before then.

Guided by an all-women trade union—the Self-Employed Women's Association (SEWA), founded in Ahmedabad in 1972—Gujarati women gradually began to exert their influence over state authorities and secured a greater voice for themselves not only within the community but also inside their own homes. The underlying strategy behind this success has been to link protecting the environment with improving livelihoods. For rural women, economic benefits often depend on the health of the natural resources they rely on. Governments, however, often treat the environment and economic development as mutually exclusive. For example, Gujarat is home to the massive Sardar Sarovar dam, which is now under construction on the Narmada River. Despite the project's goal of alleviating water shortages in rural communities, an independent review commissioned by the World Bank found that plans for the delivery of water to villagers in the drought-prone regions of Gujarat are not on track and they are not likely to happen any time soon, if at all.

In 1986, the State Water Board of Gujarat invited SEWA to increase its participation in village-level water committees. After three consecutive years of drought, the water board believed that proactive local communities might succeed where more centralized management had failed. The water works in many regions were in complete disarray. SEWA held a number of meetings where villagers expressed two urgent needs: The need to conserve water, revive traditional sources like surface wells and ponds, and create alternative water sources like roof rainwater harvesting structures. The second need was to find non-water based work, as seasonal water shortages caused a loss of jobs.

To push for these changes, SEWA encouraged women to join local water committees, called *pânî samitis*. SEWA had already organized women into about 50 business-development groups—with activities from embroidery to timber and rainwater harvesting—to help them earn more money. Giving women a voice on local water committees was the next logical step because women are primarily responsible for fetching and using water.

At first, however, women were reluctant to come forward because water "infrastructure" was regarded as a male responsibility. Most men were critical of women's participation, and several went so far as to say they would not drink water from a source created by women. But women slowly gained confidence as they began to take the lead in water activities, raised their productivity, and saw their incomes increase. The initial 42 pani samitis were to take over maintenance of the piped water system in the Santhalpur and Radhanpur sub-districts, including collecting user fees. But after the state government reversed its position on this, the village women turned to reviving and maintaining their traditional community sources of water. Pani samitis began constructing check dams, deepening existing ponds, and lining ponds with plastic sheeting to prevent salinization of the water from the region's salty soils.

By 1995 the women's association had accumulated a great deal of experience in the water sector throughout Gujarat, and its projects were yielding tangible economic, social, and environmental benefits throughout the state. The state government, recognizing SEWA's successes, invited the group to lead and implement a state-wide watershed development program. SEWA used this unprecedented opportunity to launch a more comprehensive program than the state had envisioned, one that not only promoted ecological regeneration, but fostered economic development as well. The Water, Women, and Work Millennium Campaign, as it has been called, integrates erosion controls, water conservation measures, tree-planting and forestry initiatives, dryland agriculture, and education, training, and capacity building for communities.

Between 1995 and 2001, the water campaign spread to a total of 502 villages in 9 districts. Women comprised 80% or more of the membership of most of the new water users committees, and committee activities revolved around issues of particular interest to women—fodder growing, nursery plantations, improved agriculture, rain-water harvesting and capacity-building.

Results of the water campaign in Banaskantha District have been impressive. Aquifers in 18 villages have been recharged. A total of 150 wells, including surface wells, tube wells, and farm wells, have been recharged in eight villages. In Porana village alone, a total of 25 wells have been recharged. Salinity has decreased in the treated land thanks to various innovative and low-cost mechanisms for sweetening and recharging the groundwater. Groundwater is lifted with a water pump for irrigation and farmers are able to grow three crops annually instead of one. The investment was just Rs 5,000 (US$106) for each pump system. SEWA's success has prompted villagers and civilian society groups to question India's trend toward privatizing water distribution services. There is some sign that government agencies are beginning to trust the "people's sector" to handle water supply activities, despite skepticism that poor, illiterate women could prove competent.

Apart from its work in the area of water, SEWA has expanded into other areas. Since the 1990s, SEWA has been involved with banking and providing credit to rural women, the SEWA Mahila Housing Trust helped distribute food and assisted people in rebuilding their homes after the devastating 2001 earthquake, SEWA is involved in providing health facilities, in running craft associations and dairy co-operatives, and is a partner, with the state government and UNICEF, in the Development of Women and Children in Rural Areas (DWCRA) program.

[21] BIBLIOGRAPHY

Basham, A. L., ed. *A Cultural History of India*. Oxford: Clarendon Press, 1975.

Bhatt, Narhari K. *Gujarat*. New Delhi: Publications Division, Ministry of Information and Broadcasting, Government of India, 1972.

Campbell, James M., ed. *Hindu Castes and Tribes of Gujarat*. Gurgaon, India: Vintage Books, 1988 (Reprint of *Gazetteer of the Bombay Presidency. Vol. XI. Part I. Gujarat Population: Hindus*. Bombay: Government Central Press, 1901).

Craven, Roy. C. *A Concise History of Indian Art*. New York: Praeger, 1976.

Crowell, Daniel W. *The SEWA Movement and Rural Development*. New Delhi: Sage Publications, 2003.

Möller, Ulrika. *The Prospects of Security Co-operation: A Matter of Relative Gains or Recognition? India and Nuclear Weapons Control*. Göteborg: Department of Political Science, Göteborg University, 2007.

Palit, Chittabrata and Mahua Sarkar, ed. *Indian Vistas of Environment*. Delhi: Kalpaz Publications, 2007.

Robinson, Francis, ed. *The Cambridge Encyclopedia of India, Pakistan, Bangladesh, Sri Lanka, Nepal, Bhutan and the Maldives*. Cambridge: Cambridge University Press, 1989.

Schwartzberg, Joseph E., ed. *A Historical Atlas of South Asia*. 2nd impression. New York and Oxford: Oxford University Press, 1992.

Spate, O. H. K., and A. T. A. Learmonth. *India and Pakistan: A General and Regional Geography*. 3rd rev. ed. London: Methuen, 1967.

The Statesman. *The Gujarat Holocaust: A Compilation of Caveats and Editorials from the Statesman*. Kolkata: The Statesman, 2002.

Thoothi, N. A. *The Vaishnavas of Gujarat*. London: Longmans, Green, 1935.

Verma. S. B. *Status of Women in Modern India*. New Delhi: Deep & Deep, 2005.

Wolpert, Stanley. *India*. Berkeley: University of California Press, 1991

Yagnik, Achyut and Suchitra Sheth. *The Shaping of Modern Gujarat: Plurality, Hindutva and Beyond*. New Delhi: Penguin Books, 2005

—by D. O. Lodrick.

GURUNGS

PRONUNCIATION: gur-OONGS
ALTERNATE NAMES: Tamu
LOCATION: Nepal (central Himalayan Mountain region)
POPULATION: 543,571 (2001 Census of Nepal)
LANGUAGE: Gurung; Nepali
RELIGION: Mix of Tibetan Buddhism, Hinduism, and local animistic practices

¹ INTRODUCTION

The Gurungs are a hill people living on the southern slopes of the Himalayan Mountains in central Nepal. In their own language, they call themselves "Tamu" (*Ta* means thunder, *mu* symbolizes sky). Their origins are uncertain, although they are of Mongoloid stock and their ancestors may have migrated to their current location from Tibet around 2,000 years ago.

Gurung tradition maintains that in ancient times a Gurung kingdom, ruled by a "Ghale Rājā," emerged among the numerous small kingdoms and states that existed in the Himalayan foothills. This kingdom was conquered by a neighboring *Rājā* in the 15th century AD. During the 16th century, it was incorporated into the expanding Gurkha empire of the Shah dynasty. Gurungs served as soldiers in the armies of the Shah kings, including Prithvi Narayan Shah who conquered the Kathmandu Valley in 1768 and completed the unification of Nepal.

The tradition of Gurung service in the army of the Gurkha Kingdom continued into the 19th century, and Gurungs were involved in military campaigns against both the Chinese and British. The British were so impressed with the fighting qualities of the Gurkhas following the 1814–1816 Anglo-Gurkha war that they began recruiting Gurkha soldiers into the service of the East India Company. Gurungs (along with the Magars) make up the bulk of the soldiers serving today in the Gurkha regiments of the British and Indian armies.

The Gurung, like all peoples in Nepal, have been influenced by political events in the region. Nepal was an absolute monarchy until 1990, when, faced with a people's movement against the absolute monarchy, King Birendra, agreed to large-scale political reforms by creating a parliamentary democracy with the king as the head of state and a prime minister as the head of the government. All Nepalese citizens 18 years and older became eligible to vote and in the first free and fair elections in Nepal in 1991, the Nepali Congress was victorious. However, governments in Nepal have tended to be highly unstable, no government having survived for more than two years since 1991, either through internal collapse or parliamentary dissolution by the monarch.

In February 1996 the Communist Party of Nepal (Maoist) began a violent insurgency in more than 50 of the country's 75 districts. Nearly 13,000 police, civilians, and insurgents are estimated to have been killed in the conflict since 1996. In July 2001 Prime Minister Deuba announced a cease-fire, which the Maoists pledged to observe, as part of a government effort to seek a negotiated solution to the conflict. Although Maoist-instigated intimidation and extortion continued, the killings largely subsided after the cease-fire was announced. The government and Maoists held talks in late 2001.

It is claimed that, hoping to free themselves from dominance by the Brahman-Chhetri-Newar (BCN) elite, Gurungs supported the Maoist insurgency. But Gurungs were also represented in the armed forces and police so they took casualties on both sides of the conflict. An estimated 12,800 deaths are reported during the insurgency, with a further 100,000 to 150,00 people being displaced. The government feared that Gurungs, with their military background, were providing training to insurgents in remote areas of Nepal.

On 1 June 2001, however, Crown Prince Dipendra was officially reported to have shot and killed his father, King Birendra; his mother, Queen Aishwarya; his brother; his sister, his father's younger brother, Prince Dhirendra; and several aunts, before turning the gun on himself. Gyanendra, Birendra's brother, succeeded as King, but on 1 February 2005, suspended the parliament, appointed a government led by himself, and enforced martial law. The King argued that civilian politicians were unfit to handle the Maoist insurgency. A broad coalition called the Seven Party Alliance (SPA) was formed in opposition to the royal takeover, encompassing the seven parliamentary parties who held about 90% of the seats in the old, dissolved parliament. A countrywide uprising began in April 2006, resulting in massive and spontaneous demonstrations and rallies held across Nepal against King Gyanendra's autocratic rule. Eventually, an agreement was reached by which the monarchy was to be abolished. Nepal's monarchy was abolished at the end of May 2008, thus ending 240 years of royal rule, and Nepal became the Federal Democratic Republic of Nepal with the prime minister becoming head of state.

² LOCATION AND HOMELAND

Assuming the population has increased at the national rate for Nepal since 2001, the current Gurung population is estimated at around 620,000 people. This does not include the small number of Gurungs who live in Sikkim, Bhutan and the Indian state of West Bengal. Traditional Gurung territory extends along the mountain slopes north of the Kali Gandaki River between the towns of Gorkha and Baglund. Some Gurungs are found in the upper Kali Gandaki valley itself and along the Marsyandi and Buri Gandaki rivers. Recent migrations towards the south have seen Gurungs settle in the hills of the Inner Terai zone.

The highland, or *lekhāli*, Gurungs retain a lifestyle closely tied to older traditions. They are dependent on high-altitude pastoralism and are strongly Buddhist in culture. The southern Gurungs, however, have a cereal-based economy and show a significant accommodation to Hindu cultural systems. In addition to this highland-lowland division, it is possible to distinguish between western, central, and eastern Gurungs, largely on the basis of linguistic differences.

Gurung villages are located at elevations between 1,050 and 2,150 m (approximately 3,500–7,000 ft). They often lie at the top of a hill or cling to the slopes of the steep gorges that rivers in the region have cut into the mountains. Above these, the terrain rises to the ridges and sheer cliffs that mark the southern slopes of the Annapurna, Lamjung, and Himalchuli ranges. Winters are cold and dry, although the temperature rarely drops below freezing. Differences in altitude and aspect, however, create considerable local variations in temperatures and precipitation. Mean monthly temperatures at Gorkha (elevation 1,667 m or 5,469 ft) range from about 8° to 30°c (approxi-

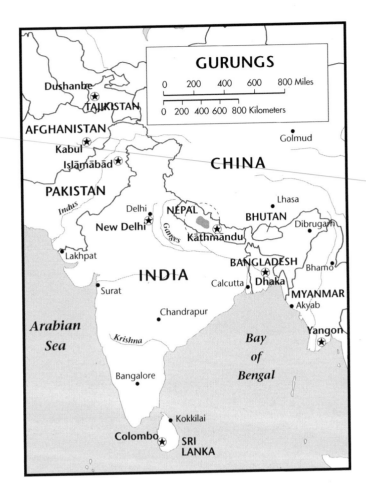

GURUNGS

continued on to the mountains where they abandoned the usual customs of their upper-caste status.

Over time, Lochan's wife gave birth to 3 sons named Ghale Mahan Gurung, Ghodane Mahan Gurung, and Lama Mahan Gurung, and a daughter. The priest fathered 2 sons—Lamechane Mahan Gurung and Plone Lamechane Gurung—and 3 daughters. The children of Lochan and the priest intermarried, and their descendants form one of the two subtribes of the Gurung, the *Chār Jāt* or "Four Clans" group. These clans are the Ghale, Ghodane, Lama, and Lamechane, in order of rank. The slave and his wife had 16 sons and 10 daughters. These married among themselves and were the forerunners of the *Solah Jāt* or "Sixteen Clans" subtribe. The Chār Jāt consider themselves superior to the Solah Jāt.

This legend serves to explain why the Gurungs, who have been strongly influenced by Hinduism, do not show the classic features of Hindu society such as a rigid caste structure and commensal (dining) restrictions. The mythical genealogy traced to a *ksatriya* ruler and the loss of former high-caste status is common among tribes who have their origins outside Hindu society. It places a tribal people firmly in a Hindu mold and provides them with a legitimizing Hindu pedigree.

5 RELIGION

The Gurungs follow Tibetan Buddhism, a form of *Mahāyāna* Buddhism that has been strongly influenced by the ancient pre-Buddhist religion of Tibet. They have also come into close contact with Hindu peoples and have adopted many Hindu religious traits. Gurung religion is thus a mix of Buddhism, Hinduism, and local animistic practices. It clearly reflects the group's tribal origins, as well as its transitional location between the Hindu and Buddhist cultural worlds.

Gurungs believe in concepts such as *karma* (the belief that actions in this life determine the nature of one's next incarnation), and worship Buddha and the *bodhisattvas* (the Savior Buddhas). Buddhist *lāmās* (priests) preside at life-cycle ceremonies such as purification rites for newborn babies, and funerals. The Gurungs also revere the major gods of Hinduism, celebrate Hindu festivals, and sometimes use Brahman priests to cast horoscopes and perform certain rituals. In addition, their world is inhabited by numerous local godlings, village deities, supernatural creatures of the forest, and spirits who have to be worshiped and appeased. Local animist shamans (priests) called *panju* and *klihbri* have the responsibility of dealing with this aspect of Gurung religion. They perform exorcisms, animal sacrifice, and other animistic rites. They help trap and expel witches. They also participate with *lāmās* in many Gurung life-cycle rituals.

6 MAJOR HOLIDAYS

Among the Hindu festivals celebrated by the Gurungs are Tihar, Dasain (the Nepali form of Dasahara), and Baisakh (Vaisakh) Purnima. In many instances, however, the Hindu festivals coincide with local Gurung festivals in their timing. This is clearly a part of the process of "Hinduization," by which non-Hindu tribal peoples are absorbed into Hindu society. It lends a degree of legitimacy to tribal celebrations by giving them a "Hindu" form.

One festival that is not of Hindu origin is the Gurung New Year, or *losar*. This is really the Tibetan New Year, but it is observed in late December or early January on a date different

mately 46°–86°f). Rainfall at Gorkha averages 193.5 cm (76 in) and is received mostly in the summer months. Vegetation is mostly temperate mixed forest, with oak, elm, and conifers. Bamboo and numerous rhododendron species are common at lower elevations.

3 LANGUAGE

Gurung, also known as Tamu or Temu, is a Tibeto-Burman language of the Sino-Tibetan linguistic family. It is similar to other languages, such as Newari and Tamang, spoken in the hills of Nepal. The Gurungs have a tradition of oral literature, but there is no written form of the language. Most Gurungs are bilingual, speaking Nepali as well as Gurung.

4 FOLKLORE

The Gurung myth of origin tells of a king of the Surya (solar) dynasty who broke with tradition by crowning his favorite younger son as his successor. As a result, the elder son, Lochan, left the kingdom to seek the life of an ascetic in the Himalayas. He took with him his wife Kali, his priest, a slave, and their wives. On their journey to the mountains, so the legend goes, the group was forced to seek shelter for a night in the company of two prostitutes. During the night, the prostitutes broke Lochan's and the priest's sacred threads, poured wine on the sleeping men's lips, and then fled. On waking, Lochan and the priest thought they had become drunk and had sexual relations with the prostitutes. Ashamed at their behavior, they

from the Tibetan and Sherpa festival. The Hindu Saraswati Pūjā, which falls in early February, marks the beginning of the dance called *ghāntu,* which is unique to the Gurungs and the neighboring Magar tribe. Ghāntu, which has both religious and social aspects, continues to be performed until the full moon that occurs in late April or early May, which marks the Baisakh Purnima festival. *Jātrās,* or fairs, are occasions on which Gurungs meet to socialize, and the sexes mingle with a considerable degree of freedom. The events usually last all night and are accompanied by dancing, singing, and the drinking of copious amounts of liquor.

7 RITES OF PASSAGE

Numerous rituals mark birth and childhood in the Gurung community. Brahman astrologers are consulted before the child is named at the *nahurān* (bathing) ceremony. Held on the 9th day after birth (7 for a girl-child), the *nahurān* involves the ritual purification of the mother and announcing of the baby's name. The rice-feeding *(pasnī)* ceremony, when the baby begins to be fed solid food, is held 5 to 6 months after birth. The ritual first cutting of the hair (*Chhaewar*) is performed when a Gurung boy is 5 or 6 years old. This is done by the boy's maternal uncle, with a lama or Brahman priest present. After this ceremony, the boy can take part in all religious and social activities of the tribe. All these ceremonies are accompanied by feasting and drinking.

Death is of great symbolic significance among Gurungs, and the funeral ritual *(Pai or Arghun)* is the most important observed in Gurung society. Immediately after a death, a white banner is raised on the roof of the house to inform the community of the death. Before rigor mortis (stiffening of the muscles) sets in, the body is placed into a seated posture in a box or a copper vessel. Both lāmās and the animist priests are called on to perform various funeral rites. The klihbri sacrifices a goat so that a blood offering may be made to buy passage of the deceased to heaven. When the rites have been completed and family, relatives, and neighbors have paid their last respects to the deceased, the body is carried in procession to its last resting place. Corpses are disposed of by cremation, burial, or water burial. On their return journey, members of the funeral procession have to step over a fire burning in the road to prevent evil spirits from following them home.

The funeral ritual is completed by an elaborate, and expensive, ceremony held a year after the death occurred. Astrologers determine an auspicious time for the ceremony, which lasts for 3 days and 2 nights. During this time, numerous rituals in which both lāmās and shamans take part are performed for the deceased. Activities include singing and dancing, the chasing away of devils with weapons such as *khukhrīs* (curved Gurkha knives), and sacrifice of animals. An effigy *(pla)* of the deceased is made and dressed in clothes and ornaments. On the last day of the ceremony, the effigy is taken to the edge of the jungle, where the deceased is told that he or she should leave the living and depart to the land of his or her ancestors. The effigy is broken up and thrown away in the jungle. A purification ceremony and a feast mark the end of the funeral rites.

8 INTERPERSONAL RELATIONS

It is considered slightly odd by Gurungs to greet people by their proper names (even if they are known). When addressing someone who is not a relative, one calls them grandmother or grandfather, mother or father, sister or brother, depending on their age. A husband or wife is never referred to directly by name.

9 LIVING CONDITIONS

Gurungs live in villages of around 150 to 200 houses, sited high on ridges and hillsides. The entrance may be indicated by a string of flowers across the path. On the outskirts of the village, there are often temples or shrines to the local gods, with flowers or the remains of sacrifices in front of them. The village itself is a maze of narrow, twisting lanes, though a small shop or a tea-stall may provide gathering places for the inhabitants.

Gurung houses are quite small and may be round, oval, or rectangular in shape. They are built of stone, cemented and plastered with mud. The roofs may be thatched or made of slate. Gurung houses are commonly two-storied, with a veranda running along one side. The upper level is used for storage, while the downstairs room is used for living and sleeping. The walls are lined with shelves to hold pots, dishes, and other household utensils. There is little furniture, and one sits or squats on the floor. People sleep on hard wooden beds or on mats on the floor. Cooking is done over a wood fire in a pit sunk into the floor, with a tripod for hanging pots over it. Few houses have latrines, and villagers go the outskirts of the village to relieve themselves. Although many villages now have piped water, in the past carrying water to the house was a time-consuming household chore.

By Nepali standards, Gurungs are fairly well off. This is largely the result of money sent home by soldiers serving in the British and Indian Gurkha regiments. This extra income, along with military pensions, allows families to accumulate cash surpluses. Many Gurungs in this position migrate from their ancestral villages to towns such as Pokhara where they have access to urban amenities and better economic opportunities.

10 FAMILY LIFE

The division of Gurung society into the Chār Jāt and the Solah Jāt subtribes is explained in the Gurung myth of origin. The two groups are endogamous (i.e., they marry only within the group). The clans within each group are exogamous, marriage partners having to be sought from outside one's own clan. Cross-cousin marriages (i.e., with the father's sister's daughter or the mother's brother's daughter) are preferred, and among some Gurungs a fine is imposed if an available cross-cousin partner is not chosen.

Marriages among the Gurungs are usually arranged, although young men and women are given full opportunity to make their own choices. After a partner has been selected, friends or male relatives are sent to the girl's house with gifts and a bottle of liquor. These are accepted and the intermediaries entertained with food and drink if the girl's family agrees to the proposed match. If the girl's family does not agree, the visitors are turned away and the matter is closed. Once the arrangements for the marriage are complete and the astrologer is consulted over the time and date of the event, the bride is brought to the groom's house for a few days. A feast is given for relatives and the villagers. Within a few days, the bride returns to her parent's home. For the next several years, the couple visits each other in their respective parents' homes. It is only after the girl gives birth to a child that she moves into her husband's

A Gurung woman carries goods in a basket, near Muktinath, Nepal. (Marco Simoni/Getty Images)

the younger generation, especially young men who have served in the military.

Gurung women wear a cotton or velvet blouse (*cholo*) that ties at the front, over a long pleated skirt (*phariyā*) that is usually dark red in color. A sash is wrapped around the waist, and a head cloth completes the outfit. The *ghalek* is a cloth hung across from one shoulder to the opposite waist, forming a bag for carrying things. Ornaments include large, heavy, silver earrings that stretch the earlobes, nose rings, and square amulets hung on a string of glass beads called *pote* necklaces. Bangles and anklets are also worn. Many women are now wearing the *sārī*.

¹² FOOD

Gurungs start their day by drinking sweetened tea. This may be as early as 4:00 or 5:00 am during the summer and around 6:00 am in the winter months. The morning meal is eaten between 9:00 and 10:00 am and consists of rice, or a dough made from millet or maize called *pengo*, with *dāl* (lentils) and vegetables. Although they may snack during the day, they will not eat again until evening, when another meal similar to the morning's is taken. In poorer households, the diet might consist of *jand*, a fermented liquid made from millet or maize, and vegetables.

Sheep are slaughtered and eaten at festival time, but meat is eaten infrequently by most people. Gurungs will not eat pork. The origin of this taboo is uncertain. Some higher-status clans, e.g., the Ghale, observe many high-caste Hindu food prohibitions and will not eat chicken, goat, or buffalo meat. Rice is considered a prestigious food, to be served to visitors and presented as offerings to the gods.

Tea is drunk throughout the day. Gurungs, both men and women, consume large quantities of beer (*chāng*) and liquor (*raksi*) made from maize, millet, or rice. Drinking is common at festivals, fairs, and social gatherings.

¹³ EDUCATION

Education has traditionally been seen by the Gurungs as the means to a desirable career in military service. Long before the Nepalese government assumed responsibility for education at the national level, the Gurung community provided strong support for village schools that prepared young men to join the Gurkhas. Once in the armed services, recruits were required to continue their education. As a consequence, literacy rates among Gurung men are among the highest in South Asia. Studies in Gurung villages place literacy rates at over 72% for the male population and even higher among servicemen and ex-servicemen. Women do not share in this advantage, however, with the corresponding value for females being only around 42.5%.

¹⁴ CULTURAL HERITAGE

Artistic expression among the Gurungs reaches its highest forms in music and folk dances. The Gurungs and the Magars of the Gandaki Zone of Nepal have a unique dance-drama called Ghāntu. The dancers are required to be virgin girls (the ghāntu), and they must abstain from eating garlic and drinking alcohol during the period of the dance. During the dance, they are believed to become possessed by the ancestor spirits. There are two forms of the dance. One can be staged at any time of the year, but the other (*Satī Ghāntu*) can be performed only be-

home permanently. At this time she receives a dowry from her family. This consists of copper and brass utensils, clothes, ornaments, and livestock.

Gurung family structure and size vary over time. A nuclear family expands as sons marry, bring their wives into the household, and have children. But, as their families grow, sons leave the household and build their own houses nearby. Inheritance is shared equally between sons.

Divorce is permitted in Gurung society and is quite common. There is no social stigma associated with divorce, and remarriage by divorcees and widows is readily accepted.

¹¹ CLOTHING

Traditional dress of Gurung men consists of a blouse-type shirt (*bhoto*) fastened with ties across the front of the body and a kilt-like garment (*jama*) that wraps around the waist and reaches to mid-thigh. A long piece of cloth is tied around the waist like a belt (into which a khukhri may be slipped). The typical Nepali cap (*topī*) completes the dress. A sheep's-wool blanket is used in winter or in wet weather to keep the wearer warm and dry. Western-style clothes are commonly worn by

tween Saraswati Pūjā and Baisakh Purnima. Satī Ghāntu tells of various events in the lives of a legendary king and queen of Gorkha, of the death of the king, and of the *satī* (burning on the funeral pyre) and resurrection of the queen. When the last performance of the season is complete, the dancers and the audience go to a nearby shrine, usually that of the mother-goddess Chandi. There they offer the dance regalia to the goddess, along with the sacrifice of a chicken.

The *Sorathī* is another Gurung dance that reenacts an ancient Gurung legend. The story, set in verse, tells of a king who had seven wives but no children. When his youngest queen bore him a daughter, the other wives were filled with jealousy and cast the baby daughter into a river. The baby was rescued by a fisherman and brought up as his own daughter. The tale ends happily as the true identity of the young princess is revealed and she is reunited with her family.

15 WORK

The Gurungs have traditionally been peasant farmers, growing hardy crops in fields terraced into hillsides. Millet and maize form their staple cereals. Wheat, buckwheat, barley, and potatoes are also grown, as are pulses, string beans, and other vegetables. Rice is becoming more important in Gurung agriculture. In the higher elevations, sheep are reared for meat and wool. Every Gurung family has a few sheep, and villages employ shepherds to tend the village flocks. The shepherds, who use mastiffs as sheep dogs, migrate with the flocks to alpine pastures in the summer. They return to the villages in time to celebrate the Dasain festival. Every family slaughters a sheep at Dasain and holds a big feast. After Dasain, the sheep are taken down to the warmth of the lower valleys.

Gurungs who do not leave their villages to serve in the Gurkha regiments of Britain and India often engage in the trans-Himalayan trade that historically has been important in Nepal's economy. Salt, wool, and livestock from Tibet are exchanged for food grains and manufactured goods from India. The surplus of cash generated from overseas employment has led many Gurungs to leave their fields and villages to live in the local towns such as Pokhara. There, they invest in property, buy shops, and operate transport companies and other businesses.

16 SPORTS

Young children play variations of draughts, hopscotch, and marbles, using stones, nuts, berries, or whatever else is close at hand. They make swings, balls from animal's bladders or old cloth, and hoops to be rolled down the road, propelled by a stick. Older boys race each other and play team games such as soccer and basketball.

17 ENTERTAINMENT AND RECREATION

Gurungs living in towns have access to urban amenities such as the cinema, but in rural areas the population is restricted to traditional forms of entertainment and recreation. These include the festivities associated with religious celebrations and the formal dance dramas such as the Ghāntu. Jātrās are occasions for socializing and merrymaking. The singing of traditional love songs and duets between young men and women are popular at such gatherings, as is dancing and beer-drinking. Nepali "pop" songs heard on the radio are popular among teenagers.

The *rodī* is an interesting Gurung institution. It is more or less a social club for boys or girls. Unlike the permanent dormitory of Indian tribes such as the Oraons or the Maria Gonds of central India, 10 or 15 young people of the same sex gather under the supervision of an adult. They sleep at the adult's house and work and play as an informal unit through their teen years. Eventually the members marry, and the rodī dissolves. Not all children in a village join a rodī, and there may be more than one such group in the larger settlements.

18 FOLK ART, CRAFTS, AND HOBBIES

Other than their traditions of music and dance, the Gurungs are not known for their folk arts and crafts. Items such as woven baskets and woolen blankets made by women, and bamboo goods fashioned by men, are essentially functional in design. Gurungs rely on local service castes for metal goods, carpentry, and tailoring.

19 SOCIAL PROBLEMS

Like many tribal societies in South Asia, the Gurungs are faced with social and economic changes that threaten their sense of community identity. Traditional Gurung society is rooted in the rhythms and rituals of a rural, agricultural society. Today, population pressure and environmental degradation is reflected in declining agricultural production and increasing poverty in rural areas. Even the tradition of service in foreign armies offers declining opportunities, as Britain is eliminating many of its Gurkha regiments. The relative affluence associated with military service and army pensions has resulted in the migration of Gurungs to towns and cities, where they lose much of their traditional culture. This process is hastened by the relatively high levels of education among Gurungs, who prefer the attractions of urban life over the village. Many Gurung children brought up in towns cannot even speak the Gurung language. As two writers put it, "What does it mean to be 'Gurung,' if one no longer practices Gurung agriculture, uses the language, or employs the Gurung priests?" (Macfarlane and Gurung 1990: 36). Whatever happens in the future, it will be many years before old men proudly sporting the crossed khukhri insignia of their Gurkha regiments disappear from the streets of towns and villages in west-central Nepal.

One feature of change, and a source of conflict among Gurungs, is the relative status of the Char Jat and the Sora Jat. The introduction of universal suffrage and the village panchayat system (local self-governing councils) has raised the aspiration of the formerly servile Sora Jat *vis-à-vis* the Char Jat.

20 GENDER ISSUES

Although some Gurung groups have adopted aspects of Hindu social values, Gurung women are much freer than their Hindu sisters. Even though marriages are arranged, they have a much greater say in marriage partners, virtually being able to choose their mate (even though cross-cousin marriage is preferred) and no stigma is attached to divorce, which is easy to obtain. Widows are allowed to remarry.

Substantial differences in gender roles exist among ethnic groups in Nepal. Gurung women are still expected to handle household chores and have little say over crop land, livestock and daily wages, but unlike in the Brahman/Chhetri and Tharu communities, Gurung women participate in community meetings and have participated in agricultural training scheme.

Literacy among Gurung women is 42.5% (almost 20 points lower than their Newar counterparts) and this limits their access to health care and inhibits upwards mobility. However, the need for literacy and self-help has been recognized and organizations such as the Nepal Gurung (Tamu) Women's Association (NGWA) (or the Nepal Gurung [Tamu] Mahila Sangh) have been established as independent, social and non-profit making organizations, to serve as a common meeting place for all Gurung women. Set up by the Gurung women themselves, the NGWA serves to promote the interests, welfare and rights of all Gurungs, and helps conserve and preserve the socio-cultural traditions, language and religion of the Gurung people.

The role of women in overall Gurung development cannot be understated. It first started when Gurung women established *Ama Samuhas* ("Mother's Groups") in the villages. The Ama Samuhas played important roles in bringing about social reforms and they have been successful in controlling and eradicating such social evils as gambling and alcohol drinking. They are also involved in the building of roads, schools, conducting literacy classes, sanitation, drinking water awareness programs, and building resting places. The concept of Ama Samuhas has now even spread to major cities such as Kathmandu, Pokhara, and Butwal Chitwan. Women's roles, initially limited to Ama Samuhas, have now taken a major step forward with the creation of the NGWA. Gurung men have been very supportive of the initiatives and endeavors of Gurung women to improve their literacy and socio-economic status.

Gurung women are aware that in terms of development, they lag far behind the rest of South Asia. Awareness of Gurung culture does not mean just wearing the Gurung dress or singing *dohori* songs (a genre of Nepali folk song). There remains the issue of improving literacy. Newari women in Nepal are far ahead in terms of education and business is dominated by Thakali women. It seems that the majority of Gurung women are contented and do not see any need to come out of their homes to seek any rights. Reasons may be that they are generally economically well taken care of by their husband's and other family members' overseas earnings or that they are simply unaware of the opportunities that they are being deprived of as they remain cocooned in their own homes. One of the main aims of the NGWA remains bringing Gurung women out of their homes and exposing them to society at large. It focuses on developing their intellectual capacity, encourages social interaction at a wider societal level, helps them become better educated, and helps to bring about a sense of self confidence. Being aware and informed will help Gurung women to guide their children properly in education, social norms and behavior.

21 BIBLIOGRAPHY

Gautam, Rajesh, and Ashoke Thapa-Magar. "Gurungs." *Tribal Ethnography of Nepal* 1 (1994): 240–261, 1994.

Macfarlane, Alan, and Indrabahadur Gurung. *Gurungs of Nepal: A Guide to the Gurungs*. Kathmandu: Ratna Pustak Bhandar, 1990.

McHugh, Ernestine. *Love and Honor in the Himalayas: Coming to Know Another Culture*. Philadelphia: University of Pennsylvania Press, 2001.

Messerschmidt, Donald. A. *The Gurungs of Nepal*. Warminster, England: Aris & Phillips, 1976.

Mumford, Stanley Royal. *Himalayan Dialogue: Tibetan Lamas and Gurung Shamans in Nepal*. Madison, Wisconsin: University of Wisconsin Press, 1989.

Regmī, Murārīprasāda. *The Gurungs, Thunder of Himal: A Cross Cultural Study of a Nepalese Ethnic Group*. Jaipur: Nirala Publications, 1990.

—by D. O. Lodrick

HAKKA

PRONUNCIATION: HAHK-uh
ALTERNATE NAMES: Han Chinese
LOCATION: China; Taiwan; Malaysia; Singapore; Thailand; Indonesia.
POPULATION: 40 million
LANGUAGE: Hakka (southern China dialect)
RELIGION: Combination of Buddhist and Daoist beliefs; ancestor worship; Christianity.
RELATED ARTICLES: Vol. 3: Han

¹ INTRODUCTION

The Hakka are ethnic Chinese (Han) who have a distinct history, language and identity. The name Hakka means "guest people," or sojourner, as if the Hakka were guests in their own land. Hakka is the Cantonese (Yue) pronunciation; the word is pronounced "Kejia" in Mandarin Chinese.

The ancient Hakka homeland was the cradle of Chinese civilization in north-central China (Shanxi and Henan provinces). The people who became known as the Hakka originated in this area and have a very long history of migration toward southern China. The first migration was to south-central China (Hubei and Jiangxi provinces) and occurred in the 4th century AD. A second migration occurred between the 9th and 10th centuries, when the Hakka reached south China (Fujian and Guangdong). Hakka dominated northern Guangdong by the end of the 13th century. The last major migration in China occurred between the 17th and 19th centuries, pushing deeper into southeast China into Fujian, Guangdong, Sichuan, and Guangxi provinces. The name Hakka was first applied by the local people (bendi) in this last migration.

The last period of migration included waves of Hakka who migrated from mainland China primarily to Taiwan and South East Asia. The Hakka first arrived on Taiwan in the 17th century during the Dutch occupation of the island. Migration to Taiwan continued until Japan took over the island in 1895. The colonization of South East Asia by European powers opened the region to Chinese immigrants, most of whom originated from southeastern coastal China, including Hakka regions in Fujian and Guangdong provinces. The modern states of Indonesia, Malaysia, Thailand, Brunei, and Singapore saw a large influx of Hakka migrants, numbering in the hundreds of thousands, who worked as miners, laborers, and shop keepers. Hakka make up a sizable minority in those countries and individual wealthy Hakka have amassed substantial financial holdings, which has led to resentment against Hakka by the non-Chinese majority. The Hakka also migrated in large numbers in the 19th and early 20th centuries to the British colony of Jamaica and French-controlled Mauritius, as well as the United States, Canada, and parts of Latin America.

Although the Hakka are a distinct ethnic group, they are considered to be Han Chinese by the mainland Chinese and, therefore, have no special minority status in the People's Republic of China. Hakka are full citizens and receive the same treatment accorded all citizens. In Taiwan and South East Asia, Hakka have developed a greater communal identity, separate from other Chinese migrant populations, and efforts to define the Hakka as distinct from Han Chinese have been made by overseas Hakka scholars.

Despite their small numbers, many Hakka have become prominent national leaders on the mainland and abroad. In the 19th century many Hakka played prominent roles in the anti-Qing Dynasty Taiping Rebellion (1850–1864), including the movements leader, Hong Xiuquan. Hakka regions in Guangdong and Fujian province were hotbeds for Communist insurgents from the 1920s to 1940s. In Taiwan in the 1940s and 1950s, the Hakka were prominent in the anti-Kuomintang resistance, and many Hakka were killed in the anti-Communist crackdown on that island. Modern important Hakka leaders include Deng Xiaoping, the former leader of the People's Republic of China; Lee Teng-hui, the former president of Taiwan; Lee Kwan Yew, the former president of Singapore; and former Thai prime minister Thaksin Shinawatra. The global Hakka diaspora has sparked a keen interest in Hakka history and culture and, in 1971, the first World Hakka Conference was inaugurated. Three decades later more than 20 World Hakka Conferences have been held and "Hakkaology," or the study of Hakka history and culture, is studied across the world.

² LOCATION AND HOMELAND

Of a population of 1.3 billion in the People's Republic of China, the 30 million Hakka are little more than 3% of the total population. Taiwan, with a population of about 22 million, is the home of approximately 2 million Hakka. Large populations of Hakka also live in Southeast Asian countries, including Malaysia, Indonesia, Singapore, and Thailand. Significant numbers of Hakka have also migrated to India, Europe, and the Americas.

Hakka traditionally migrated to rugged, mountainous districts of south China and Taiwan on land that other Chinese found too poor for agriculture. This settlement pattern developed because the best land was occupied by the time the Hakka migrants arrived in south China. The climate is hot in the summer and mild in the winter; rice, tea, citrus fruits, and vegetables all grow well. Although winter frost is uncommon, Hakka areas are subject to the devastating winds, flooding, and typhoons.

³ LANGUAGE

Hakka speak a language that linguists classify as a south China dialect. Many Hakka, however, believe that their language is closely related to Mandarin, a major northern Chinese dialect, and that they speak a purer form of Chinese than other dialects because their origin lay in the cradle of Chinese civilization. Language is the most important way that Hakka distinguish themselves from other Chinese. Unlike standard Mandarin Chinese, which has four spoken tones, Hakka has six tones.

Hakka family names (surnames) are transmitted through the father's line (patrilineally). Individuals have a personal name consisting of two syllables. When addressing someone, the surname is spoken first and the personal name follows. In families keeping a genealogy by generation, boys are often given a "generation" name as part of their personal names. The personal name can thus be used to identify the generation to which he belongs.

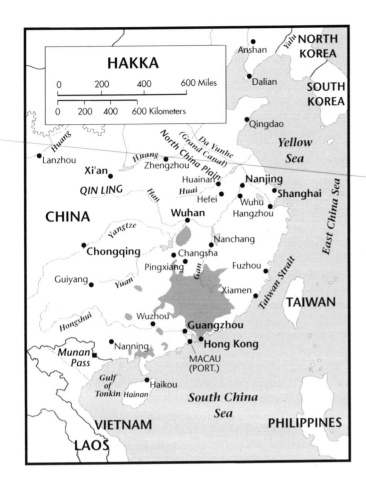

4 FOLKLORE

Many traditional Hakka believe in geomancy (*fengshui*), the belief that natural forces in the land and water can affect one's fortune and well being. People can take advantage of these forces by orienting houses, tombs, doorways, and other structures in the proper direction. Hakka also employ the ideas of yin and yang to describe the essential qualities of things. "Yin" things are thought to be chilly and wet, while objects with the "yang" quality are warm and dry. Bringing these qualities into internal balance is thought to benefit personal health. Spirit mediums (shamans) are employed to communicate with ancestors and ghosts; not all Hakka believe this practice is valid.

5 RELIGION

Hakka religion combines Buddhist and Daoist beliefs; no unifying beliefs define a distinct Hakka religion. Hakka practice a form of domestic religion called ancestor worship. They believe that the spirits of their ancestors (*zuxian*) persist and that they require care from the living. Hakka appease the ancestors by lighting incense and offering sacrifices on ritual occasions.

A local god worshiped in many Hakka village temples is the "King of the Three Mountains" (Sanshan Guowang). The legend associated with this god is that spirits inhabiting three mountains in the Hakka region of Guangdong became protectors and saved the people from disasters. People began worshipping these spirits and built temples in their honor.

Outside of mainland China many Hakka are Christian, particularly in Taiwan. In Malaysian and Indonesia a sizable percentage are Muslim.

6 MAJOR HOLIDAYS

The most important holiday in Hakka society is the lunar New Year. People return to their natal homes, and work stops for three or more days. Houses receive a thorough cleaning, and rhyming couplets with lucky phrases may be pasted on doorways. Families eat an elaborate meal featuring traditional dishes on New Year's Eve. New Year's Day is devoted to visiting other relatives, especially those in senior generations. In traditional society children received new clothes for the coming year.

Tomb-sweeping day (*qingming jie*) in April is an important holiday that is dedicated to the ancestors in the father's line (patrilineal ancestors). People prepare sacrificial foods (rice, meats, sweet rolls, and wine) and visit the family tombs as a group. The spirits of the ancestors are invited to feast on the food, strings of firecrackers are lit, and the graves are thoroughly cleaned. This ceremony emphasizes the strong bond between the living and their ancestors.

7 RITES OF PASSAGE

Mothers who have just given birth are confined to their beds for 30 days and are not allowed to wash their hair. Hakka believe that a woman's joints are prone to damage after childbirth. Newborns are tightly swaddled and are placed on their backs to sleep. The birth of a male infant may be announced to the ancestors as evidence that the family line will continue. Hakka do not mark the teenage years with any special coming-of-age ceremonies.

Hakka practice double burial. When a relative dies, a funeral is performed, and the deceased is buried in a temporary grave. After five to seven years, the skeleton is exhumed, purified, and carefully arranged in a large ceramic vessel. The vessel is then interred in a permanent site. It is not unusual in Taiwan to find large family mausoleums containing the remains of many family members. These tombs are elaborately decorated and are a central focus of family pride.

8 INTERPERSONAL RELATIONS

Hakka value family and friends very highly. The Hakka have a reputation for being reserved and stoic in their interactions with strangers or acquaintances. The standard greeting— "Have you eaten yet?"—is a polite way of inquiring after one's comfort; it is equivalent to "hello." People whose relationship is not close or whose social status is different politely greet each other by using the person's title (Mr., Miss, Teacher, or Dr.) and surname. Because of their reputation for reserve, Hakka body language is not demonstrative.

Etiquette is important. For a formal visit—as on the occasion of a senior relative's birthday, after a long absence, or to discuss personal business—a guest prepares a small gift of fruit, candy, or a local delicacy for the host. The host in turn offers tea and fruit or other light refreshment. Guests are also offered cigarettes.

Western-style dating was unknown in traditional Hakka society. Parents arranged meetings between boys and girls with the intent of finding suitable mates. Courtship was managed by parents to such an extent that the children seldom met more than a handful of times before marrying. The meetings were arranged as formal visits rather than as dates. As Chinese society changed during the last half of the 20th century, this practice has declined greatly. Young people may now date as members of a school group. This practice allows them to mix freely and gives them opportunities to identify special people. In the cities, seeing a movie, strolling in a park, or buying a small treat are popular places to go on a date.

9 LIVING CONDITIONS

Living conditions vary greatly depending on location. Most Hakka in China are rural dwellers. Until recently running water and public sewers did not exist in many locations, so people depended on wells and streams for water and on outhouses for toilets. Bottled water is now widely available, and modern bathrooms are common even in rural areas. Electricity is ubiquitous, but people still cook with wood and charcoal. Taiwan's economy is more developed; most rural Hakka have running water, public sewage, electricity and, increasingly, natural gas for cooking and hot water.

Hakka go to both traditional Chinese physicians and Western-style doctors. Herbalists operating Chinese-style pharmacies exist alongside Western drug stores. Other types of medical treatments include acupuncture, massage, folk remedies, and dietary changes.

Hakka live in modern, consumer societies and increasingly purchase the many goods that economic development and larger incomes have made possible. In the People's Republic of China, bicycles, televisions, air conditioners, washing machines, electric fans, and motorcycles are common household items. While most Hakka in rural areas cannot afford to own a car, the streets are crowded with vehicles, and many people have access to cars through their employment. In rural Taiwan, cars and air conditioners are common possessions. Living standards are rising for many, especially those who live in the cities, but daily life is not as comfortable as it is for many in the West. Houses are often not heated, so people must wear heavy clothing indoors in the winter. Increased income in China and Taiwan means a greater choice of diet in both rural and urban areas, as well as access to before unheard of luxuries, such as travel to distant domestic destinations and abroad.

A traditional Hakka farmhouse had three connected wings forming a U shape. A courtyard in the middle was used for processing harvests and other tasks. The central wing had a large room in the middle, used for eating, visiting, and household chores. The wings on the sides contained bedrooms, kitchens, storage areas, toilets, granaries, and animal pens. In areas of Guangdong and Fujian where Hakka clashed with other Chinese, an unusual type of house developed called a tulou, or earthen building. Tulou can either be rectangular or square shaped and are three to five stories high. Traditionally, the homes were built of compacted earth with very thick walls, while today the tulou are made of granite or fired bricks. Dozens of rooms built inside the walls of the structure can house as many as 80 families, and the central area functions as a courtyard. On the ground level, animals live side by side with the occupants, and families conduct daily tasks of cooking food and cleaning clothes in a common area. In Fujian province, more than 20,000 tulous have been constructed, often in clusters. Multiple generations and branches of a family often occupy a single tulou. It is thought that the unique architecture of the tulou, which includes a single entrance and gun holes, developed as a defense against banditry.

Transportation is efficient in Taiwan. Paved roads run throughout the countryside and all areas are served by public bus lines. Many rural Hakka commute to work by bus and motorcycle. Elementary, middle, and high school students also ride these buses to school.

10 FAMILY LIFE

Family life emphasizes cooperation within a hierarchy based on age and sex. Although fathers make major decisions outside the home, the relationship between the parents is more democratic in the family. Before marriage all major decisions affecting children are made by the parents. Sons are obliged to care for their parents in old age; parents usually live in the home of a married son.

Unlike other Chinese, Hakka never practiced the traditional custom of binding women's feet. Foot binding was a procedure using strips of cloth that forced the feet into small shapes. Women with bound feet were effectively crippled. Hakka women have a reputation for industry and stamina and contribute great amounts of labor on family farms.

Ideal family size among Hakka depends greatly on the social context. The population policy of the People's Republic of China allows parents to have only one or two children per family, depending on their location and economic status; abortions are common, and people generally practice birth control. Hakka outside China may have larger families, especially in agricultural communities. However, as economies industrialize and the demand for farm labor decreases, family sizes are also decreasing. A preference for male children exists; boys inherit the family name and have special obligations to the family's ancestors. Girls, it is thought, are lost to the family when they marry.

Hakka marry in their twenties. The bride and groom should have different last names (surname exogamy). Grooms are typically 2 to 10 years older than brides. Ceremonies are elaborate and focus on a sumptuous feast to which relatives and friends are invited. Large wedding feasts may have 300–500 guests. In southern China, young Hakka are allowed to date before marriage and the mass migration of millions of youth for work and school means that many Hakka marry outside of their community.

Urban families consist of parents and children (nuclear family), but parents usually live with one son (extended family). Rural family structure can be very complex, with parents sharing a compound with their married sons' families and unmarried children. Hakka also organize larger kinship groups based on the principle of descent from a common ancestor in the male line (patrilineal lineages). These kinship groups are not co-residential units but do assemble for ceremonial occasions.

11 CLOTHING

Modern Hakka do not wear distinctive clothing. Western-style pants, dresses, shirts and outerwear have replaced older Chinese styles that did not use zippers and buttons. However, women traditionally embroidered intricate, colorful patterns on strips of cloth used to fasten round hats. This style of dress is not seen in Taiwan but occurs occasionally in the People's Republic of China.

A Hakka woman smoking a pipe in Hong Kong. (Jean-Marc Truchet/Stone/Getty Images)

12 FOOD

White rice is the Hakka staple. Sweet potatoes are important where the land is not suited to wet rice. The Hakka also consume noodles made from rice, wheat, and green mung beans. Rice is steamed for lunch and supper to accompany stir-fried, steamed, and braised dishes using vegetables, meats, and fish. Rice is consumed in the morning as a thin gruel; it accompanies both pickled and fresh foods. In comparison to other regional Chinese cuisines, Hakka food is plain and not spicy. Soy sauce, salt, rice vinegar, ginger, sugar, and flavors from various preserved and pickled foods are used extensively in cooking. If there is a drink at the meal it is usually a hot soup, either a broth or a meat and vegetable combination. Like other Chinese, the Hakka do not drink tea with their meals.

Hakka have no food taboos, although some women are pious Buddhists who eat a vegetarian diet. In general, Hakka prefer a diet with high proportions of vegetables and moderate to small amounts of meat. Some Hakka will not eat beef because they believe it is morally wrong to consume animals that work in the fields to provide people with food.

13 EDUCATION

The Hakka traditionally emphasized educating boys. Before the 20th century, boys studied the Confucian teachings and other classics to cultivate the virtues associated with literacy. Exceptional students took examinations that could lead to high prestige civil service careers. Before the 20th century, Hakka girls seldom attended school; a bias against girls existed in traditional Chinese society. Modern Hakka live in societies where education is highly prized for both girls and boys; children work very hard to do well in school. In mainland China, Hakka have access to education in some of the top universities in the nation, located in Fujian and Guangdong provinces. Parents often invest heavily in their children's' education, and both boys and girls in rural areas receive education through high school. Often parents send their children to distant schools, thus many Hakka youth may spend their teen years separated from their family. Children in Taiwan finish 12 years of education, and many go to college. Both students and parents know that economic opportunities increase with advanced education. Literacy rates are very high among people born within the last 40 to 50 years. Many Hakka migrate to Western countries to pursue educations in technical and scientific fields.

14 CULTURAL HERITAGE

Hakka are famous for folk songs called "mountain songs" *(shan ge)*. Romantic mountain songs were sung to each other by women and men working in the fields. Local productions of famous historical stories presented by itinerant opera troupes also entertained people. Opera performances were often scheduled to coincide with the summer harvest and drew large crowds.

15 WORK

Hakka have the reputation of being hard workers who can persevere in the face of adversity. Most Hakka in mainland China are rural farmers living in small villages and towns. In the 19th century, female agricultural labor was especially important in locations from which men migrated to find work. Several examples of occupational specialization exist. In 19th-century Hong Kong many Hakka specialized in stone cutting. People who migrated to Calcutta, India, in the first years of the 20th century became leather tanners. In the present, most Hakka who live in Taiwan work in manufacturing, business, and government. On the mainland, most Hakka are raised in agricultural communities, but a large number of Hakka youth have migrated to urban areas, particularly in Guangdong and Fujian province, to work in manufacturing plants and in low-wage service jobs.

16 SPORTS

In school and during their free time, Hakka youth often play table tennis, badminton, and basketball. Soccer is a popular spectator sport, but not often played. Shadow boxing (taiqi) is very popular among older people as a form of relaxation and exercise.

17 ENTERTAINMENT AND RECREATION

On the mainland, Chinese movies and television programs are popular among Hakka of all ages, but few are presented in the Hakka dialect. Notable Hakka musicians and performers outside of the mainland perform almost exclusively in the language or dialect of their home country or region, usually Mandarin or Cantonese. Well known Hakka artists include Hong Kong actor and musician Jordan Chan, Hong Kong actors Chow Yun-Fat and Leslie Cheung, Hong Kong actress Cherie Chung , Taiwanese film director Hou Hsiao-Hsien, Hong Kong singers Deanie Ip and Leon Lai, Malaysian pop stars Penny Tai and Eric Moo, Hong Kong actor and director Eric Tsang, Taiwanese singer Cyndi Wang, and Singaporean actress and singer Fann Wong

18 FOLK ART, CRAFTS, AND HOBBIES

Friends often gather in the evenings and on weekends to play mahjong (majiang); children are introduced to this game in their teens. Many people take an interest in growing rare orchids and in practicing Chinese calligraphy as an art form.

19 SOCIAL PROBLEMS

Hakka are recognized in China and Taiwan as Han Chinese. The social problems that Hakka face are the same as the ones faced by other citizens. An active ethnic movement in Taiwan promotes using the Hakka language in radio and television broadcasts and supports including Hakka in public affairs. Human rights issues do not often arise in the People's Republic of China. Because of their status as an ethnic minority in non-Chinese Southeast Asian nations, Hakka may be the target of economic and political discrimination. Periodic anti-Chinese

riots in South East Asia have targeted Hakka communities, including deadly riots in Jakarta in 1998.

Drugs (opium and its derivatives) are not widely abused in Hakka society, but alcoholism is recognized as a potential problem. Excessive gambling is a problem that concerns many.

20 GENDER ISSUES

Since the economic liberalization of mainland China began under Deng Xiaoping in 1978, Hakka women have enjoyed expanded social freedoms and fallen victim to increasingly common vices. Young women from rural areas, such as the Hakka homeland, have flocked to big cities in search of employment. Often these women find low paying jobs in factories or in the service industry. The meager wages they earn at these jobs allows them to provide for their family and pursue entrepreneurial ambitions. In recent years divorce has become both legally more accessible and socially accepted, resulting in an increased number of single mothers. One of the dark sides of Chinese economic liberalization has been a marked increase in prostitution, in particular in the southern provinces where the Hakka reside. Poor young women from the countryside work in brothels for a few hundred dollars a month, exposing themselves to sexual disease and social stigmatization.

In mainland China gay rights are limited and until recently the government classified homosexuality as a mental disease. Among Hakka living outside of the mainland, the most notable gay or lesbian in recent times has been Hong Kong actor Leslie Cheung, who reached international fame before taking his life in 2003.

21 BIBLIOGRAPHY

Cohen, Myron. "The Hakka or 'Guest People'; Dialect as a Sociocultural Variable in Southeastern China." *Ethnohistory* 15, no. 3 (1968): 237–252.

Constable, Nicole. *Guest People; Hakka Identity in China and Abroad.* Seattle: University of Washington Press, 1996.

Erbaugh, Mary S. "The Secret History of the Hakkas: The Chinese Revolution as a Hakka." *The China Quarterly*, no. 132, (Dec., 1992): 937-968.

Kiang, Clyde. The Hakka Search for a Homeland. Elgin, Pennsylvania: Allegheny Press, 1991.

Martin, Howard J. "Hakka Mausoleums in North Taiwan." *Ethnology* 30, no. 1 (1981): 85–99.

———. The Hakka Ethnic Movement in Taiwan, 1986–1991. In *Guest People; Hakka Identity in China and Abroad*, edited by Nicole Constable. Seattle: University of Washington Press, 1996.

Pasternak, Burton. *Kinship and Community in Two Chinese Villages.* Stanford: Stanford University Press, 1972.

Zhou, Jianxin. "Hakka Ethnic Group Identification and Cultural Production." *Chinese Sociology and Anthropology*, vol. 40, no. 1 (Fall 2007): 83–99.

—revised by David Straub

HAN

PRONUNCIATION: HAHN
ALTERNATE NAMES: None
LOCATION: China; Taiwan; (as Overseas Chinese: Southeast Asia, Japan, North America, Oceania, and Europe)
POPULATION: 1 billion in mainland China
LANGUAGE: Mandarin Chinese
RELIGION: Taoism, Confucianism, and Buddhism
RELATED ARTICLES: Vol. 2: Chinese Americans. Vol. 3: China and Her National Minorities; Hakka.

¹INTRODUCTION

The Han are the main body of the Chinese nation, having a long history and an age-old tradition. In remote antiquity, the ancestors of the Han lived in the basin of the middle and lower reaches of the Yellow River. During long centuries of contact, conflict, and assimilation with the neighboring tribes, they formed in that area a community called Huaxia, which expanded gradually to areas along the Yangzi River. The first Emperor of Qin (r. 221 BC–AD 211) conquered the other princes of the Zhou Kingdom (1122–222 BC) and unified China in 221 BC. Shortly after, Qin was replaced by the Han Dynasty (206 BC–AD 220).

It is generally believed that the Chinese, as a unified nationality (with Huaxia as its core), came into being during the period of Han Dynasty. It was due to the political and cultural importance of this dynasty that the Chinese came to be known as the "people of Han" or simply "Han."

In the long history of China, there were several large-scale migrations of the Han Chinese to south China (south of the Yangzi River), where the population eventually exceeded that of the north about 600 years ago. Lasting for 2,000 years and more, the imperial state was finally overthrown in 1911. Since 1949, two different political systems have existed simultaneously in mainland China and Taiwan.

²LOCATION AND HOMELAND

According to the 2000 census, the Han in mainland China amount to over 1.2 billion people. They are mainly concentrated in cities and large river valleys where agriculture is most flourishing. The vast majority of people in Taiwan are also Han. In addition, quite a large population of Han ethnics have moved their residence abroad over the years as foreign citizens of Chinese origin or overseas Chinese. Most of them live in Southeast Asia, Japan, North America, Oceania, and Europe.

³LANGUAGE

Han language, usually called Chinese, has been adopted by the United Nations as an official international language. Although there are seven dialects, the written script, invented more than 3,000 years ago, is compatible with all of them.

The popularization of the northern dialect (sometimes called Mandarin Chinese), which has become the common spoken language (*putonghua*) of China, has contributed to better communication and understanding among the various peoples, nationalities, and regions of China.

⁴FOLKLORE

The ancient books of the Han people recorded thousands of myths that have been further enriched by folk tales among the people. Pangu is the god who created the world; Nüwa, the goddess who fashioned human beings; Ji, the god of all crops; Shennong, the god of herbs. Suirenshi invented the method to produce fire; Yu drained the flood; Cangjie created Han characters; Huang Di was the legendary ancestor of the Han people. The *Sanhaijing*, a book written 2,000 years ago, records the legends, folk customs, and geographical features of faraway places, blending together fact and fancy.

⁵RELIGION

Since the concept of patriarchal clan is deeply rooted in Han society, the continuity of patrilineal family is a matter of prime importance, having a great impact on attitudes and behavior even at the present. Another cultural trait deriving from the remote past is the Han belief in the idea of God's will.

The Han have historically accommodated religions of diverse origins. The first historical writings, the recently discovered inscriptions on "Oracle Bones," dating from the 14th century BC, testify to the belief of the ruling class in the deified ancestor, ancestor worship, and bone divination (to know the ancestor's will). Earlier popular oral traditions reflect beliefs in a plurality of nature gods (terrestrial and heavenly) and deified heroes.

The Han Dynasty (206 BC–AD 220), saw the formation of three religious traditions: Taoism, Confucianism, and Buddhism (based on the respective teachings of Lao zi, Confucius, and the Buddha). Buddhism, a foreign religion, exerted the greatest influence. But most Han paid homage to all three religions, thus avoiding religious conflict.

The inclusive religious attitude of the Han may perhaps be explained by the fact that the three religions were mutually complementary, Taoism centering on man's relation to nature and the cosmos, Confucianism on man's relation to society, and Buddhism on man's relation to the beyond. Islam and Christianity only came to China under the Tang Dynasty (AD 618–907) and never occupied a prominent position.

⁶MAJOR HOLIDAYS

The Han celebrate many major holidays. Among them, the most important is the Spring Festival (lunar calendar; Western calendar, between January 21 and February 20). Almost everybody travels back home, even from faraway places inside or outside China; it is estimated that hundreds of millions travel during that festive period. Generations of family members get together to share a dinner party on the eve of the lunar New Year. Fireworks and firecrackers are kindled everywhere (but have been forbidden recently in some urban districts). People dress up and have a good time for days in the cities and for weeks in the rural areas.

October 15 (lunar calendar; Western calendar, between November 6 and December 4) is the second most important day of the year for the Han people. People enjoy contemplating the full moon and eating moon cakes (originally an offering to the Moon Goddess), symbolizing the union and reunion of the family. The Lion Dance, Dragon Dance, and Dragon Boat Regatta are performed on this festival.

A Han funeral procession winds along a country road in Pingtang, China. (© Christophe Boisvieux/Corbis)

7 RITES OF PASSAGE

Since 1980, each Han couple of reproductive age in mainland China has been encouraged to have no more than one child. Childbirth, therefore, is often regarded as a major event in the family. Following the old custom, eggs cooked and dyed red are often sent to relatives and friends for celebration. Quite a number of people will have a dinner party to celebrate their baby's completion of the first month of life.

In the past, burial of the dead underground was the general practice throughout the country. Today, it has been replaced in the cities by cremation. The Qingming Festival, a day of commemorating dead relatives and paying respects to their tombs, is held on April 4, 5, or 6.

8 INTERPERSONAL RELATIONS

Paying a New Year call is a very popular tradition on the Spring Festival. The guests usually bring gifts, such as fruits, candies, cigarettes, or a bottle of wine. They can expect a warm welcome. However, greeting on the phone during festivals is becoming more and more popular in large cities today. Under the influence of Western culture, sending Christmas and New Year greeting cards is becoming a trend.

Although most young people think that the best way to find a partner is through their own efforts, there are still a number of them who are helped by their parents, relatives, or friends. On most occasions, the males take the initiative. The response of a girl invited for the first time in her life for a date is usually to postpone it until later, unless she is well acquainted with the inviter. Mutual attraction is of utmost importance in selecting a partner. Position and wealth are also important considerations.

9 LIVING CONDITIONS

Being poor and less technologically advanced, the Han for a long time exerted great efforts to guarantee and improve their means of subsistence. Following the economic development of Taiwan, mainland China adopted in 1978 the policies of reform and opening to the outside world that speeded up its own economic development and increased its gross national product (GNP) twofold and fourfold in the 1980s and mid-1990s, respectively. This ensured a relatively comfortable lifestyle for the Han, especially those living in the coastal areas.

The average life expectancy for the Han has increased to more than 70 years of age, while the mortality rate has dropped to about 7 per 1,000 in 2008. Mortality and morbidity due to infectious disease have dropped significantly. Schistosomiasis has been eliminated in the vast majority of rural areas in south China. On the contrary, sexually transmitted diseases,

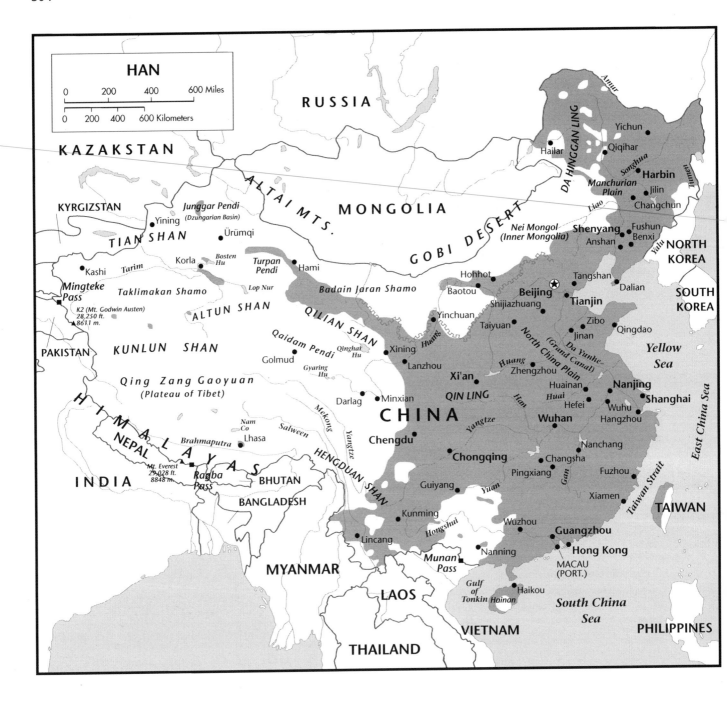

especially gonorrhea, have increased markedly since the 1980s. What merits attention is the high incidence of induced abortions (due to contraceptive failure or to sex-selection of the baby), which has had an inevitable negative impact on women's health.

With improved rural and urban incomes, Han consumer demand has turned from basic subsistence needs to various household electrical appliances, upholstery, and jewelry. However, consumers are frustrated by inflation and by the increasing number of counterfeit goods in the marketplace.

10 FAMILY LIFE

The roles of men and women in Han society of mainland China are not clearly prescribed. Han are monogamous. Men

and women marry the partners of their own choice. Although marriages are mostly stable, the incidence of divorce has been on the rise. An average Han family in urban areas will consist of a man, his wife, and their only child. In rural areas, three or more generations living together under the same roof is not uncommon. Cats and dogs are popular pets in the countryside, but they are usually forbidden in the cities. Birds are beloved pets everywhere.

11 CLOTHING

Just two decades ago, city streets were uniformly grey and dark; men and women, young and old, wore clothes of the same style and the same color. Today, in the frozen north, down jackets, woolens, and fur overcoats in red, yellow, orange, and other bright colors liven the bleak winter scene. In the south, where the climate is milder, people choose Western suits, jeans, jackets, sweaters, and other fashionable clothing to wear year-round. Famous brand names and fashions are a common sight in large cities, and they sell quite well. Cheaper and more practical clothing is also available. Similar changes also have occurred in rural areas, especially among the new class of well-to-do farmers. However, in less advanced rural areas, Han peasants still wear their "Mao suits" (the plain, two-pieced utilitarian attire named after the former Chinese leader).

12 FOOD

The main foods of the Han are rice, flour, vegetables, pork, eggs, and freshwater fish. The Han have always laid much stress on cooking skills, making Chinese cuisine (basically Han) well known throughout the world. Dumplings, wanton, spring rolls, rice, noodles, and roast Beijing duck are just examples of traditional foods.

13 EDUCATION

The Han, who invented an original system of writing more than 3,000 years ago, and the university more than 2,000 years ago, always prized education and literacy. The rate of illiteracy and semi-illiteracy in Han society is under 10%. Chinese law mandates children receive 9 years of formal education. About 98% of children enroll in school when they reach school age. More than 80% of the students who graduate from primary school and 45% of those who graduate from junior middle school continue to higher levels.

There are more than 1,000 universities and colleges and 800,000 primary and middle schools at different levels, with a total enrollment of 180 million, including 2.6 million college students and graduate students. In addition, 800,000 students are now taking home undergraduate training courses, while 14 million adult students attend classes of different levels in adult schools.

Despite progress in education, about five million school-age children do not enter school or have dropped out, and the college entrance rate is only 1.8%, below the average for developing countries. Underfunding is the primary reason for this status, and enrollment in the countryside is much lower than that in cities.

14 CULTURAL HERITAGE

The variety of traditional Han musical instruments is sufficient to form an orchestra. The most popular include the two-string violin (erhu), the lute (zheng), and the pipa. Institutions of traditional music and dance were established early in the 1950s.

The ancient literature of the Han, including poems, drama and novels, history, philosophy, and rituals, is a great world treasure. Many works have been translated into other languages and introduced into many countries. The great poets Li Bai and Du Fu, who flourished in the golden age of Chinese poetry (Tang Dynasty, 618–907), have produced works that belong to world literature. The monumental Chinese novels, starting in the 14th century with the epic Water Margin, also include Pilgrim to the West, Golden Lotus, and Dream of the Red Chamber. One should also mention philosophical masterpieces written

around the 5th century BC, namely Confucius' Analects and Lao-zi's The Way and Its Power.

The Han have also contributed greatly to world civilization by inventing paper (2nd century BC), ceramics (7th century), gunpowder (10th century), porcelain (11th century), movable printing (11th century), and the compass (12th century).

15 WORK

The economic disequilibrium of Han society is very prominent. On the one hand, scientists are engaged in nuclear power plants, while peasants in rural areas cultivate the land with primitive farming techniques. Almost all kinds of work present in both developed and developing countries can be found in China. Among them, three kinds of work go back thousands of years. Porcelain production lent the name "China," from its birthplace; China is also the homeland of sericulture (the production of raw silk), filature (reeling of silk), and silk knitting; doctors of traditional Chinese medicine prescribe herbs and acupuncture, making a great contribution to the health and population growth of the Chinese nation.

16 SPORTS

As the main ethnic body of the Chinese nation, the Han have participated in almost all the athletic contests of the Olympic Games and performed brilliantly in many sporting events. Soccer, volleyball, basketball, table tennis, badminton, jogging, and swimming are popular sports played by children and adults. Wushu and Taijiquan are two kinds of traditional shadow-boxing of the Han, which have become world-famous as methods of gymnastics and meditation.

The Chinese Government has set up a Federation of Chinese Sports to train Chinese athletes for world Olympics and for Asian Olympics. Athletes from China have performed brilliantly in many sports, especially swimming, diving, gymnastics, ping-pong, and volleyball.

17 ENTERTAINMENT AND RECREATION

Watching television is almost a daily entertainment of the Han family in the evenings. In addition, the video cassette recorder is now very popular in urban areas. The Han go to the movies just on occasion. Youngsters are often enthusiastic about dancing, karaoke, and rock music, while the aged are likely to be enchanted by Beijing opera, local drama, classical music, and mahjong tiles. Travel has become a new entertainment since the five-day work week was adopted in 1995.

18 FOLK ART, CRAFTS, AND HOBBIES

Calligraphy and traditional Chinese painting are the most popular folk arts of the Han. Paper cutting, embroidery, brocade, cloisonné, colored glaze, jadeware, clay sculpture, and dough figurines meticulously made by craftsmen are famous around the world. Chess, kite flying, and potted landscapes are hobbies among people of various ages.

19 SOCIAL PROBLEMS

China is in a period of transition, moving from a traditional to a modern society. The coexistence of the old social structure and the new, immature social system produces a number of contradictions. The widening gap of living standards between rural and urban areas draws a surplus rural labor force of 100 million and more into the coastal areas looking for jobs. This situation, which favors mobility and exchange, entails serious social disturbances. The disequilibrium of the economic development between the coastal areas and the inland, the irrational income for different occupations, the widening gap between the rich and the poor, the inflation year after year, bribery becoming more serious day by day, and the reappearance of other ugly phenomena such as gambling, drugs, prostitution, and abduction of women, are all worrisome and perplexing to the public.

20 GENDER ISSUES

The Chinese states that women have equal rights with men in all areas of life, and most legislation is gender neutral. However, there are continued reports of discrimination, sexual harassment, wage discrepancies, and other gender related problems. The gap in educational level between women and men is narrowing with women making up 47.1% of college students in 2005, but only 32.6% of doctoral students. China has strict family planning laws, and it is illegal for women to marry before 20 years of age (22 for men), and it is illegal for single women to give birth. The Family Planning Bureau can require women to take periodic pregnancy tests and enforce laws that often leave women with no real options other than abortion or sterilization.

Prostitution and the sex trade is a significant problem in China involving between 1.7 and 5 million women. It involved organized crime, businessmen, the police, and government workers, so prosecution against prostitution has limited success. In 2002, the nation removed homosexuality from its official list of mental illnesses, and though it is still a taboo topic, homosexuality is increasingly accepted, especially in large, international cities.

21 BIBLIOGRAPHY

Cambridge Encyclopedia of China. Brian Hook, ed. Cambridge: Cambridge University Press, 1982.

Chiao, Chien, Nicholas Tapp, and Kam-yin Ho, ed. "Special Issue on Ethnic Groups in China." *New Asia Bulletin,* no. 8, 1989.

China Facts and Figures Annual Handbook. Vol. 1–18. Gulf Breeze, Fla.: Academic International Press, 1978–1996.

Dreyer, June Teufel. *China's Forty Millions.* Cambridge: Harvard University Press, 1976.

Eberhard, Wolfram. *China's Minorities: Yesterday and Today.* Belmont: Wadsworth Publishing Company, 1982.

Fairbank, John King. *China: A New History.* Cambridge, Mass.: Cambridge University Press, 1992.

Gentelle, Pierre, ed. *L'État de la Chine.* Paris: La Découverte, 1989.

Gernet, Jacques. *A History of Chinese Civilisation.* transl. from the French, Cambridge: Cambridge University Press, 1985.

Greenhalgh, Susan. *Just One Child: Science and Policy in Deng's China.* Berkeley: University of California Press, c008.

Gustafsson, Bjorn A., Shi, Li, and Sicular, Terry, eds. *Inequality and Public Policy in China.* New York: Cambridge University Press, 2008.

Harrell, Stevan. *Cultural Encounters on China's Ethnic Frontiers.* Seattle: University of Washington Press, 1994.

Heberer, Thomas. *China and Its National Minorities: Autonomy or Assimilation?* Armonk, NY: M. E. Sharpe, 1989.

Keightley, David N. "Early Civilization in China: Reflections on How It Became Chinese." In *Heritage of China. Contemporary Perspectives on Chinese Civilization.* Berkeley: University of California Press, 1990.

Lebar, Frank, et al. *Ethnic Groups of Mainland Southeast Asia.* New Haven: Human Relations Area Files Press, 1964.

Lemoine, Jacques. "Les Han." In *Ethnologie régionale II* (Encyclopédie de la Pléiade). Paris: Gallimard, 1978.

Ma Yin, ed. *China's Minority Nationalities.* Beijing: Foreign Languages Press, 1989.

Pulleyblank, Edwin G. "The Chinese and their Neighbors in Prehistoric and Early Historic Times." In *The Origins of Early Chinese Civilization,* edited by David N. Keightley. Berkeley: University of California Press, 1983.

Ramsey, S. Robert. *The Languages of China.* Princeton: Princeton University Press, 1987.

Wiens, Harold J. *Han Chinese Expansion in South China.* New Haven: The Shoestring Press, 1967.

—by C. Le Blanc

HANI

ALTERNATE NAMES: Huoyi
LOCATION: China (Yunnan)
POPULATION: 1.5 million
LANGUAGE: Hani
RELIGION: Polytheism; ancestor worship; some Christianity
RELATED ARTICLES: Vol. 3: China and Her National Minorities

¹INTRODUCTION

The Huoyi tribe inhabiting the south of Dadu River (in northwest Sichuan) in the 3rd century BC was probably the ancestor of the current Hani. The Huoyi were a branch of the southward-migrating ancient Qiang. From the 4th to the 8th century, they reached southward to areas in Yunnan Province between the Lanchang Jiang River and the Yuan Jiang River where they now dwell. Since the Tang Dynasty (618–907), they paid tribute to their own elected officials. In the 18th century, the chiefs of the Hani tribes lost their authority and were replaced by Manchu or Chinese officers appointed directly by the Qing Dynasty (1644–1911).

²LOCATION AND HOMELAND

The Hani are mainly distributed in the southwest of Yunnan, between the Lanchang Jiang River and the Yuan Jiang River. There are four autonomous Hani counties; there are also large Hani populations in the Dai districts of Xishuangbanna. These areas are located in the subtropical zone, with fertile land and abundant rainfall, suitable for growing rice and other wet crops. The Hani population was 1.5 million in 2000.

³LANGUAGE

Hani language belongs to the Sino-Tibetan family, Tibeto-Burman group, Yi branch. There are three dialects and no written language. In 1957, a writing system based on Latin was created. Hani is a self-given name. The other branches have self-given names of their own. Hani is the general designation of the whole group.

⁴FOLKLORE

According to Hani mythology, there was a chaotic fog in the universe in remote antiquity. It seethed silently for a long period of time and ultimately turned into a vast expanse of water. A big fish grew up, but its head and tail were not clearly visible. The fish swung its right fin up, which turned into the sky. It swung its left fin down, which turned into the earth. When it swayed its body, 14 gods and goddesses, as well as two human beings, were sent out from its back. The man and the woman married. Later on, the woman gave birth to 21 children. The eldest was a tiger, the second an eagle, the third a dragon. The rest were men and women. The dragon brought three big bamboo tubes to its mother as gifts for her loving kindness. The first tube contained gold, silver, copper, iron, and jewelry, which she ordered to stay underground. The second contained rice, corn, cotton, grass, and trees, which she ordered to grow on earth. The third contained oxen, horses, pigs, poultry, and other animals. She ordered all the animals, except the oxen, to

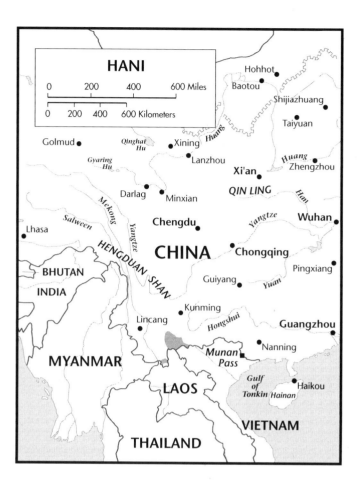

be led into the forest. The oxen were to be reserved as sacrificial offerings to the gods.

The Hani believed that seeds of the food crops were taken from the gods by a hero called Mamai, who had to pay with his own life to obtain them. That is why the Hani hold a commemorative ceremony in honor of Mamai in May or June of each year.

⁵RELIGION

The Hani are polytheistic. They believe that there is a Heaven God, an Earth God, a Tree God, as well as a Village God and a House God to protect them. They offer sacrifices to obtain their blessing and protection. Ancestor worship is also an important form of religious belief and practice. The Hani believe that some ghosts and gods bring about misfortunes; they seek the mediation of the shaman to ward off their influence and to expel them.

In Xishuangbanna District, the Hani offer sacrifices to the Village Gate, asking for the protection from the Village Gate God. There are public trees in the village as well as family trees. The shaman is usually mandated to perform the sacrificial rite for the Tree God in the context of a festive celebration of the community under the trees; on that occasion, members of the community express their best wishes for the future.

Since the beginning of the 20th century, a number of Hani have converted to Christianity.

⁶MAJOR HOLIDAYS

For the Hani, just as for the Chinese, the Spring Festival and Mid-Autumn Festival are the most important celebrations of the year. They regard the month of October (lunar calendar; Western calendar, between October 24 and November 23) as the beginning of the year. The October Festival, therefore, is their New Year. It lasts from 5 to 15 days, depending on local custom. All members of the local community participate, each household providing a course for the lively communal dinner party.

The June Festival (lunar calendar; Western calendar, between June 23 and August 20) lasts for three to five days. On the last day of the festival, in addition to sacrificial offerings, a dinner party, and recreational activities, every family lights a torch and chases the ghosts out of the home; the torches are then taken in a procession to the limits of the village so as to drive out the evil spirits from the community.

⁷RITES OF PASSAGE

A rite of joint naming of the newborn son or daughter is held on the fourth day after the infant's birth. The parents prepare rice rolls covered with cooked beans and a little piece of chicken and put them on a table for the villagers. If the infant is a male, a boy will be invited to carry a bamboo tube of glutinous rice and a hoe; he should hoe the ground three times in front of the mother and the son. If the infant is a female, a girl should be invited to hold a chopper and carry a bamboo tube of glutinous rice; she chops the firewood three times in front of the mother and the daughter. These gestures show that the boy will be good in farming and the girl good in household work when they grow up. The ritual is completed by asking for the village elder to name the baby.

The girls comb their hair into braids before marriage, but coil the braid into a bun on the top of the head after the wedding; after childbearing, they wrap their head with a turban.

They dispose of the dead by cremation.

⁸INTERPERSONAL RELATIONS

When receiving a guest, the host usually holds out a bowl of wine with both hands and offers a toast. He then takes the teapot from the firepool and pours a cup of strong tea for the guest. The guest is not free to refuse.

There are quite a few ways for boys and girls to seek each other. During breaks from manual labor, boys and girls sit in two different rows, face to face, and throw small pine twigs at each other for fun. In this playful atmosphere, they may throw the pine twigs intentionally to their preferred partner. There is then formal dating. In some areas, when a young man reaches marriage age, he will carry his knapsack and journey to different villages to look for a spouse. If he has found someone, he will have a heart-to-heart talk (mostly about love) with the girl in a public house specially provided by the village for this purpose. They might even sleep there together if they wish. If they find each other congenial, they will agree on a wedding day. When the time comes, the boy's friends will help him to steal the girl to his house and get married. In some areas, if he takes a fancy to a girl, he will snatch away her small hat from her head. The hat is made of black handwoven cloth, silver ornamented, six angles in shape. If she agrees, they will start dating. If not, she might ask him to return the hat.

⁹LIVING CONDITIONS

Most of the Hani live half-way up in the mountains. Some villages are small, with dozens of households, while others are composed of hundreds of families. Hani houses are usually made of wood and adobes, thatched with straw and built on stone foundations. Most of them have three stories: the uppermost is for storing groceries and vegetables; the second, for living and food storage; and the first, for livestock. There are variations in building styles from region to region. For instance, in the Muojiang area, houses are flat-roofed and built on adobes; but in the Xishuangbanna area, they are made of wood and bamboo and provided with a balcony. Men and women live in separate rooms; the man's is in the front, which is also the place for guest entertaining.

Different districts are connected by highways, but people have to walk in mountainous areas. Fully equipped hospitals have been established in the counties and medical clinics in the small towns.

¹⁰FAMILY LIFE

The Hani family is patrilineal. They practice the "joint name system," by which they can trace back dozens of generations along the patrilineal family tree. The last one or two syllables of the father's name are the beginnings of the sons' and daughters' names.

By tradition, the Hani family is monogamous. However, the strength of the custom varies from region to region; for instance, in Xishuangbanna District, monogamy is stringent. A man abandoning his wife and marrying again will be condemned by public opinion. In general, a concubine is allowed, though illegal, if the legal wife has had no son. Young people have full freedom to date, but marriage should be agreed to by the parents. For instance, in the Mujiang area, there is a custom called "stepping on the road." When the boy and the girl find each other congenial, their parents must walk a certain distance on the road. If they do not come across a rabbit, wolf, or some other animal, the girl is betrothed to the boy. Two or three days after the wedding, she should return to her parents and live there until the time of rice transplanting in the spring.

¹¹CLOTHING

The Hani usually wear clothes made of dark navy cloth that they weave and dye themselves. Wrapping a black or white cloth on the head, the men usually wear long pants and a garment with buttons down the front. The women's clothes vary in different districts, but usually consist of long pants and a petticoat made of a single piece of cloth and opened at the right side without any collar. The sleeve openings and the bottoms of the pants are all piped and laced. In Xishuangbanna District, the women wear barrel-like long skirts, multi-pleated skirts, or pants reaching over the knees. Earrings, necklaces, and bracelets are daily ornaments. The marital status of women can be judged by the design and color of their waistband, as well as by their hairstyle. For example, single or double braids hanging down means the girl is unmarried, while a bun made of coiled braids indicates a married woman. In some areas, when a girl becomes 17, she may wear an ornament called *ouqiuqiu* behind her head. After 18, she may keep her hair on the temples, which denotes that she is "marriageable." Married women must cover the *ouqiuqiu* with a black cloth.

Three women from the Hani dine in Yunnan Province, China. (Yann Layma/Getty Images)

12 FOOD

The staple foods of the Hani include rice and corn. Proteins are obtained from chicken, duck, eggs, pigs, and oxen. Glutinous rice and *baba* (a cake made of cooked black rice with pestle) are indispensable during festivals. Edible wild herbs and wild fowls are taken on holidays. In the second part of June (lunar calendar; Western calendar, between July 7 and August 20), the Hani celebrate the Locust Festival; all the villagers go to the fields to catch locusts, which are a delicacy for the Hani. They like sour and spicy dishes. In some areas, they pulverize brown sugar, glutinous rice, potatoes, and sophora (nut of the sophora japonica, or "scholar's tree") into a powder. They then add water to obtain a thick dough and form the mixture into balls or shapes of animals; these are fried until crispy. This delicacy is served during the New Year Festival.

13 EDUCATION

Illiteracy was prevalent in the past. Since the 1950s, many primary schools have been established in the larger villages. There are middle schools and technical schools in the small towns. The great majority of children reaching school age are enrolled in school. Although education among the Hani has developed quickly, their educational level is still below average among the national minorities.

14 CULTURAL HERITAGE

Among the traditional musical instruments of the Hani, the *bawu* is unique. It is a bamboo pipe with eight openings on the shaft and a copper reed at one end. The deep notes of this oboe-like instrument are beautiful in timbre and very pleasant to the ear.

The "Wooden Sparrow Dance" was created in a village at Yuanyang in Yunnan. According to legend, a sparrow cured a boy who was seriously ill. Thereafter, whenever a boy was born, the villagers would perform a special dance to celebrate the occasion; the dancers are usually four to six males holding a sparrow carved in wood. There is another bird dance, called the "Silvery Pheasant Dance," performed in the Hani District along the Honghe River. The silvery pheasant has been regarded as a symbol of peace and liberty by the Hani. The dancers, wearing white, with feather fans in both hands, move softly and gracefully, imitating the bird's movement in the air.

In addition to myths, legends, poems, folk tales, fables, children's folk rhymes, proverbs, and riddles, the Hani have preserved an ancient epic narrating their migrations called "Hani Ancestors crossing the River," which is the common heritage of most Hani communities.

15 WORK

The Hani are good at building terraced fields. They are able to build them in line with the local topography and the soil texture. The uninterrupted water from the streams and ravines is channeled into the terraced fields. In Hani districts, tiers upon tiers of terraced fields greet the eye on every side. Some terraces are made of hundreds of tiers, like a huge ladder stretching to the sky.

[16] SPORTS

The traditional sport of the Hani is to play on the swing. It is not an ordinary swing but rather like a small windmill. Serving as a swing seat, a board is fixed at each end of the rotating arms. Four youngsters, sitting on the boards, rotate the arms in a full swing, rising and falling with each rotation.

[17] ENTERTAINMENT AND RECREATION

Listening to the "Drinking Song" is a traditional entertainment. The song, performed by an old singer, is about stories of their ancestors.

The Hani of Muojiang in Yunnan enjoy a special recreational dance: The participants dance while beating a drum; the young men swing their arms with a rolling gait, while the girls shake their handkerchiefs and swing their legs. They often interrupt their dance to propose a toast to the surrounding people.

[18] FOLK ART, CRAFTS, AND HOBBIES

Hani girls are adept at embroidery. Various figures and flowers are embroidered on hats, clothes, leg wrappings, and waistbands. Silver ornaments, such as earrings, eardrops, necklaces, and large bracelets are carved exquisitely.

[19] SOCIAL PROBLEMS

The Hani's cultural and educational level is below the average of the national minorities of China. This is due to the low starting point, to the little attention paid to education, and to the very low income of the teachers as a result of underfunding.

[20] GENDER ISSUES

The Chinese constitution states that women have equal rights with men in all areas of life, and most legislation is gender neutral. The Hani have not achieved the same levels of education as the majority population in urban areas, but as of 2008, most Hani children were enrolled in school as of 2008. There is no significant gap in education between boys and girls.

China has strict family planning laws. It is illegal for women to marry before 20 years of age (22 for men), and it is illegal for single women to give birth. Though minority populations were previously exempt from family planning regulations, policy has changed in recent years to limit minority population growth. As of 2008 urban minority couples may have two children while rural couples may have three or four.

[21] BIBLIOGRAPHY

Chiao, Chien, Nicholas Tapp, and Kam-yin Ho, ed. "Special Issue on Ethnic Groups in China." *New Asia Bulletin* no 8 (1989).

Dreyer, June Teufel. *China's Forty Millions*. Cambridge: Harvard University Press, 1976.

Eberhard, Wolfram. *China's Minorities: Yesterday and Today*. Belmont: Wadsworth Publishing Company, 1982.

Gustafsson, Bjorn A., Shi, Li, and Sicular, Terry , eds. *Inequality and Public Policy in China*. New York: Cambridge University Press, 2008.

Heberer, Thomas. *China and Its National Minorities: Autonomy or Assimilation?* Armonk, NY: M. E. Sharpe, 1989.

Lebar, Frank, et al. *Ethnic Groups of Mainland Southeast Asia*. New Haven: Human Relations Area Files Press, 1964.

Lemoine, Jacques. "Les Hani." In *Ethnologie régionale II* (Encyclopédie de la Pléiade). Paris: Gallimard, 1978.

Ma Yin, ed. *China's Minority Nationalities*. Beijing: Foreign Languages Press, 1989.

Miller, Lucien, ed. *South of the Clouds: Tales from Yunnan*. Seattle: University of Washington Press, 1994.

Ramsey, S. Robert. *The Languages of China*. Princeton: Princeton University Press, 1987.

Shin, Leo Kwok-yueh. *The Making of the Chinese State: Ethnicity and Expansion on the Ming Borderlands*. New York: Cambridge University Press, 2006.

Wiens, Harold J. *Han Chinese Expansion in South China*. New Haven: The Shoestring Press, 1967.

—by C. Le Blanc

HAZARAS

PRONUNCIATION: huh-ZAH-ruhz
LOCATION: Afghanistan
POPULATION: 6–7 million
LANGUAGE: Dari (Khorasani Persian); Pastu; Baluchi; Turkic
RELIGION: Islam (Shia Muslim)

¹ INTRODUCTION

The Hazaras are one of the many different ethnolinguistic communities living in Afghanistan. Some of the other major ethnic groups include the Tajik, Pashtun (or Pushtun), Uzbek, Turkmen, Baluch, and Nuristani. The Hazaras, with strong Mongoloid features, consider themselves to be Moghuls (descendants of the Turko-Mongol tribes of Inner Asia). Local legends and some native historians trace their ancestry to the biblical figure Yafith (or Japheth), the son of Noah. Their ethnic origins and the exact time and historical circumstances of their appearance in Afghanistan, however, remain little understood.

Although there appears to have been considerable curiosity about the Hazaras among foreign researchers, especially during the decades preceding Soviet intervention and the civil war, a systemic and comprehensive study of their history and ethnography is yet to be attempted. For political reasons, most historians writing about Afghanistan have left out any discussion of the Hazaras in their works. Similarly, the government of Afghanistan has neglected the Hazara regions as targets for economic development and social change. It is important to note that Hazaras (excluding those in central Afghanistan) live amid a variety of different ethnolinguistic communities in the country. Hence, their cultures display some variations reflecting adaptation to local conditions and ways of living.

The Hazaras are for the most part a tribally organized society. The names of some of their major tribes and tribal units are Shaikh All, Turkuman, Qarluq, Kahgadai, Qarabatur, Daymirdad, Behsood, Jaghoori, Daychoopan, Daykhita, Aymaq, Khawjameri, Nayman, Chaichka, Daykandi, Dayzangi, Tatar, and Fooladi Hazaras.

² LOCATION AND HOMELAND

The exact number of Hazaras, like other ethnic communities in Afghanistan, is not known due to the fact that no complete national census has ever been taken in that country. The estimates of Hazara population in Afghanistan range from about 7% (or 1,519,000 people) to well over 20% (or 6,000,000–7,000,000 people) of the total Afghani population of 31 million people. Spatially, the Hazaras are more concentrated in central mountainous regions of Afghanistan, but they are also found in smaller numbers scattered in other areas of the country. In addition, a population of Hazaras dwell in Baluchistan, Pakistan. Many Hazaras have also moved to Kabul to seek a better life and today comprise about half of the population of that city.

The central portion of Afghanistan in which a high population of Hazaras live is called Hazarajat. Hazaras can be found in many different provinces. Major locations of the Hazaras include Bamyan, Ghazni, Uruzgan, Ghoor, and Zabul. Other major areas with somewhat lower Hazara populations include

Kabul, Badghees, Logar, Parwan, and Samangan. Helmand, Qandahar, Baghlan, and Joozjan are also populated with Hazaras to a lesser degree. Small populations of Hazaras can also be found in other provinces of the country. The location of the Hazaras can be found in a geographical circle in central Afghanistan and an area extending west of the circle as well. The territories inhabited by the Hazaras lie completely within Afghanistan and do not share borders with any neighboring countries.

Hazarajat generally has a cold climate, and snow lasts long on the mountains. Because Hazaras raise animals, they must prepare and store food during the summer to meet their necessities for the cold winters. Until recently, the major means of transportation among Hazaras were donkeys and horses. Motor vehicles have only recently become common in their region.

³ LANGUAGE

Most Hazaras today speak Persian (known as Dari in Afghanistan). Because of the importance of Persian for communication, economic, and educational reasons in Afghanistan, Hazaras were influenced by the language and began speaking it. In addition to Persian, some Hazaras also speak Pashtu (or Pushtu) and Baluchi. The traditional Turkic language is also used in some areas. Professor Shah Ali Akbar Shahrustani, a well-known scholar of Hazaras, wrote a book comparing Turkic and Mongolian languages. He found 1,400 Turkic and Mongolian words that were used in Hazaran Persian. Of these,

A Hazaras family in their cave in Bamiyan, Afghanistan. They were displaced from their home by the Taliban and were on the move for three years. (Tyler Hicks/Getty Images)

more than 1,000 were pure Turkic words. The Persian spoken by Hazaras is known as Khorasani Persian.

⁴ FOLKLORE

Hazaras historically have less formal education than people from other parts of the country. Hazaras believe in the superstitions that are common in the country. Some beliefs include the evil eye, ghosts, and several other superstitions about animals and nighttime.

Storytelling is a traditional Hazara habit. They tell stories of their history, their ancestors, and their heroes. Music is commonly used with poetry, epics, and love stories. The *dambura* is used to provide music. This is a bowl lute with a long neck and two strings that are plucked.

Hazaras' customs and traditions are unique. They have many different *dubaitis* (which are sung). An example of a dubaiti is:

The stars shone and I lay awake
I was behind the broken wall
As the damned cock began to crow
I was still waiting for my love.

Hazaras also have many proverbs. Examples include:

If your father owns the mill, you still must wait your turn to grind your flour.
Mirrors are not necessary at a meeting of the blind.
Don't make plans for your life on the advice of false astrologers.
The sons of wolves will be wolves.
Two people are afraid of an empty rifle: the one with the rifle, and the one without it.

⁵ RELIGION

The Islamic religion has two major sects, the Sunni and the Shia sects. Sunnis recognize the four khalifs that followed Prophet Muhammad and believe in four imams: Abu Hanifa, Malik, Shafi, and Hanbal. The Shias give more significance to the fourth khalif, Ali, and his family. The Hazaras are Shia Muslims. During the beginning of Islam in Afghanistan, the Shias were divided into three different groups: the followers of the 12 imams, the Ismaili Shias, and the Zaidi Shias. Because the Zaidi Shias were very close to the Sunni sect of Islam, they are no longer present in modern-day Afghanistan. The Shias following the 12 imams exist throughout the country.

In the past, the Sunnis and Shias of Afghanistan had very good relations with each other, including marriages between sects. Recently, however, politics have stressed their differences and have divided the two to a greater extent. During Afghanistan's civil war years (1992–1996) and the preceding years of the Soviet invasion, Hazara resistance groups were generally not allied with those of Sunni background. Hazaras were supported by Shia Iran while other Sunni groups were supported by Sunni Pakistan, and the politics involved served to further drive apart Shia Hazara and Sunni groups in Afghanistan. The majority of Muslims in the world are Sunnis, considerably outnumbering the number of Shias.

⁶ MAJOR HOLIDAYS

As Shia Muslims, Hazaras celebrate the two major Islamic holidays: Ayd-Al-Fitr, a three day holiday following Ramadan, the month of fasting; and Ayd-Al-Adha, a festival (at the time of pilgrimage) in which animals (usually goats, sheep, cattle, or camels) are sacrificed in the name of God. 'Ashura celebrations also take place among the Hazaras. One other holiday celebrated among Hazaras is Nawruz, the Afghani New Year traditionally celebrated throughout most of the Turkic-Persian world. This holiday has developed into a religious one since the advent of Islam in the country. For example, people in Mazar-i-Sharif celebrate Nawruz at the place in which the tomb of Ali is believed to be located. In Kabul, the celebration takes place around an area called Sakhi. Trees are also planted on this day.

⁷ RITES OF PASSAGE

Little girls wear bright colors and are free to go outside while they are young, but as they mature and reach puberty, they are required to cover their hair with scarves. They are also required to stay in the house more often. There are also special celebrations and practices during weddings, times of circumcision for young boys, and funerals.

⁸ INTERPERSONAL RELATIONS

The Hazara people are very hospitable and friendly to guests. They prepare special food for their guests, and the guests are honored with the best place to sit. Most of the Hazaras in Kabul and the countryside eat with their hands, rarely using utensils such as forks and knives.

Hazara women perform many household tasks, including sewing, cooking, milking animals, cleaning, and raising children. They also perform some outside tasks with the husband as well. Women are respected among men and the Hazara community, and the men are respected by Hazara women.

⁹ LIVING CONDITIONS

The living conditions of Hazaras vary considerably depending on their locations. Those living in cold climates have more difficulties than those living in warm areas. In cold areas, more clothing is necessary, there is more of a need for wood to keep warm, travel is more difficult, and agriculture is poor. (Fruits are not common in some parts of Hazarajat. They also lack vegetables as well.) Generally speaking, Hazaras are poor people, and there is little business interaction among them. In Kabul, they usually have low-paying, menial jobs such as janitorial work and are relegated to living on the outskirts of the city, with less access to clean water and electricity and other amenities than other groups.

¹⁰ FAMILY LIFE

It is customary for entire Hazara families to live together in one house. This includes grandparents and women married to the sons of the household. Daughters-in-law contribute to the household work when they move in, easing the workload of their mothers-in-law. Newborn babies are usually named by the older people of the household. Grandparents show much interest in the raising of their grandchildren. Fathers and grandfathers teach boys male tasks, while mothers and grandmothers teach girls the tasks assigned to females. Marriages are arranged, and when a daughter is married, she moves in with her husband's family. After the death of the grandparents, especially the grandfather, the sons usually begin living independently.

¹¹ CLOTHING

The most common clothing among the Hazaras is *perahan-u-tunban*, a type of clothing somewhat resembling the Western world's pajamas. Women's designs differ from those of the men. Men wear turbans, vests, overcoats, and sweaters over their perahan-u-tunbans. Their clothing is usually made from wool and/or cotton. Unlike the men, who wear simply colored clothes, the women usually wear clothes with varying bright colors and designs. The women usually wear lighter-weight clothes because they remain indoors more often. Hazaras do not have a large quantity of clothes.

¹² FOOD

The Hazaras' diet includes a large proportion of high-protein food such as meat and dairy products. They use plenty of oil when cooking. They usually eat only one type of food during a meal, not having wide selections of food at once. Exceptions are among the wealthy and at times when guests are visiting.

¹³ EDUCATION

Hazaras have two systems of education. The first one is the traditional system, which includes religious studies at mosques, education by family members at home in gender-appropriate tasks, and learning basic reading and writing skills from the local religious leaders of the villages. The second system is official education, in which the schools are administered by the Ministry of Education (from the capital of the country). After the sixth grade, only the best students are sent to Kabul to continue their education. Afghanistan has a centralized system of education.

In the years of rebuilding Afghanistan since 2001, Hazaras are often more likely to take advantage of educational opportunities that other groups in Afghanistan. Nearly all Hazaras attend school, including girls, and the literacy rate among this group is growing and is thought to be higher than the national average. Bamian State University is operating in Hazarajat, after being closed until 2004. However, marginalization does continue to exist and entrance to esteemed universities such as Kabul State University is difficult and uncommon for Hazaras.

¹⁴ CULTURAL HERITAGE

In times of celebration, Hazaras have social gatherings during which music is played and dancing takes place. Women and men dance separately, each having different styles. Poetry is read and *damburas* (lutes) are played.

Many Hazaras are proud of their cultural links to Mongols and Genghis Khan. In fact, the word Hazara comes from the Persian meaning "one thousand" and is thought to be derived from Genghis Khan's division of troops into groupings of this number. However this same heritage also creates some tensions with other Afghanis of different background.

One of the most notable features of Hazarajat were the giant Buddha statues located at Bamian, constructed 1,500 years ago by the Kushan Empire. Although the Hazara of today may not be direct descendents of those that created the Buddhas, the Buddhas for many years dominated the landscape of the homeland of the Hazaras. In 2001 the Buddhas were destroyed by the Taliban due to the fundamental Islamist proscription against idols in the human form.

15 WORK

Excluding housework, men are held responsible for managing and financially supporting the household. They work in the fields growing crops. Because of their low standard of living, Hazaras are required to perform more laborious jobs to support their families. This is apparent in Kabul, where many Hazaras have migrated and taken up menial jobs. It is common for Hazara labor migrants also to migrate to nearby countries such as Pakistan and Iran and send remittances home to support their families.

16 SPORTS

In some Hazara areas such as Bamyan, Samangan, and the northern parts of Afghanistan, *buzkashi* takes place. This is a game in which horse-riders attempt to carry a dead goat into the opposing team's goal, a marked circle on the ground. Hunting, wrestling, archery, horse-races, and a variety of children's games also take place in some areas. Because of little spare time from work, Hazaras do not spend a great deal of time playing sports.

17 ENTERTAINMENT AND RECREATION

During the winters, when they do not have as much work to do, Hazaras have some time for entertainment and recreation. They tell stories, visit with each other, and drink tea in the evenings.

18 FOLK ART, CRAFTS, AND HOBBIES

Hazaras are very well known for making handicrafts such as coats, overcoats, sweaters, jackets, shoes, hats, gloves, and scarves. Embroidery is common. These are mostly made by the women and are sold in shops in Kabul and other cities.

19 SOCIAL PROBLEMS

Despite being very social among themselves, Hazaras have many social problems in the country. Because of the level of marginalization experienced by Hazaras, they are generally not socially involved with other groups. Despite being a native group of Afghanistan, Hazaras have some differences from the other ethnic groups of the country. As Shia Muslims, they are in the minority in the largely Sunni population of Afghanistan. The Hazaras are also generally poorer and less educated than other Afghanis. These differences create tensions between the Hazaras and other Afghanis, and also limit the progress Hazaras can make in improving their standard of living. During the years the Taliban controlled most of Afghanistan (1996–2001), Hazaras were victims of ethnic cleansing and by some accounts, genocide. A fictionalized portrayal of the relationship between a Hazara boy and an Afghan boy of the upper class can be found in Khaled Hosseini's *The Kite Runner* (2003) and the movie of the same name (2007).

Hazarajat has, comparatively, avoided the large opium poppy production endemic in much of Afghanistan. However, many development projects are also not introduced to this region as to other parts of Afghanistan.

20 GENDER ISSUES

In many ways, Hazara women are able to achieve many more rights than women in other parts of Afghanistan. While nationwide numbers of girls who attend school remains low, among Hazaras the number is as high as 80%. Hazara women are not subject to the strict social mores of Pashtun and other ethnicities, and are not required to practice seclusion. As a result, they have been more likely to join the workforce and to take up farming. The first female governor in Afghanistan, Habiba Sarobi, was a Hazara and was appointed in 2005.

21 BIBLIOGRAPHY

Gharjastani, M. Isa. *New History of Hazarajat.* Kweeta, Pakistan, 1988.

Hosseini, Khaled. *The Kite Runner.* NY: Riverhead, 2003.

Khanuf, Timur. *National History of Hazara.* Translated by Aziz Tughyan. Iran: Institute of Ismaeliyan Press, 1993.

Larson, Marisa and Laura Hazelton. *Geopedia: National Geographic.* 11 February 2008.

Poladi, Hassan. *Hazaras.* Stockton, CA: Mughal Publishing Co., USA, 1989.

Sakata, Hiromi Lorraine. *Music in the Mind.* Kent, OH: Kent State University Press, 1983.

Yazdani, Husain Ali (Haj Kazim). *A Study on the History of Hazaras.* Vol. 1, 2nd ed. Gum, Iran: M. Amin Sharifi, 1993.

Zabriskie, Phil. "The Outsiders." *National Geographic*, February 2008.

—revised by M. Kerr

HILIGAYNON

PRONUNCIATION: hee-lee-GUY-nohn
ALTERNATE NAME: ILONGGO
LOCATION: Philippines (Western Visayas)
POPULATION: 5.8 million (2000)
LANGUAGE: Hiligaynon
RELIGION: Catholicism
RELATED ARTICLES: Vol. 3: Filipinos

¹INTRODUCTION

In 1569, the Spanish conquistador Legaspi transferred his headquarters from food-poor Cebu to Panay, where rice was available in abundance. Long before this time, the island's fertility permitted the Hiligaynon people to develop one of the archipelago's most advanced societies, one that engaged in international trade (as evidenced by large finds of Chinese porcelain) and that created fine work in gold and semiprecious stones. The textiles of Panay remained in high demand throughout the archipelago into the 19th century; the industry thrived until overwhelmed by cheaper British manufactures.

Among Christianized regions, the Western Visayas has been noteworthy for the persistence of pre-Christian systems of belief; here, it was *baylan*, leaders in the indigenous religion, who led revolts against the Spanish (rather than of Christian millenarian sects as in the Tagalog and other regions). Nonetheless, the church-adorned city of Iloilo on Panay became one of the great centers of Hispanicized culture in the colony (in 1993 Iloilo's baroque Miag-ao church was recognized as a UNESCO World Heritage site). Large-scale sugar production for the world market created a small, initially largely *mestizo*, elite who enjoyed an opulent lifestyle on vast plantations (and who may have provided the basis for the stereotype of Hiligaynon hedonism, also attributable to the natural bounty of the land). At the same time, economic dislocations (such as the demise of the textile industry) forced a flood of landless Hiligaynon to take ill-paid, backbreaking labor on these plantations of the formerly under populated island of Negros to the immediate east of Panay.

With the recent decades' drop in the price of sugar, much of the region has entered a steep economic decline; Negros has become one of the most impoverished regions in the country and particularly ripe for communist insurgency. Though to a lesser extent than Ilocanos and Cebuanos, Hiligaynon have settled in more sparsely populated parts of the country, such as Mindoro and Mindanao. Economic growth since the 1990s has benefited Iloilo as it has other comparable cities in the country, and one of the country's preeminent destinations for domestic and foreign tourists has developed on Boracay off Panay.

²LOCATION AND HOMELAND

Panay is one of the major rice-producing areas of the Philippines (and the most important one by far in the Visayan islands). The landscape consists of broad plains stretching between mountain ranges. Large rivers deposit the volcanic sediments that make the lowlands so fertile. The island of Guimaras in the strait between Panay and Negros is an exception; it is a coral platform.

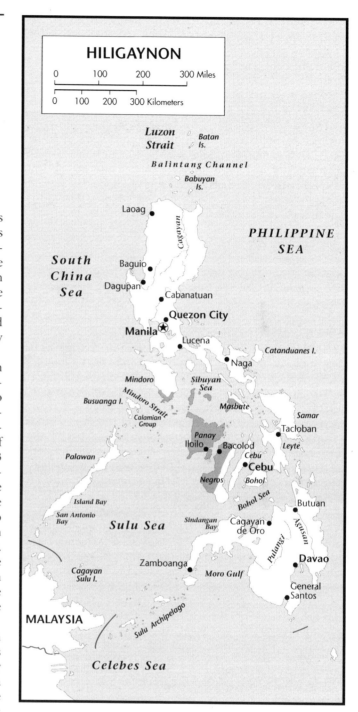

The Western Visayas region of the Philippines includes the provinces of Iloilo, Aklan, Capiz, Antique (all on Panay island), Negros Occidental, and Romblon; it includes two of the country's largest cities, Iloilo in eastern Panay and Bacolod on western Negros. The region's population numbered 6.2 million in 2000 (up from 5.4 million in 1990 and 3.6 million in 1970), of which 61.57% were speakers of Hiligaynon, concentrated on the facing coasts of Panay and Negros (72% of population of Iloilo province and 77.68% of Negros Occidental province).

According to the 2000 census, Hiligaynon speakers constituted 7.6% of the national population (5.8 million people). Beyond the Western Visayas, they can also be found in southern

Mindoro and (as recent migrants) on Palawan (13% in 2000) and Mindanao (11% of the Caraga region and 10.83% of Southern Mindanao—more than half [52%] of South Cotabato's population was Hiligaynon-speaking, and almost half [46.92%] of Sultan Kudarat's).

³LANGUAGE

The Hiligaynon language is the language of Iloilo province, which has come to be spoken throughout the Western Visayas region. Hiligaynon (as the name of both a language and an ethnic group) is also called "Ilonggo," though this generally refers specifically to the dialect and people of Iloilo. Hiligaynon intonation is noted for its gentle lilt under which, it is said, a curse may go unrecognized.

Other regions of Panay have their own distinct languages, including Capizeño, Aklanon, and Kiniray-a. Narrow straits link Panay and western Negros, and Hiligaynon is spoken on both shores. Mountains separate western from eastern Negros, whose inhabitants speak Cebuano, a language that Hiligaynon cannot readily understand.

⁴FOLKLORE

The *Maragtas* epic, an imaginative 19th century reworking of Panay folk memories, tells of the migration to the Philippines in 1250 of the Bornean *datus* (chiefs) Puti, Sumakwel, Bangkaya, Balakasusa, Paiburong, Dumangsil, Lubay, and Dumalogdog. They had led their followers there to escape the tyranny of the Srivijayan empire. The datus bought the coastal lands of Panay from the indigenous Negritos with gold, pearls, and other ornaments (the Negritos then withdrew to the interior). The meeting of the Negritos and the Borneans is commemorated in many carnival-like local festivals, foremost of which is the Ati-Atihan of Kalibo in Aklan province.

⁵RELIGION

Among the Hiligaynon, a pre-Christian belief system coexists with the Catholic one brought by the Spaniards. The two exert mutual influence on each other, as when the Santo Niño, the image of the Child Jesus as World Sovereign, is bathed to summon rain or attract good luck. The indigenous cosmogony divides the universe into three parts. The upper world houses at its zenith *(ibabaw)* the *udtohanon*, i.e., God and his favorite angels who will pass the final judgment but are otherwise remote from human affairs. Lower down in the upper world reside the *langitnon*, angelic beings that live above the clouds. In the *awan-awan* (between the clouds and the earth) live the spirits of the wind, rain, thunder, lightning, typhoons, and whirlwinds; supreme among them is the *tagurising* who lives where the sun rises. The middle world (the earth) is the home to the *dutan-on*, spirits expelled from the upper world for rebelling against God; they differentiated according to where they first landed, for example, in trees, the river, or the sea. The underworld includes hell, in front of whose gate is a hollow pit where the *engkanto*, the malevolent spirits, live with their reptilian pets; the nether regions are connected to the middle world through a tunnel called the *bungalog*.

Each community has specialists who are able to communicate with spirits and heal diseases thought to be caused by spirits, for lack of any other explanation; they also recover lost objects, predict the future, and discover the causes of misfortunes. The most important of these is the *baylan*, a medium whom a spirit has befriended and granted powers; to augment the potency of his rituals, the baylan often adds Latin prayers and Catholic sacred objects.

⁶MAJOR HOLIDAYS

See the article entitled **Filipinos**.

⁷RITES OF PASSAGE

Persons wanting to marry consult with their siblings and other relatives before approaching their parents for consent and support. The boy's kin arrange a meeting with the girl's kin to discover if the girl has already been promised to another; this serves as a public announcement to discourage other suitors. The boy's kin employ a spokesperson using allegorical language to ascertain whether the girl's parents have accepted the proposal. If they have, the arrangements, including the prospective groom's term of bride-service, are arranged at another meeting, the *padul-ong*, after which the wedding becomes binding and the girl is no longer to be seen in the company of other boys.

On the night before the wedding, both sides attend a party at the bride's parents' house. The church ceremony itself includes ritual acts that are meant to ensure the wife's subservience and fertility. Formerly, a *sinulang* (a machete dance) accompanied the couple out of the church. Arriving at the house, the couple proceeds straight to the family altar to ensure future prosperity; a feast follows. The marriage is not consummated until the second night at the groom's parents' house; on the third day, the couple returns to the bride's parents' house.

When a person is dying, relatives say prayers for the deliverance of his or her soul and to ward off evil spirits (men wave machetes in the yard). The body is washed with water mixed with ginger or bark juice to prevent odor and is laid out in the house next to an improvised altar and a tin can, in which mourners put contributions. The deceased's family refrains from making excessive noise, fighting, combing their hair, and bathing until three days after the burial. Only unmarried men may take the body out of the house; water is thrown on the threshold so that another death will not follow. The entire funeral procession must return to the deceased's house and wash their hands and feet.

Nine days of prayer follow the burial; as many as nine more days may be added, depending on the family's wealth (as all attending must be served food and drink). At a midnight ceremony on the ninth night, all family members must be awake to bid farewell to the deceased's spirit. On the death anniversary, nine days of prayer again take place. On the ninth night, a *patay-patay* (a dummy of the dead) is set up, consisting of pillows laid on a wooden trunk upon which the deceased's clothes are laid.

See also **Filipinos**.

⁸INTERPERSONAL RELATIONS

Hiligaynon share the general Filipino behavioral values, such as *hiya* (*huya* in the Hiligaynon language). Violating norms (such as insulting mediums) will earn *gaba*, supernatural punishment. Those who humiliate others will suffer the same amount of humiliation in turn, a principle called *ulin*.

⁹LIVING CONDITIONS

Houses are raised 3 to 4 m (9–13 ft) off the ground; walls are of plaited bamboo, and roofs are of nipa or coconut palm leaves or cogon grass. *Sulay,* bamboo, or timber props, are placed against all sides of a house to keep it from being blown away by typhoons. The room for receiving guests is separated from the rest of the house by a wall; a sofa and two side chairs occupy the space immediately inside the front door. Small children of both sexes sleep together, but once they are older, boys sleep near the door and girls sleep in a bedroom at the back. Animals are kept under the house, and rice is stored there (if not in a separate granary structure). The house lot is enclosed with a bamboo fence or a hedge of ornamental plants; fruit tree groves and gardens are nearby.

Average family income in the Western Visayas region amounted to 130,000 pesos (us$2,549) in 2006, relatively low for the Philippines (ranking 10th out of 17 regions), cf. the national average of ₱173,000, the National Capital Region's ₱311,000, Southern Tagalog's ₱198,000, and Central Visayas' regions, ₱144,000.

According to the 2000 census, the proportion of houses in Negros Occidental province with a roof of galvanized iron/ aluminum reached 61% (up from 26.1% in 1990), with a roof of grass or palm thatch 30%; 24.2% of houses had wooden outer walls, 40% outer walls of bamboo or thatch, and 12.9% outer walls of concrete, brick, or stone (5.21% in 1990). In 2000, 13.8% of households in the Western Visayas had access to a community faucet, 14% to a faucet of their own, 22% to a shared deep well, and 17.3% to a dug shallow well, while 9.8% obtained their water from springs, lakes, rivers, or rain. Well over half of households (57.9%) disposed of their garbage by burning it, 10.9% by dumping it into a household pit, and 7.8% by feeding it to their animals; only 14.4% had it picked up by a collection truck. 57% of houses were lit with electricity, 37.8% with kerosene lamps, and 4.2% with firewood. 725.5% possessed a radio, 42.2% a television, 23.8% a refrigerator, 15.5% a VCR, 9.2% a telephone or cell phone, 9.4% a washing machine, and 8.5% a motorized vehicle.

¹⁰FAMILY LIFE

Hiligaynon family structure conforms to the general Filipino pattern [*See* the article entitled **Filipinos** in this volume]. In wealthier families, the Spanish terms *papa* and *mama,* or even the English *mommy* and *daddy,* are preferred over the native *tatay* and *nanay.* Educated people may address their spouses with such English expressions as *honey* or *darling* (often shortened to *ling*) rather than the native *nonoy* (for the husband) or *neneng* (for the wife). Uncles and aunts are addressed as "*tay* + [name]" ("Papa ____") and "*nay* + [name]" ("Mama _____"), respectively.

A peasant couple share work responsibilities, e.g., a husband plows while the wife plants; he fishes but she sells the catch. Husbands are the dominant partner outside the house (i.e., in public or in the fields), whereas wives reign supreme within the house. Spouses refrain from showing affection publicly, exchanging only casual greetings. While village people disapprove of a man taking a mistress, saying it will bring bad luck, elite men take mistresses for the sake of prestige.

Family members lavish much attention on a child but also discipline him or her from an early age. Children will gang up on a sibling to whom the parents show favoritism. As they get older, sons become more formal with their mothers and daughters with their fathers (but with puberty, daughters become closer to their mothers). At the age of seven, a boy will start to help his father with farming or fishing.

Parents discipline children by telling them frightening tales (mentioning the *aswang* or names of old people) or by spanking or whipping them with a stick. When children misbehave, all are punished, even if only one initiates the misbehavior.

¹¹CLOTHING

For fieldwork, men wear worn-out short pants and often go shirtless. On formal occasions, however, they wear long pants, shirts, and shoes (otherwise they go barefoot).

Married women wear either a *bestida* (dress), or a *patadyong* (tube skirt) with a blouse. Traditional weaving is nearly extinct, having been a thriving industry before the 19th-century import of British manufactured cloth. For *pangalap* (magical protection), many older men wear tattoos (a crucifix, initials, or female figures). At the time of the Spanish arrival, all Visayans wore elaborate tattoos, earning them the name *Pintados,* "the painted ones," from their conquerors.

¹²FOOD

The eating pattern is either three meals a day or two meals (at 10:00–11:00 am and 4:00–5:00 pm). Between-meal snacks consist of rice cakes, boiled roots, or bananas. Family members eat at their own convenience but are encouraged to eat together. Ordinarily, people eat with their hands while sitting on the floor; silverware and tables are reserved for the use of guests. Men do not eat breakfast unless, as a gesture of hospitality, they are joining visitors who are being served breakfast.

Around 6:00 pm, men gather for *tuba* (palm wine) drinking sessions in the tree groves between houses (some women may also join) them.

¹³EDUCATION

The literacy level (population 10 years and older) in the Western Visayas was 93.02%, close to the national figure. See the article entitled **Filipinos**.

¹⁴CULTURAL HERITAGE

The Hiligaynon have an epic, the *Hinilawod. (See also* **Filipinos** in this volume).

¹⁵WORK

The Western Visayas region is dominated by two very different types of agriculture: rice cultivation by small holders, and sugar cultivation in large plantations. Swidden (shifting-cultivation) farming is still practiced in the highlands.

Tobacco has been growing in importance. Other crops grown include maize, bananas, coconuts, sweet potato, cassava, *singkamas* (jícama, similar to turnips), squash, tomatoes, beans, and red peppers. Fishing is an alternative means of livelihood. Some Hiligaynon engage in various forms of petty trade: *libod,* making the rounds of one's village, selling a product; *pahumay,* selling from one's house; *tinda,* selling at fiestas and other local events; and *tiyanggi,* operating a small variety store (*sari-sari* in Tagalog-Pilipino).

[16] SPORTS

Tumbang patis, popular with both boys and girls, involves two or more children throwing rocks at a tin can while someone who is "it" watches the can, putting it back in place when hit; if a player is caught retrieving the stone he or she has thrown, he or she becomes "it." Other popular games include: "gunfighting" with bamboo popguns; beetle- and spider-fighting; and *huyup-huyup,* blowing rubber bands out of a circle for bets. Young children catch dragonflies, dig holes in the ground, pile sticks, measure sand with bottle caps, and pull empty coconut shells or sardine cans.

[17] ENTERTAINMENT AND RECREATION

See the article entitled **Filipinos**.

[18] FOLK ART, CRAFTS, AND HOBBIES

See the article entitled **Filipinos**.

[19] SOCIAL PROBLEMS

See the article entitled **Filipinos**.

[20] GENDER ISSUES

According to the 2000 census, in the Western Visayas, the ratio of men to women was 102 to 100. Literacy was higher for women than for men (93.58% vs. 92.45%). While, overall, more overseas workers from the Western Visayas were men than women, 63% of those aged 10-24 were female.

In the past four centuries, Hiligaynon notions of gender differences have been influenced by Spanish Catholic and, later, American and modernizing national secular norms. Urban elite women, especially Spanish and Chinese mestizas, have more closely imitated foreign ideals than women of the rural lower classes. Women and men are recognized as having different characteristics, but in contrast to the case in Mediterranean gender ideologies, these differences are viewed as complementary, not as associating men with good and women with evil, nor as automatically conferring superior power to men or. Men feel no shame in deferring to an elder sister or to a strong-willed and capable wife. In colonial times, Hiligaynon men often sent their wives to discuss community issues with male Spanish officials, showing none of the concern to keep women in seclusion for the sake of family honor that was so important in Spanish culture. Hiligaynon culture generally regards women as innately more reliable and industrious than men, and there is no cultural preference for having a boy over a girl.

Female virginity is valued, but losing it does not condemn a young woman to permanent exclusion from respectable society, nor does having been a man's mistress (kerida) at one time. Premarital pregnancy is common and, if the couple marries, hardly any stigma is attached to it. Tolerance of this has been a characteristic of Hiligaynon society from earlier times, not a modern development. Modernization has brought both the model of the "liberated woman," new employment opportunities for educated women, and the removal of Spanish patriarchal legal restrictions and disabilities. However, it has also brought the realities of women being objectified in diverse contexts: U.S. military prostitution (a major phenomenon until the end of the 1980s); international mass-tourism; global consumer culture; and overseas labor recruitment, especially of domestic workers and entertainers. Government-led development programs have sought to mobilize women, highlighting the crucial role women play in society while emphasizing women's roles in the domestic sphere.

[21] BIBLIOGRAPHY

Blanc-Szanton, Cristina. "Collision of Cultures: Historical Reformulations of Gender in the Lowland Visayas." In *Power and Difference: Gender in Island Southeast Asia,* edited by Jane Monnig Atkinson and Shelley Errington. Stanford, CA: Stanford University Press, 1990.

Gordon, Raymond G., Jr. (ed.), 2005. *Ethnologue: Languages of the World, 15th edition.* Dallas, Tex.: SIL International, 2005. http://www.ethnologue.com (November 19, 2008).

Jocano, F. Landa. *The Hiligaynon: An Ethnography of Family and Community Life in Western Bisayas Region.* Quezon City: Asian Center, University of the Philippines, 1983.

LeBar, Frank M., ed. *Ethnic Groups of Insular Southeast Asia.* Vol. 2, *The Philippines and Formosa.* New Haven, CT: Human Relations Area Files Press, 1972.

National Statistics Office: Government of the Philippines. "Eight Percent of the Total Population Were From the Western Visayas." http://www.census.gov.ph/data/pressrelease/2003/pr0304tx.html (November 19, 2008).

_____. "South Cotabato: One Out of Two Persons a Hiligaynon/Ilonggo." http://www.census.gov.ph/data/pressrelease/2003/pr0363tx.html (November 19, 2008).

—revised by A. J. Abalahin

HINDUS

PRONUNCIATION: HIN-dooz
LOCATION: India; Nepal; Bangladesh; Sri Lanka; Pakistan;
  Bhutan; many other countries worldwide
POPULATION: over 1.1 billion followers
LANGUAGE: Sanskrit (sacred language); language of the region
  in which they live
RELIGION: Hinduism

¹ INTRODUCTION

Hindus are followers of a religion that has its origins on the
Punjab plains in northwestern India over 3,000 years ago. The
western boundary of early Āryan settlements in the region
was the river called Sindhu, an Indo-European word meaning
"river." The Persians pronounced the word as "Hindu," a term
that came to be applied to the peoples of the area. "Hinduism"
described the religion of these peoples. "Hindu" passed into
Greek usage as "Indos," from which is derived the names of the
Indus River and India itself.

Hindus themselves have no specific name for their religion.
One of its designations is *sanātana dharma,* which can be
loosely translated as "eternal truth." Hinduism has no founder,
no common set of beliefs or practices, no established "church,"
and no uniformity of worship. Over the centuries, Hinduism
has absorbed beliefs ranging from primitive animism to the
most sophisticated abstract philosophy. It is less of a religion
than a collection of faiths linked by some common traits. Yet
there are certain broad, distinguishing characteristics that set
Hinduism apart from other religions. These include reverence
for the *Vedas,* acceptance of the existence of God, belief in reincarnation and related doctrines, an emphasis on ritual, and
the caste system.

For many years, India was under the rule of first, the
Muslim Mughals, who established themselves in northern
India (Delhi and Agra) and then the British, but the masses remained true to Hinduism. There were conversions of Hindus,
mainly from the lower and untouchable castes to Islam, Buddhism, and Christianity, largely to escape the inequities of the
Hindu caste system, but even then Hinduism retained its tolerance for other religions. When the British left India in 1947,
they had hoped to leave a successor state that encompassed all
British possessions in mainland South Asia. However, the in-
transigence of Muhammad Ali Jinnah and the Muslim League
in demanding a homeland for Indian Muslims and the haste
of the British withdrawal from the region meant that the subcontinent was partitioned, on the basis of religion, between a
Muslim Pakistan and a predominantly Hindu India. Regions
of the subcontinent with a Muslim majority fell to Pakistan,
which was made up of a West and East Wing (now Bangladesh), separated by hundreds of miles of Indian territory, areas
with a Hindu majority were to become India, and the rulers of
the numerous princely states that were scattered across British India were to decide which country they would join (the
problem of Kashmir dates from this time). The migration of
Hindus and Muslims between India and Pakistan that accompanied this partition is estimated to have numbered around 10
million people and is thought to be the largest the world has
ever known. Partition in 1947 was also accompanied by an es-

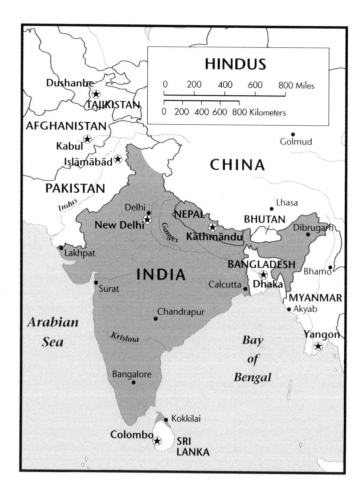

timated one million deaths of both Muslims and Hindus. Pakistan was established specifically as a homeland for Muslims in
the South Asian subcontinent. On the other hand, India, even
though it was essentially a Hindu land, remained steadfast in
its objective of remaining a secular state. Under the Nehru dynasty and, after Indira Gandhi's assassination in 1984, under
her son Rajiv Gandhi, India, even though it contained most of
the world's Hindus, remained a strongly secular democracy.

However, the rise within the last couple of decades of national political parties committed to "Hindutva" has changed
the situation. Hindutva means "Hinduness" and the word
was first coined in 1923 by Vinayak Damodar Savarkar in his
pamphlet entitled *Hindutva: Who is a Hindu?* There have been
political parties and groups, such as the Rashtriya Swayamsevak Sangh (RSS), Bajrang Dal and the Vishwa Hindu Parishad
(VHP), that have espoused Hindutva but, prior to the 1990s,
these never had power on a national scale. However, two
events that occurred towards the end of the 20th century attracted a large number of mainstream Hindus to the Hindutva
movement. The first of these was the Shah Bano case (1986) in
which Rajiv Gandhi's government, under pressure from conservative Muslims, used its large parliamentary majority to
overturn a Supreme Court verdict granting alimony to an old
Muslim woman that had angered many Muslims. (Muslims in
India are subject to "The Muslim Personal Law (Sharia) Application Act, 1937," whereas Hindus are subject to Hindu Law.)
The second was the dispute over the 16th century Mughal
Babri Masjid (Mosque) in Ayodhya—built by Babur after his

Indian Hindu devotees wait in line to make offerings to Shiva as part of Maha Shivaratri, a Hindu festival, in Amritsar, India. Hindus mark the festival by fasting and offering special prayers to Shiva, the lord of destruction. (AFP/Getty Images)

first major victory in India. Many Hindus saw it as a sacrilege that a mosque should stand on the site of the birthplace of Ram (Ram Janmabhoomi), the Hindu deity seen by many Hindus as an incarnation of Vishnu. For centuries, the mosque was a cause of tension between the Muslim and Hindu communities, with legal actions over the mosque dating back to the 19th century. In 1990, however, Lal Kriskna Advani, a leader of the Bharatiya Janata Party (BJP) (Indian People's Party, founded in 1980), undertook a *rāth yātrā* with the professed objective of building a Ram temple at the disputed site in Ayodhya. (Technically, Rath Yatra [*rāth* means "carriage" and *yātrā* means "journey"] is a Hindu festival associated with Jagannath [origin of the English word "juggernaut"] of Puri in Orissa involving a procession of towering raths being pulled through the streets of Puri by devotees, but in this case it refers to a "symbolic religious caravan" across the country) The yatra, which was accompanied by violence and bloodshed and is estimated to have been responsible for 3,000 Muslim deaths across India, failed in its avowed objectives, but in late 1992 a huge number of nationalist Hindus from all parts of India razed the mosque to the ground. The destruction of the mosque and subsequent conflict arguably lifted the BJP and Hindutva to national and international prominence. The 2002 Godhra violence in Gujarat, which pitted Hindu vs. Muslim, originated largely from the communal feelings raised by the Babri mosque issue.

The BJP was briefly in power in New Delhi during May 1996, but, having gained widespread support in the country for its political platform as a result of the events of the preceding two decades, formed the Union government between 1998 and 2004, with Atal Bihari Vajpayee as prime minister. The deputy prime minister, LK Advani, the same Advani who supported the destruction of the Babri Masjid and led the 1990 rath yatra, attributed the BJP's shocking loss of the general election in 2004 to the party straying from its platform of Hindutva.

2 LOCATION AND HOMELAND

Hinduism is one of the world's major religions, with over 1.1 billion people among its followers. Hindus make up 80% (approximately 905 million people according to the 2001 Census) of India's population. Nepal has another 22.5 million Hindus (80.2% of the population). Elsewhere in South Asia, Hindus number 11.4 million in Bangladesh (2001 Census), 1.5 million in Sri Lanka (according to government sources, though this may be a serious undercount) 30 million in Pakistan (c. 2%), and 0.25 million (25%) in Bhutan. All the preceding figures are based on 2001 census data, so allowing for population growth at the rate of national averages, and including Hindus overseas, the estimate of 1.1 billion is realistic.

Hindus have taken their religion to other parts of the world as well. Following the beginning of the Christian era, Indian colonists spread into Southeast Asia, where Hinduism strongly influenced local cultures. Although later replaced by Buddhism and Islam, Hinduism still survives in the Indonesian island of Bali. In the colonial period, the British introduced Indian labor (and thus Hinduism) into the Caribbean and Fiji. Indians also emigrated to South Africa, East Africa, and other British possessions. The later decades of the 20th century have seen a sizable immigration of Indians into Britain, Canada, and the United States.

³ LANGUAGE

Sanskrit (samskrta, "refined") is the sacred language of the Hindus. It is a later form of Vedic, the tongue in which the sacred literature of the Āryans was composed. Sanskrit dates to about 300 BC. It belongs to the Indo-Āryan branch of the Indo-European family of languages. There is a vast literature in Sanskrit, ranging from the early Vedic hymns to the numerous works (religious treatises, dramas, stories, poetry, etc.) associated with the flowering of Classical Sanskrit from the 3rd and 4th centuries AD onward. The script used today for writing Sanskrit is Nagari or Devanagari.

⁴ FOLKLORE

Hindus have an immensely rich tradition of myth and legend, ranging from the creation myths of the Vedas to the animistic beliefs surrounding local godlings. Of this vast treasury of material, only two works can be mentioned here. The *Mahābhārata*, composed probably sometime after 200 BC, is the world's longest epic poem. It tells of a great civil war in the region of modern Delhi and of the struggle between the Pandavas and the Kauravas for control of the kingdom. The centerpiece of the epic is the battle of Kurukshetra, but interwoven with the main story is a collection of myths, folk tales, and legends of Vedic gods mingled with discussions of statecraft, the science of war, and philosophy. One of the most famous sections of the epic is the *Bhagavad Gītā* ("Song of the Lord"). On the eve of the conflict, Arjuna, one of the Pandava princes, is surveying the opposing armies drawn up ready for battle. Distraught at the thought of killing his kinsmen, he seeks guidance from his charioteer, who is the god Krishna (Krsna). Krishna replies that it is his duty as a *ksatriya* (warrior) to fight his foes, and that this duty comes above all else.

The Rāmāyana, the second great Indian Hindu epic, relates the story of Rama and his wife, Sita. Sita is abducted by Ravana, who carries her off to his kingdom of Lanka (Ceylon). Rama and his brother Lakshman set out for Lanka to rescue Sita. There, with the aid of Hanuman, the monkey king, and his monkey people, they burn Lanka and free Sita. However, Sita has been associated with another man and Rama refuses to have her back as his queen, despite her protestations of innocence. After many years, Rama and Sita are reconciled. Rama is viewed as a god and his worship is universal in India. Sita is upheld as the ideal of the faithful wife.

Of all the heroes and myths of India, none are more deeply embedded in the Hindu mind than those of the Mahābhārata and the Rāmāyana. During recent broadcasts of the epics as long-running serials on Indian television, the entire country came to a standstill. Villagers even turned their television sets into shrines, performing *pūjā* (worship) before their ancient gods and heroes.

⁵ RELIGION

Central to Hindu philosophy is the concept of the soul (*ātman*). Each individual has a soul, which is a fragment of the Supreme Soul, Brahma. As such, it is the only part of human beings that is eternal and indestructible. It is, however, bound by the physical body and further surrounded by illusion (*māyā*). Furthermore, the soul is caught up in an endless cycle of rebirths (*samsāra*). The nature of each birth or incarnation is determined by actions in one's last existence (the law of *karma*). Bad deeds hinder the progress of the soul on its journey and result in rebirth as a lower form of life—perhaps as a member of an untouchable caste or as an animal. On the other hand, if one pursues righteous behavior (*dharma*), the soul returns as a higher life form, moving up the ladder of existence towards the obliteration of the physical self. Practicing noninjury to living things (*ahmsā*) is a means to this end. The ultimate aim of the Hindu is total release (*moksa*) of the soul from the physical world and its merging with the universal soul.

Such beliefs are uniquely Indian, yet other aspects of Hinduism have their origins among the Indo-European peoples who entered South Asia around 1700 BC. These invaders called themselves *Āryas* and were part of the great migrations of people that carried Indo-European culture over much of the Old World. In India, the urban civilization of the Indus Valley gave way before the simpler—though no less vigorous—Āryan culture. The Āryans were seminomadic pastoralists, depending largely on the herding of cattle. They brought with them the horse and the chariot and spoke a language that was Indo-European in origin. Their gods were male, rather than the female deities of the Harappans. But most important of all, they had a class of priests who had developed poetic techniques for composing hymns in praise of their gods. Over the centuries, these hymns were collected to form the *Veda* (literally "knowledge"), the most sacred scriptures of the Hindus.

There are four Vedas: the *Rg Veda*, the *Atharva Veda*, the *Sāma Veda*, and the *Yajur Veda*. The earliest and most important of these is the *Rg Veda*, composed between 1200 and 900 BC. Vedic religion was based on a primitive animism in which forces of nature were seen as divine and personified as gods. Thus Indra was the great war-god, riding in his chariot at the head of the Āryans against their enemies. He was a slayer of dragons, the god of thunder, and maker of rain. (Indra had replaced the original Indo-European father god Dyaus Pitr, the Zeus of the Greeks and Jupiter of the Romans.) The Vedic pantheon included Agni, god of fire; Surya, the sun god; and Soma, god of the intoxicant *soma*. Animal sacrifice was central to the Vedic religion.

Modern Hinduism, although it embraces Āryans gods and sacrifice, differs from the religion of the Vedas. The worship of mother-goddesses and tree-worship, for example, are non-Āryans and come from the Harappan cultural tradition. Some Hindu concepts appear much later than the Vedic period. But one feature of modern Hinduism can be traced directly to the Vedas, namely the division of society into distinct classes. The Sanskrit word for these categories was varna, or "color." The highest ranked class were priests (brāhmana), followed by warriors *(ksatriya)*, peasants *(vaiśya)*, and serfs *(sūdra)*. *Varna* form the basis of the caste system in India today, and many Hindus see caste as divinely ordained because of its Vedic origins.

The historical development of Hinduism is far too complex to be presented here in more than its barest outlines. By the

7th and 6th centuries BC, popular discontent with Vedic religion was widespread. This was a period of religious ferment that saw old ideas reexamined and new ones emerge. Wandering ascetics rejected the authority of the Brahmans and began reexamining the spiritual values of the Vedas. Many concepts fundamental to modern Hinduism (e.g., samsāra, karma, and ahimsā) first appear at this time in philosophical works known as the *Upanisads*.

This was also the time when Buddhism, which came to challenge Hinduism for supremacy in the Indian subcontinent, had its origins. Buddhism gained the upper hand when the Emperor Ashoka made it the state religion in the 3rd century BC, and the next millennium was one of continual struggle between Hinduism and Buddhism. It was during this period that the sanctity of the cow, a fundamental belief of modern Hinduism, came to be accepted as Hindu doctrine. There is no evidence that the cow was viewed as sacred in the Vedas. Cattle were an important economic asset in Vedic society, they were sacrificed, and their meat was eaten. Some scholars have argued that the Brahmans took the general principal of ahimsā from Buddhism and applied it specifically to the cow in their struggle to win over the mass of the population to Hinduism. By the 5th century AD, the sanctity of the cow was firmly established in Hinduism. The cow later came to be a symbol of Hindu religion and culture in the face of challenges from Islam and the Europeans.

The fortunes of Hinduism rose in the early centuries of the Christian era with what has been called the "Brahmanical revival." This was a period that saw the Brahmans assert themselves as the dominant class in Hindu society. Buddhism entered a period of decline and was to receive its death blow with the arrival of the Muslims after the 12th century AD. A reinvigorated Hinduism, however, was able to face the challenge of five and a half centuries of Muslim rule. It was also able to withstand nearly five centuries of European colonization and remain essentially unaffected by its contact with Christianity.

6 MAJOR HOLIDAYS

Holi, which is identified as the worship of Krishna, is one of the more important festivals in India. A spring celebration that falls in February–March, it clearly incorporates pre-Hindu fertility rites into its observances. The three-day festival is a time for drinking and the singing of lewd songs. Men dance in the streets, singing and carrying phallic emblems. Men and women squirt each other with colored water and red powder. The usual rules of caste behavior are relaxed, and the festival is seen by some sociologists as a "safety-valve" by which people in the rigid caste structure of Hindu society can let off steam. Bonfires are lit to celebrate the burning of the demoness Holika.

Divali, another major festival, is celebrated in the fall (October–November). The name comes from the Sanskrit *Dīpāvalī*, meaning "cluster of lights." Houses are decorated with hundreds of oil lamps (nowadays electric lights are often used). In some parts of the country, Divali marks the beginning of the New Year. It is particularly important among the mercantile castes (Jains, Vaiśyas) of western India, who worship Lakshmi, the goddess of wealth, at this time. They close their accounts for the year, begin a new set of books, redecorate their houses, and send gifts of sweets to friends and relatives. In Bengal, it is believed that the lights are intended to guide the souls of the departed ancestors. Other regions have their own legends as-

sociated with Divali. Divali is an auspicious time for gambling, and even the most respectable of women will gamble at this time.

Among other major festivals celebrated by Hindus all over India are Dasahara or Durga Pūjā (called Dasain in Nepal), Shivratri (dedicated to Shiva), and Janamashtami (Krishna's birthday). The Pongal festival of the Tamils and Kerala's Onam festival, with its snake-boat races, are important regional celebrations. In Rajasthan, the Teej festival honors the goddess Parvati.

Every Hindu temple in India has an annual festival honoring its presiding deity. Some are local events, but others are of regional, and even national, significance. One such festival is held at the Jagannath Temple at Puri in Orissa. Every year, the temple images, including that of Jagannath ("Lord of the Universe"), a form of Krishna, are taken to a "country house" some two miles away. The images are placed in cars or chariots and pulled by pilgrims. Jagannath's car is as tall as a three-storied building (roughly 14 m or 45 ft high), with wheels over 2 m (7 ft) in diameter. The English word "juggernaut" comes from Jagannath and refers to the (incorrect) belief that devotees would allow themselves to be crushed beneath the wheels of Jagannath's chariot.

Periodic fairs *(melās)* and festivals are an integral part of Hindu religious life. The most important of these is the Kumbha Mela, held every three years in turn at Nasik, Ujjain, Hardwar, and Prayag (near Allahabad). An estimated 20 million pilgrims attended the *melā* held at Prayag in 1995. Pilgrimage is one of the main religious duties of the Hindu. There are thousands of holy places in India, each sanctified by association with a deity, saint, or legend. Some may just be local shrines. Others may be sacred to specific Hindu sects (there are six major ones) such as the Vaishnavas, followers of Vishnu, or Shaivites, devotees of Shiva. Still others are of importance to all Hindus. Major sacred centers include Varanasi (Banaras), Mathura, Dwarka, and Rameshwaram. Certain rivers are considered sacred, the most important being the Ganga (River Ganges).

7 RITES OF PASSAGE

The ancient Hindu law-givers prescribed 12 important rites, from conception to marriage. Though not all of these are observed today, the name-giving ceremony is still usually performed on the tenth or twelfth day after birth. The infant's name is suggested by the family astrologer. Boys are often named after gods (e.g., Krishna, Rama, Ganesh), and girls after goddesses (Parvati, Lakshmi), flowers (Padma, meaning "lotus") or precious stones (Moti, or "pearl"). Among some groups, the ears are pierced (and, for girls, the left nostril) at this time. Other important rites at this stage of life are the first feeding of solid food and the first cutting of the hair and shaving of the head. High-caste Hindus may leave a single lock of hair uncut.

One of the most important of all Hindu rituals is the sacred-thread ceremony *(upanayana)*. Usually performed between the ages of 7 and 10, it is the initiation ceremony for males of the three higher varnas (caste-groups). The donning of the sacred thread is viewed as a symbolic rebirth, and members of the three higher caste groups are referred to as the "twice-born." The ceremony is performed by a Brahman, who consecrates the thread before placing it on the boy. The sacred thread is made of three white cotton threads, each made up of three intertwined strands of cotton (the number three is symbolic of the Hindu trinity of Brahma, Vishnu, and Shiva). It is draped over the left shoulder and tied under the right arm in a sacred knot.

Ceremonies connected with death also hold great significance for Hindus. The corpse is washed, wrapped in a shroud, garlanded with flowers, and carried in procession on a bamboo stretcher to the cremation ground. In North India, the people who accompany the body chant "Ram Nam Satya Hai," meaning "The name of [the god] Ram is truth itself." At the cremation ground, a Brahman performs certain rituals before the body is placed on the funeral pyre. The chief mourner, usually the eldest son, lights the pyre. Relatives and friends remain until the corpse is consumed. If the skull does not burst during the burning, it is broken open so that the soul can escape the body. A purificatory bath is taken by the mourners before their return home.

On the third day after the funeral, the pieces of bone are collected from the remains of the funeral pyre. Ideally, these should be taken to the sacred Ganges River, but they may be placed in any nearby stream. Sometime between the tenth and thirty-first day after the cremation, the *śrāddha* is held. This is an important (and often expensive) ceremony involving numerous rituals, a feast for relatives and friends, and the giving of gifts to Brahmans in the name of the deceased. It is believed that if the funeral rites are not performed properly, the soul of the departed will be adversely affected. As some funeral rituals have to be performed by a son, it is important for a Hindu to have male offspring.

⁸ INTERPERSONAL RELATIONS

Hindus greet each other by saying "Namaste" ("Greetings to you") while joining hands, palms together and held upright, in front of the body. In parts of India, "Namaskar" is used instead. In northern India, especially in rural areas, people commonly say, "Ram, Ram" (the name of the god Rama repeated twice), when they meet. Children may greet parents, or pupils their teachers, by bowing down and touching the feet. Hindus make the same gesture when meeting their *gurus* or important religious figures. It is usual for the person being honored in this manner to interrupt the gesture before it is complete, implying that he or she is not worthy of such homage.

⁹ LIVING CONDITIONS

Hindus mirror the living standards of Indian society at large. At one extreme, the wealthy (e.g., millionaire industrialists or some former princely ruling families) have lifestyles as luxurious as any in the world. In stark contrast is the life of the poverty-ridden rural peasant, or the destitute who live and die in the streets and slums of Calcutta or Bombay. These, of course, far outnumber the rich. An estimated 25% of India's population live below the poverty level.

¹⁰ FAMILY LIFE

A unique feature of Hindu society is the caste system, the division of the population into a hierarchy of ranked social categories. The term "caste" is a European word, derived from the Portuguese *casta,* meaning "breed" or "race." Hindus have several terms describing the same social structures. *Varna* refers to the broad division of society into four classes identified in the Vedas. *Jāti* ("birth") and the South Indian *kulam* are also

used to refer to caste. In its most restricted sense, caste refers to a kin group from which marriage partners must be selected (i.e., an endogamous kin group). There are some 3,000 castes and over 25,000 subcastes found in India.

Castes are ranked according to the number of ritually pure practices they observe. The concepts of ritual purity and pollution are important in understanding Hindu society. One is born into a caste and acquires the ritual status of that caste. This is often determined by the caste's traditional occupation. Brahmans are priests and are ritually pure, but even Brahman castes are ranked. For example, Brahmans who perform death rituals at cremations are among the lowest of the Brahman castes (but above all other castes because they still are Brahmans). Sweepers who handle human waste, or Chamars who remove animal carcasses, are ritually polluted by their occupations. They rank at the bottom of the caste hierarchy. Whether or not sweepers or Chamars follow their traditional occupation, in Hindu eyes they still partake of the pollution of their caste. If they should touch a Brahman or member of a higher caste, their touch is considered polluting. The higher-caste individual would then have to undergo a ritual purification to remove this pollution. This, of course, is the origin of the term "untouchables." Concepts of purity and pollution thus underlie many aspects of caste behavior. The higher the caste, the greater the restrictions on social activity. Among other things, caste limits the nature of social and physical contact with other peoples; it restricts the food one can eat; it limits the people one can dine with; and it defines the marriage pool from which spouses are drawn.

A Hindu marries within his or her caste or subcaste. There are, however, important differences in the selection of spouses between north and south, reflecting the Āryans-Dravidian division in India. In North India, one marries outside one's clan (*gotra),* and there is a required degree of separation in blood relations for a spouse. In South India, however, the preferred partner is one's eldest sister's daughter, or a cross-cousin (i.e., father's sister's daughter, or mother's brother's daughter). Such unions are viewed as incestuous in North India.

Hindu marriages are arranged. Though now prohibited, child marriage was common in traditional Hindu society. Once the horoscopes of the boy and girl are cast and deemed suitable, negotiations concerning details of the dowry, date of betrothal, etc., are pursued. A date and time for the marriage is determined by astrologers. There are certain "seasons" when marriages are performed, with spring being considered the most auspicious time for the ceremony. Rituals are performed at the houses of both families, followed by the *barāt,* or procession of the groom to the bride's house. Among some castes, the groom arrives on a horse (Rajputs may ride an elephant). Both bride and groom are elaborately dressed, with the bride wearing red and gold and bedecked with jewelry. The actual wedding ceremony is performed in the presence of the sacred fire by a Brahman, who recites the appropriate passages from the Vedas. In the central marriage ritual, a cloth is tied to the clothes of the bride and groom, and the groom leads the bride in the "Seven Steps" around the sacred fire. A marriage is a time of feasting and entertaining, and among the rich the ceremonies may last as long as 10 days. For the less fortunate, the marriage of a daughter may result in considerable debt (this is one reason why male children are preferred over females).

Life for the new bride may start out as anything but rosy. She moves into a new household as part of an extended joint family. She is the most junior woman in the household, which is overseen by the mother-in-law. Unless the family is wealthy enough to have servants, she is assigned household chores. The power of the mother-in-law in traditional households was such that she even determined when her married children could have sexual relations (men and women lived in different parts of the house). A woman's status in the family changes only when she gives birth to children, preferably sons. The dearest wish of a Hindu woman is to bear her husband male heirs. Divorce was rare in traditional Hindu society, though failure to bear children was one reason for returning a wife to her family, the ultimate disgrace for a woman. Modern legislation concerning Hindu marriage and divorce contains a more liberal provision for divorce.

¹¹ CLOTHING

Traditional dress for Hindus is the *dhotī* for men and the *sārī* for women. The dhotī is a single piece of cotton, wrapped around the waist for half its length and then drawn between the legs and tucked into the waist behind. In southern India, the torso is usually left bare, although in the north a shirt may be worn. Southern Indians tend to go bareheaded, while in the north turbans are common. The style of the turban often identifies the wearer as a member of a particular community (e.g., Pathan or Sikh) or from a particular region or village. The *kurtā*, a long tunic-like shirt, and the *pyjāmā*, loose baggy trousers, are common in northern India, especially in urban areas. Men in the countryside areas often wear a variety of gold or silver ornaments.

The sārī is a length of cotton or silk cloth measuring up to 10 m (approximately 30 ft) in length. It is wrapped around the waist, with one end left free and thrown over the right shoulder. This end can be drawn across the head and used to cover the face when necessary. A *cholī* a tight bodice that leaves the midriff bare, is worn under the sari. There are regional variations in the way the sārī is worn. In Maharashtra, for example, rural women draw one end of the sārī through the legs and tuck it into the waist at the small of the back. In some rural areas, women do not wear the bodice, using just the end of the sārī to cover the upper body. A married woman wears a stripe of red coloring along the parting in her hair and a *tīkā* or red dot in the center of the forehead. Nowadays, the tīkā is often worn as decoration. Women are fond of jewelry and wear a variety of earrings, bracelets, bangles, anklets, and other ornaments such as a jewel inserted in the nostril.

¹² FOOD

Hindus follow the dietary patterns of Indians as determined by broad agricultural and ecological factors. The staple in northern and western areas is cereals (wheat, millet, barley) made into flat, unleavened bread called *rotī*. This is eaten with pulses (*dāl*) and spiced dishes called "curries" (from the Tamil *karī*). In the wetter south and east, rice (*chāwal*) replaces the breads.

For Hindus, however, food is more than mere nourishment. It has ritual and symbolic meaning. The cow, for example, is considered sacred by Hindus, as are its five products (milk, curd, *ghī* or clarified butter, dung, and urine). The cow is worshipped, and its products are used in Hindu rituals. It is considered a sin to kill a cow, and the devout Hindu will avoid beef. In fact, strict adherence to ahimsā means that all animal flesh should be avoided. Yet there are Hindus such as Chamārs and other untouchable castes who eat beef, chicken, and pork. Such behavior brings ritual impurity on several counts: eating beef violates the sanctity of the cow; killing animals for food violates ahimsā; and animals such as chickens and pigs are regarded as unclean by many Hindus.

Food habits among Hindus are thus closely linked to social status and standing in the caste hierarchy. As a rule, the higher the caste, the stricter are the food taboos one must follow. Brahmans form the highest castes and are strict vegetarians, eating no animal flesh and even avoiding eggs. But they also shun foods such as onions and garlic that grow in the ground and are viewed as unclean. Some will not even eat off plates on which proscribed food has been served at some time. Alcohol is also forbidden. One outcome of this concern of the higher castes for ritual purity is strict rules of commensality (i.e., rules concerning dining with other castes).

Another dimension of food in Hindu society is the concept of "hot" and "cold" in Ayurvedic medicine, the system of medicine found in the Vedas. Foods (and diseases) are classified as possessing varying degrees of heat or cold. Hot foods (e.g., apples, radishes, or honey) are prescribed to treat diseases that are cold, and vice versa.

¹³ EDUCATION

Hindus follow the general educational and literacy patterns of India, with social and economic factors being important in determining access to modern education. In traditional Hindu society, however, formal education was limited to the Brahman male. The nature and stages of this education, which focused on the study of the Vedas, are set out in the Sanskrit texts.

¹⁴ CULTURAL HERITAGE

Sanskrit literature includes sacred texts such as the Vedas, and the various works attached to them that are called the *Brāhmanas* and *Upanisads*. Later works of importance are the epic *Mahābhārata* and Rāmāyana. The 18 *Purānas* dating from the 6th to 16th century AD are non-Vedic works that have exerted a strong influence on present-day Hinduism. *Dharma Śāstras* is the collective name of various works setting out laws governing the political, social, and religious life of the Hindus. In the tradition of secular Sanskrit literature, Kalidasa is considered to the greatest of all playwrights and poets.

Classical Hindu music and dance derive from temple performances. A 3rd century AD work called *Nātya Úāstra* is the ancient authority for these art forms. Today, the main classical dance in India is Bharata Natyam, while Kathakali is a less formal dance from southern India. Stylized hand and facial gestures are an important aspect of both dance types. Kathak and Manipuri are other dance forms. Classical Indian music attaches more importance to melody than to harmony. The "raga" is a basic melodic pattern that provides a framework within which the musician improvises. Instruments used include the *sitār* (a long-necked lute), *vīnai* (a South Indian stringed instrument), *śahnāī* (a wind instrument similar to the oboe), and *tabalā* (double hand-drums).

Architecture and sculpture in the Hindu tradition are religiously inspired art forms. The soaring towers of the North Indian temple style represent the peaks of the Himalayas, the abode of the gods. South Indian temples, with their elaborate gateways (*gopuram*), are pyramidal in shape and covered with elaborately carved figures from Hindu mythology. Famous examples of Hindu temple are the temples complex at Mahabalipuram (Tamil Nadu), the Khajuraho temples (Madhya Pradesh) with their erotic carvings, and the Sun Temple at Konarak (Orissa). The rock-cut temple at Ellora (Maharashtra) and the cave temple at Elephanta, near Bombay, are also worthy of note.

Rajput painting is the only body of Hindu painting surviving today. It covers a period from the mid-16th to the early 19th centuries and is comprised of works painted in Rajasthan and the western Himalayas under Rajput patronage. Most of the paintings are "miniatures," presenting religious and epic themes, episodes from the life of Krishna, hunting scenes, and portraits. Last, but by no means least, is an accomplishment of Hindu science. Although the matter is still debated, it is accepted by many that the concept of zero is a Hindu contribution to mathematics.

15 WORK

Hindus participate in all areas of the modern Indian economy. In traditional Hindu village society, however, castes were integrated into an economic system known as the *jajmānī* system. The focus of this system was the *jajmān* or patron, one of the landholders in the village. The patron was involved in relationships with specific families of the service castes in the village. A Brahman priest provided his services for religious ceremonies and rituals. A potter made earthenware pots and jars for the jajmān's household; a carpenter mended his carts and agricultural equipment; a Chamar removed and skinned his dead animals; and a sweeper would remove the refuse from his house. In return, they received as payment grain, food, or cash. The relationship between the patron and the service-provider (*kamīn*) was a hereditary one, passing from generation to generation. It was, moreover, more than just an economic one. The patron, for example, would be obliged to assist the kamīn at times of crisis such as sickness or death.

The jajmānī system required few cash transactions, integrated occupational castes in the village, and contributed to stability in traditional village life. The breakdown of the system and the emergence of a cash economy is one of the changes that has affected Indian village communities in modern times.

With India's economy growing at over 9% a year, many Hindus are participating in and experiencing the material benefits of this growth. While Hindus are still primarily agricultural, urban Hindus—and especially middle class urban Hindus—have access to a range of conveniences such as automobiles, refrigerators, computers and mobile telephones. This "development," however, is being achieved at a cost—air pollution is bad in Delhi and throughout northern India, while traffic congestion and environmental degradation remain major issues.

16 SPORTS

Children amuse themselves with hide-and-seek, marbles, kite-flying, and other games common among Indian children. Dice and card-playing are popular with adults, and chess is thought to have originated in India. Other pastimes include cock-fighting, camel-racing, wrestling, gambling, and hunting. Hindus, of course, participate in modern sports such as cricket, soccer, and field hockey that are popular in Indian society.

17 ENTERTAINMENT AND RECREATION

Hindus today have access to modern forms of entertainment such as radio, television, and movies.

In traditional society, entertainment was derived to a considerable degree from participation in religious fairs and festivals and in folk traditions of music and dance.

18 FOLK ART, CRAFTS, AND HOBBIES

The Hindu tradition identifies nine basic handicrafts believed to have been originated by the divine artisan Vishvakarman. These were gold working and jewelry-making; carving (of ivory, shell, and animal bones); pottery; weaving textiles; garland-making and weaving reeds and rushes; leatherworking; painting and sculpture; carpentry; and metalworking. Many of these crafts are associated with the occupational castes of India. In addition, there is a rich heritage of arts and crafts rooted in the folk traditions and regional cultures of the Hindu peoples.

19 SOCIAL PROBLEMS

Hindus, who make up the bulk of the Indian population, face the usual problems of poverty, low standards of living, and unemployment associated with developing countries. There are, however, economic and social problems that are specifically religious in origin. Hindu attitudes towards the cow and reluctance to kill cattle, even nonproductive animals, are seen by some economists as an inefficient use of resources. The fatalism associated with Hindu philosophy, it has been argued, has also been a hindrance to initiative and economic enterprise. But perhaps the most serious problems facing Hindus today are the social divisiveness of caste and the rise of Hindu fundamentalism. Caste has been made illegal in India, but it still provides the context in which Hindu society functions. With the breakdown of traditional social structures and pressure on resources as population increases, conflict (usually between higher and lower castes) has led to violent confrontation. This situation is made worse by rising Hindu fundamentalism and the increasing political strength of fundamentalist parties that would like to see India become a Hindu state. While such an achievement—though unlikely—would be a triumph for some Hindus, it goes against the longstanding tradition of Hindu tolerance for other peoples.

The rise of Hindu nationalism and Hindu nationalist political parties, such as the BJP, which specifically promote Hindu values, has introduced an element of conflict into modern India. "Hindutva" has raised tensions between Hindus and Muslims, as evidenced by the Godhra killings in 2002. The issue of fundamental Islamic terrorism remains, with Muslim groups apparently claiming responsibility for the 13 May 2008 bombings in Jaipur, the capital of Rajasthan state, which killed 63 people and injured several hundred more. Two days after the blasts, a previously unknown Islamic militant group known as the Indian Mujahideen sent an e-mail to the Indian media in which they claimed responsibility for the attacks and said they would "demolish the faith (Hinduism)" of the "infidels of India." However, Indian Home Ministry sources said that a Bangladesh-based organization, *Harkat-ul-Jihad-al-Islami* (HuJI) or "Islamic Holy War Movement," was suspected of being behind the attack. The bombings were only the latest in a series of periodic acts of violence apparently committed by Muslims against Hindus (though the indiscriminate nature of the blasts have killed Muslims as well as Hindus), *viz.* the Bombay Stock Exchange bombings (1993), the Delhi market bombings in 2005, the Bombay train bombings (2006) and the 2007 blast at the dargah of Khwaja Moinuddin Chishti in Ajmer in Rajasthan. In Kashmir, of course, where India is basically fighting a Muslim insurgency, conflict between Muslims and Hindus is commonplace.

Concerns also exist regarding the intentions of a nuclear-armed Pakistan. Muslim Pakistan, after losing the 1971 war with India, embarked on a program of developing nuclear weapons. Under the direction of Dr. Abdul Qadeer Khan, it acquired the ability to carry out a nuclear explosion in 1987. India had already tested a nuclear "device" in 1974. Of major concern is the relatively short distance between the two capitals, Islamabad and New Delhi, which are about 450 miles from each other, a distance that could easily lead to a nuclear mistake. Unlike the United States and the Soviet Union during the Cold War who had enough weapons to destroy the opposing nation several times over after surviving a nuclear strike, India and Pakistan have relatively few nuclear weapons. Pakistan is generally estimated to have between 25 and 50 nuclear weapons, with some designated for delivery by its F-16s and some outfitted for its missiles. India likely has between 30 and 60 nuclear weapons, also available for planes and missiles. The leaders of each country, despite public assurances to the contrary, may worry that the other nation could destroy its nuclear arsenal with a surprise first strike, necessitating quick trigger fingers. This problem is of greater concern for Pakistan, because without its nuclear weapons, the weaker Pakistani army might be at India's mercy. In 1999, when Pakistani freedom fighters crossed the Line of Control into Indian-held Kargil, in Kashmir and were repulsed by the Indian Army, Pakistan is thought to have prepared its intermediate-range missiles for nuclear strikes, perhaps to deter India from attacking Pakistani territory. U.S. diplomacy helped persuade then-Pakistani Prime Minister Nawaz Sharif to pull his troops out of India and temporarily head off full-scale war. Experts estimate at least 12 million dead in a nuclear exchange between the two countries and that this would result in a humanitarian crisis so great that every medical facility in the Middle East and Southwest Asia would be quickly overwhelmed.

20 GENDER ISSUES

It is difficult to generalize about the status of Hindu women, because they belong to a variety of groups, in different levels of society and each having their own customs and practices. Thus, the life of the high-caste urban Brahman woman is likely to be quite different to that of the rural untouchable. Nonetheless, Hinduism traditionally tends to treat women as second-class citizens, whose main purpose in life is to marry and have male children.

In the past, Hindu women were subject to child marriage, arranged marriages, which were often arranged by families with brides never meeting their husbands before the nuptials, the payment of dowries, the custom of *sati*, and bans on widow remarriage. Except in matriarchies, Hindu women do not inherit property, which remains in the name of male relatives.

Many traditional practices have been made illegal by state and national governments. Child marriage has, for instance, been illegal in India since the passing of the Child Marriage Restraint Act of 1929 and, in an effort to curb the practice of child marriages, the states of Rajasthan, Gujarat, Maharashtra, Karnataka, and Himachal Pradesh have passed laws that mandate the registration of all marriages in order to make them valid. But child marriage still occurs in India, mainly in rural villages and areas that usually have little legal supervision. According to the "National Plan of Action for Children 2005," published by the Department of Women and Child Development of India, a goal has been set to eliminate child marriage completely by 2010, but it is very difficult to monitor all children due to the sheer size of the Indian subcontinent and one only has to read the press on Akha Teej, a time that is favored for child marriages—some brides are as young as one year old—to see that it still goes on. A recent report by UNICEF revealed that 82% of girls in Rajasthan are married before they are 18, 15% of girls in rural areas across the country are married before 13 and a majority 52% of girls have their first pregnancy between 15 and 19. (According to the Prohibition of Child Marriage Act of 2006, it is illegal to allow or facilitate marriage of a boy under 21 and a girl under 18.) Consequences of child marriage include anemia, sacrifice of education, domestic violence, and early pregnancies, which weaken the mother and lead to higher mortality in children during their first year of life. Even though the Supreme Court of India has upheld the government's 1994 Prenatal Determination Act, which bans the use of technology, such as ultrasounds and sonograms, for the purpose of sex-selective abortion, females fetuses are still aborted, resulting in male-dominated sex ratios among Hindus in India.

Though "love" marriages do occur, marriages in India are still generally arranged by the families involved, such marriages often being as much business alliances between families as marriages between a boy and a girl. One only has to read the marriage ads in the Indian Sunday papers to see the extent to which this practice continues. It is customary for the bride's family to provide a dowry, even though this is banned by law (The 1961 Dowry Prohibition Act). It is not uncommon for the husband or husband's family to be unhappy with the amount of the dowry (demands often include items such as automobiles, scooters, and refrigerators) resulting in "dowry deaths," whereby a women's clothing "accidentally" catches fire in the kitchen. Some estimates place the number of "dowry deaths" in the country as high as 25,000 women with numerous more maimed or scarred for life as a result of attempts to kill them.

The custom of sati, when a widow burns herself on her dead husband's funeral pyre, is a thing of the past, although a sati in Rajasthan in 1987 resulted in the state government passing the Rajasthan Sati Prevention Ordinance of 1987, which makes the glorification of sati a crime.

Many groups now permit widows to remarry, but the general treatment of women in Hindu society and laws of inheritance make the lot of women in Hindu society unenviable.

Attempts to improve the lot of women have made an impact on the place of women in Hindu society. Many of the ancient customs affecting them are now illegal, women have been making strides in accessing education (studies have shown that, because more women are remaining longer in the educational system, they are delaying the age at which they marry), and among the more educated, Western concepts such as feminism and women's rights are taking root. More and more Hindu women are out in the workplace and are becoming financially more independent. But rural Hindu women still have to face problems of poverty, illiteracy, and casteism, while even in the cities women exist in a male dominated society, have to face "Eve teasers" (Eve teasing is a euphemism used for sexual harassment or molestation of women by men) and still have to prove themselves by bearing sons when they marry.

21 BIBLIOGRAPHY

Basham, A. L. *The Wonder That Was India: A Survey of the Culture of the Indian Subcontinent Before the Coming of the Muslims.* London: Sidgewick & Jackson, 1963.

Hansen, Thomas Blom and Christophe Jaffrelot, ed. *The BJP and the Compulsions of Politics in India.* New Delhi: Oxford University Press, 2001.

Harper, Edward B., ed. *Religion in South Asia.* Seattle: University of Washington Press, 1964.

Lewis, Oscar. *Village Life in Northern India.* Urbana, IL: University of Illinois Press, 1958.

Noorani, A. G., ed. *The Babri Masjid Question, 1528-2003: A Matter of National Honour.* New Delhi: Tulika Books, 2003.

Rukmani, T. S., ed. *Hindu Diaspora: Global Perspective.* New Delhi: Munshiram Manoharlal, 2001.

Sen, K. M. *Hinduism.* Harmondsworth, England.: Penguin Books, 1961.

Thomas, P. *Hindu Religion, Customs, and Manners.* Bombay: D. B. Taraporevala, 1960.

Walker, Benjamin. *Hindu World: An Encyclopedic Survey of Hindūism.* 2 vols. London: George Allen & Unwin, 1968.

—by D. O. Lodrick

HMONG

PRONUNCIATION: (H)MAWNG
ALTERNATE NAMES: Meo, Miao
LOCATION: Southern China; Viet Nam; Laos; Thailand
POPULATION: About 4 to 6 million worldwide
LANGUAGE: Hmong
RELIGION: Animism; some fundamentalist Protestant Christianity
RELATED ARTICLES: Vol. 2: Hmong Americans

1 INTRODUCTION

The Hmong (sometimes called Meo or Miao, terms the Hmong consider pejorative) are an aboriginal people of southern China. They are mentioned in Chinese records as early as 2500 BC. Traditionally they were paddy (wet rice) farmers in China. In the past two centuries, groups of Hmong have begun to filter into the mountainous north of Vietnam, Laos, and Thailand to escape the persecution and pacification campaigns of the Chinese. In Southeast Asia they settled in higher elevations, usually above 1000 m (3,280 ft), often on mountain tops where they practiced shifting slash-and-burn (swidden) agriculture—clearcutting and burning off an area of the forest, planting crops until the soil was depleted, and then shifting to a new area after a few years. The Hmong usually grow dry rice, corn, vegetables, and opium poppies. Although they traditionally grew opium poppies for their own ritual and medicinal use, they were encouraged by French colonial authorities in Vietnam and Laos to increase production for sale to the colonial opium monopoly and as payment for head taxes. Thus, opium became an important cash crop for the Hmong.

The Hmong are often at odds with the governments of the states in which they reside because of their independence, opium growing, and shifting slash-and-burn agriculture that is destructive to the environment. They are being encouraged to settle in lowland areas where they can be more easily controlled and can practice more productive wet rice agriculture. Mutual suspicion exists, however, between the Hmong and the majority populations, who tend to consider them ignorant and uncivilized.

The Hmong face a special burden in Laos, for they were divided during the Lao civil war, which was in many ways an extension of the Vietnam War. Some joined the Communist Pathet Lao while others served in the CIA-sponsored mercenary army under General Vang Pao, supporting the Royal Lao Government. The Hmong were considered fierce fighters, skillful in guerrilla warfare in mountainous terrain. Thousands of Hmong fled Laos when the Communists came to power in Laos in 1975, seeking refuge in Thailand and China. A small Hmong insurgency continued, and when Lao and Vietnamese forces were unable to secure Hmong villages with regular forces, they turned to chemical and biological warfare. New waves of Hmong refugees fled the country. Perhaps as many as 200,000 Hmong left Laos. Most were resettled in other countries, but the thousands remaining in Thai refugee camps are being unwillingly repatriated to Laos. The Thai government's hard line toward remaining Hmong is based in part on the perception that the remaining refugees are "economic migrants" rather than people fleeing in fear of their lives.

Performers of the Hmung ethnic origin dressed in traditional costume attend the opening ceremony of the 18th annual Shanghai Tourism Festival in Shanghai, China. (China Photos/Getty Images)

² LOCATION AND HOMELAND

Estimates of the Hmong population vary, but there are probably 4–6 million worldwide. An estimated 3–5 million continue to live in southern China, mostly in Yunnan. There are about 350,000 in north Vietnam, 230,000 in north and central Laos, and around 100,000 in northern Thailand, plus a few Hmong settlements in Burma (Myanmar).

The Hmong tend to live in mountainous border regions of southern China and northern Southeast Asia. They resist government controls and have paid little attention to borders, often trekking from one country to another. This makes the Hmong population a sensitive issue for governments that seek to control their peoples and their borders.

In Laos, the Hmong and others living in the higher elevations like the Akha, Phu Noi, and Mien (Yao), are called Lao Sung, or upland Lao. The Hmong make up two-thirds of the upland Lao population and about 5% of the total population of Laos, the only country where they are a significant minority. The government of the Lao People's Democratic Republic (LPDR) has tried to include the upland peoples and extend services like health and education to them. By using terms like lowland Lao (basically ethnic Lao), midland Lao (Kammu and others), and upland Lao, the LPDR has tried to de-emphasize ethnicity.

There are about 150,000 Hmong in the United States. There are 30,000 Hmong living in Fresno, California, and significant Hmong communities in other parts of California and in Minnesota, Wisconsin, and Rhode Island. The change from an illiterate agricultural life in remote mountain villages to an urban setting in the U.S. has been immense. Clan organizations have remained fairly strong and mutual help has eased the transition for many. However, the Hmong-American community is also highly factionalized, and there is a widening gap between the older generation, which tends to cling to Cold War values, and the younger generation, which is more inclined toward reconciliation with the Lao People's Democratic Republic. Some Hmong have also settled in Canada, Australia, France, and even in Argentina and mountainous areas of Surinam.

In keeping with its policy to promote stronger relations with Southeast Asia, China is reaching out to the Hmong diaspora with international conferences and other activities. This has had the effect of strengthening the Hmong sense of identity, but it has also alarmed some countries with Hmong populations, particularly in Southeast Asia.

³ LANGUAGE

The Hmong language belongs to the Sino-Tibetan group of languages. There are two major dialect and cultural groups — the Green Hmong (sometimes called the Blue Hmong) and the

White Hmong. The colors refer to women's traditional dress. The two dialects are mutually intelligible. In the past there was little intermarriage between the two dialect groups, but it has become common. One's last name is a clan name. About 18 clans have been identified in Thailand and Laos. In Laos, the government supports a Hmong radio news broadcast, the only broadcast in a minority language.

The Hmong did not have an alphabet or writing. Missionary groups have developed a romanized script for the language, but relatively few Hmong are literate in it. However, the first Hmong studies program was established in the United States in 2006 and seeks to promote literature and other works in the Hmong language. The script looks somewhat peculiar: The word "Hmong," for example, is written "Hmoob." The double letter signals a nasalized vowel, and the last consonant is an unpronounced tone marker. There are eight tones in Hmong. Here is a Hmong proverb in romanized script:

Niam-txiv piv tam lub ntuj   Parents are like the sky,
Tub-ki piv lub tem.   Children are like the earth.

The Hmong language contains many words borrowed from Chinese, Thai, Lao, French, and English. The Hmong are being educated and becoming literate in the languages of the countries where they reside.

⁴ FOLKLORE

Lacking a writing system, the Hmong have passed down their legends and ritual ceremonies orally and in crafts (especially textiles) from one generation to another.

They have many short rhyming expressions with messages of wisdom and show their outlook on the world. Here are a few examples:

You don't have to sharpen a thorn;
You don't have to explain to a smart person.

See a tiger, you will die;
See an official, you will be poor.

Tangled hair, use a comb to unsnarl it;
Complicated dispute, use an elder to solve it.

Able to weave, don't waste thread;
Able to speak, don't waste words.

The mouth tastes food;
The heart tastes words.

If the crops aren't good, you lose only one year;
If your wife isn't good, you lose a whole lifetime.

⁵ RELIGION

Most Hmong are animists and believe in a variety of spirits. The spirit of the house provides protection for the family and helps bring prosperity. An altar to this spirit is placed on the wall opposite the front door, and on the first day of the new year, a pig is sacrificed to it. The eldest male in the family conducts the ritual.

Special spirit practitioners deal with the spirits of medicine and conduct magic rituals to exorcise the spirits that cause ill-

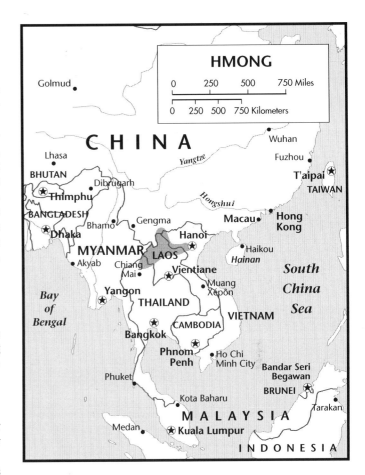

ness. Herbal specialists may also treat the patient with herbs and massage.

The spirits of nature are always on the lookout for lost or straying souls. Like the Lao, the Hmong believe that the body has many souls that sometimes stray. The *hu plig* ritual, similar to the Lao *baci,* calls the souls back to the body. The ritual is performed for someone who is sick, for a newborn on its third day of life (when body and soul are believed to come together), and for a new bride three days after marriage (to tie her soul to her husband's clan).

A shaman might be called in cases of illness that don't respond to other curing rituals. The shaman is one who can fall into trance and communicate with spirits in the sky and bargain with them for the soul of the sick person. One or more pigs are sacrificed so the shaman can trade with the spirits for the soul of the person.

At funerals, cattle are sacrificed so the deceased will have wealth in the spirit world. The Hmong believe that the well-being of the living depends on the well-being of the ancestors in the spirit world.

In Thailand and Laos, 10–20% of the Hmong have responded to missionaries and adopted fundamentalist Protestant Christianity. This is seen by other Hmong as a threat to clan solidarity, since Christians destroy their spirit altars, refuse to sacrifice at funerals, and feel less bound by clan ties.

⁶ MAJOR HOLIDAYS

The Hmong New Year is the biggest Hmong holiday, a celebration for 7–10 days in December after the harvest. It is a time for new clothes, sacrificing a pig to the ancestors, calling on the elders for blessings, eating good food, relaxing, and playing games. The household altar has been cleaned and redecorated. On the eve of the new year, the eldest male in the household calls the spirits home—the father's spirit, the mother's spirit, the children's spirits, the animals' spirits, and the spirits of the crops. The elder throws away the evil and bad words of the old year. The new year is welcomed and named after the first animal they hear cry out. The young men visit the elders, taking whiskey and food; they kneel and wish good fortune to the elders, who bless them in return.

On New Year's Day the young unmarried men and women line up opposite each other and toss a cloth ball back and forth while singing. Each person tries to throw the ball to the person who interests him or her, so it is a kind of flirting. Marriages often take place soon after the New Year.

7 RITES OF PASSAGE

The main rite of passage is marriage. Hmong marry young, usually in their teens. The girl is usually 15–17, the boy 17–20. Traditionally marriage, often between cousins, was arranged by the fathers of the couple. In more recent generations, young people generally choose for themselves. The boy sends a go-between to the girl's parents with a silver coin to ask for her hand and negotiate a bride-price. Should the girl's parents object, the traditional alternative was a mock abduction to the boy's parents' house, which is in effect an elopement. Marriage negotiations would then begin after three days. In the past, it was common for the bride-price to be 3–10 silver bars, each worth about $100. Communist governments have opposed spending much money on ceremonial and ritual expenses and the Lao government limits the payment to two silver bars. The bride-price recompenses the bride's family for the loss of her productive and reproductive capacity.

8 INTERPERSONAL RELATIONS

The household and the clan are the key units of Hmong life. Primary loyalty is to them, not to a village or region. Hmong like to live near their clan relatives, whom they can call on for social, economic, and emotional support.

Young men and women mix freely, and premarital sex is accepted as the norm, much to the horror of the dominant populations where they reside; women are expected to be chaste even if the men are promiscuous. Pregnancy usually leads to marriage. Men must marry out of their clan. Marriage outside the Hmong community is extremely rare.

Ethnic prejudice against the Hmong complicates their relations with lowland people.

9 LIVING CONDITIONS

In Laos, living conditions for Hmong are rather poor. Village houses cluster together on barren mountain tops. The house is set directly on the ground with a beaten earth floor. The walls are usually made of split bamboo and the roof of thatch. Usually 6–8 people live in a house measuring 6 x 8 m. Furnishings are minimal—a couple of stools and a table. A sleeping alcove is set a foot or two above the floor. There may be a walled-off bedroom for a couple. Much of the house may be used for storage, with a granary, tools, etc. An open hearth is used for cooking. The pigs and chickens may be brought into the house at night but wander freely in the daytime. There is usually no electricity, no running water, and no sanitary facilities. The

pigs keep the village clear of edible refuse and human waste. Access to health care is limited. Travel is usually by foot, although wealthier families may have pack horses. There are few roads. Each family tries to be as self-sufficient as possible. Despite these conditions, Hmong villages are often more prosperous than those of surrounding minorities. This is due in part to remittances from overseas Hmong. In some cases, the income discrepancies between Hmong and their poorer ethnic neighbors creates tension, particularly when Hmong are able to buy the ancestral lands of other groups.

10 FAMILY LIFE

The Hmong have large extended patrilineal families. The household can include parents, children, wives and children of married sons, and other relatives. As married sons establish their own households, the youngest son is left to care for parents and inherit their property. Polygyny, the practice of having more than one wife, is allowed by the Hmong, though governments discourage the practice. In principle, the first wife must consent and, traditionally, an additional wife is taken only if the first wife is barren or produces only female children. The daughter-in-law rises early and works hard, and new brides sometimes register their unhappiness by returning to their parents temporarily. Divorce is possible but discouraged.

The family works together to provide food. Gender roles tend to be fairly strongly differentiated. Women care for the home, cooking, water and firewood, husking rice, grinding corn, care of pigs and poultry, and weeding the fields. Men cut trees, burn the fields, hunt, care for buffalo and cows, and plow. Men punch holes for seed, which the woman puts in and covers over. Both sexes harvest and thresh and carry the crop from fields to village. Children help from an early age, netting small fish, catching edible insects, helping with the animals and gardens, and caring for younger siblings.

Men are accorded greater respect than women. The husband typically walks ahead of the wife, and if there is only one burden to carry, it is hers. But relations between spouses are generally amiable and husbands are advised to consult with their wives.

11 CLOTHING

Hmong are identified by their clothing, which indicates dialect and regional group. The Green Hmong, the White Hmong, and the smaller group of Striped Hmong are known by the traditional dress of their women. Women of the Green Hmong, sometimes called Blue Hmong, wear short, blue, indigo-dyed skirts, each done in intricate batik patterns and containing hundreds of tiny pleats. The skirts usually have cross-stitch embroidery and appliqué as well. The skirt is worn with a black long-sleeved blouse, leggings, and a black apron. An outfit takes about one year to make in one's spare time. Women also wear large silver neck rings. The men wear short, baggy black pants and black shirts, sometimes with embroidery, a long sash around the waist, and a Chinese-style black cap decorated with embroidery.

The White Hmong women wear black pants or white pleated skirts and a black blouse with an elaborately decorated collar piece at the back of the neck. Accessories include embroidered sashes, coin belts, and aprons. The men's pants are not as short and baggy as the Green Hmong outfit. The Striped Hmong women wear blouses with striped sleeves. Women's headdresses may be very elaborate and indicate regional differences. Younger people are more likely to dress like the majority population, in T-shirts and sarongs or pants.

12 FOOD

The Hmong prefer white rice to sticky rice, but grow both kinds. Sometimes they have to buy additional rice. Other food comes from their fields and gardens, supplemented by hunting, fishing, and gathering. Corn is always grown along with squash, melons, and greens of various kinds. Tubers, shoots, mushrooms, and other wild plants are found in the forest. Various rodents and insects are also eaten. Most foods are boiled and seasoned with salt and chilies. Meat is rarely part of the diet, although occasionally a hunter gets lucky. The pigs and cattle they raise are largely for sacrifices to the spirits, but they are eaten on ceremonial occasions once the offering has been made. There are usually bananas and other fruit trees and often some sugar cane. Wild foods and fish are abundant during the rainy season, but little grows in the hot dry season.

13 EDUCATION

Schools have been extended to Hmong areas only in recent years in Thailand and Laos. Many Hmong settlements are still remote from schools. Most Hmong in Laos attend school only for a year or two. Males are more likely to attend school and study longer than females. Most Hmong men can speak the national language to some extent and may have gained some literacy in it. Females are more likely to be illiterate. Education occasionally is an issue in Hmong families in the United States. Sometimes traditional parents want their teenage daughters to leave school and enter an arranged marriage, while their more Americanized daughters rebel.

14 CULTURAL HERITAGE

Because the Hmong were not a literate people, their cultural heritage had to be handed down in other ways. They are noted for their sung poetry and their story cloths. Hmong songs are poems that the singer makes up as the song is sung using rhyme and clever wordplay. Older songs may be memorized, but the singer adds his own lines to them. There are ritual songs, courting songs, and teaching songs. Songs are passed from one generation to another. Many still contain references to life in China, although the Hmong may have left there generations ago. A skilled singer gains great renown among the Hmong.

The Hmong are known in the West for the exquisite appliqué and embroidery of their story cloths, cloth panels with detailed scenes of daily village life for the Hmong: growing corn, caring for pigs and chickens, hauling rice from the fields, etc. Some have a story line that meanders across the cloth. More recent story cloths tell of war, exile, and going to America.

15 WORK

Work revolves around the agricultural calendar of planting rice, corn, vegetables, and opium poppies. Opium was once the biggest cash crop for many Hmong. It is small in volume, high in price, readily portable, and grows well at high altitudes in monsoon climates. However, opium eradication efforts in both Thailand and Laos have unsettled many Hmong communities, despite crop substitution projects. Poverty has forced some Hmong into wage labor, which is generally frowned upon since the Hmong are used to being self-sufficient. Hmong women have been selling their needlework, and their small embroidered squares are sometimes incorporated by Western fashion designers into stylish modern clothes.

16 SPORTS

The Hmong have no time for organized sports. Even young children may work long hours and have little time for recreation. Hmong boys like to play at spinning tops. Fishing is largely a task left to children and can combine elements of work and play.

17 ENTERTAINMENT AND RECREATION

Hmong sung poetry is a favorite form of entertainment. Often the songs deal with loss—of one's family, one's love, or one's homeland.

18 FOLK ART, CRAFTS, AND HOBBIES

Besides the story cloths mentioned above, the Hmong are famous for their traditional needlework squares with intricate appliquéd designs. Traditionally these were presented by a young couple to their parents and parents-in-law with a blessing. These pieces are placed in the coffin with a person after death. This type of needlework has been incorporated into modern handicraft items made for sale.

19 SOCIAL PROBLEMS

As governments have extended their control of border regions, the Hmong are under great pressure to give up their traditional way of life and settle down. Settled agriculture, wage labor, and the cash economy are replacing traditional self-sufficiency and have led to more emphasis on the individual and less on clan ties. Children exposed to lowland life are assimilating the dominant culture. Generational contrast and conflict is particularly acute for refugee families living in modern cities in the United States. It is a challenge to maintain Hmong culture and language while adapting to modern life.

20 GENDER ISSUES

Although societal discrimination against women exists in Hmong culture, several Hmong women have achieved positions of high rank in the Lao government and the Communist Party. The economic dislocation caused by opium eradication in Laos has pushed some Hmong women into prostitution, but the majority of Laotian women that are trafficked are actually lowland Lao. Nevertheless, the Hmong are suspicious of the intentions of overseas Hmong in this regard and popular folklore tends to view "rich" Hmong in the West as potential traffickers.

21 BIBLIOGRAPHY

Hein, Jeremy. *Ethnic Origins: The Adaptation of Cambodian and Hmong Refugees in Four American Cities.* New York: Russell Sage Foundation, 2006.

Ovesen, Jan. *A Minority Enters the Nation State: A Case Study of a Hmong Community in Vientiane Province, Laos.* Uppsala, Sweden: Uppsala University, 1995.

Savada, Andrea Matles, ed. *Laos: A Country Study.* Washington, D.C.: Library of Congress, 1995.

Tapp, Nicholas. *The Hmong of China: Context, Agency, and the Imaginary.* Boston: Brill, 2001.

Tapp, Nicholas, ed., et al. *Hmong-Miao in Asia.* Chiang Mai, Thailand: Silkworm Books, 2004.

Vang, Lue, and Judy Lewis. *Grandmother's Path, Grandfather's Way.* San Francisco: Zellerbach Family Fund, 1984.

—revised by C. Dalpino

HUI

PRONUNCIATION: HOO-ee
ALTERNATE NAMES: Huihui
LOCATION: China
POPULATION: 9.8 million
LANGUAGE: Chinese dialect of the area in which they live
RELIGION: Islam
RELATED ARTICLES: Vol. 3: China and Her National Minorities

[1] INTRODUCTION

The Hui are the most widely distributed of all the national minorities of China. Early in the 7th century, a great number of Arabic and Persian merchants came to China through the sea route. Setting down in Guangzhou, Quanzhou, Hangzhou, Yangzhou, and Xi'an (formerly Chang'an), quite a number of them married and multiplied in this land. They built up the first mosques and established the Muslims' graveyard.

In the 13th century, a great number of Muslims from Persia, Arabia, and Central Asia immigrated through the land route and established themselves in various parts of China, in the northwest, the Central Plains, Yunnan and the lower reaches of the Yangzi River. It was at this time that they received the name Huihui.

From the Yuan Dynasty (1271—1368) to the Ming Dynasty (1368—1644), many people of Uighur, Mongolian, and Chinese origin were assimilated to the Huihui due to intermarriage and religious affiliation. In the meantime, there were also many Huihui assimilated to the Chinese for the same reasons. A new Hui nationality gradually came into being from the reunion of Huihui of different origins. The Hui, therefore, are a nationality that took shape in China, but whose history is very different from the aboriginal nationalities living in China from time immemorial.

[2] LOCATION AND HOMELAND

The Hui are widely distributed throughout the country but are mainly concentrated in Ningxia Hui Autonomous Region; one also finds Hui in Gansu, Qinghai, Henan, Hebei, Shandong, and Yunnan provinces. Hui population was estimated at 9.8 million in 2000, representing the third-largest national minority of China after the Zhuang and the Manchus.

[3] LANGUAGE

The Hui spoke Arabic, Persian, and/or Chinese in the past. They have no specific language of their own. Today, they use the Chinese language and writing. Retaining some words of Arabic and Persian origin, they speak exactly the same Chinese dialects as the peoples among whom they live.

[4] FOLKLORE

Most of the Hui myths are related to Allah. The story of "Human Ancestor Adang" described how Hanwu married Haowa, who had 72 successive childbirths. Each time she gave birth to a boy and a girl. At the seventy-third childbearing, however, only a boy was born. Since he had no woman, he went to heaven and asked for the decree of Allah. He was kept in heaven, while 144 brothers and sisters were carried by a strong wind to all parts of the world. Human beings thus multiplied.

Another myth narrates how the goddess Duor Tea in remote antiquity was banished from Heaven by Allah because she did not fulfill her duty. She was ordered to do philanthropic works to atone for her crime. So she transformed herself into a tea tree, gave a gold axe to a poor man, and ordered him to cut the tea leaves with the axe and use them to treat various illnesses of the villagers. Finally, she returned to Heaven with her axe but not before the Hui had developed the good habit of drinking tea.

The myth of "Adang and Haowa" relates a story similar to that of "Adam and Eve." There are many other myths dealing with the origin of social and religious customs (for instance, "Adang in search of kindling material," "The Dragon Plate," and "Mohammed," are all connected with Hui belief).

⁵RELIGION

The Hui believe in Islam (also called Hui religion). The word "Islam" means obedience—to be obedient to the orders of Allah and to be the messenger of Allah. The believers are called Muslims. Islam was created by Mohammed, the messenger of Allah in Arabia in the 7th century. The Koran is the scripture of Islam. It stipulates that Muslims should recite the scripture frequently, hold the Corban Festival, fast in the daytime during September (Islamic calendar), hand in dues and go once to the Holy City Mecca to pay respects. In China, the man who takes charge of religious matters and teaches the Islamic scriptures is called *Ahung* (teacher). He is invited to preside over the ceremonies connected with birth, marriage, and death. The mosque is the place where Muslims recite the scriptures. Because of the shortage of qualified personnel of Hui religion, students have been enrolled in Shanxi and in Shandong provinces to learn the scriptures. Now, there are special universities for students learning Islamic scriptures and doing research in Islamic theology.

⁶MAJOR HOLIDAYS

In addition to the Spring Festival and the Mid-Autumn Festival of China, the Hui have three important holidays: the Fast-Breaking Festival (Lesser Bairam), the Corban Festival, and the Shengji Festival. All adult Muslims should fast during September, abstaining from food and drink from daybreak to sunset. During this period, smoking is also prohibited. Everybody restrains one's selfish desires and sincerely believes in Allah. The beginning and the end of the month of fast (Ramadan) depend on the visibility of the new moon. If the moon is not visible, the Fast-Breaking Festival should be postponed until the next day. At the end of the one-month fast, the celebration among the Hui is at its peak.

December 10 (Islamic calendar) is the Corban (sacrifice offering) Festival. Every family must clean the house, kill oxen and/or sheep, pay visits to relatives and friends, and entertain guests for dinner. The Shenji Festival is on March 12 (Islamic calendar), a memorial to Mohammed. The Hui will go to the mosque to greet each other and to participate in religious activities. There will be food and drink in the mosque for the Muslims.

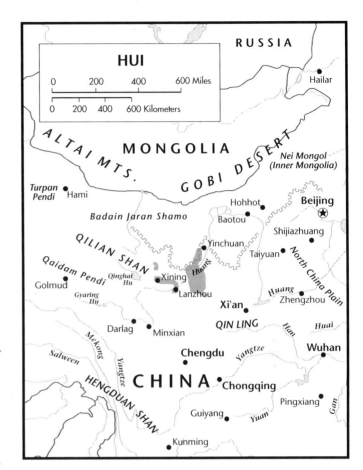

⁷RITES OF PASSAGE

At birth, the infant receives from the *Ahung* an Arabic name usually corresponding to the name of a sage or saint of the Koran. This name is called the "scripture name." To conform to the brevity of Chinese names (one or two syllables), the polysyllabic Arabic name is usually simplified, adding the Chinese suffix *zi* to the name. This custom is most prevalent in northwest China. Again following the Chinese naming system, the given Arabic name is preceded by the Chinese surname. When the child has gone through the name-giving ritual, he becomes a Muslim. The Ahung also presides at the wedding ceremony and at the funeral rites of the Hui.

Funeral rites last no more than three days. The body should be washed and wrapped with white cloth (five layers for the woman and three for the man). The Hui practice burial in the ground without a coffin. They dig a perpendicular hollow, more than 12 ft in depth, then make a pit for the body on the west wall of the hollow. The head of the body points toward the north. The body lies on its side, facing west, the direction of Mecca. The Ahung will be invited to recite scriptures during the burying and on the seventh and fortieth day after the death.

The Hui are fond of cleanliness. They take a bath or at least wash their face, mouth, nose, hands, and feet before each religious service.

Hui Muslim men rest on a roadside in Gongmachuang village, Zhengzhou, China. (AP Images/Greg Baker)

⁸INTERPERSONAL RELATIONS

When a Hui family entertains guests for dinner, the host will continue pressing more rice into the guests' bowls, even after they have eaten to satiety. The guest should receive the dish or bowl with both hands.

The Hui avoid pork; they also refrain from ox or sheep meat that has not been butchered by the Ahung. Their customs and religious beliefs discourage their young ones from dating and marrying non-Hui people. However, a growing number of young people are becoming indifferent to religious beliefs and customs and tend to adopt the way of life of the Chinese majority. Dating and intermarriage between them are on the increase.

⁹LIVING CONDITIONS

Because of their wide and scattered distribution, the living conditions of the Hui vary a great deal. They are engaged in farming in the rural areas, while in the urban areas, they engage in various trades and professions. Their living standards are similar to those of the majority Chinese. Their housing varies in the different districts.

The Hui have their own traditional prescriptions for illness. They resort both to Chinese traditional medicine and to modern medicine. There are Hui hospitals established in Hui districts and in large cities (modern facilities); these usually take the Hui religious life and customs into consideration.

¹⁰FAMILY LIFE

The Hui family is patrilineal and monogamous. The position of women in the family is usually lower than that of men. In families where both spouses work, the position of the man and the woman is the same. The aged are esteemed. There are many large families in which the parents live with their sons and daughters-in-law.

Women who work as professionals in urban areas have full freedom to choose their mate. Arranged marriage, however, is still prevalent in rural areas. Chinese law stipulates that to be legal, a marriage must be registered with the proper state authorities; however, according to Islamic customary law, a man can take a wife only if the ceremony is witnessed by the Ahung. The Hui must therefore perform a double (civil and religious) marriage ceremony.

¹¹CLOTHING

The Hui scattered in various parts of China usually wear the same clothes as those of the Chinese. Most of the men wear a white or black hat (or turban) in religious services. Some of them, such as those living in Gansu and Qinghai provinces, wear the hat every day. Hui women wear a special *gaitou* (head cover), a folded cloth (only partly sewn) covering her hair, neck, and back, leaving only her face uncovered. These kerchiefs are mainly black. Girls prefer them in green and aged women, white. Hui clothes tend to be fashionable.

[12] FOOD

The Hui take three meals a day. Their staple foods include rice, flour, corn, millet, and yams. Quite a variety of foods are taboo, mainly the flesh of animals, such as pigs, donkeys, and mules. Furthermore, the Hui do not eat the flesh of ox, sheep, or poultry that died of illness, nor flesh of ox and sheep that were not butchered by the Ahung or other Muslims. They are not allowed to eat in ordinary canteens or restaurants. Therefore, almost all schools, factories, and organizations have established particular canteens for the Hui. Also, cities have a number of Muslim restaurants. The cooks, waitresses, and ordinary workers of the Hui canteens or restaurants are exclusively Muslims.

The Hui like salted beef. They add salt and spice to fresh beef, massage it vigorously, put it in a large earthen container, cover it with a lid, and seal it. Two weeks later, they take it out and let it sit in the open air. The meat may then be fried, stewed, or cooked with rice. This is considered a high-grade dish with which to entertain guests.

The Hui like tea and usually do not indulge themselves in smoking and drinking. They also like a gruel of sweetened, fried flour. They mix flour of wheat, buckwheat, and rice together and fry, then add butter, fry again, and put the mixture in a pot to cool it down. They serve it by adding boiling water and sugar to two or three spoonfuls of fried flour in a glass.

[13] EDUCATION

The educational level of the Hui in northwest China is lower than that of the Hui living in Yunnan Province and in the cities. Quite a number of Hui professors, scientists, writers, artists, medical doctors, and lawyers are doing well. Some of them are known at home and abroad. The parents fully support the education of their children. Hui middle (junior and senior) schools, even for girls, are established in the urban areas. The Scripture College trains specialists of Islamic teachings. As a result, the educational level of the Hui is, by and large, higher than the average of national minorities in China.

[14] CULTURAL HERITAGE

Again, due to the broad regional dissemination of the Hui, their traditional culture has been integrated with that of the local nationalities. On the other hand, some of the Hui cultural traits have been adopted by the nationalities that share a common territory with the Hui. For example, the Huar folk songs, loud and clear, bold and restrained, are nowadays a common favorite of many nationalities of northwest regions. The Hui writers have produced a number of fine works, which, however, failed to attain national prominence on account of their particular features.

[15] WORK

Hui production is very similar to that of the local people with whom they share a common territory. A number of daily necessities of Hui tradition have been produced by enamel factories managed by Hui people in Ningxia Province. Also, a variety of light refreshments for Muslims appears in the markets of many cities. Muslim cooks and butchers serve their own constituencies, but are sought after by other nationalities because of their professional competence.

[16] SPORTS

The Hui generally practice the same sports as the Chinese. However, the "Wooden Ball" game is a tradition specific to the Hui of Ningxia. The ball is round or elliptic. The length of the stick is 2 ft, shaped like an ice hockey stick. The court, provided with a center line and two goals, is about 33 yds long and 22 yds wide. Each team has five players. The game lasts half an hour, divided into two periods.

[17] ENTERTAINMENT AND RECREATION

Movies and television are rapidly becoming very popular. The adults like to sing Huar songs to express their dreams about the future and their romantic feelings. The lyrics are mostly impromptu. Some are solos and some are sung in antiphonal style. The Hui often sing while dancing. There used to be gatherings of thousands of Huar fans every year in the northwest region. In recent years, the number of such gatherings has increased, other nationalities joining in for large musical and singsong events.

[18] FOLK ART, CRAFTS, AND HOBBIES

The mosque buildings have different styles, usually consisting of a main hall, a hall for scriptures, and one for bathrooms, sometimes with subsidiary buildings. The roof ridge of the main hall is usually high. The interior walls are decorated with Arabic writings of artistic quality. There is a shallow cave on the central portion of the west wall, indicating the direction of their religious homage (toward Mecca).

[19] SOCIAL PROBLEMS

The living conditions of the Hui are very diverse and depend essentially on their specific environment. Those who live in the underdeveloped northwest (Gansu, Xinjiang, Qinghai) share with their immediate neighbors the same need to catch up with the economic development of the coastal areas and areas along the Yangzi River.

[20] GENDER ISSUES

The Chinese constitution states that women have equal rights with men in all areas of life, and most legislation is gender neutral. The gap in educational level between women and men is narrowing with women making up 47.1% of college students in 2005, but only 32.6% of doctoral students.

China has strict family planning laws, and it is illegal for women to marry before 20 years of age, 22 for men, and it is illegal for single women to give birth. Though minority populations were previously exempt from family planning regulations, policy has changed in recent years to limit minority population growth. Today, urban minority couples may have two children while rural couples may have three or four.

[21] BIBLIOGRAPHY

Chiao, Chien, Nicholas Tapp, and Kam-yin Ho, ed. "Special Issue on Ethnic Groups in China." *New Asia Bulletin* no 8 (1989).

Dreyer, June Teufel. *China's Forty Millions.* Cambridge: Harvard University Press, 1976.

Eberhard, Wolfram. *China's Minorities: Yesterday and Today.* Belmont: Wadsworth Publishing Company, 1982.

Gustafsson, Bjorn A., Shi, Li, and Sicular, Terry , eds. Inequality and Public Policy in China. New York: Cambridge University Press, 2008.

Heberer, Thomas. China and Its National Minorities: Autonomy or Assimilation? Armonk, NY: M. E. Sharpe, 1989.

Lebar, Frank, et al. Ethnic Groups of Mainland Southeast Asia. New Haven: Human Relations Area Files Press, 1964.

Lemoine, Jacques. "Les Houei." In Ethnologie régionale II (Encyclopédie de la Pléiade). Paris: Gallimard, 1978.

Ma Yin, ed. China's Minority Nationalities. Beijing: Foreign Languages Press, 1989.

Ramsey, S. Robert. The Languages of China. Princeton: Princeton University Press, 1987.

Shin, Leo Kwok-yueh. The Making of the Chinese State: Ethnicity and Expansion on the Ming Borderlands. New York: Cambridge University Press, 2006.

Wiens, Harold J. Han Chinese Expansion in South China. New Haven: The Shoestring Press, 1967.

—by C. Le Blanc

IATMUL

PRONUNCIATION: YAHT-mool
ALTERNATE NAMES: Nyara
LOCATION: Papua New Guinea
POPULATION: Approximately 12,000
LANGUAGE: Iatmul (Nyara); Tok Pisin; some English
RELIGION: Traditional Iatmul; Christianity

1 INTRODUCTION

The art of Iatmul people is the most well represented of all the indigenous peoples of Papua New Guinea. Few people have much knowledge or understanding of the complex culture that produced such appealing sculptures, carvings, and masks. The Iatmul were cannibals and headhunters in the times before pacification in the 1930s. Although attempts had been made to bring a halt to the violence that was integral to the attainment of status among males in Iatmul society, it was not until public executions of "murderers" took place that men decided to forego those traditions.

2 LOCATION AND HOMELAND

The total Iatmul population is around 12,000 people. The homeland of the Iatmul is along the middle course of the Sepik River, in the East Sepik Province of the country of Papua New Guinea. There are approximately 25 Iatmul villages scattered through this portion of the Sepik River. The Sepik is a river that changes face with the change in seasons. During the rainy season that lasts for around five months, the river may rise by 12 to 18 ft and flood the surrounding lowlands. Iatmul villages become a cluster of houses perched on stilts situated within a body of muddy water. All movement has to be done by canoe during this time.

The Iatmul's location in the middle reaches of the vast river has been advantageous to them, since it enabled them to serve as middle men in the extensive trade networks that existed in the Sepik River Basin prior to the arrival of Europeans. It still serves them well, as they are able to attract a large number of tourists to their villages due to the relative ease with which the area can be reached.

A large number of Iatmul have left the Sepik region and now live in other parts of Papua New Guinea. Quite a few Iatmul live in a fishing camp on the edge of a town called Wewak in the East Sepik Province. Some estimates are as high as 50% emigration from Iatmul villages.

3 LANGUAGE

The Iatmul refer to their language by the word *nyara*. There are two mutually comprehensible dialects of the Iatmul language, which is classified by linguists as a Papuan, or non-Austronesian language that belongs to the Ndu language family. The name of this language family drives from the common word for "man," which is *ndu* in all of the related languages. The Papuan languages are spoken throughout the island of New Guinea and on a few smaller islands neighboring New Guinea in Indonesia. There is very little information on the Iatmul language, although the New Testament has been translated into Iatmul by missionary linguists. Iatmul children and many

people. Some groups recount stories of a great flood. The survivors floated down the river (the Sepik) on rafts or pieces of grass-covered ground that lodged itself and became the place of the first men's house for the Iatmul ancestors. The present-day men's houses are supposed to be representations of the original piece of earth that was to become the Iatmul world. Other myths recount the formation of the heavens and earth from the great ancestral crocodile that split in two, with his upper jaw becoming the heavens and his lower jaw becoming the terrestrial realms.

5 RELIGION

Traditional religious beliefs of the Iatmul people centered on the spirits of the rivers, forest, and swamps. There was also a concern for the ghosts of the dead and the havoc they could wreck on the living. There is a large body of myth which explains the natural and supernatural world for the Iatmul. Important in these myths are the actors and places where events took place in the mythological past. The names of the actors and places have become important items for the Iatmul and different clans have secret knowledge of the names of the actors and events in their body of myths. Clans would try to obtain the secret names of other clans. To do so was to gain power over the other group. Missionaries have been active among the Iatmul since the 1930s, and there are many converts to Christianity along the Sepik River. Some missionaries went as far as to burn the men's house and the artifacts and art that it contained. A great deal of cultural information was lost in the process.

6 MAJOR HOLIDAYS

Christian holidays are celebrated by converted Iatmul, although holidays like Christmas and Easter do not have the degree of commercial emphasis found in the United States. Santa Claus and the Easter Bunny do not visit Iatmul children. National holidays of the country are recognized, but since there are no banks or post offices in the area, most people are not directly affected by public holidays.

7 RITES OF PASSAGE

Male initiation was a common practice among the Iatmul. It involved extensive ceremonial activities that culminated in the scarification of the upper back and chest of the young initiate. Very few men still undergo this practice, not because of the pain involved, but because of the expense. It costs a few hundred dollars and several pigs to hire the older man to do the scarification. The patterns that are made are said to resemble the skin of the crocodile, the most important animal in Iatmul folklore and mythology. The Iatmul also celebrated important events in the lives of males and females, such as the first time a girl makes a sago pancake or the first time a boy carves a canoe. These celebrations were called *naven*. Naven ceremonies have all but disappeared from Iatmul culture today.

8 INTERPERSONAL RELATIONS

The Iatmul have been exposed to Western culture since the 1920s and, as a result, have adopted some of its aspects. Greetings are westernized and consist of the use of stock phrases and handshakes. Traditional greetings that took place between men of different villages who visited each other to trade con-

An Iatmul dancing or ancestor mask from the Sepik region of Papua, New Guinea. (AP Images/The (Champaign) News-Gazette, Robert K. O'Daniell)

adults are fluent in Tok Pisin, one of the national languages of Papua New Guinea.

4 FOLKLORE

Iatmul mythology states that they originated from a hole in the mud in the present-day territory of the neighboring Sawos

sisted of formalized ceremonial dialogues where men had well-defined interactional roles. The interactional styles of adult Iatmul men are often described as being aggressive, and tourists are often perplexed because when Iatmul men pose for pictures they do not smile, but instead put on a very fierce face. Iatmul women were in charge of the trade that took place with the Sawos and Chambri, two neighboring groups. The Iatmul women exchanged fish for the sago produced by the women from these neighboring groups. While men were aggressive, combative, and quick to anger, Iatmul women were the ones who maintained the cohesiveness of the community and relations with outside communities.

9 LIVING CONDITIONS

Iatmul villages vary in size from 300 to 1,200 persons. Villages traditionally centered on a men's house, which is the architectural centerpiece of the village. These buildings are massive structures and were elaborately decorated with carvings and paintings. They also house the majority of the important items of religious paraphernalia including drums, flutes, and sacred sculptures. The role of the men's house has changed over time in Iatmul villages. At the present time, most men's houses are warehouses for the storage of artifacts that are sold to tourists and art collectors, as well as being a meeting place for adult men.

Electricity and running water are not available in Iatmul villages. Without plumbing, dishes are washed in the Sepik, as are clothes and bodies. When the river is swollen but not flooded, bathing is a challenge. A person will walk upstream about 100 yards and then get in the river and wash while the current carries them to the place where they started from. Getting out of the river and staying clean is also a challenge, since the banks of the river are mounds of knee-deep mud.

10 FAMILY LIFE

Women play important roles in Iatmul daily life. Women are responsible for catching fish to trade with the neighboring villages to obtain the sago flour to make sago pancakes. Women are also the primary caregivers.

Marriage partners were determined strictly by rules in traditional Iatmul society. The marriage partners for a man included his father's mother's brother's son's daughter (a cousin), his father's sister's daughter (a cousin), or a woman that he would get in exchange for a sister he would give to another man. Anthropologists refer to this last type of marriage as "sister exchange." A married couple will take up residence in the husband's father's house. The house will also be occupied by the father's other sons and their families. Each nuclear family has its own space within the large house. Each family also has its own hearth for cooking. Husbands often sleep in the men's house.

Pet birds are kept by some people. When parrots and lorikeets are kept as pets they are not taught to talk, as most Americans try to do with pet parrots. The wings are clipped and the birds often just sit outside the house. Children sometimes play with the pet birds.

11 CLOTHING

Most Iatmul men dress in Western-style clothes consisting of athletic shorts and a T-shirt. Shoes are rarely worn. Women's dress is more varied, ranging from Western-style dresses to the use of the wrap-around *laplap* to cover the body from the waist down. Women's dress depends on what type of activity they are engaged in and who is around at the time. Children tend to dress like adults but small children go naked.

12 FOOD

The Iatmul diet consists primarily of fish and the edible palm tree called "sago." The typical Iatmul meal is not like what most Americans are used to. It is not usually the case that an entire family sits down together to eat at the dinner or kitchen table. Iatmul houses do not have tables and everyone sits on the floor. The midday meal is likely to be the only meal where everyone is together. At other times of day, people eat whenever they get hungry. The food for the day is stored in a woven basket that hangs from a carved and decorated hook near each person's sleeping area. Dried fish and sago pancakes are placed in the basket in the morning. Fruit and greens are sometimes collected from the forest. Canned curry from Indonesia and Malaysia has now become popular, as well as rice and tinned fish. These products are expensive and sometimes difficult to come by.

13 EDUCATION

Traditional education is still important to the Iatmul. Boys and girls are trained to become competent adults, able to perform the tasks that men and women do to keep the village functioning. Western school is an option for children whose parents want to send them; however, very few communities have their own school and typically children have to travel to other villages.

14 CULTURAL HERITAGE

Music in Iatmul culture was an important part of ceremonial life. Men played sacred flutes during parts of initiation rituals. These bamboo flutes were stored in the rafters of houses or in the men's house itself. The sound produced was supposed to be the voices of the ancestral spirits. Women and children were forbidden to see the flutes. The sacred flutes were also played after the death of an important man in the village. A pair of flutists would play during the night under the house of the deceased. During the day, the female relatives would also perform a kind of ritual lament that had a definite musical quality.

15 WORK

The traditional pattern of work was divided along lines of sex and age. Adult women were responsible for fishing and gardening. Women also prepared the fish that they caught, preserving a great deal of it by smoking it. Men were responsible for hunting, building, and performing most religious rituals. Boys and girls would help their mothers with her chores, but boys would not long consider performing women's work after they had passed through initiation. During initiation, boys would learn aspects of male work and ceremonial life. In the present, these patterns have remained the same, with the exception that very few boys undergo initiation. Men often seek wage labor outside the village. Some men rent their canoes and their expertise and run individual tours along the Sepik, arranging for tourists to stay with their friends and relatives in villages along the river. In many Iatmul villages, tourism is fast becoming the primary source of income. The manufacture of items for sale to tourists is an avenue for many villagers to secure cash.

16 SPORTS

For the Iatmul who still live along the Sepik River, sports are relatively unimportant. Young children play games of various sorts and boys make sling shots and propel hard, dried mud balls at birds and other living targets. Men who live in other parts of the country in towns and cities are more likely to follow rugby and soccer teams.

17 ENTERTAINMENT AND RECREATION

In an area without access to electricity, television, videos, and movies are virtually unknown. Those people who live in towns and cities with electricity go to movies and some houses have television. Traditional entertainment consisted of storytelling, ritual performances, and music.

18 FOLK ART, CRAFTS, AND HOBBIES

Artistic expression in traditional Iatmul society was completely utilitarian, and every item of daily use was decorated with carving, incision, or painting. Tourism has changed art production and appreciation in Iatmul society. Tourist art is an important money-making endeavor for the present-day Iatmul. Masks and sculpture are the most sought after item in the tourist art market.

In men's houses in Iatmul villages, there was an important ceremonial item referred to as a "debating stool." This was a free-standing sculpture with an oversized, stylized human head supported by a small body. On the back of the sculpture was a ledge that looked somewhat like a stool. The stool was used in debates which functioned to settle disputes that might otherwise end in bloodshed. The debaters from each clan would beat a bunch of specially chosen leaves while they made important points in the debate. These objects are now produced for outsiders. While a debating stool purchased in an Iatmul village on the Sepik River might cost around $100, a stool purchased from a dealer in Australia would cost around $1,500. Iatmul art has become a lucrative business for dealers in foreign countries.

19 SOCIAL PROBLEMS

Cultural change and emigration are major problems for the Iatmul today. Young people are the most likely to emigrate, and, as a result, they do not learn about the culture. They move to cities and towns and begin using Tok Pisin as their primary language. Tourism has brought major changes to the Iatmul traditional way of life. Wage earning has become important and Western items such as tennis shoes and toothpaste are becoming important cultural items for the modern Iatmul.

20 GENDER ISSUES

The Iatmul recognize two genders: *ndu* meaning 'male' and *tagwa* meaning 'female.' There are clearly defined roles and actions for men and women. It is the Iatmul men who fish with spears, who stand while in canoes, who engage in wood carving, and who, in the past, took heads and received homicide honors. On the other hand, Iatmul women fish with traps, sit while in canoes, and weave knotless net bags called *bilum* in Tok Pisin. Men and women are differentiated in Iatmul society through dress, bodily decoration, and even ways of speaking.

Iatmul boys and girls are socialized very similarly until they attain puberty. At that time, gender differentiated socialization becomes more important and boys and girls begin to separate themselves from each other. As mentioned previously, Iatmul boys were initiated into adult status through a painful set of rites involving scarification. Adult status in Iatmul society is signaled through marriage and the birth of children. Adult activities for males and females in Iatmul continue to be gender segregated.

For all members of Iatmul society, there is an idealization of motherhood, especially in its procreative and nurturing aspects. Fathers are not the primary male socializers or role model for boys. Instead, it is a boy's mother's brother (his maternal aunt) who will socialize him and provide emotional support for him. Fathers build longhouses that their sons will inherit before the fathers' deaths. It is interesting to note that upon inheriting the longhouse, a son will banish his father from continuing to live there. Fathers often live out their final years in a small, poorly constructed hut.

21 BIBLIOGRAPHY

Bateson, Gregory. *Naven*. 2nd ed. Stanford: Stanford University Press, 1954.

Ember, Carol R. and Melvin. *Encyclopedia of Sex and Gender: Men and Women in the World's Cultures*, 2 vols. New York: Springer, 2003.

Lutkehaus, Nancy, et al., ed. *Sepik Heritage: Tradition and Change in Papua New Guinea*. Durham: Carolina University Press, 1990.

—by J. Williams

IBAN

LOCATION: Malaysia (Sarawak state)
POPULATION: 657, 700 (2004)
LANGUAGE: Iban; Malay
RELIGION: Christianity; Islam; traditional beliefs

¹ INTRODUCTION

The state of Sarawak, or the Land of the Hornbills, is the largest state in Malaysia. Sarawak was a British colony from 1946 until the formation of Malaysia in 1963. Before 1841, Sarawak and its people were under the rule of the kingdom of Brunei. On 24 September 1841, the government of Sarawak was given to James Brooke as a reward for helping Brunei pacify a local revolt against the oppression by its representative in Sarawak. Sarawak was then ruled by a member of the Brooke family, commonly known as the White Rajah, until the Japanese occupation from December 1941 to August 1945. On 1 July 1946, Sarawak became a British Crown Colony. In 1963, Sarawak became one of the 13 states in the Federation of Malaysia.

As a democratic state, Sarawak ran its first general election on 7 July 1970. Since then, a general election has been called every five years to elect the state's assembly from which the state's cabinet is formed, and the chief minister is appointed as the head of the government.

² LOCATION AND HOMELAND

Sarawak occupies the northwestern coast of the island of Borneo, the third-largest island in the world after Greenland and New Guinea. The diversity of Sarawak's terrain, the variation of its soil types, and its consistently high rainfall and temperature throughout the year have resulted in the development of the most complex and luxuriant rain forests in the world. The forest is the second-most-important economic resource of Sarawak. Originally, it covered about three-quarters of the land area. Sarawak also has an intense network of meandering rivers that were the main channel of communication for its population in the past. Even though Sarawak about 124,967 sq km (48,250 sq mi) of land, it has a population of only 2.3 million people.

The Land of the Hornbills is home to at least 25 different ethnic communities. These communities can be categorized into four groups: the coastal communities, which include the Malays, Melanau, Selakau, and others; the lowland communities, which include the Iban, Bidayuh, Kayan, and Kenyah; the upland communities, which comprise the Kelabit, Penan, Lun Bawang, and many other smaller communities; and, lastly, the Chinese community.

The Iban are the largest ethnic group in Sarawak and the single-most-populous indigenous group in Malaysia, aside from the Malays. The Iban account for 29% of Sarawak's total population, while the Chinese make up 25.6%; Malays, 23.4%; Bidayuh, 8%; Melanau, 5.4%; other indigenous groups, 5.7%; and others, 0.2%; Indian, 0.2%; Non-Malaysian citizens 3.4%. The Iban mostly inhabit the lowlands of Sarawak, building their longhouses along the main rivers and smaller streams of the interior of Sarawak. The word *Iban* has various meanings, one of which is "wanderer." The Iban are a very mobile and vigorous people, moving through the hills of Borneo, farming dry-rice, fishing, gathering, and hunting, expanding in territory and numbers. They are originally from the Batang Lupar and Saribas river system of Sarawak, and from the adjoining Kapuas region of Western Kalimantan. They have gradually moved in through the Rejang Valley, traveling northward and eastward, until today they are present in every district and division of Sarawak, both in urban areas and the countryside.

SARAWAK'S POPULATION 2004

ETHNIC GROUPS	POPULATION ('000)	%
Iban	657.7	29.0
Chinese	578.7	25.6
Malay	505.8	23.4
Bidayuh	181.5	8.0
Other Indigenous Groups*	128.8	5.7
Melanau	124.3	5.4
Others	4.6	0.2
Indian	4.3	0.2
Non-Malaysian Citizens	77.0	3.4
Total	**2,262.7**	**100**

Source: Department of Statistics, 2004
Note: * Includes the Orang Ulu communities

³ LANGUAGE

The Iban speak their own language called "Iban." However, there was no written form of the language until education was introduced into Sarawak. Formerly, all information was handed down orally from one generation to the next. The Iban had to recall important events through memory, and one of the common ways used to narrate important events was through *berenong* (singing songs).

The Iban language is widely spoken in Sarawak, alongside the Malay language that has been the *lingua franca,* or common language, of the archipelago for centuries. There are significant similarities between the two languages. Although the Iban language is widely used, there are existing vernacular differences between regions or districts. For example, Iban spoken in the Miri-Bintulu region has a different accent than the Iban language spoken in the Kuching-Bau region. Despite the variations in dialects, all speakers of Iban understand each other's speech quite well.

Among the Iban, as among many other natives in Borneo, names consist of two parts: the given name, and the father's name. However, it is common practice among the Iban to insert the word *anak,* meaning "the child of," in between the given name and the father's name, for example, Ugat (given name) anak (child of) Muli (the father's name).

⁴ FOLKLORE

Although a relatively large number of Iban are now Christian, most of their beliefs, traditions, and practices are based on their native beliefs and customs. Their myths, fables, legends, and stories tell of headhunting raids, though these practices have ceased to exist. They also tell of Iban augury, a divination system in which divine guidance is sought in natural events, particularly in the behavior of birds and other natural species. Even though the Iban did not practice human sacrifice, many of them were headhunters. It was believed that the possession of an enemy's head was a sign of bravery, boldness, courage, and leadership qualities. Therefore, Iban folklore includes sto-

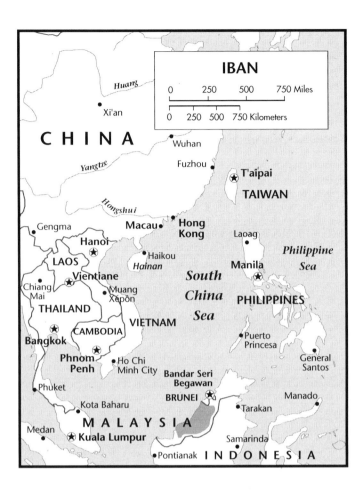

IBAN

0   250   500   750 Miles

0   250 500 750 Kilometers

CHINA

Huang
Xi'an
Yangtze
Hongshui
Wuhan
Fuzhou
T'aipai
TAIWAN
Gengma
Macau
Hong Kong
Laoag
Hanoi
Haikou
Philippine Sea
LAOS
Hainan
Manila
Vientiane
South China Sea
Chiang Mai
Muang Xépon
PHILIPPINES
THAILAND
VIETNAM
Bangkok
CAMBODIA
Puerto Princesa
Phnom Penh
Ho Chi Minh City
General Santos
Bandar Seri Begawan
Phuket
BRUNEI
Manado
Kota Baharu
Tarakan
MALAYSIA
Medan
Kuala Lumpur
Samarinda
Pontianak INDONESIA

ries of great exploits, the opening of new land settlements, and success in warfare and/or headhunting raids. The heroes and heroines of these exploits were respected during their lifetimes and have been remembered for generations in ritual invocations, legends, fables, and stories.

5 RELIGION

Over the years, many Iban became Christian, while some others became Muslim. However, a large percentage still keeps their traditional beliefs of animism, in which all beings possess a soul. This understanding underlies various rituals of the Iban. They revere mythical and legendary heroes and deities. In the past, as with many other native groups in Sarawak, the Iban relied on dreams and bird augury, particularly through the banded kingfisher, rufous piculet, and maroon woodpecker, as guidance before commencing any undertakings. For instance, they would observe the behavior of these birds and other animals, reptiles, and insects before farming, hunting, or becoming involved in a trading deal. They would not proceed with any of those undertakings if these natural events were thought to be bad omens.

6 MAJOR HOLIDAYS

Besides celebrating other Malaysian major holidays, Christmas, Hari Raya, and Chinese New Year, the Iban in Sarawak celebrate various religious festivals known as *gawai*. There are a number of *gawais* that are very important in the Iban society. These are the *gawai batu* and *gawai memali umai* (rice culti-

vation), *gawai nyintu orang sakit* (health and longevity), *gawai kenyalang* (warfare and bravery), and *gawai antu* (festival for the dead). The rituals for these festivals include *miring* (offering of food), *biau* (chanting), and *timang* (incantations) by *lemambang* (ritualists). The Sarawak government has set aside two or three days each year to observe the most important and interesting festival—the *gawai dayak*. It is a thanksgiving celebration to end the harvest season and to mark the beginning of the next farming cycle. It is an occasion to seek the blessing of the gods and spirits for the New Year. Besides observing certain rituals, this festival involves much merriment and the drinking of *tuak* (locally brewed rice-wine), as well as the display of elaborate traditional costumes.

7 RITES OF PASSAGE

A child is not immediately named when born, but will be called *ulat* (baby). A baby is normally named after his or her grandparents and/or grandparent's cousins. The bathing ceremony is performed at the river after a name is given. A girl reaches puberty when she is 10 years old and is expected to sleep by herself until she is married. Meanwhile, a boy at the same age will move to sleep in the gallery with the other bachelors. In the past, a boy had to undergo circumcision, although it is not a ceremonial event. Girls are taught to cook, pound, or unhusk rice when they attain the age of seven, while boys are expected to accompany their fathers on hunting trips. At the age of 13, girls learn to weave and boys learn to gather and split firewood with an axe. This training prepares them for marriage.

The birth of a first child marks the transition from adolescence to adulthood and signifies a change in status. The new parents cease to be called by their personal names, but are now known by relational names, that is, *apai,* "the father of," and *indai,* "the mother of," so-and-so.

When an Iban dies, she or he is said to become a spirit *(antu)*. Complicated death rites are observed after a death, to ensure the harmony of the temporary presence of the spirit among the living, and also for the future welfare of the living and the dead. Many series of rites are observed. The final rite, the *gawai antu,* is the most important of them all. At this rite, a tomb house is erected over the grave of the deceased, as a house for the dead.

8 INTERPERSONAL RELATIONS

Social interactions in the Iban community, like other communities in Sarawak, are governed by *adat. Adat* includes a variety of customs, practices, basic values, and the religious system that governs life in the longhouse, shapes relations between people and their environment, and forges a path between humans and the spirit world. It also governs interpersonal relations between individuals. Among the Iban, it is considered indecent to blow one's nose, or to spit, or even to mention something dirty while someone else is eating. When walking in front of someone who is seated in the longhouse, it is considered polite to bow one's head, place one's hands between one's knees, and say, "Please excuse me. I wish to walk in front of you." The Iban have great respect for visitors. It is polite to ask a visitor, who happens to pass the longhouse or landing place, to come up into the house and be served a snack of betel nuts. Offering betel nuts is the traditional welcome that the Iban accord to visitors in the gallery. If the visitor has not dined, she

A local Iban tribesman looks over a smouldering forest, cleared and burned for new plantation, near Balaiberkauk, West Kalimantan, Indonesia. (AP Images/Mark Fallander)

or he is served food. An Iban who does not take care of visitors is considered greedy.

⁹ LIVING CONDITIONS

Many natives in the interior of Sarawak, including the Iban, live in longhouses. However, today there are significant differences in living conditions between Iban who live in urban areas and Iban who still live in longhouses in the interior of Sarawak. A longhouse is much like a row of terraced apartments, except that the longhouse is erected on wooden pillars, 1.2 m to 2 m (4–7 ft) above the ground, for safety's sake. It consists of a series of family *bilek* (apartments) joined laterally and connected by a communicating passageway, gallery, and *ruai* (open-air veranda). Each apartment is separately owned and maintained by a single family unit, including its gallery section and the veranda. Each longhouse is governed by a *tuai rumah* (longhouse elder), who has to be a man of skill and prestige.

Even though many longhouses are supplied with tap water and electricity, some do not have these basic amenities, and have to get water from the nearest river and burn kerosene for light in the night.

From childhood, the longhouse provides a sense of belonging for the Iban. Therefore, most still owe loyalty to their longhouses after allegiance to the family unit.

¹⁰ FAMILY LIFE

An Iban family is normally small, very similar to those in European and American society. However, an Iban family is organized as an enduring group. Continuation of the Iban family or *bilek* (section of the longhouse) is highly regarded. Thus, in each generation, a son or daughter is to remain after marriage in possession of the bilek. This is to continue the family unit and to take over the temporary management of its ritual and economic estate. The family is a basic social and economic unit. It is also a very close unit, with the head of the family (normally the father) responsible for defending its interests against any encroachment. He also represents its members, should they be involved in litigation with members of other families. If any family members are found guilty of an offense, fines are usually paid out of family resources. This is because individuals have interrelated interests and are bound by kinship connection. As such, each member of the family bears the responsibility to uphold family honor.

Keeping animals as pets is very uncommon, not only among the Iban but also among many other natives on Borneo. Animals such as pigs and chicken are reared for meat, while dogs are kept for hunting. Even cats are reared as work animals, to keep mice away from the farm and the longhouse.

¹¹ CLOTHING

Today, most Iban men and women wear Western- or Malay-style clothing. The men wear shirts and pants, while the women wear blouses, skirts, or *baju kurung* and *kebaya* [see "Malaysian Malays"]. These current and daily dressing codes are very different from their traditional costumes.

The Iban prefer earthy colors of brown and brick-red, with accents of indigo-blue color pigments obtained from tree roots and leaves, as can be seen in their famous weaving of *pua kumbu* (a handspun cotton textile).

A traditional Iban woman's costume includes the *bidang* (tubular sarong-type skirt), *kain pandak* (short skirt), or *kain tating* (weighted short skirt). She may also wear a *rawai* (corset made from rattan or brass), a *sugu tinggi* (headdress made of silver), a *marik empani* (a beaded collar), a *selampai* (sash or shawl), and silver necklaces, bracelets, and anklets. The man's costume includes a *kelambi* or *baju burung* (woven cotton jacket with decorative designs) and the *sirat* (loincloth). Other accessories include the *labong* (a turban of embroidered cloth) or a rattan cap with feathers, the *dangdong* (shoulder shawl), a sword, silver bracelets, and ivory armlets.

At the *Gawai Dayak* festival, one can witness the full display of Iban traditional costume. Several young women and men are dressed in all their finery for the costume parade. A *kumang gawai* (festival princess) and a *keling gawai* (festival prince) are chosen during the parade.

The traditional woman's *rawai* is a closely fitting corset made of a series of cane hoops covered with tiny silver or brass rings, pinned together with brass wire. This encased the hips, waist, and abdomen, thus limiting body movement so that the body remained stiff and rigid. However, it was considered extremely elegant, particularly when the silver was well-polished.

¹² FOOD

As in many other Asian communities, rice is the staple food among the Iban in Sarawak and is eaten three times a day. It is normally served and eaten with wild vegetables or wild meat from the jungle. While the women collect vegetables, such as mushrooms, fern tops, and/or other young leaves of edible wild vegetation, the men are responsible for bringing back any form of meat, either from hunting or fishing activities.

The family normally gathers for dinner in the evening. They will sit together in a circle on a mat, and the dishes, which include at least a vegetable dish and a meat or fish dish, are placed in the center. The rice can be served on a plate or in leaves and can be taken by hand or spoon. The vegetable and meat dishes are served with a communal spoon from which nobody eats. Water is served and drunk after the meal. Normally, it is the women's responsibility to wash up and clean the kitchen after every meal.

Besides using brassware as cooking utensils, the Iban use bamboo and leaves to cook and serve their traditional food. Cooking meat or vegetables in bamboo is one of their exotic cuisines. The meat is marinated with salt, ginger, and lemon grass before being stuffed into a bamboo pipe 38 cm (15 in) long. The end is covered with young tapioca leaves to give a special aroma to the meat inside. The meat in the bamboo is placed on the fire and has to be constantly and consistently turned in order to avoid being burned. This dish is served with rice.

¹³ EDUCATION

The Iban know the importance of education as a means to excel in the modern world. Education is seen as a means for social security and mobility. In line with Malaysian government educational policy, the Iban children are required to go school when they are six years old, and both male and female children are deeply encouraged to attend school. As a result, the literacy rate among the Iban has increased from 3% in 1947 to 35% in 1980 and to 48.7% in 1990. Today, many Iban are literate and have obtained degrees both from local and overseas universities. With these qualifications, many Iban today are holding high positions in the public and corporate sectors. They are policy makers, corporate managers, professors, lecturers, doctors, and lawyers.

¹⁴ CULTURAL HERITAGE

Many of the musical instruments of nearly all indigenous peoples in Sarawak are made from bamboo, rattan, and woods native to the local area. However, the bronze-knobbed *gong* is widely used by the Iban and other indigenous communities in Sarawak. It is an ancient instrument appearing in many sizes and styles and used in a variety of ways at both musical and nonmusical events. The *ketebong* is another musical instrument popularly used by some Iban communities in Sarawak. It is a slightly hourglass-shaped single drumhead that is carved from the trunk of a tree. Various dances are performed to gong and ketebong music. These include the *ngajat* (performed by women), warrior dances, and the sword dance.

The Iban do not have a strong literary tradition. Most of their stories, legends, and myths are passed down orally from one generation to the next. Only quite recently have efforts been made to document and compile these stories.

¹⁵ WORK

Most Iban who live in town areas are involved in formal paid employment. This is partly as a result of Iban traditional custom known as *bejalai*, which encourages young Iban to leave their longhouses in search of prestige and new experiences. As a result, many have become professional workers and some are factory workers in places like Singapore and Johor. There are others who work on offshore oil platforms, not only in Malaysia and Brunei, but also in the Middle East and other parts of the world. This is quite different from those who still live in longhouses in the interior; they cultivate hill rice, gather wild vegetables, and fish and hunt for meat. They also rear chickens and pigs for home consumption. They are self-sufficient and self-reliant. However, some do take their produce to the market to be sold.

¹⁶ SPORTS

Various native sports and games include cock-fighting and spinning tops. Other games are played too, particularly soccer, which is becoming very popular. Individual tug-of-war (*batak lampong)*, team tug-of-war, arm-wrestling, and long-jumping, are played in the open space in front of longhouses and are also staged during festivals.

¹⁷ ENTERTAINMENT AND RECREATION

As there are no televisions or movie theatres in the villages, Iban normally entertain themselves with traditional music and dance. After working under the hot sun the whole day, the longhouse is filled with the sound of *gong*. This is very common, except during mourning periods. Women and men, old and young, dance to the music. Various dances are performed, such as sword dancing, dancing with castanets, saucer dances, war dances, and shield dances. It is considered a time to display one's dancing talents.

Among the Iban, cock-fighting is not only a sport but a form of recreation and entertainment. An annual cock-fighting season was held in the past, until it was banned because it had become a place to gamble money. Cock-fighting also has some symbolic connotations. It is a symbolic form of supernatural fights between two rivals.

[18] FOLK ART, CRAFTS, AND HOBBIES

A pride of Iban cultural heritage is the *pua kumbu*. The *pua kumbu* is a handspun textile that is made from a locally grown cotton plant called *taya*. The weaving of pua kumbu is an art that requires great skill, technique, and rich and complex ideas. Thus, Iban women are considered to be Borneo's most-skilled weavers, producing artistic masterpieces on simple backstrap looms. The secrets of making pua kumbu are passed down from mother to daughter. Producing a pua kumbu requires skill at every stage, from the preparation of the cotton yarn to the tying of threads, the dyeing process, and the selection of design. Pua kumbu is used for the women's *bidang*, the men's *kelambi*, and also as blankets.

The Iban also spend their spare time making pottery, producing clay pots for cooking. They also produce other important handicraft items such as baskets, mats, and caps from rattan, bamboo, nipah palm, bemban, screw-pine, and many other plants native to their area.

[19] SOCIAL PROBLEMS

The issue of land rights is one of the most crucial social problems faced by the Iban in Sarawak. The rapid economic development currently taking place in Sarawak, which requires the Iban to give up their land for land development, has put the Iban and the other ethnic communities in a dilemma. To be involved in "progress" and "development" requires them to give up their land to be developed into agricultural plantations. This is exacerbated by a high rate of rural-urban migration among the Iban. Many longhouses are often left empty, except during the festive seasons of gawai dayak and Christmas. Many Iban return to their longhouses on special occasions.

[20] GENDER ISSUES

Egalitarianism is one of the most central values among the Iban. It permeates almost all social relations, including relationships between men and women in the society. Therefore, as with the men, Iban women play a major role in preserving the family as a unit. Their main duties and responsibilities are to nurture the family, which includes looking after the children when they are young. Besides managing the home, Iban women are also required to work in the fields, particularly during the planting season and the harvesting season. They manage their farms together with their husbands.

[21] BIBLIOGRAPHY

Buma, Datuk Michael. *Iban Customs and Traditions*. Kuching, Sarawak: Borneo Publications Sdn. Bhd., 1987.

Chin, Lucan, and Valerie Mashman, ed. *Sarawak Cultural Legacy: A Living Tradition*. Kuching Sarawak: Society Atelier Sarawak, 1991.

Jawan, Jayum A. *The Iban Factor in Sarawak Politics*. Centre for Southeast Asian Studies, University of Hull, 1991.

Munan, Heidi. *Culture Shock: Borneo*. Singapore: Times Books International, 1988.

Ngadi, Henri Gana. *Iban Rites of Passage and Some Related Ritual Acts: A Description of Forms and Functions*. Master's thesis, Centre for Southeast Asian Studies, Hull University, 1988.

Sandin, Benedict. *Iban Way of Life*. Kuching Sarawak: Borneo Literature Bureau, 1976.

———. *Iban Adat and Augury*. Pulau Penang: Penerbit Universiti Sains Malaysia, for School of Comparative Social Sciences, 1980.

—by P. Bala

IFUGAO

PRONUNCIATION: EE-foo-gow
ALTERNATE NAMES: Igorots, Kiangan
LOCATION: Philippines (northern Luzon)
POPULATION: Over 133,000
LANGUAGE: Ifugao
RELIGION: Native beliefs
RELATED ARTICLES: Vol. 3: Filipinos; Kalinga

¹INTRODUCTION

Among highland peoples of the insular Southeast Asia, the Ifugao enjoy the rare distinction of becoming widely known not under some originally generic term for "[savage] mountaineer," but under their own name for themselves as mispronounced by their Christianized Gaddang neighbors: *i-pugaw*, "the people of the known earth." The Ifugao belong to a group of peoples inhabiting northern Luzon's Cordillera Central who are collectively known among Filipino lowlanders as "Igorots," a term that first appears in Spanish records as a label for mountaineers who came down to Pangasinan to trade gold. As these Igorots resisted Spanish colonial rule, acculturation, and Christianization for three centuries, the Spanish referred to them as infidels and fierce and independent tribes, distinguishing them from the *indios*, the tribute-paying, trouser- and dress-wearing, and church-going lowlanders.

Including the Ilongot of the Caraballo range and Sierra Madre, the Igorots are far from homogeneous, dividing into eight linguistic groups and four broad cultural types. The southern group includes the Ibaloi and the Kankanai, whose gold mines attracted more concerted Spanish attention and exposed them to more lowland influences, such as upper garments for their women; elsewhere in the highlands women traditionally went bare-chested. The northern group includes the swidden-farming (shifting-cultivation) and relatively egalitarian societies of the northern Kalinga [see **Kalinga**], Isneg (or Apayao), and Tinggianes (meaning "highlanders," a name that used to apply far more broadly). The Ilongot ("forest people," [see **Ilongot**]) comprise the Southeast group and are known for their extreme conservatism and isolationism.

Known to their mountain neighbors as "Kiangan" after their ancestral locality, the Ifugao themselves belong to the Central group along with the Bontok ("mountain"), northern Kankanai, and southern Kalinga, peoples who are world-renowned for their mountainside rice terraces. Even within this group, there are significant variations. For example, whereas Bontok society uses a village-ward *(ato)* system to subordinate individual and kin-group interests to those of the wider community, Ifugao society gives free play to competition among individuals of forceful personality and great wealth; this contentious spirit has even precluded the emergence of a Kalinga-style interregional peace-pact system [see **Kalinga**]. Ifugao culture (like Cordillera and non-Christian cultures more generally) has contributed key icons to the national identity of the predominantly Christian and Hispanized Philippines: in 1995 the rice terraces of the Cordillera (the most renowned of which are those built by the Ifugao at Banaue) were declared UNESCO World Heritage sites and in 2001 the Hudhud chants of the

Ifugao were put on the UNESCO list of the Masterpieces of the Oral and Intangible Heritage of Humanity.

The Cordillera peoples hardly lived in absolute isolation. Spanish military expeditions seeking gold or punishing lowland-raiding Igorots, as well as Catholic missionaries, penetrated the highlands from time to time, generally making little lasting impression. Of greater regularity and significance was the circulation of Ilocano traders; in the 18th century, this vigorous highland–lowland trade subverted the colonial tobacco monopoly. Ilocano towns often contracted peace-pacts with highland groups. Lowlanders and highlanders killed each other in blood feud cycles much as went on among highlanders themselves.

Possessing no gold mines and notoriously "unmanageable," the Ifugao largely escaped Spanish attention until 19th-century scholars disclosed the wonders of the rice terraces to the wider world. The Ifugao's main outside conflict was not with the Spanish directly but with the Gaddang over control of the upper Magat valley; the latter retained slave-holding chiefs for half a century after accepting Catholicism and allying with the Spanish against the Ifugao.

It was American colonial troops, followed by American schoolteachers and Protestant missionaries, who began the "integration" of the Cordillera peoples into the wider Filipino nation, though at the same time institutionalizing their status as cultural minorities. During the Japanese occupation during World War II, many Ifugao suffered from violence, hunger, and displacement; fighting extended into the Ifugao highlands. The Japanese general Yamashita surrendered to U.S. troops at Kiangan in 1945. In 1966, in recognition of highland diversity, the central government broke up the American-created Mountain Province into four separate provinces: Benguet, Mountain (Bontok), Kalinga-Apayao (now two separate provinces), and Ifugao. Currently, grouped together as the Cordillera Administrative Region, these provinces (now including Abra) enjoy a measure of autonomy that may increase to the level of that of the Autonomous Region in Muslim Mindanao.

The highland peoples face diverse and increasing pressures from lowland society. Most threatening (through the early 1990s) have been dam projects that intend to flood ancestral valleys and the spread of fighting between NPA (communist) guerrillas and the Philippine government; these have been less of an issue since the early 1990s. Agrarian reform has affected few Ifugao because landholdings tend to be very small, but the government has begun to recognize highland peoples' rights to their ancestral lands. In the past 87% of land in the Cordillera region was classified as state property and much was awarded by politicians to logging companies. International tourism, as elsewhere, has been a mixed blessing, eroding much of traditional culture at the same time as promoting certain aspects of it. In some areas, the rice terraces are falling into neglect as young people, attracted by work in cities or abroad, become less and less willing to stay in their home villages to do the arduous work of maintaining them.

²LOCATION AND HOMELAND

The Ifugao inhabit 1,940 sq km (750 sq mi) of rugged uplands in northern Luzon's Cordillera Central (which includes peaks of 2,440 m or 8,000 ft), an area drained by tributaries of the Magat River, which in turn joins the upper course of the Cagayan River. Supporting themselves on rice grown on terraces

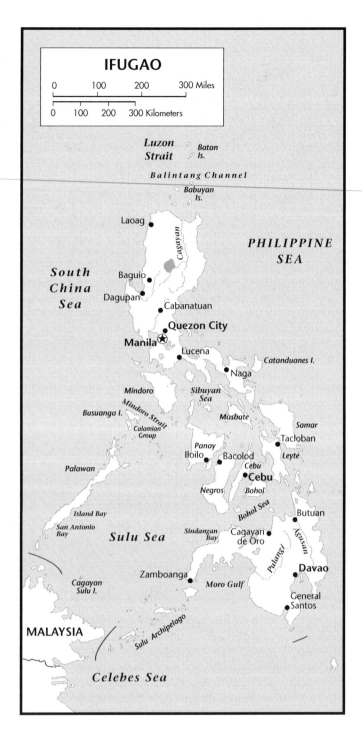

important member is Ilocano. Ifugao's immediate relations, however, are with the neighboring Cordillera languages Bontok and Kankanay from which, linguists estimate, it began to diverge 1,000 years ago.

⁴FOLKLORE

The Ifugao have a verse epic, the *Hudhud;* individual episodes are sung to relieve the tedium of harvesting, a female soloist leading and the other harvesters answering in chorus. The heroes of the epic are *kadangyan* (wealthy, high-status people), such as Bugan, a female kadangyan who fights as bravely as her brother Dinulawan and who seeks for her mate only the man who can fit her brother's sword belt. Daulayan, a poor man, fits the sword belt and eventually turns out to be of kadangyan lineage after all.

Part of the Ifugao marriage ceremony is the myth of Balitok and Bugan of Kiangan, a brother-sister couple who survive the great flood and become the ancestors of the Ifugao. In one variant, Bugan is so ashamed of becoming pregnant by her brother that she goes downstream *(lagod)* to seek destruction from the spirits there; the spirits, however, teach her how to sacrifice a male and female pig from the same litter in order to lift the curse for incest. According to another variant, Bugan is so distraught from childlessness that she goes downstream to seek death, encountering in turn Fire, a crocodile, and a shark, all of whom she impresses with her boldness and beauty. The shark passes her on to Umbumabakal, who lives in a terrifying house covered with gigantic ferns. There Bugan offers herself for Umbumabakal to devour. Umbumabakal, too, takes pity on her and takes her to Ngilin and the gods of Animal Fertility; they all return to Kiangan where they teach the priests there how to perform the *bubun* ceremony in which sacrificial meat is divided between Ambahing, the spirit who steals semen from the womb, and Komiwa, the spirit who stirs semen up in the womb.

⁵RELIGION

The Ifugao traditional religion recognizes as many as 1,500 named gods, divided into 35 categories associated with, to name the most prominent, hero ancestors, celestial bodies, natural phenomena, diseases, and agriculture. Each possesses specific attributes and powers. All are immortal, can change form, become invisible, and travel through space. They inhabit all of the five divisions of the Ifugao universe: *kabunian* (the sky world); *dalum* (the underworld); *pugao* (the "known earth," the land of the Ifugao); *daiya* (the upstream region); and *lagod* (the downstream region). Particularly exalted is the sky world deity Lidum; the uncle of Balitok, ancestor of the Ifugao, Lidum is their great teacher and lawgiver. One example of minor deities is the class of *halupe*. A person may send a halupe to harass another person by forcing an idea constantly on the latter's mind, e.g., a creditor may send a halupe to a debtor in hopes of making the latter respond peacefully to a request for repayment, or a youth may commission a halupe to make a pretty girl more receptive to his romantic overtures.

Being a priest (adult males only) is not a full-time occupation but rather a voluntary vocation learned through apprenticeship, during which one must memorize the names and characteristics of the 1,500 gods. Since the American colonial period, priests can practice beyond the circle of their kindred to which they had formerly been confined. In exchange

carved into the steep mountainsides, the Ifugao constituted 67.9% of the population of the province of Ifugao in 2000, numbering almost 110,000 (Ilocanos were 13.7%). Over 23,000 Ifugao lived in Nueva Vizcaya province. Estimates for the various Ifugao dialect-groups are as follows: Amganad, 27,000 (1987); Batad, 43,000 (1987); Mayoyao, 40,000 (1998); and Tuwali (Kiangan), 50,786 (1990). Population density is as high as 155 persons per sq km (400 per sq mi) in some locales.

³LANGUAGE

The Ifugao language is an Austronesian language, belonging to the Northern Philippine branch whose most numerically

for their services, priests receive meat and rice wine but more importantly enjoy the reputation of having a "good voice." Because ritual chanting provides an opportunity for masculine exhibitionism, as many as 15 priests can participate in a ceremony, as compared to only one or two among the Bontok.

Rituals fulfill a wide range of functions. Omens are read by examining the bile sac or livers of pigs or chickens or by interpreting birdcalls. Some rituals are used to ensure the success of hunting, farming, headhunting, peacemaking, and debt-collection, and rituals accompany prestige feasts, divorce proceedings, and sorcery. Performed under a house or granary (less commonly in a field or forest), rituals involve several hours of chanting in a fixed protocol: invoking the deities; praying to the deities; inviting the deities to possess the priests; having the deities possess the priests; and exhorting the deities to action. Priests gain power over particular deities by reciting a myth that mentions them. Invocation entails "pushing" *(tulud)* deities from their homes in kabonian, dalum, daiya, and lagod to the village where the ritual is taking place; this requires a long time as each locality (as many as 40) through which the deities must pass is named in turn. Offerings range from a little betel or a chicken claw to sacrifices of pigs or chickens; in the course of a ritual, spirits (through the drinking priests) constantly consume rice wine.

Priests also perform curing rites. Disease can be caused by sorcery or the displeasure of ancestral spirits who may allow malevolent deities to inflict suffering on offending descendants.

According to the 2000 census, 17.6% of the population of the Cordillera Administrative Region, of which Ifugao province is a part, is classified as "Other" in religious affiliation, meaning adherents of indigenous religion. The rest followed a form of Christianity: 65.8% of the region's population is Roman Catholic (much lower than the national percentage of 83%), 8.9% Evangelical, 2.9% Iglesia ni Cristo, 1.6% Jehovah's Witness, 0.8% Philippine Independent Church (Aglipayan). In the early 1990s, 54% of ethnic Ifugao identified themselves as Roman Catholic.

Thanks in particular to Christian churches' establishing schools in the Ifugao region, Ifugao associate Christianity with modern civilization and especially with the education that confers high status (and even upward mobility for some non-elite Ifugao) as well as equality with the nationally dominant lowland Filipinos. Elite, educated Ifugao identify themselves as Christian even though they continue to perform or participate in traditional Ifugao rituals (baki or bfuni), from those for healing to those for earning higher social status. Though there were Christians in all social levels among the Ifugao, those who practiced traditional religion exclusively belonged to the non-elite strata. Fundamentalist Protestant churches tended to be more condemnatory of traditional Ifugao culture than the Catholic Church. For instance, Protestant leaders strongly oppose the performance of traditional Ifugao healing rites; local Catholic Church authorities are ambivalent towards such practices, with some priests even encouraging people for whom modern medical treatments are ineffective to sponsor traditional healing rites at their homes.

⁶MAJOR HOLIDAYS

See the article entitled **Filipinos**.

⁷RITES OF PASSAGE

An adolescent boy is free to visit an adolescent girl in her *agamang* dormitory and have sex with her (a girl is not supposed to have more than one lover at a time). An individual usually experiences several "trial marriages" before committing to a permanent union. Employing *monbaga* (go-betweens), wealthy families are more careful to arrange their children's marriages with partners of equal status and to determine inheritance beforehand. The betrothal ceremony involves the exchange of pigs and gifts and initiates a close liaison. The marriage bond is formalized over a series of four wedding ceremonies including pig and chicken sacrifices, feasting, bile sac augury, and, in the last ceremony, the presentation of jars, cloth, and knives by the groom's family to the bride's. Fines for breaking off the marriage are higher after each successive wedding ceremony.

Deities may take a person's soul, causing the body to fall ill; if they do not return the soul, the person dies. With all its orifices plugged, the corpse of a person who has died a natural death is seated, tied to an honorary death chair, and guarded by fire and an undertaker. The deceased remains there for as many days (up to 13) as the family can afford to hold a nighttime wake and then is either carried by the undertaker to a hillside family sepulcher (a chamber at the end of a tunnel cut into soft rock) or put into a sealed coffin beneath the house or in a granary-like mausoleum. Children are buried in jars. Three to five years later, a second burial may be performed if the deceased is unhappy and is disturbing or harming the living. In case of wrongful death, the corpse is seated, bound to a house post, and neglected so that its spirit will seek revenge.

⁸INTERPERSONAL RELATIONS

Ifugao society looks to no chiefs, councils, or other supravillage political institutions but rather governs itself through a highly complex system of customary law. An individual identifies with the kinship group and "local area," corresponding more or less to the *himpuntona'an* (traditional agricultural district) to which he or she belongs; this core circle of trust and mutual dependence shades off gradually through areas of less and less affiliation until reaching "enemy territory," from whose alien populations heads traditionally could be taken. Wider regional solidarities began to form only with the American occupation of the highlands.

Wealth constitutes the base of status and influence in Ifugao society. The following categories are distinguished: *kadangyan,* the rich or those inheriting large areas of irrigated rice fields and prestigious heirlooms; *tumuk,* those who have sufficient rice year-round but have yet to earn the status of *kadangyan;* the *namatuk* or *mabitil,* poorer people, "those who may hunger" and be forced to incur debts with the wealthy; *nawatwat,* the "disinherited" or "passed by," who become servants or tenants of the wealthy; and, formerly, slaves, generally children sold by poor families to lowlanders to discharge debts. If bought by fellow Ifugao, they eventually were freed and their children were in any case born free.

In recent times, a new category of wealthy has emerged. The bacnang, a loanword from Ilocano meaning "rich," are people who have become rich in non-traditional ways, primarily in commercial or agricultural ventures, such as owning hotels or restaurants, by which they amass large amounts of cash. According to government statistics on family income from 1988,

A group of Ifugao women take a break from planting rice, Banaue, Philippines. (AP Images/Pat Roque)

4% of the population of Ifugao province fell into the upper-class category (earning over 60,000 pesos) and 75% in the lower-class category (earning under 30,000 pesos).

An individual qualifies for kadangyan status by amassing wealth in the form of rice lands and water buffalo (in the past also slaves). Rice lands must be of an extent sufficient to produce a surplus that can be loaned to namatuk families at high rates of interest, so high the debtors can never reach kadangyan status themselves. While hornbill headdresses, gold beads, swords, gongs, and antique Chinese jars are all signs of distinction, the essential mark of having become a kadangyan is the *hagabi*, a massive lounging bench carved from a hardwood trunk, sitting beside the house. The kadangyan-to-be must provide food and rice wine to the makers of the hagabi for the duration of the work and must hold a lengthy and expensive *uyawe* feast to install it.

Kadangyan compete in the number and quality of ritual feasts they can hold. Kadangyan status confers no formal political power, but the wealth inherent in it earns considerable influence. Community decision-making requires a consensus among all the kadangyan; this consensus is only reached after the personalities of the kadangyan have had the chance to contend in public debate.

Since there is no higher traditional authority to whom an Ifugao can appeal for redress of grievances, each must obtain his or her own justice, or rather kin-groups of injured parties seek compensation from the kin-groups of injuring parties. For instance, a kin-group could traditionally avenge the murder of one of its own by killing any member of the murderer's kin-group. To witness transactions, resolve disputes, and punish crimes, Ifugao rely on *monbaga* (go-betweens), individuals knowledgeable in genealogy and customary law who can moreover call on a large kin-group to enforce the decisions they make. Fines consist of valued goods, such as livestock (e.g., water buffalo for sacrifice at the victim's funeral), blankets, kettles, knives, and clothing and are divided between the injured party, his or her kin, and the monbaga. Fines are assessed according to the status of the parties as well as the crime's nature and intentionality. For example, a kadangyan who has committed a crime against a fellow kadangyan pays a higher fine than if the two parties are tumuk and higher still than in a case between two nawatwat. If a kadangyan commits a crime against a person of lesser status, he or she pays a lower fine than for injuring a peer, while a nawatwat wronging a social superior will pay a higher fine than if he or she had wronged an equal.

Cases between inhabitants of the same "local area" were usually settled by imposing fines, but crimes committed by one party against a party from a different "local area" generally led to feuding on the principle that "might makes right." Warfare entailed hunting for heads by ambushing a member of an enemy group found walking alone at the edge of his or her territory; raiding for women and child slaves was also common.

⁹LIVING CONDITIONS

Ifugao live in small, named hamlets of 8 to 12 houses sitting on several levels of terracing amid hillside rice fields. Hamlets may also cluster to form more extensive communities of hundreds of houses. Toward the northern edge of Ifugao territory, a village's houses are scattered over broad valley bottoms, separated by fields.

With some variation in size reflecting the wealth of the owner, houses are square, raised on four posts (with cylindrical fenders to block climbing rats), accessible by ladder, and have pyramidal roofs of thatch. The well-built wooden structures last for generations. They have few furnishings or decoration other than occasional human figures carved on the doors and, formerly, a shelf for displaying skulls of enemies and sacrificial animals. Larger communities may have stone platforms at their center on which communal celebrations are held and prestigious houses are raised. Less permanent structures, such as the *agamang*, dormitories for girls and unmarried women, are built on the ground.

Average family income in the Cordillera Administrative Region, of which Ifugao province is a part, amounted to 192,000 pesos (US$3,765) in 2006, among the highest in the country, cf. the national average of ₱173,000, the National Capital Region's ₱311,000, Southern Tagalog's ₱198,000, and those of the neighboring Cagayan Valley and Ilocos regions, ₱143,000 and ₱142,000 respectively. In 2000, Ifugao province, however, had the fourth lowest Human Development Index, 0.351 (combining measures of health, education, and income) in the country (above provinces in the Sulu archipelago, cf. the Philippines' national HDI of 0.656).

According to the 2000 census, 35.2% of households in Ifugao province had access to a community faucet, 11.5% to a faucet of their own, and 8.2% to a shared deep well, while 17.4% obtained their water from springs, lakes, rivers, or rain. Almost half of households (46.3%) disposed of their garbage by burning it, 30.2% by burying it in a pit, and 9.1% by feeding it to their animals; only 6.5% had it picked up by a collection truck. 58.5% of houses were lit with kerosene lamps, 36.8% with electricity, and 3.5% with firewood. While 34% of households lacked basic appliances of any kind, 64% possessed a radio, 15.4% a television, 10% a refrigerator, 5.4% a VCR, 1.5% a telephone or cell phone, 17.4% a washing machine, and 6.3% a motorized vehicle.

¹⁰FAMILY LIFE

An individual's kin-group extends as far as great-great-grandparents and third cousins on both the mother's and father's sides. In theory, marriage within this group is taboo, although second and third cousins can marry after the payment of fines in livestock and the performance of propitiatory sacrifices. The kin-group also assumes collective responsibility for wrongs committed by its members and is obliged to avenge wrongs done to its members.

Rice lands, forestlands, and heirlooms (e.g., jewelry, gongs, Chinese jars) are held by individuals only in "trust"; such property formally belongs to a group of persons who can claim, through either maternal or paternal lines, descent from a common ancestor. Such property can only be sold under extreme circumstances, as when needed to obtain water buffalo to sacrifice for the cure of the gravely ill or the sustenance of the deceased in the afterlife; it can only be sold, however, with the consent of other relevant kinfolk and with the performance of an *ibuy* ceremony. Houses, valuable trees, and crops of sweet potatoes are regarded as personal property whose sale demands no *ibuy* ceremony. Untilled grassland and forests distant from any settlement belong to anyone from the local area who clears and tills them; sweet potato swidden fields revert to the "public domain" after falling fallow.

Showing no preference for residence with or near either the wife's or husband's family, a couple sets up house near the largest concentration of inherited rice fields. In a house dwell the couple and their young children; children old enough to care for themselves live in an *agamang* (same-sex dormitory). Because of the severity of the incest taboo, siblings of the opposite sex deliberately avoid each other, being careful to sleep and even be buried apart, as well as refraining from making sexual jokes in each other's presence.

As marriage is considered to be a union of indefinite duration, a couple may agree to divorce at any time, although this is rare after the birth of the first child. Motives may be bad omens, childlessness, cruelty, desertion, adultery, or change of affection. Upon divorce, if there are no children, partners retain property inherited from their respective kin. If there are children, the property is assigned to the children. In the case of minors, the parent who takes the children, usually the mother, manages the property until the child marries.

Children may receive inheritances, including debt obligations, from either parent. A widow or widower may remarry after paying his or her original parents-in-law a *gibu*, the fine for extramarital relations.

¹¹CLOTHING

Traditional attire for men is the G-string, a loincloth that leaves the side of the thigh bare but hangs down in front. Women wear a short sarong (waist to knees) and formerly went barechested. Men who had yet to avenge the murder of their father let their hair grow long. Tattoos were also common.

Kadangyan (the wealthy) display their status in clothes and accessories restricted to their class: for men, an elaborate G-string, a tasseled hip-bag, kidney-shaped gold earrings, and a headdress consisting of a turban-like cloth, hornbill skull, and water buffalo horns; for women, an elegant skirt, a tasseled belt, golden earrings, four bead necklaces, strings of white and red beads to secure their long hair, and a little brass statuette.

¹²FOOD

Agricultural products provide 84% of the Ifugao diet. Rice and sweet potatoes are the staple foods, although rice is by far the more highly regarded. Ground into meal, maize (grown on the sweet potato swidden fields) is also important. Ifugao consume a wide variety of vegetables and fruits: beans, radishes, cabbage, lettuce, peas, taro, yams, cowpeas, lima beans, okra, greengrams, and other legumes, jackfruit, grapefruit, citrus, coconut, and banana. About 10% of the diet is animal protein from flooded rice fields: tilapia minnows, frogs, snails, and especially *ginga,* a kind of water clam. Sources of meat include domesticated pigs, goats, chickens, and the occasional water buffalo sacrificed in rituals, as well as wild game such as deer, buffalo, pig, civet cat, wild cat, python, iguana, cobra, and bat (only the monkey is hunted for sport alone). People also eat locusts, crickets, and ants.

The heroes of the *Hudhud* epic are often described as staggering, for the ability to withstand heavy intoxication is rare and much admired. Alcohol consumption is integral to feasts and rituals. While only the poor dilute rice wine *(bayah)* with water, the rich *kadangyan* mix bayah with sugarcane juice to make *bahi.* A press extracts the juice from the cane.

¹³EDUCATION

In 2000, literacy stood at 90.5% for the Cordillera Administrative Region, of which Ifugao province is a part. Of the population of Ifugao province over the age of five, 46.2% had attended elementary school, 21.9% high school, and 8.9% college or university (see also the article entitled Filipinos in this volume).

¹⁴CULTURAL HERITAGE

Cordillera peoples play a wide range of instruments: nose-flutes *(kalleleng),* lip-flutes *(paldong),* whistle-flutes *(olimong),* panpipes *(diwas-diwas),* buzzers *(balingbing),* tube zithers *(kolitong),* half-tube percussion *(palangug),* stamping tubes *(tongatong),* and jaws harps *(giwong).* Reflecting the primacy of Chinese over Southeast Asian trade contacts, gongs *(gangsa)* are flat rather than knobbed (strokes, slaps, and slides produce the different tones).

One important male dance is the cockfight dance performed before battle. Other male dances feature the men banging gongs as they move in circles. Female dances emphasize a rigid posture and raising outstretched hands.

¹⁵WORK

Although modern education, administration, commerce, and tourism offer some Ifugao the opportunity for nontraditional occupations, most remain farmers. The wet-rice terraces built by the Ifugao and the neighboring peoples, such as the Bontok, are engineering marvels, climbing 300 m (1,000 ft) up steep mountainsides and held up by walls of earth and stone sometimes as high as 15 m (50 ft). A grouping of adjacent fields forms a *himpuntona'an,* a traditional agricultural district (as many as 25 in a 104-sq-km or 40-sq-mi area) that is named and includes a ritual plot that is the first to be planted and harvested. Several himpuntona'an share a single water-catchment area and cooperate in regulating irrigation and land use.

Rice is the high-prestige staple, and possession of rice fields is the prime measure of status (all the more so since the end of headhunting). When flooded, rice fields also provide animal protein in the form of small minnows, frogs, etc. After the harvest, cotton, beans, radishes, cabbage, lettuce, and peas are grown on the soggy rice stalks.

In addition, Ifugao cultivate sweet potatoes, the low-prestige staple, on hillside swidden fields that also support a wide variety of vegetables as well as sugarcane and tobacco. Tree crops complete the picture: coffee, jackfruit, grapefruit, rattan, citrus, areca, coconut, and banana. Ifugao raise pigs, goats, and chickens, keeping the last in baskets under the house at night; they also import water buffalo from the lowlands to sacrifice

to their ancestors (never to use as draft animals). Hunting and the gathering of wild plants make only a minor contribution to subsistence.

Many men go down into the lowlands to trade. Coffee is the main export while imported goods include livestock, cotton, brass wire, cloth, beads, crude steel, and Chinese jars and gongs. Ifugao trade knives, pots, spears, and salt among themselves. Market gardening is increasing in importance. While in the city of Baguio (50 km [30 mi] southwest of Ifugao territory), lowlanders, including tourists from as far away as Manila, make a point of buying vegetables grown by mountain peoples.

¹⁶SPORTS

See the article entitled **Filipinos.**

¹⁷ENTERTAINMENT AND RECREATION

See the article entitled **Filipinos.**

¹⁸FOLK ART, CRAFTS, AND HOBBIES

The Ifugao practice metallurgy (using the lost-wax process), basketry, weaving, and *ikat* (tie-dyeing). Their woodcarving traditions are noted for *bulol,* cowrie-shell-eyed images of male and female gods in fighting position, weapons ready, or squatting with bowls in their outstretched hands. Other noteworthy products are canes with intricately carved handles, polished dining bowls with side compartments for condiments, chests with handles in the shape of pigs' heads, and shelves with crocodile snouts and tails worked in the design. Today, craftsmen produce objects specifically for tourist tastes (Western, generic Filipino, Chinese, Japanese), e.g. ashtrays and cell phone holders.

¹⁹SOCIAL PROBLEMS

See the article entitled **Filipinos.**

²⁰GENDER ISSUES

In 2000, the literacy level was slightly lower for women (90%) than for men (90.8%) in the Cordillera Administrative Region, of which Ifugao province is a part. In Ifugao province itself, males comprised 55.5% of those attending elementary school but only 51% of the population at large; women, however, were more numerous than men in all levels above high school; 55% of those attending college or university and 64% of academic degree holders were women.

Women's roles in Ifugao society are not conceived of as limited to that of mother; women's labor is understood as complementary to the labor of men (as in the different, but equally essential, tasks each sex takes in rice cultivation); even financially secure elite women work outside the home, and elderly women continue to do farm work, not only out of necessity but also out of love for it. Industriousness in a woman is valued over beauty. At the same time, women are considered the "weaker" sex, whose work is "lighter" than men's work and deserves less pay. In the early 1990s, the wage for a woman's agricultural labor was half that for a man's and thus well below the minimum wage. Women control family finances but feel less free to spend on themselves than do their husbands, who often spend money on drinking sessions with their male friends or on gambling, for which their wives freely criticize them.

Traditional leadership positions are monopolized by elite men. Men are believed to be inherently superior at the oratory believed necessary for leadership, and most high-ranking government officials are men. Women do serve on local community councils but are in the minority. An individual women's status is determined by more than her gender; a female kadangyan or an older woman is perceived as having more power than a man of a lower class and younger age. The influence of Christianity is reinforcing the inferior status accorded to women by traditional culture, and the spread of a cash economy where men have more opportunities to earn wages, or at least to earn higher wages, outside the home is devaluing further the unpaid work women do in the house and on family plots.

21 BIBLIOGRAPHY

Barton, R. F. *Ifugao Law.* 1919. Reprint, Berkeley: University of California Press, 1969.

Gordon, Raymond G., ed. *Ethnologue: Languages of the World,* 15th edition. Dallas, TX: SIL International, 2005. http://www.ethnologue.com/ (November 16, 2008).

LeBar, Frank M., ed. *Ethnic Groups of Insular Southeast Asia.* Vol. 2, *The Philippines and Formosa.* New Haven, CT: Human Relations Area Files Press, 1972.

Kwiatkowski, Lynn M. *Struggling with Development: The Politics of Hunger and Gender in the Philippines.* Boulder, CO: Westview Press, 1998.

Mayuga, Sylvia, and Alfred Yuson. *Philippines.* Hong Kong: APA Productions, 1987.

National Statistics Office: Government of the Philippines. "Cordillera Administrative Region: The Least Populous Region of the Philippines." http://www.census.gov.ph/data/pressrelease/2002/pr0259tx.html (November 16, 2008).

Scott, William Henry. *Barangay: Sixteenth-Century Philippine Culture and Society.* Quezon City, Manila:Ateneo de Manila University Press, 1994.

———. "Class Structure in the Unhispanized Families." In *Cracks in the Parchment Curtain.* Emended ed. Quezon City: New Day, 1985.

———. *The Discovery of the Igorots: Spanish Contacts with the Pagans of the Northern Luzon.* Rev. ed. Quezon City: New Day, 1977.

—revised by A. Abalahin

ILOCANOS

PRONUNCIATION: ee-lo-KAH-nohs
LOCATION: Philippines (northern Luzon)
POPULATION: 6.89 million (2000)
LANGUAGE: Ilocano
RELIGION: Roman Catholicism; Philippine Independent Church; Iglesia ni Kristo (Church of Christ); Protestantism
RELATED ARTICLES: Vol. 3: Filipinos

1 INTRODUCTION

When the Spanish first encountered them in 1572, the inhabitants of Ilocos (then called "Samtoy") were living in large villages at sheltered coves or river mouths and were trading with the Chinese and Japanese. Although massive churches in a distinctive style give evidence of Spanish-Ilocano collaboration, the colonial period was marked by frequent revolts; the most famous of these was that led by Diego and Gabriela Silang during the British occupation of Manila in 1762–63.

Ilocanos were prominent in the nationalist movement, and many have risen to high office in the central government. The greatest of these Ilocano success stories was President Ferdinand Marcos, who ruled for 20 years. During this time, development funds poured into the Ilocos region.

2 LOCATION AND HOMELAND

The three provinces of the Ilocano homeland (Ilocos Norte, Ilocos Sur, and La Union) stretch from Cape Bojeador at the northwestern tip of Luzon down to the Gulf of Lingayen. Most of the population is concentrated along a narrow coastal plain that has only a few good harbors. This environment yields sustenance only with difficulty, forcing Ilocanos to be hard working and thrifty and very often compelling them to seek employment outside from their homeland.

According to the 2000 census, Ilocanos numbered 6.89 million (9% of the national population). Among all Filipino ethnolinguistic groups, the Ilocanos are the most famed as migrants, settling since the 19th century in sparsely populated expanses of the northern Central Plain of Luzon (provinces of Pangasinan, Tarlac, and Nueva Ecija) and of the Cagayan Valley in the northeast. In addition, many Ilocanos have established themselves in Manila and other major cities of the country, as well as in frontier lands on Mindanao. In 2000, Ilocanos were the majority group in the Ilocos region at 66.36%. They were the largest single ethnic group in the Cordillera Administrative Region, 39.83% of the population, twice the largest indigenous group, the Kankanay, and formed 11.48% of the population of Central Luzon, with 40.9% in Tarlac, almost as numerous there as Kapampangan, and 19.3% in Nueva Ecija. In Southern Mindanao, Ilocanos formed 11.48% of the population (as high as 17.7% in Sultan Kudarat).

Working as migrant laborers on sugar plantations in Hawaii and Guam and on farms in California since the first decades of the 20th century, Ilocano males constituted the first major influx of Filipinos into the United States; every Ilocano town has its "*Hawaiianos,*" returned migrants who set up households with wives from their native place whom they have often courted by letter. Out-migration continues, though now women working as domestic servants in Hong Kong, Singapore, and the Gulf States are a significant component as well.

³LANGUAGE

The Ilocanos speak a Western Austronesian language of the Northern Philippine group, whose closest relatives are the languages of neighboring mountain peoples. Ilocano has become the lingua franca of northern Luzon, with as many as 2.3 million second-language speakers, as Ilocano traders have long provided highland peoples with their primary link to the commerce of the outside world.

⁴FOLKLORE

According to one Ilocano origin myth, a giant named Aran built the sky and hung the sun, moon, and stars in it. Under their light, Aran's companion, the giant Angalo, could see the land, which he then molded into mountains and valleys. The giants found the world they had created windswept and desolate. Angalo spat on the earth, and from his spit emerged the first man and woman. He placed them in a bamboo tube that he tossed into the sea. The bamboo washed up on the shore of the Ilocos region, and from this couple came the Ilocano people.

Like other Filipinos, Ilocanos recognize an array of supernatural beings [see **Filipinos**], such as the *katawtaw-an* (the spirits of infants, who died unbaptized and who in turn victimize newborns). The *karkarma*, the souls of living persons, leave the body at death but linger in the house until after the postfunerary offerings of food are made to the deceased; sensed as a scent of perfume, the odor of a burning candle, or a strange draft of wind, they visit relatives who have failed to come to the sickbed of the deceased. The *al-alia*, the spirit doubles of humans, appear at their human doubles' death as the groaning of the dying, the cracking of glass, the rattling of beds, and the banging of doors, or in the form (at night) of a grunting pig, howling dog, or a crowing chicken. These signs remind the living to pray to God for the forgiveness of the deceased's sins (otherwise, the al-alia may visit misfortunes upon them).

⁵RELIGION

See the article entitled **Filipinos**.

⁶MAJOR HOLIDAYS

See the article entitled **Filipinos**.

⁷RITES OF PASSAGE

Although today they are free to choose their own marriage partners, young people seek to secure the approval of both sets of parents. After gaining the consent of his own parents, who are to pay the dowry and finance the wedding, the boy makes a formal announcement *(panagpudno)* to the girl's parents of his and their daughter's intention to marry. The next stage is for the boy's parents to visit the girl's parents in order to set the date for the wedding with the aid of a *planetario,* an almanac identifying auspicious days. At a further meeting *(palalian* or *ringpas),* the boy and his kin come to the girl's house to finalize the wedding arrangements; each party employs a spokesperson who negotiates for his or her side in formal, metaphorical language. The families set the choice of wedding sponsors (an equal number [10–50] for each side), the dowry (land for the

couple, or the money to buy such land), the *sagut* (the wedding dress, jewelry, and accessories, which the groom is to provide for the bride), and the *parawad* (cash that the groom gives the bride's mother as a reward for raising his bride).

The wedding feast (following the church ceremony) includes a ritual where the groom offers the bride a plate of mung beans (symbolizing fertility). The bride refuses the dish several times before finally accepting it. Then the bride offers the beans to the groom who in turn refuses the dish until an old man calls an end to the ritual (the pleadings and feigned refusals greatly amuse the onlookers). Another highlight is the *bitor:* guests contribute cash to the newlyweds either by dropping money onto plates held by two men seated on a mat (representing the bride and groom, respectively) or by pinning bills to the couple's clothing while the two dance (groom's kin on the bride and the bride's kin on the groom). After the wedding, offerings of rice cakes are made to the spirits of departed family members.

To announce a death formally, a piece of wood *(atong)* is lit in front of the deceased's house and kept burning until after burial, at which time it is extinguished with rice wine. The corpse (kept in the house) is dressed in its best clothes and a kerchief is tied around the jaw to prevent the tongue from showing; a basin of water mixed with vinegar is placed under the bed to remove the odor of death. Money is placed in the coffin to pay the "ferry man" who brings the soul to the other world. In the days before burial, relatives keep vigil over the body, wailing and recounting the deceased's good deeds. Sometimes, professional mourners perform the lamentation *(dung-aw)*.

Before the funeral itself, each of the relatives pays their last respects by kissing the deceased's hand or raising it to his or her forehead. Extreme care is taken in bringing the body from the house to the church; any mishap or faux pas could cause premature death. After the church ceremony, the relatives pose as a group for souvenir photos with the coffin. Everyone in the procession to the cemetery must return to the deceased's home by a different route from the one taken there. Upon arrival, they must wash their faces and hands in order to remove the power of death.

See also the article entitled **Filipinos**.

[8] INTERPERSONAL RELATIONS

Ilocanos share the same basic values as other Filipinos [*see* **Filipinos**], such as *bain,* which corresponds to *hiya* or *amor propio* ("face" or "sense of shame"). The fear of gossip and the desire to avoid the envy of others serve as strong pressures for conformity. Before pushing through with his or her own plans, a person feels *alumiim,* the need to figure out how others will react first in order to avoid embarrassment. It is essential to show *panagdayaw,* proper respect for the sensitivities of others; this requires that individuals speak about themselves only in the humblest of terms. Although Ilocanos are group-oriented, they also value a certain individualism *(agwayas):* one should not reveal his or her inner intentions to others, since it is unwise to be too trusting. A person is expected to overcome life's challenges through his or her own hard work, limiting his or her dependence on others to obtaining aid from close kin. However, Ilocanos do form savings associations (including as many as 50 women in a neighborhood), mutual-aid associations (financing members' major celebrations), and labor-exchange arrangements.

Life-passage parties and fiestas provide teenage boys and girls their main opportunity to chat and joke, as girls are confined to work in the house rather than the fields. For a boy to initiate a courtship is a serious matter, as the only proper end is marriage. On his first visit to the house of the girl of his interest, the boy brings one or two companions so that he can get their opinion of the girl later. During the second visit, the companions excuse themselves to allow the boy to confess his feelings to the girl (afterwards, he visits her alone). Love notes are also an important means of courtship. A girl is careful to preserve her chastity in case the courtship does not end in marriage.

[9] LIVING CONDITIONS

Raised 0.6 m to 1 m (2–3 ft) off the ground, houses have beams of wood, walls of bamboo, and roofs of rice straw or cogon grass. Sometimes, newly married children may live in roofed extensions. On the *bangsal,* a landing on the staircase, guests wait before being admitted and wash or wipe their feet before entering the receiving room. Curtains or bamboo partitions separate the living room from the bedroom areas (most have beds but prefer sleeping mats). A separate storage room also serves for a place to change clothes. In traditional dwellings, outhouses provide toilet facilities.

Average family income in the Ilocos region was 142,000 pesos (US$2,784), while that in the Cagayan valley, the other region with an Ilocano majority, was ₱143,000 (US$2,804). These ranked respectively eighth highest in the country out of 17 regions and sixth (tied with Northern Mindanao), cf. the national average of ₱173,000, the National Capital Region's ₱311,000, Southern Tagalog's ₱198,000, and SOCCSKARGEN's (Southern Mindanao)s ₱114,000. In 2000, Ilocos Norte province in the Ilocos region and Isabela province in the Cagayan Valley had Human Development Indices (combining measures of health, education, and income) that were among the top ten in the country. Ilocos Norte ranked seventh at 0.689, higher than the national HDI of 0.656, and Isabela ranked tenth, slightly lower.

According to the 2000 census, in Ilocos Norte province (Ilocos Sur and La Union provinces have similar statistics), the proportion of houses with a roof of galvanized iron/aluminum reached 86.3% and with a roof of grass or palm thatch 10.12% (cf. 76.3% and 20.6% respectively in 1990). Over half of houses (52%, up from 27.1% in 1990) had outer walls entirely of concrete, brick, or stone, 22.9% of houses had outer walls that were half wood and half concrete, brick, or stone, 7.3% of houses had wooden outer walls, and 15.3% outer walls of bamboo or thatch.

In 2000, 8.9% of households in the Ilocos region had access to a community faucet, 16.8% to a faucet of their own, 25.7% to a shared deep well, and 23.3% to a household deep well, while 2.3% obtained their water from springs, lakes, rivers, or rain. A third of households (66.4%) disposed of their garbage by burning it, 12.5% by dumping it in a household pit, and 4.9% by composting it; only 11% had it picked up by a collection truck. 17.1% of houses were lit with kerosene lamps, 79.3% with electricity, and 2.5% with firewood. Four out of five households (79.9%) possessed a radio, over three out of five (62.3%) a television, over one out of three (34.4%) a refrigerator, one out of five (20.4%) a VCR, nearly one out of seven (13.9%) a telephone or cell phone, and one out of six a washing machine (16.5%) and a motorized vehicle (16.9%).

[10] FAMILY LIFE

The structure of the Ilocano family conforms to the general Filipino pattern [*see* **Filipinos**]. The father is the formal head of family, backing up the mother who disciplines the children and manages the house finances. The eldest child divides the chores equally among siblings. Grandparents tend to be more indulgent of grandchildren than the parents themselves.

[11] CLOTHING

Dress inappropriate for one's age or perceived wealth or status attracts gossip: "mabiag ti ruar ngem matay ti uneg" ("outwardly alive, but inwardly dying"); "uray napintas no inutang" ("even if it is nice, it is acquired through credit"). Still, one should dress well for special celebrations. Everyday wear, especially at home, consists of short pants for boys, and dusters, loose skirts, shirts, and short pants for girls. Those working in the fields wear long-sleeved shirts, long pants, and a wide-brimmed hat as protection against the sun and mud.

During the rainy season, people wear a headdress of labig leaves extending well down the back. Older women wear their hair long and knotted in a bun, while men keep it short and apply pomade on special occasions.

See also the article entitled **Filipinos**.

[12] FOOD

Ilocano food essentially resembles that elsewhere in the country [see **Filipinos**], but Ilocanos are especially fond of bagoong (a salty shrimp or fish paste). One regional specialty that has entered national cuisine is pinakbet, which is eggplant, bitter melon, okra, and green beans cooked with bagoong, tomatoes, and a little water (dried or broiled fish, meat, or shrimps can be added to enhance taste).

Other favorites are dinardaraan (cooked pig's blood, called dinuguan in Tagalog-Pilipino) and kilawen (the lean meat and intestines of water buffalo, cow, sheep, or goat, eaten raw or partially cooked with a sauce of vinegar, salt, hot pepper, and pig's bile).

Eating with their hands, family members squat around the food laid out on the floor or take food and eat in different parts of the main room. As food is regarded as a symbol of God's grace, there should be no noise, laughing, singing, or harsh words (including parents scolding children) while eating is going on. One should not drop food on the table or floor, or the food "will be angered and leave the household." Similarly, no one should leave the house while someone is still eating, for God's grace will go with him or her, out of the home.

[13] EDUCATION

In the Ilocos region, the literacy level was 95.23% in 2000, higher than the national figure; in the Cagayan Valley, it was 91.75%. See the article entitled **Filipinos**.

[14] CULTURAL HERITAGE

The Ilocanos have an epic, the Biag ni Lam-ang ("The Life of Lam-ang"), which, however, exists only in the form of a highly Hispanicized metrical romance composed in the 19th century. Ilocos is also the only place in the country where the zarzuela (operetta) is still performed.

See also the article entitled **Filipinos**.

[15] WORK

Almost all farmers (the major occupation) own the land they till, except for those who are tenants of owners who are urban professionals. The staple crop is rice, though poorer people must mix cheaper maize with their rice. Root crops are also grown both as a supplement to the diet and for sale. Watered by wet-season rains or irrigation, wet-rice fields range from small plots that can only be worked with a hoe or dibble stick to those large enough for a water-buffalo–drawn plow; dry-rice agriculture is also practiced in the hilly areas between the flatlands. Crops grown for market include tobacco, garlic (both Ilocos specialties), onions, and vegetables. Petty traders may travel as far as Manila to sell such products.

Farmers fish during the lull between planting and harvesting, usually in close offshore waters, rivers, or fishponds. An important part of the catch are ipon, small fish for bagoong (fish paste).

Cottage industries include salt making, basi-making (alcohol from molasses), pottery making (20 different types are produced in San Nicolas), weaving, basket- and mat-weaving, woodworking, and silversmithing.

[16] SPORTS

One uniquely Ilocano game is kukudisi. A stick (the an-anak) is placed on a baseline scratched into the ground. One player makes the stick jump in the air; the other player tries to catch it before it hits the ground. If the latter cannot do so, a second, longer stick (the in-ina) is laid across the baseline; the player then tries to hit it with the an-anak. The next two phases of the game involve competing to see who can hit the an-anak (which has been tossed in the air and stuck into the baseline, respectively) with the in-ina the furthest.

[17] ENTERTAINMENT AND RECREATION

Children enjoy such games as balay-balay (playing house), hide-and-seek, team-tag, jumping "hurdles" (sticks or outstretched arms or legs), and jacks.

See also the article entitled **Filipinos**.

[18] FOLK ART, CRAFTS, HOBBIES

See the article entitled **Filipinos**.

[19] SOCIAL PROBLEMS

See the article entitled **Filipinos**.

[20] GENDER ISSUES

According to the 2000 census, in the Ilocos region, the ratio of men to women was 100.76; in the Cagayan Valley, the ratio was 104.98 (possibly reflecting the latter area being one of in-migration that has been more male than female). In Ilocos, overall literacy rates were nearly as high for women (95.04%) as for men (95.41%). In a major change from the pattern from the beginning of the 20th century until the 1980s of male sojourning abroad for work, the majority of overseas workers from Ilocos in 2000 were women (61.75%); in the age bracket 20-24, 71.8% were women. Women, including female migrants from Ilocos, also heavily predominate in the work force of multinational corporations' factories in export-processing zones in other regions of the Philippines itself. With drops in the prices of the region's cash crops such as garlic and tobacco and in the demand for construction workers in the Gulf States and the continuing failure of the Philippine economy to generate sufficient urban jobs, unemployment among young men has been high in recent decades: many joke about becoming mail-order "house husbands" for Filipinas in the United States.

There is no cultural preference for having boys instead of girls. Indeed, families prefer girls because one can marry them off to other families, thereby expanding their networks of influence and assistance, without incurring the burden of paying the "male dowry" (sab-ong) for sons. Traditional Ilocano ideals of manly and womanly behavior do not entirely fit stereotypes of machismo/hyper masculinity and femininity seen in many other societies. In courtship, women appraise men's physical characteristics as freely and frankly as women do men's. Women are thought of as no less vulnerable to the seductions of male beauty and charm as men are to women's. For Ilocanos, ideal manliness includes the possession of verbal grace, used to woo a potential bride or displayed to keep an appearance of good humor when provoked in public. Young boys, who are competitive with each other, are not allowed to act aggressively towards girls. Masculinity is defined by emotional availability, rather than distance and coldness, even towards other men. It is common for groups of unmarried men in their twenties and thirties to sleep together without this thought of as homoerotic. Women share in agricultural chores, and men in household chores, including sweeping, cooking, and childcare. Women's entrepreneurship, to which women are trained from when they are little girls playing managerial games, contributes indispensably to most households, and some families are even supported primarily by the wife/mother's earnings with the husband/father staying at home to performing most of the domestic tasks.

²¹ BIBLIOGRAPHY

Gordon, Raymond G., ed. *Ethnologue: Languages of the World,* 15th edition. Dallas, TX: SIL International, 2005. http://www.ethnologue.com/ (November 16, 2008).

Jocano, F. Landa. *The Ilocanos: An Ethnography of Family and Community in the Ilocos Region.* Quezon City: Asian Center, University of Philippines, 1982.

LeBar, Frank M., ed. *Ethnic Groups of Insular Southeast Asia.* Vol. 2, *The Philippines and Formosa.* New Haven, CT: Human Relations Area Files Press, 1972.

Margold, Jane A. "Narratives of Masculinity and Transnational Migration: Filipino Workers in the Middle East." In *Bewitching Women, Pious Men: Gender and Politics in Southeast Asia,* edited by Aihwa Ong and Michael G. Peletz. Berkeley, CA: University of California Press, 1995.

National Statistics Office: Government of the Philippines. http://www.census.gov.ph (November 16, 2008).

—revised by A. J. Abalahin

ILONGOT

PRONUNCIATION: ee-LAWN-goht
ALTERNATE NAMES: Bugkalut
LOCATION: Philippines (northern Luzon)
POPULATION: 50,786 (1990)
LANGUAGE: Ilongot
RELIGION: Native beliefs; Protestantism
RELATED ARTICLES: Vol. 3: Filipinos; Kalinga; Ifugao

¹INTRODUCTION

Although sharing certain affinities with the swidden-farming (shifting-cultivation) Northern group of Cordillera peoples [see **Kalinga** and **Ifugao**], the Ilongot stand apart even from them in their extreme egalitarianism and relative cultural simplicity (in some ways comparable to the Dumagat Negritos with whom some of them have mixed). The question remains whether the culture of the "Bugkalut" (as they call themselves; the lowlander name "Ilongot" comes from *'irungut,* "forest people") is actually a largely unchanged survival of ancient north Luzon, culture or rather a version of a more complex culture pared down to the essentials in the process of the people's self-isolation.

Although Spanish soldiers and missionaries had penetrated the upper Cagayan valley by the beginning of the 17th century, they had little impact on the Ilongot whose reputation as a fierce, wild, and unsubjugated people endured well into the American period and the Japanese occupation, when a third of the group are said to have perished in fighting the new invaders. The Ilongot even avoided the trade relations with lowlanders that other independent tribes deemed indispensable.

The latter relationship is very concisely reflected in an Ilongot creation myth recorded by Laurence Wilson in the 1940s. According to this myth, the creators and guardians of all things are two quarreling brothers, Caín and Abál (the biblical Cain and Abel in Spanish). Caín is the ancestor of the Ilongot, who like him are killers and headhunters. Abál, on the other hand, is the ancestor of the lowlanders, who have inherited his mastery of water buffalo and other domesticated animals. In the Ilongot telling, Abál is the stronger of the two brothers, which explains the superior power of the lowlanders.

The arrival in recent decades of the lumbering industry and the airstrips of the New Tribes Mission (Protestant) have ended Ilongot isolation. In any case, farmers of Christian ethnic groups are encroaching inexorably upon Ilongot territory. Violent confrontations between Ilongot and settlers have been frequent and even reached the notice of the national press in the 1960s. In Nueva Vizcaya province, the Ilongot now comprise a tiny proportion of the population, less than one half of one percent in 2000 if one counts only those self-identifying as Bugkalut; though that year's census' category of "Other," largely composed of groups indigenous to the province itself, amounted to 8.2%.

²LOCATION AND HOMELAND

The Ilongot (numbering 50,786 in 1990) inhabit an 840-sq-km (325-sq-mi) area of rolling hills 0.3 m to 900 m (1–3,000 ft) above sea level in southern Nueva Vizcaya province at the point where the Cordillera Central through the Caraballo

Range connects to the Sierra Madre running down Luzon's east coast; these lands are drained by the headwaters of the Cagayan. A group of modernized Ilongot live along Baler Bay. Christian Gaddang, Isinai, Tagalog, and Ilocanos have settled the surrounding lowlands.

1970s figures estimated the number of Ilongot at around 2,500. According to the 2000 census, 1,180 inhabitants of Nueva Vizcaya province identified themselves as Bugkalut (i.e. as Ilongot). Another 2000 estimate counted 50,786 Ilongot (the discrepancy among the figures may be attributed to different criteria for defining an Ilongot—almost 30,000 people in Nueva Vizcaya province and over 14,000 in Quezon province were classified as "Other" [indigenous ethnicity] and not as Tagalogs, Ilocanos, Ifugao, Ibaloi, Ayangan, or Bugkalut, suggesting that people who might be classified as Ilongot did not identify themselves as Bugkalut).

³LANGUAGE

By linguists' estimates, the Ilongot language has developed separately from other Philippine languages for over 3,000 years (in comparison, Bontok and Ifugao were a single tongue only 1,000 years ago). Among its peculiarities is its numeral system that counts thus: numbers one through five are each expressed by distinct words, but six through nine are expressed as "five and one," etc. Higher numbers are composed along similar lines: 49, for example, is "fifty and five and four," 60 is "fifty and ten."

⁴FOLKLORE

Folktales (*dimolat*) are the principal entertainment of the Ilongot, either in a short form told by individuals taking a short rest together or otherwise meeting each other by chance, or in a long form reserved to pass long evenings or periods of torrential rains. The long form involves an old woman or man with a wealth of lore at her or his disposal singing tales that freely mix supernatural, human, and animal characters and highlight practical jokes. The storytellers embroider the basic plot with repetitions and minor happenings (often for comic relief) and draw out final syllables or add meaningless words to conform to the fixed melody; listeners enjoy the style of presentation rather than the mere content.

⁵RELIGION

Ilongot recognize a range of supernatural beings including a creator-overseer deity associated with the sun, as well as ancestral spirits. They are most concerned, however, with nature spirits and illness-giving spirits. The most powerful and feared is 'Agimeng, the "companion of the forest," guardian of hunting and headhunting but also a giver of disease; his female counterpart holds dominion over cultivated fields. Usually associated with geographical features, disease-giving spirits are identified with typical symptoms and the plants that cure them, and, as familiars, may develop an association with particular individuals.

While dreams may lead a person to health or hunting charms, visions and illness itself introduce many people to such spiritual familiars. Only a few such people become shamans qualified to perform diagnostic and curing rites, preside over special chants, and summon the souls of future headhunting victims. Those cured by a shaman can share in the power of the spiritual familiar and thus can conduct minor

rituals themselves. Other supernatural skills that individuals may possess are sucking out disease and using a bow to tell the future.

Disease usually arises from spirits licking or urinating on a victim, although harm may also come from deceased ancestors who long for the company of the living, or from guardian spirits of field and forest who feel abused by humans in some way. Healing rites first invoke the spirits and then expel them by manipulating plants (of which 700 kinds are in use); they may also entail threatening the spirits, blowing them away, steaming them out, bathing to wash them out, beating them out, or drinking to purge them out. One can also burn or beat a contagious plant in order to eliminate the symptom. Rites may also turn a sickness back on the spirit that had caused it.

Since the 1950s, Protestant missionaries have been making conversions among the Ilongot.

⁶MAJOR HOLIDAYS

Harvest rituals are the only regular communal rites. Others include occasional headhunting and peacemaking rites.

⁷RITES OF PASSAGE

A first ear-piercing takes place for girls when they are babies and for boys before their teens. At age 15, boys and girls may choose to have their teeth filed and blackened; one has this done only to beautify oneself, although feasting and oath-taking accompany the operation. As headhunters, all young men should succeed in taking a head, preferably before marrying.

Adolescents of the opposite sex may exchange betel and sleep together before being recognized as couples. An informal association involving casual field help (from the male), gifts, and sex is the prelude to formal wedding negotiations. A pregnancy generates tensions between the families, leading to both gift-giving and threats of violence, which are usually only resolved through marriage.

The *langu* or bride-price is meant to quell the anger of the woman's kinfolk and may include payments to members of distant *behrtan* that can claim a connection to her. The negotiation of langu and the protracted period of paying it gives kinfolk a chance to air grievances and settle them by mollifying the aggrieved parties with langu goods. Beginning with a *pu'rut,* an initial (often hostile) confrontation between the man's and the woman's parties, langu installments include guns, bullets, metal pots, cloth, jewelry, and knives. At a series of *pi'yat* meetings, the man's side presents meat and goods to the in-laws and finally "buys the woman." The woman's side then returns this by an *'arakad,* bringing pounded rice and liquor to the man's kin.

Each person possesses a spirit that roams away from the body during sleep and survives death as an entity dangerous to the living. Funerary rites aim to banish the deceased's spirit through ritual sweeping, smoking, bathing, and invocation.

The corpse is wrapped in bark or put in a box to be buried near the home in a sitting position or curled on its right side; valuable goods are hung on a post at the foot of the grave. The corpses of young children are enshrouded in bark and placed high in trees, for proximity to the earth is thought to be painful and perilous for them.

⁸INTERPERSONAL RELATIONS

Ilongot society has been described as an ordered anarchy where all persons are equal and recognize no authority figures. In practice, leadership in a community tends to come from a set of brothers who are skilled in oratory (*purung*) and possess knowledge of genealogy and customary law. There is no organization encompassing more than an individual community, although several settlements may recognize a common *behrtan* (local community) allegiance; in all, there are 13 such behrtan, each with its own name and dialect.

As Ilongot society has no hierarchy in which superiors command the obedience of inferiors, each man must rely on his personal eloquence to persuade his fellows to follow a course of action that he desires. At public gatherings, a man attempts to move those present toward a consensus, one to which they may individually already be inclined, as he finds out in prior discussions with each one; consensus is essential since no sanctions can be applied to compel anyone to do anything. Such discussions are exclusively a male affair, as women claim not to understand purung, much less to be capable of it.

The settling of disputes or grievances involves the exchange of betel, swearing by salt, and animal sacrifices. The victim of petty theft may demand that the accused submit to trial by ordeal.

In conferences between settlements (such as for peacemaking), those most adept at purung in one settlement pit themselves against their counterparts in the other. Bride-price negotiations provide an occasion for parties to demand redress of past grievances or recompense for contributing to previous bride-prices.

Among the Ilongot, every male is expected to headhunt, preferably before marrying, and most contemporary men have done so. Unlike in other headhunting cultures, the Ilongot do not take heads as magic to increase the fertility of the soil, to gain personal spiritual potency, to gain social distinction, nor exclusively to pursue a vendetta. A man takes heads in order to "relieve his heart" from an anxiety, the source of which may be a death in his own household or an unsettled feud. Often, a man makes a *binatan,* an oath of personal sacrifice, e.g., not to eat rice from the granary or to avoid sex until taking a head. Taking a head gives a young man the right to wear prestigious cowrie shells, feathers, and red hornbill ornaments. The act does significantly raise the young man's status, but as all males have experienced it, this merely maintains the egalitarianism of society as a whole.

Men may headhunt solo or in raiding parties of up to 40 individuals. Prior to setting out, the men gather in front of a house, and a shaman summons the souls of the victims into a bamboo receptacle. In the forest, the men listen for bird omens and may play the death-associated violin or reed flute. Distinctions to be sought include being the first to strike or shoot, to reach a felled body, to cut a head, and/or to fling the head away. The heads are not kept as in cultures where the skulls would be preserved as a status symbol or source of spiritual power, although the men may bring victims' hands back for the children to chop up. The return of the headhunters to the settlement is celebrated with singing, dancing, and slaughtering a pig.

Peace between warring parties is achieved through a series of debates and exchanges, after which members of the two groups may visit each other, enter into marriage with each other, or even go on joint raids on other groups. However, if no intermarriage takes place, hostilities resume within two generations.

⁹LIVING CONDITIONS

A settlement consists of four to nine households (five to nine nuclear families, totaling 40 to 70 persons). Initially, the houses are rarely adjacent but always within calling distance of each other. Over time, as each household abandons old fields and opens new ones, the houses relocate nearer the new fields, until the settlement becomes more and more dispersed (by the same token, as long-fallow fields are reclaimed, the houses may approach each other again). The only instance of concentrated settlements is the clusters of houses near the New Tribes Mission's airstrips.

A house *(kamari)* has a square floor plan, is raised 2 m to 5 m (6–15 ft) off the ground, and has walls of woven grass or bamboo and a pyramidal or single-ridged roof. An unpartitioned central space is edged by a slightly raised wooden platform where the hearths are located (up to three hearths, one for each resident nuclear family). The Ilongot also build smaller, temporary field houses *('abun).*

Nueva Vizcaya province is poor compared to other provinces of the Cagayan Valley region, itself tied with Northern Mindanao for sixth highest in average annual family income. According to the 2000 census, 50.8% of houses were lit with electricity, compared to 70% in neighboring Isabela province. 15.3% of households obtained water from springs, lakes, or rivers, compared to 1.9% in Isabela.

¹⁰FAMILY LIFE

Marriage between second cousins is the preferred pattern. As it is usual for a particular set of brothers to offer leadership in a community, marrying that set of brothers with a set of sisters (also their close cousins) is also common.

Peculiarities of Ilongot kinship terminology include a single term covering grandparents, parents-in-law, and children-in-law *('apu)* and a single term for a sibling's spouse and a spouse's sibling *('aum).* One must not refer to one's 'aum by name and must treat her or him with particular respect. Although sex with one's 'aum is forbidden, a surviving spouse often weds a sibling of the deceased spouse.

One to three nuclear families live under a single roof, each with its own hearth and sleeping area. These nuclear families tend to consist of the parents' family and the families of the youngest married daughters. Sons leave home when they marry, but daughters stay in the parental home, leaving only when younger daughters marry and bring in their husbands. A married couple can only return to the man's birth community when he has paid up the bride-price.

In situations such as attempting to make persuasive arguments in public debates (e.g., bride-price negotiations), an individual finds it useful to claim affiliation with one or more *behrtan.* At its simplest, the *behrtan* is a grouping of several settlements that has a collective name, usually referring to a landmark, a plant, a color, or a place, and its own dialect; it is the local group within which one tends to marry and upon whose members revenge (head-taking) can be taken for the crime of one of its members. An individual inherits the right to claim connection to a behrtan from either parent and may claim as many as four such connections (via the four grandparents). A woman prefers to take her mother's behrtan, while a man prefers not only to take his father's behrtan but also to pass it on to his children, which is only possible after he has paid up the bride-price. The behrtan, it should be stressed, is not a corporate group of any kind; very often it is merely a way of defining an interest group of the moment (such as the two parties in bride-price negotiations), and a stranger entering a discussion and asserting solidarity with one of the parties may claim a behrtan connection that no genealogy grants him or her.

¹¹CLOTHING

Traditional Ilongot clothing consists of lengths of bark pounded to the consistency of soft leather. Men wear a length of cloth passed between the legs and secured with a belt of rattan or brass wire. Women wear a short sarong (waist to knees) along with earrings, bead necklaces, and brass wire spiraling over the arms. Children go naked.

¹²FOOD

The staple food is rice eaten with vegetables (root crops are a secondary source of starch). Wild plants, such as fruits, ferns, and hearts of palm, are also gathered for food.

For animal protein, Ilongot eat wild pigs, deer, and fish but do not eat the meat of the pigs and chickens that they raise for sale to lowlanders; domestic animals are said to eat excrement and thus should not be consumed. Essential to hunting, dogs live inside the house and are never eaten.

While eating with the hands from flat lengths of leaf is found widely in Southeast Asia, the Ilongot also fashion disposable cups for vegetable broth from the *anahao* leaf.

Ilongot make *basi,* alcohol from sugarcane, and the men often get together to have drinking sessions.

¹³EDUCATION

The Ilongot isolation has meant that modern education has not reached them as it has most other Filipinos, lowlanders, and highlanders, Christian and non-Christian alike, although Protestant missions are offering some Ilongot exposure to it.

¹⁴CULTURAL HERITAGE

Musical instruments include the bamboo flute, brass gongs, a bamboo-tube zither, and a kind of violin with a body of bark and animal skin and strings of women's hair. Young men play such instruments while courting young women. Gatherings feature singing with alternating groups (antiphonal) and dances of which there are many kinds, e.g., female group dances, a male solo, or men dancing while beating hand-held gongs.

¹⁵WORK

Ilongot cultivate dry-rice, maize, and cassava side by side on swidden fields. After the harvest, they plant such fields with tobacco and vegetables. When the field is about to be abandoned, it is given over to sweet potatoes, bananas, and sugarcane. A given field may be worked from one to five years, depending on its fertility. When its fertility is exhausted, the farmer moves on to clear another plot out of the forest, going as far as 32 km (20 mi) away and returning to the first spot only after 8 to 10 fallow years. Land belongs to the individual who clears it for use and may be reopened and cultivated by anyone else at a later date. In general having little inherited property, Ilongot do not bequeath agricultural lands. Because of low population density in their territory, wild land is always available. Gathering forest plants also contributes to the diet.

Twice a week, groups of men hunt game with dogs, dividing the meat equally among the householders. The meat obtained in three- to five-day hunting expeditions without dogs is the personal property of the hunter and is dried in strips to be sold or traded. Fishing ranges from individuals using nets, traps, and spears to groups of up to 250 men cooperating to catch fish by damming streams or employing poisons. The catch is divided equally.

The Ilongot trade baskets and metalwork among themselves, but most such wares circulate as part of bride-prices or inter-kin gifts. Ilongot barter dried meat, captured fawns, pigs, and chickens for bullets, liquor, cloth, salt, and knives from lowlanders. To conduct these exchanges, Ilocano or Tagalog traders come to the borders of Ilongot territory, and Ilongot go down to the lowland towns.

¹⁶SPORTS

While girls play with rag dolls, boys enjoy shooting contests with miniature bows and arrows made by their father for them when they reach the age of four. Boys also like to climb trees and play tag in them.

Adult Ilongot are known to use a 12-m (40-ft) length of rattan with a hook at one end and a loop at the other to move through the trees. Clinging to one tree, they cast this flexible "rope" to catch on to another tree. In this way, Ilongot can travel through dense forest very rapidly. This, however, is not a sport so much as an efficient way of working (as when a man wants to cut branches from trees that will later be felled to open a field).

¹⁷ENTERTAINMENT AND RECREATION

Ilongot entertain themselves primarily by telling folktales.

¹⁸FOLK ART, CRAFTS, AND HOBBIES

Among the Ilongot, there are no specializations: each man forges his own knives, hoes, and picks and weaves his own rattan baskets; each woman weaves and sews clothing for her own family.

¹⁹SOCIAL PROBLEMS

The increasing invasion of Ilongot territory by other ethnic groups sparks violent confrontations between the Ilongot and the new settlers. This violence is bound to continue for some time to come.

²⁰GENDER ISSUES

Discussions that seek to build consensus on a common course of action are regarded as exclusively a male affair, since women claim not to understand, much less be capable of, the purung (oratory) necessary to persuade other.

According to the 2000 census, among the Ilongot self-identifying as Bugkalut, men slightly (51.7%) outnumbered women. In the Nueva Vizcaya population as a whole, more women had a college undergraduate education or higher and received more academic degrees than men by a substantial margin; elementary school completion, a measure likely more relevant to the Bugkalut, was lower for girls than for boys (53.3% of elementary school graduates were male while only 51% of the population was male). Women tend to invoke connections with their mother's behrtan, men with their father's (see "Interpersonal Relationships").

²¹BIBLIOGRAPHY

Gordon, Raymond G., Jr. (ed.). *Ethnologue: Languages of the World,* 15th ed. Dallas: Texas: SIL International, 2005. http://www.ethnologue.com (November 21, 2008).

LeBar, Frank M., ed. *Ethnic Groups of Insular Southeast Asia.* Vol 2, *The Philippines and Formosa.* New Haven, CT: Human Relations Area Files Press, 1972.

National Statistics Office: Republic of the Philippines. "Cagayan Valley: Nive in Ten Houses Amortized/Mortgaged Their Housing Units. http://www.census.gov.ph/data/pressrelease/2002/pr02192tx.html (November 23, 2008).

_____. "Nueva Vizcaya: Annual Growth Rate at 1.67 Percent." http://www.census.gov.ph/data/pressrelease/2002/pr0233tx.html (November 23, 2008)

Rosaldo, Michelle. *Knowledge and Passion: Ilongot Notions of Self and Social Life.* Cambridge, UK: Cambridge University Press, 1980.

Rosaldo, Renato. *Ilongot headhunting, 1883–1974: A Study in Society and History.* Stanford, CA: Stanford University Press, 1980.

Wilson, Laurence L. *Ilongot Life and Legends.* Baguio, Philippines: Southeast Asia Institute, 1947.

—revised by A. Abalahin

PEOPLE OF INDIA

PRONUNCIATION: IN-dee-uhns
ALTERNATE NAMES: Indians
LOCATION: India
POPULATION: About 1.32 billion (2007 est.)
LANGUAGE: Hindi (majority official language); English (co-official language); the Eighth Schedule of the Constitution of India, modified by several constitution amendments the most recent of which was in 2003, lists 22 official languages, namely Assamese, Bengali, Bodo, Dogri, Gujarati, Hindi, Kannada, Kashmiri, Konkani, Maithili, cMaithilm, Manipuri, Marathi, Nepali, Oriya, Punjabi, Sanskrit, Santhali, Sindhi, Tamil, Telugu, and Urdu. In addition, states can have their own official languages that are not necessarily listed in the Constitution. Several states have adopted official languages that are not so listed, including Kokborok in Tripura, Mizo in Mizoram, Khasi, Garo, and Jaintia in Meghalaya, and French in Pondicherry.
RELIGION: Hinduism (80.5%); Islam (13.4%); Christianity (2.3%); Sikhism (1.9%); Buddhism (0.1.5%); Jainism (0.5%); some Jews, Parsis (Zoroastrians), and animistic tribal peoples
RELATED ARTICLES: Vol. 2: Asian Indian Americans; Hindus in Guyana. Vol. 3: Ahir; Andras; Anglo-Indian; Brahmans; Chamar; Gonds; Goanese; Gujar; Jain; Jat; Khasi; Koli; Vol. 4: Lingayat; Maratha/Kunbi; Minas; Mundas; Nagas; Punjabi; Rajput; Santals; Sikh; Syrian Christians; Tamils; Todas; Veddas.

¹ INTRODUCTION

Indians are citizens of the Republic of India, the largest country in South Asia. In the past, however, the name was used for inhabitants of the entire Indian subcontinent. The word "Indian" comes from *Sindhu,* the local name for the Indus River (now in Pakistan). The Persians called the river *Hindu,* which passed to the Greeks as *Indos.* "India" was thus the region of the Indos, and "Indian" came to describe the peoples of the area. The words *Hindu* and *Hinduism* are also derived from this source. The ancient Indians called their land *Bharat* or *Bharatavarsa* ("Land of the sons of Bharata," a legendary emperor). Bharat is now the official Hindi name of modern India.

The peoples of India have a long and complex history that extends over 5,000 years. They are successors to the advanced urban civilization that flourished along the Indus Valley during the 3rd millennium BC. This Harappan civilization disappeared in the years following 1700 BC when nomadic tribes from Central Asia settled in northwestern India. These groups, referred to (somewhat loosely) as the Aryans, evolved religious, social, and economic structures that give Hindu civilization its distinctive character.

The subsequent history of India is one of waves of invaders sweeping through the northwestern mountains onto the Indo-Gangetic plains. The Persians, Greeks, Parthians, Kushans, and White Huns were some of the groups that left their imprint on the region. At times, powerful Indian states such as the Mauryan (321–181 BC) and Gupta (AD 319–c. 500) empires stemmed the flow of invaders. When they weakened, however,

their frontiers again came under threat from the northwest. It was through these same mountains that Muslim conquerors entered India at the beginning of the 11th century AD. The earliest of these incursions were merely raids led by Mahmoud of Gazni, a Turkish leader who invaded India no less than 17 times, to pillage the wealth of the Indian plains, but under Mahmoud of Ghuri, the Muslims sought to establish themselves in India. Resisted at first by the Chauhan Rajputs who controlled the northwestern India, the Ghurids eventually defeated Prithviraj Chauhan at the 2nd Battle of Tarain in 1192 and captured Delhi. For almost eight centuries from this date, Muslims ruled in north India, with their capital in Delhi. Invasions of various peoples continued through the northwest passes until 1526, when Babur captured Delhi from the Lodis and founded the Mughal dynasty. Although they were based in Delhi, the Mughals made Agra their capital from 1526 to 1685 with nearby Fatehpur Sikri, later abandoned largely because of lack of water, being Akbar's capital from 1571 to 1585. Mughals reigned in northern India until the last Mughal emperor, Bahadur Shah II, was deposed in 1857 by the British and sent into exile in Burma (Myanmar). Under the Mughals, and particularly Akbar (reigned 1556–1605), Islam made important contributions to South Asian civilization. The Taj Mahal in Agra, perhaps the finest architectural achievement of the Muslims in India and named a World Heritage Site in 1982, was completed by the Mughal Emperor Shah Jahan in 1648. India achieved an imperial greatness under Mughal rule virtually unmatched in the country's history.

The Europeans reached South Asia by sea in 1498 when the Portuguese landed at Calicut on the southwest coast of India. Their prime motivation was trade, and within the next two centuries the maritime nations of Europe (Portugal, Holland, Britain, and France) had established trading posts or "factories" on India's coasts. By the middle of the 18th century, the British East India Company had gained the upper hand over the French in India, but French (Pondicherry) and Portuguese (Goa, Daman & Diu) colonies survived on the subcontinent until the mid-20th century. Britain ultimately gained control of the entire region, either by directly administering Indian territory or by being recognized by independent native rulers as the paramount power in the region.

The political map of the Indian subcontinent, and many of its problems, originates in the country's colonial past. The inability of the British, Hindu, and Muslim leaders to reach agreement on the nature of the successor state to the British Indian Empire resulted in the partition of the subcontinent into the separate nations of India and Pakistan in 1947. A direct consequence of this has been several wars between the two countries and the ongoing problem of Kashmir. The princely states of India, of which there were several hundred in 1947, were to decide at Partition to which country they would accede. Most Hindu states joined India and Muslim states joined Pakistan. But, while the population of Kashmir was primarily Muslim, its ruler was a Hindu Rajput. The Maharaja of Kashmir, one of the largest and most powerful of the Indian princely states, wished to remain independent and delayed signing the instrument of accession as long as possible. In October 1947, however, the newly constituted nation of Pakistan sent irregular Pathan tribesmen into Kashmiri territory, at which the Maharaja appealed to Lord Louis Mountbatten for help. The Governor-General of India agreed to provide help if Kashing abductions, massacres, rape, and looting. In 1999 Pakistani troops and Kashmiri militants infiltrated across the Line of Control in Kargil, resulting in conflict between India and Pakistan. U.S. diplomacy, and perhaps the threat of Pakistan's nuclear weapons, kept the conflict from expanding beyond Kargil.

A similar situation developed in central India in 1947. Hyderabad was an important Muslim state in central India and its ruler, the Nizam, wanted to either remain independent or to join Pakistan, neither of which the new Indian government could allow. In 1948, India sent its military into Hyderabad and integrated the state into the Republic of India.

Regular Indian and Pakistani troops fought wars in 1947–48, 1965, 1971 (when Bangladesh was created from East Pakistan) and the Kargil conflict in 1999.

² LOCATION AND HOMELAND

The modern Republic of India occupies the greater part of the Indian subcontinent. Its area (3,166,414 sq km or 1,222,559 sq mi) is just over one-third the size of the United States. India's population of 1.32 billion people (2007 estimate) is the second largest in the world, behind China. The population of India is expected to exceed that of China by the year 2030.

India stretches from close to the equator to subtropical latitudes. Cape Comorin, the Indian peninsula's southern tip, lies at 8° N latitude. From there, the country extends northwards for 3,000 km (1,900 mi) to its border with China in the Himalayas and Karakoram Mountains. Pakistan lies to the west, with the international border running from the Arabian Sea through the Thar (Great Indian) Desert to the northern mountains. Some 2,900 km (1,800 mi) to the east, India shares borders with China and Myanmar (Burma). India also controls Lakshadweep and the Andaman and Nicobar islands, island groups lying in the Indian Ocean.

India falls into three broad geographical zones. In the north lie the majestic mountain ranges of the Himalayas. They run northwest to southeast for more than 2,400 km (1,500 mi) and contain many of the highest peaks in the world. Mt. Everest (on the Nepal-China border) is the world's highest mountain at 8,848 m (29,028 ft). The Himalayas are a transitional zone where the cultures of India and Central Asia meet. South of the mountains lie the Indo-Gangetic plains. With elevations mostly below 300 m (1,000 ft), these lands run in a broad arc from the Arabian Sea to the Bay of Bengal, along the valleys of the Indus and Ganges rivers. Except for the Thar Desert in the northwest, the plains are well watered and support the bulk of India's agriculture and population. The plains continue southwards along the coastal lowlands of the Indian peninsula and also eastwards along the valley of the Brahmaputra River. The third geographical region is formed by the Deccan Plateau, the uplands bordered by the Eastern and Western Ghats (mountains) that make up the interior of the Indian peninsula.

Every aspect of life in India is dominated by the seasonal rhythm of the monsoon. The winter sees bright, pleasant weather in most of the region. Mean monthly temperatures in northern areas drop below 21°C (70°F). Beginning in late February, temperatures rise steadily until May and June, when daily maximums in the northwestern plains exceed 46°C (115°F). The hot season ends with the onset of the rains. The monsoon reaches southwest India in late June and sweeps northwards, bringing torrential rains to much of the country. Cherrapun-

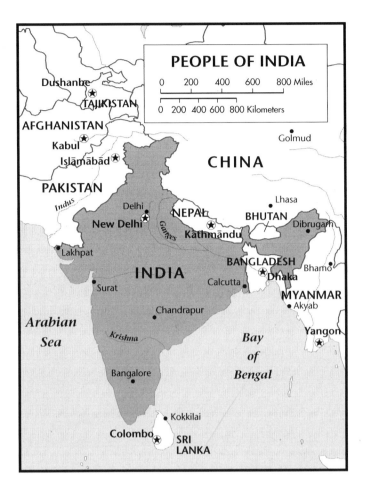

mir acceded to India, which the Maharaja did. Once the papers of accession to India were signed, Indian soldiers entered Kashmir with the order just to stop any further occupation by Pakistan but they were not allowed to drive out the invaders (by now the regular Pakistan army was involved) from the state. India took the matter to the United Nations. A UN resolution asked Pakistan to vacate the areas it had occupied and requested India to assist the UN Plebiscite Commission to organize a plebiscite (vote of the people) to determine the will of the people. Pakistan has refused to vacate the occupied areas and India has never held a plebiscite (understandably, since the majority of the Kashmiri population is Muslim). The Line of Control (LoC) divides the areas of Kashmir occupied by the two countries, with India controlling most of the former princely state of Jammu and Kashmir and Pakistan controlling some 30% of western areas of the region, in addition to what is known as the Northern Areas and Azad Kashmir (Free Kashmir). For intermittent periods between 1957, when the state approved its own Constitution, to the death of Sheikh Abdullah (Chief Minister of the State of Jammu and Kashmir) in 1982, the state had alternating spells of stability and discontent. In the late 1980s however, simmering discontent over the high-handed policies of the Indian government and allegations of the rigging of the 1987 assembly elections triggered a violent uprising that was backed by Pakistan. Since then, the region has seen a prolonged, bloody conflict between Islamist militants and the Indian army. Both the militants and the army have been accused of widespread human rights abuse, includ-

ji, in the northeast, is on record as the wettest place on earth, averaging nearly 1,150 cm (450 in) of rain annually. For three months, water is plentiful and the land is green with crops and vegetation. As September comes to a close, the rains die out and temperatures begin to drop with the approach of the cold season.

India's diverse environments are matched by the ethnic and cultural diversity of its peoples. All of the major physical types of the human race are present in the country's population. The Negritos, Negroids of small stature, are represented by the Andaman Islanders. The Proto-Australoid strain is seen in the tribal populations of southern and central India (e.g., the Mundas, the Oraons, and the Santals). The tribal peoples of the mountain belt show distinct Mongoloid features, as seen among the Bhutias of the Himalayas or the Nagas of the northeastern hills. By far the largest element in the population, however, is the Caucasoid group. The earliest Caucasoids to reach the subcontinent were moderate in stature and relatively dark complexioned. They are associated with the Dravidian languages and Dravidian culture of South India. The tall, fair, pastoralists who entered the subcontinent during the 2nd millennium BC and brought the Aryan languages with them are later Caucasoid elements in the population. They settled in northern India and are responsible for the Aryan culture of the north. Considerable mixing of peoples has occurred throughout the centuries and few "pure" racial types are found among the Indian population today.

India's ethnic diversity is accompanied by a complexity of culture that is unmatched anywhere in the world. India is less a country than a collection of countries, in the sense that there are many groups whose commitment to a regional cultural tradition is as great as, if not greater than, their identification with the nation. Thus one is a Bengali, a Tamil, a Punjabi, or a Gujarati. One speaks Bengali, Tamil, Punjabi, or Gujarati and shares in the literary, cultural, and historical traditions of the region. Each region has its own particular mix of religion, religious sects, castes, and economic and social relations that extends back over centuries.

Sizable Indian communities are found today in Nepal, Malaysia, Sri Lanka, and the Middle Eastern countries. Further afield, Indians have emigrated to South Africa, Fiji, the West Indies, the United States, Canada, and the United Kingdom.

³ LANGUAGE

Linguistic complexity is a distinguishing characteristic of Indian society. According to a Hindi proverb, "Every two miles the water doth change, and every four the dialect." The 2001 Census counted several hundred "mother-tongues." Even though this figure may include variants of the same dialect, or tongues spoken by only a small number of people, it does give some sense of the linguistic diversity of the region. Some 29 languages in India are each spoken by more than a million people.

Indian languages belong to four major linguistic families (i.e., groups of related languages that have a common ancestor). Austro-Asiatic languages (e.g., Munda, Ho, and Khasi) are spoken by tribal groups in central India and the northeastern hills. Bhotia and other languages in the mountain belt belong to the Sino-Tibetan linguistic family. Most Indians speak tongues belonging to the Aryan branch of the Indo-European family (e.g., Hindi and Bengali) or the Dravidian linguistic

family (Telugu, Kannada, Tamil, and Malayalam). The Aryan languages are found in northern India, while the Dravidian tongues are spoken in the South. Strictly speaking, "Aryan" and "Dravidian" are linguistic terms, though they are sometimes loosely used in the context of peoples or culture.

Hindi is the national language and primary tongue of 41.03% of the population. English has associate official language status and is widely used for national, political, and business purposes. In addition, India has 21 other official languages: Assamese, spoken by 1.28% of the population, Bengali (8.11%), Bodo (0.013%), Dogri (0.22%), Gujarati (4.48%), Kannada (3.69%), Kashmiri (0.24%), Konkani (0.24%), Maithili (1.18%), Malayalam (3.21%), Manipuri (0.14%), Marathi (6.99%), Nepali (0.28%), Oriya (3.21%), Punjabi (2.83), Sanskrit (0%), Santhali (0.63%), Sindhi (0.25%), Tamil (5.91%), Telugu (7.19%), and Urdu (5.01). Sanskrit is listed in the 2001 Census as the mother tongue of only 14,000 people, but it is widely studied as the classical language of North India. Tamil has recently been classified as a classical language. Urdu, while written in the Arabic script, when spoken sounds the same as Hindustani, a bazaar dialect of standard Hindi-Urdu developed in northern India.

Hindi is written in the Deva Nagari script that is the same as that used for Sanskrit. Many other languages, e,g, Gujarati and Punjabi, have their own scripts and alphabets, some derived from Deva Nagari (mainly in north India) and others, such as Tamil and Kannada, using the cursive scripts more common in the south.

⁴ FOLKLORE

The myths and folk heroes of the Indian peoples tend to be associated with specific religions or regional cultural traditions. Thus Hindus have the elaborate mythology and folklore associated with their deities and epic literature. Muslims revere their Sufi mystics, and the Sikhs have their martyred Gurus. Tribal groups have their own myths and legends. Many folk heroes are identified with specific regional folk traditions. A few historical figures such as Shivaji, the 17th-century Maratha leader who challenged Mughal power and carved out the last important Hindu empire in India, have achieved the status of heroes among Indian nationalists.

The freedom fighters involved in the struggle against British imperialism in India are viewed by many Indians as national heroes. Subhas Chandra Bose led the Indian National Army (INA), made up of Indian soldiers captured by the Japanese, against the British during World War II. Others, many of whom were jailed by the British, were supporters of Gandhi's civil disobedience movement. Mohandas Karamchand Gandhi, known as Mahatma ("Great Soul"), is surely one of the most influential world figures of the 20th century. Jawaharlal Nehru, the first prime minister of India, and his daughter Indira Gandhi (no relation to Mahatma Gandhi) are also among the most important Indian national leaders in the post-Independence era.

⁵ RELIGION

Few regions in the world show the religious diversity of India. Some 80.5% of Indians are Hindus, and certain Hindu values such as cow-protection are addressed in the Indian Constitution (Article 48). India, however, is a secular nation. Despite a rising tide of Hindutva (Hindu nationalism) that would like

Indian models display wedding dresses during a press conference in Calcutta. (Deshakalyan Chowdhury/AFP/Getty Images)

to see Hinduism become the state religion, the country prides itself on the freedom of religion guaranteed by its constitution. Religious minorities include Muslims (13.4%), Christians (2.3%), Sikhs (1.9%), Buddhists (1.5%), and Jains (0.5%). Among the remaining religious groups are Jews, Parsis (Zoroastrians), and animistic tribal peoples.

⁶ MAJOR HOLIDAYS

India officially celebrates the holidays of all the major religious communities present in the country. Thus Hindu festivals observed as holidays include Shivratri (dedicated to the god Shiva), Holi (the spring festival), Janamashtami (birthday of the god Krishna), Dasahara (the festival of the goddess Durga), and Divali (the Festival of Lights). The Muslim Id festivals (Id-ul-Fitr and Bakr-Id) and Muharram are holidays. The Christian holy days of Good Friday and Christmas are also observed, as are the birthdays of the founders of Buddhism, Jainism, and Sikhism.

Two national holidays mark the recent emergence of India as an independent nation. Independence Day on 15 August, commemorates the day in 1947 that India achieved its freedom from colonial rule. Republic Day, held on 26 January, marks the inauguration of India as a Republic in 1950. Although the holiday is celebrated throughout the country, the most spectacular festivities occur in New Delhi, with an impressive military parade and cultural performances.

The birthday of India's greatest leader of modern times, Mahatma Gandhi, is observed as a national holiday. Born on 2 October, 1869, Gandhi became a leading figure in India's independence movement and saw his ambitions realized before his assassination by a Hindu extremist in 1948. People gather at the Samadhi (cremation site) of Gandhi in Delhi to offer wreaths of flowers, pay homage to his memory, and offer prayers in his name.

⁷ RITES OF PASSAGE

Rites of passage for Indians are determined in broad outline by religion and in detail by caste, community, and region. As a predominantly Hindu population, most Indians are subject to customs and rites prescribed by the Hindu religion. For example, all Hindu groups have some form of naming and head-shaving ceremonies. Hindu males belonging to the higher castes undergo the important "Sacred Thread Ceremony" initiating them as a full member of their community. For Muslims, the circumcision of male children is the symbol of commitment to their religion, while for Christians it is baptism. Sikhs and Parsis have their own initiation ceremonies, and even tribal groups mark the passage from childhood to adulthood with certain rituals. Marriage customs conform to the norms of each community, as do methods for disposal of the dead. Hindus, Sikhs, and Buddhists cremate their dead, whereas Muslims and Christians inter their dead in cemeter-

A rickshaw puller takes children to school in New Delhi, India. (AP Images/M. Lakshman)

ies. Parsis and some Buddhist groups in the Himalayas expose their corpses to vultures. Tribal funeral customs include both cremation and burial.

8 INTERPERSONAL RELATIONS

Methods of greeting among Indians vary according to religion, social status, and the particular context of the meeting. A common greeting among Hindus is the "Namaste." This means "Greetings to you" and is said while joining one's own hands, palms together and held upright, in front of one's body. In parts of India, the word "Namaste" is replaced with "Namaskar." This form of greeting has the advantage that the persons meeting do not touch each other, which is important for Hindus. In the caste system, the mere touch of someone of a lower caste can cause one to become ritually polluted and require purification ceremonies to be undertaken. The Namaste allows one to greet a person without necessarily knowing his or her caste. It also allows one to greet a woman without touching her hand, which is considered impolite under certain circumstances. Nowadays, of course, shaking hands in the Western manner is becoming increasingly acceptable.

Another form of greeting is common between persons of unequal social standing. Children may greet their parents by bowing down and touching their feet. Pupils greet teachers in the same manner, and so do people meeting important religious figures. The person being greeted usually interrupts the gesture before it is complete, implying that he or she is not worthy of such homage.

"Salaam" or "Salaam alaikum" (Peace be with you) is the typical greeting among Muslims, while the Sikh form of salutation is "Sat Sri Akal" (God is Truth).

9 LIVING CONDITIONS

The general health of the Indian population has improved dramatically over the last half-century. Medical advances, immunization, and public health programs have raised the average life expectancy of the Indian to 64 years. However, this still lags behind the United States, where people can expect to live to 78 years of age. Leading causes of death in India include diseases of the circulatory system, infectious and parasitic diseases, respiratory diseases, and childhood diseases (measles, diphtheria, whooping cough). Some 125,000 cases of full-blown AIDS were reported from India in 2006, though this number is probably much higher, many cases being misdiagnosed or not reported at all. Inadequate sewage disposal, contaminated drinking water, and poor nutrition contribute to the health problems. Infant mortality rates are high, numbering 58 deaths per 1,000 live births (compared to 6.5 for the United States). The total fertility rate (i.e., the average births per woman of childbearing age in the population) is 2.9. The rate of natural increase of population is 1.6% per year. The last two demographic indices have been declining in recent years, an encouraging sign that the rate of India's population growth is slowing. However, the country's large base population means that the number of new mouths to feed increases by roughly the number of residents of New York State (approximately 18 million people) every year.

Although nearly three-fourths (72.2%) of Indians live in rural areas, India contains some of the largest cities in the world. Greater Bombay [Mumbai] (over 18 million people), Delhi (over 15 million) and Calcutta [Kolkata] (c. 14.5 million) rank among the top 20 urban centers of the world. Yet India is essentially a country of villages. Rural house types, settlement patterns, construction materials, furnishings, and creature comforts vary greatly according to region and economic status.

Indian standards of living range from the most luxurious to the poorest in the world. Although the world of the ruling *Mahārājās,* with their lavish lifestyles, palaces, servants, and tiger hunts, is a thing of the past, the wealthy in India still live very comfortable lives. A growing middle class is sharing in this prosperity, with access to cars, televisions, VCRs, refrigerators, and other modern conveniences. By contrast, Indians are living and dying in the streets and slums of cities such as Bombay and Calcutta (where the late Mother Teresa, winner of the Nobel Peace Prize, was known for her work with the poor). Estimates of the percentage of the population living in poverty range from 25% to 40%, although this figure is dropping. Per capita income stands at US$3,800 per year (2007). Ever since Rajiv Gandhi, with current Prime Minister Manmohan Singh as his Finance Minister, abandoned Nehru's socialist economic policies and "liberalized" India's economy in 1991, India's economy has being growing at a remarkable rate, averaging 8.5% from 2004–08. Economists have estimated 300 million Indians now belong to the middle class, one-third of them having emerged from poverty in the last 10 years, and if such growth rate can be sustained, the numbers of Indians living in poverty will decrease dramatically. At the current rate of growth, a majority of Indians will be middle-class by 2025. Nonetheless, poverty is still an issue for many Indians, especially in rural areas: a 2007 government report found that 25% of Indians lived on less than 20 rupees per day (c. $0.50) with most working in "the informal labor sector with no job or social security."

India has 3,383,344 km (2,114,600 mi) of road, 54%% of it paved. Construction of the "Golden Quadrilateral," when complete, will link India's four major cities, Delhi, Calcutta, Madras, and Bombay with high-speed, divided highways. Roads around Delhi are being improved for the Commonwealth Games, which are being held in that city in 2010. State-run and private bus services provide access to most parts of the country. The railway system, inherited from the British and further developed in the last 60 years, is a common means of long-distance travel today and, along with trucks, a major means of moving goods across the country. India's rail network is one of the densest outside of Europe. Since liberalization, a number of private airlines such as Jet Airways and Kingfisher Airlines are providing competition for the state-owned airlines, Air India and Indian Airlines. The government of India is undertaking a program of modernization of its major airports in conjunction with private companies.

¹⁰ FAMILY LIFE

Despite recent modernizing influences, the traditional joint family remains the norm among Indians. However, distinct differences in family structure and kinship patterns exist between northern and southern India. In the north, the family is patriarchal. A household consists of two or three generations of males and their dependents. In southern India, the joint family is matriarchal. It consists of one's grandmother and her brothers and sisters, one's mother and her brothers and sisters, and one's own brothers and sisters. The children of one's mother's sisters and the offspring of one's own sisters live in the household. The husbands of the women in the family live in the houses of their mothers, visiting their wives and children on occasion.

The first criterion in the selection of a marriage partner is caste. Although caste is Hindu in origin, virtually all South Asian groups (including Muslims and Christians) show its influence. Castes are endogamous groups, and as a rule one must marry within one's caste. After this, however, differences again appear between northern and southern Indians. In the north, marriage partners are usually unrelated and there are specific rules determining how close a blood-relationship is permitted. In southern India, however, cross-cousin marriage is the norm. The preferred match for a man is his maternal cross-cousin—his mother's brother's daughter. Virtually all Indian marriages are arranged and, although child marriage is prohibited by the Indian government, marriage at a young age is not uncommon. Marriages are performed according to the customs of one's community and invariably include payment of a dowry or bride-price. Marriage is essential for a woman, and any girl who is not married by a reasonable age is thought to have something wrong with her. A woman's role in Indian society is incomplete until she bears children, preferably sons. Traditionally, women have occupied an inferior social position in Indian society, although this is slowly changing as the country modernizes.

¹¹ CLOTHING

The common dress for Indian men is the *dhotī*. This is a long piece of white cotton wrapped around the waist for half its length and then drawn between the legs and tucked into the waist at the back. In southern India, the chest is usually left bare, while in the north a shirt may be worn. Turbans or some form of headdress are common in northern India. The style of the turban often identifies the wearer as a member of a particular community (e.g., Pathan or Sikh) or as being from a particular region or village. The *kurtā,* a long tunic-like shirt, and the *pyjāmā,* loose baggy trousers, are also commonly worn, especially in urban areas. People wear leather sandals, a variety of locally made shoes, or even go barefoot. Because leather is considered unclean, shoes are always taken off before entering a temple. It is also polite to take off one's shoes before entering an Indian home.

Women typically wear the *sārī,* a length of cotton or silk cloth (nowadays synthetic fabrics are also used) wrapped around the waist, with one end left free and thrown over the right shoulder. The *cholī,* a tight bodice that leaves the midriff bare, is worn under the *sārī* Regional variations exist in their manner of wearing the *sārī.* In Maharashtra, for example, rural women draw one end of the *sārī* through the legs and tuck it into the waist at the small of the back. In some rural areas, women do not wear the bodice, using just the end of the sārī to cover their upper body.

Regional variations in dress occur throughout India, reflecting differences in caste, community, and locality. In urban areas, however, Western-style clothing has become the norm, especially for males. Although women in cities, especially the younger generation, wear Western fashions, the sārī is still the preferred form of dress for most females.

12 FOOD

A typical Indian meal consists of around five or six dishes, served all at once on a *thālī*. This is a round metal tray or plate with a rim on it, on which are placed several little bowls *(katorīs)* to hold each individual dish. In some areas, food is served on banana leaves. No utensils are used. Food is eaten with the right hand, the left hand being used for personal hygiene and considered unclean.

Westerners tend to think of Indian food as "curry and rice," but this does not do justice to the rich and varied cuisine of India. The term "curry" was used by Europeans to describe the spicy dishes they found in India, but curries do not necessarily have to be hot. The "heat" in Indian food comes from chilies, which were introduced into Asia by the Portuguese in the 16th century. Other spices commonly used include cumin, coriander, turmeric, black pepper, cardamom, and cloves. Curries can be made of meat, eggs, poultry, or vegetables and are eaten with lentils *(dāl)* and an assortment of pickles and chutneys. In northern and western areas, meals are taken with flat breads *(roṭī)*. These breads are replaced by rice *(chāwal)* in the wetter east and south. Yogurt *(dahī)* may be taken with the meal, which often ends with a variety of sweets (mithāī). Milk and milk products are an important part of the Indian diet. *Pān* or betel nut served with lime and wrapped in a betel leaf is commonly taken after a meal.

Regional cuisines are as diverse as the peoples and cultures of India. Mughal-style cooking is found in the north, while dosās (thin pancakes of rice-flour) and idlīs (steamed rice-bread) are popular southern dishes. Madras is known for its fiery curries, while Bengal is famous for its fish dishes. Goan cooking shows the influence of its Portuguese past. Among Indians, food is as much a part of regional culture as dress and language.

As well as being a means of sustenance, food in India acquires ritual, religious, and even social dimensions. The Hindu view of the sanctity of the cow leads to an avoidance of beef, and many Hindus are totally vegetarian. Those Hindus who do eat meat are regarded as socially inferior, and low-caste groups try to raise their social status by abandoning meat-eating. Muslims, though meat-eaters, do not eat pork. Tribal groups avoid the flesh of animals that are their clan totems.

13 EDUCATION

The literacy rate among Indians seven years of age and over is 65.38% (2005). However, this figure masks considerable variations between males and females, urban and rural populations, and among different social groups. Primary education is free and, in most Indian states, compulsory. The poor quality of state-run secondary schools has led to an expansion of private (often English-language) schools that serve as feeders to institutions of higher education. There are numerous colleges and universities in India, some with excellent reputations.

Many of the graduates of the Indian Institutes of Technology (ITTs) and Indian Institutes of Management (IIMs) are viewed as better trained than their contemporaries in the West and are highly sought after overseas.

14 CULTURAL HERITAGE

Indians are heirs to one of the oldest continuous cultural traditions in the world. South Asian civilization has its roots in the complex urban society that flourished along the Indus Valley some 5,000 years ago. Harappan traits such as worship of mother-goddesses or trees survive in modern India, especially in the Dravidian cultures of South India. However, much of India's cultural heritage is linked in some way to the later religions of India. It is to these, and especially to Hinduism, that one must turn to see the full flowering of the Indian artistic genius.

Hindu literature written in Sanskrit includes sacred texts such as the *Vedas:* the two great epics known as the *Mahābhārata* and the Rāmāyana: political treatises such as the *Laws of Manu:* and the works of the greatest Sanskrit playwright and poet, Kalidasa. Music and dancing are the subjects of a 3rd century AD work called Nātya Śāstra, which is the ancient authority for these art forms. Today, the main form of classical dance in India is Bharata Natyam, while Kathakali is a less formal dance from southern India. The Raga forms the basis of classical Indian music.

Indian architecture and sculpture are monuments to Hinduism and the other religious traditions of India. North Indian temples replicate the peaks of the Himalayas in their soaring towers. South Indian temples on the other hand, are pyramidal in shape and covered with elaborately carved figures from Hindu mythology. Famous examples of Hindu temples are the temple complex at Mahabalipuram (Tamil Nadu), the Khajuraho temples (Madhya Pradesh) with their erotic carvings, and the Sun Temple at Konarak (Orissa). Buddhists have their own religious monuments, with the cave paintings at Ajanta being among the most impressive. The temple city of Palitana in Gujarat and the white marble temples at Dilwara (Mt. Abu) in Rajasthan are examples of Jain temple-building in India. Although Islam's contributions are seen more in miniature painting than in architecture, the distinctive blend of styles known as Indo-Islamic or Indo-Saracenic architecture can be seen throughout northern India. The Taj Mahal, built as a mausoleum by the emperor Shah Jehan for his wife, stands as the greatest architectural achievement of Islam in India.

Not all of India's artistic accomplishments lie in the distant past. Rabindranath Tagore (1861–1941), a Bengali whose work was highly regarded in Western literary circles in the early decades of the 20th century, was awarded the Nobel Prize for literature in 1913.

15 WORK

Some 61% of India's labor force is engaged in agriculture, with many farmers being subsistence cultivators. Despite this, India inherited most of the subcontinent's industrial resources and ranks among the leaders of the world's developing countries in industrial output. India's industries range from nuclear power production and nuclear research to manufacturing garments for export. Economic growth in the first 40 years after independence was slow, hampered by restrictive government economic policies and an unwieldy bureaucracy. Liberalization of the economy since 1991 under Manmohan Singh, Rajiv Gandhi's Finance Minister at the time, has seen faster growth, greater foreign investment, and expanding trade, although the direction and pace of economic change remains a matter of internal debate. The current rate of economic growth is 8.5% during the year ending March 2008, and at this rate a serious dent is being made in poverty in India. Economists estimate that, if this rate of growth can be sustained, poverty will be all but eliminated by the year 2025.

India's economy is diverse, encompassing agriculture, handicrafts, textile, manufacturing, and a multitude of services. Although nearly two-thirds of the Indian workforce still earn their livelihood directly or indirectly through agriculture, services are a growing sector and play an increasingly important role of India's economy. The advent of the digital age, and the large number of young and educated populace fluent in English, is gradually transforming India into an important "back office" destination for global outsourcing of customer services and technical support. There are many call centers in India, in locations such as Bangalore (Bengaluru) and Noidu (near Delhi). Indian "techies" from the West are returning to tech centers such as Bangalore where, despite lower wages, they can live a life-style unattainable in the West.

But India still remains a major exporter of highly-skilled workers in software and financial services, and software engineering. Other sectors like manufacturing, pharmaceuticals, biotechnology, nanotechnology, telecommunication, shipbuilding, aviation, tourism, and retailing are showing strong potentials with high growth rates.

16 SPORTS

Chess is thought to have originated in India, and dice and card-playing are of considerable antiquity. Traditional sports include pastimes such as cock-fighting, camel-racing, and wrestling. Hunting (shikār) was a favorite sport among the upper classes. Kabaddī, team wrestling, is very popular. Children's games include kite-flying, spinning tops, yo-yos, and hobby-horses. Indians have enthusiastically adopted modern sports, with cricket and field hockey being the most popular. India participates in cricket at the international level, and although its field hockey team has recently fallen on hard times, for years it was a power in international competitions. Games such as soccer, tennis, badminton, squash, table tennis, and golf are also widely played.

17 ENTERTAINMENT AND RECREATION

Until recently, all radio and television in India was controlled by the government. Programming was limited largely to Indian productions and often described as "drab and unimaginative." One smash hit, however, was the serialization of the epic *Maharabharata* on television. The whole country stopped to watch the program. There are reports that trains would interrupt their schedules to stop at a station so that passengers and crew could watch the latest episode. The advent of satellite TV and availability of VCRs and videotapes have led to a change in viewing habits. Soap operas, sports events, and movies are the most popular television programs today.

India has the world's largest film industry. Regional language films are produced in centers such as Calcutta and Madras, but the center of the industry is Bombay. "Bollywood," as it is known, produces Hindi films that fill movie theaters in cities all across India. The films tend to be melodramas, with much action, singing, dancing, and predictable plots. Film music is immensely popular. Film actors and actresses are pop idols and trend-setters, and their lives are followed with much interest. Few Indian filmmakers have achieved recognition outside of India, except for the late Satyajit Ray, who gained an international reputation.

India has a thriving, and relatively free, press, with newspapers and magazines published in Hindi and English as well as regional languages.

18 FOLK ART, CRAFTS, AND HOBBIES

Folk arts in India range from wall-painting to puppetry to regional music and dance forms. India is well known for its textiles, rugs and carpets, metalwork, bronzes, copper- and brassware, ivory and hard stone carving, pottery, woodwork, gemstones, and gold and silver jewelry.

19 SOCIAL PROBLEMS

Many of India's social problems are related to population. Despite efforts at population control, India will be the world's most populous nation sometime early in the 21st century. Existing problems such as poverty, high unemployment, illiteracy, and malnutrition can be expected to worsen, especially as over a third of the population (35.2%) is still under 15 years of age. Failure of the monsoon rains can cause famine and hardship for millions of people. An as yet unacknowledged problem is that of AIDS in India. Conservative estimates predict 1 million AIDS cases and 10 million people infected with HIV in India by the year 2000. The potential scope of the epidemic and its cost in resources and human suffering is staggering.

Another set of problems originates in the diversity of Indian society. Communal and sectarian unrest is common and ongoing. Groups in Assam, Kashmir, Punjab, Tamil Nadu, and other areas have been involved in armed conflict with the Union government, with demands varying from a greater degree of regional autonomy to outright secession from the Republic. The rise of Hindu fundamentalism on the political scene is seen by Muslims as a threat to India's commitment to secularism. It has resulted in violence between Hindus and Muslims and contains the seeds of further conflict. There is also conflict based on class distinctions. At independence, the Indian Constitution created three categories of disadvantaged groups that needed special representation and assistance. These were the Scheduled Tribes, the Scheduled Castes (mostly "untouchables"), and the Other Backward Classes (OBCs), underprivileged groups that did not fit into the first two categories. Attempts in 1990 to implement the recommendation of the Mandal Commission that 27% of central government jobs be set aside for the OBCs led to widespread unrest among caste Hindus. This "reservations policy" is as controversial in India as affirmative action policies are now in the United States. Demonstrations continue to occur both for and against, such policies. For example, in May 2008, an agitation, called by All India Gujjar Mahasabha, in support of the community's demand for Scheduled Tribe status in Rajasthan, resulted in violence, some deaths and disruption of traffic in Jaipur, Rajasthan State's capital, in the nation's capital, New Delhi, and in neighboring areas of northwestern India that have a strong Guar presence.

The BJP formed the national government from 1998 to 2004, with Atal Bihari Vajpayee as prime minister, when it shockingly lost a general election, some say by abandoning the principles of Hindutva or Hindu nationalism. The central government in 2008, with Manmohan Singh as prime minister, is formed by the United Progressive Alliance (UPA), a coalition of 12 political parties, led by the Indian Congress, but which only retains power with the support of the Left Front (which is not a part of the coalition), a group of Indian Communist parties. This has caused problems. For three decades, India has been under a nuclear trade embargo by the United States, primarily because it is not a signatory to the Nuclear Non-Proliferation Treaty. The United States has tended to favor General Pervez Musharraf and Pakistan as a result of their help in the War on Terror. In early 2006, however, President George W. Bush visited India and negotiated a treaty, highly favorable to India, which would allow for U.S. nuclear trade with India and co-operation in the areas of domestic nuclear development. However this treaty has to be ratified by the Indian Parliament, and the Left Front has threatened to withdraw its support from the government if the UPA were to bring the treaty to a vote. So, it seems that the treaty will die a natural death when Bush leaves office at the end of 2008.

Despite the problems of a weak central government and current charges of corruption in high places, Indians can approach the future with confidence. The country has survived the early decades of nationhood intact and, above all, with a continued commitment to the principles of democratic government. India is still a parliamentary democracy (the largest in the world), it has brought its birth rate under control, there is rapidly expanding middle class, its economy is flourishing, and, largely because of this, poverty is being rapidly eliminated.

20 GENDER ISSUES

Gender issues among the peoples of India arise largely from the nature of the societies found in the South Asian subcontinent. Buddhists and Christians espouse equality between men and women but, unfortunately, many adherents of these religions are of low caste converted from Hinduism and are treated very much as if they still belong to Hindu society. Even tribal societies, in which women have much greater equality and freedom than their counterparts in Hindu and Muslim societies, have been influenced by the societies amongst which they live.

Shariah (Islamic law), under which Muslims in India live, provides for differences between women's and men's roles, rights, and obligations. Muslim-majority countries give women varying degrees of rights with regards to marriage, divorce, civil rights, legal status, dress code, and education, but as a secular state, the Republic of India promotes the equality of men and women. The Constitution of India promotes equal rights and opportunities for men and women in the political, economic and social sphere, prohibits discrimination on the grounds of sex, religion, caste, or gender, empowers the State to take affirmative measures for women and provides for equality of opportunities in the matter of public appointments.

Despite this legal protection, women are generally powerless in the face of prevailing patriarchal traditions. Women lack power to decide who they will marry and are often married off as children. Legal loopholes are used to deny women inheritance rights. Women receive less health care than males.

Many women die in childbirth of easily prevented complications. Working conditions and environmental pollution further impairs women's health. In recent years, there has been an alarming rise in atrocities against women in India, in terms of rapes, assaults, and dowry-related murders. Fear of violence suppresses the aspirations of all women. Female infanticide and sex-selective abortions are additional forms of violence that reflect the devaluing of females in Indian society. Families are far less likely to educate girls than boys, and far more likely to pull them out of school, mainly to help out at home or in the fields. Women work longer hours and their work, usually as unskilled labor in agriculture, is more arduous than men's, yet their work is unrecognized. And, in 2006, a UN survey reported malnutrition among children in India is increasingly becoming a problem because tradition requires that women eat last, even when pregnant and lactating. Malnourished women give birth to malnourished children, thus perpetuating the cycle.

India has a long history of activism for women's welfare and rights, which has increasingly focused on women's economic rights. A range of government programs have been launched to increase economic opportunity for women. For instance, the National Commission for Women was set up as a statutory body in January 1992 under the National Commission for Women Act of 1990 to review the constitutional and legal safeguards for women, to recommend remedial legislative measures, to facilitate the redressing of grievances and to advise the government on all policy matters affecting women. However, there appear to be no existing programs to address the cultural and traditional discrimination against women in India.

21 BIBLIOGRAPHY

Basham, A. L., ed. *A Cultural History of India*. Oxford: Clarendon Press, 1975.

Craven, Roy. C. *A Concise History of Indian Art*. New York: Praeger, 1976.

Möller, Ulrika. *The Prospects of Security Co-operation: A Matter of Relative Gains or Recognition? India and Nuclear Weapons Control*. Göteborg: Department of Political Science, Göteborg University, 2007.

Palit, Chittabrata and Mahua Sarkar, ed. *Indian Vistas of Environment*. Delhi: Kalpaz Publications, 2007.

Robinson, Francis, ed. *The Cambridge Encyclopedia of India, Pakistan, Bangladesh, Sri Lanka, Nepal, Bhutan and the Maldives*. Cambridge: Cambridge University Press, 1989.

Schwartzberg, Joseph E., ed. *A Historical Atlas of South Asia*. 2nd impression. New York and Oxford: Oxford University Press, 1992.

Spate, O. H. K., and A. T. A. Learmonth. *India and Pakistan: A General and Regional Geography*. 3rd rev. ed. London: Methuen, 1967.

Verma. S. B. *Status of Women in Modern India*. New Delhi: Deep & Deep, 2005.

Wolpert, Stanley. *India*. Berkeley: University of California Press, 1991

—by D. O. Lodrick.

INDO-FIJIANS

PRONUNCIATION: in-do-FEE-jee-uhns
LOCATION: Fiji
POPULATION: 311,591 (38% of total Fijian population) in 2007
LANGUAGE: Fiji Hindustani (Fiji Hindi); Tamil; Punjabi; Gujarati; English
RELIGION: Hinduism; Islam; Christianity

¹ INTRODUCTION

The majority of the present-day Indo-Fijians are the descendants of indentured laborers who were brought to Fiji during the 19th century. The Indian indenture system was established to provide labor for British colonies after the abolition of slavery in Britain and her colonies in 1833. The first indentured laborers from India arrived in Fiji in 1879 and the indenture system in Fiji lasted until 1916. Other immigrants from India arrived in Fiji in the early 20th century, although they were not indentured laborers. Most of these immigrants were Punjabi or Gujarati, from northwestern India, while a number of the indentured laborers had been from southern India. The Gujaratis and Punjabis opened small shops in the coastal towns of colonial Fiji. The Indo-Fijians are part of the South Asian Diaspora that includes the Indian Ocean island of Mauritius, Trinidad in the Caribbean, Guyana in South America, South Africa, and North America.

² LOCATION AND HOMELAND

The Fijian archipelago is located in the western Pacific Ocean. The climate of Fiji is tropical with plenty of rainfall, sunshine, and high humidity. The largest islands within the 800-island group are Viti Levu and Vanua Levu. These two islands account for about 85% of the total land mass of Fiji. Around 100 of the islands in the Fijian chain are either inhabited or inhabitable. The vast majority of Indo-Fijians reside on Viti Levu.

According to the most recent population statistics, Indo-Fijians make up around 37% of the total population in Fiji. At the time before the military coup of 1987, Indo-Fijians made up close to 48% of the total population: a significant portion of the decrease is attributable to immigration to Australia, Canada, and the United States. It has been estimated that over 100,000 Indo-Fijians have left the country since the first Fijian-backed coup in 1987. In the 1960s, Indo-Fijians outnumbered the indigenous Fijians.

³ LANGUAGE

The overwhelming majority of Indo-Fijians speak a language referred to as Fiji Hindustani, or Fiji Hindi. A very small number speak other south Asian languages such as Tamil, Gujarati, Punjabi, Malayalam, and Telugu. Fiji Hindustani developed out of contact between speakers of different dialects of Hindi/Urdu and their overseers on the colonial-era sugar plantations. Although the Indian laborers could communicate fairly well across dialect boundaries, they still encountered some idiosyncratic problems. Over time, a unified dialect emerged that became the language of Indo-Fijian identity. There have been several academic studies of Fiji Hindi, and there are existing course materials available in many university libraries. Some Chinese and Fijians speak a simplified form of Fiji Hindi that differs from that spoken by the Indo-Fijians themselves. Indo-Fijians also speak English, and many older Indo-Fijians also spoke Pidgin Fijian when they were younger.

⁴ FOLKLORE

The folklore of the Indo-Fijians derives from traditional Indian folklore. Important cultural epics such as the *Râmâyana* and the *Mahâbahârata* are read, chanted, and recounted by Indo-Fijians at ceremonies and celebrations. The epic drama of Rama and Sita is performed at most religious festivals.

⁵ RELIGION

The Indian laborers brought their religions with them to Fiji. Hinduism and Islam both exist on Fiji today, alongside Christianity and indigenous forms of Fijian religious practice. The majority of indentured laborers were Hindu, and as a result, Hinduism is the major religion among Indo-Fijians. A total of approximately 77% of all Indo-Fijians follow Hinduism. The caste system is an important component of Hinduism as it is practiced in India. The caste system is one of ascribed status, whereby an individual is born into a particular socio-occupational grouping. There are restrictions on the interactions between certain groups, especially in the areas of marriage, touching, and the sharing of food. The system of indenture fundamentally modified the Hindu caste system in Fiji. Restrictions were relaxed and Indo-Fijians were able to interact more as a group. The caste component of their religion was almost completely obliterated. Temples and mosques have been constructed for religious gatherings and rituals.

Hinduism is a polytheistic religion. Hindus believe in a variety of deities, each with specific attributes, domains, functions, and powers. There are sects that are devoted to the worship of a particular deity, and shrines are created to provide offerings for the deity. These practices continue among the Indo-Fijian communities in Fiji and abroad. Although there has been considerable Christian influence in Fiji in terms of missions and mission schools, the Indo-Fijian population has not been very receptive to conversion. Less than 5% of the Indo-Fijian population is Christian.

⁶ MAJOR HOLIDAYS

Major holidays for Indo-Fijians center on the religious calendars. Hindus celebrate Diwali (the festival of lights) in early November and Holi (a festival of singing and light-hearted play). Families also sponsor *pujas,* which are ceremonies that include prayers, offerings, and feasts. Pujas take place on birthdays and other special occasions when it is appropriate to give thanks for good fortune and blessings. Muslim Indo-Fijians observe the fasting and prayer practices during the month of Ramadan. Other secular holidays include the Queen's Birthday, Boxing Day, and Fiji Day.

⁷ RITES OF PASSAGE

Indo-Fijians perform rituals at important transitional stages of the life cycle: birth, marriage, and death. The exact nature of these rituals is dictated by the religious faith of the families involved.

8 INTERPERSONAL RELATIONS

The standard greeting in Fiji Hindi is *namaste*. This greeting derives directly from Hindi as spoken in India.

Dating was unknown among unmarried Indo-Fijians until late in this century. Marriages were always arranged, as they are in most Indian communities throughout the world. Arranged marriages still continue now, but dating is seen as a means to create a marriage. Interracial dating among Indo-Fijians and Fijians is disapproved of by both groups, though Indo-Fijians do have dating relationships with other non-Fijians.

9 LIVING CONDITIONS

Fijian law dictated that non-Fijians could not live in Fijian villages. This established a precedent for segregation between the Fijians and Indo-Fijians in Fiji. Indo-Fijians established their own communities or moved to the coastal towns, which would later become the centers of commerce and trade that would provide for the economic prosperity of the Indo-Fijians.

Western-style housing made from concrete blocks or wood is the preferred style of housing for Indo-Fijians. Wattle and daub houses were built by the first waves of indentured laborers to Fiji.

10 FAMILY LIFE

In most traditional societies of India, marriages are arranged by the parents of the prospective bride and groom. In the most extreme cases, the couple had no say in the matter whatsoever. Caste distinctions and restrictions guided the arranged choices in most cases. In colonial Fiji, caste distinctions were broken down and became much less of a factor in marriage negotiations. Men greatly outnumbered women in the colonial period. In the present day, couples have more choice in their selection of mates. Male offspring generally inherit the majority of their parents' property and are expected to divide it among themselves.

11 CLOTHING

Indo-Fijians men have adopted Western-style trousers and shirts for some time now. Some women, however, still wear the traditional saris (a garment of draped cloth). Older women in particular only wear saris. Indo-Fijian women, like Indian women almost everywhere, are adorned with jewelry.

12 FOOD

Indentured Indian workers brought their styles of cooking and some of their food crops with them to Fiji in the 19th century. Roti, a staple bread served with every meal, and rice and curry dishes form the basis of Indo-Fijian cuisine. The traditional eating utensils are the hands. Pollution taboos require that only the right hand be used when eating; the left hand remains in the person's lap. Roti is used like an eating utensil to scoop up pieces of food and rice.

Indo-Fijian immigrants to Australia have opened restaurants that are popular with Indians, Australians, and Indo-Fijians alike. The spices and the use of coconut products in many of the curries belie the south Indian ancestry of many of the Indo-Fijians.

13 EDUCATION

Formal education for the children of indentured Indian laborers in Fiji did not begin until 1898. These schools were opened by the Catholic and Methodist missionaries who had also opened mission schools for the Fijian children much earlier. Indo-Fijians stress the importance of education with their children and many go on to complete advanced degrees at universities and colleges abroad.

14 CULTURAL HERITAGE

Traditional music and film music are both important in Fiji among Indo-Fijians. Almost all of the cultural entertainment that Indo-Fijians consume is produced outside of Fiji. The importation of Indian film music provides the latest hits from the most popular film stars of India. Most shops carry a wide selection of cassettes and videos, along with imported Indian foods. Traditional music and dance are also performed in certain contexts.

15 WORK

After the period of indenture, Indo-Fijians began to specialize in certain occupations in Fiji. They grew sugar cane, which was and still is an important cash crop, controlled transportation, and also were in charge of most of the craft and retail trade. Although they held little land, the Indo-Fijian population acquired control of the Fijian economy. This situation did not please the traditional Fijian chiefs and ultimately led to the 1987 military coup. The majority of those Indo-Fijians that left following the coup were shop owners and other retail merchants and bankers.

16 SPORTS

Cricket is a popular spectator and participant sport among Indo-Fijians. Other sports that have large followings in Fiji, like rugby, are not as important to Indo-Fijians.

17 ENTERTAINMENT AND RECREATION

Traditional south Asian forms of entertainment, including classical forms of music and dance, are enjoyed and practiced within the Indo-Fijian community. Music and dance academies have also been established by the Indo-Fijians that have left Fiji and moved to Sydney, Australia.

18 FOLK ART, CRAFTS, AND HOBBIES

Rural folk arts accompanied those south Asians that came to Fiji as indentured laborers. Artistic specialization was caste-associated in India and few ascribed artists were present in the early society. On the plantations, there was little time for the production of painting and sculpture. Pottery production and the painting and sculpting of religious images for local consumption were minimal during the early stages of Indo-Fijian settlement history. Nowadays, religious images and other Indian products are imported directly from India.

19 SOCIAL PROBLEMS

Indo-Fijians still face difficulties living in Fiji. Although relations between the Indo-Fijians and Fijians have improved considerably since 1988, there is still resentment and anger on both sides. The coup adversely affected the tourist industry, which has to yet regain the ground it had prior to the coups.

The exodus of Indo-Fijians resulted in loss of over one-third of the nation's doctors, one-half of its lawyers, and a great number of teachers and nurses.

20 GENDER ISSUES

Many occupations in Indo-Fijian society are traditionally held by males only. Musicians, religious functionaries, and cooks for public functions like weddings and pujas are typically male. There is a marked preference for male offspring since daughters incur more costs at marriage, and also leave the family at marriage to live with their husbands. Male children are also usually given much more freedom and independence than are female children. Like the societies in India from which Indo-Fijian society sprang, descent is traced through the father's line and offspring become members of the patriline.

The cultural construction of gender in Indo-Fijian society is influenced by the conceptualization of gender in Hinduism. While in Indo-Fijian society there are two recognized gender categories, male and female, in the Hindu pantheon these two categories are mixed and transformed. In Hindu myths, there are several accounts of deities who transformed genders, who are bisexual, and who are transsexual and transgendered.

The onset of menstruation marks puberty for females in Indo-Fijian society. Depending on the family and the sect of Hinduism that the family follows, rituals may follow a girl's first menstruation and a set of restrictions will be placed upon her during her menstrual periods. Many of the strict observances that were part of rural life in India have been relaxed in Indo-Fijian society. However, for rural families, the observances can still greatly restrict the movement and actions of menstruating women.

For both males and females, adulthood is symbolized by marriage. The state of marriage is characterized by increasing responsibilities to family and work. By middle age, children should be grown and married, with married sons perpetuating the father's lineage.

21 BIBLIOGRAPHY

Donniger, Wendy. *Splitting the Difference: Gender and Myth in Ancient Greece and India.* Chicago: University of Chicago Press, 1999.

Lamb, S. *White Saris and Sweet Mangoes: Aging, Gender, and Body in North India.* Berkeley: University of California Press, 2000.

Mayer, Adrian. *Indians in Fiji.* London: Oxford University Press, 1963.

Siegel, Jeff. *Language Contact in a Plantation Environment: A Sociolinguistic History of Fiji.* New York: Cambridge University Press, 1987.

—by J. Williams

INDONESIANS

PRONUNCIATION: in-do-NEE-zhuns
LOCATION: Indonesia
POPULATION: 238 million
LANGUAGE: Bahasa Indonesia (official language); otherwise, the languages spoken by the various ethnic groups
RELIGION: Islam (88%); Protestantism (5%); Catholicism (3%); Hinduism (2%); Buddhism (1%)
RELATED ARTICLES: Vol. 3: Achenese; Ambonese; Balinese; Banjarese; Batak; Bugis, Makassarese, and Mandarese; Javanese; Vol. Madurese; Malays in Indonesia; Minahasans; Minangkabaus; Ngaju Dayaks; Niasans; Sasak; Sumbanese; Sumbawans

1 INTRODUCTION

Who are the Indonesians? This is no easier a question than "Who are the Americans?" Although administration and mass education have made all but the most isolated peoples of Indonesia aware of being "Indonesian," it is still true that as one moves outwards from the national capital, Jakarta, into the rural areas where almost 55% of Indonesians still live, an individual's ethnic group (*suku bangsa* in the national language) determines more and more his or her identity and way of life. By one estimate, there are more than 250 distinct cultural groups (sukus), speaking as many as 700 mutually unintelligible languages, and representing a wide range of physical types. Striving to maintain a delicate balance between preserving each suku's distinctive heritage and propagating a modern, development-oriented national culture, the republic takes as its motto, *"Bhinneka Tunggal Ika,"* an Old Javanese expression meaning "The Many Are One."

In addition to being crossed by the world's prime trade routes, the archipelago was itself the source of the world's most coveted commodities: spices. Beginning as early as the 2nd century AD, leaders who controlled the flow of trade goods and the production of rice (especially in Java and Bali) established kingdoms whose civilizations freely integrated foreign influences with indigenous traditions. For the antecedents of their nation, Indonesians look beyond Dutch colonialism to the greatest of those Hindu-Buddhist states, the empires of Srivijaya (South Sumatra, 7th–12th centuries) and Majapahit (East Java, late 13th–late 15th centuries), which stood as overlords of many lesser kingdoms in the archipelago.

In time, these same trade routes also introduced Islam and Arabo-Persian culture. From the late 13th century until the early 17th century, kingdom after kingdom converted to Islam. Beginning in the early 16th century, the spices of the Moluccas and the stranglehold the Malayan port of Malacca, Srivijaya's successor, held on international commerce attracted first the Portuguese and Spaniards and later the Dutch and English. The modern state of Indonesia had its beginnings in a scattering of fortified outposts established by the Holland-based VOC (Dutch East India Company) in the early 17th century. The VOC eventually succeeded in excluding European competitors from the spice trade and in dominating native rulers, but not without getting mired in a territorial expansion, which would bankrupt it by the end of the 18th century.

By the 1830s, the modern Dutch colonial state was founded, initially as a royal monopoly intent on squeezing as much prof-

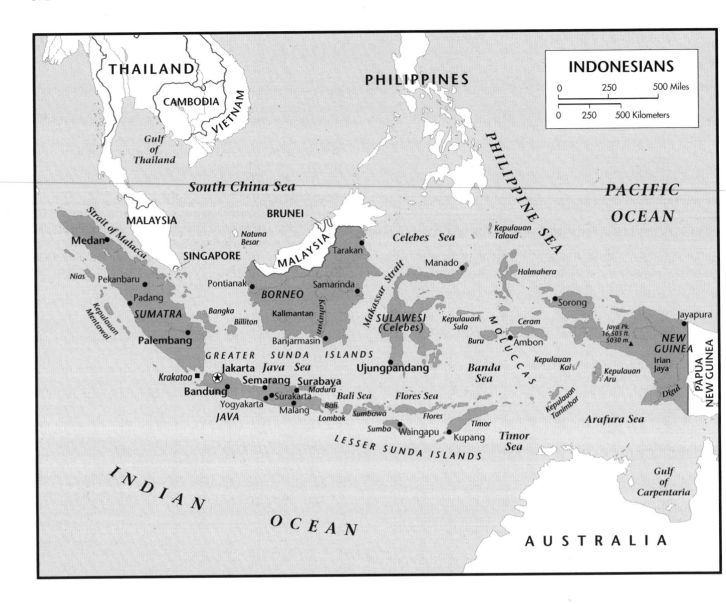

it as possible out of Java's peasants under the infamous Cultivation System. Over the next century, the power of this state and of a global capitalism hungry for the Indies' sugar, oil, rubber, and other natural riches expanded throughout the archipelago and penetrated deeper into the lives of more and more indigenes. It was within the framework of a common Dutch administration and European-style education that in the early years of the 20th century a small but rapidly growing group of "natives" began to imagine a community encompassing all the archipelago's peoples and to struggle to free an "Indonesian nation."

In early 1942, the Japanese, fresh from defeating the Americans and British elsewhere in Southeast Asia, took the Netherlands Indies with hardly any resistance from the Dutch; while brutally exploiting the colony for the resources needed by its own war effort, the new occupier gave Indonesian nationalist leaders, suppressed under the Dutch since the 1920s, opportunities to mobilize the population. On 17 August 1945, after the atomic bombings of Hiroshima and Nagasaki, the two most prominent, Sukarno and Hatta, proclaimed Indonesian independence. It would take years of bloody struggle before the re-

turned Dutch formally recognized the Indonesian republic on 17 December 1949.

In the 1950s, an experiment with parliamentary democracy failed amid the economic chaos produced in the previous two decades by world depression, world war, anti-colonial revolution, and post-revolutionary rebellions. President Sukarno attempted to restore stability through "Guided Democracy," a highly personalized style of rule wherein Sukarno's charisma was supposed to reconcile the differences among increasingly antagonistic political parties (Muslim, secular nationalist, and Communist) and a politicized army. As hyperinflation drove millions to the edge of starvation by the mid-1960s, this political competition intensified, sharpening rural conflicts over land. On the night of 30 September 1965, leftist junior officers abducted and killed six prominent generals. Major General Suharto stepped in to save the nation from what the military termed a "Communist coup," eventually forcing the left-leaning Sukarno to hand supreme power over to him on 11 March 1966. A nationwide bloodletting followed the coup and counter-coup, one of the 20th century's worst: local vigilantes under army sponsorship massacred as many as 400,000 Communists, leftist nationalists, and the victims of local mass "settling of scores."

By 1997, after more than 30 years of Suharto's "New Order," Indonesia had gone from being an economic "basket case" and diplomatic "renegade"/"pariah" to becoming a favored destination for foreign investment and a regional power whose voice carried ever more weight. However, social changes generated by rapid development were already threatening the stability of the very authoritarian system that had fostered economic growth. Despite massive corruption (most notoriously that of Suharto's own children) and pervasive repression of labor activism and other opposition, the general population seemed willing to recognize the regime's legitimacy as long as it delivered rising standards of living. When the Asian/global emerging markets financial crisis of 1997–98 threw millions of Indonesians into poverty, massive popular protests forced Suharto to resign. The sudden end of the New Order regime unleashed interethnic and interreligious conflicts that government suppression (as well as manipulation) had only intensified (riots against ethnic Chinese, including murder and rape, drove many to emigrate). In many parts of Indonesia, as the nation began experimenting with shifting more power into the hands of local governments, Christianized indigenous communities and Muslim transmigrants shed each other's blood, the latter often at the instigation of military factions and of international radical Islamist networks.

Since 1998, economic growth has resumed. The unemployment level, however, has not been substantially reduced and food and fuel prices are rising, making the lot of the poor even harder. Corruption, moreover, remains a massive problem: according to Transparency International, in 2007 Indonesia ranked 143 in a scale of 179, the same as Russia and only slightly better than Angola and Nigeria. Nonetheless, democracy has taken root, with free parliamentary elections held for the first time in almost four decades in 1999 and free direct presidential elections in 2004 (with an impeachment in between). The sequence of Indonesia's post-Suharto presidents represents the contemporary political spectrum: Muslim technocrats (B. J. Habibie), moderate Islamic parties (Abdurrahman Wahid), Sukarnoist secular nationalists (Megawati Sukarnoputri), and the military (ex-general Bambang Yudhoyono). Tensions persist, inherent in the discrepancies between Indonesia's realities and the ideals embodied in the Pancasila (the Five Principles), the state ideology: (1) belief in one Supreme God; (2) a noble and civilized humanity; (3) the unity of Indonesia; (4) democracy guided by the principles of consensus and representation; and (5) social justice for the entire Indonesian people.

² LOCATION AND HOMELAND

In the Indonesian national language, the usual expression for the "homeland," *Tanah Air Kita,* translates as "Our Land and Water." This phrase expresses most succinctly the central fact of Indonesia's geography: the country consists of more than 17,000 islands, of which 6,000 are permanently inhabited (the total land area equals that of Mexico). The principal islands and island groups are Sumatra, Java, Bali, the Lesser Sundas (in Indonesian, *Nusa Tenggara,* the "Southeastern Islands," including Lombok, Sumbawa, Flores, Roti, and Timor), Irian Jaya (Indonesian New Guinea), the Moluccas (including Ambon and Halmahera), Sulawesi, and Kalimantan (Indonesian Borneo).

The extraordinary fertility of much of the country's soil derives from the fact that the archipelago belongs to the "Ring of Fire," which circles the Pacific Ocean with a chain of insular and continental volcanoes. Indonesia's islands straddle the equator in a broad belt, which is actually longer than the east–west span of Europe or the continental United States. Proximity to warm water ensures that the overall climatic temperature varies little, remaining hot and humid all year round. Most of Indonesia experiences only two seasons: a dry season and a wet season. In January and February for western Indonesia, and April to July in the Moluccas, the monsoon winds bring torrential rains.

Indonesia, with its 238,000,000 inhabitants (September 2008 estimate), is the fourth–most populous country in the world (after China, India, and the United States). The most striking characteristic of Indonesia's population is its radically uneven distribution: Java, whose area (about that of New York State) amounts to no more than 7% of the Indonesian total, possesses nearly 60% of the population, and population densities overall vary from 980 people per sq km (1,550 per sq mi) in Central Java to less than 12 in Central Kalimantan and 6 in Papua. Because of the government's vigorous promotion of contraception over the past three decades, the population growth rate has been reduced to 1.18% per year. Nonetheless, the population (33.6% under age of 18) is still predicted to increase by nearly a quarter in the next four decades, reaching 294 million by the year 2050. The population, moreover, is becoming increasingly urbanized: the proportion of Indonesians living in cities rose from only 30% in 1990 to 45.6% in 2003 and is estimated to increase to 67.7% by 2030. Teeming with 15.1 million people (12,635 people per sq km [2000]) and sprawling over a vast stretch of coastal northwestern Java, the urban agglomeration centered on Jakarta, Indonesia's capital, ranks as the world's 14th most populous megacity, ahead of Beijing and London. Indonesia possesses seven other cities with populations of over a million; of these cities, Surabaya, Medan, and Makassar (Ujung Pandang) serve as regional centers for east Java/eastern Indonesia, Sumatra, and eastern Indonesia respectively.

Throughout Indonesia, rapid population growth has increased human demands on land and water, resulting in severe ecological problems: deforestation (with its inevitable companions, soil erosion, river siltation, reef death, and massive wildfires spewing heavy smog that affects not only western Indonesia but also Malaysia and Singapore); water pollution from sewage, pesticides, and offshore drilling; and depletion of fishing stocks. Ironically, "transmigration," the government-organized transfer of landless peasants from Java and Bali to sparsely peopled regions of Sumatra, Kalimantan, Sulawesi, and Indonesian (western) New Guinea (Papua, formerly Irian Jaya) has all too often introduced a method of agriculture that is ruinous of the local soils.

³ LANGUAGE

Although Indonesians speak between 250 and 700 distinct mother languages, there is only one official language of government, commerce, education, and mass media: Bahasa Indonesia (literally, the "Indonesian language"), a dialect of Malay. Although Malay is the mother tongue of less than 10% of the population, forms of Malay had long been in use throughout the archipelago as a medium of interethnic communication, a fact recognized by the Dutch colonial administration and by Indonesian nationalists' 1928 "Youth Oath" *(Sumpah Pemuda)*.

For the majority of Indonesians, Bahasa Indonesia is the language of the public sphere, while a regional language is used for private, family, and local community life. Outside of Jakarta, where 90% of households report Bahasa Indonesia as the primary language of the home, monolingualism in Bahasa Indonesia is growing rapidly in the major multiethnic cities of the archipelago, such as Medan and Ujung Pandang, as well as in regions of traditionally great linguistic diversity, such as the Minahasa area of North Sulawesi and many islands in the Moluccas.

While Malay was and (to a limited extent) still is written in Arabic script, Bahasa Indonesia uses a Latin script. In 1972, a spelling reform was promulgated to unify the orthographies of Bahasa Indonesia and Bahasa Malaysia.

Except for several separate families of Papuan languages spoken in Irian Jaya and some other eastern islands, the tongues spoken in Indonesia belong to several branches of the Austronesian language family. This language family includes the closely related languages of Madagascar, Malaysia, and the Philippines, as well as the more distant tongues of Melanesia, Micronesia, Polynesia, and aboriginal Taiwan. Austronesian languages were brought by Southern Mongoloid farming and seafaring peoples who entered Indonesia from the Philippines beginning 5,000 to 4,000 years ago. However, the farther east one travels in the Moluccas and the Lesser Sundas, the more pronounced becomes the Papuan genetic and linguistic legacy.

The major ethnolinguistic groups in Indonesia were as follows (population figures from the 2000 census, whose criterion for membership in an ethnicity was self-identification, supplemented by estimates from the 1990s if these are significantly different):

Java: Javanese (83.9 million people, in the center and east, 41.7% of the national population, the first largest ethnic group, western Java's 4.1 million Bantenese and 1.9 million Cirebonese, who speak dialects of Javanese, were counted as separate ethnicities in the 2000 census); Sundanese (31 million, in the west, 15.4% of the national population, the second largest ethnic group); Madurese (6.7–14 million in the east and on the nearby island of Madura); and Betawi (5 million), the "indigenous" people of Jakarta ("Batavia" under the Dutch), descended from slaves settled there by the VOC.

Sumatra: Acehnese (3 million, on the far northern tip); Gayo (in the highlands immediately south of the Acehnese); Toba Batak and Dairi Batak (respectively, 2 million and 1.2 million, in the highlands of the north, other Batak subgroups are the Karo, Mandailing, Angkola, and Simalungan, all groups total 6.1 million); Minangkabau (5.5–7.5 in the west); Nias and Mentawai (on islands off the west coast); Rejang and Lampung (respectively, 1 million and 1.5 million in southernmost Sumatra); and Malay (7–10 million, the third largest ethnic classification, scattered from the east coast of Sumatra through the Riau archipelago and on to the coasts of Kalimantan; also the dominant population of West Malaysia and present on the coasts of East Malaysia

and in Brunei and Singapore; the Riau-Johor dialect is the basis of Bahasa Indonesia and Bahasa Malaysia).

Kalimantan: Banjarese (3.9–5 million people in southeastern Kalimantan); and a great diversity of inland, animist peoples generally known as "Dayak" but who can be subdivided into such distinct groupings as the Ngaju, Maanyan, Ot Danum, Penan, and Kenyah.

Sulawesi: on the southwestern peninsula, Bugis (5 million in South Sulawesi), Makassarese (2 million), and Mandar; in the central highlands, a great diversity of groups, of which the best known are the Sa'dan Toraja and Pamona; on the northern peninsula, the Tomini, Gorontalo, Bolaang Mongondow, and the nationally prominent Minahasa; and in the east and on offshore islands, the Mori, Bungku, Muna, and Butonese.

The Lesser Sundas (only the better-known groups, names roughly corresponding to islands except as noted): Balinese (3–4 million people); Sasak (2.6 million, on Lombok); Sumbawans; Bimanese; Sumbanese; Savunese; on Flores, Manggarai, Ngada, Endenese, Sikanese; and on Timor, Tetum, Atoni, Helong; Rotinese.

The Moluccas: Non-Austronesian, Ternatans; Tidorese; and in northern Halmahera, Tobelorese, Galelarese, and other small groups; Austronesian, in southern Halmahera, small language groups such as Sawai; in the southern islands, Tanimbarese, Aru, and Kei; and the most important culture in the central islands, Ambonese.

Papua (Irian Jaya): although this province is home to less than 1% of the national population, the number of mutually unintelligible speech forms there may well approach the number in all the rest of the archipelago. Austronesian languages are spoken along the north and west coasts, while Papuan languages are spoken elsewhere (e.g., Asmat and Dani).

Chinese: numbering 1.7–7.5 million, they form the most important "nonindigenous" group (though most have resided in Indonesia for generations). The great majority are urban, although there are sizable rural populations in West Kalimantan and in the Riau Archipelago. Chinese-Indonesians are far from homogeneous, divided between the nonindigenized and the indigenized (i.e., acculturated to various local societies, the most prominent example being the peranakan of Java) as well as among home-region language groups (Hokkien, Teochiu, Cantonese, and Hakka). Under both colonial and post-colonial regimes, the Chinese have been set apart from the indigenous population. They are both granted privileges and subjected to discrimination and controls. Their economic prominence and cultural distinctiveness have long been the target of popular resentment; the 2000 census likely under-reports the number of Chinese because many Chinese were reluctant to identify themselves as such.

Names

Practices of naming vary from ethnic group to ethnic group as well as across class and religious lines. The most commonly encountered type of name is an Arabic one associated with Islam.

Indonesian workers paint traditional Javanese textile, batik, in central Java. (AP Images/Tatan Syuflana)

On Java, however, names of Sanskrit origin are favored, either alone or in combination with Arabic ones. Similarly, throughout the country, Christians add European names to names from their own ethnic languages. Outside of a few suku, such as the Batak and the Minahasa, family names are not used. In recent decades, Chinese have been under pressure to adopt "Indonesian" names for official purposes; in keeping with their own traditions, Chinese often pass on these adopted names as surnames to their children.

In general, Indonesians are fond of nicknames, usually based on the last syllable of the full name, e.g., the male name "Hermawan" becomes "Wawan," or the female name "Hermawati" becomes "Titi." On the other hand, etiquette requires that titles be used at all times to indicate respect. In Bahasa Indonesia, one addresses persons of greater age or status with the word "Bapak" for men and "Ibu" for women (literally, "Father" and "Mother," but meaning "Sir" and "Madam," and used instead of words for "you," which imply the speaker's equal or superior rank). The shortened forms "Pak" and "Bu" precede names and nicknames.

⁴ FOLKLORE

The nationalist movement and, later, the central government have honored a long list of "national heroes," who are commemorated not only in monuments but also in pictures hung in elementary school classrooms and in the names of streets, airports, universities, and other public institutions. Below are a few of the best-known figures:

Gajah Mada, the 14th-century Majapahit prime minister who is reputed to have prefigured Indonesian nationalism by vowing not to rest until he united the entire archipelago; the Javanese prince Diponegoro (1785–1855) and the Minangkabau cleric Imam Bonjol (1772–1864) who led an armed resistance to Dutch power; and Raden Ajeng Kartini (1879–1905), a Central Javanese noblewoman who advocated modern education and women's emancipation, and who is revered as a pioneer of Indonesian nationalism.

⁵ RELIGION

Religion plays a central role in defining individual identity and community life throughout Indonesia. One's religious affiliation is an essential fact noted on all official documents, including identity cards. All Indonesians must register as adherents of one of five recognized religions: Islam, Protestantism, Catholicism, Hinduism, or Buddhism. Atheism, associated with the banned Communist movement, is not an option. An elaborate bureaucracy oversees the operations of each of the five religious communities. No Indonesian Muslim may leave for the pilgrimage to Mecca *(Hajj)* without joining an official travel group (to avoid this constraint, some Indonesian Muslims depart for Mecca from other countries, such as Egypt). Legislation discourages marriage between members of different religious communities: one of the prospective partners must officially convert to the religion of the other. In the interests of confessional harmony, religious communities are forbidden to seek converts from each other's memberships, though they are welcome to proselytize among peoples "who do not yet have religion," e.g., animist tribespeople or many ethnic Chinese.

The vast majority (88%) of the population adheres to Islam, making Indonesia the largest Muslim nation on earth, with more Muslims than all the Arab countries put together. Practice ranges from "purist" (conforming to the standards of Middle Eastern orthodoxy) to "syncretist," including a wide range of pre-Islamic beliefs, especially characteristic of much Javanese Islam (for *kebatinan,* Javanese mystical sects, which often distinguish themselves from Islam, *see* **Javanese**). Among purists, there is a further distinction between "traditionalists" and "modernists," the former supporting and the latter rejecting local Muslim practices, as well as being open to techniques of Western education and organization.

Protestantism claims 5% of the population. Although the VOC was by no means a missionary enterprise, some populations associated with the Dutch converted to Calvinism: Minahasa, Ambonese, and Indos (Eurasians). In the 19th century, the colonial government permitted Protestant proselytization among the remaining non-Muslim peoples, with the most significant successes among the Batak of North Sumatra and peoples of Central Sulawesi. Catholicism (3%) was first introduced by the Portuguese in the 16th century; Flores and Timor are surviving enclaves. Missionary work in the 19th–20th century has propagated the religion in West Kalimantan and Papua. Especially in the last few decades, great numbers of Chinese have converted to either Protestantism or Catholicism.

Hinduism (2% of the population) in Indonesia means almost exclusively the religion of Bali, which is not a direct transplant of the Indian religion but rather a synthesis of indigenous and Indian elements. In addition, some ethnic groups have succeeded in legitimizing their own animist religions by having them reclassified as "Hinduism," e.g., the Aluk To Dolo of the Sa'dan Toraja, and the Kaharingan of the Dayak. Buddhism (no more than 1% of the population) claims mostly Chinese adherents, whose traditional practices combine Mahayana Buddhism with Taoism and Confucianism.

6 MAJOR HOLIDAYS

The Department of Religion authorizes a list of 12 public holidays (on which government offices and schools are closed). Two are purely secular: New Year's Day and Independence Day (August 17). The others are feasts observed by the five recognized religions: Nyepi, the Hindu-Balinese New Year; Waisak, the birth of the Buddha; Christmas, Good Friday, and Ascension Thursday for Christians; and five Muslim holidays, including the Islamic New Year, the Birth of Muhammad, the Night of the Ascent (Muhammad's visit to heaven), Idul Fitri (the end of the fasting month of Ramadan), and Idul Adha (recalling Abraham's willingness to sacrifice his son Ishmael at God's command).

Every year, Independence Day is celebrated with great fanfare. Each village and city neighborhood is decorated with red and white national flags, ceremonial gateways, and colorful paintings commemorating the Revolution. Parades, speeches, and performances of traditional music, dance, and theater also mark the day.

During the month of Ramadan, Muslims may not eat, drink, or smoke during the daylight hours. The end of these four weeks of self-denial is marked by a great celebration, called variously Idul Fitri, Lebaran, or Hari Raya. Through-

out Indonesia, special feasts are prepared, heralded by the mass weaving of *ketupat,* small palm-leaf containers for rice cooked in the previous days. Idul Fitri is the occasion for family reunions: migrants return to their hometowns (all intercity roads and the buses on them are packed at this time) to clean ancestral graves and sprinkle them with flower petals. Even non-Muslims observe the custom of making calls on family members, friends, neighbors, colleagues, and superiors to ask forgiveness for the offenses of the past year.

7 RITES OF PASSAGE

Life cycle rituals differ greatly according to ethnic group, religion, and social class. Although for many, particularly the urban poor, modernization in everyday life has simplified the rites of passage, the trend, beginning during the New Order, has been for affluent families to display their status by holding traditional rituals as elaborately as they can afford, often reviving forgotten customs with the help of ritual experts. Celebrations are public affairs to which the extended family (who often assist the hosts), friends, workmates, professional associates, and local officials are invited; indeed, they are generally open to the entire neighborhood or village, all of whom must be fed. The most important celebrations accompany births, circumcisions (for Muslim boys), weddings, and funerals. Weddings usually consist of the legally required religious ceremony (usually Muslim or Christian) and rites following ethnic custom, followed by a large reception held in a family home, a hotel, or a rented hall. Among the Muslim majority, funerals tend to be somewhat more uniform from ethnic group to ethnic group, including washing and enshrouding of the body and burial within 24 hours. Mourners in truckloads accompany the body to the cemetery and, after collective prayer, each mourner tosses a handful of earth into the grave.

8 INTERPERSONAL RELATIONS

Although traditional codes of behavior differ considerably from ethnic group to ethnic group (and group stereotypes exaggerate these differences), interpersonal relations throughout Indonesia are governed by a concern to preserve social harmony and personal honor ("face"); respect for hierarchy is considered essential to both. In their interactions with others, Indonesians take great care to show deference to those of higher status, whether from greater age, nobler ancestry, superior educational attainment, or higher organizational rank.

In general, Indonesian life tends to be group, rather than individual oriented. In a society where individuals have little personal space, rarely having even a bed to themselves, privacy is largely an alien concept; solitude is most commonly associated with defenselessness. Subordinating one's interests to the group's interest is a village value that has been carried over into many aspects of modern urban life. Great care (more in some regions, like Java, than in others) is taken to avoid the overt expression of disagreement within the group. Fear of bringing shame upon one's family and other groups to which one belongs in the face of outsiders powerfully conditions personal decisions. Indonesian etiquette stresses the interdependence of individuals, not their independence of one another.

Greetings and body language

The Islamic greeting, *"Wassalamu alaikum (warakhmatulla-hi wabarakatuh),"* which means "Peace upon you (and God's

A vendor cooks traditional snacks in downtown Jakarta. (Bay Ismoyo/AFP/Getty Images)

blessings),” has become the standard greeting in public life, even for non-Muslims, often accompanied by the shaking of hands, concluded by bringing the right palm to one’s own chest. The most common informal greeting is “*Dari mana?*” (“Where are you coming from?)” which is a question that is not felt to be intrusive and that no one is obliged to answer in specifics. Even in relatively informal situations, great importance is placed on asking leave to depart (a common phrase is the Dutch-derived “*Permisi?*”).

In offering or receiving things, one extends the right hand, showing particular deference by placing the left hand under the right elbow while doing so. While passing in front of older or higher-status people, it is customary to bow low, extend the right hand in front of oneself, and walk forward slowly. The left hand, used with water for cleaning oneself after defecation, is taboo for the above purposes; when one is forced to use the left hand in front of others, one excuses oneself (“*Ma’af kiri,*” “Forgive, the left.”). Especially in Java, the index finger is taboo; pointing is done with the right thumb, and one beckons others to come with a downward, inward movement of the right palm. Similarly, it is offensive to point the soles of one’s feet at others while sitting, a situation avoided by traditional modes of sitting cross-legged (*bersila,* men) or with legs folded to one side (*bersimpuh,* women). Folding one’s arms over one’s chest or holding them akimbo while speaking can appear to be aggressive.

Visiting and dating customs

Unannounced visits may be made in the late afternoon between siesta and dinnertime (4:00–6:00 PM). Visitors are served tea and snacks; one leaves a little food on the plate to show one wants no more. Indonesian attitudes toward punctuality are reflected in the expression “*jam karet*” (“rubber time”). Lateness to appointments is the norm; however, Indonesians tend to rise early, as well as retire early, perhaps as a function of the tropical climate.

Although there is considerable variation in this regard, interaction between members of the opposite sex tends to be closely monitored by elders and peers: dating and premarital sex are not condoned (early marriage is the traditional outlet). In many regions, the honor of the family is invested in its women’s reputation for chastity (which may entail the women avoiding any eye contact with males who are not their relatives), and the family’s men take quite seriously their responsibility to protect that honor. Public displays of affection between the sexes (such as holding hands or kissing) are taboo. Physical contact between members of the same sex, however, (such as walking arm in arm) is common, not being considered homosexual. One common way teenagers meet is for the boy to loiter by the front gate of the girl’s house, hoping to be admitted by a servant or family member who will chaperone the ensuing conversation.

⁹ LIVING CONDITIONS

At US$3,843 per year, Indonesia's per capita GDP (adjusted for Purchasing Power Parity, all figures are from 2005, unless otherwise noted) places it in the category of lower middle income nations. Its ranking in the United Nations Human Development Index is 107 (out of 177 countries ranked). Countries with similar HDIs are Vietnam, Syria, the Occupied Palestinian Territories, Turkmenistan, and Nicaragua. Its HDI ranking is six places higher than its ranking according to GNP per capita (PPP), indicating that its population is somewhat better off in terms of health and education than per capita income alone would provide for (South Africa's per capita GDP, adjusted for PPP, is almost three times that of Indonesia's, yet South Africa's HDI index is slightly lower).

More than half the population (52.4%) lives on less than two dollars equivalent a day, and 7.5% on less than a dollar a day. The proportion of the population living below the national poverty line (earning less than the amount needed to provide oneself a daily intake of 2,100 calories and other basic needs) has declined dramatically over the years, from 40.1% in 1976 to 16.58% in 2007. As measured by its Gini coefficient of 34.3, income inequality in Indonesia is not particularly severe by world standards. It is greater in the United States (40.8), far greater in Brazil (57), and not much less in Japan (29.9). Still, the richest 20% earns 5.2 times as much as the poorest 20%. (a slight improvement over seven times in the 1990s). Moreover, there is wide variation in the standard of living from region to region and between urban and rural areas. For instance, on average, rural people spend more of their income on food than urbanites do, despite higher food prices in cities (in 2005 residents of the national capital region spent 37.72% of their income on food, while residents of heavily rural Nusa Tenggara Timur spent 62.24% (the national average had been 54.59% in 2004).

Given the high average family size, Indonesian houses tend to be crowded; in 2006, 44.9% of houses were under 50 sq m in size, 21.3% under 9 sq m (1990s figures record 6% of houses as having no separate bedroom). Some 37.78% had walls of materials other than brick (down from 51.77% in 1990). Roofs are of tile (66% of all houses according to 1990s figures), zinc, or thatch (4.65%, down from 8.75% in 1990). About 16% of houses had an earthen floor in 2006 (down from 24% in 1990). The layout of a well-off family's house does not differ from that of Western houses, having separate rooms for receiving guests, eating dinner, etc. About 60% of houses had their own toilet in 2006, up from 47% in 1990. Most bathrooms, however, differ from Western ones in having squat toilets and an open tank to scoop water out of for bathing and flushing. Many poorer Indonesian homes lack such facilities, forcing their owners to use public areas such as riversides. While nearly all houses in Jakarta have electricity, the national figure is only 54% (47.3% in the 1990s). 28.5% of households use biomass (firewood, etc) or waste material for fuel. Overall, per capita carbon dioxide emissions are still low, at 1.7 tons in 2004 (up from 1.2 in 1990).

In the early 1990s, just over 11% of houses had their garbage picked up by sanitation workers. The rest disposed of it themselves by burning or piling it in their yards, or throwing it in public dumps, gutters, canals, or rivers. Only 13% of houses (mostly urban) enjoyed running water (not generally drinkable); most people obtained water from streams, canals, ponds, and wells that were usually polluted to some degree (in 1990, only 16.37% received piped or bottled water). By 2006, 46.6% had access to safe drinking water from pump, well, or spring.

Life expectancy (according to 2008 figures) has been rising: 67.98 years for men and 73.07 years for women; 58.4 years for men and 62 years for women in 1990, up from 51.1 years for men and 54.4 years for women in 1980. Infant mortality is also falling: 31.04 from 105 deaths per 1,000 live births in 1980 to 75.2 deaths in 1990. Modern pharmaceuticals and physicians are expensive, so most people use traditional herbal remedies (*jamu,* much of which are now mass-manufactured) and consult traditional healers (*dukun*) more frequently. As part of an extensive public clinic system stressing preventative care (immunization, contraception, and natal care), doctors make weekly visits to villages.

Ownership of an automobile (25 per 1,000 people in 2005) or motorcycle (130 per 1,000 people) is a luxury unavailable to all but upper class and some middle-class families (up from 1990s figures of 5 and 30 respectively). Most people rely on buses for travel within and between cities; Java also has a well-used rail network. Minivans run within cities and through the countryside (where horse-drawn carriages are still common). Except in Jakarta where *bajaj* (motorcycle cabs) are used instead, *becak* (tricycles with a seating carriage in front of the peddler) carry people and goods through side streets and roads. As an alternative to expensive airplanes, large passenger ships provide the principal means of interisland travel for most people; sailing ships are still in wide use for fishing and carrying merchandise.

Telephone access is spreading rapidly; the number of telephone landlines per 1,000 people rose from 6 in 1990 to 213 in 2005. More than 1 out of 5 people had a cell phone subscription in 2005. The number of Internet users is growing fast, tripling from 11.2 million in 2004 to 33.2 million in 2008 (UN figures estimated 73 Internet users for every 1000 people in 2005).

¹⁰ FAMILY LIFE

The family is the central institution of Indonesian society, and the model for other social relations. Although kinship patterns differ from ethnic group to ethnic group, some common features can be seen throughout the country. The family household includes not only parents and children but also grandparents, other unmarried relatives, and servants. Child care responsibilities are shared among mothers, grandmothers, older daughters, and others. The father is often the ultimate authority figure, though often a distant one, while the mother manages the family money. Remaining at home, children remain dependent on their parents until, and often well into, marriage. Children are duty-bound to take care of their parents in old age, and older siblings likewise help their juniors, even going as far as financing the latter's education.

Indonesians keep cats and dogs as well as songbirds as pets.

¹¹ CLOTHING

Context and class determine the choice between modern and traditional clothes. For instance, while a male office worker wears a Western-style shirt and trousers to work, he often relaxes at home, does his prayers, or is wed in some kind of sarong. Shorts are not worn by adults, except by becak drivers and other low-status laborers. In their everyday clothing, members of the elite follow Western fashions closely. For example, young people commonly wear jeans and t-shirts. For ceremonial purposes, however, they lavish great expense on traditional costumes. A small number of Muslim women wear a head covering in public (i.e., in the presence of men who are not their kin or very close friends): this may be either a more traditional scarf *(kudung)* or, the modernist preference, a full veil exposing only the face *(jilbab)* and often worn with items of Western-style clothing like jeans.

Under the New Order, a standard "national costume" came into vogue for use on formal occasions. For men, the black felt *peci* cap, originally associated with Muslims, was first popularized as a symbol of nationalism by Sukarno in the 1920s. In current practice, this is worn with a batik shirt (untucked) and trousers. Women wear a sarong and a *kebaya* (tight-sleeved, collarless shirt) and put their hair up into a bun (or tuck it under a wig of the required shape). For work, many jobs require a uniform: soldiers, elementary school students, and civil servants all wear uniforms.

12 FOOD

Indonesian cuisine has been influenced by Indian, Middle Eastern, Chinese, Portuguese, and even Dutch cooking.

Throughout the country (with the partial exception of dry eastern islands where maize, cassava, taro, and sago are important, if not esteemed, starch sources), rice is the staple, the definition of a "full meal" being "cooked rice *(nasi)* with side dishes *(lauk-pauk)*." Depending on one's budget, these side dishes can range from the most modest (some boiled vegetables with or without a piece of dried fish) to the most extravagant (several fried and stewed dishes including meat curries, heavily spiced, especially with chilies). Outside of well-off families, meat (goat, mutton, beef for Muslims, also pork and in some regions dog for non-Muslims) is consumed only on special occasions. Chicken, seafood, and soybean products provide a cheaper protein source acceptable to all.

The traditional mode of eating for all ethnic groups has been to scoop up food from flat dishes with the fingers of the right hand (the left hand being reserved exclusively for washing oneself after defecation). An alternative associated with sitting at a Western-style table is to use a spoon and fork (i.e., using the fork in the left hand to push food on to the spoon in the right hand). Individual portions are not separated; rather, everyone takes from common dishes laid out at once in the center of the table or dining mat. Ordinary meals are usually consumed quickly without conversation.

Most Indonesians do not eat a distinct breakfast, apart from leftovers of the previous evening's meal, should there be any. Middle-class people will eat bread with coffee or tea; this bread is usually bought from men sent around neighborhoods by bakeries at dawn. For lunch and dinner, upper- and middle-class people eat rice and side dishes prepared by their maids. For lunch, office workers and students will either go to *warung* or *kedai* (small food stalls) or buy dishes like *bakso* (meatball soup) from mobile street vendors. For those who can afford them, afternoon snacks (e.g., *rujak*, a fresh fruit salad) are also common. In city neighborhoods, a great variety of street vendors make the rounds well into the night. Especially popular are stalls that set up for the evening around plazas or along major thoroughfares, closing up after midnight. Throughout the country, Chinese restaurants can be found, as well as those serving Padang food (that of the far-migrating Minangkabau of West Sumatra).

Outside animist and Christian areas, because of Islamic strictures, the consumption of alcohol (mostly beer) is limited to some particularly Westernized members of the elite. As untreated water is usually unsafe, tea and coffee are drunk in great quantities, usually with sugar and sometimes milk. Soft drinks, including bottled tea and bottled water, are also popular. 58% of men and 3% of women smokes (up from 30% in the 1990s); Indonesians favor cigarettes *(kretek)* flavored with cloves.

13 EDUCATION

Literacy (2004 estimate) stands at 90.4 % overall, 94% for males, and 86.8% for females, a substantial increase from 1990s figures of 77%, 84%, and 68% respectively. Schooling is free of charge and compulsory for ages 7 to 15. About 81% of the age-eligible students are enrolled in all levels of education; 94% of age-eligible students are enrolled in elementary education, and 61% in secondary education (2005). About 75% of students reach fifth grade (2004). Between 1980 and 1990, the proportion of the population that had graduated from senior high school doubled, reaching 13.7%.

Curriculum in primary and secondary schools is determined by the central government. Major goals of the educational system include teaching the national language, instilling the state ideology of Pancasila, and supplying religious instruction. Teaching methodology stresses rote memorization. For poorer families, sending a child to a public school is often a financial burden because of supplementary fees and other costs, such as textbooks and uniforms (a uniform costs Rp10,000 or us$9, almost one-eighth of the average monthly industrial wage).

Over 2.58 million were enrolled in tertiary education in 2007. Only one in five applicants to state institutions is admitted (a decrease from one in four in the 1990s). The requirement of a written thesis *(skripsi)* prevents most students from earning their degrees on time. Many must interrupt their study in order to work to support themselves and finance further coursework.

While only about 7.6% of students enrolled in primary education attends private (mostly Islamic schools), about 40% of students enrolled in secondary education does (2007). At *pesantren* (Islamic schools of the traditional type), students learn the Arabic language, scripture, and religious law but without specific graduation requirements; students who live at the usually rural schools may leave study at any time.

14 CULTURAL HERITAGE

No dance styles can be said to be truly national, but three urban-based music genres have won nationwide popularity. *Kroncong,* a melancholy music for voice and strings, ultimately of Portuguese origin via the Eurasians of the VOC towns, is still widely heard though considered old-fashioned (during the Revolution, it was the medium for patriotic songs). Favored by the self-consciously "cosmopolitan" upper and middle classes is *pop Indonesia,* modeled on American-European pop music. *Dangdut,* characterized by high-pitch vocals and an insistent beat derived from Indian film music, on the other hand, has its base in the urban poor. Holiday fairs will feature large tents where hundreds of young people crush together gyrating to live *dangdut* singing.

Literature in Bahasa Indonesia (as distinct from writing in Classical Malay) had its beginnings in late 19th-century "penny dreadfuls" produced for the Sino-Indonesian and Eurasian urban market. More substantial novels, such as Marah Roesidi's *Sitti Noerbaja* (1922), as well as poetry, have been written since the early years of the 20th century, often published by Balai Pustaka, a still extant printing house established by the Dutch government in 1908. Indonesia's internationally famous writer has been Pramoedya Ananta Toer (1925–2006), a leftist author, imprisoned for years under the New Order, whose tetralogy, "This Earth of Mankind," "Child of All Nations," "Footsteps," and "House of Glass," explores the birth of Indonesian nationalism.

15 WORK

With more than 70% of the population living in rural areas, agriculture employed more than half of Indonesia's workforce. Only 13% of cultivated land belongs to large plantations, the rest divided among tens of millions of smallholders. Although the high economic growth of recent years has benefited many rural families, many peasants do not own enough land to survive, or have none at all and are forced to work others' land. One out of four rural families has at least one member working in the cities.

Rice grown in irrigated fields *(sawah)* is by far the most important food crop, particularly in Java and Bali, but maize, cassava, taro, sago, soybeans, peanuts, and coconuts are also widely grown. Sugar, coffee, tea, cloves (for domestic cigarettes), and rubber are important cash crops. Cattle, goats, chickens, and, in non-Muslim areas, pigs are the main livestock species. In the Outer Islands, a decreasing number of people still practice slash-and-burn agriculture *(ladang)*. Fishing employed 1.5 million in the 1990s.

Official figures put the unemployment rate at 8.46% in 2008, but many of the "working" can be classified as "underemployed," engaged in small tasks for minimal pay. In 2005–2006, the nominal monthly wage in a manufacturing job ranged between Rp 876,600 to Rp1,029,200, in a hotel job between Rp 723,900 and Rp 931,700 (at an average of Rp10,800 per us$1). Over 43% of the work force works in the "informal sector," at jobs requiring little skill or capital. In the 1990s, petty traders, including half of all non-farming women, make up most of the 16% of the work force then engaged in commerce. In 2005, 44% of the population was employed in agriculture. Industry employed 18% (up from 11% in the 1990s), including great numbers of young women who work in textile factories. 38% work in the service sector (compared to only 13% in the previous decade); these include those employed in the bureaucracy and the military. With only a little over 300,000 active duty personnel, this is a relatively low proportion by world standards. Indonesia, though the fourth largest country by population, only has the fourteenth largest military, approximately the same size as Thailand's, a country only one-fifth as populous.

According to government figures from 2006, 2.7 million Indonesians were working legally abroad (only 2.8% of the labor force), mostly in the Middle East but also increasingly in neighboring Asian countries with labor shortages, such as Singapore and Taiwan. The world's second largest flow of illegal workers (after that from Mexico into the United States) is from Indonesia into Malaysia.

16 SPORTS

Part of the Dutch colonial heritage, the most popular modern sport is soccer, which is played on large open spaces in towns throughout the country. In 1994, the whole nation stayed up night after night to watch live telecasts of the World Cup being played in Atlanta. The other two most widely played sports are basketball and badminton, the latter often played in the middle of the street without a net.

Martial arts are also widely practiced, be they the indigenous *silat* or imported East Asian forms, such as *kung fu* or *taekwando*. With the government stressing calisthenics, many people can be seen jogging or otherwise exercising in streets and public squares and parks, particularly on Sunday morning. A common excursion for young people is to go hiking in large groups through mountain areas.

17 ENTERTAINMENT AND RECREATION

There were 130 radios and 57 televisions for every 1,000 people. Numerous radio stations broadcast programs in the national and regional languages and play regional (traditional), national, and foreign music (Heavy Metal, for instance, appeals to a wide teenage audience). Until 1989, only one government-run channel was available, beamed in by Indonesia's own Palapa satellite, but at present there are 11 national broadcast channels (all but two are private) and many more local ones. Programming includes the government-produced news, comedies set in middle-class Jakarta homes, historical dramas, music concerts, and old movies; dubbed or subtitled foreign imports consist of American series, Japanese anime and melodramas, and Latin American soap operas. Many well-to-do households receive a wide selection of foreign channels through a satellite dish *(parabola)* or cable and often allow neighbors to pay to tap in. In the countryside, families wealthy enough to purchase a television set regularly invite fellow villagers to watch.

In cinemas, elite audiences prefer to watch subtitled American movies, or dubbed or subtitled Hong Kong kung fu films (all censored of sexually explicit footage). The masses watch Indonesian, Hong Kong, and Indian movies. Films produced by the declining Indonesian film industry resort to predictable plots, violence, and as much exposed flesh as the censors will allow.

Other popular urban pastimes include window-shopping in malls and department stores, browsing in night markets, and eating at evening-only food stalls.

18 FOLK ART, CRAFTS, AND HOBBIES

A variety of crafts are practiced by individual Indonesian ethnic groups, including woodcarving, weaving textiles, baskets, and mats, metalworking (gold, silver, copper, and iron), pottery and stone carving, leatherworking, tie-dying and batiking, glass painting, boat building, and gardening.

19 SOCIAL PROBLEMS

Rapid development has not brought comparable benefits to all sectors of the population. Despite the success of contraception programs, the large and growing population continues to strain national resources. Although living standards have risen, economic growth has widened the gap between the rich and the poor, especially the rural landless. The security net provided by traditional social networks is weakening, exposing many people to exploitation. The conflict between traditional values and those of modernity, both as defined by the national state and by international consumer culture, is intensifying, leading many to espouse religious fundamentalism as an alternative.

Political liberalization since the end of the New Order has given an opening to groups seeking to impose Sharia (Islamic law) on many localities. In October 2008, a national anti-pornography bill was passed in the face of strong opposition, including from women's groups and from non-Muslim ethnic groups, such as the Balinese (who felt their religious images might be threatened); the legislation's targets include public displays of affection, such as kissing relatives in greeting and public performances that "excite sexual desire," as well as pop concerts where dangdut stars' dancing involve gyrating on stage. Many feared that the law would legitimize violent actions taken by radical Islamist vigilante groups against places deemed "immoral," such as brothels and pool halls.

20 GENDER ISSUES

The country's Gender Related Development Index (2005) is 0.721, slightly less than its Human Development Index of 0.728. In comparison with their counterparts in Middle Eastern Muslim societies, Indonesian women play a more prominent public role, from petty trading to the professions. Under bilateral kinship, the mother's line is potentially as important as the father's line in channeling inheritance and status. Women are active in organizations, such as those for the wives of civil servants or army officers. In Indonesian Islam, women are not segregated from men in the mosque. Indonesians are currently debating the legality of polygamy (allowed by Islam but not common and even forbidden to civil servants).

Life expectancy for women is higher (71.6 years) than for men (67.8). Adult literacy, however, is lower for women (86.8%) than for men (94%), as is enrollment in all levels of education (67% vs. 70%, there are about 8 women for every 10 men in university and other tertiary educational institutions). The country has had a woman president (Megawati Sukarnoputri, the daughter of Indonesia's first president), and women hold 11.3% of the seats in parliament. On average, women earn 46% of the income that men do. 1 million women are employed as domestic workers overseas, most commonly in Saudi Arabia or Malaysia, and are vulnerable to exploitation and abuse from their employers.

Abortion is prohibited except in the case of danger to the life of the mother. In 2000–2005, the fertility rate stood at 2.4 births per woman (down from 5.3 three decades earlier). 89% of women from the richest 20% of society were attended by a skilled health professional while giving birth; the proportion was only 21% for the poorest 20% of society. During 1990–2004, 310 women died in childbirth for every 100,000 live births. For the richest 20% of society, infant mortality ran to 23 per 1,000 live births and under five mortality to 29 per 1,000 live births; for the poorest 20 % of society, the figures were respectively 78 and 109 (population overall, 28 and 36).

The government's approach towards prostitution is ambivalent. On the one hand, prostitutes (officially termed "WTS," short for "wanita tuna susila," "women without morals") are concentrated in government-supervised "lokalisasi," brothel districts; on the other, these lokalisasi are subject to being shut down by the same government, and the prostitutes are subject to harassment. Enforcing anti-prostitution regulations, however, very often means that police detain non-prostitutes simply for being out on city streets at night. The trafficking of women and children within the country and to foreign countries is a major problem (entertainers and mail order brides often suffer abuse). Underage marriage is common (the legal age for marriage is 16 but exceptions can be made with parental consent, 33% of marriages in rural areas and 15% in urban areas are underage). High rates of underage marriage and of divorce leave many women with few options other than going into prostitution or falling prey to human traffickers holding forth promises of jobs in cities or abroad.

Human Rights Watch regards Indonesia as failing to back up fully its rhetoric in promoting women's rights.

21 BIBLIOGRAPHY

Badan Pusat Statistik (Statistics Indonesia). www.bps.go.id.

———. Statistik Indonesia. *Statistical Yearbook of Indonesia.* Jakarta: Biro Pusat Statistik, 1994.

Cummings, Joe, et al. Indonesia: *A Travel Survival Kit.* Hawthorn, Australia: Lonely Planet Publications, 1990.

Dalton, Bill. *Indonesia Handbook.* Chico, CA: Moon Publications, 1991.

Departemen Pendidikan Nasional Republik Indonesia (Ministry of National Education). www.depdiknas.go.id

Draine, Cathie, and Barbara Hall. *Culture Shock Indonesia.* Singapore: Times Books International, 1986.

Euromonitor International. "Indonesia Statistics." www.euromonitor.com.

Federal Research Division, Library of Congress, 1993

Gordon, Raymond G., Jr. (ed.), 2005. *Ethnologue: Languages of the World,* 15th edition. Dallas, Tex.: SIL International. Online version: www.ethnologue.com.

Human Rights Watch. "Regional Overview of Women's Rights in Asia." www.hrw.org/women/overview-asia.html (3 November 2008).

International Catholic Migration Commission. *Trafficking of Women and Children in Indonesia.* www.icmc.net/pdf/traffreport_en.pdf (3 November 2008).

Ricklefs, M. C. *A History of Modern Indonesia since c.1300,* 3rd ed. Stanford, CA: Stanford University Press, 2001.

Schwarz, Adam. *A Nation in Waiting: Indonesia in the 1990s.* St. Leonards, England: Allen and Unwin, 1994.

Transparency International. "Corruption Perceptions Index 2008." www.transparency.org/policy_research/surveys_indices/cpi/2008 (3 November 2008).

United Nations Children's Fund. "At a Glance: Indonesia—Statistics." http://www.unicef.org/infobycountry/indonesia_statistics.html (7 September 2008).

United Nations Development Programme. Human Development Reports. "2007–2008 Report: Indonesia." hdrstats.undp.org/countries/data_sheets/cty_ds_IDN.html (3 November 2008).

World Values Survey. "Inglehart-Welzel Cultural Map of the World." www.worldvaluessurvey.org (5 November 2008).

—by A. J. Abalahin

IRANIANS

PRONUNCIATION: i-RAHN-ee-uhns
LOCATION: Iran
POPULATION: 69,400,000 (2005 estimate)
LANGUAGE: Farsi (Persian)
RELIGION: Islam (Shia Muslim)

¹ INTRODUCTION

Iran, known since ancient times as Persia, has had a long and turbulent history. Iran's location at the crossroads of Europe and Asia resulted in many invasions and migrations. Cultural influences have thus been great, with Afghans, Arabs, Chinese, Greeks, Indians, Russians, and Turks all leaving behind traces of themselves.

Archaeologists have determined that Iran was inhabited as far back as 100,000 BC. Knowledge about this era is sparse, however. There is evidence that Iran played a role in the emergence of civilization 10,000 years ago. It is known that settled communities and villages had engaged in farming, pottery, metalworking, and other activities on the Iranian plateau around 6000 BC. A kingdom known as Elam dominated southwest Iran around 3000 BC, establishing a very advanced culture. This culture could write, and had a system of kingship and an organized priesthood. During the Iron Age, around 1500 BC, members of the Aryan (Indo-European) peoples began migrating in waves through the Caucasus Mountains across Central Asia into Iran. Around 1000–900 BC, the forerunners of present-day Iranians began arriving in the country. These included the Bactrians, Medes, and Parthians. A group settled in the southern area then known as Parsa. They were given the name of Persians, and Persia then became the name of the entire region of Iran. In 553 BC, the leader of the Achaemenid clan of Parsa, Cyrus the Great, established the first Persian Empire, which extended to Egypt, Greece, and Russia. Under the Achaemenids, Persia extended the realm of civilization, giving distant countries the opportunity to learn art and culture from one another and to trade goods.

The Achaemenids were overthrown in 336–330 BC by Alexander the Great, of Greece. Persia became part of the Greek Empire and, for several centuries, was the focus of much fighting between the Greeks and Romans. Upon Alexander's death in 323 BC, control of Persia was seized by General Seleucus, who established Seleucid rule for almost a century. In the 3rd century BC, a group known as the Parni (immigrants from Central Asia) assumed power and set up the Parthian Empire, which later collapsed in the 3rd century AD. From AD 226 until 641, Iran was ruled by the Sassanids, a dynasty of local rulers who encouraged Persian art and literature to flourish. Sculptures commemorating Sassanid military victories still adorn hills and cliffs in Iran.

From the 7th through the 9th centuries AD, Iran was conquered by Muslims from Arabia whose goal was the spread of the Muslim religion. They were successful in converting many Persians from their native religion of Zoroastrianism (which dated from the 7th–6th centuries BC) to Islam. Most of the Zoroastrians who did not convert to Islam left the country and settled in India. The Arab rulers were followed by various Turkish Muslim rulers. Then, in the 13th to 14th centuries,

Mongol leader Genghis Khan and his army subjected Persia to fierce destruction and killing. Between 1220 and 1258, one-fourth of Iran's population died as a result of the Mongol conquest. In 1380, Tamerlane (Timur the Lame), one of the last Mongol leaders, established the Timurid dynasty over Iran and Afghanistan. This was replaced centuries later, during the 16th century, by the Safavids, a local clan who were finally able to rid Iran of outside control. Under the rulership of these native Iranians, the arts once again flourished. Mosques and palaces built by the Safavids in their capital city, Esfahan, still stand in Iran. The Safavids were then conquered by Afghan invaders in 1722. An Iranian named Nadir Shah drove them out and established the Afshar dynasty in 1736. Another Turkish tribe, the Qajars, took power in the late 18th century.

The periodic foreign rule ended in 1921, when Reza Khan, an Iranian army officer, deposed the Qajars and established the Pahlavi dynasty. He became the emperor or *shah,* with the name Reza Shah Pahlavi. In 1935, the Shah changed the country's name to Iran, a variation on "Ariana," which means "country of the Aryan people." During World War II (1939–45), Shah Pahlavi, angered by British and Russian troop deployments in Iran, sided with Germany instead of with the Allied powers. In 1941, the Allied powers forced him to abdicate his throne. Pahlavi's son, Muhammad Reza Shah Pahlavi, then ruled Iran until the Islamic Revolution of 1979. Under the Pahlavis, Western cultural influences grew, and Persia's oil industry was developed. By the 1950s, Iran was a world leader in petroleum production.

Muhammad Reza Shah Pahlavi was a staunch advocate of Westernization. In the 1960s he introduced Iran to the "White Revolution," which replaced many of Iran's traditions with Western influences. He tried to propel Iran out of its traditions of agriculture and Islam into modern industrialization and Western culture. While the Shah enacted many measures for the benefit of Iranians, he also became increasingly dictatorial and restricted many freedoms. In 1975, the Shah outlawed all political parties except his own. His secret police force (SAVAK) became increasingly repressive and cruel. People who opposed the government, such as religious opponents, were jailed and tortured.

In 1978, Islamic opposition forces and Communist forces acted together to demonstrate and riot for political change in Iran. Their rebellion grew into a major revolution against the Westernization and oppression inflicted on Iran by the Shah. Shah Pahlavi fled the country and abdicated his throne under pressure. After a stay in the United States, he sought refuge in Egypt, where he and his wife were welcomed by President Anwar Sadat. The ailing Shah later died in July 1980 in Egypt. The Islamic Revolution of 1979 was organized under the leadership of Ayatollah Ruhollah Khomeini, a prominent religious leader who returned from exile in Paris. On 11 February 1979, the twenty-second day of the Muslim month of *Bahman,* Khomeini and his supporters succeeded in replacing the secular government of the Shah with an Islamic republic. Symbolically, the words "God is Great" are repeated 22 times on the Iranian flag.

The Islamic Revolution targeted Western influences for having corrupted Iranian Islamic traditions. The United States, in particular, was seen as the evil nation whose culture was pervading Iran. In November 1979, revolutionary students seized control of the U.S. embassy in Tehran and held 53 Americans

Iranians play ball in a park to mark the 13th day of Norouz, commencing the start of spring, in Tehran, Iran. Norouz is the first day of the new year according to the Persian calendar and is a Zoroastrian tradition, still celebrated by Iranians even after Islam.
(Behrouz Mehri/Staff/Getty Images)

hostage. In response to the hostage crisis, the United States froze Iranian assets that were banked or invested in the United States. The hostages were held for 14 months, and the crisis created extreme hostility between the two countries. The hostages were released in January 1981 following an agreement negotiated by Algeria, as the United States' leadership was changing hands from President Jimmy Carter to President Ronald Reagan.

Under the leadership of Ayatollah Khomeini, Iran became a theocracy with the name of the Islamic Republic of Iran. Religious standards thus became the guiding principles for the government and society, and religious leaders known as *mullahs* led Iran along the Islamization route. Many Iranians holding secular views saw the strict religious system as an infringement on their personal liberties. Those who wanted to protect their Western ways of life left Iran and went to Europe and the United States. Khomeini was ruthlessly intolerant of those who opposed his theocracy, and thousands of his opponents were assassinated or arrested during his 10-year reign. Most Jews and Christians, fearing religious persecution, fled the country during the 1980s.

From 1980 until 1988, Iran fought a severe and costly war with its neighbor Iraq. The war began when Iraq invaded Khuzistan, in southwestern Iran, to resolve a longstanding dispute over control of the Shatt al-Arab waterway. Iraqi forces seized southwestern Iranian territory and an oil refinery along the Shatt al-Arab, resulting in a full-scale war between the two countries. More than 500,000 Iraqis and Iranians died, and, although Iran was able to expel Iraq from Khuzistan, neither side could really claim a victory. International access to Middle Eastern oil was adversely affected, as both Iran and Iraq attacked one another's oil freighters in the Persian Gulf. The United States and the Soviet Union, in the mid-1980s, arranged for Kuwaiti oil freighters to operate in the Gulf under protection of the American and Soviet flags, with both countries' naval forces positioned in the Gulf. The United States got involved in the battle in the late 1980s. First, an Iraqi bomber accidentally attacked a U.S. ship in 1987. Then, a floating mine damaged an American tanker, and an Iranian passenger plane was accidentally shot down by a U.S. warship in 1988. The war ended in the summer of 1988, with Iran and Iraq signing a cease-fire agreement arranged by the United Nations.

In June 1989, spiritual leader and head-of-state Ayatollah Khomeini died. Some 2 million Iranians attended Khomeini's funeral in Tehran. Thousands of mourners were injured, and several died in the chaos and hysteria that filled the streets. Shortly after Khomeini's death, Ali Khamenei replaced him as spiritual leader, and Ali Akbar Hashemi Rafsanjani became president. Rafsanjani was reelected to the presidency in June 1993 and remained in office until 1997.

Struggles for power between reformists and conservatives in Iran grew increasingly bitter during Rafsanjani's presidency. Rafsanjani favored economic and political reforms, but conservatives in Iran's legislature, known as the Majlis, often prevented his policies from taking effect. In Iran, the president, prime minister, and cabinet ministers do not make decisions on their own. They answer to the *faqih,* or spiritual leader, and to a group of religious scholars and judicial authorities whom the faqih appoints. In addition, the Majlis, which is elected by the people every four years, enacts laws that must be in keeping with the Islamic faith. A council made up of six clergy and six lawyers oversees the work of the Majlis. The power of religious leaders in Iran's government slowed the effort to introduce reforms through the mid 1990s.

Conservatives suffered a defeat in 1997 when reformist Muhammad Khatami won a landslide victory in the presidential election and when his supporters gained a majority in the Majlis in 2000. Khatami was then re-elected in 2001, despite conservative clerics who used their power to bring many of the reformists to trial on alleged political charges. Clerics then began a concerted effort to stop reforms. Nearly 100 reform proposals were blocked between 2000 and early 2004. Conservatives regained control of the Majlis in 2003, and Iranian voters began to regard the reformists as individuals who could not effectively create change.

While reformists and conservatives battled for political power in Iran, U.S. president George W. Bush began to accuse Iran of developing nuclear weapons. The American president labeled Iran as a member of an "axis of evil," a statement that turned many of the conservatives in Iran against the United States. Rafsanjani ran for president in July 2005 in an effort to regain support for the reformist movement. However, he was defeated by a hardline conservative Mahmoud Ahmadinejad. Soon after taking office, Ahmadinejad assumed a strident anti-American stance and announced in April 2007 that he was enriching uranium, a process that often leads to the building of nuclear weapons. The United Nations has responded by imposing sanctions on Iran. The election in August 2007 of Rajsanjani to the Assembly of Experts ensures that the reformist movement has not died out entirely because the Assembly of Experts has the power to dismiss Iran's highest authority. However, Ahmadinejad remains popular among Iranians who have embraced the conservative stance of their president.

² LOCATION AND HOMELAND

Iran is located in southwest Asia. It is bordered to the north by Azerbaijan, Turkmenistan, and the Caspian Sea, by Turkey to the northwest, Iraq to the west, and by Afghanistan and Pakistan to the east. Kuwait, Saudi Arabia, Bahrain, Qatar, and the United Arab Emirates are to Iran's south and southwest, separated from Iran by the Persian (or Arabian) Gulf. Oman is to the southeast, separated from Iran by the Gulf of Oman and the Arabian Sea. Iran's location led to invasions and cultural influences by many ethnic and national communities. One of the major influences was a direct result of Iran's proximity to Saudi Arabia, known in the 7th century AD as the Hejaz. After the death of the Prophet Muhammad, Arab Muslims from the Hejaz spread their new Islamic religion to Iran, converting most Iranian Zoroastrians to Islam by the 9th century AD.

With an area of 1,647,063 sq km (635,932 sq mi), Iran is slightly larger than the U.S. state of Alaska. Iran's geography

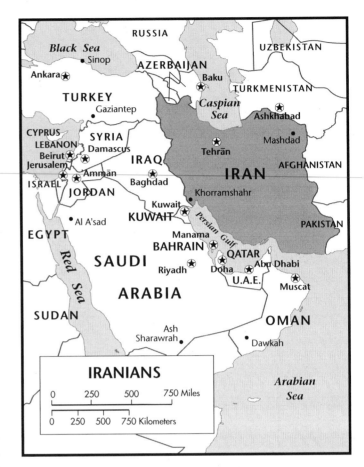

has three types of terrain. A vast, dry plateau in the center of the country is encircled by a ring of snow-topped mountain ranges that cover about half of Iran's area. Outside of the mountains to the north and south is coastal lowland. The rocky central plateau is a high plain with an average height of 1,200 m (4,000 ft) above sea level, covered with low hills. In northwest Iran, streams flowing down the slopes of mountains have facilitated the establishment of large cities. This region is the location of the capital city, Tehran, and Isfahan and Qom.

To the south and east of Tehran, on the plateau, lie two deserts: the Dasht-e-Kavir (Great Salt Desert), and the Dasht-e-Lut. The deserts, which make up about 25% of Iran's total land area, consist of very salty soil. Following rain, the soil dries into a white crust of salt crystals. Below the surface is salty quicksand, making travel over the desert dangerous. The Dasht-e-Lut has been described as a hostile wasteland, whereas the Dasht-e-Kavir has an occasional oasis. Iran has three major mountain ranges. The Zagros Mountains in the west have a height of up to 4,242 m (14,000 ft). The Elburz Mountains in the north have the highest peaks, with Mount Damavand reaching 5,736 m (18,934 ft). The Khorasan Mountains in the east have productive farmland and grasslands. Small mountain ranges are located in the south and southeast.

The climate of northern and eastern Iran is generally more moderate than in the southern and western parts. While the summers get very hot nationwide, in the areas of high elevation the evenings are cool and breezy, and even the days are comfortable. In the lower elevations, the climate is hot in the summer. It is hottest around the Persian Gulf, where temperatures reach 60°C (140°F) in the summer. In the winter, the Persian Gulf region sees high temperatures of 20°C to 30°C (70°–85°F).

Iran, considered an arid country, has several creeks, rivers, and lakes, many of which fill up with rain and melted snow in the spring, and then dry up during the summer. Even the Caspian Sea loses much of its water to evaporation. Lake Urmia in the northwest, Iran's largest inland body of water, covers an area of 5,200 sq km (2,000 sq mi). The three principal rivers are the Karun, the Atrek, and the Safid. Of these, only the Karun is navigable. It travels from the Zagros Mountains to the Shatt al-Arab, and then into the Persian Gulf. The lakes are salty and thus of little use for irrigation or drinking, but the rivers provide usable water. Underground irrigation tunnels carry water from springs, streams, and snow-topped hills. These canals are critical to this country with a water scarcity.

The name "Persian" is now used to refer to all Iranians (with a total population of about 69,400,000 people). Only 51% (or 35,954,000) of Iranians, however, are actually Persians, i.e., descendants of the Aryans who emigrated from Central Asia. Persians, the largest ethnic group, live either in the developed farm areas or in the large cities of the northern and western plateau. Another large ethnic group is the Azerbaijanis, descendants of Turkish settlers from the 10th century AD. They live in the northwest part of Iran and make up 24% of the population (or 16,600,000 people). The Zagros Mountains are home to several ethnic groups, such as the Kurds, who make up 7% of the total population (or 4,848,000 people), and the Lurs and the Bakhtiari, each of whom makes up 2% of the population (or 1,380,000 people).

The Kurds are a nomadic people whose origins are located in territory that extends into parts of Iraq, Syria, and Turkey, with 33% of the Middle East's Kurdish population residing in Iran. They are also part of a political dilemma involving all of these states, because they wish to establish their own state of Kurdistan over Kurdish-populated territories. In fact, the Kurds, who are Sunni Muslims, demanded independence from Iran following the Shia Islamic Revolution of 1979. Relations between the Kurds and the government have gotten better.

The Lurs (or Luri) live in an area known as Luristan, and the Bakhtiari live west of Shiraz, in the mountains. Both are nomadic peoples, although the Iranian government since the 1960s has tried to modernize their lifestyle by settling them in farming villages. Another 2% of the population (or 1,380,000 people) are of the Baluchi tribe—farmers living in the Baluchistan region in southeastern Iran. Arabs make up 3% of the population (or 2,082,000 people). They live in Iranian islands in the Persian Gulf and in Khuzistan. Other ethnic groups include the Qashqai, Turkomans, Khamsheh, Mamasani, Shahsevan, Armenians, Brahui, Syrians, Afghans, and Pakistanis. The overwhelming majority of Iranians are Muslims, belonging to the Shia school of Islam. However, there are a significant number of minority religious groups in Iran, including Sunni Muslims, Zoroastrians, Armenian and Chaldean Christians, and Jews. The 1979 constitution guarantees religious freedom, and is widely respected.

Iran had as many as 3 million refugees residing within its borders in the 1990s, as a result of the civil war in Afghanistan. The total number was less than 1 million in 2007. This drop in the refugee population resulted from the government's effort to return refugees from Afghanistan, following the fall of the Taliban regime in 2002 in that country. Other refugees were Shia Muslims from Iraq, who began returning to Iraq after the fall of Iraqi leader Saddam Hussein, who was Sunni. Refugees from southeastern Turkey and Azerbaijan also have entered Iran.

³ LANGUAGE

Iran's official language is Farsi, which is also known as Persian. Farsi, also spoken in parts of Turkey and Afghanistan, was brought to Iran when the Aryan people of Central Asia migrated across Iran's northern border. Farsi has since been influenced by other languages, predominantly Arabic. The Farsi alphabet is very similar to the Arabic alphabet and, like the latter, is written from right to left. Many Iranians understand Arabic, an important language since the Quran, the holy book of Muslims, is written in Arabic. The Azerbaijanis speak a Turkish dialect known as Azeri. The Lurs and Bakhtiari both speak the Luri language. The Baluchis speak an Indo-European language, and the Kurds speak a language known as Kurdish.

⁴ FOLKLORE

Many Muslims believe in *jinns,* spirits who can change shape and be either visible or invisible. Muslims sometimes wear amulets around their necks to protect them from jinns. Stories of jinns are often told at night, like ghost stories around a campfire.

⁵ RELIGION

Shia Islam is the state religion of Iran. Shia is one of the two schools of Islam. Sunni Islam is the major school, with a far greater number of adherents worldwide. Followers of the Prophet Muhammad in the 7th century AD engaged in a dispute, after his death, as to who the rightful successor to the Prophet's leadership was. Those who believed that the Prophet's son-in-law 'Ali should become *khalifa* (caliph), the Islamic leader, formed the Shia school, which took root in Iran and has dominated religious thinking there through the present day.

The overwhelming majority of Iranians (about 98%) are Muslims. Most Iranians (about 89%) belong to the Shia school of Islam, while the remaining population is Sunni Muslim (9%) or Zoroastrian, Armenian and Chaldean Christian, or Jewish. The latter groups make up about 2% of the population. The 1979 constitution guarantees religious freedom and is widely respected. However, non-Muslims must follow civil laws in Iran that are formed on the basis of Islamic principles.

Before the advent of Islam, most Iranians were Zoroastrians. The Zoroastrian faith developed in Iran around the 7th to 6th centuries BC. Zoroastrians followed a teacher named Zoroaster or Zarathustra. They worshiped a god of good known as Ahura Mazda and believed in a god of evil known as Ahriman. Most Zoroastrians converted to Islam starting in the 7th century AD. Over the centuries, most of the remaining Zoroastrians fled Iran and resettled in India.

⁶ MAJOR HOLIDAYS

The major secular holiday is Now Ruz (or Nawruz), the ancient Persian New Year. The festival begins on March 21, which is also the first day of spring, and continues through March 24. Much socializing takes place on this very festive day. A gong is sounded or a cannon is fired in the cities to signal the beginning of the new year. Children are given money and gifts, and dancers perform at festivals. Oil Nationalization Day (March 20) commemorates the day in 1951 when Iran assumed ownership of the Iranian oil industry, which had been controlled principally by Great Britain. Other national holidays include Islamic Republic Day (April 1) and Revolution Day (June 5).

Iran is on the lunar Islamic calendar, so the dates of religious holidays change every year. Some of Iran's major religious holidays commemorate the birthdays of imams, or religious leaders, who were famous in history. One of these is the birthday celebration of an imam of particular importance to Iranians, known as the Twelfth Imam.

One major Muslim holiday comes at the end of Ramadan, the month of fasting. During the month, Muslims refrain from eating, drinking, or having sexual relations during the daytime in order to reflect on God and on the plight of the unfortunate who do not have enough food. Another major Muslim holiday commemorates the willingness of the Prophet Abraham, as well as his son, to obey God's command in all things, even when Abraham was about to sacrifice his son. This holiday signals the end of the Muslim pilgrimage to Mecca, or *hajj*, which every Muslim must undertake at least once during his or her lifetime.

Another significant month, particularly to the Shia Muslims of Iran, is the Islamic month of Muharram. During this month, the grandsons of the Prophet Muhammad, Husayn and Hasan, were killed. Iranians mourn their death throughout the month, sometimes mourning in street processions in which they beat themselves. Those who can afford to do so give money, food, and goods to the poor. No weddings or parties can be held during the month of Muharram.

7 RITES OF PASSAGE

Marriage is the most important stage in a person's life, marking the official transition to adulthood. In the Islamic Republic, a woman traditionally could have been betrothed at age nine and a man at age fourteen. Iran's present day Civil Law sets the minimum age of marriage at fifteen for women and at eighteen for men. However, the law also allows for earlier marriage if a woman's legal guardian, and a judge or medical doctor felt that she was mature enough for marriage. For these reasons, most Iranian men and women marry between the ages of eighteen and twenty-five. Although dating is not common in rural areas, college students and other couples who live in cities often will get to know a future spouse by going to movies, eating out in restaurants, or socializing together before marriage. Iranian laws also allow for couples to have a *sigheh* or temporary marriage in which men and women are able to test whether they wish to remain together. Many women enter such marriages for the sake of financial support.

There are two ceremonies in the marital tradition: the *agd*, and the *arusi*. The engagement is the arusi and is usually a very intimate and private affair among the families involved. The actual ceremony is the agd, which can involve the entire community. Iranian society is built on the importance of the family, and marriage is often arranged among families that have long-established ties. A potential suitor must seek the approval of the father before even speaking to his prospective wife. Women and men are raised to see marriage as their social and religious obligation, and it is valued as such.

The birth of a child is an important event. Relatives and friends typically will bring a gift. Children's birthday parties are attended mostly by adults, and children gather to eat and play traditional games. Girls traditionally will have a party at school at age nine and fifteen.

Respect toward the deceased is also an important ritual. Loved ones gather at the home of the recently deceased to sit and quietly pray or reflect. Those who knew the deceased casually pay their respects at the mosque. The death of a community member in urban areas is announced in the local paper. Mourning lasts for 40 days, and special dark attire is worn to show grief for the deceased.

8 INTERPERSONAL RELATIONS

It is customary to greet others with a handshake and slight bow of the head in Iran. Men, however, will not shake the hand of a woman unless the woman offers her hand first. It is also customary to stand when an elder individual or prominent person enters the room.

Most people in Iran employ an elaborate system of courtesy, known in Farsi as *taarof*. Polite and complimentary phrases are used to create an atmosphere of trust and mutual respect. For example, when an Iranian finds he or she has had their back to someone, which is considered offensive body language, he or she will apologize. The other person will usually reply, "A flower has neither back nor front." At times, taarof can complicate or delay things, such as when two people each insist that the other should proceed first through a door. Since it brings honor to the one who insists, there could be a long struggle before one person finally gives in.

Another aspect of taarof is the elaborate display of courtesy when one entertains a guest. For example, a host will always offer a guest food or other treats, even on a brief visit. Hungry or not, a guest will most often take the offering in order to please the host. A host will make sure to make the guest feel comfortable and well-liked. The host will go to great lengths to please the guest, but the guest also must behave with the utmost courtesy and politeness toward the host.

Iranians, like many people of the Middle East, are very hospitable. They serve their guests as much as they can afford. Iranians typically place a large basket of fruit on their table for guests and family to consume. This display symbolizes abundance and mirth, which all Iranians want to share. Women in the family cook for the enjoyment of their guests. Tea is boiled in a metal (usually copper) urn known as a *samovar* and is served to guests in small glasses with lots of sugar. Visitors return the courtesy by removing their shoes when they enter the carpeted areas of a home.

Iranians are very demonstrative with their facial and hand gestures. Some gestures that have specific meanings in the United States are interpreted differently in Iran. For example, the American hand gesture meaning "come here," with the forefinger pointed outward and waved toward one's body, in Iran is a gesture used by men to beckon suggestively to women. The American "thumbs up" gesture, indicating something well done, in Iran is an aggressive gesture that can create ill feeling.

9 LIVING CONDITIONS

Almost 70% of Iran is uninhabited because of the harshness of the deserts and mountains. The population density is about 148 persons per sq km (92 per sq mi). Most of the population lives in the western and northern parts of the country, with the highest concentration of people in Tehran, the capital city, which has a population of 7,315,000. The second-largest city is Mashhad, with a population of 2,150,000. The third-largest cities are Tabriz and Isfahan, each with a population of about 1,350,000. Other highly populated areas are in Azerbaijan in the northwest and along the coast of the Caspian Sea in the north. The population of more than 69,400,000 is highly urban. About 67.5% of Iranians lived in cities in 2007 compared with about 31% in 1951. The cities, however, are finding it difficult to keep up with the needs of the migrants. Sanitation and housing in the cities are thus inadequate.

A rise in the number of young Iranians has accompanied the migration of people from rural to urban areas. The average life expectancy at birth for Iranians was 70.7 years in 2004 compared with 55.3 years in the early 1970s. As a result, nearly one-third (29.8%) of the population was under age 15 in 2004. This large percentage of youth has created a large workforce, with 23.1 million workers as of March 2007. About 600,000 new job-seekers enter the labor market each year. Although Iran's economy is rich with oil reserves, the country is finding it difficult to employ its young people. As a result, more than 200,000 Iranians leave the country each year in search of better work opportunities in Europe and the United States.

The cities of Iran are very spacious, and the streets are lined with trees. Despite the space, city streets are often very congested with automobiles. Larger cities have many high-rise apartments built during the Shah's renovations, and some have modern supermarket complexes that are several stories high. Tehran underwent extensive modernization during the 20th century, resulting in modern skyscrapers overlooking ancient mosques. Tehran is the industrial and cultural center of Iran. Cities also have marketplaces, or bazaars. Tehran's bazaar has more than 6,000 businesses. Wooden houses are common along the Caspian coast and square houses made of mud brick are found on the slopes in the mountain villages. Nomadic tribes in the Zagros Mountains live in round black tents made of goat hair. The people of Baluchistan, in the southeast, are farmers who live in huts.

Although Iran exports oil, fuel for use in homes is not always available. Appliances used for cooking include grill-like charcoal heaters and coal stoves. Hydroelectric power has increasingly been made available in the country.

10 FAMILY LIFE

In the cities, the family unit is the extended family, including one's aunts, uncles, cousins, and grandparents. The concerns of all members of the extended family have a bearing on the nuclear family, consisting of the mother, father, and children. Although large families were traditionally prized, the Iranian government has been taking steps to reduce the country's population. Couples must now attend a family planning course before they marry, and men are only allowed more than one wife if they are able to provide for each spouse equally. Government policies have helped reduce the average size of the nuclear family to about six children per family.

The tribe ruled by a tribal chief is the basic social unit among nomads. Tribes have elaborate customs that govern individuals' behavior. In the villages, clans and families are the most important social units. This creates a strong sense of belonging in the villages, as all the families share much in common.

The father is the head of the Iranian household, yet there is a tacit recognition of the mother's role and preeminence. There is a respect within the family for males and a ranking by age, with the young showing respect toward older siblings. Respect, especially toward one's elders, is an integral part of the family structure. However, Iranians extend their respect beyond their immediate and extended families. For instance, an Iranian is expected to rise to her or his feet when any person of equal or greater age or status enters the room.

There is no pension system and little state welfare for the elderly. Aging parents are taken care of by their children until death. The elderly are venerated for their wisdom and place at the head of the family. Thus, taking care of them is seen as their children's responsibility.

Because most workers and students take two-hour lunch breaks, families are able to spend time together in the afternoons, as well as in the evenings. They also see much of each other on Fridays, the Muslim day of rest and prayer. It is typical on Fridays for families to go on an outing, usually to the park to watch children play, talk about current events, and eat prepared food. Schools and government offices close early on Thursdays to honor this tradition.

11 CLOTHING

Iranians value personal cleanliness, a value that is reflected in how they dress. Western clothing for both men and women was popular until the Islamic Revolution of 1979. Since then, women have been forced to cover their hair and wear the Iranian *chador*, a long cloak, when in public. Although the chador most often seen in Western images of Iran is black, many Iranian women wear very colorful chadors. Some women wear only a head-covering or use the chador to cover more fashionable, Western-style clothing. It also is common for Iranian women to wear make-up.

Most men wear slacks, shirts, and jackets. Most usually do not wear ties, because religious leaders have condemned the accessory as a symbol of Western influence. Some men, especially religious leaders, wear floor-length, jacket-like garments, and cover their heads with turbans.

Mountain-dwellers continue to wear their traditional clothing. For Kurdish men, this consists of a long-sleeved cotton shirt over baggy pants that taper down to fit tightly at the ankles. A thick belt of cloth, much like a cummerbund, is wrapped around the waist, and a turban adorns the head. Some tribal women wear long, embroidered vests, and skirts or dresses adorned with beads. They wear an elaborate head covering with coin trimming. In general, great importance is placed on one's presentability. This being the case, both women and men dress in their best clothing to create a good impression.

12 FOOD

There is no doubt that the multitude of invasions and migrations by foreign peoples contributed to Iranian cuisine. The influence of Turkey, Greece, India, and Arab countries is seen, respectively, in shish kabob, stuffed grape leaves, spicy curry stews, and dishes made of lamb, dates, and figs. Iranian bread and rice are a must at the table. Breads come in a wide variety of shapes and sizes. *Sang-gak* is made of whole meal flour and baked over hot stones. *Nan* is a round, flat bread that can either be baked or cooked over a bed of small stones. Iranians make a popular skewered kabob known as *chelo kebab*. Boneless cubes of lamb are marinated in spicy yogurt and arranged with vegetables on metal skewers. These are then grilled over hot coals and served on a bed of rice.

One of Iran's most popular dishes is sweet orange-peel rice, also known as "wedding rice." The color and taste of the rice make it an appropriate dish to serve to wedding guests. The cook prepares a sauce made of orange peel, shelled almonds and pistachios, sugar, butter, saffron, cinnamon, nutmeg, and orange juice. The sauce is cooked for about five minutes and then added to partially cooked (steamed) rice. The rice is then cooked for another 30 minutes.

Yogurt is a main part of the Iranian diet. It is rich and creamy and is used in many different ways. It can be used to marinate meats, it is added to salads, it is used in soups, and it is enjoyed as a cool drink in the summer. Tea, the national beverage, is grown in the Caspian region and on the slopes of mountains. Tea is made in metal urns called *samovars*. It is served in glasses. Iranians have a particular tea-drinking method: they place a cube of sugar on the tongue and sip the tea through the sugar. Pork and alcoholic beverages are forbidden in Islam.

13 EDUCATION

Iran underwent large-scale educational reform in the 1960s, building many schools and colleges. Emphasis was placed on training teachers, and by 1968, some 35,000 Literacy Corps teachers had been trained to teach adults and young children. Illiteracy has dropped from 70% in the 1960s to about 33% as of 2002. There is a gender gap in literacy rates, with only about 70.4% of women able to read and write, compared to 83.5% of men. Iran's younger children enjoy much higher literacy rates than adults, with 96.5% of those between ages six and twenty-nine able to read and write as of 2005.

The school year begins in September and ends in June. There is a two-week holiday in March. July and August are the months of summer vacation. Students attend school from Saturday morning until Thursday at noon. Elementary schooling lasts five years and is required for children between the ages of seven and twelve. Schools are operated by the state. Elementary schools are free, with pupils also receiving free textbooks.

After the compulsory period ends, students take a major qualifying examination to determine if they qualify to attend secondary school. These schools are free except for small fees. Secondary schools are academically demanding, and students take a major examination at the end of each school year. Failing one of the subjects could mean repeating the whole year. About three-fourths of all children enter secondary school, which consists of three years of general education and three years of high school. After completing the six years of school, students have the option to take a seventh year of "pre-college" schooling.

Universities in Iran also are free. After the 1979 Islamic revolution, two Islamic universities were built: the Free Islamic University, and the International University of Islamic Studies. The universities have suffered from financial problems, and many wealthy Iranian families send their children overseas for education.

14 CULTURAL HERITAGE

Iran is known for its magnificent mosques and architecture commissioned by rulers throughout history. One of the most

beautiful of these buildings is a mosque located in the city of Mashhad that was built by Tamerlane's daughter-in-law. The mosaics of tile that embellish the mosque are brilliantly colored. The city of Isfahan is known for the blue tiles of some of its historic buildings, such as the mosque named Masjid-i-Shah. This 17th-century mosque has an intricately patterned domed ceiling that is intensely geometric in design.

Iran also has palaces and monuments built centuries ago that document both the tremendous influences of foreigners and the power of the ancient Persian Empire. Carved stone structures depict various aspects of Persian life and history. The ruins of Persepolis, the capital city of the Persian Empire that was built in 520 BC, are located near Shiraz in south-central Iran. The ruins consist of rock slabs and pillars with elaborate carvings. One stone pillar is topped with a large sculpture of an animal's head. Carved soldiers and courtiers bedeck some of the stone remains, providing much information about the ancient customs of Persia.

One of the most fascinating items of Iranian artwork is the *Peacock Throne*, on which all Iran's kings since the 18th century have sat. It is part of the priceless crown jewels collection, which is now the property of the state. The throne bears more than 20,000 precious gems and serves as the backing for Iran's currency.

Many writers known around the world have contributed to a very rich literary tradition among Iranians, and Iranian music is often inspired by the country's rich heritage of poetry. By far the most famous of Iranian poets was a man named Firdawsi (AD 940–1020), who wrote Iran's national epic, the *Shahnameh* (Book of Kings). A fictional poem based on facts, the 120,000-line story relates the adventures of four ancient Iranian dynasties. Many of the copies made of this epic are illustrated with miniature art. Another internationally known Iranian poet was Omar Khayyam (11th century AD), who was also a mathematician and astronomer. His four-line rhyming verses, known as *ruba'is,* became famous when Edward Fitzgerald, a British writer, translated 101 of the poems in his volume *The Rubaiyat of Omar Khayyam.* One of the more famous of the translated verses is:

The Moving Finger writes; and, having writ,
Moves on; nor all the Piety nor Wit
Shall lure it back to cancel half a Line,
Nor all thy Tears wash out a Word of it.

The city of Shiraz was home to two other great poets: Sadi (13th century AD) and Hafez (14th century AD). Sadi's poems were among the first examples of Persian literature introduced to Europe. Hafez wrote a collection of about 700 poems, which is known as the *Divan.*

15 WORK

About one-fourth of Iran's work force is composed of industrial employees. They engage in petroleum extraction and refinery; mineral mining (coal, chromite, copper, iron ore, lead, manganese, salt, sulfur, and zinc); production of steel; food processing; and many other industries. One of the most important industries is cement production.

About one-third of the work force is employed in agriculture. This category includes farming, raising livestock, forestry, and fishing. Fishers off the Caspian coast provide about 20% of the world's supply of caviar. Iran's major cultivated crops include barley, cotton, dates, raisins, rice, sugar beets, tea, tobacco, and wheat.

The remainder of Iran's work force is engaged in the service sector. The typical Iranian urban work-day is eight hours long, often starting at 7:00 am. Workers commonly take a two-hour lunch break. During the hot summer months, workers might take longer lunch breaks and then work later into the evening when it is not so hot. Farmers and herders work from sunrise to sunset. They rely predominantly on manual labor; modern mechanical equipment is uncommon. While some farmers have the luxury of animals to assist in plowing and other fieldwork, in some regions such animals are unavailable, so the farmer relies on his own and his family's efforts.

16 SPORTS

Iran's most popular sports are wrestling, weight lifting, soccer, martial arts, basketball, volleyball, table tennis, and horse-racing. The *Zur Khaneh,* or House of Strength, is a physical training and wrestling center where young men undergo vigorous training with heavy clubs and perform in wrestling matches for spectators. Tennis and squash are popular, especially among urban Iranians. Gymnastics is encouraged in schools and is becoming popular. Camel- and horse-racing are popular in rural areas.

17 ENTERTAINMENT AND RECREATION

In rural areas, people are entertained by traveling groups of actors who recite poetry and perform plays. Generally, the plays tell stories about Iran's history, reliving important episodes and highlighting the lives of famous Iranians.

In urban areas, men enjoy spending their leisure time in teahouses, socializing and smoking the *hookah,* or water pipe. Going to movies also is becoming more popular. Women enjoy entertaining family and friends in the home. They often spend time engaged in leisurely craftwork. Iranians enjoy the game of chess, and many argue that chess was invented in their country. Many Iranians attend the mosque every Friday, both for prayer and to socialize with friends.

18 FOLK ART, CRAFTS, AND HOBBIES

Iranians have long been recognized as a people of artistic distinction, renowned for the crafts made by their goldsmiths during the Sassanid dynasty of the 3rd to 7th centuries AD. The city of Isfahan is famous for its abundance of artists and craftspeople. The cities of Shiraz and Tabriz are famous for their rugs. Iran's handwoven carpets and rugs are made of either silk or wool and use special knots dating from the Middle Ages. They come with many designs and patterns that vary from region to region, with geometric shapes being the most common. Persian carpets are sold in all parts of the world. Shiraz and Isfahan are famous also for their tradition of crafting metal, such as silver and copper, into ornamental plates, cups, vases, trays, and jewelry. Picture frames and jewelry boxes are embellished with a form of art known as *khatam.* This involves the use of ivory, bone, and pieces of wood to create geometric patterns.

Calligraphy (ornate writing) is also a fine art in Iran, as it is in much of the Islamic world. Verses from the Quran are skillfully handwritten and painted in beautifully flowing lettering. The calligraphy has adorned many books and manuscripts produced in Iran through the centuries. Iranians, influenced by a Chinese art style, developed an art of painting very detailed small images on their manuscripts. Known as "miniature painting," this art form was especially prized during the 15th century. Masterpieces created at that time by an artist named Bihzad are now prized the world over.

19 SOCIAL PROBLEMS

Iran's development has fluctuated considerably since the Islamic Revolution of 1979. In the early 21st century, the government's opposition to the United States and its war against Islamic terrorists has led to many reactionary practices. The 2008 Amnesty International report on the state of the world's human rights noted that Iranian authorities shut down media outlets critical of the Islamic regime, jailed journalists, and closed many non-governmental organizations operating in Iraq. Nearly 350 people were executed in 2007 and harsh punishments of flogging, stoning, and amputation were handed down by the courts.

One of Iran's greatest challenges in the early 21st century has been balancing the country's older cultural and social traditions against the attitudes of its younger citizens who are more influenced by Western ideas and globalization. Nearly one-third of Iran's population is under age 25. Young people often challenge the Islamic clergy's rules on attire and socialization between the sexes by wearing Western clothing and gathering together in streets, particularly in Tehran. The government has responded by arresting those who defy Islamic based laws.

The war in Iraq (begun in 2003) has made Iranians vulnerable to external threats, as well as to threats from militants who are said to be hiding in Iran. Despite a modest increase in per capita GNP, unemployment is a severe problem, swelling the numbers of urban and rural poor. Women in rural areas particularly have suffered from the economy, where handicrafts and other commodities are given a small market value and where they have to compete with men for work. In addition, U.S. pressure on Iran's economy (through sanctions) has curbed Iran's potential for investment and growth. Overall efforts are being made by the Iranian government to compensate for this loss of revenue.

The state of the Iranian press and intellectuals in Iran today is a source of concern for human-rights activists both within and abroad. Members of the Iranian intelligentsia are frequently arrested and tortured for their so-called "un-Islamic" writings, and most live in fear for their lives. In spite of this, visitors to Iran have observed the active efforts within the intellectual community to solve various problems in the Islamic Republic, and to contribute to a lively discourse.

20 GENDER ISSUES

Information on the status of women in Iran can often be colored by Western prejudice against the Islamic Revolution. However, numerous accounts documented the repression of women accused of such things as improper veiling. The condition of women in Iranian society began to improve in the 1990s and women have gained more educational opportunities, employment options, and rights to seek compensation from their former husbands in the event of divorce. In addition, rules on the dress code for women began to relax in the 1990s. In 1995, a journalist asked President Rajsanjani why women's veils had to be black. The president suggested that women could wear veils in any color of their choice. Iranian women responded by donning veils of numerous colors, including light blue and pink. The example illustrates how many women are willing to push for more social freedoms while still remaining respectful of Islamic traditions.

The advances have been pushed back with the new dominance of conservatives loyal to fundamentalist Islamic clerics in Iran. Amnesty International reported that thousands of women were arrested in 2007 for not complying with the Islamic dress code. In early 2008, the Iranian government shut down the feminist magazine *Zanan* for publishing articles that the government found detrimental to Iranian society. The magazine had been in circulation for 16 years and was among 42 publications that the government had suspended since 2005.

Iranian women continue to seek an end to legalized discrimination through the Campaign for Equality. The activist group has been trying to collect a million signatures in Iran in support for their cause. The government responded in 2007 by arresting several women working with the campaign.

21 BIBLIOGRAPHY

"A man for nearly all seasons." *The Economist (US)* 3 June 2000, 46.

Amnesty International Report 2008: State of the World's Human Rights. http://thereport.amnesty.org/eng/Homepage (retrieved August 3, 2008)

Economist Intelligence Unit: Country Profile: Iran. Economist Intelligence Unit Inc., 2007

Iran: A Country Study. Washington, D.C.: Library of Congress, 1989.

Islamic Republic of Iran. Culture Grams: World Edition. Ann Arbor, Mich.: ProQuest LLC, 2008.

"The house of strength; Tehran diary; Our correspondent admires Iranian tradition." *Global Agenda* (3 July 2007).

Mackey, Sandra. *The Iranians: Persia, Islam and the Soul of a Nation.* New York: Penguin Books, 1996.

Rajendra, Vijeya, and Gisela Kaplan. *Cultures of the World: Iran.* New York: Times Books, 1993.

Sanders, Renfield. *Iran.* New York and Philadelphia: Chelsea House Publishers, 1990.

Seelhoff, Cheryl Lindsey. "Government closes down leading feminist magazine," *Off Our Backs* 37.4 (April 2008): 5(2)

Tremayne, Soraya. "Modernity and early marriage in Iran: a view from within." *JMEWS: Journal of Middle East Women's Studies* 2:1 65(30), 2006

—revised by H. Gupta-Carlson

IRAQIS

PRONUNCIATION: i-RAH-keez
LOCATION: Iraq
POPULATION: 28,221,180 (2008 estimate)
LANGUAGE: Arabic; Kurdish; Turkoman (a Turkish dialect); Assyrian; Armenian
RELIGION: Islam (Shi'ite, 60-65%; Sunni, 32-37%); Christianity

1 INTRODUCTION

Iraqis are among the world's most economically devastated peoples. Iraqis have lived under conditions of war nearly continuously since 1980. Nevertheless, the people have a long and proud history and some of the world's oldest civilizations originated in what is present-day Iraq.

Iraq (the Arabic word for "cliff") contains the ancient land of Mesopotamia, or "the land between the rivers." The rivers are the Tigris and the Euphrates, which originate in the mountains of Turkey and flow southward through Syria into Iraq. Between these two rivers lies a fertile plain where, as far as is known, the first human civilization flourished. By 4000 BC, the Sumerians had established cities and government institutions, the earliest known on the planet. Writing, mathematics, and science also began in Sumer. The Akkadians conquered Sumer in 2334 BC, but a mere 200 years later, the Sumerians regained control of the region. From then on, a series of peoples invaded and conquered this fertile land. The Babylonians gained control in 1900 BC and ruled for 300 years, during which King Hammurabi developed his famous law code. The Assyrians followed the Babylonians, then the Chaldeans took over in the 7th century BC. Perhaps the best-remembered Chaldean leader was Nebuchadnezzar II, who reigned from 605 to 562 BC from the capital city of Babylon. The Persians invaded in 550 BC, then Alexander the Great conquered the Persians and claimed Mesopotamia for the Greeks in 331 BC. The Greeks introduced metropolitan cities and scientific rationalism and improved irrigation methods, trade, and commerce. In 126 BC, the Persian Parthians took command and ruled for about 300 years. The Romans occupied the land briefly two different times: once from AD 98–117 and again from AD 193–211. The next conquerors were the Iranian Sasanids, who took charge in AD 227, and then Islamic troops, who entered the country in AD 636. Arab tribes, some of whom were Christian, lived in the area at that time and often acted as paid armies for the Persians. The Arab tribes from the Arabian Peninsula, having recently converted to Islam, were sent to invade the area now known as Iraq. The Christian Arab tribes and others switched allegiances en masse and "converted" to Islam. They then joined the Arab troops from the Arabian Peninsula in attacking the Persians. By AD 650, Iraq was an Islamic state.

The Golden Age of Iraq occurred during the reign of the Abbasid Caliphate, from AD 750 to 1258. In 762, Baghdad became the capital and the center of political power and culture in the Middle East. The Abbasids, however, tried to control more territory than their resources would allow. This problem was further complicated by the inherent problems of hereditary rule. By the time of the Mongol invasion of the Middle East, the Abbasid empire had fragmented into many small realms that showed allegiance to Bagdad in name only. This made it easy for the superior military forces of the Mongols to formally bring to an end the Abbasid Caliphate with the sacking of Baghdad in 1258. The Ottoman Turks eventually added Iraq to their empire in the 16th century. Iraq remained part of the Ottoman Empire until World War I, when Britain invaded and conquered it in 1917–18. In 1920, at the end of the war, an Iraqi Arab state under British mandate was created. Twelve years later, in October 1932, Iraq was recognized as an independent monarchy.

Independence did not spell the end of Iraq's troubles, however. Beset by internal conflicts and plagued by foreign powers, the monarchy finally fell to a military coup on 14 July 1958. A series of coups followed over the next 10 years, until the Ba'ath Party seized control in 1968. Saddam Hussein, named vice-president in 1968, became president of what was renamed the socialist Republic of Iraq in 1979. Iran and Iraq were at war from 1980–1988. Although Iraq declared itself the victor, the war destroyed the country's economy, heavily militarized the society, and spurred rebellion among Kurds living in the country's northern mountains. Hussein responded to the Kurdish rebellion with a chemical weapons attack that killed several thousand Kurdish civilians.

Iraq invaded Kuwait in August 1990, but a U.S.-led coalition acting under United Nations (UN) resolutions launched an invasion of Iraq in January 1991 and expelled Iraqi troops from Kuwait by February 1991. After the war, known as the 1991 Persian Gulf War, Kurds in the north and Shia Muslims in the south rebelled against Hussein's government. Hussein responded with a brutal military assault. Over the next decade, Hussein ruled Iraq as a dictator, and repressed both Shia Muslims as well as Kurds. His Ba'ath government also enacted several damaging environmental and agricultural policies that resulted in a draining of Iraq's southern marshes and extinction of a people known as the Ma'dan (or Marsh Arabs). Hussein's actions caused the United States, Great Britain, and France to set up no-fly zones over the country and requirements from the United Nations' Security Council to surrender weapons of mass destruction. Hussein refused to cooperate with the U.N. orders, and international sanctions were imposed against the country. These measures led to a U.S.-led invasion of the country in March 2003, and removal of the Ba'ath regime from power. Hussein went into hiding but was captured in December 2003 and was brought to trial and executed in late 2006. A U.S.-led coalition established an occupational government in 2003 known as the Coalition Provisional Authority and established what was initially an interim Iraqi government and, as of 2008, a transitional government. A new constitution was approved in 2006, but U.S. troops continue to occupy Iraq and war-like conditions continue to plague Iraq. Serious conflicts between the country's Shi'ite majority, Sunni minority, and Kurds threaten Iraq's long-term stability and as of 2008 the country remained at risk of falling into civil war.

² LOCATION AND HOMELAND

Iraq is located in southwestern Asia, in the heart of the Middle East. It is bounded by Turkey to the north, Syria and Jordan to the west, Iran to the east, and Kuwait and Saudi Arabia to the south. There is a short coastline in the southeast on the Arabian (or Persian) Gulf. The total land area is about 437,072 sq km (168,754 sq mi), including half of a neutral zone that Iraq administers with Saudi Arabia to make it easier for the no-

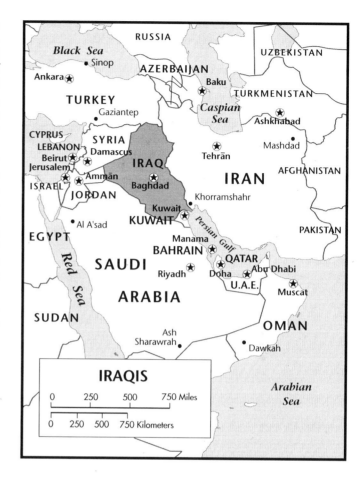

madic Bedu to move between the two countries. For comparison's sake, Iraq is just a little larger than the state of California. Within Iraq are four distinct regions. The Delta region of the southeast is a broad alluvial plain. West of the Delta are the Steppe-Desert Plains, part of the dry Syrian Desert, made up of sand and stony plains. The northern foothills between the Tigris and Euphrates rivers contain a fertile area of grassy flatlands and rolling hills. In the Kurdish Country of the northeast, the land rises steeply into the Zagros Mountains where the Kurds live.

The climate varies from region to region. In the north it is temperate in the summer and freezing in the winter. The east and southeast have a tropical climate with high humidity. The west is dry and desert-like. Temperatures also vary by region, with summer highs ranging from 22°C (72°F) in the north to 43°C (110°F) in the south and west, and winter lows of 0°C (32°F) or less in the north to 15.5°C (60°F) in the south and west. Iraq has two seasons. Summer lasts from May to October and is generally hot and dry, and winter stretches from November to April and is cooler and wetter. About 90% of the yearly rainfall occurs during the winter. On average, Iraq is a dry country. In most regions, the annual rainfall averages only 10–18 cm (4–7 in), although up to 101 cm (40 in) can fall in the mountains. Even the fertile lands between the rivers receive only 38–63.5 cm (15–25 in) of rain per year. In the summer, a dry, dusty northwesterly wind known as the *shamal* frequently blasts the landscape, lasting for several days at a time, and it is often accompanied by fierce dust storms. A winter wind called the *sharqi* comes from the south and southeast, bringing cool, moist air from the sea, which is a welcome change.

Plant and animal life differs by region. For its size, Iraq has very little wildlife. The most common tree is the date palm. Before the 1980–88 Iran-Iraq war, Iraq had more than 30 million date palms, each of which produced about 1,000 dates per year, and more than 80% of the world's date supply was grown in Iraq. Two decades of war have harmed the country's date industry seriously, and fewer than 3 million date palms are estimated to remain in the country.

The people who live in Iraq include a number of ethnic groups, physical types, and languages. According to 2008 estimates, the total population of Iraq was 28,221,180. About 75% to 80% of the population is Arab, and Kurds make up the largest ethnic minority at 15% to 20% of the population. Other ethnic groups in Iraq include Turkoman and Assyrian peoples. About 40% of the total population of Iraq is under the age of 15. Most Iraqis (75%) live in cities. Baghdad, the capital and largest city, has a population of 6 million people. The next largest cities, in descending order, are Basra, Mosul, and Kirkuk.

A distinct subgroup of Iraqi Arabs called the Ma'dan, or Marsh Arabs, once inhabited 15,540 sq km (6,000 sq mi) of marshy area just above the point at which the Tigris and Euphrates rivers flow together. Their lifestyle, however, has become virtually extinct as a result of the wars and Iraqi government programs to drain the marshlands.

3 LANGUAGE

The official languages of Iraq are Arabic and Kurdish. Kurdish is spoken primarily in the mountainous regions of the north. Other languages spoken in Iraq are Turkoman, Assyrian, and Armenian. Arabic has two different forms, spoken and written. Spoken Arabic has developed many dialects that often differ from one country to another, and those who speak different dialects may not always be able to understand each other. The written form of Arabic is called Classical Arabic or, for today's literature and press, Modern Standard Arabic. It is the same for all literate Arabs, regardless of how different their spoken forms are. Arabic is written from right to left in a unique alphabet that has no distinction between upper and lower cases. It is not necessary for the letters to be written on a straight line, as English letters must be. Punctuation conventions are also quite different from English. Kurdish uses an Arabic-based alphabet, but it is an Indo-European language in origin.

Arabic speakers tend to use emotional appeal, exaggeration, repetition, and words instead of action (for example, making threats with no intention to follow through on them). They are more interested in the poetry of the language than in communicating cold, hard facts. "Hello" in Arabic is *marhaba* or *ahlan*, to which one replies, *marhabtayn* or *ahlayn*. Other common greetings are *As-salam alaykum*, "Peace be with you," with the reply of *Walaykum as-salam*, "and to you peace." *Ma'assalama* means "goodbye." "Thank you" is *Shukran* and "You're welcome" is *Afwan*; "yes" is *na'am* and "no" is *la'a*. The numbers one to ten in Arabic are: *wahad, itnin, talata, arba'a, khamsa, sitta, saba'a, tamania, tisa'a,* and *ashara*.

Iraqi Arabs have very long names, consisting of their first name, their father's name, their paternal grandfather's name, and finally their family name. Following Islamic custom, a woman does not take her husband's name when she marries, but maintains her family identity. First names usually indicate

an Iraqi's religious affiliation. Muslims use names with Islamic religious significance, such as *Muhammad* and *Fatima*.

4 FOLKLORE

The most famous collection of Arab folktales, *The Thousand and One Nights*, was probably put together in Iraq sometime around AD 1000–1500, during the reign of the Abbasid Caliphate. The premise of the collection is that a king keeps killing his wives until the beautiful woman Scheherazade marries him. She tells him a story each night with a cliffhanger ending so that he must keep her alive to find out the ending. This goes on for one thousand and one nights, until finally the king decides to let her stay alive forever as his wife. Among the stories she tells are the well-known tales of "Ali Baba and the Forty Thieves," "Aladdin and the Magic Lamp," and "The Voyages of Sinbad the Sailor."

Another famous story originating in ancient Iraq (then known as Mesopotamia) is the Akkadian hero-tale, the *Epic of Gilgamesh*. Gilgamesh was the name of a ruler of Erech, but it is unknown whether this is the same Gilgamesh as the one in the epic poem. The poem tells of Gilgamesh's struggles to achieve immortality.

Some common superstitions in Iraq are beliefs in omens and signs. For example, it is considered good luck if a stork chooses to build its nest on the roof of your home. Also, precautions are taken at birth celebrations to ensure the protection of the child from bad luck, such as not allowing women who have had no children or people with blue eyes to attend.

5 RELIGION

The majority of Iraqis, about 95%, are Muslim. Of these, 60% to 65% are Shi'ite, and the remainder is Sunni. Most Kurds are Sunni Muslim but consider themselves distinct from Iraq's Sunni Arab population. Orthodox Christians, Catholic Christians, Mandaeans, and Yazaidis also live in Iraq. Ancient Mesopotamia was originally a Jewish region, and the Jews actually left and returned to Mesopotamia many times with various conquering armies, including the Greeks and the Persians. The few Jews who stayed on in Mesopotamia created a small band of descendants in Iraq, most of whom migrated to Israel when it became an independent Jewish state in 1948. Iraqi Christians are mostly Catholic. They consider themselves the original Iraqis since they were there before the Islamic invasion. When Islam arrived in the 7th century AD, many gods and goddesses were being worshiped by the people of present-day Iraq. The Islamic conquerors brought most of the people together under one god, Allah.

The difference between Sunni and Shi'ite Muslims, which has played such an important part in Iraqi history, has to do with the early history of the religion. After Muhammad's death, the entire Muslim community was divided over who should become the first political successor, or caliph. A strong minority believed that Ali, Muhammad's cousin and son-in-law, should be caliph. The rest accepted Abu Baker as the first caliph. Abu Baker assumed the caliphate and eventually obtained the allegiance of Ali.

Ali did not become caliph until after the death of Uthman, the third caliph. At that time, Mu'awiyah, the governor of Syria and a relative of Uthman, challenged Ali for the caliphate using Syrian troops personally loyal to him. The battles between the caliph and Mu'awiyah were inconclusive, and Ali remained in control over most areas except Greater Syria until his death. At that time, Mu'awiyah was able to defeat a number of challenges from Muslims of Muhammad's family and friends to firmly establish himself as caliph. He instituted a system of hereditary rule for his family, thus establishing the Umayyed dynasty. Those Muslims who continued to refuse to recognize the legitimacy of Mu'awiyah's caliphate and the Umayyed dynasty were called the followers of Ali, or *Shi'iat Ali*. The supporters of the Umayyeds were known as *Shi'iat Uthman*. Eventually the followers of Ali became known as the Shi'ites.

Although there are doctrinal differences, the fundamental difference between the sects is an argument about authority, not doctrine. The Shi'ites believe that the successors of Muhammad should have been from his close family (or *Ahl al-Bayt*) and that Ali should have been first caliph. The Sunnis believe that, although Ali was justified in defending the caliphate from Mu'awiyah, once the Umayyeds took control, it was more important to maintain political stability than to risk the chaos that might have resulted from a civil war. These political differences have developed into substantial theological differences over the centuries.

6 MAJOR HOLIDAYS

Iraqi Muslims celebrate Muslim holidays, and Christians celebrate Christian holidays. Because Iraq is not officially an Islamic state, Muslim holidays are not official state holidays. But, since the overwhelming majority of Iraqis are Muslim, their holidays become essentially state holidays. Friday is the Islamic day of rest, so most businesses and services are closed on Fridays. Muslim holidays follow the lunar calendar, moving back by 11 days each year, so their dates are not fixed on the standard Gregorian calendar.

The main Muslim holidays are: *Ramadan*, the ninth month of the Muslim year, during which Muhammad received his first revelations—celebrated by complete fasting from dawn until dusk each day of the entire month; *Ayd Al-Fitr*, a three-day festival at the end of *Ramadan*; *Ayd Al-Adha*, a three-day feast of sacrifice at the end of the month of pilgrimage to Mecca (known as the *Haj*)—families who can afford it slaughter a lamb and share the meat with poorer Muslims; the First of *Muharram*, or the Muslim New Year; *Mawoulid An-Nabawi*, the prophet Muhammad's birthday; and *Ayd Al-Isra wa Al-Miraj*, a feast celebrating the nocturnal visit of Muhammad to heaven.

Ahura, which is only commemorated by Shi'ites, is a formal day of mourning for the anniversary of when Muhammad's grandson, Husayn, and a small band of loyal followers were massacred by Yazid, the son of Mu'awiyah, who was named caliph by the Umayyeds after Mu'awiyah's death. Yazid was almost universally despised by the Muslims for his impiety and oppression but maintained a strong army personally loyal to him. The massacre occurred at Karbala' in Iraq. The Muslims who had asked Husayn to oppose Yazid failed to show up at Karbala' to help him against Yazid's army. Today, the holiday has political overtones as Shi'ites cry and lament the failure of the Muslims to defend Muhammad's family and celebrate the bravery of Husayn in opposing an unjust ruler despite terrible odds. For this reason, Iraq's former leader Saddam Hussein had outlawed the commemoration of this important Shi'ite holiday.

Christian holidays center on Christmas (December 25) and Easter (depending on the lunar cycle, occurring sometime in late March or early April). Several secular holidays that were celebrated under Saddam Hussein's regime are no longer officially observed, and the government of Iraq had not established new national holidays as of 2008.

7 RITES OF PASSAGE

The birth of a child is an occasion for a big celebration, especially if the child is a boy. Boys are usually circumcised at birth. Three days after the birth, family members and friends come to visit and bring gifts for the child. Sometime between 9 and 13 years old, children begin the *al'Khatma*, or the "reading of the Quran." A child studies for a year or more to prepare for this difficult task. When ready, boys read to men and girls read to women. Those who read without an error earn the title of *hafiz*. After a successful reading, the family holds a celebration in the child's honor, usually a luncheon or a tea. Relatives give the child gifts and money, and everyone wears colorful clothes.

After children reach puberty, they generally are segregated by gender. Young men and young women attend separate schools and are rarely seen together in public. Early marriage is encouraged, and marriage is considered the start of adulthood. Unmarried daughters and sisters are carefully protected by the male members of their families, and marriages are often arranged. Marriage is considered a contract between families. Dating is relatively rare. In all circumstances, the groom is required to pay a large dowry to the bride's family, but this money is often used to buy furniture for the new couple. Weddings consist of a brief ceremony and several days of parties. After the parties, guests escort the newlywed couple to their new home or to a hotel. Cars following in a procession, honking horns, and in rural areas, bullets are sometimes fired into the air.

Islamic law allows men to have up to four wives, but most Iraqi men have only one wife. Divorce is rare.

Young Iraqi adults expect to take care of parents as they age. As a result, few retirement homes exist in Iraq. When an Iraqi Muslim dies, the body is buried in a grave facing Mecca. After burial, a collective prayer seeking forgiveness for the deceased is offered.

8 INTERPERSONAL RELATIONS

Iraqis are very generous and loyal, and very polite to their friends. If a friend asks for a favor, it is considered very rude to say no. It is taboo to wish bad luck on someone because it might come true. While having a conversation, it is rude to turn one's foot out so that the sole is facing the other person. The left hand is considered "unclean" so it is never used when eating. If someone praises one of an Iraqi's possessions, he or she will insist that the other take it; therefore, it is rude to praise another's things too much.

When talking, Iraqis touch each other much more often and stand much closer together than Westerners do. People of the same sex will often hold hands while talking, even if they are virtual strangers. (Members of the opposite sex, even married couples, never touch in public.) Iraqis talk a lot, talk loudly, repeat themselves often, and interrupt each other constantly. Conversations are highly emotional and full of gestures. Some common Iraqi gestures are:

eyebrows raised and head tilted back = "No."
clicking the tongue = "No."
right forefinger moving right-to-left repeatedly = "No."
right hand moving up and down with the palm facing down = "Be quiet!"
right hand moving away from the body with the palm down = "Go away!"
right hand out while opening and closing the hand = "Come here!"
right hand on heart after shaking hands = show of sincerity
fist with thumb pointing upwards = sign of victory

9 LIVING CONDITIONS

Living conditions among Iraqis are in disarray as a result of nearly three decades of war. Iraqi society typically consisted of three classes: the upper class, composed of well-known, influential families and government officials; the middle class, composed of government employees, professionals, merchants, small landowners, etc.; and the lower class, comprising the peasants and laborers, rural farmers, and the unemployed. The middle and upper classes traditionally have lived in much better conditions than the lower class. The lower class, mostly rural people, lived in reed and mud huts, generally without electricity or running water. However, all classes have suffered greatly from the war.

Most Iraqis still decorate their homes with religious art, including Quranic verses written in Arabic calligraphy, religious icons, and pictures of the holy Islamic cities of Mecca and Medina in Saudi Arabia. Homes usually are set up so that a husband and wife occupy one bedroom, and so that girls and boys each sleep in separate quarters. Homes are built of stone and fired bricks. In more peaceful times, Iraqis would sleep on their roofs on hot nights.

Before the 2003 U.S.-led invasion, about 60% of Iraqis relied on the United Nations' "oil-for-food" program for basic nutrition. This program allowed Iraq to bypass economic sanctions that had been imposed against Saddam Hussein's government in order to sell oil to purchase food, medicine, and other basic supplies. Since the beginning of the 2003 war, much of that relief has come from humanitarian aid agencies. The country's hospitals are understaffed, and many basic medications are in short supply. Drinking water has been contaminated, and diseases, such as typhoid and cholera, are common. Widespread poverty, malnutrition, and pollution have caused infant mortality to rise in recent years. The infant mortality rate was estimated at 45.43 deaths for every 1,000 live births in 2008, with males less likely to survive childhood than females. Iraqi life expectancy rates also are lower than that of much of the world. The average life expectancy is 68 years for men and 71 years for women. These factors have produced a very young population of Iraqis, with a median age of 20.2 years.

10 FAMILY LIFE

The family is the most important social unit in Iraq, and family loyalty is one of the most important values. Honor, both personal and family, is also very important. It is considered a disgrace to speak badly about a family member, or tell non-family members about bad things that have happened in the family. A "family" consists of all related kin and can include hundreds of people. Rural families live with or near each other.

Although urban families do not always live together, they are always willing to help out a family member in need. The traditional household of a typical man in his 40s consists of himself, his wife, their unmarried sons and daughters, their married sons with their wives and children, the man's mother if she is still alive, and frequently his unmarried sisters, if he has any. Very probably, the most powerful force in the household is the man's mother: her sons revere her, and her daughters-in-law must do her bidding. The structure of Arab society is such that financial power is in the hands of the husband, although his wife is not completely without influence. Women have a great deal of power at home and over their children, including their grown sons. Sex roles are very clearly defined in Iraq. Men wield public authority and are the stern disciplinarians at home, whereas women rule in domestic affairs and are the loving, nurturing force at home (often to the point of spoiling their children). In rural areas, this strict division of labor and sex roles causes the sexes to be almost completely segregated except when eating and sleeping.

Most marriages are still arranged by families, but a couple must approve a match. Traditionally, first or second cousins are preferred for marriage partners. Divorce is fairly easy under Islamic law and has no stigma attached to it; even so, it rarely occurs. Children belong to their father's family, and in the case of divorce the father is automatically awarded custody.

Young children are adored and indulged, though they are strictly punished for misbehavior. Older boys are allowed to attend the gatherings of the men, and by listening they absorb many of the cultural values and attitudes that will shape their public behavior. Older girls are very carefully protected. They learn domestic skills through participation. Children are expected to obey their parents and grandparents. Iraqis believe that wisdom increases with age, so the elderly are deeply revered.

11 CLOTHING

Urban Iraqis, for the most part, wear Western-style clothing, although there is a resurgence of fundamentalism that has led some to return to more traditional Arab dress (such as veils for women). Most rural Iraqis wear traditional clothing. Traditional dress for women consists of a veil, which girls begin to wear after their first menstrual period, and a dark robe called an *abaaya*, which is an outer cloak that covers the body from head to ankle. Under the abaaya, they wear brightly colored dresses. Veils are only removed at home or in female-only groups. For men, traditional dress consists of a caftan and a head cloth. A caftan is an ankle-length robe with long sleeves. Caftans used to be colorful but are plain-colored now. Light cotton caftans are worn in summer, and heavy woolen ones in winter. Head cloths are either wrapped around the head like a turban (rural men) or draped over the head and held in place with a cord (urban men). Kurdish women wear pants under their dresses, while men wear baggy trousers tied with sashes.

12 FOOD

Staple foods in Iraq are wheat, barley, rice, and dates. Iraqis cook almost every part of an animal, including the kidneys, liver, brain, feet, eyes, and ears. The meat is usually cut into strips and cooked with onions and garlic, or it is minced for a stew served with rice. Sheep and goats are the most common meat animals, although cows, chickens, fish, and camels are also eaten. Islam forbids the eating of pork. Lamb and mutton are traditionally used for special feasts.

Coffee is prepared in a unique way in Iraq. The beans are ground, then the drink is heated and cooled nine times before it is served. It is believed that this process removes all impurities from the imported product. Iraqis usually drink their coffee with sugar and cream or milk. Coffee and tea are the favorite drinks, served before and after (not during) meals. Ice water is drunk frequently in the summer, and Western soft drinks are popular in the cities. Islam forbids the consumption of alcohol.

An Iraqi meal has several courses, starting with appetizers, such as *kebabs,* which are cubes of marinated meat cooked on skewers, and soups, which are drunk from the bowl and not eaten with a spoon. A simple main course follows, such as lamb with rice, and ends with a salad and *khubaz,* which is a flat wheat bread served buttered with fruit jelly spread on top. Iraqis love desserts, especially one called *ma'mounia,* dating from the 9th century. A recipe for ma'mounia follows.

Ma'mounia

3 cups water
2 cups sugar
1 teaspoon lemon juice
½ cup sweet butter
1 cup semolina
whipped cream
1 teaspoon ground cinnamon

Put sugar and water in a large saucepan over low heat, and stir constantly until sugar dissolves. Bring mixture to a boil while adding lemon juice. After the syrup boils, reduce heat and let simmer until syrup thickens slightly (about 10 minutes). In another saucepan, melt butter and add semolina. Stir until semolina is lightly fried. Then add the syrup from the other pan, and let the mixture simmer another 10 minutes, stirring constantly. Remove from heat and let cool 20 minutes. Spoon ma'mounia into individual serving bowls, top with whipped cream, and sprinkle with cinnamon.

Makes 4 servings.

(Adapted from Susan M. Hassig, Cultures of the World: Iraq, p.119.)

¹³ EDUCATION

Before the 1991 Gulf War, the government invested heavily in Iraqi education. Literacy rates increased substantially and more Iraqis had access to higher education. Since then, schools have fallen into disrepair and teachers have been forced to leave jobs that often pay only a few dollars a month. When schools have been able to operate, students sit in overcrowded classrooms and share books. In addition, security concerns have prompted many families to keep their children at home. About one in six students who are eligible to receive free public education are able to do so under the war-like conditions. As of 2000, about one-quarter of the adult population was illiterate.

¹⁴ CULTURAL HERITAGE

Iraq has a rich cultural history dating back to the Sumerians, thought to be the first advanced civilization on Earth. Storytelling has been important since the very beginning. Mesopo-

Iraqi Shiite pilgrims march to the holy Shiite city of Karbala, Baghdad, Iraq. (Wathiq Khuzaie/Getty Images)

tamian stories have influenced other literature and art in the world, including Biblical stories, such as Adam and Eve, the Song of Songs, and the Psalms, and Greek epics and myths, such as *The Iliad* and *Aesop's Fables.* The most famous literary works to emerge from this vast cultural history are the *Epic of Gilgamesh* (an Akkadian hero-tale) and *The Thousand and One Nights* (a collection of Arab folktales). Modern Iraqi literature is becoming Westernized in its form and content, turning from the romantic, poetic epics of traditional Arabic literature to short stories about everyday life and non-rhyming poetry on personal subjects.

Visual art in Iraq has been greatly influenced since the 7th century AD by the Islamic prohibition against depicting human or animal forms. Iraqi visual art has, therefore, focused on intricate geometric and floral patterns, as well as calligraphy. The rich legacy of Islamic architecture can be seen particularly in Iraq's mosques, with their detailed mosaics, graceful lines, and beautifully carved golden domes and minarets. Iraq is also famous for its carpets, woven from fine threads in brilliant colors. Painting and sculpture have traditionally been the favored visual arts in Iraq, with television and film-making gaining popularity in recent years.

¹⁵ WORK

Iraq was once an agricultural nation, but after oil was discovered it quickly grew to become the principal industry. More than 90% of Iraq's exports are now in the form of crude oil. By 1986, only 30% of Iraqis were still farmers. Wheat, barley, tobacco, and dates are the major crops. Only 10% of the population works in small manufacturing. These industries include textiles, cement, paper products, food processing, and leather. Rural children usually follow in their parents' footsteps. The son of a blacksmith, for example, will become a blacksmith.

16 SPORTS

Soccer is the favorite sport in Iraq. Besides soccer, there is growing interest in boating, basketball, volleyball, weightlifting, and boxing. The continual warfare of the past few decades has prevented Iraq from developing competitive international sports teams.

17 ENTERTAINMENT AND RECREATION

Outdoor activities are popular in the mountains of the north, and swimming and fishing are favorite recreations in the Tigris and Euphrates rivers during the summer. Rural men hunt and fish with friends and shop together for food and drinks at the markets and bazaars of the towns. Rural women visit with each other and talk, cook, or make handicrafts. In the cities, people visit museums, haggle over prices in the bazaars, or shop in large shopping complexes with their families and friends. Men frequent teahouses, and everyone enjoys watching television. The most noteworthy fact about Iraqi entertainment and recreation is that it is nearly always done in the company of others. Iraqis are extremely social people.

18 FOLK ART, CRAFTS, AND HOBBIES

Handicrafts are very popular in Iraq, and there are hundreds of arts and crafts fairs each year to handle the volume of handicrafts produced. Most crafts are in the form of jewelry, rugs, blankets, leather, and pottery. Village women love to make handicrafts in their leisure time. Several households may chip in together to buy a pottery wheel and share the use of it.

19 SOCIAL PROBLEMS

The 1980–88 Iran-Iraq war, the 1991 Gulf War, and the 2003 U.S.-led invasion have produced poverty and social upheaval for Iraqis. It remains to be seen whether the country will recover and thrive under its 2005 constitution or whether internal strife between Sunni, Shi'ite, and Kurdish factions will force Iraqi society to crumble under civil war. Since 1991, the Iraqi middle class has virtually collapsed.

Violence continues in Iraq. The human rights group Amnesty International noted in its *2008 Human Rights Watch Report* that thousands of civilians, including many children, were killed in sectarian fighting. Human rights violations were committed by armed militias, Iraq's military forces, and U.S.-led forces. An estimated 2 million Iraqis are believed to have been killed in war-related violence, and about 2.8 million Iraqis are living as refugees within the country. An additional 2.2 million have fled the country in search of safer living conditions abroad. Among those who have stayed, unemployment rates are approximately 40%.

20 GENDER ISSUES

Ongoing violence in Iraq has made conditions in the country increasingly unsafe for women. Although Islamic principles have long enforced such practices as public segregation of individuals by gender, many Iraqi women worked outside the home and enjoyed a great deal of authority in the running of households. This independence has been hampered by death threats, domestic violence, and "honor killings." Many women have been forced to leave jobs or seek refuge abroad. Early marriage continues to be encouraged for women, especially in rural areas, and women who marry outside their religious sect face an increasing threat of violence.

21 BIBLIOGRAPHY

Amnesty International. *Amnesty International Report 2008: State of the World's Human Rights.* http://thereport.amnesty.org/eng/Homepage (October 28, 2008).

Background Note: Iraq. http://www.state.gov/r/pa/ei/bgn/6804.htm (October 28, 2008).

Economist Intelligence Unit. *Country Profile: Iraq,* www.economist.com (October 28, 2008).

Foster, Leila Merrell. *Enchantment of the World: Iraq.* Chicago: Children's Press, 1991.

Hassig, Susan M. *Cultures of the World: Iraq.* New York: Marshall Cavendish, 1993.

Iraq. CultureGrams: World Edition. Ann Arbor, Mich.: ProQuest LLC, 2008.

Iraq...in Pictures. Minneapolis: Lerner Publications Co., 1990.

Nolan, Clare. "Lessons from Iraqi Refugees." *National Catholic Reporter,* Jul 25, 2008. 44:24 (11-12).

"The change in Iraq: Is it turning the corner?" *The Economist,* June 12, 2008, www.economist.com (October 28, 2008).

The Iraqis: Their History and Culture. CAL Refugee Fact Series No. 11. Washington, DC: Refugee Service Center, Center for Applied Linguistics, 1995.

Vesely, Milan. "A delicacy of war. (Dubai Dates)." *The Middle East* July 2003: 62-63.

—revised by H. Gupta-Carlson

ISRAELIS

PRONUNCIATION: iz-RAY-leez
LOCATION: Israel
POPULATION: 7.2 million (2007 estimate, includes approximately 350,000 settlers living in Palestinian territories of Gaza Strip and the West Bank, as well as in the Israeli-occupied territories of East Jerusalem and Golan Heights)
LANGUAGE: Hebrew; Arabic; English
RELIGION: Judaism; Islam; Christianity; Druze
RELATED ARTICLES: Vol. 3 Palestinians; Vol. 4: Traditional Orthodox Jews

¹ INTRODUCTION

The history of the land of Israel and the Jewish people spans 35 centuries, although the state of Israel is only a few decades old. The modern state of Israel was established in 1948 as a homeland for the Jewish people, who had been living in exile for 2,000 years. Jews from all over the world have been encouraged to immigrate to Israel in what is known as the "ingathering of exiles," thus creating a very diverse society. The population of Israel more than doubled in the first four years of its existence (1948–1952) as Jews from Eastern and Western Europe flocked to a land where they would no longer be persecuted. From 1989 to 1992, some 500,000 new immigrants arrived, mostly from the former Soviet Union, plus almost the entire population of Ethiopian Jews. In terms of percentage of population, this would be the equivalent of the United States taking in 25 million more people.

Israel also has a sizable population of non-Jews to integrate into its society, most of whom are Arabs: Muslim, Druze, and Christian. The world center for the Baha'i faith is in Israel, and there is also a small but significant population of Bedouin Arabs (former nomadic herders who are now trying to make the transition to a settled life). Arabs in Israel are challenged to create and maintain a sense of identity. They are Israeli, but they have family, cultural, and religious ties to Arabs (especially to West Bank Palestinians) in other Middle East states. Yet, Arabs in other states are sometimes wary of Israeli Arabs because they are citizens of Israel, a country with which neighboring Arab states have been at war for many, many years. Muslim and Christian Arabs feel that they also have claims to the land of Israel, as it is the historical and spiritual center of their religions as well, and struggles for statehood and land rights have dominated Israeli politics through the early 21st century. These struggles have created tremendous tensions within Israeli society. Many programs are in place to try to reduce these tensions by breaking down stereotypes, encouraging cooperation among different elements of the Israeli population, and improving conditions for disadvantaged minorities.

The Holy Land, of which the present-day state of Israel is a part, has a long history of rule by different powers. A Hebrew kingdom was established from 12 tribes of Israel that left Egypt with Moses. King David ruled this kingdom some three thousand years ago. After his son Solomon's reign, the kingdom split into two states:Israel and Judah. These states were subsequently destroyed by Assyria and Babylonia. At this point, the peoples living in the area were forced to disperse. Jews re-

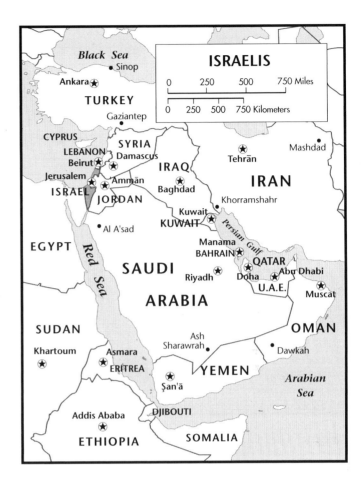

turned to the Holy Land after the Persian conquest of the Middle East but suffered great persecution under Greek, Roman, Byzantine, and eventually Muslim rule until World War I.

In the 1890s, a Hungarian named Theodor Herzl founded Zionism. The ideology grew into an international movement to restore the Land of Palestine to the Jews. The British gained control of the territory after World War I when the Ottoman Empire collapsed. During World War II, as Jews suffered genocide in Germany, many immigrated to Palestine, seeking safety. Some 600,000 Arabs also resided in the territory, and when the war ended, the international community faced the task of trying to reconcile claims for statehood by the Jews with the traditional practices of Arabs living in the area. In 1947, the United Nations voted to divide the area into two states, one Arab and one Jewish. In May 1948, Israel was proclaimed an independent state. Neighboring Arab nations almost immediately declared war and attacked the new nation. Subsequent wars were fought in 1956, 1967, and 1973. Israel occupied territories conquered in the 1967 War: the Sinai Peninsula and the Gaza Strip from Egypt, the Golan Heights from Syria, and the West Bank and East Jerusalem from Jordan. A series of peace agreements have resulted in Israel giving up some of those lands. Israel returned Sinai to Egypt in 1982 surrendered much of the Gaza Strip and West Bank to Palestinians through a withdrawal process that began in 1993, and withdrew troops from southern Lebanon in 2000.

Treaties with Egypt and Lebanon have helped restore some relationships between Israel and its neighbors. However, relationships between the two groups who reside in Israel, the

Israeli ultra-Orthodox Jews wear sac cloth in order to appear humble before God during a religious ritual at the Wailing Wall in east Jerusalem. (Yoav Lemmer/AFP/Getty Images)

mostly Jewish Israelis and the mostly Muslim Palestinians, remain tense. Much of the tension stems from the establishment of the Jewish state of Israel itself. The state was created through international treaties that paid little attention to the Arab communities, who now are known as Palestinians, living in the land. Palestinians often have experienced discrimination in educational and workplace facilities in Israel and began a long, often violent movement known as intifada in 1982 to establish a permanent state. As part of that effort, U.S. President George W. Bush and other diplomatic leaders created a treaty that called for the eventual creation of a Palestinian state within Israeli territories. As part of that process, Israel withdrew from the Gaza Strip in 2005, and that area, along with parts of the West Bank, has been known more recently as the Palestinian territories. However, the efforts to achieve peace between Israelis and Palestinians have been stalled through the first decade of the 21st century.

Israelis have regarded their nation-state as a place of refuge for diasporic Jews, and Israeli law allows all Jews to immigrate to Israel, provided that they can prove that they either were born into a Jewish family or have been recognized as converts to the religion. However, for the first time in 2,000 years, a generation of Jews is growing up as the majority in their homeland. Known as Sabras (native-born Israelis), this new generation is developing a very different understanding of themselves than that of their parents and grandparents. Many Sabras think of themselves not as Jews, but as Israelis. Their nationalistic identity has further fueled tensions between Jews residing in Israel and their Palestinian counterparts. That identity also has be-

gun to make more Jews outside of Israel regard the nation as spiritually uninviting.

² LOCATION AND HOMELAND

Israel is a small, narrow country, and its continually disputed borders are constantly subject to change. As of 2008, Israel is approximately 20,770 sq km (8,020 sq mi) in size, which makes it slightly smaller than the U.S. state of New Jersey. The tiny country shares borders with Egypt, Lebanon, Syria, Jordan, and the Palestinian territories of Gaza Strip and the West Bank. The area, despite its size, contains an amazing diversity of landscape, from mountains (Golan Heights) to desert (Negev) to a fertile river valley (Jordan). The lowest point on Earth is in Israel; the Dead Sea is 400 m (1,300 ft) below sea level. The waters of the Dead Sea are the saltiest and densest in the world. (It is almost impossible to sink in the Dead Sea.) Located at the junction of three continents—Europe, Asia, and Africa—and their natural life zones, Israel has a tremendous variety of plants and animals for its small size. The rainy season, from November to March, does not provide enough moisture to last through the dry season, from April to October, so lack of water is always a problem. Sophisticated irrigation and water-transportation and conservation techniques have been developed, highlighted by the National Water Carrier—a huge system of pipes, aqueducts, canals, reservoirs, dams, and so on—to carry water from the fertile north to the drier south. Through these sophisticated techniques, Israel has managed to create enough arable land to grow almost all the food needed by its people.

Approximately 7.2 million people live in Israel, the Israeli-occupied territories, and the Palestinian territories. Within the current boundaries of Israel, more than 90% of residents live in cities. The other 10% live in *kibbutzim* and *moshavim* (communal farms) or in small villages. There are about 110,000 Bedouin Arabs (former nomadic herders who now live mostly settled lives) scattered throughout the Negev desert, living in tents and cooking over open fires. The median age in Israel is about 28 years old. About 82% of the population is Jewish and 16% is Arab. The largest cities are Jerusalem, a mixture of ancient and modern; Tel Aviv–Yafo, the commercial and financial center, located on the Mediterranean coast; and Haifa, a busy Mediterranean port city.

3 LANGUAGE

The official languages of Israel are Hebrew and Arabic. English is widely used in commerce. Hebrew is the language of the majority, and more Arabs speak Hebrew than Jews speak Arabic. Most Israelis also speak English, particularly in business dealings.

Both Arabic and English are taught in schools, beginning in the fifth grade. The Israeli government sponsors classes for immigrants to Israel to learn Hebrew. However, proficiency in the language is no longer considered crucial for survival in Israel. Most Israelis speak at least two languages, often because they or their parents emigrated after 1948, and languages such as Russian often appear on food labels and in ads.

Modern Hebrew is a very young language, born only about 100 years ago. After the Exile of the Jews from ancient Israel, Hebrew was used only for religious writings and liturgical purposes for 2,000 years. For everyday use, Jews learned to speak the language of whatever country they ended up in. In the late 19th century, Eliezer Ben Yehuda (1858–1922) moved to the Holy Land with his family and decided that they would never speak a word in any language but Hebrew again. This forced them to coin many new words, and modern Hebrew was born. Yehuda compiled the first modern Hebrew dictionary and is considered to be the "father" of modern Hebrew. The Orthodox Jewish community of his time excommunicated Yehuda for "defiling" the holy language by bringing it into everyday use, and some ultra-Orthodox Israelis still refuse to speak modern Hebrew. Other Hebrew purists are frustrated by the Israeli people's persistence in using cognates from other languages, such as *democratia, sveder* ("sweater"), and *breks* ("brakes"). But in a language that was used for two millennia solely for religious communication, a great deal of borrowing from other languages for modern and technological terms is to be expected.

Hebrew uses a unique alphabet with no vowels. It is read from right to left, except for numerals, which are read from left to right. Some common words in Hebrew are *toda*, ("thank you"), *ken*, ("yes"), and *lo* ("no"). The numbers from one to ten in Hebrew are: *ehad, shtayim, shalosh, arba', hamesh, shesh, sheva', shmoney, taysha'*, and *esser*. Common male names are *Menahem, Avraham, Moshe, Benyamin,* and *Shlomo.* Common female names are *Esther, Hannah, Sareh, Rachel,* and *Galit.*

4 FOLKLORE

Most of Israeli folklore and legend reflects their history of exile in other lands, their return to the land of their ancestors, and the modern-day battles over establishing and maintaining statehood. The traditional stories, rooted in the Jewish faith, give prominence to the Jews as God's Chosen People and to their yearning for the Promised Land.

For example, the story of Passover, or *Pesach*, is a reference to the deliverance of the children of Israel from over two centuries of bondage in Egypt. It refers to the Jewish exodus from Egypt more than 3,000 years ago. Exodus (chapters 1–15) recounts the story of the Israelites' oppressive servitude to the Pharaoh of Egypt and their escape with the help of Moses and his brother, Aaron. The Torah calls Passover the "season of our freedom," for it is the time when the plague that struck Egypt passed over the Israelites without destroying them.

Another important event in the history of Judaism is the *zman matan Torateinu*, "the season of the giving of our Torah." This commemorates the Revelation of the Ten Commandments, seven weeks after the Israelites escaped from Egypt, as they camped at the foot of Mount Sinai. The exact nature of God's communication with Moses has been subject to various opinions, but the event itself is considered to have given the Jews their unique character.

Some modern-day Israeli heroes include Theodor Herzl, who convened the first Zionist Congress, held in Basel, Switzerland, in 1897, and the author of *The Jewish State;* Chaim Weizmann, Israel's first president; and David Ben-Gurion, Israel's first prime minister, who announced the independence of Israel in 1948.

5 RELIGION

The modern state of Israel was established in 1948 as a homeland for Jews, so it is not surprising that 82% of the population is Jewish. Nevertheless, the city of Jerusalem and many other areas in Israel played an important role in the development of three of the world's major religions: Judaism, Christianity, and Islam. Jerusalem is holy to all three religions and is a source of conflict among them. Of the 18% who are non-Jews, 77% (or 13.8% of the Israeli population) are Muslim Arabs, most of them Sunni Muslims. About 130,000 Israelis (2.6% of the population) are Christian, most of them Arab, and the other 1.6% (or 80,000 people) are Druze. The Baha'i world center is also located in Israel, in the Mediterranean coastal city of Haifa. The Baha'i religion developed out of the mystical Islamic movement around AD 1850. Religious freedom is guaranteed by the state, but there is little separation between "church and state," as the Jewish faith and rabbinical law are intricately entwined with the political and public spheres. Consequently, there is constant tension between the religious and secular worlds in Israel.

Jews, Muslims, and Christians all view the land of Israel as their birthplace and the first five books of the Bible as holy scripture. Despite this common foundation, these three religions have developed in very different and often contradictory ways that bring them into almost constant conflict with each other. For example, the Muslim day of rest is on Friday, the Jewish on Saturday, and the Christian on Sunday. Muslim men and women pray separately, Jewish men and women sit separately while praying, and Christian men and women sit and pray together. Jews worship in a synagogue, where a quorum (*minyan*) of 10 adult males is needed to begin. All heads are covered, and prayers happen three times daily. In contrast, at a Muslim mosque, prayers occur five times a day, facing Mecca, with shoes removed. During prayer, men bare their heads, while women cover theirs. In contrast to traditional Christian services at a church, which have music and choral singing, Jewish and Muslim worship (while it similarly includes a sermon) features unaccompanied chanting. Holy days for the three religions differ, although some occur at similar times of the year (such as the Jewish Hanukkah and Christian Christmas). Because Muslim holy days follow a lunar calendar, sometimes they occur around Hanukkah and Christmas, and sometimes they do not.

6 MAJOR HOLIDAYS

Because the majority of the Israeli population is Jewish, Jewish holidays become, in effect, state holidays. During the Jewish *shabbat*, or Sabbath, from sunset Friday to sunset Saturday each week, almost all public and commercial enterprise stops. On *Yom Kippur*, the Day of Atonement, which occurs ten days after *Rosh Hashana*, the Jewish New Year, the whole country comes to a standstill while observant Jews complete 25 hours of total fasting and prayer. No Jewish hotels or restaurants will serve bread or fermented foods during the week of *Pesach*, or Passover, which commemorates the exodus of the Jews from Egypt during Biblical times.

At *kibbutzim* and *moshavim* (communal farms), a distinctive cultural life has developed with celebrations based on traditional Jewish holidays combined with ancient earth-cycle customs, such as first fruits and harvest feasts.

Independence Day is observed on May 15.

7 RITES OF PASSAGE

Most Israelis observe Jewish rituals and traditions. Boys are named after eight days, at the time of circumcision. The *brit milah* (circumcision ritual) is both a Jewish and Muslim ritual that has been performed for 4,000 years, since the days of the prophet Abraham. The ritual Jewish circumcision, performed eight days after birth, involves prayers, is performed by a Jew, and expresses the intent of bringing the son into the covenant with God. The son is named at circumcision. Muslim circumcisions take place either at birth or during the boy's youth. They are followed by a feast in celebration. Girls are generally named three days after birth and are given their names in a synagogue.

Both boys and girls celebrate the onset of adolescence with a formal ceremony. For girls, the celebration is known as the Bat Mitzvah (literally, "daughter of the commandments") and generally takes place at age 12. For boys, a Bar Mitzvah ("son of the commandments") takes place at age 13. Bar Mitzvah also means "he who is subject to the commandments" and signifies a boy's attainment of maturity. During the service, the boy reads from the Torah and speaks on a Biblical theme from memory. Both ceremonies are festive affairs attended by many extended family members and friends. All Israeli youth, regardless of their gender, serve in the military for two to three years. Although the mandatory military service is required of Israeli Jews, Israeli Arabs also are encouraged to volunteer for military service.

Dating is quite common among Israelis, but marriage is a highly religious matter. No civil marriages are permitted in Israel; all couples must be married by an authority within their religious faith. For Jews, the religious authority performing marriages is a rabbi. Muslim marriages are performed by a khadi and Christian marriages are performed by members of their clergy. A Jewish bride remains veiled until after the wedding ceremony. During the first part of the ceremony, the sanctification or *kiddushin*, the groom places a ring upon the bride's finger and recites, "Be sanctified to me with this ring in accordance with the law of Moses and Israel." The bride gives her consent in the presence of two witnesses and thus becomes the man's wife. At weddings, a glass is broken to symbolize the destruction of the ancient Temple in Jerusalem (AD 70) by the Romans. A wedding contract requires a husband to support his wife. Both men and women attend the ceremony, but during the feast and afterwards, the two sexes are separated by a *mehitzah*, or dividing wall. Muslim marriages in Israel are similar to those among the Palestinians. They consist of a religious ceremony and a wedding reception at which guests and family eat, sing, and dance.

When a Jew dies, the body must be cleansed and then dressed in white robes. Males are also wrapped in a *tallit*. Embalming is forbidden because blood must be buried as part of the dead individual. Burial must take place as soon as possible following death, but Jews cannot be buried on the Sabbath. The deceased is mourned during three consecutive periods. The first period, the *shiva*, lasts seven days. At its end comes the *shloshim*, a 30-day period. The *avelut* period of mourning then begins, and it ends after the conclusion of 12 months from the day of death. To comfort a bereaved family, Jews recall the loss of Jerusalem with the following prayer: "May the Lord comfort you, together with all who mourn for Zion and Jerusalem." A son must recite the *Kaddish* prayer each day for an 11-month period after a parent's death. Sons and daughters are expected to contribute to charity in memory of a deceased parent.

Muslims also bury their dead as soon as possible. Generally, only the men attend the funeral procession. There is a three-day mourning period, during which condolences are given and Quranic verses are recited. This is followed by another Quranic recitation after 40 days. Black (unsweetened) Turkish coffee is traditionally served during mourning.

8 INTERPERSONAL RELATIONS

Given the extremely diverse population of Israel, it is difficult to define any standard Israeli ways of relating to one another. Native-born Israelis (known as Sabras), however, tend to be very straightforward, plain-talking people, even to the point of rudeness. They detest sentimentality of any kind and love a good argument. They are fierce and articulate, friendly and hospitable, self-confident, ambitious, and proud. Sabras are high-achievers. "Creative" drivers, Sabras make their way through the seriously congested streets of Haifa and Tel Aviv–Yafo by using their horns frequently. Because Sabras love to argue and drink coffee so much, it is considered perfectly acceptable to sit at a streetside cafŽ (the center of Israeli social life) and talk for hours over just a cup of coffee and a piece of cake.

Other Israelis are known for showing respect toward each other and taking an active role in their communities. The early years of Israel's existence as a nation-state focused on the cooperative spirit of nation building through *kibbutzim* development. The *kibbutzim* are communities where land and the means of production are commonly owned. Decisions are made by a general assembly of members, meals are prepared and served in a common dining hall, and children live, eat, and study together. About 3% of Israelis live in *kibbutzim* today, but the community spirit lingers even in urban apartment

lar heating panels, large windows, and a *merpeset* (balcony or patio) on which people often relax in the late afternoon and evening. In the crowded urban corridor between Tel Aviv and Haifa, most people own or rent apartments in low-rise buildings. Houses are generally covered with ceramic tiles or plastered and painted white or a pastel color. A law that dates back to Ottoman rule requires that the front of all buildings in Jerusalem be made of white, cream, or rose-pink limestone.

About 3% of the population lives in some 270 *kibbutzim*. *Kibbutzim* were traditionally the backbone of Israeli agriculture, but they are now branching out into some light industry as well. Another rural communal arrangement is the *moshav*, where about 60 individually owned family farms cooperate in purchasing, marketing, and community services. There are some 450 *moshavim* in Israel, totaling about 3.5% of the population. These supply much of Israel's farm produce.

Small villages in Israel are mostly inhabited by Arabs. In northern Israel, there are a few villages of Druze. Bedouin Arabs live in tent communities in the Negev desert, cooking over open fires and tending sheep and goats. Bedouins used to be nomadic but are now making the shift to a more settled lifestyle.

The quality of health care in Israel is high, with high-tech medical equipment and facilities. About 95% of the population has health insurance, and there are clinics for the disadvantaged. Health problems are basically the same as in the Western world: cancer and heart disease cause 66% of the deaths in Israel. Water pollution is a serious problem, with efforts underway to rehabilitate the waterways, but the water is drinkable. Air pollution is not a major problem because most of Israel's heavy industry was initiated after the awakening of environmental awareness. Life expectancy for Israelis is comparable to most industrialized nations, about 79 years for men and 80 years for women.

Almost all areas of Israel, even the most remote, are accessible by roadways, and most people drive wherever they want to go. Highways are very congested in the major cities, however, so many people use public transport there. Haifa has the only subway system, which is a line with only six stops that takes nine minutes to travel from one end to the other.

10 FAMILY LIFE

Religious and cultural traditions shape family relationships. There are four types of Jews in Israel: ultra-Orthodox, national religious, traditional, and nonobservant. Each of these four types follows rabbinical law to a different degree and interprets religious and cultural traditions in a different way. The ultra-Orthodox family lives in a separate neighborhood with other ultra-Orthodox families, follows religious law and tradition strictly, sends its children to a school run by ultra-Orthodox Jews, dresses in traditional clothing, and has well-defined, separate roles for men and women. National religious Jews follow rabbinical law closely as well, but they are fully active in the public life of the state (political, economic, and social), rather than living separately as the ultra-Orthodox do. The majority of Jewish Israelis are traditional Jews who follow rabbinical law to a greater or lesser extent and treat women and men as equals in all areas of life. Nonobservant Jews live an essentially liberal Western way of life with varying degrees of respect for religious ideas.

An Orthodox Jewish mother and daughter swim in the Mediterranean Sea at the religious beach for women in Tel Aviv, Israel. The beach has a separate area for men and women, which is required by the Orthodox Jewish religion. (Paula Bronstein/Getty Images)

complexes. All residents are likely to know the other inhabitants by name. Most Israelis view the family and community as more important than its individual members. Most Israelis view material possessions as less important than a strong family.

The common greeting is *"Shalom,"* which means both "hello" and "goodbye" as well as "peace" and "good health." For the Arabs of Israel, *"Salam"* also means "peace and good health," and *"as-salamu 'alaykum"* means "peace be with you," also used as a common greeting. *"Toda"* means "thanks," to which the reply is usually *"bevakasha"* ("please") or *"alo davar"* ("it's nothing"). *"Lehitra'ot"* is "See you!"

9 LIVING CONDITIONS

The Israeli government oversaw construction between 1948 and 1970 as vast numbers of Jews immigrated to Israel. Most government housing was of low quality, and today, most homes are built by private companies. A typical home has so-

Traditional Arab families have been exposed to huge changes since the establishment of the Israeli state in 1948. New laws protecting the rights of women and prohibiting polygamy and child marriage, plus compulsory education, have ripped into the age-old cultural practices of many Arabs and created turmoil in their families. New participation in the economic and political life of the state, and the shift from an agricultural way of life to one based on employment in industry, business, and the professional sector, have also upset the former balance of Arab families. The new generation is growing up very different from the old, and this puts tremendous pressure on the family.

Generally, the family is highly important to Israeli life, and children receive much care and attention. Parents work hard to prepare and provide for a child's future, and married children often expect to care for elderly parents. Families come together on holidays, especially Passover, and for big celebrations.

11 CLOTHING

Daily wear in Israel is generally informal and Western-style. Few men wear suit jackets and ties in the summer, except for important business occasions. Ultra-Orthodox Jews wear traditional clothing every day. Some Orthodox males wear their hair in sidelocks called *payes*. It is an Orthodox custom to give a boy his first haircut at the age of three. Married Orthodox women often wear a wig called a *shietel* and a scarf tied to the back. Men wear long black or gray coats over a shirt and pants and a black hat on their heads.

Muslim men and women dress similarly to Palestinians, with the *kaffiyyeh* (scarf-like headdress) worn by many of the more traditional and elderly men. The kaffiyyeh is folded in a triangle, laid over the head, and then secured to the head with a double-coiled rope called an *I'gal*. Most Muslim women in Israel no longer wear the traditional *thob* of the Palestinians, choosing Western attire instead.

12 FOOD

Because of the great diversity in the Israeli population, there is no such thing as Israeli cuisine. The meeting of cultures in Israel has brought about some interesting food combinations, such as felafel (or falafel) and chips, goulash and *couscous*, or chicken soup and *kubbe*. Israelis love to eat and do it often, starting the day with a huge breakfast and continuing to eat frequently throughout the day. Because of kosher restrictions, Jewish Israelis tend to eat a main "meat" meal at midday and a lighter "dairy" meal in the evening, since meat and dairy cannot be eaten together. Eggplant is eaten in many different ways by all Israelis, and pita bread (a flat bread with an air pocket in the middle) has become a favorite. The dietary restrictions of Judaism, known as *kashrut* ("right" or "fit"), are considered a personal matter in modern Israel. Meat and dairy products cannot be consumed at the same meal or from the same utensils. Camels, pigs, and hares are forbidden in the Jewish diet. Animals that have cloven hoofs and chew cud are permitted, such as sheep, cattle, and deer. Similarly, lobsters, oysters, shrimp, clams, and crabs are forbidden. Only fish with both fins and scales are permitted.

By far the most widely popular food in Israel is *felafel, which is* deep-fried balls of ground chickpeas. All along city streets, one finds felafel stands (not unlike hot dog stands in the United States) where a large variety of things to put with felafel in pita bread are available. The best-known felafel center is Tel Aviv's Shuk Betzalel, where there is an entire street of felafel vendors, offering the largest selection of salads east of the Mediterranean. Other popular foods include pizza, open sandwiches, hamburgers, *kebab* (skewered meats and vegetables), and Russian borscht (beet soup). A vegetable salad, often mixed with olive oil, lemon juice, or spices, is usually eaten daily. Poultry and fish are eaten more frequently than beef. Fruits and vegetables are plentiful, and fruit juices are often part of lunch or dinner. Milk products, such as yogurt and cheese, are eaten with breakfast or dinner.

13 EDUCATION

Israel is a land of the educated. Schooling is highly valued, and Israeli students are high achievers. According to 2004 estimates, 97.1% of Israelis were literate, and most complete at least 15 years of schooling prior to attending college. The government of Israel provides both religious and secular school systems, and Israelis are allowed to choose between schools where the instruction is in Hebrew and where the instruction is in Arabic. Many schools hold classes six days a week, and education is free through the 10th grade. Israel has eight colleges and universities, which enroll approximately 350,000 students. Most Israelis are over 21 when they begin college because of the compulsory military service required of them after high school.

14 CULTURAL HERITAGE

Israel has become one of the most active music centers in the world, with a dynamic and unique folk-music scene stemming from the diverse backgrounds of its various immigrant groups. Israeli folk dance is also a unique blend of Jewish and non-Jewish folk dances from around the world. Classical "art" dance was not introduced in Israel until the 1920s, when Moscow-trained ballerina Rina Nikova moved there. Classical music did not appear as a professional activity until the 1930s, when it arrived with European immigrants fleeing Nazism. Now, it is an extremely popular pastime, with subscriptions to the Israeli Philharmonic Orchestra handed down from parents to children as a coveted inheritance.

Visual artists struggle to define an Israeli style, although the content of their artwork is often based on the Israeli environment. Israeli cinema is also struggling to define itself and move beyond the local market to a more global involvement. Poetry and literature, on the other hand, are vibrant and vital expressions of the Israeli spirit, despite the fact that modern Hebrew is such a new language that only 4 to 5 million people speak it and even fewer read it. An estimated 10,000 new poems are published each year in Israel. In 1966, Shmuel Yosef Agnon (1888–1970) was the first author writing in modern Hebrew to win the Nobel Prize for Literature. Amos Oz, the author of *Perfect Peace, The Slopes of Lebanon,* and *In the Land of Israel,* and other Hebrew writers have become known worldwide. A number of Arab Israeli authors have also achieved success.

15 WORK

Working conditions have minimum requirements established by law, such as a 47-hour maximum work week, minimum wages, overtime compensation, severance pay, and paid vacation and work leave. Laws also exist to protect working women, particularly those with children or giving birth. Women are legally entitled to equal pay as men, but in practice it does not always work out that way. Wages for everyone are determined through negotiations between the government (Israel's largest employer), the Histadrut (a federation of trade unions—Israel's largest nongovernment employer), and the Bureau of Economic Organizations (representing all other employers). At the end of 1991, the average monthly wage was NIS (New Israeli Shekels) 2,911, or about US$1,200.

16 SPORTS

Soccer and basketball are Israel's most popular sports. Training takes place mostly at sports organizations, such as Maccabi, Betar, Hapoel, and Elizur. The Tel Aviv Maccabi basketball team has won the European championship twice. Mass sporting events, such as the Jerusalem March, the swim across Lake Kinneret (Sea of Galilee), and various marathons are also very popular. Jewish athletes from around the world compete in the Maccabiah Games (also known as the "Jewish Olympics"), which have been held in what is now Israel every four years since 1932. Israel sent its first delegation to the International Olympic Games in 1952. Twenty years later, at the 1972 Munich Games, eleven Israeli athletes were killed by PLO (Palestine Liberation Organization) terrorists. Despite this tragedy, Israeli athletes continue to compete in the Olympic Games.

17 ENTERTAINMENT AND RECREATION

Many of Israel's urban centers, most notably Tel Aviv, are home to dozens of art galleries, theatrical companies, movie theaters, and concert halls. The Mann Auditorium in Tel Aviv is the home of the Israel Philharmonic Orchestra (IPA). The IPA has more subscribers and supporters per capita than any other orchestra in the world. Classical music is a favorite in Israel, and Israelis take pride in their native musicians, such as violinists Yitzhak Perlman and Pinchas Zukerman. Hebrew pop music is also popular. In it, one senses a merging of the many Israeli ethnic backgrounds, including Arabic, Latin, and North American.

One of the favorite Israeli pastimes is eating out. Outdoor vendors and sit-down restaurants offer a wide range of food choices, from Middle Eastern felafel to pizza and McDonald's. Israelis of all cultures enjoy strolling through the streets of Jerusalem and Tel Aviv, cracking the shells of sunflower seeds and watermelon seeds between their teeth.

Reflecting the diversity of the Israeli population is the diversity of sporting activities. European soccer is one of the most popular sports, and the population gets quite excited over national tournaments. Basketball has been brought to Israel by North American immigrants, and cricket arrived with Australians, English, and Indians.

Israelis are beachgoers, enjoying swimming in Eilat in southern Israel and at Tel Aviv's beach, as well as floating on the salty waters of the Dead Sea, where the concentration of salt helps even non-swimmers remain buoyant.

18 FOLK ART, CRAFTS, AND HOBBIES

Not surprisingly, Israel is the world center for the production of Judaica, crafts relating to Jewish religious life. There are no design restrictions in Jewish law on these objects, so artists can exercise their own creativity. Hanukkah lamps, wine cups, candlesticks, and spice boxes for the Sabbath and other holidays, and *mezuzot* (parchment scrolls hung on every Jew-

ish doorpost) cases, are found in abundance in Israeli craft and folk-art shops.

The national hobby is archaeology. With more than 3,500 archeological sites in an area the size of the state of Maryland, there is plenty of opportunity for amateur and professional archaeologists. Finds date back as far as 150,000 BC. Many Israelis are amateur archaeologists, and all have an opinion about it.

19 SOCIAL PROBLEMS

Israel's social problems stem primarily from the newness of the state (60 years old, as of 2008), the tensions between the Jewish and Palestinian residents, and the tremendous diversity of its population. The huge, ongoing influx of immigrants creates overcrowding, unemployment, and cultural confusion. Schools constantly have to accommodate more and more students who speak different languages and come from different backgrounds. Some of the immigrant groups come from illiterate, subsistence-farming communities and have a very difficult time adapting to a fast-paced technological society. Ashkenazi (European) Jews founded the modern state of Israel and so have traditionally occupied the top positions in society. When the Sephardic ("Oriental") Jews arrived in the 1950s, they were ghettoized and finally rebelled in the 1960s. Since then, programs have been put in place to improve conditions for Sephardic Jews, and they are now becoming a more integrated part of Israeli society. The Ethiopian Jews who were brought in during the 1980s are still marginalized due to their nontechnological background and the continuing debates among the rabbinical authorities as to whether or not they are "true" Jews.

The other major problem in Israel is the lack of resolution over Palestinian statehood. The human rights group Amnesty International notes that the Israeli government continues to use military force in the Palestinian territories, even as the two groups attempt to negotiate a path to peace. In 2007 alone, Amnesty International reports that Israeli forces killed more than 370 Palestinians and destroyed more than 100 Palestinian homes. A blockage on the Gaza Strip prevented 1.5 million Palestinians living in the territory from leaving, even in search of urgent medical treatment. In the West Bank territory, Israeli authorities are building a wall separating Palestinian land from Israel, despite protests that the measure violates international law. Israeli jails also held approximately 9,000 Palestinians, some who had not been charged with a crime or brought to trial for years. Despite efforts to promote Jewish-Arab friendliness, many Israeli children grow up with the same prejudices that their parents held toward Arabs. Overcoming these prejudices in all sectors of society is the biggest challenge facing Israelis in the early 21st century.

20 GENDER ISSUES

The equality of women is protected under law in Israel, but in some cases, religious and cultural traditions constrain how much power women have. The traditional *kibbutzim* placed a great deal of emphasis on the equality of all individuals, and cooperation among all to build a strong nation. That spirit of equality and cooperative effort continues to exist among Israeli Jews today. Women make up about 35% of the labor force. Women also are required to serve two years in the Israeli military alongside men. Although the head of the Israeli family is considered to be the father, women make many decisions on family matters.

In November 2005, an Israeli court ruled that a lesbian spouse could officially adopt a child born to her current partner by artificial insemination from an anonymous sperm donor. Although Israel has not yet sanctioned gay marriage, it does recognize same-sex marriages that have been performed elsewhere.

Judaism does allow for divorce, but a civil court divorce is not enough to dissolve a religious marriage. If one remarries without having attained a religious divorce performed by three rabbis, the new relationship is considered adulterous, and any children born of the second marriage are considered illegitimate.

21 BIBLIOGRAPHY

Amnesty International. *Amnesty International Report 2008: State of the World's Human Rights.* http://thereport.amnesty.org/eng/Homepage (October 25, 2008).

Economist.com. *Country Briefings: Israel.* www.economist.com/countries/Israel/profile.cfm?folder=History%20in%20brief (October 25, 2008).

Facts about Israel. Jerusalem: Israel Information Center, 1993.

Ganor, Avi, and Ron Maiberg. *Taste of Israel: A Mediterranean Feast.* New York: Rizzoli International, 1990.

Israel. Amsterdam: Time-Life Books, 1986.

Israel. CultureGrams: World Edition. Ann Arbor, Mich.: ProQuest LLC, 2008.

Israel Today. Jerusalem: Ahva Press, 1993.

A Letter from Israel. Jerusalem: Israel Information Center, 1991.

Melrod, George, ed. *Insight Guides: Israel (including the West Bank and Gaza Strip).* Boston: Houghton Mifflin, 1994.

Willard, Jed, ed. *Let's Go: The Budget Guide to Israel and Egypt, 1996.* New York: St. Martin's Press, 1996.

—revised by H. Gupta-Carlson.

JAINS

PRONUNCIATION: JINES
LOCATION: India
POPULATION: 4,225,043 (Census of India 2001)
LANGUAGE: Language of the region in which they live
RELIGION: Jainism
RELATED ARTICLES: Vol. 3: Hindus; People of India

1 INTRODUCTION

Jains are followers of Jainism, a South Asian religion that predates Christianity by over five centuries or more. The Jains derive their name from *Jina* (conqueror), or "one who conquers worldly passions." Although it has much in common with Hinduism, Jainism emerged during the 6th century BC as a reaction against the Hindu religion as practiced at the time. The geographical origins of Jainism lie in the Indian state of Bihar and southern Nepal, a region that also saw the emergence of Buddhism at about the same time. Unlike Buddhism, however, which has spread around the world, Jainism is an ethnic religion. Ethnic religions have little appeal outside their immediate cultures, and most remain localized in the lands of their birth. Jainism remains today a religion of India.

Over the centuries, the center of Jainism gradually shifted from eastern India, first to Mathura and Ujjain to the west, and then southwards. With the patronage of kings and ruling houses, Jainism firmly established itself throughout much of the Indian peninsula (Andhra, Tamil Nadu, Karnataka, and Maharashtra). For over a thousand years, it was the principal religion among the Kannada-speaking peoples of Mysore. Western areas such as Rajasthan and Gujarat also became strongholds of Jaina beliefs.

Jainism reached its greatest geographical extent, as well as its highest levels of scholarship and intellectual activity, in the period from roughly the 8th to the 10th centuries AD. The impact of Jaina thinking and the Jain way of life was felt in all parts of the country at this time. Thereafter, the religion entered a period of decline, especially in the south. Jains gave ground before a strong Hindu revival movement in what are now Tamil Nadu, Andhra Pradesh, and parts of Karnataka, even facing persecution from Brahmans. But Jainism continued to make gains in the west. Kumarapala, King of Gujarat in the 12th century, is said to have established Jainism as the state religion and to have promoted Jaina values. The end of the 13th century, however, saw western India invaded by Muslim powers from the north. Gujarat was conquered by Ala-uddin Khalji around 1298, and Jainism, its followers persecuted and its temples destroyed by the Muslims, was never to regain its former prominence.

Jainism accounts for only 0.5% of India's total population (2001 Census of India). Mere numbers, however, reveal little of Jainism's influence on the philosophy, art, history, and culture of India.

2 LOCATION AND HOMELAND

There are problems in determining the exact number of Jains in India today. The Census of India reports a population of c. 4.2 million people in 2001 and if that figure is accurate, the population of Jains in India is either declining or has been enumerated inaccurately. However, if Jains account for 0.05% of India's population, as reported by the Census, the numbers for 2008 would be around 6.5 million. Some estimates place the population at 10 million, which one suspects is too high. A realistic estimate of the current Jain population in India would be between around 5 million, assuming growth rates reflect the national average, or, at most, just less than 6 million people. Jains have a strong presence in Gujarat and Rajasthan and are also found in the northern region of Madhya Pradesh around Ujjain. Another area of high population concentration is the region of Mysore (the modern Karnataka State) that has historically been a Jain stronghold. The city of Bombay has a large Jain community, and Jains are found throughout much of the rest of Maharashtra State. It is interesting to note that today there are few Jains in eastern India, where Jainism had its beginnings.

During the last century, a number of Jains have migrated to East Africa, Great Britain, and the United States. They are mostly Gujarati in origin and are engaged in business and commercial ventures. Jains living in the West are often quite successful, and in many areas they have set up temples and associations to promote Jain culture.

3 LANGUAGE

There is no specific language associated with the Jain religion. Jains use the language and script of their region.

4 FOLKLORE

Jainism holds that the universe has existed through all eternity and will continue to exist forever. Thus, there is no need for a creator-god, or a creation myth. Indeed, in its original form Jainism had no gods and did not worship idols (in direct contrast to Hindu practices). The 24 Jain *Tirthankaras* ("fordmakers") were to be revered, but they were men, not gods. They had attained perfect knowledge, and their appearance in the world was tied to the moral and religious decay of the people and the need for a reawakening and revival of religious values.

Lacking gods, the Jains soon raised the Tirthankaras to deified status, and their literature describes the mythological lives of these saints (only two are known to be historical personages). Today, many Jains have even adopted gods from the Hindu pantheon, although they are ranked lower than the Tirthankaras. The Jaina world of myth and legend is perhaps best illustrated by a display in an imposing two-story hall behind the Jain temple (the Lal Mandir or "Red Temple") in Ajmer in Rajasthan. The hall shows scenes of the birth and death of Rishabdeva, the first Tirthankara. Included in this display, which takes up the entire hall, is the sacred city of Ayodhya, with its palaces and mansions for the nobles. The Tribeni, the sacred confluence of three rivers at Allahabad, is also shown, with the sacred banyan tree, and Rishabdeva in contemplation. Suspended from the ceiling are gods sailing the skies in brightly colored airships. This is, in fact, a huge model of the mythological world of the Jains.

5 RELIGION

The founder of Jainism is generally regarded to be Mahavira, who was born in Vaisali (in Basarh in northern Bihar) in the 6th century BC. *Mahavira* literally means "great victor" and is the name given by Jains to Vardhamana, the son of a *ksatriya* (warrior-caste) chieftain. Mahavira most likely lived from

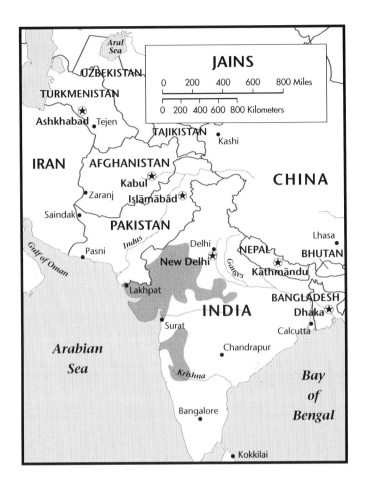

599 to 527 BC, although some sources give 549–477 BC as his dates. The Jains claim that rather than being the founder of their religion, he was but the twenty-fourth in a line of prophets and teachers stretching back through time. There is historical evidence for the existence of Parsvanatha, the twenty-third Tirthankara, who lived in the 8th century BC. Some Jain scholars even claim that Jainism was present in the Harappan civilization, a thousand years earlier (the swastika, a religious symbol of the Jains, is found in Harappan culture).

As his parents were followers of Parsvanatha, it seems certain that Mahavira was brought up in the Jain tradition. Even though he married and had a daughter, at the age of thirty he became an ascetic. He gave up his family, his high caste status, and all his worldly possessions, and for 12 years he wandered the countryside, naked, meditating, and searching for the truth. Mahavira was a contemporary of Buddha, who was born and lived in the same region, but as far as is known the two never met. At the age of 42, Mahavira achieved a state of perfect knowledge. One who attains this level is certain to achieve the state of ultimate perfection (*moksa*) upon death. Mahavira continued to travel through parts of what are now northern Bihar, West Bengal, and Uttar Pradesh, preaching his message. He died at the age of 72 in Pavapuri in Bihar.

In the years following its appearance, Jainism experienced the divisions that are so common in the history of any religion. One, dating to the very beginning of the 3rd century BC, continues to divide the Jain community today. During a 12-year famine, a prominent Jain teacher led a migration of Jains to southern India, eventually reaching the hills of Shravana Belgola in Mysore. This site remains a holy place for Jains today. On their return to their homeland, the migrants found that the monks they had left behind had abandoned the rule of nudity and other observances taught by Mahavira. They regarded this as heretical, and the subsequent dispute led to the division of the Jains into the *Svetambara* ("white-clad") and *Digambara* ("sky-clad") sects. The Svetambara sect are the descendants of those who remained behind during the great migration south and took to wearing clothes. They are found today mostly in northern India. The Digambara continue to go naked, although in practice only ascetics adhere strictly to the rule of nudity. The Digambaras, who are found mainly in South India, also hold that women can never achieve sainthood. They are not allowed to become nuns or even enter Digambara temples.

The central themes of Mahavira's teachings were truth, nonviolence, and nonattachment to the material world. For the Jain, all living things (and even some inanimate objects) have an immortal soul *(jiva)*. This soul passes through a never-ending cycle of rebirths, acquiring a spiritual and even material presence because of the accumulation of *karma*. Karma is envisaged as a form of atomic matter that is attracted to the soul in this and past lives through desires and actions. To free the soul from this endless cycle of reincarnations, one has to eliminate existing karma by following an austere lifestyle. The accumulation of new karma can be avoided by nonattachment and lack of desires. Only then can the state of ultimate perfection be reached.

Nonviolence *(ahimsa)* is a means by which Jains can avoid the accumulation of karma. Technically, ahimsa means the "negation of the desire to injure any living thing," and the concept is found in Hinduism and Buddhism as well as in Jainism. But it is in Jainism that ahimsa has its greatest impact. The philosophy underpins almost all aspects of Jaina life and society. The first of 12 vows taken by the Jain layperson is that of ahimsa. This and the vows taken against falsehood, dishonesty, unchaste behavior, and covetousness form the code by which the Jain lives.

The "Five Great Vows" taken by Jaina ascetics, though similar to those of the laity, hold them to much stricter standards of behavior. For instance, even the accidental death of an insect caused by inhaling it is a sin. To prevent this, Jain monks (or nuns) wear a mask over their mouth and nose. They must not eat after dark in case they accidentally eat an insect. They should not travel after dark in case they tread on an insect they cannot see. When traveling, monks and nuns often sweep their path to avoid violating ahimsa. Hair is pulled out rather than cut, to avoid accidentally harming life. Jains are, of course, vegetarians, but the dietary restrictions on ascetics can extend beyond the eating of animal flesh. In Jaina belief, even plants have life and many vegetables are forbidden them as well. Though rare, strict adherence to ahimsa has led monks and nuns to suicide through starvation, an act that is seen as meritorious.

Jainism in its original form was a sect of wandering holy ascetics. It had no temples or idols. Today, however, Jains worship in temples that contain images of the Tirthankaras (in Digambara temples the idols are nude, while in Svetambara temples they are adorned with loincloths). Temple rituals are similar in form to those of the Hindus and include *puja* (worship), ritual bathing of the idols, anointing of the idols with colored powder, and the offering of special foods. *Arati*, or the ritual waving of lamps around the idols, is performed during evening worship. Unlike Hindus, Jains have no priestly caste to officiate at religious ceremonies, though some groups employ Brahmans (Hindu priests) for this purpose. One modern sect, the Sthanakavasis, continues the traditional Jain ideal of having no temples or idols.

⁶ MAJOR HOLIDAYS

Jainism is a religion with a strong element of asceticism and it is therefore not surprising that Jain festivals often lack the gaiety, color, and elaborate rituals characteristic of many Hindu celebrations. Jains observe their religious holy days with fasting, offerings of prayer, pilgrimages, and sober feasting.

Pajjusana, which is celebrated in August and closes the Jain year, is an important Jain festival. It is observed by fasting and meditation for a period of 8 to 10 days. On the last day, Jains ask forgiveness of all living things for any harm that they might have done them in thought, word, and deed. It is customary for Jains to seek forgiveness from neighbors and friends, for family elders to ask pardon from younger members, and for employers to seek the forgiveness of their workers. Alms and food are distributed to the poor, and Jain idols are taken through the streets in elaborately decorated *rathas* or processional carts.

Mahavira Jayanti celebrates the birth of Mahavira. Jains offer prayers at temples, worship the Tirthankaras, and make pilgrimages to sacred places. Images of Mahavira are carried through the streets in processions. The death of Mahavira is celebrated at Deva Divali, which falls soon after the Hindu Divali festival. One unusual ceremony is Jnana-Panchami, when all the Jain sacred texts are dusted, cleaned, and worshipped.

An aspect of Jain religious observances that is often undertaken to coincide with major festival days is pilgrimage to Jaina sacred sites. These include Vaisali (Mahavira's birthplace), the Hill of Parsvanatha in Bihar, Mt. Abu in Rajasthan, Girnar and Mt. Shatrunjaya in Gujarat, and the ancient Karnatak site at Shravana Belgola. At Shatrunjaya, with its temple-city built on top of a hill, the most meritorious pilgrimage involves climbing the thousands of steps to the summit, circling a temple, and descending again, 99 times. This takes about three months to complete. Every 15 years, a major ritual takes place at Shravana Belgola involving the anointing of the head of a statue of Gomatesvara, a Jain saint. The statue is over 17 m (57 ft) in height, or nearly as tall as a six-story building. Jains from all over the country make the journey to be present at the ceremony. Pilgrimages are not undertaken during the monsoon months, however, as the Jains believe that traveling might result in harm to the abundant insect life that flourishes during the rainy season.

⁷ RITES OF PASSAGE

Jains follow regional customs; thus, rituals associated with birth, marriage, and death vary around the country. There are broad similarities—for instance, Jains cremate their dead, and their death ceremonies in general follow Hindu patterns—but in detail their death rites differ from region to region. Similarly, in some areas no special ceremonies mark the attaining of adulthood, but in others boys undergo the sacred thread ritual as would a high-caste Hindu. Essentially, Jains in Gujarat follow Gujarati practices, those in Rajasthan follow Rajasthani customs, and so on.

⁸ INTERPERSONAL RELATIONS

Jains follow regional patterns in matters of interpersonal relations, greetings, and visiting customs. They are enjoined by their religion to be truthful and compassionate in social and business dealings, not to lie, and to live chaste, humble lives.

⁹ LIVING CONDITIONS

Jains, as a prosperous urban community, generally enjoy much higher standards of living and greater material comforts than the average Indian. They have access to all the amenities available in modern Indian towns and cities. They also have a strong tradition of involvement in charitable giving, supporting welfare organizations, educational institutions, and even homes and hospitals for animals (*pinjrapols*).

¹⁰ FAMILY LIFE

Although it originated, in part, as a reaction against the Hindu caste system, modern Jainism has its own castes. They are social rather than religious divisions, however, and lack the hierarchy of the Hindu caste system, yet they are still important in matters of marriage. The Agrawala, Oswala, Srimali, Chaturtha, and Panchama are some of the more important Jain castes. Some castes such as the Oswala are divided into major endogamous groups such as Bisa and Dasa, and these are even further divided into exogamous clans or *gotras,* and over 500 subclans. In marriage patterns, family size, and family structure, Jain communities tend to follow regional patterns and practices.

¹¹ CLOTHING

Jains dress according to local customs and are hardly distinguishable from local peoples of similar social standing. However, they are still subject to the restrictions of the ahimsa philosophy. Jains do not wear furs, feathers, silk, or wool because the obtaining of these products causes harm to insects, animals, and birds. They are required to restrict the use of leather goods to a minimum, and to ensure that such leather they do use comes from animals that died a natural death and not from slaughtered animals. There are no restrictions on the wearing of ornaments, however. Given the Jains' involvement in the jewelry business, women usually wear quite spectacular gems and gold ornaments when dressed for formal occasions.

It is the custom of Digambara ("sky-clad") monks to go naked, while Jain monks and nuns often wear masks to prevent the accidental inhalation of insects and use brooms with which to sweep the road, so they do not tread on insects and thus accidentally do harm to living things.

¹² FOOD

As a consequence of the vow of ahimsa, Jains are strict vegetarians and avoid all animal flesh, eggs, and even certain types of root vegetables (e.g., potatoes, carrots, onions, and beetroots) and fruits. They are enjoined to drink strained water and are prohibited from using intoxicants and stimulants. Honey is not eaten because bees are killed when it is collected.

Fasting, though an ascetic practice, is also popular among the Jaina laity, especially women. It is undertaken as a vow rather than a penance and is a means of demonstrating one's piety and commitment to Jain ideals. It is common at the time of festivals, on full-moon days, and during the four-month rainy season.

¹³ EDUCATION

Jains have a tradition of education and have schools (*gurukuls*) that provide both a religious and a secular education for Jains. Jains are also open to modern education and have achieved great prominence in areas of business and industry, finance, scholarship, and government service.

¹⁴ CULTURAL HERITAGE

Mahavira preached his message in Ardhamagadhi, the language of the area of his birth (which was called Magadha). The Jain scriptures originally were written in this language so that the common people could have access to their sacred texts without the need for a class of priests or scholars to interpret them. Jain scriptures are called *Sutras* and the most important of these, the *Kalpasutra,* contains the life and teachings of Mahavira. Jain sacred texts have been written in other vernacular languages and also in Sanskrit, the classical language of North India. The Jains have some of the oldest libraries of ancient manuscripts in India. Jain writings have also enriched regional literary traditions such as those of Gujarat and Karnataka.

Architecture is another area where Jains have left their imprint on India. The past commercial success of the Jain merchant community in western India is reflected in the numerous *havelis* (mansions) and temples they constructed. The intricately carved white marble temples of Dilwara and Ranakpur in Rajasthan, the temple complex of Girnar, and the walled, temple-city atop Mt. Shatrunjaya are part of a Jain tradition of temple-building that goes back to the 11th century AD. The earliest surviving examples of a Jaina school of palm-leaf painting in western India also date to this time.

¹⁵ WORK

The Jains' commitment to ahimsa effectively bars them from activities that might result in injury or death to living creatures. Thus, occupations such as butcher, leatherworker, or flour-miller are prohibited. Pastoralism violates ahimsa, since it takes sustenance out of the mouth of calves. Agriculture is prohibited, because ploughing the land could result in harm to insects and other creatures living in the soil (although the Chaturthas of southern India are an agricultural community). Similarly, the operating of machinery could result in harm to insects and flying creatures, so manufacturing industries are avoided.

As a result of such occupational restrictions, Jains have devoted their energies to business, trade, and similar urban professions. They are typically an important and prosperous element in the "Bania," or business community, of any Indian city. They are mainly bankers, moneylenders, jewelers, traders, cloth-merchants, and, more recently, highly successful industrialists. They have entered the legal, medical, teaching, and engineering professions and also hold important positions in state and central governments.

¹⁶ SPORTS

There are no sports uniquely associated with the Jains.

¹⁷ ENTERTAINMENT AND RECREATION

There are no forms of entertainment or recreation identified specifically with the Jain community.

¹⁸ FOLK ART, CRAFTS, AND HOBBIES

Given their emphasis on commercial activities, the Jains are not engaged in folk arts and crafts.

¹⁹ SOCIAL PROBLEMS

The Jain community in Delhi, where there are almost 500,000 adherents to the religion, is currently agitating for minority status on par with the Buddhists, Christians, Sikhs, Muslims, and Parsis, listed as notified minority groups under the Delhi Minorities Commission Act, 1999. Members of the community say they want minority status primarily because they want to incorporate Jainism, the religion of the community, as a subject in Jain schools. The capital and its adjoining areas have eight Jain schools. They are not able teach Jainism to their children because most of the Jain schools in Delhi are partially funded by the government, which doesn't allow the teaching of any particular religion at schools unless it belongs to a minority community. Delhi is one of the few states in India where the Jain community has not been granted official minority status. According to Article 30 of the Indian Constitution, non-Hindu groups are entitled to certain benefits that Hindus are not. The most important of these is the exclusive right to run state funded educational institutions free of governmental interference. In light of this, many religious sects that are typically classified as Hindu have tried to obtain the non-Hindu status in order to be able to obtain state funding for their private institutions. "Hindu," as defined in the Constitution, originally included Jains, and there has been a debate in the Jain community as to whether or not to seek minority status.

As a relatively small, affluent, urban community, the Jains do not face the social and economic problems so typical of many groups in India. Rather, the problem—if it can be called a problem—is one of identity. As an offshoot of Hinduism, Jainism has retained many Hindu characteristics and Jains are often seen as just another caste of Hindus. Some observers argue that Jainism, as a small minority religion, is rapidly losing its separate identity. Others see in Jaina religion and society a distinctiveness that will ensure its continued survival. For the Jains, however, there is no question. Mahavira gave Jainism its current existence. Mahapadma, the next Tirthankara or fordmaker to come, will ensure that it lives forever.

²⁰ GENDER ISSUES

Theoretically, in Mahavira's Jainism, there was no distinction of caste, color, creed, or sex. Thus, for some, Jainism is a religion of equality, but for others, a woman's very femaleness creates spiritual inequality. The Digambara Jain sect believes that women cannot achieve liberation without being reborn as men first. Digambara Jains hold this view because they believe that nakedness is an essential element of the road to liberation. Since women are not allowed to be naked in public they cannot achieve liberation directly and so are seen as second-class citizens. This ban on female nakedness is partly intended to protect both men and women: if women went around naked it would cause men to experience sexual desire and the desire produced would hinder the man's progress to liberation. Digambaras also believe that women are inherently *himsic* (which is best translated as harmful). This comes partly from a belief that menstrual blood kills micro-organisms living in the female body. The killing of the micro-organisms is said to show that a female body is less non-violent than a male body—

although that idea doesn't have any scientific support and isn't found in modern Jain thinking.

Some Jain texts say that menstrual blood is a sign of impurity (this view is mirrored in Hinduism also), but the idea that women are spiritually impure because of menstruation is a rather odd basis for a Jain argument, since Jainism usually concerns itself with thinking, speaking, and acting rightly—there isn't any other area where Jainism says that involuntary bodily functions are a spiritual obstacle.

Another argument is that because a woman's nature is to care for children and other dependents, she will find it much more difficult to break free from these earthly attachments, and unless she does this, she cannot achieve liberation.

The Svetambaras have a different view of women, and indeed, there are famous nuns in both the Svetambara and Digambara traditions. Sadhvi, for instance, is a modern Svetambara nun well known for social reform and for her charitable works.

Jains exist in a specific social context, however, and, especially away from areas of Jain concentrations, have come to the influenced by local (usually Hindu) societies. When this author was talking to Jain families in the Brahmaputra River Valley of Assam, where Jains are few in number, they expressed the view that they were but another caste of Hinduism, whereas in Rajasthan and Gujarat, Jains saw their religion as quite distinct from Hinduism.

As one author observes, Jain women in India have legal and constitutional protection and that, whereas in the majority of Jain families in Uttar Pradesh the status of women used to be inferior to that of men, the impact of education, western culture, and the breakdown of the joint family have tended to loosen the stranglehold that "outmoded social mores" exerted over the freedom of Jain women. Literacy rates among Jain women at 90.6% are the highest of any religion, but female work participation (9.2%) is the is lowest of any group, suggesting that education is a means of attracting good husbands, and that the primary role of Jain women in society remains, in general, taking care of the home and their husbands, and raising male children.

²¹ BIBLIOGRAPHY

Dundas, Paul. *The Jains.* London and New York: Routledge, 1992.

Jain, Satish Kumar and Kamal Chand Sogani, ed. *Perspectives in Jaina Philosophy and Culture.* New Delhi: Ahimsa International, 1985.

Jaini, Padmanabh S. ed. *Collected Papers on Jaina Studies.* Delhi: Motilal Banarsidass, 2000.

———. *The Jaina Path of Purification.* Berkeley and Los Angeles: University of California Press, 1970.

Kumar, Rajjan. *Different Aspects of Jainism.* Delhi: Sunrise Publications, 2006.

Lodrick, Deryck O. "*Ahimsa*, Man and Animals: Aspect of Religion in the Cultural Landscape of Western India." In *India: Cultural Patterns and Processes,* edited by Allen G. Noble and Ashok K. Dutt. Westview Press: Boulder, Co., 1982.

Sangave, Vilas Adinath. *Jaina Community: A Social Survey.* Bombay: Popular Prakashan, 1980.

—by D. O. Lodrick

JAPANESE

PRONUNCIATION: jap-uhn-EEZ
LOCATION: Japan; small numbers in Hawaii, North and South America
POPULATION: 127 million
LANGUAGE: Japanese
RELIGION: Shinto; Buddhism; Confucianism; Christianity
RELATED ARTICLES: Vol. 2: Japanese Americans

¹ INTRODUCTION

The Japanese islands have been inhabited by humans since Paleolithic times and archaeologists have discovered there some of the oldest pottery known; below is a summary of Japan's centuries of history.

Neolithic Japan

10,000 BC–300 BC: Jomon Period
300 BC–AD 300: Yayoi Period

Early Japan

300–710: Yamato Period: Political consolidation; Chinese cultural influence; Literacy and Buddhism introduced.

Civilian Court Rule

710–794: Nara Period: Emperor-centered court at the first permanent capital city, Nara. Buddhist influence is strong.

794–1185: Heian Period: Court at the new capital, Heian-kyo (Kyoto), dominated by Fujiwara clan, which legitimizes power by intermarriage with the imperial family. There is great production of literature.

Warrior (samurai) Rule

1185–1333: Kamakura Period: After Gempei War (1180–85) between rival warrior clans, head of victorious Minamoto Clan claims the title Shogun, which implies he is an agent of the emperor, and establishes a military government (bakufu) in Kamakura. Power shifts to warriors. Zen is introduced and two Mongol invasions are repelled (1274, 1281).

1333–1336: Kemmu Restoration: Emperor Go-Daigo attempts to reclaim political power for the emperor.

1336–1568: Muromachi Period: Warrior Ashikaga Takauji forces abdication of Go-Daigo and replaces him with a new emperor. Takauji becomes Shogun and bases bakufu in the Muromachi section of Kyoto. This era is also called the "Ashikaga Period," for the family of shoguns. Art (ink painting) and literature (Noh theater) flourish. Bakufu loses control of the warriors. Protracted civil war called "Warring States Period" (1467–1573). The first Europeans reach Japan in the 1540s.

1568–1600: Reunification: Three warriors, Oda Nobunaga (d. 1582), Toyotomi Hideyoshi (d. 1598), and Tokugawa Ieyasu (d. 1616) reunify Japan. Hideyoshi launches an invasion of Korea (1592–98).

1600–1868: Edo Period: Tokuqawa Ieyasu is victorious at the Battle of Sekigahara (1600). Ieyasu becomes Shogun and founds bakufu at Edo (now Tokyo). This era is also called the "Tokugawa Period," for family of the shoguns. Severe laws imposed to prevent relapse into anarchy include secluding Japan from contact with outside world, ferocious suppression of Christianity, and division of society into four classes (samurai, peasant, artisan, merchant). Peace allows rapid economic growth and the spread of literacy. Merchants dominate culture, producing haiku, novels, theater (kabuki, puppet drama), and art (woodblock prints).

Modern Period

1868–1912: Meiji Period: Matthew Perry reopens Japan to the outside world (1853–54). The ensuing crisis over Japanese response to the challenge of Western powers leads to the overthrow of Tokugawa bakufu and a return to emperor-centered government (Meiji Restoration, 1868), although the actual political role of the emperor is limited. The teenage emperor Mutsuhito (d.1912) moves the imperial capital from Kyoto to Tokyo, takes the title "Meiji." The government launches a modernization campaign to master Western technology, military developments, education system, business practices, and governmental structures. The samurai class and institutions are swept away, Japan creates a cabinet style government, promulgates its constitution (1889), holds its first national election (1890) of representatives to a new national parliament (Diet). Japan defeats China (1894–95) and Russia (1904–05) and takes Taiwan and Korea as colonies.

1912–1926: Taisho Period: During the reign of the son of the Meiji Emperor, Japan experiments with relatively liberal concepts of democracy but suffers a post-World War I economic crisis. Tokyo and Yokohama are devastated by earthquake (1923).

1926–1989: Showa Period: Here begins the reign of the Showa Emperor, Hirohito (d.1989). In 1926–40 economic depression and reaction against liberalism lead to a repressive political climate. Military aggression in China leads to war. Japan attacks the United States and Great Britain in 1941. Defeat in World War II (1941–45) strips Japan of its overseas empire and military, devastates its economy and most of its large cities, including Hiroshima and Nagasaki, which were destroyed by atomic bombs. Allied (overwhelmingly American) military forces occupy Japan (1945–52) and impose sweeping reforms to democratize and demilitarize Japan. A new constitution (1947) declares the emperor as the symbol of Japanese unity, vests sovereignty in the people, and gives women the right to vote. After the occupation Japan rebuilds and rejoins the family of nations. The Tokyo Olympics (1964) are viewed by the Japanese as the end of post-war recovery. Japan grows dramatically as an economic force, its gross national product (GNP) now the world's second largest and its standard of living very high. In the 1980s Japan becomes the world's leading creditor nation and the biggest donor of foreign aid. Much of the Japanese economic success involves large-scale exporting, often disrupting importing nations' industries, embroiling Japan in trade confrontations. Japan's Asian neighbors benefit from massive Japanese investment, but worry about great Japanese influence. Despite rejecting military power, Japan is once again a major power due to its economic impact abroad.

1989–present: Heisei Period: Akihito becomes emperor in 1989. Economic stagnation begins in 1990, which, combined with scandals, undermine confidence in the government. In 1993 the Liberal Democratic Party (LDP) loses its majority in the Diet's lower house after 38 years. In 1995 mismanagement of relief efforts for the Kobe earthquake and poison gas attacks on the Tokyo subway by the Aum Shinrikyo cult further unsettle Japanese self-confidence. Beginning in the early 1990s the Japanese economy has been mired in a period of slow growth, recession, and occasional deflation, while facing with a resurgent China, which threatens to eclipse Japan as the economic and military regional power. While social order and high standards of living remain intact, Japan is undergoing a major self examination, seeking answers to domestic problems and a new role in the world at large.

Migration has not been a major feature in Japan's history. Since the dawn of history the Japanese have been a mixture of northeast Asians with others from the China coast, Southeast Asia, and Polynesia. By the Heian Period the dominant Japanese population extended control over northern Honshu, displacing the indigenous Ainu. Hokkaido was settled by the majority Japanese in the 19th century.

Politically, Japan is a parliamentary democracy modeled on the British system. Representatives are elected to the Diet, a parliament with two legislative chambers. The majority party in the lower house, the House of Representatives, elects its Prime Minister, who forms a cabinet. The conservative Liberal Democratic Party (LDP) is the largest party. In 1993 the Social Democratic Party broke the LDP's longstanding monopoly on power and ruled under a coalition government. In 1996 the LDP regained control of the government and today holds the largest number of seats in the Diet. An elite career bureaucracy manages most of the operations of the government and has considerable influence over policy in their ministries' fields of competence.

Mythology says that the imperial line descended from the Shinto sun goddess; since the late Yamato Period, one family has occupied the throne—the world's oldest dynasty. During most of that time the emperor exercised no political power but served to validate the rule of others who claimed to act in his name. The Meiji government created a state cult around the emperor to rally popular support and focus nationalist sentiment. This culminated in the excesses of emperor worship in the wartime 1930s and 1940s. Since World War II the emperor has publicly denied his divinity, mythology has been removed from school history texts, and the emperor is defined as the symbol of Japanese unity in the 1947 constitution. The current crown prince is Naruhito, son of Emperor Akihito, who is anticipated to succeed his father to the throne.

² LOCATION AND HOMELAND

Japan's population is about 127 million. Practically all Japanese speakers live in Japan. Small communities have emigrated to Hawaii and North and South America, but most of their descendants no longer speak Japanese.

Japan is an archipelago of approximately 3,000 islands off the eastern coast of Asia. Throughout history the main islands of Honshu, Kyushu, and Shikoku have been the homeland of the Japanese. During the 17th century political influence was extended southward over the Ryukyu Islands, including Okinawa. These are occupied by a closely related population that speaks a variant of Japanese. The Ryukyus became part of Japan in the 19th century. Hokkaido was fully annexed in the 19th century.

Approximately two-thirds of the land area is too mountainous for development. This compresses the population into a few large plains, the Kanto (around Tokyo), the Kansai (around Osaka), and the Nobi (around Nagoya), mountain basins, and coastal strips. The population is overwhelmingly urban, drawn by jobs and city life.

Japan suffers great seismic activity. It has many active volcanoes and experiences numerous earthquakes. Most earthquakes cannot be felt but major quakes can be deadly. A huge earthquake on 1 September 1923 destroyed Tokyo and Yokohama and killed approximately 130,000 people. Kobe was devastated by an earthquake on 17 January 1995, which took over 5,000 lives. In 2007 a 6.8 magnitude earthquake triggered a fire at the Kashiwazaki nuclear power plant; though the fire did not lead to a leakage of nuclear radiation, it sparked fears of a nuclear disaster in a nation that is still haunted by the Hiroshima and Nagasaki atomic bombings that ended WWII. Earthquakes off the coast of Japan and in the Pacific Rim occasionally result in tsunamis that can devastate coastal communities and cause massive loss of life. The deadliest tsunami in the history of Japan occurred on 15 June 1896 when an earthquake off the coast of Sanriku triggered a tsunami that destroyed 10,000 homes and killed more than 20,000. Japan also endures seasonal typhoons. While often destructive, these storms cause little loss of life.

³ LANGUAGE

The Japanese language is essentially limited to Japan. It is an Altaic language and its nearest relative is Korean. It is not related to Chinese.

Japanese words are polysyllabic and agglutinative—that is, they are composed of many syllables, and endings are attached to change tense, form a negative, or otherwise modify meaning. The standard sentence order is subject, object, verb. Grammatical particles are placed after words to indicate the topic (*wa*), subject (*ga*), and object (*wo*), or to serve like prepositions in English (*kara* = from; *ni* = in and on). Modifiers precede the words they modify.

Writing was learned from China, and Chinese characters (*kanji*), each with a meaning and multiple pronunciations, are part of the writing system. Two phonetic syllabaries (characters representing syllables) of 48 characters each allow particles, inflections, and words not well represented by kanji to be written. These syllabaries are called *kana*, and include fluid *hiragana* and angular *katakana*. They are two duplicate systems that represent the same sounds. Katakana is used for borrowed words and proper names from foreign languages. Written Japanese is a mixture of kanji and the two kana systems.

STANDARD PHRASES AND WORDS

Ohayoo-gozaimasu	good morning
Kon-nichi wa	good day
Kon-ban wa	good evening
O genki desu-ka	How are you?
O-kagesama de	I'm well, thank you.
Sayoonara	goodbye (formal)
Doozo	please (when offering something)
Onegaishimasu	please (when requesting something)
Arigatoo-gozaimasu	thank you
Doo itashimashite	you are welcome

Family names come first and given names second. Hence, Tanaka Junko is a female name for Junko of the Tanaka family. Titles of respect follow a name. *San* is a universal title of respect equal to Mr., Miss, Mrs.; therefore Tanaka-san could mean Mr. Tanaka, Ms. Tanaka, Miss Tanaka, or Mrs. Tanaka.

The Ainu language is spoken by the indigenous Ainu people of Hokkaido Island. Ainu is considered a *language isolate* that has no proven affiliation with other extant languages. During the Meiji period the use of Ainu was actively discouraged as part of an official policy to assimilate the Ainu and the language was gradually replaced by Japanese. Standard Ainu vocabulary includes words that are distinct from Japanese, including *habo*, or mother, and *ihabo*, father. In recent decades, Ainu language and culture have experienced a revival, reinforced by Ainu language schools, and the Ainu population speaks both Japanese and Ainu.

A father takes photos of his wife and children in kimono as they visit Tokyo's Hie Shrine on Culture Day. Japanese families mark the day by visiting shrines and offering prayer for the healthy growth of their children. (AP Images/Koji Sasahara)

⁴ FOLKLORE

Japanese folklore combines Shinto religious myths, stories of nature spirits, Buddhist tales, and historical figures to whom mythical deeds are attributed. For example, Minamoto Yoshitsune helped his half brother, Minamoto Yoritomo, win the Gempei War (1180–85). He was a brilliant general, who supposedly learned warrior skills as a boy from *tengu*, half-man, half-bird figures that live in mountain forests. Later, Yoshitsune used these skills to defeat a giant Buddhist warrior-monk, Benkei, in a duel on the Go-jo Bridge in Kyoto. Benkei, overwhelmed by Yoshitsune's skill, surrendered and became his loyal follower. Benkei has become a paragon of loyalty. They died in a battle against Yoritomo, who became jealous of Yoshitsune and turned against him.

Japanese folklore is rich in strange beings that inhabit nature. Tengu were mentioned above. *Kappa* are water demons about three feet tall, which have bird beaks and turtle shells on their backs. They often lure people into the water to drown. They love cucumbers, and you can protect yourself from kappa by carving your name on a cucumber and tossing it into the local stream. When out of the water, kappa carry water in a depression on their heads. If you encounter one, bow, and it will return your bow, spilling the water, becoming too weak to harm you.

Myths include Shinto tales collected in the oldest surviving Japanese book, the *Kojiki* (712). These describe the creation of the world and the Japanese islands by Izanagi and Izanami, a pair of male and female deities. The primary deity is the sun goddess, Amaterasu. Upon her descendant's departure to rule Japan, she gave him three sacred treasures: a bronze mirror, a sword, and a string of comma-shaped jewels called *magatama*. These imperial regalia are still associated with the imperial family. Amaterasu is honored at the Ise Grand Shrine, where the original mirror is supposedly enshrined.

5 RELIGION

Traditional Japanese religion includes Shinto, Buddhism, and Confucianism.

Shinto ("The Way of the Gods") is the name given to religious practices that were indigenous to Japan before Buddhism was introduced. It is not a systematic body of beliefs, but includes nature worship, animism, shamanism, fertility cults, ancestor worship, and creation myths. It is concerned with humanity's relationship to nature, to agriculture, and to society. Prayers and offerings petition deities (*kami*) for health, a good crop, children, and safety. Harvest festivals are Shinto events. Shinto also concerns itself with community relationships; hence, marriages are usually Shinto ceremonies.

Shinto is more concerned with pollution than morals. For this reason Shinto offerings are free of blood and include rice wine (*sake*), rice cakes (*mochi*), and entertainments such as dances and wrestling. Shinto shrines are marked by a *torii* gateway. The deity is usually represented at a shrine by a symbol such as a mirror.

The richness of Buddhism and its ties to Chinese culture helped it gain support at the Japanese court. Buddhism also answered spiritual needs that Shinto neglected, such as questions of morals and life after death. By the Nara Period, the court supported the spread of Buddhism and sought to link secular government to the grandeur of institutional Buddhism. Thus the emperor, who claimed descent from the Shinto goddess, also supported the spread of Buddhism. This was possible because these religions were not seen as mutually exclusive. Shinto deities were explained as being local manifestations in Japan of the universal beings represented by the many Buddhas. In addition, while Shinto dealt with issues of this world (crops, social relations, clan ancestors), Buddhism concentrated on ethical and metaphysical issues. This division still works for many Japanese. Weddings may be Shinto ceremonies, but Buddhism deals with morality, funerals, and questions about the future life of the human soul.

Confucianism is a social ethic imported from China. The Tokugawa bakufu based its social order on Confucianism. There is little institutional evidence of Confucianism in Japan, but its values have powerfully influenced Japanese society. Confucianism emphasizes the need for one to find one's place within the greater social order, starting with one's own family, and to be a responsible member of the social units to which one belongs. Confucianism is hierarchical: in social relations one party is superior, the other inferior. It is the duty of the superior to teach, protect, and nurture the inferior. The inferior should respect and learn from the superior. Ideally, Confucianism leads to a highly ethical, supportive social order. It also stresses study, a value widely accepted in Japan.

Christianity was introduced to Japan by St. Francis Xavier in 1549. Catholic missionaries had considerable success for nearly one century before the bakufu expelled them in 1587, slaughtered the local Christian population, and made Christianity a crime punishable by death. Christianity was again made legal in the 1870s. At that time Catholic, Protestant, and Orthodox missions were established, and they are active throughout the country today, especially in education and charity work. Only 1% of Japanese are Christians, but Christian teachings, especially its social ethics, have influenced Japanese thinking.

Many new religious cults have arisen in the past century. Most are devotional cults centered around a charismatic figure and blend ideas from Shinto and Buddhism with features inspired by Christianity, Hinduism, and other faiths. They attract devoted followers and are appealing, in part, because of the sense of dislocation suffered by many people in Japan's urban society. In 1995 the cult movement Aum Shinrikyo carried out a sarin gas attack on the Tokyo subway that resulted in a dozen deaths and hundreds of injuries. The movement incorporated aspects of Yoga, Buddhism, and Christianity as interpreted by its leader, Shoko Asahara, who in 2004 received a death sentence for the attack. At the time of the attack the movement claimed a global following that numbered in the tens of thousands and today Aum Shinrikyo is estimated to have several thousand members.

6 MAJOR HOLIDAYS

Holidays celebrated by the Japanese include the following:

1 January, New Year's Day: The major holiday of the year with three days off from work. Buddhist temple bells are rung 108 times at midnight. People eat noodles for long life and visit Shinto shrines, friends, relations.

15 January, Coming of Age Day: Honors all who have become legal adults at age 20.

11 February, National Foundation Day: Anniversary of the enthronement of the mythical first emperor, Jimmu Tenno.

3 March, Hina Matsuri: Not a legal holiday, but girls display elaborate sets of dolls representing a prince, princess, and their court.

21 March, the Vernal Equinox: Has Buddhist origins, is used to visit and tend family graves.

29 April, Greenery Day: Previously marked the Showa Emperor's birthday; later it was changed to foster appreciation of nature after his death.

3 May, Constitution Day: Commemorates the 1947 Constitution.

5 May, Children's Day: Celebrates Japan's children. Families with children fly carp-shaped streamers. Many companies take off 1 May. This concentration of holidays, 29 April through 5 May, is called "Golden Week."

13–15 July (13–15 August in some areas), Bon Festival: Not a legal holiday but traditionally considered second only to New Year's Day. This Buddhist festival honors de-

A vendor checks crabs at Nijo Ichiba market in downtown Sapporo, Japan. Local residents and tourists can buy fresh seafood and vegetables in the market. (Toru Yamanaka/AFP/Getty Images)

ceased family, and visits to the ancestral home, tending family graves, and prayer services are part of the celebrations. Publicly there is the bonodori, communal dancing during the three evenings of the festival.

15 September, Respect the Aged Day: Honors Japan's elderly.

23 September, The Autumnal Equinox: Similar to 21 March.

10 October, Sports Day: Commemorates the 1964 Tokyo Olympics and encourages good health through sports.

3 November, Culture Day: Fosters cultural activities.

23 November, Labor Thanksgiving Day: Commemorates those who work and expresses thanks for the fruits of their effort.

23 December, the Emperor's Birthday: Current emperor's birthday.

In this non-Christian country Christmas is celebrated as a gift-giving holiday for children, though it has no religious sig-

nificance for the majority of the population. In the Japanese version of Valentine's Day (February 14) women give presents, usually chocolate, to men. On March 14 men in turn give gifts to women on "White Day," the male equivalent of Valentine's Day.

⁷ RITES OF PASSAGE

One hundred days after birth an infant is presented at a local Shinto shrine for blessing.

15 November is "Shichi-Go-San," or "7, 5, 3," on which children of those ages are taken to a Shinto shrine to be blessed. Originally this was for girls three or seven years old and boys five years old.

The beginning of formal schooling is celebrated. The child is presented with a leather backpack for books and may receive a private study desk. School entrance ceremonies are attended by formally dressed parents. Graduations are also celebrated and considered significant social events. University entrance examinations are a major turning point in a teenager's life. Admission to a good university can be critical to an individual's future, and much is made of preparation, the exam, and the results.

15 January is "Coming of Age Day." All who have turned 20 are recognized as legal adults. Fancy dress, usually a kimono for young women, is worn to ceremonies that are often followed by celebration parties. The new adult usually receives significant gifts.

Most people join a company as employees on 1 April following high school or university graduation. Formal company ceremonies induct new employees.

Marriage is usually celebrated at a commercial wedding hall that orchestrates the event. Shinto ceremonies are conducted in private with the couple, priest, witnesses, and parents. In place of vows, cups of sake are exchanged and drunk. Christian church weddings strike many Japanese as romantic, and many wedding halls have an imitation church in which a church-style ceremony can be enacted before guests. The ceremony is followed by an elaborate dinner with multiple speeches and the formal cutting of a Western-style wedding cake.

Retirement is usually marked with some ceremony, and 15 September is a holiday honoring the elderly.

Death is usually associated with Buddhist rituals. Visitors honor the dead at a wake, in which guests dressed in white burn incense in front of a photo of the deceased. The body is cremated. Ashes are placed in a family grave, which has space for numerous urns under a single tombstone. A plaque bearing the posthumous Buddhist name of the deceased is added to the family Buddhist altar, and memorial ceremonies are held over several years to pray for the person.

8 INTERPERSONAL RELATIONS

Japan is more ceremonial and formal than in Western countries, and phrases and forms of polite exchange are more fixed. Manners require that the speaker use honorific language to elevate the other party, while being self-denigrating. Japanese society pays great attention to who is superior to whom in any relationship. This is reflected in language and gestures.

Japanese bow to greet each other. The person of lower status bows lower and should initiate the greeting. Shaking hands is rare among Japanese, who usually do not engage in physical contact. Distinctive gestures include pointing to one's nose to indicate oneself. Women cover their mouths with their hands when laughing. Men, when embarrassed, scratch the back of their heads.

Because houses are very small, Japanese usually entertain outside the home. Home visits are usually confined to a brief meeting over tea. The guest brings some gift such as flowers, fruit, or pastries. Such gifts are used to reinforce relationships with relatives, friends, teachers, doctors, business contacts, etc. Two gift-giving seasons, New Year and midsummer, are marked by a large-scale buying and giving of gift packages.

Dating is usually confined to high school students and young adults. Schools actively discourage it. Group dating is common and takes the form of outings, picnics, karaoke parties, or visits to amusement parks. Japanese students rarely work (many schools forbid it) and often have limited disposable incomes. This and busy study schedules restrict dating options. Dating among working adults is common. Most marriages today are based on romantic attachments rather than the arranged marriages that were the norm in the past.

9 LIVING CONDITIONS

Japanese generally enjoy good health and have the greatest life expectancy in the world—77 years for men and 82 for women. Medical care is generally good and includes both modern scientific and traditional Chinese-style herbal medicines. A national health insurance system supports low-cost care but labors under massive debt.

Ninety-five percent of the Japanese population is urban and housing is a major problem in the country's crowded cities. While Japanese prefer independent houses, the enormous cost of land prevents them from having any real yard; as many as 40 houses are built on one acre. Small apartments are very common. The average dwelling space for a middle-class household in 2001 was just above 350 sq ft. Traditional housing was furnished with wall-to-wall straw mats (tatami), but recent trends are toward carpet or wooden floors and Western-style furniture.

The country's aging population and low number of births had led to wide predictions that Japan will experience a demographic decline by the middle of the 21st century. In 2006 Japan's fertility rate was only 1.29, far below the 2.1 needed to prevent a population drop. The Japanese ministry of health has forecasted that the country's population could fall below 90 million by 2050, at which time more than 40% of Japanese are expected to be older than 65 years of age.

The Japanese standard of living is very high. Material possessions are comparable to those in the United States and the general safety of Japanese city streets adds a sense of well-being. The major problems are the restricted living space and the limited personal time left by demanding work and study hours. Japanese consumers are conscious of fads and fashions and major Japanese cities host large shopping districts.

Japan has excellent public transportation, which most people use for commuting to work and school in the major cities. Trains and subways are very crowded but reliable. Long distance travel is dominated by the Bullet Trains and other expresses, and there is a network of domestic air routes. Most Japanese households own a car and many have two, but roads are often heavily congested.

10 FAMILY LIFE

Traditionally, Japanese families have conformed to the nuclear family structure, but in recent decades, as Japan has modernized, family trends have followed patterns similar to Western nations. Economic prosperity has led to couples marrying at later ages, fewer children per couple, and a higher divorce rate, all of which have contributed to a decline in traditional Japanese social mores.

In the last century Japanese family size has dramatically declined, due in part to Japanese couples marrying at a later age and thus having fewer children. In 2004 the average age of first marriage in Japan was 29.6 years for husbands and 27.8 for wives, compared with 28.9 and 27.5 respectively in 1995, and there were only 5.7 marriages per 1,000 people, the lowest on record. The practice of the eldest son's family living with his parents in a three-generation household is rapidly declining.

Women traditionally played a subservient role in the family, but modern Japanese wives have increasingly sought independence from their husbands. The divorce rate in Japan has nearly doubled since 1990 to 27%. This is due in part to the increased freedom Japanese have obtained. As women have enrolled in the workforce in greater numbers, they have resisted the role of housewife, leading them to marry at a later age and leave their husbands at an increased rate.

Some Japanese have pet dogs and cats, but many are prevented from having them by small living space. Goldfish and birds are popular. Some keep crickets for their song.

11 CLOTHING

Traditional clothing is the kimono, a robe that is wrapped around the body, left side over right, for men and women, and tied with a sash (obi). Women's kimonos vary from the simple everyday designs preferred by older women, to the elaborate painted silk robes worn for ceremonial occasions. Traditionally Japanese kimonos were made of fine silk and included embroideries of gold and silver thread. A kimono style known as junihitoe, or a "twelve-layer robe" with elegant and complex designs, was worn by court ladies in historic times. Men rarely wear kimonos except for formal occasions and when performing traditional arts. The light summer cotton style (yukata) remains very popular for relaxing at home, resorts, and summer festivals.

Traditional footwear is sandals (zori) or wooden clogs (geta) with a thong that passes between the big toe and the second toe. Tabi, a split-toed sock that accommodates the thong, is worn with these. In the past, the standard footwear of the common people of Japan was the waraji, or sandals made from straw rope, which today are mostly worn by monks.

Most Japanese wear Western clothing for daily use. Japanese tend to dress more formally and neatly than Americans. Jeans are popular with the young. Middle and high school students wear dark blue or black uniforms with badges that indicate their school and grade.

12 FOOD

Japanese eat a wide range of foods, including imports from China and the West, as well as traditional Japanese cuisine. The staple of their diet is rice, which is usually eaten plain from a bowl without seasoning, butter, etc. Rice (gohan) is complemented with other dishes: fish, meat, vegetables, various pickled vegetables, and soup. Japanese eat much seafood. Some fresh fish is eaten raw with soy sauce as sashimi, or combined raw with rice in sushi. However, most fish is cooked, often grilled or deep fried in batter (tempura).

Buddhism discouraged the eating of meat, but this taboo has largely disappeared. Japanese eat chicken, pork, and beef, but servings are small. Soup is made from fermented soy bean paste (miso) or dried bonito shavings (katsuobushi). Men-rui (noodles) in various forms are a common main dish. Traditional dishes derived from Buddhist cuisine are known as kaiseki and only include salt as seasoning.

Popular styles of cuisine include teppan-yaki, or frying beefsteaks and a variety of seafoods and vegetables prepared on a large hot-plate in front of the diners; teriyaki, foods broiled or grilled in a sweet soy sauce marinade; and oden, traditional stew that consists of chunks of seafood and vegetables cooked in soy-based soup stock.

Japanese food is served in numerous small dishes. Pieces are cut to be eaten with chopsticks. Soup is drunk from the bowl and often takes the place of beverages during meals. It is very impolite to stick chopsticks upright in your rice bowl or pass food from one pair of chopsticks to another as these are

gestures associated with cremation ceremonies. The national beverage is green tea, and there are elaborate ceremonial tea traditions developed in accordance with Shinto and Buddhists practices. Sake, or wine made from fermented rice, is consumed along with sakana side dishes, which consist of grilled skewered meats and vegetables and pickled dishes.

Sweets are served separately with tea or coffee. Japanese sweets are often based on sweet bean paste. Western baked goods are widely available. Milk and dairy products, a recent addition to the Japanese diet, are ubiquitous, as are other western imports, such as soda, coffee and beer.

Most Western foods can be found in Japan. Hamburgers and pizza are popular and many American restaurant chains are well represented. Meals do not include desserts. Japanese brand fast-food restaurants are numerous, including Ajisen Ramen, which specializes in ramen noodle soup dishes, and Yoshinoya, which is popular for its gyudon, or rice bowl topped with beef and onion. Many of these chain restaurants have opened branches overseas.

13 EDUCATION

Japanese place great value on education and see it as the major path toward self-improvement and launching a successful career. This reflects Confucian values and the degree to which education has created a true meritocracy in Japanese society. Japan claims a 100% literacy rate.

The academic year begins in April and ends in March. Japanese children begin kindergarten at age four and elementary school at age six. Compulsory education covers only elementary school (six grades) and middle school (three grades), but 94% go on to high school (three grades). Most schools are coeducational. Elementary education stresses basic skills, especially reading and math, and seeks to develop the individual into a socially responsible group member. Elementary school teachers establish strong ties with their students, and children often find early education an enjoyable experience.

Middle and high school becomes increasingly rigorous as emphasis shifts to intensive study with limited electives. For a white-collar career a university degree is essential, but university entry is by competitive examination. Preparation for these exams, called "examination hell," drives much of Japanese middle and high school education. Students often supplement regular classes by attending a "juku" (cram school) after hours. Parents, particularly mothers, support their children's educational endeavors. Critics rightly charge that Japanese education stresses memorization for university examinations, but Japanese schools also cultivate problem-solving and group work skills more than is usually recognized.

One-third of high school graduates enter college or university and most of those graduate. Two-year colleges are common for women and for studying vocational subjects. Four-year universities are similar to those in the United States, but many students arrive burned out by "examination hell" and exert minimal effort. Graduate study is not as common as in the United States. English language classes are common in Japan and native-English speakers are often recruited to teach in schools and language training centers. Though Japanese students begin English instruction in elementary school, English language proficiency remains low.

14 CULTURAL HERITAGE

Japan is part of the Chinese sphere of cultural influence; its traditional culture includes many areas in which a Chinese model has been adopted and adapted to suit Japanese tastes. There is also a dynamic folk tradition that has its origins in Japan.

Classical musical instruments include the *koto* (13 string, horizontal harp), the *shakuhachi* (vertical bamboo flute), and the *shamisen* (three-stringed banjo-like instrument). The shakuhachi usually plays solo or with the koto. The koto is frequently played solo or in group ensembles. The shamisen is a popular folk instrument that is played solo, accompanies vocalists, appears in ensembles, and accompanies theater performances.

Western instruments such as the piano, violin, or guitar are more popular now than traditional instruments. Modern popular music reflects strong Western influences and Western classical music is well known in Japan.

In dance, stately classical forms continue to be studied, while a dynamic folk tradition preserves lively dances, including recent additions to the repertoire. The annual Bon Festival includes communal dancing open to all.

Japan's literary heritage is very rich. The oldest surviving text, *Kojiki*, blends Shinto myth and history. Poetry anthologies date back to the Nara Period *Manyoshu*. The Heian Period produced a rich outpouring of literature, especially by court women. Sei Shonagon wrote a lively compilation of miscellaneous observations, the *Pillow Book;* her contemporary, Murasaki Shikibu, wrote the Heian masterpiece novel, the *Tale of Genii*. During the Middle Ages military tales were popular, the greatest being the *Tale of the Heike*. The Muromachi Period produced poetic Noh play texts that often reflect Buddhist values. Most poetry was written in the *tanka* form, five lines of 5-7-5-7-7 syllables. The first three lines of the tanka gave rise to the 17-syllable haiku, the most famous author of which was Basho. The Tokugawa Period gave rise to the *bunraku* puppet drama and kabuki theater, for which Chikamatsu wrote tragedies. In the 19th century, Western influences inspired many autobiographical novels. Natsume Soseki's *Kokoro* is an early 20th-century favorite. Japanese writers are read overseas in translation and Kawabata Yasunari and Oe Kenzaburo have won Nobel Prizes for literature.

15 WORK

Traditionally, most men joined a company directly after graduating from high school (for blue-collar jobs) or college (for white-collar work) and were expected to remain with one firm until retirement at about 60. In return for loyalty and long hours of work, the company made a commitment to preserve the jobs of their employees. This "lifetime employment" ideal has become increasingly uncommon as Japanese companies have adjusted to stagnant economic growth and have begun to lay off workers. In addition, many younger Japanese question the lack of mobility required by lifetime employment and seek more risky and potentially rewarding career paths over security.

The work environment in Japan is group-oriented, and employers expect employees to put company interests before personal concerns. Long hours are characteristic of office workers and it is not uncommon for employees to be expected to work six days a week and excessively long hours. Underlings must demonstrate a great deal of respect for superiors in the work place and it is common for workers to bow to their boss. The workplace is a male-dominated atmosphere. Popular forms of entertainment for businessmen include karaoke and golf.

Wages start very low and rise with longevity; the average per capita income in Japan is higher than in America, but many things, especially housing, are more costly than in the United States. Japan has seen increased unemployment as companies have moved manufacturing facilities overseas, mostly to China and South East Asia.

16 SPORTS

The Japanese are great sports enthusiasts. High school physical education classes include an elective in one of Japan's traditional martial arts such as judo, karate, and archery. Baseball is extremely popular, and the annual national high school baseball tournament in August is followed throughout Japan. The teams of Japan's universities compete in baseball, rugby, martial arts, and other sports.

The most popular professional sport in Japan is baseball. Games in the two leagues, the Pacific and the Central, draw large crowds including noisy but well-organized fan clubs. In the past decade some of Japan's top baseball stars have joined Major League Baseball teams in the United States. Noted Japanese baseball stars in America include Hideki Matsui of the New York Yankees, Daisuke Matsuzaka of the Boston Red Sox, and Ichiro Suzuki of the Seattle Mariners.

Sumo wrestling is a native sport centered upon six annual fifteen-day tournaments. Two wrestlers seek to force each other out of a circle or to touch the ground with some part of their bodies (other than the soles of their feet). A striking feature is the huge size of the wrestlers; top ranked wrestlers usually exceed 300 pounds and can weigh over 500 pounds. In recent decades foreigners have risen to the top ranks in Sumo and in 2007 the grand champion was a Mongolian. Judo, translated as "gentle way," is a martial art developed in the 19th century from traditional Samurai defense techniques. Judo practitioners wear a white uniform called a *judogi*. In a match Judo competitors attempt to throw or trip a player to the ground and use grappling and choking to force an opponent to concede victory.

Popular participatory sports include golf, tennis, skiing, hiking, swimming, and fishing. Gateball, similar to croquet, is popular with elderly Japanese.

17 ENTERTAINMENT AND RECREATION

The Japanese are fans of television and have more television sets per capita than the United States. Song and variety shows and celebrity quiz shows are popular, and there are extensive sports and news broadcasts. Movies are a popular entertainment form, but depend heavily upon imports. Japan's own movie industry is productive but has faded since it achieved international fame for its art and sophistication in the 1950s and '60s. The director Akira Kurosawa made a lasting international impression with films such as *Rashomon* and *Seven Samurai*.

Traditional live theater forms survive. Stately Noh drama has a small but dedicated following. The Bunraku puppet plays and live kabuki theater attract a broader audience and mix traditional fare with more current experimentation. The Japanese also attend concerts, including classical Western music and pop groups.

A popular form of participatory entertainment is karaoke. This form of singing along with recorded orchestral accompaniment to popular songs began as entertainment in bars and has since spread overseas. Japanese children are prolific fans of computer video games and the companies Sony and Nintendo dominate the video game industry in Japan and abroad.

Major festivals attract huge crowds, and famous sites for admiring plum and cherry blossoms, irises, azaleas, chrysanthemums, and the bright leaves of fall draw many visitors who come to view the sights and to party outdoors among the flowers.

18 FOLK ART, CRAFTS, AND HOBBIES

Japan is a land in which many handicrafts have been raised to the level of arts. Japan has many regional variations on pottery. While some fine pottery is noted for delicate form and finely detailed decoration, there is also a strong tradition of heavier folk pottery that aspires to a rustic simplicity of color and shape. The aesthetic values of "*wabi cha*" (poverty tea) of the Tea Ceremony encourages this style of pottery.

Handmade paper, produced from mulberry bark, remains a popular art form, and special papers with distinct textures and patterns are prized for letter writing, calligraphy, and wrapping. Decorating the panels of silk used for women's kimonos has produced a variety of dying, painting, and decorative styles and methods. Tie-dying is also employed.

In the late 19th century, as Japanese rapidly modernized, traditional craftsmen were forced to adapt their skills to develop new art forms. Many smiths and artisans were traditionally employed in producing swords and armor for the Samurai class. These artisans turned their skills towards making elaborate bronzes inlaid with gold and silver that were sold for export and today are prized by collectors around the globe. Japanese ceramics have a long tradition and range in design from *satsuma* ware, earthenware pottery with highly decorative motifs, to *bizen* ware, noted for its reddish brown color and coarse surface.

The Japanese government cherishes these arts, recognizing masters as "National Living Treasures" to honor and support their work.

19 SOCIAL PROBLEMS

Social problems in Japan mostly stem from the fact that Japanese society is largely homogenous and governed by strong social mores that encourage conformity. Civil rights are a problem for some small minority groups. Resident aliens (less than 1% of the population), primarily Koreans, may have been born and raised in Japan but are required to register as foreign residents and have been excluded from certain jobs. A campaign to remove these barriers is gradually moderating restrictions.

Another minority group (about 2% of the population) is the *burakumin* (hamlet people). Physically indistinguishable from the majority Japanese, these are descendants of outcasts who suffered severe discrimination in pre-modern times. Despite attempts to legislate equality, they are subject to widespread discrimination. The tiny population of Ainu on Hokkaido are an indigenous people who were swamped by the majority Japanese population. Most have intermarried with the majority Japanese.

The resident Koreans, burakumin, and Ainu have formed groups to end discrimination and promote pride. Though progress has been made, these groups are small, relatively invisible in Japanese society, and not given much attention by the national press.

Japanese society tolerates and even encourages considerable drinking, and alcoholism is a problem. Relieving stress and renewing personal bonds over a drink after work is common in Japan, and leads to heavy drinking. Japan's island geography has helped to restrict the inflow of hard drugs and firearms to very low levels, but there are signs that these problems may be on the rise.

Suicide remains a stubbornly lethal problem that takes more than 30,000 Japanese lives each year. In 2003 Japan's suicide rate was the second highest in the industrialized world, at 25.5 per 100,000. The high profile suicide of Japan's farm minister in 2007 prompted government officials to call for more measures to curb Japan's suicide crisis. Japan has long had a tradition of taking one's life, which was seen as an acceptable method of responding to public shame. As Japan's economic crisis worsened in the 1990s, suicides grew to record rates and the trend has yet to abate. The advent of the Internet has led to a problem of "suicide clubs," websites where those contemplating suicide can find a pact partner who will agree to take their lives together.

20 GENDER ISSUES

In traditional Japanese society women are relegated to a secondary status, but even in families that conform to customary mores, women enjoy considerable autonomy and power. Japanese schooling treats boys and girls equally, guaranteeing well educated women. Traditionally the wife has charge of the house and oversees the children. This is her full-time job and includes two important responsibilities, money and education. The wife keeps the family's budget, manages savings and large purchases, and even gives her husband his weekly allowance. She also monitors the children's education. Most Japanese children have few household chores, but devote regular time to study under their mother's watchful eye.

In modern Japanese society most women work outside of the home in retail, service, or clerical jobs. They are expected to quit work upon marrying or when their first child is due. These women represent an affluent portion of the Japanese public and many enjoy their status prior to marriage. After raising children, many return to work. Until recently, true career options were not open to many women in corporations. Teaching and some government offices provided careers, but corporations only began to recruit women executives seriously in the 1980s and they are still rare in many industries.

Legally, Japanese women enjoy considerable protection. However, Japanese society discourages confrontational litigation and this restricts the use of the law as a tool for force social change. Social values tend to emphasize gender-based career paths. While many Japanese women appear content with their status, those who wish to pursue careers previously limited to men find the door only partially open.

In Japan there are no laws that prohibit homosexual activity. Historically homosexuals have not been socially ostracized, and same-sex relationships have been depicted in art and literature. Civil rights laws have not been extended to gays and lesbians at the national level, but some local governments have banned discrimination based on sexual orientation.

21 BIBLIOGRAPHY

Gordon, Andrew. *The Modern History of Japan: From Tokugawa Times to the Present.* New York: Oxford University Press, 2003.

Mente, Boye Lafayette de and Boye De Mente. *Dining Guide to Japan.* North Clarendon, V.T.: Tuttle, 2007.

Morton ,William Scott and J. Kenneth Olenik. *Japan: Its History and Culture.* New York: McGraw-Hill, Inc. 2005.

Okamoto, Shigeko and Janet S. Shibamato Smith eds. *Japanese Language, Gender, and Ideology: Cultural Models and Real People.* New York: Oxford University Press, 2004.

Robertson, Jennifer. *Takarazuka: Sexual Politics and Popular Culture in Modern Japan.* Berkeley: University of California Press, 1998.

Smith, Robert J. and Richard K. Beardsley eds. *Japanese Culture: Its Development and Characteristics.* New York: Routledge, 2004.

Siddle, Richard. *Race, Resistance and the Ainu of Japan.* New York: Routledge, 1996.

—by F. A. Moyer and M. C. Moyer; revised by D. Straub

JATS

PRONUNCIATION: JAHTS
ALTERNATE NAMES: Baluch; Pathan; Rajput
LOCATION: India; Pakistan
POPULATION: About between 33 and 43 million (estimate)
LANGUAGE: Language of the region in which they live
RELIGION: Hinduism; Islam; Sikhism

1 INTRODUCTION

The Jats (Jâts) are a peasant caste widely distributed throughout northern India and Pakistan. They form geographically separate endogamous groups that have become integrated into the local community as distinct castes. These groups are possibly of differing origins and go by various names. In some regions they call themselves Baluch, Pathan, or Rajput, rather than Jat. They are, however, quite separate from the communities of peddlers, artisans, and entertainers of Afghanistan who are also designated by the name Jat.

The origin of the Jats is a matter of much conjecture. Some authorities see them as being of Aryan stock and entering the subcontinent as part of the great Aryan migrations of the past. Others hold that they are Indo-Scythians who arrived from their home along the Oxus River during the 2nd and 1st centuries BC. Still others argue that they are a Rajput tribe. Whatever their origins, they spread across a wide area of the northern plains and rapidly emerged as the dominant cultivators in the regions they settled.

In 1699, the Jats around Mathura, in Uttar Pradesh, rebelled against the powerful Mughal rulers in Delhi, essentially as a result of political provocation aggravated by the economic discontent, and further aggravated by religious persecution and discrimination. Although defeated by the Mughals, Jat resistance resumed in 1707 in the disorder following Aurangzeb's death. The Jats under Badan Singh (1722–1756) established a kingdom centered at Deeg, from which Jat rule was extended over Agra and Mathura and much of the neighboring area of the Ganges plain. Suraj Mal, described as one of the greatest Jat rulers, moved his capital from Deeg to Bharatpur in 1733 and Rustam, a Jat king of the Sogariya clan, laid the foundation of the modern city of Bharatpur. Bharatpur has the distinction of being one of the few states in India to defeat the British, who unsuccessfully besieged the city under Lord Lake in 1805. During the British Raj, the princely state of Bharatpur covered an area of 5,123 square kilometers, and its rulers enjoyed a salute of 17 guns. The state of Bharatpur, now a part of Rajasthan State and site of the famous Keoladeo Ghana Bird Sanctuary, which was designated a World Heritage Site in 1985, acceded unto the dominion of India in 1947.

2 LOCATION AND HOMELAND

There is no accurate data available concerning the number of Jats in South Asia. In the late 1980s, the Jat populations of India and Pakistan were estimated at 8 million and 13 million, respectively. Assuming these initial estimates are accurate, and that growth rates for the Jat communities has approximated that for their respective countries, Jats in India must number around 12 million, and in Pakistan over 21 million, for a total Jat population of over 33 million. However, some estimates place the Jat population in 1988 at 31 million, which would place their current population at around 43 million. At best, these are crude estimates.

Jats are distributed across the northern and western plains of the Indian subcontinent in a belt extending from the middle Ganges valley to Sind. They form the bulk of the population in the Punjab (both Indian and Pakistani), in the land between the Ganges (Ganga) and Jumna (Yamuna) rivers, and in a belt extending through the western and central districts of Uttar Pradesh. They are the most-numerous caste over much of the western half of Rajasthan. Significant Jat communities are also found in northern Kashmir and in Sind (in Pakistan). The physical environments occupied by the Jats consist mostly of the alluvial plains and *doab* (land between rivers) of the Indus, Ganges, and Jumna rivers, or the semiarid and desert regions of Rajasthan and Sind. Climate and vegetation conform to the broad patterns found in these areas of the subcontinent. In recent years, increasing population pressure has led to significant emigration of Jats to North America, the United Kingdom, Malaysia, and the Middle East.

3 LANGUAGE

Jats speak the languages and dialects that are current in the regions where they live. Thus, Jats in Sind speak Sindhi, an Indo-Aryan tongue with a large number of Persian and Arabic words, written in a script similar to that used for Urdu. In Pakistan's Punjab Province, they speak Punjabi and use the Perso-Arabic script introduced to the region during the Muslim conquests. Jats in the Indian Punjab speak Punjabi but write in the Lahnda script, which is related to Devanagari, or the Gurmukhi script in which the Sikh sacred books are written. In Rajasthan, local Rajasthani dialects are spoken and written with the Devanagari (Hindi) script.

4 FOLKLORE

Tejaji is a local folk hero revered by Jats in Rajasthan. Tejaji, it is said, was a Jat who lived about 900 years ago. One day he noticed that a Brahman's cow was in the habit of going into the jungle, where milk from her udder fell into the hole of a snake. Tejaji undertook to supply the snake with milk every day so that the Brahman would not suffer a loss. One day, when Tejaji was preparing to visit his father-in-law, he forgot to give the snake any milk. The snake appeared to Tejaji and declared he would have to bite him. Tejaji asked for permission to complete his visit, to which the snake agreed. On his journey, Tejaji rescued the village cattle from a gang of robbers but was desperately wounded in the encounter. With much difficulty he presented himself to the snake, as he had promised. However, he was so badly wounded that the snake could not find a spot on his body to bite. Tejaji put out his tongue for the snake to bite, which he did, and Tejaji subsequently died. Today, Tejaji is worshiped as a protector against snake-bite. He is represented as a man on horseback with a snake biting his tongue, and this image is common on local shrines throughout the region. Tejaji is revered not only by Jats but by the local population as well.

5 RELIGION

Jats may be Hindu, Muslim, or Sikh by religion. Hindu Jats (47% of all Jats) know and worship the gods of the Sanskrit tradition and, like all Hindus, hold the cow in high regard. But

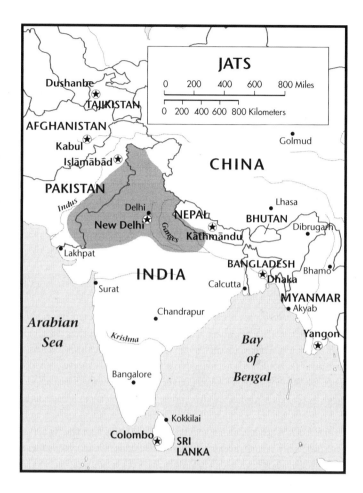

they also follow many local religious practices and observances, and worship local deities. Ancestor worship is also an important part of Jat religious life. The Jats of western Uttar Pradesh pay homage to their ancestors during the festival of Kanagat (September-October). At this time, offerings of water are made to the spirits of the deceased. The head of the family, assisted by a Brahman priest who performs rituals and recites Sanskrit hymns, presents offerings (*pindas*) to the clan ancestors, who are believed to look after the welfare of their descendants. Jats in the Indian Punjab are mostly Sikh (c. 20% of Jats), though they preserve many Hindu elements in their ritual life. The tradition of *pir* (saint) worship is widespread among Muslim Jats (c. 33%), who belong mainly to the Sunni sect of Islam.

6 MAJOR HOLIDAYS

Jats throughout South Asia observe the holidays and festivals of their respective religious communities. Thus, Muslims celebrate the two great religious festivals of Id ul-Fitr, celebrating the end of Ramadan, and Bakr-Id, the Feast of Sacrifice. Sikh festivals include Vaisakhi, which marks the beginning of the new year in the Punjab, and the gurpurbs, holidays related to events from the life of the gurus. Hindu Jats keep Holi, Divali, and other festivals of the Hindu calendar. In addition, many regional festivals such as the Urs of Sufi saints are celebrated at the saints' shrines. These local festivals are often celebrated by the community at large. Sakhi Sarwar, for instance, is a Jat saint worshiped in the Punjab, but he is revered by Hindus and Sikhs as well.

7 RITES OF PASSAGE

Rites of passage conform to the customs of the community to which each Jat belongs. Thus, male babies among Muslim Jats are circumcised, Sikhs are baptized into their religion, and Brahmans officiate at Hindu rituals. However, many ceremonies are common to all Jats, whatever their religion. Many Sikhs, for example, follow Hindu marriage rites and even use Brahmans for some of their ceremonies. Sikhs and Hindus cremate their dead, while Muslims resort to burial.

8 INTERPERSONAL RELATIONS

Jats use greetings such as "Salaam," "Sat Sri Akal," or "Ram Ram," according to their religious affiliations and local customs.

9 LIVING CONDITIONS

Jat settlements and house-types conform to broad regional patterns. Over much of the northern plains, villages are compact clusters of houses situated in the middle of agricultural land. In Pakistan's Punjab, grid-patterned "canal colony" villages are added to the mix. Houses are *kacca* (built of mud or unfired brick) or *pukka* (made with fired brick), reflecting the economic standing of their owners. In mixed villages, the houses of different castes (including Jats) are segregated into distinct neighborhoods. A Jat house in the *doab* (land between rivers) of the Sutlej and Jumna (Yamuna) rivers typically consists of a courtyard around which are the women's quarters, a room used exclusively by men, and cattle sheds. The more-prosperous villagers may have two-story houses and refinements such as studded wooden doors and Moorish-style arches. By contrast, nomadic Jats in Sind live in tents or flimsy, easily collapsible structures built of reed mats. Household furnishings vary according to the resources of the individual.

10 FAMILY LIFE

Jats are organized into clans, with clan members living in villages in a fairly compact area. Each clan has a hereditary leader called a *Chaudhry*. Clans are divided into lineages *(thok)*, sublineages, and minimal lineages *(khandan)*. The minimal lineage comprises the families of living brothers whose father is deceased. The Jat family may be an independent nuclear family or an extended joint family. Among Sikh and Hindu Jats, one cannot marry a woman if any of her four grandparents comes from the same clan as oneself. Muslims Jats, however, are not subject to such restrictive rules of exogamy. Until recently, Jats practiced polygyny (i.e., a man could have more than one wife at the same time), but in India this has been declared illegal. Under Islamic law, however, a man may have up to four wives. Today, most Jats are monogamous. Marriage ceremonies follow Muslim, Sikh, or Hindu patterns. Divorce is not common and often leads to conflict between the two lineages involved. Widow remarriage is permitted by all Jat groups.

11 CLOTHING

Jat clothing reflects regional dress-styles. Punjabi men wear tight-legged trousers covered by a long shirt *(kurta)* worn hanging down outside the trousers. This is accompanied by a turban, the style of which is determined by where one comes from and whether one is a Sikh, Muslim, or Hindu. Women of all denominations wear trousers and a tunic *(salwar-kamiz)*, accompanied by a scarf *(dupatta)* thrown over their shoulders or around their heads. In Uttar Pradesh, men wear Western-type shirts over trousers or a cotton *dhoti* (a long piece of cloth wrapped around the waist, then drawn between the legs). Women in Uttar Pradesh dress in full, wide, colorful skirts *(ghaghri),* a kurta or a bodice, and a shawl. Their clothes are sometimes decorated with rhinestones and mirrors.

12 FOOD

The Jat diet is determined in part by agricultural ecology, and in part by culture. As Jat populations are found in the drier wheat-growing areas of the subcontinent, wheat and other cereals form their staple starch. *Roti* (flat bread made from wheat or millet) is eaten every day, along with a vegetable curry, lentils, curds, and—for those who can afford it—*ghi* (clarified butter). Hindu Jats are usually vegetarian, while Sikhs and Muslims eat meat. Many Sikhs, however, share Hindu attitudes towards beef-eating, while pork is banned by the Muslim religion.

13 EDUCATION

Attitudes toward education vary among Jat populations. A study in a village near Delhi, for example, showed 92% of Jat boys between 6 and 15 years of age attend school. The percentage dropped to 40% for girls, this difference reflecting the relative positions of males and females in Jat society, and indeed in South Asian society in general. Yet even the figure for Jat girls compares favorably with those of the Bhangis (0%), Kumhars (10%), and other castes in the village. Access to educational facilities for groups such as the nomadic Jats of Sind in Pakistan is clearly limited.

14 CULTURAL HERITAGE

Hinduism, Islam, and Sikhism all have ancient traditions of music, dance, and literature. Jat communities share in this cultural heritage. They also share in the folk culture of the regions in which they live. Thus, Hindu Jats living in the middle Ganges valley are familiar with the great traditions of Brahmanical Hinduism. But in regions such as Braj, southeast of Delhi, where folk culture is closely tied to the life of Krishna, they also participate in Krishna-related rituals and practices that are localized in nature. Similarly, the writings of the Sikh gurus, Sikh sacred music, and Sufi mysticism are part of the heritage of the Punjabi Jats—as are dances such as the Bhangra, and the Punjabi folk tunes that are popular in the region. Muslim Jats are the successors to centuries of Islamic cultural dominance in northwestern India. This is seen not only in religious practices and social customs, but in areas such as the Indo-Islamic style of architecture, and the poetry and music of the Sufis. Music forms such as the *qawwali* and *ghazal* continue to be popular among the Muslim population today.

15 WORK

Jats are known throughout northern India and Pakistan as skilled and industrious agriculturalists. They are the dominant landowning caste in many areas. Jats make up the bulk of the farming community in the Punjab, one of the most agriculturally productive regions in the entire subcontinent. They are open to change and receptive to innovation in farming techniques. It is no accident that the advances in agriculture of the

A Jat girl smiles at the camera in Orissa, India. (© Tiziana and Gianni Baldizzone/Corbis)

late 1960s and early 1970s known as the Green Revolution were implemented in the Punjab. Some Jats are pastoralists, raising water buffaloes and camels for sale. The Jats were viewed by the British as one of the martial races of northern India, and many served in Jat regiments in the British Indian Army. This tradition of military service has carried over into the armed forces and police forces of India and Pakistan. Today, many Sikh Jats are heavily involved in the trucking business.

In Pakistan, the word "Jat" is used as an occupational term for "landlord," so the Sikh and Muslim Jats in Pakistan who originate from the Punjab may be different in appearance from "Jats" in the rest of the country, who belong to local communities.

16 SPORTS

Games played by children are typical of those found throughout India. These include hide-and-seek, various games of tag, marbles, kite-flying, spinning tops, and *gulli-danda* (Indian cricket). Wrestling and team wrestling *(kabaddi)* are popular among youth and young adults. Traditional rural pastimes among men include gambling, cockfighting, partridge-fighting, and camel-racing. Hunting *(shikar)* is a favorite sport among the well-to-do classes. Young people have taken enthusiastically to modern sports such as cricket, field hockey, and soccer.

17 ENTERTAINMENT AND RECREATION

With the advent of the mass media, Jats throughout northern and western India are able to receive radio and television broadcasts. Moreover, with the advent of cable and satellite television, those who can afford it can access overseas networks such as CNN. Movies and sports events are the most commonly watched programming. Movie theaters are found in almost all towns of any size. It is only the most isolated and economically depressed Jat groups, such as the nomadic pastoralists of Sind, who have to rely heavily on traditional pastimes for their entertainment.

18 FOLK ART, CRAFTS, AND HOBBIES

Folk arts and crafts vary from region to region. The nomadic Jats of the delta region of the Indus are known for their elaborate embroidery work and mirrored textiles.

19 SOCIAL PROBLEMS

Problems facing the Jats vary according to location and the specific communities involved. Relatively affluent landowning Jats in Uttar Pradesh, for example, do not face the problems of economic hardship, illiteracy, and lack of access to schools and other amenities that confront the nomadic Jat pastoralists in Sind. In such communities, internal factions and caste relations are often of greater concern than social ills. In Sind, expansion of agriculture has reduced grazing areas, and many pastoral Jats have had to turn to other occupations. Sikh Jats in the Punjab, on the other hand, have had to live through the unrest, violence, and political instability generated by the Sikh separatist movement over the last two decades (many Sikh Jats actively supported the movement, as well).

As agriculturalists, Jats in India, especially in the upper Ganges plains where they are concentrated, were negatively affected by Prime Minister Jawarhala Nehru's agricultural policies. Chaudhary Charan Singh opposed Nehru's socialistic and collectivist land-use policies. A politician from Uttar Pradesh, Singh was born into a Jat family in 1902 and served as India's sixth prime minister from 28 July 1979 until 14 January 1980, leading the Bharatiya Lok Dal party. His association with the causes dear to farming communities in the North caused his memorial in New Delhi to be named Kisan Ghat (in Hindi, Kisan is the word for farmer).

The Jat people have a discrete and distinct cultural history that can be historically traced back to ancient times. However, to a large extent, because of their diversity, the question of a Jat identity remains an issue. Several religious traditions played an important role in shaping Jat identity. The Jats had no patience for the intricate symbols and elaborate practices of orthodox Hinduism. They described their religion as "kachha mazhab"—simple and earthy—as contrasted with the "pukkaa mazhab" of the high castes. Second, the reformist tradition in the Jat community had a pronounced non-Brahmanical orientation. There was nothing sacred about the Ganga or the Yamuna for them. Idols and temples were emblems of superstition, and the Brahmans had no role to play in their rituals and ceremonies. The Naths, followers of Gorakhnath, an 8th century Hindu sage, who are well-represented among the Jats in some areas, eat meat and drink alcohol. Such practices resulted in Jats being placed on the lower rung of the Hindu social order and they had no illusion of belonging to the twice-born Hindu varnas till the advent of the Arya Samaj (Ârya Samâj), which tried to engineer a basic shift in the Jat psyche. Whatever the current notions about the superiority of the Jat "quom" (community), Jats were stigmatized by the higher castes. The Brahmans treated the Jats as Shudras and denied them the right to wear the sacred thread. The Jats were largely free from the Brahmanical orthodoxy and caste rigidity. The Arya Samaj's attack on Brahmanical rituals, orthodoxy, superstitions, and caste rigidity had a natural appeal for the Jats and they easily took to it.

The Arya Samaj is a Hindu reform movement, dating back to the late 19th century, that denies traditional Brahmanical dominance in Hindu society, but that also promotes Hindu values. For instance, cow-protection societies form a major plank of the Arya Samaj movement in north India and the cow-slaughter theory is specifically used to justify violence against the Dalits and Muslims by Jats. The brutal lynching in 2002 of five Dalits in Jhajjar in Haryana State by Jats reflects the growing success of the Hindutva forces in the State. The "cow" has suddenly emerged as the principal symbol for the mobilization of dominant caste groups into the Hindutva fold. The Dalit victims have become the culprits; the Jats have emerged as warriors, like the Rajputs, defending the cow against the depredation of non-Hindus or low caste Hindus. Popular ballads and stories abound, highlighting the virtues of kshatriya values embodied in acts of saving the cow from the assaults of Muslim butchers, who were allegedly supplied cows by Chuhras and Chamars (low caste Hindu groups). One of the most powerful images in the Jat belt is that of a gaurakshak (cow-protector), who is venerated for protecting the community through an act of saving the cow, and killing the "culprits" and "infidels." Protection of the cow has become a centerpiece of the emerging Jat identity.

Many Jats see themselves as equal to the martial Rajputs and some regard themselves as belong to the "twice-born" castes, i.e. the three upper levels of the Hindu caste system, but in general they are looked down upon by the higher castes in India. In fact, in 1999 the Vajpayee government in New Delhi included Jats in the Center's list of Other Backward Castes (OBCs) and they are also classed as OBCs in the states of Haryana, Uttar Pradesh, Rajasthan, and Madhya Pradesh. Designation as an OBC indicates a caste needs assistance in the sphere of socio-economic development and gives a group access to reserved quotas (27%) in public sector employment and places in educational institutions, as well as special political representation. Such as designation is, of course, subject to political patronage and causes much resentment in the community at large, other castes having to compete with the Jats, whom they see as successful and economically prosperous. The agitation in 2008 amongst Gujars in Rajasthan for classification as a Scheduled Tribe stems, in part, from Jats being classed as an OBC in the state and the Gujars having to compete with them in the areas of employment and access to education.

In general, while there are some who live in poverty and are economically disadvantaged, Jats are a prosperous farming caste who form the backbone of the rural communities where they are found.

20 GENDER ISSUES

Gender issues among Jat depend to a large extent on the community to which women belong. Thus among Hindu Jats, traditional Hindu constraints prevail. A recent study in Shahargaon, an urbanizing Jat village just south of Delhi in Haryana State, found that sex-selective abortion was practiced within a system of patriarchy, manifested in terms of preference for sons over daughters. Although the overall impact has been a decrease in family size, the sex ratio in the village increasingly favors males. Even among Sikhs, whose *gurus* preached gender equality, there is a preference for sons. In Nanowal village, part of Fategarh Sahib district in Punjab State, in which 70% of the families are landed Jat Sikhs, 18 boys and six girls were born in 2003, the latter all belonging to the Scheduled Castes. According to the 2001 census, Fatehgarh Sahib district recorded the country's lowest sex ratio of 754 girls per 1,000 boys in the age group of 0–6 years. The State of Punjab has legislation preventing ultrasound sex-determination being used for sex-selective abortion, although clearly this does occur.

Literacy among Hindu Jat women is only 27.5 % though it is even less for Sikh Jats (20%) and Muslim Jats (14%). In Pakistan, of course, Muslim Jat women are subject to *purdah* and wearing the *burqa* in public. While many Jat communities are quite prosperous, poverty and illiteracy are problems among rural groups of lower socio-economic standing, where women tend to be actively involved in agricultural activities.

21 BIBLIOGRAPHY

Dabas, Bal Kishan. *The Political and Social History of the Jats.* Delhi: Sanjay Prakashan, 2001.

Lewis, Oscar. *Village Life in Northern India.* New York: Random House, 1958.

Pradhan, M. C. *The Political System of the Jats in Northern India.* Delhi: Oxford University Press, 1966.

Singh, Jagbir. *The Jat Rulers of Upper Doab.* Jaipur: Aavishkar Publishers, 2002.

Singh, Vir. *The Jats: Their Role & Contribution to the Socio-economic Life and Polity of North & North-West India.* 2 vols. Delhi: Originals, 2006.

Westphal-Hellbusch, Sigrid, and Heinz Westphal. *The Jat of Pakistan.* Islamabad: Lok Virsa Publishing House, 1986.

—by D. O. Lodrick

JAVANESE

PRONUNCIATION: JAHV-uh-neez
LOCATION: Indonesia (Java)
POPULATION: 100 million
LANGUAGE: Javanese
RELIGION: Islam; Protestantism: Catholicism; folk religion
RELATED ARTICLES: Vol 3: Indonesians

1 INTRODUCTION

To medieval geographers, the name "Java" was virtually synonymous with the entire sweep of islands between China and India. From Mecca's viewpoint, every Muslim from "below the winds," that is, Southeast Asia, was "*jawi.*" While Bali might monopolize Indonesia's tourist brochure image, Java and the Javanese in many ways dominate Indonesia's reality. Non-Javanese Indonesians often complain of a Javanese "colonialism" having replaced the Dutch version, but, from the viewpoint of a multiethnic Jakarta elite oriented towards development and modernity, Javanese culture is just another regional culture, albeit one with far greater power than others to influence national culture in its turn. More importantly, Javanese culture is riven (and enlivened) by the same tensions that obsess Indonesian society as a whole. Javanese Muslim purists find kindred spirits more easily among Malays, Minang, or Bugis than among fellow Javanese whose secularism or syncretism allies them rather to the Balinese, Dayak, or Torajan.

The Austronesian ancestors of the Javanese arrived perhaps as early as 3000 BC from the Kalimantan coast. The name "Java" may have itself originally meant "outlying island," from the point of view of Borneo or Sulawesi. Having acquired metallurgical skills about 2,000 years ago, the Javanese developed complex supra-village polities before choosing to adopt (and recombine and transform) elements of Indian religion, art, and statecraft. From the 7th century, inscriptions and Chinese annals record kingdoms in central Java (two centuries later than in west Java). Despite the value of maritime trade, Mataram, the first great kingdom on Java, emerged in the agrarian interior of central Java, powerful and wealthy enough to raise the "holy mountains" of Borobudur (Mahayana Buddhist) and Prambanan (Sivaite Hindu), monuments surpassing in scale any in India itself. By this time, Java's influence radiated as far as Indochina; the Khmer prince who founded the Angkorean empire had been a captive in Java.

In the 10th century, the vital political and cultural heart of Hindu-Javanese civilization shifted to the Brantas valley in eastern Java, driven from central Java by some unknown (volcanic?) calamity, as well as drawn by greater access to maritime trade. By the end of the 13th century, centered not far inland from modern Surabaya, rose Majapahit, a kingdom whose glorious memory inspired not only Javanese of later centuries but also the Balinese and other peoples of the archipelago. Since Majapahit, like all native Javanese states before and after, was a fragile coalition of regional lords under a paramount dynasty often embroiled in bloody succession struggles, its effective authority could hardly have extended as far as its propaganda claimed. Nonetheless, the list of its far-flung "tributaries" indicates that Majapahit at its height was at the center of a trading network that the Dutch East India Company (VOC), the direct forerunner of modern Indonesia, would later enter and colonize.

In the 15th century, Java's north coast ports fell into the orbit of Muslim Malacca (then the center of international commerce) and under the rule of the descendants of non-Javanese Muslim merchants. These Islamized states, led by Demak, vanquished the remnants of a by then already declining Majapahit and propagated the new religion in the interior. By the following century, in central Java, a new Mataram emerged with a hybrid culture that integrated Islam with the legacy of the old Hindu-Buddhist civilization.

The greatest Mataram ruler, Sultan Agung, might have achieved the unification of Java had it not been for the opposition of the VOC, newly established on the coast. After Agung's death in 1646, Mataram slipped into over a century of civil wars and foreign invasions. The only long-term beneficiary was the ever-intervening VOC, which acquired the north coast and finally oversaw the permanent division of the remaining realm into two equally subjected courts at Surakarta (Solo) and Yogyakarta (Yogya) in 1755.

After the over-extended VOC declared bankruptcy in 1799, the Dutch government took firm control of Java only in the 1830s, after taking half a decade to subdue a rebellion led by the Yogyanese prince, Diponegoro. Colonial pacification deprived Javanese rulers of political power, leaving them the arts as the only theater in which to express authority. Under the Cultivation System, the Dutch, utilizing the native aristocracy and Chinese intermediaries, forced peasants to discharge their tax obligations by growing cash crops (especially sugar) on a portion of their rice lands. Coupled with a population explosion that turned 3 million Javanese in 1800 to 28.4 million by 1900, these exactions impoverished the peasantry.

Resistance took diverse forms: the elite retreated into a world fashioned of arts and etiquette where Javanese refinement remained superior to Dutch "brutishness"; peasants in the Samin movement practiced nonviolent noncooperation, recognizing no obligation to pay taxes. In time, however, the steamship, the railroad, the telegraph, the newspaper, and European racism created an arena for struggle stretching far beyond Java, even beyond the Netherlands Indies. Javanese took the lead in the Islamic, communist, and nationalist movements that challenged colonialism from early in the 20th century. Surakarta was the birthplace in 1911 of Sarekat Islam, the first mass political organization in the Dutch East Indies, and Surabaya was the site of a communist revolt in 1917 among the soldiers and sailors at the naval base there and of fierce resistance in 1945 to British forces come to reimpose Dutch rule after the Japanese occupation. Under the new republic, Yogyakarta, out of recognition for its sultan's support for the struggle for independence, was not integrated into the province of Central Java but rather was granted province-level status in its own right. All but one of Indonesia's presidents have been Javanese, the exception being B. J. Habibie, a Bugis. Sukarno was a partial exception, being half-Balinese.

Java, along with Bali, suffered the great majority of the killings during the anti-leftist massacres of 1965-1966; one of the most important factors leading to the bloodshed was conflict over land in rural Java between landowning peasants aligned with Islamic parties and landless peasants aligned with the Communist party. In promoting the growth of export industries in Java's cities, development under Suharto's New Order regime increased the importance of Java in Indonesia's overall economy, long heavily dependent on the export of petroleum and other natural resources from the Outer Islands. Despite much small-scale, "routine" collective violence (including vigilante exercises of "popular justice" against "immoral elements," attacks on black-magic practitioners [dukun santet], and church burnings), more than in other parts of Indonesia, Java has not seen episodes of ferocious ethnic/religious conflict resulting in thousands of dead and tens of thousands displaced as have occurred in the Moliccas and Kalimantan, though Surakarta was the site of major anti-Chinese rioting in May 1998.

See also the article entitled **Indonesians**.

²LOCATION AND HOMELAND

The Britain-sized island of Java formed eons ago along the line where the Indo-Australian plate meets the continental shelf of Asia. Their collision folded Java along two parallel east-west lines of plateaus and hills. Along the intervening trough, a series of volcanoes broke through; well-spaced, their peaks slope gradually down to broad plains, ideal for rice terraces. Some 63% of the island is cultivated (as compared to 10–20% of the other Indonesian islands); 25% of the surface is devoted to wet-rice paddies. Fragmented into rice-fields that give way to fish-ponds and saltpans and dotted with ports, the northern coastal plain faces the shallow and busy Java Sea. Along the southern shore, in contrast, plateaus fall sharply down to a deep and desolate Indian Ocean.

According to the 2000 census, Javanese comprised 41.7% of Indonesia's total population, thus numbering 83.9 million. No other Southeast Asian national population and no European one outnumbers them. Speaking dialects of Javanese but counted separately were the Bantenese (4.1 million) and Cirebonese (1.9 million) of western Java. Java's population density ranges from 850 persons per sq km (2,200 per sq mi) to as high as 2,000 persons per sq km (5,180 per sq mi) in the countryside around Yogyakarta. According to 2005 figures, Central Java's population density stood as high as 982 per sq km, East Java's at 757, far higher than West Sumatra's 106 for West Sumatra and Central Kalimantan's 12. Urban crowding is even more striking, given that single-story housing rather than high-rises is the norm.

The Javanese homeland consists of the provinces of Central Java and East Java, minus the island of Madura, and the Special Region of Yogyakarta. Javanese have also settled for centuries along the northern coast of West Java, particularly in the area of Cirebon and Banten. Javanese perceive several regional subcultures. The major division is between the *kejawen* and the *pesisir*. Extending over the north coast and including distinct centers, such as Cirebon, Demak-Kudus, and Surabaya, the *pesisir* is more oriented towards maritime commerce and partakes more directly in Islamo-Malay civilization. Centered on the old royal cities of Surakarta (Solo) and Yogyakarta (Yogya), the *kejawen* of the interior, on the other hand, emphasizes an indigenous synthesis of Islamic and the older Hindu-Buddhist cultures. This subculture includes the "outlying territories" *(mancanegara)* of the Bengawan Solo and Brantas valleys, as well as the Banyumas area bordering the Sundanese cultural zone. Depopulated by Mataram's wars, much of contemporary East Java presents a highly mixed landscape, including Madurese, "Westerners" (*tiyang kilenan*, migrants from cen-

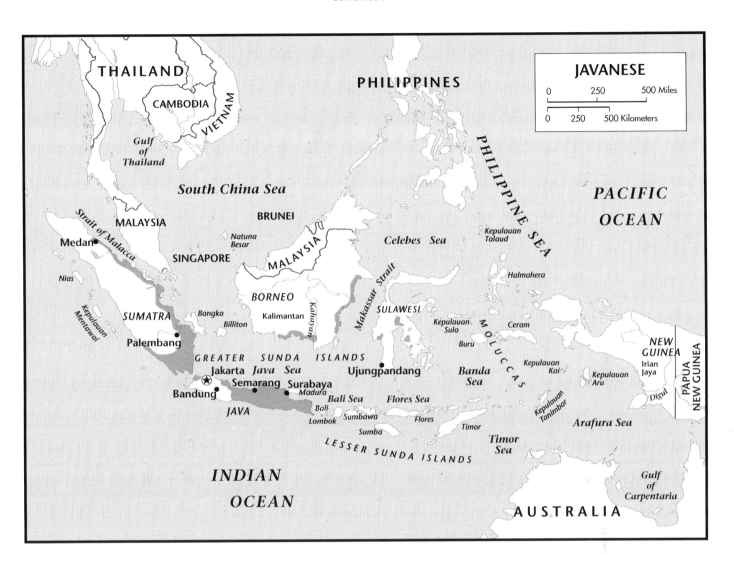

tral Java), Hindu-Buddhist Tenggerese, and the Balinese-influenced *tiyang Osing* of the eastern salient.

Migration from Java is a longstanding phenomenon. Javanese, from merchant princes to artisans and servants, filled 15th-century Malacca. Since the 19th century, the land scarcity attendant upon overpopulation has driven tens of thousands to emigrate, first as coolies, later as transmigrants, to the southern and eastern coasts of Sumatra, to Kalimantan, and to Sulawesi. For instance, Javanese comprise 62% of the population in Lampung province (on Sumatra across the Sunda Strait from Java), 32% in North Sumatra, 30% in East Kalimantan, and 12% in Papua; more than one in three residents of the national capital Jakarta is Javanese. Transmigration is in part responsible for the reduction in the proportion of Indonesia's population living on Java and Madura—from 68.5% in 1960 to 58.7% in 2005. In the late 19th century, different colonial powers imported Javanese labor (like Chinese and Indian) to work in Malaya, South Africa, Suriname, Curaçao, and New Caledonia. About 15% of Suriname's current population is Javanese. After more than a century, some of these communities retain their ancestor's language and culture.

³LANGUAGE

The Javanese language is Austronesian, most similar to neighboring Sundanese and Madurese (less so to Malay). It divides into several regional dialects. The people of Solo and Yogya regard their own speech as the most refined and view other dialects as corruptions (other Javanese often agree).

To a level comparable only to Japanese and Korean among major languages, every exchange in the Javanese language systematically defines the hierarchical relations between the speakers. A speaker must adjust his or her "speech level" according to the status of the person addressed, expecting the same courtesy in return. Although there are many fine gradations between them, there are basically two "speech levels": *ngoko* and *kromo*. *Ngoko* is the language in which a person thinks and, thus, is only appropriately used with people of equal status whom one knows intimately and with social inferiors. *Kromo* is spoken to older people, people of higher status, and those whose status relative to one is not yet known.

While the great majority of vocabulary items do not change between levels, the ones that do are the most common. Thus, the most basic sentences differ completely, e.g., "where [are you] coming from?" is *"Soko ngendi?"* in *ngoko* and *"Saking pundi?"* in *kromo*. "I cannot do [it]" translates as either *"Aku*

Two Indonesians ride a bicycle past an abandoned old Dutch-era building in Jakarta's Old Town, Jakarta, Indonesia.
(Dimas Ardian/Getty Images)

ora iso" or *"Kulo mboten saged."* Moreover, the very texture of the two levels contrasts: *ngoko* can sound rough, even harsh, and is very precise (as in numerous onomatopoeic words, such as *gregel,* "nervous to the point of quivering and dropping things"); *kromo,* on the other hand, is always spoken softly and slowly and is deliberately vague.

Mastering *kromo* is an acquired skill; in the past, peasants with little *kromo* kept silent in front of aristocrats or communicated to them through *kromo*-fluent intermediaries. Today, when unable to speak *kromo* or unwilling to elevate other people over themselves, all but the most uneducated and village-confined Javanese can avoid clearly insulting others by resorting to Indonesian (which takes on the character of a new *kromo*).

Although Islamo-Arabic names are common (e.g. Abdurrahman Wahid, the name of a recent Indonesian president), Javanese just as typically takes names of Sanskrit origin. Javanese do not use surnames and, as with Sukarno and Suharto, go only by a single personal name. Many Muslims combine Arabic and Sanskrit names, and the Christian minority generally combines Latin names with Sanskrit ones, e.g. the name of the head of the Roman Catholic Church in Indonesia, Yulius Riyadi Dharmaatmaja (Latin-Arabic-Sanskrit).

⁴FOLKLORE

Javanese recognize several classes of supernaturals. *Memedis* are frightening spirits, such as *sundal bolong* [*see* **Banjarese**] and the playful *gendruwo*. The latter appear to people as familiar relatives in order to abduct them, making them invisible; if the victim accepts food from the gendruwo, he or she will remain invisible forever. *Lelembut* are possessing spirits. *Tuyul* are spirit familiars one can enlist through fasting and meditation. *Demit* are the spirits of spooky spots, and *danyang* are the guardian spirits of villages, palaces, and other places. The greatest spirit is Ratu Kidul, the Queen of the South Sea, believed to be the mystical bride of Java's rulers; her favorite color is green, so young men should avoid wearing this color while at the Indian Ocean shore, otherwise, they may be pulled down into Ratu Kidul's underwater realm.

In the past, parents inculcated values in their children through tales from the *wayang* shadow play. The characters provided a wide range of personality types and behavioral models and anti-models: e.g., the pure king Yudistira who has a gambling problem; the refined Arjuna, the perfect warrior and lover; the mighty and irreverent Bima; and the headstrong Srikandi and the retiring Sumbadra, both female paragons. The more laughable human follies appear in the clown-servants (not part of the original Indian epic) Petruk, Gareng, Bagong, and their father Semar. The last is an ugly and rotund old man, who is actually the supreme god in disguise (as well as danyang of all Java). There are also two female clown-servants, the tall and thin Cangik and her short and fat daughter, Limbuk.

Another set of legendary figures are the *wali songo*, the nine holy men (variously of Arab, Egyptian, Persian, Uzbek, and Chinese origin) who brought Islam to Java (from Malacca, Champa, and the Middle East); they are credited with magical powers, such as flying and with developing ways to propagate Islam to the Javanese through their own cultural forms, such as Sunan Bonang who used Javanese sung poetry and the music of the Javanese gamelan orchestra to communicate Islamic teaching. To this day, their graves, located in cities all along Java's north coast, are popular sites of pilgrimage, especially those of Sunan Giri at Gresik near Surabaya, of Sunan Kudus in Kudus, and Sunan Gunung Jati in Cirebon. Another Muslim figure who attracts pilgrims to his shrine is the spirit of Sam Po Kong (Zheng He), the Yunnan-born admiral of the massive Ming Chinese fleets that made seven voyages to lands around the Indian Ocean in the early 15th century; both non-Muslim Chinese and Muslim Javanese visit his temple in Semarang, the great port on the north coast of Central Java.

⁵RELIGION

All but a fraction of Javanese are Muslim. However, only a portion regularly follow the "five pillars of Islam" and other practices of orthodox, Middle Eastern Islam; they have come to be called *santri*, a term originally referring only to those taking formal instruction from Islamic teachers. These "purist" Muslims divide further into conservatives, those who keep to orthodox Islam as it has been practiced in Java for centuries; and modernists, who reject local traditions and espouse a more scriptural faith supported by Western-style educational institutions. Both groups have strong organizations (once functioning as official political parties), Nahdatul Ulama and Muhammadiyah, respectively.

Non-santri Javanese Muslims, popularly termed *abangan* or *Islam kejawen,* revere Gusti Allah and Kangjeng Nabi ("the Venerable Prophet," Muhammad) but do not perform the five daily prayers, fast during the month of Ramadan, or go or want to go on the pilgrimage to Mecca. Their religious life focuses not on communal prayer in the mosque but on *slametan,* ritual meals held during rites of passage, village "spiritual cleansings" and harvest festivals, Islamic holidays, and special occasions, such as the inauguration of a new house or rites to protect an only child from the ogre Batara Kala *(ruwatan).* They also leave offerings, such as flowers, incense, coins, and rice cakes on a bamboo tray or banana leaf, for the spirits at crossroads, under bridges, in big trees, and elsewhere. They respect the spiritual potency *(kesakten)* residing in respected heirloom objects, such as gongs, *kris* swords, and royal carriages. Abangan believe paying homage to rulers and other exceptional people of the past at their tombs will confer spiritual and material benefits. These notions and practices are, however, widespread among santri as well. For example, conservatives regularly make pilgrimages to the graves of Islamic "saints" (legendary holy men), something modernists denounce as "idolatrous." Both abangan and santri consult *dukun,* diverse magical specialists, including spirit mediums, masseurs, acupuncturists, herbalists, midwives, sorcerers, and numerologists.

Fatalism suffuses much of Javanese thinking. One must be accepting *(nerimo),* have fortitude *(sabar),* and free oneself from emotions and desires to reach serenity *(ikhlas).* Earthly life is but a moment in eternity, the soul "stopping to have a drink" *(mampir ngombe).* Mystical practices, such as meditation in a secluded place, are common ways to accumulate spiritual power and a major preoccupation of the aristocracy. Explicitly distancing themselves from conventional Islam, numerous mystical sects command a considerable following and have sought unsuccessfully to have the government recognize their beliefs (called *kebatinan,* "innerness") as an official religion.

As much as 12% of the population of the island of Java (including Chinese and migrants from other islands) adhere to religions other than Islam. There are several hundred thousand Christians. Roman Catholics are particularly numerous; their church has used *gamelan* in the mass and taught biblical stories through *wayang,* and Javanese make the traditional sign of homage, palms placed together over the forehead, at the moment of Eucharistic consecration.

On the slopes of the east Javanese volcano Bromo live the Tenggerese, an archaic Javanese subgroup, who practice a folk religion derived from Majapahit Hinduism and highlighting the honoring of Joko Seger, Bromo's guardian spirit.

⁶MAJOR HOLIDAYS

Javanese combine the seven-day Islamic-Western week (Saturday to Friday: *Sabtu, Minggu, Senin, Selasa, Rebo, Kemis, Jum'at*) with a five-day indigenous week (*Legi, Paing, Pon, Wage, Kliwon*). Each day is identified by its place in both weeks (e.g., *Selasa Pon* or *Rebo Legi*), a conjunction that recurs every 35 days; birthdays, rituals, and performances are celebrated every time a particular day-pair returns.

The first day (beginning at sunset) of the Islamic year (1 Sura) is regarded as mystically charged. On this night, people stay up all night, watching processions, such as the *kirab pusaka* (parading the royal heirlooms) in Solo or meditating on mountains or beaches (one means of gaining spiritual potency is to stand in the cold water of a stream all night). The birthday of Muhammad (12 Mulud) is celebrated in Yogya and Solo by the holding of the Sekaten fair (the whole preceding week), the playing of ancient *gamelans* brought out only for the festival, and, on the day itself, a procession of three or more glutinous rice "mountains" ("male," "female," and "baby").

See also the article entitled **Indonesians**.

⁷RITES OF PASSAGE

Arranged marriages still occur in villages, but most people choose their own partners. The process begins with the man making a formal inquiry of the father or the *wali*, a paternal relative who can take a dead father's place, as to whether or not the woman is spoken for, followed later by the presentation of the gifts to the woman's side. On the night before the wedding (*midadareni*, when heavenly nymphs descend to bless the marriage), the woman's kin visit the graves of their ancestors to ask for their blessing, and the woman's kin, neighbors, and friends come for a *slametan* feast; the kin stay up all night, making palm-leaf decorations (*janur*). A *dukun manten* dresses and adorns the bride for the ceremony.

The wedding ceremony itself is the conclusion of the Islamic marriage contract between the groom and the bride's father or *wali.* The groom, with his party, proceeds to the bride's house, meets the bride, and is seated on the bridal dais. The groom's parents then arrive to the sound of the *gamelan* piece "Kebo Giro" (nowadays usually from a cassette). The couple bows *(sungkem)* to their parents and to other older relatives. The guests then eat and watch dancing by young female relatives of the couple. The groom can take the bride away only after five days; then, they can visit his kin and neighbors for a simpler reception *(ngunduh temanten).* Immediately after Indonesian independence, the move was to simplify wedding ceremonies, but under the New Order the trend reversed, with wealthy families displaying status through reviving the more elaborate traditional ceremonies (including rich costumes).

Javanese hold *slametan* for the repose of the deceased on the third, seventh, fortieth, 100th, and 1,000th day after death. On every Selasa Kliwon and Jum'at Kliwon, offerings (flower petals in a half-full water glass) are made to the spirits of the dead. On Ramadan, people go to strew flowers on the graves of their departed.

[8] INTERPERSONAL RELATIONS

In the old Javanese kingdoms, descendants of rulers formed the elite *(ningrat or priyayi).* During the colonial period, *priyayi* came to refer to all educated people, generally those employed in white-collar jobs, whatever their descent. This term distinguished them from the *wong cilik* ("little people"), peasants and laborers. *Ulama* (Islamic scholars), their students, and merchants formed a distinct *santri* elite of their own.

Peasants recognized their own hierarchy with *wong baku* (house-owners and the descendants of village founders) at the top, followed by *kuli gandok* (married men continuing to live with their parents) and *joko* or *sinoman* (unmarried men living with parents or others). Heading each village is a *lurah* (also called *petinggi, bekel,* or *glondong*), elected by the villagers, and receiving the right to use communal land to support himself and his staff. The villagers cooperate on common works, such as the construction and upkeep of roads, bridges, and public buildings, and the village spiritual *(bersih desa)* cleansing rites.

Javanese say of children who have not yet learned to control their emotions and to behave in a dignified and respectful way that they are *durung jawa,* "not yet Javanese." The ideal condition of the individual and society is an uneventful tranquility. Thus, Javanese avoid confrontation at all costs, reacting even to disturbing news with a resigned smile and soft words and never giving any request a direct refusal (Javanese are adept at giving and taking hints). In addition to polite speech, proper respect requires appropriate body language: bowing and slow, graceful movements.

[9] LIVING CONDITIONS

Javanese villages *(desa)* may cluster amid fields (in the highlands) or stretch out along roads (in the lowlands), the individual houses and yards enclosed by bamboo fences. Paths no wider than 2 m (6.5 ft) connect the *dukuh* (its various constituent hamlets). Each village has a *balai desa* (community meeting hall), several *langgar* (prayer halls) or a mosque, and a school. Entrance gates are seen everywhere, also defining city wards. There are open areas for a weekly market, stops for buses, and parking for minivans *(bemo, kol, daihatsu)* and pedicabs *(becak)* waiting for passengers.

Village houses sit on the ground and have earthen floors. They have a framework of bamboo, palm trunks, or teak; walls of plaited bamboo *(gedek),* wood planks, or bricks; and roofs of dried palm leaves *(blarak)* or tiles. Inside, rooms are made with movable gedek partitions. Traditional houses have no windows, light and air entering through chinks in the wall or holes in the roof. Roof shape was used to reflect social status. Ordinary villagers had a *serotong* roof with two slopes on two sides only. Descendants of the village founders possessed a *limasan* roof with a double slope on four sides. Marking an aristocratic house was the *joglo* roof with three slopes on four sides; such residences also had a large pavilion (pendopo) in front for receiving guests and petitioners.

Central Java has a Human Development Index (combining measures of income, health, and education) of 69.8 (2005 score), just above Indonesia' national HDI 69.6, while East Java's HDI's is significantly lower, 68.5 as is Banten's, 68.8. However, the Special Region of Yogyakarta (province-level status) had among the highest HDI's in the country, 73.5. Central Java's GDP per capita is us$6,293, relatively low for Indonesia (for instance, below West Sumatra's us$9,784 and North Sulawesi's us$8,360, though above East Nusa Tenggara's us$3,427). East Java's GDP per capita, however, is relatively high, us$ 11,090). The level of infant mortality (2000 figures) in East Java, 47.69 deaths out of 1,000 live births, is almost twice that in Jakarta; Central Java's figure is a little better, at 43.69, and Yogyakarta's is the same as the national capital's (compare all these with 88.55 for West Nusa Tenggara).

[10] FAMILY LIFE

The nuclear family *(kuluwarga* or *somah)* is the basic unit of Javanese society, including a couple, their unmarried children, and sometimes other relatives and married children and their families. Javanese recognize kin obligations on both the mother's and father's sides. Descendants of a common great-grandparent form a *golongan* or *sanak-sadulur,* whose members help each other hold major celebrations and gather on Islamic holidays. Larger still is the *alurwaris,* a kinship group directed towards the care of the graves of a common ancestor seven generations back; a descendant living in the village where the grave is located is responsible for mobilizing the scattered kin for this work.

Marriages between first cousins, especially the children of two brothers, and between a man of a younger generation than the woman's, are taboo. A married couple prefers to set up a separate household if they can afford to; otherwise, they usually move in with the wife's parents. Taking more than one wife is rare (kings and other aristocrats formerly kept harems). The divorce rate is high among village folk and poorer city folk; after divorce, children follow the mother or, if she marries again, they may go to live with other relatives. An inheritance may be divided through *perdamaian,* by deliberation among the children and close kin with the object of providing for those who have the least. The child who has remained in the family home to take care of the parents may also inherit the bulk of the property.

While Javanese mothers continue to provide direct emotional support to their children throughout life, fathers become more distant after children reach the age of four. They become the first "public authority" figures to whom individuals must be reserved and respectful. Although fathers are regarded as the heads of the house, the mother exercises more real control, being able, as a woman, to be more direct; the inevitable display of emotion would compromise a man's image of dignity, the source of his power. Two-thirds of Javanese are reported as speaking *kromo* (the language of respect) to their parents while greeting or asking for help, and half use *kromo* even during relaxed conversation with them.

While parents are supposed to be constantly correcting and advising their children, however old the child is, children never criticize or correct their parents except in the most indirect ways.

¹¹CLOTHING

For everyday wear, Javanese follow the Indonesian style of dress; men and women wearing sarongs in public are also common. Ceremonial clothing for men includes a sarong, high-collared shirt, jacket, and a *blangkon*, a head cloth wrapped to resemble a skullcap. Women wear the sarong, *kebaya* (long-sleeved blouse), *selendang* (sash over the shoulder), and *sanggul* (long hair in a thick, flat bun at the back, often achieved with a wig addition); handbags have become obligatory. One variation for both sexes is to wear a short sarong over pajama-like trousers (men add a high fez). Traditional dance costumes and wedding attire leave the chest bare for men and the shoulders bare for women.

¹²FOOD

Meals consist of rice and, at their simplest, stir-fried vegetables, dried salted fish, *tahu* (tofu), *tempe* (a bar of preserved whole soybeans), *krupuk* (fish or shrimp crackers), and *sambel* (chili sauce). Common dishes include *gado-gado* (a salad of parboiled vegetables eaten with a peanut sauce), *sayur lodeh* (a vegetable and coconut milk stew), *pergedel* (fat potato fritters), and *soto* (soup with chicken, noodle, and other ingredients). Regional specialties include Yogya's *gudeg* (chicken and young jackfruit stewed in coconut milk), Solo's *nasi liwet* (rice cooked in coconut milk), and *nasi rawon* (rice with a rich beef soup). Dishes of Chinese origin are very popular, such as *bakso* (meatball soup), *bakmi* (fried noodles), and *cap cay* (stir-fried meat and vegetables). Snack foods include crackers: *emping* (from the *mlinjo* nut) and *rempeyek* (from peanut). Common desserts are *gethuk* (cassava that is steamed, mashed, mixed with coconut milk and sugar, and colored pink, green, or white) and various glutinous rice preparations (*jenang, dodol, klepon,* and *wajik*). Javanese often buy prepared food from peddlers making the rounds of neighborhoods and enjoy *lesehan,* late-night dining on mats provided by sidewalk food vendors.

¹³EDUCATION

In 2005, the level of literacy in Central Java stood at 87.41%, in East Java at 85.84%, and in Yogykarta at 86.72%, low by Indonesian national standards (the national level is 90.4% according to 2004 figures) but comparable with other provinces with large numbers of poor, such as Bali and South Sulawesi (*see also the article entitled* **Indonesians** *in this volume*).

¹⁴CULTURAL HERITAGE

An integral part of traditional rituals, festivities, and theater, the classical Javanese orchestra (*gamelan*) consists of bronze gongs, keyed metallophones, drums, a flute, a spike-fiddle (*re-*

bab), and a zither (*celempung*), along with male and female vocalists. Making little use of recently invented notation systems, the music (either loud or soft styles) includes hundreds of named compositions (*gending*) in diverse forms. Street performers can also play *gamelan* music with a bamboo-tube gong and box-and-rubber-band zither. *Kroncong* ensembles can also interperet *langgam jawa,* folk and contemporary songs in the Javanese scale. Finally, there is also *pop* and *dangdut* in the Javanese language [*see* **Indonesians**].

Traditional dance emphasizes precise and measured control of the body, particularly in exquisitely graceful hand movements. Once confined to the palaces but now widely taught outside, the most revered dances are the *bedoyo* and *srimpi* in which young women enact unrecognizably stylized combat. Other female dances are the coquettish *golek* and *gambyong,* which are refinements of the dances of *taledek* or *ronggeng* (itinerant performers, generally regarded as little different from prostitutes). The latter consist of flirtation dances (*tayub*) in which the performer dances in front of a male audience, coaxing individual men to join her. Male dancing includes the *tari topeng* in which solo performers portray refined as well as violent characters from the Panji tales. A very common popular dance form (and mini-drama) is the trancelike *kuda lumping (jarang kepang),* which highlights hobby-horse dancers.

Although Javanese today use the Latin alphabet to write their language, some use is still made of *hanacaraka,* an Indian-derived script that can be traced back to the 8th century, and *pegon,* a modified Arabic script. Javanese literature goes back to the 11th century, beginning with adaptations in Kawi, the Old Javanese language, of the Hindu epics *Ramayana* and *Mahabharata.* By the 14th century, original masterpieces, such as the *Nagarkrtagama,* describing a royal tour of Majapahit, were being produced. The earliest surviving literature in modern Javanese (though still impossibly archaic to modern ears) dates from well into the Islamic period and includes *babad,* semi-mythical poetic chronicles, such as the *Babad Tanah Jawi* on Java's history. Once commonly heard, the singing of verse (*tembang macapat*) is a dying art. Novels and short stories are produced in Javanese but must compete with more widely marketable works in Indonesian.

¹⁵WORK

Some 60% of Javanese earn a living from agriculture, growing wet-rice and dry-field (*tegalan*) crops (cassava, maize, yams, peanuts, and soybeans); in mountain areas, many peasants engage in market gardening (vegetables and fruits, including temperate-zone species like carrots).

Traditionally, Javanese disdain manual labor and commercial occupations, preferring white-collar jobs and, most of all, aspiring to bureaucratic service. However, most nonfarming Javanese work as artisans or as petty traders (most of the latter are women). Although on Java, the bigger business owners tend to be Chinese or sometimes Arab, in much of the rest of Indonesia not only the civil servants and soldiers but also the merchants tend to be Javanese. With Indonesia's recent rapid economic development, more Javanese (especially young women from the villages) are taking factory or service jobs. Landlessness and underemployment have compelled many Javanese to take low-status work, such as being a maid, prostitute, beggar, street-peddler, *kenek* (fare-collector on a minivan or bus, usually young men or boys), "parking attendant" (men, usually old, who help people parallel park their cars on Java's crowded streets), or *ngamen* (street musicians who play on sidewalks or on buses between stops).

[16] SPORTS

See the article entitled **Indonesians**.

[17] ENTERTAINMENT AND RECREATION

On the whole, urban middle-class Javanese prefer to spend their leisure time enjoying the products of international and national pop culture rather than the traditional performing arts, which many have only glimpsed on television. Court circles (and those wishing to connect themselves to them, members of the new elite and the Indonesian state as a whole) and the peasantry (and by extension many of the urban poor), however, are still attached to the traditional performing arts

Java's master art form is the *wayang kulit* shadow-puppet play, an adjunct to life-passage ceremonies as well as either ritual or entertainment in itself. In it, a *dalang* manipulates flat, highly stylized puppets against a screen lit by a lamp or electric bulb over his head. Sitting from mid-evening until near daybreak without getting up, he speaks all the parts, intones narration, sings, and conducts the *gamelan* orchestra that provides background and accompaniment. Based on the Hindu epics *Mahabharata* and *Ramayana* and improvised within set frameworks, the plays encompass intrigues, romance, philosophizing, comic interludes, subtle social commentary, pitched combat, and heartbreaking tragedy. Watching either the puppets or their shadows, spectators are free to come and go according to their taste in scenes. Today, wayang is broadcast on the radio, blaring from open-air eateries, and people giving celebrations can play recorded wayang (several cassettes) to approximate the atmosphere.

The most traditional of Java's theater forms is *wayang orang,* which substitutes human actors or dancers for the puppets. Far more popular today is central Javanese *ketoprak,* which emphasizes spoken comedy and melodrama over music and dance and draws stories from Javanese history, Chinese, and Arab tales. Employing male performers for female as well as male parts, the east Javanese *ludruk* is even earthier and more contemporary.

[18] FOLK ART, CRAFTS, AND HOBBIES

Alongside *gamelan* and *wayang,* batik textiles are the signature art of Java. The intricate designs are created in several dyeings, with the space not to be dyed in a particular color covered with wax. The wax can be applied with copper stamps or, far more laboriously and beautifully, with a *canting* dipper. Batik styles differ radically between the *kejawen* (Yogya-Solo) and the *pesisir* (Pekalongan), the former emphasizing dense geometric patterns in brown, indigo, and white, while the latter prefer delicate floral patterns in red and other bright colors.

Other important or noteworthy crafts are leatherwork (wayang puppets), woodcarving (dance masks, furniture, and screens), pottery, glass-painting, and ironsmithing (*kris* swords).

[19] SOCIAL PROBLEMS

With the clearing long ago of the last virgin land, an equal inheritance system has meant that Javanese peasants must support themselves on small landholdings. Many lose their land altogether and must enter tenancy, sharecropping, or wage-labor arrangements with richer peasants who can afford fertilizers and some machinery. Customs, such as permitting the poorest to glean grains that remain in fields after reaping, are being abandoned. During the New Order period (1966-1998), the government pushed ahead with dams and other development projects despite the opposition of the peasants who would be displaced by them. Similarly, the military assisted industrialists in suppressing labor unrest in the factories multiplying in Java's crowded cities.

[20] GENDER ISSUES

Central Java's Gender-Related Development Index (combining measures of women's health, education, and income relative to men's) is 58.7, East Java's 56.3, and Banten's 54.9, significantly below Indonesia's national GDI of 59.2. Yogyakarta's, however, was higher, at 65.2, a little lower than Jakarta's. Gender Empowerment Measures (reflecting women's participation and power in political and economic life relative to men's) are 51 for Central Java, 54.9 for East Java, 48.6 for Banten, and 56.1 for Yogyakarta (cf. the national GEM of 54.6).

Javanese notions of gender difference are complex. Men, particularly priyayi (elite) men, on the one hand, are regarded as more capable of the emotional and behavioral self-control (including the intricacies of Javanese linguistic etiquette) so valued in Javanese culture, self-control that grants the individual the spiritual potency to attract the deference and submission of others without overt coercion. At the same time, men on the other hand are regarded as far less capable of controlling their desires, especially for sex and money, than women are, thus, for instance, making women more successful as traders in the marketplace and in financial matters in general (for this reason, husbands hand over most or all of their earnings to their wives who single-handedly manage the household). Javanese women have available to them contrasting, but equally legitimate, models for behavior, both a submissive and demure one (epitomized by Sumbadra, a wife of the wayang hero Arjuna) and an aggressive and bold one (epitomized by Srikandi, another of his wives). Differences between women and men are often described as a contrast between women as kasar (coarse) and men as halus (refined), and, yet, the male ideal (as represented by heroes like Arjuna) is characterized by the same grace and gentleness that the female ideal projects; both are the fruits of inner discipline and can in no way be confused with mere passivity.

[21] BIBLIOGRAPHY

Ayatrohaedi, et al. *Tatakrama di Beberapa Daerah di Indonesia* [Etiquette in Some Regions of Indonesia]. Jakarta: Department of Education and Culture, 1989.

Badan Pusat Statistik: *Statistik Indonesia.* http://demografi.bps.go.id (November 9, 2008).

Brenner, Suzanne. "Why Women Rule the Roost: Rethinking Javanese Ideologies of Gender and Self-Control." In *Bewitching Women, Pious Men: Gender and Politics in Southeast Asia*, edited by Aihwa Ong and Michael G. Peletz. Berkeley, CA: University of California Press, 1995.

Geertz, Clifford. *The Religion of Java.* Chicago: University of Chicago Press, 1960.

Hughes-Freeland, Felicia. "Performance and Gender in the Javanese Palace Tradition." In *"Male" and "Female" in Developing Southeast Asia*, edited by Wazir Jahan Karim. Oxford, UK: Berg, 1995.

Hutton, Peter. *Insight Guides: Java*. Hong Kong: APA Publications, 1993.

Keeler, Ward. *Javanese Shadow Plays, Javanese Selves*. Princeton: Princeton University Press, 1987.

Koentjaraningrat. *Javanese Culture*. Singapore: Oxford University Press, 1985.

Kodiran. "Kebudayaan Jawa." In *Manusia dan Kebudayaan di Indonesia* [Man and Culture in Indonesia], edited by Koentjaraningrat. Jakarta: Djambatan, 1975.

Kullanda, Sergey. "Nushântara or Java? The Acquisition of the Name." *Indonesia and the Malay World* Vol. 34, No. 98 (March 2006).

LeBar, Frank M., ed. *Ethnic Groups of Insular Southeast Asia*. Vol. 1, *Indonesia, Andaman Islands, and Madagascar*. New Haven, CT: Human Relations Area Files Press, 1972.

Oey, Eric, ed. *Java: Garden of the East*. Lincolnwood, IL: Passport Books, 1991.

Suyenaga, Joan. *Insight Pocket Guides: Yogyakarta*. Hong Kong: APA Publications, 1991.

—revised by A. J. Abalahin

JEWS OF COCHIN

PRONUNCIATION: Jews of KOH-chin
LOCATION: India (state of Kerala)
POPULATION: FEWER THAN 5 (2008 estimate)
LANGUAGE: Malayalam; Hebrew for religious purposes
RELIGION: Judaism

¹ INTRODUCTION

South Asia is home to several distinct communities of Jews. Some, such as the Baghdadi Jews, are relative latecomers, arriving in the late 18th century. They came mostly from Iraq, but also from Syria and Iran. They spoke Arabic and Persian, and reflected a continuation of Jewish interests in trade between the Middle East and South Asia. Baghdadi Jews settled mainly in the great port cities of the subcontinent. Two other Jewish communities, however, are of greater antiquity. The Bene Israel are descended from immigrants whose arrival is dated anywhere between 800 BC and AD 1300. They settled in the Konkan region around Bombay (Mumbai), spoke Marathi, and integrated with the local village populations. The other Jewish community of South Asia is found in Cochin in Kerala, on the Arabian coast of the Indian peninsula.

The Cochin Jews have differing traditions concerning the date of their arrival in India. One view suggests that Jewish merchants reached there during the reign of King Solomon (10th century BC) and took back ivory, monkeys, apes, and peacocks for his temple. Some Hebrew words for these objects appear to be derived from Sanskrit or Tamil. For example, the Hebrew for "ivory" is *shenhabbim,* or "elephant's tooth," a literal translation of the Sanskrit *ibhadanta*. Another account suggests the Cochin Jews were descendants of Jews taken captive by Nebuchadnezzar in the 6th century BC. The most likely theory, however, holds that the Jews reached the Malabar coast sometime in the 1st century AD, following the destruction of Jerusalem by the Romans.

The earliest certain reference to the Cochin Jews is found on the famous "Jewish copperplates" that are now in the care of the Paradeshi synagogue in Cochin. The Jewish community traditionally assigns them to AD 379, although recent scholarship dates them to around AD 1000. Written in Tamil and inscribed on sheets of copper, they record various privileges granted by the local ruler to Joseph Rabban, leader of the Cochin Jews and "proprietor of the Anjuvannam." This last name is taken to identify a trading corporation or a Jewish guild. The copperplates gave Joseph Rabban and his heirs numerous rights, including exemption from certain taxes and the right to collect tolls from boats and other vehicles.

The Cochin Jews existed as a thriving community until the middle of the 20th century. Deteriorating economic conditions in India after 1947, however, combined with the creation of a Jewish homeland in Palestine, led to the mass migration of Cochin Jews to Israel. In 1953–54, some 2,400 Cochin Jews—almost the entire population—left India, leaving only about 100 Jews behind. In Israel, Cochin Jews settled in several *moshavim* (agricultural settlements). Nevatim, Mesillat Zion, Ta'oz, Aviezer, and Kfar Yuval are still primarily Cochini in population. At first, adjustment to an agricultural life was difficult, but the Jews from Kerala soon prospered in Is-

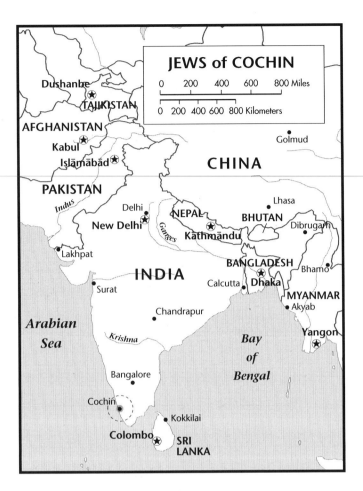

JEWS of COCHIN

0   200   400   600   800 Miles

0   200 400 600 800 Kilometers

people, and today, Jews have all but disappeared from Cochin (Kochi).

The Cochin Jews are traditionally divided into two castes. The "White" Jews (also called Paradeshi or "foreign" Jews) are descendants of immigrants who arrived from the Middle East and Europe from the 16th century on. The "Black" Jews, or Malabar Jews, are converts from the local population, or the offspring of marriages between the Jews and the local people ("Brown" Jews). Ironically, virtually all of the Black Jews emigrated to Israel, where their numbers are increasing. They continue to preserve the traditional religious customs they took with them from Cochin. The few White Jews who remained in India are rapidly disappearing as a community.

Cochin Jews live on the Malabar coast, the lush, fertile, tropical lowlands that lie along the shores of the Arabian Sea in India's southern state of Kerala. The coastal plains are well watered, with inland lagoons, backwaters, and canals forming a network of waterways that crisscross the area. Inland, the Western Ghats form a barrier to eastward movement, so Malabar has always looked west to the sea. The monsoon wind patterns across the Arabian Sea were "discovered" by the Greek Hippalus in the 2nd century BC, but must have been known to experienced navigators in the region long before this. Ships could sail from Africa to India on the southwest monsoon and return on the northeast monsoon. Known in ancient times for its spices (cinnamon, cardamom, ginger, and especially pepper), sandalwood, and teak, the Malabar coast has long attracted merchants and traders seeking to share in the country's riches. Arab, Greek, Roman, Portuguese, Dutch, French, and British are among the many peoples who have trod the shores of Malabar. The Jews of Cochin are one of these communities that stayed and made India its home.

³ LANGUAGE

The Cochin Jews speak Malayalam, the Dravidian language that is the native tongue of the peoples of Kerala. Hebrew is used for religious purposes.

⁴ FOLKLORE

A series of 10 paintings were commissioned for the celebrations in 1968 of the 400th anniversary of the founding of the Cochin synagogue. In essence, they are a record of the myths, legends, and history of the Jews of Cochin. The first painting shows a bazaar filled with spices and ivory, a trading port of the ancient world. It is the Jews' ancestral home in Kerala, known to them as Shingly and actually the modern port of Cranganur. It establishes a link between the Jews of India and the splendor of King Solomon's Palestine. The next 3 paintings capture the birth of the Cochin Jewish community—Herod's Temple ablaze in AD 70, a ship full of Biblical-looking Jews about to land at Shingly, and the Raja of Cranganur waiting to greet them. The fifth painting shows Joseph Rabban receiving the "Jewish copperplates" from the Maharaja of Cochin.

The sixth painting addresses internal strife in the Jewish community. According to tradition, two of the original silver trumpets used in the Second Temple at Jerusalem had been brought to Shingly. They were blown by Levites on the eve of the Sabbath. On one occasion the Levites were late, and non-Levites blew the trumpets. In the ensuing quarrel the trumpets were destroyed. This may well be an allegory for the loss of Shingly as a result of internal conflict among the Jews and

rael, Nevatim even constructing its synagogue in the Keralan style. But Cochinis, originally being part of the Sephardic diaspora, stated that they could more easily follow their religion in India than in Ashkenazi-dominated Israel. This view was also expressed by Jews who remained behind in India, even though dwindling numbers have precluded them from holding daily prayers and more recently, most Shabbat services, in the synagogue. Although exact numbers are not available, it is estimated some 4,000 Cochinim live in Israel today. Cochini neighborhoods are found in Rishon LeZion, Ashdod, Beersheba, and Jerusalem, and in some of these neighborhoods there are synagogues in which the traditional Cochin liturgy is followed. Cochin Jews in Israel get together to celebrate Simhat Torah and other holidays that are Cochini in character. Some feel that even though the Jewish community in Cochin is disappearing, the Cochini community is thriving in Israel.

In Kerala, the 2001 Census estimated around 8,000 Jews in the population, but this included "Black" and "Brown" Jews, as well as "White" Jews. The ancient Jewish community of Cochin, the "White" Jews, has all but died out today, with at most five members of the community left.

² LOCATION AND HOMELAND

In 1948, there were about 2,500 members of the Jewish community of Cochin. They lived mainly in coastal towns, such as Ernakulam, Mallah, Mattancheri, and Parur. Jews in the city of Cochin, the so-called "White Jews," lived in an area called "Jew Town." By the early 1990s, the population had fallen to 22

Rabbi Leah Novick, leader of the Jewish Renewal Movement, lights a traditional lamp as part of the inauguration ceremony of an Interfaith Conference at the venue of the Amritavarsham 50 festival in Cochin. (AFP/Getty Images)

the move of some of the Jewish community to Cochin. The remaining paintings show the building of the Cochin synagogue, the sack of Shingly by the Portuguese in 1524, and various audiences between the Jews and the Cochin *Maharajas*.

5 RELIGION

The religious beliefs of the Jews of Cochin conform in every way with the norms of the Jewish faith as set out in the *Halakha* or Jewish Legal Code. They accept the concept of one true deity, Yahweh, whose will is revealed in the Torah, and who exists in a special relationship with his "chosen people." They observe the Sabbath, worship in synagogues, and observe the Jewish dietary codes. The community maintained its Jewish identity through frequent contact with the main centers of Judaism over the centuries. However, the Cochin Jews adopted certain features of local society that make them as much Indian as Jewish. At least one of these traits, the acceptance of a caste structure, violates and even defies the standards of the Halakha.

The life of the Cochin Jews centers around their synagogues. Each synagogue—known in Malayalam as *Juta-palli*, "gather-

ing-place for Jewish worship"—has three functions. It is a legal body that owns common property; it is the place where the Beit Din, the religious authority in matters of marriage, inheritance, etc., is convened; and it is a place of worship. The Cochin Jews have no rabbis; each synagogue is run by the elders of the community. Each community has its cantor, scribe, Hebrew teacher, and ritual slaughterer.

6 MAJOR HOLIDAYS

The Cochin Jews observe all the festivals of the Jewish calendar, from Rosh Hashanah (the New Year) to Tisha be-Av (the Fast of Av). However, in Cochin there are festivals that are found only in India, or that are celebrated in a manner unique to the country. Simchat Kohen, for example, is a little-known Sephardic holiday that may be kept only in India. It is explained as a celebratory feast of the priests *(kohanim)* at the time of the Temple after their arduous ritual activities of Kippur. It is the custom of the Cochin kohanim to host a party for their friends on the day after Kippur. In days past, when the Jewish community was at full strength, Simchat Torah, a non-Biblical celebration of the end of the yearly cycle of Torah reading and the beginning of the new cycle, was celebrated with great style. Perhaps one of the most distinctive Jewish celebrations in Cochin, Simchat Torah was observed by one Sassoon Hallegua in a unique way. People recall he mixed up a "milk punch," which, of course, was not milk at all but arrack and a mixture of other spirits. Then, early in the morning of the day of Simchat Torah, he would visit his friends on Synagogue Lane, insisting they partake of the "punch."

For the Cochin Jews, Passover or *Pesah* has the usual Jewish meaning, i.e., the celebration of the Exodus from Egypt. Jews in Cochin would also incur great expense at this time in the annual repainting or whitewashing of their homes, the stripping and repolishing of their furniture and draining and scrubbing of their wells and water tanks. However, Pesah also has meaning in the context of the community's integration into broader Indian society. Passover practices throughout the Jewish world involve avoiding leaven (any substance such as yeast that causes dough to rise). But Cochin customs concerning food taboos and ritual concerns for purity at this time go far beyond normal Jewish practices. This has been interpreted as a Jewish co-option of Indian concerns for caste status. By displaying the same restrictive dietary practices as high-caste Hindus, the Cochin Jews periodically reassert their high-caste status in the local community.

7 RITES OF PASSAGE

Birth rituals of the Jews of Cochin are the same as for any Jewish community. A male undergoes circumcision and passes through the usual stages in the life of a young Jewish boy. His education begins at the age of 3. His first public reading takes place at the age of 5 or 6, unlike in most Jewish communities where this occurs at the boy's *bar mitzvah* around 13 years of age. This provides another example of the role of South Indian belief and custom in the life of the Cochin Jews. In Hindu thought, 5 years is a complete cycle and by this age a child is seen to have passed infancy and the dangers associated with it. The *bar mitzvah* (known in Cochin as the *bar minyan*) and ordination as a lay cantor complete the rituals of childhood.

Burial practices among the Cochin Jews closely follow those of the Middle Eastern Sephardic community. The body is washed and dressed in fine clothes, and lit candles are placed around it. Members of the family gather for the funeral, which takes place within a few hours. After a second washing, bits of earth from Jerusalem and Cranganur (Shingly) are placed in the eyes and mouth of the corpse. The body is then dressed in a white linen shroud, sprinkled with rose water, and placed in a wooden coffin. The coffin is carried to the cemetery, to the accompaniment of dirges and Psalm 91. Following the burial, the family begins a seven-day period of mourning called *sheva*.

8 INTERPERSONAL RELATIONS

Cochin Jews use typical Jewish greetings (e.g., "Shalom") among themselves, and Malayalam forms in their dealings with others.

9 LIVING CONDITIONS

Cochin Jews are urban-dwellers, often residing together in a particular neighborhood near their synagogue. In Cochin's Jew Town, the Paradeshi synagogue lies at the end of a narrow cul-de-sac known as Synagogue Lane. The street is lined with large, Dutch-style colonial homes, a throwback to medieval times. At one time, higher-class White Jews lived at the end of the street closest to the synagogue, while the socially inferior Malabar or Black Jews had their homes at the other end. Today, most of these building are no longer occupied by Jews but are used as warehouses or for other purposes.

10 FAMILY LIFE

The system of local observances (*minhag*) of the Cochin Jews contains many borrowings from their Hindu neighbors. Like most of the other non-Hindu communities that have survived for any length of time in India, the Cochin Jews evolved a social structure that mirrors the caste system of Hinduism. The White Jews and Black Jews function very much like castes—they do not enter each other's synagogues, they do not interdine, and they do not intermarry. Even the subgroups that exist within the White and Black Jews, the *meyuschasim* (the "privileged") and non-*meyuschasim* ("non-privileged") do not intermarry. There are separate cemeteries for White and Black Jews.

Marriage is perhaps the most important social occasion for the Cochin Jews. In the past, marriages were arranged, with the typical South Indian pattern of cross-cousin marriage being favored. The actual marriage ceremony follows the Jewish rite, but the celebrations accompanying marriage show a definite Hindu influence. This ranges from the lavish scale of the event (in the past, it often involved the entire Jewish community and lasted as long as 15 days) to the singing of traditional Malayalam wedding songs by women. The Jewish tradition of smashing a glass is conspicuous by its absence, the bridal couple having ashes smeared on their forehead instead. This is interpreted as a sign of mourning for the Temple, but it also mirrors the Hindu custom of wearing sacred ash on the forehead. The Cochin wedding, an occasion for much joy, revelry, singing, dancing, feasting, and drinking, continues for a week.

11 CLOTHING

Everyday dress for both men and women is the *mundu,* a long piece of cloth wrapped around the waist and reaching to the ankles. Men put on a shirt with this, while women wear a blouse or jacket. For festive occasions, women wear colorful and elaborately embroidered mundus, often of silk and worked with silver or gold thread. In the synagogue, men wear prayer shawls and skullcaps (*yarmulkas*) known in Cochin as *kippa*. Western-style dress is commonly worn by men, and women may adopt the Indian *sari* for formal occasions.

12 FOOD

Cochin Jews observe the normal Jewish dietary taboos, avoiding pork and eating kosher foods. Otherwise, they are nonvegetarian, eating meat, poultry, and fish (to ensure such food is kosher, however, it is eaten only in the home or at community gatherings). The food is prepared in curries and eaten with seasonal vegetables and dishes such as yellow rice and *biryani* (rice mixed with meat or vegetables). Fish, a symbol of fertility, is often served at wedding banquets. Sweet dishes and fruits such as pineapples, bananas, guavas, melons, and pomegranates complete the meal. Cutlery and napkins may be placed on the table before a meal, but they are removed before the meal starts. The diners eat with their hands, as is the local custom. *Arrack* (a local liquor), beer, rum, brandy, and whiskey are popular drinks, especially on festive occasions.

There are many special foods prepared for ritual occasions. Specialties at Rosh Hashanah, for example, include rich "wedding cakes" and baked goods made from semolina. *Massa* (matzoh) is prepared at Passover. *Pastels,* a pastry filled with chicken or egg, are a special Sabbath treat. Eggs, a symbol of rebirth, are eaten at the feast celebrating the rite of circumcision, as well as during the period of mourning following a death.

13 EDUCATION

Education was always part of the Jewish tradition in Kerala. Girls as well as boys were registered in Jewish schools in Cochin as early as 1821, and most leaned English as a second language.

Children become proficient in Hebrew at an early age, taught by a Hebrew teacher supported by the community. In general, Cochin Jews are open to secular education and take advantage of the opportunities available to them. Literacy among the community is high, and in modern times many individuals have obtained university degrees or professional qualifications.

14 CULTURAL HERITAGE

The heritage of Cochin Jews reflects a unique blend of Jewish tradition and Indian culture. The community's memories and legends, tales of antique origins, and symbolic identification with the ancient Jewish homeland are combined with customs that clearly assign the Jews the status of a high caste in Keralan society. This is exemplified by the theme of royalty that underlies the Jew Town wedding observances, a theme that is borrowed from the Hindus. Certain unique Hebrew prayers and hymns, known as "Shingly tunes," hark back to the community's early home and perhaps even to Mesopotamia. At the same time, folk songs are sung in Malayalam at weddings and other festive occasions. It is in large part their adaptation to local society that has allowed the Cochin Jews to maintain their identity for almost 2,000 years. It is also the longstanding memory of the community's origins that has led to their emigration to Israel.

Some community elders privately hold the view that the "curse" of Jew Town is responsible for the exodus of Jews from Cochin. After all, they argue, with no experience of ill-will or persecution in India, what else can explain the Jews' departure from the land they loved?

Cochin Jews adopted many Hindu practices, yet scrupulously ensured that their religious patterns did not violate any Jewish legal or ethical principles. In doing so, they did what Jews around the world have done—adapted to their cultural milieu while maintaining a distinct identity. Some of their customs, such as dietary codes, the existence of a sacred language, concern for family purity and the avoidance of menstruating women, are found in both the Hindu and Jewish tradition, but some customs have clearly been borrowed from the Nambudiris, Kerala's Brahman caste. Jew Town mimics the various "Brahman Towns" found in Kerala, with houses aligned in a particular way and the houses interconnected on the second story. Jews, like the Nambuduris, placed great emphasis on purity of descent, the corporate identity of the community and the importance of networks.

15 WORK

Many Cochin Jews engage in trade, keeping small shops in front of their houses and selling foodstuffs, dry goods, and other wares. Some work as artisans—carpenters, masons, and the like. A few have become successful and prosperous merchants. During the early decades of the 20th century, for example, the Koder family emerged as the owners of a leading business house, providing employment for a considerable number of Cochin Jews. They also were one of the leading families in the Jewish community.

16 SPORTS

A unique custom of Tisha be-Av is a board game for men, played with colored cowry shells. Known as "the royal game of Ur," it is believed to date to the Babylonian captivity.

17 ENTERTAINMENT AND RECREATION

The social life of the Cochin Jews centers on their synagogues and on the celebrations accompanying religious festivals and life-cycle events.

18 FOLK ART, CRAFTS, AND HOBBIES

There are no arts, crafts, or hobbies found specifically among the Cochin Jews.

19 SOCIAL PROBLEMS

The Cochin Jews, like other foreign communities in Kerala, were received cordially by the local *rajas*. They enjoyed royal patronage and lived as a high-caste community among the local people. There is no record of anti-Semitism in their relations with their Hindu neighbors. However, internal differences between White and Black Jews often led to discord and bitter disputes within the community. Though never very numerous, the Cochin Jewish community has existed in India for nearly 2,000 years. Mass emigration to Israel, however, has reduced the numbers of the "White" Jews to a handful of elderly people. It is doubtful that the community will survive long into the 21st century.

20 GENDER ISSUES

The major problem with the White Jew community of Cochin is one of numbers rather than of gender. The community has sunk below the population level that makes it viable. In the recent past, an issue for females has clearly been finding suitable husbands within the community with the result that women have been marrying local Indian males and leaving the Jewish community for others. The remaining few (less than five) people are quite elderly and are mainly women, so one suspects that the White Jews, despite their long and storied history in Kerala, will be extinct within the next few years. Jew Town and the Jewish synagogue in Cochin will become just another tourist attraction.

21 BIBLIOGRAPHY

Blady, Ken. *Jewish Communities in Exotic Places*. Northvale, N.J.: Jason Aronson, 2000.

Katz, Nathan. *Kashrut, Caste, and Kabbalah: The Religious Life of the Jews of Cochin*. New Delhi: Manohar Publishers, 2005.

———, ed. *Studies of Indian Jewish Identity*. New Delhi: Manohar Publishers, 2004.

Katz, Nathan, and Ellen S. Goldberg. *The Last Jews of Cochin: Jewish Identity in Hindu India*. Columbia, SC: University of South Carolina Press, 1993.

Segal, J. B. *A History of the Jews of Cochin*. London: Valentine Mitchell, 1993.

Timberg, Thomas A., ed. *Jews in India*. New York: Advent Books, 1986.

—by D. O. Lodrick

JORDANIANS

PRONUNCIATION: jawr-DAY-nee-uhns
LOCATION: Jordan
POPULATION: 6.1 million
LANGUAGE: Arabic; English
RELIGION: Islam (majority Sunni Muslim)

¹ INTRODUCTION

The land of Jordan lies along an ancient and well-used trade route, making it very valuable geographically. Many powers have ruled the land, under many different names. The modern Hashemite Kingdom of Jordan, however, was established relatively recently, on 25 May 1946, when it finally reached full independence and King Abdullah Hussein, of the Hashemite line descended from the prophet Muhammad, took the throne. The current King Abdulla is Abdullah's great grandson and has reigned since his father's death in 1999. His father King Hussein's rule lasted 46 years and began when he was barely 18 years old. King Hussein survived many near-disasters and threats to his rule to create a fairly stable, growing nation based on a constitutional monarchy with a democratically elected parliament. Both King Hussein and King Abdulla have pushed for further strides toward democracy because they know that long-term stability and progress for Jordan depend on the participation of its people, not on military strength, foreign aid, or the personal and political contacts of its monarch.

² LOCATION AND HOMELAND

Jordan is located on the East Bank of the Jordan River, with the Palestinians as its neighbors on the West Bank. South of the West Bank, Jordan shares a border with Israel. To the north lies Syria, and to the east and south lies Saudi Arabia. Iraq shares a northeastern border with Jordan. Jordan has three distinct natural zones: the Jordan River valley, which is green and fertile; mountainous regions in the north and south, which have a cool, Mediterranean climate; and the main bulk of the country, which is an arid desert. Among the 6 million people who populate Jordan, there is a centuries-old distinction between the peoples of the desert (descended from fiercely independent desert tribes who strictly controlled and protected their territories) and the people who live in the Jordan River valley, the "valley people" (taller and more heavily built than the desert people, believed to be descended from the ancient Canaanites with a blending of other cultures). The desert people are believed to be "pure" lineage, thought to be indistinguishable from the desert populations of Syria and Saudi Arabia. This difference of "blended" versus "pure" extends also to the local national culture: the valley people have absorbed aspects of the surrounding cultures, whereas the desert people have remained firmly committed to their own traditions. Those considered the "truest" Jordanians are the Bedouins (*see Bedu*), the nomadic sheep and goat herders of the desert, who are regarded as Jordan's indigenous people. In addition to this native Jordanian segment of the population, there is a large population of Palestinians in Jordan. Tens of thousands of Palestinian refugees were either forcibly exiled or fled to Jordan following the establishment of the state of Israel in 1948, during the ensuing war and again following the Israel annexation of the

West Bank in 1967. They lived in tent camps that were eventually replaced by homes of galvanized steel, aluminum, and asbestos. Most of the refugee camps are located in northwestern Jordan near major cities.

The land of Jordan was not always so arid, but serious deforestation has led to desertification. During the 7th century AD, the Omayyad caliphs (who ruled from 638–658) built castles in the midst of the forest as big-game hunting lodges. Now, those castles stand in barren desert. The severe water shortage became even worse after a drought of the 1970s. Surface water, wells, and streams are extremely scarce. A new environmental awareness is beginning to take hold in Jordan, and it has declared a National Environment Strategy, the first Middle East country to do so. The Royal Society for the Conservation of Nature puts a high priority on reforestation and saving what woodlands are left, and a severe shortage of water has led to urgent studies on water conservation and preservation. Jordan has also played a key part in saving the Arabian oryx from extinction through a program of captive breeding and reintroduction to the wild.

³ LANGUAGE

The official and most commonly spoken language of Jordan is Arabic, a language spoken by up to 422 million people worldwide, both as native and non-native speakers. Arabic has many distinct dialects, so that people living as few as 500 km (about 310 mi) apart may not be able to entirely understand one another. The written form of Arabic is called Classical Arabic, or, for today's literature and press, Modern Standard Arabic. It is the same for all literate Arabs, regardless of how different their spoken dialects are. Arabic is written from right to left in a unique alphabet that makes no distinction between capital and lower-case letters. It is not necessary for the letters to be written in a straight line, as English letters must be. Punctuation rules are also quite different from those of English.

Many Jordanians also speak English. "Hello" in Arabic is "*marhaba*" or "*ahlan,*" to which one replies, "*marhabtayn*" or "*ahlayn.*" Other common greetings are "*As-salam alaykum*" ("Peace be with you"), with the reply of "*Walaykum as-salam*" ("and to you peace"). "*Ma'assalama*" means "Goodbye." "Thank you" is "*Shukran,*" and "You're welcome" is "*Afwan.*" "Yes" is "*na'am*" and "no" is "*la'a.*" The numbers one to ten in Arabic are: *wahad, itnin, talata, arba'a, khamsa, sitta, saba'a, tamania, tisa'a,* and *ashara.*

Common names for boys are *Talal, Muhammad,* and *'Abdullah.* Common names for girls are: *Fadwa, Leila, Fatima, Noor,* and *Reem.* The queen's name is *Rania.*

⁴ FOLKLORE

Jordanians are superstitious people and firm believers in fate and omens. When someone is sick or injured, it may be attributed to *ghire* (jealousy) and *hassad* (envy). "Coffee ladies" read fortunes in the dregs of a cup of coffee, and to ward off the "evil eye," incense is burned, a lamb is offered to the poor, and a blue eye-shaped amulet medallion is worn around the neck. This is also common to many Middle Eastern cultures. To fend off hassad, some families guard their homes by stamping the exterior walls or doors with a palm of lamb blood.

Jordanian folk tales, particularly those of the Bedouin (Bedu), often feature themes of honor, generosity, and hospitality, all considered important Arab attributes. One folk story

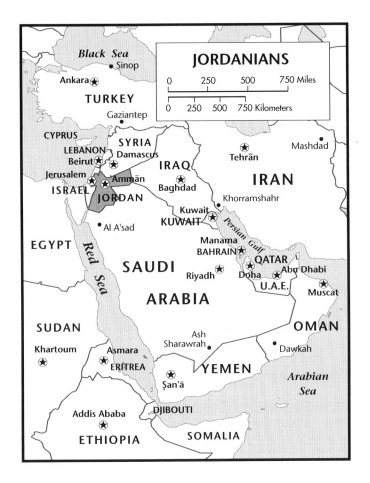

Islam is the youngest of the world's main monotheist religions, having begun in the early seventh century AD when the prophet Muhammad received his revelations from Allah, the one true God (according to Islam). Within just a few years of Muhammad's death in AD 632, Islam had spread throughout the entire Middle East, gaining converts at a dynamic rate.

Born into the Koreish tribe of Mecca (c. AD 570), Muhammad was later driven from the city because of his outspoken denunciation of the pagan idols worshipped there (idols that attracted a lucrative pilgrim trade). The year of Muhammad's flight from Mecca, called the *Hegira*, is counted as Year One in the Muslim calendar. Eventually, Muhammad returned to Mecca as a triumphant religious and political leader, destroyed the idols (saving the Black Stone, an ancient meteorite housed in the *Kaaba*, or Cube, building, which has become a focal point of Muslim worship), and established Mecca as the spiritual center of Islam. All prayers are said facing Mecca, and each Muslim is expected, and greatly desires, to make a pilgrimage there (called a *Haj* or *Hadj*) at least once in his or her lifetime.

Islam is a simple, straightforward faith with clear rules for correct living. It is a total way of life, inseparable from the rest of one's daily concerns. Therefore, religion and politics and faith and culture, are one and the same for Muslims. There is no such thing as the "separation of church and state" or any distinction between private religious values and public cultural norms in an Islamic country such as Jordan. The Hashemite family of King Hussein traces its descent from the prophet Muhammad himself and, in the Muslim mind, it is this lineage that makes the Hashemites qualified to rule.

The lack of separation of religion and politics is exemplified by the recent inclusion of the Muslim Brotherhood party in parliamentary elections. The Brotherhood wishes to see more Islamic legislation enacted in Jordan. Members of the party have won parliamentary seats and have been placed in political positions within which they can influence national policy on education and social matters.

6 MAJOR HOLIDAYS

Friday is the Islamic day of rest, so most businesses and services are closed on Fridays. Muslim holidays follow the lunar calendar, moving back 11 days each year, so their dates are not fixed on the standard Gregorian calendar. The main Muslim holidays are: *Ramadan*, the ninth month of the Muslim year, during which Muhammad received his first revelations, celebrated by complete fasting from dawn until dusk each day of the entire month; *Ayd Al-Fitr*, a three-day festival at the end of *Ramadan*; *Ayd Al-Adha*, a three-day feast of sacrifice at the end of the month of pilgrimage to Mecca (known as the *Haj*)—families who can afford it slaughter a lamb and share the meat with poorer Muslims; the First of *Muharram*, or the Muslim New Year; *Mawoulid An-Nabawi*, the prophet Muhammad's birthday; and *Ayd Al-Isra wa Al-Miraj*, a feast celebrating the nocturnal visit of Muhammad to heaven.

Fixed public holidays in Jordan include the secular New Year on January 1, Tree Day (January 15), Arab League Day (March 22), Labor Day (May 1), Independence Day (May 25), Arab Renaissance Day (commemorating the Arab Revolt) and Army Day (both on June 10), King Hussein's accession to the throne (August 11); King Hussein's birthday (November 14); and Christmas (December 25).

revolves around the legendary Hatim al-Ta'i, whose name is synonymous with generosity. Before Hatim's birth, when his mother was newly married, she dreamt that she was offered a choice: She could either bear ten brave sons or she could have one son, Hatim, who would possess superior generosity. She chose to have Hatim, and indeed he proved to be highly generous. When Hatim was sent to take the family's camels to pasture, Hatim proudly returned to tell his dismayed father that he had given away every one of the camels, and that this no doubt would bring fame to the family name. This story typifies the importance that Jordanians place on generosity.

There are several dances and musical genres specific to Jordan, most of which are adaptations of the *dabke* (a group line dance that involves stomping and jumping in unison) and various tribal dance sequences that incorporate the sword. The bagpipe has quickly become a symbol of the Jordanian army's regalia and is often played at ceremonies to indigenous and folkloric tunes.

Also much of the Jordanian folklore of the past several decades has been greatly influenced by the large Palestinian population in the country.

5 RELIGION

More than 90% of Jordanians are Sunni Muslim, the majority sect of Islam, whose followers believe that the caliph (ruler) must be a member of the Koreish, the tribe of Muhammad. The remaining minority belong to a wide range of Muslim and Christian sects.

Members of the camel corps stand in front of the archaeological site of Petra in Arabah, Jordan. Petra has been a World Heritage Site since 1985 and was named in 2007 as one of the New Seven Wonders of the World by the New Open World Corporation. (Tim Graham/Getty Images)

7 RITES OF PASSAGE

Weddings are the most important event in a Jordanian's lifetime, and the cost of the celebration is second only to that of buying a home. The guest list can number anywhere from 200 to 2,000 people. Even though social and religious customs encourage people to marry when they are in their 20s, many men from middle- and low-income families must wait until they are in their 30s because they cannot afford the cost of a wedding until then. Births are also joyfully celebrated, with the mother's family providing the child's first wardrobe and furniture. The circumcision of males used to be part of the rite of passage into adulthood, performed by a local barber when a boy was 13 years old, followed by a huge party. Now, it is usually done in a hospital shortly after birth.

The *aza*, or condolence period, following a death is a very important ritual in Jordanian society. It is essential to attend the *aza* of a neighbor or colleague, or even the relative of a neighbor or colleague. During the *aza*, men and women sit in separate rooms in the house of the deceased or a mosque and drink black, unsweetened Arabic coffee. For 40 days after the death, the *aza* is reopened every Monday and Thursday at the deceased's home. Jordanians wear black for mourning, contrary to the Islamic custom of white or beige.

8 INTERPERSONAL RELATIONS

Jordanians may appear to foreigners as introverted and conservative, yet they are extremely hospitable. *Marhaba* and *Ahlan wa-sahlan*, words for "welcome," are a constant refrain. When invited to a Jordanian home, a guest is not expected to bring a house gift. In personal encounters, Jordanians are formal and polite. Saltis (people from the city of Salt) are the frequent butt of jokes because of their unique mannerisms, as are the people of Tafilie, who have a similar reputation.

9 LIVING CONDITIONS

Before 1979, few houses had piped water. Most houses have home storage tanks and rely on water deliveries by truck. Because of a severe water shortage, rationing is in effect. A major water and sewage improvement project was initiated in 1979 with an emphasis on long-term needs.

Today, Jordan has a good highway network. Most roads are paved, and international roadways connect Jordan to Iraq, Syria, and Saudi Arabia. Bridges connect Jordan with the West Bank. Most Jordanians live in stone masonry houses called "villas" or cement-based apartments. Most of the villas are modest in appearance, but many are large and luxurious and reflect the wealth of their owners. Hotels, including Marriott and Sheraton, are plentiful throughout Jordan, catering to the tourists who come to see the Dead Sea, Petra (Biblical Sela that is now one of the modern world wonders), and the Gulf of al-'Aqaba on the Red Sea, and to ease their aches and pains in the spas and springs of the Ma'in Spa Village resort area, located southwest of Amman.

Although it is a relatively young country, Jordan has managed to develop quickly into a technological society with decent housing, excellent roadways, efficient postal and communications services, and good health care. About 70% of Jordanians live in urban areas, most of them in the capital city of Amman (considered one of the cleanest and most efficient cities of the Arab world). Jordan is among the top 10 countries of the world in reducing infant mortality, and life expectancies are fairly high: 67 years for men and 71 years for women.

However, unemployment and poverty are widespread problems, and many Jordanians must struggle for a living. Because of the difficulty in finding employment in Jordan, particularly for skilled workers, many Jordanians go abroad in search of work. The majority go to the Gulf oil states, whose small populations require them to import laborers from neighboring states. Working in the Gulf allows Jordanians to earn steady incomes, which are sent in the form of remittances to family members in Jordan, thus helping the Jordanian economy. Similarly, Jordan allows laborers from neighboring states such as Egypt, to seek employment in Jordan. It has been found that the income derived from remittances sent to Jordan far exceeds that sent out by foreign workers; thus, the exchange has been favorable for Jordan. Jordan is a technologically advanced country.

¹⁰ FAMILY LIFE

Family values are of top priority to Jordanians, leading to a strict moral code that ensures a low crime rate. Prostitution is illegal (and the law is strongly enforced), public drunkenness is not tolerated, gambling is illegal, and even belly dancing is restricted to a few large hotels. Very few nightclubs exist, and a "good family" would never allow a daughter to marry a man seen frequenting them. Marriages usually result from family introductions, if not outright matches, but couples are almost never forced to marry against their will. Upper-middle-class couples court each other in the Western style. Suitable brides and grooms must be from proper families with a respectable lineage, have decent wealth and education, be of the same religion, and never have been married before. Brides also must be "virtuous" (never had sexual intercourse), although this restriction may not apply as rigorously to the grooms. Less than 1% of marriages today are polygamous, largely because of the prohibitive cost of weddings.

One out of five marriages ends in divorce, and divorced women are faced with the uphill battle of combating the stigma of a failed marriage to go into wedlock again. The average Jordanian family has seven children, giving Jordan one of the highest birth rates in the world. Because sons are often more spoiled than daughters, girls tend to grow up and become independent more quickly than boys. Women are guaranteed equal rights in the Jordanian constitution, but social custom and religious interpretation often undermine this. There are a few women in the Jordanian Parliament, suggesting their improved status.

Two men chat outside their shops at a market in central Amman, Jordan. Poverty, unemployment, and inflation are fundamental problems in Jordan, but King Abdallah has undertaken some broad economic reforms in a long-term effort to improve living standards. (Jewel Samad/AFP/Getty Images)

Homes are built so that floors can be added when sons marry; the son brings his bride home and they raise their family there. Most Jordanians live in three- or four-story homes containing extended families that eat together. Daughters-in-law are expected to do most of the cooking. Until recently men were not expected to cook or share in the household labor.

¹¹ CLOTHING

The tradition of women covering their faces with veils is being revived as a result of a spiritual quest for identity on the part of Arab women and as a rejection of Western values. Everyday Jordanian dress is generally conservative, particularly for women, who do not wear tight clothes, sleeveless blouses, shorts, short skirts, or low-cut backs on shirts or dresses.

There are basically three styles of clothing for women in Jordan. "Westernized" women, of whom there are many, dress in the typical Western style with dresses, skirts, and slacks, while avoiding overly revealing or suggestive clothing. Very religious women (increasingly more common in Jordan), wear an outfit called the *libis shar'i* or *jilbab*. This is a floor-length, long-sleeved, button-front dress worn with the hair covered by a scarf. Stores catering to religious women have sprouted up all over Jordan, and women from other parts of the Middle East, particularly from the West Bank, purchase *shar'i* clothing while visiting Jordan. The third type of attire is the traditional dress or national costume. This is a hand-made dress with embroidered and cross-stitched patterns that vary from region to region. In northern Jordan (around Irbid and Ramtha), women wear a black cotton dress whose bodice is stitched with triangular, multicolored borders. In central Jordan (i.e., in Salt), women's traditional dresses are made of 16 m (52 ft) of fabric, with sleeves measuring 3 m (10 ft) in length. Around the sleeves and the hem, blue panels are stitched. The costume of southern Jordan is made from a variety of silk fabrics in a combination of colors. A silk cloak, called a *'abaya,* is draped over the head.

Jordanian men dress in basically Western clothing, with suits and ties being the preferred attire for the office, and casual slacks and shirts worn for informal socializing. Some men wear a Jordanian *kaffiyyeh,* or scarf-like headpiece. The Jordanian kaffiyyeh is red and white, in contrast to the black and white Palestinian kaffiyyeh. The kaffiyyeh is folded in a triangle and laid over the head. It is secured to the head with a double-coiled rope called an *i'gal.*

12 FOOD

Jordan has one of the world's most elaborate and sophisticated cuisines, largely borrowed from its neighbors. Few dishes are unique to Jordan; one unique dish is *mansaf,* chunks of stewed lamb in a yogurt-based sauce served with rice. Mansaf, also called *fatiyyeh,* is the traditional Jordanian meal served for special occasions. *Jameed* is required for the preparation of mansaf. Jameed is made of yogurt seasoned with salt. The yogurt is drained, molded or shaped into balls that fit into the palm of a hand, and then allowed to dry until the balls harden into rocks. A recipe for mansaf follows.

Mansaf

3 balls jameed
3 pounds lamb chunks
2 quarts water
1 large onion, finely chopped
4 loaves pita bread, or 2 loaves shraj bread
3 cups cooked white rice
½ cup sautéed pine nuts
¼ teaspoon black pepper
1 teaspoon ground allspice
dash of salt

Soak balls of jameed overnight to soften; purée them in a blender with a quart of water and a dash of salt. Cook lamb chunks in a quart of water. Once the water boils, add chopped onion to the water and meat. Add black pepper and ground allspice. When the lamb chunks are tender (about 1 hour), add the puréed jameed to the stewed lamb and water. Cook for another hour.

In the meantime, cut up pieces of thin pita bread (or, if available, shraj, a paper-thin bread). Spread the bread in 2 layers in a large round pan until the bottom is covered. Cover the bread with about 2 cups of the cooked jameed sauce, and allow to soak 10 minutes. Spread rice over the soaked bread. Sprinkle another cup of jameed sauce over the entire pan, and cover the rice with all of the lamb chunks. Sprinkle pine nuts over the lamb.

At home, all courses are served together, but in restaurants, *mezze* or *muqabalat* (appetizers) are brought first. Typical mezze are *hummus* (puréed chickpeas with tahina [sesame paste], lemon juice, and garlic), *baba ghanouj* (puréed eggplant mixed with tahina, lemon, garlic, and salt), and *taboula* (a salad of chopped fresh parsley, tomatoes, green onions, and fresh mint mixed with soaked bulgur wheat and lemon juice). Then, a meat or fish course is served. The meal usually ends with seasonal fruit.

Jordanians love sweets and eat lots of them. A favorite kind of sweet is layers of filo pastry filled with nuts or creams, similar to *baklava.*

13 EDUCATION

Jordanians are very well educated, and their country has the highest number of university graduates per capita in the Arab world. Its main export is skilled labor and professionals to other Arab countries. At 82% (with a target of 95% by the year 2005), Jordan also has one of the highest literacy rates in the Arab world. One-third of Jordan's population is students, partly due to the fact that more than half of Jordan's population is under the age of 16. Education is free and compulsory from grades one through ten, and then it continues to be free for another two years. Literacy training is free to all Jordanian residents. To make sure that Jordan keeps pace with the rest of the world, computer studies are mandatory in the 10th grade and optional in the 11th and 12th grades. Girls must attend school through the 10th grade and are encouraged to finish secondary and even higher education. More than half of the 39,000 students at the University of Jordan in Amman are women, whom enroll in 18 faculties.

14 CULTURAL HERITAGE

The Islamic prohibition against the depiction of the human figure has significantly shaped Jordanian art. Western-style fine arts became popular in the late 20th century as more Jordanians traveled abroad. Recently, however, there has been a revival of more traditional Jordanian art forms, especially stylized Islamic calligraphy.

The traditional dance of Jordan is the *dabkeh,* a group dance performed by both men and women, either together or separately. Traditional musical instruments include the *qassaba* and *nay,* woodwinds; the *rababa,* a one-stringed instrument; the *kamanja,* resembling a violin; the *oud* (lute), with five double strings; the *qanun,* a zither-like instrument with 26 strings; and the *daff* and *durbakkeh,* percussion instruments.

Arabic literature abounds with stories of love, honor, generosity, hospitality, exile, political turmoil, war, lost lands, and lost identities. The Arabic word for poet is *sha'ir,* which translates literally into "he who feels."

15 WORK

Working conditions are regulated by law, including minimum wages, minimum age for employment, vacation and sick leave, maternity leave, health benefits, social security and retirement pensions, maximum hours and overtime compensation, advance notice before firing or layoffs and severance pay, worker's compensation for job-related injuries, and labor disputes. There is no compulsory retirement age. Unions are legal.

Although women are guaranteed equal rights in Jordan's constitution and are just as well educated as men, women make up only 12.5% of the labor force due to the traditional belief that a woman's job is to marry well and have many children (particularly sons). Unemployment has become a serious problem since about 300,000 expatriates returning from Kuwait in 1991 (after the Gulf War) glutted the labor pool. Many Jordanians now take jobs for which they are overqualified simply to survive.

16 SPORTS

The most popular sports in Jordan are soccer and basketball. Also enjoyed are horse and camel racing. The Royal Jordanian State Stud is a stable devoted to maintaining the purity of the Arabian breed of horse. Stud services are offered worldwide in a highly regulated way in order to prevent the breed from being lost through crossbreeding.

In the 1950s, car rallying was begun as a weekend sport attracting a few spectators. It has since developed into one of Jordan's major sporting events. The royal family strongly supports the car races, with King Hussein himself having raced in the rallies. King Hussein's eldest son, Prince 'Abdullah, also competes in the national rallies. Competitions are international, with most racers representing countries of the Middle East, such as Qatar, Kuwait, Oman, and the United Arab Emirates.

17 ENTERTAINMENT AND RECREATION

All films in Jordan, both in cinemas and in video form, are censored for kissing and sex scenes. Martial arts and low-grade action movies are popular among Jordanian youth.

Jordan has two domestic television stations, one providing Arabic entertainment and news, and the other providing foreign-language programming. The latter features predominantly English-language programming, but also provides French cartoons, dramas, and news broadcasts. Jordanians film many of their own shows. A particular favorite is a soap-opera-like drama, called a *musalsal,* which is shown in sequels every night. Often, the theme of the drama is love and honor among the Bedouins, and the stories take place in Bedouin tents. Jordanians also produce dramatic shows with religious themes, which are predominantly nonfiction representations of prominent figures and stories in Islamic history. Jordan is also a major hub for the production and translation of Arabic language children's programs. Most animations from Japan and the United States are translated in Jordanian studios and then broadcast to all 22 Arab countries.

English-language programming includes domestically produced news and a myriad of American and British shows. These include *Dynasty, Murder She Wrote, The Benny Hill Show, 90210, 24, The Bill Cosby Show, Fresh Prince of Bel Air.* Cartoons, including Disney productions and classics, such as *Tom and Jerry,* remain popular among Jordanian children.

Jordan receives Arabic radio broadcasts from around the Middle East and also has its own domestic stations. A favorite among young people is the English-language Jordanian station, for it plays all of the latest music that is enjoyed in the West. "Radio Monte Carlo" and U.S.-based Radio Sawa also play Western music. Jordanians listen more to European-based pop music than American, but the billboard top hits remain popular among teenagers. Today, Jordanians have access to hun-

dreds of satellite stations from around the world that makes their options for entertainment television virtually unlimited.

18 FOLK ART, CRAFTS, AND HOBBIES

There are many traditional folk arts and crafts in Jordan, among them pottery, silver and gold jewelry making, glass blowing, and basket weaving. Textile arts are women's crafts, particularly embroidery and cloth weaving. As young girls learn embroidery stitches from older women, they are initiated into the culture. Patterns, colors, and fabrics show the village, tribe, social status, wealth, and period in which the woman lives (or lived). Until very recently, almost every Jordanian girl embroidered her own trousseau, consisting of six to twelve loosely cut robes to be worn over a lifetime, her bridal dress (which would also serve for other special occasions), cushions and pillows for bed and sofa, and often even her burial shroud. It is often said of Jordanian women that they are never idle, their hands ever busy stitching and sewing while chatting with each other.

19 SOCIAL PROBLEMS

Jordan's economy is struggling due to a lack of resources, the sudden influx of expatriates and refugees after both the 1967 war with Israel (in which Jordan lost the West Bank territory) and the Gulf War in 1990–91, and massive foreign debt. Almost one-third of the population lives below the poverty level, and the percentage is increasing. A severe water shortage also causes difficulties in both the public and private sectors.

There is an ongoing conflict between the government's desire to maintain ties with Western powers and popular support for the Palestinians and Iraq. Support for the Palestinians is necessary because more than 60% of the population is Palestinian, about 2.7 million inhabitants of Jordan. Palestinians serve on the parliament, thus exerting an influence over political policies. Because Jordan is on the East Bank of the Jordan River and Palestine is on the West Bank, there is a strong emotional bond that makes Jordanians particularly sensitive to the plight of the Palestinians. This makes the forging of peace between Israel and Jordan a sensitive matter to Jordanians, who wish to see justice for the Palestinians enacted in any peace agreement. Jordan has now signed a peace agreement with Israel and, generally speaking, this has gone smoothly. Some emotionally sensitive matters, such as whether or not Jordan should permit Israelis to purchase Jordanian land while Palestinian land remains under Israeli control, lead to fervent debate in the parliament. The king's father, Hussein, also found himself in a complicated situation with the Palestinian population in his country. In his opposition to the growing Palestinian resistance within his country, he took several drastic measures to eliminate this presence. The outcome led to the killing of many Palestinian Liberation Organization (PLO) members and militias by the Jordanian army, often described as "Black September," which drove the organization out of Jordan and into Lebanon.

The U.S.-led war in Iraq, which commenced in March 2003, is similarly important to Jordanians. Iraq has been home to thousands of Jordanian and Palestinian expatriates, providing jobs that have been vital to the Jordanian and Palestinian economies. Historically, Iraq has also been a major source of oil for Jordan. Thus, when Iraq invaded Kuwait in 1990, the Jordanian government announced its opposition to the invasion and refused to participate in Operation Desert Storm, which was organized by the United States. Jordan wished—and wishes—to maintain its good ties with Iraq, and this has caused tension between Jordan and the United States, an important ally.

[20] GENDER ISSUES

Jordanian women have received much media attention in the last two decades for several notable examples of honor killings, which were strongly condemned by the human rights groups and the international community. This topic has since subsided as several high profile campaigns against honor killings have been launched nationwide.

Today, the public visibility of women in the Jordanian royal family has changed the tone of discussion about Jordanian women. Queen Noor, the wife of the late King Hussein, and Queen Rania, the wife of King Abdullah, both have very public portfolios and are extremely vocal and involved in issues pertaining to women's rights domestically, regionally, and globally. They serve on the board of advisors of many organizations working in the area of public awareness and advocacy for women's issues. Queen Rania recently created her own online video channel, allowing people worldwide to post videos responding to her questions or allowing her to respond to the world's questions. This is thought to be a unique way of bridging the intercultural divide.

[21] BIBLIOGRAPHY

Facts About Jordan: Factsheet No. 1. Washington, D.C.: Jordan Information Bureau, n.d.

The Hashemite Kingdom of Jordan: Facts and Figures. Washington, DC: Jordan Information Bureau, n.d.

Jordan: Issues and Perspectives. No. 16, November/December 1993. Washington, DC: Jordan Information Bureau, 1993.

Massad, Joseph A. *Colonial Effects: The Making of Modern Identity in Jordan.* New York: Columbia University Press, 2001.

Noor, Queen. *Leap of Faith: Memoirs of an Unexpected Life.* New York: Miramax, 2003.

Stannard, Dorothy, ed. *Insight Guides: Jordan.* Boston: Houghton Mifflin, 1994.

Welles, Sam, ed. *The World's Great Religions.* New York: Time, Inc., 1957.

—revised by Amal Daraiseh and Adel Iskandar

KACHINS

PRONUNCIATION: KAH-CHINS
LOCATION: Northern Myanmar (Burma); China; India; Thailand
POPULATION: 1.5 million
LANGUAGE: Kachin
RELIGION: Christianity (Baptist and Catholicism); Buddhism; Animism

[1] INTRODUCTION

The people known collectively as Kachins, who live in mountainous northern Burma (renamed Myanmar by the military government in 1989), are a group of seven tribes: the Atsi, Jinghpaw, Lashi, Lisu, Maru, Nung, and Rawang.

The tribes share similar Tibeto-Burman languages, a clan system, and many customs. They migrated into Burma from China to the northwest and established highland settlements governed by independent chieftains. The Kachins were fierce warriors who never acknowledged the dominance of Burma's various empires until the arrival of the British. Initially the Kachins fought the colonizers, but then joined Britain's Imperial Army. Kachin guerrillas proved indispensable to the Allied forces in the Second World War, fighting in their native forests against the Japanese invasion.

Some rebellion, aimed at establishing an independent Kachin nation, occurred soon after Burmese independence, but it was after the military takeover of Burma's government in 1962 that large-scale Kachin insurgency occurred. One of Burma's biggest anti-government armies was recruited from the hill people and financed by trade in locally-mined jade and gold. Called the Kachin Independence Organization, it continues to hold considerable territory, although it has observed a ceasefire with government forces since 1994. A much smaller militia called the Kachin Defense Army also has a ceasefire agreement with the Myanmar government.

The Kachin Independence Organization (KIO) was allowed to participate in constitutional conventions held by Myanmar's military government. KIO participation in the conventions was seen as a political compromise by many former supporters in Kachin State and overseas exiles. The KIO issued statements supporting the Myanmar government's policies and engaged in commercial joint ventures in logging and gold mining, which gave the KIO the image of having abandoned its original revolutionary goals. A few small Kachin underground or exile political and environmental groups have emerged in recent years as potential alternatives to the KIO.

[2] LOCATION AND HOMELAND

The Kachin State of Myanmar borders China, Tibet, and India. Myanmar has an estimated 1.5 million Kachins, about 100,000 of whom live in the Shan State. Kachin-related indigenous people also live in China, India, and Thailand.

The huge Irrawaddy River flows south from Tibet through Kachin State, past the main cities of Myitkyina and Bhamo. Ranges of Himalayan foothills rise as high as snowcapped Hkakabo Razi (19,314 ft), Southeast Asia's highest mountain, near the border with Tibet.

A Kachin couple look out from a hut during the celebration of Myanmar's national festival of Shapawng Yawng Manau Poit near Gauhati, India. Kachins from Myanmar joined Kachins from India for the two-day festival. (AP Images/Anupam Nath)

³ LANGUAGE

Kachins speak a Tibeto-Burman language, in seven main dialects, and with many regional variations. A written version of Kachin using the Roman alphabet (without F, Q, V, and X) was devised by American missionary Olaf Hansen in 1895. The writing system is hard to use because of the lack of accents showing the different tones of voice that alter the meanings of words in Kachin.

The typical greeting in Kachin's Jinghpaw dialect is *"Kaja ai I?"* meaning "Are you well?" Another common greeting expression is *"Shatsa sa ni?"* (Have you eaten?). To take leave, you say, *"Naw wa sa na"* (I am going), and the reply is *"Angwi sha wa u"* (go back slowly).

⁴ FOLKLORE

Kachins traditionally believed that the original ancestor of their tribes was a blacksmith. They thought that the moon was the spirit of a young girl, and some girls are thought to be able to foretell the future by communicating with the moon. Particularly among Animist Kachins, there is a belief in malicious witches called *phi*, including the *Yu Phi*, who disguise themselves as animals or insects to harm people or animals.

⁵ RELIGION

About two-thirds of the Kachins are Christians, mostly Baptists and Catholics. The rest are Buddhists or Animists, who worship the spirits in nature. Spirits are always present in the Kachins' mountain homeland, and even Christian or Buddhist Kachins often believe in a group of spirits called *Nats*. There are good and bad Nats: the good ones include a merciful spirit called *Hpan wa ningsan chye wa ning san*, who (known as *Karai Kasang*) is also the god worshipped by Christians. This Nat accepts only live offerings that the worshippers set free, such as birds. There are also good Nats of the earth and heaven, and household Nats. A series of bad Nats bring harm to hunters, fishermen, or women in labor and cause accidents or other misfortune.

The Kachins have intermediaries to the world of the Nats, such as high priests who know a special vocabulary and take part only in major ceremonies, including weddings; priests who conduct ceremonies with offerings; and assistants who perform animal sacrifices. There are also interpreters of the Nats' wishes, spirit mediums, and interpreters of the natural world, who function like Chinese *Feng Shui* specialists.

Missionaries from the United States and Europe introduced the Kachins to Christianity during the British colonial days, and Kachin evangelists then spread the new religion through the hills. Christianity was adopted without discarding Kachin traditions such as the clan system. Actual churches are rare outside of the few cities and towns, so church services are held on Sundays and holidays in village meeting halls or homes. Kachin Christians sometimes have difficulties holding large meetings or conventions, as those need to be approved by the military government, which is suspicious of Christian gatherings.

⁶ MAJOR HOLIDAYS

In traditional Kachin society, ceremonies were held in connection with the planting of rice and other crops. Before planting the fields, offerings were made to the spirits of the earth, and the farmers rested for a few days. Harvest ceremonies were also held. Because Christianity is now so widespread among the Kachins, holidays such as Christmas and Easter are important celebrations, with music, community feasts, and church services in cities, towns, and villages.

⁷ RITES OF PASSAGE

Many Kachin mothers now give birth in a clinic or hospital, if there is one nearby; otherwise, their babies are born at home. Infant and child mortality rates are high in most areas of the Kachin State, mainly due to malaria, except where the elevation and cold temperatures prevent malaria-carrying mosquitoes.

Young people help their parents in the fields or shops. In the towns and cities, it is common for teenagers to be active in church groups, and some even travel to other parts of Burma for church meetings and to seek converts to Christianity.

Traditionally, Kachins are buried a week after death. For Animists, special ceremonies are performed to make sure that the spirit of the dead person goes away from the living. Funeral music may be played on slightly broken instruments. Christians hold a prayer service and often mark graves with a cross.

[8] INTERPERSONAL RELATIONS

Kachins shake hands when introduced and when greeting or saying goodbye. They are generous hosts and always offer food, or at least tea, to visitors. The guest is expected to politely refuse the refreshments at least once—perhaps several times to be "overcome" by the hosts' insistence. Then they will please the hosts if they eat large amounts of the food offered. Particularly honored guests, such as those who have endured great difficulty to travel from far away, may be given a special welcoming ceremony. They are presented with bamboo cups of rice wine and a basket containing cooked chicken and rice wrapped in leaf packets, to be shared, and may be given a sword and shoulder bag (if male) or Kachin clothing (if female).

Kachins are raised to value cooperation and an uncomplaining spirit. Children are discouraged from fighting with each other and encouraged to share their possessions and food. Although they have been known as brave, tough warriors in battle, adult Kachins rarely seem to argue among themselves.

[9] LIVING CONDITIONS

The Kachins are living in an ongoing health crisis. They have been subject to unchecked epidemics of cholera, plague, and HIV/AIDS. Malaria, including the deadly blackwater fever, is rife in low-lying areas, as are tuberculosis and other lung diseases throughout the Kachin State. With very few trained doctors available, fake "injection doctors" roam the hills in their place, giving malnourished people vitamin shots with dirty needles, thereby spreading the HIV/AIDS virus and other ailments among unknowing people. Traditional healers can be more beneficial, and the many medicinal plants of the Kachin State provide the hope of cures for many diseases—if logging does not destroy the forests before they can be properly studied.

A massive increase in logging in recent decades has decimated the great temperate rainforests of the Kachin State in all but the most remote regions of the far north. Logging trucks move back and forth, day and night, carrying hardwood logs from Kachin forests for sale in neighboring China and India. Environmental concerns have also been raised about gold mining by companies from China that enter Kachin State in joint ventures with Myanmar's military government or the KIO. The gold miners use highly toxic mercury when processing ore dredged from the rivers, and gold mining also erodes river banks.

Most Kachins live in houses built of bamboo and wood, up on stilts or low to the ground with dirt floors. The hills are cold and foggy, sometimes even snowy, so houses have wood stoves or open hearths inside them. In stilt houses, people sit and sleep on the floor; in the single-level houses, they sit on wood or rattan chairs and sleep on bamboo platforms. Much of what is used by the Kachins is crafted by them of bamboo or wood, but trade goods do enter from China and India. The Kachin State has few road, railway, or air links. Heavy trucks, motorcycles, elephants, ponies, and mules are typical modes of transportation over the many hills and mountain passes.

What wealth Kachins manage to acquire is usually in the form of jewelry, which is easily portable. A family's "bank account" takes the form of rings or earrings made of the gold and colorful jade or amber found in Kachin State, and sometimes elaborate silver wedding jewelry. In general, the Kachins place more value on friendships and kinship than on material possessions, and even small children would usually rather play games with other children than play with toys.

[10] FAMILY LIFE

Marriage usually occurs in the late teens or early twenties. Few Kachins remain single and large families—six or more children—are the norm. Some Kachins believe that since their ethnic group is few in numbers, having many children is important to their survival as a culture. The clan system determines who marries whom. With everyone belonging to one of the main clans, it is common knowledge which clans a girl or boy can marry into, and which are taboo. When outsiders are adopted as Kachins, they are assigned to one of the clans and given a Kachin name that, in part, comes from their birth-order in their family.

Some Kachin families own pack-ponies or even elephants, and they take good care of them. Many keep dogs for hunting and as pets.

[11] CLOTHING

The Kachin tribes traditionally wear homespun thick cotton jackets with baggy trousers for men and wrap-around sarongs for women. The special occasion outfit for Jinghpaw women, which is nowadays worn for weddings and dance performances, is highly ornamented. Large silver disks decorate a black velvet jacket, worn with an embroidered red sarong and leggings, many silver necklaces and bracelets, and rattan wrapped around the waist and hips. These heirloom costumes are becoming quite rare.

For everyday wear, most Kachin men now wear shirts, trousers or sarongs, and often sweaters or heavy jackets, as the climate can be quite cold. Kachin women in most areas wear sarongs with blouses or T-shirts. They often knit their own sweaters with yarn imported from China, and also knit warm outfits for children and babies. Children often wear several layers of clothing to school in the mountains because the buildings are unheated. Girls wear lipstick and either cut their hair short or style it in intricate French braids. A type of Kachin sarong with traditional embroidery on a black cotton background became a symbol of democracy throughout Myanmar when opposition leader Aung San Suu Kyi wore it.

[12] FOOD

The Kachins grow some cold-climate foods such as potatoes, which are not so common elsewhere in Myanmar. These crops are combined in Kachin cooking with wild game such as boar and venison, domestically raised chicken and goat, and edible plants gathered in the forest. Rice is grown in hillside fields or brought as a trade commodity from China. The Kachins are known for eating large quantities of rice and whatever accompanying curry they can afford. If they can afford it, they typically eat a few bowls of rice with their late-morning breakfast and a few more with the late-afternoon supper. Tea or coffee (a luxury) is served with fruit, crackers, or cookies during the rest of the day.

[13] EDUCATION

Educational opportunities are few in the Kachin State. There is a severe shortage of schools, teachers, and educational materials, especially in rural areas. There is discrimination against

Kachin students in Myanmar's educational system, and few opportunities for higher education exist in the Kachin State. Some high school graduates attend Bible study academies in the cities. Little is written in the Kachin language, so most of the school texts are in Burmese and very outdated. Kachin parents often express the hope that their children will get more of an education than they were able to. In 2008 Kachin students in Myitkyina were active campaigners for a "No" vote on a national constitutional referendum held by Myanmar's military government, which was pressuring the population to vote "Yes."

14 CULTURAL HERITAGE

Kachin traditional music, using the repetitive rhythms of metal gongs, is played mostly for dancing. The best-known dance is the *ton-kha,* in which lines of men and women form a circle and step in and out holding kerchiefs in their hands. Western-influenced hymns are sung at Christian church services. Some churches have electronic keyboards, and guitars may accompany the hymn-singing. International pop and rock songs are also well-liked by many Kachins. The Kachin rebel forces had small marching bands with bagpipes, like those of Scottish troops who served in Burma in the days of the British Empire.

The centerpiece of traditional Kachin culture is the *Manau* ceremony, which combines religion, dance, and visual arts. This elaborate celebration is usually sponsored by a *duwa,* a member of the traditional aristocracy. They hold a Manau for various reasons: celebrating prosperity or warding off ill-health or evil spirits, and inviting a good *Nat* to a new community. The Manau involves all members of society from throughout a district and provides a place for young people to meet and for distant relatives to reunite. It is an expensive production and takes a year to prepare (and a year to recover from it, say the Kachins).

The Manau is led by high-ranking Animist priests who make offerings for the good of the community. The priests wear elaborate robes of brightly-colored embroidered silk and woven rattan headdresses topped with tall peacock and pheasant feathers. Offerings, prayers, music, and dance take place in an open ground. The area is decorated with pennants and streamers, and Manau poles are set up where the priests preside. The poles, 10 ft tall or higher, are painted in bright colors with abstract patterns of triangles, diamonds, and spirals.

15 WORK

The Kachins are mostly farmers. The mountainous climate and rocky soil make agriculture hard work in most areas, although a variety of cold-climate crops could profitably be introduced in the future. In Putao's valley (warm although far in the north) oranges and other fruits are grown.

Joining the military has long been a favored occupation for young Kachins. In the colonial period they joined the British Army, and at independence, the Burmese Army. Thousands still are enrolled in the Kachin Independence Organization's armed forces, although a ceasefire is in effect. For those less interested in the military life, religious studies are popular.

Jade is very important to the Kachins. Jadeite, the most precious kind of jade, is found in large quantities only in Kachin State. The bright green jade is best known, but it also comes in white, lavender, blue, and honey-colored shades. Huge boulders and tiny pieces of jade are brought out through government controlled areas, for sale around the world. Kachins working at the big jade mines have often been mistreated and are especially susceptible to drug and alcohol abuse.

16 SPORTS

Kachins enjoy playing and watching soccer, volleyball, and badminton. Some study martial arts such as kung fu. Children run races and play jump-rope games, making their own ropes by looping together collections of rubber bands.

17 ENTERTAINMENT AND RECREATION

In some areas people have DVD players and karaoke machines, which are usually powered by a small generator, as electricity is in short supply in Kachin State. They often show "homemade" DVD dramas produced and acted by people in Myitkyina or Bhamo. In some places satellite dishes have been rigged up, so Kachins can watch international television such as the BBC World News and Asian MTV. Otherwise, short-wave radios are relied on for information on the outside world, as well as word on developments in Myanmar. There is very little Internet access in Kachin State, but the cities have some cafes where computer games can be played. Kachins also enjoy getting together to sing hymns or pop songs, accompanied by guitar players. Sometimes church youth groups will travel from village to village presenting Christian music shows.

18 FOLK ART, CRAFTS, AND HOBBIES

Kachins are talented jewelers, making ornaments from the local gold, silver, amber, and jade. They also make traditional swords with embossed silver scabbards, baskets, and bamboo drinking cups. Kachin embroidery, often using diamond-shaped designs that symbolize the mountains, is distinctive, and different patterns can identify tribes or regions.

19 SOCIAL PROBLEMS

During the late 20th century, widespread human rights violations by Myanmar's military, including massacres, village burnings, rape, torture, and forced labor, uprooted tens of thousands of Kachins. While these abuses have been less widespread since the KIO 1994 ceasefire ended open warfare, they do continue in many parts of Kachin State, and refugees still flee to other countries.

In the cities and jade mining region, many have turned to heroin abuse. The HIV/AIDS epidemic has spread through the most remote parts of the Kachin State, largely from injections of heroin and other drugs with shared needles. The Kachin Independence Organization responded in 1991 by banning opium growing and heroin trading; they successfully substituted food crops for opium poppies, but in the Burmese government-controlled areas, the drug trade is still carried on openly. There is little educational material about AIDS in the Kachin language, and the whole population of the ethnic group is under threat from the epidemic.

20 GENDER ISSUES

In old Kachin society, women's status was considerably lower than men's, but this is changing as women seek more education and stand up for themselves. Kachin women often own small shops or restaurants, and in KIO-controlled areas they are particularly active in education and healthcare, as well as serving as soldiers. In those areas they have formed a women's organization that runs kindergartens and promotes good nutrition and economic empowerment. In the cities and towns, women are active in church activities and some are in popular Christian singing groups. Kachin society tends to be conservative and somewhat disapproving of gender identities other than heterosexuality.

[21] BIBLIOGRAPHY

All Kachin Students and Youth Union (AKSYU), Kachin Development Networking Group (KDNG). *Valley of Darkness: Gold Mining and Militarization in Burma's Hugawng Valley.* Chiang Mai, Thailand: AKSYU and KDNG, http://www.aksyu.com/2007/AKSYU-Books/ValleyofDarkness.pdf (23 April 2008)

Brackenbury, Wade. *The Last Paradise on Earth: The Vanishing Peoples and Wilderness of Northern Burma.* Singapore: Flame of the Forest Publishing, 2005.

Global Witness. *A Conflict of Interest: The Uncertain Future of Burma's Forests.* London: Global Witness, 2003 www.globalwitness.org/media_library_detail.php/113/en/a_conflict_of_interest_english (23 April 2008)

Kachin News Group. www.kachinnews.com (23 April 2008)

La Raw, Maran. "The Nation-State of Burma and the Victimization of its Co-founders." *Burma.* III, no. 6 (Nov/Dec 1996).

Leach, Edmond. *Political Systems of Highland Burma.* Cambridge: Harvard University Press, 1954.

LeBar, Frank, ed. *Ethnic Groups of Mainland Southeast Asia.* New Haven, Ct: Human Relations Area Files , 1964.

Lintner, Bertil. *Land of Jade: A Journey Through Insurgent Burma.* Edinburgh: Kiscadale, 1990.

Mirante, Edith. *Down the Rat Hole: Adventures Underground on Burma's Frontiers.* Bangkok: Orchid Press, 2005.

Schramm-Evans, Zoe. *Dark Ruby: Travels in a Troubled Land.* London: Pandora, 1997.

Scott-Clark, Cathy and Levy, Adrian. *The Stone of Heaven: Unearthing the Secret History of Imperial Green Jade.* New York: Little, Brown, 2002.

Smith, Martin. *Ethnic Groups in Burma.* London: Anti-Slavery International, 1994.

Tucker, Shelby. *Among Insurgents: Walking Through Burma.* London: IB Taurus, 2000.

—by E. Mirante

KADAZAN

PRONUNCIATION: kah-tah-CHAN
ALTERNATE NAMES: Dusun
LOCATION: Malaysia (Sabah state)
POPULATION: 514.400 (2004)
LANGUAGE: Kadazandusun
RELIGION: Christianity; Islam; animistic beliefs

[1] INTRODUCTION

Sabah, known as "The Land Below the Wind," is the second-largest state in Malaysia. It is situated on the northern tip of the island of Borneo, bordered by Sarawak on its southwestern side and by Kalimantan to the south. Archeological findings show that Sabah was inhabited by people as early as 28,000 years ago. Certain scholars believe that about 5,000 years ago Sabah was settled by Mongoloid-type peoples, and by the 1st millennium BC, Malayic and other related Mongoloid groups migrated from mainland Asia.

It is believed that Sabah's early inhabitants settled in the coastal areas but were slowly driven inland by the later arrival of other settlers. These later settlers were mainly from Malaya and neighboring islands, settling along the coast and along the banks of rivers when they arrived. The descendants of the displaced groups are believed to be today's Kadazan of Sabah, sometimes known as the Dusun. These displaced peoples over the years remained isolated and insulated from outside influences until the late 17th century.

Prior to the formation of the North Borneo Company in 1877, by an Austrian baron in partnership with a British firm, Sabah was divided under the influences of sultans of Brunei and Sulu. In 1881 the North Borneo Company was upgraded into a Chartered Company, giving it official recognition to rule the 73,300 sq km (28,300 sq mi) of North Borneo until the Japanese invasion in 1942. After the war, Sabah became a British Crown Colony until 31 August 1963, when it obtained self-government from the British. On the 16 September 1963, Sabah, together with Sarawak, Singapore, and Malaya, became the Federation of Malaysia.

[2] LOCATION AND HOMELAND

Sabah is not only rich in natural beauty and resources, but also in the cultural heritage of its people. It is endowed with a heterogeneous population and is considered to be a melting pot of many indigenous and immigrant groups. It is estimated that there are some 30 indigenous communities using more than 50 indigenous languages and not less than 80 dialects in Sabah. The largest ethnic group is the Kadazandusun, numbering about 514.400 in 2004, who make up 25% of Sabah's population. The group consists of both Kadazan and Dusun and other subgroups. The other main ethnic groups are the Muruts, Bajau, Paitan, and Chinese. The largest non-indigenous group is the Chinese. They dominate trade and commerce. Nonetheless, many of these ethnic groups share similar oral histories, languages, and traditions.

The Kadazandusun are a collection of ethnic groups who speak similar languages and dialects known as Dusunic family, as well as share a common belief system with variations in customs and practices. Within this group exist at least 10 distinct languages with possibly 30 or more dialects. This includes the various subgroups such as the Kadazan of Penampang and Papar, the Lotud, Dusun, Kwijau, Bisaya, Dumpas, Mankaak, Minokok, Maragang, Tangaah, Liwan, Tatanah, Sino-Natives, the Rungus, and other subgroups from Tempusuk, Tambunan, Ranau, and other districts. The Kadazandusun can be found in all districts, but they are mainly in the western half of Sabah.

POPULATION OF SABAH 2004

ETHNIC SUBGROUPS	('000)
Kadazandusun	514.4
Other Bumiputera	421.7
Bajau	381.5
Malay	330.6
Chinese	277.3
Others	127.4
Murut	94.0
Indian	10.7
Non-Malaysian citizens	704.8
Total	**2862.3**

Source: Department of Statistics, 2004

3 LANGUAGE

The various subgroups of Kadazan are speakers of the Dusunic languages with dialectical differences in pronunciation and description of words. The differences are a result of poor communication facilities and environmental evolution in the past. Like most other indigenous groups on the island of Borneo, the Kadazan did not possess a written language until the introduction of formal education in the 18th century, therefore oral traditions were very important among the Kadazan. Most of their knowledge was passed down by oral tradition from generation to generation.

The structure of a Kadazan's name is divided into two parts: the first name is the child's name, and the second is the father's first name. Some common male names are Gimbang, Kunul, Kerupang, Galumau, Gantoung, Empurut, Ampingan, and Sangan. Typical female names are Semitah, Rangkumas, Ansayu, Baimin, Salud, Amin, Halimah, Nani, and Mainah.

4 FOLKLORE

As is true with many other indigenous people on the island of Borneo, Kadazan folklore plays a major role in Kadazan traditions, customs, and worldviews. One of their most popular folk tales is the myth of their origin. According to legend, all the tribes are believed to have come from one common place called Nunuk Ragang, meaning "Red Casuarina Tree," a fig tree located at the confluence of the Liwagu and Kogibangan rivers in the heart of Sabah. Nunuk Ragang grew in plenty at the Liwagu River in Ranau. It is believed that their ancestors used to swim in the river and climb on the branches of the Nunuk Ragang to sun themselves. Red sap from the Nunuk Ragang roots was thought to have curative elements for different kinds of diseases. The Kadazan lived in abundance at Nunuk Ragang, and as their numbers increased, it became difficult to find enough food for every family within the limited area. In order to solve the problem, the leaders exhorted their followers to move and spread out in search of land and space.

5 RELIGION

Today, the majority of the Kadazan peoples are Christian, though some profess Islam, while others are followers of their ancestors' animistic beliefs. Even though a large number have converted to Christianity and Islam, many Kadazans still have ritual specialists to perform certain ceremonies. This is particularly true during the Harvest Festival. On the other hand, many of the old customs and traditions, such as headhunting, have ceased among the Kadazan.

According to the Kadazan's traditional beliefs, the spiritual universe is presided over by two supreme deities: *kinohoringan* (male/husband) and *umunsumundu* (female/wife). They are husband and wife. Under the command of these two deities are the lesser good and evil spirits that dwell within all objects and the natural environment—the forest, mountains, rivers, caves, and the earth itself—that need to be respected. These spirits must be appeased by means of ceremonial observances. Otherwise, the *rogon* (evil spirit) will inflict sickness and disease on the people or interfere and withhold blessings in secular world. Therefore, the spirits are presented with offerings and are called to attend the feast. These spirits can be encountered in the forest or sought in sacred places, and they also can be contacted in dreams and through mediums, ritual specialists, or priestesses who are called *Babalian* or *Bobohizan* (depending on dialect).

Bobolians or bobohizans play a major role in Kadazan ceremonial rituals. Incantations, prayers, singing, trances and animal sacrifices are common practices at these rituals, some of which can last for days. A bobolian plays a variety of roles. As medium, she beseeches spirits to stay away from newborn babies. As healer, she is engaged to exorcize sicknesses brought by evil spirits. At funerals, she heads the rites that guide the deceased spirit towards its final journey up Mount Kinabalu, which stands at 4,101 m (13,455 ft). It is one of the highest mountains in Southeast Asia. It is believed to be the resting place of the souls of the departed Kadazan peoples.

6 MAJOR HOLIDAYS

The Harvest Festival, known as *Magavau* among the Kadazan of Sabah, is celebrated annually on May 13 and 14. In 1960, the festival was proclaimed as a public holiday by the state government. It is a festival of celebration in honor of the spirit of rice called "Bambaazon," giving thanks to the spirit for the good harvest. It is both a public and private celebration that involves huge parties, traditional dancing, and beauty contests in various parts of town. However, it is important to note that the celebration of Magavau varies in accordance with the different dialects and districts of the state.

7 RITES OF PASSAGE

In the past, childbirth was usually done at home with the help of a local midwife or experienced elder. Today, many Kadazan babies are born in hospitals or clinics, though there are others who are still delivered in the traditional method. It is a common practice that when a child is born, a *bobolian* (priestess) will invoke the spirits and pray over the child for its well-being. This is particularly true among those who still practice the traditional religion. When the newborn child is about a month old, the hair-cutting (*momuga*) ceremony takes place. It is an announcement of the arrival of a new member in the community. Goats, pigs, and chickens are always slaughtered for this occasion.

Traditionally, there are three stages to a marriage. A marriage enquiry known as *monohuku* is made when the boy is only 12 years old and the girl is 11. The second stage is *momuaboi* (engagement) when the proposal is accepted. The final stage is called as *matod* by the Kadazan. When the parents think that the time has come for their children to be married, normally when the girl is 16 and the boy is 17, the wedding date is fixed mutually between both sets of parents and the couple. During the engagement period, the couple stays with their respective parents. During this time, the boy is obliged to help in his future mother-in-law's house, doing chores, such as collecting firewood, plowing the field, etc. Similarly, the girl is expected to help her future mother-in-law in the kitchen and in planting rice in the fields. This is done to prepare the couple for their life together.

A death in a family or village is announced to relatives and neighbors by the monotonous, fast beat of the gong, or by firing a carbide or kerosene bamboo cannon at frequent intervals. The corpse is draped in a clean white cloth and laid on a mat on the floor in a convenient place in the house. Relatives, neighbors, and friends are expected to pay their last respects to the dead person. Usually, a buffalo is killed and portions of the meat are distributed to visiting mourners, or it is cooked to be served with rice to those present at the funeral.

8 INTERPERSONAL RELATIONS

It is considered impolite to walk upright in front of those who are seated in the house or longhouses. The usual way is to walk with knees slightly bent, holding both hands stiffly at the sides to avoid one's clothes touching other people, or to put both hands palm-to-palm between your knees, and wedge yourself in.

Visitors and friends are always welcome in a Kadazan home. There is no fixed time for visiting, especially among relatives and friends. Upon arrival at the house, a visitor is expected to take off his or her shoes unless told otherwise. He or she will then be offered betel nut, tobacco, or a cigarette. A visitor is usually asked to stay for the night, even if the visitor does not indicate his or her intention to stay. It is to be noted, however, that when a male visitor pays frequent visits to a house where the house owner has a daughter, it may be taken to mean he is interested in marrying the daughter.

Dating among the Kadazan differs from dating in the West. Even when they are engaged, a boy and a girl are "supervised" or observed by their parents and older siblings. A boy may visit his fiancée's house whenever he likes. The girl may do likewise, but she has to be accompanied by her mother, an aunt or an elder sister. If the boy has an elder sister, the boy is allowed to invite his fiancée to stay a night or two at his parents' house. At the same time if either one of them breaks the rules, a penalty will be exacted. However, it is important to note that many of these customs have changed over the years.

9 LIVING CONDITIONS

Modernization, education, and improved infrastructure have begun to have impact on Sabah's population. Nonetheless, living standards and conditions among the Kadazandusun vary according to their location. Many continue to live in their traditional areas and maintain a longhouse lifestyle, whereby several families live together under one roof. Meanwhile, those who live in suburban areas have living standards comparable to those found in suburban areas in the United States. They have access to modern health services, tap water, electricity, good public transportation services, and other modern amenities. Most Kadazandusun who live in villages, however, have yet to experience a high standard of living. They still rely on the river for water, kerosene for light, and their feet to get from place to place.

Except for Kadazan and Rungus in Kudat, most have long abandoned their longhouses for individual homes, although the houses are still built of wood, bamboo, and thatch. In recent years, a growing affluence is changing this, replacing thatch with tiles and zinc. However, in places where bamboo is in abundance, some houses are made entirely from bamboo, including the pillars, the roof, the walls, and the floor. This is true in the Tambunan District.

10 FAMILY LIFE

The nuclear family generally provides the basic social unit of Kadazan society and the basis of the household. It is close-knit in terms of personal obligation and responsibility toward one another. The misfortune or disgrace of one member of the family is deeply felt by all kin; likewise, the good luck and prosperity of one are shared by all. Nonetheless, the high rate of rural-urban migration has led to more intermarriage with other non Kadazandusun groups.

A family consists of a husband, a wife, and their children. Sometimes a household includes other members of the extended family, such as grandparents, uncles, and aunts. A woman's primary role is to raise her children and to see daily that the family has enough food to eat. She is responsible for collecting jungle vegetables like fern tops, mushrooms, and young leaves for the evening, while her husband contributes fish or meat to the pot. Every evening the wife is responsible for preparing a good meal for her family.

Like most other native marriage customs in Borneo, the Kadazan marriage is fiercely monogamous. Adultery committed by either the husband or wife is severely punished.

A family may rear chickens, pigs, dogs, and cats not as house pets but for other purposes. Pigs, ducks, and chicken are reared for domestic consumption, while dogs are reared for hunting and cats to chase or kill rats and mice in the house and farms.

11 CLOTHING

Most of the traditional costumes worn by Kadazan men and women are predominantly dark or black in color. However, today a modern adaptation to the original attire is rich decoration done with colorful embroidery, glittering sequins, and imported gold lace trimming, as well as handmade lace from imported gold thread or yarn. The women's skirts reach down 5 cm (2 in) above the kneecap, with red embroidery running down the sides. Silver coin belts, rattan or beaded waist bands, beaded necklaces, and other silver ornaments and accessories are worn with these costumes. The color of the rattan waist band worn around the waist holds special meaning. Red denotes that the wearer is not a mother, while black denotes that she is, and white signifies that the wearer is a grandmother.

For their headgear, the women wear hats and/or scarves, while the men wear a head cloth called *sigah* or *kain dasar,* a piece of cloth draped, folded, and tied according to the style and pattern of the district. It is important to note that dress codes vary from one district to another.

Today, Kadazan women and men wear Western-style clothing for everyday use. This includes skirts, blouses, shirts, pants, tank tops, etc.

¹² FOOD

As in most societies in Asia, rice forms the staple food of the Kadazandusun diet. Rice is eaten at every meal, with meat and/or vegetable dishes. In the village the woman is responsible for collecting vegetables such as young ferns, mushrooms, bamboo shoots, etc., for breakfast, lunch, and dinner. The man is responsible for bringing meat or fish for the meals. Young ferns are one of the Kadazan's traditional foods. There are normally stir-fried with garlic, onion, and shrimp paste, and are served with steamed rice. Nowadays, most Kadazan's kitchen utensils include pans, pots, plates, forks, spoons, etc., which are available in department stores. In the old days, most of their utensils were made from bamboo, wood, and rattan.

¹³ EDUCATION

The Kadazan have responded positively to the Malaysian government's effort to encourage education. This is because education can raise living standards by creating wider job opportunities. Consequently, many are able to read and write in both Malay and English. Children at the age of six are required to go to elementary school, and continue on to lower and upper secondary schools. Many obtain the Malaysian Education Certificate, which is equal to a high school diploma in the United States, and some go on to obtain degrees from local or foreign universities or other higher learning institutions. Parental support and encouragement have been driving forces behind the academic success of many Kadazan. Formal education is seen as an avenue toward success in the modern world.

¹⁴ CULTURAL HERITAGE

Music and dance are closely related among the Kadazan. Both are vital parts of nearly every social event, particularly at the village level. Music is played during wedding celebrations, engagement parties, harvest festivals, first birthday parties and animistic religious ceremonies. A Kadazan wedding sees a rare airing of traditional instruments such as the bronze *kulintangan* (gongs) and *gendang* (drums made from wood and leather or calfskin). The *sompotan*, a mouth organ, is another instrument that is popular among the Kadazan. Made from a dried bitter gourd, it is produced in Tambunan and traded throughout Sabah. Sumazan is a dance between a male and female performed by couples or a group of couples to a symphony of *kulintangan*.

Since the Kadazan did not have a written language in the past, their stories, songs, history, legends, and myths were passed down orally. Only in recent years have measures been taken to document these stories in books, articles, and journals.

¹⁵ WORK

Although the Kadazan were originally farmers or agriculturalists, many have migrated to urban centers and have become prominent figures in the civil service and other professions.

In the interior, rice planting is the most common occupation, although, with the introduction of other cash crops such as rubber and coffee, this is likely to change. In hilly areas, some Kadazan still practice shifting rice cultivation. However, this is gradually dying out. Government efforts to modernize and improve socioeconomic status have enabled the Kadazandusun to become part of mainstream society. As a result, a number of them are now political leaders, entrepreneurs, and professionals.

¹⁶ SPORTS

In the past, swimming in the river and climbing trees were the popular sports among the children. Today, both children and adults are becoming more acquainted with sports such as soccer, volleyball, and basketball. In the evening, after they return home from their farms, they get together to play a game in the yard.

¹⁷ ENTERTAINMENT AND RECREATION

The type of entertainment or recreation that Kadazan enjoy depends on their locality. Kadazan in urban areas have easy access to movies, television, etc., comparable to residents of major cities in the United States or United Kingdom, and their forms of entertainment are very different from those Kadazan who still live in the village. Traditional music, songs, and dance are some forms of entertainment that are still very popular in the village. However, television and videos are becoming an increasingly widespread form of entertainment.

¹⁸ FOLK ART, CRAFTS, AND HOBBIES

The availability of local materials, such as bamboo and wood, has greatly influenced the nature of handicrafts of the Kadazan. Bamboo is used for making different kinds of household utensils, baskets, and mats. It is also widely used to build houses and fences. Wood and rattan are two durable materials widely used by the interior people for making huts, baskets, and decorative wall hangings. Rattan is also useful for tying pieces of wood or bamboo together. The weaving of baskets, mats, and other household utensils is done mostly by women during their free time.

¹⁹ SOCIAL PROBLEMS

The Kadazan and most natives of Borneo are facing one common problem: obtaining legal rights over their ancestral lands. They are faced with the dilemma of having to give up their rights to the land in favor of land development programs, usually initiated by the state or federal government. Although the socioeconomic status of the Kadazandusun has improved in recent years, they have to cope with changes to their traditional values. For instance, extended families with several generations staying together are being replaced by nuclear families. This has implications on traditional social and support network.

²⁰ GENDER ISSUES

Like the Iban of Sarawak, the Kadazandusun maintain an egalitarian society with a bilateral descent system. In this sense, men and women has equal standing in the society. However, there is a clear sense of division of labor between men and women. In the village, for instance, the woman is responsible for collecting vegetables, such as young ferns, mushrooms, bamboo shoots, etc., for breakfast, lunch, and dinner. The man is responsible for bringing meat or fish for the meals.

[21] BIBLIOGRAPHY

Chay, Peter. *Sabah: The Land below the Wind.* Kuala Lumpur, Malaysia: Foto Teknik Sdn. Bhd, 1988.

Regis, Patricia. "Classification and identity of Sabah's indigenous groups," In *The Encyclopedia of Malaysia, Peoples and Traditions,* edited by Hood Sellah, 108–109. Kuala Lumpur: Editions Didier Millet, 2006.

Sabah Museum. *Sabah's Heritage: A Brief Introduction to Sabah's History and Heritage.* Kota Kinabalu: Sabah Museum, 1992.

Teo, Albert C. K., and A. G. Sullivan. *Sabah: Land of the Sacred Mountain.* Kota Kinabalu, Malaysia: Sabah Handicraft, 1988.

—by P. Bala

KALINGA

PRONUNCIATION: kuh-LING-uh
LOCATION: Philippines (northern Luzon)
POPULATION: 112,000 (2000)
LANGUAGE: Kalinga
RELIGION: Native spirit beliefs
RELATED ARTICLES: Vol. 3: Filipinos; Ifugao; Vol. 4: Manuvu'

[1] INTRODUCTION

Although at present speaking mutually intelligible dialects and possessing a strong sense of ethnic identity nurtured by a peace-pact system, the Kalinga display much cultural diversity among themselves. This is because of their division into small endogamous territories *(boboloy)* and perhaps also to their disparate origins as relatively recent refugees from the lower Abra valley to the west and the Cagayan valley to the east. The name Kalinga itself is a negative marker. It comes from the word for "enemy" in Ibanag, the language of Christianized Cagayan lowlanders. Major differences exist between the Kalinga north and south of the Pacil River; the southerners grow wet-rice on terraces and share many cultural elements with the Bontok and Ifugao, who depend on the same type of agriculture.

Substantial external influence commenced only in the 19th century with the opening of a Spanish trail between Abra and Cagayan through Kalinga territory; this trail introduced Tinggianes (fellow highlanders) and lowland Ilocano traders. Replacing spears, machetes, and axes, guns obtained from these increased contacts made the endemic feuding infinitely more murderous and threatened to annihilate Kalinga society. This fear motivated the emergence of the peace-pact system that the American colonial regime, intent on abolishing head-hunting, was to endorse.

The Americans introduced sanitation and schools, and educated Kalinga were soon able to fill the local administrative positions initially occupied by lowland Filipinos; the Kalinga passion for individual distinction predisposed them to enthusiastic participation in Filipino electoral politics. World War II flooded the highlands (as it did the Philippine countryside in general) with firearms, and since then "mutually assured destruction" has kept the peace between well-armed Kalinga groups. As a substitute for headhunting, private revenge continues to be part of everyday life. With some of their lands threatened by government dam projects, the Kalinga, along with the Bontok, have been among the most assertive of what are currently termed "cultural communities" (formerly "cultural minorities" or "non-Christian tribes").

See also the article entitled **Ifugao**.

[2] LOCATION AND HOMELAND

The Kalinga occupy a northern section of northern Luzon's Cordillera Central, which is drained by the middle Chico River and its tributaries. The territory of the Isneg people of the Apayao basin intervenes between the Kalinga and the sea. Towards the southern edge of Kalinga territory, ridges rise to 1,830 m (6,000 ft), while the mountains are lower in the northern area. Pine trees crown the ridge tops, cogon grass blankets the steep slopes, and dense semitropical vegetation covers the

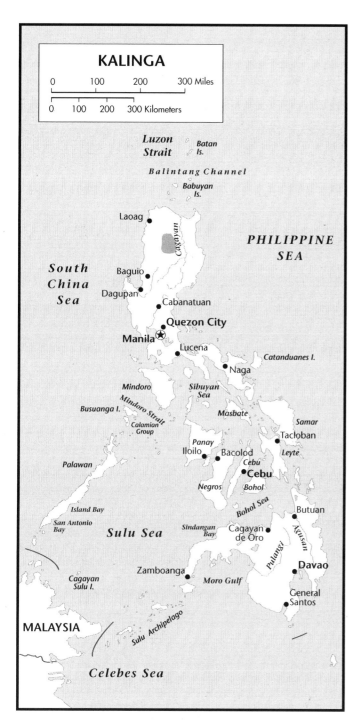

KALINGA

0   100   200   300 Miles

0   100   200   300 Kilometers

Luzon Strait

Batan Is.

Balintang Channel

Babuyan Is.

Laoag

Cagayan

PHILIPPINE SEA

South China Sea

Baguio

Dagupan

Cabanatuan

Quezon City

Manila

Lucena

Catanduanes I.

Naga

Mindoro

Sibuyan Sea

Busuanga I.

Mindoro Strait

Calamian Group

Masbate

Samar

Tacloban

Panay

Iloilo   Bacolod

Cebu

Leyte

Palawan

Cebu

Negros

Bohol

Island Bay

Bohol Sea

San Antonio Bay

Butuan

Sulu Sea

Sindangan Bay

Cagayan de Oro

Agusan

Pulangi

Davao

Zamboanga

Cagayan Sulu I.

Moro Gulf

General Santos

MALAYSIA

Sulu Archipelago

Celebes Sea

valley bottoms where settlements are located (still 610 m or 2,000 ft above sea level).

In the 1970s, the Kalinga numbered 40,000, with the heaviest concentration in the south where wet-rice is grown. According to the 2000 census, the population of Kalinga province stood at 174,023, of which 64.4% (or nearly 112,000) identified themselves as Kalinga (24% identified themselves as Ilocanos, 2.5% as Kankanay). Estimates for various Kalinga dialect groups are as follows: Limos, 20,000 (1977); Mandukayang, 1,500 (1990); Butbut, 8,000 (1998); Lower Tanudan (1998); Upper Tanudan (1998); Lubuagan, 14,003 (2000); Southern Kalinga, 13,000 (2000).

³LANGUAGE

The Kalinga speak mutually intelligible dialects of the same Austronesian language; Kalinga is more closely related to Tinggian, Isneg, Gaddang, Ibanag, and Ilocano than to Bontok, Kankanai, and Ifugao. The dialects may currently be converging under the influence of a phonetically simplified, heavily Ilocano-influenced form of Kalinga. In fact, Ilocano is so widely understood that it is used to record the terms of peace-pacts between Kalinga groups (instead of or along with English, a language in which a few people in the larger communities are literate).

Children are given the name of a dead or living grandparent, in order to receive qualities of that person.

⁴FOLKLORE

Among supernaturals, Kalinga believe in the *ngilin,* a malevolent water spirit in the form of a human pigmy who prevents women from conceiving; it also victimizes newborns. Also feared are the *alan* or *kotmo,* giant ghouls who feed on corpses.

⁵RELIGION

Anito are supernatural beings in general. The Kalinga recognize a creator god, Kaboniyan, but invoke him only in moments of extreme and sudden crisis, such as an accidental death or the destruction of the rice crop by a storm. They take for granted the good will of the *mandodwa* (benevolent spirits) and focus their prayers, chants, and sacrifices on appeasing malevolent spirits who, if neglected, bring illness and misfortune on humans by capturing their souls. Kalinga must also show respect to their village guardian spirit, *sangasang,* who resides in a *podayan* shelter housing sacred *bayog* stones. In addition, they make offerings to deceased ancestors at funeral ceremonies, which are more elaborate among the southerners who follow the Ifugao and Bontok in emphasizing the ancestral cult. While fear of witchcraft is weak, that of poisoning is widespread and often attributed as the work of old childless women, who are believed to be vindictive because of their misfortune.

Formerly, male priests officiated at headhunting rites, but now female mediums (*mangalisig* in southern Kalinga and *mandadawak* or *manganito* in northern Kalinga) are more prominent, leading rites for curing, community welfare, and the life-cycle. Before receiving instruction from a practicing medium, a future medium must be called first to her vocation (by disturbing dreams, trembling fits, or nausea after eating certain foods like eel or dog). A medium possesses spirit helpers (familiars), a repertoire of chants, and standard paraphernalia, which includes a *bayobong* turban, a Chinese plate and a bamboo stick to beat it with during rituals, and a basket to contain everything.

In the 1990s, Christian conversion (mostly to Catholicism) remained limited because of the daunting geographical barriers to missionary penetration. According to the 2000 census, 17.6% of the population of the Cordillera Administrative Region, of which Kalinga province is a part, was classified as "Other" in religious affiliation, meaning adherents of indigenous religion. The rest followed a form of Christianity: 65.8% of the region's population is Roman Catholic (much lower than the national percentage of 83%), 8.9% Evangelical, 2.9% Iglesia ni Cristo, 1.6% Jehovah's Witness, 0.8% Philippine Independent Church (Aglipayan).

6 MAJOR HOLIDAYS

See the article entitled **Filipinos**.

7 RITES OF PASSAGE

For a month after a birth, the family refrains from eating beef, cow's milk, eel, frogs, taro, and dog meat; the father may not leave the village; and no one who does not habitually sleep in the house may enter it. At the end of the month, a medium sweeps the house with an *anaao* (a palm-frond raincoat) and removes the four reeds that have been placed at the four corners of the house as a sign of the taboo period. Over the first year and a half of its life, six *kontad* ceremonies are held for the child, involving pig and chicken sacrifices, chanting, the taking of pig's liver omens, and the erecting of a spirit house or platform.

Now that free-choice matches are more prevalent, the traditional contract marriage proceeds in the following stages. In some regions soon after a boy's birth, his parents pick a suitable girl and commission go-betweens to take omens and present valuable beads to her family at a *banat* feast. The go-betweens return with gifts for the boy's parents and for themselves (henceforth, the two families invite each other to their respective feasts and give each other a share of the meat). At the age of 12, the boy may begin light bride-service for the girl's family. At the age of 17, the boy's uncles and aunts escort him to the girl's house because for the parents to do so would appear to be indifference toward the boy and would invite victimization by malevolent spirits, i.e., illness. The girl's side prepares a feast and gives the escorts meat to take back to the boy's kin. Two weeks later, after the boy's family gives the girl's family Chinese beads and plates, the couple begins to sleep together. The Kalinga apply less pressure on the couple to consummate the union than other highlanders, such as the Ibaloi go-betweens, who strip an unwilling pair, bind them together, and wrap them in a water buffalo hide. Five months later, a feast to which both kin groups are invited seals the marriage contract; this includes competitive gift-giving between the sides and the handing over of a portion of the inheritances coming to the newlyweds.

After death, the deceased is seated on a death chair for up to 10 days, with the surviving spouse guarding it and relatives preparing rice wine for the wake, which also requires the slaughter of pigs and water buffalo. While children are buried near the house or under the granary, adults are interred in graves faced with small stones smoothed over with lime plaster; big stone slabs are laid over the body, the slabs are then covered with dirt, and a thatch arbor is then erected on top of the dirt for offerings (rice bread hung for the dead, and betel, charcoal, and lemon leaves to repel malevolent spirits). Today, wealthy southerners raise concrete family mausoleums. Nine days later, in some areas, personal belongings are placed on the grave. A year of mourning follows an adult's death, during which relatives may neither sing nor dance, must wear a black or brown strip, and let their hair grow long and unoiled. A surviving spouse may not remarry during this period and may eat only fruits and greens and may neither gather food nor cook. A morning-to-morning *kolias* feast concludes the mourning; singing, dancing, and boasting keep the mood fes-

A Kalinga couple wear traditional dress in Luzon, Philippines. The Kalinga are known for their bright colors and accessories. (© Paul Almasy/Corbis)

tive, for weeping would attract another death. If individuals cannot stop grieving, they restore themselves to normal life by exhuming the bones and reburying them or by taking a long journey that includes crossing a wide river.

8 INTERPERSONAL RELATIONS

Beyond the immediate kin, an individual traditionally identified only with the *boboloy*, the area inhabited by overlapping kin-groups, within which one generally married and outside of which no one could be trusted. In recent times, peace-pacts have weakened this localism to a considerable extent but have far from eliminated it. Northern boboloy consist of 10 to 12 hamlets (500–700 people), while southern ones encompass even larger numbers.

In former times, authority gravitated towards *mangngol*, renowned warrior-headhunters (also wealthy and well-spoken) who avenged wrongs done to their kinfolk [*see* **Manuvu**]. Currently, regional power issues from the ability to arbitrate disputes (imposing fines that take into consideration public opinion and the kin-groups involved) and serve as a pact-holder; individuals with the required wealth, wisdom, and charisma are called *pangngat* (*lakay* in the north). Despite distinguishing poor (*kapos*) from rich (*baknang*; in the south, also *kadangyang*), Kalinga culture stresses equal treatment for all individuals irrespective of status (e.g., servants are treated as well as adopted children and may even appeal to pangngat if mistreated by their masters). At the same time, Kalinga exhibit a strong drive towards personal distinction, as expressed in the boasting sessions that are integral to all gatherings (though rice-land and livestock wealth have replaced headhunting exploits as the source of pride).

Within the boboloy, pangngat arbitrate disputes. Between boboloy, however, conflicts generally escalated in the past to reciprocal headhunting raids (feuding for blood vengeance). Since the colonial abolition of headhunting, pitched battles *(botad)* now provide the outlet for revenge-taking; their firearm-increased murderousness has led to the peace-pact *(bodong)* system.

A bodong is contracted between two individuals (generally pangngat) but is binding on both boboloy. The first stage is a "tasting" *(simsim* or *singlip)* where the sides gather, review grievances, and settle disputes. After this, at a large gathering *(lonok)* the *pagta* or provisions of the bodong are written out, detailing how to punish crimes committed by a member of one boboloy against a member of the other, e.g., punishing killings or woundings by fines, counter-killing, or symbolic counter-injury. Also set down are rules of courting, the return of lost or stolen articles, and hospitality, including how to handle the death, accident, or illness within one's territory of a person from the other boboloy. Renewed at *dolnat* gatherings and transferable to new pact-holders, peace-pacts permit trade and even migration between boboloy territories.

The southern Kalinga follow the Bontok-Ifugao practice of having children from the age of six or seven sleep in a unisex dormitory (girls sleep in a widow's house and boys in a vacant house *[obog]).* Boys may visit the girls at night, but only engaged couples may have sex. The northern Kalinga, on the other hand, expect their adolescent children to stay in the home of a close relative; sexual contact must be kept secret from parents. A girl who has sex with a boy with whom she is not contracted to marry, or a man who is already married, will be whipped (the male, unless he raped the girl, is only fined).

Courting procedures leading to love-match unions have long coexisted with contract marriages. A boy may intercept a girl on her way to fetch water. As talking to each other would violate etiquette, they exchange signals, the girl expressing approval with a subtle wink, a raised eyebrow, or a sudden lowering of her eyes. Thus encouraged, the boy presents himself at her house in the evening, serenading her with courting songs or flute-playing in the presence of her parents. Afterwards, the girl arranges to meet the boy while parents are away.

9 LIVING CONDITIONS

Kalinga live in hamlets of 6–30 houses in the north and of over 200 in the south. The wood-plank or bamboo-plaiting houses are on piles, are entered by stairs or a ladder, and have thatched grass or reed roofs. The floor plan is rectangular or square in the north, and octagonal in the south, with a single room. In more traditional homes, floors consist of split-bamboo mats over a grating of slender beams; the mats are removed and washed in a stream every two or three days. A bit off-center in the single room is a fire pit enclosed in a 10–15-cm-high (4–6-in-high) wooden box full of sand and ash; above it hangs a rack for drying wood, food, and clothing. Today, each village has at least one or two houses of hewn-wood planks with galvanized iron roofs. These are more prestigious, but hotter than a thatched one. A traditional house may be kept alongside for use as a kitchen; this new house-type will eventually dominate.

Average family income in the Cordillera Administrative Region, of which Kalinga province is a part, amounted to 192,000 pesos (US$3,765) in 2006, among the highest in the country, cf. the national average of ₱173,000, the National Capital Region's ₱311,000, Southern Tagalog's ₱198,000, and those of the neighboring Cagayan Valley and Ilocos regions, ₱143,000 and

₱142,000 respectively. In 2000, 32% of households in Kalinga had access to a community faucet, 12% to a faucet of their own, and 21.6% to a shared deep well, while 11.7% obtained their water from springs, lakes, rivers, or rain. Almost half of households (48.6%) disposed of their garbage by burning it, 21.9% by burying it in a pit, and 11.7% by feeding it to their animals; only 6.3% had it picked up by a collection truck. 50% of houses were lit with kerosene lamps, 44.3% with electricity, and 3.5% with firewood. While 29% of households lacked basic appliances of any kind, 68.9% possessed a radio, 21.9% a television, 12.9% a refrigerator, 7% a VCR, 2% a telephone or cell phone, 6.6% a washing machine, and 8.2% a motorized vehicle.

10 FAMILY LIFE

Each individual recognizes his or her personal kindred as including the descendants of both paternal and maternal great-grandparents (i.e., counting second cousins) among the northern Kalinga. In the more densely populated south, kindred includes only grandparents and first cousins, although the wealthy there may recognize bilateral descent groups [*see* **Ifugao**].

The nuclear family includes a married couple, their younger children, and occasionally grandparents and, among the wealthy, servants. Adolescents live together in same-sex dormitories. Two to four related nuclear families work together in agriculture and other economic activities; this extended household is actually emphasized more than its components. Face-to-face interaction among more distant kin is diminishing with the greater mobility of modern times. In the south where larger towns offer individuals greater economic independence from kin, people tend to address relatives with personal names rather than with kinship terms such as are still regularly used in the north.

Formerly, it was a strongly enforced rule for an individual to marry within his or her *boboloy* (barrio); third-cousin marriage was permitted, but second-cousin marriage met with disapproval. Marriage by contract between the parents while the children are still young was the norm but is now giving way to free-choice matches. The ideal, still followed in the south, is for a new couple to join the wife's parents' extended household. Wealthy men might take concubines *(dagdagas),* especially in order to seal peace-pacts with other localities. Half of the marriages in north Kalinga end in divorce. The primary reason for the divorce is childlessness (and occasionally the poor hospitality or laziness of the wife).

Relations between parents and children are markedly less prolonged and intense among the Kalinga than among other highland peoples, but grandparents and grandchildren are very close, often given to mildly teasing each other. The grandparents act as babysitters while the parents are working away from the house (a still strong grandfather will carry his grandchild in a sling to roam about watching the activities in village and field). Grandchildren also learn ritual procedures from grandparents and take care of them as well as their own parents in old age and, via offerings, in the afterlife. Parents regard safeguarding inheritance and making a good match for them as their main duties to their children. Children tend to be indulged; adults rarely resort to whipping and prefer to scare children into behaving with stories about "strangers" (indeed, inflicting corporal punishment on another's child would incur fines from the incensed relatives).

[11] CLOTHING

Northern Kalinga traditional male clothing is of brightly colored cotton and consists of a G-string with beads or buttons, a short jacket with beads and tassels, a tube sarong worn over one shoulder, a turban with blossoms and feathers stuck in it, earplugs, an agate-bead choker, and an ornamental betel-bag. Women's traditional clothing includes sarongs, shirts, agate-bead necklaces, and brass and mother-of-pearl earrings, and hair grown long (augmented with switches of hair from departed or living relatives).

Today, northern Kalinga men wear lowland-style trousers and cut-offs with or without an old shirt, and the women wear cotton dresses. Traditional clothing is still commonly worn in the south, where colors are more subdued and accessories are kept to a minimum [for southern women's attire, *see* **Ifugao**].

[12] FOOD

The staple food is rice supplemented by vegetables and some meat.

[13] EDUCATION

In 2000, literacy stood at 90.5% for the Cordillera Administrative Region, of which Kalinga province is a part. In Kalinga province itself, of people five years or older 45.79% had attended elementary school, 23% high school, and 11.19% college; 4% held academic degrees. (see also the article entitled **Filipinos** in this volume).

[14] CULTURAL HERITAGE

See the article entitled **Ifugao**.

[15] WORK

Although some Kalinga receive enough modern education to become schoolteachers (a most esteemed profession among them), municipal employees, or Baguio or Manila office workers, most Kalinga remain subsistence farmers. Only in the southern area adjacent to the Bontok has wet-rice cultivation on terraces been the dominant form (though now it is spreading in the north); Kalinga terraces slope gently at an angle and are not held back by stone walls as are those of the Bontok or Ifugao. The northern Kalinga grow dry-rice on swidden (shifting-cultivation) fields along with beans, sweet potatoes, maize, sugarcane, taro, betel, tobacco, and coffee.

Animal protein comes from a variety of sources: wild pig, deer, fowl, dogs, birds, fish, mussels, and eels. Livestock includes a few horses and cattle as well as pigs and chickens for sacrifice and meat distribution at ritual celebrations. Kept for slaughter, water buffalo are also important as a measure of wealth and the means to buy rice-land.

Guaranteed by highly formalized and ritualized pacts *(abuyog)* between potentially warring regions, traditional trade patterns resembled those of the Ifugao [*see* **Ifugao**].

[16] SPORTS

Children between the ages of 3 and 10 play at the riverside bathing place while their older female relatives wash and do other chores. A common game for single- or mixed-sex groups is hide-and-seek. Boys between 7 and 15 enjoy spinning tops.

[17] ENTERTAINMENT AND RECREATION

Kalinga are fond of putting on plays or skits at public gatherings; the source material derives from school lessons, such as the life of Filipino national hero Jose Rizal. Parents teach their children to perform public recitations of pieces that they themselves learned in school.

[18] FOLK ART, CRAFTS, AND HOBBIES

See the article entitled **Ifugao**.

[19] SOCIAL PROBLEMS

See the article entitled **Filipinos**.

[20] GENDER ISSUES

Although Kalinga couples do not automatically prefer boys over girls, not to have any sons at all is regarded as a great misfortune, because men, through combat, can defend the family and win it prestige. From an early age, girls assume the heavier tasks, such as taking care of younger children, pounding and winnowing rice, scrubbing mats, toting water, and helping in the fields. By contrast, when boys are not fetching firewood from the potentially dangerous forest, they just sit around and gossip. A boy already promised in marriage, however, may also help around his in-laws' house. In the past, this was so that the young men could be ready to defend the community at any time, but in these relatively peaceful times, they have little to do and fall into insulting relatives, quarreling, vandalizing, and theft. As adults, women work year-round all day and into the night, whereas men work only in the daytime, clearing and plowing fields, and in the dry season, they travel to increase the family's wealth and prestige.

In 2000, the literacy level was slightly lower for women (90%) than for men (90.8%) in the Cordillera Administrative Region, of which Kalinga province is a part. Of those who had attended elementary school, 54.03% were males, slightly higher than their proportion of the population, 52.8%. Of those who had attended college and those who held post-baccalaureate degrees, the majority were women.

[21] BIBLIOGRAPHY

Dozier, Edward P. *The Kalinga of Northern Luzon, Philippines.* New York: Holt, Rinehart and Winston, 1967.

Gordon, Raymond G., ed. *Ethnologue: Languages of the World*, 15th ed. Dallas, TX: SIL International, 2005. http://www. ethnologue.com (November 16, 2008)

LeBar, Frank M., ed. *Ethnic Groups of Insular Southeast Asia.* Vol 2, *The Philippines and Formosa.* New Haven, Conn.: Human Relations Area Files Press, 1972.

National Statistics Office: republic of the Philippines. "Cordillera Administrative Region: The Least Populous Region of the Philippines." http://www.census.gov.ph/data/pressrelease/2002/pr0259tx.html (November 16, 2008).

——"Females Better Educated in Kalinga (Results from the 2000 Census of Population and Housing, NSO)." http://www.census.gov.ph/data/pressrelease/2002/pr0259tx.html (November 16, 2008).

—revise by A. Abalahin

KAMMU

PRONUNCIATION: kah-MOO
ALTERNATE NAMES: Khamu; Khmu
LOCATION: Laos, Thailand, Vietnam, and China.
POPULATION: About 500,000
LANGUAGE: Kammu
RELIGION: Animism; some Buddhism and Christianity

¹ INTRODUCTION

The Kammu (also written Khamu, Khmu, and Kmhmu), who make up the largest minority group in Laos, are believed to be the original inhabitants of the country. They are an Austro-Asiatic people who moved north from the area of Indonesia in prehistoric times. The Kammu practiced paddy rice agriculture in the valleys along the Mekong River until they were displaced around the 14th century by the Lao moving southward from what is today southern China. Pushed out of the fertile river valleys where wet rice agriculture was possible, the Kammu settled on mountain slopes and in small, narrow upland valleys in northern and central Laos and in northern Thailand. There they practiced swidden (slash-and-burn) agriculture, clear cutting and burning off areas of the forest, farming the fields for a few years until the soil was depleted, and then burning off a new area and letting the old fields lie fallow. Sometimes they relocated their villages to find suitable land.

The Kammu have traditionally been at the bottom of Laotian society. Members of the ethnic Lao majority frequently refer to the Kammu with contemptuous terminology, including the word *kha,* or slaves. Ethnic Kammu regions of the country have historically received less funding for roads, schools, and government services than Lao majority areas. Many Kammu joined the Communist Pathet Lao (Lao Nation) movement and the Lao People's Liberation Army in the 1960s and 1970s, during the Lao civil war because the Communists promised them respect and education and technical training in Vietnam if they joined the cause. During the war years some Kammu areas were heavily bombed by the United States as the Laotian civil war was linked to the Vietnam War, which was also being fought in Laos. After the Pathet Lao won control of the country in 1975, some Kammu Communist cadres gained positions of prestige within the government. However, the majority of ethnic Kammu have remained impoverished and have had few opportunities for economic or social advancement.

The Lao People's Democratic Republic (LPDR), established in 1975, has tried to do away with ethnic labels and now refers to "lowland Lao," "midland Lao," and "upland Lao." The Kammu are classified as midland Lao because they tend to live on the mountain slopes. The LPDR government has tried to end slash-and-burn agriculture and has encouraged the Kammu to resettle in lowland areas. Some Kammu had already relocated to escape war related violence. The Kammu, like other midland Lao, are among the poorest people in what is already a very poor country. Their low levels of education and geographic isolation, together with continued prejudice from the ethnic Lao, have been barriers to their integration.

² LOCATION AND HOMELAND

The Kammu are considered as one of the indigenous populations of Laos and represent the country's largest minority group. There are roughly 500,000 Kammu in Laos and smaller numbers of Kammu in northern Thailand, northern Vietnam, and southern China. A few thousand Kammu fled as refugees after the Communists came to power in 1975, and they have resettled mostly in the United States.

The Kammu live in scattered villages in mountainous areas of north and central Laos and in border regions of neighboring countries. Often villages are small, with only 20–30 families, but some villages can include several hundred households. Neighboring villages may belong to different ethnic groups lumped together with the Kammu as midland Lao, but with their own cultures and languages that are mutually incomprehensible. Young Kammu men often leave their mountain homes to find unskilled jobs in towns and cities for a few years to earn money for a bride-price. During the Lao civil war, many young men went to Thailand to escape forced conscription into the Laotian armed forces. The government has pressured Kammu to switch to settled lowland farming rather than shifting slash-and-burn cultivation, but the land offered to Kammu farmers has often been poor for agricultural cultivation.

³ LANGUAGE

The Kammu have their own language, which belongs to the Mon-Khmer family of languages, but it is not a written language. Kammu words are mostly monosyllabic, though disyllabic words are still numerous. The normal word order in Kammu is subject-verb-object, though the object may appear at the beginning of a phrase for emphasis. Kammu contains many Laotian and Thai loan words, and Kammu who live in Thai urban areas often adopt the more simplistic syntax of Thai.

The Laotian government's efforts to reclassify Kammu as "midland Lao" has resulted in few references to Kammu in Laotian historical texts and, until recent decades, there were few significant works about the Kammu in Western literature. Variation in the Kammu language is common, as the Kammu are spaced over a wide area with limited contact with more distant settlements. The language includes an increasing number of loan words from Lao.

The majority of Kammu are illiterate, as few have had access to education. Agreements are oral and are made before village elders, who memorize the terms and will arbitrate any disputes. Children use their father's first name as their last name, so last names change every generation. Once a person becomes a parent, he or she is referred to as the father or mother of their child.

⁴ FOLKLORE

The Kammu have a rich folklore that has been transmitted orally. They are well regarded by other groups for their knowledge of folk medicines made from plants gathered in the forest.

The Kammu consider Luang Prabang, which served as the Lao royal capital, as their city, and they have a legend that explains how the city was founded by a Kammu.

> The old people say that long, long ago people wished to build the city of Luang Prabang, but an enormous tree grew on the site that nobody was able to cut down. Each

man that tried fell ill and fled. Then a man by the name of Wang said, "I will cut the tree if you will taboo the day of my death forever." The people promised and Wang cut the tree, but he dropped dead when the tree fell. Once they buried Wang, the Kammu began to build the city of Luang Prabang.

When the city was finished, they looked for a man to be their king. They all went to a cliff overlooking the place where the Ou River flows into the Mekong River, and the people said, "Any man brave enough to jump off this cliff, we will elect king."

The people boarded seven boats and seven rafts in the waters below the cliff and called for the men who wished to be king to jump. Looking down from the dizzying heights, one man after another was afraid and ran away. Finally just one man remained, a relative of Wang, who had cut the tree. This man had tucked a quiver into his belt, and as he leaned over to look down from the top of the cliff, his quiver struck against something and he lost his balance and fell into the river. The people hurried to help him get in a boat, and they praised his courage and elected him king. To this day the Kammu taboo the day Wang cut the tree and the day Wang was buried, and on these days no work is undertaken.

The Kammu played a significant role in annual ceremonies in the Lao court of Luang Prabang until fairly recent times. The ceremonies indicated the Kammu's prior claim to the land through a symbolic payment to the Kammu representatives, who in turn acknowledged the legitimacy of the King of Luang Prabang.

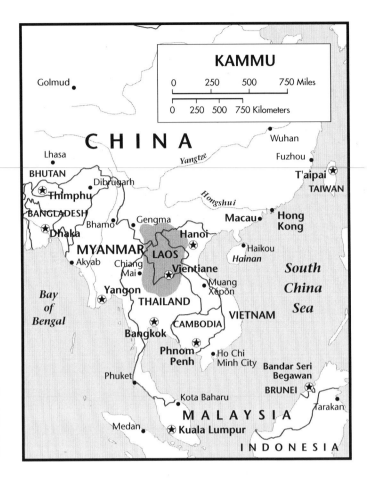

5 RELIGION

The majority of Kammu are animists, with smaller numbers of Buddhists and Christians. The Kammu believe there are hundreds of different spirits, helpful and harmful, that reside in natural settings. An important aspect of Kammu spiritual beliefs is the notion of reincarnation based upon merit. Individuals are engaged in a struggle between good and evil forces that plays itself out through the interaction of spirits.

Each village has its own shaman to propitiate the spirits that cause illness and accidents, and a priest (*lkuun*) to perform the village ceremony for the ancestor spirits. A shaman can be either male or female, but the priest holds a hereditary office passed on to the eldest son of the priestly family, even if the individual is only a child at the time. One becomes a shaman by apprenticing to a shaman and learning the magic formulas to be recited on different occasions. The shaman must also be a person of good character who follows many specific rules or the magic formulas will not work to drive away evil spirits.

Living far from health centers and access to modern medicine, the Kammu often attribute illness to evil spirits and call on a shaman to exorcise them and bring back the soul of the patient. Minor diseases are treated by a medicine man, an expert in herbal remedies. It is believed that conception of a child is determined by the ancestors of the wife. If a woman does not become pregnant after marriage, then her father will sacrifice a pig as an offering to his ancestors.

Rituals and taboos are a common part of Kammu spirituality and daily life. The Kammu have a calendar that operates on a 60-day cycle that includes many taboo days when various kinds of work cannot be done and strangers cannot enter the village. During special ceremonies, woven wicker squares and bamboo arrows are placed along paths and trails leading to the village to warn outsiders not to enter. The Kammu also believe that spirits in important places must be placated. For example, before setting out traps or beginning to hunt, a man must perform a ceremony to ask permission from the spirits that reside in the hunting grounds.

6 MAJOR HOLIDAYS

The most important holiday for the Kammu is the three-day series of ceremonies once a year to sacrifice to the village ancestor spirits, remake the village common house where the spirits reside, and ritually renew the village. The village spirits are considered benign, helping people lead good and happy lives so long as proper rituals are observed. There is no set day to sacrifice to the village spirits, but the ceremony is usually performed just after sowing the rice so the spirits will bring rain, or just before harvest, so they will chase away evil spirits like the spirits of accidents or the spirits of waste. The house where the spirits reside is cleaned and remade with a new thatched roof, then a black pig is killed and its blood smeared on the altar. The spirits are offered pork, rice, and rice wine, and then the whole village eats and drinks.

The next day a sacrifice is made to the water spirits. Villagers dress up and parade to the village well with drums and gongs. There is a ritual cleaning of the well, and fresh water is fetched from the well in a decorated water container and placed in the house of the spirits.

On the third day each family places a basket under the water container, which the priest shoots with an arrow from a crossbow. Those baskets sprinkled with a lot of water are a sign of luck and a good harvest, while those baskets the water does not reach presage a poor harvest. There is then a procession to a stream to float away the bad spirits. The young people engage in horseplay with mud fights and pushing each other in the water. A communal meal is eaten at noon, and in the evening the villagers parade home and celebrate with lots of food and rice wine.

7 RITES OF PASSAGE

For most men the main rite of passage is preparing for marriage, usually by leaving home to work as a laborer for a few years to get money for a bride-price. Each family has a totem and is grouped by totems (plants, birds, four-legged creatures) into a system of marriage alliances. There are three such groups in each village, with a circular pattern of one group taking wives from a second group and giving wives to a third group. The man can choose a bride only from the wife-giving group in his marriage alliance system, or it is believed dire misfortune will result. Ideally there is matrilineal cross-cousin marriage, in which a man marries his mother's brother's daughter (the brother might be a real brother or a clan brother). Within the constraints of the marriage alliance system, the bride and groom are free to choose, but their parents will negotiate the bride-price. Sometimes a man can work for his bride's parents for a few years in lieu of a bride-price.

8 INTERPERSONAL RELATIONS

Kammu interpersonal relations are based on family lineage. The eldest man in the family is treated with great respect. The marriage alliance system also involves patterns of respect. For example, the father of the bride has a higher ritual status than the father of the groom because the wife brings children to the family. A father-in-law must be treated with great respect. It is even common to call an elderly man father-in-law as a term of respect.

Living in isolated villages, the Kammu must depend upon their neighbors for mutual help—so relations are relatively egalitarian. Although most families farm individually owned plots, in some Kammu villages the land was owned collectively. After the rise to power in 1975 of the communist LPDR government, numerous Kammu communities were successfully converted to collectivized farms, while communal agriculture proved a failure in many other Kammu villages. The closure of all stores resulted in the development of a barter system among the Kammu for trading foodstuffs.

9 LIVING CONDITIONS

Laos is one of the poorest nations in East Asia and living conditions are harsh for most Kammu. The Kammu tend to be among the most impoverished people in the country and Kammu communities in Thailand, Vietnam, and China live far below the national economic average. Governments have been slow to extend roads, education, and health services to the hill areas. In the aftermath of the Communist takeover of Laos, diseases like malaria, dysentery, and pneumonia were common, and there were high rates of infant mortality and malnutrition. Most Kammu are subsistence farmers, and each day is spent farming, hunting, or fishing. People don't go into the forest alone, however, because they worry about wild animals, snakes, and accidents.

Kammu houses are built close together on pilings in the villages, located on a hilltop or halfway up a mountain at elevations near 1,000 ft. The village is usually surrounded by a thick band of old forest, which separates homes from the fields. The large old trees are believed to have souls, and they serve to protect the village from storms and from fire when the fields are burned off. Houses are built on piles 1–2 m (3–7 ft) above the ground, usually with frame and floors of wood, walls of bamboo matting, and a roof of thatch. There is an open porch on one side of the house and a kitchen hearth built over a box of dirt toward the back. Domestic animals, including chickens, ducks, and pigs, are raised underneath the house in fenced areas. Buffalo are highly valued for plowing fields, as food, and for sacrifice, though few Kammu can afford to own them. Dogs are commonly kept as pets. In most Kammu villages there is no running water or electricity, nor are there any sanitary facilities.

10 FAMILY LIFE

A household usually numbers 6–7 people but can be much larger. A single dwelling may include parents, children, daughters-in-law, and grandchildren. Much of the work of the household is gender-specific, with women working longer hours than men and responsible for the hard work of hauling water and firewood and husking the rice. Traditionally, young boys left the family home between age six and eight, to live in the nearest village common house with older boys, unmarried men, and male guests in the village. However, newer villages set up in lowland areas have dispensed with common houses for men. Children are engaged in helping the family get enough food from an early age. Boys learn to fish and make snares to catch rodents and small game. Girls help their mothers garden and go in a group to the forest to look for edible shoots, tubers, and other plants. It is the responsibility of the women in the household to ensure there is enough water and firewood, while men provide for the family's meat and fish. The family could not function without the labor of all, so there is mutual respect for the contribution each person makes to the household.

11 CLOTHING

In the past, clothing was most often rough homespun cloth made from their own cotton that the women spun and wove, but today manufactured fabric or store-bought clothes are increasingly common. Women wear a long-sleeved blouse that fastens to one side and a sarong, while men wear a shirt and pants. Rubber sandals serve as shoes. Both sexes may carry woven or knit bags. In addition, there are special clothes for ritual occasions.

12 FOOD

The staple food of the Kammu is sticky (glutinous) rice, which is eaten at every meal. The Kammu generally do not purchase food, but grow or hunt what they eat. Besides rice, Kammu farmers grow corn, tobacco, maize, sugarcane, and occasionally cotton and opium. The men fish, hunt small game with rifles and crossbows, and set snares for rodents and other small animals. Frogs and various insects are also eaten. Fish and meat are smoked and dried over the fires that are continuously maintained in common houses reserved for men. Large game is usually shared within the community. The women gather bamboo shoots, mushrooms, and other wild plants in the forest. Deforestation has made supplementing the daily diet through hunting and gathering more difficult. Although most families have a water buffalo or cow, these animals are rarely eaten except on ceremonial occasions, when an animal is sacrificed to propitiate the spirits. Fruit trees, including bananas, citrus, and jackfruit, are planted around the village. Eggs are considered a special food, and gifts of eggs are given to a bride's family. Black sticky rice is used for traditional ceremonial meals. It represents safety, so a small packet of black sticky rice is always carried by people when they travel. Kammu meals tend to be rather simple and are seasoned with salt and chilies.

13 EDUCATION

Few Kammu have had any formal education in a classroom. Although schools are being extended into Kammu areas, schools remain scare and tend to have very low standards. Lessons are conducted in Lao, a foreign tongue to many of the pupils. Teachers sent to Kammu areas often consider the assignment a hardship. Compulsory school attendance laws, such as those in Thailand, are rarely enforced and do not apply in any case to children living at a great distance from a school. More than half of the Kammu never attend school. Kammu boys are more likely to be sent to school than girls. Few Kammu are able to afford the cost of sending their children to schools in urban areas.

In villages Kammu receive practical education in daily chores from their parents and older siblings. Boys learn from older male residents, while girls hone their skills with the family's females. Because of the pattern of males leaving the village to work in cities or in northern Thailand for a few years, men are more likely to speak a national language like Thai or Lao.

14 CULTURAL HERITAGE

The Kammu have a musical tradition, but instruments are usually played for ceremonial purposes in conjunction with prayer and sacrifice. Their instruments include long wooden drums, kettlegongs, knobbed gongs, cymbals, bamboo beaters, flutes, and buffalo horns. Musical instruments are often ritual gifts. Bamboo clappers are a gift from the bride's family to the family of the groom, while the highly valued long wooden drum is usually a gift given by the groom's family to that of the bride.

There are songs appropriate to various ritual occasions, and different types of music for every season of the farming year. Music thus plays a ritual role in securing a sufficient supply of food.

15 WORK

The majority of Kammu are subsistence farmers and fishermen who reside in villages in mountainous regions. While Kammu are unable to accumulate great wealth, most villagers are able to provide for their daily needs, and some villagers are capable of keeping dozens of animals, including highly prized water buffalo. Within the villages, men tend the fields, hunt, and fish, while the women raise children and sew clothes. Children help their parents and both boys and girls may help with the care of young siblings. When the rice develops ears in the autumn, young people stay in small field huts for days to scare away the birds and wild animals that come to eat the rice. Teenagers enjoy this period away from the village and grownups. Grandparents help with cooking, childcare, and small chores near the house.

In recent decades, Kammu men from Laos have increasingly migrated to Thailand in search of work. Young Kammu men find employment in Thai factories and shops, as well as in the logging industry. During the war years, many youths fled to Thailand to avoid military conscription. Traditionally, men would work abroad until they saved sufficient money for a bride price and then return to their home village, but now many Kammu men have married Thai women and have become Thai citizens.

16 SPORTS

The regions of South East Asia that the Kammu reside in are impoverished, and there are no traditions of organized sports among the Kammu. For children, play typically involves preparation for adult tasks. Thus, boys are often found fishing, catching insects, and practicing with bows and arrows, and children of both sexes often swim in rivers and streams.

17 ENTERTAINMENT AND RECREATION

Singing and storytelling are popular forms of entertainment. Folk tales include creation stories, tales of magic and the supernatural, stories of plants and animals, and tales of mischief and trickery.

Music plays an important role in Kammu ceremonies. During the ritual calling of spirits by shamans, chanting and the playing of gongs are used to communicate with the deceased and natural spirits. Songs and the playing of musical instruments often accompany weddings, the building of new houses, harvests and New Year celebrations. When Kammu entertain guests in their home, grain alcohol is consumed, songs are sung, and musical instruments are played. Bronze drums are often played during ceremonies, especially for summoning rain.

Kammu in urban areas have access to the kinds of entertainment enjoyed by the majority population, including theater, bars, and festivals.

18 FOLK ART, CRAFTS, AND HOBBIES

The Kammu are very skillful in the use of bamboo, which they use to make a wide variety of objects ranging from baskets, musical instruments, water containers, and snares to a complete house. Traditional Kammu musical instruments (constructed by Kammu villagers) include two kinds of bamboo flutes (pii and tot), lutes (saw), Jew's harps, bamboo beaters (klt), clappers (taaw taaw), gongs, and bronze drums.

19 SOCIAL PROBLEMS

Lack of education and geographic isolation has resulted in economic and social stagnation in Kammu populated regions. While the economies of Laos, Thailand, Vietnam, and China have experienced double digit growth in the last two decades, the Kammu villages situated in the rural mountains remain underdeveloped and have seen a lack of government investment in infrastructure. The Kammu tradition of slash-and-burn agriculture has fallen out of favor for environmental reasons, and local governments have pressured the Kammu to resettle in lowland areas. In addition, illegal loggers and corrupt local officials have colluded to expel Kammu villagers from the forests adjoining their villages that have traditionally been used for hunting and gathering. The Kammu still face prejudice and discrimination. Many ethnic Lao still casually use the pejorative term "slave" in speaking of the Kammu and other midland minorities, despite the efforts of the LPDR government to call all people "Lao" and to stress the multiethnic nature of Lao society.

The Kammu who have settled in lowland areas are threatened by cultural assimilation by the majority culture. Kammu children in these regions are educated in the national language and gradually adopt the culture of the dominant group. Acculturation and assimilation are common among Kammu migrants in towns in northern Thailand who work and marry local women. Their children are raised as Thai, and the Kammu migrants adopt the language and culture of the Thai.

[20] GENDER ISSUES

In Kammu villages work tends to be gender-specific. Men clear and burn the swidden fields, weave baskets, repair farm tools, care for large animals, trap, and hunt. They are also more likely to be involved in trade, selling livestock, forest products, and, more recently, scrap metal left over from the war. Men often migrate to find work as farmhands on Lao-own farms and as laborers in urban areas. Many Kammu men find work in Thailand, where they can earn comparatively higher wages and purchase goods otherwise unavailable in their home villages. Women cook, care for children, husk rice, haul water, and firewood, care for gardens and pigs and poultry, gather edible plants, weave cloth, and sew. They may engage in small trade with vegetables and chickens. One area of labor where men and women work together is in the planting of crops. Men poke holes in the field to plant seeds, and women follow after to drop in the seed and cover it over. Both sexes weed, although this hard and fairly continuous chore is more likely to be done by women. Both sexes also harvest.

Sexuality is overtly expressed in Kammu folk tale traditions. In the Kammu language, sexual imagery does not elicit shame and folk story tellers freely mention the sexual lives of characters in stories. In one folk tale recorded in Thailand, The Orphan Makes a Field, the hero succeeds in successfully tricking his seven wives into going to bed with him. Despite sex not being a taboo subject, Kammu folk tales lack explicit and graphic sexual descriptions.

[21] BIBLIOGRAPHY

Damrong Tayanin. *Being Kammu: My Village, My Life*. Ithaca, N.Y.: Cornell University, 1994.

Lindell, Kristina, et al. A Kammu Story-Listener's Tales. London: Curzon Press, 1977.

———. Folk Tales from Kammu II. London: Curzon Press, 1980.

———. *The Kammu Year: Its Lore and Music*. London: Curzon Press, 1982.

———. *Tribe Kammu of Northern Laos and Thailand: Folklore and Folkliterature*. Taipei: Chinese Association for Folklore, 1984.

Mansfield, Stephan. *Lao Hill Tribes: Traditions and Patterns of Existence*. New York: Oxford University Press, 2000.

Suwilai Premsrirat. "Aspects of Inter-Clausal Relations in Khmu." In *J.H.C.S Davidson ed. Austroasiatic Languages* London: School of Oriental and African Studies. University of London, 1991.

Uchida, Ruriko and Amy Catlin. "Music of Upland Minorities in Burma, Laos, and Thailand." in *Terry E. Miller Sean Williams The Garland Encyclopedia of World Music*. Vol. 4. New York: Routledge, 1998: 546-47.

—Revised by David Straub

KARAKALPAKS

PRONUNCIATION: kar-uh-kuhl-PAKS
ALTERNATE NAMES: Qoraqolpoqlar
LOCATION: Uzbekistan (territory of Karakalpakistan);
    Kazakhstan; Russia; Turkmenistan
POPULATION: 350,000
LANGUAGES: Karakalpak; Russian
Religion: Islam (Sunni Muslim)

¹ INTRODUCTION

Karakalpak means Òblack hatÓ in the Karakalpak language. When the ancestors of present-day Karakalpaks (who call themselves *Qoraqolpoqlar*) settled in the area during the 10th and 11th centuries ad, they came upon Turkic Qipchoq (sometimes spelled Kipchak) people, who referred to the newcomers from the Irtysh River areas in southern Siberia as ÒKarakalpaks,Ó supposedly because they wore black wool or high felt hats. From that time onward, the development of Karakalpak language, religion, and cultural practices has been influenced by the extremes of harsh desert and steppe existence as well as by military attacks by invading peoples such as the Mongols, Timurids, Kalmyks, Khorezmian Uzbeks, and Russians. With the exception of the Russians, who colonized the Karakalpak during the latter half of the 19th century, the other invaders were all Central Asian peoples of similar ethnic and cultural backgrounds who had formed themselves into diverse political states and conquering armies.

Various historical records prove that a Karakalpak people living essentially in today's Karakalpak lands existed by the 16th and 17th centuries. These people became a part of the Noghai horde (ÒarmyÓ or ÒconfederacyÓ in Mongol), whose forefathers had come into the area with Genghis Khan's forces from Mongolia. Scholars today acknowledge that the Karakalpaks are a composite of three cultural-geographical areas: the Khorezm oasis of southern Karakalpakistan; the Qipchoq desert steppe along the lower course of the Syr River, which is a part of Kazakhstan today; and the east European cultural areas including parts of the Ural mountains, the Volga river area, and the North Caucasus mountains.

² LOCATION AND HOMELAND

The Karakalpak are a people of Central Asia, who lived within the Uzbek Soviet Socialist Republic of the USSR until it was dissolved in 1991. Today their territory is under the rule of independent Uzbekistan. Approximately 2.3 million people reside in Karakalpakistan, of whom approximately 350,000 are Karakalpaks. Most Karakalpaks live concentrated in the southern part of their republic in the Amu River delta. Other Karakalpak people live in the surrounding countries of Uzbekistan, Kazakhstan, Russia, and Turkmenistan. Karakalpak territory occupies nearly 40% of Uzbekistan's overall territory. Karakalpakistan (*Qoraqolpoqiston*) lies in the northwestern part of Uzbekistan and is bordered by Kazakhstan to the north and Turkmenistan to the southwest. Much of its geography was dominated until recently by the Aral Sea, which took up a large portion of north-central and northeastern Karakalpakistan. Today, however, the Aral is drying up at a very fast rate.

The Aral Sea desiccation (evaporation) has become an international tragedy, so much so that any mention of the Karakalpaks immediately causes people to ask about the Aral. Indeed, the death of the Aral has destroyed the lives and livelihoods of tens of thousands of Karakalpaks, who depended both directly and indirectly on the sea. Its degradation has affected the lives of nearly 2 million people in both the Karakalpak and Kazak areas. Agricultural chemicals that were transported to the Aral via the Amu and Syr Rivers now blow across the land. Much of the fertilizer, pesticides, and defoliants used in agricultural production for decades eventually washed into the artificial network of canals that has served much of the primary farming lands of Central Asia, and those chemicals were deposited into the Aral Sea. In addition, salts from the sea have blown across farm lands and into local drinking supplies. Although many international agencies and experts have researched and attempted to solve the problem of the slow death of the Aral Sea, no real solution is has been found, and health problems and economic decline continue to plague the region.

³ LANGUAGE

The Karakalpak language is part of the Turkic linguistic family, so it shares structural and grammatical similarities, as well as a vocabulary, with modern languages such as Turkish, Kazak, Kyrgyz, Turkmen, and Uzbek. However, the Turkic family of languages is quite varied, and differences between them may be as pronounced as differences between the Romance languages. Therefore, there are further linguistic subdivisions. Karakalpak is part of the Western branch of this family and is considered a part of the Noghai-Qipchoq subgroup, so that its roots are found in the languages spoken by much earlier inhabitants of the Karakalpak area. Modern Karakalpak most closely resembles modern Kazak in the north and Khorezmian Uzbek in the south. Although there was no written Karakalpak language until the 1920s, the contemporary language is written in a modified Cyrillic alphabet (the alphabet used by Russians, Serbians, and Bulgarians).

Because language was always learned and passed on orally, literacy among Karakalpaks included a developed knowledge of songs, poems, and tales. Through such artistic oral expression, Karakalpak people were able to preserve their history and customs from generation to generation. This was not merely a matter of repetition and memorization. Those who learned well were able to engage and excite others as they spoke of the subjects and events important to their own people.

Nearly all adult Karakalpaks can read and write their language, and most people learned some Russian in school as part of the Soviet educational legacy. Newspapers, journals, and books are printed in the Karakalpak language. Although Russian remains an important second language for educated Karakalpak people, many young people are now studying other foreign languages such as English, French, and Arabic because they are international languages of commerce and diplomacy.

⁴ FOLKLORE

Folklore is divided into the lyrical tales and epics (*zhyr* and *dostan*), and Karakalpaks consider themselves among the first poets and singers of the steppe. Most folkloric tales deal with realistic matters. In the famous tales of Tarzshi, a bald orphan with few impressive qualities is able to pull the wool over the eyes of greedy and arrogant landlords and corrupt leaders. A

KARAKALPAKS

0   250   500   750 Miles

0 250 500 750 1000 Kilometers

RUSSIA

KAZAKSTAN

UZBEKISTAN

Zaysan

TURKMENISTAN

Tashkent

KYRGYSTAN

Almaty
(Alma-Ata)

Ashkhabad   Tejen

Dushanbe

TAJIKISTAN

CHINA

IRAN

AFGHANISTAN

Kabul

Zaranj

Islāmābād

Saindak

PAKISTAN

Indus

Gulf of Oman

Pasni

New Delhi

NEPAL

BHUTAN

Kathmandu

Ganges

Arabian
Sea

Lakhpat

INDIA

Dhaka

BANGLADESH

Surat

process was relatively rapid in comparison to the conversion of Central Asian peoples who lived in more remote or inaccessible areas. Deserts, mountains, and the steppes of Central Asia, historically home to nomadic pastoralist and semi-nomadic peoples such as the Karakalpaks, converted to Islam gradually. Among the Karakalpak, most conversions probably occurred from the 10th to the 13th centuries.

The Karakalpaks observe disciplined piety and have long been influenced by Sufism, which is a very tolerant and ecstatic branch of Islam. Universal Muslim holidays such as Ramadan (the month of fasting) and *Kurban Bayram* (The Feast of the Sacrifice based on Abraham) have long been among the most important. Until the collapse of the USSR and the economic and health consequences associated with the Aral Sea destruction, one could argue that religious practice and teaching played a minor role in the lives of most Karakalpaks. This has begun to change, however, as people search for answers, solutions, and comfort during a terrible period of deprivation and illness. Faith in Soviet Communist ideals is being supplanted by faith in the Muslim religion.

Many Karakalpak beliefs relate to the natural world. These are not a part of the Muslim religion, but rather connect to cults of saints or patrons who watch out for herds, fisherman, farmers, and so on. Many people believe that each type of herd or flock has its own patron. For cattle, the patron is Zangibaba, and people concerned for their herd may visit his grave outside Nukus to pray for help. Another example of a traditional belief here concerns the time at which shepherds release their flocks onto open meadows to graze for the summer. Many will not do so until they have been blessed by women who bring them yellow sashes to tie around their overcoats. They believe this provides protection for their flocks.

6 MAJOR HOLIDAYS

Four major nonreligious or state holidays are celebrated by the Karakalpaks and Uzbeks together. *Novruz* (New Day), celebrated throughout Iran, the Caucasus, and Central Asia, coincides with the beginning of spring on March 20 or 21. Although many Central Asians believe *Novruz* to be a Muslim holiday, its origins date back more than 2,000 years, long before there was a Muslim religion. The holiday is marked by festivals, contests, game playing, and especially eating. Schoolchildren celebrate with their teachers and put on a variety of skits. Afterwards, communities gather in the central square of their towns to continue the celebration. People dress in their very best clothing. Speeches commemorate the cultural heritage of the Central Asian peoples who are linked through this holiday. The favorite food of this holiday is *sumalak*, which is made from young wheat plants that are boiled communally in huge cauldrons. It takes about 24 hours to prepare this sweet, tasty pudding. Each year, one family will take on the responsibility of preparing enough *sumalak* for several families, and members of each family gather where the *sumalak* is being prepared, to take turns stirring the thick, bubbling mass and feeding the enormous fire needed to keep it boiling for so many hours. *Sumalak* parties are a standard part of the *Novruz* festivities. This particular food is considered vitamin-rich and portends the coming of all the new agricultural foods that warmer weather will bring.

Victory Day celebrations commemorating World War II take place on May 9. This day is associated with both solem-

similar set of stories make up the tales of Aldarkose, who is another boy everybody tries to outsmart, but who always comes out on top. There are also allegorical tales about animals such as the cunning fox, who can trick just about anyone and anything. Other tales involve wolves, tigers, and occasionally even God himself.

What makes the epics different from the tales is not only their length and poetic construction, but also the fact that they almost always concern historical events and heroic figures—political leaders and rulers—as well as the mythical origins of Karakalpak triumphs over invaders. The most famous examples of these epics are *Kyrk Qiz*, *Er-Shora*, *Koblan*, and *Maspatsha*. Epic heroes often turn out to be women. In *Kyrk Qiz* (The Forty Maidens), the heroine Gulaim defends her homeland from invading Kalmyks. *Maspatsha* is the story of Aiparshir, a woman of rich beauty and unparalleled courage. Themes and values from Karakalpak life, such as love of one's homeland, defense of one's people, and a willingness to sacrifice on behalf of others, are all emphasized. An epic is typically composed of more than 20,000 lines of verse.

5 RELIGION

The religion of the Karakalpaks is Sunni Islam, which is the dominant school of Islamic belief throughout the world. As early as the 7th century, Arabs entered Central Asia to spread and propagate Islam, to which they had converted themselves only a century earlier. The first large-scale conversions in Central Asia were concentrated in cities and oasis areas, and the

nity and merriment. Parades of military personnel and World War II veterans take place. Later, people go off with family and friends to celebrations of their own. Victory Day is celebrated by all the former Soviet peoples because of the enormous sacrifices and suffering they endured in their defeat of Nazi Germany.

Uzbekistan Independence Day, September 1, has been celebrated since 1991. This day features parades and carnival-like events in all cities and towns throughout Uzbekistan. Political speeches, poems, songs, dances, and games are featured. Everyone in the community participates in the town square and outside municipal administrative buildings. Food is served to all, and most people dress in fine clothes out of respect for and pride in the new independent status of their nation.

Constitution Day, December 8, is another holiday that commemorates the creation of the Uzbekistan constitution in 1992. Most people treat this day simply as one to relax, and most workplaces and businesses are closed.

7 RITES OF PASSAGE

Parents with newborns visit relatives constantly for the first few months as they introduce the infant far and wide. Boys undergo circumcision at approximately age five, and a big celebration known as the *sunnat toi* occurs.

The most major event of adulthood is one's wedding. Called the *kelin toi,* this is the biggest celebration and rite of passage an individual ordinarily experiences. Marking the joining of families and the continuation of family lines, the *kelin toi* is marked by feasts, dances, music, and speeches that continue for days at various locations of both the groom and bride's families.

Death and funerals are marked by ritual wailings and outpourings of grief at the home of the deceased. Mourners come and cry purposely to empathize and commiserate with the bereaved. Afterward a local clergyman called a *molla* leads a procession of men or women (depending upon the sex of the deceased) to the local cemetery, where the closest relatives perform the actual burial after prayers are said.

8 INTERPERSONAL RELATIONS

It is customary for one person approaching another at rest or in a stationary position to offer the first greeting. This practice is typical of Karakalpaks and other Central Asian semi-nomads. Typically, the greeting is *"Assalomu alaikum!"* (Arabic for ÒMay peace be upon you!Ó). The person being greeted responds with, *"Valaikum assalom!"* (ÒAnd may peace be upon you, too!Ó) Then men will shake hands, using either one or two hands, depending upon their personal closeness or the respect they have for one another. Women typically hug one another after greeting. Ordinarily, men and women may exchange greetings, but there will be no further physical contact between them. A rapid succession of questions concerning health and family usually follows. A younger person typically bows slightly and may cover the lower part of the chest with the right hand to show reverence for an older person. Respect for older people, even those who are only a few years older, is an extremely serious matter in Central Asia. Another common gesture, associated with leave-taking, is for the person leaving to wrap his arms around himself as he nods to the person exiting. This is a gesture of deference and respect.

Visiting neighbors, friends, and family members is an essential part of Karakalpak life. It expands the concept of the home. Karakalpaks enjoy guests and, like other Central Asians, are always ready to welcome any number of guests into their homes. When visiting, Karakalpaks always bring presents or food. Neighbors constantly visit with one another to chat and snack, and sometimes to borrow food or bring food to families who may be in need. Dating, especially among teenagers and young adults, is rare among the Karakalpaks, save for in large cities such as Nukus. Ordinarily, parents keep a careful watch over the children's outside activities.

The health of the Karakalpak population began a steady decline more than 30 years ago. All of the problems have been associated with the drying of the Aral Sea, intensive irrigation for cotton, and the use of pesticides such as DDT and defoliants. The residues from these chemicals, along with the salts from the evaporating sea, have led to a variety of cancers, eye illnesses, internal organ poisonings, and so on. Hospital facilities are poorly staffed and stocked, and neonatal care is practically nonexistent. The major result of the ecological devastation is that Karakalpaks have moved away from the worst zones, especially near the sea, to other cities in Uzbekistan, including the capital Tashkent.

9 LIVING CONDITIONS

The economic deterioration of post-Soviet Karakalpak life has affected nearly everyone, and few people are able to afford more than the bare essentials such as tea, rice, vegetables, occasional meat, and the most necessary housewares and clothing. It used to be that people spent a great deal on wedding parties, but even those elaborate celebrations have become a thing of the past. Today most of the monies are spent on foodstuffs, and the diet is heavy in carbohydrates, including rice, bread, pasta, and potatoes.

The people of Karakalpakistan suffer from acute health problems due to the spread of fertilizers, pesticides, and defoliants that have been blown about from the dry parts of the Aral Sea bed. These chemicals were transported to the Aral via the Amu and Syr Rivers, the main sources for artificial irrigation throughout much of Central Asia. Diseases such as tuberculosis, hepatitis, and leprosy have increased at unprecedented rates among the Karakalpak compared to other peoples of the former Soviet Union. The latest statistics show that more than 70% of Karakalpaks suffer poor health and illnesses. Karakalpakistan once had the highest growth rate of any Soviet territory, but it now has the highest death rate.

Traditionally, Karakalpaks lived in flat, clay homes resembling those of southwestern Native Americans. Most homes had two or three central rooms with an attached kitchen area. The house would be surrounded by a wall of mud that enclosed a small garden plot. Within the enclosure, there was also space for the dome-shaped felt tent, known as a *yurt.* Yurts contain a wooden-lattice frame over which huge pieces of felt are thrown and then carefully arranged. They are ideal for summer living, because they keep people cool indoors and they keep mosquitoes away. The felt acts as a good insulator. Inside Karakalpak homes, some European-style furniture is found, but most people relax and sleep on thick, dense quilts called *kurpas.* Kurpas are often placed on raised platforms built into the home, and this is where a family will take its meals, listen to music, and watch television. Kurpas are easily moved and stored. Large

*Young women who have been affected by agricultural chemical and salt damage stand for the camera in Karakalpakistan, Uzbekistan. (©
Kazuyoshi Nomachi/Corbis)*

wooden cabinets known as *sandal* are used as storage chests. Sometimes the sandals are decorated with carvings or painted designs.

Buses have served as the chief means for traveling from village to village as well as between cities and villages. Developed rail travel also exists, but it is more expensive, less frequent, and does not make nearly the number of stops as buses do. Ozbekiston Havo Iolari is the new national airline company, and flights from major Uzbekistani cities such as Tashkent, Andijon, and Samarqand to Nukus are available, although they are too expensive for the average citizen. During a period when gasoline and spare parts are increasingly expensive and hard to come by, many Karakalpak people are turning to bicycles, piling into friends' cars, or riding on the backs of motorcycles.

¹⁰ FAMILY LIFE

Karakalpak families are generally large, with anywhere from 4 to 10 children; however, most women prefer to have 4 or 5 children. Extended family living is common, and a family of four generations may reside in a single home. Beyond the extended family is the *koshe*, a loose organization uniting a number of families who claim descent from a common male ancestor four or five generations ago. The *koshe* enables people to claim a common territory. Several *koshe* make up an *uru*, a kind of

clan. One finds these formations on modern Karakalpak collective farms today. More than 20 clans claim origins to ancient tribes that are among the ethnographic groups of today's Karakalpaks. People marry exogamously, which means to people outside of their own clans. This may be very difficult for the brides, who often are treated as servants initially by their new in-laws.

The residence patterns after marriage are uxorilocal, which means that the bride moves in with her husband's family. This often makes the situation for young wives difficult as the husband's mother often rules her life with a strong hand. In the domestic sphere, women do most of the work that deals with cooking, cleaning, and rearing children. Women work outside of the home, too, in agricultural fields and as teachers, doctors, accountants, and so on. The working sphere for men is in agriculture and administration, but men are also usually responsible for most market shopping, the preparation of certain feast dishes, and fixing up or repair work that needs to be done around the house, especially electrical or carpentry work.

Girls marry early, usually from the age of 16, and these marriages are arranged through consenting sets of parents. Women are given dowries by their parents and are presented with all sorts of bride gifts by the groom's parents, including clothing, porcelain tea sets, jewelry, and household wares. Boys and men are usually of the same age or a bit older than the girls they marry. Although polygyny (the practice of marrying more than one woman) is illegal, some men do it secretly. On the whole, this is rare because it costs a great deal. A second wife entails a great deal of extra economic support.

Karakalpaks may keep dogs or cats, but they don't treat them as pets. They are instead working domestic animals, serving the purposes of guard duty and pest control. Some men train eagles to hunt rabbits and other birds on the steppe and in the Kyzyl Kum (Red Sand) desert.

11 CLOTHING

Karakalpaks often wear a mix of traditional and European-style clothing. Boys do not wear shorts, even in the hottest weather. Girls never wear dresses cut much above their knees; nor will they wear sleeveless dresses. Some sort of headwear for both men and women is almost always essential due to the extreme temperatures and merciless sun. Men wear silk or cotton embroidered skullcaps (*duppi*) or thick sheep hair hats (the namesake *karakalpak*). Women wear long cotton or woolen scarves (*rumol*) that cover their heads, ears, backs, and shoulders. The usual foot coverings for older people are leather boots and rubbers (*etik va kalosh*), whereas younger people wear more fashionable sandals, sneakers, and dress shoes.

Koilek (a long, loose white shirt with an open collar and no buttons) and loose trousers tucked into boots compose the man's typical summer outfit. If men spend a great deal of time outdoors during the winter months watching cattle or flocks of sheep, they wear an enormously heavy *pustin*, which is a sheepskin and sheep hair overcoat with extremely long sleeves. Lighter, long quilted coats known as *sholpan* are worn around the home and outdoors when the weather is not quite so cold. These come in numerous colors and patterns.

Women wear the *kiimeshek*—white is worn by older women and red by the younger. This is a long dress with a head covering but no sleeves whatsoever. It has a cape-like quality and is made of wool with geometrical patterns. Tunic-like shirts and baggy trousers are also typical women's garments. Many Karakalpak women today wear the famously colorful *atlas* tie-dyed silk dresses in summer. These patterns and styles come from the Uzbeks.

12 FOOD

Historically, the Karakalpak diet is quite varied. People have tended to rely on grains, especially rice, sorghum, barley, and millet. From these grains, wonderful breads, noodles, and dumplings are made. Bread-baking (*Nan-iapish*) is done in the *tandir*, the ubiquitous outdoor, spherical oven that is used throughout Central and South Asia. Women stick bread dough on the internal curved clay walls of the fiery ovens, and when the bread is ready, it practically falls off the sides of the oven.

Fruits and vegetables, while not quite as plentiful in other oases areas of Uzbekistan, still include onions, carrots, plums, pears, grapes, apricots, and all kinds of melons and squashes. Pumpkin is often included in turnovers prepared in the *tandir*, and they are known as *samsa*. Milk products include yogurt, butter, cream, and curd cheeses. Cow's milk is the preferred type.

Meats have never been a part of ordinary daily fare but were eaten in honor of guests or during wedding and male circumcision parties. Boiled beef, mutton, and smoked horsemeat are among the favorites. Beef and mutton are also ingredients in *palov*, which is the favorite dish of millions of Central Asians. The best *palov* recipes consist of rice, meat, carrots, garlic, steamed quinces, and mutton tail fat (*dumba*) (The fat ranks as a real delicacy.) In the past, Aral fish were very popular, and fried dishes included bream, grey mullet, wild pike, and sheat fish. Today breakfast is an important meal, but it is often very simple. Children often head off to school with tea and bread in their stomachs and occasionally cream, raisins, grapes, or a few almonds. Summer and fall breakfasts feature a richer variety.

Following is a recipe for *durama* (shredded mutton):

Use sorghum groats and mutton and boil separately. Next, the men begin carefully shredding the meat. Then carefully shred the boiled dumplings separately. After that, carefully combine your shredded foods. You are now ready to add a bit of broth to the top, and for extra flavor add *duzlyk*, a mix of chopped green onions and boiled fat.

As Muslims, Karakalpaks do not eat certain foods, with pork being one of the most prominent dietary restrictions. Other food taboos have little to do with religion, but more to do with customs. For example, a pregnant woman must not eat a rabbit's head for fear her newborn will have a harelip, and the consumption of camel meat for a pregnant woman may result in a longer than normal term pregnancy. Children must not use large spoons for eating liquids, as the result may be marriage to someone with a large and unattractive nose.

Karakalpaks eat most meals with their hands, so ritual washing beforehand is imperative. After three washings, one must use one's own hands to wipe off the excess water. To shake off the excess is a sign that one's hands are dirty and one is spreading uncleanliness. No one should begin to eat until the eldest person at table begins.

13 EDUCATION

The Soviet educational system remains in place, so almost all children receive a high school education. Some then go on for technical and university training. Karakalpakistan has only one university, located in Nukus. Recently, *medresses*, schools for higher religious instruction, have opened. Most parents want both boys and girls to obtain higher education, or receive some technical training, if possible. A small percentage of parents would rather their girls get married and start a family directly after finishing high school. In recent years, Karakalpaks have received less and less education in Russian and more in English as their primary foreign language. However, the overall education decline since the Soviet period has led many to speak only Karakalpak or Karakalpak and some Uzbek.

14 CULTURAL HERITAGE

For a people who had no literacy until relatively recently, the Karakalpaks have a rich oral tradition of folktales and epic poems. Select and talented individuals would roam from village to village as bards, reciting stories and verses to music performed on the stringed instruments such as the two-stringed *dutar*, and the *qobyz* and *ghypzhek*, which were played with bows. In fact, music, singing, and storytelling were usually one in the same thing.

Two of the greatest traditional Karakalpak literary figures—Azhiniaz Kosybai uly and Berdakh Kargabai uly—have been ranked among the greatest Central Asian litterateurs. Both poets lived during the 19th century. Azhiniaz's famous work is *Boz-Atau,* a poem that recalls the capture and enslavement of the Karakalpak people at the hands of Khivan (of the Khivan Khanate or Kingdom, located in Khorezm) and Turkmen invaders. Berdakh-shair wrote many verses dedicated to the dark side of life that affected poor people. Modern writers have adopted Western literary genres such as novels, short stories, and plays.

Dance was never a part of Karakalpak cultural heritage, although the Soviets created a dance for them.

15 WORK

Prior to the Soviet period, the economy of the Karakalpaks was characterized primarily by agriculture, cattle herding, and fishing, depending on the terrain and climate of a particular area. Those living in the oases near the Amu river in the south practiced agriculture, which included cultivation of grains and fruits, such as rice, sorghum, wheat, millet, melons, and squashes. Those living out on the steppe and in desert regions kept herds of sheep, goats, camels, and cattle. Those living in the Aral region fished.

The majority of work in Karakalpakistan is agricultural, and almost 70% of the population is rural. The only real industrial jobs are centered around the cotton industry, and these jobs include ginning, baling, and pressing cotton seeds for their oil.

Silk manufacture also plays a significant role in the local agricultural economy. Farming people feed silkworms mulberry leaves from nearby trees. The worms in turn create cocoons, which people then bring to regional cocoon collection centers. Profits, depend on the quality of the cocoons. Silkworm feeding is very arduous. The insects require constant attention, and most people would rather not spend the long hours this work requires, but in today's economy every extra bit of income is vital. Death of the fisheries industry has led to rising unemployment.

Agricultural workers work 12 to 15 hours a day at harvest time. They will work seven days a week, no matter how inclement the weather. Work for the Karakalpaks is cyclical: during late fall, winter, and part of spring, work is minimal and takes place primarily around the household. Professionals and administrative workers work year-round and receive about six weeks paid vacation each year taken during July and August.

16 SPORTS

Sports for the young are similar to those of Westerners. Volleyball and soccer are popular at school, and boys also test their strength at a kind of wrestling that involves grabbing one another around the back of the neck and thigh. The object is to force one's opponent to lose his grip, and thus his balance. This is known as *Qurash.* Unfortunately, girls and women are rarely if ever encouraged in sports.

17 ENTERTAINMENT AND RECREATION

Movies and television are popular and have become dominated by imports from the West, especially action movies and Latin American soap operas. Karakalpak television tends toward the lackluster, with much in the way of folk, music, documentaries about refining cotton planting techniques, and long-winded talk shows with camera-shy scientific guests. Theatrical plays on humorous or historical themes that are Karakalpak-centric are popular and well-attended.

Adults entertain themselves by getting together with friends at rap sessions known as *gap,* which means ÒtalkÓ Here men and women meet separately, perhaps twice monthly, to eat, play games, sing songs, catch up on community happenings, and offer advice to one another.

Pop music is as important to Karakalpak young people as it is throughout the world. Both international and local stars are widely appreciated. Iulduz Usmanova is one of the most popular young singers, and many of her songs deal with the human condition in contemporary society.

Children enjoy an elaborate game of riddles called *askiia.* Two children try to outsmart one another with a series of questions about a particular thing. One child starts with a description, and the other must ask relevant questions about what is being described or else be quickly lead astray by the describer.

18 FOLK ART, CRAFTS, AND HOBBIES

Some of the greatest traditional representations of Karakalpak folk arts are in the applied arts, especially in rug-making and jewelry production. Most rug materials are used to adorn yurts. A number of geometrical and antler-horn motifs reflect regional styles that in some way parallel the development of famous Turkmen tribal rugs. Karakalpak rugs are narrow and not usually used as floor coverings. They are hung as doors to the entrance of yurts and used as wall coverings or saddlebags. Vibrant blues, yellows, and greens are common colors.

Jewelry is mostly silver, consisting of various plaited or mesh patterns from which baubles dangle. Muted blue and red stones, such as lapis lazuli, are often inlaid. Necklaces, earrings, and bracelets are most common. Men never wear jewelry.

Men specialize as smiths, woodworkers (especially carvers), and shoemakers. Hat makers may be either men or women, but almost all sewn skullcaps are made by women. Some of the most revered craftsmanship goes into the woodcarving of house doors and on the top and bottom of building support beams. Central Asian wood carving distinguishes itself by unique floral and geometric patterns that require incredible dexterity and concentration on the part of the craftsmen.

Hobbies are common among Karakalpaks as they are among Westerners. Stamps, coins, pop star photos, and tape and CD collections are the stuff of young people's hobbies. Some young people have pen pals.

19 SOCIAL PROBLEMS

During the Soviet period, agriculture and fisheries were developed and emphasized to the detriment of cattle rearing and the raising of food crops. In agriculture, cotton became a major industrial cash crop at the expense of food crops and the area's water supply, much of which was used for the intensive irrigation required for cotton growing. During the 1950s, the Aral Sea provided about 7% of all the fish consumed in the USSR. Unfortunately, a non-diversified economy, combined with the intensity of the effort, has left Karakalpakistan in a ruined state. Few people have safe drinking water, and local food production is inadequate. Not only do people suffer from acute health problems associated with their poisoned environment and inadequately balanced diet, but alcoholism and drug addiction (primarily heroin) are growing problems for the middle aged and young, many of whom suffer from depression. Criminal activity—from petty theft to organized drug smuggling and mafia-style murders—is dramatically higher than it was before the breakup of the Soviet Union.

The Uzbekistani state is itself a police state, and the government is authoritarian. There is little tolerance for dissent with official views or for independent political activity. Since 2001 the Uzbek government has become increasingly repressive toward any expressions of economic or religious expression, and minority groups, such as the Karakalpak, face discrimination. For this reason, when Karakalpaks are among Uzbeks they often try to hide their identity. For the tens of thousands of impoverished Karakalpaks, the only real relief from the stagnation of the economy in Uzbekistan has been to seek work abroad; labor migration is the latest social phenomenon in this area. Unconfirmed reports indicate that more than half of the able-bodied population spends at least some part of the year working abroad, in countries such as Kazakhstan and Russia. The future of the population of Karakalpakistan—especially its cultural continuity—hangs in the balance now, and the near future does not seem to be particularly positive. The government of Uzbekistan has shown very little inclination to maintain the distinctiveness and territorial integrity of these people.

20 GENDER ISSUES

Because Karakalpak culture is similar to the Kazakhs, there historically has been slightly greater gender equity among Karakalpak men and women than one finds, say, among the Uzbeks. Nevertheless, older girls and women are hardly treated as equals by men. Domestic chores still remain the purview of women, and, as mentioned above, Karakalpak women fare poorly when first married, especially as they no longer live among their own clansmen. While most girls receive an education just as boys do, there is little expectation that girls should go on to university or enter professions, although one certainly finds more professional women in the capital Nukus as opposed to the countryside.

The historical and Soviet gender relations have given way of late because of the mass exodus of Karakalpak owing to labor migration. This process causes the breakdown of gender relations to some extent as women necessarily are more in control of what they do if they decide to go abroad for work. While migration gives women greater autonomy as well as wealth, its effects also can cause havoc within families, especially when children have to do without a mother and father for lengthy periods of time.

One phenomenon that has been on the increase since the late 1990s, and that we also see among the Kazakhs and Kyrgyz, is bride kidnapping. Just as the term implies, young women are taken by men in order to marry with no courtship or formal family arrangements. To some degree, this is due to the terrible financial predicament most people find themselves in. Weddings are costly affairs, and by kidnapping a young woman many of the expenses of traditional weddings can be avoided, and a family gets a new member for its own workforce. Still, young women can and do successfully resist these efforts. If the value of education continues to wane, it is unlikely to see any gains in gender equity soon.

21 BIBLIOGRAPHY

Akiner, Shirin. *Islamic Peoples of the Soviet Union*. London: Kegan Paul International, 1983.

Burghart, Daniel L., and Theresa Sabonis-Helf, eds. *In the Tracks of Tamerlane: Central Asia's Path to the 21st Century*. Washington, D.C.: Center For Technology and National Security Policy, National Defense University, 2004.

Etnografiia Karakalpakov XIX-nachalo XX veka (Materialy i Issledovaniia) (Ethnography of the Karakalpaks from the 19th to the early 20th centuries). Tashkent, Uzbekistan: Izdatel'stvo ÒFANÓ Uzbekskoi SSR, 1980.

Freidrich, Paul and Norma Diamond, ed. *Encyclopedia of World Cultures. Vol. VI, Russian and Eurasia/China*. Boston: G. K. Hall, 1994.

Hughes, James, Gwendolyn Sasse, eds. *Ethnicity and Territory in the Former Soviet Union: Regions in Conflict*. London: Frank Cass, 2002.

Muslim Peoples: A World Ethnographic Survey. 2nd rev. ed. Ed. Richard V. Weekes. Westport, CT: Greenwood, 1984.

Narody Srednei Azii i Kazakhstana I (The Peoples of Central Asia and Kazakhstan, Vol. I). Ed. S. P. Tolstov. Moscow: Izdatel'stvo Akademii Nauk, 1962.

Ro'i, Yaacov. *Democracy and Pluralism in Muslim Eurasia*. London: Frank Cass, 2004.

Schlyter, Birgit N. "The Karakalpaks and Other Language Minorities under Central Asian State Rule," in *Prospects for Democracy in Central Asia*. London: I.B.Tauris, 2005.

—by R. Zanca

KARENS

PRONUNCIATION: kuh-RENS
LOCATION: Southern and eastern Myanmar (Burma); Thailand
POPULATION: 5 to 7 million
LANGUAGE: Pwo and Sgaw dialects of Karen; Burmese
RELIGION: Buddhism; animism; Christianity (Baptist, Catholicism)

¹ INTRODUCTION

The Karens are a large and dispersed ethnic group of Southeast Asia. They trace their origins to the Gobi Desert, Mongolia, or Tibet. Karens settled, perhaps as far back as the 8th century, in Myanmar's southern Irrawaddy Delta area and in the hills along the Salween River in eastern Myanmar. In the 1700s, Karens also began living in neighboring Siam (now called Thailand).

There are numerous Karen sub-groups: the Pwo Karens (mostly delta rice-growers), the Sgaw Karens of the mountains; and the Kayahs (also called Karennis), Pa-Os, and Kayans (also called Padaungs), who live in the Karenni and Shan States of Myanmar. These varied people lived mainly in tribal societies, governed by chiefs or princes. They sometimes came into conflict with the Burmese (Burman) dynastic rulers, or with other ethnic groups inclined to wage war.

The advent of British colonization in the mid-to-late 19th century brought a new sense of security to the Karens. Contact with American and European Christian missionaries, and associated literacy and education, was welcomed. The British administrators recruited many Karens into their police and armed forces. When the Second World War came to Myanmar, those Karens became loyal guerrilla fighters for the Allies against Japanese occupiers.

As Britain granted Myanmar independence after the war, Karen politicians hoped for their own nation. Karennis, who had never ceded authority, enjoying "protectorate" status with the British Empire, also expected their nationhood to be recognized. Instead Karens, along with other ethnic populations, were to be absorbed into the new Union of Burma (renamed Union of Myanmar in 1989.) Problems began almost immediately, when troops of the predominantly Burmese (Burman) government killed Karen villagers. A Karen insurgency sprang up and rapidly gained momentum until it threatened to seize control of the capital, Rangoon. The Karen rebels were driven back by the government troops, and the military came to dominate the country, eventually taking over power in 1962, pledging to quell rebellion and unify the country by force.

Counter-insurgency tactics intended to subdue the rebellion by denying it support from civilians actually drove more Karens into joining the rebel Karen National Union, and other Karen peoples such as the Karennis and Pa-Os took up arms against the central military government as well. A consistent pattern of deliberate human rights violations by the government forces against the ethnic minority civilians has continued to this day, driving tens of thousands of Karens to Thailand as refugees and making the Karen conflict the world's longest running insurgency. Sporadic attempts to broker a ceasefire arrangement between the Karen National Union and Myanmar government never bore results, and low-intensity rural guer-

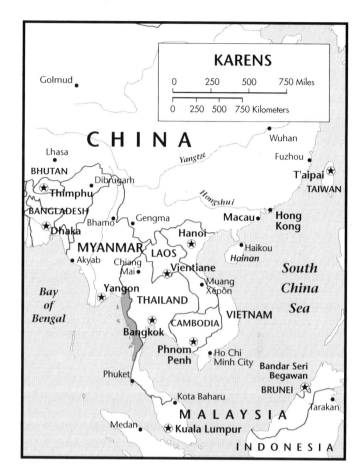

rilla warfare continued into the 21st century. General Bo Mya, the longtime chairman of the Karen National Union died at age 79 in 2006. In 2008 Padoe Mahn Sha, the rebel group's Secretary General was assassinated near the Thailand/Myanmar border.

² LOCATION AND HOMELAND

Estimates of the Karen population of Myanmar vary greatly, as there has been no census in decades. Perhaps as many as 6 million Pwo and Sgaw Karens live there, along with some 150,000 Kayahs, 600,000 Pa-Os, 80,000 Kayans, and other related groups. Another 400,000 Karen-ethnic peoples have roots in Thailand, and thousands of others live there as refugees. In the early 21st century, Karen refugees have increasingly settled in the United States, with a large community coming to live in and around St. Paul, Minnesota.

Karen people live in several parts of southern and eastern Myanmar. The largest Karen population is in the Irrawaddy Delta area, a vast agricultural lowland whose main city is Bassein. On 2 May 2008, Cyclone Nargis devastated the Irrawaddy Delta region, killing tens of thousands of people, making over a million homeless, and flooding rice-growing land with saltwater. Myanmar's government delayed aid delivery after the cyclone, and there were reports that Karen villagers in the Delta were discriminated against in relief distribution.

Another significant region for the Karens is the eastern border with Thailand, where the Dawna Mountain Range stretches down to the Tenasserim River. The area along the Salween also is inhabited by Karens. Thaton, Papun and Pa-an are towns with major Karen populations. Kayahs and Kayans live in a rugged, mountainous area where the main city is Loikaw. The Pa-Os live on the plateau of the southern Shan State. According to international human rights organizations, as many as 3,000 villages in predominantly Karen areas of eastern Myanmar were destroyed by Myanmar government forces between 1996 and 2006, with the civilian inhabitants hiding as internally displaced people or fleeing as refugees to neighboring Thailand.

³ LANGUAGE

The languages of the Karens are generally considered to be of the Tibeto-Burman family, and the main dialects are Pwo and Sgaw. Many Karen people in isolated hill areas remain illiterate, and those in the Delta region often can speak only Burmese. Their language does, however, remain a feature of Karen cultural pride. Baptist missionaries developed scripts based on Burmese for Pwo Karen (with 25 letters) and for other Karen languages. An old Pwo script known as "chicken scratch," because of the shapes of its letters, was devised by Karen Buddhists as well.

In Sgaw Karen, an informal greeting ("How's it going?") is "*Madee leh?*" and a farewell is "*Leh mu mu*" ("Go pleasantly"). "Thank you" in Sgaw Karen is "*Dah bluet.*"

⁴ FOLKLORE

Karen folklore impressed early Christian missionaries with its similarity to the Book of Genesis in the Bible. The tribal mythology also told of the Karen language being kept in a book, which was lost in the mass migration south from "the river of sand." There is a sense in their old stories of being preyed upon by other ethnic groups, and of wishing to regain some past glories through miracles or supernaturally gifted leaders. Sometimes Karens have become cult followers of messianic leaders who assure them that special clothing or tattoos will make them impervious from harm. In traditional animist, spirit-worshipping belief systems, the Karens must make offerings to natural forces such as "the Lord of Land and Water." Even Christian Karens still have their skin adorned with tattoos as a form of magical protection. Buddhist Karens often wear amulets (small metal, stone, or clay Buddha images) around their necks.

The Kayan people are known for the neck rings made of brass worn by girls and women. Over time, more and more coils are added to the rings, which pushes the collarbones down, giving the appearance of an elongated neck (hence their Burmese name, Padaung, meaning "long-neck"). Kayan society is traditionally a matriarchy and the rings around necks, arms, and knees are sometimes explained as a traditional protection against tiger bites. Many Kayans have become refugees in recent years, and women with neck rings have been exploited as "freak show" tourist attractions in Thailand and Myanmar.

⁵ RELIGION

Most of the Pwo and Sgaw Karens are Buddhists or animists. There are also significant populations of Christians, mainly Baptists, and the Karen National Union leadership is largely Christian. Many Kayahs and Kayans are Catholic, and most of the Pa-Os are Buddhists.

There is considerable interplay between animist rituals and Buddhist practices among the Karens. Animists believe in helpful female guardian spirits called "ther myng khae," the "lord of land and water," and local spirits, as well as beneficial and malicious ghosts. The Christians emphasize Bible study and prayer services with hymn singing. Villages tend to be predominantly one or the other of the three religions, while there is a mixture of faiths and houses of worship in the towns. Christian Karens have tried to convert the Buddhists and animists, and Myanmar's military government has encouraged conflict between Buddhist Karens and the Christian-led Karen National Union.

⁶ MAJOR HOLIDAYS

The Karen New Year in January is celebrated as a national holiday in Myanmar and is often the occasion for traditional dances and music. Christian Karens celebrate Christmas with parties and caroling trips from village to village. Buddhist Karens hold festivals to mark their religious New Year (mid-spring) and the end of Lent (post-monsoon). Animists hold crop-protection festivals during the monsoon and after harvest.

⁷ RITES OF PASSAGE

Traditional Karen society has various taboos for pregnant women, such as not drinking liquor and not going to funerals. Births usually take place at home, assisted by family members or a village "midwife" (often a man). After the birth, the mother eats a special diet of rice and chicken, and the baby has strings tied around its wrists to protect it from evil spirits. Deaths in childhood and infant mortality are very common among the Karens. In rural areas there is little understanding of hygiene and mother-child nutrition, but Karen medical practitioners are working to spread information that can save lives.

Among Buddhist Karens, young boys often become novice monks for a short period of time. Teenaged Karen boys sometimes get tattooed with magical symbols to show their bravery and protect them from harm. Kayan girls may begin to wear coils of brass around their necks as young as six years old, and keep adding to the coils during their teenage years until the neck piece stretches as long as 10 in.

Karens have a variety of funeral customs, according to their religions. The animist Karens believe in an afterlife and dress the corpse to be accepted in the land of *Khu See-du,* the Lord of the Dead. The body may be cremated or buried. Buddhist Karens hold cremation ceremonies with prayers to ease the deceased person into the next incarnation. Christian Karens hold a funeral prayer service and bury the body, usually with a wooden cross to mark the grave.

⁸ INTERPERSONAL RELATIONS

For a polite greeting, a Karen holds his or her right elbow in their left hand, and shakes hands with the right. They use the same gesture to give or offer objects to other people. Introductions will include the honorifics Karens use with their names, usually "Saw" for men and "Naw" for women.

Karens are very hospitable and will expect any guests to eat with them and, if possible, stay overnight or longer at their house. In traditional Karen bamboo houses, sleeping quarters for guests are on the verandah.

Boys and girls usually meet in school, at Buddhist festivals, or in Christian youth groups. In traditional animist villages, funerals have been the scene of much boy-girl socializing.

A Kayan family, refugees from Burma, came to Thailand to escape the civil war and now reside in Thailand. (AP Images/Ben Bohane)

When a young couple gets involved, love letters and secret messages are often exchanged. Sometimes a game is played between groups of boys and girls, with the boys asking poetic questions and the girls replying with a rhyming answer. The questions and answers are about romance, but are subtle and symbolic.

⁹ LIVING CONDITIONS

Warfare and forced relocation campaigns by the Myanmar government have displaced much of Myanmar's Karen population. Villagers are compelled to leave their family homes and move to resettlement camps near government army bases (where they are used for forced labor), or they flee to forest areas or across the border to Thailand. As they leave their towns and villages, the rate of infection with malaria, typhoid, cholera, hepatitis, dysentery, and other diseases increases. Many Karens, especially children, die from such infectious illnesses. Several foreign non-governmental aid agencies assist Karen refugees in Thailand's camps, and some aid groups of Karen exiles and foreigners risk crossing the Thailand/Myanmar border to try to help displaced Karens hiding out inside Myanmar. Also, a few foreign aid organizations have attempted to reduce diseases such as malaria among Karens in the Delta region.

Malnutrition is widespread among the Karens, many of whom subsist on rice with chili pepper, and perhaps some fish sauce and greens gathered from the forests. Anemia and vitamin deficiency are common. In addition to forced relocation, the widespread taking of farmers for forced labor by the government military has made it hard for them to grow their crops. Rampant deforestation as the Myanmar government sold off frontier teak forests to Thai logging firms has decreased the Karens' sources of wild game and edible and medicinal plants, as well as causing climate changes and landslides.

For many generations, the Karen people had lived in harmony with the forest. Only if teak trees reached a certain size could they be harvested. They were replanted and the logs were transported by elephants and river rafts. Forest-dwelling Karens built their houses from bamboo with some wood, on stilts with a thatched roof. The stilts are said to be especially high if it is the house of an elephant-owning family, so that the verandah can be used for loading and unloading the animal. In the bamboo houses, the family will sit and sleep on woven mats on the floor. In larger houses of teak or other wood, they sit on benches at tables and sleep on raised wooden beds with mosquito netting. Baths are taken, wearing sarongs, in a river or by pouring water from a village pump or an urn of rainwater. Sections of bamboo or plastic buckets are used to carry water from nearby streams for cooking and washing. Toilets are usually small pit latrines with a bamboo shelter.

The ox-cart is still the usual means of transport for goods and people, along with motorized river long-boats, motorbikes, and elephants. The Karens are well known for their work with elephants, which they capture, train, and use for hauling and transport. Pa-Os and Kayahs often raise ponies or mules for transportation.

¹⁰ FAMILY LIFE

Traditionally, either a boy or girl can propose marriage, and the whole village is allowed a say in whether their marriage would be appropriate and not offensive to any spirits. Weddings are festive occasions when both the bride's and groom's villages come together. The bride changes from her unmarried woman's long dress to a married woman's two-part outfit. Marriage is considered to be for life, and among Karens of all faiths, adultery is considered extremely taboo—as an unnatural act that can bring catastrophe on the whole village. Karens have an average of four or five children, but infant and child mortality rates are very high.

Karen families keep dogs for hunting and as pets. Sometimes they have birds or baby forest animals such as squirrels or gibbons. Karen elephant tamers "adopt" one elephant, train it, and take care of it for life.

¹¹ CLOTHING

Many Karen men now wear mass-produced shirts and T-shirts with trousers, and women wear sarongs of factory-woven batik cloth. Younger women sometimes wear blue jeans or long skirts, especially if they are in a town or city. However, traditional Karen clothing is still popular, especially in mountain areas and for special occasions. Traditionally, Pwo and Sgaw Karens wear tunics and sarongs of homespun cotton, dyed red, blue, and black. Men and married women wear a loose tunic over a wrapped sarong. The women's tunics are often elaborately embroidered with colored thread and seed-beads. The men's are plainer with fringed hems. Unmarried girls wear simple long white dresses called "*hsay mo htoo*" in Sgaw Karen. Men and women often wear turbans, and Pwo men sometimes have very long hair worn in side swept ponytails or loose. Pwo and Sgaw women wear masses of bead necklaces and a great many silver bracelets on their wrists and upper arms.

The Kayans wear similar clothing to the Pwo Karens, but usually in natural off-white homespun, and the Pa-O people dress in black cotton tunics with trousers or sarongs. Kayahs are often known as Karennis ("red Karens") because of their predominantly red homespun clothing. The women wear a short sarong wrapped up over one shoulder with a belt or sash and cords of thin black rattan wrapped around their legs.

¹² FOOD

Karens are known for eating a huge variety of foods, including jungle products such as snake, bat, monkey, grubs, bee larvae, ants, palm sugar, wild honey, forest herbs, frog, and lizard. Many types of birds and fish are consumed, and Karens raise chickens, ducks, pigs, cattle, corn, and pumpkins for food. A favorite dish for Karens in the forest is *takataw,* made by adding a handful of rice and some shreds of dried meat (such as venison or wild boar) to boiling water, letting it cook until the meat and rice are soft like porridge, and then adding some chopped vegetables.

Because of deforestation, crop confiscation, and rural dislocation, nowadays many Karens have trouble obtaining enough nutrition for their families. Karen refugees and poor villagers typically live on rice, chili peppers, some fish paste, and whatever greens they can gather. The Karens normally eat several helpings of rice at meals and for snacks. They eat mostly polished white rice now, which is less nutritious than red or brown rice. For flavoring, many people use monosodium glutamate powder, which comes from Thailand.

Karens often chew betel nut, which comes from a species of palm and is combined with leaves and lime paste; it is a mild stimulant and stains the mouth bright red.

¹³ EDUCATION

During the British colonial period, missionaries in Bassein and elsewhere helped the Karens to start Christian-staffed village schools, which were supported by Buddhist and animist parents as well. Myanmar's military government took over those schools in the 1960s, changing to a national rather than Karen curriculum. In Karen National Union-held areas, a series of schools up to the secondary level was established, but most of these are gone now, as the rebels have lost most of their territory to the government. Even in refugee camps, the Karens try to have formal education for their children, but those makeshift schools, like the refugee health clinics, have mostly been destroyed in cross-border raids. Textbooks, often decades old, and school materials are in very short supply, and what schools there are tend to be understaffed. Another difficulty in Karen education is that the schoolchildren are often traumatized by their experience of human rights abuse and are malnourished and beset by malaria and other diseases. In recent years, some young people have been able to receive "backpack medical" or alternative technology training while in refugee camps.

¹⁴ CULTURAL HERITAGE

Karen music includes traditional songs (many of which were love songs) and Western-influenced Christian hymns. In the rebel areas there are also political songs and military marching music played by drum and flute corps. Music that uses the repetitive beat of metal gongs accompanies such dances as the rice-planting dance and the bamboo dance, as well as wedding processions. In the bamboo dance, sets of 8 to 12 long bamboo poles are placed in a grid. Participants kneel on the ground and bang the poles together in time to the music, while dancers step in and out of the openings in the grid.

The Karens have several musical instruments of importance. The Karen drum is a symbol of the people's culture. It is round and made of cast bronze, often with figures of frogs and elephants decorating it. The Karens play a harp called the *t'na,* which has five or six strings and is tuned with pegs along the neck. Another stringed instrument is the large, wooden guitar-like *haw tu.* The *pa ku* is a bamboo xylophone played with hammers, and there are bamboo panpipes and mouth-harps of various sizes. Karens also use imported instruments such as guitars and electric keyboards, especially for Christian church music.

The Karen literary tradition is mostly in oral form. Folktales abound, often about a poor orphan boy who falls in love with a girl of a wealthy family. Books by Karens written since World War II include *Memoirs of the Four-Foot Colonel* by Smith Dun, a high ranking officer in the British Army, and *The Golden Book*, a Christian interpretation of ancient Karen prophetic poems. Kayan writer Pascal Khoo Thwe's *From the Land of Green Ghosts*, a memoir of his childhood and life as a refugee won acclaim when it was published in Britain in 2003. Foreign aid workers have also written about their experiences with the Karens. Sylvester Stallone's 2008 movie *Rambo* was a fictional depiction of the war and human rights abuse affecting Karen villages. A 2002 Thai movie, *Blissfully Yours,* directed by Apichatpong Weerasethakul, featured a Karen refugee protagonist. *Total Denial,* a 2006 film documented the efforts of Karen environmental activist Ka Hsaw Wa, founder of EarthRights International, and his group's lawsuit against Unocal, a petroleum company doing business in Myanmar.

¹⁵ WORK

The Karens have long been rice farmers in wet, irrigated fields in the Delta or in hill fields in the mountains. To cultivate rice in the highlands, villagers burn down plots of forest. This system, called "swidden cultivation," worked well when populations were small and stable, and forests were hardly touched by logging. Now, with the forest size drastically decreased by voracious timber companies and large segments of the Karen population involuntarily on the move, this slash-and-burn method contributes to erosion and loss of wildlife habitat.

Karens also make their living through fishing in coastal areas, working in tin or wolfram mines, and gathering forest products like rattan and honey. There are some educated professionals among the Karens, but many of them live overseas as exiles. When they reach other countries, they often have to take any job available, in spite of their education.

¹⁶ SPORTS

Soccer, volleyball, and a type of kickball called *chinlone* are popular with Karen young people. Even in mountainous areas, Karen villages often have one flat open space where such sports can be played. Karens sometimes play a game they call *mahket* in which the large seeds from a vine are rolled to knock over other seeds. In places where television is available, soccer is the favorite spectator sport.

¹⁷ ENTERTAINMENT AND RECREATION

In their free time, Karens enjoy musical activities, movies and DVD shows, and taking walks around their town or village in the evening when the air cools down. People rise at or before dawn and often take an afternoon siesta.

¹⁸ FOLK ART, CRAFTS, AND HOBBIES

Karen women are known for their fine cotton weaving of clothing, blankets and shoulder bags. The weaving is usually done on a small loom set up with a strap that wraps around the waist at one end, but in some areas there are large wooden frame looms as well. The thread is dyed with natural or artificial colors, sometimes with a pattern tie-dyed in. Some woven items are now produced for overseas sale as a means for refugee women to support their families. The Karens also produce etched silver jewelry, baskets, and embroidery.

¹⁹ SOCIAL PROBLEMS

The Karens feel particularly persecuted after several decades of widespread abuse by military forces of the Myanmar government. The consistent pattern of human rights violations includes forced labor as army equipment porters, human mine-sweepers, human shields, and road and railway builders;

destruction of entire villagers; torture of civilians suspected of rebel sympathies; and massacres and executions without trial. Government military abuse of Karen women, particularly rape of village girls by troops, is especially common. These events have made the usually stable Karens into terrified nomads and have turned many into stubborn rebel fighters. Some are third or fourth generation guerrilla soldiers who have grown up knowing nothing but war. For many Karens, the highest priority has become finding a way to escape Myanmar as a refugee, and then obtaining resettlement from Thailand's camps to a third country, in order to start a new life with hopes of peace and education for their children. For others, staying close to their homeland is the goal, even if that means hiding in the forest and moving from place to place to avoid the Myanmar government's soldiers.

²⁰ GENDER ISSUES

In Karen societies, other than the Kayan matriarchy, women have been considered inferior or subservient to men. Women did a great deal of difficult farm work, but had little status or decision-making power. This has been changing since World War II, as more Karen women have become educated and have taken noteworthy roles in fields such as teaching and health. Dr. Cynthia Maung, a Karen physician, is admired for her brave work in bringing medical care to remote, war-torn regions. Many older women have become village leaders when men have been taken away for forced labor. Refugee women's groups have been formed, emphasizing self-help programs and economic empowerment through the sale of weaving and other crafts. Although Karen society is rather conservative, some individuals who look or behave in ways unconventional to their gender behavior have been tolerated and accepted.

²¹ BIBLIOGRAPHY

Anderson, Edward F. *Plants and People of the Golden Triangle: Ethnobotany of the Hill Tribes of Northern Thailand.* Dioscorides Press, 1993.

Falla, Jonathan. *Truelove and Bartholomew: Rebels on the Burmese Border.* Cambridge: Cambridge University Press, 1991.

Karen Human Rights Group. www.khrg.org (18 April 2008)

Lewis, Paul and Elaine. *Peoples of the Golden Triangle.* New York: Thames and Hudson, 1984.

Mirante, Edith T. *Burmese Looking Glass: A Human Rights Adventure.* New York: Grove Press, 1993.

Rebecca, Naw. "Karen Education: Children on the Front Line." *Cultural Survival Quarterly* 13, no. 4 (1989).

Smith, Martin. *Ethnic Groups in Burma.* London: Anti-Slavery International, 1994.

Thornton, Phil. *Restless Souls: Rebels, Refugees, Medics and Misfits on the Thai-Burmese Border.* Bangkok: Asia Books, 2006.

Thwe, Pascal Khoo. *From the Land of Green Ghosts: A Burmese Odyssey.* New York: HarperCollins, 2002

"Total Denial," DVD, directed by Milena Kaneva. Italy: MK Production, 2007.

—by E. Mirante

KASHMIRIS

LOCATION: Kashmir in the northwest of the Indian
   subcontinent
POPULATION: Greater Kashmir c. 15 million (estimate)
LANGUAGE: Kashmiri (including the Dardi, Shrinya and
   Khowar dialects)
RELIGION: Islam, Hinduism, Buddhism

1 INTRODUCTION

Kashmiris occupy the northwestern region of the Indian subcontinent. Until the mid-19th century, the term "Kashmir"
referred only to the Vale of Kashmir lying between the Great
Himalayas and the Pir Panjal range. Since then, however, it
has been used to refer to a larger area that includes the Indian-
administered state of Jammu and Kashmir (consisting of the
Kashmir valley, Jammu, and Ladakh), the Pakistani-admin-
istered provinces of the Northern Areas (including Gilgit and
Baltistan) and Azad Kashmir ("Free Kashmir"), and the Chi-
nese-administered region Aksai Chin.

In the Indian Epic (15th-10th centuries BC), Kashmir is
mentioned as a focus of Sanskrit learning and, by the first half
of the first millennium BC, Kashmir was an important center
of Hinduism. However, the Indian Emperor Ashoka, who converted to Buddhism, is credited with having founded the city
of Srinagar, and Kashmir became a seat of Buddhist learning,
with the Sarvāstivādan school dominating. East and Central
Asian Buddhist monks are recorded as having visited the kingdom. In the late 4th century AD, the famous monk Kumārajīva,
who helped take Buddhism to China, studied in Kashmir.

Islam was introduced into Kashmir in the 8th century AD,
when Muslims started gaining high positions in the Kashmiri
army. The Hindu ruler Chandrapida gave territory to the Arab
military commander Muhammad Alafi to live along with his
hundreds of followers. The employment of hundreds of Muslim captains in the armies of the Kashmiri Kings at the turn of
the 11th century alludes to the presence of a sizeable Muslim
population in Kashmir more than 200 years before the establishment of Muslim rule. By the beginning of the 13th century
Muslims formed an important section of the Kashmiri population and had made great strides. However, the conversion
of Buddhist ruler Rinchana Sadr-ud-Din (AD 1320–1323) to
Islam marked a turning point in the history of Kashmir. He
converted after having discussions with Hindu, Buddhist, and
Muslim religious personages of the period. His conversion
was followed by that of a large number of people including the
prime minister, Rawanchandra.

During the 14th century, Islam was the dominant religion
in Kashmir. The Muslims and Hindus of Kashmir lived in relative harmony, since the Sufi-Islamic way of life of ordinary
Muslims in Kashmir complemented the Rishi tradition of the
Hindu Kashmiri Pandits. This led to a syncretic culture where
Hindus and Muslims revered the same local saints and prayed
at the same shrines. However, some Muslim Kashmiri rulers
were intolerant of Hinduism. For instance, the *Tarikh-i-Firish-
ta* records that Sultan Sikandar Butshikan of Kashmir (AD
1389–1413) persecuted Hindus and issued orders proscribing
the residence of any other than Muslims in Kashmir.

The Princely State of Kashmir and Jammu (as it was then
called) was constituted between 1820 and 1858 and was "somewhat artificial in composition and it did not develop a fully coherent identity, partly as a result of its disparate origins and
partly as a result of the autocratic rule which it experienced
on the fringes of Empire." It combined disparate regions, religions, and ethnicities: to the east, Ladakh was ethnically and
culturally Tibetan, and its inhabitants practiced Buddhism;
to the south, Jammu had a mixed population of Hindus, Muslims, and Sikhs. In the heavily populated central Kashmir
valley, the population was overwhelmingly Sunni Muslim,
however, and there was also a small but influential Hindu minority, the Kashmiri Brahmans or Pandits. To the northeast,
sparsely populated Baltistan had a population ethnically related to Ladakh, but which practiced Shia Islam, while to the
north, also sparsely populated, Gilgit Agency, was an area of
diverse, mostly Shia groups. In the west, Punch was Muslim,
but of different ethnicity than Muslims in the Kashmir valley.

The British acquired Kashmir from the Sikhs (who had annexed the state in 1820) in 1846 following the First Anglo-Sikh
War and allowed the Dogra (Rajput) Maharaja Gulab Singh,
ruler of Jammu, to purchase the state for a large sum of money. So, the princely state of Jammu and Kashmir, in which the
majority of the population was Muslim, came to be ruled by a
Hindu maharaja.

At the time of Independence in 1947 the princely states of
India were to accede to either Muslim Pakistan or India. It was
anticipated that, with a Muslim population of some 77% and a
common border with Pakistan, the ruler of Jammu and Kashmir would accede to Pakistan, but when Maharaja Hari Singh,
ruler of one of the most powerful princely states in India, hesi-
tated, perhaps trying to attain an independent status, Pakistan
sent Pathan and Pashto tribesmen into Kashmir in a guerrilla
onslaught meant to frighten its ruler into submission. Instead,
the Maharaja appealed to Louis Mountbatten for assistance
and the Governor-General of British India agreed to provide
this on the condition that the ruler accede to India. Once the
Maharaja signed the Instrument of Accession, Indian soldiers
entered Kashmir (only one road from Jammu provided access
to the Vale of Kashmir) and drove the Pakistani-sponsored ir-
regulars from all but a small section of the state. Pakistan responded by sending in its regular army, and a full scale war
was fought between India and Pakistan (fortunately it did not
spread beyond Kashmir). India approached the United Nations
Security Council to mediate the quarrel. In a UN-sponsored
cease fire, the opposing forces stopped in 1949 at what is now
called the Line of Control, which is today the de facto border between Pakistan and India in Kashmir. Thus, although
there was a clear Muslim majority in Kashmir before the 1947
partition and its economic, cultural, and geographic contigu-
ity with the Muslim-majority area of the Punjab (in Pakistan)
could be convincingly demonstrated, Pakistan was left with
territory that, although basically Muslim in character, was
thinly populated, relatively inaccessible, and economically underdeveloped. The largest Muslim group, situated in the Vale
of Kashmir and estimated to number more than half the population of the entire region, lay in Indian-administered territory, with its former outlets to the Punjab, via the Jhelum valley
route, blocked. The Indian Prime Minister Jawaharlal Nehru
promised a plebiscite under UN supervision, which never happened because one of the pre-conditions for this was that Paki-

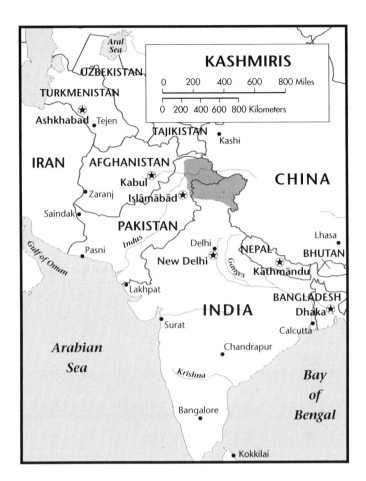

occupied and administered by China. To the south of the Pir Panjal range lie the lowlands of Jammu, an extension of the Indo-Gangetic plains to the foot of the mountains.

To the west of the Vale is Azad Kashmir ("Free Kashmir"), Pakistani-occupied territory separated from Indian-controlled Kashmir by the Line of Control. To the north lies the Northern Areas of Pakistan, Baltistan and Gilgit, mountainous terrain crossed by the Karakoram Mountains and containing some of the highest mountains in the world (K-2, at 6,811 m [28,251 ft] second only to Everest, and Nanga Parbat, 8,125 m [26,658 ft]), ranked the 9th highest peak in the world.

Kashmir occupies a region where Pakistan, India, Afghanistan, and China come together and thus has been strategically important in the history of the subcontinent. The 2001 Census of India reports the population of Jammu and Kashmir as 10,143,700 persons. Add to this perhaps 3 million people in Azad Kashmir, the population of the other areas of Pakistan that fall into "greater Kashmir" and factor in natural increase, and the population of greater Kashmir is close to 15 million people.

³ LANGUAGE

Kashmiri is a Dardic language, a linguistic sub-grouping belonging to the Indo-European Language Family. It is spoken primarily in the valley of Kashmir and has about 5 million speakers in India. The 105,000 or so speakers of Kashmiri in Pakistan are mostly immigrants from the Kashmir Valley to Pakistan. Traditionally, Kashmiri was written in the Perso-Arabic script but today is written in either the Perso-Arabic script (with some modifications) or the Devanagari script. It is the official state language of Jammu and Kashmir and is also one of India's 23 national languages. Some Kashmiri speakers use English or Urdu as a second language, though in the past few decades Kashmiri has been introduced as a subject at the university and the colleges of the valley. At present, attempts are underway for inclusion of Kashmiri in the school curriculum.

Kashmiri has a literary tradition that dates back to the 14th century AD. Kashmiri literature consists largely of poetry particularly rich in the lyrics of life and nature, besides compositions in the mystic vein of both the Brahmanical (Shaivite) and Islamic (Sufi) traditions. There are works of modern Kashmiri literature, with Ghulam Ahmed Mahjoor (1885–1952) considered to be one of the greatest of modern Kashmiri poets, short story writers such as Akthar Mohi-ud-Din, Hari Krishnan Kaul, and Amin Kamil, and contributions in the area of non-fiction by the likes of Jawaharlal Nehru.

⁴ FOLKLORE

As is to be expected, the diverse regions of "Kashmir" each have their own traditions of folklore. Thus, areas like Baltistan and Ladakh have their own folklore, with the former having a veneer of Islamization and the latter reflecting its Buddhist character. Similarly, the folklore in southern areas shows the influence of the Pakistani Punjab, with variants of the epic *Heera Ranjha*, in addition to ballads, folktales, folk music, and dance

In Kashmir proper, however, perhaps Hatim's Tales are in a class by themselves in the folklore tradition. A spell-binding story-teller, Hatim Talawon was a legend in his lifetime. He recited, intoned, sang, and talked to his listeners in the towns and villages of the picturesque Kashmir valley. His tales were

stan should withdraw all military forces from the region of Kashmir.

Every time India and Pakistan have fought a war since 1949 (i.e. in 1965, 1971), Kashmir has remained a focal point of the conflicts. Most recently, in 1999, Indian and Pakistani forces fought each other in Kargil, India, claiming that regular Pakistani troops and Kashmiri militants, in a plan devised by the then Pakistani Army Commander, General Pervez Musharraf, entered Indian territory in Kargil. Later in 1999, Musharraf seized power in Pakistan in a military coup and became president.

² LOCATION AND HOMELAND

The heart of Kashmir is the Vale of Kashmir, an ancient lake bed lying between the Pir Panjal mountain range and the main Himalayas to the northeast. The valley is 85 mi (140 km) long, 20 mi wide, and set at an altitude of 1,620 m (5,300 ft) high. Drained by the upper Jhelum River, the valley is lined by 3,600–5,000 meters-high mountains (c. 12,000–16,000 ft) that help shelter it from the wet southwest monsoon. It is the centre of population for Kashmir. The main city in the Vale, Srīnagar, is the capital of the Indian state of Jammu and Kashmir. The fertile alluvial soil yields rice, corn (maize), fruit, and vegetables, and the scenic mountains and lakes (notably Wular and Dal) used to attract many tourists to the region.

To the east lie the mountains of Ladakh and still further to the east is the Aksai Chin, physically a part of the Tibetan Plateau claimed by India but, since the 1962 Indo-Chinese War,

drawn from history, mythology, traditional narratives, and original stories devised by Hatim himself. They were part of the Kashmir's oral tradition that survived in memory and by word of the mouth and were gathered and published by Sir Aurel Stein in 1918.

5 RELIGION

Over three quarters of Kashmir's population is Muslim, mainly following the Sufi customs commonly found in India. Kashmiri Muslims fall into four groups: the Sheikh, the Sayed, the Mughal, and the Pathan. The Sheikhs are by far the most numerous and are thought to be descended from Hindus. They have clans, which are called *krāms*. There appear to be few marriage restrictions according to krām, though many scholars suggest that the krām are descended from Hindu groups and, indeed, in some ways there appears to be a kind of hierarchical structure not unlike the Hindu caste system. The Dar boatmen and the Dums, gardeners and butchers by trade, are, for instance, viewed as being socially inferior. But, as some writers observe, the social system is very plastic, and prosperity and a little wealth soon erase humble origins. The Sayeds tend to marry among themselves. They are either holy men, in which case they are given the title *Mir*, or (and this includes the bulk of the Sayeds) they are agriculturalists, in which case the name Mir is used as a suffix. There are a few Mughals, who settled Kashmir at the time of Mughal rule and the Pathans, found in the southwest of the valley, and date to Durrani rule (18th century), or who were brought in to Kashmir by Maharah Gulab Singh (1846–1857) for service on the frontier. The Pathans tend to speak Pashto, maintain their own dress, and carry weapons, although they are now rapidly assimilating into Kashmiri society.

Numerous Hindu groups are found in Kashmir, the most important of which are the Kashmiri Pandits (the first Prime Minister of an independent India, Jawaharlal Nehru, belonged to this community). Of the Brahman caste, the Pandits have played a long and important role in the history of Kashmir. Even though they follow Hindu rituals, the Pandits, for many years, co-existed with the Kashmiri Muslims in the spirit of *Kashmiriyat* (Kashmiri tolerance). Other Hindu castes, who tend to be found mainly in Jammu, include the Dogra Rajputs, the Gaddis (sheep and goat herders), Khattris (traders), and Thakkars.

It is often difficult to distinguish, from a religious perspective, between Kashmiri Muslims and Hindus. They respect the same saints and worship at the same shrines. However, another distinctive element in the population is Buddhism. The religion was introduced into the Vale of Kashmir when Ashoka conquered the region in the 3rd century BC and even though today Buddhists make up only just over 1% of Kashmir's population, the region has, in the past, been an important center for the development and spread of the religion. Numerous Buddhist monks from Kashmir were responsible for carrying Buddhism north of the Himalayas and into China and Tibet.

6 MAJOR HOLIDAYS

Major festivals in Kashmir reflect the mix of Islamic, Hindu, and Sikh peoples found in the region. Thus, typical Hindu festivals include Navaratra, or New Year's Day, which is celebrated on the first day of the new moon in the month of Chaitra (March/April). In every Hindu home, it begins with an invoca-

tion to Lakshmi, the goddess of wealth. In all families, a young lady lays a large plate with paddy, sugar, curds, fruits, walnut, coins, a mirror, ink-holder, and the New Year scroll and shows it to every family member, thus seeking the blessings of the goddess for moral and material development of members of the family. In April, Durga Ashtami, Ramnavami (Rama's birthday), and Baisakhi (the Spring festival) are observed. Holi, Diwali, and Dussehra, major festivals on the Hindu calendar, are also kept in Kashmir. Some festivals are observed by both Hindus and Muslims. For instance, the anniversary of Rishi Pir, a Hindu saint, held on the fifth day of the full moon of Baisakh at his home in Srinagar is attended by Muslims also.

The Navroz festival of the Shia Muslims falls a week after the Hindu New Year's Day. The Urs (or Ziarats) is a typical Kashmiri festival. It is held annually at the shrines of Muslim saints on their death anniversaries. There is a saying that goes, "It snows when the Urs of Meesha Sahib is held, it is windy when the Urs of Batamol Sahib takes place, it rains on the occasion of the Urs of Bahauddin." These Urs are popular despite the rigors of weather. They are celebrated in different parts of Srinagar, not only by Muslims but also by Hindus and Sikhs. An interesting feature of the Urs celebrations at Batamaloo (the locality in Srinagar named after the saint Batamol Sahib) and in Anantag (Rishi Mol's anniversary) is that both Muslims and Hindus abstain from taking meat during the course of the festival.

Muslim festivals that are celebrated nationally include Shab-i Mairaj, which is followed by Shab-i-Barat, Muharram, the month of Ramadan, and the Ids. The dates of these festivals change in accordance with the appearance of the moon and shift by 10 days each year. During the night of Shab-i-Barat the Muslims keep vigil. Legend goes that on this night the Holy Prophet visits each house and relieves the pains of suffering humanity.

The Birthday of Guru Nanak Dev in November is a very auspicious day for the Sikhs of Kashmir. They visit Chati Patshahi near Hari Parbat. Epistles from the Granth Sahib (the Sikh scripture) are recited throughout the day.

A typically Kashmiri festival known as Khichri Amavasya falls in the month of Posh (December/January). Kashmir is believed to have been the abode of Yakshas in ancient times. The Yaksha spirit is invited to relish *khichri* (rice cooked with dal and ghee). Kashmiris leave khichri out along with a fish, and it is believed that during the night the yaksha comes and tastes the food.

The festival cycle in other parts of Kashmir differ slightly. Thus, in Jammu, in addition to the usual festivals celebrated by Hindus throughout India (e.g. Holi, Diwali, Dussehra), the Lohri festival, marking the culmination of the cold season, is celebrated with zest every where. The Gurupubs, birthdays of the Sikh saints, are celebrated in the region, as is the anniversary of the birth of Buddha. In Ladakh, the festival calendar is, naturally, dominated by Buddhist festivals, such as the one held at Hemis, near Leh.

7 RITES OF PASSAGE

The rites of passage of the Kashmiris follow those of the specific community to which an individual belongs. Thus, Muslims, whether in Pakistani or Indian Kashmir, follow the outlines of ritual prescribed by Islamic law (the *Shariah)*, but they often combine these rites with local customs. Newborns are sancti-

Kashmiri Muslims row on the waters of Dal Lake in Srinagar, Kashmir. (Rouf Bhat/AFP/Getty Images)

fied by prayer and undergo head-shaving and naming ceremonies. All males undergo the ritual of circumcision (*sunnat*). Among some Muslims, a ceremony known as *Bismillah* marks the beginning of a child's education in religious matters. Ceremonies associated with death and burial combine practices from the *Shariah* with local customs. The body is ritually bathed and wrapped in a white shroud in preparation for burial. The body is brought out of the house and the face of the deceased person is shown to relatives and neighbors. Mourners, led by a priest, say prayers over the body, which is then taken in procession to the graveyard and buried facing Mecca.

Hindus follow Hindu practices. Thus, for the Kashmiri Pandit, life is ruled by the Hindu concept of *dharma* (known locally as *bhattil*). In the name-giving ceremony, the donning of the sacred thread, the marriage ceremony and the various stages of a householder's life, the Pandit is governed by the Hindu scriptures. At the time of death, the body is washed with water to which some Ganges water has been added, cotton balls are inserted into the ears and nostrils, and a coin is placed at the lips. The corpse is placed in a white shroud, which is tied with a thread, and the body taken in procession, led by the eldest son, to the cremation grounds to be burned. Various rituals are performed on certain days after the death.

8 INTERPERSONAL RELATIONS

Again, greetings in Kashmir are determined by the ethnic communities to which the individuals involved belong and whether the context is formal or informal. In the former case, the response is virtually pre-determined. Thus, a Hindu greeting a Hindu would, as elsewhere in India, say "namaste" or "namaskar," while bringing the palms together in front of the body and making a slight bow. The reply would be the same. A Hindu meeting a Muslim, and *vice versa*, would say "ādāb" ("brother") and expect the same response. A Muslim greeting a Muslim would use the traditional greeting "Salaam Aleikum" ("Peace be with you"), to which the response should be "Vailaikum Salaam" ("And unto you be peace").

But in an informal context, the usual greeting is "vāray chivā" ("Are you fine?"), which indicates concern about the health and prosperity of the individual. It can elicit a variety of responses, which, from elders, usually involves the invocation of blessings from the Almighty, gods and goddesses, and saints.

9 LIVING CONDITIONS

Living conditions vary according to where in Kashmir one lives. In Ladakh, for instance, houses are built of mud brick and are similar in appearance to houses in Tibet, reflecting the strong Tibetan cultural influence in the region. In Baltistan, the villages are in clusters of huts, usually located where-ever flat land exists near sources of water and built of stone and wood. In many hamlets, there is a tower three stories high. Most of the huts are diminutive, with rooms only eight or ten feet in diameter and an entrance door two feet wide and two-

and-a-half feet high. In the lower rooms one can barely stand up, but there is a notched pole used as a ladder to an upper room, which is less cave-like. Many of the upper rooms are made in wattle, sometimes plastered over with clay.

In the Kashmir Valley, however, the typical dwelling in a village is a two or three-storey house made of wood and unburned brick with a thatched roof (the region is relatively dry, so keeping out rain is a minor issue). In Srinigar and in urban areas, modern construction uses fired brick and corrugated iron for roofs. The dimensions, decoration, and quality of materials used in the construction of the rooms vary according to socio-economic status. People generally prefer to keep cattle in the lower rooms at night (as protection against the weather), though it is not uncommon, where large numbers of the animals are involved, to see cattle sheds and stables scattered around the landscape. The room in which cattle and other livestock are kept is called *gan*. People live on the upper floors, but generally do not make use of furniture and sit and sleep on the floor, which is covered with rugs or carpets. Houses are not heated, but Kashmiris use a *kangra* (firepot filled with burning charcoal) for individual heating. This is worn under one's clothes and, as might be expected, the potential for accidental burns is considerable.

¹⁰ FAMILY LIFE

Customs regarding family life also vary according to one's community. Thus, the life of most Kashmiris is governed by Muslim law, while Kashmiri Pandits are ruled by Hindu law, and Sikhs, Buddhists, and Christians follow the dictates of their religion. Traditionally, the joint extended family was the norm, but the situation is changing, with the nuclear family becoming more common. The majority of the people in the valley are Muslims, many of them being converted Hindus, and while they have no formal caste system, the custom of the payment of a dowry (*mehar*) is common. It is usual among the Muslim peasants to marry a daughter to a near relative (this keeps property within the family) but, if this is not possible, a go-between, or *Manzimyur*, is used. Muslim (and Hindu) laws of inheritance do not allow women to inherit land or property.

¹¹ CLOTHING

The traditional dress of Kashmiris is simple, and there is not much difference between that of a man or a woman. Both wear a *phiran*, a kind of gown that is made of wool during the winter and of cotton during the summer. Muslim and Pandit men wear the gown differently, while the phirans of Muslim women may be brocaded on the chest with attractive designs. Hindu women wear a cotton *lungi* around the waist over the top of the phiran and the outfit is completed by headgear, a brocaded cap (*qasaba*) in the case of Muslim women, or a woolen *taranga* by Hindu women. Men often wear a brocaded cap, though typical headwear for the modern Kashmiri male is the *qaraguli* (karakal) cap made of lamb's wool, the kind often sported by Jawaharlal Nehru. A *kurta, pyjama,* or *shilwar* is worn by all under the phiran. In winter, the personal *kangra* is worn under the phiran for warmth. Of course, modern western clothes are becoming quite popular and are commonly seen in urban areas and amongst the young.

¹² FOOD

Kashmiri cuisine is famous for its vegetarian as well as non-vegetarian dishes. There are also variants between Hindu and Muslim cooking. Traditional Kashmiri food includes *dum aloo* (boiled potatoes with heavy amounts of spice), *tzaman* (a solid cottage cheese), *rogan josh* (lamb cooked in heavy spices), *zaam dod* (curd), *yakhayn* (lamb cooked in curd with mild spices), *hakh* (a spinach-like leaf), *rista-gushtava* (minced meat balls in tomato and curd curry), and, of course, the signature rice that is particular to Asian cultures. Even Kashmiri Pandits, who are Brahmans, enjoy mutton and fish. Muslim cooking makes heavy use of onions and garlic, though this was traditionally avoided by the Kashmiri Pandits. Meat is almost always cooked in curd. The traditional *wazwan* feast involves cooking meat or vegetables, usually mutton, in several different ways.

Alcohol is not widely drunk in Kashmir. There are two famous teas from the region: *nun chai*, or salt tea, which is pink in color and popular with locals and *kahwah*, a green tea made with spices (cinnamon, cardamom, and saffron), nuts, such as almonds or pistachios, sweetened by sugar or honey, and presented without milk.

¹³ EDUCATION

Educational standards vary throughout Kashmir. In Pakistani areas, distance, the lack of quality schools, and the dominant socio-cultural ethos of the tribal peoples in the area result in low levels of literacy and generally poor levels of education. Some authors have suggested the influence of Islamic fundamentalism has had a negative effect on education, especially for women. In the Indian state of Jammu and Kashmir, where the 2001 census return was notoriously unreliable, only 60% of the men were recorded as being literate, with the corresponding value for women being 45%. This, of course, is not only below the average for India as a whole, but it also masks considerable variations between urban areas and the more remote outlying districts.

¹⁴ CULTURAL HERITAGE

Communities in the different regions of broader Kashmir have their own cultural heritage. Thus, for Ladakhis, the devil dance, performed by monks dressed up in elaborate costumes at the time of Buddhist festivals to drive away evil spirits, is part of the heritage of Tibetan, or *Mahāyāna,* Buddhism. Muslims living in Baltistan or Gilgit share the views of honor and proper behavior that are held by tribal peoples in the north west of the Indian subcontinent.

However, in Kashmir proper, i.e. the Vale of Kashmir, history tends to shape the cultural heritage of the people. Thus, up to the 14th century, Buddhism and Shaivism dominated the Kashmir region and strongly influenced the region's early cultural history. The role of Buddhist monks from Kashmir in carrying the religion to China has already been noted. Kashmir has a rich architectural tradition that dates to this time, as well as having its scholars contribute to Sanskrit manuscripts (e.g. Kalhana's *Rajatarangini* and Somadeva's collection of stories called *Kathasaritsagar*). Even today, Shaivism *bhakti* (devotionalism) and *Tantrism* form a distinct undercurrent in the ritualistic worship of the Pandit community. The arrival of the Muslims in the early 14th century and the conquest by the Sikhs in the 19th century also added distinctive elements to the cultural heritage of Kashmir. Though some writers see *Kashmiriyat* as a myth, the peaceful co-existence of four of the world's great religions (Buddhism, Hinduism, Islam, and Sikhism), at least until the communal troubles that followed Partition, is seen by many as one of the great achievements of Kashmiri culture.

The existence of branches of the Silk Road across Kashmir is another aspect of the region's history. Not only did silk, ivory, gold, and gems move along this great Trans-Asian highway linking Rome with distant China, so did art, culture, and religion. Buddhist and Christian missionaries traveled along the Silk Road into Central Asia, as did aspects of Kashmiri art and sculpture. Many centuries later, Kashmir played a significant role in the "Great Game," that reflected British concerns that Russia would move into the region. The modern version of the Great Game, reflecting Kashmir's strategic location, is seen, perhaps, in the continued confrontation of India and Pakistan in Kashmir.

15 WORK

The traditional occupations of the Kashmiri were agriculture, tourism, and handicrafts. However, overseas tourism has virtually dried up since the communal troubles began in Kashmir in the 1980s and even though tourists from India still visit the region, the arts and crafts industry has basically been eliminated from Kashmir. Foreign tourists used to stay on houseboats on Lake Dal, but no longer. One consequence is that now Kashmir's economy is centered around agriculture. Traditionally, the staple crop of the valley is rice, which forms the chief food of the people. In addition, Indian corn (maize), wheat, barley, and oats were also grown. Given its temperate climate, Kashmir is suited for crops like asparagus, artichoke, broad beans, beetroot, cauliflower, and cabbage. Fruit trees are common in the valley and the cultivated orchards yield pears, apples, peaches, and cherries, and a variety of nuts.

Agriculture in Kashmir faces many problems, not the least of which is the average size of land-holdings. One result of the inheritance system is extreme fragmentation of the land with the average land holding in Indian-administered Jammu and Kashmir amounting to 0.66 hectares (just over 1.6 acres), a figure that has declined in recent decades. According to the 2001 Census of India, 49% of the labor force in Kashmir is either a cultivator or agricultural laborer, even though only 5% of the land in Kashmir can be farmed.

In Pakistani Kashmir, virtually the entire population is engaged in subsistence agriculture, cultivating whatever flat land is found near in the river valleys, or terracing the land along the lower portion of the valleys and bringing water from the slopes to the fields using small scale, home-built irrigation systems. With the land in most of Pakistani Kashmir occurring at higher altitudes, the crops grown (and the length of the growing season) reflect the climatic environment. These include maize, barley, potato, buck wheat, and millet, while the mainstay of the livestock population are goats, sheep, and types of cattle such as the yak or dzo that are adapted to high altitudes.

In Ladakh, subsistence irrigated agriculture similar to that of Tibet is practiced, while agriculture in Jammu mirrors that found on the nearby Indo-Gangetic plains.

16 SPORTS

Although polo is popular in Baltistan, and Gilgit and Ladakh have their devil dances, there is no sport that is unique to Kashmir.

17 ENTERTAINMENT AND RECREATION

Before hunting was banned throughout India by the government, hunting (*shikar*) was popular in Kashmir, with groups coming in from around the world to shoot local wildlife. In the Vale of Kashmir, the Bhands or minstrels are professional actors and singers (and beggars), who entertain the people, and they even travel as far afield as the Punjab to perform before Kashmiri audiences. Religious festivals are a main source of entertainment among the different Kashmiri communities. For instance, in Ladakh, the Buddhist devil dances performed at various festivals are popular. During the summer, young children in Kashmir play *Zangtār* and *Guti*, the latter involving tossing coins or nuts into a shallow hole in the ground (the guti) from a distance of 10–12 feet. Kite-flying is a popular pastime during certain seasons of the year while, as everywhere in India, Hindi movies are popular in urban areas.

18 FOLK ART, CRAFTS, AND HOBBIES

Kashmir is renowned for its arts and crafts the world over. It is known for its textiles, carpets made from silk or wool, which take families months to make. It is also known for its lacquered *paper maché* work and painting on paper maché goods or on wood. Kashmiris are also known for their delicate wood carvings. An entirely indigenous form of woodwork, known as *khatam bandi*, is used for the decoration of ceilings and is usually done in panels of pinewood in various geometrical designs fitted together in grooves. Wicker objects, *pashmina* shawls (made from fine cashmere wool that comes from the pashmina goat), embroidery, wooden boxes and toys, metalwork, and fine woolen goods round out the handicrafts for which Kashmiris are famous.

One problem facing traditional craftsmen in Kashmir is that with the decline of tourism due to the unrest in the state, they have difficulty accessing markets, and many have had to abandon their traditional occupations. Some have adjusted by moving to places such as Delhi where they do have access to tourists and continue in their traditional activities, but clearly this is not an ideal solution.

19 SOCIAL PROBLEMS

An ongoing problem in Kashmir is the continued conflict between Muslim and Hindu and the partition of Kashmir into Pakistani and Indian territory. With a majority Muslim population, any plebiscite would see Kashmir opt for Pakistan, but India cannot afford to see Kashmir accede to Pakistan. However, elections held in Indian Jammu and Kashmir brought to power the popular Muslim leader Sheikh Abdullah Muhammad, who with his party, the National Conference, by and large supported India. The elected Constituent Assembly met for the first time in 1954 and confirmed the accession of the state to the Union of India. The state's own Constitution came into force on 26 January 1957 under which the elections to the State Legislative Assembly were held for the first time on the basis of adult franchise the same year. This Constitution also ratified the state's accession to India. However, this was not recognized by Pakistan, which has continued to press for a plebiscite to ascertain the wishes of the people.

Though sporadic violence occurred before this, 1989 is usually the year assigned the beginning of the insurgency in Kashmir. This coincides with the end of the Afghan-Russian conflict and saw Afghan *mujahideen* fighters enter Kashmir (India claims with active Pakistani support). Since then violence has increased significantly in strength and separatists have carried out attacks on Indian civilians and Indian army installations in response to what they see as an Indian army of occupation. Estimates of deaths during the conflict vary from 35,000 to more than 85,000, with 1994 representing a peak in militancy and over 6,000 incidents in that year. Nongovernmental organizations (NGOs) have reported numerous human rights violations by both sides in the conflict. Some groups, such as the All Parties Hurriyat Conference and the Jammu and Kashmir Liberation Front, demand an independent Kashmir. Other militant groups, such as Lashkar-e-Toiba and Jaish-e-Muhammad (organizations that no longer operate under these names after they were banned by the Indian and Pakistani government) favor a Pakistani Kashmir. Of the larger militant groups, the Hizbul Mujahideen, a militant organization based in Indian-administered Kashmir, is believed to number thousands rather than hundreds. Several new separatist organizations have also emerged.

In 2005 a 7.6-magnitude earthquake hit northern parts of Pakistan and India and left an estimated 80,000 people dead and more than 3 million homeless. The epicenter was located near the city of Muzaffarabad in the Pakistani region of Azad Kashmir. Areas of Pakistan's North-West Frontier Province (NWFP) and India's Jammu and Kashmir state were also heavily damaged by the quake. Many countries, international organizations, and nongovernmental organizations offered relief aid to the region, in the form of donations as well as supplies of food, medicines, tents, and blankets, and rescue and relief workers were sent to the region, along with their equipment, including helicopters and rescue dogs, from different parts of the world. However, the remoteness of many areas affected by the earthquake and the onset of winter in the mountains (the earthquake occurred in early October) hampered relief efforts and no doubt led to even more casualties, who were not able to access aid or medical supplies.

Violence continued in Kashmir in 2008. Commentators saw the pitched battles between civilians and the police in the Kashmir Valley in June 2008 and the paralysis of the administration as a throwback to the turbulent 1990s, when Kashmiri resentment against the Indian government's policies led to a virtual civil war in Kashmir. The immediate cause of this violence was the transference of some forest land to a Hindu shrine by the Kashmiri government.

The civil unrest in Kashmir has virtually seen an end to Kashmiri tourism and has impacted the market for the sale of arts and crafts.

[20] GENDER ISSUES

Kashmiri women, in addition to having to face restrictions imposed by their own Hindu and Muslim communities, have had to deal with the civil and communal unrest that has affected the state since the 1980s. Militant Islamic separatist guerrillas have tried to ban beauty parlors, cinema halls, and wine shops and demanded that Muslim women follow the Islamic dress code and wear *burqas* or the veil. The Indian Army is viewed by many in Kashmir as an army of occupation, and it has been accused of numerous violations of human rights. In fact, an Islamic women's separatist group said it would begin training Muslim women in martial arts and called on them to carry daggers to fend off sexual attacks by Indian soldiers. More and more Kashmiri women are being seen as *mukhbirs*, or informers, and becoming targets of the militants.

Thus, not only do women in Kashmir have to live in dominant patriarchal social systems, they have to face poverty, illiteracy, arranged marriages, dowry deaths, a lack of inheritance, and economic discrimination. In addition, they have to live with the depredations of both soldiers of the Indian army and the militants in Kashmir in the context of the ongoing civil unrest.

[21] BIBLIOGRAPHY

Bhati, Avanti, ed. *Kashmiri Pandits: Problems and Perspectives.* New Delhi: Rupa, 2005.

Dhar, Triloki Nath. *Kashmiri Pandit Community: A Profile.* New Delhi: Mittal Publications, 2006.

Hassnain, Fida Mohammad Khan. *Historic Kashmir.* Srinagar: Gulshan Publishers, 2002.

Kaul, Gwasha Lal. *Kashmir Through the Ages(5000 BC to 1965 AD).* Srinagar: Chronicle Publishing House, 1963.

Kaw, M. K. *Kashmir and Its People.* New Delhi: A. P. H. Publishing Corporation, 2004.

Lawrence, Walter R. *Provincial Gazetteers of Kashmir and Jammu.* New Delhi: Rima Publishing House, reprinted 1985.

Qadri, Shafi Ahmad. *Kashmiri Sufism.* Srinagar: Gulshan Publishers, 2002.

Rahman, Mushtaqur. *Divided Kashmir: Old Problems, New Opportunities for India, Pakistan, and the Kashmiri People.* Boulder, CO: Lynne Rienner Publishers, 1996.

—by D. O. Lodrick

KAZAKH CHINESE

PRONUNCIATION: kuh-ZAHK chigh-NEEZ
ALTERNATE NAMES: Wusun, Turks, Geluolo, Huihu, Kerei, Naiman
LOCATION: China; Kazakstan; Uzbekistan; Turkmenistan; Kyrgyzstan; Tajikistan
POPULATION: 1.25 million
LANGUAGE: Kazakh
RELIGION: Islam
RELATED ARTICLES: Vol. 3: China and Her National Minorities; Kazaks

¹INTRODUCTION

The Kazakh have common historical origins with the ancient tribes of the Wusun (2nd century BC–2nd century AD), Turks (mid-6th century), Geluolo and Huihu (10th-12th century), and Kerei and Naiman (12th-13th century). They all lived in the Ili River Valley and areas around the Lake Issyk, which had been governed in the past by the central government of China. Up to the present, there are still tribes of Kazakh that retain the ancient tribal names. In the 13th century, conquering a number of countries in central and west Asia, Genghis Khan had established quite a few Khan dependencies. Later on, some of the tribes moved to the Talas River Valley and established there a Kazakh Khan. After the 17th century, a part of the Kazakh was conquered by Russia. The other part became one of the national minorities of China.

²LOCATION AND HOMELAND

The Kazakh live in the northern part of Xinjiang Uighur Autonomous Region, including Ili Kazakh Autonomous Prefecture, Mori and Burqin Kazakh Autonomous County. The rest of them are distributed in Aksay Kazakh Autonomous County. The population was 1.25 million in 2000.

³LANGUAGE

The Kazakh language belongs to the Altaic family, Turkic group. There is not much difference among the various dialects. The Kazakh living in the above-mentioned countries could have a lively conversation without any serious language problems. The name Kazakh was self-given, meaning "free man," "refugee," and "separator." Kazakh writing, based on Arabic characters, has been used since the last century. Owing to the difference between the phonetic systems of Arabic script and Kazakh language, the People's Republic of Kazakh of the former USSR reformed the writing system quite a few times, based on Arabic (1917 and 1924), based on Latin (1929), and based on Russian (1940). In China, a new writing system based on Latin was designed in 1959, but it proved unsuccessful. In 1982, they reverted to their original writing system.

⁴FOLKLORE

The folklore of the "White Swan" has been so widespread that some believe that it was created by the Kazakh. It was said that there was an orphan shepherd who dreamed one night of a white swan coming from the sky singing and dancing before him. The next day, his dream came true. Unfortunately,

a windstorm appeared from nowhere and dispersed all his sheep. With the help of the swan, he finally found them. In fact, he was also rescued by the swan. To his surprise, the swan turned into a beautiful lady, who married the shepherd and gave birth to a number of children, the Kazakh. A similar story states that a general was rescued by a white swan from the desert. It turned into a beautiful lady. They married and had a son who grew up, married, and had three sons—the ancestors of the three largest tribes of Kazakh.

In addition, a myth describes how the Kazakh God of Creation made a man and a woman from mud. But, a demon thwarted their marriage. The God shot the demon with his bow and arrow, thunder being the sound of his shooting and lightning being the sparks flying from the arrows. The God planted the Tree of Life. Every leaf represented a soul. A new leaf appeared on somebody's birth, and a fallen leaf indicated somebody's death.

⁵RELIGION

The Kazakh believe in Islam, although remnants of primitive shamanistic beliefs and reverence for the fire and sun still exist. In pastoral areas mosques are few, but the Muslim priest, called *mulla*, should be invited to recite scriptures on festivals, weddings, and funerals, or in case of illness. Of course, he will be paid.

⁶MAJOR HOLIDAYS

The main holidays of the Kazakh are related to their religion. According to Islamic stipulations, December 10 (Islamic calendar) is the Corban Festival. The word *corban* in Arabic means sacrificial offering. When the day comes, the Kazakh kill oxen or sheep as sacrifice. They all dress up, extend greetings to each other, entertain guests, and present gifts to their friends or relatives. A variety of traditional sports will be held. The Festival of Fast-Breaking (Lesser Bairam) is the day ending the Ramadan. In September (Islamic calendar) every year, every adult Kazakh abstains from food and drink from daybreak to sunset. The beginning and the end of the month of fast depend on the new moon being visible. On the next day, all festive activities will be held in a lively atmosphere. The Nuoluzi Festival in January (lunar calendar; Western calendar, between January 21 and March 19) is also ceremonious. It is similar to the Spring Festival of the Chinese. To ring out the old year and ring in the new, every family will take *kuji*, a meal made of seven ingredients including beef, barley, wheat, and milk products.

⁷RITES OF PASSAGE

The birth of a baby is a particularly happy event for the Kazakh and a reason to entertain guests at dinner. The Kazakh, men and women, are adept in horsemanship; horsemanship, therefore, plays an important role in their festivals. One particular festival, extremely popular with the young people, is called "Women's Pursuit." Young men and women, each mounting his or her own horse, stride slowly in pairs toward a designated place; the lad is allowed to tease the girl whom he likes, and she should not get angry. But, as soon as they arrive at the designated place and start to get back, the girl pursues the lad in mock revenge. The game is designed to foster love between the two.

The Kazakh funeral follows Islamic stipulations. The body should be washed with clean water, wrapped in white cloth, and buried three days after death. On the seventh day and the fortieth day after the funeral, sacrificial offerings are mandatory. The horse used by the deceased during his or her lifetime is not allowed to be mounted any longer. The horse tail should be cut after the master's death. The horse should be killed one year later for sacrifice. When Kazakh migrate to new pasture lands, the hat and clothes of the deceased should be put on horseback and moved with the family. The women of the household sing a mournful song when they pass each nomadic colony.

[8] INTERPERSONAL RELATIONS

Long-separated friends usually embrace when meeting again. Usually, they talk about their livestock first, then the families greet each other. The Kazakh are warm, sincere, and straightforward. They will spare no effort to assist a member of the clan who is in trouble. A traveler, no matter what his nationality may be, will be put up for the night in any Kazakh's *yurt*. On account of Kazakh hospitality, one finds no beggars among them. "As long as there are Kazakh on the way, you may travel for a year without a cent or a grain in your bag," goes a saying. Another proverb states: "One could never wipe out the disgrace of letting guests leave at sunset." They offer their best food to the guests; for distinguished ones, they will kill a live sheep with yellow head and white body. Respectfully, the host will offer a tray containing the sheep head. The guest receives it, cuts a slice of meat from its right cheek and puts it on his own plate. He should then cut an ear, give it to the youngest one at the banquet, and return the sheep head to the host. The guests sit cross-legged on the felt rug. They must not straighten their legs. It is very impolite to take off one's shoes and point the sole of the foot to people.

[9] LIVING CONDITIONS

The great majority of the Kazakh engage in nomadic animal husbandry; only a small number engage in agriculture and settle down. The herdsmen move from place to place in search of water and grass. In spring, summer, and autumn, they live in a *yu*, a round-shaped yurt that may be dismantled and carried on horseback when they migrate. The framework of the yurt is made from locally grown Chinese tamarisk. They enclose the paling (fence-like framework) with splendid achnatherum, a kind of grass with long, narrow leaves, grown in grassy shoals. Then, they cover the side with a layer of felt rug. There is a skylight for ventilation at the top of the conic roof of the yurt. The yurt usually opens to the east. Inside the yurt, the horse gear, hunting gear, food and cooking utensils are placed on each side of the door, with the plank beds overhead. Opposite the door are the suitcases, covered with sitting cushions.

After the fall, they move to their adobe house for the winter pasture.

[10] FAMILY LIFE

Before 1950, the well-to-do and the nobles were polygamous. Now, they practice monogamy. The man is the person of authority in the family. The wife must obey her husband. Sons and daughters must obey their father. The women have neither power nor property. The marriage of children and the distribution of property are all decided by the father. As soon as a male has grown up and married, he leaves his parents, builds his own yurt, and receives a part of the property from his fa-ther. The family property will ultimately be inherited by the youngest son.

In the past, a wedding required betrothal gifts from the bridegroom to the bride's family—in particular, dozens of heads of livestock. As a result, poor families would exchange their daughters, thus canceling the need for betrothal gifts. A widow had to marry her brother-in-law or another member of the clan. Although a married woman had no right to ask for divorce, a man was allowed to abandon his wife any time at will. Nowadays, according to the new dispositions of the law, Kazakh women are free to marry and to divorce.

[11] CLOTHING

The herdsmen's clothes are mainly made of fur, usually loose for the convenience of horse-riding. In winter, the men usually wear a durable, single-layered, sheepskin overcoat or camel's wool waded topcoat. They have a leather belt with figures on the waist and wear a sword on the right. Their trousers are mostly made of sheepskin. The women wear dresses, mostly red. In winter, they add a cotton-padded overcoat. Young girls like to wear silver ornaments or coins and embroidered cotton trousers. Men in different districts wear different hats. Married women almost always wear a long scarf with colored figures. All Kazakh like to wear boots, with a pair of felt stockings in winter.

[12] FOOD

Most foodstuffs come from livestock. There are a variety of milk products, including cheese, butter, and skin on boiled milk. In spring or summer, the herdsmen pour a mare's milk into a leather bag, stir frequently, and wait for fermentation. The final product is a semi-transparent sour mare's milk wine, a favorite beverage in summer. Another popular beverage is a special hot milk tea made of tea, butter, salt, and cow or camel milk. Food made of rice and flour includes crusty *nang* (shaped like bagels and pancakes), "rice taken by hand" (cooked and steamed rice with raisins, sliced onions and carrots, and small cubes of fried beef), fried dough, etc. The Kazakh eat a lot of mutton, mostly cooked in water and taken by hand. They make smoked meat in the late fall. Sausage made of mare's meat has a special flavor and can be preserved for a long time. The herdsmen eat fewer vegetables and fruits.

[13] EDUCATION

Because of the nomadic way of life of the Kazakh, there are many mobile primary schools. The teacher visits the yurt and teaches the children on the spot. This explains the high rate of illiteracy in pastoral areas. In farming areas close to the cities, there are many schools for formal education. High schools and universities have been established in Tacheng, Altay, and Ili. Overall, the cultural and educational level of the Kazakh is higher than the average level of the national minorities in China.

[14] CULTURAL HERITAGE

Kazakh music and dance have distinctive features and are noticeable by the large number of participants in each performance. The Kazakh are good at singing and dancing. A two-stringed, guitar-like instrument, the *dongbula*, is very popular with the men. Because of illiteracy in the past, the ancient poems, stories, proverbs, and fables were all handed down orally. A group of folksingers, called *aken*, visit the grazing lands to collect and collate oral literature. Kazakh writers have begun the publication of their ancient literature.

¹⁵WORK

For centuries the Kazakh have led a nomadic life, their main occupation being animal husbandry (ox, sheep, horses, and camel). Only a small number of them engaged in farming. There were very few craftsmen and very little handicraft industry. Almost all productive tools and daily necessities were fashioned by family members at home or purchased through barter for grains, tea, cloth, and household utensils. In the last few decades, the Kazakh have begun to combine agriculture and stockraising, gradually settling down and abandoning their nomadic ways. Small-scaled tannery, wool mill, and oil press factories have been established. The mode of production of the Kazakh is now in transition.

¹⁶SPORTS

Wrestling and "Snatching the Lamb" (*diaoyang*) are popular sports that attract large crowds; they are part of every festival. In the game of "Snatching the Lamb," a venerable elder puts a headless lamb on the grass. At a full gallop, five to eight horsemen try to grab the lamb with one hand. The winner is the first horseman who brings the lamb to a designated place.

¹⁷ENTERTAINMENT AND RECREATION

With the gradual introduction of movies and television into Kazakh colonies, villages, and towns, their traditional singing and dancing have become more and more restricted to festive occasions. Film projection teams frequently visit the herdsmen's colonies, thus enabling them to enjoy the modern entertainment of movies.

¹⁸FOLK ART, CRAFTS, AND HOBBIES

Kazakh artisans are well-known for the quality of their felt products (hats, shoes, and boots) and embroideries (especially women's clothes and hats). Folk art also includes wooden articles, ironware, bone implements, and ornaments made of gold, silver, and jade.

¹⁹SOCIAL PROBLEMS

The grassland environment of the Kazakh does not favor a diversified economy. The combination of agriculture and stockraising has already improved the living conditions of the Kazakh. One promising avenue for further development is border trade with the Kazakh on the other side of the Chinese border.

²⁰ GENDER ISSUES

The Chinese constitution states that women have equal rights with men in all areas of life, and most legislation is gender neutral. However, among the Kazakhs certain traditions persist to deny women equal rights in practice.

Since 1950, the practice of polygamy has been discontinued, but the man of the household retains ultimate authority and all family members, including the wife, must obey him. While according to law, women have equal rights, in Kazakh society women traditionally hold no property and the family property is inherited by the youngest son. As China modernizes, these traditions are changing slowly. In the past, married women had no access to divorce, while a man was free to abandon his wife. With the guarantees afforded by Chinese law, Kazakh women are increasingly taking action to marry and to divorce according to their own interests.

China has strict family planning laws. It is illegal for women to marry before 20 years of age (22 for men), and it is illegal for single women to give birth. Though minority populations were previously exempt from family planning regulations, policy has changed in recent years to limit minority population growth. Today, urban minority couples may have two children while rural couples may have three or four.

²¹ BIBLIOGRAPHY

Chiao, Chien, Nicholas Tapp, and Kam-yin Ho, ed. "Special Issue on Ethnic Groups in China." *New Asia Bulletin* no 8 (1989).

Dreyer, June Teufel. *China's Forty Millions.* Cambridge: Harvard University Press, 1976.

Eberhard, Wolfram. *China's Minorities: Yesterday and Today.* Belmont: Wadsworth Publishing Company, 1982.

Gustafsson, Bjorn A., Shi, Li, and Sicular, Terry, eds. *Inequality and Public Policy in China.* New York: Cambridge University Press, 2008.

Heberer, Thomas. *China and Its National Minorities: Autonomy or Assimilation?* Armonk, NY: M. E. Sharpe, 1989.

Lebar, Frank, et al. *Ethnic Groups of Mainland Southeast Asia.* New Haven: Human Relations Area Files Press, 1964.

Lemoine, Jacques. "Les Kazakh." In *Ethnologie régionale II* (Encyclopédie de la Pléiade). Paris: Gallimard, 1978.

Ma Yin, ed. *China's Minority Nationalities.* Beijing: Foreign Languages Press, 1989.

Ramsey, S. Robert. *The Languages of China.* Princeton: Princeton University Press, 1987.

Schwarz, Henry G. *The Minorities of Northern China: A Survey.* Bellingham, WA: Western Washington University Press, 1989.

Shin, Leo Kwok-yueh. *The Making of the Chinese State: Ethnicity and Expansion on the Ming Borderlands.* New York: Cambridge University Press, 2006.

—by C. Le Blanc

KAZAKHS

PRONUNCIATION: kuh-ZAKS
LOCATION: Kazakhstan
POPULATION: 10.8 million
LANGUAGES: Kazakh; Russian
RELIGION: Islam (Sunni Muslim)
RELATED ARTICLES: Vol. 3: Kazakh Chinese

¹ INTRODUCTION

At the foundation of traditional Kazakh culture was the nomadic way of life, which was typical until the early 20th century. The Kazakhs are closely related to the Kyrgyz in ethnicity, culture, and language. The Kazakhs traditionally divided themselves into three territorial *zhüz* (tribal unions, or hordes): Greater, Central, and Lesser. The Greater Horde occupied much of what is now southern Kazakhstan and consisted of the Sary Uisin, Kangli, Dulat, Alban, Suan, Zhalayir, and other smaller tribes. The Central Horde occupied the northern and eastern parts of modern Kazakhstan and consisted of the Argyn, Naiman, Kerei, and Kongrat tribes. The Lesser Horde was composed of three united tribes—Zheti Ru, Alim Uly, and Bai Uly—who migrated in 1801 to the land between the Ural and Volga Rivers. Since the Kazakhs were nomads, during the 1800s it was possible for large numbers of Slavic settlers to move into and seize the land inhabited by the Kazakhs.

² LOCATION AND HOMELAND

The Kazakh homeland, although covering 2.6 million sq km (more than 1 million sq mi) is not topographically diverse. Approximately 80% of the area consists of lowlands, plains, and plateaus, and strong winds often sweep through these flat lands. The only mountains are the Tien Shan and Altai ranges in the east and southeast. The climate within Kazakhstan varies significantly, which means that the types of plants and animals found in Kazakhstan also vary significantly from region to region. Parts of Kazakhstan become bitterly cold in the winter and intensely hot during the summer. The massive Kara Kum Desert occupies much of central Kazakhstan. The Kara Kum ("black sand") is the world's fourth largest desert, and much of it extends into other nations of Central Asia. There are two large inland seas, the Caspian Sea and the Aral Sea. Both of these great seas, however, contain significantly less water than in the recent past because of heavy irrigation use during the Soviet era. From 1960 to 1975, the shores of the Aral Sea moved more than 100 km (60 mi) inward as the total volume of water shrank (and became more salty). The Aral Sea today is only one-third of its original size and is divided into two parts. The larger part lies in Uzbekistan and is considered a dead sea; there is some hope for revitalizing the smaller part that lies in Kazakhstan, and efforts have been made to separate the two. As of 2008, these efforts had not been successful.

There are currently more than 10 million Kazakhs, 80% of whom live in Kazakhstan. The Kazakhs were for many years a minority within their own homeland, accounting for only 42% of the population as recently as the mid 1990s. Today the Kazakh government has been successful in creating policies to encourage growth of ethnic Kazakh population, including policies to encourage ethnic Kazakhs to move to Kazakhstan.

This combined with out-migration of Russians and other non-titular nationalities has contributed to an increase in the Kazakh population, to 60%. Ethnic Russians have been settling in the Kazakh homeland since the 18th century and presently account for about 30% of the population in the Kazakh homeland. Approximately 100 other nationalities account for the remainder of the population; many of them were deported to Kazakhstan during World War II. The birth rate of Kazakhs is higher than that of Russians in Kazakhstan, which means that the percentage of Kazakhs should continue to rise. There are approximately one million ethnic Kazakhs living in the Sinkiang-Uygur Autonomous Region of China.

³ LANGUAGE

Kazakh is a central Turkic language. More specifically, it belongs to the Nogai group in the Kipchak division of the Turkic branch of Ural-Altaic languages. Modern Kazakh has many words borrowed from Russian, Arabic, Persian, Mongol, Chinese, Tatar, and Uzbek. There are three primary dialects that correspond to the three historic Kazakh hordes. Written Kazakh, which dates back only to the late 19th century, is based on the dialect of the Central Horde.

The Kazakh language was originally influenced by a nomadic way of life. A person who did not migrate, such as a *balykshi* (fisherman) or a *eginshi* (grain-grower) was atypical. Livestock, such as the *at* or *jilqi* (horse), *qazaqi qoy* (fat-tailed sheep), *ayïr tüye* (Bactrian camel), and *yeshki* (goat) also played a central role in the development of the Kazakh language, with numerous terms and idioms focusing on livestock and their breeding. A traditional Kazakh greeting that is still sometimes used in rural areas literally translates as: "Are your livestock and your soul still healthy?" A traditional Kazakh wish for good fortune is literally translated as; "May God give you one thousand sheep with lambs, eighty camels, and eight married sons."

The Kazakh language used Arabic script until 1930, when the Soviet government replaced it with the Latin alphabet. Just before World War II, the government switched from the Latin to the Cyrillic alphabet, which is used for the Russian language. With the Cyrillic alphabet came the large-scale incorporation of Russian terms and Russian-sounding place-names among the Kazakhs. Today, approximately 40% of all ethnic Kazakhs speak Russian as a second language. Approximately 70% of Kazakhstan's population regularly speaks Russian. Since independence, the government of Kazakhstan has declared in the constitution that Kazakh was the state language and Russian the official language. The government has begun to change the Russian names of some places back to the original Kazakh names.

⁴ FOLKLORE

As with the folklore of other nomadic peoples, the oral tradition forms the basis of Kazakh folklore. Over the centuries, sagas were passed down by memory from one generation to the next. Most of the stories are heroic epics where the *batir* (warrior) and his trusty horse save the clan and its livestock from danger. There are also stories about Alash, the legendary first Kazakh. The most famous heroic stories are *Koblandy-Batir, Er Sain*, and *Er Targyn*, all of which are from the 15th or 16th century and involve clashes between the Kazakhs and the Kalmyks. The most famous lyric epics are *Kozy Korpesh–Bain Sulu* and *Aiman–Sholpan*. The most famous Kazakh love story

KAZAKHS

0   500   1000 Miles

0   500   1000 Kilometers

RUSSIA

Moscow

Nizhniy Novgorod

Kazan'

Perm'

Ufa

Yekaterinburg

Samara

Chelyabinsk

Omsk

Rostov

Novokuznetsk

Caspian Sea

KAZAKHSTAN

Alma Ata

UZBEKISTAN

TURKMENISTAN

KYRGYZSTAN

TAJIKISTAN

IRAN

AFGHANISTAN

CHINA

PAKISTAN

INDIA

Severnaya Zemlya

Kara Sea

Poluostrov Yamal

Gydanskiy Poluostrov

ZAPADNO

SIBIRSKAYA

RAVNINA

Ob'

Irtysh

Yenisey

URAL MOUNTAINS

Ural

Volga

Don

Kama

Central Asia, although there has recently been a religious revival among young Kazakhs.

6 MAJOR HOLIDAYS

The Republic of Kazakhstan celebrates the following national holidays: New Year's Day (January 1), celebrated in the Russian fashion with the decorating of the tree and a visit from a Santa Claus-like *Ded Moroz*; International Women's Day (March 8), *Nauryz* (the day of the vernal equinox), the traditional Persian-Turkic new year; May Day or Unity Day of the Kazakh Nation (May 1), Victory Day (May 9), celebrating the Soviet Union's defeat of Nazi Germany in World War II, Capital Day (May 10), Constitution Day (August 30),Independence Day (October 25), and Democracy Day (December 16). Additionally, Muslim Kazakhs celebrate the traditional Muslim holidays Eid al Fitr and Eid al Adha (Kurban Eid in the Kazakh language) and many choose to observe Ramadan as well.

7 RITES OF PASSAGE

Kazakhs typically have large birthday parties with many relatives and friends, and several Kazakh festivities mark various rites of passage during a person's life. Celebrations are held for a birth, a baby's fortieth day of life, the first day of school, and graduation. Voting and driving privileges come at 18 years of age.

Weddings are very important in Kazakh society, not only for honoring the married couple, but also as an event to assemble an extended family or clan together. The traditional wedding festival ceremonial is called the *toi*. In the past, arranged marriages were common, and the payment of *kalym* (a dowry) was expected upon betrothal.

8 INTERPERSONAL RELATIONS

Hospitality is an important part of Kazakh culture. A Kazakh host will be quite offended if the guest does not have some refreshments or at least a cup of traditional tea. Asking a guest lots of questions is considered bad manners. Guests in a Kazakh home are customarily allowed to rest after their journey and given some fermented mare's milk to drink. When a Kazakh host has finished attending to the guest, cordial conversation can then begin.

When a Kazakh greets an elderly person, both hands are used in a handshake as a sign of respect. It is considered impolite for a young person to shake hands with an elder using only one hand. Cohabitation without marriage is considered a dishonor to both families. Women and men are expected to stay chaste until marriage, but a double standard is common, with women held more accountable than men.

9 LIVING CONDITIONS

During the Soviet era, medical care was provided by the government. The medical system now is in a state of transition.

At one time, the nomadic Kazakhs lived in *yurts*, cone-shaped tents of white felt stretched over a framework of wooden poles. Yurts are light and easy to assemble, dismantle, and transport. Today, yurts are only used as temporary shelters by shepherds in remote, seasonal pastures. The modern Kazakh home is typically an apartment in the city or a permanent single dwelling in rural areas. Kazakh interior design emphasiz-

in the lyric tradition is *Kiz-Jhibek*, which contains historic information about Kazakh betrothal and marriage customs and ceremonies.

5 RELIGION

Most Kazakhs are Sunni Muslims. Islam, however, has not historically been as centralized among the Kazakhs as it has among other Central Asian peoples. Even though Islam had been adopted by the Kazakhs as early as 1043, it was not until the late 1700s that many of the popular Islamic religious practices became common among Kazakhs. Islam was historically most popular in the cities and towns of Central Asia, where there were mosques and seminaries. However, since the Kazakhs were primarily nomads and had minor contact with urban areas, many of them had little knowledge of the religion. The Kazakhs were introduced to Islam through contact with the Tatars, who traditionally were not as conservative as other Muslim peoples in Central Asia. For this reason, the imperial Russian government preferred that the Kazakhs associate with the Tatars.

Because the Kazakhs were wanderers who depended on livestock for their survival, animals were at the core of the ancient Kazakh religion. Until the mid-1800s, elements of this ancient animist belief system (including shamanism and ancestor worship) were still widely practiced among many Kazakh Muslims. This historical background, together with the fusion of Russian and other cultures, means that the Kazakh society of today is perhaps more secular than elsewhere in

es the use of stucco artwork and wall facings as well as ornate carpets.

The main means of transportation is public bus. In larger towns and cities, people often use trolleys and streetcars. However, in villages and rural areas it is not unheard of for people to travel short distances by horse. People commonly take trains when traveling long distances within Kazakhstan. Kazakhs have international air service from their homeland through foreign airlines such as Lufthansa, Aeroflot, and Turkish Airlines.

10 FAMILY LIFE

Women play a significant role in economic, social, and cultural life in Kazakhstan. Most married women work outside the home. Within the family, Kazakh women have equal rights with men, but they usually consider the husband the head of the family. In Kazakh custom, women prepare and serve the meals and watch over the children. The husband's role in assisting with housework varies from family to family.

The average urban Kazakh family has two children, and the typical rural one has three or four. By tradition, every Kazakh is supposed to know the names of his or her ancestors going back seven generations. Many Kazakhs today might not know all seven generations, but they are sure to know from which tribe and *zhüz* (tribal union) they are descended.

Before the Soviet period, there were several possible ways for Kazakhs to get married. One of the most famous was the tradition of a man to "steal" the girl from her parents. This type of elopement is still practiced in some of the southern regions of Kazakhstan. Another traditional method of marriage was for parents to seek a fixed marriage when they thought their son was an adult. The parents of the bride usually tried to find a bachelor who came from a family with a financial position similar to their own. According to custom, a Kazakh girl is supposed to compose her own wedding song before getting married. A popular tradition at weddings, anniversaries, and holidays is the *kyz-kuu* (girl chase). A *kyz-kuu* is a light-hearted social event involving a man and wife or a boyfriend and girlfriend. A man on horseback chases a woman on horseback and tries to catch her in order to steal a kiss. The woman tries to flee, and even uses a small horsewhip to keep the man or his horse away from her.

Extended families are common in the country, less so in the cities. Children, regardless of age, typically live with their parents until marriage. Elderly parents usually move in with children, as it is considered dishonorable to permit one's parents to live in a nursing home. Men who reach their thirties without having married are often looked upon with suspicion, and may even suffer from discrimination in society and the workplace.

11 CLOTHING

In the past, women typically wore long dresses with stiff collars and loose baggy pants cinched at the ankles. Men traditionally wore robes made of wool or cotton over large white shirts and broad trousers. Today, some women in rural areas wear the traditional dress, but most young women and men wear European-style clothes. The clothes worn today are often brightly colored and very stylish, with a greater emphasis on form than on function.

12 FOOD

Kymyz is a fermented beverage made from mare's milk and served in a *piala* (Oriental teacup). Other Kazakh drinks include *boza*, an alcoholic beverage made from millet, and *musalla*, a nonalcoholic type of grape juice. Fruit is mainly grown in *mewäzar bagh* (orchards). *Orik* (apricots), *shäftali* (peaches), *qawun* (melons), and *uzum* (grapes) are the most popular fruits. *Almä* (apples) are not as popular a fruit among Kazakhs as they are for export. (The name of the former capital and largest city of Kazakhstan, Almaty derives from its previous name Alma Ata or Alma Aty, means "mountain of apples.") A unique Kazakh culinary custom is the *dastarkhan*, a feast for special occasions consisting primarily of meat dishes and dairy products. For a *dastarkhan*, an entire animal (usually a sheep) is slaughtered, and the oldest member of the family gets the honor of carving the head and serving the family. The various parts of the animal symbolize desired traits for those eating them. For example, children are often served the ears as a symbol to be better listeners. Someone who is served the tongue should be more eloquent, and the person who receives the eye should seek wisdom.

Horse meat and mutton are popular items, because those animals were historically raised when the Kazakhs were nomadic herders. Examples of Kazakh dishes include *shuzhuk* (a type of kielbasa made from fresh or smoked horse meat); other horse meat dishes such as *kazy, karta, zhaya*, and *zhal. Kuirdak* is prepared from a freshly slaughtered horse, sheep, or cow and consists of the animal's liver, heart, kidneys, and other organs cut into pieces, boiled in oil, and served with onions and pepper. *Beshbarmak* is a type of boiled dough. The dough is rolled into thin strips and cooked in the broth that is left over from boiled mutton. It is served with mutton on top, and is garnished with garlic and onions. *Beshbarmak* is a light dish that many Kazakhs eat when they are sick.

13 EDUCATION

The Kazakh educational system consists of the following stages: kindergarten (not required), secondary school (11 years), higher education institute (4–5 years), graduate research program (2 years), and post-graduate program (3 years). There also is a system of professional three-year colleges. Kazakhstan has more than 60 higher education institutions, including the Kazakh National University, Almaty State University, the Kazakh University of World Languages, Polytechnic University , and others. In the early 1990s, approximately 1,000 Kazakhs were studying abroad, and this number has grown, as the Kazakh government promotes study overseas through a program that provides scholarships. Higher education carries much prestige, and parents strongly encourage children to earn their diplomas. In Kazakhstan, 90% of boys and girls attend primary school, and nearly that many attend secondary school. Over 99% of the population is literate. The Kazakh educational system is currently in a state of transition, because the values of society have drastically changed since Kazakhstan became a democratic state. Many schools' language of instruction is Russian; however, Kazakh is becoming more prevalent.

14 CULTURAL HERITAGE

The ancient Kazakh homeland has produced numerous talented musicians and singers. Music is a part of everyday Kazakh life from birth to death. Music is played for military expeditions, weddings, funerals, parties, and games. Almost every Kazakh knows how to sing and play a musical instrument by ear. A traditional form of Kazakh music is the *sazgen*, a folk music quintet that includes traditional string and percussion instruments. The most popular folk instrument is the *dombra*, which has two strings and is played by plucking. Other traditional instruments include the *sybyzgy* and *uran* (wind instruments), the *dangyra* and *dabyl* (percussion instruments), and the *sherter* and *kobyz* (other stringed instruments). The *aitys* is a musical tradition in which two poet/composers duel with each other. This tradition remains very popular in Kazakhstan. The most popular contemporary Kazakh singers are Bibigul Tulegenova, Vermek Serkebaev, Alibek Dnishev, R. Bapov, and Roza Rymbaeva.

The 15th-century poetry of Asan Kaigy, and the 17th-century poems of Zhyrau and Dosmambet are highly revered among the Kazakh people. The founder of modern Kazakh literature was the humanist and poet Abai Ibragim Kunanbayev (1845–1904), who wrote the famous *Teachings* during 1890–98 as a collection of philosophical thoughts and proverbs. Prominent Kazakh writers during the Soviet years included Zhambyl Zhabaev, Saken Seifullin, Mailin, Ilias Dzansugurov, Sabit Mukanov, and Mukhtar Auezov, who wrote *Abbay*, a famous novel about 19th-century Kazakh life on the steppe. During the Soviet era, however, the names of many talented dissident writers, poets, and scientists (such as Ahmed Baitursunov, Makzhan Zhumabaev, and Zhusibek Aimautov) were buried in oblivion. Contemporary writers who have enriched Kazakh literature since the 1960s include I. Esenberlin, M. Makataev, O. Suleimenov, K. Myrzaliev, and F. Ongarsynova.

15 WORK

During the Soviet years, many Kazakhs worked on large state-run farms growing *maqta* (cotton). A very high birth rate among the Kazakhs during the 1980s has led to a large rate of unemployment in the late 1990s, creating a large labor force of young Kazakhs but not enough entry-level jobs for them. Since 2000 the unemployment rate in Kazakhstan, while still high, dropped considerably, and in 2006 was at 7%. This may be in part due to an economy stimulated by oil revenues, although this wealth is not shared by the entire population. However, by 2008, the worldwide economic downturn was causing a new rise in the numbers of unemployed in Kazakhstan.

16 SPORTS

Soccer is a popular sport to play in the warmer months, and hockey is popular during the winter. The national sport of Kazakhstan is Kazakh-style wrestling, which is similar to judo. In the country, horse racing and equine events are common. Although the risk of an avalanche is fairly high, skiing in the Tien Shan Mountains is becoming popular. Recently, the slopes have received international attention as a future site for expert and world-class skiing. Skiers are flown by helicopter to the tops of slopes.

17 ENTERTAINMENT AND RECREATION

City dwellers often spend the weekends with their families in recreational parks, which can be found in almost any Kazakh town. Urban Kazakhs frequently go to the movies or watch videos. (Pirated videotapes of current movies are popular as well.) A popular Kazakh event for entertainment is the *itys*, a

A young Kazakh boy waits for customers on the Tianshan Mountain, Xinjiang, China. Kazakh herdsmen in Xinjiang make money by offering their services to tourists.
(AP Images/Xinhua)

formal or informal competition of wit between two singers of either gender. During the *itys*, each singer plays the *dombra* (a two-stringed instrument) and cleverly makes up the lyrics as he or she sings, which requires a rich knowledge of the Kazakh language. Usually the singer will brag about aspects of his or her hometown or region (e.g., the fattest sheep, the best milk, the most beautiful people), and make fun of the other person's. The loser is the first person who can't sing a comeback quickly enough. Rural and city Kazakhs often visit in order to relax. Kazakhs enjoy drinking tea with neighbors or family.

18 FOLK ART, CRAFTS, AND HOBBIES

In recent years, there has been a revival in Kazakh folk art and crafts, including carpet and jewelry making. Jewelry with traditional Kazakh symbols and designs is popular among women, especially silver jewelry. Collecting stamps and small pins are also popular hobbies.

¹⁹ SOCIAL PROBLEMS

Since the 1970s, nationalist attitudes among the Kazakhs have been on the rise, leading many times to violence. In 1979, Kazakhs rioted in Tselinograd because there were rumors that the government was going to set aside land for local Germans who wanted to create their own autonomous region. Suspicion and antagonism against ethnic Russians increased during the late 1980s because the Soviet Union had often given them preference in leadership positions. Today, the situation is in many ways reversed and ethnic Russians resent new Kazakh language policies.

Atomic testing in northern Kazakhstan in the 1950s weakened the health of many residents. These people and their descendants are often born with deficient immune systems, a condition similar to AIDS. Some researchers have estimated that it will take another 50 years for the condition to reverse through intermarriage with people from unaffected families.

Narcotics use has become a serious social problem for Kazakhstan since independence. This is in part because of its location between the major producer of the world's heroin, Afghanistan, and the markets in Russia and the rest of Europe. As Kazakhstan became a trafficking route, the number of drug users increased. In 2006 there were 53,172 registered drug users, with the actual numbers of drug users projected to be as much as four times as high. Along with the increased numbers of drug users has come an increased number of HIV/AIDS infections. In 2003 as many as 23,000 people were thought to be living with HIV, although because there is a strong stigma against those with the disease, actual numbers are difficult to confirm.

²⁰ GENDER ISSUES

In many ways the situation of women in Kazakhstan is better than that in many parts of the world, and especially better than that in some other Central Asian countries. Women are active in the workplace, they hold government positions, and they can be successful in business. This is possibly due to the traditionally nomadic lifestyle of the Kazakhs, which required that women be more active in everyday life for survival of the family. The introduction of Soviet values also encouraged women to join the workforce alongside men. The Kazakh constitution prohibits discrimination based on sex. However, women generally do not hold the highest government positions. Women are often victims of domestic violence, and there are few resources for these women to turn to for help. Bride kidnapping is practiced in some rural areas. Women are more likely to be unemployed than their male counterparts in the workforce, despite the fact that women tend to be better educated than men.

Gays and lesbians should also be protected under the Kazakh constitution's prohibition of discrimination on the basis of sexuality, but in practice this is not the case. While there is a small gay community in large cities such as Almaty, homosexuality is still very much stigmatized by relatively traditional Kazakh society. Reports have surfaced of gay men being fired from their jobs. The community is so secretive that it is difficult to make contact with members to obtain information about the community.

²¹ BIBLIOGRAPHY

Allworth, Edward, ed. *Central Asia: 130 Years of Russian Dominance, A Historical Overview*. Durham, NC: Duke University Press, 1994.

Country Factsheets, Eurasian Narcotics-Kazakhstan. Uppsala, Sweden and Washington, D.C.: Silk Road Studies Program, 2004.

Greenall, Robert. "Kazakh Women See Familiar Limits." *BBC News*. http://news.bbc.co.uk/2/hi/asia-pacific/4485204.stm (27 May 2008).

International Women's Rights Action Watch. "Kazakhstan Country Report." http://iwraw.igc.org/publications/countries/kazakhstan.htm (27 May 2008).

LeVine, Steve. *The Oil and the Glory: The Pursuit of Empire and Fortune on the Caspian Sea*. New York: Random House, 2007.

Moore, Kathleen. "Gays Struggle for Acceptance." *Radio Free Europe/Radio Liberty*. http://www.rferl.org/featuresarticle/2006/02/ff60f904-cbaa-4311-934d-656122e68809.html (27 May 2008).

Olcott, Martha Brill. *The Kazakhs*. Stanford, CA: Hoover Institution Press, 1987.

The Republic of Kazakhstan. "The Kazakhstan National Commission for UNESCO." http://www.natcom.unesco.kz/about/about_kz.html (27 May 2008).

Sahadeo, Jeff, and Russell Zanca. *Everyday Life in Central Asia: Past and Present*. Bloomington: Indiana University Press, 2007.

UNESCO Institute for Statistics. "Education in Kazakhstan, UIS Statistics in Brief." http://stats.uis.unesco.org/unesco/TableViewer/document.aspx?ReportId=121&IF_Language=eng&BR_Country=4020b (27 May 2008).

U.S. Department of State. Overseas Security Advisory Council. "Unemployment in Astana, Kazakhstan Raises Security Issues." https://www.osac.gov/Reports/report.cfm?contentID=79606 (27 May 2008).

Waters, Bella. *Kazakhstan in Pictures*. Minneapolis, MN: Twenty-First Century Books, 2007.

—revised by M. Kerr

KELABIT

PRONUNCIATION: kuh-LAH-buht [biht]
LOCATION: Malaysia (Sarawak state)
POPULATION: About 5,200 (in 2000)
LANGUAGE: Kelabit
RELIGION: Christianity
RELATED ARTICLES: Vol. 3: Iban

¹ INTRODUCTION

See the article entitled **Iban**.

² LOCATION AND HOMELAND

The Kelabit, with a population of approximately 5,200 people in 2000, is one of the smallest ethnic groups in Sarawak. They are highland people that inhabit the Kelabit Highlands area, which is located at the farthest reaches of the Baram and Limbang rivers in the remote interior of northern Sarawak. The unofficial capital of the Kelabit Highlands is Bario with 16 villages in the area. This includes Pa'Umur, Pa' Ukat, Pa' Lungan, (located along the Depbur basin), Long Dano, Pa Dalih, Ramudu (located along Kelapang basin), and Pa Ramapuh Benah, Pa Ramapuh Dita, Pa Derung, Ulung Palang Dita, Ulung Palang Benah, Padang Pasir, Kampung Baru, Arur Layun, Bario Asal, and Arur Dalan, in the Merariu river basin. There are four other Kelabit settlements located further down the tributaries of the Baram River: Long Peluan, Long Seridan, Long Lellang, and Long Napir.

Like many other indigenous communities in Sarawak, the Kelabit used to live in longhouses in the highlands of Central Borneo. However, due to economic and social factors, many have migrated to live in urban areas since the 1980s. It is estimated that only about 1,200 Kelabit are still living on the highlands. Many of the younger generation have moved out, mostly to get further education and to get jobs that suit their qualifications in towns and cities like Miri, Kuching, Sibu, Bintulu, Kuala Lumpur, and other places overseas.

³ LANGUAGE

The Kelabit speak their own language, which is called "Kelabit." Today, many have learned to speak English and Malay languages. Unfortunately, this has affected the usage of the Kelabit language very badly. It is decreasingly used, particularly by the younger generations. The Kelabit did not have a written form of their language until education was introduced on the highlands in the 1950s and 1960s. A recent effort was made to document the language in a dictionary, partly to preserve the language.

Basically, a Kelabit name has two parts: the given name, and the father's name. Some common male Kelabit names are Lian, Agan, Giak, and Apui. Some common female names are Supang, Sigang, Rinai, Dayang, and Ruran. A common Kelabit name would be Supang (given name) Lian (father's name).

The Kelabit practice an elaborate and fascinating relational-name system, thus distinguishing them from the other tribes in Sarawak. This practice requires new parents and new grandparents to change their names completely and permanently, making their old names redundant. These new sets of names

have to be announced to the community at the *Irau Mekaa Ngadan* (Changing Name Ceremony).

⁴ FOLKLORE

Over a century ago, the Kelabit were involved in headhunting raids, not so much for ritual purposes but as a means to prove one's courage, bravery, or valiancy, and to get even with an enemy. Thus, a person who succeeded in headhunting exploits was hailed as a hero and looked upon as a role model. Stories of successful exploits are narrated in various forms of oral stories. One of these heroes is Agan Tadun. His fame and achievement are recounted in legends, myths, and traditional songs.

One popular myth among the Kelabit is that all humans were originally from the highlands, until a big flood covered the whole earth. Many people had to build rafts to survive and were brought to the coastal areas by the water. However, some had built big and heavy rafts and were therefore stranded on the highlands. That is why and how the Kelabit remained on the highlands.

⁵ RELIGION

Most Kelabit are fervent Christians. A spiritual revival arose among them in 1973, causing the whole tribe to embrace Christianity. As a consequence, they have abandoned most of their traditional beliefs. They believe that Christianity has brought them freedom from the old religion which restricted their activities.

Formerly, the Kelabit had to rely on bird augury and dreams as guidance before beginning an important journey or starting the agriculture cycle. Certain rituals and practices were observed before commencing any undertaking. Sometimes these rituals required them to abandon a field that had been cleared for farming, or to leave their ripened rice to rot. With their conversion to Christianity, these rituals ceased to be observed by the Kelabit. Instead of these rituals, today many Kelabit say (Christian) prayers before embarking on major tasks on their farms.

⁶ MAJOR HOLIDAYS

Two major holidays for the Kelabit are Christmas and Easter. They celebrate both occasions as a community, not merely as a family affairs. Opening one's home to visitors is one of the main features of Christmas. Visitors are served with a variety of cakes, cookies, and drinks. Longhouse communities also get together for a meal either on Christmas Eve or for Christmas lunch, or both, after Christmas services.

The Easter celebration lasts for four days at least. The whole community will get together at the central church to worship and socialize together. Special speakers are invited to give sermons. It is an occasion most people look forward to attending. In addition to Christian holidays, and like other Malaysians, the Kelabit also observe other national public holidays or festivals which include New Year's Day, Hari Raya Puasa or Hari Raya Aidil Fitri (end of Ramadan), Thaipusam (celebrated by Hindus on the 10th month of the Hindu calendar), Chinese New Year (celebrated over 15 days beginning on the first day of Chinese Lunar Calendar), Wesak Day, Gawai Dayak (harvest festival), Deepavali, and Christmas.

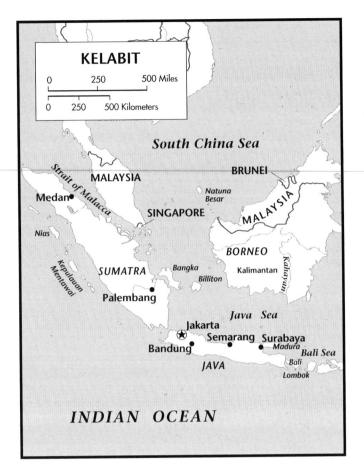

8 INTERPERSONAL RELATIONS

A hospitable and friendly person is highly respected and valued by the Kelabit. It is considered rude not to offer hospitality to any visitors at the longhouse. Everybody is expected to greet one another by shaking hands and asking simple questions like "Where are you going?" "Where are you from?" "Who came with you?" and "How are you?" A person who does not greet others, particularly elderly people, is considered rude, unfriendly, and, to a certain extent, bad-mannered.

It is considered improper to wear shoes or slippers in the house. Helping the host or hostess with cooking or cleaning up is most welcomed. Taking gifts when visiting a friend or relative is highly favored.

9 LIVING CONDITIONS

The Kelabit, like many other ethnic groups on the island of Borneo, used to live in longhouses. This situation has changed and continues to change since more and more Kelabit in the Highlands are residing in detached-single houses. Furthermore, many Kelabit have migrated to live in towns and cities. The longhouses and houses in the villages are always kept clean. This is encouraged by constant inspections by the health officers. All the longhouses have tap water, and some longhouses have generators to give light in the night, while the others have to depend on kerosene lamps or candles. In order to be safe to drink, the tap water must be boiled.

Most Kelabit in the highlands are free of common diseases that can be found elsewhere in the tropical interior. Their constant involvement in vigorous work on the farm keeps most of them physically fit. The consistent supply of fresh fruit, vegetables, meat, and fish keeps them healthy. They buy or barter these goods from each other. This said, it is important to note that there is increasing dependence on foodstuff from nearby cities and towns. These groceries are air-flown to Bario on a daily basis.

A government clinic with a hospital assistant is stationed in the highlands. The villagers have a constant supply of medication, except for major or serious illnesses and accidents. In these cases, the patients are sent down by aircraft to the nearest town for better medical care.

10 FAMILY LIFE

Family life is highly valued among the Kelabit. The family is not only a social unit, but also an economic one. A large family consists of 6 to 12 children. Often the grandparents will live with the family, and sometimes other members of the extended family live with the family as well. Consequently, there are cases where a family consists of 12 to 15 members. However, this has changed over the years, as many children have migrated to urban areas.

The husband is considered the head of the household. He is responsible for making political or leadership decisions for the family. This involves being the spokesman for the family. If any members of the family have problems, e.g., misunderstandings with other members of the community, the father is responsible for making peace. The wife, however, makes most of the economic decisions. She decides when to start the farming each year. While the husband is responsible for bringing back meat and fish for the family meals, it is the wife's job to collect vegetables and mushrooms for the meals. Their children are trained from a young age to help carry out these tasks. A

7 RITES OF PASSAGE

An infant is normally delivered by a midwife or an experienced older woman. In the past, a child was required to go through different stages of ceremonies or rituals as she or he grew to be a teenager. One of these ceremonies was the Initiation of the Child. It involved the slaughtering of one or more pigs, and the examinations of the livers and gall bladders to discern the fate and fortune of the child concerned. Today, these ceremonies are not observed at all, except for the *Irau Mekaa Ngadan* (Name Changing Ceremony).

As a teenager, a child is trained by her or his parents, grandparents, aunts, and uncles to do chores. While a girl is trained by her mother, grandmother, and aunts about cooking, washing, and working on the field, a boy is trained by his father, grandfather, and uncles how to hunt, fish, collect firewood, and build huts or houses.

The birth of the first child among the Kelabit signifies a transition in an individual's life. This is marked by the Irau Mekaa Ngadan, which is held to affirm one's transition to parenthood and grandparenthood. The new parents and grandparents are required to take up new names to mark their new status. These new names are chosen and announced at the Irau Mekaa Ngadan which involves the whole community. Guests at the ceremony are served a big feast by the hosts (the new parents and grandparents).

A death among the Kelabit is often followed by a lot of mourning and weeping. Relatives and friends come from all over to pay their last respects. A dead person is normally buried within 24 hours.

A young girl of the Kelabit tribe of Sarawak dances at the 6th Rainforest World Music Festival in Malaysia. The festival brings together renowned world musicians from all continents and indigenous musicians from the interiors of Borneo. (© Reuters/Corbis)

son will help his father, and a daughter is expected to help her mother.

Not many families keep animals as pets. Some raise cats to keep pests away, and some raise dogs for hunting. Poultry such as chicken and ducks are kept for their meat and eggs. Water buffalo are kept to prepare the fields for farming and also to carry heavy loads.

11 CLOTHING

Traditionally the Kelabit wore very simple clothing. A man used to wear a loincloth and a jacket made from tree bark. A woman used to wear a knee-length skirt, and adorned herself with bead necklaces and a bead cap. However, today the Western style of dress is very common among the Kelabit.

12 FOOD

The Kelabit always have a supply of fresh meat and vegetables from the jungle or garden. They collect wild vegetables from the jungle and hunt or fish for their protein. Each family also has farms for growing their own rice, not only for domestic consumption, but also for sale. Poultry such as chicken and ducks are reared for domestic consumption. The encroachment of urbanization is changing the food supply chains among the

Kelabit. With easier access to cash and modern transportation, the Kelabit in Bario are also getting their daily food supplies from nearby towns like Miri and Marudi.

The Kelabit also produce their own salt, called Kelabit or Bario salt. This salt is obtained by evaporating salty water from salt springs which are found in the highlands. The salty water is boiled until all the water is evaporated, leaving the salt at the bottom of the *kawang* (big cooking utensil). The remaining water is completely dripped from the salt before it is put in bamboo pipes to be burnt in the fire. This is to harden the salt, which is later wrapped in big leaves to be kept in dry and safe places. The salt is used in cooking and also to preserve meat.

Traditionally the Kelabit used clay pots, made locally by women, to cook or prepare their food. However, today most of their kitchen utensils, such as spoons, forks, plates, and metal cooking pots, are obtained from urban areas.

Labo Belatuh (smoked meat) is a traditional Kelabit food. Meat, particularly wild boar and venison, is salted and smoked over an open fire. The meat will later be boiled and pounded into small strips and eaten with rice.

[13] EDUCATION

The first school was opened in the highlands in 1946 by Tom Harrison, a former British soldier who lived with the Kelabit for two years after World War II. He was assisted by Paul Kouhan who was originally from the island of Roti but later married and settled in Bario. There were only 46 students in the school when it first started. A few other schools were opened later on to cater to the needs of the Kelabit, who were coming to see the importance of formal education. Both sons and daughters were encouraged to go to school. Some students had to walk five to seven days through the thick rain forest to get to the nearest school. Access to education is one of the main reasons why many young people have migrated to urban areas.

The literacy rate among the Kelabit is quite high, particularly among the younger generations. Many of them have at least obtained a Malaysian Education Certificate. Of the 5,200 Kelabit, about 250 have obtained university degrees locally and abroad. Many others have attended professional courses and are working with governmental and private sectors across the country. In other words, the Kelabit, considering the difficult terrain of the highlands and the fact that they must leave their homes as soon as they go to school, have been very successful in their quest for formal education. Many have had to leave their home at the age of six or seven to attend boarding school.

Kelabit parents have played a crucial role in promoting formal education for their children. They see education as the means to improve their children's social condition. As a result, many highly educated Kelabit attribute their success to the encouragement of their parents.

[14] CULTURAL HERITAGE

Even though the Kelabit have gone through rapid social and economic changes within the very short span of 50 years, they have managed to maintain certain aspects of their culture which are still very unique, particularly their music and dance. A traditional musical instrument is the *sape*, a plucked lute instrument. It is carved from a tree trunk in an elongated rectangular shape, with a neck extending from one end of the body. Formerly, its three or four strings were made from finely split rattan, but today they are made of wire.

The Kelabit also play the *pagang* (tube zither), which is made from a length of bamboo tube, closed at both ends by its natural bamboo nodes. The strings are finely cut strips from the surface of the bamboo tube itself, which are still attached to the tube at either end.

The Kelabit use the sape and pagang music to dance their lovely hornbill and warrior dances, long dances, and single dances. The hornbill dance is performed in imitation of the hornbill bird. Hornbill birds are beautiful, shy, and very gracious. Many natives in Sarawak adore them, so they try to imitate their movements.

The Kelabit, like many other indigenous people in the Borneo island, do not have a written language. So most of their stories were passed down orally. However, recent efforts have been made by the local people to record this invaluable knowledge.

[15] WORK

Most Kelabit in the highlands are rice cultivators. Historically, the Kelabit permanent wet-rice cultivation has distinguished them from the other natives in Sarawak, except for the Lun Bawang. They cultivate the famous Bario rice, which is well known for its sweet aroma and pleasant taste. Besides cultivating rice, they also grow citrus fruits for domestic consumption. Unlike those who remain in the highlands, Kelabit migrants to cities and towns are professionals, religious leaders, and intellectuals who play important roles in the wider Malaysian society.

[16] SPORTS

Most Kelabits' traditional games and sports are slowly being abandoned by the younger generation. They have learned new games like basketball, volleyball, and soccer. In recent years, these sports have been promoted within the Kelabit community through and during the annual Highlanders Games Carnival. During the carnival, game competitions are carried out to ensure participation by Kelabit from different cities, towns, and villages. In the past, children spent most of their time swimming in the river, or playing in the shrubs surrounding the longhouses. Unfortunately, today most of these games are abandoned.

Soccer as a sport has become very popular among the Kelabit. Most Kelabit young men and boys are enthralled with the game. Another sport which has become popular among the Kelabit is golf. Tournaments are often organized to promote and maintain interests in the sport among urban Kelabit.

[17] ENTERTAINMENT AND RECREATION

Since the highlands are quite isolated in the interior of Sarawak, television and movies were unknown in the highlands until recently. The installation of generators in most Kelabit longhouses has enabled them to watch movies on television and video. Some families do have satellite dishes, which make it possible for them to receive television channels from all over the world.

Occasionally, the Kelabit get together in the night to sing, dance, and talk, after working hard in the rice field during the day. Various dances are danced to the *sape* music. The women sometimes get together to sing Christian songs, or traditional songs. These occasions are always joyous and delightful.

[18] FOLK ART, CRAFTS, AND HOBBIES

The Kelabit make many handicraft items, many of them for everyday use. Most of these items, however, are made with little ornamentation and no carving. Nonetheless, many of them are beautifully made, with great skill.

Bamboo and rattan are the two common materials used to make Kelabit crafts. Rattan is easily obtained from the primary forest, and bamboo is acquired from the secondary forest, i.e., from areas which have at some time in the past been used for agriculture. Many cooking utensils, tools in the kitchen, baskets for storage and carrying, fish traps, and rice winnowing trays are some items that are made of these materials.

The Kelabit also use other materials like grass, bark, or other plant materials to make mats, brooms, sun hats, knife sheaths, and rain capes. Nylon cord and thread are sometimes used together with the other materials.

[19] SOCIAL PROBLEMS

One of the acute social problems faced by the Kelabit in the highlands is the increasing and rapid migration of the younger generations into urban areas. This inevitable trend has left the old people to tend the rice fields. In order to overcome the shortage of labor to work in the rice fields, the Kelabit are hiring laborers from their neighboring communities.

The rapid economic progress in Sarawak has benefited the Kelabit in many ways. However, the increasing encroachment of commercial logging and demand for agricultural land development has put the Kelabit in a dilemma. They have to decide whether to give up their land for large-scale land development and timber concessions, or to maintain their traditional farming system.

20 GENDER ISSUES

The Kelabit stress the fundamental equality of the sexes and the complementarities of their work. Nonetheless there are differences between men and women. This is especially with regards to their roles, responsibilities, functions and activities in the society. Female's functions and feminine roles include nurturing the family through cooking, cleaning, and working on the household farm, activities which reflect and at the same time reinforce feminine qualities such as motherliness, gentleness, friendliness and kindness. In contrast, activities which demand greater physical prowess, such as hunting, travelling and headhunting, are deemed to be men's activities. They involve and develop qualities that are considered to be masculine traits, such as strength industriousness, and physical ability and prowess. In its essence, the Kelabit gender system reflects a pattern, in which roles and activities are assigned for the purposes of accomplishing particular tasks and with a view to each individual's differing abilities and opportunities in performing them. Social differences between men and women in this case are defined by and based on the activities that they are engaged in. Nowadays gender roles have changed as a result of high rate of rural-urban migration and the arrival of formal education which facilitated women's increased labor force participation.

21 BIBLIOGRAPHY

Bala, Poline. *Changing Borders and Identities in the Kelabit Highlands: Anthropological Reflections on Growing up in a Kelabit Village near the International Border.* Dayak Studies Contemporary Series, No. 1, The Institute of East Asian Studies, Universiti Malaysia Sarawak, 2002.

Janowski, Monica Hughes. "The Making of Earthenware Cooking Pots in the Kelabit Highlands." In *Sarawak Cultural Legacy: A Living Tradition*, edited by Lucas Chin and Valerie Mashman. Kuching, Sarawak: Society Atelier Sarawak, 1991.

Saging, Robert Lian, and Lucy Bulan. "Kelabit Ethnography (A Brief Report)." *Sarawak Museum Journal 11,* no. 6 (1989): 89–118.

Talla, Yahya. *The Kelabits of the Kelabit Highlands, Sarawak.* Provisional Research Report, No. 9. Pulau Pinang: Social Anthrosection School of Comparative Social Sciences, University Sains Malaysia, 1979.

—by P. Bala

KHASI

PRONUNCIATION: KAH-zee
ALTERNATE NAMES: Ki Khasi; Ri Lum
LOCATION: India (Meghalaya state)
POPULATION: 1.34 million (estimate)
LANGUAGE: Khasi
RELIGION: Christianity; native animist beliefs
RELATED ARTICLES: Vol. 3: People of India

1 INTRODUCTION

The name *Khasi* identifies a group of tribes and subtribes presently inhabiting the Khasi and Jaintia Hills in Meghalaya State in northeastern India. The Khasi call themselves Ki Khasi or Ri Lum. The name *Khasi* was probably given to them by the people of the surrounding plains. In its broad sense, Khasi includes several neighboring groups such as the Jaintia, Pnar, Lyngam, Bhoi, War, and Khynriam. In Bangladesh, in the hills of Sylhet, Khasis sometimes refer to themselves as the Hynniewtrep, the "Seven Huts," which refers to the original seven families from which all Khasi believe they are descended.

Early Khasi history remains a mystery, although linguistic and other evidence suggests a probable Southeast Asian origin. By the mid-16th century, numerous small Khasi chiefdoms existed in the Khasi and Jaintia hills. British expansion into Assam in the early 19th century led to contact with the Khasi tribes. Periodic conflict with the Khasi eventually led to the British extending their control into the Khasi and Jaintia Hills. Between 1826 and 1835, the 25 Khasi states in the region accepted British protection. Relations were formalized in 1862, when treaties were signed between the British and the Khasi, granting the latter autonomy and freedom from British taxation. Shillong was made the capital of the British province of Assam in 1874, exposing the Khasi to significant Western cultural influences. At India's independence in 1947, the Khasi and Jaintia Hills were designated an autonomous tribal area under the administration of the government of Assam. The region achieved full statehood as Meghalaya State in 1972.

The majority of the Khasi population live in Meghalaya State, although there is a significant minority (c. 29,000) found in Assam. Small numbers of Khasi are also found in Bangladesh and in the Indian states of West Bengal, Mizoram, Tripura, Maharashtra, Tamil Nadu, Aunachal Pradesh and the Andaman and Nicobar Islands.

2 LOCATION AND HOMELAND

According to census returns, the Khasi population in Meghalya numbered 1.12 million in 2001. The current estimated total population of the Khasi is around 1.34 million. The homeland of the Khasi lies on the Assam or Meghalaya plateau, an upland area some 240 km by 100 km (150 mi by 60 mi) located between the Brahmaputra Valley to the north and the alluvial plains of Bangladesh to the south. With summit levels at 1,370–1,830 m (4,500–6,000 ft), the region experiences a temperate climate. Maximum temperatures during the hottest month average around 27°c (80°f), while during the winter months temperatures rarely drop below 5°c (40°f). The plateau stands right in the path of monsoon winds blowing in from the Bay of Bengal, and the region experiences heavy rainfall dur-

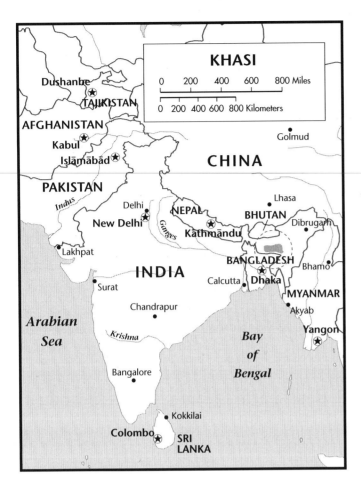

KHASI

0   200   400   600   800 Miles

0 200 400 600 800 Kilometers

Dushanbe

TAJIKISTAN

AFGHANISTAN

Kabul

Islamabad

PAKISTAN

Indus

Delhi

New Delhi

Ganges

Lakhpat

INDIA

Surat

Chandrapur

Arabian Sea

Krishna

Bangalore

Kokkilai

Colombo   SRI LANKA

Golmud

CHINA

Lhasa

NEPAL   BHUTAN

Kathmandu   Dibrugarh

BANGLADESH   Bhamo

Calcutta   Dhaka

MYANMAR

Akyab

Bay of Bengal

Yangon

the stall and trampling on his goods. The dog complained to the principal beasts at the market and also to the tiger, who was priest of the market. He was told he would be fined for selling such foul-smelling goods in the market, and they, also, kicked and trampled his wares. The dog eventually went to a human, who said, "Come and live with me, and I will arise with you to seek revenge on all the animals who have wronged you." Since that day, humans have hunted with the assistance of the dog. Dogs know how to track animals because they can scent in their footprints the rotten peas that they trampled at the market at Lura-Luri.

5 RELIGION

Khasi religion may be described as animistic, focusing on the propitiation of spirits—both good and evil—especially in times of trouble. The particular spirit to be appeased is identified through an egg-breaking ritual, and the appropriate sacrifice is performed. Fowl and goats are the principal sacrificial victims, although human sacrifice was not unknown in the past. The priest (*lyngdoh*), who is appointed from a special priestly clan, is the principal person responsible for performing ritual functions. However, the presence of a female priest (*ka-soh-blei* or *ka-lyngdoh*) is necessary at all sacrifices. This is, perhaps, a reflection of the matriarchal nature of Khasi society, as is the assigning of a feminine gender to the Khasi creator goddess. Other religious practitioners, such as diviners and elders skilled in sorcery, play a role in Khasi religious life. Family ceremonies are performed by the head of the family or clan. Ancestor worship and the worship of natural forces and gods and goddesses of nature form an integral part of Khasi religious practices.

Although many aspects of traditional Khasi religion survive, the majority of Khasi have adopted Christianity. Missionary work began in the region during the late 19th century and has been so successful that today over 80% of Khasi profess to be Christian, belonging mostly to the Presbyterian or Roman Catholic churches, although there are a few Unitarians in the mix. There are a few Hindus and Muslims among the Khasi, the latter coming primarily as traders from other parts of India and intermarrying with local Khasi women.

6 MAJOR HOLIDAYS

The most important of the many festivals celebrated by the Khasi is the Nongkrem Dance. This is held in late spring (usually in May) and is part of a ceremony performed by the Syiem (chief) of Khyrim State (one of the former Khasi states) and his priests. Goats are sacrificed to Ka Blei Synshar, the ruling goddess of the Khasi, for an abundance of crops and for the prosperity of the people. Various ritual dances, some performed by the chief and his entourage, are part of the ceremonies. This is followed by the great dance by Khasi girls and men before the house of the high priestess. People come from all over the region to participate in the festival and its activities.

7 RITES OF PASSAGE

The naming ceremony for a child is held the day after its birth. Several names are suggested to the elderly man who is called to perform the naming *puja* (ceremony). He recites the names while pouring liquor from a gourd onto the ground. The name on his lips when the last drop of liquor adheres to the spout of the gourd is the one selected. Certain other rituals complete

ing the summer months. Cherrapunji, southwest of Shillong and on the south-facing slope of the hills, is on record as the wettest place on earth, averaging nearly 1,150 cm (450 in) of rain annually. As a result of the heavy rains, much of the plateau is deeply dissected and is also covered with dense forests.

3 LANGUAGE

The Khasi language and its dialects belong to the Mon-Khmer branch of the Austro-Asiatic language family. Mon-Khmer languages are widely spoken in Cambodia, Vietnam, and Burma, indicating possible Southeast Asian origins for the Khasi tribes. Khasi represents the westernmost occurrence of the Mon-Khmer group. Some scholars see it as a link between the Southeast Asian languages and those of central India belonging to the Munda branch of the Austro-Asiatic family, spoken by the Munda, Santals, and other tribes.

4 FOLKLORE

The Khasi possess a rich and varied folklore. The dog is considered the friend of humans and, unlike some of their neighbors, the Khasi do not eat dog flesh. One tale tells of how the dog came to live with humans. Many, many years ago, when the world was very young, so the legend goes, all the beasts lived happily together. They bought and sold goods at a market located at Luri-Lura in the territory of the Bhoi Khasi, in the northeastern part of the region. One day a dog came to the market to sell rotten peas. The animals around the dog's stall objected to the unpleasant odor of his wares, knocking over

the naming ceremony, including the placing of the placenta in a pot and hanging it on a tree outside the village. Among some groups, egg-breaking forms part of the naming ritual. Traditional rituals associated with birth are not observed by Christians.

Death rituals of the Khasi are quite elaborate and involve the sacrifice of several types of animals. At death, the body is washed, dressed in white cloth, and laid out with an egg placed on the stomach. A cock is sacrificed to scratch a path for the spirit to the next world. A bull is then sacrificed for a man, or a cow for a woman. On the day of the funeral, pigs are sacrificed by relatives and friends of the deceased. The dead are cremated, with pieces of bone collected from the funeral pyre and placed in the clan bone repository (along with some bones from the sacrificed animals). For three days after cremation, the family is in mourning and under various taboos. After a month, a pig or fowl is sacrificed to complete the funeral rites. Among Christian Khasi, the dead are buried according to the rites of the Christian Church.

An unusual feature of the Khasi is their custom of erecting memorial stones. These are huge, upright stone monoliths, some as high as 8 m (27 ft), that may be seen standing in groups throughout the Khasi and Jaintia Hills. They serve as memorials to the dead or to mark places of particular importance or sanctity to the Khasi.

8 INTERPERSONAL RELATIONS

Khasi are a cheerful people by nature. They seem to thoroughly appreciate a joke, and even women are not reluctant to indulge in lighthearted exchanges with total strangers. It is customary not to mention names of immediate relations, perhaps for fear of attracting the attention of evil spirits. A person may be addressed as the "mother of so and so" or the "father of so and so" rather than by their real name. Actual names may eventually be entirely forgotten through lack of use.

9 LIVING CONDITIONS

Khasi villages are built a little below the summits of hills to protect them from the elements. A marketplace and a sacred grove of trees may be found outside the village, along with numerous Khasi memorial stones. The village itself may contain schools and Christian churches, as well as homes. The Khasi house is an oval-shaped, thatched structure, with walls of timber or stone. It is usually divided into three rooms: a porch, a living room, and sleeping quarters. Furnishings are a mixture of traditional and modern, reflecting the strong influence of the British in the region. Wealthier families have more substantial houses, with comfortable European-style furniture.

10 FAMILY LIFE

The Khasi are divided into a number of clans, each of which trace their descent from an ancestress known as *kiaw* (grandmother). The clans are exogamous, with marriage within a clan strictly prohibited. Members of a clan are bound together by ties of religion, ancestor worship, and funeral rites, and even Christian Khasi preserve their clan structure. Descent is traced through the female line. Marriage is by choice and usually takes place during early adulthood. Omens are read and an auspicious day fixed for the marriage ceremony. The ceremony itself is performed by a priest and is accompanied by animal sacrifice, feasting, and much drinking. In the Christian community, the marriage ceremony is performed according to the rites of the Church.

The newlyweds usually reside with the bride's mother until children are born, when they set up their own household. The Khasi are monogamous in their marriage relationships. However, divorce is frequent and easily obtained, and remarriage of divorcées is permitted. The youngest daughter inherits ancestral property, and daughters receive preference in any division of property.

Women enjoy a high social status and play a significant role in managing the household's social and economic affairs.

11 CLOTHING

The traditional dress of a Khasi man consists of a sleeveless coat (*jymphong*) that leaves the arms and neck bare. It fastens across the front with frogs (braided loops that slip over buttons) and has tassels on the chest and a fringe at the bottom. This is worn over a loincloth that wraps around the waist and is drawn though the legs, with one end hanging down in front like an apron. A black cap completes the outfit. Elderly men sometimes replace the cap with a white turban. Males wear earrings, armlets, and necklaces made of gold, silver, and semiprecious stones.

For women, typical clothing is a short piece of cloth wrapped around the waist that hangs to the knees. Over this is worn a long piece of cloth, knotted at the shoulders, that hangs down to the ankles. Another long piece of cloth, often striped or brightly colored, is thrown around the shoulders like a cloak and tied at the front. A wrap is worn over the head and shoulders. Women wear a variety of jewelry made from gold, silver, and stones such as coral and carnelian.

12 FOOD

Khasi usually take two meals a day, one in the early morning and the other in the evening. They are nonvegetarians, eating pork, beef, and chicken, as well as the flesh of many wild animals. They are said to enjoy a curry made from a particular kind of green frog. Dried fish with rice is a staple of the Khasi diet. When rice is not available, millet or Job's tears (the seeds of the grass *Coix lacryma-jobi*) is used instead. The inner bark of the wild sago palm is dried and made into a sweet, reddish flour and mixed with rice or eaten in the form of cakes. Milk and milk products are not used, a trait common among peoples of Mongoloid descent. This no doubt reflects the high incidence of lactose malabsorption (the inability of the body to use milk) that is found among peoples of this ethnic background. Beer made from rice or millet is widely consumed by the Khasi, as well as being used for ritual purposes. Some clans among the Khasi have specific food taboos originating, most likely, from totemic considerations.

13 EDUCATION

Compared to other tribal peoples in the Indian subcontinent, the Khasi have made good progress in the field of education, partly, perhaps, a result of the influence of missionaries in the past. Nearly two-thirds of the population is literate (66.1% in 2001), with women having a slightly higher literacy than men (the reverse of the norm in South Asia) and participating more in the educational process, although their involvement in higher education declines relative to men.

A Khasi woman and her child waits for customers to sell fruits in Nongpoh, Gauhati, India. (AP Images/Anupam Nath)

¹⁴ CULTURAL HERITAGE

Having no written script until 1842, when the Roman alphabet was introduced by a missionary, the Khasi lack any significant body of literature. However, this is more than made up for by their oral folk traditions. Singing and dancing are of particular importance, accompanied by music played on drums, pipes, flutes, and stringed instruments like guitars. Dancing accompanies all Khasi festivities and plays a role in some of their religious ceremonies. Only unmarried girls participate in the dance of the women. They don spectacular costumes, dressing in rich silk clothes that extend from their neck to the ground. They are laden with a profusion of jewelry, bead necklaces, silver and gold chains, bracelets, and earrings. On their heads, they wear a gold or silver crown. The girls dance in a circle, taking tiny steps to the beat of the music, barely lifting their feet off the ground. The hands are held straight down at the sides, with the eyes downcast. The men dance around the circle of girls, waving fly-whisks and prancing around with huge, ungainly steps. There are also dances performed only by men.

¹⁵ WORK

Although many Khasi have entered other occupations, agriculture remains the main economic activity among the community. A variety of crops, produced by methods ranging from

intensive paddy cultivation to shifting agriculture *(jhum)*, are cultivated for consumption and sale. Crops grown by the Khasi include rice, maize (corn), millet, pulses, chilies, potatoes, vegetables (e.g., eggplants, pumpkins, and gourds) and fruits (pineapples and oranges). Agricultural produce is sold at weekly markets and through marketing societies. The Khasi raise livestock for economic and ritual purposes (goats, pigs, and chickens are important sacrificial animals), and also engage in hunting and fishing. Bees are kept for larvae, wax, and honey.

¹⁶ SPORTS

Games played by children include spinning tops, a kind of hopscotch, kite-flying, marbles using stone pebbles, and wrestling. The principal sport of Khasi men is archery. The Khasi believe that archery originated at the creation of the world, when the first Khasi woman taught her two sons to shoot arrows. Villages challenge each other to archery meets, and archery competitions accompany many festivals. Betting on the outcome of a contest is commonplace.

¹⁷ ENTERTAINMENT AND RECREATION

The Khasi enjoy pastimes such as hunting and archery, as well as their folk traditions of singing and dancing. Modern mass media such as radio and television are becoming increasingly popular.

¹⁸ FOLK ART, CRAFTS, AND HOBBIES

Although they manufacture items ranging from simple metal agricultural implements to cane baskets and sieves, Khasi can hardly be said to have any distinctive arts or crafts. They are skilled in basketry, net-making, carpentry, weaving cotton and silk cloth, and the manufacture of various utilitarian goods.

¹⁹ SOCIAL PROBLEMS

The Khasi, like many other tribes in India, are undergoing changes that have led to internal social stresses as well as to problems in relations with other ethnic groups. The community is designated as a Scheduled Tribe and is entitled to the benefits that accompany this status under the Indian Constitution. The predominantly "tribal" nature of Meghalaya, however, has led to problems with nontribal groups. Aggressive organizations such as the Khasi Students Union (KSU) and the Federation of Khasi, Jaintia, and Garo Peoples (FKJGP) actively support policies that are aimed at preventing nontribal peoples from living and working in the state. The need to present a united tribal front, however, has to some degree clouded internal social tensions. The undifferentiated Khasi society of former times has now become stratified, with new classes of landlords, white-collar professionals, and agriculturalists all competing for limited resources. There is particular resentment by traditional Khasi against the Christian Khasi, who are seen as becoming increasingly dominant in the political, economic, and social arenas. This accounts for the rise of movements such as Seng Khasi, aimed at preserving the traditional Khasi religion.

²⁰ GENDER ISSUES

Khasi society is matrilineal and so women enjoy many advantages they lack in other South Asian societies. A 2007 study from Germany concluded that the tribes of Meghalaya, such as the Khasi, whose societies are organized on matrilineal and matrifocal principles have obtained much greater gender equality than the other societies of South Asia (e.g. Hindu and Muslim) that are organized on the patriarchal principles. Khasi women enjoy a high social status and play a significant role in socio-economic matters and household management. Many Khasi women have taken up professions in the civil service and in industries besides agriculture.

Khasi women are divided into several matrilineal clans such as Mawlong, Khongweer and Symley. The youngest daughter inherits the ancestral property and daughters are given preference in the division of property while males can own only self-acquired property. Even Christians are known to pass down their ancestral property through the female line.

Even so, there are many male heads of families among the Khasi and women tend to lag behind in terms of socio-economic standing. It is possible for males who have no living female relatives to adopt a female as a younger daughter (a Khasi custom known as *Rap-iing*) to ensure property passes down from generation to generation (viz. Khasi Hills Autonomous District [Khasi Social Custom of Lineage] Act of 1997).

Though females in Meghalaya are aware of their rights and position in society, hardly any Khasi women actively participate in the world of politics. Khasi society does not even allow women to participate in political decision-making. Few women are heads of a *dorbar* (the equivalent of a panchayat in the plains) and only recently, despite their status in society, have women been allowed to participate much in a dorbar meeting. The dorbar continues to be dominated by males.

Though women in Khasi society are relatively free, with authority, title, inheritance, the right to maintain matrilocal residence after marriage and succession traced through the female line, still there is discrimination (for instance, many Khasi women wait to eat until after their husbands have eaten) and in rural areas many Khasi women feel that the reservation of a seat for them in a dorbar is not beneficial to them. Of course most females exercise their franchise in the elections and that percentage increases with the rise in educational levels.

However, in general, women in Khasi society enjoy an enviable freedom and equality vis- à-vis males compared to other women in South Asia.

21 BIBLIOGRAPHY

Bareh, Hamlet. *The History and Culture of the Khasi People*. Calcutta: Naba Mudran Private Ltd., 1967.

Das Gupta, P. K. *Life and Culture of a Matrilineal Tribe of Meghalaya*. New Delhi: Inter-India Publications, 1984.

Gurdon, P. R. T. *The Khasis*. Delhi: Cosmo Publications, 1974 [1914].

Lest we forget. Shillong: Khasi National Celebration Committee: Sevenhuts Enterprise, 1994.

Lyngdoh, Mary Pristilla Rina. *The Festivals in the History and Culture of the Khasi*. New Delhi : Har-Anand Publications, 1991.

Sen, Soumen. *Khasi-Jaintia folklore: Context, Discourse, and History*. Chennai: National Folklore Support Centre, 2004.

—by D. O. Lodrick

KHMER

PRONUNCIATION: kuh-MER
ALTERNATE NAMES: Cambodians
LOCATION: Cambodia
POPULATION: About 8 million
LANGUAGE: Cambodian
RELIGION: Theravada Buddhism; Islam; Roman Catholicism; traditional beliefs; Taoism

1 INTRODUCTION

For much of the past century, the State of Cambodia has been largely unknown to most of the world except as the home of Angkor Wat, one of the wonders of the world. Not until the Vietnam War did Cambodia come to the world's attention, when its strategic location to the west of Vietnam, where it shared a border hundreds of miles long, brought it unwanted involvement in the War.

Cambodians are called Khmer and their language, culture, and appearance reflect many centuries of Hindu influence from India, Chinese from China, and other groups from prehistoric Cambodia, Malaysia, and Europe.

Cambodians value tradition, as revealed in a common proverb that states, "Don't choose a straight path and don't reject a winding one. Choose the path your ancestors followed." Cambodians eat rice and fish, raise pigs and water buffalo, and live in stilt houses, as have their ancestors for millennia. It is also probable that present-day Cambodian practices, such as wearing tattoos for protection, chewing betel, and games played at the New Year, have been part of daily life for centuries, perhaps for thousands of years. Some beliefs, such as believing in water spirits, associating ancestor spirits with the lunar calendar, and natural phenomena like rocks and soil, may be thousands of years old.

Cambodians are quick to note that their nation was once the heart of a great empire that stretched over much of Southeast Asia. In the late 1800s the French colonized Cambodia in an effort to protect its holdings in Vietnam, which it considered potentially more lucrative than Cambodia. France was also interested in having Cambodia serve as a buffer between France's possessions and Thailand, also interested in the resources of Cambodia.

In 1953 Cambodia gained independence with King Norodom Sihanouk as head of state. For the next decade and a half, Sihanouk tried to keep his country neutral and out of the war that was spreading in neighboring Vietnam. He was unsuccessful and was overthrown in 1970. Cambodia has been ruled by four governments since 1953, each having gained power by overthrowing the previous one until the 1993 election, supervised by the United Nations. The first government was run by General Lon Nol, who allowed the United States to fight the Vietnam War from Cambodia. As the war continued, corruption, bombing, economic disruption, and the displacement of over half the population from their homes destroyed much of Cambodia and facilitated the overthrow of the country in 1975 by Communist rebels.

The Communists or "Khmer Rouge" attempted to remake society. Intent on a Maoist "cultural revolution," they evacuated the cities, turned everyone into laborers, dissolved banks, the

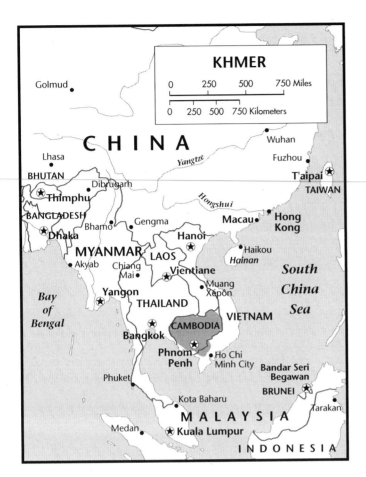

KHMER

0   250   500   750 Miles

0 250 500 750 Kilometers

C H I N A

Golmud

Lhasa
BHUTAN
Thimphu
BANGLADESH
Dhaka
MYANMAR
Akyab
Yangon
THAILAND
Bangkok
Phuket
Medan
Kuala Lumpur
M A L A Y S I A
I N D O N E S I A

Dibrugarh
Bhamo
Gengma
Chiang
Mai
Bay
of
Bengal

Wuhan
Fuzhou
T'aipai
TAIWAN
Macau
Hong
Kong
Hanoi
Haikou
Hainan
LAOS
Vientiane
Muang
Xépôn
VIETNAM
CAMBODIA
Phnom
Penh
Ho Chi
Minh City
Bandar Seri
Begawan
BRUNEI
Kota Baharu
Tarakan

South
China
Sea

Hongshui
Yangtze

postal service, the airlines, and other institutions. They closed schools and hospitals and tore down temples and churches. In three and a half years of Khmer Rouge rule, at least one million Cambodians died from execution, starvation, torture, and disease, and the numbers are still being revised upward as new gravesites are uncovered with the help of satellite mapping.

In December 1978, Vietnam invaded and chased the Khmer Rouge to the Thai border. For the next decade the country was ruled by a government installed by the Vietnamese. Resistance armies including the Khmer Rouge—one led by Sihanouk and another led by non-Communists—attempted to take over the country. In 1993 the United Nations oversaw reconciliation between resistance groups and the government and held elections. Cambodians are now experiencing more peace, security, and prosperity than most have since at least 1970.

² LOCATION AND HOMELAND

The population of Cambodia in 2008 was approximately 8 million people, although the continued war between government troops and the Khmer Rouge make a complete census of the country impossible.

Approximately 90% of the Cambodian population is ethnic Khmer. Another 5% of the population is Chinese-Cambodians.

There is also a significant Vietnamese minority, although observers differ on the number. This is because virtually all birth records were destroyed during the Khmer Rouge era and, in the post-KR years, ethnic Vietnamese have been reluctant to come forward and identify themselves. Most Vietnamese live

in the capital of Phnom Penh or near the border with Vietnam. They are still subject to considerable discrimination, particularly during Cambodian election campaigns, when politicians seem all too willing to play the "racist card."

Hill people, called "Khmer Loeu" by other Cambodians, also live in Cambodia. These are scattered tribes who live in remote plateaus and mountainous areas on the Western, northern, and eastern periphery of Cambodia. There are also Cham, the descendants of a once-great empire that dominated from central Vietnam. The Cham speak their own language and practice Islam. Most are fishermen or rice farmers.

Cambodia is a small country, about the size of Oregon, hugged between the two larger, more populous countries of Vietnam and Thailand. Physically, three-quarters of Cambodia lie in a flat basin that forms the center of the country, surrounded by plateaus and mountains.

This central plain is Cambodia's "rice bowl." The rice bowl has fed Cambodians for millennia, for it is home to rice fields in the flooded areas and vegetables and fruit in the drier areas.

Cambodia is a monsoon country with two seasons. The monsoons from the southwest bring the rainy season from May to October. During the wet season, there are torrential downpours almost every day. The rest of the time is generally cloudy and humid.

From November to April, the monsoons come from the opposite direction, the northeast, bringing sunshine and little rain. The weather is dry and hot, with the heat increasing into April making the coming of the rainy season a welcome event.

During the rainy season, Cambodia is home to a truly amazing phenomenon. Tonle Sap Lake is a long narrow lake located in west central Cambodia connected to the Mekong River by the Tonle Sap River. During the rainy season, the Mekong swells with flood waters as it travels over 4,023 km (2,500 mi) from its source in China. The surplus water is pushed up the Tonle Sap River, reversing its normal southward rush to the sea and pushing it back into the Tonle Sap Lake. However, this pattern has been disrupted by changes to the Mekong as the upper riparian nations –especially China–construct dams in keeping with their economic development plans. The Cambodian government and environmental groups are beginning to express concern. Fish from the lake provide Cambodians with a quarter of their protein.

Cambodia's population of wild animals includes spotted leopards, tiger, black panthers, bears, boar, and many species of monkeys. These animals frequent the forests, which are avoided by most Cambodians. Snakes abound. Three of the world's most dangerous—the cobra, king cobra, and banded krait—also live in Cambodia but are rarer. Numerous species of birds also reside in Cambodia. These include peacocks, wild duck, and pheasant. A land of water, Cambodia is also home to fish-eating birds, such as cormorants, egrets, and pelicans.

Between 500,000 and 700,000 Khmer live in southern Vietnam, where most continue to speak their language and practice Cambodian Buddhism. Most are rice farmers, as were their ancestors when southern Vietnam was part of the large Khmer kingdom. Another quarter-to half-million live in Thailand just across the border from west and northwest Cambodia.

In addition, Cambodian migrants now live in more than 20 countries throughout the world. This diaspora of the Khmer people began before the Khmer Rouge takeover in 1975 as Cambodians fled to Vietnam and Thailand. Most fled in 1979, after the Vietnamese chased the Khmer Rouge from power. Approximately 150,000 Cambodians have been resettled in the United States. In contrast to the Vietnamese and Laotian diasporas, which are hampered by political tensions born in the Cold War, many overseas Cambodians are involved in Cambodia's recovery and development, and some have returned to work in the country. This is due in part to policies by the United Nations and Western donors to try to use overseas Khmer as consultants and project managers whenever possible.

³ LANGUAGE

The official language of the State of Cambodia is Cambodian. It is probable that 2,000 years ago the inhabitants of Cambodia were speaking a language related to the modern Cambodian language that the Khmer speak. Pockets of people speaking languages related to Cambodian exist all over Southeast Asia and probably represent an older linguistic and cultural tradition that was eventually pushed into the highlands by invading lowlanders.

Cambodian has borrowed extensively from the administrative, military, and literary vocabulary of Sanskrit. Theravada Buddhism brought additional Pali words. In addition, Cambodians have borrowed words from Thai, French, Chinese, and Vietnamese. English words are becoming more common.

The Cambodian language is atonal in contrast to both Vietnamese and Thai. Cambodian also has a number of disyllabic words, adding prefixes and infixes to modify the basic syllable.

The Cambodian script is quite exotic looking to Westerners and is based on an ancient Brahmi script from South India. The earliest evidence of this script comes from the 2nd or 3rd century. The widespread destruction of books and other documents during the Khmer Rouge period created a great deficit in available Cambodian literature, but international projects to return materials in Khmer that had been held overseas have helped to address this deficit.

⁴ FOLKLORE

The first hero of Cambodia was Kaundinya, who is also the legendary first Cambodian. Cambodians trace their origin to the marriage of a handsome prince who traveled to Cambodia with a magical bow. When a dragon princess rowed out to meet him, he shot an arrow at her boat. Frightened, she agreed to marry him. In exchange for the clothes he gave the naked princess, her father drank up the water that covered the land that became Cambodia.

It has been more difficult for Cambodians to admire present-day leaders, especially for any length of period. Undoubtedly the most important and most revered Cambodian in recent times has been Norodom Sihanouk. Appointed King by the French in the 1940s, he later became Prince so that he could continue to act as a political rather than a monarchical leader. In 1970 he was deposed and continued until 1993 as a leader around whom opposition groups of various persuasions collected. After the United Nations-sponsored elections, he returned to Cambodia as its figurehead leader. Especially honored by older peasants, Sihanouk continues to be a pivotal figure in his country.

⁵ RELIGION

Most Cambodians are Theravada Buddhists. Theravada Buddhism is one of the two main Buddhist sects and is practiced also in Thailand and Laos. Cambodians are so Buddhist that they often say, "To be Cambodian is to be Buddhist." Khmer Buddhists believe in karma and reincarnation. They believe that the acts they do today will affect their lives in the future, either in this or future lives. The Buddhist religion allows Cambodians a way to gain merit so they may be reborn to a better life. They gain merit by a myriad of good acts and religious deeds, which include acting properly, celebrating holy days, and taking food to the monks at the temple. No one can earn as much merit as a man who becomes a monk, whose merit accrues to him and his relatives, primarily his parents. Both Buddhism and some Hindu influences, which continue to be seen in Cambodia, originated in India and were brought into Cambodia at the beginning of the Christian era.

Most Cambodians also follow the traditional practices of their forefathers, which have probably been practiced in Cambodia for millennia. Most believe in a wide pantheon of spirits. These spirits must be fed, placated, and informed of family events; thus, every wedding includes a ceremony to notify family spirits that a new member is joining the family.

Cambodian Cham are Muslims, many Vietnamese are Roman Catholic, the hill tribes are primarily traditionalists, and the Chinese Cambodians are Taoist or Buddhists.

⁶ MAJOR HOLIDAYS

All holidays in Cambodia are both religious and secular events. The most important festivals are Buddhist festivals. Among them are the celebration of the birth, enlightenment, and death of the Buddha, the monks' entry into and exit from the rainy season retreat; the Festival of the Dead; and offerings to the monks, called Kathin.

One of the most important holidays of the Cambodian year is New Year, which is celebrated at the beginning of the lunar month, usually in April. This is the time when most Cambodians begin preparing their rice fields for planting and sowing their rice seedbeds. The New Year celebration lasts several days and is an extremely joyous time. There are religious ceremonies, dancing, music, and games.

The Festival of the Dead, or Prachum Ben, occurs in the fall. During the fortnight of celebration, offerings are made to the ancestors in the hope they will protect their descendants.

⁷ RITES OF PASSAGE

The birth of a child is a wonderful and dangerous time for Cambodian families. While they welcome the coming of a new member of the family, they worry about spirits who are especially threatening to pregnant women, women in childbirth, and newborn babies. Women, and often their husbands, especially in rural areas, observe a number of rules to protect their family. After the birth, the woman drinks a special concoction of herbs, water, and alcohol to help her regain her physical equilibrium, while bracelets and anklets blessed by the monks or healers are placed on their babies.

Toddlers are nursed until two to four years of age and are treated with considerable lenience. At about four, children are expected to feed, bathe, and control themselves, and shortly thereafter to care for their younger siblings.

For many Cambodian children, parents continue to exert almost complete control over them until they are married. Even then, the influence of their parents is heavy. Children are expected to show great respect to their parents and elders and are severely punished for any lapse. While the Khmer Rouge loosened the traditional control of parents over their children, and modernization in urban areas continues to threaten traditional respect and obedience toward parents, most Cambodians continue to observe traditional family behavior. Children become full adults when they have jobs and their own households, spouses, and children. Even then, they are expected to follow the advice of their elders.

Most Cambodians are cremated at death and their ashes are put in a repository, or *stupa*, at the local Buddhist temple. If initially buried, the body is exhumed after several years, and the bones are taken to a stupa. In addition to having a funeral, Cambodians celebrate anniversary ceremonies after the death of a family member.

8 INTERPERSONAL RELATIONS

When Cambodians meet, they greet each other with the *sampeah*: joining their palms together, their fingers pointing up or slightly tilted toward the other person, they bring their hands up to their chest or forehead. The higher the status of the person they are greeting, the higher their hands go. They may also bow their head as they sampeah.

Cambodians place great importance on hierarchy and proper behavior. Women must respect men, children must respect their elders, and everyone must respect their superiors, which includes anyone with higher status, greater wealth, or a more important job. Inferiors greet their superiors with greater respect, a deeper bow, or greater stoop when offering food or passing by. Cambodians thus tend to be more reserved before those they consider their superiors, or with strangers. Visitors, both familiar and strange, are treated to the best the household has to offer.

Few young people date. Virginity remains highly valued for brides, although premarital sex is becoming more accepted in urban areas, especially among young professional Cambodians. Girls and boys have the opportunity to talk and flirt only on special occasions, surrounded by relatives and neighbors.

Most men marry between 19 and 25 years of age; women are slightly younger, usually between 16 and 22. Most young people continue to court as did their parents. It remains much more common for a young man to ask his parents' permission and assistance in obtaining a wife than to do so on his own. His parents, or a matchmaker, approach the young woman's family to see if they are interested in a match. If the response is positive, the families negotiate the terms and time of the marriage.

After an exchange of gifts, the young couple marry. It is still common for many young couples to spend the first year of marriage in the home of the woman's parents. After the parents are assured of their son-in-law's stability, or after the birth of the first child, the young couple commonly moves into a new house built for them by their families.

9 LIVING CONDITIONS

Health care in the country has been devastated by the events of the past decades. Unable to obtain health care during the second half of the 1970s, the inadequate food, cruelty, and horrors of those years has had dreadful consequences on Cambodians, both physically and mentally. One legacy from this period is the high level of personal violence seen in Cambodia, which runs the gamut from spousal relations to politics. The subsequent isolation of Cambodia from much of the international community and the embargo against most imports and aid meant that Cambodians went another decade without even reaching minimum standards of modern health care.

International health assistance has improved services to many people, but much of this aid has been cut back in recent years. Cambodians continue to patronize local healers and spiritual leaders for most health needs. Modern medicine is expensive, with patients having to pay before being seen for services and medicines supposedly offered without fee.

While Cambodians long for the amenities of modern culture, with which they are becoming increasingly familiar through television and periodic visits or work trips to the larger cities, most cannot afford these items. The most important and frequently seen consumer items are imported from Vietnam, Thailand, and other Southeast Asian countries and are generally inexpensive. Most Cambodians own few objects they have not made themselves, while a tiny percentage of the urban population enjoy luxuries, including expensive villas, furnishings, cars, servants, clothing, and liquors.

Most rural Cambodians live in small villages of 200 or 300 people. Their houses are typically aligned along a river, stream, canal, or road. Houses are built on stilts to keep them above the floods of the rainy season. Poorer Cambodians live in single-room dwellings with thatched roofs and walls. With additional money, Cambodians add wooden walls, another room or two, windows, and tile roofs. Newer houses may have sheet metal roofs. The kitchen is attached to the side of the house.

Furniture is simple. Beds are woven plastic or thatch mats, rolled up and stored leaning against the wall or up in the rafters during the day. There may be a small desk, a chair or two, and a storage cabinet. Most families have little furniture, instead sporting baskets, water jugs, kitchen utensils, and a book or two. An altar to the spirits and ancestors, also high on the wall, may have a small glass of alcohol or water, a dish of fruit or sticky rice, a candle, and incense sticks.

Much living occurs under the house, where platforms provide sitting and siesta space. Both humans and animals benefit from the shade during the hot season and protection from the rain during the rainy season. Cambodians work, visit, eat, and sleep under the house during the daytime and retreat to their houses in the cool and darkness of the evening.

In the cities, Cambodians live in houses ranging from villas to a rag on the sidewalk. Wealthier Cambodians live in two- and three-story houses and apartments with electricity and running water. Less affluent Cambodians live in smaller apartments, often with many family members to a room.

The vast majority of Cambodians have never ridden in an airplane, car, bus, or motorized boat. Most, however, have paddled a boat. Many consider themselves lucky if their family owns a bicycle, and the dream of most youth and adults is to be able to purchase a motorbike. It is not unusual in the cities to see a whole family out for a ride, all on one motorbike: the father driving, a child sandwiched between him and his wife behind him, another on the handlebars, another in his wife's arms, and yet another in his lap. Everywhere in Cambodia, however, the commonest form of transport continues to be by foot.

¹⁰ FAMILY LIFE

The husband is the head of the family and its public spokesperson. He is responsible for providing the family's shelter and food. In the countryside, his duties include plowing and harrowing the rice field, threshing rice, caring for animals and household tools, and working at additional jobs if necessary to support the family. In the city, he generally works outside the house.

The Cambodian wife controls her family's purse strings, handling money and determining income and expenditures. In the countryside, her duties include caring for children and home, transplanting, harvesting and winnowing the rice, and caring for the garden. In the city, she may work out of the home, most commonly as a tradesperson. The Khmer wife is also considered the ethical and religious heart of her family. Cambodians say as she acts, so do her children.

Cambodian families have traditionally been smaller than Chinese or Vietnamese families, with the ideal of most being to have about five children. Cambodians value children and rely on them for assistance with supporting the family when they are young and their parents when they are old. Women especially, however, appreciate birth control information and contraceptive technology, if only to better control the timing of their family's growth.

Like the first Cambodian, Kaundinya, in much of Cambodia a young man is expected to gain the approval of his future parents-in-law by living and working with them before or after his marriage to their daughter. The traditional wedding is long and elaborate; Cambodians complain that expenses now cause weddings to be much shorter, cut from three to one or one-and-a-half days. The ceremony, which includes a blessing by the local healer, monks, family elders, and neighbors, is followed by a banquet as elegant as the family can afford.

In the past, both divorce and multiple wives were the luxury of rich people. Now, however, divorce is more common. It continues to be easier for men than women, and, since the relative number of women is higher than men, men are able not only to abandon a wife, they may have multiple wives.

The primary economic, cooperative, and emotional unit is a husband, wife, and their children. The nuclear family is surrounded by the personal kindred of the husband and wife, which extends back two or three generations. Beyond that are the *nek ta*, or family spirits, who continue to watch over their descendants. Cambodians form close relationships also with neighbors and hold monks and healers in high regard.

Few Cambodian children have pets; instead, animals, like people, have jobs. Domesticated animals, such as water buffalo, oxen, pigs, and fowl, are used to support the family, and children are thus discouraged from treating them as pets. Even cats and dogs have jobs: dogs to guard the home, cats to kill the rats. Only a few of the wealthier people in the cities view animals as pets.

¹¹ CLOTHING

Many Cambodians continue to wear traditional clothing. Women wear a sampot and men a sarong. Both are wraparound cotton or silk skirts that fall to the knee. With the sampot Khmer women wear a white blouse or shirt, while men go bare-chested or wear a light-colored shirt over their sarong.

Many Cambodians, especially men, prefer to wear Western trousers and shirts, usually short-sleeved. Women also, especially in urban areas, are shifting to Western-style dresses, trousers, and tops.

The quintessential Cambodian piece of clothing is a *krama*, a long slender scarf worn in a multitude of ways. Krama is most commonly worn around the neck, but also as a head turban or scarf, a skirt, blouse, purse, or baby sling. The everyday krama is usually checkered, but fancier ones may be made of silk and come in a variety of colors and styles. Nearly every Cambodian owns a krama and many Western visitors as well.

Since the terrible Khmer Rouge years, when people were forced to wear dark clothes and were punished or killed for wearing colors or jewelry, and the years following, when they were too poor to buy what they wanted, Cambodians have delighted in the return of a prospering economy and brightly-colored and printed fabric and clothing in the marketplaces. Still, poverty is widespread, and most Cambodians can purchase only imported second-hand clothing.

Most Cambodian children wear Western-style clothing: their best shorts or skirts and shirts for school, old ones for home and work. Children go barefoot, while their parents wear rubber thongs or sandals.

¹² FOOD

Rice is the most important Cambodian food. Eaten at virtually every meal, it forms the basis of most Khmer dishes. Cambodians distinguish rice by species, taste, area, and growing season.

Fish is almost as important and is eaten fresh, dried, and salted. Cambodians fish for lake chub, carp, eels, and numerous other species. The Tonle Sap itself is one of the richest freshwater fisheries in the world. Fish abound in these waters and can be easily taken, especially when the waters begin to recede, and the fish are left literally high and dry. When the Tonle Sap River again begins to flow to the sea, tens of thousands of fishermen rush to the Lake. With dams and traps, they capture the millions of fish caught in the area of decreasing water. As noted above, however, recent changes to the lake threaten this important source of food and livelihood for Cambodia.

Vegetables are a vital part of the Cambodian diet. Cambodians grow a number of crops in their gardens, including onions, peppers, eggplant, tomatoes, and potatoes. Many homes are also surrounded by coconut and banana trees and numerous other plants. An especially loved treat is the durien fruit, horrid-smelling but delicious in taste. Other fruits include mangoes, papayas, jack fruit, and palm fruit. The sugar palm also yields syrup, which is used in cooking.

A typical traditional meal that continues to be part of Cambodians' main diet is a bowl of steamed rice eaten with a sauce containing bits of fish, fowl or meat, eggs, vegetables, and spices, such as onions, chilies, garlic, mint, ginger, or lemon grass. On special occasions Cambodians eat fried rice, noodles, Vietnamese pou soup, chicken curry, barbecued shrimp, duck eggs served with the almost-hatched ducklings still inside, roasted sunflower seeds, and rice cakes containing beans or banana. Tea is served by everyone who can afford it, although soft drinks and beer are becoming more common, especially in urban areas.

The most traditional of Cambodian foods is *prahok*, fermented fish, which is used as a thick sauce condiment with other dishes. Betel nut is another favorite, a seed that is wrapped in leaves and chewed for its mild narcotic effect. Chewers, primarily older women, are obvious from the dark red juice they spit, which stains their gums and teeth.

Cambodians usually eat an early meal of left-over rice, cakes, or fruit either at home or in the field. The big meal of the day is lunch around midday, followed by supper at twilight.

Cambodians eat together, usually with the family seated in a circle on the floor of their house. Each has a bowl of rice, and all take bites of food from several dishes sitting in the middle of the group. When eating on the job, away from the house, or under the house, Cambodians may eat sitting in a squatting position, their feet flat on the ground, their knees bent sharply, and their bottoms hanging almost to the ground. Whether squatting or sitting on the ground, the men cross-legged or, like the women, with their legs folding back to one side, Cambodians can sit for hours in positions that are uncomfortable for Westerners after just a few minutes.

Most Cambodians eat with two basic eating utensils, a spoon and a fork. Others, however, including some urban Cambodians, Chinese Cambodians, and Vietnamese living in Cambodia, use chopsticks. Many urban Khmer use spoons and forks at home, and chopsticks at restaurants and at Vietnamese soup shops on the street.

Cambodians seldom fail to share a bit of their meal with the spirits, putting a small amount of food, fruit, or liquid in a receptacle before the indoor altar or outdoor spirit house.

13 EDUCATION

Traditionally, education was provided primarily to boys at temple schools. There they were taught religion and the religious language of Pali by Buddhist monks. After independence and before the 1970s, Cambodia developed an educational system built on the French model. Elementary and secondary schooling was expanded enormously for both boys and girls throughout the country. Colleges and technical schools were built in large numbers and attendance increased from a mere handful to over 9,000. Most boys and some girls learned to read and write a little Khmer.

During the war of the early 1970s and Khmer Rouge rule, traditional and Western-style education came to a virtual standstill. Schools were destroyed, and those who had been teachers or students and those caught attempting to teach or learn religious or Western knowledge were severely punished or killed. Cambodia had to begin again to build a system of education.

Most children begin school at age seven or eight and receive some schooling for at least several years. While parents want their children to become educated, seeing education as the path to better employment and freedom from poverty, families can ill afford to pay their children's school fees, books, or clothing, or to free their children from household chores.

14 CULTURAL HERITAGE

During the Khmer Rouge regime of the late 1970s, Cambodians were not allowed to sing or dance on pain of death. It was a loss that hurt them deeply, for Cambodians say that to dance and to listen to Cambodian music is one of life's sweetest pleasures. Most Cambodians sing, and traditional orchestras, with their various kinds of guitars, xylophones, violins, gongs, and drums, are greatly appreciated.

Traditional dance has been the pride of Cambodians for a thousand years. Children undergo years of training in order to execute the intricate moves of court and classical dance. Their costumes are elaborate and expensive, so tightly fitted that the dancers must be dressed, even sewn into their outfits of silk and velvet. Their hand gestures and body movements mirror those seen on buildings of Angkor built over 800 years ago.

In the villages, troupes of costumed young men and women perform various folk dances. Everywhere throughout the country on special occasions, Cambodians dance the traditional circle dance, moving slowly several steps forward, then back, all the time twirling their arms and hands in the air.

Cambodian plays, which include both dance and music, tell ancient stories of Hindu gods and heroes, folktales about beautiful and wealthy royalty, greedy merchants, and noble youth, and comic stories that delight everyone.

Cambodian literature begins with inscriptions from the 7th century and continues through the classical work of the 16 and 17th centuries. Traditional texts were memorized by professional storytellers, who traveled from place to place performing. Many of these oral traditions were written down in the mid-20th century and used as textbooks in classrooms. Cambodian literature also includes tales of the Buddha's lives, verses that contain advice for daily life called *chbap*, and folktales.

Traditional Cambodian literature is being overshadowed by modern radio and movies, and especially by television and videos. From city-dwellers to inhabitants of the more remote villages, most Cambodian youth would rather watch a martial arts video from Hong Kong than listen to a storyteller relate ancient stories.

Cambodian pride in ancient heritage has resulted in sharp tension with neighbors in recent years. A remark by a Thai soap opera actress impugning the origins of Ankor Wat resulted in anti-Thai riots in Phnom Penh that ultimately resulted in the destruction of the Thai embassy and led the Thai government to evacuate Thai citizens from the city. Cambodia and Thailand have also taken a dispute over ownership of an ancient temple to an international court.

15 WORK

Most Cambodians are rice farmers who also grow vegetables and fruit in family gardens around the house. Others cultivate cash crops, either on a small scale or on large plantations. Most Cambodian farmers also raise domestic animals, most commonly water buffalo or oxen, which are used to plow the fields, pigs, ducks, and chickens.

Cambodians spend much of the slack season from cultivating rice in crafting items they will use to support their family in the coming seasons: stringing fish nets, twisting vines into string or rope, and making pots for carrying water or cooking.

As the economy improves, however, more Cambodians are buying plastic or metal tools and utensils in the marketplace rather than making them for themselves from the vines and wood around them. Thus, colorful plastic utensils and enduring metal tools are replacing the handicrafts Cambodians have practiced for centuries. A village that has "since long ago" made earthenware pots is now selling them for pennies to tourists because, as the people say, Cambodians can buy modern pots imported from Thailand and Vietnam cheaper in the market.

In the cities, Cambodians hold all the jobs seen in most cities of the world: government officials, construction workers, taxi cab drivers, waiters and maids, retailers. However, in contrast to some Southeast Asian countries, there are few Cambodian financiers. This is because the financial sector had been dominated by ethnic Chinese prior to 1975. Many Cambodians are soldiers, many coming from former resistance armies. Demobilization of the armed forces only began in earnest in the late 1990s and reintegrating soldiers into Cambodian society has proved to be a complex undertaking. This has been made more difficult by political struggles between Cambodian politicians, all of whom are reluctant to give up the forces that had been pledged to them during the decades of civil war.

16 SPORTS

In Cambodian villages, children spend a few years of their lives in school. The rest of their time is spent helping their families make a living. Even the smallest children help their parents fish, cook, gather firewood, and do a variety of chores. Both boys and girls help with younger children, and it is not uncommon to see boys carrying a baby sister for hours at a time.

Children are often responsible for caring for the animals. Boys herd the water buffalo and oxen when they are not being used for plowing, and girls feed the pigs and chickens. Boys climb up sugar palm or coconut trees seeking syrup or coconuts. In some parts of the country they hunt for rats, lizards, snakes, small fish, and crabs to supplement the family diet.

Children usually turn these subsistence activities into play and games. In addition, they enjoy swimming and running. A popular village game is played with rubber thongs. The boys draw a line in the dirt, then stand back and throw their sandals at the line. The boy who gets the closest is the winner. Girls and smaller children play a similar game with rubber bands, and the winner wears his captured bands around his wrist. Girls also play hopscotch.

The most popular spectator and participant sport is soccer. Volleyball is also a favorite and both are seen frequently in rural and urban Cambodia. Other sports include boxing, basketball, and bicycle races. A few Cambodians in urban areas also play tennis and swim. Kite-flying and canoe-racing, although not as popular as before the Khmer Rouge period, remain desirable activities, and communities not yet able to afford either look forward to the day when they can.

17 ENTERTAINMENT AND RECREATION

Movies, television, and videos are extremely popular in both the urban and rural areas, although they are more accessible in the cities where people have more money and there are numerous theaters. Televisions are becoming more common in the villages, most battery-operated since electricity in rural areas is nonexistent or rare. Villagers carry their batteries to a recharging store with a generator and pick them up again in the early evening so the family may watch television together at night.

Also popular are videos, which circulate from family to family. Village cafes and bars charge patrons to watch videos. These draw large crowds, many including children standing outside and into the roadway hoping to catch a glimpse of martial arts films made in Hong Kong, Singapore, and other neighboring countries.

Karaoke is popular and can be found in the fanciest clubs in the capital of Phnom Penh to the humblest village. For the price of a beer, Cambodians, usually men, sing along to the music and lyrics printed on the video and played over the television set.

In the villages, local festivals remain the most common and popular leisure activity. Eating, music by local or traveling bands, videos, games, drinking, and dancing fill the hours.

Government officials estimated that by 1967 almost every Cambodian home had a transistor radio. This vastly increased the contact Cambodians had with their government and their sense of being one nation. The Khmer Rouge destroyed virtually all of these radios, and it has taken some time for Cambodia to regain the communication network it had prior to the 1970s. This process was given a boost by the United Nations in the early 1990s as the UN relied upon radio to communicate with the population in the lead-up to the 1993 election. As of 2008 television and radio link most Cambodians to their government, popular culture, and imported entertainment.

18 FOLK ART, CRAFTS, AND HOBBIES

The greatest handiwork of Cambodians was crafted during the Angkorean Period, from the 9th to the 14th centuries, when Cambodian rule spread from Vietnam to Burma. During those centuries, Cambodian architects designed and Cambodian slaves built a number of temples and palaces in the Angkor region of northwest Cambodia. Included in these is what most consider to be the grandest of all, a priceless jewel of artistic work, the temple mausoleum of Angkor Wat.

Traditional crafts include carvings in stone and wood, jewelry-making, and gold-and-silver working. Artists often copy ancient religious designs: statues of the Buddha, Hindu gods, scenes from the Ramayana, an ancient Hindu epic, and designs from the ancient temples of Angkor. Silk weaving is another craft practiced by many Cambodians, who weave gorgeous and colorful fabric for *sampot* and *karma*, which are sold in the marketplace to both Cambodians and tourists.

19 SOCIAL PROBLEMS

Members of a hierarchical Buddhist society, Cambodians have always viewed their lot in life as the consequence of activities in previous lives. Thus, Cambodians have traditionally accepted their position in life with more equanimity than non-Buddhists.

During the Khmer Rouge regime, human and civil rights in Cambodia were nonexistent. Most nations consider the Democratic Kampuchean government to have been one of the cruelest of modern times. With the end of the Khmer Rouge as a political force and efforts by the United Nations to bring the remaining KR to a war crimes tribunal, Cambodians have found themselves reliving some of the Khmer Rouge era days—at least psychologically—as the trials go forward.

Most Cambodians view politicians as venal and rapacious and often take a resigned approach to corruption. The dominant party, which dates back to the Vietnamese occupation of the 1980s, has managed to regain almost total control. This is due not only to the party's own authoritarian practices but also to the weaknesses of other parties. Although human and civil rights are still under siege in Cambodia, the legacy of the United Nations period is still seen in terms of human rights advocacy groups, the press, and the overall non-governmental sector, all of which compare favorably to some other states in the region. Apart from these issues, however, Cambodians are experiencing more peace than they have for decades and value that highly. In 2003 a public opinion survey showed that a majority of Cambodians associate peace with the concept of democracy, rather than electoral politics.

20 GENDER ISSUES

There are two distinct problems involving gender issues in Cambodia. First, despite the influence of Western donors and the fact that decades of war have made Cambodia a female-majority country, in comparison to neighboring countries, Cambodian women have not achieved high positions in government, commerce, or education. This implies a lack of social mobility in the country as a whole. Secondly, although both domestic violence and human trafficking are illegal, Cambodia suffers from high levels of both problems. Rape is more common than in other Southeast Asian countries. Although trafficking of women has been a serious problem since the 1990s, many accounts of this problem do not reflect that fact that more ethnic Vietnamese women in Cambodia are forced into prostitution than ethnic Khmer.

21 BIBLIOGRAPHY

Chandler, David P. *A History of Cambodia.* Boulder, CO: Westview Press, 1983.

Coates, Karen J. *Cambodia Now: Life in the Wake of War.* Jefferson, N.C.: McFarland, 2005.

Ebihara, M. M. Svay. "A Khmer Village in Cambodia." Ph.D. diss., Columbia University, 1968.

Ebihara, M. M., C. A. Mortland, and J. Ledgerwood. *Cambodian Culture since 1975. Homeland and Exile.* Ithaca, NY: Cornell University Press, 1994.

Edmonds, I. G. *The Khmers of Cambodia. The Story of a Mysterious People.* New York: The Bobbs-Merrill Company, Inc., 1970.

Mortland, Carol A. "Khmer," In *Refugees in America in the 1990s. A Reference Handbook.* D. W. Haines, ed. Westport, CT: Greenwood Press, 1996.

Ollier, Leakthina Chau-Pech and Tim Winter, eds. *Expressions of Cambodia: The Politics of Tradition, Identity, and Change.* New York: Routledge, 2006.

Ross, Russell R. *Cambodia. A Country Study.* Washington D.C.: U.S. Government Printing Office, 1990.

Vecchia, Stefano. *Khmer: History and Treasures of an Ancient Civilization.* Vercelli, Italy: White Star, 2007.

—revised by C. Dalpino

KOLIS

PRONUNCIATION: KOH-leez
LOCATION: India (primarily Maharashtra and Gujarat states)
POPULATION: About 12 million
LANGUAGE: Dialects of Marathi or Gujarati, or the language of the region of India in which they live
RELIGION: Hindu; small numbers of Muslims
RELATED ARTICLES: Vol. 3: Hindus; People of India; Vol. 4: Muslims in South Asia

1 INTRODUCTION

Koli is a vague term covering the tribal populations living in parts of western India. Although traditionally classed as a tribe inferior in status to the Kunbis, the cultivating caste of the region, Kolis have now been designated as a Hindu caste in some areas. It is possible that the name of the tribe is derived from the Sanskrit *kula,* meaning "clan." There are numerous groupings and sub-groupings among the Kolis, who tend to be endogamous, i.e. they do not intermarry with the Kolis of other regions. Kolis are thus a group of tribes or castes, rather than a monolithic entity. Some writers suggest that the English word *coolie,* meaning porter or hired laborer, comes from *Koli.*

The origin of the Kolis remains a matter of debate. One view holds that they entered the region from Sindh and were part of the White Huns. Another theory links them to the Kol and Munda tribes of east-central India. One branch of the Kolis, the Son Kolis or Sea Kolis, are thought to have settled in the region of Bombay (Mumbai) during the 12th century ad, where, today, they are usually fishermen. The other branch of the Kolis, the Hill Kolis, acquired a widespread reputation as "hill robbers." Kolis are generally held to be of low social status and are classified either as Dalits ("Untouchables"), Sudras or as a Scheduled Tribe. In some localities, however, Kolis claim Rajput blood, follow Rajput customs, and have a relatively high social position. Thus the Khant, Bariya, and Thakore Kolis of Gujarat give brides to Rajputs, converted Rajputs, and Muslims, but never give their daughters to lower caste Kolis such as the Pagis and Kotwals.

2 LOCATION AND HOMELAND

The Kolis form one of the largest tribal groups in the western part of India. A current estimate of total Koli population is about 12 million, though this figure may well include groups that once were Koli but are now considered as other castes. Kolis are spread through the states of Maharashtra and Gujarat, with small communities also found in Rajasthan, Madhya Pradesh, and Orissa. The Son Kolis are concentrated in the coastal areas around Bombay. Other Koli groups are found in the interior of Gujarat and the upland regions of Maharashtra and Madhya Pradesh. Kolis are also found in Sindh and areas of the Thar Desert east of the river in the lower Indus Valley in Pakistan. They are primarily Hindu, a relic of pre-Partition days, and culturally and linguistically they are very similar to the nomadic Rabari and other peoples in the region. Kolis in that region of Pakistan include the Parkari Koachchhi, the Wadiyara Koli, the Kutchhi Kohli (or Lohar), and the Tharadari Koli. Koli communities in Pakistan also view their social standing somewhat differently. Thus the Kutchhi Kohli, even though they are classed as a Scheduled Tribe in Gujarat State, consider themselves to be superior to other Hindus, and at least equal with Brahmans.

³ LANGUAGE

Kolis speak the language of their localities. Thus, most speak one of the numerous dialects of Marathi or Gujarati, both of which belong to the Indo-Aryan language family. These languages are written in the Devanagari and Gujarati scripts, respectively.

⁴ FOLKLORE

According to legend, the Kolis are the descendants of the black dwarf who is believed to have emerged from the body of King Vena. The *Mahabharata* and other ancient texts tell that Vena was a wise and just king who ruled many tribes and peoples in eastern India. However, he became corrupted and abandoned the true faith, prohibiting all worship and sacrifice, except to himself. His religious advisers tried in vain to reason with him, but to no avail. Finally, in exasperation, they killed him with blades of the sacred *kusa* grass that miraculously became swords in their hands. To secure a successor to rule the country, the rishis rubbed Vena's thigh and there emerged a dark, dwarfish man, representing the evil nature of the King. This dwarf is said to be the ancestor of the Kolis.

⁵ RELIGION

Except for a small number of converts to Islam, Kolis are Hindu and their religious practices conform to Hindu norms. They retain, however, many aspects of their former animism. For instance, the Talapada Kolis of Gujarat worship numerous *devi* or goddesses who appear tribal rather than Hindu in origin. These goddesses protect against various kinds of diseases and ailments, and their help is sought in making decisions in daily life. Goddess-worship has acquired aspects of the *sakti* cult, and every household has its family goddess or *Mata*. These family goddesses may be known by different names, but they are all represented by terra-cotta figures that are basically triangular in shape and smeared with red coloring. Swords kept alongside the figure are supposed to belong to the goddess, being used by her to drive away evil. In Gujarat, individuals known as *bhua* go into a trance and are thought to communicate directly with the goddess, answering questions put to her by the gathered audience. The bhua are also consulted in the case of sickness, as the Kolis believe that disease is caused by malevolent spirits.

Regional deities are of some importance. The Son Kolis of Maharashtra, for instance, worship the god Khandoba, who is believed to be an incarnation of Shiva. The Kolis of Nimar in Madhya Pradesh worship the goddess Bhawani, and every family has a silver image of the deity in the house.

⁶ MAJOR HOLIDAYS

Kolis celebrate the important festivals of the Hindu calendar cycle. In addition, they observe various festivals that are agricultural in nature. There are, however, festivals that are exclusively Koli. Among the Talapada Kolis of central Gujarat, for instance, Attam is the occasion when special foods and prayers are offered to the family goddess. People gather at the family *math* or shrine, which is redecorated for the event. Special food

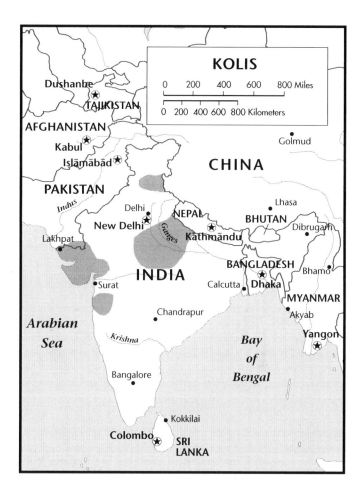

(molasses, rice, lentils, wheat, and peanut oil) are offered to the deity and then cooked for a family feast. Coconuts are broken open to ensure health and prosperity for the family. Other Koli celebrations, such as Hutasni, are Hindu festivals to which the Kolis have attached their own beliefs and rituals.

⁷ RITES OF PASSAGE

No special diet or restrictions are imposed on Koli women in Gujarat during pregnancy. The child is delivered with the aid of the village midwife. After delivery, the umbilical cord is cut with a sickle, and the afterbirth is buried in the courtyard of the house along with some salt. Mother and child are subject to a period of ritual pollution (*sutak*) lasting 37 days, after which various purification ceremonies are undertaken. Subsequently, the child undergoes the naming ceremony and the ear- and nose-piercing ceremony. It is common for both boys and girls to be tattooed, usually between the ages of 8 and 12, but definitely before marriage.

After death, the corpse is bathed. A sacred *tulsi* (basil) leaf and a piece of silver are placed in the mouth to purify the body. The body is dressed in white clothes and, if the deceased was unmarried, anointed with turmeric as a ritual of marriage. Marriage is necessary for the departed to be a full-fledged member of the community. Those who have not achieved this status are symbolically married as part of the funeral rites. The body is carried to the cremation grounds and placed on the funeral pyre facing north, the direction in which Paradise is believed to lie. On the eleventh or thirteenth day after death, the final rites of *karj* are performed. This expensive ceremony requires that various goods such as food, cooking utensils, clothes, and household items be offered to the deceased through a Brahman priest. It is through the Brahman, the purest of caste, that these goods will reach the dead. The funeral rites are completed by a lavish feast for friends and relations. The eldest son feeds a crow delicacies prepared on this occasion. It is thought that this bird is the only creature that can reach the city of the dead.

8 INTERPERSONAL RELATIONS

Although Kolis are often forced to leave their native villages in search of employment, they exhibit strong kinship ties with deep roots in the worship of family deities. It is usual for family members to return to the family home at the time of festivals honoring the family goddesses.

9 LIVING CONDITIONS

The typical Koli house is enclosed by four high walls, with access from the street through a wooden door that opens into a courtyard. Along one side of the yard is a shed for cattle and other livestock, and areas for storing fodder and the cow-dung cakes used for fuel. On the opposite side of the courtyard from the cattle sheds, steps lead up to the family's living quarters. The focus of this is the *math*, the shrine where the family gods and household idols are kept. In addition, there are the kitchen and rooms used for living and sleeping. Most rooms in Koli houses are lined with shelves holding household utensils. Wooden cots *(charpai)* are used for sleeping and resting. Women are not segregated to any particular part of the house, and married men sleep with their wives and children in the same room. Daughters-in-law maintain *purdah* (seclusion) from male members of the family by covering their face.

10 FAMILY LIFE

Kolis are divided into numerous branches such as the Talapada Kolis, the Mahadeo Kolis, and the Dhor Kolis. These are essentially regional groupings that are endogamous and do not intermarry. Each endogamous group, however, is organized into exogamous clans. One does not marry within one's clan, and before a marriage Kolis ascertain that the families are unrelated up to four ascending generations. Marriages are arranged, and girls marry at a young age. The actual ceremony is performed by a Brahman and in general follows Hindu rites. A bride-price is commonly paid to the family of the girl. Sometimes a wealthy father refuses to accept the bride price, an action that raises his social standing in the community. The new bride enters the household of her husband, where she assumes her role as the dutiful daughter-in-law.

11 CLOTHING

Koli clothing reflects regional patterns in dress. In the Saurashtra region of Gujarat, for example, Koli men wear pants like pajamas that are skintight from the knee downwards and loose and baggy above. A sleeveless waistcoat called a *bandi* is worn in the summer. In the winter, however, this is replaced by a full-sleeved, high-necked blouse. This is fitted under the armpits but then flares out to the waist in pleats. This dress, which is typically Gujarati, is invariably white in color. A white turban or *pagri* is worn on the head. Men wear heavy leather shoes, with pointed toes, that are heavily sequined with brass.

Traditional dress for Koli women consists of a blouse and a full-length, slitted skirt with an embroidered edge. A length of cloth 2.5 m (8 ft) long known as *odhni* is tucked in at the waist and drawn over the head. Sometimes women wear the traditional Indian *choli* and *sari*. Koli women are fond of jewelry and cosmetics and wear an assortment of ornaments in the ear and nose and bangles on the arms and legs. The most prominent feature of Koli personal adornment is tattooing, although this is more extensive on women than on men. The motifs vary from flowers, birds, and figures of gods and goddesses to geometric designs. A girl who is not tattooed before marriage reflects poorly on her family.

12 FOOD

Kolis in Gujarat eat a light breakfast and two meals during the day. Breakfast, taken in the early morning, consists of *bajra-ki-roti* (unleavened millet bread) left over from the previous evening's meal and tea. Goat's milk is used for the tea because it is cheaper than cow's milk. The afternoon meal consists of millet bread and vegetables. Poorer families eat a paste of garlic and chilies with the bread rather than vegetables. In the evening, *khichri* (a dish of lentils and rice boiled together) is eaten with the bread. If available, buttermilk is taken with both meals. For festive occasions, *puris*—deep-fried bread made with wheat flour and stuffed with potato curry—are prepared. In Gujarat, most Kolis are vegetarian, but elsewhere they eat meat. Kolis eat chicken and pork but usually abstain from beef. The Dhor Kolis, however, eat beef and carrion. Fish is a significant element in the diet of the Son Kolis. Fermented liquor and opium are used by Koli men.

13 EDUCATION

The traditional concept of education among Kolis was essentially functionally oriented. Boys were given full freedom to play until they were about five years, at which time they were sent to school—assuming the village had a school and the parents wanted a formal education for their child. Even then, boys were allotted domestic duties, which taught them the basics of cultivation. When farm work became heavy, they used to leave school and work in the fields. As girls were to be married, education for them was deemed superfluous. They used to stay at home, carrying out domestic chores.

Educational levels vary among the Koli tribes, depending on their location and their status. For example, even though literacy among the Dhor Koli (or Kholi Dhor) group in Dadra and Nagar Haveli, a Union Territory on India's west coast, has improved over the last few decades, it is still quite low, especially among females. The Koli in Dadra are classed as a Scheduled Tribe and female literacy among Scheduled Tribes is only 27%. By contrast, literacy among the Mahadeo Koli in Maharashtra is 62.8%, and among females, the 52.9% literacy recorded by the 2001 Census is the highest among the Scheduled Tribes in the State.

Figures for attendance at school are generally quite low for Kolis—in Gujarat State this is 33.4%, the lowest value for any of the Scheduled Tribes. Even though free schooling is provided by the state through the secondary level, for many Koli it is more important to have children help in the field. In Gujarat literacy levels among Kolis are also very low according to the 2001 Census (38.4% and 12.8% for males and females, respectively).

¹⁴ CULTURAL HERITAGE

The Kolis have their own traditions of song and dance and also share in regional cultural traditions. The Kolis of Gujarat, for instance, have incorporated the Gujarati *garba* and *dandya ras* dances into their religious and social ceremonies. Unmarried girls participate in the garba, dancing in a circle while balancing a lighted oil lamp on their heads and singing garba songs. Dandya ras is a stick dance usually performed by men.

¹⁵ WORK

The Kolis fall into two main groups: the Son Kolis, who are skilled fishers, and the Hill Kolis, who engage in numerous occupations. The Chunvalia Kolis were once known for their criminal activities but today are mainly engaged in cultivation or work as agricultural laborers. The traditional occupation of the Dhor Kolis is the tanning of animal hides. Some Kolis have taken to occupations as domestic servants, village watchmen, baggage-handlers, and porters. A few, who have some education, work in government offices and schools.

¹⁶ SPORTS

Games played by children include blind-man's bluff, skipping, and "jacks" played with pebbles or stones. Boys enjoy fighting with bamboo sticks. Males play various board games with cowry shells as game tokens. The "boards" are often just drawn with the fingers on the ground. Hockey and cricket are popular games learned by children in school.

¹⁷ ENTERTAINMENT AND RECREATION

Mass media such as radio, television, and movies are available throughout India. However, access to this entertainment is often limited by economic resources. For many of the poorer classes, and especially those living in more isolated areas, the main forms of recreation are still to be found in festivals, folk traditions, and social events such as marriages.

¹⁸ FOLK ART, CRAFTS, AND HOBBIES

Koli women are particularly adept at embroidery. Girls are taught various types of stitching at a young age. They decorate clothes and make mirrored wall hangings. They also engage in decorative beadwork.

¹⁹ SOCIAL PROBLEMS

While some Koli groups are successful peasant cultivators, many suffer the problems of the depressed classes in any developing society—landlessness, poverty, malnutrition, illiteracy, the burden of rural debt, and lack of the means to escape their situation. Some have left their villages and joined the migration of the rural poor to cities such as Bombay, where they swell the ranks of the urban underclasses. However, a recent study in Pune in Maharashtra State suggests that some Kolis have bettered themselves by moving to the city. The sample Koli population studied in Pune was characterized by a higher standard of living, effective use of birth control, better educational levels, and better nutrition than other groups. While this suggests that for some the flight to the city may be a positive move, it remains to be seen whether this is the exception

to rule. The Kolis remain a tribal community ranked near the lowest economic and social levels of Hindu society.

Although Kolis are primarily agricultural, in Bombay the fishing Kolis face competition from other fishing groups. Thus in the spring of 2004 several fish vendors from the north of India brought a legal suit in the Bombay high court claiming that Koli women did not allow them to enter Bombay's wholesale fish market and that the police had failed to redress their grievances. The Koli Mahila Sangharsha Samiti, a Koli women's organization, had launched an agitation in Mumbai demanding the boycott of North Indian fish vendors at the city's wholesale fish markets. Koli women observed a day-long strike and held several meetings to protest against the entry of the North Indians into the trade.

²⁰ GENDER ISSUES

The relative position of Koli women varies from place to place. In states where Kolis are classified as Scheduled Tribes (Gujarat, Maharashtra, Karnataka, Rajasthan, and the Union Territory of Dadra & Nagar Haveli), Koli women are better off than amongst groups that have been Hinduized. They reap the benefits of being classed as a Scheduled Tribe for which they are eligible (whether or not they take advantage of this) and are generally much freer in their personal lives than their Hindu counterparts.

Even so, marriages among the Koli are usually arranged and the females are often legally children, being married below the age of 18 years (the traditional age for Koli marriage was 5 to 10 years for the girl). Since a bride price is paid to the girl's family it is important that the girl is appropriate and that her family is in good economic standing. In Pakistan even Hindu Kolis adopt *purdah*, and there is considerable friction between the Muslim and Hindu communities.

Hinduized Kolis tend to show patterns of behavior that reflect society at large. Thus there have been reports of bride burning amongst the Kolis, often for failing to bear male children. In 2005 the press reported a case of a pregnant Koli woman who was burned to death because her unborn fetus would have been her third girl child. The husband and mother-in-law were subsequently arrested for murder. Even among Christian Kolis, bigamy—for the purpose of having a son—is not uncommon.

The central government passed the Pre-Natal Diagnostic Techniques (Regulation and Prevention of Misuse) Act in 1996, but abortion of females is still a major issue amongst Kolis. The 2001 Census of India show the Koli Mahadeo to have the lowest sex ratio for over 6 year-olds (964 women to 1000 males) of all the Scheduled Tribes in Maharashtra State, this despite the state passing legislation in 1988 banning selective sex abortion.

Poverty, illiteracy, low socio-economic standing, and cultural norms remain the main obstacles facing Koli women in their attempts to better themselves.

²¹ BIBLIOGRAPHY

Gare, G. M. "Process of Social Change in a Scheduled Tribe: A Case Study of the Mahadeo Kolis in Poona City." *Indian Journal of Social Work* 34, no 2 (July 1973): 131–39.

Ghurye, G. S. *The Mahadeo Kolis*. Bombay: Popular Book Depot, 1963.

Ferreira, J. V. *The Koknas and the Malhar Kolis of the Thane District: A Case Study in the Larger Socio-Cultural Context.* Bombay: Dept. of Sociology, University of Bombay, 1982.

Punekar, Vinaja B. *The Son Kolis of Bombay.* Bombay: Popular Book Depot, 1959.

Roy Burman, J. J. *Sacred Groves among Communities: the Mahadeo Kolis and the Kunbis of the Western Ghats.* New Delhi: Mittal Publications, 2003.

Roy, Shibani. *Koli Culture.* New Delhi: Cosmo Publications, 1983.

Singh, K. S., ed. "Koli." In *People of India.* Vol. 3, *The Scheduled Tribes.* Delhi and Oxford: Oxford University Press with the Anthropological Survey of India, 1994.

—by D. O. Lodrick

KOLS

PRONUNCIATION: KOHLS
LOCATION: India (Madhya Pradesh region)
POPULATION: c. 200,000 (estimate)
LANGUAGE: Local dialect of Hindi; Kol
RELIGION: Hindu; small numbers of Muslims
RELATED ARTICLES: Vol. 3: Hindus; People of India; Vol. 4: Muslims in South Asia

[1] INTRODUCTION

At one time, the name "Kol" was used to identify a group of primitive aboriginal tribes thought to be descended from Negrito and Australoid peoples who had entered India in prehistoric times. These tribes are concentrated in central India and the northeastern regions of the Deccan plateau. They speak related languages described as "Kolarian," which are known today as the Munda languages. The tribes include the Santal, Munda, and Ho. But in modern usage, the term "Kol" is used in a more restricted sense to identify a specific tribe among these Munda-speaking peoples.

The name "Kol" may come from the Mundari word *ko*, meaning "they." Alternatively, it may be derived from *koro* or *horo* (meaning "men,"), a term the Kol use to identify themselves. In legend, the Kol trace their origins to a Sheori or Savari, calling her the "Mother of all Kols." Some try to relate the name "Savari" to the Savaras mentioned in the *Mahabharata* epic, but the name most likely comes from the *Ramayana*. There once was a woman named Sheori, so the story goes. Some people called her "Kolni" (-*ni* is a feminine suffix, so "Kolni" means "a "Kol woman") and others called her "Bhilni." Sheori was a devotee of Bhagwan ("God"), gathering jungle plums for him. Pleased with her devotion, one day Bhagwan offered Sheori favor: she could have a kingdom or a family. Sheori chose a family and gave birth to five sons. The sons eventually went away to various regions and founded the various subdivisions of the Kol. It is interesting to note that some Kol believe they once inhabited the hills of Rajasthan where, with the Bhils, they helped Rana Pratap Singh in his struggle with the Moguls (Mughals).

[2] LOCATION AND HOMELAND

Reliable data on the Kol population is unavailable. The 1981 census reported a population of 132,232 persons. The current population would be approximately about 200,000, assuming growth rates that mirror the national average. The Kol are concentrated in the northern districts of Madhya Pradesh around Jabbalpur and Rewa. Small Kol populations are also found in Orissa and Maharashtra. The region of Madhya Pradesh occupied by the Kol lies in the highlands that define the northern edge of the Indian peninsula. It includes the eastern Vindhya Range, the Bhandar Plateau, and the Kaimur Range. The plateaus and escarpments of the region are crossed by the upper reaches of rivers such as the Narmada, the Son, and the lesser streams draining north to the Ganges. Rainfall averages around 120 cm (47 in). Because the area lies in the interior of the subcontinent, temperatures reach extremes of both heat and cold. Maximum temperatures in May, the hottest month, average over 40°c (104°f), and winter minimums drop below

10°c (50°f). Before roads were built, the terrain and the heavy forest cover made travel to the region difficult. Because of this, it has served as a refuge where some of the oldest peoples in India have survived relatively undisturbed until modern times.

3 LANGUAGE

The Kol language belongs to the Munda languages. However, few Kol speak the Kol language today. In the 2001 census, only some 12,200 persons were identified as Kol speakers, and this total had probably dropped considerably by 2008. The Kol speak local dialects of Hindi and use the Devanagari script for writing. A few Kol are bilingual, speaking Kol and another language such as Hindi or Oriya.

4 FOLKLORE

The Kol have a myth that explains how the cat became a household pet. Once upon a time, so the story goes, Mahadeo (the god Shiva) sent a cat to spy on a certain home. He wanted to know if there was a fire in the house at that time. The cat, which had being staying with Mahadeo for a long time, went to the house. There, she found a fire burning and milk warming beside it and butter on the floor. Eating the butter and drinking the milk, the cat curled up by the fire and went to sleep. She never left the home; she preferred it to the treatment she had received while living with Mahadeo. Since that time, the cat has been a household animal. It is considered a great sin to kill a cat, since it came directly from the god Mahadeo.

5 RELIGION

The Kol identify themselves as Hindus, although their religion has little in common with the higher forms of Hinduism. The Kol believe in a Supreme Deity, Bhagwan, but he is seen as a passive, distant entity. On the rare occasions when he must be approached, the Kol employ Brahmans to intercede on their behalf. Worship of Hindu deities and even of forces of nature is secondary to the worship of village and household gods (*deotas*) and goddesses (*devis*). These deities are believed to influence every aspect of life, and they are central to Kol religious life. They are too numerous to mention by name, but the one most frequently worshipped by the Kol is Khermai. She protects the village, wards off evil spirits, guards against disease, and helps the Kol in their business ventures. Other Kol deities include Shitalamai, the goddess of smallpox, Shardamai and her six sisters, and Gwalbansa Baba, a household god. Each village has its priest (*panda*), who officiates at religious ceremonies, performs sacrifices, and when possessed by the goddess becomes her mouthpiece. Animals (chickens, pigs, goats, and occasionally sheep) are offered as sacrifices to village and household deities. The Kol believe in magic and witchcraft, spirits and ghosts, and the evil eye.

6 MAJOR HOLIDAYS

The Kol observe Hindu festivals such as Holi, Dasahara, and Divali. The Jawara festival, however, appears to be an ancient Kol agricultural festival that later acquired some Hindu characteristics. The name is derived from the *juari* plant, a type of millet. Jawara is held twice a year, in the fall just before the sowing of the winter crop, and in the spring after it has been harvested. The festival lasts for nine days and is celebrated with feasting, singing, and dancing. People worship the village gods

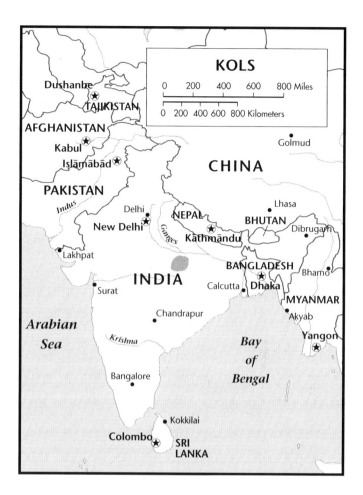

and sacrifice animals at their shrines. Jawara is a time when, it is believed, possession by spirits is common. The focus of the fall festival is the ritual growing of seedlings in the house, partly to predict the coming harvest and possibly as magic to ensure a good one.

7 RITES OF PASSAGE

The Kol have adopted Hindu life-cycle rituals, although older traditions are often apparent in their actual customs and practices. For instance, the Kol take precautions to protect mother and child from the influences of evil spirits. The Kol greatly fear the nightjar, a bird they believe drinks milk from the nursing mother's breast, sometimes causing the death of both baby and mother. Doors are kept closed and branches of the *nim* (margosa) tree are hung over the doorway to protect against the bird. The Chhatthi, or Sixth Day, ceremony marks the end of the period of impurity believed to follow childbirth. Other childhood ceremonies include the naming ceremony, the haircutting ceremony, and the first feeding ceremony. Girls have their ears and nose pierced and they are tattooed when they are between the ages of ten and twelve. No particular initiation rites mark the reaching of puberty, although girls are kept in seclusion during their first menstruation.

When a person is dying, he or she is usually placed on the ground so there is close contact with Mother Earth. The Kol utilize both burial and cremation in their funeral rites, which take place as soon as possible after a death. The body is carried to the burial ground or burning ghat in a procession. Lamentation and weeping are expected to occur, but there should be no singing, chanting, or music of any kind. Once at the place of burial, the body is washed, anointed with oil, and dressed in new white clothes. The grave is dug in a north-south direction, and the body is buried with its head toward the north. The feet point south because that is the direction in which the soul must travel to the land of the dead. If it is cremated, the body is aligned in the same direction on the funeral pyre. The ashes are to be scattered in a sacred river such as the Ganges or the Narmada. If this is not possible, they are placed in a "tank" (reservoir) or a stream, with a small amount kept to be taken to one of the holy rivers in the future. Various purification and mourning rites are carried out. These include the custom of "feeding the dead" for ten days, during which the spirit of the dead person is believed to return to familiar places. A feast on the tenth day (the ninth for a woman) ends the funeral observances.

8 INTERPERSONAL RELATIONS

The Kol greeting takes the form of an embrace. When two men meet, they put their arms around each other and touch the left shoulder to the left shoulder, and then the right to the right. Next they touch each other's knees, first the left and then the right, usually using both hands. As a final gesture, they grasp each other's right hand. Because their houses are small, the Kol do not entertain frequently. A visiting relative is given a place to sleep, eats with the family, and is made as comfortable as possible. Hospitality is usually not extended to or expected by strangers.

9 LIVING CONDITIONS

The traditional Kol village is set in a clearing in the forest and consists of a few houses built on either side of a winding pathway. Each village has its central shrine, an open platform built around the base of a tree, preferably a nim tree. There may also be shrines to other deities in other places in the village. The graveyard is located on the south side of the settlement. The boundaries of the village are usually not clearly defined.

Situated immediately in the front of each house, facing the path, is a small courtyard plastered with mud and cow dung. The houses themselves are rectangular and small, usually no more than a single room in which as many as five or six people may live. The walls are of grass or mud and the roof is thatched, although the better-off people have tiled roofs. There may be a small veranda, or porch, and a shed for cattle. One enters the house through a single door, and there are no windows. Inside the house, there is an area set aside for cooking, with a hearth, a stone mill, and a few cooking utensils. A large earthen jar holds grain, and baskets and discarded cans and bottles are used for storing other things. Furnishings are sparse. The Kol do not use beds and chairs, and they sleep on the floor on mattresses. One corner of the room is devoted to the household's shrine.

10 FAMILY LIFE

The Kol are divided into numerous subgroups called *kurhis*, which form the basic divisions of the tribe; people must marry within their own kurhi. There is little agreement on exactly how many *kurhis* there are, and the marriage rules are not always strictly observed. The Rautiya consider themselves to be the highest ranking *kurhi*. Some groups, such as the Rautiya,

who are married by Brahman priests, are more Hinduized than others. Marriages are arranged (although elopement is possible), and brides usually come from outside the village. A bride-price is paid, although the dowry is now becoming common. Many of the rituals related to marriage appear to be borrowed from the Hindus. A man who can afford it may keep more than one wife. The nuclear family appears to the norm among the Kol, with households averaging four persons. The main duties of the wife are caring for the house, cooking food, and raising the children. In addition, she is expected to contribute to the family income by working for wages, gathering wood and so forth. Kol society permits divorce and the remarriage of widows.

11 CLOTHING

Although in the past they may have worn little in the way of clothing, today Kol resemble their Hindu neighbors in dress. Men wear the *dhoti*, sometimes going bare-chested, sometimes with a *kurta*, or shirt. They sometimes wear a turban. The sari, worn with or without a bodice, or blouse, is the standard dress for women. Among the more Hinduized Kol, the end of the sari is used to cover the head. Women wear whatever necklaces, earrings and other jewelry as they can afford. They also often have tattoos on their bodies as another form of ornamentation. This is said to have some religious significance.

12 FOOD

Like most villagers in India, the Kol have two meals a day, one around noon and the other late at night. Early in the morning, they may eat leftover chapatis or rice. There is little variation in the menu. A meal consist of rice or of chapatis made from wheat or millet, whichever is cheaper, with a small amount of vegetable curry and some *dal*. The vegetables include *sag* (leafy greens such as spinach), eggplant, pumpkin, potatoes, and certain roots and leaves gathered in the jungle. The Kol are not vegetarians, but the high cost of meat means that it is rarely eaten. Almost any animal flesh is consumed, although the Kola avoid beef in deference to Hindus and avoid carrion, because it is a food of the untouchable castes. Although the more Hinduized Kol avoid pork, a pig is sometimes sacrificed to the goddess at Kol festivals and then eaten ceremonially. The parrot, crow, sparrow, and kite (a hawklike bird) are never killed or eaten. The Kol use liquor at feasts and festivals; they buy it rather than distill it themselves.

13 EDUCATION

In recent years, the Kol have begun to send their male children to school. However, dropout rates after the middle-school level are very high, and around half the Kol population (47.9%) do not have any formal schooling at all. Only 6.6% of Kols complete high school. The 2001 census showed a literacy rate for the Kol in Madhya Pradesh of only 35.9%. Literacy among males is considerably higher than for females (the census reports literacy among females to be 22.2%).

14 CULTURAL HERITAGE

The Kol have a legacy of legend and tribal lore. But the highlight of Kol culture is a passion for music, song, and dance. The Kol use mainly percussion instruments such as drums and cymbals. Their songs include songs of worship (*bhagats* and *bhajans*), obscene songs performed at the Holi festivals, love songs, and songs to be sung at the time of childbirth, marriage, or other festive occasions. Dancing is also important at social events and festivals. Among the Kol, only the women dance, while the men play instruments and sing along with them. The *dadra*, accompanied by the appropriate songs, is the most popular of the Kol dances.

15 WORK

The Kol are mostly a landless people, and nearly three-quarters of them (70.4%) work as agricultural laborers for local landowning castes. Some work in factories, mines, quarries, and construction. A 2004 report by the International Labor Office in Geneva indicates that some Kols have lost their land, are in debt and serve as bonded labor. A few make a living by gathering forest products and wood for fuel. Rather than purchasing wood from forest department depots, merchants from Jabalpur recruited Kol tribals as suppliers of cheap illegal timber. Kol tribals, who are adapt at cutting timber, responded to this new economic activity with enthusiasm. Some members of Kol Lohar, a small Kol community in Orissa, follow their traditional occupation as blacksmiths.

16 SPORTS

No sports or games are known to be identified with the Kol community.

17 ENTERTAINMENT AND RECREATION

The main source of entertainment for the Kol is their festivals and the music, song, and dance that accompany religious and social celebrations.

18 FOLK ARTS, CRAFTS, AND HOBBIES

Arts and crafts are poorly developed among the Kol. Their houses are occasionally decorated with crude paintings of peacocks and other figures, but these are also found on the houses of non-Kol peoples. There are no taboos associated with the peacock, and the designs appear to be purely decorative. The Kol seem to be lacking handicrafts of any sort: they make no baskets, cloth, ornaments, or musical instruments.

19 SOCIAL PROBLEMS

The Kol are designated a Scheduled Tribe, that is, a disadvantaged community recognized as needing special representation and assistance in the context of modern India. The greatest challenge facing the Kol is poverty and its related problems. The Kol possess little land, and the land they do own is relatively unproductive. Many live in conditions of near-starvation. The forests, once a major resource for the Kol, are increasingly subject to government restrictions on their use. Debt is widespread, and once they are in the hands of moneylenders, it is hard for the Kol to get out of debt. The attitude of caste Hindus toward the Kol has traditionally been a desire to dominate and exploit them. Many Kol have no health care facilities, or even basic amenities such as safe drinking water. Illiteracy and a lack of education make it extremely difficult for the Kol to break out of the vicious cycle of poverty in which they live.

Many Kols are landless. The government of India allows landless tribals who have been "squatting" on land for a period of time to be regularized under the new Recognition of Forest Rights Act of 2006. However, on 19 April 2008, in the remote Ghateha village in the Rewa district of the Madhya Pradesh, a large contingent of police and forest department personnel descended on some 1,500 landless tribal families who had settled on a stretch of land near the village and evicted them using firing and tear gas. The local group Birsa Munda Bhumi Adhikar Manch and activists of the National Forum of Forest People and Forest Workers claimed that the settlers had been on this land since 2003, but local forest officials have denied this point, stating that the settlers had moved on the land only a month earlier. Landlessness and poverty, as well as lack of social assistance (such as welfare) and political representation, remain issues for the Kols.

20 GENDER ISSUES

As is the case with most tribal women in South Asia, Kol women are, except where they have been Hinduized, considerably freer than women in the Hindu societies amongst which they live. Although they are responsible for the household, experience arranged marriages, and suffer sometimes from child marriage, Kol society allows divorce and widow remarriage. Payment of a bride price, which is usually quite low, is more common than the dowry system found among Hindus.

However, partly as a result of the areas where they live and partly because women are expected to contribute to the household income, women have a low literacy rate and are generally limited access to education and health facilities.

Tribal women are specifically targeted by the Madhya Pradesh Government's District Poverty Initiatives Project (DPIP). The DPIP takes affirmative action in favor of tribal people within project structures and processes at the village, district, and state levels, focuses on activities of immediate relevance and importance to the income security and livelihood portfolios of tribal people in villages and makes strategic linkages with development organizations working with tribals and development programs or opportunities specifically addressing the needs of tribal men and women. Kols are one of the major tribes represented in Rewa, Panna, and Sidhi Districts, which fall under the DPIP scheme.

The critical role women play in collecting and processing forest products and the contribution of their activities to the household economy means that local governments are becoming increasingly aware of the need for their participation in the success of forest management projects. The government of Madhya Pradesh, for instance, has made provisions for women's representation on certain executive committees. However, many of the activities under joint forest management (JFM) in Jabalpur District, in Madhya Pradesh State, actually operate against women. (Joint forest management [JFM] is a system adopted by the government of India in 1990, in which forestry departments and local communities share both responsibilities related to forest management and benefits in terms of the proceeds.) Most non-timber forest products (NTFP) collection is conducted by women, but their efforts are disproportionately taxed under the JFM scheme.

Part of the proceeds of JFM are placed in a collective fund that is used as a source of credit to villagers, lending money to them at up to 5% lower interest than the local money lenders. The fund is a source of pride for many villagers and is used to construct temples and make purchases, such as musical instruments, for the community as a whole. But as yet the collective fund has not provided any specific benefits to Kol women, and the purchase of cooking utensils for providing meals for community gatherings has in fact increased their costs. Although gender inequity may not endanger the JFM process in the short term, if the concerns of women—and in particular Kol women—are not addressed, this could lead to disproportionate costs being shouldered by this segment of the community and consequently the creation of a dynamic that facilitates the rejection of both conservation and equity goals.

21 BIBLIOGRAPHY

Griffiths, Walter G. *The Kol Tribe of Central India.* Calcutta: Royal Asiatic Society of Bengal. Monograph Series, Vol. II, 1946.

Hasan, Amir. *The Kols of Patha.* Allahabad, India: Kitab Mahal, 1972.

Pandey, G. D. and Tiwary, R. S. "Impact of Migration on KAP and MCH of Family Welfare Service: A Study on the Kol Tribe of Madhya Pradesh." In *Tribal Situation and Development in Central India.* ed. S. K. Tiwari. Delhi: MD Publications, 1995.

Russell, R. V., and Hira Lal. "Kol." In *The Tribes and Castes of the Central Provinces of India.* Vol. 3., pp. 500-519. London: Macmillan, 1916.

Singh, Pramod. "Tribal Women: A Case Study of Kol Tribe of Patha Area of Manikpur and Mau Blocks of Banda District." In *Rural Reconstruction Ecosystem and Forestry.* ed. Pramod Singh. Delhi: MD Publications, 1993.

Singh, K. S. ed. *Peoples of India: Maharashtra.* Part Two. Vol. XXX. Bombay: Anthropological Survey of India and Popular Prakashan, 2004.

—by D. O. Lodrick

KONDS

PRONUNCIATION: KAHNDS
ALTERNATE NAMES: Khond; Kondh; Kandha; Ku (self-reference)
LOCATION: India (Orissa region)
POPULATION: 1.8 million (estimate)
LANGUAGE: Kui; Kuvi
RELIGION: Animism; small number of Christians
RELATED ARTICLES: Vol. 3: People of India

1 INTRODUCTION

The Konds are a tribal group found in the hills and jungles of Orissa in eastern India. The name *Kond* (also *Khond, Kondh,* or *Kandha*) translates as "mountaineer" and probably comes from the Dravidian word *konda* meaning "hill." The Konds refer to themselves in their own tongue as *Ku.*

Several theories have been put forward to explain the origins of the Konds. The Konds themselves believe they originated in Orissa and have always lived in their present location. Based on this, some scholars have argued that the Konds are remnants of the pre-Dravidian aboriginal population of the subcontinent who have survived subsequent Dravidian and Aryan invasions because of their physical isolation. Another theory sees the Konds as Dravidians who were pushed back into the hills by Aryan invaders as they occupied the fertile coastal plains of eastern India. Still another view proposes that the Konds were a Dravidian tribe from South India who were expelled by superior agricultural peoples and settled in their current locale around 500 BC.

Today, Konds fall into two broad divisions. The Hill or Maliah Konds, who are numerically the dominant group, inhabit the interior uplands and have retained much of their original tribal culture. The Plains Konds have had extended contact with the Oriya-speaking peoples of the lowlands and have adopted many aspects of Hindu religion and culture. The Kond tribe has a number of sub-tribes, for instance, the Dongria, Kovi, Kuttia, Languli, Penga, and Jharnia. Raj Konds are virtually a caste or sub-caste of Konds who are landowners.

2 LOCATION AND HOMELAND

The 2001 Census of India records just over 1.4 million Konds in Orissa. Currently this figure is closer to 1.5 million of the nearly 1.8 million Konds in the country. The Kond population is concentrated in the southern hills of the state and the Mahanadi River basin, and some are also found in the Srikakulam, Vizianagaram, and Visakhapatnam districts of the neighboring Andhra Pradesh State. The Eastern Ghats in southern Orissa form a hilly tract up to 200 km (125 mi) wide. The land varies between 450 m and 900 m (1,500–3,000 ft) in altitude, with a maximum elevation of 1,515 m (4,970 ft) near the headwaters of the Nagavali River. The rugged hills, expanses of trackless jungle, forests, and deep water courses of the region provided a safe refuge in which the Konds were able to preserve their traditional way of life relatively untouched by outsiders (until recently). The climate is typical of India, with a winter cold season, summer hot season, and monsoonal rains from mid-June to September. Higher altitudes experience lower temperatures than do the neighboring coastal plains. Annual rainfall varies between 120 cm and 160 cm (47–63 in).

³ LANGUAGE

Konds speak a language called Kui and its southern dialect, Kuvi. These belong to the Dravidian language family and have strong similarities to Telugu, Tamil, and Kannada. The language has no script of its own, with the Oriya script used for writing Kui, and the Telugu script used for Kuvi. Some Konds speak only Oriya, having lost all knowledge of their mother tongue. Other Konds are bilingual, speaking Oriya or other regional languages in addition to the Kond language. In more remote areas, people may speak only Kui or Kuvi.

⁴ FOLKLORE

A mythical account of Kond origins relates that, once upon a time, the ground was all wet, and there were only two females on earth. They were named Karaboodi and Tharthaboodi, and each was blessed with a single male child. The two children were named Kasarodi and Singarodi. All of these individuals had sprung up from the interior of the earth. They depended for their existence on two plants, called nangakoocha and badokoocha, which had also sprung up from the earth's interior. Subsequently, the wet soil dried up, and from it all kinds of animals and trees came into existence. Kasarodi and Singarodi were given in marriage to the two daughters of Buru Pennu, the supreme being and Creator God of the Konds. The Konds believe that they are the children resulting from this union.

⁵ RELIGION

Kond religion is animistic in nature. The Sun is worshiped as Bura Pennu, the chief of the Kond deities and the source of all good in the world. Tari Pennu, the Earth-Goddess, is his consort, though she later became the source of all evil. All the Kond deities *(Pennu)* are said to be descended from Bura Pennu and Tari Pennu, who are also responsible for creating the universe and all that is in it. The gods and goddesses are believed to be very sensitive to neglect, disobedience, and violation of taboos. They react by ruining a crop, sending a tiger to attack cattle, or making the offender sick. They have to be propitiated by blood-offerings, and so sacrifice is an integral part of Kond religion. Priests officiate at sacrificial rituals, which in former times included human victims as well as animal ones. The Meriah or human sacrifice was stamped out by the British in the late 19th century.

Worship of the spirits of dead ancestors is also an important aspect of traditional Kond religion. Contact with Hindu peoples has led the Konds to adopt Hindu deities into their pantheon. For instance, Kali and Durga are worshiped in a variety of guises, but always with the sacrifice of buffaloes, goats, or fowl. Christian missionary activity among the Konds is reflected in the roughly 3% of the population who claim the Christian faith.

⁶ MAJOR HOLIDAYS

Important festivals *(jatras)* are celebrated to mark events such as the gathering of the new bean crop in November (Semi Jatra) or the beginning of the rice harvest in September (Chawal Dhuba Jatra). All important festivals are accompanied by animal sacrifice. Following the suppression of the Meriah human

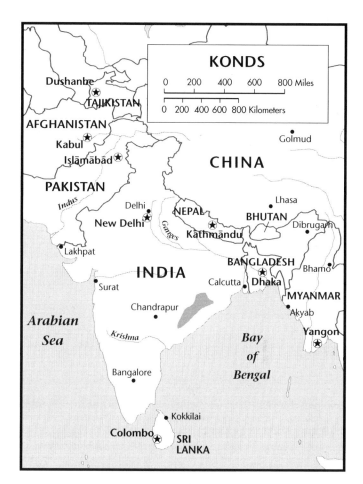

sacrifice, the Konds accepted buffaloes as substitute victims. Thus the Meriah festival, which is held between March and May, is still celebrated with buffaloes sacrificed as an offering to the Earth Goddess.

⁷ RITES OF PASSAGE

Rites of passage are occasions of ceremony and solemnity among the Konds. The birth of a child is cause for celebration (although some Kond groups practiced infanticide until this was suppressed by the British). A few days before the expected delivery date, husband and wife leave the house and move to a separate room specially built for the purpose. In the case of a first confinement, the husband or his father sacrifices a pig and offers rice and strong drinks to the spirits of the ancestors so that nothing goes wrong. After birth, the cord is cut and the placenta buried near the house. Among the Kuttia Konds of the interior hills, the head of an arrow is used to cut the cord of a male child. Birth rituals include smearing the infant with paste made from oil and turmeric until she or he reaches one month old. Many Konds name children after one of their ancestors, although how the name is selected varies from group to group. In the Kuttia Kond ritual, the father or a priest holds a bunch of leaves while reciting the name of the child's ancestors. When the baby touches the leaves, it is felt that the soul of the ancestor whose name is being spoken at the time enters the child's body, and the infant takes on that name.

The Konds feel that death is not the direct responsibility of Bura Pennu, but rather is caused by Jomereri Pennu, evil spirits, or through a person's sorcery and witchcraft. Corpses are burnt, although infants, women who died in childbirth, and those who die of smallpox or cholera are usually buried. Funeral rites include the sacrifice of buffaloes and pigs, dancing, feasting, and drinking.

⁸ INTERPERSONAL RELATIONS

The Konds believe that the first duty imposed on them by the gods was hospitality. Any neglect of this duty, violation of an oath, or denial of a debt is seen as sinful and likely to bring down divine retribution through poverty, disease, and even death.

⁹ LIVING CONDITIONS

Konds build their villages on the slopes of valleys, overlooking their cultivated fields. The houses usually form two rows, built along a curved road and closed at both ends by strong wooden barriers for defense. At the center of the village is a cotton tree, planted by the priest and dedicated to the village. Houses or huts are rectangular in shape, with the walls made of timber and plastered over with mud. The floor is of hardened dirt, and the low roof is built of bamboo thatched with grass. The huts are small, consisting mostly of one room, which is shared with the livestock. Furnishings are sparse, with the occupants sleeping on wooden cots or reed mats. Only the father, mother, and younger children sleep in the house. Around the age of eight or so, Kond girls and boys leave home to live in segregated village dormitories under the supervision of an elderly female. As in many tribal societies, the dormitory system lends itself to a somewhat casual attitude to premarital sex among Kond youth.

¹⁰ FAMILY LIFE

Konds are divided into exogamous clans, each of which claim descent from a common ancestor. As a rule, these groups inhabit villages in a limited geographical area. All the families in a village may be members of a subclan, which are commonly named after their totems. These may be plants, animals, or natural objects. Typical names of subclans are Hikoka (horse), Kelka (kingfisher), and Kadam (a tree). The Konds are a warlike people, and in the past clans were continually fighting one another. Conflicts were usually over land or women. Various eyewitness accounts are available of Kond battles in the 19th century.

The Kond family is typically patrilineal and nuclear in structure. Women are highly respected and are entitled to almost the same privileges as are men. Women manage the household, plant and weed the rice paddies, and raise the young, but they are also consulted before decisions are made in domestic affairs. Women attend the village council, where they can voice their opinion on matters relating to community affairs. Wives are acquired in several ways—by mutual consent, by purchase, by elopement, by capture, or through an arranged marriage to which both parties consent. Kond marriage rituals show the assimilation of many Hindu customs into traditional tribal practices. Both divorce and widow remarriage are permitted.

¹¹ CLOTHING

The traditional dress of Kond men is a long cloth, a few inches wide, that is wrapped around the waist and drawn between the legs. The ends of the garment are brightly colored, and hang down at the back like a tail. Although the head is left bare, the hair is oiled and combed and tied into an elaborate knot. The feathers of the peacock, blue jay, or white crane, colored combs, and ornamental hairpins are used to adorn the hair. Women wear a short skirt reaching from the waist to the knee, leaving the breasts bare. Married women have their ears pierced in 8 to 10 places and wear the corresponding number of earrings. A variety of necklaces, bangles, and anklets complete the ensemble. Men also wear jewelry. Girls of marriageable age have designs tattooed on the face, arms, and legs.

¹² FOOD

Rice is the staple food of the Konds. It is eaten with lentils and with wild leafy vegetables gathered in the jungle. The diet is rather bland compared to the spicy curries eaten by other peoples in India. Konds are nonvegetarian, eating eggs, chicken, buffalo, goat, pork, and even beef. The Konds do not use milk. Wild game is hunted in the forest to supplement the diet. Konds enjoy alcohol, drinking rice-beer, sago palm toddy, or liquor made from *mahua* flowers (*Bassia latifolia*).

¹³ EDUCATION

Access to educational facilities has always been a problem for Konds living in the remote interior of the Eastern Ghats. Although some 30% of Kond children attend government schools today, many drop out because of economic hardship and the need to help support their families. The drop-out rate by Grade 5 is close to 80%. Literacy among Konds is low, with the rates (2001) among the Dongria Konds, who live in the Niyamgiri ranges of Orissa, being 29% for men and 14% for women, respectively. Yet, as noted elsewhere, many Kond are bilingual, speaking the local dialect as well as Kui.

¹⁴ CULTURAL HERITAGE

Music, song, and dance play an important role in traditional Kond culture. Instruments include trumpets, drums, and the shepherd's pipe. The *deka*, a two-stringed violin made with a bamboo stick and gourd, provides the musical accompaniment as the poet sings, or rather chants, the verses. There are songs for every occasion—love songs, songs to be sung on the eve of the Meriah sacrifice, at marriages, at the time of plowing, and at the time of death. Of greater importance is the Kond dance. Every village has a place set aside for dancing. In a dance of the Kuttia Konds, boys and girls stand in a row facing each other. They link arms and shuffle back and forth in time to the music, getting more agitated and excited as the tempo of the dance quickens. Konds arm themselves with weapons for the war dance, in which they mimic a battle scene. In a hunting dance, a man wearing the horns and skin of a wild animal is chased and captured by a party of "hunters." Dancing accompanies festivals, marriages, and other important events and may continue day and night until the dancers are exhausted.

¹⁵ WORK

Although originally hunters and gatherers, most Konds are now engaged in agriculture. They practice shifting cultivation, as well as settled cultivation and animal husbandry. Rice, maize (corn), and pulses are important food crops, while turmeric, mustard seed, and legumes are grown as cash crops.

Many Konds work as agricultural laborers, while some still hunt or gather forest products such as teak. Of particular interest are the relationships of the Konds with the Panas and Doms. These are peoples who live in the Kond hill country, sometimes even in Kond villages, who act as traders, moneylenders, and intermediaries between the Konds and the Hindus. They also carry out certain ritual functions, which the Konds are forbidden to perform themselves.

In the past, Konds sacrificed humans for the good of the crops, though today buffalo are substituted for humans in this blood sacrifice. The practice of human sacrifice, which occurred until the middle of the nineteenth century, was stamped out by the British.

¹⁶ SPORTS

The Konds are fond of hunting, using bows and arrows and battle-axes as their weapons. They are skilled at tracking and pursuing deer and other large game.

¹⁷ ENTERTAINMENT AND RECREATION

Konds find their entertainment in their festivals and the singing, dancing, and revelry that accompanies their celebration of social occasions.

¹⁸ FOLK ART, CRAFTS, AND HOBBIES

Kond folk arts include tattooing, the carving of hairpins and similar objects out of animal bone, and jewelry-making. Konds are known for their skill in creating figures of animals and people out of brass and bronze. Other examples of Kond art are masks carved out of wood or gourds, elaborately carved wooden pillars formerly used in the Meriah sacrifice, and carvings on the doors of Kond houses.

¹⁹ SOCIAL PROBLEMS

As a tribal people inhabiting some of the more isolated hills and jungles of eastern India, the Konds are typical of the country's many underdeveloped communities. They are classified by the governments of Orissa and other states as a Scheduled Tribe and as such are deemed in need of special help in overcoming their economic and social problems. While social evils of the past, e.g., infanticide and human sacrifice, have long been abandoned, other tribal customs have survived. Today, many Konds are landless and locked in a cycle of poverty and illiteracy from which escape is difficult. The community remains socially marginalized and essentially isolated from the social and economic gains that Indian society in general has achieved since the time of independence.

Orissa has abundant mineral resources, and a major social issue for the Dongria Konds in the Niyamgiri ranges is the intrusion of mining companies into traditional Kond territory. Even though construction of refineries creates jobs and advances the local economy, Konds object to the accompanying pollution and destruction of their pristine, and sometimes, sacred lands (the Konds worship the Nyamgiri Mountains as a living deity). Thus, in 2004, in anticipation of official permission being granted by the Indian government, a bauxite company constructed a refinery in the Niyamgiri hills, which contains an estimated 73 million tons of bauxite. The 10,000 tribal Konds who live in the area view the plan to mine bauxite in their territory as a threat to their way of life. Conserva-

tionists predict the bauxite mine will pollute the eco-sensitive Niyamgiri hills, causing mass displacement and the end of a traditional livelihood based on farming millet and beans, hunting and gathering fruits. In the past decade, more than 1.4 million Indians have been removed from 10 million acres of land in four states to pave the way for industry and infrastructure projects, according to a recent report by ActionAid, an international anti-poverty agency. Kond tribals made the trip to Orissa's state capital, Bhubaneshwar, in eastern Orissa to lobby state officials. The establishment of the refinery was taken all the way to the usually business-friendly Supreme Court of India, which rejected the mining company's proposal and fined it for "blatant violation" of the law, but also invited it submit another proposal, which included environmental safeguards and channeling some of the operation's profits into tribal welfare. NGOs are skeptical of this, saying similar safeguards have been enacted before, but are rarely implemented. Vedanta, the company involved, says that it is giving tribals more generous compensation than the law requires, has built rehabilitation camps for the displaced villagers, and that much of the area's water sources and rare plants and animals will be protected.

Vedanta Alumina's plans hit another snag at the end of 2007 when environmentalists filed an intervener petition with the Supreme Court, highlighting the plight of the local Dongria Konds. However, even though a ban on mining has been sought in view of social, cultural, religious, and ethnic rights of Dongria Kondhs and also their livelihood, which protected under Article 21 and other provisions of the Constitution, related laws and international conventions to preserve tribal communities, the project has commenced "trial production," although it is yet to be granted a mining lease in Kalahandi, pending decision in the Supreme Court. The state-owned Orissa Mining Corporation intends to mine 3 million tons of bauxite annually to sell the same to Vedanta, its joint venture partner, for its alumina refinery at Lanjigarh and smelter plant at Jharsuguda. In September 2004 the ministry of environment and forests had granted environmental clearance for the refinery, but the Central Empowered Committee (CEC), appointed by the Supreme Court, noted that the clearance was obtained by concealing material particulars, principally that no forest land was involved in the project whereas about 660 hectares of forest land was involved.

Similar situations arise elsewhere in Orissa and also in neighboring mineral-rich Chhattisgarh, Jharkhand and Bihar, with protests by tribals often turning violent and involving fatalities.

Local agencies such as the Dongria Kond Development Agency (DKDA) and the Kutia Kond Development Agency are involved in representing the Konds on local tribal and environmental issues.

²⁰ GENDER ISSUES

As with many tribal groups, women among the Kond are respected and are virtually on an equal footing with men, even though Kond society is patriarchal. Divorce is allowed, as is widow remarriage. Even with arranged marriages, both parties must give their consent. Kond girls are tattooed on their face at 10 years of age—if they do not submit to this, they are viewed as unsuitable for marriage. Although child marriage was common among some Kond groups, real gender issues are to be found among plains groups that have come into close contact with their Hindu neighbors and adopted many of their customs, such as demanding dowries at the time of marriage.

Another problem for Kond women arises from displacement and loss of traditional land due to mining activities. Not only have there been deaths among the menfolk, but in the post-displacement landscape, women and girls often end up working for daily wages or as domestic helps or prostitutes. The women also have to cope with alcoholism and domestic violence.

[21] BIBLIOGRAPHY

Banerjee, Sukumar. *Ethnographic Study of the Kuvi-Khanda*. Calcutta: Anthropological Survey of India, 1969.

Boal, Barbara M. *The Konds: Human Sacrifice and Religious Change*. Warminster: Aris & Philips, 1982.

———. "Kond Ritual Practices and Prayers: Conservation and Change," *Journal of Indian Folklorestics*, vol. 2, 1979: 89-110.

Padel, Felix. *The Sacrifice of Human Being: British Rule and the Konds of Orissa*. Delhi: Oxford University Press, 1995.

Patnaik, Nihar Ranjan. *History and Culture of Khond Tribes*. New Delhi: Commonwealth Publishers, 1992.

Sharma, Krishnan. *The Khonds of Orissa*. New Delhi: Concept Publishing Company, 1979.

—by D. O. Lodrick

KOREAN CHINESE

PRONUNCIATION: kaw-REE-uhn chigh-NEEZ
ALTERNATE NAMES: None
LOCATION: China (Jilin province)
POPULATION: 2 million
LANGUAGE: Korean
RELIGION: Shamanism, Buddhism, Confucianism, and Christianity
RELATED ARTICLES: Vol. 3: China and Her National Minorities; Vol. 4: South Koreans

[1] INTRODUCTION

The immigration of Koreans into China began at the end of the 17th century. At that time, they were limited in number. In the mid-19th century, due to widespread famine in north Korea, a sizable Korean population crossed the border and settled in Yanbian and adjacent areas of northeast China, mixing with the native Manchu and Chinese residents. Later on, new waves of Korean immigrants settled in the same area. Under the Qing Dynasty (1644–1911), the Koreans in Yanbian district amounted to more than 10,000 and those who dwelled in Jian, Linjiang, and Xinbin counties numbered more than 37,000. In 1885, the Qing Dynasty allotted to the Korean immigrants an area of about 3,500 sq mi along the north bank of the Tumen River. After the annexation of the Korean peninsula by Japan in 1910, vast numbers of Koreans entered China, reaching more than 360,000 by 1918. At first, the Qing Dynasty imposed restrictions on their immigration, but changed to a policy of "recruiting for land reclamation" shortly after. Land reclamation bureaus were set up in cities and counties near the border; Korean immigrants recruited to reclaim wastelands were recognized as Chinese. From then on, they opened up virgin soil and built up large Korean communities in northeastern Manchuria. This policy continued under the Republican government after the demise of the Qing Empire in 1911.

[2] LOCATION AND HOMELAND

The Koreans dwelled mainly in Jilin province. They also scattered in Heilongjiang and Liaoning provinces, Inner Mongolia Autonomous Region, and some inland cities of north and northeast China. Yanbian Korean Autonomous Prefecture of Jilin Province is the most populated area among the compact Korean communities. It is located in hilly land around Baitou, the highest peak in Changbai Mountains, which dominate one of China's largest forest reserves. The forest, covering 494,000 acres, is divided into a semiprotected area and an area off-limits to both guns and axes. More than 300 species of medicinal herbs, including ginseng, grow in habitats that range from alpine to heath. Ethnic Korean population in the People's Republic of China reached 2 million in 2002.

[3] LANGUAGE

The Korean language belongs to the Ural-Altaic family, Tungusic branch. With the spread of Confucianism and Buddhism, Koreans began using Chinese characters as a writing system from the 4th century AD. Scholars estimate that about 70% of present-day Korean vocabulary is of Chinese origin. From the

10th century onward, the Koreans devised their own phonetic alphabet and syllabary and gradually abandoned the use of the Chinese ideographic characters. The official alphabet used in the Korean Peninsula, called Hangul, was developed in the 15th century and consists of 24 phonetic signs; these are sometimes combined with Chinese characters. However, Koreans living in China use a 40-character phonetic alphabet and have completely abandoned Chinese characters.

⁴FOLKLORE

The Tanjun myth, narrating the origin of the Korean people, is widespread among the Koreans living in China. The youngest son of the Emperor of Heaven wished to move down to the earth. His father acquiesced and awarded him a blessed parcel of land. The gods of winds, rain, and clouds ensured the prosperity of all living things on this parcel of land. Now, there was a tiger and a bear living together in a cavern. The son sent the two animals each *lingzhi* (glossy ganoderma—a type of fungus) and 20 bulbs of garlic and told them that whichever had eaten them within 100 days would become a human being. A few days later, the tiger, unable to eat anymore, abandoned the contest, while the bear continued and ultimately turned into a girl. She prayed to the gods to give her a man. The son of the Emperor of Heaven changed himself into a man and married the girl. From this union Tanjun was born and, thereafter, human beings multiplied. Tanjun built up a country called Korea and made Pyongyang the capital. He lived to be 1,908 years of age and was finally transformed into a mountain god.

⁵RELIGION

There have been four major religions among the Koreans of the Korean Peninsula: Shamanism, Buddhism, Confucianism, and Christianity. Most Koreans who migrated to China in the 19th and early 20th centuries shared in the beliefs of one or more of these religious traditions, but since the Communist takeover many have abandoned religious beliefs and practices. Large segments of Koreans living in rural areas still hold the Christian faith, while the older generations still believe in Confucianism; geomantic beliefs (divination by means of geographic features) related to the location of a house or a tomb are widespread among the ethnic Koreans living in China.

⁶MAJOR HOLIDAYS

On the Spring Festival (lunar New Year; Western calendar, between January 21 and February 20), in addition to singing, dancing, and dinner parties at home, people add to the fun by kindling bonfires in the fields and engaging in outdoor activities.

The fifteenth of January (lunar calendar; Western calendar, between February 6 and March 6), the Chinese Lantern Festival is also an important holiday for the Koreans, especially in the rural areas. Each household cooks five kinds of rice, barley, red beans, and husked sorghum and puts a small quantity of each before an ox to see which one is eaten first; this will indicate which variety of grain will have a bumper crop this year. An important activity will be held in the evening: "greeting the moon." More than 10 oak rods, each 12 ft in length, tied up at one end, are erected in the form of a circular cone before the village. Pine branches are piled up at the bottom. As soon as the moon appears, they kindle the cone. In a moment, a deafening sound of gongs and drums welcomes the

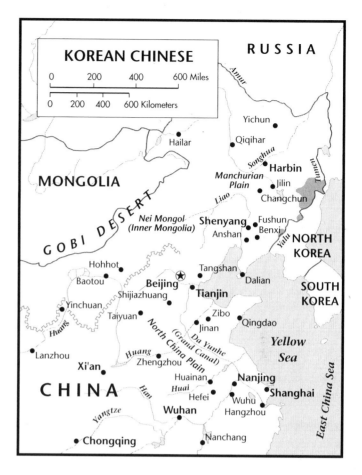

full moon. Children have long, thin bags filled with charcoal, made by their parents beforehand. At this moment they light them up and hang them on the trees. The girls move around holding odd-shaped paper lanterns.

September 3 is the anniversary of the founding of the Yanbian Korean Autonomous Prefecture. Families dress up, call on their relatives' homes, and participate in various recreational activities.

⁷RITES OF PASSAGE

On a child's first birthday, relatives and friends are invited to dinner. A rite of "putting on the hat" will be held when a boy comes of age at 20. According to Korean custom, the rite should be held three times within a few days. During the first rite, the boy should take off his clothes and wear a garment made of white linen trimmed with black silk. Then, his hair is combed into a bun, covered by a hairnet, and finally by a hat. During the second rite, his hat and garment should be changed again. During the third rite, a kerchief is added to the hat. The boy should go to the ancestral hall and salute the elder members of his family.

A family will hold a special celebration on a person's sixtieth birthday because of the symbolism of the 60-year cycle obtained by combining the 12 "Heavenly Stems" and the 10 "Earthly Branches." This computing system was invented by the Chinese in the second millennium bc. For the same reason, the sixtieth wedding anniversary is an important family festival. On this occasion children, grandchildren, relatives, friends, and neighbors all come to celebrate, usually for two days.

When a senior person dies, family members should wear mourning dress and abstain from eating cooked rice, haircutting, and face washing for three days. Paying homage to the dead, the visitor should kowtow twice, then exchange kowtow twice with the family members. The burial should be held within three days and strictly on odd days. New clothes should be put on and the old ones burned. The location of the tomb is usually selected by a geomancer, often on the sunny side of a slope. After the funeral, the memorial ceremony should be held for three successive days and repeated on the deceased's birthday, on the anniversary of the death, the Festival for the Dead (*Qingming*), and the Mid-Autumn Festival. Most of the customs surrounding funerary rites were borrowed by the Koreans from the Chinese long before they migrated into China.

8 INTERPERSONAL RELATIONS

The Koreans are very warm and courteous. When celebrating at home, all the family members sing and dance, making for very lively entertainment. On June 20 (lunar calendar; Western calendar, between July 13 and August 12), everybody dresses up in the Korean national costume and crowds gather on the square. They express good wishes to the aged, commend parents-in-law who live in harmony with their daughters-in-law, and vice versa. This festival shows the attention and importance the Koreans pay to interpersonal relations among the generations. Young people have full freedom to choose their spouses. They find many opportunities to meet each other during social meetings.

9 LIVING CONDITIONS

Ethnic Korean villages are usually located on the flatlands below mountain slopes. Villages, a few kilometers from each other, are usually rather small, comprising a few dozen households. Houses have no courtyard, face south, southeast, or southwest, and are whitewashed both inside and outside. The roof, covered with straw or tiles, slopes down on all four sides. There are four doors at the front that also serve as windows. The house usually consists of a bedroom, a living room, a kitchen and a storeroom. The platform bed, made of adobe bricks and stones covered by wooden boards, also serves as a table. The interior is usually tastefully furnished. Koreans are particular about tidiness and cleanliness. When entering the house, everybody takes off his or her shoes at the door. The chief modes of transportation are bicycle, motorcycle, car, or train. Highways and railways crisscross in all directions from the districts inhabited by the Koreans.

10 FAMILY LIFE

Families may be as small as three or four or as many as a dozen. Men engage in agriculture, while women take care of household chores. Usually, it is the responsibility of the eldest son to live with the parents, even after marriage. The younger sons live apart after marriage. The eldest son inherits the legacy, but a part is reserved for the younger sons, while the daughters have none. Korean families are monogamous. According to their customs, marriage is not allowed between people of the same clan, the same surname, or between close relatives. Marrying too early is still a problem. Following age-old traditions, women rarely ask for divorce and widows rarely remarry.

11 CLOTHING

The Koreans are fond of white or plain-color clothes. Women's blouses are very short. Adult women wear long, multipleated skirts or a sari-like cloth winding down their bodies; young girls wear short skirts cut well over the knees. Both men and women like their traditional boat-like shoes all made of rubber. Men wear loose pants, short tops, and vests. They usually wear a long overcoat outdoors. "Mao's suits" and Western-style clothes are popular today.

12 FOOD

The Koreans' staple foods include rice and millet. They are fond of rice, glutinous rice cakes, cold noodles in sauce, soup made from soya beans and flour, pickled vegetables, and dog flesh. They like sour and spicy dishes. Meals are seldom without pickles and the soup mentioned above; the pickles are made of Chinese cabbage, radish, garlic, pepper, ginger, and salt. Cold noodles are made of buckwheat and sweet potato powder, together with beef, chicken, pork, eggs, pepper, sesame and its oil, pears, and apples. They like tea and wine.

13 EDUCATION

Because of their long-standing Confucian tradition, the Koreans value education very highly. Since the 1930s many schools have been established. Yanbian University was set up in 1949. Currently, there are six universities and five adult colleges in Yanbian Korean Autonomous Prefecture. Education in primary school and middle (junior and senior) school is practically universal. There are newspapers and broadcasting in the Korean language. The educational and cultural level of the Koreans is first among all nationalities in China, including the Chinese, and compares favorably with the world average, being lower only than that of North America and Europe.

14 CULTURAL HERITAGE

Jiayeqin is a traditional plucked stringed instrument, said to have been prevalent in a small country called Jiaye as early as the 6th century. The player (usually a woman) puts the left end of the instrument on her knee and the right end on the ground. It may be used for solos as well as for accompanying songs. *Changgu* is a long drum, narrowing toward the middle, usually hung over the front of the chest. The player beats the drum with his left hand and with four bamboo twigs held in the right hand.

Koreans make it a point of honor to master their traditional dances. They dance on every happy occasion. For example, a Korean wedding begins with feasting and ends hours later with prolonged dancing. There are quite a few unique dance styles for specific occasions.

15 WORK

The area of northeast China inhabited by the Koreans is in the "cold belt." The frost-free period lasts only about one-third of the year. Rice and other grains must be grown and harvested during this short period. So, the Koreans developed special irrigation techniques, which are very productive. The rice they produce is white, tasty, and nutritious; it is famous throughout China. Another important contribution of the Chinese Koreans is the raising of sika deer, whose pilose antlers (covered with soft hair) are sought for their curative and strengthening virtues.

¹⁶SPORTS

Korean men are fond of soccer and wrestling. The former is the most popular sport of men. From primary school to university, each class organizes a team of its own. Soccer games held on every festival and holiday attract large numbers of people, sometimes living dozens of kilometers away. The favorite sport of women is the springboard game. Five meters in length, the board is about one meter above the ground. Two girls standing on each end of the board jump alternately, propelling the each other higher and higher in the air. The highest jumper is the winner.

¹⁷ENTERTAINMENT AND RECREATION

The Korean community has been very active in producing Korean-language movies and television programs. Chinese and foreign films and television programs dubbed into Korean are also popular. The Koreans like to actively participate in many forms of entertainment. For instance, during breaks in their manual work, as soon as a person sings or beats the drum, fellow workers will spontaneously join in the singing or dancing.

¹⁸FOLK ART, CRAFTS, AND HOBBIES

One of the most sophisticated crafts of the Chinese Koreans is the handmade musical instrument *jiayeqin*. There were originally two types. The standard instrument was 67 in long and 12 in wide with 12 strings. The popular instrument was shorter and narrower. Both instruments had some limitations, including weak volume and incomplete scales. After 1949, a new version of the *jiayeqin* with 18 strings corrected these limitations.

¹⁹SOCIAL PROBLEMS

The success of Chinese Korean education and economic development is in sharp contrast with the low position of Korean women. Chinese Korean society is male-oriented both in public and at home. The revolution does not seem to have modified in a significant way the traditional social values based on patriarchal structures and Confucianism.

²⁰ GENDER ISSUES

The Chinese constitution states that women have equal rights with men in all areas of life, and most legislation is gender neutral. While Chinese Koreans rank first in educational attainment among all Chinese ethnic groups, a gap in educational level persists between women and men. Though the statistics for ethnic Korean women are above the average, they still face significant gender stereotypes in their private and professional life.

China has strict family planning laws. It is illegal for women to marry before 20 years of age (22 for men), and it is illegal for single women to give birth. The Family Planning Bureau can require women to take periodic pregnancy tests and enforce laws that often leave women with no real options other than abortion or sterilization. Though minority populations were previously exempt from family planning regulations, policy has changed in recent years to limit minority population growth. Today, urban minority couples may have two children while rural couples may have three or four.

²¹ BIBLIOGRAPHY

Chiao, Chien, Nicholas Tapp, and Kam-yin Ho, ed. "Special Issue on Ethnic Groups in China." *New Asia Bulletin* no 8 (1989).

Dreyer, June Teufel. *China's Forty Millions.* Cambridge: Harvard University Press, 1976.

Eberhard, Wolfram. *China's Minorities: Yesterday and Today.* Belmont: Wadsworth Publishing Company, 1982.

Gustafsson, Bjorn A., Shi, Li, and Sicular, Terry, eds. *Inequality and Public Policy in China.* New York: Cambridge University Press, 2008.

Heberer, Thomas. *China and Its National Minorities: Autonomy or Assimilation?* Armonk, NY: M. E. Sharpe, 1989.

Lebar, Frank, et al. *Ethnic Groups of Mainland Southeast Asia.* New Haven: Human Relations Area Files Press, 1964.

Ma Yin, ed. *China's Minority Nationalities.* Beijing: Foreign Languages Press, 1989.

Ramsey, S. Robert. *The Languages of China.* Princeton: Princeton University Press, 1987.

Schwarz, Henry G. *The Minorities of Northern China: A Survey.* Bellingham, WA: Western Washington University Press, 1989.

Shin, Leo Kwok-yueh. *The Making of the Chinese State: Ethnicity and Expansion on the Ming Borderlands.* New York: Cambridge University Press, 2006.

—by C. Le Blanc

KURDS

PRONUNCIATION: KURDS
LOCATION: Turkey, Iraq, Iran, Armenia, and Syria
POPULATION: 30 million to 35 million (2008 estimate)
LANGUAGE: Kurdish
RELIGION: Islam

¹ INTRODUCTION

The Kurds are an Indo-European people and constitute the fourth largest ethnic group in the Middle East. However, they have never had their own nation. The traditional life of Kurds was nomadic. Tribes would move throughout the Mesopotamian plains and Turkish and Iranian highlands on a seasonal basis, herding sheep and goats. The end of World War I and the breakup of the Ottoman Empire led to the development of nation-states in the Middle East. This geo-political change forced the Kurds to abandon their traditional ways.

Although Kurds called the land they traveled through Kurdistan, they historically have been incorporated into either the old Islamic empires or the new Middle Eastern nation states. In AD 1514, their lands were divided between the Ottoman Turkish and Shi'ite Persian Empires, who kept control of them for the next 400 years. After World War I, the Kurds had a brief taste of self-rule. The Treaty of Sèvres, signed on 10 August 1920, recognized an independent Kurdistan. Unfortunately, the European powers dividing the Middle East after the defeat of the Ottoman Empire decided to divide the area known as Kurdistan among various states, in which Kurds would be the minority. The Kurds were forced to rely on foreign European support for protection, which guaranteed the promotion of European policies. Thus, three years later, on 24 July 1923, the Treaty of Lausanne was signed, once again dividing Kurdistan between the Turks and Persians in the states now known as Turkey and Iraq. The Kurds had another taste of independence after World War II when they were allowed a small homeland in western Iran in 1946, with the capital at Mahabad. The Shah of Iran soon came into power, however, and crushed the Kurdish state less than a year after it was established. Once again, the Kurds were without a land to call their own.

Kurdish history since 1946 has been a continuation of the struggle to maintain their cultural identity in the face of persecution and pressure to assimilate in every country where they live. Guerrilla fighters called *peshmerga* ("one who faces death") hide in the hills and fight for Kurdistan. A peshmerga uprising in Iraq in 1991 led to a disastrous defeat, and many Kurds fled to Iran. The long years of war and hostility between Iran and Iraq have put the Kurds in a very difficult position, because they live in both countries, and are constantly caught in the middle of the fighting. Kurdish resistance fighters have sometimes tried to use the hostilities between the two countries to their own advantage, so far without success. In Turkey, the Kurdistan Workers Party (PKK) is a radical communist paramilitary group campaigning for Kurdish independence. Not all Kurds agree with the methods and political aims of the peshmerga or PKK, but all want to have homes where they are safe and free to be themselves. Nearly 44,000 people had died in activities related to the PKK.

Kurds generally have had more national rights in Iraq than in the other modern nation-states in which they currently reside. Iraqi governments beginning in the 1930s allowed the use of Kurdish in schools, recognized the existence of a distinct Kurdish ethnic identity, and allowed for some political autonomy in the Kurdish regions of northern Iraq. Kurds suffered brutal repression under the Ba'ath political regime led by Iraqi leader Saddam Hussein. The overthrow of Hussein's government in 2003, however, has created a sort of "nation within a nation" for Kurds in three northern provinces. The Kurdistan Regional Government allows for Kurd leaders to make decisions for the provinces with limited interference from Iraq's new government. Kurds also have been given equal voice in Iraq's central government with the country's Arab Sunnis and Arab Shi'ite populations. In addition, Iraq recognizes Kurdish as one of its two official national languages.

² LOCATION AND HOMELAND

Population estimates for the Kurds range from 30 million to 35 million. It is difficult to get an accurate count because the Kurds live in remote mountain areas, many are refugees and flee from one place to another to escape persecution, and governments want to downplay their numbers and significance. The largest numbers of Kurds live in Turkey (approximately 15 million to 20 million, according to estimates from the *CIA World Factbook*). Large numbers of Kurds also live in Iran (8.5 million), Iraq (5.5 million), Pakistan (2.6 million to 3.9 million), and Syria (1.6 million to 1.9 million). Kurds are the second-largest ethnic group in Turkey, Iraq, and Syria. They are the third-largest group (after Azerbaijanis) in Iran. Kurds also live in Lebanon, Armenia, and Azerbaijan, as well as Germany (about 400,000) and other places across Europe, the United States, Canada, Australia, and elsewhere. Although they live among them, Kurds are unrelated to Turks, Arabs, and Iranians.

"Kurdistan" is generally thought of as the mountainous area at the junction of the Iraqi, Iranian, Turkish, Syrian, and Armenian borders. The average altitude is 6,000 ft and much of the territory is so convoluted that it is inaccessible. The climate is severe: temperatures can range from –29°C (–20°F) in winter to 38°C (100°F) in summer. What little precipitation there is usually falls in winter in the form of snow. The mostly barren hillsides are seriously overgrazed and, as political restrictions on the Kurds' traditional nomadic herding increase, the problem only worsens. River valleys in the Kurdish lands are fertile, supporting fruit orchards and vineyards.

³ LANGUAGE

The Kurdish language is related to Persian (or Farsi), the language spoken in Iran. The main Kurdish dialects are the northern Kurmanji, spoken in Turkey, Syria, and the Caucasus region (of the former Soviet Union); and the southern Sorani, spoken in Iraq and Iran. Kurmanji is more widely used than Sorani. Kurdish, like Persian, has also borrowed many words from the Arabic language. Written Kurdish differs from region to region: Iraqi Kurds use a written form of Sorani; Syrian and Turkish Kurds write Kurmanji with the Latin alphabet; and Kurds of the Caucasus region finally settled on Kurmanji written with the Cyrillic alphabet, after trying Arabic, Armenian, and Latin alphabets. Kurdish has no "th" sounds; they are considered very un-Kurdish.

Most Kurds also speak the official language of the nation-state in which they happen to live. Arabic, Turkish, and Persian are two of the most common second languages used.

The skillful use of language is highly valued by Kurds. Witty repartee and a command of poetry are considered important social assets. In Turkey, however, it was illegal to speak Kurdish, except at home, until 1991. It is not illegal to speak Kurdish in Iran or Iraq. Iraq, until recently, allowed the Kurds a greater range of cultural autonomy than did Turkey or Iran. At school and in public, Kurds must use the language of the country where they live. So they can only practice their Kurdish language arts at home.

Modern Kurdish names are mostly Arabic with Islamic significance, or Persian names of heroes of Persian history and legend. There are very few uniquely Kurdish names. A mother usually names a child. Kurds did not traditionally use surnames, so most modern surnames are tribal designations or geographic locations.

⁴ FOLKLORE

Modern-day Kurds are descendants of ancient Indo-European peoples known as the Medes who moved into the Middle East 4,000 years ago. The Medes were fierce warriors, and the Kurds continue in that tradition. The Muslim hero Saladin (Salah Ad-Din Yusuf Ibn Ayyub, AD 1137–93) was a Kurd, as were many of his soldiers. Saladin and his army fought against the Crusaders, and Saladin became the sultan of Egypt and Syria in 1174.

⁵ RELIGION

The Kurds at first resisted the Islamic invasion during the 7th century AD. But they eventually gave in after the Islamic victory near the modern-day Iraqi city of Sulaimaniya in AD 643. Most Kurds are now Sunni Muslims. About one-fifth is Shi'ite, especially in Iran. Many Kurds also belong to Sufi (Islam mystic) brotherhoods and meet to chant and dance together to worship Allah. The Sufi brotherhoods are very important in Kurdish village life. There are a million or so Kurdish Alevis in Turkey, and 40,000–70,000 Yazidis (an independent sect combining aspects of Islam, Judaism, and Christianity), mostly in Armenia and Azerbaijan. A very few Kurds are Christian.

⁶ MAJOR HOLIDAYS

The most important Kurdish holiday is the *nwerroz*, or Persian New Year, at the time of the spring equinox (21 March). There are special foods, fireworks, dancing, singing, and poetry recitations, all with an emphasis on Kurdish ethnicity. Even though many Kurds no longer live the nomadic life of herders, Kurds continue to have seasonal celebrations at lambing time, before moving the herds to summer pastures, shearing time, and the time of return to the village in the fall. Islamic holidays vary in importance among individual Kurds, although the Prophet Muhammad's birthday is the most important.

⁷ RITES OF PASSAGE

The greatest occasion for celebration in a Kurd's life is marriage. Kurds marry at a relatively early age (17 or 18). The bride is decked in gold bracelets, earrings, and necklaces, with new dresses and shoes. The highlight of the wedding is the public procession from the home of the bride to the home of the

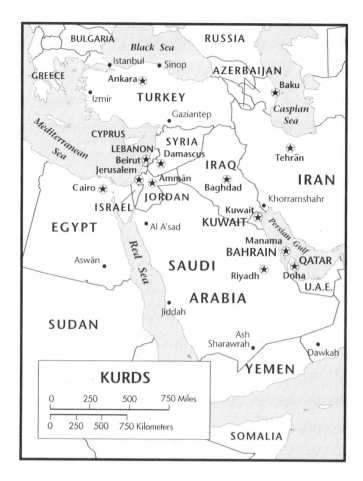

KURDS

| 0 | 250 | 500 | 750 Miles |
| 0 | 250 | 500 | 750 Kilometers |

groom. Everyone joins in the parade, with lots of fanfare. After they reach the groom's home, the bride enters the house and sits quietly veiled in a corner of the room while the guests feast and dance outside. In some areas, there are horse-riding displays.

Parents and relatives hold a feast for the birth of a child, especially the birth of a first son. Boys are circumcised by the local religious leader during the first week after birth. In some more traditional Kurdish communities, boys are circumcised at age 10, followed by a huge party.

⁸ INTERPERSONAL RELATIONS

The Kurds are a patrilineal society whose various lineages have been preserved over the generations by a high degree of endogamy resulting from the frequent marriage of first cousins (a man generally marries the daughter of a paternal uncle). This practice promotes unity among kin but allows distance to develop between different lineages.

While tribal leadership among the Kurds is inherited, local leaders are chosen for their personal qualities, including integrity, generosity, and skill at dealing with government officials.

⁹ LIVING CONDITIONS

Most Kurds live in small villages in remote mountain regions. Some live in the valleys or on the plains. A typical Kurdish house is made of mud-brick with a wooden roof. In the summer, Kurds sleep on the roof where it is cooler. In some mountain villages, the houses are built so close together that those

Kurdish children in the village of Sierye, Iraq. (Safin Hamed/AFP/Getty Images)

on higher elevations use their lower neighbors' roofs for extra living space. Some homes have underground rooms to use in the winter to escape the cold. There is rarely indoor plumbing; water is carried into the house in jars and cans from a central village well. There is no central heating. The few remaining nomadic Kurds live in tents made of blackened hides, and extended family members cluster their tents together in small communities.

Kurds are generally sheep- and goat-herders. Breeding horses used to be important, with the horses used for transportation, but mules and donkeys have become more common now. Families grow wheat and barley for subsistence, or rice in some areas, and raise chickens for eggs and meat. There are only a few Kurdish towns: Diyarbakir (a sort of capital for Kurds) and Van in Turkey; Erbil and Kirkuk in Iraq; and Mahabad in Iran.

10 FAMILY LIFE

Kurds marry fairly young and choose their own marriage partners. Few Kurds marry non-Kurds. Couples may continue to live with one or the other's family after marrying, but they have rooms of their own and separate housekeeping arrangements. Men and women both work in the fields, and boys and girls start helping at an early age. Kurdish women were traditionally not veiled except during parts of the marriage ceremony. They freely associated with men in most social interactions.

If there was no qualified male heir, a woman assumed tribal leadership. Even today, when Kurdish women have had to bow to the more conservative Islamic conventions of the countries where they live, many Kurdish women fight alongside the men as *peshmerga* (guerrilla fighters). More than 1,000 peshmerga are women. The radical Kurdistan Workers Party (PKK) encourages freedom for women.

11 CLOTHING

Traditionally, Kurdish women wear colorful skirts and blouses, and men wear baggy pants, vests, a red sash around the waist, and a blue silk turban on the head. Men also like to wear daggers. The typical Kurdish hat used to be a conical shape made of white felt, but today it is usually only worn by children. Nomadic Kurdish men shave their heads and wear long moustaches.

Traditional dress is becoming rarer as Kurds choose to dress like the people of the countries where they are living. In Iran, they must obey the laws of the Muslim government, so women must wear the black *chador*—a cloth covering their hair and clothes. In contrast, the government of Turkey has banned women from covering their hair in universities and public jobs, and so women are forced to wear more Western-style clothing. In Iraq, men wear woolen coats and vests, checkered headscarves, and baggy pants. Women wear the Muslim-style dress, often with baggy trousers underneath.

12 FOOD

Bulghur (cracked wheat) used to be the staple food for Kurds, but rice is becoming more popular where it is available. The Kurdish diet includes a wide variety of fruits and vegetables (cucumbers are especially common). In the valleys where grapes are grown, raisins and grape jam are common. Meat is only eaten on special occasions. The usual beverage is tea. Particular Kurdish specialties are a type of wafer bread eaten for breakfast and any kind of grain cooked in whey. A recipe for Bulghur Bread follows.

Nane Casoki (Bulghur Bread)

2 cups bulghur
1 teaspoon salt
½ cup minced onion
2 cups boiling water
approximately 2 cups unbleached white flour

In a medium-sized bowl, combine the bulghur, salt, and onion. Pour the boiling water over the mixture and let stand for 30 minutes. Put in a food processor and process for about 20 seconds. Add 1 cup of flour and process again until it is a smooth texture. (You can also work the flour in by hand, if you do not have a food processor.) Turn the mixture out onto a well-floured surface and knead it, adding flour as necessary to keep the dough from sticking, for about 3 to 4 minutes. Cover the dough and let it rest for at least 15 minutes, or up to 3 hours.

Place a large baking sheet (or two small ones) on the bottom rack of the oven, leaving an inch of space between the sheet and the walls of the oven. Preheat the oven to 450°F. After the dough has rested, divide it into 8 pieces and flatten each piece on the well-floured surface. With a rolling pin, roll out a piece of dough to a very thin round about 8 to 10 inches in diameter. Place the bread on a baking sheet and bake for 1½ to 2 minutes. Turn the bread over and bake for another minute, or until the bread begins to brown around the edges. (If you like a crispier bread, you may bake it longer, until it is spotted with brown all over.) Stack the baked bread and wrap in a clean kitchen towel to keep warm while you roll out and bake the rest of the dough. Serve warm or at room temperature.

Makes 8 breads.

(Adapted from Alford & Duguid, Flatbreads & Flavors, p. 175–6.)

13 EDUCATION

Schools are not widely available in most of the Kurdish territory. Where they are available, they are not much help. Because classes are taught in the official language of the Kurds' countries of residence, not in Kurdish, many Kurdish children find school very difficult and drop out. The Kurdish literacy rate is therefore very low. Girls often do not attend school at all because tradition holds that they are needed at home.

14 CULTURAL HERITAGE

Kurdish culture has a rich oral tradition, especially in epic poetry called *lawj*, which often tells of adventure in love or battle. Kurdish literature first appeared in the 7th century AD. In 1596, Sharaf Khan, Emir of Bitlis, composed a history of the Kurds in Persian called the *Sharafnama*. Almost 100 years later, in 1695, a great national epic called the *Memozin* was written in Kurdish by Ahmed Khani.

A Kurd named Ibrahim Mawsili founded the first Muslim Conservatory of Music after introducing Kurdish music to the ruler's court in the 8th century AD.

15 WORK

Most Kurds are farmers and sheep- and goat-herders. They sell products from their flocks such as leather, goat cheese, and wool. Women make crafts to sell such as carpets and cloth. Some Kurds grow tobacco to sell, and Turkish Kurds grow cotton for the market. A few mountain Kurds are still nomadic herders.

In towns, Kurds work as shopkeepers, plumbers, teachers, bankers, and so on. Kurds work as unskilled laborers in large Turkish cities, as well as in Baghdad and Mosul in Iraq, and Tehran in Iran. Some urban Kurds build on their traditional skills and specialize as bricklayers, butchers, cattle dealers, and small traders. The oil fields in Turkey and Iraq have attracted many Kurdish workers in recent times. Those Kurds who are able to go abroad find a variety of jobs and send the money back home.

16 SPORTS

See articles entitled **Armenians, Iraqis, Syrians**, and **Turks**.

17 ENTERTAINMENT AND RECREATION

Only men go out at night. They often sit at teahouses and cafés and play backgammon or dominoes. A favorite pastime is to listen to tapes or live singers at cafés. Singers have only recently been allowed to sing publicly in Kurdish.

18 FOLK ART, CRAFTS, AND HOBBIES

Carpet weaving is by far the most significant Kurdish folk art. Other crafts are embroidery, silk-weaving, leather-working, and metal ornamentation (especially copper inlay).

19 SOCIAL PROBLEMS

The greatest problem for the Kurds is the unwillingness of nations in which they live to allow them cultural autonomy. Although some Kurdish groups continue to fight for an independent Kurdistan, most Kurds wish only to be allowed to maintain their own language and culture within the states in which they live. Persecution of the Kurds has been especially traumatic in the age of nation-states. The concept of one nation with one people and one language has been adopted by the governments of Turkey, and this has led to great oppression of the Kurds in an attempt to make them conform. In Iraq, Kurds also faced persecution, although the Iraqi government did recognize their cultural autonomy. During the Iran–Iraq War (1980–88), the government engaged in systematic genocide to stop the Kurds from allying with Iran. Thousands of villages were destroyed and tens of thousands of Kurds were murdered and buried in mass graves. The Iraqi government also used nerve gas purchased from European governments against Kurdish civilians and Iranian troops, killing thousands more. One of the worst massacres occurred in the Iraqi Kurd town of Halabja, in which the entire population was killed by nerve gas. Because most countries tacitly supported

Iraq against Iran, no substantial pressure was placed on the Iraqi government to stop its offensive. After the Gulf War and the unsuccessful Kurdish and Iraqi rebellion against Saddam Hussein's power, thousands more Kurds were forced into refugee camps, although part of the Kurdish territory in northern Iraq has been declared off limits by Western countries. Since 1991, Turkey has attacked Kurdish civilian centers inside the "safe haven" zone in Iraq to punish Kurds for supporting the Kurdistan Workers Party (PKK). Because Turkey is needed to enforce the embargo against Iraq, little pressure has been placed on its government to stop these invasions. Many thousands of Kurds have now fled to Iran, and the government there is hard-pressed to provide support to literally millions of refugees from Iraq, Azerbaijan, and Afghanistan. Compounding the humanitarian tragedy is the fact that Kurdish leaders remain politically divided and unsure of a common strategy to demand their rights.

At least 44,000 people, mostly Kurds, had died in clashes between Kurdish rebels and the Turkish government as of 2008, and Turkey had spent $300 billion battling the terrorists. Kurds in Syria are not allowed to assert a sense of identity. Legal restrictions in Syria prohibit them from using their language in public, while the Iranian government continues to arrest Kurd journalists and activists for asserting rights for independence. The situation for Kurds has improved considerably in northern Iraq, where Kurds are building a regional government and encouraging tourism. Despite the instability in the rest of Iraq, the Kurdish regions are peaceful and offer hope for a future Kurdistan.

[20] GENDER ISSUES

An international conference on Kurdish women in 2007 raised many issues that challenge Kurdish women in the early 21st century. Most of the conference attendees emphasized that equalizing relationships between men and women was an important aspect of the international struggle for Kurdish independence.

Kurdish women lack educational opportunities and often face discrimination in workplaces. Because most Kurds are Muslim, religious practices also constrain women from working independently and from expressing themselves in the literary and creative arts. Kurdish women often face domestic abuse and suffer the risk of honor killings not only in the Middle East but also in the European countries that many have migrated to. The conference established a steering committee to organize future activities, passed resolutions to urge the Kurdish Regional Government in Iraq to make services for domestic violence available, and to work to increase social and political rights for women.

[21] BIBLIOGRAPHY

Alford, Jeffrey, and Naomi Duguid. *Flatbreads & Flavors: A Baker's Atlas*. New York: William Morrow & Co., 1995.

Amnesty International Report 2008: State of the World's Human Rights. http://thereport.amnesty.org/eng/Homepage (retrieved October 30, 2008).

Katzman, Kenneth and Alfred B. Prados, "The Kurds in Post-Saddam Iraq," *Congressional Research Service Report for Congress*, March 15, 2005. http://fpc.state.gov/documents/organization/44128.pdf (October 30, 2008).

King, Dr. John. *Kurds*. New York: Thomson Learning, 1994.

The Kurds, CAL Fact Sheet Series #4. Washington, DC: Language and Orientation Resource Center, Center for Applied Linguistics, 1981.

Linzey, Sharon. "International Conference on Kurdish Women for Peace and Equality, March 8, 2007, Erbil, Southern Kurdistan." *JMEWS: Journal of Middle East Women's Studies* 3.3 (Fall 2007): 103-105.

Moss, Joyce, and George Wilson. *Peoples of the World: The Middle East and North Africa*, 1st ed. Detroit: Gale Research, 1992.

"Mountains and Waterfalls: An Unconventional Holiday in 'the Other Iraq'," *The Economist* July 11, 2008, http://www.economist.com/displaystory.cfm?story_id=11695930&CFID=27666117&CFTOKEN=19845424 (October 30, 2008).

"Terror in the Mountains: Renewed Violence Raises Questions About Turkey's Treatment of its Kurds," *The Economist* October 16, 2008, http://www.economist.com/world/europe/displaystory.cfm?story_id=12429572 (October 30, 2008).

"Who Are The Kurds?" *washingtonpost.com*, 1999. http://www.washingtonpost.com/wp-srv/inatl/daily/feb99/kurdprofile.htm (October 30, 2008).

—revised by H. Gupta Carlson

KUWAITIS

PRONUNCIATION: koo-WAIT-eez
LOCATION: Kuwait
POPULATION: 3.2 million (30% of whom are Kuwaiti citizens)
LANGUAGE: Arabic (official); English
RELIGION: Islam (Sunni, 70%; Shi'ite, 30%)

¹ INTRODUCTION

Kuwait has one of the world's largest proven oil fields, an oil field that the Iraqis did their best to control and later attempted to destroy in their 1990-91 invasion and occupation of Kuwait. One of the wealthiest nations in the world before the invasion, Kuwait has undergone a significant recovery from the widespread infrastructural and cultural destruction inflicted on the country by six months of Iraqi occupation.

Archaeological study shows evidence of human settlements in Kuwait dating back to 5000 bc. The Dilmun civilization occupied the area from 4000 to 2000 BC, controlling the trade route to India. The Babylonians took over, then the Persians; after this, the Greeks established a colony on Falaika Island and then expanded inland around 300 BC. Greek rule lasted about 200 years, after which the Romans entered. The Islamic revolution swept through the area during the 7th century AD. Not much is known about Kuwait from the time of the Islamic revolution until the 18th century.

Modern-day Kuwait was founded in 1722 by the Utub tribe of Arabs, who moved there to flee the drought across the inland Arabian Peninsula at that time. The name Kuwait is the diminutive form of the Arabic word *kut,* meaning "a fortress built near water." The few native inhabitants already there mingled with the Utub, and they all made their living by trading, fishing, and pearling. Sabah bin Jabir was elected sheikh (leader) of the Kuwaiti Utub in 1756, and the Sabah family has ruled Kuwait ever since.

Kuwait has a history of friendly relations with Britain, and it became a British-protected state in 1899. Kuwait was granted self-rule in 1914, but it remained a British protectorate until 19 June 1961, when it became officially independent. The Kuwaiti government is a constitutional monarchy that has a provision for an elected parliamentary body, the National Assembly, but the monarchy has rarely allowed it to exist. In 1992, elections were held for a new Assembly, and a majority of those elected are considered to be in opposition to the monarchy.

A small but wealthy state, Kuwait has suffered continual conflicts with its larger neighbors, Iraq and Iran. On 2 August 1990, Saddam Hussein led an Iraqi invasion of Kuwait, occupying the country until 26 February 1991. Relations between the two nations had soured some months prior to the invasion over disputed border oilfields and growing Iraqi discontentment with an economically-crippling military debt to Kuwait and Saudi Arabia amassed during Iraq's eight-year war with Iran. During the occupation, Iraqi soldiers ravaged the country, and much of the nation's wealth was looted and transferred to Iraq. There are conflicting accounts regarding the extent of the human rights violations committed by the Iraqi military invasion, with Kuwait claiming that the arbitrary arrest, beating, torture, rape, and murder of Kuwaiti citizens was widespread. Iraqis have contested this and argued that these claims were exaggerated by the Kuwaiti regime in exile to make a more compelling and emotionally-appealing case for UN-backed military intervention. Following the passing of a landmark resolution in the Security Council, a United Nations coalition force from 38 nations (including eight Arab countries) came to Kuwait's defense on 16 January 1991 and drove out the Iraqis a month later. On their way out, the Iraqis conducted a scorched earth campaign, bombing and burning Kuwait's oil wells, roads, buildings—virtually everything in their path. Most of Kuwait's oilfields were set ablaze and took months to extinguish. This has had a severe toll on the Kuwaiti environmental conditions, both marine and terrestrial. Since the invasion, Kuwait has made a significant leap forward and recovered from all but one of the traumas of the invasion—the emotional one. Kuwait's currency stands unrivaled as one of the strongest in the world, the nation's population has swelled to twice its size two decades ago, and with souring oil prices, the country has been experiencing an economic renaissance.

² LOCATION AND HOMELAND

Kuwait is located in the desert on the northwestern coast of the Arabian (or Persian) Gulf. It is bordered to the north and west by Iraq, to the south and southwest by Saudi Arabia, and to the east by the Gulf. Directly across the Gulf is Iran. Kuwait's total land area is about 17,820 sq km (6,880 sq mi), just slightly smaller than that of the U.S. state of New Jersey. Several islands are included within Kuwait's borders; the island of Failaka is the most densely populated. The largest island is Bubiyan, but it is uninhabited because it is low-lying and marshy. Kuwait Bay is a protected harbor on the Gulf that has been much used for millennia. Kuwait's capital city, Al-Kuwait, is located at the harbor. The rest of Kuwait is flat desert, with a couple of low ridges (about 122 m, or 400 ft above sea level) where the oil is located. Because the oil is in ground that is higher than the rest of the country, it does not have to be pumped, but simply flows with the force of gravity into collecting tanks.

What little plant and animal life there was before the Iraqi invasion is now almost totally destroyed. Military vehicles churned up the delicate desert soil, and oil flooding from bombed wells and spreading in a slick on the Gulf waters has killed most wild sea, land, and air life. Recovery efforts are slow, and some damage may never be repaired. Oil spills, significant percentages of acid precipitation, widespread ordinances, and residues of the war arms continue to pose significant threats for the revival of the country's terrestrial and marine flora and fauna.

The climate in Kuwait is hot and humid, with summer temperatures reaching as high as 49°C (120°F) or more. Frequent sandstorms occur from May to July, and August and September are extremely humid. Winters are cooler, with temperatures ranging from 10° to 16°C (50°–60°F). Average rainfall is only 2.5 to 18 cm (1–7 in) yearly, all of which falls during the winter months, from October through April.

Kuwait's total population, based on a 1999 census, is 2,273,842 persons, of whom only 792,000 are Kuwaiti citizens. The rest are foreign workers in the oil, medical, educational, and construction industries, as well as significant numbers in skilled labor. Foreign workers are not allowed citizenship, even if they work in Kuwait all their adult lives. Even children born in Kuwait to foreign workers are not granted Kuwaiti citizenship. After a career of service in Kuwait, a foreign

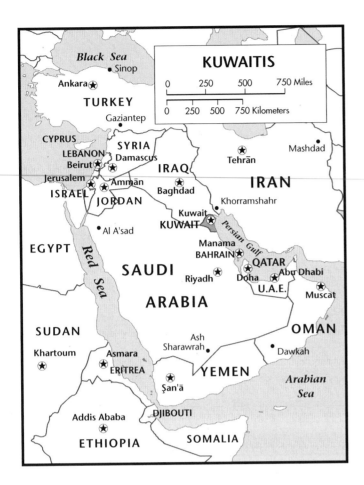

3

LANGUAGE

Arabic is the official language of Kuwait and is the language spoken by all Kuwaiti citizens. Kuwaiti students are taught English as a second language. Arabic, spoken by 422 million people worldwide, has many distinct dialects, so that people living as few as 500 km (about 310 mi) apart may not be able to understand one another. The written form of Arabic is called Classical Arabic, or, for today's literature and press, Modern Standard Arabic. It is the same for all literate Arabs, regardless of how different their spoken dialects are. Arabic is written from right to left in a unique alphabet that makes no distinction between capital and lower-case letters. It is not necessary for the letters to be written in a straight line, as English letters must be. Punctuation rules are also quite different from those of English.

"Hello" in Arabic is *marhaba* or *ahlan*, to which one replies, *marhabtayn* or *ahlayn*. Other common greetings are *As-salam `alaykum*, "Peace be with you," with the reply of *Wa `alaykum as-salam*, "and to you peace." *Ma`assalama* means "Goodbye." "Thank you" is *Shukran*, and "You're welcome" is *`Afwan*; "yes" is *na`am* and "no" is *la`a*. The numbers one to ten in Arabic are *wahad, ithnayn, thalatha, arba`a, khamsa, sitta, saba`a, thamanya, tisa`a,* and *`ashara*.

Arab names consist of their first name, their father's name, and their paternal grandfather's name. Women do not take their husband's name when they marry but rather keep their father's family name as a sign of respect for their family of origin. First names usually indicate an Arab's religious affiliation: Muslims often use names with Islamic religious significance, such as Muhammad and Fatima, while Christians often use Western names, as well as Arabic Christian names, such as Elias and Butrus.

Kuwaitis speak a dialect of Arabic known as Khaleeji (Gulf Arabic) that is spoken with some variation throughout the Gulf countries including Iraq, Saudi Arabia, Qatar, Bahrain, United Arab Emirates, and Oman. Khaleeji dialects are comprehensible to all their speakers but may not be understood completely in other regions of the Arab world, such as the Levant (Syria, Lebanon, Jordan and Palestine) or the North Africa region. These dialects are spoken rather than written although there is a move towards textually documenting these oral languages in the form of literature and poetry for fear of their loss due increased reliance on foreign-produced media content.

4

FOLKLORE

Kuwaiti folk beliefs and rituals are strongly linked to Islam, to which Kuwaitis turn for daily guidance, as well as explanations for many aspects of their current lives and past history. Prior to the discovery of oil, the people of Kuwait relied primarily on desert herding and fishing for sustenance. These have had a substantial impact on the country's folklore and culture with many songs, theatrical performance, literature, and poetry and musical compositions and often serve as inspiration for the stories in these artistic expressions. Bedouin and desert nomadic culture has also left its mark in the traditional garb worn by men and women both casually and on special occasions including weddings, funerals, ceremonies, celebrations and formal meetings.

worker is asked to leave the country immediately after retiring or upon the expiration of their work permits. Of the foreigners, about 35% are Arab; 10% are Iranian; 10% are Indian; 15% are Bangladeshi and Pakistani; and 10% are Egyptian, 10% are Palestinian (numbers halved following the liberation due to political reasons); and the remaining 10% are from a variety of countries. In May 1991, following liberation from the Iraqi invasion, it was reported that 900 persons were being investigated for their activities during the Iraqi invasion. The Kuwaiti prime minister acknowledged that non-Kuwaitis had been abducted and tortured. Some were arrested and tried as collaborators with the Iraqis; many were forced to leave the country.

Most of the Kuwaiti population is urban, with estimates reaching 96%. According to the 1999 census, 30,958 people live in the capital, Kuwait City. The largest town is Salmiyya, with a population of 150,452. Jalib al-Shuyukh has 160,289 persons, and Hawalli has 93,000. Before the Iraqi occupation, new towns were being built to house the growing population. Since the liberation, reconstruction has rebuilt much of the country's destroyed areas and new residential areas, both urban and suburban enclaves have emerged throughout. The demographic distribution of the country shows a geographic and socioeconomic disparity between residential areas for Kuwaitis and those for expatriates, with the latter occupying smaller urban apartments whilst the prior live in luxurious suburban property.

⁵ RELIGION

The original inhabitants of Kuwait were pantheistic, worshiping various goddesses and gods. A temple to Artemis, the Greek virgin moon goddess of the hunt, was located on the island of Falaika. In AD 313, the emperor Constantine made Christianity the official religion of the Roman Empire, of which Kuwait was then a part, so Kuwait became a Christian state. When the Islamic revolution swept through the area in the 7th century AD, virtually all Kuwaitis converted to Islam. Today, about 70% of Kuwaiti citizens are Sunni Muslims, while 30% are Shi'ite Muslims.

Islam is the youngest of the world's three Abrahamic religions, having begun in the early 7th century AD when the prophet Muhammad received his revelations from Allah (God). Within just a few years of Muhammad's death in AD 632, Islam had spread through the entire Middle East, gaining converts at a dynamic rate.

Born into the Koreish tribe of Mecca (c. AD 570), in what is now Saudi Arabia, Muhammad was later driven from the city because of his vigorous denunciation of the pagan idols worshiped there (idols that attracted a profitable pilgrim trade). The year of Muhammad's flight from Mecca, AD 622 (July 16), called the *Hijra,* is counted as the year one in the Muslim calendar. Muhammad fled to the city now known as Medina, another of the holy sites of modern-day Saudi Arabia. Eventually, Muhammad returned to Mecca as a triumphant religious and political leader, destroyed the idols (saving the Black Stone, an ancient meteorite housed in the Kaaba, or Cube, building, which has become a focal point of Muslim worship), and established Mecca as the spiritual center of Islam.

The Islamic religion has five so-called "pillars": (1) Muslims must pray five times a day; (2) Muslims must give alms, or *zakat,* to the poor; (3) Muslims must fast during the month of Ramadan; (4) Muslims must make the pilgrimage, or hajj, to Mecca; and (5) each Muslim must recite the *shahada:* "ashhadu an la illah ila Allah wa ashhadu an Muhammadu rasul Allah,"* which means "I witness that there is no god but Allah and that Muhammad is the prophet of Allah." Muslims say all their prayers facing in the direction of Mecca. Both men and women are expected, and greatly desire, to make the pilgrimage at least once in their lifetime. Ramadan, the ninth month of the Muslim year, during which Muhammad received his first revelations, is observed by complete fasting from dusk until dawn each day of the entire month.

Islam is a simple, straightforward faith with clear rules for correct living; it is a total way of life, inseparable from the rest of one's daily concerns. Therefore, religion and politics and faith and culture, are one and the same for Muslims. There is no such thing as the separation of church and state. In theory, there should be no distinction between private religious values and public cultural norms in an Islamic country; in actuality, history, geography, and daily life have influenced the cultures of Islamic countries, resulting in standards of social behavior and interaction that are not always in agreement with religious codes of conduct.

The difference between the Sunni and Shi'ite Muslims, which has played such an important part in Arab history, has to do with the early history of the religion. After Muhammad's death, the entire Muslim community recognized the legitimacy of the next three successors, or caliphs. The fourth caliph was 'Ali, Muhammad's cousin and son-in-law. His legitimacy was challenged by Mu'awiyah, the governor of Syria, and after the Battle of Siffin in 657, 'Ali was forced to withdraw. He moved his capital to Iraq and was murdered shortly thereafter. His followers refused to recognize the legitimacy of Mu'awiyah's caliphate and established the Shi'ite sect. Although there are doctrinal differences, the fundamental difference between the sects, therefore, is an argument about authority, not doctrine: the Shi'ites believe that caliphs must be direct descendants of Muhammad and that 'Ali was the legitimate fourth successor, while the Sunnis believe that caliphs should be elected by the people and therefore that Mu'awiyah and his successors were legitimate. Because there are more Sunnis than Shi'ites worldwide, the Sunnis refer to themselves as the orthodox sect.

⁶ MAJOR HOLIDAYS

Secular holidays in Kuwait include New Year's Day (January 1) and National Day (February 25). Liberation Day (February 26), commemorating the expulsion of Iraqi forces from Kuwait, is not recognized as an official holiday, but Kuwaitis seem to treat it as one. In deference to Kuwaitis still missing in Iraq after the occupation and to their families, no ceremonies or celebrations are held to mark the National Day or the Liberation Day.

Because Kuwait is an Islamic state, its official religious holidays are Muslim ones. Muslim holidays follow the lunar calendar, moving back by eleven days each Western year, so their dates are not fixed on the standard Gregorian calendar. The main Muslim holidays are *Eid Al-Fitr,* a three-day festival at the end of Ramadan; *Eid Al-Adha,* a three-day feast of sacrifice at the end of the month of pilgrimage to Mecca, during which families who can afford it slaughter a lamb and share the meat with poorer Muslims; the First of *Muharram,* or the Muslim New Year; *al-Mawlid An Nabawi,* the prophet Muhammad's birthday; and *Eid Al-Isra' wa Al-Mi'raj,* a feast celebrating Muhammad's nocturnal visit to heaven. Friday is the Islamic day of rest, so most businesses and services are closed on Fridays. All government offices, private businesses, and schools are closed also during *Eid Al-Fitr* and *Eid Al-Adha.*

⁷ RITES OF PASSAGE

Births are the occasion for celebration, particularly if the child is a boy. Kuwaiti boys are circumcised on the seventh day after their birth. This is usually accompanied by a banquet *(Aqiq),* for which sheep are slaughtered and relatives and friends are invited in for a festive meal. After giving birth, a mother is expected to stay in bed for 40 days *(nifas),* to recuperate and regain her strength.

Weddings are perhaps the most elaborately celebrated occasions, with great feasts and dancing. In the past, girls could be betrothed at the age of 14. Today, the average age for marriage is 20 to 25. There are two rituals in the marital tradition, the *milka,* or marriage contract, and the *'urs,* or marriage ceremony. Kuwaiti society is built on the importance of the family, and marriages are often arranged between families with long-established ties.

Respect toward the dead is also an important ritual. The burial takes place on the same day as the death. The body is washed and wrapped in a white shroud and then taken to a nearby mosque, where special prayers *(Salat al-Janaza)* are recited. After the burial, the relatives, friends, and acquaintances gather at the home of the grieving family to pay their respects and read aloud parts of the Quran. Mourning lasts for three days.

8 INTERPERSONAL RELATIONS

During the Iraqi invasion and occupation (1990–91), the usual social barriers and divisions, such as age, religious differences, and gender segregation, disappeared as Kuwaitis banded together to resist and/or survive. During more peaceful times, men and women do not mix socially, except in family groups, and Shi'ite and Sunni Muslims keep their distance from each other.

The *diwaniyas,* private clubs for men, played an important role during the Iraqi occupation. Traditionally, functioning as meeting places where men sit and talk over coffee or tea, making business contacts, discussing government policy with influential persons who can then make the suggested changes, and making deals with each other, the diwaniyas became the hub of the resistance movement. Men gathered there (as well as in mosques) and organized their resistance efforts against the Iraqis. In post-liberation Kuwait, these congregations have become a forum for political organizing that has led to recent crackdowns on some of the diwaniyas that reflect opposition to the Al-Sabah family rule.

In general, Arab hospitality reigns in Kuwait. When talking, Arabs touch each other much more often, and stand much closer together, than Westerners do. People of the same sex will often hold hands while talking or walking. (In earlier days, members of the opposite sex, even married couples, never touched in public; this is changing today.) Arabs tend to be social, gregarious, highly conversant, and insistent and have different conversational and interpersonal rules than Westerners. Interrupting a person speaking is not seen as offensive, and speaking with a high volume is acceptable. Most conversations appear to involve emotion and are replete with non-verbal gestures.

With a new generation of Kuwaiti youth being influenced by foreign travel and exposure to international media, there is greater mixing between males and females, with a growing number of private co-ed British and American schools and universities setting the standards in education and creating an environment where popular cultural youth trends are explored. Large shopping centers have become a place where youth meet, congregate, or simply people watch and now serve as some of the most public spaces for socialization.

Given the high income levels in Kuwait, the country has a very hierarchical system of socioeconomic classes, which affects interpersonal relations. Interactions between Kuwaiti and other nationalities are governed by this hierarchy. Domestic workers are common in Kuwait, and most citizens have several employees in the household who are expatriate laborers sponsored by the host/employer family. Most such workers are citizens of countries in South Asia, East and North Africa, or the Philippines. With more than half the population of the country being comprised of non-Kuwaitis, communication between various ethnic, national, and racial communities makes for an intriguing intercultural interpersonal environment.

9 LIVING CONDITIONS

During the Iraqi invasion and occupation (1990–91), conditions in Kuwait were horrendous. During the incredibly hot summer months, most of Kuwait's citizen population is given extended leaves from work and permitted to travel to more temperate climates. With a high GDP, most Kuwaiti citizens own property or second homes outside of their country that serve as places of summer vacation. The Iraqi invasion occurred during the summer of 1990 when the population of Kuwait had shrunk to half its size. For the small numbers of Kuwaitis and the remaining expatriate population that remained and had not fled, life was extremely difficult and dangerous. There was little food and no running water. Utilities (electricity, gas, water, and so forth) were cut off and other services closed down. The Iraqis stole everything that could be hauled away—from homes, stores, offices, even hospitals. Kuwaitis and anyone deemed suspicious were arrested arbitrarily with many cases of rape, torture, or murder reported. When the UN forces drove the Iraqis out of Kuwait, the Iraqis conducted a scorched earth campaign: they bombed and/or burned everything in their path as they were leaving. Kuwait was left in flaming rubble. In the years since, a massive rebuilding effort has brought Kuwait back to its modern, well-developed, pre-invasion state.

Health care and education through the university level are free to all Kuwaiti citizens. Foreign workers are entitled to most of the benefits but are restricted from admission to some programs. The infant mortality rate is low; life expectancy is high: 73 years for men, and 77 years for women. Modern health-care centers are conveniently located throughout the country and tend to be of high quality. Several exceptional medical research and service facilities have emerged in the last quarter century including a world-class medical genetics center, a top cancer treatment center, and a network of rehabilitation and support agencies for those with mental and physical disabilities.

The government sponsors social welfare programs for disabled persons, the elderly, students' families, widows, unmarried women over 18, orphans, the poor, and prisoners' families. Housing is subsidized, as are utilities. Telephone services are free. TV broadcasting began in 1961, with satellite communications established in 1969.

Kuwaitis' per capita (per person) income is one of the highest in the world. About one-fourth of all Kuwaitis own a car, usually an expensive one. On the other end of the economic scale, some laborers receive small earnings and live in dormitory-like apartments, sending most of their incomes as remittances to their families in their home countries.

Kuwait has an advanced highway system that connects all corners of the country but tends to be dangerous with high frequencies of accidents due to reckless driving. However, as the population of Kuwait continues to swell, the government is considering building a rail system within the capital city of Al-Kuwait and its suburbs to alleviate traffic congestion.

The press is censored less in Kuwait than in other Arab countries, but it is still controlled by the government. Kuwait has a ministry of information that monitors, advises and occasionally censors all forms of media in the country although the print press tends to be independent both in ownership and in coverage with several daily newspapers espousing clear oppositional views to the government. Recently, Kuwait was ranked the freest of all Arab media systems but remains hopelessly behind many countries in the world. Nonetheless, Kuwait has made a name for itself in the Arab digital and video media industry, producing several cutting-edge animation television series, producing high-end children's programming and leading the dubbing industry along with Jordan and Lebanon.

A Kuwaiti woman buys straw baskets and trays at a shop in downtown Kuwait. Kuwaitis use baskets to distribute sweets during the holy month of Ramadan. (Yasser Al-Zayyat/AFP/Getty Images)

¹⁰ FAMILY LIFE

The family unit is more important to Kuwaitis than the individual, the larger community, or the state. Families tend to be large; the government encourages large families in its effort to increase the percentage of native Kuwaitis in the overall population. The government even pays over $7,000.00 to each couple at the time of their marriage and offers child support to families for every child born, with a sliding scale if the child has a disability or is in need of special medical care.

Extended families usually live together, except in some urban areas where the houses are too small. In this case, relatives live near each other. A typical Kuwaiti household consists of a husband, his parents, his wife, his sons and their wives and children, and his unmarried sons and daughters. Parents arrange marriages, usually between extended-family members. First cousins are an acceptable match among urban Kuwaitis and preferred among Bedouin Kuwaitis. Marrying and having children, particularly sons, increases a woman's status in society. Most girls marry young; 29% of Kuwaiti women are married by the time they are 20 years old.

¹¹ CLOTHING

In Kuwait's urban centers, Western-style clothing is becoming popular, particularly with young people. However, many Kuwaitis still wear traditional Arab clothing, such as the *dishdasha* (ankle-length robe) with a *ghutra* (head scarf), usually white, worn over a skull cap and held in place with an *ʿaqal* (wool rope) for men. Women are veiled according to Islamic law, with the covering being of varying degrees, from hair-covering, to the niqab (showing only the eyes), to the burqa' (full face and head-cover). Kuwaiti men and women are very fond of luxury products and commodities, often preferring the most expensive western designer accessories for watches, sunglasses, perfume, etc. Today, Kuwaitis comfortably and delicately balance the complexities of traditional attire with high-end western style in an often unique amalgam.

¹² FOOD

As a wealthy country, Kuwait is able to import foods from all over the world. Their desert climate supports almost no agriculture, making importation absolutely necessary. As Muslims, Kuwaitis cannot eat pork or drink alcohol, and all meats must be slaughtered according to Islamic tradition to ensure purity and cleanliness, which is known as halal (meaning permitted). Coffee and tea are the most popular beverages and are often mixed with spices, coffee with cardamom and tea with saffron or mint. Food and drink are always taken with the right hand. Etiquette of hospitality requires that hosts continue offering refills on drinks and food regardless of the guest's wishes.

The Kuwaiti cuisine offers a variety of dishes that reflect the country's Bedouin traditions and long history of contacts with other cultures, such as those of India, Iraq, and Iran. In addition to the simple Bedouin meals of dates and yogurt, Kuwaitis favor meat, fish, and rice. Spices are an essential part of the Kuwaiti cuisine. Among the most commonly used spices are coriander, cardamom, saffron, and turmeric. Most Kuwaitis eat in large groups and enjoy entertaining others including neighbors, extended families and clans. In the household and for traditional meals, Kuwaitis share food from a colossal single serving plate and customarily prefer using their bare hands over utensils.

When it comes to non-traditional foods, Kuwaitis' hefty budgets have led to discerning palates. As they prefer only the best of world fare, restaurants in Kuwait are exceptional compared to their counterparts elsewhere in the world.

13 EDUCATION

Education is a primary focus of the Kuwaiti government. It puts a tremendous amount of money into providing good, free education for all its citizens. Because of this emphasis, the literacy rate in Kuwait is quite high compared to those of other Arab countries: 74% of Kuwaitis are literate. The percentage is significantly lower for older women who grew up during a time when girls were not encouraged to obtain a formal education. The literacy rate is higher for young Kuwaitis: 87% of Kuwaiti children age 10 to 14 can read and write.

Education is compulsory for all Kuwaiti children 6 to 14 years of age. Schools teach in Arabic, and English is taught as a second language to all students 10 years of age and older. Boys and girls attend separate schools. Every child is trained to become computer-literate in primary and early secondary school. Since the mid 1970s the number of English language private all-grade schools has grown exponentially. These institutions differ from public schools in being co-ed and multinational in composition as they attract many children of expatriates. They also follow the British or American school curricula rather than that of the state's Ministry of Education.

Education is free through the university level; the government also pays for students to study abroad. All expenses, including books, tuition, transportation, uniforms, and meals, are paid by the government. The government also pays families of students an allowance to help cover any other education-related expenses. This has led to an explosion in the number of Kuwaitis with graduate degrees and upper-level qualifications in all industries and supported the government's campaign of takweet (Kuwaitization) of all sectors to ensure that reliance on expatriate expertise declines.

A law passed in 1981 in Kuwait requires all adults who cannot read to attend literacy classes. To round out Kuwaitis' education, the government has put in place a strong arts program.

14 CULTURAL HERITAGE

To help promote and encourage the arts in Kuwait, the Kuwaiti government founded the National Council for Culture, Arts, and Letters in 1974. Painting and sculpture are relatively recent developments on Kuwait's cultural scene. The National Museum building formerly contained the Al-Sabah Collection, which was considered one of the most important collections of Islamic arts in the world. During the Iraqi invasion, however, the entire museum was looted by the occupying forces.

The Sadu House is a cultural foundation and a museum that is entirely dedicated to the preservation of Bedouin art heritage, particularly weaving. In all other respects, Kuwait shares the cultural heritage of other Arab countries generally.

Arab music is rich and diverse. The oud, a popular instrument, is an ancient stringed instrument that is the ancestor of the European lute. Another traditional instrument originally from southern Egypt is the *rebaba,* a one-stringed instrument. The sea chantey is the most distinctive Kuwaiti folk song; chanteys were traditionally sung as work songs on pearling ships.

A traditional Arab dance is the *ardha,* or men's sword dance. Men carrying swords stand shoulder to shoulder and move forward and to the sides together to the rhythm of drums, while verses are sung by a poet. From among them a poet sings verses while drummers beat out a rhythm. Traditional Bedouin dances performed by men and women in national attire incorporate sheep and camel-skin drums, elaborate rhythmic clapping, various unique dance movements including the swinging of Kuwaiti women's long black hair from side to side to the beat of the music. Most nationalistic songs proclaim reverence to the ancestors of Kuwait and their minimalistic lifestyle, love and commitment to the nation and its sovereignty, and loyalty to its royal family, while proclaiming a desire to develop and progress.

Compared to that of other Gulf states, the Kuwaiti theater is highly professional.

Islam forbids the depiction of the human form, so Kuwaiti Islamic art is based on geometric and abstract shapes. Contemporary art in Kuwait has recently flourished with a growing faculty of fine arts at the country's national university. Traditional Islamic calligraphy is a sacred art, with passages from the Quran being the primary subject matter. Muslim visual art finds its greatest expression in the adornment of mosques.

The Islamic reverence for poetry and the poetic richness of the Arabic language inform much of Kuwait's cultural heritage.

15 WORK

The main source of employment and income in Kuwait is the oil industry. At the current rate of production, proven reserves are expected to last another 250 years. Kuwait was the first OPEC (Organization of Petroleum Exporting Countries) nation to explore outside its national boundaries for oil. Along with the oil are huge reserves of natural gas.

Even with these sources of substantial guaranteed income for perhaps another two centuries, Kuwait is trying to encourage the development of other industries so that it will not remain entirely dependent on oil and natural gas. The government offers low-interest loans, tax breaks, and subsidies for electricity and water to businesses that are starting out. Other industries remain small, however. Fishing is one of the oldest industries in Kuwait, as are pearling and shipbuilding.

Trade unions are not permitted in Kuwait, and the oil industry is totally government-run. In the 1990s over 43% of non-Kuwaiti women in Kuwait worked outside the home, while fewer than 14% of native Kuwaiti women did. Recent changes in Kuwaiti society have transformed these numbers completely and now qualified Kuwaiti women are represented in almost every industry.

16 SPORTS

Soccer is the most popular sport in Kuwait. The National Soccer Team has won both Arab and international competitions including a notable appearance in the 1982 World Cup in Spain. Kuwait has also had international success in the traditional sport of horse racing. Other traditional sports include falconry and camel racing. Water sports are popular in the Arabian (or Persian) Gulf, although jellyfish prevent swimming there. Kuwaitis tend to enjoy summer months by the many pools in their homes or public clubs. These government-run sports clubs have facilities for swimming, tennis, equestrian and other sports.

17 ENTERTAINMENT AND RECREATION

Kuwaitis, as well as tourists to Kuwait, spend a great deal of time relaxing on the beaches along the Gulf coast. Water sports are a popular form of recreation. One of the biggest attractions in Kuwait is Entertainment City, modeled after Disneyland in the United States and several other theme parks of comparable quality service every part of the country. These tend to house recreational and educational facilities as well as exhibits. There are several movie theaters in Kuwait cities, which show Arab, Indian, Pakistani, and English-language films, although most of these Hollywood and Bollywood films are heavily edited for anything deemed offensive to Islam or local culture by the state's censorship office.

18 FOLK ART, CRAFTS, AND HOBBIES

The best-known folk art in Kuwait is that of the Bedu (or Bedouins—see **Bedu**), particularly weavings done with brightly colored wool on a loom called a *sadu*. Other popular artifacts, ornaments and gifts include the argila (waterpipe used to smoke flavored tobacco), traditional engraved incense burners, miniatures of wooden fishing boats (boom), and elaborate fragrant and scented extracts forms of herbs and plants.

19 SOCIAL PROBLEMS

Even before the massive, widespread destruction caused by the Iraqi invasion and occupation (1990–91), Kuwait suffered from severe ecological problems caused by human population growth, industrialization, and especially the oil industry, which has leaked about 250,000 barrels' worth of oil into the Gulf each year. Only 3 out of 27 species of mammals in Kuwait are not endangered. They are the house rat, brown rat, and house mouse.

Following the scorched earth campaign accompanying the Iraqi retreat from Kuwait in 1991, the ecological catastrophe has worsened greatly. The Iraqis deliberately spilled four to six million barrels of oil into the Gulf, creating the largest oil slick ever on the planet. The slick covered about 1,550 sq km (about 600 sq mi) of sea surface and coated about 480 km (about 300 mi) of coastline. The Iraqis also bombed 749 oil wells, many of which caught fire. It took almost a year to put out the flames. The plume of oil smoke from the burning wells rose over 6,700 m (about 22,000 ft) into the air and spread for more than 2,400 km (1,500 mi), dropping soot and oil in its path. When the fires were still burning, everything in Kuwait was covered with oil and soot, including the people. Children who played outside became black with grime. It was impossible to keep clean.

The sulfur dioxide released in the smoke is a major component of acid rain. The blasted wells also leaked oil into lakes on the desert surface. At least 20,000 wild birds were killed by the oily lakes and the oil slick on the Gulf (when birds become coated with oil, they cannot fly and are no longer able to take care of themselves). The lakes of oil also killed all plant and animal life beneath them, and it is feared the oil may have seeped into the groundwater, allowing toxic metals to enter the food chain. These toxic metals can cause brain damage, cancer, and cardiac problems in humans and other animals. Medical research in Kuwait's centers has confirmed a significant and alarming rise in all these conditions in the past 17 years.

Another casualty of the war with Iraq was the fragile desert soil, churned up by the heavy military vehicles. It may take centuries for the soil structure to repair itself—if it can. This damage may lead to drifting sand dunes and more severe sandstorms. What little agriculture the desert land could support before the war has been made nearly impossible now. In other places, oil and soot dropped by the plume of smoke from the burning oil wells turned the desert surface into a blackened, brittle crust. Where the oil slick washed ashore, entire beaches turned black and grimy.

Before the Iraqi invasion, there was a sharp division between Kuwaiti citizens (the minority) and foreign workers (the majority). After the war, those tensions increased. The Kuwaiti government rounded up many foreign workers and forced them to leave the country. Those who remain still cannot become citizens, even children born in Kuwait to foreign workers. After a lifetime of working in Kuwait, a foreigner is asked to leave the country immediately upon retiring. This creates a great deal of ill will among the long-term foreign workers in Kuwait.

Since the Iraqi invasion, another division has occurred in Kuwaiti society, between the "insiders"—those who stayed in Kuwait during the occupation—and the "outsiders"—those who fled the country and have since returned. Insiders feel that they should have more say in the running of the country now, since they stayed to defend their homes. Outsiders include the royal family and ruling members of the government, who hesitate to give up much of their power. The government did finally allow elections for a new National Assembly in 1992, giving the people a greater say in their governance.

One of the most difficult social problems in Kuwait is the emotional and psychological scarring from the horrors of the Iraqi invasion and occupation. At least 100,000 persons—Kuwaitis and others—died in the war, and another 300,000 were wounded. Many Kuwaitis were kidnapped and taken to Iraq. Others were arrested, tortured, raped, killed, or forced to watch members of their family being raped or killed. Some Kuwaitis simply "disappeared," never to be seen again. Most of the reconstruction effort in Kuwait has focused on physical and industrial reconstruction, ignoring people's emotional wounds. These wounds will take far longer to heal, and no amount of money will cure them.

However, the most complicated of all social problems in Kuwait has been the perennial condition of a subset of Kuwaitis who have been denied citizenship. Known commonly as the Bidoon (the withouts), they are descendents of tribes that have lived and roamed the land that is Kuwait for decades, if not centuries. While numbers vary, estimates are often listed around 120,000 persons. The Bidoon receive few of the privileges afforded to citizens and have been increasingly vocal in their protests of this disparity. During the Iraqi invasion, their loyalty to the sovereignty of the Kuwaiti state and its independence was called into question as some chose to align themselves with the Iraqis at the expense of the Kuwaiti royal family, which they hold reservations about. In the post-liberation period, the government has adopted various measures to try and integrate this population and allowed a small proportion to become citizens. Despite this, the issue remains a sore often aggravated by various issues.

20 GENDER ISSUES

For decades, girls received training in home and child care as well as vocational training for jobs considered acceptable for women: secretary, receptionist, teacher, and so forth. If they continued through to a college education, they were not encouraged to take engineering courses and other vocations perceived as masculine, but they were able to become medical doctors. This resulted in an upsurge of women doctors, with about one-third of all Kuwaiti doctors being women. Interestingly, Kuwaiti women exceed men in every faculty at Kuwait University and at several new private accredited American and British universities. Women have attained some of the top professional positions in the country including judges, deans, engineers, and notable literary figures.

Women are more independent in Kuwait than in most other Arab countries, but they are still usually segregated from men and were not allowed to vote until 2005. In a recent upsurge of gender equality, suffrage and candidacy were decreed universal for all able eligible Kuwaiti citizens of age. This resulted in several Kuwaiti women running in the first parliamentary elections in 2008. Although none secured a seat in the all-male parliament, it led to wide-ranging debates in the country about the role of women in a rapidly-modernizing Kuwait, with support from progressive citizens and sharp criticism from traditionalists and Islamists. Today, women have also built networks of solidarity in the form of diwaniyas, which are increasingly popular and common given the growing influence of women in the Gulf emirate. Recently, the emir of Kuwait appointed to his cabinet two women ministers, which was considered a significant move towards incorporating women into the political system.

21 BIBLIOGRAPHY

Abercrombie, Thomas J. "The Persian Gulf: Living in Harm's Way." *National Geographic* 173, no. 5 (May 1988): 648–671.

Background Notes: Kuwait. Washington, D.C.: United States Department of State, Bureau of Public Affairs, Office of Public Communication, November 1994.

Farag, Talaat I. (2006, January). "The Young Man that Inspired a Nation: How a Kuwaiti with Down Syndrome Child Moved his Parents, Community, Scholars, and me." *Ambassadors Online Magazine*, Vol 9, Issue 1.

Farag, Talaat I. "Community Genetics in Kuwait: A 25-Years Experience." *Ambassadors Online Magazine*, Vol 9, Issue 2: July 2006

Mallos, Tess. *The Complete Middle East Cookbook.* Boston: Charles E. Tuttle Company, Inc., 1993.

Sluglett, Peter, and Marion Farouk-Sluglett. *Tuttle Guide to the Middle East.* Boston: Charles E. Tuttle Co., 1992.

Tétreault, Mary Ann. "Kuwait: The Morning After." *Current History: The Middle East, 1992.* 91, no. 561 (January 1992): 6–10.

Vine, Peter and Paula Casey. *Kuwait: A Nation's Story.* London: Immel Publishing, 1992.

—reviewed by S. Abed-Kotob; reviewed by Adel Iskandar

GLOSSARY

a capella: singing without musical accompaniment.

aboriginal: the first inhabitants of a country. A species of animals or plants which originated within a given area.

acupuncture: ancient practice of treating disease or relieving pain by inserting needles into pressure points on the body. The Chinese are associated with this medical treatment.

adobe: a clay from which bricks are made for use in making houses.

adult literacy: the capacity of adults to read and write.

agglutinative tongue: a language in which the suffixes and prefixes to words retain a certain independence of one another and of the stem to which they are added. Turkish is an example of an agglutinative tongue.

agrarian economy: an economy where agriculture is the dominant form of economic activity.

active volcano: a large rock mass formed by the expulsion of molten rock, or lava, which periodically erupts.

acute accent: a mark (') used to denote accentual stress of a single sound.

agglutinative tongue: a language in which the suffixes and prefixes to words retain a certain independence of one another and of the stem to which they are added. Turkish is an example of an agglutinative tongue.

agrarian economy: an economy where agriculture is the dominant form of economic activity.

agrarian society: a society where agriculture dominates the day-to-day activities of the population.

All Saints' Day: a Christian holiday on 1 November (a public holiday in many countries). Saints and martyrs who have no special festival are commemorated. In the Middle Ages, it was known as All Hallows' Day; the evening of the previous day, October 31, was called All Hallow Even, from which the secular holiday Halloween is derived.

All Souls' Day: a Christian holiday. This day, 2 November, is dedicated to prayer for the repose of the souls of the dead.

allies: groups or persons who are united in a common purpose. Typically used to describe nations that have joined together to fight a common enemy in war.

Altaic language family: a family of languages spoken by people in portions of northern and eastern Europe, and nearly the whole of northern and central Asia, together with some other regions, and divided into five branches, the Ugrian or Finno-Hungarian, Samoyed, Turkish, Mongolian, and Tungus.

altoplano: refers to the high plains of South American mountain ranges on the Pacific coast.

Amerindian: a contraction of the two words, American Indian. It describes native peoples of North, South, or Central America.

Amerindian language group: the language groups of the American Indians.

Amish: Anabaptist Protestants originally from Germany. Settled in Pennsylvania and the American Midwest.

Anabaptist: Christian sect that was founded in Switzerland during the 16th century. Rejected infant baptism as invalid.

ancestor worship: the worship of one's ancestors.

Anglican: pertaining to or connected with the Church of England.

animism: the belief that natural objects and phenomena have souls or innate spiritual powers.

anthropologist: one who studies the characteristics, customs, and development of mankind.

anti-miscegenation laws: prohibition of marriage or sexual relations between men and women of different races.

anti-Semitism: agitation, persecution, or discrimination (physical, emotional, economic, political, or otherwise) directed against the Jews.

apartheid: the past governmental policy in the Republic of South Africa of separating the races in society.

appliqué: a trimming made from one cloth and sewn onto another cloth.

aquaculture: the culture or "farming" of aquatic plants or animals.

arable land: land which can be cultivated by plowing, as distinguished from grassland, woodland, common pasture, and wasteland.

archipelago: any body of water having many islands, or the islands themselves collectively.

arctic climate: cold, frigid weather similar to that experienced at or near the North Pole.

arid: dry; without moisture; parched with heat.

aristocracy: a small minority that controls the government of a nation, typically on the basis of inherited wealth. Political power is restricted to its members. Also may referred to any privileged elite of a country.

artifacts: objects or tools that date back to an ancient period of human history.

Ash Wednesday: a Christian holiday. The first day of Lent, observed 46 days before Easter, is so called from the practice of placing ashes on the forehead of the worshipper as a sign of penitence. In the Roman Catholic Church, these ashes are obtained from burning palm branches used in the previous year's Palm Sunday observation. (Palm Sunday commemorates the entry of Jesus into Jerusalem a week before Easter Sunday, and it begins Holy Week.) On Ash Wednesday, the ashes are placed on the forehead of the communicant during Mass. The recipient is told, "Remember that you are dust, and unto dust you shall return" or "Turn away from sin and be faithful to the Gospel."

Ashura: a Muslim holiday. This fast day was instituted by Muhammad as the equivalent of the Jewish Yom Kippur but later became voluntary when Ramadan replaced it as a holiday of penance. It also commemorates Noah's leaving the ark on Mt. Ararat after the waters of the Great Flood had subsided. In Iran, the martyrdom of Husayn, grandson of Muhammad, is commemorated with passion plays on this day.

assembly: in government, a body of legislators that meets together regularly.

Assumption: a Christian holiday. This holiday, observed on 15 August in many countries, celebrates the Roman Catholic and Eastern Orthodox dogma that, following Mary's death, her body was taken into heaven and reunited with her soul.

atheist: a person who denies the existence of God, or of a supreme intelligent being.

atherosclerosis: a disease of the arteries. Characterized by blockages that prevent blood flow from the heart to the brain and other parts of the body.

atoll: a coral island, consisting of a strip or ring of coral surrounding a central lagoon. Such islands are common in the Pacific Ocean and are often very picturesque.

aurora borealis: the northern lights, consisting of bands of light across the night sky seen in northern geographical locations.

Australoid: pertains to the type of aborigines of Australia.

Austronesian language: a family of languages which includes Indonesian, Melanesian, Polynesian, and Micronesian sub-families.

B

Babushka: a head scarf worn by women.

Baltic States: the three formerly communist countries of Estonia, Latvia, and Lithuania that border on the Baltic Sea.

Bantu language group: a name applied to the south African family of tongues. The most marked peculiarity of these languages is their prevailing use of prefixes instead of suffixes in derivation and inflection. Some employ clicks and clucks as alphabetic elements.

baptism: any ceremonial bathing intended as a sign of purification, dedication, etc. Baptisms are performed by immersion of the person in water, or by sprinkling the water on the person.

Baptist: a member of a Protestant denomination which practices adult baptism by immersion.

barren land: unproductive land, partly or entirely treeless.

barter: Trade in which merchandise is exchanged directly for other merchandise or services without use of money.

bilingual: able to speak two languages. Also used to describe anything that contains or is expressed in two languages, such as directions written in both English and Spanish.

boat people: a term used to describe individuals (refugees) who attempt to flee their country by boat.

Bolshevik Revolution: pertaining to the Russian revolution of 1917. Russian communists overthrew Tsar Nicholas II and ended the feudal Russian empire.

borscht: cold beet soup, topped with sour cream.

Brahman: a member of the sacred caste among the Hindus. There are many subdivisions of the caste, often remaining in isolation from one another.

bratwurst: seasoned fresh German sausage. Made from pork or veal.

bride price: the price paid to the family of the bride by the young man who seeks to marry her.

bride wealth: the money or property or livestock a bride brings to her marriage. *See* **dowry**.

Buddhism: the religious system common in India and eastern Asia. Founded by and based upon the teachings of Gautama Buddha, Buddhism asserts that suffering is an inescapable part of life. Deliverance can only be achieved through the practice of charity, temperance, justice, honesty, and truth.

bureaucracy: a system of government which is characterized by division into bureaus of administration with their own divisional heads. Also refers to the institutional inflexibility and red tape of such a system.

bush country: a large area of land which is wild with low, bushlike vegetation.

Byzantine Empire: an empire centered in the city of Byzantium, now Istanbul in present-day Turkey.

C

Cajun: name given to Canadians who emigrated to Louisiana from Acadia, the old name for Nova Scotia. Contraction of the name Accadian.

Calvinist: a follower of the theological system of John Calvin.

Candlemas: a Christian holiday. A national holiday on 2 February in Liechtenstein, this observation is now called the Presentation of the Lord, commemorating the presentation of the infant Jesus in the Temple at Jerusalem. Before a 1969 Vatican reform, it commemorated the Purification of Mary 40 days after giving birth to a male child in accordance with a Jewish practice of the time.

capital punishment: the ultimate act of punishment for a crime; the death penalty.

capitalism: an economic system in which goods and services and the means to produce and sell them are privately owned, and prices and wages are determined by market forces.

cash crop: a crop that is grown to be sold, rather than kept for private use.

caste system: one of the artificial divisions or social classes into which the Hindus are rigidly separated according to the religious law of Brahmanism. The privileges and disabilities of a caste are passed on to each succeeding generation.

Caucasian: the "white" race of human beings, as determined by genealogy and physical features.

Caucasoid: belonging to the racial group characterized by light skin pigmentation. Commonly called the "white race," although it can refer to peoples of darker skin color.

celibate: a person who voluntarily abstains from marriage. In some religious practices, the person will often take a vow of abstention from sexual intercourse as well.

censorship: the practice of withholding certain items of news that may cast a country in an unfavorable light or give away secrets to the enemy.

census: an official counting of the inhabitants of a state or country with details of sex and age, family, occupation, possessions, etc.

Central Powers: in World War I, Germany and Austria-Hungary, and their allies, Turkey and Bulgaria.

centrally planned economy: an economic system in which all aspects are supervised and regulated by the government.

cerebrovascular: pertains to the brain and the blood vessels leading to and from the brain.

chancellery: the office of an embassy or consulate.

chaperone: an older married person, usually female, who supervises the activities of young, unmarried couples.

chattel: refers to the movable personal property of an individual or group. It cannot refer to real estate or buildings.

cholera: an acute infectious disease characterized by severe diarrhea, vomiting, and often, death.

Christianity: the religion founded by Jesus Christ.

Christmas: a Christian holiday. The annual commemoration of the nativity of Jesus is held on 25 December. A midnight Mass ushers in this joyous celebration in many Roman

Catholic churches. The custom of distributing gifts to children on Christmas Eve derives from a Dutch custom originally observed on the evening before St. Nicholas' Day (6 December). The day after Christmas—often called Boxing Day, for the boxed gifts customarily given—is a public holiday in many countries.

Church of England: the national and established church in England. The Church of England claims continuity with the branch of the Catholic Church which existed in England before the Reformation. Under Henry VIII, the spiritual supremacy and jurisdiction of the Pope were abolished, and the sovereign was declared head of the church.

chaplet: a wreath or garland of flowers placed on a woman's head.

cistern: a natural or artificial receptacle or reservoir for holding water or other fluids.

city-state: an independent state consisting of a city and its surrounding territory.

civil law: the law developed by a nation or state for the conduct of daily life of its own people.

civil rights: the privileges of all individuals to be treated as equals under the laws of their country; specifically, the rights given by certain amendments to the U.S. Constitution.

civil unrest: the feeling of uneasiness due to an unstable political climate or actions taken as a result of it.

civil war: a war between groups of citizens of the same country who have different opinions or agendas. The Civil War of the United States was the conflict between the states of the North and South from 1861 to 1865.

coca: a shrub native to South America, the leaves of which produce alkaloids which are used in the production of cocaine.

cohabitation: living together as husband and wife without being legally married.

cold war: refers to conflict over ideological differences that is carried on by words and diplomatic actions, not by military action. The term is usually used to refer to the tension that existed between the United States and the USSR from the 1950s until the breakup of the USSR in 1991.

collard greens: a hearty, leafy green vegetable. Popular part of southern American and West Indian cuisine.

collective farm: a large farm formed from many small farms and supervised by the government; usually found in communist countries.

collective farming: the system of farming on a collective where all workers share in the income of the farm.

colloquial: belonging to the language of common or familiar conversation, or ordinary, everyday speech; often especially applied to common words and phrases which are not used in formal speech.

colonial period: in the United States, the period of time when the original thirteen colonies were being formed.

colonist: any member of a colony or one who helps settle a new colony.

colony: a group of people who settle in a new area far from their original country, but still under the jurisdiction of that country. Also refers to the newly settled area itself.

commerce: the trading of goods (buying and selling), especially on a large scale, between cities, states, and countries.

commodity: any items, such as goods or services, that are bought or sold, or agricultural products that are traded or marketed.

common law: a legal system based on custom and legal precedent. The basic system of law of the United States.

common law spouse: a husband or wife in a marriage that, although not legally formalized through a religious or state-sanctioned ceremony, is legally acknowledged based on the agreement of the two people to consider themselves married.

communicable disease: referring to infectious or contagious diseases.

communion: 1. The act of partaking of the sacrament of the Eucharist; the celebration of the Lord's Supper. 2. A body of Christians who have one common faith, but not necessarily ecclesiastical union; a religious denomination. 3. Union in religious worship, or in doctrine and discipline.

communism: a form of government whose system requires common ownership of property for the use of all citizens. All profits are to be equally distributed and prices on goods and services are usually set by the state. Also, communism refers directly to the official doctrine of the former USSR.

compulsory education: the mandatory requirement for children to attend school until they have reached a certain age or grade level.

condolence: expression of sympathy.

Condomblé: American name for the Yoruba pantheon of 401 gods and goddesses.

Confucianism: the ethical system taught by the Chinese philosopher Confucius. It was enlarged upon by his contemporary Mencius so that political systems would be tested with the same ethical standards. (*See* **Taoism**)

constitution: the written laws and basic rights of citizens of a country or members of an organized group.

consumer goods: items that are bought to satisfy personal needs or wants of individuals.

Coptic Christians: members of the Coptic Church of Egypt, formerly of Ethiopia.

Corpus Christi: a Christian holiday. This holiday in honor of the Eucharist is observed on the Thursday or Sunday after Trinity Sunday, which is the Sunday after Pentecost. In the Roman Catholic and Eastern Orthodox Churches, the Eucharist is a sacrament in which the consecrated bread and wine become the body and blood of Jesus Christ, a belief stemming from New Testament accounts of the Last Supper.

corrugated steel: galvanized metal with furrows that give added strength. This metal is often used as roofing materials on houses in tropical countries because of its strength.

coup d'état: a sudden, violent overthrow of a government or its leader.

covert action: secret, concealed activities carried out without public knowledge.

cricket (sport): a game played by two teams with a ball and bat, with two wickets being defended by a batsman.

criminal law: the branch of law that deals primarily with crimes and their punishments.

crown colony: a colony established by a commonwealth over which the monarch has some control, as in colonies established by the British Commonwealth.

Crowning of Our Lady of Altagracia: a Christian holiday in honor of Mary, this day is celebrated in the Dominican Republic on 15 August with a pilgrimage to her shrine. (Altagracia Day, 21 January, is also a holiday in the Dominican Republic.)

Crusades: military expeditions by European Christian armies in the 11th, 12th, and 13th centuries to win land controlled by the Muslims in the Middle East.

cuisine: a particular style of preparing food, especially when referring to the cooking of a particular country or ethnic group.

cultivable land: land that can be prepared for the production of crops.

cursive script: a style of writing in which the letters are joined together in a flowing manner.

Cushitic language group: a group of Hamitic languages which are spoken in Ethiopia and other areas of eastern Africa.

cyclone: any atmospheric movement, general or local, in which the wind blows spirally around and in towards a center. In the northern hemisphere, the cyclonic movement is usually counter-clockwise, and in the southern hemisphere, it is clockwise.

Cyrillic alphabet: an alphabet adopted by the Slavic people and invented by Cyril and Methodius in the 9th century as an alphabet that was easier for the copyist to write. The Russian alphabet is a slight modification of it.

D

Day of Our Lady of Mercy (Las Mercedes): a Christian holiday in honor of Mary, this observance on 24 September is a holiday in the Dominican Republic.

Day of Santa Rosa of Lima: a Christian holiday. The feast day in honor of the first native-born saint of the New World, declared patron saint of South America by Pope Clement X in 1671, is 23 August, but in Peru, she is commemorated by a national holiday on 30 August.

Day of St. Peter and St. Paul: a Christian holiday. This observance, on 29 June, commemorates the martyrdom of the two apostles traditionally believed to have been executed in Rome on the same day (c. AD 67) during the persecution of Christians ordered by Emperor Nero.

deforestation: the removal of a forest ecosystem.

deity: a being with the attributes, nature, and essence of a god; a divinity.

delta: triangular-shaped deposits of soil formed at the mouths of large rivers.

democracy: a form of government in which the power lies in the hands of the people, who can govern directly, or indirectly by electing representatives.

demography: that department of anthropology which relates to vital and social statistics and their application to the comparative study of races and nations.

desegregation: the act of removing restrictions on people of a particular race that keep them separate from other groups, socially, economically, and, sometimes, physically.

détente: the official lessening of tension between countries in conflict.

developed countries: countries which have a high standard of living and a well-developed industrial base.

diacritics: as in diacritical marks, a dot, line, or other mark added or put adjacent to a letter or sign in order to give it a different sound or to indicate some particular accent, tone, stress, or emphasis. An example of diacritical marks would be those used in dictionaries to aid in pronunciation of words.

dialect: One of a number of related forms of speech regarded as descending from a common origin. The speech pattern of a locality or social class as distinguished from the generally accepted literary language.

dictatorship: a form of government in which all the power is retained by an absolute leader or tyrant. There are no rights granted to the people to elect their own representatives.

direct descendant: the offspring in an unbroken line of ancestors.

divine origin: having originated directly, or by direct descendant, from a divine being.

dogma: a principle, maxim, or tenet held as being firmly established.

domicile: a place of residence of an individual or family; a place of habitual abode.

dowry: the sum of the property or money that a bride brings to her groom at their marriage.

druid: a member of a Celtic religion practiced in ancient Britain, Ireland, and France.

Druze: a member of a religious sect of Syria, living chiefly in the mountain regions of Lebanon.

ducal: Referring to a duke or a dukedom.

dysentery: painful inflammation of the large intestine.

E

Easter: the chief Christian holiday is Easter, the annual celebration of the resurrection of Jesus Christ. Like Passover, the Jewish feast from which it is derived, the date of observation is linked to the phases of the moon. Since the Christian calendar is a solar one rather than a lunar one, the date of Easter changes from year to year. Easter is celebrated on the first Sunday after the first full moon following the spring equinox; in the Gregorian calendar, it can occur as early as 22 March or as late as 25 April. The Easter date determines the date of many other Roman Catholic holidays, such as Ash Wednesday, Ascension, and Pentecost.

Easter Monday: a Christian holiday. The day after Easter is a public holiday in many countries.

empire: a group of territories ruled by one sovereign, or supreme ruler.

Epiphany of Our Lord: a Christian holiday. Traditionally observed on 6 January but now observable on the Sunday falling between 2 January and 7 January, this feast commemorates the adoration of the Magi, who journeyed to the place of Jesus' birth. In the Orthodox churches, however, it is the feast celebrating Jesus' baptism.

episcopal: belonging to or vested in bishops or prelates; characteristic of or pertaining to a bishop or bishops.

equestrian culture: a culture that depends on horses for its livelihood. Mastery of the horse is an essential part of the culture's identity.

escarpment: a steep cliff formed from a geological fault or erosion.

ethnographic: referring to the division of anthropology which studies primitive cultures.

ethnolinguistic group: a classification of related languages based on common ethnic origin.

exodus: the departure or migration of a large body of people or animals from one country or region to another.

extinction: dying out of a species of animals or a culture of people.

F

fauna: referring to species of animals found in a specific region.

Feast of Our Lady of Angels: a Christian holiday. This feast, on 2 August, is celebrated as a national holiday in Costa Rica in honor of the Virgin Mary. Pilgrimage is made to the basilica in Cartago, which houses a black stone statue of the Virgin.

fetishism: the practice of worshipping a material object which one believes has mysterious powers residing in it or is the representation of a deity to which worship may be paid and from which supernatural aid is expected.

feudal society: In medieval times, an economic and social structure in which persons could hold land given to them by a lord (nobleman) in return for service to that lord.

Finno-Ugric language group: a subfamily of languages spoken in northeastern Europe, including Finnish, Hungarian (Ugric, Magyar), Estonian, Lapp, and others.

flora: referring to native plant life in a specific region.

folk religion: a religion with origins and traditions among the common people of a nation or region; relevant to their particular lifestyle.

folk tale: an oral story that is passed from generation to generation. Folktales are cultural records of the history and progress of different ethnic groups.

free-market economy: an economic system that relies on the market, as opposed to government planners, to set the prices for wages and products.

fundamentalist: a person who holds religious beliefs based on the complete acceptance of the words of the Bible or other holy scripture as the truth. For instance, a fundamentalist would believe the story of creation exactly as it is told in the Bible and would reject the idea of evolution.

G

gastroenteritis: inflammation of the stomach and small intestines.

geometric pattern: a design of circles, triangles, or lines on cloth.

geriatrics: the study and treatment of diseases of old age.

Germanic language group: a large branch of the Indo-European family of languages including German itself, the Scandinavian languages, Dutch, Yiddish, Modern English, Modern Scottish, Afrikaans and others. The group also includes extinct languages such as Gothic, Old High German, Old Saxon, Old English, Middle English and the like.

glottal stop: a sound formed in speech by a brief but complete closure of the glottis, the opening between the vocal cords. It is a typical sound in certain British dialects.

godparent: a male or female adult who is asked by the parents of a newborn child to assume responsibility for the care and rearing of the child in the event of the death of the parents. Godparents sometimes contribute school tuition, gifts on birthdays and holidays, as well as take an active part in the child's life.

Good Friday: a Christian holiday. The day after Holy Thursday, it is devoted to remembrance of the crucifixion of Jesus and is given to penance and prayer.

Greek Catholic: a person who is a member of an Orthodox Eastern Church.

Greek Orthodox: the official church of Greece, a self-governing branch of the Orthodox Eastern Church.

H

haiku: a form of Japanese poetry, consisting of three lines. Each line has a specific measurement of syllables.

Hanukkah: a Jewish holiday. The Festival of Lights, corresponding roughly to the winter solstice, is celebrated over an eight-day period beginning on 25 Kislev, the third month. Also known as the Feast of Dedication and Feast of the Maccabees, Hanukkah commemorates the rededication of the Temple at Jerusalem in 164 BC. According to tradition, the one ritually pure container of olive oil, sufficient to illuminate the Temple for one day, miraculously burned for eight days, until new oil could be prepared. A feature of the Hanukkah celebration is the lighting in each Jewish home of an eight-branched candelabrum, the menorah. This festival, though not a public holiday in Israel, is widely observed with the lighting of giant menorahs in public places.

harem: in a Muslim household, refers to the women (wives, concubines, and servants in ancient times) who live there and also to the area of the home they live in.

harmattan: an intensely dry, dusty wind felt along the coast of Africa between Cape Verde and Cape Lopez. It prevails at intervals during the months of December, January, and February.

Hinduism: the religion professed by a large part of the inhabitants of India. It is a development of the ancient Brahmanism, influenced by Buddhistic and other elements. Its forms are varied and numerous.

Holi: a Hindu holiday. A festival lasting 3 to 10 days, Holi closes the old year with processions and merriment. It terminates on the full moon of Phalguna, the last month, corresponding to February or March.

Holocaust: the mass slaughter of European civilians, the vast majority Jews, by the Nazis during World War II.

Holy (Maundy) Thursday: a Christian holiday. The Thursday preceding Easter commemorates the Last Supper, the betrayal of Jesus by Judas Iscariot, and the arrest and arraignment of Jesus. In Rome, the pope customarily performs a ceremony in remembrance of Jesus' washing of his apostles' feet (John 13:5–20).

Holy Roman Empire: a kingdom consisting of a loose union of German and Italian territories that existed from around the ninth century until 1806.

Holy Saturday: a Christian holiday. This day commemorates the time during which Jesus was buried and, like Good Friday, is given to solemn prayer.

homeland: a region or area set aside to be a state for a people of a particular national, cultural, or racial origin.

homogeneous: of the same kind or nature, often used in reference to a whole.

homophonic: music that has a single part with no harmonies.

Horn of Africa: the Horn of Africa comprises Djibouti, Eritrea, Ethiopia, Somalia, and Sudan.

human rights issues: any matters involving people's basic rights which are in question or thought to be abused.

humanist: a person who centers on human needs and values, and stresses dignity of the individual.

hydrology: the science of dealing with the earth's waters and their distribution above and below ground.

I

Id al-Adha: a Muslim holiday. The Great Festival, or Sacrificial Feast, celebrates the end of the special pilgrimage season, or Hajj, to Mecca and Medina, an obligation for Muslims once in their lifetime if physically and economically feasible. The slaughter of animals pays tribute to Abraham's obedience to God in offering his son to the Lord for sacrifice; a portion of the meat is supposed to be donated to the poor. The feast begins on 10 Dhu'l-Hijja and continues to 13 Dhu'l-Hijja (14 Dhu'l-Hijja in a leap year). In Malaysia and Singapore, this festival is celebrated as Hari Raya Haji; in Indonesia, Lebaran Haji; in Turkey, Kurban Bayrami.

Id al-Fitr: a Muslim holiday. The Little Festival, or Breaking-Fast-Festival, which begins just after Ramadan, on 1 Shawwal, the 10th month, is the occasion for three or four days of feasting. In Malaysia and Singapore, this festival is called Hari Raya Puasa; in Turkey, Seker Bayrami.

Iemanja: Brazilian name for Yoruba river goddess, Yemoja. Represented as a mermaid.

Immaculate Conception: a Christian holiday. This day, 8 December, celebrates the Roman Catholic dogma asserting that Mary's conception, as the future mother of God, was uniquely free from original sin. In Paraguay, it is observed as the Day of Our Lady of Caacupé.

incursion: a sudden or brief invasion or raid.

indigenous: born or originating in a particular place or country; native to a particular region or area.

indigent: person without any means of economic support.

indigo: a blue dye that is extracted from plants.

Indo-Aryan language group: the group that includes the languages of India; within a branch of the Indo-European language family.

Indo-European language family: the large family of languages that includes those of India, much of Europe, and southwestern Asia.

indulgence: a Catholic blessing given for a person's soul after death.

infant mortality: infant deaths.

infant mortality rate: the number of deaths of children less than one year old per 1,000 live births in a given year.

infanticide: the act of murdering a baby.

infidel: one who is without faith, or unbelieving; particularly, one who rejects the distinctive doctrines of a particular religion, while perhaps remaining an adherent to another religion.

inflective: refers to a language in which differences in tone and pitch give meaning to words and indicate grammatical constructions.

interferon: a drug used in the treatment of cancer in Mexico.

Inuit: an indigenous people of northwestern Canada. They are sometimes mistakenly called Eskimos.

Islam: the religious system of Mohammed, practiced by Muslims and based on a belief in Allah as the supreme being and Mohammed as his prophet. The term also refers to those nations in which it is the primary religion.

isthmus: a narrow strip of land with connecting large bodies of water on either side.

J

Jehovah's Witness: a member of a Christian sect that believes that the end of the world is near and that God should establish a theocracy on earth.

Judaism: the religious system of the Jews, based on the Old Testament as revealed to Moses and characterized by a belief in one God and adherence to the laws of scripture and rabbinic traditions.

Judeo-Christian: the dominant traditional religious makeup of the United States and other countries based on the worship of the Old and New Testaments of the Bible.

Juneteenth: an African American holiday that celebrates the freeing of slaves in America. It is thought to coincide with the surrender of the Confederacy to the Union armies.

Junkanoo: a holiday celebrated around December in the Caribbean and South America. It also has been observed in the United States in Alabama. The holiday has West African origins. Also known as John Canoe and Yancanu.

K

kale: Another hearty, green leafy vegetable that is sometimes mixed with spinach and collard greens to vary the flavor of these vegetables.

khan: a title given Genghis Khan and his successors who ruled over Turkey and Mongolia in the Middle Ages.

kielbasa: seasoned Polish sausage. Made from beef or pork.

L

lagoon: a shallow body of water connected to a larger body of water. It is sometimes separated from the larger body by reefs.

lama: a celebrated priest or ecclesiastic belonging to that variety of Buddhism known as Lamaism. The Dalai-Lama and the tesho- or bogdo-lama are regarded as supreme pontiffs.

land reforms: steps taken to create a fair distribution of farm land, especially by governmental action.

latke: potato pancake.

Leeward Islands: northern islands of the Lesser Antilles in the Caribbean that stretch from Puerto Rico southward.

leprosy: an infectious disease of the skin or nerves which can cause ulcers of the skin, loss of feeling, or loss of fingers and toes.

life expectancy: an individual's expected lifespan, calculated as an average.

lingua franca: Originally, a mixed language or jargon of Mediterranean ports, consisting of Italian mixed with Arabic, Turkish, Greek, French, and Spanish. Nowadays, the phrase is used to denote any hybrid tongue used similarly in other parts of the world; an international dialect.

linguist: a person skilled in the use of languages.

linguistic group: a group of related languages.

literacy: the ability to read and write.

lox: kosher smoked salmon.

Lutheran: of or pertaining to Martin Luther (1483–1546), the reformer, to the Evangelical Protestant Church of Germany which bears his name, or to the doctrines taught by Luther or held by the Evangelical Lutheran Church.

M

macron: a horizontal mark placed over a vowel to indicate its pronunciation as long.

maize: another name (Spanish or British) for corn or the color of ripe corn.

Malayo-Polynesian language group: also referred to as the Austronesian language group, which includes the Indonesian, Polynesian, Melanesian, and Micronesian subfamilies.

mangrove: a kind of evergreen shrub growing along tropical coasts.

marimba: a type of xylophone found in Central and South America.

massif: a central mountain-mass or the dominant part of a range of mountains. A part of a range which appears, from the position of the depression by which it is more or less isolated, to form an independent whole.

matriarchy: a society in which women are recognized as the leaders of the family or tribe.

matrifocal: a society in which women are the focus of activity or attention.

matrilineal (descent): descending from, or tracing descent through, the maternal line.

Mayan language family: the languages of the Central American Indians, further divided into two subgroups: the Maya and the Huastek.

Mecca (Mekkah): a city in Saudi Arabia; a destination of pilgrims in the Islamic world.

Mennonite: a member of the Christian denomination which originated in Friesland, Holland in the early part of the 16th century and upholds the doctrine of which Menno Simons (1492–1559) was the chief exponent.

mestizo: the offspring of a person of mixed blood; especially, a person of mixed Spanish and American Indian parentage.

metamorphosis: referring to the shamanic practice of changing from a person to an animal.

Methodist: a member of the Christian denomination founded by John Wesley (1703–1791). The name was first applied to Wesley and his companions on account of their methodical habits in study and in religious life.

millennium: any one-thousand-year period, but also refers to a real or imagined period of peace and happiness.

missionary: a person sent by ecclesiastical authority to work to spread his religious faith in a community where his church has no self-supporting organization.

Mohammed (or Muhammed or Mahomet): an Arabian prophet, known as the "Prophet of Allah" who founded the religion of Islam in 622, and wrote The Koran, the scripture of Islam. Also commonly spelled Muhammed, especially by Islamic people.

Mongol: one of an Asiatic race chiefly resident in Mongolia, a region north of China proper and south of Siberia.

Mongoloid: having physical characteristics like those of the typical Mongols (Chinese, Japanese, Turks, Eskimos, etc.).

monogamy: the practice of marrying one spouse.

monolingual: speaking one language only.

monsoon: a wind occurring in the alternation of the trade-winds in India and the north Indian Ocean. They occur between April and October when the regular northeast trade-winds are reversed and, with occasional interruptions, the wind blows at almost a steady gale from the southwest. In some areas, as in China, the change of the monsoons is followed with storms and much rain.

Moors: one of the Arab tribes that conquered Spain in the 8th century.

Mormon: an adherent of the religious body the Church of Jesus Christ of Latter-day Saints founded in 1830 by Joseph Smith.

Moslem: a follower of Mohammed (spelled Muhammed by many Islamic people), in the religion of Islam.

mosque: a Mohammedan place of worship and the ecclesiastical organization with which it is connected.

mother tongue: a tongue or language to which other languages owe their origin. One's native language.

Motown: nickname for Detroit. A contraction of Motor City Town.

mujahideen or **mujahedeen:** *see* **mujahidin.**

mujahidin: rebel fighters in Islamic countries, especially those supporting the cause of Islam.

mulatto: one who is the offspring of parents of whom one is white and the other is black.

multicultural: awareness of the effect and existence of more than one cultural viewpoint within one's value system and world view.

multilingual: having the ability to speak several languages. Also used to describe anything that contains or is expressed in several languages, such as directions written in English, Spanish, and French.

mummify: ancient method used to preserve the dead. Associated with ancient Egyptian culture.

Muslim: same as Moslem.

Muslim New Year: a Muslim holiday. Although in some countries 1 Muharram, which is the first month of the Islamic year, is observed as a holiday, in other places the new year is observed on Sha'ban, the eighth month of the year. This practice apparently stems from pagan Arab times. Shab-i-Bharat, a national holiday in Bangladesh on this day, is held by many to be the occasion when God ordains all actions in the coming year.

N

native tongue: one's natural language. The language that is indigenous to an area.

Nobel Laureate: a person awarded a prize for lifetime achievement in literature, sciences, economics, or peace. Prize founded by Swedish industrialist Alfred Nobel, inventor of dynamite.

nomad: a wanderer; member of a tribe of people who have no fixed place or abode, but move about from place to place depending on the availability of food sources.

novena: a series of prayers in honor of a saint for a specific reason.

O

obsidian: a black, shiny volcanic rock, resembling glass.

official language: the language in which the business of a country and its government is conducted.

Ottoman Empire: a Turkish empire founded by Osman I in about 1603, that variously controlled large areas of land around the Mediterranean, Black, and Caspian Seas until it was dissolved in 1918.

outback region: the rural interior region of the continent of Australia. It is sparsely populated, mainly by aboriginal peoples.

overgrazing: allowing animals to graze in an area to the point that the ground vegetation is damaged or destroyed.

P

pagan: a person who worships more than one diety. Sometimes refers to non-Christians.

pagoda: in the Far East, a sacred tower, usually pyramidal in outline, richly carved, painted, or otherwise adorned, and of several stories. They can be, but are not always, connected to a temple.

Paleoasiatic languages: languages that date back to a prehistoric or unwritten era in linguistic history.

parochial: an institution supported by a church or parish.

parody: dance or song ridiculing a serious subject in a silly manner. Usually focuses on the person or people who dominate another cultural group.

Parsi: one of the descendants of those Persians who settled in India about the end of the seventh century in order to escape Mohammedan persecution, and who still retain their ancient religion. Also Parsee.

Passover (Pesach): a Jewish holiday. Pesach, lasting seven days in Israel and eight outside it, begins on 15 Nisan, at roughly the spring equinox, and recalls the exodus of the Hebrews from Egypt and their delivery from bondage. The chief festival of Judaism, Pesach begins with a ceremonial family meal, or seder, at which special foods (including unleavened bread, or matzoh) are eaten and the Passover story (Haggadah) is read.

pastoralist: a nomadic people who move with their herds of sheep or cattle, searching for pasture and water.

patois: a dialect peculiar to a district or locality, in use especially among the peasantry or uneducated classes; hence, a rustic, provincial, or barbarous form of speech.

patriarchal system: a social system in which the head of the family or tribe is the father or oldest male. Kinship is determined and traced through the male members of the tribe.

patrilineal (descent): Descending from, or tracing descent through, the paternal line.

patrilocal: a society in which men take the larger role in activities and receive greater attention.

peccary: a pig-like animal native to North and South America and the Caribbean Islands. Noted for its musky smell, sharp tusks, and gray color.

pentatonic: music consisting of a five tone scale.

Pentecost Monday (Whitmonday): a Christian holiday. This public holiday observed in many countries occurs the day after Pentecost (derived from the ancient Greek pentekostos, "fiftieth"), or Whitsunday, which commemorates the descent of the Holy Spirit upon Jesus' apostles on the seventh Sunday after Easter and is derived from the Jewish feast of Shavuot. It was an important occasion for baptism in the early church, and the name "Whitsunday" originated from the white robes worn by the newly baptized.

Pentecostal: having to do with Pentecost, a Christian holiday celebrated the seventh Sunday after Easter, marking the day that the Holy Spirit descended upon the Apostles.

peyote: the tops of the small spineless mescal cactus. Native to the southwestern United States and northern Mexico.

phoneme: slightly different sounds in a language that are heard as the same by a native speaker.

pierogie: a Polish dumpling made from pastry dough. It contains various fillings, such as meat and potatoes.

pilgrimage: a journey to a sacred place in order to perform some religious vow or duty, or to obtain some spiritual or miraculous benefit.

polygamy: the practice of having two or more spouses at the same time.

polygyny: the practice of having two or more wives and/or mistresses.

polyphonic: combining a number of harmonic sounds. Music that has more than one sound.

polytheism: belief and worship of many gods.

post traumatic stress disorder: psychological disorder that accompanies violent or tragic experiences. Known as shell-shock during World War I.

Prayer Day: a Christian holiday. This Danish public holiday is observed on the fourth Friday after Easter.

Presbyterian: of or pertaining to ecclesiastical government by elders or by presbyteries.

Prophet Muhammed: *see* **Mohammed**.

proselytizing: inducing or persuading someone to become the adherent of some religion, doctrine, sect, or party. To convert.

Protestant: a member or an adherent of one of those Christian bodies which descended from the Reformation of the sixteenth century. Originally applied to those who opposed or protested the Roman Catholic Church.

province: an administrative territory of a country.

Purim: a Jewish holiday. This holiday, celebrated on 14 Adar (Adar Sheni in a leap year), commemorates the delivery of the Jews from potential annihilation at the hands of Haman, viceroy of Persia, as described in the Book of Esther, which is read from a scroll (megillah). The day, though not a public holiday in Israel, is widely marked by charity, exchange of edible gifts, and feasting.

R

rabbi: a Jewish religious leader; head of a congregation.

racial integration: to remove all restrictions and barriers preventing complete access to society to persons of all races.

racially homogeneous: composed of persons all of the same race.

rain forest: a tropical vegetation in the equatorial region of the world which consists of a dense growth of a wide variety of broadleaf evergreen trees and vines.

Raksha Bandhan: a Hindu holiday. During this festival, which usually falls in August, bracelets of colored thread and tinsel are tied by women to the wrists of their menfolk, thus binding the men to guard and protect them during the year. It is celebrated on the full moon of Sravana.

Ramadan: a Muslim holiday. The first day of Ramadan (the ninth month) is a public holiday in many countries, although the religious festival does not officially begin until the new moon is sighted from the Naval Observatory in Cairo, Egypt. The entire month commemorates the period in which the Prophet received divine revelation and is observed by a strict fast from sunrise to sundown. This observance is one of Islam's five main duties for believers.

Rastafarian: a member of a Jamaican cult begun in 1930 as a semi-religious, semi-political movement. Rastafarians are usually lower class men who are anti-white and advocate the return of blacks to Africa.

refugee: one who flees to a refuge, shelter or place of safety. One who in times of persecution or political commotion flees to a foreign country for safety.

respiratory: pertaining to the lungs and other breathing passages.

Roman alphabet: the alphabet of the ancient Romans from which the alphabets of most modern western European languages, including English, are derived.

Roman Catholic Church: the designation of the church of which the pope or bishop of Rome is the head, and which holds him, as the successor of St. Peter and heir of his spiritual authority, privileges, and gifts, as its supreme ruler, pastor, and teacher.

Romance language: the group of languages derived from Latin: French, Spanish, Italian, Portuguese and other related languages.

Rosh Hashanah: a Jewish holiday. The Jewish New Year is celebrated on 1 Tishri, the first month. In synagogues, the sounding of the shofar (ram's horn) heralds the new year. Rosh Hashanah begins the observance of the Ten Penitential Days, which culminate in Yom Kippur. Orthodox and Conservative Jews outside Israel celebrate 2 Tishri, the next day, as well.

runic music: music that is ancient, obscure, and mystical.

Russian Orthodox: the arm of the Orthodox Eastern Church which was the official church of czarist Russia.

S

Sacred Heart: a Christian holiday. The Friday of the week after Corpus Christi is a holiday in Colombia. The object of devotion is the divine person of Jesus, whose heart is the symbol of his love for mankind.

Samaritans: a native or an inhabitant of Samaria; specifically, one of a race settled in the cities of Samaria by the king of Assyria after the removal of the Israelites from the country.

samba: a Brazilian dance and musical tradition based on two beats to the measure.

sambo: indicates a person of visible African ancestry. Familiar form of address for an uncle from the Foulah language of West Africa.

Santer'a: Christian religion with West African origins. It merges Christian saints with Yoruban dieties.

savanna: a treeless or near treeless plain of a tropical or subtropical region dominated by drought-resistant grasses.

schistosomiasis: a tropical disease that is chronic and characterized by disorders of the liver, urinary bladder, lungs, or central nervous system.

sect: a religious denomination or group, often a dissenting one with extreme views.

self-determination: the desire of a culture to control its economic and social development.

Semitic tongue: an important family of languages distinguished by triliteral verbal roots and vowel inflections.

Seventh-day Adventist: one who believes in the second coming of Christ to establish a personal reign upon the earth. They observe the seventh day of the week as the Sabbath and believe in the existence of the spirit of prophecy among them.

shaman: holy man or woman said to have the power to heal diseases. Also thought to have magical powers.

shamanism: a religion centered on a belief in good and evil spirits that can be influenced only by shamans.

Shavuot: a Jewish holiday. This festival, on 6 Sivan, celebrates the presentation of the Ten Commandments to Moses on Mt. Sinai and the offering of the first harvest fruits at the temple in Jerusalem. The precursor of the Christian Pentecost, Shavuot takes place on the 50th day after the first day of Passover.

Shia Muslim: member of one of two great sects of Islam. Shia Muslims believe that Ali and the Imams are the rightful successors of Mohammed (also commonly spelled Muhammed). They also believe that the last recognized Imam will return as a messiah. Also known as Shiites. (*Also see* **Sunni Muslim**.)

Shiites: *see* **Shia Muslim**.

Shintoism: the system of nature- and hero-worship which forms the indigenous religion of Japan.

Shivarati (Mahashivarati): a Hindu holiday. Dedicated to the god Shiva, this holiday is observed on the 13th day of the dark half of Magha, corresponding to January or February.

Shrove Monday and Shrove Tuesday: a Christian holiday. These two days occur just prior to the beginning of Lent (a term which derives from the Middle English lente, "spring"), the Christian season of penitence that ends with Easter Sunday. These are days of Carnival, public holidays of feasting, and merriment in many lands. Shrove Tuesday is also known as Mardi Gras.

shunning: Amish practice of not interacting in any way with a person who has been cast out by the church and the community.

sierra: a chain of hills or mountains.

Sikh: a member of a politico-religious community of India, founded as a sect around 1500 and based on the principles of monotheism and human brotherhood.

Sino-Tibetan language family: the family of languages spoken in Eastern Asia, including China, Thailand, Tibet, and Burma.

slash-and-burn agriculture: a hasty and sometimes temporary way of clearing land to make it available for agriculture by cutting down trees and burning them.

slave trade: the transportation of black Africans beginning in the 1700s to other countries to be sold as slaves-people owned as property and compelled to work for their owners at no pay.

Slavic languages: a major subgroup of the Indo-European language family. It is further subdivided into West Slavic (including Polish, Czech, Slovak and Sorbian), South Slavic (including Bulgarian, Serbo-Croatian, Slovene, and Old Church Slavonic), and East Slavic (including Russian Ukrainian and Byelorussian).

Society of Friends: a religious sect founded about 1650 whose members shun military service and believe in plain dress, behavior and worship. Also referred to as the Quaker religion by those outside it.

Solemnity of Mary, Mother of God: a Christian holiday. Observed on 1 January, this celebration was, before a 1969 Vatican reform, the Feast of the Circumcision of Our Lord Jesus Christ.

sorghum: a type of tropical grass that is grown for grain, syrup, and livestock feed.

St. Agatha's Day: a Christian holiday. Celebrated on 5 February, it is the feast day of the patron saint of San Marino. St. Agatha is also the patron saint of nurses, firefighters, and jewelers.

St. Dévôte Day: a Christian holiday. Observed on 27 January in Monaco in honor of the principality's patron saint, this day celebrates her safe landing after a perilous voyage, thanks to a dove who directed her ship to the Monaco shore.

St. James's Day: a Christian holiday. Observed on 25 July, this day commemorates St. James the Greater, one of Jesus' 12 apostles. St. James is the patron saint of Spain.

St. Joseph's Day: a Christian holiday. The feast day in honor of Mary's husband is observed on 19 March as a public holiday in several countries.

St. Patrick's Day: a Christian holiday. This holiday, observed on 17 March, is celebrated in Ireland to honor its patron saint.

St. Stephen's Day: a Christian holiday. The feast day in honor of the first martyred Christian saint is 26 December, the day after Christmas. St. Stephen is the patron saint of Hungary.

steppe: a level tract of land more or less devoid of trees. It is a name given to certain parts of European and Asiatic Russia, of which the most characteristic feature is the absence of forests.

stigmatize: branding someone as a disgrace because of his or her behavior.

straits: a narrow passage of water connecting two bodies of water.

stroganoff: Russian beef stew. Sauce made from sour cream and wine.

subcontinent: a landmass of great size, but smaller than any of the continents; a large subdivision of a continent.

subsistence farming: farming that provides the minimum food goods necessary for the continuation of the farm family.

Sudanic language group: a related group of languages spoken in various areas of northern Africa, including Yoruba, Mandingo and Tshi.

Sufi: a Mohammedan mystic who believes (a) that God alone exists, and all visible and invisible beings are mere emanations from Him; (b) that, as God is the real author of all the acts of mankind, man is not a free agent, and there can be no real difference between good and evil; (c) that, as the soul existed before the body, and is confined within the latter as in a cage, death should be the chief object of desire, for only then does the soul return to the bosom of the divinity; and (d) that religions are matters of indifference, though some are more advantageous than others, and Sufism is the only true philosophy.

Sukkot: a Jewish holiday. This ancient Jewish harvest festival, which begins on 15 Tishri, recalls the period in which harvesters left their homes to dwell in the fields in sukkot, or booths—small outdoor shelters of boards, leaves, and branches—in order to facilitate gathering the crops before the seasonal rains began. In religious terms, it commemorates the 40 years of wandering in the desert by the ancient Hebrews after their exodus from Egypt. The 8th day of Sukkot (and the 22d day of Tishri) is Shmini Azeret/Simhat Torah, a joyous holiday in which the annual cycle of reading the Torah (the Five Books of Moses) is completed and begun anew. Outside of Israel, Simhat Torah and the beginning of a new reading cycle are celebrated on the next day, 23 Tishri.

sultan: a king of a Muslim state.

Sunni Muslim: Member of one of two major sects of the religion of Islam. Sunni Muslims adhere to strict orthodox traditions and believe that the four caliphs are the rightful successors to Mohammed, founder of Islam. (Mohammed is commonly spelled Muhammed, especially by Islamic people.) (*Also see* **Shia Muslim.**)

surname: a person's last name. Generally different from his or her first name.

T

taboo: a system, practice, or act whereby persons, things, places, actions, or words are placed under ban, curse, or prohibition, or set apart as sacred or privileged in some specific manner.

taiga: a coniferous forest in the far northern areas of Canada, Alaska, and Eurasia.

Taoism: the doctrine of Lao-Tzu, an ancient Chinese philosopher (about 500 BC) as laid down by him in the Tao-te-ching.

Thaipusam: a Hindu holiday. A holiday in Malaysia, Thaipusam honors Subrimaya, son of Shiva and an important deity in southern India. The three-day festival is held in the month of Magha according to when Pusam, a section of the lunar zodiac, is on the ascendant.

Tibeto-Burman language group: a subgroup of the Sino-Tibetan language family which includes Tibetan and Burmese.

Tishah b'Av: a Jewish holiday. This holiday, which takes place on 9 Av, commemorates the destruction of the First Temple by the Babylonians (Chaldeans) in 586 BC and of the Second Temple by the Romans in AD 70. It is observed by fasting.

toboggan: a kind of sled without runners or a steering mechanism.

topography: an accurate drawing representing the surface of a region on maps and charts.

toucan: a brightly colored, fruit-eating bird of tropical America with a distinctive beak.

trachoma: contagious, viral infection of the cornea. Causes scarring in the eye.

tribal society: a society based on tribal consciousness and loyalties.

tribal system: a social community in which people are organized into groups or clans descended from common ancestors and sharing customs and languages.

tsetse fly: any of the several African insects which can transmit a variety of parasitic organisms through its bite. Some of these organisms can prove fatal to both human and animal victims.

tundra: a nearly level treeless area whose climate and vegetation are more characteristically arctic due to its northern position. Although the region attains seasonal temperatures warm enough to allow a thin layer of soil on the surface to unthaw enough to support the growth of various species of plants, the subsoil is permanently frozen.

tutelary: a god or spirit who acts a guardian that watches over a person or group of people.

typhoon: a violent hurricane occurring in the China Sea or Philippine region, principally between the months of July and October.

U

unemployment rate: the overall unemployment rate is the percentage of the work force (both employed and unemployed) who claim to be unemployed. The natural unemployment rate is the lowest level at which unemployment in an economy can be maintained and still reflect a balance of the labor market and the product market.

untouchables: in 19th century India, members of the lowest caste in the caste system, a hereditary social class system.

They were considered unworthy to touch members of higher castes.

urban center: a city.

USSR: an abbreviation of Union of Soviet Socialist Republics.

V

veldt: in South Africa, an unforested or thinly forested tract of land or region, a grassland.

Vesak: this last full moon day of Visakha highlights a three-day celebration of the birth, enlightenment, and death of the Buddha. It falls in April or May.

voodoo: a belief system which is based on sorcery and other primitive rites and the power of charms and fetishes, originating in Africa.

W

wadi(s): the channel of a watercourse which is dry except in the rainy season. Also called wady.

Windward Islands: a southern group of islands stretching south to Trinidad. Part of the Lesser Antilles, but does not include Barbados.

Y

Yom Kippur: a Jewish holiday. The Day of Atonement, spent in fasting, penitence, and prayer, is the most solemn day in Judaism. It takes place on 10 Tishri.

yucca: a plant native to Mexico, Central and South America, and the southwestern United States. Can grow to the 12 feet in height.

yurt: a framework tent of stretched felt or skins. Associated with Siberia and Mongolia.

Z

Zoroastrianism: the system of religious doctrine taught by Zoroaster and his followers in the Avesta; the religion prevalent in Persia until its overthrow by the Muslims in the 7th century.